READINGS
IN THE PHILOSOPHY
OF LAW

Third Edition

READINGS IN THE PHILOSOPHY OF LAW

John Arthur
Binghamton University—State University of New York

William H. Shaw
San Jose State University

Prentice
Hall

Upper Saddle River, New Jersey 07458

Library of Congress Cataloging-in-Publication Data

Readings in the philosophy of law / [edited by] John Arthur and William H. Shaw.—3rd ed.
  p. cm.
  ISBN 0-13-027741-X
  1. Law—Philosophy. 2. Law—United States. I. Arthur, John (date) II. Shaw, William
H. (date)

K235.R39 2000
340′.1—dc21   00-026709

Editor in Chief: Charlyce Jones-Owen
Acquisitions Editor: Ross Miller
Assistant Editor: Katie Janssen
AVP, Director of Manufacturing
  and Production: Barbara Kittle
Senior Managing Editor: Jan Stephan
Production Liaison: Fran Russello
Project Manager: Linda B. Pawelchak
Manufacturing Manager: Nick Sklitsis
Prepress and Manufacturing Buyer: Sherry Lewis
Cover Director: Jayne Conte

Acknowledgments begin on page 666, which constitutes
a continuation of this copyright page.

This book was set in 10/11 Janson Text
by Pub-Set, Inc. and was printed
and bound by RR Donnelley & Sons Company.
The cover was printed by Phoenix Color Corp.

©2001, 1993, 1984 by Prentice-Hall, Inc.
A Division of Pearson Education
Upper Saddle River, New Jersey 07458

Printed in the United States of America
10 9 8 7 6 5 4 3 2

ISBN 0-13-027741-X

Prentice-Hall International (UK) Limited, *London*
Prentice-Hall of Australia Pty. Limited, *Sydney*
Prentice-Hall Canada Inc., *Toronto*
Prentice Hall Hispanoamericana, S.A., *Mexico*
Prentice-Hall of India Private Limited, *New Delhi*
Prentice-Hall of Japan, Inc., *Tokyo*
Pearson Education Asia Pte. Ltd., *Singapore*
Editora Prentice-Hall do Brasil, Ltda., *Rio de Janeiro*

CONTENTS

PART II ❖ THE NATURE OF LAW

PART III ❖ PHILOSOPHICAL ISSUES IN CRIMINAL LAW

PART IV ❖ PHILOSOPHICAL ISSUES IN CIVIL LAW

PART V ❖ PHILOSOPHICAL ISSUES IN CONSTITUTIONAL LAW

PREFACE

We have been gratified by the reception that the first two editions of *Readings in the Philosophy of Law* have received. Each edition went through several printings, and many friends and colleagues have written to offer comments and suggestions. Like its predeccesors, this new edition reflects the conviction that legal philosophy is its own subject, best approached by paying attention to how the law is organized and to the particular issues it raises. The book is, therefore, not a book in applied ethics, nor one in political philosophy; it is its own subject with its own fascinating set of problems.

This text can be used in many different ways. It is designed so that each section stands on its own, enabling instructors to address the topics in any order and to skip certain topics if they wish. Readers familiar with the earlier editions will find in the third edition much continuity in the themes and issues treated. Believing it to be the soundest organizational structure, we continue to follow the traditional divisions among different fields of law. Initial sections on legal practice, legal reasoning, and the nature of law are followed by discussions of criminal, tort, contract, property, and constitutional law. These make up the major subdivisions in the book.

We have also expanded and redefined the early sections to deal with an array of topics either ignored or inadequately covered in other texts. In particular, we found it useful to begin undergraduate courses in philosophy of law with discussions of legal practice, the adversary system, the rule of law, obedience to law, and legal reasoning. Many philosophy of law students plan to attend law school, so these topics are a natural way to introduce them to the subject. We have been especially careful in selecting this introductory material to use readings that are accessible and interesting to discuss. The introductory section, "The Practice of Law," brings together four widely different viewpoints on the role and responsibilities of lawyers in an adversary system, while the readings on the rule of law focus on the practical problem of how to deal legally with people who worked with a previous, Nazi-like regime.

Readers will also notice many other new topics and essays in this edition. Part II, "The Nature of Law," now includes greatly expanded discussions of "Law and Economics" as well as "Critical Legal Theory and Feminist Jurisprudence." Material on criminal law now includes an essay on the O. J. Simpson trial, jury nullification, and racial politics, along with readings on the battered woman's defense and the cultural defense in criminal cases. Part V, on constitutional law, has also been revised and expanded. It now includes more focused discussions of the justification of judicial review and the nature of constitutional interpretation, as well as an essay comparing the American understanding of constitutionalism with that of the French and British. We have added an essay and cases on religious freedom. The last section, "Equality and the Constitution," begins with two new essays on the ideal of equality itself, it also includes new cases on sexual harassment and hate speech.

While seeking to present the readings in a coherent and interrelated format, we have at the same time sought to provide a textbook with ample resources to allow a variety of different courses to be taught, in different ways, and to different student audiences. These and related editorial decisions grow out of our experience in teaching courses in philosophy of law at several colleges and universities, both private and public, to undergraduates with varying degrees of philosophical background and academic preparedness. One of us teaches philosophy of law

PART I

LAW IN ACTION

❖

1
THE PRACTICE OF LAW

We begin this book with essays on the nature of the practice of law for two reasons. First, the selections are of great practical and moral interest: Many who study the philosophy of law will be thinking about becoming lawyers. The oft-heard criticisms of lawyers and of the practice of law will be all too familiar to them. We all know that lawyers often bear the brunt of jokes about the practice of law. They are also frequently accused of demonstrating a lack of integrity or a willingness to do what may seem to be immoral acts. Why, for instance, does society tolerate the confidentiality of the lawyer–client relationship when it means that useful information is being withheld from the police? Or why do the activities of lawyers make truthful people appear to be liars and liars appear to be truthful? Second, beyond these practical and moral issues, the essays in this section also begin our inquiry into some of the other important topics that arise throughout the text, which include the justification of the legal practices of excluding relevant evidence in certain cases, the connections between the law and politics, and the essential nature of the law.

Lawyers' Ethics in an Adversary System

Monroe H. Freedman

In this selection from his book Lawyers' Ethics in an Adversary System, *Monroe H. Freedman, professor of law and dean of the Hofstra University School of Law, examines the obligations of criminal defense lawyers in three difficult, morally troubling cases: whether to keep knowledge of a client's crime confidential, whether to allow a client to present perjured testimony, and whether to destroy a truthful witness through tough cross-examination. Freedman notes the conflicting obligations facing the conscientious attorney, but he defends zealous and aggressive advocacy in these cases as a necessary part of our adversarial criminal justice system.*

WHERE THE BODIES ARE BURIED: THE ADVERSARY SYSTEM AND THE OBLIGATION OF CONFIDENTIALITY

In a recent case in Lake Pleasant, New York, a defendant in a murder case told his lawyers about two other people he had killed and where their bodies had been hidden. The lawyers went there, observed the bodies, and took photographs of them. They did not, however, inform the authorities about the bodies until several months later, when their client had confessed to those crimes. In addition to withholding the information from police and prosecutors, one of the attorneys denied information to one of the victims' parents, who came to him in the course of seeking his missing daughter.

There were interesting reactions to that dramatic event. Members of the public were generally shocked at the apparent callousness on the part of the lawyers, whose conduct was considered typical of an unhealthy lack of concern by lawyers with the public interest and with simple decency. That attitude was encouraged by public statements by the local prosecutor, who sought to indict the lawyers for failing to reveal knowledge of a crime and for failing to see that dead bodies were properly buried. In addition, the reactions of lawyers and law professors who were questioned by the press were ambivalent and confused, indicating that few members of the legal profession had given serious thought to the fundamental questions of administration of justice and of professional responsibility that were raised by the case.

One can certainly understand the sense of moral compulsion to assist the parents and to give the dignity of proper burial to the victims. What seems to be less readily understood—but which, to my mind, throws the moral balance in the other direction—is the obligation of the lawyers to their client and, in a larger sense, to a system of administering justice which is itself essential to maintaining human dignity. In short,

not only did the two lawyers behave properly, but they would have committed a serious breach of professional responsibility if they had divulged the information contrary to their client's interest. The explanation of that answer takes us to the very nature of our system of criminal justice and, indeed, to the fundamentals of our system of government. . . .

A trial is, in part, a search for truth. Accordingly, those basic rights are most often characterized as procedural safeguards against error in the search for truth. Actually, however, a trial is far more than a search for truth, and the constitutional rights that are provided by our system of justice may well outweigh the truth-seeking value—a fact which is manifest when we consider that those rights and others guaranteed by the Constitution may well impede the search for truth rather than further it. What more effective way is there, for example, to expose a defendant's guilt than to require self-incrimination, at least to the extent of compelling the defendant to take the stand and respond to interrogation before the jury? The defendant, however, is presumed innocent; the burden is on the prosecution to prove guilt beyond a reasonable doubt, and even the guilty accused has an "absolute constitutional right" to remain silent and to put the government to its proof.

Thus, the defense lawyer's professional obligation may well be to advise the client to withhold the truth. As Justice Jackson said: "Any lawyer worth his salt will tell the suspect in no uncertain terms to make no statement to police under any circumstances." Similarly, the defense lawyer is obligated to prevent the introduction of evidence that may be wholly reliable, such as a murder weapon seized in violation of the Fourth Amendment, or a truthful but involuntary confession. Justice White has observed that although law enforcement officials must be dedicated to using only truthful evidence, "defense counsel has no comparable obligation to ascertain or present the truth. Our system assigns him a different mission. . . .

[W]e . . . insist that he defend his client whether he is innocent or guilty." . . .

Before we will permit the state to deprive any person of life, liberty, or property, we require that certain processes be duly followed which ensure regard for the dignity of the individual, irrespective of the impact of those processes upon the determination of truth.

By emphasizing that the adversary process has its foundations in respect for human dignity, even at the expense of the search for truth, I do not mean to deprecate the search for truth or to suggest that the adversary system is not concerned with it. On the contrary, truth is a basic value, and the adversary system is one of the most efficient and fair methods designed for determining it. That system proceeds on the assumption that the best way to ascertain the truth is to present to an impartial judge or jury a confrontation between the proponents of conflicting views, assigning to each the task of marshalling and presenting the evidence in as thorough and persuasive a way as possible. The truth-seeking techniques used by the advocates on each side include investigation, pretrial discovery, cross-examination of opposing witnesses, and a marshalling of the evidence in summation. Thus, the judge or jury is given the strongest possible view of each side, and is put in the best possible position to make an accurate and fair judgment. Nevertheless, the point that I now emphasize is that in a society that honors the dignity of the individual, the high value that we assign to truth-seeking is not an absolute, but may on occasion be subordinated to even higher values.

The concept of a right to counsel is one of the most significant manifestations of our regard for the dignity of the individual. No person is required to stand alone against the awesome power of the People of New York or the Government of the United States of America. Rather, every criminal defendant is guaranteed an advocate—a "champion" against a "hostile world," the "single voice on which he must rely with confidence that his interests will be protected to the fullest extent consistent with the rules of procedure and the standards of professional conduct." In addition, the attorney serves in significant part to assure equality before the law. Thus, the lawyer has been referred to as "the equalizer," who "places each litigant as nearly as possible on an equal footing under the substantive and procedural law under which he is tried."

The lawyer can serve effectively as advocate, however, "only if he knows all that his client knows" concerning the facts of the case. Nor is the client ordinarily competent to evaluate the relevance or significance of particular facts. What may seem incriminating to the client, may actually be exculpatory. For example, one client was reluctant to tell her lawyer that her husband had attacked her with a knife, because it tended to confirm that she had in fact shot him (contrary to what she had at first maintained). Having been persuaded by her attorney's insistence upon complete and candid disclosure, she finally "confessed all"—which permitted the lawyer to defend her properly and successfully on grounds of self-defense.

Obviously, however, the client cannot be expected to reveal to the lawyer all information that is potentially relevant, including that which may well be incriminating, unless the client can be assured that the lawyer will maintain all such information in the strictest confidence. "The purposes and necessities of the relation between a client and his attorney" require "the fullest and freest disclosures" of the client's "objects, motives and acts." If the attorney were permitted to reveal such disclosures, it would be "not only a gross violation of a sacred trust upon his part," but it would "utterly destroy and prevent the usefulness and benefits to be derived from professional assistance." That "sacred trust" of confidentiality must "upon all occasions be inviolable," or else the client could not feel free "to repose [confidence] in the attorney to whom he resorts for legal advice and assistance." Destroy that confidence, and "a man would not venture to consult any skillful person, or would only dare to tell his counselor half his case." The result would be impairment of the "perfect freedom of consultation by client with attorney," which is "essential to the administration of justice." Accordingly, the new Code of Professional Responsibility provides that a lawyer shall not knowingly reveal a confidence or secret of the client, nor use a confidence or secret to the disadvantage of the client, or to the advantage of a third person, without the client's consent. . . .

That is not to say, of course, that the attorney is privileged to go beyond the needs of confidentiality imposed by the adversary system, and actively participate in concealment of evidence or obstruction of justice. For example, in the *Ryder* case, which arose in Virginia several years ago, the attorney removed from his client's safe deposit box a sawed-off shotgun and the money from a bank robbery and put them, for greater safety, into the lawyers's own safe deposit box. The attorney, quite properly, was suspended from practice for 18 months. (The penalty might well have been heavier, except for the fact that Ryder sought advice from senior members of the bench and bar, and apparently acted more in ignorance than in venality.) The important difference between the *Ryder* case and the one in Lake Pleasant lies in the active role played by the attorney in *Ryder* to conceal evidence. There is no indication, for example, that the attorneys in Lake Pleasant attempted to hide the bodies more effectively. If they had done so, they would have gone beyond maintaining confidentiality and into active participation in the concealment of evidence.

The distinction should also be noted between the attorney's knowledge of a past crime (which is what we have been discussing so far) and knowledge of a crime to be committed in the future. Thus, a major exception to the strict rule of confidentiality is the "intention of his client to commit a crime, and information necessary to prevent the crime." Significantly, however, even in that exceptional circumstance, disclosure of the confidence is only permissible, not mandatory. Moreover, a footnote in the Code suggests that the exception is applicable only when the attorney knows "beyond a reasonable doubt" that a crime will be committed. There is little guidance as to how the lawyer is to exercise the discretion to report future crimes. At one extreme, it seems clear that the lawyer should reveal information necessary to save a life. On the other hand, as will be discussed [below], the lawyer should not reveal the intention of a client in a criminal case to commit perjury in his or her own defense.

It has been suggested that the information regarding the two bodies in the Lake Pleasant case was not relevant to the crime for which the defendant was being prosecuted, and that, therefore, that knowledge was outside the scope of confidentiality. That point lacks merit for three reasons. First, an unsophisticated lay person should not be required to anticipate which disclosures might fall outside the scope of confidentiality because of insufficient legal relevance. Second, the information in question might well have been highly relevant to the defense of insanity. Third, a lawyer has an obligation to merge other, unrelated crimes into the bargained plea, if it is possible to do so. Accordingly, the information about the other murders was clearly within the production of confidentiality. . . .

In summary, the Constitution has committed us to an adversary system for the administration of criminal justice. The essentially humanitarian reason for such a system is that it preserves the dignity of the individual, even though that may occasionally require significant frustration of the search for truth and the will of the state. An essential element of that system is the right to counsel, a right that would be meaningless if the defendant were not able to communicate freely and fully with the attorney.

In order to protect the communication—and, ultimately, the adversary system itself—we impose upon attorneys what has been called the "sacred trust" of confidentiality. It was pursuant to that high trust that the lawyers acted in Lake Pleasant, New York, when they refrained from divulging their knowledge of where the bodies were buried. . . .

PERJURY: THE CRIMINAL DEFENSE LAWYER'S TRILEMMA

Is it ever proper for a criminal defense lawyer to present perjured testimony? . . . That question cannot be answered properly without an appreciation of the fact that the attorney functions in an adversary system of criminal justice which . . . imposes special responsibilities upon the advocate.

First, the lawyer is required to determine "all relevant facts known to the accused," because "counsel cannot properly perform their duties without knowing the truth." The lawyer who is ignorant of any potentially relevant fact "incapacitates himself to serve his client effectively," because "an adequate defense cannot be framed if the lawyer does not know what is likely to develop at trial."*

Second, the lawyer must hold in strictest confidence the disclosures made by the client in the course of the professional relationship. "Nothing is more fundamental to the lawyer-client relationship than the establishment of trust and confidence." The "first duty" of an attorney is "to keep the secrets of his clients." If this were not so, the client would not feel free to confide fully, and the lawyer would not be able to fulfill the obligation to ascertain all relevant facts. Accordingly, defense counsel is required to establish "a relationship of trust and confidence" with the accused, to explain "the necessity of full disclosure of all facts," and to explain to the client "the obligation of confidentiality which makes privileged the accused's disclosures."

Third, the lawyer is an officer of the court, and his or her conduct before the court "should be characterized by candor."

As soon as one begins to think about those responsibilities, it becomes apparent that the conscientious attorney is faced with what we may call a trilemma—that is, the lawyer is required to know everything, to keep it in confidence, and to reveal it to the court. Moreover, the difficulties presented by those conflicting obligations are particularly acute in the criminal defense area because of the presumption of innocence, the burden upon the state to prove its case beyond a reasonable doubt, and the right to put the prosecution to its proof.

Before addressing the issue of the criminal defense lawyer's responsibilities when the client indicates to the lawyer the intention to commit perjury in the future, we might note the

somewhat less difficult question of what the lawyer should do when knowledge of the perjury comes after its commission rather than before it. Although there is some ambiguity in the most recent authorities, the rules appear to require that the criminal defense lawyer should urge the client to correct the perjury, but beyond that, the obligation of confidentiality precludes the lawyer from revealing the truth. . . .

If we recognize that professional responsibility requires that an advocate have full knowledge of every pertinent fact, then the lawyer must seek the truth from the client, not shun it. That means that the attorney will have to dig and pry and cajole, and, even then, the lawyer will not be successful without convincing the client that full disclosure to the lawyer will never result in prejudice to the client by any word or action of the attorney. That is particularly true in the case of the indigent defendant, who meets the lawyer for the first time in the cell block or the rotunda of the jail. The client did not choose the lawyer, who comes as a stranger sent by the judge, and who therefore appears to be part of the system that is attempting to punish the defendant. It is no easy task to persuade that client to talk freely without fear of harm. . . .

Assume the following situation. Your client has been falsely accused of a robbery committed at 16th and P Streets at 11:00 P.M. He tells you at first that at no time on the evening of the crime was he within six blocks of that location. However, you are able to persuade him that he must tell you the truth and that doing so will in no way prejudice him. He then reveals to you that he was at 15th and P Streets at 10:55 that evening, but that he was walking east, away from the scene of the crime, and that, by 11:00 P.M., he was six blocks away. At the trial, there are two prosecution witnesses. The first mistakenly, but with some degree of persuasiveness, identifies your client as the criminal. At that point the prosecution's case depends upon that single witness, who might or might not be believed. The second prosecution witness is an elderly woman who is somewhat nervous and who wears glasses. She testifies truthfully and accurately that she saw your client at 15th and P Streets at 10:55 P.M. She has corroborated the erroneous testimony

---

*American Bar Association Canons of Professional Ethics, 15.

of the first witness and made conviction extremely likely. However, on cross-examination her reliability is thrown into doubt through demonstration that she is easily confused and has poor eyesight. Thus, the corroboration has been eliminated, and doubt has been established in the minds of the jurors as to the prosecution's entire case.

The client then insists upon taking the stand in his own defense, not only to deny the erroneous evidence identifying him as the criminal, but also to deny the truthful, but highly damaging, testimony of the corroborating witness who placed him one block away from the intersection five minutes prior to the crime. Of course, if he tells the truth and thus verifies the corroborating witness, the jury will be more inclined to accept the inaccurate testimony of the principal witness, who specifically identified him as the criminal.

In my opinion, the attorney's obligation in such a situation would be to advise the client that the proposed testimony is unlawful, but to proceed in the normal fashion in presenting the testimony and arguing the case to the jury if the client makes the decision to go forward. Any other course would be a betrayal of the assurances of confidentiality given by the attorney in order to induce the client to reveal everything, however damaging it might appear. . . .

For example, how would [one] resolve the following case? The prosecution witness testified that the robbery had taken place at 10:15, and identified the defendant as the criminal. However, the defendant had a convincing alibi for 10:00 to 10:30. The attorney presented the alibi, and the client was acquitted. The alibi was truthful, but the attorney knew that the prosecution witness had been confused about the time, and that his client had in fact committed the crime at 10:45. (Ironically, that same attorney considers it clearly unethical for a lawyer to present the false testimony on behalf of the innocent defendant in the case of the robbery at 16th and P Streets.) Should the lawyer have refused to present the honest alibi? How could he possibly have avoided doing so? Was he contributing to wise and informed judgment when he did present it?

The most obvious way to avoid the ethical difficulty is for the lawyer to withdraw from the case, at least if there is sufficient time before trial for the client to retain another attorney. The client will then go to the nearest law office, realizing that the obligation of confidentiality is not what it has been represented to be, and withhold incriminating information or the fact of guilt from the new attorney. In terms of professional ethics, the practice of withdrawing from a case under such circumstances is difficult to defend, since the identical perjured testimony will ultimately be presented. Moreover, the new attorney will be ignorant of the perjury and therefore will be in no position to attempt to discourage the client from presenting it. Only the original attorney, who knows the truth, has that opportunity, but loses it in the very act of evading the ethical problem.

The difficulty is all the more severe when the client is indigent. In that event, the client cannot retain other counsel, and in many jurisdictions it is impossible for appointed counsel or a public defender to withdraw from a case except for extraordinary reasons. Thus, the attorney can successfully withdraw only by revealing to the judge that the attorney has received knowledge of the client's guilt, or by giving the judge a false or misleading reason for moving for leave to withdraw. However, for the attorney to reveal knowledge of the client's guilt would be a gross violation of the obligation of confidentiality, particularly since it is entirely possible in many jurisdictions that the same judge who permits the attorney to withdraw will subsequently hear the case and sentence the defendant. Not only will the judge then have personal knowledge of the defendant's guilt before the trial begins, but it will be knowledge of which the newly appointed counsel for the defendant will very likely be ignorant.

Even where counsel is retained, withdrawal may not be a practical solution either because trial has begun or it is so close to trial that withdrawal would leave the client without counsel, or because the court for other reasons denies leave to withdraw. Judges are most reluctant to grant leave to withdraw during the trial or even shortly before it because of the power that that would give to defendants to delay the trial date or even to cause a series of mistrials. . . .

Since there are actually three obligations that create the difficulty—the third being the attorney's duty to learn all the facts—there is, of course, another way to resolve the difficulty. That is, by "selective ignorance." The attorney can make it clear to the client from the outset that the attorney does not want to hear an admission of guilt or incriminating information from the client. That view, however, puts an unreasonable burden on the unsophisticated client to select what to tell and what to hold back, and it can seriously impair the attorney's effectiveness in counselling the client and in trying the case.

For example, one leading attorney, who favors selective ignorance to avoid the trilemma, told me about one of his own cases in which the defendant assumed that the attorney would prefer to be ignorant of the fact that the defendant had been having sexual relations with the chief defense witness. As a result of the lawyer's ignorance of that fact, he was unable to minimize its impact by raising it with potential jurors during jury selection and by having the defendant and the defense witness admit it freely on direct examination. Instead, the first time the lawyer learned about the illicit sexual relationship was when the prosecutor dramatically obtained a reluctant admission from the defense witness on cross examination. The defense attorney is convinced that the client was innocent of the robbery with which he had been charged, but the defendant was nevertheless found guilty by the jury—in the attorney's own opinion because the defendant was guilty of fornication, a far less serious offense for which he had not been charged.

The question remains: what should the lawyer do when faced with the client's insistence upon taking the stand and committing perjury? It is in response to that question that the Standards present a most extraordinary solution. If the lawyer knows that the client is going to commit perjury, Section 7.7 of the Standards requires that the lawyer "must confine his examination to identifying the witness as the defendant and permitting him to make his statement." That is, the lawyer "may not engage in direct examination of

the defendant . . . in the conventional manner." Thus, the client's story will become part of the record, although without the attorney's assistance through direct examination. The general rule, of course, is that in closing argument to the jury "the lawyer may argue all reasonable inferences from the evidence in the record." Section 7.7 also provides, however, that the defense lawyer is forbidden to make any reference in closing argument to the client's testimony.

There are at least two critical flaws in that proposal. The first is purely practical: The prosecutor might well object to testimony from the defendant in narrative form rather than in the conventional manner, because it would give the prosecutor no opportunity to object to inadmissible evidence prior to the jury's hearing it. The Standards provide no guidance as to what the defense attorney should do if the objection is sustained.

More importantly, experienced trial attorneys have often noted that jurors assume that the defendant's lawyer knows the truth about the case, and that the jury will frequently judge the defendant by drawing inferences from the attorney's conduct in the case. There is, of course, only one inference that can be drawn if the defendant's own attorney turns his or her back on the defendant at the most critical point in the trial, and then, in closing argument, sums up the case with no reference to the fact that the defendant has given exculpatory testimony. . . .

It would appear that the ABA Standards have chosen to resolve the trilemma by maintaining the requirements of complete knowledge and of candor to the court, and sacrificing confidentiality. Interestingly, however, that may not in fact be the case. I say that because the Standards fail to answer a critically important question: Should the client be told about the obligation imposed by Section 7.7? That is, the Standards ignore the issue of whether the lawyer should say to the client at the outset of their relationship: "I think it's only fair that I warn you: If you should tell me anything incriminating and subsequently decide to deny the incriminating facts at trial, I would not be able to examine you in the ordinary manner or to argue your untrue testimony to the jury." The Canadian Bar

Association, for example, takes an extremely hard line against the presentation of perjury by the client, but it also explicitly requires that the client be put on notice of that fact. Obviously, any other course would be a betrayal of the client's trust, since everything else said by the attorney in attempting to obtain complete information about the case would indicate to the client that no information thus obtained would be used to the client's disadvantage.

On the other hand, the inevitable result of the position taken by the Canadian Bar Association would be to caution the client not to be completely candid with the attorney. That, of course, returns us to resolving the trilemma by maintaining confidentiality and candor, but sacrificing complete knowledge—a solution which, as we have already seen, is denounced by the Standards as "unscrupulous," "most egregious," and "professional impropriety."

Thus, the Standards, by failing to face up to the question of whether to put the client on notice, take us out of the trilemma by one door only to lead us back by another. . . .

Taking into account, therefore, . . . the practical and constitutional difficulties encountered by any of the alternatives to strict maintenance of confidentiality, . . . I continue to stand with those lawyers who hold that "the lawyer's obligation of confidentiality does not permit him to disclose the facts he has learned from his client which form the basis for his conclusion that the client intends to perjure himself." What that means—necessarily, it seems to me—is that the criminal defense attorney, however unwillingly in terms of personal morality, has a professional responsibility as an advocate in an adversary system to examine the perjurious client in the ordinary way and to argue to the jury, as evidence in the case, the testimony presented by the defendant. . . .

CROSS-EXAMINATION: DESTROYING THE TRUTHFUL WITNESS

More difficult than the question of whether the criminal defense lawyer should present known perjury, is the question of whether the attorney should cross-examine a witness who is testifying accurately and truthfully, in order to make the witness appear to be mistaken or lying. The issue was raised effectively in a symposium on legal ethics through the following hypothetical case.

The accused is a drifter who sometimes works as a filling station attendant. He is charged with rape, a capital crime. You are his court-appointed defense counsel. The alleged victim is the twenty-two-year-old daughter of a local bank president. She is engaged to a promising young minister in town. . . .

You learn that the victim has had affairs with two local men from good families. Smith, one of these young men, admits that the victim and he went together for some time, but refuses to say whether he had sexual intercourse with her and indicates he has a low opinion of you for asking. The other, Jones, apparently a bitterly disappointed and jealous suitor, readily states that he frequently had intercourse with the victim, and describes her behavior toward strange men as scandalous. He once took her to a fraternity dance, he says, and, having noticed she had been gone for some time, discovered her upstairs with Smith, a fraternity brother, on a bed in a state of semiundress. He appears eager to testify and he states that the girl got what she'd always been asking for. You believe Jones, but are somewhat repelled by the disappointed suitor's apparent willingness to smear the young woman's reputation.

Suppose the accused, after you press him, admits that he forced himself on the victim and admits that his first story was a lie. He refuses to plead guilty to the charge or any lesser charge. He says that he can get away with his story, because he did once before in California.

Should the defense lawyer use the information supplied by Jones to impeach the young woman and, if necessary, call Jones as a witness? . . .

That case takes us to the heart of my disagreement with the traditional approach to dealing with difficult questions of professional responsibility. That approach has two characteristics. First, in a rhetorical flourish, the profession is committed in general terms to all that is good and true. Then, specific questions are answered by uncritical reliance upon legalistic norms, regardless of the context in which the lawyer may be acting, and regardless of the motive and the consequences of the act. Perjury is wrong, and therefore no lawyer, in any circumstance, should knowingly present perjury. Cross-examination, however, is good, and therefore any lawyer, under any circumstances and regardless of the consequences, can properly impeach a witness through cross-examination. The system of professional responsibility that I have been advancing, on the other hand, is one that attempts to deal with ethical problems in context—that is, as part of a functional sociopolitical system concerned with the administration of justice in a free society—and giving due regard both to motive and to consequences. In that respect, the debate returns us to some fundamental philosophical questions that have not been adequately developed in the literature of professional responsibility. . . .

One of the major flaws in the traditional approach to legal ethics is that it seeks to answer the difficult questions in a legalistic fashion at the personal level, but begs completely the critical questions raised at the systemic level. Thus, if you say to a lawyer: "Lawyers are under a moral duty not to participate in the presentation of perjury, and therefore you are required to act in a way contrary to your client's interest if the client insists upon committing perjury," the lawyer is entitled to respond: "Let us consider your maxim. If it is embodied into the system as a universal law to be applied to all lawyers in all circumstances, would the maxim destroy itself and be destructive of the system?"

As we have seen [previously], the system requires the attorney to know everything that the client knows that is relevant to the case. In order to enable the lawyer to obtain that information, the system provides for an obligation of confidentiality, designed to protect the client from being prejudiced by disclosures to the attorney. In addition, the attorney is required to impress upon the client the obligation of confidentiality in order to induce the client to confide freely and fully.

Let us return, then, to the case involving the street robbery at 16th and P Streets, in which the defendant has been wrongly identified as the criminal, but correctly identified by the nervous, elderly woman who wears eyeglasses, as having been only a block away five minutes before the crime took place. If the woman is not cross-examined vigorously and her testimony shaken, it will serve to corroborate the erroneous evidence of guilt. On the other hand, the lawyer could take the position that since the woman is testifying truthfully and accurately, she should not be made to appear to be mistaken or lying. But if a similar course were to be adopted by every lawyer who learned the truth through confidential disclosures from the client, such disclosures would soon cease to be made. The result, for practical purposes, would be identical with the practice, disapproved in the ABA Standards, of "selective ignorance," in which the client is warned not to reveal to the lawyer anything that might prove embarrassing and prevent the lawyer from doing a vigorous job of presenting evidence and cross-examining. Of course, if that is the result we want, it would be far better that lawyers take a direct and honest approach with their clients, telling them to be less than candid, rather than lying to their clients by impressing upon them a bond of trust that the lawyers do not intend to maintain. Thus, when we examine the problem in a systemic context, we reach the conclusion . . . supporting cross-examination of the prosecutrix in the rape case.

Obviously, however, the rape case is a much harder one, because the injury done to the prosecutrix is far more severe than the more limited humiliation of the public-spirited and truthful witness in the case of the street robbery. In addition, in the rape case, the lawyer is acting pursuant to a manifestly irrational rule, that is, one that permits the defense to argue that the prosecutrix is the kind of person who would have sexual intercourse with a stranger because she has had sexual relations with two men whom she knew in wholly different social circumstances. Irrational or not, however, in those jurisdictions in which the defense of unchastity is still the law, the attorney is bound to provide it on the client's behalf. For the lawyer who finds the presentation of that defense, and perhaps others in rape cases, to go beyond what he or she can in good conscience do, there are two courses that should be followed. The first is to be active in efforts to reform the law in that regard; the second is to decline to accept the defense of rape cases, on the grounds of a conflict of interest (a strong personal view) that would interfere with providing the defendant with his constitutional rights to effective assistance of counsel.

REVIEW AND DISCUSSION QUESTIONS

1. What moral and professional conflict is raised by the Lake Pleasant, buried-bodies case? Explain how Freedman appeals to our adversarial system to defend confidentiality. What are the limits to what an attorney may do to assist a client? How does the *Ryder* case differ from the Lake Pleasant case?

2. What does Freedman mean by the "lawyer's trilemma"? Why does he criticize the treatment of the issue by the American Bar Association (ABA) Standards?

3. Should an attorney allow a client to present perjured testimony to the court? Is the Canadian Bar Association's rule an improvement over the system that Freedman defends?

4. How ought an attorney handle the cross-examination of the truthful witness?

5. Does Freedman's defense of the adversary system tip the balance too much in favor of criminal defendants?

6. Freedman discusses criminal cases, but our society also uses an adversary system for handling civil cases. To what extent can Freedman's arguments be used to defend zealous advocacy and aggressive legal tactics in civil cases?

Building Power and Breaking Images: Critical Legal Theory and the Practice of Law

Peter Gabel and Paul Harris

In this essay Gabel and Harris explore a model of legal practice radically at odds with the traditional one. Rather than protecting rights, they argue, the current legal system is more accurately understood if seen simply as part of a structure designed to maintain power and prevent serious social change. Using two famous cases as illustrations, the authors describe an alternative approach to legal practice that would politicize legal cases and empower those who are normally made powerless under the current legal system.

INTRODUCTION

In this essay we present [an] optimistic approach to radical law practice that is based on a view of the legal system different from . . . both the orthodox Marxist view that the law is simply a "tool of the ruling class" and the liberal-legalist view that powerless groups in society can gradually improve their position by getting more rights. Instead we argue that the legal system is an important public arena through which the State attempts—through manipulation of symbols, images, and ideas—to legitimize a social order that most people find alienating and inhumane. Our objective is to show the way that the legal system works at many different levels to shape popular consciousness toward accepting the political legitimacy of the status quo, and to outline the ways that lawyers can effectively resist these efforts in building a movement for fundamental social change. Our basic claim is that the very public and political character of the legal arena gives lawyers, acting together with clients and fellow legal workers, an important opportunity to reshape the way that people understand the existing social order and their place within it. . . .

1. A POWER-ORIENTED APPROACH TO LAW PRACTICE

A first principle of a "counter-hegemonic" legal practice must be to subordinate the goal of getting people their rights to the goal of building an authentic or unalienated political consciousness. This obviously does not mean that one should not try to win one's cases; nor does it necessarily mean that we should not continue to organize groups by appealing to rights. But the great weakness of a rights-oriented legal practice is that it does not address itself to a central precondition for building a sustained political movement—that of overcoming the psychological conditions upon which both the power of the legal system and the power of social hierarchy in general rest. In fact an excessive preoccupation with "rights-consciousness" tends in the long run to reinforce alienation and powerlessness, because the appeal to rights inherently affirms that the source of social power resides in the State rather than in the people themselves. . . .

A legal strategy that goes beyond rights-consciousness is one that focuses upon expanding political consciousness through using the legal system to increase people's sense of personal and political power. This can mean many different things depending upon the political visibility of any given case and the specific social and legal context within which a case arises. But in any context, a "power" rather than a "rights" approach to law practice should be guided by three general objectives that are as applicable to minor personal injury cases as to major cases involving important social issues. First, the lawyer should seek to develop a relationship of genuine equality and mutual respect with her client. Second, the lawyer should conduct herself in a way that demystifies the symbolic authority of the State as this authority is embodied in, for example, the flag, the robed judge, and the ritualized

professional technicality of the legal proceeding. Third, the lawyer should always attempt to reshape the way legal conflicts are represented in the law, revealing the limiting character of legal ideology and bringing out the true socio-economic and political foundations of legal disputes. Reaching these objectives may have a transformative impact not only upon the lawyer and client working in concert, but also upon others who come into contact with the case, including the client's friends and family, courtroom participants such as jurors, stenographers, and public observers, and, in some cases, thousands or even millions of people who follow high-visibility political cases through the media. Of course, any particular lawyer's action in a single case cannot lead to the development of an anti-hierarchical social movement; we believe, however, that if lawyers as a group begin to organize themselves around the realization of these goals, their impact on the culture as a whole can be much greater than they currently believe is possible. . . .

If one looks at the institutions of the legal system from a power-oriented rather than a rights-oriented perspective, the very nature of these institutions takes on a different appearance from that portrayed in the conventional model. Instead of seeing the judiciary, for example, as an integrated hierarchy of trial and appellate courts organized for the purpose of establishing the proper scope of procedural and substantive rights, one sees diverse locuses of state power that are organized for the purpose of maintaining alienation and powerlessness. In this perspective the lower state courts, for example, are designed primarily to provide administrative control over the minor disturbances of everyday life in local communities in order to maintain social order at the local level. It is for this reason that lower court judges are often indifferent to the intricacies of legal doctrine and are more concerned with the efficient management of high-volume court calendars through plea-bargaining and the informal mediation of civil disputes. One might say that at this level the manifestation of restrained force and symbolic authority is much more important than legal ideology as such, and an excessive

Luis." Earlier in the trial, Garcia had reacted violently to the judge's decision to disallow testimony about the emotional trauma of rape. She leaped up from the counsel table and said: "Why don't you just find me guilty? Just send me to jail. . . . I killed the fucking guy because he raped me!" Obviously, after that, the jury could not accept the attempted portrayal of Garcia as a demure and innocent woman who was so overcome that she could not be held responsible for her acts.

Garcia's conviction was reversed on appeal because of an improper jury instruction. In the retrial she was represented by radical-feminist attorney Susan Jordan. The defense was a creative combination of the traditional rules of self-defense and the historical reality of the victimization of women by men. The task Jordan faced was to translate the male-oriented rule of self-defense into a form that would capture the real experience of a woman facing possible attack by a man. She also had to combat, within the confines of the courtroom, the sexist myths that would influence the jurors.

The rule of self-defense is based on one's right to use reasonable force if, and only if, one reasonably perceives that there will be an imminent attack. The heart of the defense is the defendant's state of mind—it is necessary to convince a jury that the defendant acted in a reasonable manner given the circumstances.

In Garcia's situation, the juror's understanding of whether Garcia acted "reasonably" would almost certainly be influenced by cultural myths about the act of rape. The rape myths are that women invite it, that they encourage it, and they like it, and that ultimately the rape is their own fault. Jordan directly confronted these stereotypes by the creative use of voir dire. The jurors were questioned individually, one by one in the judge's chambers. Each juror was asked questions which were designed to bring out any underlying sexist stereotypes. Although this was a painful process, initially opposed by the judge, and irritating to some jurors, the process paid off. The final jury of ten men and two women was able to view the rape not as a sexual act caused by male-female flirting, but rather as a violent assault. This view of rape as an act of violence was key to the acceptance of the self-defense theory.

Jordan also faced the problem of Garcia's obvious anger at the men who raped her. If this anger was viewed by the jury as the motive for her shooting, then it would negate self-defense and lead to a verdict of manslaughter. The defense, therefore, attempted to show that the anger was a justified and reasonable response to her rape. Expert witnesses testified to the psychological effects of rape, especially a rape committed on a latina, Catholic woman. Instead of the traditional tactic of trying to hide the woman's anger, the defense affirmed this anger and explained it in human terms which broke through the male prejudices embodied in the law's traditional view of the reasonable person. The result was a complete acquittal.

The two trials of Inez Garcia demonstrate that in the right circumstances it is possible to win a case with a political approach when a more conventional legal approach would fail. Inez Garcia took the action that she did at a time when the women's movement was actively challenging the forms of patriarchal domination characteristic of man-woman relations throughout the social structure, and the central symbol of this domination was the act of forcible rape itself. With a male attorney in her first trial in effect apologizing for her action and the anger that produced it, Garcia was separated from the movement supporting her, and indeed from her own self. In pleading "impaired consciousness" she was forced to deny the legitimacy of her own action and simultaneously the legitimacy of the "unreasonable" rage that women throughout the country were expressing in response to their social powerlessness in relation to men. The form of the first trial turned Garcia into an isolated object of the legal system, a mere "defendant" requesting mercy from a "masculine" legal structure. Even a victory in the first trial would have had negative political consequences because it would have affirmed the wrongness of both her action and the feeling that provoked it, while legitimizing the authority of a benevolent State.

The most important feature of the second trial was that it reversed the power relations upon which the first trial was premised. The defense both affirmed the validity of Garcia's action, and allowed Jordan to join Garcia as co-advocate for a vast popular movement, to speak to the jury not as a State-licensed technician "representing" an abstract "defendant," but as a woman standing together with another woman. Together, the two women were able to put the act of rape itself on trial and to address the jurors, not as "jurors" but as human beings, about the meaning of being a woman in contemporary society. The effect of this was to transform the courtroom into a popular tribunal and to divest the prosecutor and the judge (who, as men, could not abstract themselves entirely from the evident signs of their own gender) of some of the symbolic authority upon which the legitimacy of the "legal form" of the proceeding depended. This shift in the vectors of power within the room also allowed the jurors to escape their own reification, to discover themselves as politically responsible for making a human, rather than a merely formal, decision based on an application of existing law. Thus the conduct of the second trial, coupled with the widespread publicity attendant to it, served to expand the power of the movement from which the political basis of the case derived, and to delegitimate the apparent necessity of existing legal consciousness. This last point deserves special emphasis, for breaking through the sedimented authoritarian forms of a legal proceeding in an overtly political case has radical implications beyond those of the particular case itself: it signifies that the existing order is *merely possible*, and that people have the freedom and power to act upon it. In the special context of a public trial, such action demonstrates the living disintegration of symbolic State power in a heavily ritualized setting, one that is normally a principal medium for the transmission of authoritarian imagery.

REVIEW AND DISCUSSION QUESTIONS

1. Describe the "rights" approach to legal practice, and then indicate why the authors think it is inadequate.

2. Compare the authors' understanding of the judiciary with the "rights-oriented" perspective.

3. What are the strategies the authors suggest to implement the "power-oriented" approach to legal practice?

4. How did the lawyers in the Chicago Eight and Inez Garcia trials exemplify the authors' approach?

5. Describe Monroe Freedman's approach to legal practice, and then compare it with the one advocated by Gabel and Harris. To what extent can the differences between Freedman's and these authors' approaches be traced to their different attitudes toward the U.S. political system?

6. Suppose a client wants to plea bargain rather than run the risks of being found guilty at trial, or does not share the lawyer's political commitment. What would these authors say about such a situation? What would Freedman say?

The Lawyer as Friend

Charles Fried

In this well-known essay, Harvard law professor Charles Fried begins with a discussion of two familiar criticisms of the adversary system: that it wastes resources and that it requires (or at least allows) lawyers to perform actions that are dangerous or costly to society. Fried then weighs the utilitarian claim that in fact it is always wrong to favor the interests of those close to us, such as family and friends. He contends, rather, that both one's sense of self and individual liberty support the conclusion that we are not obligated to maximize our own happiness but instead should often pay special attention to the well-being of family and friends. He concludes by arguing that the lawyer-client relationship closely resembles that of a "special purpose" friend, and that by maintaining the friendship, the lawyer helps the client preserve and protect his or her autonomy.

Advocatus sed non ladro, Res miranda populo. . . .

Medieval anthem honoring St. Ives

I. THE CHALLENGE TO THE TRADITIONAL CONCEPTION

A. THE TWO CRITICISMS

Two frequent criticisms of the traditional conception of the lawyer's role attack both its ends and its means. First, it is said that the ideal of professional loyalty to one's client permits, even demands, an allocation of the lawyer's time, passion, and resources in ways that are not always maximally conducive to the greatest good of the greatest number. Interestingly, this criticism is leveled increasingly against doctors as well as lawyers. Both professions affirm the principle that the professional's primary loyalty is to his client, his patient. A "good" lawyer will lavish energy and resources on his existing client, even if it can be shown that others could derive greater benefit from them. The professional ideal authorizes a care for the client and the patient which exceeds what the efficient distribution of a scarce social resource (the professional's time) would dictate.

That same professional ideal has little or nothing to say about the initial choice of clients or patients. Certainly it is laudable if the doctor and lawyer choose their clients among the poorest or sickest or most dramatically threatened, but the professional ideal does not require this kind of choice in any systematic way—the choice of client remains largely a matter of fortuity or arbitrary choice. But once the client has been chosen, the professional ideal requires primary loyalty to the client whatever his need or situation. Critics contend that it is wasteful and immoral that some of the finest talent in the legal profession is devoted to the intricacies of, say,

corporate finance or elaborate estate plans, while important public and private needs for legal services go unmet. The immorality of this waste is seen to be compounded when the clients who are the beneficiaries of this lavish attention use it to avoid their obligations in justice (if not in law) to society and to perpetuate their (legal) domination of the very groups whose greater needs these lawyers should be meeting.

The second criticism applies particularly to the lawyer. It addresses not the misallocation of scarce resources, which the lawyer's exclusive concern with his client's interests permits, but the means which this loyalty appears to authorize, tactics which procure advantages for the client at the direct expense of some identified opposing party. Examples are discrediting a nervous but probably truthful complaining witness[1] or taking advantage of the need or ignorance of an adversary in a negotiation. This second criticism is, of course, related to the first, but there is a difference. The first criticism focuses on a social harm: the waste of scarce resources implicit in a doctor caring for the hearts of the sedentary managerial classes or a lawyer tending to the estates and marital difficulties of the rich. The professional is accused of failing to confer benefits wisely and efficiently. By the second criticism the lawyer is accused not of failing to benefit the appropriate, though usually unidentified, persons, but of harming his identified adversary.

B. EXAMPLES

Consider a number of cases which illustrate the first criticism: A doctor is said to owe a duty of loyalty to his patient, but how is he to react if doing his very best for his patient would deplete the resources of the patient's family, as in the case of a severely deformed baby who can only be kept alive through extraordinarily expensive means? Should a doctor prescribe every test of distinct but marginal utility for every patient on public assistance, even if he knows that in the aggregate such a policy will put the medical care system under intolerable burdens? Should he subject his patients to prudent testing of new remedies because he knows that only in this way can medicine make the strides that it has in the past?

These problems are analogous to problems which are faced by the lawyer. The lawyer who advises a client how to avoid the effects of a tax or a form of regulation, though it is a fair tax or a regulation in the public interest, is facing the same dilemma and resolving it in favor of his client. So does the public defender who accedes to his client's demands and takes a "losing" case to trial, thereby wasting court time and depleting the limited resources of his organization. We tolerate and indeed may applaud the decision of a lawyer who vigorously defends a criminal whom he believes to be guilty and dangerous.[2] And I for one think that a lawyer who arranges the estate of a disagreeable dowager or represents one of the parties in a bitter matrimonial dispute must be as assiduous and single-minded in fulfilling his obligation to that client as the lawyer who is defending the civil liberties case of the century.

Illustrative of the second criticism (doing things which are offensive to a particular person) are familiar situations such as the following: In a negotiation it becomes clear to the lawyer for the seller that the buyer and his lawyer mistakenly believe that somebody else has already offered a handsome price for the property. The buyer asks the seller if this is true, and the seller's lawyer hears his client give an ambiguous but clearly encouraging response. Another classic case is the interposition of a technical defense such as the running of the statute of limitations to defeat a debt that the client admits he owes.

There is another class of cases which does not so unambiguously involve the lawyer's furthering his client's interests at the direct expense of some equally identified, concrete individual, but where furthering those interests does require the lawyer to do things which are personally offensive to him. The conventional paradigms in the casuistic literature deal with criminal defense lawyers who are asked improper questions by the trial judge ("Your client doesn't have a criminal record, does he?" or "Your client hasn't offered to plead guilty to a lesser offense, has he?"), a truthful answer to which would be damningly prejudicial to the client, but [to] which the lawyer must lie in defense of his client's interests even though lying is personally and professionally offensive to him. The defense lawyer who cross-examines a complaining rape victim (whom he knows to be telling the truth) about her chastity or lack thereof in order to discredit her accusing testimony faces a similar moral difficulty. In some respects these cases might be taken to illustrate both principal criticisms of the traditional conception. On the one hand, there is harm to society in making the choice to favor the client's interests: a dangerous criminal may escape punishment or an appropriately heavy sentence. On the other hand, this social harm is accomplished by means of acting towards another human being—the judge, the complaining witness—in ways that seem demeaning and dishonorable.

II. THE LAWYER AS FRIEND

A. THE THESIS

In this essay I will consider the moral status of the traditional conception of the professional. The two criticisms of this traditional conception, if left unanswered, will not put the lawyer in jail, but they will leave him without a moral basis for his acts. The real question is whether, in the face of these two criticisms, a decent and morally sensitive person can conduct himself according to the traditional conception of professional loyalty and still believe that what he is doing is morally worthwhile.

It might be said that any one whose conscience is so tender that he cannot fulfill the prescribed obligations of a professional should not undertake those obligations. He should not allow his moral scruples to operate as a trap for those who are told by the law that they may expect something more. But of course this suggestion merely pushes the inquiry back a step. We must ask then not how a decent lawyer may behave, but whether a decent, ethical person can ever be a lawyer. Are the assurances implicit in assuming the role of lawyer such that an honorable person would not give them and thus would not enter the profession? And, indeed, this is a general point about an argument from obligation: It may be that the internal logic of a particular obligation demands certain forms of conduct (e.g., honor among thieves), but the question remains whether it is just and moral to contract such obligations.

I will argue in this essay that it is not only legally but also morally right that a lawyer adopt as his dominant purpose the furthering of his client's interests—that it is right that a professional put the interests of his client above some idea, however valid, of the collective interest. I maintain that the traditional conception of the professional role expresses a morally valid conception of human conduct and human relationships, that one who acts according to that conception is to that extent a good person. Indeed, it is my view that, far from being a mere creature of positive law, the traditional conception is so far mandated by moral right that any advanced legal system which did not sanction this conception would be unjust.

The general problem raised by the two criticisms is this: How can it be that it is not only permissible, but indeed morally right, to favor the interests of a particular person in a way which we can be fairly sure is either harmful to another particular individual or not maximally conducive to the welfare of society as a whole?

The resolution of this problem is aided, I think, if set in a larger perspective. Charles Curtis made the perspicacious remark that a lawyer may be privileged to lie for his client in a way that one might lie to save one's friends or close relatives. I do not want to underwrite the notion that it is justifiable to lie even in those situations, but there is a great deal to the point that in those relations—friendship, kinship—we recognize an authorization to take the interests of particular concrete persons more seriously and to give them priority over the interests of the wider collectivity. One who provides an expensive education for his own children surely cannot be blamed because he does not use those resources to alleviate famine or to save lives in some distant land. Nor does he blame himself. Indeed, our intuition that an individual is authorized to prefer identified persons standing close to him over the abstract interests of humanity finds its sharpest expression in our sense that an individual is entitled to act with something less than impartiality to that person who stands closest to him—the person that he is. There is such a thing as selfishness to be sure, yet no reasonable morality asks us to look upon ourselves as merely plausible candidates for the distribution of the attention and resources which we command, plausible candidates whose entitlement to our own concern is no greater in principle than that of any other human being. Such a doctrine may seem edifying, but on reflection it strikes us as merely fanatical.

This suggests an interesting way to look at the situation of the lawyer. As a professional person one has a special care for the interests of those accepted as clients, just as his friends, his family, and he himself have a very general claim to his special concern. But I concede this does no more than widen the problem. It merely shows that in claiming this authorization to have a special care for my clients I am doing something which I do in other contexts as well.

B. The Utilitarian Explanation

I consider first an argument to account for fidelity to role, for obligation, made most elaborately by the classical utilitarians, Mill and Sidgwick. They argued that our propensity to prefer the interests of those who are close to us is in fact perfectly reasonable because we are more likely to be able to benefit those people. Thus, if everyone is mainly concerned with those closest to him, the distribution of social energies will be most efficient and the greatest good of the greatest number will be achieved. The idea is that the efforts I expend for my friend or my relative are more likely to be effective because I am more likely to know what needs to be done. I am more likely to be sure that the good I intend is in fact accomplished.

One might say that there is less overhead, fewer administrative costs, in benefiting those nearest to us. I would not want to ridicule this argument, but it does not seem to me to go far enough. Because if that were the sole basis for the preference, then it would be my duty to determine whether my efforts might not be more efficiently spent on the collectivity, on the distant, anonymous beneficiary. But it is just my point that *this* is an inquiry we are not required, indeed sometimes not even authorized, to make. When we decide to care for our children, to assure our own comforts, to fulfill our obligations to our clients or patients, we do not do so as a result of a cost-benefit inquiry which takes into account the ease of producing a good result for our friends and relations.

Might it not be said, however, that the best means of favoring the abstract collectivity is in certain cases not to try to favor it directly but to concentrate on those to whom one has a special relation? This does not involve tricking oneself, but only recognizing the limitations of what an individual can do and know. But that, it seems to me, is just Mill's and Sidgwick's argument all over again. There is no trickery involved, but this is still a kind of deliberate limitation of our moral horizon which leaves us uncomfortable. Do I know in a particular case whether sticking to the narrow definition of my role will *in that case* further the good of all? If I know that it will not further the general good, then why am I acting as the role demands? Is it to avoid setting a bad example? But for whom? I need not tell others—whether I tell or not could enter into my calculation. For myself then? But that begs the question, since if short-circuiting the role-definition of my obligation and going straight for the general good is the best thing to do in that case, then the example I set myself is not a bad example, but a good example. In short, I do not see how one can at the same time admit that the general good is one's only moral standard, while steadfastly hewing to obligations to friends, family, and clients. What we must look for is an argument which shows that giving some degree of special consideration to myself, my friends, my clients is not merely instrumentally justified (as the utilitarians would argue) but to some degree intrinsically so.

I think such an argument can be made. Instead of speaking the language of maximization of value over all of humanity, it will speak the language of rights. The stubborn ethical datum affirming such a preference grows out of the profoundest springs of morality: the concepts of personality, identity, and liberty.

C. Self, Friendship, and Justice

Consider for a moment the picture of the human person that would emerge if the utilitarian claim were in fact correct. It would mean that in all my choices I must consider the well-being of all humanity—actual and potential—as the range of my concern. Moreover, every actual or potential human being is absolutely equal in his claims upon me. Indeed, I myself am to myself only as one of this innumerable multitude. And that is the clue to what is wrong with the utilitarian vision. Before there is morality there must be the person. We must attain and maintain in our morality a concept of personality such that it makes sense to posit choosing, valuing entities—free, moral beings. But the picture of the moral universe in which my own interests disappear and are merged into the interests of the totality of humanity is incompatible with that, because one wishes to develop a conception of a responsible, valuable, and valuing agent, and such an agent must first of all be dear to himself. It is from the kernal of individuality that the other things we value radiate. The Gospel says we must love our neighbor as ourselves and this implies that any concern for others which is a *human* concern must presuppose a concern for ourselves. The human concern which we then show others is a concern which first of all recognizes the concrete individuality of that other person just as we recognize our own.

It might be objected that the picture I sketch does not show that each individual, in order to maintain the integral sense of himself as an individual, is justified in attributing a greater value to his most essential interests than he ascribes to the most essential interests of all other persons. Should not the individual generalize and attribute in equal degree to all persons the value which he naturally attributes to himself? I agree with those who hold that it is the essence of morality for reason to push us beyond inclination to the fair conclusion of our premises. It *is* fair conclusion that as my experience as a judging, valuing, choosing entity is crucial to me, I must also conclude that for other persons their own lives and desires are the center of their universe. If morality is transcendent, it must somehow transcend particularity to take account of this general fact. I do not wish to deny this. On the contrary, my claim is that the kind of preference which an individual gives himself and concrete others is a preference which he would in exactly this universalizing spirit allow others to exhibit as well. It is not that I callously overlook the claim of the abstract individual, but indeed I would understand and approve were I myself to be prejudiced because some person to whom I stood in a similar situation of abstraction preferred his own concrete dimensions.

Finally, the concreteness which is the starting point of my own moral sensibility, the sense of myself, is not just a historical, biographical fact. It continues to enter into and condition my moral judgments because the effects which I can produce upon people who are close to me are qualitatively different from those produced upon abstract, unknown persons. My own concreteness is important not only because it establishes a basis for understanding what I and what all other human beings might be, but because in engaging that aspect of myself with the concrete aspects of others, I realize special values for both of us. Quite simply, the individualized relations of love and friendship (and perhaps also their opposites, hatred and enmity) have a different, more intense aspect than do the cooler, more abstract relations of love and service to humanity in general. The impulse I describe, therefore, is not in any sense a selfish impulse. But it does begin with the sense of self as a concrete entity. Those who object to my thesis by saying that we must generalize it are not wholly wrong; they merely exaggerate. Truly I must be ready to generalize outward all the way. That is what justice consists of. But justice is not all of morality; there remains a circle of intensity which through its emphasis on the particular and the concrete continues to reflect what I have identified as the source of all sense of value—our sense of self.

Therefore, it is not only consonant with, but also required by, an ethics for human beings that one be entitled first of all to reserve an area of concern for oneself and then to move out freely from that area if one wishes to lavish that concern on others to whom one stands in concrete, personal relations. Similarly, a person is entitled to enjoy this extra measure of care from those who choose to bestow it upon him without having to justify this grace as either just or efficient. We may choose the individuals to whom we will stand in this special relation, or they may be thrust upon us, as in family ties. Perhaps we recognize family ties because, after all, there often has been an element of choice, but also because—by some kind of atavism or superstition—we identify with those who share a part of our biological natures.

In explicating the lawyer's relation to his client, my analogy shall be a friendship, where the freedom to choose and to be chosen expresses our freedom to hold something of ourselves in reserve, in reserve even from the universalizing claims of morality. These personal ties and the claims they engender may be all-consuming, as with a close friend or family member, or they may be limited, special-purpose claims, as in the case of the client or patient. The special-purpose claim is one in which the beneficiary, the client, is entitled to all the special consideration *within* the limits of the relationship which we accord to a friend or a loved one. It is not that the claims of the client are less intense or demanding; they are only more limited in their scope. After all, the ordinary concept of friendship provides only an analogy, and it is to the development of that analogy that I turn.

D. SPECIAL-PURPOSE FRIENDS

How does a professional fit into the concept of personal relations at all? He is, I have suggested, a limited-purpose friend. A lawyer is a friend in regard to the legal system. He is someone who enters into a personal relation with you—not an abstract relation as under the concept of justice. That means that like a friend he acts in your interests, not his own; or rather he adopts your interests as his own. I would call that the classic definition of friendship. To be sure, the lawyer's range of concern is sharply limited. But within that limited domain the intensity of identification with the client's interests is the same. It is not the specialized focus of the relationship which may make the metaphor inapposite, but the way in which the relation of legal friendship comes about and the one-sided nature of the ensuing "friendship." But I do insist upon the analogy, for in overcoming the arguments that the analogy is false, I think the true moral foundations of the lawyer's special role are illuminated and the utilitarian objections to the traditional conception of that role overthrown.

1. The Professional Role as Socially Defined: The Content of the Relation. The claims that are made on the doctor or lawyer are made within a social context and are defined, at least in part, by social expectations. Most strikingly, in talking about friendship the focus of the inquiry is quite naturally upon the free gift of the donor; yet in professional relationships it is the recipient's need for medical or legal aid which defines the relationship. So the source of the relationship seems to be located at the other end, that of the recipient. To put this disquiet another way, we might ask how recognizing the special claims of friendship in any way compels society to allow the doctor or the lawyer to define his role on the analogy of those claims. Why are these people not like other social actors designated to purvey certain, perhaps necessary, goods? Would we say that one's grocer, tailor, or landlord should be viewed as a limited-purpose friend? Special considerations must be brought forward for doctors and lawyers.

A special argument is at hand in both cases. The doctor does not minister just to any need, but to health. He helps maintain the very physical integrity which is the concrete substrate of individuality. To be sure, so does a grocer or landlord. But illness wears a special guise: it appears as a critical assault on one's person. The needs to which the doctor ministers usually are implicated in crises going to one's concreteness and individuality, and therefore what one looks for is a kind of ministration which is particularly concrete, personal, individualized. Thus, it is not difficult to see why I claim that a doctor is a friend, though a special purpose friend, the purpose being defined by the special needs of illness and crisis to which he tends.

But what, then, of the lawyer? Friendship and kinship are natural relations existing within, but not declined by, complex social institutions. Illness too is more a natural than social phenomenon. The response here requires an additional step. True, the special situations—legal relations or disputes—in which the lawyer acts as a limited-purpose friend are themselves a product of social institutions. But it does not follow that the role of the lawyer, which is created to help us deal with those social institutions, is defined by and is wholly at the mercy of the social good. We need only concede that at the very least the law must leave us a measure of autonomy, whether or not it is in the social interest to do so. Individuals have rights over and against the collectivity. The moral capital arising out of individuals' concrete situations is one way of expressing that structure of rights, or at least part of it. It is because the law must respect the rights of individuals that the law must also create and support the specific role of legal friend. For the social nexus—the web of perhaps entirely just institutions—has become so complex that without the assistance of an expert adviser an ordinary layman cannot exercise that autonomy which the system must allow him. Without such an adviser, the law would impose constraints on the lay citizen (unequally at that) which it is not entitled to impose explicitly. Thus, the need which the lawyer serves in his special-purpose friendship may not be, as in the case of the doctor, natural, pre-social. Yet it is a need which has a moral grounding analogous to the need which the physician serves: the need to maintain one's integrity as a person. When I say the lawyer is his client's legal friend, I mean the lawyer makes the client's interests his own insofar as this is necessary to preserve and foster the client's autonomy within the law. This argument does not require us to assume that the law is hostile to the client's rights. All we need to assume is that even a system of law which is perfectly sensitive to personal rights would not work fairly unless the client could claim a professional's assistance in realizing that autonomy which the law recognizes.

2. The Asymmetry of Motive and Duty: The Form of the Relation.

The institutional origin of the lawyer-client relationship is not its only characteristic which suggests that the analogy to natural friendship is vulnerable. In natural friendship the ideal relation is reciprocal; in legal friendship it is not. The lawyer is said to be the client's friend insofar as he is devoted to his client's interests, but it is no part of the ideal that the client should have any reciprocal devotion to the interests of his lawyer. Furthermore, I have argued that our right to be a friend to whomever we choose is a product of our individual autonomy. But in legal friendship the emphasis has been on the autonomy of the client, and it is the client who chooses the lawyer; yet it is the lawyer who acts as a friend in the relation. And as a final contrast to natural friendship, the usual motive for agreeing or refusing to provide legal services is money. Indeed, when we speak of the lawyer's right to represent whomever he wishes, we are usually defending his moral title to represent whoever pays.

But recall that the concept of legal friendship was introduced to answer the argument that the lawyer is morally reprehensible to the extent that he lavishes undue concern on some particular person. The concept of friendship explains how it can be that a particular person may rightfully receive more than his share of care from another: he can receive that care if he receives it as an act of friendship. Although in natural friendship I emphasized the freedom to bestow, surely that freedom must imply a freedom to receive that extra measure of care. And it is the right of the client to receive such an extra measure of care (without regard, that is, to considerations of efficiency or fairness) as much as the lawyer's right to give it, that I have been trying to explicate. Thus, the fact that the care in legal friendship systematically runs all one way does not impair the argument.

Yet the unease persists. Is it that while I have shown that the lawyer has a right to help the "unworthy" client, I have not shown that whenever the lawyer exercises this right he does something which is morally worthy, entitling him to self-respect? I may have shown that the law is obliged to allow the "unworthy" client to seek legal help and the lawyer to give it. But have I also shown that every lawyer who avails himself of this legal right (his and the client's legal right) performs a *morally worthy* function? Can a good lawyer be a good person?

The lawyer acts morally because he helps to preserve and express the autonomy of his client vis-à-vis the legal system. It is not just that the lawyer helps his client accomplish a particular lawful purpose. Pornography may be legal, but it hardly follows that I perform a morally worthy function if I lend money or artistic talent to help the pornographer flourish in the exercise of this right. What is special about legal counsel is that whatever else may stop the pornographer's enterprise, he should not be stopped because he mistakenly believes there is a legal impediment. There is no wrong if a venture fails for lack of talent or lack of money—no one's rights have been violated. But rights *are* violated if, through ignorance or misinformation about the law, an individual refrains from pursuing a wholly lawful purpose. Therefore, to assist others in understanding and realizing their legal rights is always morally worthy. Moreover, the legal system, by instituting the role of the legal friend, not only assures what it in justice must—the due liberty of each citizen before the law—but does it by creating an institution which exemplifies, at least in a unilateral sense, the ideal of personal relations of trust and personal care which (as in natural friendship) are good in themselves.

Perhaps the unease has another source. The lawyer does work for pay. Is there not something odd about analogizing the lawyer's role to friendship when in fact his so-called friendship must usually be bought? If the lawyer is a public purveyor of goods, is not the lawyer–client relationship like that underlying any commercial transaction? My answer is "No." The lawyer and doctor have obligations to the client or patient beyond those of other economic agents. A grocer may refuse to give food to a customer when it becomes apparent that the customer does not have the money to pay for it. But the lawyer and doctor may not refuse to give additional care to an individual who cannot pay for it if withdrawal of their services would prejudice that individual. Their duty to the client or patient to whom they have made an initial commitment transcends the conventional quid pro quo of the marketplace. It is undeniable that money is usually what cements the lawyer–client relationship. But the content of the relation is determined by the client's needs, just as friendship is a response to another's needs. It is not determined, as are simple economic relationships, by the mere coincidence of a willingness to sell and a willingness to buy. So the fact that the lawyer works for pay does not seriously undermine the friendship analogy.

* * *

CONCLUSION

I do not imagine that what I have said provides an algorithm for resolving some of these perennial difficulties. Rather, what I am proposing is a general way of looking at the problem, a way of understanding not so much the difficult borderline cases as the central and clear ones, in the hope that the principles we can there discern will illuminate our necessarily approximate and prudential quest for resolution on the borderline. The notion of the lawyer as the client's legal friend, whatever its limitations and difficulties, does account for a kind of callousness toward society and exclusivity in the service of the client which otherwise seem quite mysterious. It justifies a kind of scheming which we would deplore on the part of a lay person dealing with another lay person—even if he were acting on behalf of a friend.

But these special indulgences apply only as a lawyer assists his client in his legal business. I do not owe my client my political assistance. I do not have to espouse his cause when I act as a citizen. Indeed, it is one of the most repellent features of the American legal profession—one against which the barrister–solicitor split has to some extent guarded the English profession—that many lawyers really feel that they are totally bought by their clients, that they must identify

with their clients' interests far beyond the special purpose of advising them and operating the legal system for them. The defendants' antitrust lawyer or defendants' food and drug lawyer who writes articles, gives speeches, and pontificates generally about the evils of regulation may believe these things, but too often he does so because it is good for business or because he thinks that such conduct is what good representation requires. In general, I think it deplorable that lawyers have specialized not only in terms of subject matter—that may or may not be a good thing—but in terms of plaintiffs or defendants, in terms of the position that they represent.[3]

There is a related point which cuts very much in the opposite direction. It is no part of my thesis that the *client* is not morally bound to avoid lying to the court, to pay a just debt even though it is barred by the statute of limitations, to treat an opposite party in a negotiation with humanity and consideration for his needs and vulnerability, or to help the effectuation of policies aimed at the common good. Further, it is no part of my argument to hold that a lawyer must assume that the client is not a decent, moral person, has no desire to fulfill his moral obligations, and is asking only what is the minimum that he must do to stay within the law. On the contrary, to assume this about anyone is itself a form of immorality because it is a form of disrespect between persons. Thus in a very many situations a lawyer will be advising a client who wants to effectuate his purposes within the law, to be sure, but who also wants to behave as a decent, moral person. It would be absurd to contend that the lawyer must abstain from giving advice that takes account of the client's moral duties and his presumed desire to fulfill them. Indeed, in these situations the lawyer experiences the very special satisfaction of assisting the client not only to realize his autonomy within the law, but also to realize his status as a moral being. I want to make very clear that my conception of the lawyer's role in no way disentitles the lawyer from experiencing this satisfaction. Rather, it has been my purpose to explicate the less obvious point that there is a vocation and a satisfaction even in helping Shylock obtain his pound of flesh or in bringing about the acquittal of a guilty man.

Finally, I would like to return to the charge that the morality of role and personal relationship I offer here is almost certain to lead to the diversion of legal services from areas of greatest need. It is just my point, of course, that when we fulfill the office of friend—legal, medical, or friend *tout court*—we do right, and thus it would be a great wrong to place us under a general regime of always doing what will "do the most good." What I affirm, therefore, is the moral liberty of a lawyer to make his life out of what personal scraps and shards of motivation his inclination and character suggest: idealism, greed, curiosity, love of luxury, love of travel, a need for adventure or repose; only so long as these lead him to give wise and faithful counsel. It is the task of the social system as a whole, and of all its citizens, to work for the conditions under which everyone will benefit in fair measure from the performance of doctors, lawyers, teachers, and musicians. But I would not see the integrity of these roles undermined in order that the millennium might come sooner. After all, it may never come, and then what would we be left with?

NOTES

[1] For a defense of an attorney's use of such tactics, see Monroe H. Freedman, *Lawyers' Ethics in an Adversary System* 43–49 (1975). *See also* Curtis, "The Ethics of Advocacy," 4, *Stan L. Rev.* 3 (1951).

[2] *See* M. Freedman, *supra* note 1, at 43–49.

[3] In England barristers are regularly hired by the government in all manner of litigation, thereby accomplishing the many-sidedness I call for here. *See* Q. Johnstone and D. Hopson, *Lawyers and Their Work* 374–75 (1967). Why should this not be done in the United States? Perhaps there is fear that this might simply become the occasion for a suspect form of patronage.

REVIEW AND DISCUSSION QUESTIONS

1. Explain the two challenges to the traditional understanding of the role of the lawyer.

2. What is the "utilitarian explanation" of the idea of the lawyer as friend? Why does Fried reject it?

3. Explain the notion of a "special-purpose" friend, as opposed to the ordinary idea of friendship. Why does Fried say lawyers are justified in acting like special-purpose friends?

4. Explain whether or not you think Fried has answered the objections that are often raised against lawyers whose actions are wasteful and dangerous to society.

The Lost Lawyer

Anthony Kronman

In this selection from his book The Lost Lawyer, *Yale law professor Anthony Kronman discusses the role of lawyers and the quality of their lives. The successful life, he argues, is that of the "lawyer statesman," who exemplifies prudence or practical wisdom. But, because of changes in the legal profession, Kronman argues, that idea of the lawyer as statesman has been substantially undermined. After a brief discussion of the unique expertise lawyers bring to political and legal discussions, Kronman concludes by contrasting the ideal of the lawyer-statesman with the advocacy model and the public-spirited lawyer—neither of which, he contends, can provide the practitioner with the satisfying career of the lawyer-statesman.*

REALITIES

Suppose that someone you do not know asks for your advice at a moment of crisis in his life. Assuming you lack the time to get acquainted, what kind of advice can you give him? One possibility is simply to take as given his own statement of what he believes his present needs to be—however incomplete or contradictory that statement may appear—and then help him frame a plan for meeting these needs in the most efficient way. Alternatively, you can help him devise a strategy that makes sense whatever his interests may be, and whether, in particular, they are what he believes them to be or not: a strategy, for example, of delay, if it seems likely that matters will be clearer later on and there is little cost to waiting. There is one thing, however, that you are likely to find quite difficult to do, and that is to advise the person who has sought your help as to what his interests should be. For advice of this sort generally requires a more extensive knowledge of the person's character, habits, and history—the sort of knowledge that friends often have and that sometimes even makes it plausible for one friend to claim a better understanding of another's interests than that person himself possesses.

Something like this is also true of institutions, including the commercial ones that make up the clientele of most large law firms. It is, of course, a fiction to speak of the aims and interests of an institution, for in reality these can never be anything more than the aims and interests of the individuals who compose it. But that does not make it nonsensical to say that questions can arise concerning an institution's ends. For there may be uncertainty within the minds of the individuals who are responsible for managing it as to what its ends should be, or conflict between different individuals, or groups of individuals, who each have some share in this responsibility. In either case, it may become important to decide which of the conflicting conceptions of an institution's aims and interests is the best one, and this is most likely to happen at extraordinary moments of crisis or disruption, as in the lives of individuals.

The lawyer who is asked to help his corporate client through such a crisis is likely to find, however, that he has little to contribute to this decision if he is meeting the client for the first time and thus lacks a context of routine encounters in which to assess conflicting claims about the client's aims—for the same reason that a stranger will in general have less to contribute than a friend to another person's deliberations concerning his own ends. A lack of familiarity with the person or institution in question prevents one, in each case, from entering as fully as one might into the process of third-personal deliberation, the process of deliberating with and for another about the other's ends. That is not to say that lawyers whose practice is essentially transactional are incapable of offering such help. But the more the relationship to a client approximates a one-time encounter between strangers, the more difficult it becomes for a lawyer to provide deliberative assistance of this kind in a dependable way. And to the extent that is true, the more the help a lawyer does offer is likely to be of an exclusively instrumental sort.

In some cases, to be sure, instrumental help is all, and in every case it is a part, of what a lawyer is expected to provide. To be helpful in this way, moreover, is often both a challenge and (where one succeeds) a satisfaction. But this is not the only kind of help for which lawyers are commonly asked, nor do I think it either the most challenging or most satisfying kind to provide. The most demanding and also most rewarding function that lawyers perform is to help their clients decide what it is they really want, to help them make up their minds as to what their ends should be, a function that differs importantly from the instrumental servicing of preestablished goals. It is this enterprise of co-deliberation that the lawyer-statesman ideal places at the center of the lawyer's professional life. The new transactional style of large-firm practice, with its emphasis on the exceptional and its detachment from the routine, makes this enterprise more difficult by narrowing the field within which it can be responsibly pursued. To that extent, the growing dominance of this style, though unavoidable, perhaps, in economic terms, represents a threat to the core of the lawyer-statesman ideal.

The second way in which the work of large-firm lawyers has grown narrower—its increasing restriction to specific subject-matter specialties—has similar implications. The demand for greater specialization is pervasive in the law today, and one sees its effects at every level and in every institutional setting. In the most general sense, this demand is simply a response to the law's growing volume and complexity, to changes in the legal culture that no lawyer can avoid. But at large firms this general pressure is further aggravated by the transformation of the lawyer-client relationship along the lines I have described. For the more transactional this relationship becomes, the more likely it is that any individual lawyer will in his or her practice see only one kind of problem, over and over again, rather than a wide range of problems, as might be expected if dealings with clients were (as they used to be) more continuous and routine.

Even more than most, lawyers in large firms are thus encouraged to become subject-matter specialists by the kind of practice they now have. One important consequence of this is a decrease in the ability of any single lawyer to see a client's problem whole and to address all the issues it presents. To provide their clients with full coverage, therefore, most large firms must now assemble teams of specialists, each of whose members contributes some focal expertise and has responsibility for a discrete part of the client's total situation.

But though a firm can offer its clients full coverage in this sense, there is something that a generalist possesses which a team of specialists does not: the capacity to synthesize, to integrate from a single point of view all the considerations that the client's case presents. The more narrowly specialized his advisers become, the more likely it is that the client will have to provide this point of view himself, and decide what should be made of the various specialized recommendations he receives. In one sense, of course, that decision is always the client's, whatever his lawyers are like, since he must decide, in every case, whether to accept their advice or not. Still, what most clients, including corporate clients,

want from their lawyers is not just a string of discrete judgments about various aspects of their problem, but deliberative advice as to what they should do, all things considered. The ability to give such advice is what distinguishes the wise counselor from the technocrat. But to give responsible advice of this sort, a lawyer needs, among other things, an understanding of the client's entire situation, not just some portion of it. And that is precisely what the subject-matter specialization of large-firm practice has made more difficult to attain.

Without a comprehensive understanding of the client's situation, the only advice a lawyer can offer is conditional or hypothetical: "If you wish to do this or that, then I advise you to pursue the following course of action." What one cannot do is recommend, unconditionally, that a client whose ends are conflicting embrace one goal rather than another. To make that sort of recommendation, a lawyer must be able to see the client's predicament from a single integrative point of view, in the same way that the client himself does or at least aspires to. That, however, is just the kind of advice clients often want, and the lawyer who cannot give it because he cannot see a client's problem whole must resign himself to playing the role of a technician: not, of course, an unhelpful role, but a different and more limited one than that of a lawyer-statesman.

The point that I am making can be stated simply. In recent years, large-firm law practice has narrowed in two ways. It has become more episodic or transactional, with contact between firm and client being limited increasingly to extraordinary situations with few routine dealings in between. For many of the lawyers involved, it has become more specialized along subject-matter lines as well. Each of these changes has narrowed the kind of advice that corporate clients are likely to demand from outside firms and that the lawyers in these firms are competent to give. Deliberative advice—advice about the ends a client ought to choose, as opposed to the means for reaching ends already chosen—presupposes a familiarity with the client's past and a breadth of understanding of his or her present situation, which the movement toward a more transactional and specialized form of law practice has gone a long way toward destroying in the country's largest firms. As a result, lawyers in these firms are today less often called upon than they were a generation ago to give advice that requires real prudence as distinct from technical knowledge. . . .

[Editor's Note: Kronman earlier explained practical wisdom as follows: "To have practical wisdom, I have said, a lawyer must be able to combine the opposing qualities of sympathy and detachment, and while some, perhaps, find this easy to do, most learn how only through a process of discipline and training that runs against the grain of other, more primitive feelings. The object of this process is to force the person undergoing it to entertain the widest possible diversity of points of view, and to explore these in a mood of deepening sympathy, while retaining the spirit of aloofness on which sound judgment also critically depends. Breadth of experience, real or vicarious, is an essential component of this process. Hence the narrower a lawyer's experience—before law school, in it, or afterward—the less developed his or her capacity for joining these two attitudes is likely to be."]

Prudence or practical wisdom is a trait of character that can be acquired, moreover, only through the experience of having to make the sorts of decisions that demand it—only through an extended apprenticeship in judgment. The fewer the occasions on which a lawyer is required to exercise practical wisdom, the less likely he is to develop it. That, I think, is what is happening in the country's large law firms today. The lawyers in these firms are becoming transactional specialists whose narrow relationships with their clients give the clients little reason to ask for the lawyers' deliberative advice, and the lawyers themselves limited experience at providing it. Today, the corporations that constitute the core of the large firm's clientele often look to others for advice of this sort—for example, to investment bankers, who in this generation have assumed many of the general advisory functions that lawyers once performed. The lawyers in these firms have been left, as a result, with a more limited role to play in the transactions on which they work, a largely technical

role that demands less practical wisdom and offers fewer opportunities for its development. Eventually, perhaps, the lawyer who sees his professional function in these terms may even begin to wonder whether practical wisdom has any value at all, and openly reject the ideal of the lawyer-statesman—which seems irrelevant to his work—in favor of the very different ideal of the expert with its emphasis on knowledge and technique and its disregard for character.

Of course many lawyers in large firms are not yet prepared to abandon the first of these ideals for the second, at least in a candid and self-conscious way. For they understand, if only viscerally, that such a substitution of ideals would strike at the heart of their own professional self-respect. But the twofold narrowing of the lawyer–client relationship that has reshaped the nature of large-firm practice is nonetheless pushing steadily in this direction and has created an environment in which the lawyer-statesman ideal is less likely to survive, whether its demise be viewed with approval or regret. . . .

What lawyers are particularly trained to do and can generally do better than philosophers and economists is think about cases—imaginary future cases, as in my example, but real past ones too. The ability to fashion hypothetical cases and empathically to explore both real and invented ones is the lawyer's professional forte. It is what his case-centered education and experience give him special competence at doing—unlike philosophers and economists, whose disciplines are on the whole more concerned with the construction of abstract systems of thought. And it is what defines the distinctive vantage point from which lawyers tend to see things: the point of view of those who see the world through the lens of individual cases and are temperamentally inclined to assess the abstract claims of philosophy and economics from the particularistic standpoint they afford.

If lawyers have a distinctive expertise of their own, it thus consists in the art of handling cases. There is, in fact, no other candidate for the position. For this art is the only one in which lawyers have a professional advantage over experts in the various nonlegal fields on whose relevance to law the advocates of policy science insist. A philosopher or an economist may of course have some facility in deliberating about cases, just as a lawyer may have some understanding of the concepts and methods they employ. But if he is an amateur in their fields, they are amateurs in his, and when it comes to the imaginative probing of specific cases, it is the lawyer who is best equipped, by training and temperament, to lead the way. A well-educated lawyer will be aware of the theories circulating in other disciplines and, in general terms at least, will understand their application to the law. But it is not his knowledge of these theories that defines the lawyer's expertise or the core of his professional persona. That is to be found, instead, in his ability to deliberate well about cases—a valued trait and one the law promotes in special measure.

Thus if we think of the lawyer as a jack-of-all-trades with a dilettante's understanding of many fields but no expertise of his own, whose special function is to serve as an intermediary between other disciplines like philosophy and economics, his position will be a subordinate one marked by deference toward the real experts in these areas—not a very elevated or inspiring ideal for lawyers to embrace. If, on the other hand, we start with the assumption that lawyers do possess a distinctive expertise equal in dignity to that of those in other fields, and then inquire what this expertise may be, the best answer remains the old one: that lawyers are experts at dealing with cases and possess to an exceptional degree the special imaginative powers this requires. But that is of course precisely the answer the decaying ideal of the lawyer-statesman has always given.

Those who maintain that the lawyer of the future must be a multidisciplinary social engineer and who claim that this new model of professional excellence offers an appealing alternative to the lawyer-statesman ideal are thus mistaken, whichever of these two views we adopt. For on the first there is nothing appealing to lawyers in the model they propose. And on the second their alternative to the ideal of the lawyer-statesman proves in the end to be indistinguishable from it. On neither view, therefore, is it plausible to think that the concept of a policy

science of law can provide a new rallying-point for the profession—a new and satisfying foundation on which the identity of lawyers may once again be based. For if it is not an elevated conception, no one will rally to it. And if at its heart it is simply a modified version of the lawyer-statesman ideal, it offers no more hope than that ideal does of surviving the identity crisis in which the profession is now caught.

There is one final reason for doubting whether the void left by the collapse of the lawyer-statesman ideal can be filled by even the most visionary program of policy science—perhaps the most important reason of all.

The lawyer-statesman ideal is an ideal of character. It calls upon the lawyer who adopts it not just to acquire a set of intellectual skills, but to develop certain character traits as well. It engages his affects along with his intellect and forces him to feel as well as think in certain ways. The lawyer-statesman ideal poses a challenge to the whole person, and this helps to explain why it is capable of offering such deep personal meaning to those who view their professional responsibilities in its light.

The ideal set up by the proponents of policy science is by contrast narrowly intellectual. It is an ideal directed at the thinking part of the soul only. To achieve the mastery of other disciplines that this ideal so highly values is a purely intellectual feat that a person can perform without undergoing the more elementary change in affect that every ideal of character contemplates. Learning a subject like philosophy or economics is of course bound to produce a legitimate sense of accomplishment. But an understanding of even the most complex intellectual discipline cannot by itself convey the deeper satisfaction that comes with the attainment of a valued trait of character like practical wisdom. For this does more than increase a person's knowledge of the world. It alters one's dispositional attitude toward it and thereby modifies one's personality in an essential way. The ideal of the lawyer-statesman made it easy for lawyers to identify with their role because it promised a deeper satisfaction of this kind. No program of policy science can do the same. And that is the most important reason why it is incapable in the end of offering a really fulfilling alternative to the lawyer-statesman ideal, however well suited to the conditions of our age such a program appears to be.

AN OLD IDEAL RESTORED?

If the ideal of the lawyer-statesman cannot be replaced, perhaps its central values, at least, may be restored. That is the hopeful suggestion implicit in the new republicanism and one that Robert Gordon, in particular, has advanced with considerable force. Those who hold this view do not share the enthusiasm for policy science that many contemporary legal writers display; indeed, they tend to be quite skeptical of its claims. They trace their intellectual roots instead to the federalist-republican culture of the early nineteenth century and its historical successors (progressivism in particular). At the core of this tradition, they say, is the simple but potent idea that lawyers have an obligation to serve the public good—consciously to promote not only their clients' private interests but also the integrity of the rules and institutions that form the framework within which these interests exist. On their view, for a lawyer to lead a responsible professional life, he must keep one eye on the legal arrangements that define the broad background of his everyday work. He must take an active interest in the betterment of these arrangements and be prepared to contribute to their improvement and repair. Failing this, the practice of law loses its status as a calling and degenerates into a tool with no more inherent moral dignity than a hammer or a gun.

Through all its permutations, they maintain, the republican tradition has adhered to this idea, which today remains as valid as before. To be sure, various intellectual and institutional developments have placed its relevance in doubt. The declining independence of lawyers and the acceptance by many of a view of advocacy that depreciates all direct concern for the public good have been especially important in this regard. But there is no reason to believe these doubts cannot be overcome. The advocacy model of law practice that in its strong form is so dismissive of

the need for public-spiritedness has been substantially weakened by recent criticisms of it. And while it is true that some lawyers are in certain ways today more dependent on their clients, in others they are freer than before. One should not despair, therefore, about the possibility of reviving the legal profession's ethic of public service. The conditions for doing so exist. What is mainly needed is will—a renewed commitment to this ethic and the courage to make the sacrifices it demands. The key to restoring the profession's failing sense of identity is thus not some new set of refined intellectual techniques (as the proponents of policy science suggest). The crucial factor is resolve: the ability to make and stand by a commitment to serve the public good. That is not easy to do, even under the best of circumstances. And the forces that conspire against it—including, most importantly, the ethos of commercialism that now dominates the country's leading firms—are exceptionally strong. But the republican revival that has been so influential in the world of legal scholarship has inspired some to hope that even at this late hour the ethic of public service may be restored to a central place in the consciousness of practicing lawyers and, with encouragement from the organized bar, renew the sense of moral purpose that dignified their work in the past.

This hopeful view is clearly right in two respects. First, unless the practice of law is tempered by a concern for the public good, it can never be anything but an amoral tool for the satisfaction of private needs. And second, the level of public-spiritedness within the profession is today dismally low and needs to be increased. Lawyers should spend more time on law reform and the *pro bono* representation of worthy causes and clients. Whether they will or not is largely a question—as this view also rightly suggests—of courage and resolve.

But is such a change in outlook, however desirable, capable of restoring to lawyers the confident sense that their professional role is an intrinsically fulfilling one, as the lawyer-statesman ideal implied? Not, I think, by itself. Although a devotion to the public good is essential to the law's standing as a morally honorable calling, it is not enough to ensure that even those lawyers who feel this devotion most deeply will find intrinsic satisfaction in their work. For that, something more is required.

Suppose, for example, that a lawyer takes an interest in the public good and works with determination to advance it, making significant material sacrifices along the way. Suppose, even, that this interest is the dominant one in his professional life. It is what motivates him to go to law school and then afterward to pursue the particular career he does. Such a lawyer certainly lives up to the highest standards of public-spiritedness. But he may still view his own professional role in narrowly instrumental terms. For it is entirely possible that he sees his legal skills merely as an asset to be used in the campaign for a better world and judges the soundness of his investment in them strictly in terms of how much betterment they produce. The lawyer who views his work in this way resembles the one who sees the practice of law merely as a means for making money. The ends the public-spirited lawyer pursues may be more praiseworthy than those of his selfish counterpart. These two are not on a moral par in every way. But the attitude they take toward their work is in one respect the same, for its value to each derives from a goal external to the work itself.

There is, of course, no necessity that a public-spirited lawyer see things in this way. He may, indeed, view his role in a very different light, as possessing an intrinsic value of its own. Thus, though committed to the public good, he may believe that disputes about its meaning often raise questions to which no clear answer exists; that the settlement of these disputes requires prudence as well as public-spiritedness; that the exercise of prudence is a component of good politics and not just a prelude to it; and that the practice of law is an activity that fosters the development of deliberative wisdom to an exceptional degree. The lawyer who believes these things will be public-spirited too, but he is less likely to view his professional role in strictly instrumental terms. He is less likely to see it as a means to an external goal than as a part of the good he is seeking, and thus more likely to find some measure of intrinsic satisfaction in his work.

But if he is to do so, two conditions must be met. First, his work must require certain powers or capacities whose exercise he values for their own sake and not just because they produce an independently desirable outcome, even of a morally praiseworthy kind. And second, these powers must figure importantly in his conception of himself. They cannot be mere skills he may acquire or discard without changing in a significant way. They must be part of his identity—elements in his personality—that bear on who he is as well as what he does. They must be traits of character.

The lawyer-statesman ideal satisfied these two conditions and therefore gave its adherents reason to hope they might find intrinsic fulfillment in their work. But the neorepublican ethic of public service does not. For this ethic is, in essence, an abbreviated version of the lawyer-statesman ideal from which everything but the latter's emphasis on civic duty has been stripped. In particular, the new republicans give no weight to the character-virtue of practical wisdom, which the ideal of the lawyer-statesman stressed. That is because of their strongly egalitarian outlook. Deliberative wisdom is a virtue that people possess to different degrees, making the distinction between excellence and mediocrity unavoidably relevant to it. Devotion to the public good, by contrast, requires only an act of will that every citizen is in principle able to perform. Given their commitment to a will-based conception of equality, it is unsurprising that the new republicans should emphasize the second element of the lawyer-statesman ideal while ignoring the first entirely. But if we eliminate this aspect of the ideal and reduce it to the element of public service alone, we are left with a conception of the lawyer's role that is too thin to explain why it is an inherently fulfilling one to play.

Only this narrowing of the lawyer-statesman ideal, moreover, gives us any grounds to hope for its revival. Even today, a lawyer working in a large firm or other complex organization may be a dedicated activist if his or her will is strong and steady. The demand that lawyers in such settings devote more time and energy to the pursuit of the public good is therefore not an unreasonable one to make. But the barriers these same institutions put in the way of restoring other elements of the lawyer-statesman ideal—those the new republicans reject—are far more difficult to surmount. For their very size and structure make these institutions deeply inhospitable to the cultivation of deliberative judgment. A re-ally serious revival of public-spiritedness in the country's leading firms would be hard enough to achieve, but far easier than the structural reforms now needed to provide a supportive setting for the broader version of the lawyer-statesman ideal I have defended in this book. . . .

REVIEW AND DISCUSSION QUESTIONS

1. Describe what Kronman means by "practical wisdom."

2. Why does Kronman believe that the ideal of the lawyer-statesman has been largely lost?

3. The expertise of economists and philosophers is sought in public discourse, but what is the unique expertise that lawyers can contribute to public discussion?

4. Explain why Kronman believes the lawyer-statesman role is preferable to that of the pure advocate and the publicly minded lawyer.

5. How realistic is Kronman's ideal in the contemporary world?

6. Compare the different visions of legal practice defended in this section. What are the philosophical assumptions and arguments lying behind each of them?

2

THE RULE OF LAW

Essays in this section share a common theme, which has been of interest to philosophers and legal theorists since they first began thinking about the law: the idea of the rule of law itself. Using a real-life problem of how a newly chosen, democratic government should deal with "grudge informers"—those who had used the authority of the previous Nazi regime as an instrument of revenge—the authors explore the nature of the rule of law itself, how it can best be protected, and why it is important that it be maintained.

Magnitude and Importance of Legal Science

David Dudley Field

The following remarks were delivered at the dedication ceremonies of what was eventually to become Northwestern University Law School very near the time Christopher Columbus Langdell took over as dean at Harvard. In his speech, Field not only indicates his general agreement with Langdell on the "science" of law but also explains in eloquent terms why law, viewed as a science, is critical to any society. Field was both a lawyer and legal reformer. He is best known for his authorship of the "Field Code" and his leadership of the movement to codify the common law by setting forth its principles in clear, coherent, and concise language.

There are undoubtedly several topics, which might properly be considered, in connection with the establishment of this school—as, for example, its relations to the public, to the university and to its own pupils, or the most advisable course of study; but I shall only ask you to consider with me now the magnitude and importance of legal science. And though all knowledge has value, and all the arts their uses, yet, as there are differences in value as in use, I hope to show you that, of all the sciences and all the arts, not one can be named greater in magnitude or importance than . . . the science of the law.

Law is a rule of property and of conduct prescribed by the sovereign power of a state. The science of the law embraces, therefore, all the rules recognized and enforced by the state, of all the property and of all the conduct of men in all their relations, public and private. . . . No engagement can be entered into, no work undertaken, no journey made, but with the law in view. . . . This science, therefore, is equal in duration with history, in extent with all the affairs of men.

We can measure it best by tracing its progress. When men dwelt in tents and led a pastoral life, their laws might have been compressed in a few pages. They had, of course, some part of our law of personal rights, the law of succession, and of boundaries between the occupiers of adjoining pastures. This was the condition of the race in the primitive ages, and is even yet the condition of some parts of it. . . .

The next stage in the civilization of the race was the fixed habitation and the cultivation of the soil; and this brought with it the next stage in the development of the legal system—the law of land and of permanent structures—a department which, though it teaches of the most permanent of earthly things, has not partaken of their permanence, but has fluctuated with political condition. The distribution of the land has determined the policy and the fate of governments, and these in their turn have encouraged the aggregation or subdivision of estates, as they inclined to aristocratic or democratic institutions.

. . . To possess land, to own an estate, to found a family, and to make for it an ancestral home, are objects of ambition almost universal. We seem to ourselves to be more firmly fixed when we are anchored in the soil. . . . And, not withstanding the enormous increase of personal property in our modern society, the larger portion of man's wealth is still in the land. . . .

For these reasons, the law, which regulates the possession, enjoyment, and transfer of real property, has always been the subject of special attention. It has oscillated, as governments have swayed back and forth; at one time allodial, at another fuedal, sometimes comparatively simple; then excessively complex; in one country natural, in another artificial. But in all countries . . . the law of real property has ever been and must be large and difficult. The acquisition and use of land, the different kinds of ownership, the exclusive and perpetual, or the joint or temporary title, the conflicting interests of adjoining owners, the relative rights of landlord and tenant, and a thousand other conditions and incidents, can only be regulated upon a careful and minute analysis, by a series of rules adjusted with nice discrimination. . . .

In the next stage of civilization, the products of the soil were wrought into new forms, and manufactured fabrics added to the wealth and comfort of man. Manufactures required the purchase and collection of materials, the employment of workmen, and the sale of the fabric. Commerce led to navigation. Each of these operations added a new chapter to the law.

Of these three stages in civilization and in law, the ancient world was witness, but not in their highest development, though in forms of which the records will last for ever. The accumulation of lawbooks became so burdensome that, thirteen hundred years ago, it was found necessary to reduce them by substituting digests and codes. . . . Since then, however, materials have accumulated, greater by far than those out of which the Roman Codes were constructed.

. . . Who that has studied the government of a country, though occupying but a single department in its laws, but wonders at the magnitude of the subject? A lifetime seems scarcely sufficient for its mastery. Political philosophy and history are its adjuncts. Take our political code, survey it generally, enter into its details, study its history, consider how many good and wise men have participated in its framing, how cautiously it has been contrived, amended, added to, debated, at every step in its progress, and then stand reverently before it as the grandest monument of human genius. Time would fail me if I were to attempt recounting even the principal epochs in its history; the long and hardy training of our forefathers beyond the sea, where their institutions were purified by blood and fire, the transplanting of those institutions hither, their curtailment of the monarchical portions, the amelioration which time and experience have wrought, the principle of federation, its origin and development, and the final completion of the vast structure of our Government, Federal and State, through all its parts. . . . Large must be the book which shall even describe adequately this double Government of ours—larger still that which shall contain all the laws by which it moves and all the functions which it performs; its various departments, legislative, executive, and judicial, the powers and duties of all its public officers, its revenues, and the different branches of the public service. . . .

. . . Let us select for example a single department and follow out its subdivisions. Take if you will the contract of sale, and see into how many branches it divides itself. Whether the contract be written or unwritten, whether there be an actual transfer, or only an agreement to transfer, whether the thing agreed upon be already made or only to be made, whether it be sound or defective or deficient in quantity, whether there be fair dealing, concealment, or misrepresentation as to quality, existence, or value, whether the thing has been delivered or paid for in whole or in part, whether the seller or the purchaser ever, and if so when and upon what terms, may rescind the contract and be reinstated—all these, and many more, are considerations affecting the transaction, which the law has carefully provided for, by an appropriate rule.

The law may be compared to a majestic tree that is ever growing. It has a trunk heavy with centuries, great branches equal themselves to other trees, with their roots in the parent trunk; lesser-branches, and from those lesser branches still, till you arrive at the delicate bud, which in a few years will be itself a branch, with a multitude of leaves and buds. . . . [T]he law appears infinite in its manifestations; the shelves of law libraries groan under the accumulation of their volumes. The curious in such matters have computed that the number of cases in the English Courts relating to practice alone equals twenty-five thousand, and that the common law has two million rules!

Compare this science with any of the other sciences; with those which are esteemed the greatest in extent, and the most exalted in subject. Take even astronomy, that noble science which . . . weighs the sun and the planets, measures their distances, traces their orbits, and penetrates the secrets of that great law which governs their motions. Sublime as this science is, it is but the science of inanimate matter, and a few natural laws; while the science which is the subject of our discourse governs the actions of human beings, intelligent and immortal, penetrates into the secrets of their souls, subdues their wills, and adapts itself to the endless variety of their wants, motives, and conditions.

Will you compare it with one of the exact sciences—as, for example, with mathematics? . . . Clear, precise, simple in its elements, far-reaching and sublime in its results, [mathematics] has disciplined and exalted some of the greatest minds of our race, and been the nursery of other sciences, and of the mechanic arts. . . . But the science of calculation is occupied with a single principle. This it may go on to develop more and more, till the mind is almost lost in its immensity; yet the development of that one principle can never reach in extent, comprehensiveness, and variety the development of all the principles by which the actions of men toward each other are governed in all their relations. The law, it will be remembered, is the rule of all property and all conduct. . . .

This rapid survey may serve to give us some idea, imperfect, indeed, of the magnitude of legal science. Though it may be the most familiar of all things, it is also the most profound and immense. It surrounds us everywhere like the light of this autumnal day, or the breath of this all-comprehending air. It sits with us, sleeps beside us, walks with us abroad, studies with the inventor, writes with the scholar, and marches by the side of every new branch of industry and every new mode of travel. The infant of an hour old, the old man of threescore and ten, the feeble woman, the strong and hardy youth, are all under its equal care, and by it alike protected and restrained. . . .

We have considered thus far the magnitude of legal science. Its importance is more than commensurate with its magnitude. Without it there could be no civilization and no order. Where there is no law, there can be no order, since order is but another name for regularity, or conformity to rule. Without order, society would relapse into barbarism. The very magnitude of the law is a proof of its necessity. It is great, because it is essential. There is a necessity, not only for law, but for a system, with arrangement and a due relation of parts; for, without this system, the administration of government, both in its judicial and its administrative departments, would fall into irretrievable confusion. . . .

'I'he science of the law is our great security against the maladministration of justice. If the decision of litigated questions were to depend upon the will of the Judge or upon his notions of what was just, our property and our lives would be at the mercy of a fluctuating judgment, or of caprice. The existence of a system of rules and conformity to them are the essential conditions of all free government, and of republican government above all others. The law is our only sovereign. We have enthroned it. In other governments, loyalty to a personal sovereign is a bond for the State. . . . We have substituted loyalty to the State and the law for what with others is loyalty to the person. In place of a government of opposing interests, we have a double government of written Constitutions. The just interpretation of these Constitutions and the working of the double machinery, so that there may be no break and no jar, are committed in a great degree, how great few ever reflect, to the legal profession, and are dependent upon their knowledge of the science of law in all its departments, political, civil, penal, and remedial. Precisely, therefore, as free government and republican institutions are valuable, in the same proportion is the science of the law valuable as a means of preserving them.

REVIEW AND DISCUSSION QUESTIONS

1. Field titled his speech the "Magnitude and Importance of Legal Science." In what does he think its magnitude consists?

2. Why is law so important, according to Field?

3. Field argues that the better the civilization, the more complete will be its law. What does he mean by that?

4. Field says law is our sovereign. What does he mean by that?

5. Some have suggested that, contrary to Field, the more just the society the *less* law there will be: In heaven there would be no law, and in hell there would be nothing but law, as Grant Gilmore wrote in his book *The Ages of American Law* (1977). Who is right?

6. Does Field assume history progresses, in a way that Gilmore or others in the early twenty-first century might find difficult to accept? In what ways have both history and the law progressed or not progressed?

Eight Ways to Fail to Make Law

Lon Fuller

The task of making a law may seem simple, with the only real problem being how to decide which laws to make. But in this tale, Lon Fuller illustrates that making law at all is often a difficult task that may or may not be effectively accomplished. Implicit in this story is another, deeper issue about the nature of law and the ideal of the rule of law. Lon Fuller was professor of law at Harvard Law School.

[A] law which a man cannot obey, nor act according to it, is void and no law: and it is impossible to obey contradictions, or act according to them.

—Vaughan, C. J. in *Thomas v. Sorrell*, 1677

It is desired that our learned lawyers would answer these ensuing queries . . . whether ever the Commonwealth, when they chose the Parliament, gave them a lawless unlimited power, and at their pleasure to walk contrary to their own laws and ordinances before they have repealed them?

—Lilburne, *England's Birth-Right Justified*, 1645

This chapter will begin with a fairly lengthy allegory. It concerns the unhappy reign of a monarch who bore the convenient, but not very imaginative and not even very regal sounding name of Rex.

EIGHT WAYS TO FAIL TO MAKE LAW

Rex came to the throne filled with the zeal of a reformer. He considered that the greatest failure of his predecessors had been in the field of law. For generations the legal system had known nothing like a basic reform. Procedures of trial were cumbersome, the rules of law spoke in the archaic tongue of another age, justice was expensive, the judges were slovenly and sometimes corrupt. Rex was resolved to remedy all this and to make his name in history as a great lawgiver. It was his unhappy fate to fail in this ambition. Indeed, he failed spectacularly, since not only did he not succeed in introducing the needed reforms, but he never even succeeded in creating any law at all, good or bad.

His first official act was, however, dramatic and propitious. Since he needed a clean slate on which to write, he announced to his subjects the immediate repeal of all existing law, of whatever kind. He then set about drafting a new code. Unfortunately, trained as a lonely prince, his education had been very defective. In particular he found himself incapable of making even the simplest generalizations. Though not lacking in confidence when it came to deciding specific controversies, the effort to give articulate reasons for any conclusion strained his capacities to the breaking point.

Becoming aware of his limitations, Rex gave up the project of a code and announced to his subjects that henceforth he would act as a judge in any disputes that might arise among them. In this way under the stimulus of a variety of cases he hoped that his latent powers of generalization might develop and, proceeding case by case, he would gradually work out a system of rules that could be incorporated in a code. Unfortunately the defects in his education were more deep-seated than he had supposed. The venture failed completely. After he had handed down literally hundreds of decisions neither he nor his subjects could detect in those decisions any pattern whatsoever. Such tentatives toward generalization as were to be found in his opinions only compounded the confusion, for they gave false leads to his subjects and threw his own meager powers of judgment off balance in the decision of later cases.

After this fiasco Rex realized it was necessary to take a fresh start. His first move was to subscribe to a course of lessons in generalization. With his intellectual powers thus fortified, he resumed the project of a code and, after many hours of solitary labor, succeeded in preparing a fairly lengthy document. He was sill not confident, however, that he had fully overcome his previous defects. Accordingly, he announced to his subjects that he had written out a code and would henceforth be governed by it in deciding cases, but that for an indefinite future the contents of the code would remain an official state secret, known only to him and his scrivener. To Rex's surprise this sensible plan was deeply resented by his subjects. They declared it was very unpleasant to have one's case decided by rules when there was no way of knowing what those rules were.

Stunned by this rejection Rex undertook an earnest inventory of his personal strengths and weaknesses. He decided that life had taught him one clear lesson, namely, that it is easier to decide things with the aid of hindsight than it is to attempt to foresee and control the future. Not only did hindsight make it easier to decide cases, but—and this was of supreme importance to Rex—it made it easier to give reasons. Deciding to capitalize on this insight, Rex hit on the following plan. At the beginning of each calendar year he would decide all the controversies that had arisen among his subjects during the preceding year. He would accompany his decisions with a full statement of reasons. Naturally, the reasons thus given would be understood as not controlling decisions in future years, for that would be to defeat the whole purpose of the new arrangement, which was to gain the advantages of hindsight. Rex confidently announced the new plan to his subjects, observing that he was going to publish the full text of his judgments with the rules applied by him, thus meeting the chief objection to the old plan. Rex's subjects received this announcement in silence, then quietly explained through their leaders that when they said they needed to know the rules, they meant they needed to know them *in advance* so they could act on them. Rex muttered something to the effect that they might have made that point a little clearer, but said he would see what could be done.

Rex now realized that there was no escape from a published code declaring the rules to be applied in future disputes. Continuing his lessons in generalization, Rex worked diligently on a revised code, and finally announced that it would shortly be published. This announcement was received with universal gratification. The dismay of Rex's subjects was all the more intense, therefore, when his code became available and it was discovered that it was truly a masterpiece of obscurity. Legal experts who studied it declared that there was not a single sentence in it that could be understood either by an ordinary citizen or by a trained lawyer. Indignation became general and soon a picket appeared before the royal palace carrying a sign that read, "How can anybody follow a rule that nobody can understand?"

The code was quickly withdrawn. Recognizing for the first time that he needed assistance, Rex put a staff of experts to work on a revision. He instructed them to leave the substance untouched, but to clarify the expression throughout. The resulting code was a model of clarity, but as it was studied it became apparent that its new clarity had merely brought to light that it was honeycombed with contradictions. It was reliably reported that there was not a single provision in the code that was not nullified by another provision inconsistent with it. A picket again appeared before the royal residence carrying a sign that read, "This time the king made himself clear—in both directions."

Once again the code was withdrawn for revision. By now, however, Rex had lost his patience with his subjects and the negative attitude they seemed to adopt toward everything he tried to do for them. He decided to teach them a lesson and put an end to their carping. He instructed his experts to purge the code of contradictions, but at the same time to stiffen drastically every requirement contained in it and to add a long list of new crimes. Thus, where before the citizen summoned to the throne was given ten days in which to report, in the revision the time was cut to ten seconds. It was made a crime, punishable by ten years' imprisonment, to cough, sneeze, hiccough, faint or fall down in the presence of the king. It was made treason not to understand, believe in, and correctly profess the doctrine of evolutionary, democratic redemption.

When the new code was published a near revolution resulted. Leading citizens declared their intention to flout its provisions. Someone discovered in an ancient author a passage that seemed apt: "To command what cannot be done is not to make law; it is to unmake law, for a command that cannot be obeyed serves no end but confusion, fear and chaos." Soon this passage was being quoted in a hundred petitions to the king.

The code was again withdrawn and a staff of experts charged with the task of revision. Rex's instructions to the experts were that whenever they encountered a rule requiring an impossibility, it should be revised to make compliance possible. It turned out that to accomplish this result every provision in the code had to be substantially rewritten. The final result was, however, a triumph of draftsmanship. It was clear, consistent with itself, and demanded nothing of the subject that did not lie easily within his powers. It was printed and distributed free of charge on every street corner.

However, before the effective date for the new code had arrived, it was discovered that so much time had been spent in successive revisions of Rex's original draft, that the substance of the code had been seriously overtaken by events. Ever since Rex assumed the throne there had been a suspension of ordinary legal processes and this had brought about important economic and institutional changes within the country. Accommodation to these altered conditions required many changes of substance in the law. Accordingly as soon as the new code became legally effective, it was subjected to a daily stream of amendments. Again popular content mounted; an anonymous pamphlet appeared on the streets carrying scurrilous cartoons of the king and a leading article with the title: "A law that changes every day is worse than no law at all."

Within a short time this source of discontent began to cure itself as the pace of amendment gradually slackened. Before this had occurred to any noticeable degree, however, Rex announced an important decision. Reflecting on the misadventures of his reign, he concluded that much of the trouble lay in bad advice he had received from experts. He accordingly declared he was reassuming the judicial power in his own person. In this way he could directly control the application of the new code and insure his country against another crisis. He began to spend practically all of his time hearing and deciding cases arising under the new code.

As the king proceeded with this task, it seemed to bring to a belated blossoming his long dormant powers of generalization. His opinions began, indeed, to reveal a confident and almost exuberant virtuosity as he deftly distinguished his own previous decisions, exposed the principles on which he acted, and laid down guide lines for the disposition of future controversies. For Rex's subjects a new day seemed about to dawn when they could finally conform their conduct to a coherent body of rules.

This hope was, however, soon shattered. As the bound volumes of Rex's judgments became available and were subjected to closer study, his subjects were appalled to discover that there existed no discernible relation between those judgments and the code they purported to apply. Insofar as it found expression in the actual disposition of controversies, the new code might just as well not have existed at all. Yet in virtually every one of his decisions Rex declared and redeclared the code to be the basic law of his kingdom.

Leading citizens began to hold private meetings to discuss what measures, short of open revolt, could be taken to get the king away from the bench and back on the throne. While these discussions were going on Rex suddenly died, old before his time and deeply disillusioned with his subjects.

The first act of his successor, Rex II, was to announce that he was taking the powers of government away from the lawyers and placing them in the hands of psychiatrists and experts in public relations. This way, he explained, people could be made happy without rules.

THE CONSEQUENCES OF FAILURE

Rex's bungling career as legislator and judge illustrates that the attempt to create and maintain a system of legal rules may miscarry in at least eight ways; there are in this enterprise, if you will, eight distinct routes to disaster. The first and most obvious lies in a failure to achieve rules at all, so that every issue must be decided on an ad hoc basis. The other routes are: (2) a failure to publicize, or at least to make available to the affected party, the rules he is expected to observe; (3) the abuse of retroactive legislation, which not only cannot itself guide action, but undercuts the integrity of rules prospective in effect, since it puts them under the threat of retrospective change; (4) a failure to make rules understandable; (5) the enactment of contradictory rules or (6) rules that require conduct beyond the powers of the affected party; (7) introducing such frequent changes in the rules that the subject cannot orient his action by them; and, finally, (8) a failure of congruence between the rules as announced and their actual administration.

A total failure in any one of these eight directions does not simply result in a bad system of law; it results in something that is not properly called a legal system at all, except perhaps in the Pickwickian sense in which a void contract can still be said to be one kind of contract. Certainly there can be no rational ground for asserting that a man can have a moral obligation to obey a legal rule that does not exist, or is kept secret from him, or that came into existence only after he had acted, or was unintelligible, or was contradicted by another rule of the same system, or commanded the impossible, or changed every minute. It may not be impossible for a man to obey a rule that is disregarded by those charged with its administration, but at some point obedience becomes futile—as futile, in fact, as casting a vote that will never be counted. As the sociologist Simmel has observed, there is a kind of reciprocity between government and the citizen with respect to the observance of rules.[1] Government says to the citizen in effect, "These are the rules we expect you to follow. If you follow them, you have our assurance that they are the rules that will be applied to your conduct." When this bond of reciprocity is finally and completely ruptured by government, nothing is left on which to ground the citizen's duty to observe the rules.

The citizen's predicament becomes more difficult when, though there is no total failure in any direction, there is a general and drastic deterioration in legality, such as occurred in Germany under Hitler.[2] A situation begins to develop, for example, in which though some laws are published, others, including the most important, are not. Though most laws are prospective in effect, so free a use is made of retrospective legislation that no law is immune to change ex post facto if it suits the convenience of those in power. For the trial of criminal cases concerned with loyalty to the regime, special military tribunals are established and these tribunals disregard, whenever it suits their convenience, the rules that are supposed to control their decisions. Increasingly the principal object of government seems to be, not that of giving the citizen rules by which to shape his conduct, but to frighten him into impotence. As such a situation develops, the problem faced by the citizen is not so simple as that of a voter who knows

with certainty that his ballot will not be counted. It is more like that of the voter who knows that the odds are against his ballot being counted at all, and that if it is counted, there is a good chance that it will be counted for the side against which he actually voted. A citizen in this predicament has to decide for himself whether to stay with the system and cast his ballot as a kind of symbolic act expressing the hope of a better day. So it was with the German citizen under Hitler faced with deciding whether he had an obligation to obey such portions of the laws as the Nazi terror had left intact.

In situations like these there can be no simple principle by which to test the citizen's obligation of fidelity to law, any more than there can be such a principle for testing his right to engage in a general revolution. One thing is, however, clear. A mere respect for constituted authority must not be confused with fidelity to law. Rex's subjects, for example, remained faithful to him as king throughout his long and inept reign. They were not faithful to his law, for he never made any. . . .

. . . Do the principles expounded in my second chapter represent some variety of natural law *[Which holds that law and morality are necessarily linked—Ed.]*? The answer is an emphatic, though qualified, yes.

What I have tried to do is to discern and articulate the natural laws of a particular kind of human undertaking, which I have described as "the enterprise of subjecting human conduct to the governance of rules." These natural laws have nothing to do with any "brooding omnipresence in the skies." Nor have they the slightest affinity with any such proposition as that the practice of contraception is a violation of God's law. They remain entirely terrestrial in origin and application. They are not "higher" laws; if any metaphor of elevation is appropriate they should be called "lower" laws. They are like the natural laws of carpentry, or at least those laws respected by a carpenter who wants the house he builds to remain standing and serve the purpose of those who live in it.

. . . Now clearly the ability to prophesy presupposes order of some sort. . . . If we are to predict intelligently what the courts will do in fact, we must ask what they are trying to do. We must indeed go further and participate vicariously in the whole purposive effort that goes into creating and maintaining a system for directing human conduct by rules. If we are to understand that effort, we must understand that many of its characteristic problems are moral in nature. Thus, we need to put ourselves in the place of the judge faced with a statute extremely vague in its operative terms yet disclosing clearly enough in its preamble an objective the judge considers plainly unwise. We need to share the anguish of the weary legislative draftsman who at 2:00 A.M. says to himself, "I know this has got to be right and if it isn't people may be hauled into court for things we don't mean to cover at all. But how long must I go on rewriting it?"

A concentration on the order imposed by law in abstraction from the purposive effort that goes into creating it is by no means [rare]. Professor Friedmann, for example, in an attempt to offer a neutral concept of law that will not import into the notion of law itself any particular ideal of substantive justice, proposes the following definition:

the rule of law simply means the "existence of public order." It means organized government, operating through the various instruments and channels of legal command. In this sense, all modern societies live under the rule of law, fascist as well as socialist and liberal states.[3]

Now it is plain that a semblance of "public order" can be created by lawless terror, which may serve to keep people off the streets and in their homes. Obviously, Friedmann does not have this sort of order in mind, for he speaks of the "organized government, operating through the various instruments and channels of legal command." But beyond this vague intimation of the kind of order he has in mind he says nothing. He plainly indicates, however, a conviction that, considered just "as law," the law of Nazi Germany was as much law as that of any other nation. This proposition, I need not say, is completely at odds with the analysis presented here.

NOTES

[1]*The Sociology of Georg Simmel* (1950), trans. Wolff, § 4. "Interaction in the Idea of 'Law,' " pp. 186–89; see also Chapter 4, "Subordination under a Principle," pp. 250–67. Simmel's discussion is worthy of study by those concerned with defining the conditions under which the ideal of "the rule of law" can be realized.

[2]I have discussed some of the features of this deterioration in my article, "Positivism and Fidelity to Law," 71 *Harvard Law Review* 630, 648–57 (1958). This article makes no attempt at a comprehensive survey of all the postwar judicial decisions in Germany concerned with events occurring during the Hitler regime. Some of the later decisions rested the nullity of judgments rendered by the courts under Hitler not on the ground that the statutes applied were void, but on the ground that the Nazi judges misinterpreted the statutes of their own government. See Pappe, "On the Validity of Judicial Decisions in the Nazi Era," 23 *Modern Law Review* 260–74 (1960). Dr. Pappe makes more of this distinction than seems to me appropriate. After all, the meaning of a statute depends in part on accepted modes of interpretation. Can it be said that the postwar German courts gave full effect to Nazi laws when they interpreted them by their own standards instead of the quite different standards current during the Nazi regime? Moreover, with statutes of the kind involved, filled as they were with vague phrases and unrestricted delegations of power, it seems a little out of place to strain over questions of their proper interpretation.

[3]*Law and Social Change* (1951), p. 281.

REVIEW AND DISCUSSION QUESTIONS

1. List the ways Rex failed to make law.
2. In what sense has Fuller shown there is an inherent "morality" of law?
3. How might Fuller be said to provide an account of the ideal of the rule of law?
4. How does law differ from mere maintenance of order, according to Fuller?

The Problem of the Grudge Informer

Lon Fuller

Conflicts between individual conscience and the demands of law are often wrenching, as the Vietnam War demonstrated, and as Dworkin argued it can also be controversial whether a law is even valid. In the following essay, Lon Fuller discusses a related issue that is often confronted as societies undergo rapid political change such as has been experienced in Eastern Europe. The specific question he poses, whether to prosecute grudge informers from a prior regime, raises complex questions about the meaning and importance of the rule of law and about the nature and purpose of law itself. Lon Fuller was professor of law at Harvard Law School.

By a narrow margin you have been elected Minister of Justice of your country, a nation of some twenty million inhabitants. At the outset of your term of office you are confronted by a serious problem that will be described below. But first the background of this problem must be presented.

For many decades your country enjoyed a peaceful, constitutional and democratic government. However, some time ago it came upon bad times. Normal relations were disrupted by a deepening economic depression and by an increasing antagonism among various factional groups, formed along economic, political, and religious lines. The proverbial man on horseback appeared in the form of the Headman of a political party or society that called itself the Purple Shirts.

In a national election attended by much disorder the Headman was elected President of the Republic and his party obtained a majority of the seats in the General Assembly. The success of the party at the polls was partly brought about by a campaign of reckless promises and ingenious falsifications, and partly by the physical intimidation of nightriding Purple Shirts who frightened many people away from the polls who would have voted against the party.

When the Purple Shirts arrived in power they took no steps to repeal the ancient Constitution or any of its provisions. They also left intact the Civil and Criminal Codes and the Code of Procedure. No official action was taken to dismiss any government official or to remove any judge from the bench. Elections continued to be held at intervals and ballots were counted with apparent honesty. Nevertheless, the country lived under a reign of terror.

Judges who rendered decisions contrary to the wishes of the party were beaten and murdered. The accepted meaning of the Criminal Code was perverted to place political opponents in jail. Secret statutes were passed, the contents of which were known only to the upper levels of the party hierarchy. Retroactive statutes were enacted which made acts criminal that were legally innocent when committed. No attention was paid by the government to the restraints of the Constitution, of antecedent laws, or even of its own laws. All opposing political parties were disbanded. Thousands of political opponents were put to death, either methodically in prisons or in sporadic night forays of terror. A general amnesty was declared in favor of persons under sentence for acts "committed in defending the fatherland against subversion." Under this amnesty a general liberation of all prisoners who were members of the Purple Shirt party was effected. No one not a member of the party was released under the amnesty.

The Purple Shirts as a matter of deliberate policy preserved an element of flexibility in their operations by acting at times through the party "in the streets," and by acting at other times through the apparatus of the state which they controlled. Choice between the two methods of proceeding was purely a matter of expediency. For example, when the inner circle of the party decided to ruin all the former Socialist-Republicans (whose party put up a last-ditch resistance to the new regime), a dispute arose as to the best way of confiscating their property. One faction, perhaps still influenced by prerevolutionary conceptions, wanted to accomplish this by a statute declaring their goods forfeited for criminal acts. Another wanted to do it by compelling the owners to deed their property over at the point of a bayonet. This group argued against the proposed statute on the ground that it would attract unfavorable comment abroad. The Headman decided in favor of direct action through the party to be followed by a secret statute ratifying the party's action and confirming the titles obtained by threats of physical violence.

The Purple Shirts have now been overthrown and a democratic and constitutional government restored. Some difficult problems have, however, been left behind by the deposed regime. These you and your associates in the new government must find some way of solving. One of these problems is that of the "grudge informer."

During the Purple Shirt regime a great many people worked off grudges by reporting their enemies to the party or to the government authorities. The activities reported were such things as the private expression of views critical of the government, listening to foreign radio broadcasts, associating with known wreckers and hooligans, hoarding more than the permitted amount of dried eggs, failing to report a loss of identification papers within five days, etc. As things then stood with the administration of justice, any of these acts, if proved, could lead to a sentence of death. In some cases this sentence was authorized by "emergency" statutes; in others it was imposed without statutory warrant, though by judges duly appointed to their offices.

After the overthrow of the Purple Shirts, a strong public demand grew up that these grudge informers be punished. The interim government, which preceded that with which you are associated, temporized on this matter. Meanwhile it has become a burning issue and a decision concerning it can no longer be postponed. Accordingly, your first act as Minister of Justice has been to address yourself to it. You have asked your five Deputies to give thought to the matter and to bring their recommendations to

conference. At the conference the five Deputies speak in turn as follows:

FIRST DEPUTY: "It is perfectly clear to me that we can do nothing about these so-called grudge informers. The acts they reported were unlawful according to the rules of the government then in actual control of the nation's affairs. The sentences imposed on their victims were rendered in accordance with principles of law then obtaining. These principles differed from those familiar to us in ways that we consider detestable. Nevertheless they were then the law of the land. One of the principle differences between that law and our own lies in the much wider discretion it accorded to the judge in criminal matters. This rule and its consequences are as much entitled to respect by us as the reform which the Purple Shirts introduced into the law of wills, whereby only two witnesses were required instead of three. It is immaterial that the rule granting the judge a more or less uncontrolled discretion in criminal cases was never formally enacted but was a matter of tacit acceptance. Exactly the same thing can be said of the opposite rule which we accept that restricts the judge's discretion narrowly. The difference between ourselves and the Purple Shirts is not that theirs was an unlawful government—a contradiction in terms—but lies rather in the field of ideology. No one has a greater abhorrence than I for Purple Shirtism. Yet the fundamental difference between our philosophy and theirs is that we permit and tolerate differences in viewpoint, while they attempted to impose their monolithic code on everyone. Our whole system of government assumes that law is a flexible thing, capable of expressing and effectuating many different aims. The cardinal point of our creed is that when an objective has been duly incorporated into a law or judicial decree it must be provisionally accepted even by those that hate it, who must await their chance at the polls, or in another litigation, to secure a legal recognition for their own aims. The Purple Shirts, on the other hand, simply disregarded laws that incorporated objectives of which they did not approve, not even considering it worth the effort involved to repeal them. If we now seek to unscramble the acts of the Purple Shirt regime, declaring this judgment invalid, that statute void, this sentence excessive, we shall be doing exactly the thing we most condemn in them. I recognize that it will take courage to carry through with the program I recommend and we shall have to resist strong pressures of public opinion. We shall also have to be prepared to prevent the people from taking the law into their own hands. In the long run, however, I believe the course I recommend is the only one that will insure the triumph of the conceptions of law and government in which we believe."

SECOND DEPUTY: "Curiously, I arrive at the same conclusion as my colleague, by an exactly opposite route. To me it seems absurd to call the Purple Shirt regime a lawful government. A legal system does not exist simply because policemen continue to patrol the streets and wear uniforms or because a constitution and code are left on the shelf unrepealed. A legal system presupposes laws that are known, or can be known, by those subject to them. It presupposes some uniformity of action and that like cases will be given like treatment. It presupposes the absence of some lawless power, like the Purple Shirt Party, standing above the government and able at any time to interfere with the administration of justice whenever it does not function according to the whims of that power. All of these presuppositions enter into the very conception of an order of law and have nothing to do with political and economic ideologies. In my opinion law in any ordinary sense of the word ceased to exist when the Purple Shirts came to power. During their regime we had, in effect, an interregnum in the rule of law. Instead of a government of laws we had a war of all against all conducted behind barred doors, in dark alleyways, in palace intrigues, and prisonyard conspiracies. The acts of these so-called grudge informers were just one phase of that war. For us to condemn these acts as criminal would involve as much incongruity as if we were to attempt to apply juristic conceptions to the struggle for existence that goes on in the jungle or beneath the surface of the sea. We must put this whole dark, lawless chapter of our history behind us like a

bad dream. If we stir among its hatreds, we shall bring upon ourselves something of its evil spirit and risk infection from its miasmas. I therefore say with my colleague, let bygones be bygones. Let us do nothing about the so-called grudge informers. What they did do was neither lawful nor contrary to law, for they lived, not under a regime of law, but under one of anarchy and terror."

THIRD DEPUTY: "I have a profound suspicion of any kind of reasoning that proceeds by an 'either-or' alternative. I do not think we need to assume either, on the one hand, that in some manner the whole of the Purple Shirt regime was outside the realm of law, or, on the other, that all of its doings are entitled to full credence as the act of a lawful government. My two colleagues have unwittingly delivered powerful arguments against these extreme assumptions by demonstrating that both of them lead to the same absurd conclusion, a conclusion that is ethically and politically impossible. If one reflects about the matter without emotion it becomes clear that we did not have during the Purple Shirt regime a 'war of all against all.' Under the surface much of what we call normal human life went on—marriages were contracted, goods were sold, wills were drafted and executed. This life was attended by the usual dislocations—automobile accidents, bankruptcies, unwitnessed wills, defamatory misprints in the newspapers. Much of this normal life and most of these equally normal dislocations of it were unaffected by the Purple Shirt ideology. The legal questions that arose in this area were handled by the courts much as they had been formerly and much as they are being handled today. It would invite an intolerable chaos if we were to declare everything that happened under the Purple Shirts to be without legal basis. On the other hand, we certainly cannot say that the murders committed in the streets by members of the party acting under orders from the Headman were lawful simply because the party had achieved control of the government and its chief had become President of the Republic. If we must condemn the criminal acts of the party and its members, it would seem absurd to uphold every act which happened to be canalized through the apparatus of a government that had become, in effect, the alter ego of the Purple Shirt Party. We must therefore, in this situation, as in most human affairs, discriminate. Where the Purple Shirt philosophy introduced itself and perverted the administration of justice from its normal aims and uses, there we must interfere. Among these perversions of justice I would count, for example, the case of a man who was in love with another man's wife and brought about the death of the husband by informing against him for a wholly trivial offense, that is, for not reporting a loss of his identification papers within five days. This informer was a murderer under the Criminal Code which was in effect at the time of his act and which the Purple Shirts had not repealed. He encompassed the death of one who stood in the way of his illicit passions and utilized the courts for the realization of his murderous intent. He knew that the courts were themselves the pliant instruments of whatever policy the Purple Shirts might for the moment consider expedient. There are other cases that are equally clear. I admit that there are also some that are less clear. We shall be embarrassed, for example, by the cases of mere busybodies who reported to the authorities everything that looked suspect. Some of these persons acted not from desire to get rid of those they accused, but with a desire to curry favor with the party, to divert suspicions (perhaps ill-founded) raised against themselves, or through sheer officiousness. I don't know how these cases should be handled, and make no recommendation with regard to them. But the fact that these troublesome cases exist should not deter us from acting at once in the cases that are clear, of which there are far too many to permit us to disregard them."

FOURTH DEPUTY: "Like my colleague I too distrust 'either-or' reasoning, but I think we need to reflect more than he has about where we are headed. This proposal to pick and choose among the acts of the deposed regime is thoroughly objectionable. It is, in fact, Purple Shirtism itself, pure and simple. We like this law, so let us enforce it. We like this judgment, let it stand. This law we don't like, therefore it never was a law at all. This governmental act we disapprove, let it

be deemed a nullity. If we proceed this way, we take toward the laws and acts of the Purple Shirt government precisely the unprincipled attitude they took toward the laws and acts of the government they supplanted. We shall have chaos, with every judge and every prosecuting attorney a law unto himself. Instead of ending the abuses of the Purple Shirt regime, my colleague's proposal would perpetuate them. There is only one way of dealing with this problem that is compatible with our philosophy of law and government and that is to deal with it by duly enacted law, I mean, by a special statute directed toward it. Let us study this whole problem of the grudge informer, get all the relevant facts, and draft a comprehensive law dealing with it. We shall not then be twisting old laws to purposes for which they were never intended. We shall furthermore provide penalties appropriate to the offense and not treat every informer as a murderer simply because the one he informed against was ultimately executed. I admit that we shall encounter some difficult problems of draftsmanship. Among other things, we shall have to assign a definite legal meaning to 'grudge' and that will not be easy. We should not be deterred by these difficulties, however, from adopting the only course that will lead us out of a condition of lawless, personal rule."

FIFTH DEPUTY: "I find a considerable irony in the last proposal. It speaks of putting a definite end to the abuses of the Purple Shirtism, yet it proposes to do this by resorting to one of the most hated devices of the Purple Shirt regime, the ex post facto criminal statute. My colleague dreads the confusion that will result if we attempt without a statute to undo and redress 'wrong' acts of the departed order, while we uphold and enforce its 'right' acts. Yet he seems not to realize that his proposed statute is a wholly specious cure for this uncertainty. It is easy to make a plausible argument for an undrafted statute; we all agree it would be nice to have things down in black and white on paper. But just what would this statute provide? One of my colleagues speaks of someone who had failed for five days to report a loss of his identification papers. My colleague implies that the judicial sentence imposed for that offense, namely death, was so utterly disproportionate as to be clearly wrong. But we must remember that at that time the underground movement against the Purple Shirts was mounting in intensity and that the Purple Shirts were being harassed constantly by people with false identification papers. From their point of view they had a real problem, and the only objection we can make to their solution of it (other than the fact that we didn't want them to solve it) was that they acted with somewhat more rigor than the occasion seemed to demand. How will my colleague deal with this case in his statute, and with all of its cousins and second cousins? Will he deny the existence of any need for law and order under the Purple Shirt regime? I will not go further into the difficulties involved in drafting this proposed statute, since they are evident enough to anyone who reflects. I shall instead turn to my own solution. It has been said on very respectable authority that the main purpose of the criminal law is to give an outlet to the human instinct for revenge. There are times, and I believe this is one of them, when we should allow that instinct to express itself directly without the intervention of forms of law. This matter of the grudge informers is already in process of straightening itself out. One reads almost every day that a former lackey of the Purple Shirt regime has met his just reward in some unguarded spot. The people are quietly handling this thing in their own way and if we leave them alone, and instruct our public prosecutors to do the same, there will soon be no problem left for us to solve. There will be some disorders, of course, and a few innocent heads will be broken. But our government and our legal system will not be involved in the affair and we shall not find ourselves hopelessly bogged down in an attempt to unscramble all the deeds and misdeeds of the Purple Shirts."

As Minister of Justice which of these recommendations would you adopt?

REVIEW AND DISCUSSION QUESTIONS

1. Describe the five alternatives that the various deputies defend.

2. Fuller's dialogue raises two issues. The first is whether or not a state may legitimately punish someone when what he or she did was wrong, though not illegal. How would you answer that question?

3. The article also raises questions about the validity of laws during the reign of the Purple Shirts. In light of your own understanding of what it is that makes a law valid, and the deputy's arguments, is the law of the Purple Shirts valid? Were laws from the previous constitutional regime still valid? How does that question bear on the choice between the five deputies' positions?

4. How would you answer the question raised at the end of the article? Explain why you reject the advice of each deputy whose position you think is mistaken.

5. Fuller's article shows that this is a dilemma in which each position leads to the next, and the final back to the first. Explain.

Grudge Informers and the Rule of Law

H. L. A. Hart

Using the example of people who used Nazi law and power to work out grudges against other citizens, H. L. A. Hart continues the consideration of a range of issues that will occupy us in later sections. These issues include the rule of law, the relationship between law and morality, and the ideal of the rule of law. H. L. A. Hart was professor of jurisprudence at Oxford University.

Gustav Radbruch was a German legal philosopher who had shared the "positivist" doctrine until the Nazi tyranny. Prior to his recantation of positivism, he held that resistance to law was a matter for the personal conscience, to be thought out by the individual as a moral problem, and the validity of a law could not be disproved by showing that its requirements were morally evil or even by showing that the effect of compliance with the law would be more evil than the effect of disobedience. . . .

Radbruch, however, had concluded from the ease with which the Nazi regime had exploited subservience to mere law—or expressed, as he thought, in the "positivist" slogan "law is law"—and from the failure of the German legal profession to protest against the enormities which they were required to perpetrate in the name of law, that "positivism" (meaning here the insistence on the separation of law as it is from law as it ought to be) had powerfully contributed to the horrors.

After the war Radbruch's conception of law as containing in itself the essential moral principle of humanitarianism was applied in practice by German courts in certain cases in which local war criminals, spies, and informers under the Nazi regime were punished. The special importance of these cases is that the persons accused of these crimes claimed that what they had done was not illegal under the laws of the regime in force at the time these actions were performed. This plea was met with the reply that the laws upon which they relied were invalid as contravening the fundamental principles of morality. Let me cite briefly one of these cases.

In 1944 a woman, wishing to be rid of her husband, denounced him to the authorities for insulting remarks he had made about Hitler while home on leave from the German army. The wife was under no legal duty to report his acts, though what he had said was apparently in violation of statutes making it illegal to make statements detrimental to the government of the Third Reich or to impair by any means the military defense of the German people. The husband was arrested and sentenced to death, apparently pursuant to these statutes, though he was not executed but was sent to the front. In 1949 the wife was prosecuted in a West German court for an offense which we would describe as illegally depriving a person of his freedom. This was punishable as a crime under the German Criminal Code of 1871 which had remained in force continuously since its enactment. The wife pleaded that her husband's imprisonment was pursuant to the Nazi statutes and hence that she had committed no crime. The court of appeal to which the case ultimately came held that the wife was guilty of procuring the deprivation of her husband's liberty by denouncing him to the German courts, even though he had been sentenced by a court for having violated a statute, since, to quote the words of the court, the statute "was contrary to the sound conscience and sense of justice of all decent human beings." This reasoning was followed in many cases which have been hailed as a triumph of the doctrines of natural law and as signaling the overthrow of positivism. The unqualified satisfaction with this result seems to me to be hysteria. Many of us might applaud the objective—that of punishing a woman for an outrageously immoral act—but this was secured only by declaring a statute established since 1934 not to have the force of law, and at least the wisdom of this course must be doubted. There were, of course, two other choices. One was to let the woman go unpunished; one can sympathize with and endorse the view that this might have been a bad thing to do. The other was to face the fact that if the woman were to be punished it must be pursuant to the introduction of a frankly retrospective law and with a full consciousness of what was sacrificed in securing her punishment in this way. Odious as retrospective criminal legislation and punishment may be, to have pursued it openly in this case would at least have had the merits of candour. It would have made plain that in punishing the woman a choice had to be made between two evils, that of leaving her unpunished and that of sacrificing a very precious principle of morality endorsed by most legal systems. Surely if we have learned anything from the history of morals it is that the thing to do with a moral quandary is not to hide it. Like nettles, the occasions when life forces us to choose between the lesser of two evils must be grasped with the consciousness that they are what they are.

REVIEW AND DISCUSSION QUESTIONS

1. Describe the facts relating to the woman accused of being a grudge informer.
2. What solution to the problem does Hart recommend? Why does he recommend it?
3. Explain why Hart thinks that retrospective legislation, whatever its disadvantages, is better than the alternative(s).
4. Do you think that "positivism" was a relevant factor in the German experience, as Radbruch did? Explain.

The Rule of Law and Its Virtues

Joseph Raz

In this essay, Joseph Raz begins with a discussion of the nature of the ideal of the rule of law itself: What, precisely, does that ideal mean? His answer leads to a discussion of various principles that can be derived from the basic idea of the rule of law. He then describes the values of the rule of law and concludes with a brief critique of the attempt by Lon Fuller to establish a link between law and morality. Joseph Raz is professor of philosophy at Oxford University.

. . . The rule of law is a political ideal which a legal system may lack or may possess to a greater or lesser degree. That much is common ground. It is also to be insisted that the rule of law is just one of the virtues which a legal system may possess and by which it is to be judged. It is not to be confused with democracy, justice, equality (before the law or otherwise), human rights of any kind or respect for persons or for the dignity of man. A nondemocratic legal system, based on the denial of human rights, on extensive poverty, on racial segregation, sexual inequalities, and religious persecution may, in principle, conform to the requirements of the rule of law better than any of the legal systems of the more enlightened Western democracies. This does not mean that it will be better than those Western democracies. It will be an immeasurably worse legal system, but it will excel in one respect: in its conformity to the rule of law.

Given the promiscuous use made in recent years of the expression 'the rule of law' it is hardly surprising that my claim will alarm many. We have reached the stage in which no purist can claim that truth is on his side and blame the others for distorting the notion of the rule of law. . . .

1. THE BASIC IDEA

'The rule of law' means literally what it says: the rule of the law. Taken in its broadest sense this means that people should obey the law and be ruled by it. But in political and legal theory it has come to be read in a narrower sense, that the government shall be ruled by the law and subject to it. The ideal of the rule of law in this sense is often expressed by the phrase 'government by law and not by men'. No sooner does one use these formulas than their obscurity becomes evident. Surely government must be both by law and by men. It is said that the rule of law means that all government action must have foundation in law, must be authorized by law. But is not that a tautology? Actions not authorized by law cannot be the actions of the government as a government. They would be without legal effect and often unlawful. . . .

. . . If government is, by definition, government authorized by law the rule of law seems to amount to an empty tautology, not a political ideal.

The solution to this riddle is in the difference between the professional and the lay sense of 'law'. For the lawyer anything is the law if it meets the conditions of validity laid down in the system's rules of recognition *[i.e., its accepted test of legal validity—Ed.]* or in other rules of the system. This includes the constitution, parliamentary legislation, ministerial regulations, policemen's orders, the regulations of limited companies, conditions imposed in trading licenses, etc. To the layman the law consists only of a subclass of these. To him the law is essentially a set of open, general, and relatively stable laws. Government by law and not by men is not a tautology if 'law' means general, open, and relatively stable law. In fact, the danger of this interpretation is that the rule of law might set too strict a requirement, one which no legal system can meet and which embodies very little virtue. It is humanly inconceivable that law can consist only of general rules and it is very undesirable that it should. Just as we need government both by laws and by men, so we need both general and particular laws to carry out the jobs for which we need the law.

The doctrine of the rule of law does not deny that every legal system should consist of both general, open, and stable rules (the popular conception of law) and particular laws (legal orders), an essential tool in the hands of the executive and the judiciary alike. As we shall see, what the doctrine requires is the subjection of particular laws to general, open, and stable ones. It is one of the important principles of the doctrine that *the making of particular laws should be guided by open and relatively stable general rules.*

This principle shows how the slogan of the rule of law and not of men can be read as a meaningful political ideal. The principle does not, however, exhaust the meaning of 'the rule of law' and does not by itself illuminate the reasons for its alleged importance. Let us, therefore, return to the literal sense of 'the rule of law'. It has two aspects: (1) that people should be ruled by the law and obey it, and (2) that the law should be such that people will be able to be guided by it. As was noted above, it is with the second aspect that we are concerned: the law must be capable of being obeyed. A person conforms with the law to the extent that he does not break the law. But he obeys the law only if part of his reason for con-

forming is his knowledge of the law. Therefore, if the law is to be obeyed *it must be capable of guiding the behaviour of its subjects.* It must be such that they can find out what it is and act on it.

This is the basic intuition from which the doctrine of the rule of law derives: the law must be capable of guiding the behavior of its subjects. It is evident that this conception of the rule of law is a formal one. It says nothing about how the law is to be made: by tyrants, democratic majorities, or any other way. It says nothing about fundamental rights, about equality, or justice. It may even be thought that this version of the doctrine is formal to the extent that it is almost devoid of content. This is far from the truth. Most of the requirements which were associated with the rule of law before it came to signify all the virtues of the state can be derived from this one basic idea.

2. SOME PRINCIPLES

Many of the principles which can be derived from the basic idea of the rule of law depend for their validity or importance on the particular circumstances of different societies. There is little point in trying to enumerate them all, but some of the more important ones might be mentioned:

(1) All Laws Should Be Prospective, Open, and Clear. One cannot be guided by a retroactive law. It does not exist at the time of action. Sometimes it is then known for certain that a retroactive law will be enacted. When this happens retroactivity does not conflict with the rule of law (though it may be objected to on other grounds). The law must be open and adequately publicized. If it is to guide people they must be able to find out what it is. For the same reason its meaning must be clear. An ambiguous, vague, obscure, or imprecise law is likely to mislead or confuse at least some of those who desire to be guided by it.

(2) Laws Should Be Relatively Stable. They should not be changed too often. If they are frequently changed people will find it difficult to find out what the law is at any given moment

and will be constantly in fear that the law has been changed since they last learnt what it was. But more important still is the fact that people need to know the law not only for short-term decisions (where to park one's car, how much alcohol is allowed duty free, etc.) but also for long-term planning. Knowledge of at least the general outlines and sometimes even of details of tax law and company law are often important for business plans which will bear fruit only years later. Stability is essential if people are to be guided by law in their long-term decisions.[1]

. . . [C]onformity to the rule of law is often a matter of degree, not only when the conformity of the legal system as a whole is at stake, but also with respect to single laws. A law is either retroactive or not, but it can be more or less clear, more or less stable, etc. It should be remembered, however, that by asserting that conformity to the principles is a matter of degree, it is not meant that the degree of conformity can be quantitatively measured by counting the number of infringements, or some such method. Some infringements are worse than others. . . .

(3) The Making of Particular Laws (Particular Legal Orders) Should Be Guided by Open, Stable, Clear, and General Rules.

. . . Racial, religious, and all manner of discrimination are not only compatible but often institutionalized by general rules.

The formal conception of the rule of law which I am defending does not object to particular legal orders as long as they are stable, clear, etc. But of course particular legal orders are mostly used by government agencies to introduce flexibility into the law. A police constable regulating traffic, a licensing authority granting a licence under certain conditions, all these and their like are among the more ephemeral parts of the law. As such they run counter to the basic idea of the rule of law. They make it difficult for people to plan ahead on the basis of their knowledge of the law. This difficulty is overcome to a large extent if particular laws of an ephemeral status are enacted only within a framework set by general laws which are more durable and which impose limits on the unpredictability introduced by the particular orders. . . .

(4) The Independence of the Judiciary Must Be Guaranteed.

It is of the essence of municipal legal systems that they institute judicial bodies charged, among other things, with the duty of applying the law to cases brought before them and whose judgments and conclusions as to the legal merits of those cases are final. Since just about any matter arising under any law can be subject to a conclusive court judgment, it is obvious that it is futile to guide one's action on the basis of the law if when the matter comes to adjudication the courts will not apply the law and will act for some other reasons. The point can be put even more strongly. Since the court's judgment establishes conclusively what is the law in the case before it, the litigants can be guided by law only if the judges apply the law correctly. Otherwise people will only be able to be guided by their guesses as to what the courts are likely to do—but these guesses will not be based on the law but on other considerations.

The rules concerning the independence of the judiciary—the method of appointing judges, their security of tenure, the way of fixing their salaries, and other conditions of service—are designed to guarantee that they will be free from extraneous pressures and independent of all authority save that of the law. They are, therefore, essential for the preservation of the rule of law.

(5) The Principles of Natural Justice Must Be Observed.

Open and fair hearing, absence of bias, and the like are obviously essential for the correct application of the law and thus, through the very same considerations mentioned above, to its ability to guide action.

(6) The Courts Should Have Review Powers over the Implementation of the Other Principles.

This includes review of both subordinate and parliamentary legislation and of administrative action, but in itself it is a very limited review—merely to ensure conformity to the rule of law.

(7) The Courts Should Be Easily Accessible.

Given the central position of the courts in ensuring the rule of law (see principles 4 and 6) it is obvious that their accessibility is of paramount importance. Long delays, excessive costs, etc., may effectively turn the most enlightened law into a dead letter and frustrate one's ability effectively to guide oneself by the law.

(8) *The Discretion of the Crime-Preventing Agencies Should Not Be Allowed to Pervert the Law.* Not only the courts but also the actions of the police and the prosecuting authorities can subvert the law. The prosecution should not be allowed, for example, to decide not to prosecute for commission of certain crimes, or for crimes committed by certain classes of offenders. The police should not be allowed to allocate its resources so as to avoid all effort to prevent and detect certain crimes or prosecute certain classes of criminals. . . .

This list is very incomplete.[2] My purpose in listing them was merely to illustrate the power and fruitfulness of the formal conception of the rule of law. It should, however, be remembered that in the final analysis the doctrine rests on its basic idea that the law should be capable of providing effective guidance. The principles do not stand on their own. They must be constantly interpreted in the light of the basic idea.

The eight principles listed fall into two groups. Principles 1 to 3 require that the law should conform to standards designed to enable it effectively to guide action. Principles 4 to 8 are designed to ensure that the legal machinery of enforcing the law should not deprive it of its ability to guide through distorted enforcement and that it shall be capable of supervising conformity to the rule of law and provide effective remedies in cases of deviation from it. All the principles directly concern the system and method of government in matters directly relevant to the rule of law. Needless to say, many other aspects in the life of a community may, in more indirect ways, either strengthen or weaken the rule of law. A free press run by people anxious to defend the rule of law is of great assistance in preserving it, just as a gagged press or one run by people wishing to undermine the rule of law is a threat to it. But we need not be concerned here with these more indirect influences.

3. THE VALUE OF THE RULE OF LAW

One of the merits of the doctrine of the rule of law I am defending is that there are so many values it does not serve. Conformity to the rule of law is a virtue, but only one of the many virtues a legal system should possess. This makes it all the more important to be clear on the values which the rule of law does serve.

The rule of law is often rightly contrasted with arbitrary power. Arbitrary power is broader than the rule of law. Many forms of arbitrary rule are compatible with the rule of law. A ruler can promote general rules based on whim or self-interest, etc., without offending against the rule of law. But certainly many of the more common manifestations of arbitrary power run foul of the rule of law. A government subjected to the rule of law is prevented from changing the law retroactively or abruptly or secretly whenever this suits its purposes. The one area where the rule of law excludes all forms of arbitrary power is in the law-applying function of the judiciary where the courts are required to be subject only to the law and to conform to fairly strict procedures. No less important is the restraint imposed by the rule of law on the making of particular laws and thus on the powers of the executive. The arbitrary use of power for personal gain, out of vengeance or favouritism, is most commonly manifested in the making of particular legal orders. These possibilities are drastically restricted by close adherence to the rule of law. . . .

. . . Since it is universally believed that it is wrong to use public powers for private ends any such use is in itself an instance of arbitrary use of power. As we have seen the rule of law does help to curb such forms of arbitrary power.

But there are more reasons for valuing the rule of law. We value the ability to choose styles and forms of life, to fix long-term goals and effectively direct one's life towards them. One's ability to do so depends on the existence of stable, secure frameworks for one's life and actions. The law can help to secure such fixed points of reference in two ways: (1) by stabilizing social relationships which but for the law may disintegrate or develop in erratic and unpredictable ways; (2) by a policy of self-restraint designed to make the law itself a stable and safe basis for individual planning. This last aspect is the concern of the rule of law.

This second virtue of the rule of law is often . . . identified as the protection of individual freedom. This is right in the sense of freedom in which it is identified with an effective ability to choose between as many options as possible. Predictability in one's environment does increase one's power of action.[3] If this is freedom, well and good. . . . But it has no bearing on the existence of spheres of activity free from governmental interference and is compatible with gross violations of human rights.

More important than both these considerations is the fact that observance of the rule of law is necessary if the law is to respect human dignity. Respecting human dignity entails treating humans as persons capable of planning and plotting their future. Thus, respecting people's dignity includes respecting their autonomy, their right to control their future. A person's control over his life is never complete. It can be incomplete in any one of several respects. The person may be ignorant of his options, unable to decide what to do, incapable of realizing his choices or frustrated in his attempts to do so, or he may have no choice at all (or at least none which is worth having). All these failures can occur through natural causes or through the limitations of the person's own character and abilities. . . .

The law can violate people's dignity in many ways. Observing the rule of law by no means guarantees that such violations do not occur. But it is clear that deliberate disregard for the rule of law violates human dignity. It is the business of law to guide human action by affecting people's options. The law may, for example, institute slavery without violating the rule of law. But deliberate violation of the rule of law violates human dignity. The violation of the rule of law can take two forms. It may lead to uncertainty or it may lead to frustrated and disappointed expectations. It leads to the first when the law does not enable people to foresee future developments or to form definite expectations (as in cases of vagueness and most cases of wide discretion). It

leads to frustrated expectations when the appearance of stability and certainty which encourages people to rely and plan on the basis of the existing law is shattered by retroactive law-making or by preventing proper law-enforcement, etc. The evils of uncertainty are in providing opportunities for arbitrary power and restricting people's ability to plan for their future. The evils of frustrated expectations are greater. Quite apart from the concrete harm they cause they also offend dignity in expressing disrespect for people's autonomy. The law in such cases encourages autonomous action only in order to frustrate its purpose. When such frustration is the result of human action or the result of the activities of social institutions then it expresses disrespect. Often it is analogous to entrapment: one is encouraged innocently to rely on the law and then that assurance is withdrawn and one's very reliance is turned into a cause of harm to one. A legal system which does in general observe the rule of law treats people as persons at least in the sense that it attempts to guide their behaviour through affecting the circumstances of their action. It thus presupposes that they are rational autonomous creatures and attempts to affect their actions and habits by affecting their deliberations.

Conformity to the rule of law is a matter of degree. Complete conformity is impossible (some vagueness is inescapable) and maximal possible conformity is on the whole undesirable (some controlled administrative discretion is better than none). It is generally agreed that general conformity to the rule of law is to be highly cherished. But one should not take the value of the rule of law on trust nor assert it blindly. Disentangling the various values served by the rule of law helps to assess intelligently what is at stake in various possible or actual violations. Some cases insult human dignity, give free rein to arbitrary power, frustrate one's expectations, and undermine one's ability to plan. Others involve only some of these evils. The evil of different violations of the rule of law is not always the same despite the fact that the doctrine rests on the solid core of its basic idea.

4. THE RULE OF LAW AND ITS ESSENCE

Lon Fuller has claimed that the principles of the rule of law which he enumerated are essential for the existence of law. This claim if true is crucial to our understanding not only of the rule of law but also of the relation of law and morality. I have been treating the rule of law as an ideal, as a standard to which the law ought to conform but which it can and sometimes does violate most radically and systematically. Fuller, while allowing that deviations from the ideal of the rule of law can occur, denies that they can be radical or total. A legal system must of necessity conform to the rule of law to a certain degree, he claims. From this claim he concludes that there is an essential link between law and morality. Law is necessarily moral, at least in some respects. . . .

Clearly, the extent to which generality, clarity, prospectivity, etc., are essential to the law is minimal and is consistent with gross violations of the rule of law. But are not considerations of the kind mentioned sufficient to establish that there is necessarily at least some moral value in every legal system? I think not. The rule of law is essentially a negative value. The law inevitably creates a great danger of arbitrary power—the rule of law is designed to minimize the danger created by the law itself. Similarly, the law may be unstable, obscure, retrospective, etc., and thus infringe people's freedom and dignity. The rule of law is designed to prevent this danger as well. . . . A person who cannot communicate cannot claim any moral merit for being honest. A person who through ignorance or inability cannot kill another by poison deserves no credit for it. Similarly, that the law cannot sanction arbitrary force or violations of freedom and dignity through total absence of generality, prospectivity, or clarity is no moral credit to the law. It only means that there are some kinds of evil which cannot be brought about by the law. But this is no virtue in the law just as it is no virtue in the law that it cannot rape or murder (all it can do is sanction such actions).

Fuller's attempt to establish a necessary connection between law and morality fails. In so far as conformity to the rule of law is a moral virtue it is an ideal which should but may fail to become a reality. There is another argument, however, which establishes an essential connection between the law and the rule of law, though it does not guarantee any virtue to the law. Conformity to the rule of law is essential for securing whatever purposes the law is designed to achieve. This statement should be qualified. We could divide the purposes a law is intended to serve into two kinds: those which are secured by conformity with the law in itself and those further consequences of conformity with the law or of knowledge of its existence which the law is intended to secure. Thus a law prohibiting racial discrimination in government employment has as its direct purpose the establishment of racial equality in the hiring, promotion, and conditions of service of government employees (since discriminatory action is a breach of law). Its indirect purposes may well be to improve race relations in the country in general, prevent a threat of a strike by some trade unions, or halt the decline in popularity of the government.

Conformity to the rule of law does not always facilitate realization of the indirect purposes of the law, but it is essential to the realization of its direct purposes. These are achieved by conformity with the law which is secured (unless accidentally) by people taking note of the law and guiding themselves accordingly. Therefore, if the direct purposes of the law are not to be frustrated it must be capable of guiding human behaviour, and the more it conforms to the principles of the rule of law the better it can do so.

In section 2 we saw that conformity to the rule of law is one among many moral virtues which the law should possess. The present consideration shows that the rule of law is not merely a moral virtue—it is a necessary condition for the law to be serving directly any good purpose at all. Of course, conformity to the rule of law also enables the law to serve bad purposes. That does not show that it is not a virtue, just as the fact that a sharp knife can be used to harm does not show that being sharp is not a good-making characteristic for knives. At most it shows that from the point of view of the present consideration it is not a moral good. Being sharp is an inherent good-making characteristic of knives. A good knife is, among other things, a sharp knife. Similarly, conformity to the rule of law is an inherent value of laws, indeed it is their most important inherent value. It is of the essence of law to guide behaviour through rules and courts in charge of their application. Therefore, the rule of law is the specific excellence of the law. Since conformity to the rule of law is the virtue of law in itself, law as law regardless of the purposes it serves, it is understandable and right that the rule of law is thought of as among the few virtues of law which are the special responsibility of the courts and the legal profession.

Regarding the rule of law as the inherent or specific virtue of law is a result of an instrumental conception of law. The law is not just a fact of life. It is a form of social organization which should be used properly and for the proper ends. It is a tool in the hands of men differing from many others in being versatile and capable of being used for a large variety of proper purposes. As with some other tools, machines, and instruments a thing is not of the kind unless it has at least some ability to perform its function. A knife is not a knife unless it has some ability to cut. The law to be law must be capable of guiding behaviour, however inefficiently. Like other instruments, the law has a specific virtue which is morally neutral in being neutral as to the end to which the instrument is put. It is the virtue of efficiency; the virtue of the instrument as an instrument. For the law this virtue is the rule of law. Thus the rule of law is an inherent virtue of the law, but not a moral virtue as such.

The special status of the rule of law does not mean that conformity with it is of no moral importance. Quite apart from the fact that conformity to the rule of law is also a moral virtue, it is a moral requirement when necessary to enable the law to perform useful social functions; just as it may be of moral importance to produce a sharp knife when it is required for a moral purpose. In the case of the rule of law this means that it is virtually always of great moral value. . . .

NOTES

[1]Of course, uncertainty generated by instability of law also affects people's planning of action. If it did not, stability would not have any impact either. The point is that only if the law is stable are people guided by *their knowledge of the content of the law.*

[2]For a list similar to mine see Lon Fuller's *The Morality of Law,* 2nd ed., ch. 2. His discussion of many of the principles is full of good sense. My main reason for abandoning some of his principles is a difference of views on conflicts between the laws of one system.

[3]But then welfare law and governmental manipulation of the economy also increase freedom by increasing—if successful—people's welfare. If the rule of law is defended as the bulwark of freedom in this sense, it can hardly be used to oppose in principle governmental management of the economy.

REVIEW AND DISCUSSION QUESTIONS

1. What is the basic idea of the rule of law, according to Raz?

2. Describe the different principles that Raz thinks are implicit in the idea of the rule of law.

3. What are the values that Raz argues the rule of law serves? What values does it not guarantee?

4. Describe why Raz rejects Fuller's claim that there is a necessary connection between law and morality.

5. Using Raz's a metaphor that the law should be a sharp knife, discuss how he understands the importance of conformity to the rule of law and the importance of obeying law.

3

THE MORAL FORCE OF LAW

Essays in this section focus on two interrelated topics: legal obligation and civil disobedience. Is there reason to obey the law, merely because it is the law? To introduce this topic, we chose what is probably the best known discussion of legal obligation in the history of Western philosophy: Plato's *Crito*. The two subsequent essays explore the related topic of civil disobedience: What is it? When is it justified? Is it fair to those who do not disobey the law that officials charged with enforcing the law always prosecute civil disobedients? Embedded in these discussions are other topics that will emerge in later sections, including the nature of law itself and the connections between a law's being unjust and its status as valid law.

Crito

Plato

Plato was born into an aristocratic family in Athens around 427 B.C. Socrates (470–399 B.C.) was a friend of Plato's family from the time Plato was a schoolboy. Although a young Athenian of Plato's class would normally have pursued a political career, Plato chose philosophy instead and achieved fame as Socrates' most talented student and one of the world's greatest philosophers.

In 387 B.C., Plato founded the Academy, a school of higher education and research, which existed for more than 900 years, and he continued as its head until his death in 347 B.C. at the age of eighty. Plato wrote some twenty-five dialogues, including "Crito" and the book-length Republic.

"Crito" begins after Socrates has been condemned to death for corrupting the youth through his teaching. Friends try to convince Socrates to allow them to save his life by breaking him out of jail, but

Socrates will agree only if he can be convinced that violating the law would be just. "Crito" thus sets the stage for centuries of debate over the nature and extent of a citizen's legal obligation. (Socrates, in fact, refused to disobey the law and was executed.)

SCENE: *THE PRISON OF SOCRATES*

SOCRATES: Why have you come at this hour, Crito? it must be quite early?

CRITO: Yes, certainly.

SOCRATES: What is the exact time?

CRITO: The dawn is breaking.

SOCRATES: I wonder that the keeper of the prison would let you in.

CRITO: He knows me, because I often come, Socrates; moreover, I have done him a kindness.

SOCRATES: And are you only just come?

CRITO: No, I came some time ago.

SOCRATES: Then why did you sit and say nothing, instead of awakening me at once?

CRITO: Why, indeed, Socrates, I myself would rather not have all this sleeplessness and sorrow. But I have been wondering at your peaceful slumbers, and that was the reason why I did not awaken you, because I wanted you to be out of pain. I have always thought you happy in the calmness of your temperament; but never did I see the like of the easy, cheerful way in which you bear this calamity.

SOCRATES: Why, Crito, when a man has reached my age he ought not to be repining at the prospect of death.

CRITO: And yet other old men find themselves in similar misfortunes and age does not prevent them from repining.

SOCRATES: That may be. But you have not told me why you come at this early hour.

CRITO: I come to bring you a message which is sad and painful; not, as I believe, to yourself, but to all of us who are your friends, and saddest of all to me.

SOCRATES: What! I suppose that the ship has come from Delos, on the arrival of which I am to die?

CRITO: No, the ship has not actually arrived, but she will probably be here today, as persons who have come from Sunium tell me that they left her there; and therefore to-morrow, Socrates, will be the last day of your life.

SOCRATES: Very well, Crito; if such is the will of God, I am willing; but my belief is that there will be a delay of a day.

CRITO: Why do you say this?

SOCRATES: I will tell you. I am to die on the day after the arrival of the ship?

CRITO: Yes; that is what the authorities say.

SOCRATES: But I do not think that the ship will be here until tomorrow; this I gather from a vision which I had last night, or rather only just now, when you fortunately allowed me to sleep.

CRITO: And what was the nature of the vision?

SOCRATES: There came to me the likeness of a woman, fair and comely, clothed in white raiment, who called to me and said: O Socrates,

The third day hence to Phthia shalt thou go.

CRITO: What a singular dream, Socrates!

SOCRATES: There can be no doubt about the meaning, Crito, I think.

CRITO: Yes; the meaning is only too clear. But, Oh! my beloved Socrates, let me entreat you once more to take my advice and escape. For if you die I shall not only lose a friend who can never be replaced, but there is another evil: people who do not know you and me will believe that I might have saved you if I had been willing to give money, but that I did not care. Now, can there be a worse disgrace than this—that I should be thought to value money more than the life of a friend? For the many will not be persuaded that I wanted you to escape, and that you refused.

SOCRATES: But why, my dear Crito, should we care about the opinion of the many? Good men, and they are the only persons who are worth considering, will think of these things truly as they happened.

CRITO: But do you see, Socrates, that the opinion of the many must be regarded, as is evident in your own case, because they can do the very greatest evil to any one who has lost their good opinion.

SOCRATES: I only wish, Crito, that they could; for then they could also do the greatest good, and that would be well. But the truth is, that they can do neither good nor evil: they can not make a man wise or make him foolish; and whatever they do is the result of chance.

CRITO: Well, I will not dispute about that; but please to tell me, Socrates, whether you are not acting out of regard to me and your other friends: are you not afraid that if you escape hence we may get into trouble with the informers for having stolen you away, and lose either the whole or a great part of our property; or that even a worse evil may happen to us? Now, if this is your fear, be at ease; for in order to save you, we ought surely to run this, or even a greater risk; be persuaded, then, and do as I say.

SOCRATES: Yes, Crito, that is one fear which you mention, but by no means the only one.

CRITO: Fear not. There are persons who at no great cost are willing to save you and bring you out of prison; and as for the informers, you may observe that they are far from being exorbitant in their demands; a little money will satisfy them. My means, which, as I am sure, are ample, are at your service, and if you have a scruple about spending all mine, here are strangers who will give you the use of theirs; and one of them, Simmias the Theban, has brought a sum of money for this very purpose; and Cebes and many others are willing to spend their money too. I say therefore, do not on that account hesitate about making your escape, and do not say, as you did in the court, that you will have a difficulty in knowing what to do with yourself if you escape. For men will love you in other places to which you may go, and not in Athens only; there are friends of mine in Thessaly, if you like to go to them, who will value and protect you, and no Thessalian will give you any trouble. Nor can I think that you are justified, Socrates, in betraying your own life when you might be saved; this is playing into the hands of your enemies and destroyers; and moreover I should say that you were betraying your children; for you might bring them up and educate them; instead of

which you go away and leave them, and they will have to take their chance; and if they do not meet with the usual fate of orphans, there will be small thanks to you. No man should bring children into the world who is unwilling to persevere to the end in their nurture and education. But you are choosing the easier part, as I think, not the better and manlier, which would rather have become one who professes virtue in all his actions, like yourself. And indeed, I am ashamed not only of you, but of us who are your friends, when I reflect that this entire business of yours will be attributed to our want of courage. The trial need never have come on, or might have been brought to another issue; and the end of all, which is the crowning absurdity, will seem to have been permitted by us, through cowardice and baseness, who might have saved you, as you might have saved yourself, if we had been good for anything (for there was no difficulty in escaping); and we did not see how disgraceful, Socrates, and also miserable all this will be to us as well as to you. Make your mind up then, or rather have your mind already made up, for the time of deliberation is over, and there is only one thing to be done, which must be done, if at all, this very night, and which any delay will render all but impossible; I beseech you therefore, Socrates, to be persuaded by me, and to do as I say.

SOCRATES: Dear Crito, your zeal is invaluable, if a right one; but if wrong, the greater the zeal the greater the evil; and therefore we ought to consider whether these things shall be done or not. For I am and always have been one of those natures who must be guided by reason, whatever the reason may be which upon reflection appears to me to be the best; and now that this fortune has come upon me, I can not put away the reasons which I have before given: the principles which I have hitherto honored and revered I still honor, and unless we can find other and better principles on the instant, I am certain not to agree with you; no, not even if the power of the multitude could inflict many more imprisonments, confiscations, deaths, frightening us like children with hobgoblin terrors. But what will be the fairest way of considering the question? Shall I return to your old argument about the opinions of men some of which are to be regarded, and others, as we were saying, are not to be regarded? Now were we right in maintaining this before I was condemned? And has the argument which was once good now proved to be talk for the sake of talking;—in fact an amusement only, and altogether vanity? That is what I want to consider with your help, Crito:—whether, under my present circumstances, the argument appears to be in any way different or not; and is to be allowed by me or disallowed. That argument, which, as I believe, is maintained by many who assume to be authorities, was to the effect, as I was saying, that the opinions of some men are to be regarded, and of other men not to be regarded. Now you, Crito, are a disinterested person who are not going to die to-morrow—at least, there is no human probability of this, and you are therefore not liable to be deceived by the circumstances in which you are placed. Tell me then, whether I am right in saying that some opinions, and the opinions of some men only, are to be valued, and other opinions and the opinions of other men, are not to be valued. I ask you whether I was right in maintaining this?

CRITO: Certainly.

SOCRATES: Very good; and is not this true, Crito, of other things which we need not separately enumerate? In the matter of just and unjust, fair and foul, good and evil, which are the subjects of our present consultation, ought we to follow the opinion of the many and to fear them; or the opinion of the one man who has understanding, and whom we ought to fear and reverence more than all the rest of the world: and whom deserting we shall destroy and injure that principle in us which may be assumed to be improved by justice and deteriorated by injustice;—is there not such a principle?

CRITO: Certainly there is, Socrates.

SOCRATES: Take a parallel instance:—if, acting under the advice of men who have no understanding, we destroy that which is improvable by health and deteriorated by disease—when that has been destroyed, I say, would life be worth having? And that is—the body?

CRITO: Yes.

SOCRATES: Could we live, having an evil and corrupted body?

CRITO: Certainly not.

SOCRATES: And will life be worth having, if that higher part of man be depraved, which is improved by justice and deteriorated by injustice? Do we suppose that principle, whatever it may be in man, which has to do with justice and injustice, to be inferior to the body?

CRITO: Certainly not.

SOCRATES: More honored, then?

CRITO: Far more honored.

SOCRATES: Then, my friend, we must not regard what the many say of us; but what he, the one man who has understanding of just and unjust, will say, and what the truth will say. And therefore you begin in error when you suggest that we should regard the opinion of the many about just and unjust, good and evil, honorable and dishonorable.—Well, some one will say, "but the many can kill us."

CRITO: Yes, Socrates; that will clearly be the answer.

SOCRATES: That is true: but still I find with surprise that the old argument is, as I conceive, unshaken as ever. And I should like to know whether I may say the same of another proposition—that not life, but a good life, is to be chiefly valued?

CRITO: Yes, that also remains.

SOCRATES: And a good life is equivalent to a just and honorable one—that holds also?

CRITO: Yes, that holds.

SOCRATES: From these premises I proceed to argue the question whether I ought not to try and escape without the consent of the Athenians: and if I am clearly right in escaping, then I will make the attempt; but if not, I will abstain. The other considerations which you mention, of money and loss of character and the duty of educating children, are, as I fear, only the doctrines of the multitude, who would be as ready to call people to life, if they were able, as they are to put them to death—and with as little reason. But now, since the argument has thus far prevailed, the only question which remains to be considered is, whether we shall do rightly either in escaping or in suffering others to aid in our escape and paying them in money and thanks, or whether we shall not do rightly; and if the latter, then death or any other calamity which may ensue on my remaining here must not be allowed to enter into the calculation.

CRITO: I think that you are right, Socrates; how then shall we proceed?

SOCRATES: Let us consider the matter together, and do you either refute me if you can, and I will be convinced; or else cease, my dear friend, from repeating to me that I ought to escape against the wishes of the Athenians: for I am extremely desirous to be persuaded by you, but not against my own better judgment. And now please to consider my first position, and do your best to answer me.

CRITO: I will do my best.

SOCRATES: Are we to say that we are never intentionally to do wrong, or that in one way we ought and in another way we ought not to do wrong, or is doing wrong always evil and dishonorable, as I was just now saying, and as has been already acknowledged by us? Are all our former admissions which were made within a few days to be thrown away? And have we, at our age, been earnestly discoursing with one another all our life long only to discover that we are no better than children? Or are we to rest assured, in spite of the opinion of the many, and in spite of consequences whether better or worse, of the truth of what was then said, that injustice is always an evil and dishonor to him who acts unjustly? Shall we affirm that?

CRITO: Yes.

SOCRATES: Then we must do no wrong?

CRITO: Certainly not.

SOCRATES: Nor when injured injure in return, as the many imagine; for we must injure no one at all?

CRITO: Clearly not.

SOCRATES: Again, Crito, may we do evil?

CRITO: Surely not, Socrates.

SOCRATES: And what of doing evil in return for evil, which is the morality of the many—is that just or not?

CRITO: Not just.

SOCRATES: For doing evil to another is the same as injuring him?

CRITO: Very true.

SOCRATES: Then we ought not to retaliate or render evil for evil to any one, whatever evil we may have suffered from him. But I would have you consider, Crito, whether you really mean what you are saying. For this opinion has never been held, and never will be held, by any considerable number of persons; and those who are agreed and those who are not agreed upon this point have no common ground, and can only despise one another when they see how widely they differ. Tell me, then, whether you agree with and assent to my first principle, that neither injury nor retaliation nor warding off evil by evil is ever right. And shall that be the premiss of our argument? Or do you decline and dissent from this? For this has been of old and is still my opinion; but, if you are of another opinion, let me hear what you have to say. If, however, you remain of the same mind as formerly, I will proceed to the next step.

CRITO: You may proceed, for I have not changed my mind.

SOCRATES: Then I will proceed to the next step, which may be put in the form of a question:—Ought a man to do what he admits to be right, or ought he to betray the right?

CRITO: He ought to do what he thinks right.

SOCRATES: But if this is true, what is the application? In leaving the prison against the will of the Athenians, do I wrong any? or rather do I not wrong those whom I ought least to wrong? Do I not desert the principles which were acknowledged by us to be just? What do you say?

CRITO: I can not tell, Socrates, for I do not know.

SOCRATES: Then consider the matter in this way:—Imagine that I am about to play truant (you may call the proceeding by any name which you like), and the laws and the government come and interrogate me: "Tell us, Socrates," they say; "what are you about? are you going by an act of yours to overturn us—the laws and the whole state, as far as in you lies? Do you imagine that a state can subsist and not be overthrown, in which the decisions of law have no power, but are set aside and overthrown by individuals?" What will be our answer, Crito, to these and the like words? Any one, and especially a clever rhetorician, will have a good deal to urge about the evil of setting aside the law which requires a sentence to be carried out; and we might reply, "Yes; but the state has injured us and given an unjust sentence." Suppose I say that?

CRITO: Very good, Socrates.

SOCRATES: "And was that our agreement with you?" the law would say; "or were you to abide by the sentence of the state?" And if I were to express astonishment at their saying this, the law would probably add: "Answer, Socrates, instead of opening your eyes: you are in the habit of asking and answering questions. Tell us what complaint you have to make against us which justifies you in attempting to destroy us and the state? In the first place did we not bring you into existence? Your father married your mother by our aid and begat you. Say whether you have any objection to urge against those of us who regulate marriage?" None, I should reply. "Or against those of us who regulate the system of nurture and education of children in which you were trained? Were not the laws, who have the charge of this, right in commanding your father to train you in music and gymnastic?" Right, I should reply, "Well then, since you were brought into the world and nurtured and educated by us, can you deny in the first place that you are our child and slave, as your fathers were before you? And if this is true you are not on equal terms with us; nor can you think that you have a right to do to us what we are doing to you. Would you have any right to strike or revile or do any other evil to a father or to your master, if you had one, when you have been struck or reviled by him, or received some other evil at his hands?— you would not say this? And because we think right to destroy you, do you think that you have any right to destroy us in return, and your country as far as in you lies? And will you, O professor of true virtue, say that you are justified in this? Has a philosopher like you failed to discover that our country is more to be valued and higher and holier far than mother or father or any ancestor, and more to be regarded in the eyes of the gods and of men of understanding? Also to be soothed, and gently and reverently entreated when angry, even more than a father, and if not persuaded, obeyed? And when we are punished by her, whether with imprisonment or stripes, the punishment is to be endured in silence; and if she lead us to wounds or death in battle, thither we follow as is right; neither may any one yield or retreat or leave his rank, but whether in battle or in a court of law, or in any other place, he must do what his city and his country order him; or he must change their view of what is just: and if he may do no violence to his father or mother, much less may he do violence to his country." What answer shall we make to his, Crito? Do the laws speak truly, or do they not?

CRITO: I think that they do.

SOCRATES: Then the laws will say: "Consider, Socrates, if this is true, that in your present attempt you are going to do us wrong. For, after having brought you into the world, and nurtured and educated you, and given you and every other citizen a share in every good that we had to give, we further proclaim and give the right to every Athenian, that if he does not like us when he has come of age and has seen the ways of the city, and made our acquaintance, he may go where he pleases and take his goods with him; and none of us laws will forbid him or interfere with him. Any of you who does not like us and the city, and who wants to go to a colony or to any other city, may go where he likes, and take his goods with him. But he who has experience of the manner in which we order justice and administer the state, and still remains, has entered into an implied contract that he will do as we command him. And he who disobeys us is, as we maintain, thrice wrong; first, because in disobeying us he is disobeying his parents; secondly, because we are the authors of his education; thirdly, because he has made an agreement with us that he will duly obey our commands; and he neither obeys them nor convinces us that our commands are wrong; and we do not rudely impose them, but give them the alternative of obeying or convincing us;—that is what we offer, and he does neither. These are the sort of accusations to which, as we were saying, you, Socrates, will be exposed if you accomplish your intentions; you, above all other Athenians." Suppose I ask, why is this? they will justly retort upon me that I above all other men have acknowledged the agreement. "There is clear

Few twentieth-century philosophers have had as much influence on our thinking about these issues as John Rawls. His seminal work, A Theory of Justice, *offers a new and important work in the social contract tradition. Rawls argues that principles governing a constitution and laws enacted under it should be chosen behind a "veil of ignorance" in which people ignore their social class, race, and religion, as well as any other facts that are morally arbitrary and that, if known, would allow the laws to be tailored so as to advantage one group over another. He calls the theory "justice as fairness" because the veil of ignorance (corresponding to the traditional social contract) assures that the chosen principles are fair. Forced to choose a constitution and laws behind such a veil of ignorance, Rawls argues that people would secure for themselves basic rights, assure equality of opportunity, and allow economic inequality only if everybody benefits from it, including the least advantaged.*

In the following essay, John Rawls discusses the related questions of legal obligation and civil disobedience within the context of social contract theory. Even assuming the constitution is just, there is no assurance laws enacted in accordance with its procedures will also be just. Nonetheless, Rawls argues, citizens may have an obligation to obey that is based on their having benefited from the (generally) just regime. He concludes with a discussion of the role of civil disobedience in a constitutional democracy, including the circumstances in which it would be justified. John Rawls is emeritus professor of philosophy at Harvard University.

INTRODUCTION

I should like to discuss briefly, and in an informal way, the grounds of civil disobedience in a constitutional democracy. Thus, I shall limit my remarks to the conditions under which we may, by civil disobedience, properly oppose legally established democratic authority; I am not concerned with the situation under other kinds of government nor, except incidentally, with other forms of resistance. My thought is that in a reasonably just (though of course not perfectly just) democratic regime, civil disobedience, when it is justified, is normally to be understood as a political action which addresses the sense of justice of the majority in order to urge reconsideration of the measures protested and to warn that in the firm opinion of the dissenters the conditions of social cooperation are not being honored. This characterization of civil disobedience is intended to apply to dissent on fundamental questions of internal policy, a limitation which I shall follow to simplify our question.

THE SOCIAL CONTRACT DOCTRINE

It is obvious that the justification of civil disobedience depends upon the theory of political obligation in general, and so we may appropriately begin with a few comments on this question. The two chief virtues of social institutions are justice and efficiency, where by the efficiency of institutions I understand their effectiveness for certain social conditions and ends the fulfillment of which is to everyone's advantage. We should comply with and do our part in just and efficient social arrangements for at least two reasons: first of all, we have a natural duty not to oppose the establishment of just and efficient institutions (when they do not yet exist) and to uphold and comply with them (when they do exist); and second, assuming that we have knowingly accepted the benefits of these institutions and plan to continue to do so, and that we have encouraged and expect others to do their part, we also have an obligation to do our share when, as the arrangement requires, it comes our turn. Thus, we often have both a natural duty as well as an obligation to support just and efficient institutions, the obligation arising from our voluntary acts while the duty does not.

Now all this is perhaps obvious enough, but it does not take us very far. Any more particular conclusions depend upon the conception of justice which is the basis of a theory of political obligation. I believe that the appropriate conception, at least for an account of political obligation in a constitutional democracy, is that of the social contract theory from which so much of our political thought derives. If we are careful to interpret it in a suitably general way, I hold that this doctrine provides a satisfactory basis for political theory, indeed even for ethical theory itself, but this is beyond our present concern. The interpretation I suggest is the following: that the principles to which social arrangements must conform, and in particular the principles of justice, are those which free and rational men would agree to in an original position of equal liberty; and similarly, the principles which govern men's relations to institutions and define their natural duties and obligations are the principles to which they would consent when so situated. It should be noted straightway that in this interpretation of the contract theory the principles of justice are understood as the outcome of a hypothetical agreement. They are principles which would be agreed to if the situation of the original position were to arise. There is no mention of an actual agreement nor need such an agreement ever be made. Social arrangements are just or unjust according to whether they accord with the principles for assigning and securing fundamental rights and liberties which would be chosen in the original position. This position is, to be sure, the analytic analogue of the traditional notion of the state of nature, but it must not be mistaken for a historical occasion. Rather it is a hypothetical situation which embodies the basic ideas of the contract doctrine; the description of this situation enables us to work out which principles would be adopted. I must now say something about these matters.

The original doctrine has always supposed that the persons in the original position have equal powers and rights, that is, that they are symmetrically situated with respect to any arrangements for reaching agreement, and that coalitions and the like are excluded. But it is an essential element (which has not been sufficiently observed although it is implicit in Kant's version of the theory) that there are very strong restrictions on what the contracting parties are presumed to know. In particular, I interpret the theory to hold that the parties do not know their position in society, past, present, or future; nor do they know which institutions exist. Again, they do not know their own place in the

distribution of natural talents and abilities, whether they are intelligent or strong, man or woman, and so on. Finally, they do not know their own particular interests and preferences or the system of ends which they wish to advance: they do not know their conception of the good. In all these respects the parties are confronted with a veil of ignorance which prevents any one from being able to take advantage of his good fortune or particular interests or from being disadvantaged by them. What the parties do know (or assume) is that Hume's circumstances of justice obtain: namely, that the bounty of nature is not so generous as to render cooperative schemes superfluous nor so harsh as to make them impossible. Moreover, they assume that the extent of their altruism is limited and that, in general, they do not take an interest in one another's interests. Thus, given the special features of the original position, each man tries to do the best he can for himself by insisting on principles calculated to protect and advance his system of ends whatever it turns out to be.

I believe that as a consequence of the peculiar nature of the original position there would be an agreement on the following two principles for assigning rights and duties and for regulating distributive shares as these are determined by the fundamental institutions of society: first, each person is to have an equal right to the most extensive liberty compatible with a like liberty for all; second, social and economic inequalities (as defined by the institutional structure or fostered by it) are to be arranged so that they are both to everyone's advantage and attached to positions and offices open to all. In view of the content of these two principles and their application of the main institutions of society, and therefore to the social system as a whole, we may regard them as the two principles of justice. Basic social arrangements are just insofar as they conform to these principles, and we can, if we like, discuss questions of justice directly by reference to them. But a deeper understanding of the justification of civil disobedience requires, I think, an account of the derivation of these principles provided by the doctrine of the social contract. Part of our task is to show why this is so.

THE GROUNDS OF COMPLIANCE WITH AN UNJUST LAW

If we assume that in the original position men would agree both to the principle of doing their part when they have accepted and plan to continue to accept the benefits of just institutions (the principle of fairness), and also to the principle of not preventing the establishment of just institutions and of upholding and complying with them when they do exist, then the contract doctrine easily accounts for our having to conform to just institutions.

[Editor's Note: Rawls has argued elsewhere that legal obligation rests on the duty of "fair play." Though not absolute, the obligation exists whenever there is a "mutually beneficial and just scheme of cooperation" in which the advantages depend on the willing cooperation of nearly everyone. According to Rawls, because social cooperation requires sacrifice on the part of everybody, including a restriction on personal liberty, and because the benefits are "free" in the sense that each person can benefit individually as long as others do their part whether or not he does his part, each citizen is therefore bound to do his fair share, which in a constitutional democracy means obeying the law.]

But how does it account for the fact that we are normally required to comply with unjust laws as well? The injustice of a law is not a sufficient ground for not complying with it any more than the legal validity of legislation is always sufficient to require obedience to it. Sometimes one hears these extremes asserted, but I think that we need not take them seriously.

An answer to our question can be given by elaborating the social contract theory in the following way. I interpret it to hold that one is to envisage a series of agreements as follows: first, men are to agree upon the principles of justice in the original position. Then they are to move to a constitutional convention in which they choose a constitution that satisfies the principles of justice already chosen. Finally they assume the role of a legislative body and guided by the principles of justice enact laws subject to the constraints and procedures of the just constitution.

The decisions reached in any stage are binding in all subsequent stages. Now whereas in the original position the contracting parties have no knowledge of their society or of their own position in it, in both a constitutional convention and a legislature, they do know certain general facts about their institutions, for example, the statistics regarding employment and output required for fiscal and economic policy. But no one knows particular facts about his own social class or his place in the distribution of natural assets. On each occasion the contracting parties have the knowledge required to make their agreement rational from the appropriate point of view, but not so much as to make them prejudiced. They are unable to tailor principles and legislation to take advantage of their social or natural position; a veil of ignorance prevents their knowing what this position is. With this series of agreements in mind, we can characterize just laws and policies as those which would be enacted were this whole process correctly carried out.

In choosing a constitution the aim is to find among the just constitutions the one which is most likely, given the general facts about the society in question, to lead to just and effective legislation. The principles of justice provide a criterion for the laws desired; the problem is to find a set of political procedures that will give this outcome. I shall assume that, at least under the normal conditions of a modern state, the best constitution is some form of democratic regime affirming equal political liberty and using some sort of majority (or other plurality) rule. Thus it follows that on the contract theory a constitutional democracy of some sort is required by the principles of justice. At the same time it is essential to observe that the constitutional process is always a case of what we may call imperfect procedural justice: that is, there is no feasible political procedure which guarantees that the enacted legislation is just even though we have (let us suppose) a standard for just legislation. In simple cases, such as games of fair division, there are procedures which always lead to the right outcome (assume that equal shares is fair and let the man who cuts the cake take the last piece). These situations are those of perfect procedural justice. In other cases it does not matter what the outcome is as long as the fair procedure is followed: fairness of the process is transferred to the result (fair gambling is an instance of this). These situations are those of pure procedural justice. The constitutional process, like a criminal trial, resembles neither of these; the result matters and we have a standard for it. The difficulty is that we cannot frame a procedure which guarantees that only just and effective legislation is enacted. Thus even under a just constitution unjust laws may be passed and unjust policies enforced. Some form of the majority principle is necessary but the majority may be mistaken, more or less willfully, in what it legislates. In agreeing to a democratic constitution (as an instance of imperfect procedural justice) one accepts at the same time the principle of majority rule. Assuming that the constitution is just and that we have accepted and plan to continue to accept its benefits, we then have both an obligation and a natural duty (and in any case the duty) to comply with what the majority enacts even though it may be unjust. In this way we become bound to follow unjust laws, not always, of course, but provided the injustice does not exceed certain limits. We recognize that we must run the risk of suffering from the defects of one another's sense of justice; this burden we are prepared to carry as long as it is more or less evenly distributed or does not weigh too heavily. Justice binds us to a just constitution and to the unjust laws which may be enacted under it in precisely the same way that it binds us to any other social arrangement. Once we take the sequence of stages into account, there is nothing unusual in our being required to comply with unjust laws.

It should be observed that the majority principle has a secondary place as a rule of procedure which is perhaps the most efficient one under usual circumstances for working a democratic constitution. The basis for it rests essentially upon the principles of justice and therefore we may, when conditions allow, appeal to these principles against unjust legislation. The justice of the constitution does not insure the justice of laws enacted under it; and while we often have both an obligation and a duty to comply with what the majority legislates (as long as it does not exceed certain limits), there is, of course, no corresponding obligation or duty to regard what the majority enacts as itself just. The right to make law does not guarantee that the decision is rightly made; and while the citizen submits in his conduct to the judgment of democratic authority, he does not submit his judgment to it. And if in his judgment the enactments of the majority exceed certain bounds of injustice, the citizen may consider civil disobedience. For we are not required to accept the majority's acts unconditionally and to acquiesce in the denial of our and others' liberties; rather we submit our conduct to democratic authority to the extent necessary to share the burden of working a constitutional regime, distorted as it must inevitably be by men's lack of wisdom and the defects of their sense of justice.

THE PLACE OF CIVIL DISOBEDIENCE IN A CONSTITUTIONAL DEMOCRACY

We are now in a position to say a few things about civil disobedience. I shall understand it to be a public, nonviolent, and conscientious act contrary to law usually done with the intent to bring about a change in the policies or laws of the government. Civil disobedience is a political act in the sense that it is an act justified by moral principles which define a conception of civil society and the public good. It rests, then, on political conviction as opposed to a search for self or group interest; and in the case of a constitutional democracy, we may assume that this conviction involves the conception of justice (say that expressed by the contract doctrine) which underlies the constitution itself. That is, in a viable democratic regime there is a common conception of justice by reference to which its citizens regulate their political affairs and interpret the constitution. Civil disobedience is a public art which the dissenter believes to be justified by this conception of justice and for this reason it may be understood as addressing the sense of justice of the majority in order to urge reconsideration of the measures protested and to warn that, in the sincere opinion of the dissenters, the conditions of social cooperation are not being honored. For the principles of justice express precisely such conditions, and their persistent and deliberate violation in regard to basic liberties over any extended period of time cuts the ties of community and invites either submission or forceful resistance. By engaging in civil disobedience a minority leads the majority to consider whether it wants to have its acts taken in this way, or whether, in view of the common sense of justice, it wishes to acknowledge the claims of the minority.

Civil disobedience is also civil in another sense. Not only is it the outcome of a sincere conviction based on principles which regulate civic life, but it is public and nonviolent, that is, it is done in a situation where arrest and punishment are expected and accepted without resistance. In this way it manifests a respect for legal procedures. Civil disobedience expresses disobedience to law within the limits of fidelity to law, and this feature of it helps to establish in the eyes of the majority that it is indeed conscientious and sincere, that it really is meant to address their sense of justice. Being completely open about one's acts and being willing to accept the legal consequences of one's conduct is a bond given to make good one's sincerity, for that one's deeds are conscientious is not easy to demonstrate to another or even before oneself. No doubt it is possible to imagine a legal system in which conscientious belief that the law is unjust is accepted as a defense for noncompliance, and men of great honesty who are confident in one another might make such a system work. But as things are such a scheme would be unstable; we must pay a price in order to establish that we believe our actions have a moral basis in the convictions of the community.

The nonviolent nature of civil disobedience refers to the fact that it is intended to address the sense of justice of the majority and as such it is a form of speech, an expression of conviction. To engage in violent acts likely to injure and to hurt is incompatible with civil disobedience as a mode of address. Indeed, an interference with the basic rights of others tends to obscure the civilly disobedient quality of one's act. Civil disobedience is nonviolent in the further sense that the legal penalty for one's action is accepted and that resistance is not (at least for the moment) contemplated. Nonviolence in this sense is to be distinguished from nonviolence as a religious or pacifist principle. While those engaging in civil disobedience have often held some such principle, there is no necessary connection between it and civil disobedience. For on the interpretation suggested, civil disobedience in a democratic society is best understood as an appeal to the principles of justice, the fundamental conditions of willing social cooperation among free men, which in the view of the community as a whole are expressed in the constitution and guide its interpretation. Being an appeal to the moral basis of public life, civil disobedience is a political and not primarily a religious act. It addresses itself to the common principles of justice which men can require one another to follow and not to the aspirations of love which they cannot. Moreover by taking part in civilly disobedient acts one does not foreswear indefinitely the idea of forceful resistance; for if the appeal against injustice is repeatedly denied, then the majority has declared its intention to invite submission or resistance and the latter may conceivably be justified even in a democratic regime. We are not required to acquiesce in the crushing of fundamental liberties by democratic majorities which have shown themselves blind to the principles of justice upon which justification of the constitution depends.

THE JUSTIFICATION OF CIVIL DISOBEDIENCE

So far we have said nothing about the justification of civil disobedience, that is, the conditions under which civil disobedience may be engaged in consistent with the principles of justice that support a democratic regime. Our task is to see how the characterization of civil disobedience as addressed to the sense of justice of the majority (or to the citizens as a body) determines when such action is justified.

First of all, we may suppose that the normal political appeals to the majority have already been made in good faith and have been rejected, and that the standard means of redress have been tried. Thus, for example, existing political parties are indifferent to the claims of the minority and attempts to repeal the laws protested have been met with further repression since legal institutions are in the control of the majority. While civil disobedience should be recognized, I think, as a form of political action within the limits of fidelity to the rule of law, at the same time it is a rather desperate act just within these limits, and therefore it should, in general, be undertaken as a last resort when standard democratic processes have failed. In this sense it is not a normal political action. When it is justified there has been a serious breakdown; not only is there grave injustice in the law but a refusal more or less deliberate to correct it.

Second, since civil disobedience is a political act addressed to the sense of justice of the majority, it should usually be limited to substantial and clear violations of justice and preferably to those which, if rectified, will establish a basis for doing away with remaining injustices. For this reason there is a presumption in favor of restricting civil disobedience to violations of the first principle of justice, the principle of equal liberty, and to barriers which contravene the second principle, the principle of open offices which protects equality of opportunity. It is not, of course, always easy to tell whether these principles are satisfied. . . . When minorities are denied the right to vote or to hold certain political offices, when certain religious groups are repressed and others denied equality of opportunity in the economy, this is often obvious and there is no doubt that justice is not being given. . . .

Third, civil disobedience should be restricted to those cases where the dissenter is willing to affirm that everyone else similarly subjected to the same degree of injustice has the right to protest in a similar way. That is, we must be prepared to authorize others to dissent in similar situations and in the same way, and to accept the consequences of their doing so. Thus, we may hold, for example, that the widespread disposition to disobey civilly clear violations of fundamental liberties more or less deliberate over an extended period of time would raise the degree of justice throughout society and would insure men's self-esteem as well as their respect for one another. Indeed, I believe this to be true, though certainly it is partly a matter of conjecture. As the contract doctrine emphasizes, since the principles of justice are principles which we would agree to in an original position of equality when we do not know our social position and the like, the refusal to grant justice is either the denial of the other as an equal (as one in regard to whom we are prepared to constrain our actions by principles which we would consent to) or the manifestation of a willingness to take advantage of natural contingencies and social fortune at his expense. In either case, injustice invites submission or resistance; but submission arouses the contempt of the oppressor and confirms him in his intention. If straightway, after a decent period of time to make reasonable political appeals in the normal way, men were in general to dissent by civil disobedience from infractions of the fundamental equal liberties, these liberties would, I believe, be more rather than less secure. Legitimate civil disobedience properly exercised is a stabilizing device in a constitutional regime, tending to make it more firmly just. . . .

The final condition, of a different nature, is the following. We have been considering when one has a right to engage in civil disobedience, and our conclusion is that one has this right should three conditions hold: when one is subject to injustice more or less deliberate over an extended period of time in the face of normal political protests; where the injustice is a clear violation of the liberties of equal citizenship; and provided that the general disposition to protest similarly in similar cases would have acceptable consequences. These conditions are not, I think, exhaustive but they seem to cover the more obvious points; yet even when they are satisfied and one has the right to engage in civil disobedience, there is still the different question of whether one should exercise this right, that is, whether by doing so one is likely to further one's ends. Having established one's right to protest one is then free to consider these tactical questions. We may be acting within our rights but still foolishly if our action only serves to provoke the harsh retaliation of the majority; and it is likely to do so if the majority lacks a sense of justice, or if the action is poorly timed or not well designed to make the appeal to the sense of justice effective. . . .

CONCLUSION: SEVERAL OBJECTIONS CONSIDERED

. . . It is natural to object to this view of civil disobedience that it relies too heavily upon the existence of a sense of justice. Some may hold that the feeling for justice is not a vital political force, and that what moves men are various other interests, the desire for wealth, power, prestige, and so on. Now this is a large question the answer to which is highly conjectural and each tends to have his own opinion. But there are two remarks which may clarify what I have said: first, I have assumed that there is in a constitutional regime a common sense of justice the principles of which are recognized to support the constitution and to guide its interpretation. In any given situation particular men may be tempted to violate these principles, but the collective force in their behalf is usually effective since they are seen as the necessary terms of cooperation among free men; and presumably the citizens of a democracy (or sufficiently many of them) want to see justice done. Where these assumptions fail, the justifying conditions for civil disobedience (the first three) are not affected, but the rationality of engaging in it certainly is. In this case, unless the costs of repressing civil dissent injures the economic self-interest (or whatever) of the majority, protest may simply make the position of the minority worse. No doubt as a tactical matter civil disobedience is more effective when its appeal coincides with other interests, but a constitutional regime is not viable in the long run without an attachment to the principles of justice of the sort which we have assumed.

Then, further, there may be a misapprehension about the manner in which a sense of justice manifests itself. There is a tendency to think that it is shown by professions of the relevant principles together with actions of an altruistic nature requiring a considerable degree of self-sacrifice.

But these conditions are obviously too strong, for the majority's sense of justice may show itself simply in its being unable to undertake the measures required to suppress the minority and to punish as the law requires the various acts of civil disobedience. The sense of justice undermines the will to uphold unjust institutions, and so a majority despite its superior power may give way. It is unprepared to force the minority to be subject to injustice. Thus, although the majority's action is reluctant and grudging, the role of the sense of justice is nevertheless essential, for without it the majority would have been willing to enforce the law and to defend its position. Once we see the sense of justice as working in this negative way to make established injustices indefensible, then it is recognized as a central element of democratic politics.

Finally, it may be objected against this account that it does not settle the question of who is to say when the situation is such as to justify civil disobedience. And because it does not answer this question, it invites anarchy by encouraging every man to decide the matter for himself. Now the reply to this is that each man must indeed settle this question for himself, although he may, of course, decide wrongly. This is true on any theory of political duty and obligation, at least on any theory compatible with the principles of a democratic constitution. The citizen is responsible for what he does. If we usually think that we should comply with the law, this is because our political principles normally lead to this conclusion. There is a presumption in favor of compliance in the absence of good reasons to the contrary. But because each man is responsible and must decide for himself as best he can whether the circumstances justify civil disobedience, it does not follow that he may decide as he pleases. It is not by looking to our personal interests or to political allegiances narrowly construed, that we should make up our mind. The citizen must decide on the basis of the principles of justice that underlie and guide the interpretation of the constitution and in the light of his sincere conviction as to how these principles should be applied in the circumstances. If he concludes that conditions obtain which justify civil disobedience and conducts himself accordingly, he has acted conscientiously and perhaps mistakenly, but not in any case at his convenience.

In a democratic society each man must act as he thinks the principles of political right require him to. We are to follow our understanding of these principles, and we cannot do otherwise. There can be no morally binding legal interpretation of these principles, not even by a supreme court or legislature. Nor is there any infallible procedure for determining what or who is right. In our system the Supreme Court, Congress, and the President often put forward rival interpretations of the Constitution. Although the Court has the final say in settling any particular case, it is not immune from powerful political influence that may change its reading of the law of the land. The Court presents its point of view

by reason and argument; its conception of the Constitution must, if it is to endure, persuade men of its soundness. The final court of appeal is not the Court, or Congress, or the President, but the electorate as a whole. The civilly disobedient appeal in effect to this body. There is no danger of anarchy as long as there is a sufficient working agreement in men's conceptions of political justice and what it requires. That men can achieve such an understanding when the essential political liberties are maintained is the assumption implicit in democratic institutions. There is no way to avoid entirely the risk of divisive strife. But if legitimate civil disobedience seems to threaten civil peace, the responsibility falls not so much on those who protest as upon those whose abuse of authority and power justifies such opposition.

REVIEW AND DISCUSSION QUESTIONS

1. Describe what Rawls means by justice as "fairness."

2. Why does Rawls think that the basic principles used to select a constitution and laws governing citizens' rights and opportunities should be chosen behind a "veil of ignorance"?

3. "Even a just constitution can lead to unjust laws." Explain using the analogy of a criminal trial.

4. Rawls thinks that the obligation to obey the law (assuming a just constitution) rests on the duty

of fair play. Explain what he means.

5. How does Rawls define civil disobedience? What role does civil disobedience play in a constitutional democracy?

6. Under what circumstances does Rawls think civil disobedience is justified?

7. How does Rawls respond to those who suggest his view is naive because it is based on the view that civil disobedience is an appeal to a majority's "sense of justice"?

On Not Prosecuting Civil Disobedience

Ronald Dworkin

Besides legal obligation, civil disobedience raises further philosophical questions about the nature of law itself and whether civil disobedients should be prosecuted. Ronald Dworkin begins with a familiar argument, that since society could not function if everybody were allowed to pick and choose the laws that he or she wishes to obey, fairness *demands uniform prosecution of all acts of civil disobedience. But in order to assess the argument, Dworkin maintains, we must first ask ourselves what we expect fellow citizens to do when they sincerely believe a law is unjust or immoral. In the American constitutional system, according to Dworkin, law and morality are not easily separated, which means that the validity of law is itself often an issue in civil disobedience cases and therefore that officials should think of civil disobedients differently from ordinary criminals. Ronald Dworkin teaches philosophy and law at London University and New York University.*

How should the government deal with those who disobey the draft laws out of conscience? Many people think the answer is obvious: the government must prosecute the dissenters, and if they are convicted it must punish them. Some people reach this conclusion easily, because they hold the mindless view that conscientious disobedience is the same as lawlessness. They think that the dissenters are anarchists who must be punished before their corruption spreads. Many lawyers and intellectuals come to the same conclusion, however, on what looks like a more sophisticated argument. They recognize that disobedience to law may be *morally* justified, but they insist that it cannot be *legally* justified, and they think that it follows from this truism that the law must be enforced. Erwin Griswold, the Solicitor General of the United States, and the former dean of the Harvard Law School, appears to have adopted this view in a recent statement. "[It] is of the essence of law," he said, "that it is equally applied to all, that it binds all alike, irrespective of personal motive. For this reason, one who contemplates civil disobedience out of moral conviction should not be surprised and must not be bitter if a criminal conviction ensues. And he must accept the fact that organized society cannot endure on any other basis." . . .

But the argument that, because the government believes a man has committed a crime, it must prosecute him is much weaker than it seems. Society "cannot endure" if it tolerates all disobedience; it does not follow, however, nor is there evidence, that it will collapse if it tolerates some. In the United States prosecutors have discretion whether to enforce criminal laws in particular cases. A prosecutor may properly decide not to press charges if the lawbreaker is young, or inexperienced, or the sole support of the family, or is repentant, or turns state's evidence, or if the law is unpopular or unworkable or generally disobeyed, or if the courts are clogged with more important cases, or for dozens of other reasons. This discretion is not license—we expect prosecutors to have good reasons for exercising it—but there are, at least *prima facie*,

some good reasons for not prosecuting those who disobey the draft laws out of conscience. One is the obvious reason that they act out of better motives than those who break the law out of greed or a desire to subvert government. Another is the practical reason that our society suffers a loss if it punishes a group that includes—as a group of draft dissenters does—some of its most thoughtful and loyal citizens. Jailing such men solidifies their alienation from society, and alienates many like them who are deterred by the threat.

Those who think that conscientious draft offenders . . . should always be punished must show that these are not good reasons for exercising discretion, or they must find contrary reasons that outweigh them. What arguments might they produce? . . . Dean Griswold and those who agree with him seem to rely on a fundamental moral argument that it would be unfair, not merely impractical, to let the dissenters go unpunished. They think it would be unfair, I gather, because society could not function if everyone disobeyed laws he disapproved of or found disadvantageous. If the government tolerates those few who will not "play the game," it allows them to secure the benefits of everyone else's deference to law, without shouldering the burdens, such as the burden of the draft.

This argument is a serious one. It cannot be answered simply by saying that the dissenters would allow everyone else the privilege of disobeying a law he believed immoral. In fact, few draft dissenters would accept a changed society in which sincere segregationists were free to break civil rights laws they hated. The majority want no such change, in any event, because they think that society would be worse off for it; until they are shown this is wrong, they will expect their officials to punish anyone who assumes a privilege which they, for the general benefit, do not assume.

There is, however, a flaw in the argument. The reasoning contains a hidden assumption that makes it almost entirely irrelevant to the draft cases, and indeed to any serious case of civil disobedience in the United States. The argument assumes that the dissenters know that they are breaking a valid law, and that the privilege they assert is the privilege to do that. Of course, almost everyone who discusses civil disobedience recognizes that in America a law may be invalid because it is unconstitutional. . . .

Doubtful law is by no means special or exotic in cases of civil disobedience. On the contrary. In the United States, at least, almost any law which a significant number of people would be tempted to disobey on moral grounds would be doubtful—if not clearly invalid—on constitutional grounds as well. The constitution makes our conventional political morality relevant to the question of validity; any statute that appears to compromise that morality raises constitutional questions, and if the compromise is serious, the constitutional doubts are serious also.

[Editor's Note: Dworkin illustrates this by pointing out that moral objections to the Vietnam War—for example, that the United States was using immoral weapons, that Congress had never officially declared war, and that it had been made a crime to "counsel" draft resistance—have parallels in law, for example, international treaties we signed banning certain weapons, Congress's exclusive power to declare war, and First Amendment protections of free speech. These moral/legal arguments thus provide the basis for thinking that, in fact, the laws in question are invalid.]

. . . We cannot conclude from these arguments that the draft (or any part of it) was unconstitutional. . . . But the arguments of unconstitutionality were at least plausible and a reasonable and competent lawyer might think that they present a stronger case, on balance, than the counter arguments. . . .

Therefore we cannot assume, in judging what should have been done with the draft dissenters, that they were asserting a privilege to disobey valid laws. We cannot decide that fairness demanded their punishment until we try to answer further questions: What should a citizen do when the law is unclear, and when he thinks it allows what others think it does not? I do not mean to ask, of course, what it is *legally* proper

for him to do, or what his *legal* rights are—that would be begging the question, because it depends upon whether he is right or they are right. I mean to ask what his proper course is as a citizen, what, in other words, we would consider to be "playing the game." That is a crucial question, because it cannot be unfair not to punish him if he is acting as, given his opinions, we think he should.[1]

There is no obvious answer on which most citizens would readily agree, and that is itself significant. If we examine our legal institutions and practices, however, we shall discover some relevant underlying principles and policies. I shall set out three possible answers to the question, and then try to show which of these best fits our practices and expectations. The three possibilities I want to consider are these:

1. If the law is doubtful, and it is therefore unclear whether it permits someone to do what he wants, he should assume the worst, and act on the assumption that it does not. He should obey the executive authorities who command him, even though he thinks they are wrong, while using the political process, if he can, to change the law.

2. If the law is doubtful, he may follow his own judgment, that is, he may do what he wants if he believes that the case that the law permits this is stronger than the case that it does not. But he may follow his own judgment only until an authoritative institution, like a court, decides the other way in a case involving him or someone else. Once an institutional decision has been reached, he must abide by that decision, even though he thinks that it was wrong. (There are, in theory, many subdivisions of this second possibility. We may say that the individual's choice is foreclosed by the contrary decision of any court, including the lowest court in the system if the case is not appealed. Or we may require a decision of some particular court or institution. I shall discuss this second possibility in its most liberal form, namely that the individual may properly follow his own judgment until a contrary decision of the highest court competent to pass on the issue, which, in the case of the draft, was the United States Supreme Court.)

3. If the law is doubtful, he may follow his own judgment, even after a contrary decision by the highest competent court. Of course, he must take the contrary decision of any court into account in making his judgment of what the law requires. Otherwise the judgment would not be an honest or reasonable one, because the doctrine of precedent, which is an established part of our legal system, has the effect of allowing the decision of the courts to change the law. Suppose, for example, that a taxpayer believes that he is not required to pay tax on certain forms of income. If the Supreme Court decides to the contrary, he should, taking into account the practice of according great weight to the decisions of the Supreme Court on tax matters, decide that the Court's decision has itself tipped the balance, and that the law now requires him to pay the tax.

Someone might think that this qualification erases the difference between the third and the second models, but it does not. The doctrine of precedent gives different weights to the decisions of different courts, and greatest weight to the decisions of the Supreme Court, but it does not make the decisions of any court conclusive. Sometimes, even after a contrary Supreme Court decision, an individual may still reasonably believe that the law is on his side; such cases are rare, but they are most likely to occur in disputes over constitutional law when civil disobedience is involved. The Court has shown itself more likely to overrule its past decisions if these have limited important personal or political rights, and it is just these decisions that a dissenter might want to challenge.

We cannot assume, in other words, that the Constitution is always what the Supreme Court says it is. Oliver Wendell Holmes, for example, did not follow such a rule in his famous dissent in the *Gitlow* case. A few years before, in *Abrams*, he had lost his battle to persuade the court that the First Amendment protected an anarchist who had been urging general strikes against the government. A similar issue was presented in *Gitlow*, and Holmes once again dissented. "It is true," he said, "that in my opinion this criterion was departed from [in *Abrams*] but the

convictions that I expressed in that case are too deep for it to be possible for me as yet to believe that it . . . settled the law." Holmes voted for acquitting Gitlow, on the ground that what Gitlow had done was no crime, even though the Supreme Court had recently held that it was.

Here then are three possible models for the behavior of dissenters who disagree with the executive authorities when the law is doubtful. Which of them best fits our legal and social practices?

I think it plain that we do not follow the first of these models, that is, that we do not expect citizens to assume the worst. If no court has decided the issue, and a man thinks, on balance, that the law is on his side, most of our lawyers and critics think it perfectly proper for him to follow his own judgment. Even when many disapprove of what he does—such as peddling pornography—they do not think he must desist just because the legality of his conduct is subject to doubt.

I think it plain that we do not follow the first of these models, that is, that we do not expect citizens to assume the worst . . . [and that] he must desist just because the legality of his conduct is subject to doubt.

It is worth pausing a moment to consider what society would lose if it did follow the first model or, to put the matter the other way, what society gains when people follow their own judgment in cases like this. When the law is uncertain, in the sense that lawyers can reasonably disagree on what a court ought to decide, the reason usually is that different legal principles and policies have collided, and it is unclear how best to accommodate these conflicting principles and policies.

Our practice, in which different parties are encouraged to pursue their own understanding, provides a means of testing relevant hypotheses. If the question is whether a particular rule would have certain undesirable consequences, or whether these consequences would have limited or broad ramifications, then, before the issue is decided, it is useful to know what does in fact take place when some people proceed on that rule. (Much anti-trust and business regulation law has developed through this kind of testing.)

If the question is whether and to what degree a particular solution would offend principles of justice or fair play deeply respected by the community, it is useful, again, to experiment by testing the community's response. The extent of community indifference to anti-contraception laws, for example, would never have become established had not some organizations deliberately flouted those laws.

If the first model were followed, we would lose the advantages of these tests. The law would suffer, particularly if this model were applied to constitutional issues. When the validity of a criminal statute is in doubt, the statute will almost always strike some people as being unfair or unjust, because it will infringe some principle of liberty or justice or fairness which they take to be built into the Constitution. If our practice were that whenever a law is doubtful on these grounds, one must act as if it were valid, then the chief vehicle we have for challenging the law on moral grounds would be lost, and over time the law we obeyed would certainly become less fair and just, and the liberty of our citizens would certainly be diminished. . . .

We must also reject the second model, that if the law is unclear a citizen may properly follow his own judgment until the highest court has ruled that he is wrong. This fails to take into account the fact that any court, including the Supreme Court, may overrule itself. In 1940 the Court decided that a West Virginia law requiring students to salute the Flag was constitutional. In 1943 it reversed itself, and decided that such a statute was unconstitutional after all. What was the duty as citizens, of those people who in 1941 and 1942 objected to saluting the Flag on grounds of conscience, and thought that the Court's 1940 decision was wrong? We can hardly say that their duty was to follow the first decision. They believed that saluting the Flag was unconscionable, and they believed, reasonably, that no valid law required them to do so. The Supreme Court later decided that in this they were right. The Court did not simply hold that after the second decision failing to salute would not be a crime; it held (as in a case like this it almost always would) that it was no crime after the first decision either.

Some will say that the flag-salute dissenters should have obeyed the Court's first decision, while they worked in the legislatures to have the law repealed, and tried in the courts to find some way to challenge the law again without actually violating it. That would be, perhaps, a plausible recommendation if conscience were not involved, because it would then be arguable that the gain in orderly procedure was worth the personal sacrifice of patience. But conscience was involved, and if the dissenters had obeyed the law while biding their time, they would have suffered the irreparable injury of having done what their conscience forbade them to do. It is one thing to say that an individual must sometimes violate his conscience when he knows that the law commands him to do it. It is quite another to say that he must violate his conscience even when he reasonably believes that the law does not require it, because it would inconvenience his fellow citizens if he took the most direct, and perhaps the only, method of attempting to show that he is right and they are wrong.

Since a court may overrule itself, the same reasons we listed for rejecting the first model count against the second as well. If we did not have the pressure of dissent, we would not have a dramatic statement of the degree to which a court decision against the dissenter is felt to be wrong, a demonstration that is surely pertinent to the question of whether it was right. We would increase the chance of being governed by rules that offend the principles we claim to serve. . . .

Thus the third model, or something close to it, seems to be the fairest statement of a man's social duty in our community. A citizen's allegiance is to the law, not to any particular person's view of what the law is, and he does not behave unfairly so long as he proceeds on his own considered and reasonable view of what the law requires. Let me repeat (because it is crucial) that this is not the same as saying that an individual may disregard what the courts have said. The doctrine of precedent lies near the core of our legal system, and no one can make a reasonable effort to follow the law unless he grants the courts the general power to alter it by their decisions. But if the issue is one touching fundamental personal or political rights, and it is arguable that the Supreme Court has made a mistake, a man is within his social rights in refusing to accept that decision as conclusive. . . .

. . . I have been talking about the case of a man who believes that the law is not what other people think, or what the courts have held. This description may fit some of those who disobey the draft laws out of conscience, but it does not fit most of them. Most of the dissenters are not lawyers or political philosophers; they believe that the laws on the books are immoral, and inconsistent with their country's legal ideals, but they have not considered the question of whether they may be invalid as well. Of what relevance to their situation, then, is the proposition that one may properly follow one's own view of the law?

To answer this, I shall have to return to the point I made earlier. The Constitution, through the due process clause [government cannot deprive citizens of "life, liberty, or property without due process of law"], the equal protection clause [states cannot deny citizens the "equal protection of the laws"], the First Amendment [government cannot "abridge freedom of speech" or make a law "respecting the establishment of religion, or prohibiting the free exercise thereof"], and the other provisions I mentioned, injects an extraordinary amount of our political morality into the issue of whether a law is valid. The statement that most draft dissenters are unaware that the law is invalid therefore needs qualification. They hold beliefs that, if true, strongly support the view that the law is on their side; the fact that they have not reached that further conclusion can be traced, in at least most cases, to their lack of legal sophistication. If we believe that when the law is doubtful people who follow their own judgment of the law may be acting properly, it would seem wrong not to extend that view to those dissenters whose judgments come to the same thing. No part of the case that I made for the third model would entitle us to distinguish them from their more knowledgeable colleagues.

We can draw several tentative conclusions from the argument so far: When the law is uncertain, in the sense that a plausible case can be made on both sides, then a citizen who follows his own judgment is not behaving unfairly. Our practices permit and encourage him to follow his own judgment in such cases. For that reason, our government has a special responsibility to try to protect him, and soften his predicament, whenever it can do so without great damage to other policies. It does not follow that the government can guarantee him immunity—it cannot adopt the rule that it will prosecute no one who acts out of conscience, or convict no one who reasonably disagrees with the courts. That would paralyze the government's ability to carry out its policies; it would, moreover, throw away the most important benefit of following the third model. If the state never prosecuted, then the courts could not act on the experience and the arguments the dissent has generated. But it does follow that when the practical reasons for prosecuting are relatively weak in a particular case, or can be met in other ways, the path of fairness lies in tolerance. The popular view that the law is the law and must always be enforced refuses to distinguish the man who acts on his own judgment of a doubtful law, and thus behaves as our practices provide, from the common criminal. I know of no reason, short of moral blindness, for not drawing a distinction in principle between the two cases.

I anticipate a philosophical objection to these conclusions: that I am treating law as a "brooding omnipresence in the sky." I have spoken of people making judgments about what the law requires, even in cases in which the law is unclear and undemonstrable. I have spoken of cases in which a man might think that the law requires one thing, even though the Supreme Court has said that it requires another, and even when it was not likely that the Supreme Court would soon change its mind. I will therefore be charged with the view that there is always a "right answer" to a legal problem to be found in natural law or locked up in some transcendental strongbox.

The strongbox theory of law is, of course, nonsense. When I say that people hold views on the law when the law is doubtful, and that these views are not merely predictions of what the courts will hold, I intend no such metaphysics. I mean only to summarize as accurately as I can many of the practices that are part of our legal process.

Lawyers and judges make statements of legal right and duty, even when they know these are not demonstrable, and support them with arguments even when they know that these arguments will not appeal to everyone. They make these arguments to one another, in the professional journals, in the classrooms, and in the courts. They respond to these arguments, when others make them, by judging them good or bad or mediocre. In so doing they assume that some arguments for a given doubtful position are better than others. They also assume that the case on one side of a doubtful proposition may be stronger than the case on the other, which is what I take a claim of law in a doubtful case to mean. . . .

Our legal system pursues these goals (the development and testing of the law through experimentation by citizens and through the adversary process) by inviting citizens to decide the strengths and weaknesses of legal arguments for themselves, or through their own counsel, and to act on these judgments, although that permission is qualified by the limited threat that they may suffer if the courts do not agree. Success in this strategy depends on whether there is sufficient agreement within the community on what counts as a good or bad argument, so that, although different people will reach different judgments, these differences will be neither so profound nor so frequent as to make the system unworkable, or dangerous for those who act by their own lights. I believe there is sufficient agreement on the criteria of the argument to avoid these traps, although one of the main tasks of legal philosophy is to exhibit and clarify these criteria. In any event, the practices I have described have not yet been shown to be misguided; they therefore must count in determining whether it is just and fair to be lenient to those who break what others think is the law.

I have said that the government has a special responsibility to those who act on a reasonable judgment that a law is invalid. It should make accommodation for them as far as possible, when this is consistent with other policies. It may be difficult to decide what the government ought to do, in the name of that responsibility, in particular cases. The decision will be a matter of balance, and flat rules will not help. . . .

Some lawyers will be shocked by my general conclusion that we have a responsibility toward those who disobey the draft laws out of conscience, and that we may be required not to prosecute them, but rather to change our laws or adjust our sentencing procedures to accommodate them. The simple Draconian propositions, that crime must be punished, and that he who misjudges the law must take the consequences, have an extraordinary hold on the professional as well as the popular imagination. But the rule of law is more complex and more intelligent than that and it is important that it survive.

NOTE

[1] I do not mean to imply that the government should always punish a man who deliberately breaks a law he knows is valid. There may be reasons of fairness or practicality, like those I listed in the third paragraph, for not prosecuting such men. But cases like the draft cases present special arguments for tolerance; I want to concentrate on these arguments and therefore have isolated these cases.

REVIEW AND DISCUSSION QUESTIONS

1. Describe how Dworkin understands the relationship between morality and law. Why is it often difficult to know whether a law is valid?

2. What service does Dworkin think civil disobedients provide in our system?

3. Dworkin argues that it is not unfair to refuse to prosecute civil disobedients. His argument relies on a discussion of three courses of action open to citizens who object to law, and what we as a society reasonably expect of our fellow citizens. Explain his argument.

4. What does Dworkin mean in rejecting the "strongbox" view of law? If law and morality are connected, as he suggests, how is the law to be tested and legal arguments assessed?

5. In light of one or two of the cases you have read, is Dworkin's description of the connections between law and morality an accurate one?

4

THE ELEMENTS OF LEGAL REASONING

Through essays and cases, this section explores the basic elements of legal reasoning involved in case law and in statutory interpretation (constitutional interpretation is reserved for a later section). Although the process of reasoning and argumentation used by lawyers and judges appears in some ways as a paradigm of analysis and argumentation, it differs strikingly from the form of reasoning that characterizes philosophy on the one hand or science on the other. For example, reliance on precedent, so distinctive of law, has no counterpart in other areas of intellectual inquiry. Among the topics raised here are the nature of—and justification for—following precedent and the importance of legislative intent to statutory interpretation. Not only is an understanding of legal argumentation—and of the debates over its proper nature—of inherent interest, but such an understanding also provides fascinating background for many of the issues explored in the rest of the book.

On Interpretation: The Adultery Clause of the Ten Commandments

Sanford Levinson

Using an ingenious example drawn from his own course in constitutional law, Sanford Levinson describes a variety of problems confronting anybody who undertakes to interpret broad concepts with ancient roots, such as the Ten Commandments. Professor Levinson teaches at the University of Texas Law School.

Author's Note: . . . I have for many years introduced my first-year constitutional law course with the following hypothetical exercise. It has proved useful in helping students to grasp the kinds of interpretive issues that analysis of the constitutional text necessarily raises.

Consider the following problem:

In 1970, a number of concerned citizens, worried about what they regarded as the corruption of American life, met to consider what could be done. During the course of the discussion, one of the speakers electrified the audience with the following comments:

> The cure for our ills is a return to old-time religion, and the best single guide remains the Ten Commandments. Whenever I am perplexed as to what I ought to do, I turn to the Commandments for the answer, and I am never disappointed. Sometimes I don't immediately like what I discover, but then I think more about the problem and realize how limited my perspective is compared to that of the framer of those great words. Indeed, all that is necessary is for everyone to obey the Ten Commandments, and our problems will all be solved.[1]

Within several hours the following plan was devised: As part of the effort to encourage a return to the "old-time religion" of the Ten Commandments, a number of young people would be asked to take an oath on their eighteenth birthday to "obey, protect, support, and defend the Ten Commandments" in all of their actions. If the person complied with the oath for seventeen years, he or she would receive an award of $10,000 on his or her thirty-fifth birthday.

The foundation for the Ten Commandments was funded by the members of the 1970 convention, plus the proceeds of a national campaign for contributions. The speaker quoted above contributed $20 million, and an additional $30 million was collected, $15 million from the convention and $15 million from the national campaign. The interest generated by the $50 million is approximately $6 million per year. Each year since 1970, 500 persons have taken the oath. *You* are appointed sole trustee of the Foundation, and your most important duty is to determine whether the oath-takers have complied with their vows and are thus entitled to the $10,000.

It is now 1987, and the first set of claimants comes before you:

1. Claimant *A* is a married male. Although freely admitting that he has had sexual intercourse with a number of women other than his wife during their marriage, he brings to your attention the fact that "adultery," at the time of Biblical Israel, referred only to the voluntary intercourse of a married woman with a man other than her husband. He specifically notes the following passage from the article *Adultery*, I JEWISH ENCYCLOPEDIA 314:

> The extramarital intercourse of a married man is not *per se* a crime in biblical or later Jewish law. This distinction stems from the economic aspect of Israelite marriage: The wife as the husband's possession . . . , and adultery constituted a violation of the husband's exclusive right to her; the wife, as the husband's possession, had no such right to him.

A has taken great care to make sure that all his sexual partners were unmarried, and thus he claims to have been faithful to the original understanding of the Ten Commandments. However we might define "adultery" today, he argues, is irrelevant. His oath was to comply with the Ten Commandments; he claims to have done so. (It is stipulated that *A*, like all the other claimants, has complied with all the other commandments; the only question involves compliance with the commandment against adultery.)

Upon further questioning, you discover that no line-by-line explication of the Ten Commandments was proffered in 1970 at the time that *A* took the oath. But, says *A*, whenever a question arose in his mind as to what the Ten Commandments required of him, he made conscientious attempts to research the particular issue. He initially shared your (presumed) surprise at the results of his research, but further study indicated that all authorities agreed with the scholars who wrote the *Jewish Encyclopedia* regarding the original understanding of the Commandment.

2. Claimant *B* is *A*'s wife, who admits that she has had extramarital relationships with other men. She notes, though, that these affairs were entered into with the consent of her husband. In response to the fact that she undoubtedly violated the ancient understanding of "adultery," she states that that understanding is fatally outdated:

a. It is unfair to distinguish between the sexual rights of males and females. That the Israelites were outrageously sexist is no warrant for your maintaining the discrimination.

b. Moreover, the reason for the differentiation, as already noted, was the perception of the wife as property. That notion is a repugnant one that has been properly repudiated by all rational thinkers, including all major branches of the Judeo-Christian religious tradition historically linked to the Ten Commandments.

c. She further argues that, insofar as the modern prohibition of adultery is defensible, it rests on the ideal of discouraging deceit and the betrayal of promises of sexual fidelity. But these admittedly negative factors are not present in her case because she had scrupulously informed her husband and received his consent, as required by their marriage contract outlining the terms of their "open marriage."

(It turns out, incidentally, that *A* had failed to inform his wife of at least one of his sexual encounters. Though he freely admits that this constitutes a breach of the contract he had made with *B*, he nevertheless returns to his basic argument about original understanding, which makes consent irrelevant.)

3. *C*, a male (is this relevant?), is the participant in a bigamous marriage. *C* had no sexual encounters beyond his two wives. (He also points out that bigamy was clearly tolerated in both pre- and post-Sinai Israel and indeed was accepted within the Yemenite community of Jews well into the twentieth century. It is also accepted in a variety of world cultures.)

4. *D*, a practicing Christian, admits that he has often lusted after women other than his wife. (Indeed, he confesses as well that it was only after much contemplation that he decided not to sexually consummate a relationship with a coworker whom he thinks he "may love" and with whom he has held hands.) You are familiar with Christ's words, *Matthew* 5:28: "Whosoever looketh on a woman to lust after, he hath committed adultery with her already in his heart." (Would it matter to you if *D* were the wife, who had lusted after other men?)

5. Finally, claimant *E* has never even lusted after another woman since his marriage on the same day he took his oath. He does admit, however, to occasional lustful fantasies about his wife. *G*, a Catholic, is shocked when informed of Pope John Paul II's statement that "adultery in your heart is committed not only when you look with concupiscence at a woman who is not your wife, but also if you look in the same manner at your wife." The Pope's rationale apparently is that all lust, even that directed toward a spouse, dehumanizes and reduces the other person "to an erotic object."

Which, if any, of the claimants should get the $10,000? . . .

NOTE

[1]*Cf.* Statement of President Ronald Reagan, Press Conference, Feb. 21, 1985, reprinted in *N.Y. Times*, Feb. 22, 1985 §1, at 10, col. 3: "I've found that the Bible contains an answer to just about everything and every problem that confronts us, and I wonder sometimes why we won't recognize that one Book could solve a lot of problems for us."

REVIEW AND DISCUSSION QUESTIONS

1. Describe the situation Levinson envisions.
2. Summarize the arguments of each of the five claimants.

3. Which of the five, if any, should get the money? Explain.

Stare Decisis: The Use of Precedent

C. Gordon Post

Everyone knows that lawyers and judges rely on legal "precedents," but what precisely does that mean? In this essay C. Gordon Post, professor of political science at Vassar College, discusses what precedents are, why following them is thought important, the ways judges eliminate old precedents and establish new ones, and the form of reasoning that is employed by judges when they appeal to a precedent. Along the way he describes a wide variety of legal cases and opinions from both England and the United States that illuminate these important questions.

In the resolution of conflicts a court invokes and applies rules of law to proven facts. A question arises: Just where does a court find these rules?

There are two *chief* sources of law: *statutes* and *precedents*. The former, of course, come from the legislature which consists of the elected representatives of the people. The latter come from the courts; precedents are the products of earlier decisions. To the latter, we should add the decisions of an increasing number of administrative bodies and the precedents established thereby, but of this matter we shall speak later.

Most everybody knows what a statute is, but what is a precedent? In a general, nonlegal way, precedent plays an important role in our lives. Often, we do things as our parents did them and cite their experience as precedent for what we do now; out of some continuing or repetitive situation there comes a rough rule of thumb. When a father is questioned as to why he spanked his son for some infraction of the household rules he might reply that as a boy in like circumstances he had been spanked as had his father before him. He might go on to explain that such treatment was an application of the rule of experience, "Spare the rod and spoil the child."

When a mother solicits the aid of her protesting children in doing the household chores, she might declare that children have always helped their parents, and in support of this experience she quotes the rule, "Many hands make light work." On the other hand, when the children clamor to help her make a cake for the church bazaar, she more than likely will decline the proffered aid and repeat the ancient adage, "Too many cooks spoil the broth."

A young man, intending a change from one job to another, is cautioned by his father, who tries to dissuade him with the rule, hoary with time, that "A rolling stone gathers no moss," or no money, as the case may be. The son, wanting a change of work, answers with another ancient rule, "Nothing ventured, nothing gained."

In all of these instances, there is the application of a rule of experience to a given situation. These are homely examples. Clubs, business organizations, boards of trustees, student groups—all have their rules, some written, some unwritten, which are often invoked as precedent for doing, or not doing, one thing or another. And a precedent here is defined by Webster as "something done or said that may serve as an example or rule to authorize or justify a subsequent act of the same or analogous kind."

JUDICIAL PRECEDENT

A judicial precedent is defined in the same dictionary as "a judicial decision, a form of proceeding, or course of action that serves as a rule for future determinations in similar or analogous cases."

The driver of a wagon loaded with buckskin goods stopped for the night at a certain inn. He was received as a guest and the innkeeper took charge of his property. During the night a fire broke out which resulted in the destruction of horses, wagon and goods. The owner of the property thus destroyed sued the innkeeper for damages.

Let us suppose that this was a case of first impression, that is, a situation which is before an American court for the first time. After hearing the evidence from both sides, the judge does not simply say, "I decide for the plaintiff," or "I decide for the defendant." He decides for one or the other and gives his reasons. He will speak as follows: "An innkeeper is responsible for the safe keeping of property committed to his custody by a guest. He is an insurer against loss, unless caused by the negligence or fraud of the guest, or by the act of God or the public enemy." The judge looks to the English common law and finds that the liability of innkeepers was expressed tersely in *Cross v. Andrews:* "The defendant, if he will keep an inn, ought, *at his peril*, to keep safely his guests' goods"; and at greater length by Coke in *Calye's Case:* "If one brings a bag or chest, etc., of evidences into the inn as obligations, deeds, or other specialities, and by default of the innkeeper they are taken away, the innkeeper shall answer for them."

The judge will go on to explain the reason for the rule. He will say that the rule has its origin in public policy.

Every facility should be furnished for secure and convenient intercourse between different portions of the kingdom. The safeguards, of which the law gave assurance to the wayfarer, were akin to those which invested each English home with the legal security of a castle. The traveller was peculiarly exposed to depredation and fraud. He was compelled to repose confidence in a host, who was subject to constant temptation, and favored with peculiar opportunities, if he chose to betray his trust. The innkeeper was at liberty to fix his own compensation, and enforce summary payment. His lien, then as now, fastened upon the goods of his guest from the time they came to his custody. The care of the property was usually committed to servants, over whom the guest had no control, and who had no interest in its preservation, unless their employer was held responsible for its safety. In case of depredation by collusion, or of injury or destruction by neglect, the stranger would of necessity be at every possible disadvantage. He would be without the means either of proving guilt or detecting it. The witnesses to whom he must resort for information, if not accessories to the injury,

would ordinarily be in the interest of the innkeeper. The sufferer would be deprived, by the very wrong of which he complained, of the means of remaining to ascertain and enforce his rights, and redress would be well-nigh hopeless, but for the rule of law casting the loss on the party entrusted with the custody of the property, and paid for keeping it safely.[1]

STARE DECISIS

Let us suppose that a year or so later, another driver with a wagon load of hides spends the night at an inn. Again, the horses, the wagon, and the hides, are turned over to the innkeeper; and again, a fire occurs during the night and the property of the guest is burned up. The owner of the property then sues the innkeeper for damages. The situation here is exactly the same as in the earlier case.

The judge in the second case, according to the theory, will apply the rule or principle (which is the precedent) and decide in favor of the plaintiff. The precedent or authority of the first case is precise and fits the facts of the second case very nicely. This application by courts of rules announced in earlier decisions is spoken of as *stare decisis*, which means "let the decision stand." This has been, and is, a fundamental characteristic of the common law, although in American jurisdictions it is the practice upon occasion for a high court to overrule its own precedents.

Obviously, a legal system in which judges could decide cases any which way, manifesting prejudice, whimsy, ignorance and venality, each decision being an entity in itself unconnected with the theory, practices and precedents of the whole, would be a sorry system, or, one might say, no system at all, and a source of little comfort either to attorneys or litigants. Speaking of *stare decisis* many years ago, Judge Maxwell of the Supreme Court of Nebraska said: "In the application of the principles of the common law, where the precedents are unanimous in the support of a proposition, there is no safety but in a strict adherence to such precedents. If the court will not follow established rules, rights are sacrificed, and lawyers and litigants are left in doubt and uncertainty, while there is no certainty in regard to what, upon a given state of facts, the decision of the court will be."

One concludes, after a little thought, that *stare decisis* is "the instrument of *stability* in a legal system," that it "furnishes a legal system with *certainty* and *predictability*," and "clothes a legal system with *reliability*"; in addition, it "assures all persons of *equality and uniformity of treatment*" and judges with "an instrument of *convenience and expediency*." In short, "*Stare decisis* preserves the judicial *experience* of the past."[2]

After a little more thought, however, one also sees that *stare decisis* is an instrument of conservatism, of immobility, of eyes-in-the-back-of-the-head, of stultification. The application of the same rule, decade after decade, long after changed conditions have robbed the rule of its validity, makes the rule a troublesome fiction.

But, American high courts do not hesitate to overrule their own precedents when social, economic, or political change demand a corresponding change in the law. Cardozo has said that "If we figure stability and progress as opposite poles, then at one pole we have the maxim of *stare decisis* and the method of decision by the tool of a deductive logic; at the other we have the method which subordinates origins to ends. The one emphasizes considerations of uniformity and symmetry, and follows fundamental conceptions to ultimate conclusions. The other gives freer play to considerations of equity and justice, and the value to society of the interests affected. The one searches for the analogy that is nearest in point of similarity, and adheres to it inflexibly. The other, in its choice of the analogy that shall govern, finds community of spirit more significant than resemblance in externals. 'Much of the administration of justice,' says Pound, 'is a compromise between the tendency to treat each case as one of a generalized type of case, and the tendency to treat each case as unique.' Each method," concludes Cardozo, "has its value, and for each in the changes of litigation there will come the hour for use. A wise eclecticism employs them both."[3]

PRECEDENT AND FACTS

In the two cases outlined above, it has been assumed that the facts were identical, but only rarely are fact situations exactly alike. And from a different fact situation there may arise a different precedent or rule of law. Professor Rodell, taking as an example a collision of two automobiles, points out the difficulties:

Suppose a man driving a 1939 Cadillac along the Lincoln Highway toward Chicago runs into a Model T Ford, driven by a farmer who has just turned onto the Highway from a dirt road, and demolishes the Ford but does not hurt the farmer. The farmer sues, and a local judge, on the basis of various principles of Law which are said to "control" the case, awards him $100. A week later, another man driving a 1939 Cadillac along the Lincoln Highway toward Chicago runs into a Model T Ford driven by another farmer who has just turned onto the Highway from the same dirt road, and demolishes the Ford but does not hurt the farmer. This farmer also sues. The facts, as stated, seem to make this case quite similar to the previous case. Will it then fall into the same group of fact situations? Will it be "controlled" by the same principles of Law? Will the second farmer get $100?

That all depends. For of course [as in the innkeeper's case] there will be other facts in both cases. Some may still be similar. Others, inevitably, will be different. And the possibilities of variation are literally endless.

Maybe the first Cadillac was doing sixty miles an hour and the second one thirty. Or maybe one was doing forty-five and the other one forty. Or maybe both were doing forty-five but it was raining one week and clear the next. Maybe one farmer blew his horn and the other didn't. Maybe one farmer stopped at the crossing and the other didn't. Maybe one farmer had a driver's license and the other didn't. Maybe one farmer was young and the other was old and wore glasses. Maybe they both wore glasses but one was nearsighted and the other farsighted.

Maybe one Cadillac carried an out-of-state license plate and the other a local license plate. Maybe one of the Cadillac drivers was a bond salesman and the other a doctor. Maybe one was insured and the other wasn't. Maybe one had a girl in the seat beside him and the other didn't. Maybe they both had girls beside them but one was talking to his girl and the other wasn't.

Maybe one Cadillac hit its Ford in the rear left wheel and the other in the front left wheel. Maybe a boy on a bicycle was riding along the Highway at one time but not the other. Maybe a tree at the intersection had come into leaf since the first accident. Maybe a go-slow sign had blown over.[4]

In the second case of the innkeeper and the guest a difference in the fact situation, no matter how similar it may be to that of the first case, may lead a court to *distinguish* the one case from the other and to apply therefore a different precedent or rule.

James P. Tallon was employed as a guard on one of the trains of the Interborough Rapid Transit Company. He lived at 146th Street in Manhattan and it was his duty to report for duty each morning at the Transit Company's station at 177th Street and Third Avenue. To get to and from work, he was provided with a pass by the company which allowed him free passage. One morning on his way to work and in the uniform of a guard, a collision of trains occurred which resulted in Tallon's death.

Tallon's wife brought suit against the company for damages, alleging negligence on the part of the company, and claiming that her husband was a passenger on one of the defendant's trains and not an employee within the meaning of the Workmen's Compensation Law.

The defendant insisted in the trial that, "Tallon was injured in an accident arising out of and in the course of his employment and that this action could not be maintained." The trial judge ruled as a matter of law that Tallon had been a passenger and "the negligence being admitted, left to the jury solely the question of damages."

The Appellate Division reversed the judgment of the trial court and dismissed the complaint on the ground that the only relief for Mrs. Tallon was under the Workmen's Compensation Law, since Tallon, at the time of his death, was within the terms of that law in that "he was injured in an accident arising out of and in the course of his employment."

The Court of Appeals, speaking through Judge Crane, reversed the Appellate Division

and affirmed the judgment of the trial court. Judge McLaughlin, dissenting, and supporting the judgment of the intermediate court, was of the opinion that "at the time of the collision Tallon occupied the status of an employee and, therefore, relief should have been sought under the Workmen's Compensation Law. At the time of the accident he was riding on a pass which entitled him to free transportation to and from his work. Such transportation was an incident of the employment. It was a part of the contract of employment and enforcible by him as such. The facts bring the case directly within the principle laid down in *Matter of Littler v. Fuller Co.*"

Littler was a bricklayer. He worked for the Fuller Co. which was constructing a residence in Great Neck, some two miles from the railroad station. The workmen who came out to Great Neck by train had refused to continue to work unless the employer would furnish them with free transportation from the railroad station and back again at the end of a day's work. The employer hired a truck to transport the men. Littler was injured when the truck, making its way back to the station, turned over in a ditch.

Littler sued the Fuller Company, arguing that his injury did not arise out of or in the course of employment. The Court of Appeals thought otherwise. "The vehicle," said Judge Pound, "was provided by the employer for the specific purpose of carrying the workmen to and from the place of the employment and in order to secure their services. The place of injury was brought within the scope of the employment because Littler, when he was injured, was 'on his way . . . from his duty within the precincts of the company.' . . . The day's work began when he entered the automobile truck in the morning and ended when he left it in the evening. The rule is well established that in such cases compensation should be awarded." Judge Pound goes on to say that the "case would be different if at the time of the accident" Littler "had been on the railroad train on his way to or from Great Neck."

Judge Crane, speaking for the majority in the Tallon case, *distinguished* the Littler case from the matter at hand. He said,

The cardinal underlying fact is that Tallon's employment did not actually begin until he reported for work at One Hundred and Seventy-seventh Street and Third avenue. He had to get there, and get there on time, and to facilitate his arriving on time the defendant gave him the right to ride in its passenger trains free of charge, but I cannot see how this in any way changes the reality, the existing fact, that the employment commenced at One Hundred and Seventy-seventh Street and Third avenue at the time of reporting. It would cause no such change, had Tallon paid his fare on defendant's train or had ridden in another conveyance, the defendant paying his fare. The pass alone, even though it be a part of his compensation, cannot create a fictitious relationship.

But there is still the Littler case to be considered, which Judge McLaughlin in his dissent thought applicable in this matter. Judge Crane, therefore, *distinguished* the Littler case as follows: "Now this case differs materially from those cases where the employer in order to get his employees to and from their work, provide conveyances exclusively for their use which in no sense are public conveyances and in which the employees undertaken to ride as part of their contract of employment in going to and from their work. Such a case was *Matter of Littler v. Fuller Co.*"

Thus, Littler had to accept an award under Workmen's Compensation while Mrs. Tallon would receive damages from the wealthy construction company. Between the majority view and the dissenting view of the facts there was a decided difference; each view elicited a different precedent and each produced a different result.

IMPRECISE PRECEDENTS

The Tallon matter might be called a run-of-the-mill case, and it is an example of the kind of thing courts do every day. They "distinguish" or they "follow" precedents. But what happens when the precedents do not fit the facts or two precedents might well and equally, but not exactly, cover a situation?

It was customary some years ago for young boys to swim in the United States Ship Canal, a narrow body of water separating Manhattan and the Bronx. They would cross from the Manhattan side and climb the bulkhead belonging to the New York Central Railroad and to which was attached, by whom or when no one knew, a rough plank which served as a diving board. This plank extended several feet beyond the line of the railroad's property. As sixteen-year-old Harvey Hynes stood poised on the board ready to dive, a high tension wire belonging to the railroad fell upon him and swept him to his death below. Hynes' mother brought an action for damages against the company.

The complaint brought by Mrs. Hynes alleged that the defendant's neglect in improperly erecting, constructing, and maintaining its poles and appurtenances and the wires attached thereto was responsible for the death of her son.

In the court of first instance, a jury awarded the plaintiff, Mrs. Hynes, eight thousand dollars. The defendant, the railroad, at once appealed to the Supreme Court of New York to set aside the verdict of the jury and to grant a new trial, and the Supreme Court so ordered. Mrs. Hynes then appealed from this order to the Appellate Division of the Supreme Court.

Before the Appellate Division, the defendant argued that Hynes, in climbing the bulkhead and standing in readiness to plunge from the diving board into the water, was a trespasser. True, the railroad was duty bound "to use reasonable care that bathers swimming or standing in the water should not be electrocuted by wires falling from its right of way," but that there was no duty to a boy on the springboard unless any injury he might receive was "the product of mere wilfulness or wantonness."

The court accepted his argument. The majority held that one who trespasses on a riparian owner's land and goes from there onto a springboard extending out over public waters is still a trespasser even though he is on that part of the board beyond the technical boundary of the riparian owner.

Two of the Appellate Division judges did not agree with the majority and one of them wrote a dissenting opinion. His argument was that Hynes was not a trespasser in the usual sense. Ordinarily, in like cases, the accident would not

In the old days a farmer who desired to have wheels made for an ox-cart would be apt to inspect the timber before it was painted, before the wheel was ironed and the defects covered up, in order that he might know what he was buying. He would realize that the oxen, in case of an accident or fright, as he would say, "might go pretty fast," and that if a wheel broke serious damage might occur to him or to others. . . . An ordinary man, in buying a pitchfork, a golf club, an axe-helve, or an oar for a boat, will look at the timber, "heft it," and otherwise endeavor to ascertain whether it is made of suitable material.

Since the ultimate purchaser is not qualified to make such an examination, or even to examine the quality of the wood, it is incumbent upon the manufacturer to do it for him.

The court held that under the circumstances, the Buick Company "owed a duty to all purchasers of its automobiles to make a reasonable inspection and test to ascertain whether the wheels purchased and put in use by it were reasonably fit for the purposes for which it used them, and if it fails to exercise care in that respect it is responsible for any defect which would have been discovered by such reasonable inspection and test."

The Buick Company appealed to the New York Court of Appeals. The sole question to be determined was "whether the defendant owed a duty of care and vigilance to anyone but the immediate purchaser," that is, the retail dealer. . . .

The general rule, you will remember, was well expressed by Judge Cooley. An exception to the general rule is the doctrine, if such it may be called, of the "inherently dangerous instrument." If the article is "inherently" or "imminently" dangerous, then the manufacturer is liable to third parties; if it is not within the category of "inherently dangerous," then the manufacturer is not liable to third parties. The Buick Company struggled to the bitter end to persuade the court not to include an automobile in this category, while the respondent sought to persuade the court to keep the car in the category in line with the lower court opinion.

The Court of Appeals, speaking through Judge Cardozo, affirmed the judgment of the Appellate Division. First he reviewed the precedents. That a manufacturer may be liable to a third party was established in New York in the case of *Thomas v. Winchester*, decided in 1853. A druggist had purchased a bottle of what was supposedly extract of dandelion from Winchester, who operated a pharmaceutical business in New York City. The bottle, through the negligence of one of Winchester's employees, had been incorrectly labeled extract of dandelion although the bottle did in fact contain belladonna, a poison. A Mr. Thomas bought a small quantity of this liquid from the druggist for his wife, who, after taking a few spoonfuls, became violently sick. Mrs. Thomas sued Winchester, not the druggist, and recovered damages. "The defendant's negligence," said the Court, "put human life in imminent danger." With regard to this early case, Cardozo said, "A poison falsely labeled is likely to injure anyone who gets it. Because the danger is to be foreseen, there is a duty to avoid the injury."

In 1882, in *Devlin v. Smith*, the Court of Appeals had under consideration a case in which the defendant, a contractor, contracted to build a scaffold for a painter. The painter's workmen were injured when the scaffold collapsed, and the contractor was held liable although there was no privity of contract between him and the workmen. The defendant, said Cardozo, "knew that the scaffold, if improperly constructed, was a most dangerous trap. He knew that it was to be used by the workmen. . . . Building it for their use, he owed them a duty, irrespective of his contract with their master, to build it with care."

Cardozo then considers another case in which the rule of *Thomas v. Winchester* was followed: *Statler v. Ray Manufacturing Company*. Here the manufacturer of a coffee urn was held liable when one of his urns, installed in a restaurant, exploded and injured the plaintiff. The court declared that the urn "was of such a character inherently that, when applied to the purposes for which it was designed, it was liable to become a source of great danger to many people if not carefully and properly constructed."

To the argument that things imminently dangerous to life were poisons, explosives, and deadly weapons, and that (reasoning by analogy) the automobile was not like any of these, Cardozo said: "Whatever the rule in *Thomas v. Winchester* may once have been, it has no longer that restricted meaning. A scaffold . . . is not inherently a destructive instrument. It becomes destructive only if imperfectly constructed. A large coffee urn . . . may have within itself, if negligently made, the potency of danger, yet no one thinks of it as an implement whose normal function is destruction." After a review of New York court decisions, Judge Cardozo declared that the rule of *Thomas v. Winchester* was not limited to "poisons, explosives, and things of like nature. . . ." He goes on to state the rule: "If the nature of a thing is such that it is reasonably certain to place life and limb in peril when negligently made, it is then a thing of danger. Its nature gives warning of the consequences to be expected. If to the element of danger there is added knowledge that the thing will be used by persons other than the purchaser, and used without new tests, then, irrespective of contract, the manufacturer of this thing of danger is under a duty to make it carefully. That is as far as we are required to go for the decision of this case."

Cardozo then goes on to clarify the rule. "There must be knowledge of a danger," he said, "not merely possible, but probable. It is *possible* to use almost anything in a way that will make it dangerous if defective. That is not enough to charge the manufacturer with a duty independent of his contract." . . .

The MacPherson and Smith cases, as compared with *Thomas v. Winchester,* reveal an enlargement of a rule of society as manifested by the courts. Certainly, in this area the law was brought more "in line with social considerations." Unlike a hundred years ago, the enlarged ruling recognized the new position of the buyer vis-à-vis the manufacturer. The meat, the canned or frozen fruits and vegetables, the bottled waters—these come from distant places and merely pass through the hands of the retailer to the consumer. If a young man buys a bottle of ginger beer from a retailer for his girl and she drinks the concoction only to find the remains of a decomposed snail in the bottom of the bottle and becomes deathly sick, are we, in this day and age,

to say that the poisoned consumer has no remedy against the negligent manufacturer?

As Mr. Holmes said, with some tenderness for a felicitous statement, the life of the law has not been logic, it has been experience. Perhaps this is not altogether true, but the cases do reflect the changing attitudes of courts to the changing facts of social life. And, as Professor Levi says, to contrast "logic and the actual legal method [reasoning by example] is" to do "a disservice to both. Legal reasoning has a logic of its own. Its structure fits it to give meaning to ambiguity and to test constantly whether the society has come to see new differences or similarities. Social theories and other changes in society will be relevant when the ambiguity has to be resolved for a particular case."[6]

In the absence of statute, courts as a general rule will follow precedent or the rules announced by judges in earlier cases. As often as not, new facts do not adapt themselves precisely to existing precedent and, therefore, courts must make distinctions, analogies must be drawn, and in some cases precedents are overruled and new ones created. Where the legislature by statute moves in on territory occupied by precedent, the statute prevails, as we have seen in the labor cases. But statutes are not always crystal-clear and admit of various interpretations which may even allow the continuance of a common law rule it was presumably the intention of the legislature to abolish.

NOTES

[1]*Hulett v. Swift* (1865) 33 N.Y. 572–573.

[2]Robert A. Sprecher, "The Development of the Doctrine of *Stare Decisis* and the Extent to which it should be Applied," in 31 *American Bar Association Journal* (Oct., 1945), p. 501.

[3]Benjamin N. Cardozo, *The Parodoxes of Legal Science* (New York: Columbia University Press, 1928), p. 8.

[4]Fred Rodell, *Woe Unto You, Lawyers!* (New York: Pageant Press, 1957), pp. 116–118.

[5]Benjamin N. Cardozo, *The Growth of the Law* (New Haven: Yale University Press, 1927), pp. 100–101.

[6]Edward H. Levi, *An Introduction to Legal Reasoning* (Chicago: The University of Chicago Press, 1949), pp. 73–74. In the foregoing section, the writer is greatly indebted to Professor Levi's stimulating and enlightening study.

1. Explain the various reasons for thinking *stare decisis* is important.

2. As Post explains, precedents can be (1) distinguished, (2) overturned, or (3) revised (limited or expanded). Give examples of each of these from his essay.

3. Given the importance of following precedents, why may it be important to revise or overturn them?

Rules of Interpretation

William Blackstone

American law took as its foundation English law, and the major source of Americans' knowledge of English law was William Blackstone's Commentaries on the Laws of England. *Blackstone had already argued for a definition of law, which he understood to be "the rule of conduct prescribed by supreme power in the state commanding what is right and wrong." In this selection from his* Commentaries, *Blackstone discusses the correct method of interpreting statutes, including especially the importance of understanding the intention of the legislature.*

ROMAN METHOD

When any doubt arose upon the construction of the Roman laws, the usage was to state the case to the emperor in writing and take his opinion upon it. This was certainly a bad method of interpretation. To interrogate the legislature to decide particular disputes is not only endless, but affords great room for partiality and oppression. The answers of the emperor were called his rescripts, and these had in succeeding cases the force of perpetual laws. . . . The emperor Macrinus, as his historian Capitolinus informs us, had once resolved to abolish these rescripts, and retain only the general edicts: he could not bear that the hasty and crude answers of such princes as Commodus and Caracalla should be reverenced as laws. But Justinian thought otherwise, and he has preserved them all. . . .

INTENT AS EXPRESSED

The fairest and most rational method to interpret the will of the legislator is by exploring his intentions at the time when the law was made, by signs the most natural and probable. And these signs are either the words, the context, the subject matter, the effects and consequence, or the spirit and reason of the law. Let us take a short view of them all:

1. Laws are generally to be understood in their usual and most known signification; not so much regarding the propriety of grammar, as their general and popular use. Thus the law mentioned by Puffendorf which forbade a layman to lay hands on a priest, was adjudged to extend to him, who had hurt a priest with a weapon. . . .

2. If words happen to be still dubious, we may establish their meaning from the context, with which it may be of singular use to compare a word or a sentence, whenever, they are ambiguous, equivocal or intricate. Thus the proeme, or preamble is often called in to help the construction of an act of parliament. Of the same nature and use is the comparison of a law with other laws, that are made by the same legislator, that have some affinity with the subject, or that expressly relate to the same point. Thus, when the law of England declares murder to be felony without benefit of clergy, we must resort to the same law of England to learn what the benefit of clergy is. . . .

3. As to the subject matter, words are always to be understood as having a read thereto, for that is always supposed to be in the eye of the legislator, and all his expressions directed to that end. Thus, when a law of our Edward III forbids all ecclesiastical persons to purchase provisions at Rome, it might seem to prohibit the buying of grain and other victuals; but, when we consider that the statute was made to repress the usurpations of the papal see, and that the nominations to benefices by the pope were called provisions, we shall see that the restraint is intended to be laid upon such provisions only.

4. As to the effects and consequence, the rule is, that where words bear either none, or a very absurd signification, if literally understood, we must a little deviate from the received sense of them. Therefore the Bolognian law, mentioned by Puffendorf, which enacted "that whoever drew blood in the streets should be punished with the utmost severity," was held after long debate not to extend to the surgeon, who opened the vein of a person that fell down in the street with a fit.

5. But, lastly, the most universal and effectual way of discovering the true meaning of a law, when the words are dubious is by considering the reason and spirit of it or the cause which moved the legislator to enact it. For when this reason ceases, the law itself ought likewise to cease with it. An instance of this is given in a case put by Cicero, or whoever was the author of the treatise inscribed to Herennius. There was a law, that those who in a storm forsook the ship should forfeit all property therein; and that the ship and lading should belong entirely to those who stayed in it. In a dangerous tempest all the mariners forsook the ship, except only one sick passenger, who, by reason of his disease, was unable to get out and escape. By chance the ship came safe to port. The sick man kept possession, and claimed the benefit of the law.

Now here all the learned agree that the sick man is not within reason of the law; for the reason of making it was, to give encouragement to such as should venture their lives to save the vessel; but this is a merit which he could never pretend to, who neither stayed in the ship upon that account, nor contributed anything to its preservation.

From this method of interpreting laws, by the reason of them, arises what we call equity, which is thus defined by Grotius as "the correction of that wherein the law, by reason of its universality, is deficient." For, since in laws all cases cannot be foreseen or expressed, it is necessary that, when the general decrees of the law come to be applied to particular cases, there should be somewhere a power vested of defining those circumstances, which (had they been foreseen) the legislator himself would have expressed. And these are the cases which according to Grotius, "*lex non exacte definit, sed arbitrio boni viri permittit*" (The law does not define exactly, but leaves something to the discretion of a just and wise judge).

Equity thus depending, essentially, upon the particular circumstances of each individual case, there can be no established rules and fixed precepts of equity laid down, without destroying its very essence, and reducing it to a positive law. And, on the other hand, the liberty of considering all cases in an equitable light must not be indulged too far, lest thereby we destroy all law, and leave the decision of every question entirely in the breast of the judge. And law, without equity, though hard and disagreeable, is much more desirable for the public good than equity without law; which would make every judge a legislator, and introduce most infinite confusion; as there would then be almost as many different rules of action laid down in our courts as there are differences of capacity and sentiment in the human mind.

REVIEW AND DISCUSSION QUESTIONS

1. What was the method used in Rome to interpret the laws of the emperor?

2. Why does Blackstone think another method should be used to interpret the intent of legislation?

3. Describe the approach that Blackstone argues should be followed in interpreting a statute.

4. What role does equity play in interpretation, according to Blackstone?

A Case Study in Interpretation:
The Mann Act

Edward H. Levi

In this essay, Edward H. Levi begins by distinguishing case-law reasoning from statutory interpretation. Central to deciding what a statute means is the question of the intention of the legislature. He then illustrates these problems by describing the legislative history of the Mann Act (sometimes called the "White Slave Traffic Act"). Edward H. Levi was professor of law at the University of Chicago.

It is customary to think of case-law reasoning as inductive and the application of statutes as deductive. The thought seems erroneous but the emphasis has some meaning. With case law the concepts can be created out of particular instances. . . .

The application of a statute seems to be in great contrast. The words are given. They are not to be taken lightly since they express the will of the legislature. The legislature is the law-making body. It looks like deduction to apply the word to the specific case.

The difference is seen immediately when it is realized that the words of a statute are not dictum. The legislature may have had a particular case uppermost in mind, but it has spoken in general terms. Not only respect but application is due to the general words the legislature used. The rules for statutory construction make the same point. They are words which tell one how to operate a given classification system. The problem is to place the species inside the genus and the particular case inside the species. The words used by the legislature are treated as words of classification which are to be applied. Yet the rules [of construction] themselves show that there may be some ambiguity in the words used. The words are to be construed in the light of the meaning given to other words in the same or related statute. The specification of particular instances indicates that similar but unmentioned instances are not to be included. But the specification of particular instances, when in addition a word of a general category is used, may be the indication that other like instances are also intended.

Thus in the application of a statute the intent of the legislature seems important. The rules of construction are ways of finding out the intent. The actual words used are important but insufficient. The report of congressional committees may give some clue. Prior drafts of the statute may show where meaning was intentionally changed. Bills presented but not passed may have some bearing. Words spoken in debate may now be looked at. Even the conduct of the litigants may be important in that the failure of the government to have acted over a period of time on what it now suggests as the proper interpretation throws light on the common meaning. But it is not easy to find the intent of the legislature.

Justice Reed has given us some Polonius-sounding advice on the matter.

There is, of course, no more persuasive evidence of the purpose of a statute than the words by which the legislature undertook to give expression to its wishes. Often these words are sufficient in and of themselves to determine the purpose of the legislature. In such cases we have followed their plain meaning. When that meaning had led to absurd or futile results, however, this Court has looked beyond the words to the purpose of the act. Frequently, however, even when the plain meaning did not produce absurd results but merely an unreasonable one "plainly at variance with the policy of legislation as a whole" this Court has followed that purpose rather than the literal words. . . . Obviously there is danger that the courts' conclusion as to legislative purpose will be unconsciously influenced by the judges' own views or by factors not considered by the enacting body. A lively appreciation of the danger is the best assurance of escape from its threat but hardly justifies an acceptance of a literal interpretation dogma which withholds from the courts available information for reaching a correct conclusion. Emphasis should be laid too upon the necessity for appraisal of the purposes as a whole of Congress in analyzing the meaning of clauses of sections of general acts. A few words of general connotation appearing in the text of statutes should not be given a wide meaning, contrary to settled policy, "except as a different purpose is plainly shown."[1]

The words of advice force one to re-examine whether there is any difference between case law and statutory interpretation. It is not enough to show that the words used by the legislature have some meaning. Concepts created by case law also have some meaning, but the meaning is ambiguous. It is not clear how wide or narrow the scope is to be. Can it be said that the words used by the legislature have any more meaning than that, or is there the same ambiguity? One important difference can be noted immediately. Where case law is considered, there is a conscious realignment of cases; the problem is not the intention of the prior judge. But with a statute the reference is to the kind of things intended by the legislature. All concepts suggest, but case-law concepts can be re-worked. A statutory concept, however, is supposed to suggest what the legislature had in mind; the items to be included under it should be of the same order. We mean to accomplish what the legislature intended. This is what Justice Reed has said. The difficulty is that what the legislature intended is ambiguous. In a significant sense there is only a general intent which preserves as much ambiguity in the concept used as though it had been created by case law.

This is not the result of inadequate draftsmanship, as is so frequently urged. Matters are not decided until they have to be. For a legislature perhaps the pressures are such that a bill has to be passed dealing with a certain subject. But the precise effect of the bill is not something upon which the members have to reach agreement. If the legislature were a court, it would not decide the precise effect until a specific fact situation arose demanding an answer. Its first pronouncement would not be expected to fill in the gaps. But since it is not a court, this is even more true. It will not be required to make the determination in any event, but can wait for the court to do so. There is a related and an additional reason for ambiguity. As to what type of situation is the legislature to make a decision? Despite much gospel to the contrary, a legislature is not a fact-finding body. There is no mechanism, as there is with a court, to require the legislature to sift facts and to make a decision about specific situations. There need be no agreement about what the situation is. The members of the legislative body will be talking about different things; they cannot force each other to accept even a hypothetical set of facts. The result is that even in a non-controversial atmosphere just exactly what has been decided will not be clear.

Controversy does not help. Agreement is then possible only through escape to a higher level of discourse with greater ambiguity. This is one element which makes compromise possible. Moreover, from the standpoint of the individual member of the legislature there is reason to be deceptive. He must escape from pressures at home. Newspapers may have created an atmosphere in which some legislation must be passed. Perhaps the only chance to get legislation through is to have it mean something not understood by some colleagues. . . . And if all this were not sufficient, it cannot be forgotten that to speak of legislative intent is to talk of group action, where much of the group may be ignorant or misinformed. Yet the emphasis should not be on this fact, but on the necessity that there be ambiguity before there can be any agreement about how unknown cases will be handled.

But the court will search for the legislative intent, and this does make a difference. Its search results in an initial filling-up of the gap. The first opinions may not definitely set the whole interpretation. A more decisive view may be edged toward, but finally there is likely to be an interpretation by the court which gives greater content to the words used. In building up this interpretation, the reference will be to the kind of examples that the words used, as commonly understood, would call to mind. Reasoning by example will then proceed from that point.

There is a difference then from case law in that the legislature has compelled the use of one word. The word will not change verbally. It could change in meaning, however, and if frequent appeals as to what the legislature really intended are permitted, it may shift radically from time to time. When this is done, a court in interpreting legislation has really more discretion than it has with case law. For it can escape from prior cases by saying that they have ignored the legislative intent.

There is great danger in this. Legislatures and courts are cooperative law-making bodies. It is important to know where the responsibility lies. If legislation which is disfavored can be interpreted away from time to time, then it is not to be expected, particularly if controversy is high, that the legislature will ever act. It will always be possible to say that new legislation is not needed because the court in the future will make a more appropriate interpretation. If the court is to have freedom to reinterpret legislation, the result will be to relieve the legislature from pressure. The legislation needs judicial consistency. Moreover, the court's own behavior in the face of pressure is likely to be indecisive. In all likelihood it will do enough to prevent legislative revision and not much more. Therefore it seems better to say that once a decisive interpretation of legislative intent has been made, and in that sense a direction has been fixed within the gap of ambiguity, the court should take that direction as given. In this sense a court's interpretation of legislation is not dictum. The words it uses do more than decide the case. They give broad direction to the statute.

The doctrine which is suggested here is a hard one. In many controversial situations, legislative revision cannot be expected. It often appears that the only hope lies with the courts. Yet the democratic process seems to require that controversial changes should be made by the legislative body. This is not only because there is a mechanism for holding legislators responsible. It is also because courts are normally timid. Since they decide only the case before them, it is difficult for them to compel any controversial reform unless they are willing to hold to an unpopular doctrine over a sustained period of time.

The difficulties which administrative agencies have in the face of sustained pressure serve as a warning. When courts enter the area of great controversy, they require unusual protection. They must be ready to appeal to the constitution.

Where legislative interpretation is concerned, therefore, it appears that legal reasoning does attempt to fix the meaning of the word. When this is done, subsequent cases must be decided upon the basis that the prior meaning remains. It must not be re-worked. Its meaning is made clear as examples are seen, but the reference is fixed. It is a hard doctrine against which judges frequently rebel. The Mann Act is a good example.

On June 25, 1910, the Mann Act, which recites that it "shall be known and referred to as the 'White Slave Traffic Act,'" went into effect. The Act provides in part: "Any person who shall knowingly transport or cause to be transported, or aid or assist in obtaining transportation for, or in transporting, in interstate or foreign commerce or in any territory or in the District of Columbia, any woman or girl for the purpose of prostitution or debauchery, or for any other immoral purpose, or with the intent and purpose to induce, entice or compel such woman or girl to become a prostitute, or to give herself up to debauchery, or to engage in any other immoral practice . . . shall be deemed guilty of a felony." The Act was not passed in haste. Indeed, the matter was much debated and prior reports about it had been written. The Secretary of Commerce and Labor had discussed the problem in his 1908 report; so had an Immigration Commission in a preliminary report for 1909. There were international aspects to the problem, and a treaty had been concluded. The President had directed the attention of Congress to the need for legislation, and the proposed bill had been considered in majority and minority congressional committee reports.

The Mann Act was passed during a period when large American cities had illegal but segregated "red-light" areas. It was believed that women were procured for houses of prostitution by bands of "white slavers" who "were said to operate from coast to coast, in town and country, with tentacles in foreign lands, east and west and across the American borders. The most sensational of these were said to be the French, Italian, and Jewish rings who preyed on innocent girls of their respective nationalities at ports of entry into the United States or ensnared them at the ports of embarkation in Europe and even in their home towns." It was thought that the girls were young; many of them were supposed to be scarcely in their teens." They were forced or lured into the business. It was thought that they had previously been virtuous, and while supposedly many of them had been aliens, it was also believed that they represented "our" women. Once captured, the woman disappeared from her own community, was brutally treated, whipped with rawhide, and became, as the House Report said, practically a slave in the true sense of the word.

To meet this assumed situation, the White Slave Traffic Act made it a crime to transport a woman "for the purpose of prostitution, or debauchery or for any other immoral purpose."

While Representative Richardson said that the bill was "impractical, vague, indistinct and indefinite in every respect," the debates show that Congress had in mind some very fundamental issues. On one side were those who were in favor of home rule or the powers of the states. . . . On the other side were those who argued that "public health and public morals appeal to us." They were the ones who said, "The proposed legislation is constitutional, and it is related to moral considerations of the most compelling force. If it were not true that our penal legislation were related to moral questions, and moral considerations, then the whole fabric of that legislation would lose its power to command the approbation of the country." They were careful to insist, however, that "the sections proposed do not amount to an interference with the police powers of the States."

In a way the bill must surely have been about the "white-slave traffic." Congressman Mann at the end of the debate emphasized the subject matter by declaring: "Congress would be derelict in its duty if it did not exercise [power], because all the horrors which have been urged, either truthfully or fancifully, against the black-slave traffic pale into insignificance as compared with the horrors of the so-called 'white-slave

traffic.'" Congressman Peters said: "The considerations which prompt the support of this bill are so widespread and its objects are so well understood and meet with such universal approval that no explanation or repetition of them need be made to this House. The bill aims to aid in the suppression of the white-slave traffic. . . ." The majority report of the House Committee had defined the white-slave trade as the "business of securing white women and girls and selling them outright or exploiting them for immoral purposes." It had stressed the international character of the trade and the large earnings involved.

Yet while it was said that "the traffic at which this bill strikes is admitted to be abhorrent to all men," and "the time will never arrive when there will be a change of sentiment with respect to its infamy and depravity," there was confusion both as to the facts and as to the legislation proposed.

For example, Congressman Richardson said he knew of the complaint about the traffic but "it may be that there is a good deal of exaggeration about it." Many of the situations described in the House Report had to do with conditions in Illinois. But the "law in Illinois has been strengthened and there had been many prosecutions under it." Congressman Adamson noted that "the Chairman of the Committee on Immigration and Naturalization . . . stated . . . that the white slave traffic had practically been stamped out of our large cities." An examination of the instances cited, Adamson thought, would show that they could be handled under existing laws. And despite the descriptions of immorality, the truth was that society was getting better and "we are vastly better morally than the rest of the world." On the other hand, Congressman Russell, as his contribution on the facts, told the House the story of a Negro who was supposed to have purchased his third white wife "out of a group of twenty-five that were offered for sale in Chicago."

Whatever the evil, presumably the legislation was molded to cure it. The Act speaks of "prostitution," "debauchery," and of "other immoral practice" or "purpose." So far as prostitution was concerned, the report of the House Committee had said that "the bill reported does not endeavor to regulate, prohibit or punish prostitution or the keeping of places where prostitution is indulged in." Congressman Adamson noted that the purpose of the bill "is not to stamp out prostitution, nor do its advocates so contend." He realized that many good men and women, and some good congressmen, thought the purpose was to stamp out prostitution and immorality, but this was an error. But the House Report clearly said that the bill reaches the transportation of women "for the purpose of prostitution." And Representative Peters joined the three elements of white-slave traffic, transportation, and prostitution together in his statement that "the bill aims to aid in the suppression of the white slave traffic by making it a felony to purchase interstate transportation for any woman going to a place for purposes of prostitution. . . .

Except for the charge that the provisions of the bill were "liable to furnish boundless opportunity to hold up and blackmail and make unnecessary trouble without the corresponding benefit to society," there seemed to be general agreement that the women involved were victims. The women were under control of keepers and were unable to communicate with the outside world without permission. It was said that the evidence "shows, that many victims of this traffic, have been coerced into leading lives of shame, by the use of force, deceit, fraud and every variety of trickery. In many instances they are most unwilling victims, who are literally compelled to practice immorality, and are held to its pursuit by means of violence and restraint." The House Report said that in many cases the women "are practically slaves in the true sense of the word.". . .

There was hardly any discussion of the meaning of "other immoral practice" or "purpose." It was known to some that in 1908, in the *Bitty* case, the Supreme Court had construed similar language in a related statute which dealt with alien women imported for the purpose of prostitution or "any other immoral purpose" to include the importation of a woman for the purpose of concubinage.

The Mann Act was passed after there had been many extensive governmental investigations. Yet there was no common understanding of the facts, and whatever understanding seems to have been achieved concerning the white-slave trade in retrospect seems incorrectly based. The words used were broad and ambiguous. There were three key phrases: "prostitution," "debauchery," and "for any other immoral purpose." The Act was now ready for interpretation.

NOTE

[1]*United States v. American Trucking Ass'n*, 310 U.S. 534, 542 (1940).

REVIEW AND DISCUSSION QUESTIONS

1. Explain why Levi thinks the intent of the legislature is important to interpreters of statutes.

2. Why does he think statutory interpretation differs from interpreting case law?

3. What motivated Congress to pass the Mann Act?

Cases Interpreting the Mann Act

Caminetti v. United States

Passed in 1909, the Mann Act (which Congress said should be "known and referred to as the 'White-Slave Traffic Act'") made it a crime to transport across a state line "any woman or girl for the purpose of prostitution or debauchery, or for any other immoral purpose, or with the intent and purpose to induce, entice or compel such woman or girl to become a prostitute, or to give herself up to debauchery, or to engage in any other immoral practice." The Mann Act was upheld by the U.S. Supreme Court in Hoke v. United States *(1913) under the power given to Congress to regulate interstate commerce.*

In this case, Caminetti v. United States, *four men had been convicted under the act. Two of them had taken their mistresses across a state line; two others coerced an eighteen-year-old girl to go from Oklahoma to Kansas, intending that she engage in prostitution. In this selection the Supreme Court focuses on the first two, asking if by taking their mistresses into another state they violated the act.*

Mr. Justice Day delivered the opinion of the Court:

It is contended that the Act of Congress is intended to reach only "commercialized vice" or the traffic in women for gain, and that the conduct for which the several petitioners were indicted and convicted, however reprehensible in morals, is not within the purview of the statute when properly construed in the light of its history and the purposes intended to be accomplished by its enactment. In none of the cases was it charged or proved that the transportation was for gain or for the purpose of furnishing women for prostitution for hire, and it is insisted that, such being the case, the acts charged and proved, upon which conviction was had, do not come within the statute.

It is elementary that the meaning of a statute must, in the first instance, be sought in the language in which the act is framed, and if that is plain, and if the law is within the constitutional authority of the law-making body which passed it, the sole function of the courts is to enforce it according to its terms.

Where the language is plain and admits of no more than one meaning the duty of interpretation does not arise and the rules which are to aid doubtful meanings need no discussion. There is

no ambiguity in the terms of this act. It is specifically made an offense to knowingly transport or cause to be transported, etc., in interstate commerce, any woman or girl for the purpose of prostitution or debauchery, or for "any other immoral purpose," or with the intent or purpose, to induce any such woman or girl to become a prostitute or to give herself up to debauchery, or to engage in any other immoral practice.

Statutory words are uniformly presumed, unless the contrary appears, to be used in their ordinary and usual sense. . . . To cause a woman or girl to be transported for the purposes of debauchery, and for an immoral purpose, to-wit, becoming a concubine or mistress . . . or to transport an unmarried woman, under eighteen years of age, with the intent to induce her to engage in prostitution, debauchery and other immoral practices . . . would seem by the very statement of the facts to embrace transportation for purposes denounced by the act, and therefore fairly within its meaning.

While such immoral purpose would be more culpable in morals and attributed to baser motives if accompanied with the expectation of pecuniary gain, such considerations do not prevent the lesser offense against morals of furnishing transportation in order that a woman may be debauched, or become a mistress or a concubine from being the execution of purposes within the meaning of this law. To say the contrary would

242 U.S. 470 (1917).

shock the common understanding of what constitutes an immoral purpose. . . .

. . . [I]t may be observed that while the title of an act cannot overcome the meaning of plain and unambiguous words used in its body, the title of this act embraces the regulation of interstate commerce "by prohibiting the transportation therein for immoral purposes of women and girls, and for other purposes." It is true that §8 of the act provides that it shall be known and referred to as the "White-slave traffic Act," and the report accompanying the introduction of the same into the House of Representatives set forth the fact that a material portion of the legislation suggested was to meet conditions which had arisen in the past few years, and that the legislation was needed to put a stop to a villainous interstate and international traffic in women and girls. Still, the name given to an act by way of designation or description, or the report which accompanies, cannot change the plain import of its words. . . .

Reports to Congress accompanying the introduction of proposed laws may aid the courts in reaching the true meaning of the legislature in cases of doubtful interpretation. But, as we have already said, and it has been so often affirmed as to become a recognized rule, when words are free from doubt they must be taken as the final expression of the legislative intent, and are not to be added to or subtracted from by considerations drawn from titles or designating names or reports accompanying their introduction, or from any extraneous source. In other words, the language being plain, and not leading to absurd or wholly impracticable consequences, it is the sole evidence of the ultimate legislative intent. . . .

The judgment in each of the cases is

Affirmed.

Mr. Justice McKenna, with whom concurred the Chief Justice [White] and Mr. Justice Clarke, dissenting:

Undoubtedly in the investigation of the meaning of a statute we resort first to its words, and when clear they are decisive. The principle has attractive and seemingly disposing simplicity, but that it is not easy of application or, at least, encounters other principles, many cases demonstrate. The words of a statute may be uncertain in their signification or in their application. If the words be ambiguous, the problem they present is to be resolved by their definition; the subject-matter and the lexicons become our guides. But here, even, we are not exempt from putting ourselves in the place of the legislators. If the words be clear in meaning but the objects to which they are addressed be uncertain, the problem then is to determine the uncertainty. And for this a realization of conditions that provoked the statute must inform our judgment. . . .

The transportation which is made unlawful is of a woman or girl "to become a prostitute or to give herself up to debauchery, or to engage in any other immoral practice." Our present concern is with the words "any other immoral practice," which, it is asserted, have a special office. The words are clear enough as general descriptions; they fail in particular designation. . . . "Immoral" is a very comprehensive word. It means a dereliction of morals. In such sense it covers every form of vice, every form of conduct that is contrary to good order. It will hardly be contended that in this sweeping sense it is used in the statute. But if not used in such sense, to what is it limited and by what limited? If it be admitted that it is limited at all, that ends the imperative effect assigned to it in the opinion of the court. But not insisting quite on that, we ask again. By what is it limited? By its context, necessarily, and the purpose of the statute.

For the context I must refer to the statute; of the purpose of the statute Congress itself has given us illumination. It devotes a section to the declaration that the "Act shall be known and referred to as the 'White-slave traffic Act.'" And its prominence gives it prevalence in the construction of the statute. It cannot be pushed aside or subordinated by indefinite words in other sentences, limited even there by the context. . . . The designation "White-slave traffic" has the sufficiency of an axiom. If apprehended, there is no uncertainty as to the conduct it describes. It is commercialized vice, immoralities having a mercenary purpose, and this is confirmed by other circumstances.

The author of the bill was Mr. Mann, and in reporting it from the House Committee on Interstate and Foreign Commerce he declared for the Committee that it was not the purpose of the bill to interfere with or usurp in any way the police power of the States, and further that it was not the intention of the bill to regulate prostitution or the places where prostitution or immorality was practiced, which were said to be matters wholly within the power of the States and over which the federal government had no jurisdiction. And further explaining the bill, it was said that the sections of the act had been "so drawn that they are limited to cases in which there is the act of transportation in interstate commerce of women for purposes of prostitution." And again:

... The legislation is needed to put a stop to a villainous interstate and international traffic in women and girls. ... It does not attempt to regulate the practice of voluntary prostitution, but aims solely to prevent panderers and procurers from compelling thousands of women and girls against their will and desire to enter and continue in a life of prostitution. ...

In other words, it is vice as a business at which the law is directed, using interstate commerce as a facility to procure or distribute its victims. ...

This being the purpose, the words of the statute should be construed to execute it, and they may be so construed even if their literal meaning be otherwise.

REVIEW AND DISCUSSION QUESTIONS

1. Describe the reasoning of Justice Day in upholding the conviction.

2. How does Justice Day think the Court should decide the meaning of a statute?

3. Why does Justice McKenna dispute Day's argument?

4. Which position, the majority or the dissent, is more sound? Explain.

5. In what ways, if any, is Levi's discussion of the legislative history of the Mann Act relevant to this case?

Mortensen v. United States

Mr. and Mrs. Mortensen ran a house of prostitution in Nebraska. Unfortunately for them, however, they took two of their employees on vacation to Salt Lake City and Yellowstone Park. The ladies resumed their work after returning to Nebraska, again in the employ of the Mortensens. The Mortensens were convicted under the Mann Act, though there was no indication the women had been involved in prostitution while on vacation or that the Mortensens had coerced the women to return to Nebraska.

Mr. Justice Murphy delivered the opinion of the Court:

The penalties of §2 of the Act are directed at those who knowingly transport in interstate commerce "any woman or girl for the purpose of prostitution or debauchery, or for any other

322 U.S. 369 (1944).

immoral purpose, or with the intent and purpose to induce, entice, or compel such woman or girl to become a prostitute or to give herself up to debauchery, or to engage in any other immoral practice." The statute thus aims to penalize only those who use interstate commerce with a view toward accomplishing the unlawful purposes. To constitute a violation of the Act, it is essential that the interstate transportation have for its object or be the means of effecting or facilitating the proscribed activities. An intention that the women or girls shall engage in the conduct outlawed by §2 must be found to exist before the conclusion of the interstate journey and must be the dominant motive of such interstate movement. And the transportation must be designed to bring about such result. Without that necessary intention and motivation, immoral conduct during or following the journal is insufficient to subject the transporter to the penalties of the act. . . .

It may be assumed that petitioners anticipated that the two girls would resume their activities as prostitutes upon their return to Grand Island. But we do not think it is fair or permissible under the evidence adduced to infer that this interstate vacation trip, or any part of it, was undertaken by petitioners for the purpose of, or as a means of effecting or facilitating, such activities. The sole purpose of the journey from beginning to end was to provide innocent recreation and a holiday for petitioners and the two girls. . . . What Congress has outlawed by the Mann Act, however, is the use of interstate commerce as a calculated means for effectuating sexual immorality. In ordinary speech an interstate trip undertaken for an innocent vacation purpose constitutes the use of interstate commerce for that innocent purpose. Such a trip does not lose that meaning when viewed in light of a criminal statute outlawing interstate trips for immoral purposes.

The fact that the two girls actually resumed their immoral practices after their return to Grand Island does not, standing alone, operate to inject a retroactive illegal purpose into the return trip to Grand Island. Nor does it justify an arbitrary splitting of the round trip into two parts so as to permit an inference that the purpose of the drive to Salt Lake City was innocent while the purpose of the homeward journey to Grand Island was criminal. The return journey under the circumstances of this case cannot be considered apart from its integral relation with the innocent round trip as a whole. There is no evidence of any change in the purpose of the trip during its course. If innocent when it began it remained so until it ended. . . .

To punish those who transport inmates of a house of prostitution on an innocent vacation trip in no way related to the practice of their commercial vice is consistent neither with the purpose nor with the language of the Act. Congress was attempting primarily to eliminate the "white-slave" business. . . . To accomplish its purpose the statute enumerates the prohibited acts in broad language capable of application beyond that intended by the legislative framers. But even such broad language is conditioned upon the use of interstate transportation for the purpose of, or as a means of effecting or facilitating, the commission of the illegal acts. Here the interstate round trip had no such purpose and was in no way related to the subsequent immoralities in Grand Island. . . .

The judgment of the court below is

Reversed.

Mr. Chief Justice Stone:
Mr. Justice Black, Mr. Justice Reed,
Mr. Justice Douglas and I think
the judgment should be affirmed.

Courts have no more concern with the policy and wisdom of the Mann Act than of the Labor Relations Act or any other which Congress may constitutionally adopt. Those are matters for Congress to determine, not the courts. . . .

The fact that petitioners, who were engaged in an established business of operating a house of prostitution in Nebraska, took some of its women inmates on a transient and innocent vacation trip to other states, is in no way incompatible with the conclusion that petitioners, in bringing them back to Nebraska, purposed and intended that they should resume there the practice of commercial vice, which in fact they did promptly resume in petitioners' establishment. The record is without evidence that they engaged or intended to engage in any other activities in Nebraska, or that anything other than the practice of their profession was the object of their return.

1. Describe the reasons Justice Murphy gives for reversing the conviction.

2. On what basis do the dissenters claim the convictions should be upheld? Which side do you think is correct?

3. Discuss the relevance for this case of the legislative history of the Mann Act described by Edward Levi.

4. Is this decision compatible with *Caminetti?* Explain.

Cleveland v. United States

This case raised still further questions about the reach of the Mann Act. Six members of the Mormon Church were convicted for violating the act by transporting their wives across state lines. The reason for their conviction was that the Mormons practiced polygamy.

Mr. Justice Douglas delivered the opinion of the Court:

The Act makes an offense the transportation in interstate commerce of "any woman or girl for the purpose of prostitution or debauchery, or for any other immoral purpose." The decision turns on the meaning of the latter phrase, "for any other immoral purpose." . . .

It is argued that the *Caminetti* decision gave too wide a sweep to the Act; that the Act was designed to cover only the white slave business and related vices; that it was not designed to cover voluntary actions bereft of sex commercialism; and that in any event it should not be construed to embrace polygamy which is a form of marriage and, unlike prostitution or debauchery or the concubinage involved in the *Caminetti* case, has as its object parenthood and the creation and maintenance of family life. . . .

While *Mortensen v. United States* [1944] rightly indicated that the Act was aimed "primarily" at the use of interstate commerce for the conduct of the white slave business, we find no indication that a profit motive is a *sine qua non* to its application. Prostitution, to be sure, normally suggests sexual relations for hire. But debauchery has no such implied limitation. In common understanding the indulgence which that term

329 U.S. 14 (1946).

suggests may be motivated solely by lust. And so we start with words which by their natural import embrace more than commercialized sex. What follows is "any other immoral purpose." Under the *ejusdem generis* [of the same class or kind] rule of construction the general words are confined to the class and may not be used to enlarge it. But we could not give the words a faithful interpretation if we confined them more narrowly than the class of which they are a part.

That was the view taken by the Court in [earlier] cases. We do not stop to reexamine the *Caminetti* case to determine whether the Act was properly applied to the facts there presented. But we adhere to its holding . . . that the Act, while primarily aimed at the use of interstate commerce for the purposes of commercialized sex, is not restricted to that end.

We conclude, moreover, that polygamous practices are not excluded from the Act. They have long been outlawed in our society. As stated in *Reynolds v. United States* [1879]:

Polygamy has always been odious among the northern and western nations of Europe, and, until the establishment of the Mormon Church, was almost exclusively a feature of the life of Asiatic and of African people. At common law, the second marriage was always void (2 Kent, Com. 79), and from the earliest history of England polygamy has been treated as an offence against society. . . .

. . . Polygamy is a practice with far more pervasive influences in society than the casual, isolated transgressions involved in the *Caminetti* case. The establishment or maintenance of polygamous households is a notorious example of promiscuity. . . . We could conclude that Congress excluded these practices from the Act only if it were clear that the Act is confined to commercialized sexual vice. Since we cannot say it is, we see no way by which the present transgressions can be excluded. These polygamous practices have long been branded as immoral in the law. Though they have different ramifications, they are in the same genus as the other immoral practices covered by the Act. . . .

It is also urged that the requisite criminal intent was lacking since petitioners were motivated by a religious belief. That defense claims too much. If upheld, it would place beyond the law any act done under claim of religious sanction. But it has long been held that the fact that polygamy is supported by a religious creed affords no defense in a prosecution for bigamy. *Reynolds v. United States*. Whether an act is immoral within the meaning of the statute is not to be determined by the accused's concepts of morality Congress has provided the standard. The offense is complete if the accused intended to perform, and did in fact perform, the act which the statute condemns. . . .

Affirmed.

Mr. Justice Murphy, dissenting:

Today another unfortunate chapter is added to the troubled history of the White Slave Traffic Act. It is a chapter written in terms that misapply the statutory language and that disregard the intention of the legislative framer. It results in the imprisonment of individuals whose actions have none of the earmarks of white slavery, whatever else may be said of their conduct. . . .

It is not my purpose to defend the practice of polygamy or to claim that it is morally the equivalent of monogamy. But it is essential to understand what it is, as well as what it is not. Only in that way can we intelligently decide whether it falls within the same genus as prostitution or debauchery.

There are four fundamental forms of marriage: (1) monogamy; (2) polygyny, or one man with several wives; (3) polyandry, or one woman with several husbands; and (4) group marriage. The term "polygamy" covers both polygyny and polyandry. Thus we are dealing here with polygyny, one of the basic forms of marriage. Historically, its use has far exceeded that of any other form. It was quite common among ancient civilizations and was referred to many times by the writers of the Old Testament; even today it is to be found frequently among certain pagan and non-Christian peoples of the world. We must recognize, then, that polygyny, like other forms of marriage, is basically a cultural institution rooted deeply in the religious beliefs and social mores of those societies in which it appears. It is equally true that the beliefs and mores of the dominant culture of the contemporary world condemn the practice as immoral and substitute monogamy in its place. To those beliefs and mores I subscribe, but that does not alter the fact that polygyny is a form of marriage built upon a set of social and moral principles. . . .

The Court states that polygamy is "a notorious example of promiscuity." The important fact, however, is that, despite the differences that may exist between polygamy and monogamy, such differences do not place polygamy in the same category as prostitution or debauchery. When we use those terms we are speaking of acts of an entirely different nature, having no relation whatever to the various forms of marriage. It takes no elaboration here to point out that marriage, even when it occurs in a form of which we disapprove, is not to be compared with prostitution or debauchery or other immoralities of that character.

The Court's failure to recognize this vital distinction and its insistence that polygyny is "in the same genus" as prostitution and debauchery do violence to the anthropological factors involved. Even etymologically, the words "polygyny" and "polygamy" are quite distinct from "prostitution," "debauchery," and words of that ilk. There is thus no basis in fact for including polygyny within the phrase "any other immoral purpose" as used in this statute.

REVIEW AND DISCUSSION QUESTIONS

1. Why does Justice Douglas think polygamous practices are included in the act?

2. How is the precedent found in *Reynolds v. United States* relevant to the case, according to Justice Douglas?

3. Summarize briefly the reasons Justice Murphy dissents.

4. Explain what role (if any) is played in the opinions by the justices' attitudes toward polygamy.

5. Trace the development of the Court's thinking about the meaning of the Mann Act from *Caminetti* to this case. Is there a single, consistent pattern here?

6. Which of the three Mann Act cases is most incompatible with the legislative history Levi describes?

7. Why is it important for courts to rely on the intent of the legislature when they interpret a statute?

Can a Murderer Inherit?

Riggs v. Palmer

Here the specific issue before the Court is whether a grandson who murdered his grandfather may nonetheless keep the inheritance provided in his grandfather's will. As with the Mann Act cases, however, there is deep disagreement between the judges over how the statute should be interpreted, as well as over the correct methods of statutory interpretation.

Earl, J.:

On the 13th day of August, 1880, Francis B. Palmer made his last will and testament, in which he gave small legacies to his two daughters, Mrs. Riggs and Mrs. Preston, the plaintiffs in this action, and the remainder of his estate to his grandson, the defendant Elmer E. Palmer, subject to the support of Susan Palmer, his mother, with a gift over to the two daughters, subject to the support of Mrs. Palmer in case Elmer should survive him and die under age, unmarried, and without any issue. The testator, at the date of his will, owned a farm, and considerable personal property. . . . At the date of the will, and subsequently to the death of the testator, Elmer lived with him as a member of his family, and at his death was 16 years old. He knew of the provisions made in his favor in the will, and, that he might prevent his grandfather from revoking such provisions, which he had manifested some intention to do, and to obtain the speedy enjoyment and immediate possession

22 N.E. 188 (1889).

of his property, he willfully murdered him by poisoning him. He now claims the property, and the sole question for our determination is, can he have it?

The defendants say that the testator is dead; that his will was made in due form, and has been admitted to probate; and that therefore it must have effect according to the letter of the law. It is quite true that statutes regulating the making, proof, and effect of wills and the devolution of property, if literally construed, and if their force and effect can in no way and under no circumstances be controlled or modified, give this property to the murderer. The purpose of those statutes was to enable testators to dispose of their estates to the objects of their bounty at death, and to carry into effect their final wishes legally expressed; and in considering and giving effect to them this purpose must be kept in view. It was the intention of the law-makers that the donees in a will should have the property given to them. But it never could have been their intention that a donee who murdered the testator to make the will operative should have any benefit under it. If such a case had been present to their minds, and it had been supposed necessary to make some provision of law to meet it, it cannot be doubted that they would have provided for it. It is a familiar canon of construction that a thing which is within the intention of the makers of a statute is as much within the statute as if it were within the letter; and a thing which is within the letter of the statute is not within the statute unless it be within the intention of the makers. The writers of laws do not always express their intention perfectly, but either exceed it or fall short of it, so that judges are to collect it from probable or rational conjectures only, and this is called "rational interpretation;" and Rutherford, in his Institutes, (page 420,) says: "Where we make use of rational interpretation, sometimes we restrain the meaning of the writer so as to take in less, and sometimes we extend or enlarge his meaning so as to take in more, than his words express." Such a construction ought to be put upon a statute as will best answer the intention which the makers had in view. . . .

> By an equitable construction a case not within the letter of a statute is sometimes holden to be within the meaning, because it is within the mischief for which a remedy is provided. The reason for such construction is that the law-makers could not set down every case in express terms. In order to form a right judgment whether a case be within the equity of a statute, it is a good way to suppose the law-maker present, and that you have asked him this question: Did you intend to comprehend this case? Then you must give yourself such answer as you imagine he, being an upright and reasonable man, would have given. If this be that he did mean to comprehend it, you may safely hold the case to be within the equity of the statute; for while you do no more than he would have done, you do not act contrary to the statute, but in conformity thereto. 9 Bac. Abr. 248.

In some cases the letter of a legislative act is restrained by an equitable construction; in others, it is enlarged; in others, the construction is contrary to the letter. . . . If the lawmakers could, as to this case, be consulted, would they say that they intended by their general language that the property of a testator or of an ancestor should pass to one who had taken his life for the express purpose of getting his property? . . . [I]f an act of parliament gives a man power to try all causes that arise within his manor of Dale, yet, if a cause should arise in which he himself is party, the act is construed not to extend to that, because it is unreasonable that any man should determine his own quarrel. There was a statute in Bologna that whoever drew blood in the streets should be severely punished, and yet it was held not to apply to the case of a barber who opened a vein in the street. It is commanded in the decalogue that no work shall be done upon the Sabbath, and yet giving the command a rational interpretation founded upon its design the Infallible Judge held that it did not prohibit works of necessity, charity, or benevolence on that day.

What could be more unreasonable than to suppose that it was the legislative intention in the general laws passed for the orderly, peaceable, and just devolution of property that they should have operation in favor of one who murdered his ancestor that he might speedily come into the possession of his estate? Such an intention is inconceivable. We need not, therefore, be much troubled by the general language contained in the laws. Besides, all laws, as well as all contracts, may be controlled in their operation and effect by general, fundamental maxims of the common law. No one shall be permitted to profit by his own fraud, or to take advantage of his own wrong, or to found any claim upon his own iniquity, or to acquire property by his own crime. These maxims are dictated by public policy, have their foundation in universal law administered in all civilized countries, and have nowhere been superseded by statutes. . . .

Here there was no certainty that this murderer would survive the testator, or that the testator would not change his will, and there was no certainty that he would get this property if nature was allowed to take its course. He therefore murdered the testator expressly to vest himself with an estate. Under such circumstances, what law, human or divine, will allow him to take the estate and enjoy the fruits of his crime? The will spoke and became operative at the death of the testator. He caused that death, and thus by his crime made it speak and have operation. Shall it speak and operate in his favor? If he had met the testator, and taken his property by force, he would have had no title to it. Shall he acquire title by murdering him? If he had gone to the testator's house, and by force compelled him, or by fraud or undue influence had induced him, to will him his property, the law would not allow him to hold it. But can he give effect and operation to a will by murder, and yet take the property? To answer these questions in the affirmative it seems to me would be a reproach to the jurisprudence of our state, and an offense against public policy. Under the civil law, evolved from the general principles of natural law and justice by many generations of jurisconsults, philosophers, and statesmen, one cannot take property by inheritance or will from an ancestor or benefactor whom he has murdered. . . . Just before the murder he was not an heir, and it was not certain that he ever would be. He might have died before his grandfather, or might have been disinherited by him. He made himself an heir by the murder, and he seeks to take property as the fruit of his crime. What has before been said as to him as legatee applies to him with equal force as an heir. He cannot vest himself with title by crime. My view of this case does not inflict upon Elmer any greater or other punishment for his crime than the law specifies. It takes from him no property, but simply holds that he shall not acquire property by his crime, and thus be rewarded for its commission.

Our attention is called to *Owens v. Owens*, as a case quite like this. There a wife had been convicted of being an accessory before the fact to the murder of her husband, and it was held that she was nevertheless entitled to dower. I am unwilling to assent to the doctrine of that case. The statutes provide dower for a wife who has the misfortune to survive her husband, and thus lose his support and protection. It is clear beyond their purpose to make provision for a wife who by her own crime makes herself a widow, and willfully and intentionally deprives herself of the support and protection of her husband. As she might have died before him, and thus never have been his widow, she cannot by her crime vest herself with an estate. The principle which lies at the bottom of the maxim *volenti non fit injuria* should be applied to such a case, and a widow should not, for the purpose of acquiring, as such, property rights, be permitted to allege a widowhood which she has wickedly and intentionally created.

. . . The judgment of the general term and that entered upon the report of the referee should therefore be reversed, and judgment should be entered as follows: That Elmer E. Palmer and the administrator be enjoined from using any of the personalty or real estate left by the testator for Elmer's benefit; that the devise and bequest in the will to Elmer be declared ineffective to pass the title to him; that by reason of the crime of murder committed upon the grandfather he is deprived of any interest in the estate left by him; that the plaintiffs are the true owners of the real and personal estate left by the testator. . . .

Gray, J., dissenting:

[If] I believed that the decision of the question could be effected by considerations of an equitable nature, I should not hesitate to assent to views which commend themselves to the conscience. But the matter does not lie within the domain of conscience. We are bound by the rigid rules of law, which have been established by the legislature, and within the limits of which the determination of this question is confined. . . . Modern jurisprudence, in recognizing the right of the individual, under more or less restrictions, to dispose of his property after his death, subjects it to legislative control, both as to extent and as to mode of exercise. . . . To the statutory restraints which are imposed upon the disposition of one's property by will are added strict and systematic statutory rules for the execution, alteration, and revocation of the will, which must be, at least substantially, if not exactly, followed to insure validity and performance. . . . The capacity and the power of the individual to dispose of his property after death, and the mode by which that power can be exercised, are matters of which the legislature has assumed the entire control, and has undertaken to regulate with comprehensive particularity.

. . . I concede that rules of law which annul testamentary provisions made for the benefit of those who have become unworthy of them may be based on principles of equity and of natural justice. It is quite reasonable to suppose that a testator would revoke or alter his will, where his mind has been so angered and changed as to make him unwilling to have his will executed as it stood. But these principles only suggest sufficient reasons for the enactment of laws to meet such cases.

The statutes of this state have prescribed various ways in which a will may be altered or revoked; but the very provision defining the modes of alteration and revocation implies a prohibition of alteration or revocation in any other way. The words of the section of the statute are: "No will in writing, except in the cases hereinafter mentioned, nor any part thereof, shall be revoked or altered otherwise," etc. Where, therefore, none of the cases mentioned are met by the facts, and the revocation is not in the way described in the section, the will of the testator is unalterable. I think that a valid will must continue as a will always, unless revoked in the manner provided by the statutes. Mere intention to revoke a will does not have the effect of revocation. The intention to revoke is necessary to constitute the effective revocation of a will, but it must be demonstrated by one of the acts contemplated by the statute. As Woodworth, Jr., said in *Dan v. Brown*, 4 Oow. 490: "Revocation is an act of the mind, which must be demonstrated by some outward and visible sign of revocation." The same learned judge said in that case: "The rule is that if the testator lets the will stand until he dies, it is his will; if he does not suffer it to do so, it is not his will." . . . The finding of fact of the referee that presumably the testator would have altered his will had he known of his grandson's murderous intent cannot affect the question. We may concede it to the fullest extent; but still the cardinal objection is undisposed of—that the making and the revocation of a will are purely matters of statutory regulation, by which the court is bound in the determination of questions relating to these acts.

Two cases—in this state and in Kentucky—at an early day, seem to me to be much in point.

Gains v. Gains, 2 A. K. Marsh. 190, was decided by the Kentucky court of appeals in 1820. It was there urged that the testator intended to have destroyed his will, and that he was forcibly prevented from doing so by the defendant in error or devisee; and it was insisted that the will, though not expressly, was thereby virtually, revoked. The court held, as the act concerning wills prescribed the manner in which a will might be revoked, that, as none of the acts evidencing revocation were done, the intention could not be substituted for the act. In that case the will was snatched away, and forcibly retained. In 1854, Surrogate Bradford, whose opinions are entitled to the highest consideration, decided the case of *Leaycraft v. Simmons*, 3 Bradf. Sur. 35. In that case the testator, a man of 89 years of age, desired to make a codicil to his will, in order to enlarge the provisions for his daughter. His son, having the custody of the instrument, and the one to be prejudiced by the change, refused to produce the will at testator's request, for the purpose of alteration. The learned surrogate refers to the provisions of the civil law for such and other cases of unworthy conduct in the heir or legatee, and says: "Our statute has undertaken to prescribe the mode in which wills can be revoked [citing the statutory provision]. This is the law by which I am governed in passing upon questions touching the revocation of wills. The whole of this subject is now regulated by statute; and a mere intention to revoke, however well authenticated, or however defeated, is not sufficient." And he held that the will must be admitted to probate.

. . . The appellants' argument practically amounts to this: that, as the legatee has been guilty of a crime, by the commission of which he is placed in a position to sooner receive the benefits of the testamentary provision, his rights to the property should be forfeited, and he should be divested of his estate. To allow their argument to prevail would involve the diversion by the court of the testator's estate into the hands of persons whom, possibly enough, for all we know, the testator might not have chosen or desired as its recipients. Practically the court is asked to make another will for the testator. The laws do not warrant this judicial action, and mere presumption would not be strong enough to sustain it. But, more than this, to concede the appellants' views would involve the imposition of an additional punishment or penalty upon the respondent. What power or warrant have the courts to add to the respondent's penalties by depriving him of property? The law has punished him for his crime, and we may not say that it was an insufficient punishment. In the trial and punishment of the respondent the law has vindicated itself for the outrage which he committed, and further judicial utterance upon the subject of punishment or deprivation of rights is barred. We may not, in the language of the court in *People v. Thornton*, "enhance the pains, penalties, and forfeitures provided by law for the punishment of crime." The judgment should be affirmed, with costs.

REVIEW AND DISCUSSION QUESTIONS

1. Why does Judge Earl think Elmer should not inherit?

2. On what basis does Judge Gray conclude that the inheritance should be given to Elmer despite his crime?

3. Describe the different approaches the two judges take to statutory interpretation.

4. Judge Earl relies heavily on the notion of "principles" that although not explicit in any statute should nevertheless be given consideration when applying statutes to cases. Where does he think those principles originate? If challenged, how might he defend their soundness?

5. Does Judge Gray also rely on political principles? Explain.

PART II

THE NATURE OF LAW

❖

Aquinas undertook this task, developing an all-embracing philosophical system that sought a synthesis of faith and reason. He died at the age of fifty, and in 1879, the Roman Catholic Church declared his writings to be its official teaching.

In this brief selection from his classic work, Summa Theologica, *Aquinas first provides a definition of law and then describes the four types of law along with the interrelationships among them. As background, Aquinas assumes with Aristotle that each creature has its own natural purpose or end and that fulfilling that purpose defines its good. Just as one cannot understand a knife or an eye without appreciating its purpose, so too for Aristotle it is impossible to understand a legal or a political system without first thinking about the natural good of human beings, as well as the purpose of law itself.*

QUESTION 90: ON THE ESSENCE OF LAW

WHETHER LAW IS ALWAYS DIRECTED TO THE COMMON GOOD?

As we have stated above, law belongs to that which is a principle of human acts, because it is their rule and measure. Now as reason is a principle of human acts, so in reason itself there is something which is the principle in respect of all the rest. Hence to this principle chiefly and mainly law must needs be referred. Now the first principle in practical matters, which are the object of the practical reason, is the last end: and the last end of human life is happiness or beatitude, as we have stated above. Consequently, law must needs concern itself mainly with the order that is in beatitude. Moreover, since every part is ordained to the whole as the imperfect to the perfect, and since one man is a part of the perfect community, law must needs concern itself properly with the order directed to universal happiness. Therefore the Philosopher [Aristotle], in the above definition of legal matters, mentions both happiness and the body politic, since he says that we call those legal matters *just which are adapted to produce and preserve happiness and its parts for the body politic.* For the state is a perfect community, as he says in *Politics* i.

Now, in every genus, that which belongs to it chiefly is the principle of the others, and the others belong to that genus according to some order towards that thing. Thus fire, which is chief among hot things, is the cause of heat in mixed bodies, and these are said to be hot in so far as they have a share of fire. Consequently, since law is chiefly ordained to the common good, any other precept in regard to some individual work must needs be devoid of the nature of a law, save in so far as it regards the common good. Therefore every law is ordained to the common good. . . .

WHETHER THE REASON OF ANY MAN IS COMPETENT TO MAKE LAWS?

. . . A private person cannot lead another to virtue efficaciously; for he can only advise, and if his advice be not taken, it has no coercive power, such as the law should have, in order to prove an efficacious inducement to virtue, as the Philosopher says. But this coercive power is vested in the whole people or in some public personage, to whom it belongs to inflict penalties, as we shall state further on. Therefore the framing of laws belongs to him alone.

. . . As one man is a part of the household, so a household is a part of the state; and the state is a perfect community, according to *Politics* i. Therefore, just as the good of one man is not the last end, but is ordained to the common good, so too the good of one household is ordained to the good of a single state, which is a perfect community. Consequently, he that governs a family can indeed make certain commands or ordinances, but not such as to have properly the nature of law.

WHETHER PROMULGATION IS ESSENTIAL TO LAW?

As was stated above, a law is imposed on others as a rule and measure. Now a rule or measure is imposed by being applied to those who are to be ruled and measured by it. Therefore, in order that a law obtain the binding force which is proper to a law, it must needs [be] applied to the men who have to be ruled by it. But such application is made by its being made known to them by promulgation. Therefore promulgation is necessary for law to obtain its force.

Thus, . . . the definition of law may be gathered. Law is nothing else than an ordinance of reason for the common good, promulgated by him who has the care of the community.

. . . The natural law is promulgated by the very fact that God instilled it into man's mind so as to be known by him naturally.]

. . . Those who are not present when a law [is] promulgated are bound to observe the law, in so far as it is made known or can be made known to them by others, after it has been promulgated. . . .

QUESTION 91:
ON THE VARIOUS KINDS OF LAW

WHETHER THERE IS AN ETERNAL LAW?

Objection. It would seem that there is no eternal law. For every law is imposed on someone. But there was not someone from eternity on whom a law could be imposed, since God alone was from eternity. Therefore no law is eternal. . . .

On the contrary, Augustine says: *That Law which is the Supreme Reason cannot be understood to be otherwise than unchangeable and eternal.*

I answer that . . . law is nothing else but a dictate of practical reason emanating from the ruler who governs a perfect community. Now it is evident, granted that the world is ruled by divine providence, . . . that the whole community of the universe is governed by the divine reason. Therefore the very notion of the government of things in God, the ruler of the universe, has the nature of a law. And since the divine reason's conception of things is not subject to time, but is eternal, according to *Prov.* viii. 23, therefore it is that this kind of law must be called eternal. . . .

WHETHER THERE IS IN US A NATURAL LAW?

. . . Law, being a rule and measure, can be in a person in two ways: in one way, as in him

that rules and measures; in another way, as in that which is ruled and measured, since a thing is ruled and measured in so far as it partakes of the rule or measure. Therefore, since all things subject to divine providence are ruled and measured by the eternal law, as was stated above, it is evident that all things partake in some way in the eternal law, in so far as, namely, from its being imprinted on them, they derive their respective inclinations to their proper acts and ends. Now among all others, the rational creature is subject to divine providence in a more excellent way, in so far as it itself partakes of a share of providence, by being provident both for itself and for others. Therefore it has a share of the eternal reason, whereby it has a natural inclination to its proper act and end; and this participation of the eternal law in the rational creature is called the natural law. . . . [T]he light of natural reason, whereby we discern what is good and what is evil, which is the function of the natural law, is nothing else than an imprint on us of the divine light. It is therefore evident that the natural law is nothing else than the rational creature's participation of the eternal law. . . .

WHETHER THERE IS A HUMAN LAW?

. . . A law is a dictate of the practical reason. Now it is to be observed that the same procedure takes place in the practical and in the speculative reason, for each proceeds from principles to conclusions, as was stated above. Accordingly, we conclude that, just as in the speculative reason, from naturally known indemonstrable principles we draw the conclusions of the various sciences, the knowledge of which is not imparted to us by nature, but acquired by the efforts of reason, so too it is that from the precepts of the natural law, as from common and indemonstrable principles, the human reason needs to proceed to the more particular determination of certain matters. These particular determinations, devised by human reason, are called human laws, provided that the other essential conditions of law be observed, as was stated above.

. . . The human reason cannot have a full participation of the dictate of the divine reason, but according to its own mode, and imperfectly. Consequently, just as on the part of the speculative reason, by a natural participation of divine wisdom, there is in us the knowledge of certain common pinciples, but not a proper knowledge of each single truth, such as that contained in the divine wisdom, so, too, on the part of the practical reason, man has a natural participation of the eternal law, according to certain common principles, but not as regards the particular determinations of individual cases, which are, however, contained in the eternal law. Hence the need for human reason to proceed further to sanction them by law. . . .

WHETHER THERE WAS ANY NEED FOR A DIVINE LAW?

. . . Besides the natural and the human law it was necessary for the directing of human conduct to have a divine law. And this for four reasons. First, because it is by law that man is directed how to perform his proper acts in view of his last end. Now if man were ordained to no other end than that which is proportionate to his natural ability, there would be no need for man to have any further direction, on the part of his reason, in addition to the natural law and humanly devised law which is derived from it. But since man is ordained to an end of eternal happiness which exceeds man's natural ability, as we have stated above, therefore it was necessary that, in addition to the natural and the human law, man should be directed to his end by a law given by God.

Secondly, because, by reason, of the uncertainty of human judgment, especially on contingent and particular matters, different people form different judgments on human acts; whence also different and contrary laws result. In order, therefore, that man may know without any doubt what he ought to do and what he ought to avoid, it was necessary for man to be directed in his proper acts by a law given by God, for it is certain that such a law cannot err.

Thirdly, because man can make laws in those matters of which he is competent to judge. But man is not competent to judge of interior movements, that are hidden, but only of

exterior acts which are observable; and yet for the perfection of virtue it is necessary for man to conduct himself rightly in both kinds of acts. Consequently, human law could not sufficiently curb and direct interior acts, and it was necessary for this purpose that a divine law should supervene.

Fourthly, because, as Augustine says, human law cannot punish or forbid all evil deeds, since, while aiming at doing away with all evils, it would do away with many good things, and would hinder the advance of the common good, which is necessary for human living. In order, therefore, that no evil might remain unforbidden and unpunished, it was necessary for the divine law to supervene, whereby all sins are forbidden. . . .

QUESTION 92: ON THE EFFECTS OF LAW

WHETHER IT IS AN EFFECT OF LAW TO MAKE MEN GOOD?

. . . A law is nothing else than a dictate of reason in the ruler by whom his subjects are governed. Now the virtue of any being that is a subject consists in its being well subordinated to that by which it is regulated; and thus we see that the virtue of the irascible and concupiscible powers consists in their being obedient to reason. In the same way, *the virtue of every subject consists in his being well subjected to his ruler,* as the Philosopher says. But every law aims at being obeyed by those who are subject to it. Consequently it is evident that the proper effect of law is to lead its subjects to their proper virtue; and since virtue is *that which makes its subject good,* it follows that the proper effect of law is to make those, to whom it is given, good, either absolutely or in some particular respect. For if the intention of the lawgiver is fixed on a true good, which is the common good regulated according to divine justice, it follows that the effect of law is to make men good absolutely. If, however, the intention of the lawgiver is fixed on that which is not good absolutely, but useful or pleasurable to himself, or in opposition to divine justice, then law does not make men good absolutely, but in a relative way, namely, in relation to that particular government. In this way good is found even in things that are bad of themselves. Thus a man is called a good robber, because he works in a way that is adapted to his end.

. . . A tyrannical law, through not being according to reason, is not a law, absolutely speaking, but rather a perversion of law; and yet in so far as it is something in the nature of a law, its aim is that the citizens be good. For it has the nature of law only in so far as it is an ordinance made by a superior to his subjects, and aims at being obeyed by them; and this is to make them good, not absolutely, but with respect to that particular government. . . .

QUESTION 93: THE ETERNAL LAW

. . . Just as in every artificer there pre-exists an exemplar of the things that are made by his art, so too in every governor there must pre-exist the exemplar of the order of those things that are to be done by those who are subject to his government. And just as the exemplar of the things yet to be made by an art is called the art or model of the products of that art, so, too, the exemplar in him who governs the acts of his subjects bears the character of a law, provided the other conditions be present which we have mentioned above as belonging to the nature of law. Now God, by His wisdom, is the Creator of all things, in relation to which He stands as the artificer to the products of His art, as was stated in the First Part. Moreover, He governs all the acts and movements that are to be found in each single creature, as was also stated in the First Part. Therefore, just as the exemplar of the divine wisdom, inasmuch as all things are created by it, has the character of an art, a model or an idea, so the exemplar of divine wisdom, as moving all things to their due end, bears the character of law. Accordingly, the eternal law is nothing else than the exemplar of divine wisdom. As directing all actions and movements. . . .

Since, then, the eternal law is the plan of government in the Chief Governor, all the plans of government in the inferior governors must be derived from the eternal law. But these plans of inferior governors are all the other laws which are in addition to the eternal law. Therefore all laws, in so far as they partake of right reason, are derived from the eternal law. Hence Augustine says that *in temporal law there is nothing just and lawful but what man has drawn from the eternal law.*

. . . Human law has the nature of law in so far as it partakes of right reason; and it is clear that, in this respect, it is derived from the eternal law. But in so far as it deviates from reason, it is called an unjust law, and has the nature, not of law, but of violence. Nevertheless, even an unjust law, in so far as it retains some appearance of law, through being framed by one who is in power, is derived from the eternal law; for all power is from the Lord God, according to *Rom* xiii, I.

. . . Human law is said to permit certain things, not as approving of them, but as being unable to direct them. And many things are directed by the divine law, which human law is unable to direct, because more things are subject to a higher than a lower cause. Hence the very fact that human law does not concern itself with matters it cannot direct comes under the ordination of the eternal law. It would be different, were human law to sanction what the eternal law condemns. Consequently, it does not follow that human law is not derived from the eternal law; what follows is rather that it is not on a perfect equality with it. . . .

QUESTION 94: THE NATURAL LAW

WHETHER THE NATURAL LAW CONTAINS SEVERAL PRECEPTS OR ONLY ONE?

. . . The precepts of the natural law are to the practical reason what the first principles of demonstrations are to the speculative reason, because both are self-evident principles. Now a thing is said to be self-evident in two ways: first, in itself; secondly, in relation to us. Any proposition is said to be self-evident in itself, if its predicate is contained in the notion of the subject; even though it may happen that to one who does not know the definition of the subject, such a proposition is not self-evident. For instance, this proposition, *Man is a rational being*, is in its very nature, self-evident, since he who says *man*, says *a rational being;* and yet to one who does not know what a man is, this proposition is not self-evident. Hence it is that, [as Boethius says, certain axioms or propositions are universally self-evident to all; and such are the propositions whose terms are known to all, as, *Every whole is greater than its part*, and, *Things equal to one and the same are equal to one another.*] But some propositions are self-evident only to the wise, who understand the meaning of the terms of such propositions. Thus to one who understands that an angel is not a body, it is self-evident that an angel is not circumscriptively in a place. But this is not evident to the unlearned, for they cannot grasp it.

. . . Now as *being* is the first thing that falls under the apprehension absolutely, so *good* is the first thing that falls under the apprehension of the practical reason, which is directed to action (since every agent acts for an end, which has the nature of good). Consequently, the first principle in the practical reason is one founded on the nature of good, viz., that *good is that which all things seek after.* Hence this is the first precept of law, that *good is to be done and promoted, and evil is to be avoided.* All other precepts of the natural law are based upon this; so that all the things which the practical reason naturally apprehends as man's good belong to the precepts of the natural law under the form of things to be done or avoided.

Since, however, good has the nature of an end, and evil, the nature of the contrary, hence it is that all those things to which man has a natural inclination are naturally apprehended by reason as being good, and consequently as objects of pursuit, and their contraries as evil, and objects of avoidance. Therefore, the order of the precepts of the natural law is according to the order of natural inclinations. For there is in man, first of all, an inclination to good in accordance with the nature which he has in common with all

substances, inasmuch, namely, as every substance seeks the preservation of its own being, according to its nature; and by reason of this inclination, whatever is a means of preserving human life, and of warding off its obstacles, belongs to the natural law. Secondly, there is in man an inclination to things that pertain to him more specially, according to that nature which he has in common with other animals; and in virtue of this inclination, those things are said to belong to the natural law *which nature has taught to all animals*, such as sexual intercourse, the education of offspring and so forth. Thirdly, there is in man an inclination to good according to the nature of his reason, which nature is proper to him. Thus man has a natural inclination to know the truth about God, and to live in society; and in this respect, whatever pertains to this inclination belongs to the natural law: *e.g.*, to shun ignorance, to avoid offending those among whom one has to live, and other such things regarding the above inclination.

. . . All these precepts of the law of nature have the character of one natural law, inasmuch as they flow from one first precept.

. . . All the inclinations of any parts whatsoever of human nature, *e.g.*, of the concupiscible and irascible parts, in so far as they are ruled by reason, belong to the natural law, and are reduced to one first precept, as was stated above. And thus the precepts of the natural law are many in themselves, but they are based on one common foundation. . . .

QUESTION 95: HUMAN LAW

WHETHER IT WAS USEFUL FOR LAWS TO BE FRAMED BY MEN?

. . . As we have stated above, man has a natural aptitude for virtue; but the perfection of virtue must be acquired by man by means of some kind of training. . . . Now it is difficult to see how man could suffice for himself in the matter of this training, since the perfection of virtue consists chiefly in withdrawing man from undue pleasures, to which above all man is inclined, and especially the young, who are more capable of being trained. Consequently a man needs to receive this training from another, whereby to arrive at the perfection of virtue. And as to those young people who are inclined to acts of virtue by their good natural disposition, or by custom, or rather by the give of God, paternal training suffices, which is by admonitions. But since some are found to be dissolute and prone to vice, and not easily amenable to words, it was necessary for such to be restrained from evil by force and fear, in order that, at least, they might desist from evildoing, and leave others in peace, and that they themselves, by being habituated in this way, might be brought to do willingly what hitherto they did from fear, and thus become virtuous. Now this kind of training, which compels through fear of punishment, is the discipline of laws. Therefore,

in order that man might have peace and virtue, it was necessary for laws to be framed. . . .

WHETHER EVERY HUMAN LAW IS DERIVED FROM THE NATURAL LAW?

. . . As Augustine says, *that which is not just seems to be no law at all*. Hence the force of a law depends on the extent of its justice. Now in human affairs a thing is said to be just from being right, according to the rule of reason. But the first rule of reason is the law of nature, as is clear from what has been stated above. Consequently, every human law has just so much of the nature of law as it is derived from the law of nature. But if in any point it departs from the law of nature, it is no longer a law but a perversion of law.

REVIEW AND DISCUSSION QUESTIONS

1. Describe the nature or essence of law, according to Aquinas, indicating its connection with the common good.
2. How does he define "law"?
3. Describe briefly each of the types of law

he distinguishes.
4. "Lawmaking is purposive and rational." Explain, indicating what Aquinas thinks its purpose is and why law cannot be arbitrary.

The Province of Jurisprudence Determined

John Austin

Along with Jeremy Bentham, John Austin was among the most influential of the early utilitarian philosophers. In this selection, taken from his important work on law, Austin explains his positivist conception of law as a species of command and argues that the question of a law's status as law is distinct from the question of whether it is just or compatible with divine law.

LECTURE 1

The matter of jurisprudence is positive law: law, simply and strictly so called: or law set by political superiors to political inferiors. . . .

A law, in the most general and comprehensive acceptation in which the term, in its literal

meaning, is employed, may be said to be a rule laid down for the guidance of an intelligent being by an intelligent being having power over him. Under this definition are concluded, and without impropriety, several species. It is necessary to define accurately the line of demarcation which separates these species from one

Superiority is often synonymous with *precedence or excellence.* . . .

But, taken with the meaning wherein I here understand it, the term *superiority* signifies *might:* the power of affecting others with evil or pain, and of forcing them, through fear of that evil, to fashion their conduct to one's wishes.

For example, God is emphatically the *superior* of Man. For His power of affecting us with pain, and of forcing us to comply with His will, is unbounded and resistless.

To a limited extent, the sovereign One or Number is the superior of the subject or citizen: the master, of the slave or servant: the father, of the child.

In short, whoever can *oblige* another to comply with his wishes, is the *superior* of that other, so far as the ability reaches: The party who is obnoxious to the impending evil, being, to that same extent, the *inferior.*

The might or superiority of God, is simple or absolute. . . .

A member of a sovereign assembly is the superior of the judge: the judge being bound by the law which proceeds from that sovereign body. But, in his character of citizen or subject, he is the inferior of the judge: the judge being the minister of the law, and armed with the power of enforcing it.

It appears, then, that the term *superiority* (like the terms *duty* and *sanction*) is implied by the term *command.* For superiority is the power of enforcing compliance with a wish: and the expression or intimation of a wish, with the power and the purpose of enforcing, are the constituent elements of a command.

"That *laws* emanate from *superiors*" is, therefore, an identical proposition. For the meaning which it affects to impart is contained in its subject. . . .

According to an opinion which I must notice *incidentally* here, though the subject to which it relates will be treated *directly* hereafter, *customary laws* must be excepted from the proposition "that laws are a series of commands."

By many of the admirers of customary laws . . . they are thought to oblige legally (independently of the sovereign or state), *because*

the citizens or subjects have observed or kept them. . . .

At its origin, a custom is a rule of conduct which the governed observe spontaneously, or not in pursuance of a law set by a political superior. The custom is transmitted into positive law, when it is adopted as such by the courts of justice, and when the judicial decisions fashioned upon it are enforced by the power of the state. But before it is adopted by the courts, and clothed with the legal sanction, it is merely a rule of positive morality: a rule generally observed by the citizens or subjects; but deriving the only force, which it can be said to possess, from the general disapprobation falling on those who transgress it.

Now when judges transmute a custom into a legal rule (or make a legal rule not suggested by a custom), the legal rule which they establish is established by the sovereign legislature. A subordinate or subject judge is merely a minister. The portion of the sovereign power which lies at his disposition is merely delegated. The rules which he makes derive their legal force from authority given by the state: an authority which the state may confer expressly, but which it commonly imparts in the way of acquiescence. For, since the state may reverse the rules which he makes, and yet permits him to enforce them by the power of the political community, its sovereign will "that his rules shall obtain as law" is clearly evinced by its conduct, though not by its express declarations. . . .

LECTURE 5

. . . Now it follows from these premises, that the laws of God, and positive laws are laws proper, or laws properly so called.

The laws of God are laws proper, inasmuch as they are *commands* express or tacit, and therefore emanate from a *certain* source.

Positive laws, or laws strictly so called, are established directly or immediately by authors of three kinds:—by monarchs, or sovereign bodies, as supreme political superiors: by men in a state of subjection, as subordinate political superiors:

by subjects as private persons, in pursuance of legal rights. But every positive law, or every law strictly so called, is a direct or circuitous command of a monarch or sovereign number in the character of political superior: that is to say, a direct or circuitous command of a monarch or sovereign number to a person or persons in a state of subjection to its author. And being a *command* (and therefore flowing from a *determinate* source), every positive law is a law proper, or a law properly so called.

Besides the human laws which I style positive law, there are human laws which I style positive morality, rules of positive morality, or positive moral rules.

The generic character of laws of the class may be stated briefly in the following negative manner.—No law belonging to the class is a direct or circuitous command of a monarch or sovereign number in the character of political superior. In other words, no law belonging to the class is a direct or circuitous command of a monarch or sovereign number to a person or persons in a state of subjection to its author. . . .

The existence of law is one thing; its merit or demerit is another. Whether it be or be not is one enquiry; whether it be or be not conformable to an assumed standard, is a different enquiry. A law, which actually exists, is a law, though we happen to dislike it, or though it vary from the text, by which we regulate our approbation and disapprobation. This truth, when formally announced as an abstract proposition, is so simple and glaring that it seems idle to insist upon it. But simple and glaring as it is, when enunciated in abstract expressions the enumeration of the instances in which it has been forgotten would fill a volume.

Sir William Blackstone, for example, says in his "Commentaries," that the laws of God are superior in obligation to all other laws; that no human laws should be suffered to contradict them; that human laws are of no validity if contrary to them; and that all valid laws derive their force from that Divine original.

Now, he *may* mean that all human laws ought to conform to the Divine laws. If this be his meaning, I assent to it without hesitation. The

evils which we are exposed to suffer from the hands of God as a consequence of disobeying His commands are the greatest evils to which we are obnoxious; the obligations which they impose are consequently paramount to those imposed by any other laws, and if human commands conflict with the Divine law, we ought to disobey the command which is enforced by the less powerful sanction; this is implied in the term *ought:* the proposition is identical, and therefore perfectly indisputable—it is our interest to choose the smaller and more uncertain evil, in preference to the greater and surer. If this be Blackstone's meaning, I assent to his proposition, and have only to object to it, that it tells us just nothing.

Perhaps, again, he means that human lawgivers are themselves obliged by the Divine laws to fashion the laws which they impose by that ultimate standard, because if they do not, God will punish them. To this also I entirely assent. . . .

But the meaning of this passage of Blackstone, if it has a meaning, seems rather to be this: that no human law which conflicts with the Divine law is obligatory or binding; in other words, that no human law which conflicts with the Divine law is a *law*, for a law without an obligation is a contradiction in terms. I suppose this to be his meaning, because when we say of any transaction that it is invalid or void, we mean that it is not binding: as, for example, if it be a contract, we mean that the political law will not lend its sanction to enforce the contract.

Now, to say that human laws which conflict with the Divine law are not binding, that is to say, are not laws, is to talk stark nonsense. The most pernicious laws, and therefore those which are most opposed to the will of God, have been and are continually enforced as laws by judicial tribunals. Suppose an act innocuous, or positively beneficial, be prohibited by the sovereign under the penalty of death; if I commit this act, I shall be tried and condemned, and if I object to the sentence, that it is contrary to the law of God, who has commanded that human lawgivers shall not prohibit acts which have no evil consequences, the Court of Justice will demonstrate the inconclusiveness of my reasoning by hanging me up, in pursuance of the law of which I have impugned the validity. An exception, demurrer, or plea, founded on the law of God was never heard in a Court of Justice, from the creation of the world down to the present moment.

But this abuse of language is not merely puerile, it is mischievous. When it is said that a law ought to be disobeyed, what is meant is that we are urged to disobey it by motives more cogent and compulsory than those by which it is itself sanctioned. If the laws of God are certain, the motives which they hold out to disobey any human command which is at variance with them are paramount to all others. But the laws of God are not always certain. . . . In quiet times the dictates of utility are fortunately so obvious that the anarchical doctrine sleeps, and men habitually admit the validity of laws which they dislike. To prove by pertinent reasons that a law is pernicious is highly useful, because such process may lead to the abrogation of the pernicious law. To incite the public to resistance by determinate views of *utility* may be useful, for resistance, grounded on clear and definite prospects of good, is sometimes beneficial. But to proclaim generally that all laws which are pernicious or contrary to the will of God are void and not to be tolerated, is to preach anarchy, hostile and perilous as much to wise and benign rule as to stupid and galling tyranny. . . .

LECTURE 6

. . . Every positive law, or every law simply and strictly so called, is set by a sovereign person, or a sovereign body of persons, to a member or members of the independent political society wherein that person or body is sovereign or supreme. Or (changing the expression) it *is* set by a monarch, or sovereign number, to a person or persons in a state of subjection to its author. Even though it sprung directly from another fountain or source, it is a positive law,

or a law strictly so called, by the institution of that present sovereign in the character of political superior. . . .

The superiority which is styled sovereignty, and the independent political society which sovereignty implies, is distinguished from other superiority, and from other society, by the following marks or characters.—1. The bulk of the given society are in a *habit* of obedience or submission to a *determinate* and *common* superior: let that common superior be a certain individual person, or a certain body or aggregate of individual persons. 2. That certain individual, or that certain body of individuals, is *not* in a habit of obedience to a determinate human superior. Laws (improperly so called) which opinion sets or imposes, may permanently affect the conduct of that certain individual or body. To express or tacit commands of other determinate parties, that certain individual or body may yield occasional submission. But there is no determinate person, determinate aggregate of persons, to whose commands, express or tacit, that certain individual or body renders habitual obedience. . . . By "an independent political society," or "an independent and sovereign nation," we mean a political society consisting of a sovereign and subjects, as opposed to a political society which is merely subordinate: that is to say, which is merely a limb or member of another political society, and which therefore consists entirely of persons in a state of subjection.

In order that a given society may form a society political and independent, the two distinguishing marks which I have mentioned above must unite. The *generality* of the given society must be in the *habit* of obedience to a *determinate* and *common* superior: whilst that determinate person, or determinate body of persons must *not* be habitually obedient to a determinate person or body. It is the union of that positive, with this negative mark, which renders that certain superior sovereign or supreme, and which renders that given society (including that certain superior) a society political and independent.

REVIEW AND DISCUSSION QUESTIONS

1. Laws are rules, according to Austin, but rules are really just a form of command. How does Austin define a command?

2. Many of us give orders or commands, but these commands are not laws because we are not the "sovereign." How does Austin understand the sovereign?

3. How does Austin understand the notion of an obligation?

4. Which is superior, legal obligations or religious obligations? Explain.

5. Austin argues that in a democratic government the electorate is sovereign. Do you agree? Explain.

6. If Austin is correct that people are sovereign in a democracy, does it then make sense to think of law as orders?

7. How can Austin account for common or judge-made law?

8. Suppose a judge, noticing there is no relevant statute, applies a customary rule that people have followed for generations and holds a ship liable for not coming to the aid of another at sea. Who is the sovereign in that case? Was the customary rule law *before* the judge applied it, according to Austin?

9. Given his theory of obligation, do positive laws that contradict divine law establish obligations? If not, can they really be laws at all?

6

FORMALISM AND LEGAL REALISM

Judges and lawyers often disagree about how a statute or precedent should be interpreted. Such disagreements raise important questions. Is there really a right or best answer to legal questions, or are there instead only different, subjective opinions? Are past precedents, statutes, and other legal materials sufficient to determine the correct legal outcome in a given case? Or is it instead merely a matter of a particular judge's political opinions? These important questions engage the authors presented in this section, but they will also emerge in various other contexts throughout the book. The term "formalist" is often used to describe those who think that if properly interpreted, the law speaks with a single voice, so there is in theory always a right legal answer. This formalist position is represented by Christopher Columbus Langdell and Joseph Beal. Opposing the formalist view is a school of thinking known as legal "realism." Realists deny that the law is determinate. In the early decades of the twentieth century, legal realism emerged as a distinctive and radical school of jurisprudence in the United States, and today it continues to exert an important influence on legal philosophy and legal scholarship. Legal realists reacted against what they saw as the "mechanical" and "nonpolitical" approach of those who saw the law as a logical and consistent system of rules and principles. Realists such as Oliver Wendell Holmes and Jerome Frank thus adopted a more pragmatic approach to law, an approach frequently informed by the social sciences and eager to acknowledge the extent to which various social forces external to the law influence its development. Realists see the law as consisting of decisions, not rules. Judges do not apply the law. They make it. The section concludes with a discussion of the nature of interpretation and its formal character by Tony Honoré.

Preface to *Cases on the Law of Contracts*

Christopher Columbus Langdell

Although both Harvard's and Yale's law schools date from the 1820s, the study of law in those days was almost entirely done through apprenticeships with practicing lawyers. Admission to the law schools was easier than to the colleges, and neither school was able to establish its importance as an institution of legal education until Langdell arrived as dean of Harvard in 1869. Determined to raise the law school's stature and improve legal education, he was forced to confront the question of how law can be taught other than through the normal method of working alongside an already established practitioner. The following selection is taken from the preface to his original casebook on contracts. In it he describes why cases are necessary to the study of law and the nature of "legal science" itself.

I entered upon the duties of my present position, a year and a half ago, with a settled conviction that law could only be taught or learned effectively by means of cases in some form. I had entertained such an opinion ever since I knew any thing of the nature of law or of legal study; but it was chiefly through my experience as a learner that it was first formed, as well as subsequently strengthened and confirmed. . . .

Now, however, I was called upon to consider directly the subject of teaching, not theoretically but practically. . . . I was expected to take a large class of pupils, meet them regularly from day to day, and give them systematic instruction in such branches of law as had been assigned to me. . . . How could this . . . object be accomplished? Only one mode occurred to me which seemed to hold out any reasonable prospect of success; and that was, to make a series of cases, carefully selected from the books of reports, the subject alike of study and instruction. But here I was met by what seemed at first to be an insuperable practical difficulty, namely, the want of books. . . .

It was with a view to removing these obstacles, that I was first led to inquire into the feasibility of preparing and publishing such a selection of cases as would be adapted to my purpose as a teacher. The most important element in that inquiry was the great and rapidly increasing number of reported cases in every department of law. In view of this fact, was there

any satisfactory principle upon which such a selection could be made? It seemed to me that there was. Law, considered as a science, consists of certain principles or doctrines. To have such a mastery of these as to be able to apply them with constant facility and certainty to the ever-tangled skein of human affairs, is what constitutes a true lawyer; and hence to acquire that mastery should be the business of every earnest student of law. Each of these doctrines has arrived at its present state by slow degrees; in other words, it is a growth, extending in many cases through centuries. This growth is to be traced in the main through a series of cases. . . . But the cases which are useful and necessary for this purpose at the present day bear an exceedingly small proportion to all that have been reported. The vast majority are useless and worse than useless for any purpose of systematic study. Moreover, the number of fundamental legal doctrines is much less than is commonly supposed; the many different guises in which the same doctrine is constantly making its appearance, and the great extent to which legal treatises are a repetition of each other, being the cause of much misapprehension. . . . It seemed to me, therefore, to be possible to take such a branch of the law as Contracts, for example, and, without exceeding comparatively moderate limits, to select, classify, and arrange all the cases which had contributed in any important degree to the growth, development, or establishment of any of its essential doctrines; and that such a work could not fail to be of material service to all who desire to study that branch of law systematically and in its original sources.

It is upon this principle that the present volume has been prepared. It begins the subject of Contracts, and embraces the important topics of Mutual Consent, Consideration, and Conditional Contracts. Though complete in itself, it is my expectation that it will be followed by other volumes upon the same plan.

REVIEW AND DISCUSSION QUESTIONS

1. On what basis does Langdell say he chose the cases for his book from among the many thousands that are "reported" (i.e., published)?
2. Describe Langdell's view of the nature of law. Does he think law is theoretically separable from sound moral principles?
3. Does he seem to think individual judges exercise discretion, and if so, in what sense?

A Treatise on the Conflict of Laws

Joseph H. Beale

In this brief selection from his treatise discussing how the law addresses conflicts among its various compartments and jurisdictions, Joseph Beale summarizes some of the central features of the formalist's picture of law. Properly understood, law is a system or body that includes various sorts of standards, rules, and principles of conduct. Taken together, these constitute a "single, homogeneous philosophical system." While law and legal principles can be changed either by legislation or by bad judicial decisions, Beale argues that these are not pervasive enough to render the entire system incoherent but instead represent what is "local" about each system. Beale concludes with a discussion of the general characteristics of a legal system: generality, universality, continuity, and predictability.

Body of Principles, Standards, and Rules. The particular law of a state is made up of several elements, some of them quite arbitrary in their operation. These accidental elements prevent the law from becoming, like the common law a scientific system.

The principles which form the largest portion even of the particular law of a state are general premises of law which can be used for deduction and for analogy. Such principles are: "A conveyance of any interest in land is governed as to its validity by the law of the state of situs." "The existence of a cause of action for a tort is governed by the law of the place of wrong."

A standard is a rule which is stated as a degree of a continuously changing series to be reached, in order for a legal result to follow; the application of the standard requires therefore not merely the finding of facts but the finding of this peculiar fact, the reaching of a particular degree in events which are capable of a continuous series. Examples of standards are: a negligence is the lack of *due care*; a result of an act of which there was *appreciable risk* is proximate.

A rule means a statement of law applicable only to a narrowly defined class of cases and incapable of extension by deduction or analogy. Instances of rules are: the rule in Shelley's case; the rule that one must stop, look, and listen before crossing a railroad track; the rule that one must turn to the right to pass a vehicle coming in an opposite direction. Most statutory law is of this sort. . . .

Definition of Law. The writers of the analytical school of jurisprudence, emphasizing the positive character of law as an expression of sovereign will, have proposed definitions which fit one portion of the law only; that is, the rules made by the legislative body.

* * *

These definitions appear to ignore the principal element of law, the so-called "unwritten law." So important is this portion of the law, and so widespread is the distinction, that in other languages than English different terms are used to distinguish the two. The positive law formulated and fixed by a legislative body is called *lex, loi, Gesetz*; the general unwritten law is called *ius, droit, Recht*.

The definitions of the analytic school are properly applicable only to *lex*. Austin, realizing this defect, fitted the facts to his theory by assuming a tacit command by the sovereign to his judges to express the rules of law which they lay down in their decisions; thus assimilating judicial to statute law.

A second objection to these definitions, even extended (by a fiction) to cover the unwritten law, is that they all ignore that quality of the law which is absolutely characteristic: that it tends to form a single homogeneous philosophical system. Any definition of law which treats each part of it as an isolated thing, instead of as part of an embodied system, misses its nature altogether. . . .

The authors whose opinions have been examined neglect, or at least too little emphasize, the one most important feature of law: that it is not a mere collection of arbitrary rules, but a body of scientific principle. That part of the law which in other languages is known as *ius, Recht, droit*, is a branch of practical philosophy; by which, through the use of reason and experience, legal generalizations may be made. Purity of doctrine may be lost through wrong decisions of courts, thus warping legal principle by bad

precedent; but wrong decisions are after all uncommon, and the law is not seriously affected by them. The application of general principles may be inhibited by legislation: but the amount of legislation which affects ordinary private law is relatively small, and doctrine is not greatly changed by statute. Much the largest and most important part of the law, therefore, is this body of principle, or as it is almost invariably called by European writers, *doctrine*. The changes in principle made by legislation and by wrong decisions constitute the greater part of the peculiar local law of any jurisdiction, as distinguished from the general doctrine of the prevailing legal system.

Law, therefore, is made in part by the legislature; in part it rests upon precedent; and in great part it consists in a homogeneous, scientific, and all-embracing body of principle; and a correct definition of law in general must apply to all these varieties of law. . . .

The Characteristics of Law. An essential characteristic of law is its generality; since justice requires equality of treatment for all persons, and this means generality. It is, as has been seen, a body of general principles, not a collection of special commands. A set of rules for the action of a particular person would lack this character of generality. Thus, the decision and judgment of a court, determining a particular controversy and laying an order upon one party to it, lacks this element and can in no sense be regarded as in itself law. . . . Law being a general principle applying indifferently to all cases which in the future can arise under it, the decision of a court can be law only if the court has power in its decision to lay down binding rules for future conduct. . . .

Another characteristic of law is universality. It is unthinkable in a civilized country that any act should fall outside of the domain of law. If law be regarded as a command, then every act done must either be permitted or forbidden. . . .

Another characteristic of law is continuity. "From the day of its promulgation to the day of its repeal the law must always be heard and obeyed."[1]

There can be no break or interregnum in law. From the time law comes into existence with the first felt corporateness of a primitive people, it must last until the final disappearance of human society. Once created, it persists until a change takes place, and when changed it continues in such changed condition until the next change, and so on forever. . . .

The social need of continuity in law is most clearly felt because society needs to know the law in advance of judicial action upon it. In order that law may help rather than hinder the carrying on of the work of society it must be possible for every person, of his own knowledge or by the help of others' knowledge, to discover the application of the law to any contemplated act. He must be in some way secured against unexpected legal consequences of his actions. Business could not go on, industry could not be maintained unless it were possible for the producer or the merchant to learn how he could conform his activities to the law. For this purpose it must be possible for one learned in the law to speak with authority on the application of law to the proposed acts and to predict with reasonable degree of certainty the decision of courts in case the legality of the acts should be called in question. If there were any discontinuity in the law,— if, for instance, a judicial tribunal had the power to change the law as it liked, or the discretion as to the application of law to the facts,—the client would seek advice in vain, for counsel however learned could only vaguely guess what the law would be at the time of possible future litigation. . . .

In order that it may be possible, then, for the law to function, it should be predicable; that is, in a case not previously passed on by a court, competent counsel should be able to predict what the action of a court in the case will be. Predicability can be secured only by a union of regularity, system, and reason. *[Beale does not include a separate discussion of "reason" apart from "regularity" and "system"—Ed.]*

a. Regularity. An administrative tribunal may guess at the "very right" of the particular case before it; but since each man's reaction to the idea of right is subjective to himself, it is practically impossible in a given case to predict the reaction of some as yet undetermined body of men to a given state of fact. To be predicable,

therefore, the result of judicial action must not lie in mere judicial discretion. That dictum of the fourteenth-century judge, that law is the will of the judges, his more experienced colleague at once corrected by pointing out a criterion of the decision: "By no means; it is the rule of right."[2] The court must have a rule to guide it, or its judgment, being merely discretionary, will be impredicable.

b. System. It is not enough, however, that law should be regular; for a merely regular law fails to meet the needs of modern civilization. A mass of rules is necessarily limited in its application; no legislator can formulate rules which will cover all future cases. Law must have the power of extension to novel facts. An example of this need occurred when streetcars were first introduced. A street-car line between Charlestown and Boston was opened about 1856, at a time when one man enjoyed a monopoly of public conveyance between the cities by omnibus and dray. The drays thereupon drove slowly along the tracks of the street-cars, while the busses hurried by. No formulated rule applied to the case, for it could not have been foreseen and guarded against. If the law had been regular but non-systematic, like the folk-law that preceded the common law, the wrong lacking a formal remedy, must have been unredressed. But the common law was systematic; that is, it consisted of a system of thought based upon principles which covered every possible occurrence. Every human act was either permitted or forbidden; every act either changed or left unchanged existing rights. Under this system of rights the act of a drayman in delaying the street-car was either forbidden or permitted by the law, whether the rule that determined the answer had ever been formulated or not; and the court was able to say that legal principle forbade the act of the drayman.

NOTES

[1]*Commonwealth v. Temple*, 80 Mass. (14 Gray) 69 (1860) (Shaw, C. J.).
[2]Ibid.

REVIEW AND DISCUSSION QUESTIONS

1. Beale claims that law includes rules and principles. How does he distinguish the two?

2. Why does Beale think that those who see law as the expression of rules of the legislative body or of the sovereign will have a too narrow view of the law?

3. Explain the importance of the unwritten law, for Beale.

4. Describe the essential characteristics of the law, according to Beale. Why does he call it a "system"?

The Path of the Law

Oliver Wendell Holmes

Written in 1897, this much-discussed essay has seemed to many to capture the central tenets of what came to be called legal realism. In it, Oliver Wendell Holmes offers a perspective on law at variance with both the formalists who had gone before and the traditional positivists, such as John Austin. According to Holmes, the law is, in fact, nothing more than past decisions plus predictions of what future judges will do. In making that claim, he sets himself against not only those who see law as a coherent, complete system of rules and principles, but also against people who seek to understand the law in terms of orders of a sovereign power.

When we study law we are not studying a mystery but a well known profession. We are studying what we shall want in order to appear before judges, or to advise people in such a way as to keep them out of court. The reason why it is a profession, why people will pay lawyers to argue for them or to advise them is that in societies like ours the command of the public force is intrusted to the judges in certain cases, and the whole power of the state will be put forth, if necessary, to carry out their judgments and decrees. People want to know under what circumstances and how far they will run the risk of coming against what is so much stronger than themselves, and hence it becomes a business to find out when this danger is to be feared. The object of our study, then, is prediction, the prediction of the incidence of the public force through the instrumentality of the courts.

The means of the study are a body of reports, of treatises, and of statutes, in this country and in England, extending back for six hundred years, and now increasing annually by hundreds. In these sibylline leaves are gathered the scattered prophecies of the past upon the cases in which the axe will fall. These are what properly have been called the oracles of the law. Far the most important and pretty nearly the whole meaning of every new effort of legal thought is to make these prophecies more precise, and to generalize them into a thoroughly connected system. The process is one, from a lawyer's statement of a case, eliminating as it does all the dramatic elements with which his client's story has clothed it, and retaining only the facts of legal import, up to the final analyses and abstract universals of theoretic jurisprudence. The reason why a lawyer does not mention that his client wore a white hat when he made a contract, while Mrs. Quickly would be sure to dwell upon it along with the parcel gilt goblet and the sea-coal fire is that he forsees that the public force will act in the same way whatever his client had upon his head. It is to make the prophecies easier to be remembered and to be understood that the teachings of the decisions of the past are put into general propositions and gathered into text-books, or that statutes are passed in a general form. . . .

The number of our predictions when generalized and reduced to a system is not unmanageably large. They present themselves as a finite body of dogma which may be mastered within a reasonable time. . . .

The first thing for a business-like understanding of the matter is to understand its limits, and therefore I think it desirable at once to point out and dispel a confusion between morality and law, which sometimes rises to the height of conscious theory, and more often and indeed constantly is making trouble in detail without reaching the point of consciousness. You can see very plainly that a bad man has as much reason as a good one for wishing to avoid an encounter with the public force, and therefore you can see the practical importance of the distinction between morality and law. A man who cares nothing for an ethical rule which is believed and practised by his neighbors is likely nevertheless to care a good deal to avoid being made to pay money, and will want to keep out of jail if he can. [I take it for granted that no hearer of mine will misinterpret what I have to say as the language of cynicism. The law is the witness and external deposit of our moral life. Its history is the history of the moral development of the race.] The practice of it, in spite of popular jests, tends to make good citizens and good men. When I emphasize the difference between law and morals I do so with reference to a single end, that of learning and understanding the law. For that purpose you must definitely master its specific marks, and it is for that that I ask you for the moment to imagine yourselves indifferent to other and greater things. . . .

. . . If you want to know the law and nothing else, you must look at it as a bad man, who cares only for the material consequences which such knowledge enables him to predict, not as a good one, who finds his reasons for conduct, whether inside the law or outside of it, in the vaguer sanctions of conscience. The theoretical importance of the distinction is no less, if you would reason on your subject aright. The law is full of phraseology drawn from morals, and by the mere force of language continually invites us to pass from one domain to the other without perceiving it, as we are sure to do unless we have the boundary

constantly before our minds. The law talks about rights, and duties, and malice, and intent, and negligence, and so forth, and nothing is easier, or, I may say, more common in legal reasoning, than to take these words in their moral sense, at some stage of the argument, and so to drop into fallacy. For instance, when we speak of the rights of man in a moral sense, we mean to mark the limits of interference with individual freedom which we think are prescribed by conscience, or by our ideal, however reached. Yet it is certain that many laws have been enforced in the past, and it is likely that some are enforced now, which are condemned by the most enlightened opinion of the time, or which at all events pass the limit of interference as many consciences would draw it. Manifestly, therefore, nothing but confusion of thought can result from assuming that the rights of man in a moral sense are equally rights in the sense of the Constitution and the law. No doubt simple and extreme cases can be put of imaginable laws which the statute-making power would not dare to enact, even in the absence of written constitutional prohibitions, because the community would rise in rebellion and fight; and this gives some plausibility to the proposition that the law, if not a part of morality, is limited by it. But this limit of power is not coextensive with any system of morals. For the most part it falls far within the lines of any such system, and in some cases may extend beyond them, for reasons drawn from the habits of a particular people at a particular time. I once heard the late Professor Agassiz say that a German population would rise if you added two cents to the price of a glass of beer. A statute in such a case would be empty words, not because it was wrong, but because it could not be enforced. No one will deny that wrong statutes can be and are enforced, and we should not all agree as to which were the wrong ones.

The confusion with which I am dealing besets confessedly legal conceptions. Take the fundamental question, What constitutes the law? You will find some text writers telling you that it is something different from what is decided by the courts of Massachusetts or England, that it is a system of reason, that it is a deduction from principles of ethics or admitted axioms or what not, which may or may not coincide with the decisions. But if we take the view of our friend the bad man we shall find that he does not care two straws for the axioms or deductions, but that he does want to know what the Massachusetts or English courts are likely to do in fact. I am much of his mind. The prophecies of what the courts will do in fact, and nothing more pretentious, are what I mean by the law.

Take again a notion which as popularly understood is the widest conception which the law contains;—the notion of legal duty, to which already I have referred. We fill the word with all the content which we draw from morals. But what does it mean to a bad man? Mainly, and in the first place, a prophecy that if he does certain things he will be subjected to disagreeable consequences by way of imprisonment or compulsory payment of money. But from his point of view, what is the difference between being fined and being taxed a certain sum for doing a certain thing? That his point of view is the test of legal principles is shown by the many discussions which have arisen in the courts on the very question whether a given statutory liability is a penalty or a tax. On the answer to this question depends the decision whether conduct is legally wrong or right, and also whether a man is under compulsion or free. Leaving the criminal law on one side, what is the difference between the liability under the mill acts or statutes authorizing a taking by eminent domain and the liability for what we call a wrongful conversion of property where restoration is out of the question? In both cases the party taking another man's property has to pay its fair value as assessed by a jury, and no more. What significance is there in calling one taking right and another wrong from the point of view of the law? It does not matter, so far as the given consequence, the compulsory payment, is concerned, whether the act to which it is attached is described in terms of praise or in terms of blame, or whether the law porports to prohibit it or allow it. . . .

Nowhere is the confusion between legal and moral ideas more manifest than in the law of contract. Among other things, here again the so called primary rights and duties are invested with a mystic significance beyond what can be assigned and explained. The duty to keep a contract at common law means a prediction that you must pay damages if you do not keep it,—and nothing else. If you commit a tort, you are liable to pay a compensatory sum. If you commit a contract, you are liable to pay a conpensatory sum unless the promised event comes to pass, and that is all the difference. But such a mode of looking at the matter stinks in the nostrils of those who think it advantageous to get as much ethics into the law as they can. . . .

. . . We talk about a contract as a meeting of the minds of the parties, and thence it is inferred in various cases that there is no contract because their minds have not met; that is, because they have intended different things or because one party has not known of the assent of the other. Yet nothing is more certain than that parties may be bound by a contract to things which neither of them intended, and when one does not know of the other's assent. Suppose a contract is executed in due form and in writing to deliver a lecture, mentioning no time. One of the parties thinks that the promise will be construed to mean at once, within a week. The other thinks that it means when he is ready. The court says that it means within a reasonable time. The parties are bound by the contract as it is interpreted by the court, yet neither of them meant what the court declares that they have said. . . .

. . . I hope that my illustrations have shown the danger, both to speculation and to practice, of confounding morality with law, and the trap which legal language lays for us on that side of our way. For my own part, I often doubt whether it would not be a gain if every word of moral significance could be banished from the law altogether, and other words adopted which should convey legal ideas uncolored by anything outside the law. We should lose the fossil records of a good deal of history and the majesty got from ethical associations, but by ridding ourselves of an unncessary confusion we should gain very much in the clearness of our thought.

So much for the limits of the law. The next thing which I wish to consider is what are the forces which determine its content and its growth. You may assume, with Hobbes and Bentham and Austin, that all law emanates from the sovereign, even when the first human beings to enunciate it are the judges, or you may think that law is the voice of the Zeitgeist, or what you like. It is all one to my present purpose. Even if every decision required the sanction of an emperor with despotic power and a whimsical turn of mind, we should be interested none the less, still with a view to prediction, in discovering some order, some rational explanation, and some principle of growth for the rules which he laid down. In every system there are such explanations and principles to be found. It is with regard to them that a second fallacy comes in, which I think it important to expose.

The fallacy to which I refer is the notion that the only force at work in the development of the law is logic. . . . The danger of which I speak is not the admission that the principles governing other phenomena also govern the law, but the notion that a given system, ours, for instance, can be worked out like mathematics from some general axioms of conduct. This is the natural error of the schools, but it is not confined to them. I once heard a very eminent judge say that he never let a decision go until he was absolutely sure that it was right. So judicial dissent often is blamed, as if it meant simply that one side or the other were not doing their sums right, and, if they would take more trouble, agreement inevitably would come.

This mode of thinking is entirely natural. The training of lawyers is a training in logic. The processes of analogy, discrimination, and deduction are those in which they are most at home. The language of judicial decision is mainly the language of logic. And the logical method and form flatter that longing for certainty and for repose which is in every human mind. But certainty generally is illusion, and repose is not the destiny of man. Behind the logical form lies a judgment as to the relative worth and importance of competing legislative grounds, often an inarticulate and unconscious judgment, it is true, and yet the very root and nerve of the whole proceeding. You can give any conclusion a logical form. You always can imply a condition in a contract. But why do you imply it? It is because of some belief as to the practice of the community or of a class, or because of some opinion as to policy, or, in short, because of some attitude of yours upon a matter not capable of exact quantitative measurement, and therefore not capable of founding exact logical conclusions. Such matters really are battle grounds where the means do not exist for determinations that shall be good for all time, and where the decision can do no more than embody the preference of a given body in a given time and place. We do not realize how large a part of our law is open to reconsideration upon a slight change in the habit of the public mind. No concrete proposition is self-evident, no matter how ready we may be to accept it, not even Mr. Herbert Spencer's Every man has a right to do what he wills, provided he interferes not with a like right on the part of his neighbors.

Why is a false and injurious statement privileged, if it is made honestly in giving information about a servant? It is because it has been thought more important that information should be given freely, than that a man should be protected from what under other circumstances would be an actionable wrong. Why is a man at liberty to set up a business which he knows will ruin his neighbor? It is because the public good is supposed to be best subserved by free competition. Obviously such judgments of relative importance may vary in different times and places. . . .

REVIEW AND DISCUSSION QUESTIONS

1. Explain how Holmes understands the essential nature of the law. What, finally, is law, according to him?

2. Why does Holmes suggest that the best way to look at the law is from the perspective of the bad man?

3. How does Holmes explain the distinction between moral and legal duty?

4. What value or values do you think underlie the law, according to Holmes?

5. How do you think Holmes would respond to legal formalists such as Langdell and Beale?

Realism and the Law

Jerome Frank

Legal realism arose as a distinctive school of American jurisprudence in the early decades of this century. Describing their opponents as "formalists," legal realists argued that the law is essentially normative and that judges exercise wide discretion; a judge's values and beliefs about society have a large impact, they argued, on how cases are decided. Law is not a "seamless web" and, more important, it places few rational restraints on how judges rule. Jerome Frank, who served as an appeals court judge, was among the most outspoken of the legal realists. In the following essay, taken from his book Law and the Modern Mind, *he first describes the "conventional" view of law, which fails to acknowledge that judges often make new law. He then describes how the judge's personality affects the laws he or she makes, and attacks the "myth" that precedents and reason control judges. He concludes with a brief discussion of the nature of law from the perspective of the legal realist.*

JUDICIAL LAW-MAKING

Have judges the right and power to make law and change law? Much good ink has been spilled in arguing that question. A brief survey of the controversy will illuminate our thesis.

The conventional view may be summarized thus:

Law is a complete body of rules existing from time immemorial and unchangeable except to the limited extent that legislatures have changed the rules by enacted statutes. Legislatures are expressly empowered thus to change the law. But the judges are not to make or change the law but to apply it. The law, ready-made, pre-exists the judicial decisions.

Judges are simply "living oracles" of law. They are merely "the speaking law." Their function is purely passive. They are "but the mouth which pronounces the law." They no more make or invent new law than Columbus made or invented America. Judicial opinions are evidence of what the law is; the best evidence, but no more than that. When a former decision is overruled, we must not say that the rule announced in the earlier decision was once the law and has now been changed by the later decision. We must view the earlier decision as laying down an erroneous rule. It was a false map of the law just as a pre-Columbian map of the world was false. Emphatically, we must not refer to the new decision as making new law. It only seems to do so. It is merely a bit of revised legal cartography.

If a judge actually attempted to contrive a new rule, he would be guilty of usurpation of power, for the legislature alone has the authority to change the law. The judges, writes Blackstone, are "not delegated to pronounce a new law, but to maintain and expound the old law"; even when a former decision is abandoned because "most evidently contrary to reason," the "subsequent judges do not pretend to make new law, but to vindicate the old one from misrepresentation." The prior judge's eyesight had been defective and he made "a mistake" in finding the law, which mistake is now being rectified by his successors.

Such is the conventional notion. There is a contrary minority view, which any dispassionate observer must accept as obviously the correct view:

"No intelligent lawyer would in this day pretend that the decisions of the courts do not add to and alter the law," says Pollock, a distinguished English jurist. "Judge-made law is real law," writes Dicey, another famous legal commentator, "though made under the form of, and often described by judges no less than jurists, as the mere interpretation of law. . . . The amount of such judge-made law is in England far more extensive than a student realizes. Nine-tenths, at least, of the law of contract, and the whole, or nearly the whole, of the law of torts are not to be discovered in any volume of the statutes. . . .

Whole branches, not of ancient but of very modern law, have been built up, developed or created by action of the courts."

Judges, then, do make and change law. The minority view is patently correct; the opposing arguments will not bear analysis. What, then, explains the belief so tenaciously held that the judiciary does not ever change the law or that, when it does, it is acting improperly? Why is it that judges adhere to what Morris Cohen has happily called "the phonographic theory of the judicial function"? What explains the recent remark of an eminent member of the Bar: "The man who claims that under our system courts make law is asserting that the courts habitually act unconstitutionally"? Why do the courts customarily deny that they have any law-making power and describe new law which they create to deal with essentially contemporary events, as mere explanations or interpretations of law which already exists and has existed from time immemorial? Why this obstinate denial of the juristic realities?

We revert to our thesis: The essence of the basic legal myth or illusion is that law can be entirely predictable. Back of this illusion is the childish desire to have a fixed father-controlled universe, free of chance and error due to human fallibility. . . .

But if it is once recognized that a judge, in the course of deciding a case, can for the first time create the law applicable to that case, or can alter the rules which were supposed to exist before the case was decided, then it will also have to be recognized that the rights and obligations of the parties to that case may be decided retroactively. A change thus made by a judge, when passing upon a case, is a change in the law made with respect to past events,—events which occurred before the law came into existence. Legal predictability is plainly impossible, if, at the time I do an act, I do so with reference to law which, should a lawsuit thereafter arise with reference to my act, may be changed by the judge who tries the case. For then the result is that my case is decided according to law which was not in existence when I acted and which I, therefore, could not have known, predicted or relied on when I acted.

If, therefore, one has a powerful need to believe in the possibility of anything like exact legal predictability, he will find judicial lawmaking intolerable and seek to deny its existence.

Hence the myth that the judges have no power to change existing law or make new law. . . .

THE JUDGING PROCESS AND THE JUDGE'S PERSONALITY

. . . As the word indicates, the judge in reaching a decision is making a judgment. And if we would understand what goes into the creating of that judgment, we must observe how ordinary men dealing with ordinary affairs arrive at their judgments.

The process of judging, so the psychologists tell us, seldom begins with a premise from which a conclusion is subsequently worked out. Judging begins rather the other way around—with a conclusion more or less vaguely formed; a man ordinarily starts with such a conclusion and afterwards tries to find premises which will substantiate it. If he cannot, to his satisfaction, find proper arguments to link up his conclusion with premises which he finds acceptable, he will, unless he is arbitrary or mad, reject the conclusion and seek another.

In the case of the lawyer who is to present a case to a court, the dominance in his thinking of the conclusion over the premises is moderately obvious. He is a partisan working on behalf of his client. The conclusion is, therefore, not a matter of choice except within narrow limits. He must, that is if he is to be successful, begin with a conclusion which will insure his client's winning the lawsuit. He then assembles the facts in such a fashion that he can work back from this result he desires to some major premise which he thinks the court will be willing to accept. The precedents, rules, principles and standards to which he will call the court's attention constitute this premise.

While "the dominance of the conclusion" in the case of the lawyer is clear, it is less so in the case of the judge. For the respectable and traditional descriptions of the judicial judging process admit no such backward-working explanation. In theory, the judge begins with some rule or principle of law as his premise, applies this premise to the facts, and thus arrives at his decision.

Now, since the judge is a human being and since no human being in his normal thinking process arrives at decisions (except in dealing with a limited number of simple situations) by the route of any such syllogistic reasoning, it is fair to assume that the judge, merely by putting on the judicial ermine, will not acquire so artificial a method of reasoning. Judicial judgments, like other judgments, doubtless, in most cases, are worked out backward from conclusions tentatively formulated.

As Jastrow says, "In spite of the fact that the answer in the book happens to be wrong, a considerable portion of the class succeeds in reaching it. . . . The young mathematician will manage to obtain the answer which the book requires, even at the cost of a resort to very unmathematical processes." Courts, in their reasoning, are often singularly like Jastrow's young mathematician. Professor Tulin has made a study which prettily illustrates that fact. While driving at a reckless rate of speed, a man runs over another, causing severe injuries. The driver of the car is drunk at the time. He is indicted for the statutory crime of "assault with intent to kill." The question arises whether his act constitutes that crime or merely the lesser statutory crime of "reckless driving." The courts of several states have held one way, and the courts of several other states have held the other.

The first group maintain that a conviction for assault with intent to kill cannot be sustained in the absence of proof of an actual purpose to inflict death. In the second group of states the courts have said that it was sufficient to constitute such a crime if there was a reckless disregard of the lives of others, such recklessness being said to be the equivalent of actual intent.

With what, then, appears to be the same facts before them, these two groups of courts seem to have sharply divided in their reasoning and in the conclusions at which they have arrived. But upon closer examination it has been revealed by Tulin that, in actual effect, the results arrived at in all these states have been more or less the same. In Georgia, which may be taken as representative of the second group of states, the penalty provided by the statute for reckless driving is far less than that provided, for instance, in Iowa, which is in the first group of states. If, then, a man is indicted in Georgia for reckless driving while drunk, the courts can impose on him only a mild penalty; whereas in Iowa the judge, under an identically worded indictment, can give a stiff sentence. In order to make it possible for the Georgia courts to give a reckless driver virtually the same punishment for the same offense as can be given by an Iowa judge, it is necessary in Georgia to construe the statutory crime of assault with intent to kill so that it will include reckless driving while drunk; if, and only if, the Georgia court so construes the statute, can it impose the same penalty under the same facts as could the Iowa courts under the reckless driving statute. On the other hand, if the Iowa court were to construe the Iowa statute as the Georgia court construes the Georgia statute, the punishment of the reckless driver in Iowa would be too severe.

In other words, the courts in these cases began with the results they desired to accomplish: they wanted to give what they considered to be adequate punishment to drunken drivers; their conclusions determined their reasoning.

But the conception that judges work back from conclusions to principles is so heretical that it seldom finds expression. Daily, judges, in connection with their decisions, deliver so-called opinions in which they purport to set forth the bases of their conclusions. Yet you will study these opinions in vain to discover anything remotely resembling a statement of the actual judging process. They are written in conformity with the time-honored theory. They picture the judge applying rules and principles to the facts, that is, taking some rule or principle (usually derived from opinions in earlier cases) as his major premise, employing the facts of the case as the minor premise, and then coming to his judgment by processes of pure reasoning.

Now and again some judge, more clear-witted and outspoken than his fellows, describes (when off the bench) his methods in more homely terms. Recently Judge Hutcheson essayed such an honest report of the judicial process. He tells us that after canvassing all the available material at his command and duly cogitating on it, he gives his imagination play,

> and brooding over the case, waits for the feeling, the hunch—that intuitive flash of understanding that makes the jump-spark connection between question and decision and at the point where the path is darkest for the judicial feet, sets its light along the way. . . . In feeling or 'hunching' out his decisions, the judge acts not differently from but precisely as the lawyers do in working on their cases, with only this exception, that the lawyer, in having a predetermined destination in view,—to win the law-suit for his client—looks for and regards only those hunches which keep him in the path that he has chosen, while the judge, being merely on his way with a roving commission to find the just solution, will follow his hunch wherever it leads him. . . .

And Judge Hutcheson adds:

> I must premise that I speak now of the judgment or decision, the solution itself, as opposed to the apologia for that decision; the decree, as opposed to the logomachy, the effusion of the judge by which that decree is explained or excused. . . . The judge really decides by feeling and not by judgment, by hunching and not by ratiocination, such ratiocination appearing only in the opinion. The vital motivating impulse for the decision is an intuitive sense of what is right or wrong in the particular case; and the astute judge, having so decided, enlists his every faculty and belabors his laggard mind, not only to justify that intuition to himself, but to make it pass muster with his critics. [Accordingly, he passes in review all of the rules, principles, legal categories, and concepts] which he may find useful, directly or by an analogy, so as to select from them those which in his opinion will justify his desired result.

We may accept this as an approximately correct description of how all judges do their thinking. But see the consequences. If the law consists of the decisions of the judges and if those decisions are based on the judge's hunches, then the way in which the judge gets his hunches is the key to the judicial process. Whatever produces the judge's hunches makes the law.

What, then, are the hunch-producers? What are the stimuli which make a judge feel that he should try to justify one conclusion rather than another?

The rules and principles of law are one class of such stimuli. But there are many others, concealed or unrevealed, not frequently considered in discussions of the character or nature of law. To the infrequent extent that these other stimuli have been considered at all, they have been usually referred to as "the political, economic and moral prejudices" of the judge. A moment's reflection would, indeed, induce any openminded person to admit that factors of such character must be operating in the mind of the judge. . . .

ILLUSORY PRECEDENTS

Lawyers and judges purport to make large use of precedents; that is, they purport to rely on the conduct of judges in past cases as a means of procuring analogies for action in new cases. But since what was actually decided in the earlier cases is seldom revealed, it is impossible, in a real sense, to rely on these precedents. What the courts in fact do is to manipulate the language of former decisions. They could approximate a system of real precedents only if the judges, in rendering those former decisions, had reported with fidelity the precise steps by which they arrived at their decisions. The paradox of the situations is that, granting there is value in a system of precedents, our present use of illusory precedents makes the employment of real precedents impossible.

The decision of a judge after trying a case is the product of a unique experience. "Of the many things which have been said of the mystery of the judicial process," writes Yntema, "the most salient is that *decision is reached after an emotive experience in which principles and logic play a secondary part.* The function of juristic logic and the principles which it employs seem to be like that of language, to describe the event which has already transpired. These considerations must reveal to us the impotence of general principles to control decision. Vague because of their generality, they mean nothing save what they suggest in the organized experience of one who thinks them, and, because of their vagueness, they only remotely compel the organization of that experience. The important problem . . . is not the formulation of the rule but the ascertainment of the cases to which, and the extent to which, it applies. And this, even if we are seeking uniformity in the administration of justice, will lead us again to the circumstances of the concrete case. . . . The reason why the general principle cannot control is because it does not inform. . . . It should be obvious that when we have observed a recurrent phenomenon in the decisions of the courts, we may appropriately express the classification in a rule. But the rule will be only a mnemonic device, a useful but hollow diagram of what has been. It will be intelligible only if we *relive again the experience of the classifier.*"

The rules a judge announces when publishing his decision are, therefore, intelligible only if one can relive the judge's unique experience while he was trying the case—which, of course, cannot be done. One cannot even approximate that experience as long as opinions take the form of abstract rules applied to facts formally described. Even if it were desirable that, despite its uniqueness, the judge's decision should be followed, as an analogy, by other judges while trying other cases, this is impossible when the manner in which the judge reached his judgment in the earlier case is most inaccurately reported, as it now is. You are not really applying his decision as a precedent in another case unless you can say, in effect, that, having relived his experience in the earlier case, you believe that he would have thought his decision applicable to the facts of the latter case. And as opinions are now written, it is impossible to guess what the judge did experience in trying a case. The facts of all but the simplest controversies are complicated and unlike those of any other controversy; in the absence of a highly detailed account by the judge of how he reacted to the evidence, no other person is capable of reproducing his actual reactions. The rules announced in his opinions are therefore often insufficient to tell the reader why the judge reached his decision.

Dickinson admits that the "personal bent of the judge" to some extent affects his decisions.

But this "personal bent," he insists, is a factor only in the selection of new rules for unprovided cases. However, *in a profound sense the unique circumstances of almost any case make it an "unprovided case" where no well-established rule "authoritatively" compels a given result.* The uniqueness of the facts and of the judge's reaction thereto is often concealed because the judge so states the facts that they appear to call for the application of a settled rule. But that concealment does not mean that the judge's personal bent has been inoperative or that his emotive experience is simple and reproducible. . . .

Every lawyer of experience comes to know (more or less unconsciously) that in the great majority of cases, the precedents are none too good as bases of prediction. Somehow or other, there are plenty of precedents to go around. A recent writer, a believer in the use of precedents, has said proudly that "it is very seldom indeed that a judge cannot find guidance of some kind, direct or indirect, in the mass of our reported decisions—by this time a huge accumulation of facts as well as rules." In plain English, . . . a court can usually find earlier decisions which can be made to appear to justify almost any conclusion.

What has just been said is not intended to mean that most courts arrive at their conclusions arbitrarily or apply a process of casuistical deception in writing their opinions. The process we have been describing involves no insincerity or duplicity. The average judge sincerely believes that he is using his intellect as "a cold logic engine" in applying rules and principles derived from the earlier cases to the objective facts of the case before him.

A satirist might indeed suggest that it is regrettable that the practice of precedent-mongering does not involve *conscious* deception, for it would be comparatively easy for judges entirely aware of what they were doing, to abandon such conscious deception and to report accurately how they arrived at their decisions. Unfortunately, most judges have no such awareness. Worse than that, they are not even aware that they are not aware.

. . . Swayed by the belief that their opinions will serve as precedents and will therefore bind the thought processes of judges in cases which may thereafter arise, they feel obliged to consider excessively not only what has previously been said by other judges but also the future effect of those generalizations which they themselves set forth as explanations of their own decisions. When publishing the rules which are supposed to be the core of their decisions, they thus feel obliged to look too far both backwards and forwards. Many a judge, when unable to find old worn-patterns which will fit his conclusions, is overcautious about announcing a so-called new rule for fear that, although the new rule may lead to a just conclusion in the case before him, it may lead to undesirable results in the future—that is, in cases not then before the court. Once trapped by the belief that the announced rules are the paramount thing in the law, and that uniformity and certainty are of major importance and are to be procured by uniformity and certainty in the phrasing of rules, a judge is likely to be affected, in determining what is fair to the parties in the unique situation before him, by consideration of the possible, yet scarcely imaginable, bad effect of a just opinion in the instant case on possible unlike cases which may later be brought into court. He then refuses to do justice in the case on trial because he fears that "hard cases make bad laws." And thus arises what may aptly be called "injustice according to law." . . .

The judge, at his best, is an arbitrator, a "sound man" who strives to do justice to the parties by exercising a wise discretion with reference to the peculiar circumstances of the case. He does not merely "find" or invent some generalized rule which he "applied" to the facts presented to him. He does "equity" in the sense in which Aristotle—when thinking most clearly—described it. "It is equity," he wrote in his Rhetoric, "to pardon human failings, and to look to the law giver and not to the law; . . . to prefer arbitration to judgment, for the arbitrator sees what is equitable, but the judge only the law, and for this an arbitrator was first appointed, in order that equity might flourish." The bench and bar usually try to conceal the arbitral function of the judge. (Dicey represents the typical view. A judge, he says, "when deciding any case must act, *not as an arbitrator, but strictly as a judge; . . . it is a judge's business to determine not what may be fair as between A and X in a given case*, but what according to some principle of law, are the respective rights of A and X.") But although fear of legal uncertainty leads to this concealment, the arbitral function is the central fact in the administration of justice. . . .

. . . We may now venture a rough definition of law from the point of view of the average man: For any particular lay person, the law, with respect to any particular set of facts, is a decision of a court with respect to those facts so far as that decision affects that particular person. Until a court has passed on those facts no law on that subject is yet in existence. Prior to such a decision, the only law available is the opinion of lawyers as to the law relating to that person and to those facts. Such opinion is not actually law but only a guess as to what a court will decide.

Law, then, as to any given situation is either (a) actual law, *i.e.*, a specific past decision, as to that situation, or (b) probable law, *i.e.*, a guess as to a specific future decision.

Usually, when a client consults his lawyer about "the law," his purpose is to ascertain not what courts have actually decided in the past but what the courts will probably decide in the future. He asks, "Have I a right, as a stockholder of the American Taffy Company of Indiana, to look at the corporate books?" Or, "Do I have to pay an inheritance tax to the State of New York on bonds left me by my deceased wife, if our residence was in Ohio, but the bonds, at the time of her death, were in a safety deposit box in New York?" Or, "Is there a right of 'peaceful' picketing in a strike in the State of California?" Or, "If Jones sells me his Chicago shoe business and agrees not to compete for ten years, will the agreement be binding?" The answers (although they may run "There is such a right," "The law is that the property is not taxable," "Such picketing is unlawful," "The agreement is not legally binding") are in fact prophecies or predictions of judicial action. It is from this point of view that the practice of law has been aptly termed an art of prediction. . . .

While the majority of lawyers deny that judges make law, a vigorous minority assert, realistically, that they do. But when does a judge make law? The minority here splits into two groups.

John Chipman Gray is typical of the first group. His contribution to hard-headed thinking about law was invaluable. He compelled his readers to differentiate between *law* and the *sources* of law. "The Law of the State," he wrote, "is composed of the rules which the courts, that is the judicial organs of that body, lay down for the determination of legal rights and duties." He felt it absurd to affirm the existence of law which the courts do not follow: "The Law of a State . . . is not an ideal, but something which actually exists." His thesis was that "the Law is made up of the rules for decision which the courts lay down; that all such rules are Law; that *rules for conduct which the courts do not apply are not Law; that the fact that courts apply rules is what makes them Law; that there is no mysterious entity 'The Law' apart from these rules; and that the judges are rather the creators than the discoverers of the Law.*"

According to Gray, the "law of a great nation" means "the opinions of a half-a-dozen old gentlemen. . . ." For, "if those half-a-dozen old gentlemen form the highest tribunal of a country, then no rule or principle which they refuse to follow is Law in that country." Of course, he added, "those six men seek the rules which they follow not in their own whims, but the derive them from *sources* . . . to which they are directed, by the organized body (the State) to which they belong, to apply themselves."

And those sources of law—*i.e.*, sources of "the rules for decision which the courts lay down"—are statutes, judicial precedents, opinions of experts, customs and principles of morality (using the term morality to include "public policy"). That none of these factors is, in and of itself, Law is best exemplified by a consideration of a most important source—statutes. For, says Gray, after all it is only words that the legislature utters when it enacts a statute. And these words can get into action only through the rules laid down by the courts: it is for the courts to say what those words mean. There are limits to the courts' power of interpretation, but those limits are vague and undefined. And that is why statutes are not part of the Law itself, but only

a source of law: "It has sometimes been said that the Law is composed of two parts—legislative law and judge-made law, but in truth all the Law is judge-made law. The shape in which a statute is imposed on the community as a guide for conduct is that statute as interpreted by the courts. The courts put life into the dead words of the statute. To quote . . . from Bishop Hoadly: 'Nay, whoever hath an *absolute authority* to *interpret* any written or spoken laws, it is *He* who is truly the Law Giver to all intents and purposes, and not the Person who first wrote and spoke them.'"

Gray was indeed a hardy foe of the Realist fundamentalists. Judges, he saw, make the law and, until they make it, there isn't any law, but only ingredients for making law. When a handful of old gentlemen who compose the highest court announce the law, that is the Law, until they change it, whether anyone else, however wise, thinks it good or bad, right or wrong. *But,* for all his terse directness, you will detect more than a trace of the old philosophy in Gray's views. You will note his constant reiteration of the words "rules" and "principles." Gray defines law not as what courts decide but as the *"rules* which the courts lay down for the determination of legal rights and duties" or "the *rules of decision* which the courts lay down." If a court in deciding a particular case fails to apply the "rule generally followed," that decision is not law. The rule for decisions usually laid down by the courts in Massachusetts is that a payment made on Sunday discharges a debt. "A judge in Massachusetts once decided that payment on Sunday was no discharge of a debt, but that has never been the Law of Massachusetts," said Gray. Judges make law, according to Gray, when they make or change the rules; lawmaking is legal rule-making, the promulgation by a judge of a new rule for decision.

Now this stress on generality as the essence of law is a remnant of the old myth. And a vigorous remnant. It is found in the thinking of perhaps ninety percent of even those who, like Gray, scoff at the idea that law making occurs anywhere except in the court-room. Unless, they say, a court announces a new rule—announces it expressly or impliedly—it is not making law. Law equals legal rules—rules which the courts use, not anyone else's rules, but rules nevertheless; such judge-made rules constitute the law.

But in 1897 a new attitude was expressed when Holmes wrote, "A legal duty so called is nothing but a prediction that if a man does or omits certain things he will be made to suffer in this or that way by a judgment of the court; and so of a legal right. . . . *If you want to know the law and nothing else, you must look at it as a bad man, who cares only for the material consequences which such knowledge enables him to predict.* . . . What constitutes the law? You will find some text writers telling you that it is something different from what is decided by the courts of Massachusetts or England, that it is a system of reason, that it is a deduction from principles of ethics or admitted axioms or what not. But if we take the view of our friend the bad man we shall find that he does not care two straws for the axioms or deductions, but that he does want to know what the Massachusetts or English courts are likely to do in fact. I am much of his mind. *The prophecies of what the courts will do in fact, and nothing more pretentious, are what I mean by law.*"

That was in 1897. In 1899 Holmes said, "We must think things not words, or at least we must constantly translate our words into the facts for which they stand if we are to keep to the real and the true. I sometimes tell law students that the law schools pursue an inspirational method combined with a logical method, that is, the postulates are taken for granted upon authority without inquiry into their worth, and then logic is used as the only tool to develop the results. It is a necessary method for the purpose of teaching dogma. But inasmuch as the real justification of a rule of law, if there be one, is that it helps to bring about a social end which we desire, it is no less necessary that those who make and develop the law should have those ends articulately in their mind. . . . *A generalization is empty so far as it is general. Its value depends on the number of particulars which it calls up to the speaker and the hearer.*"

Holmes's description of law can be stated as a revision of Gray's definition, thus: Law is made up not of rules for decision laid down by the courts but of the decisions themselves. All such decisions are law. The fact that courts render

these decisions makes them law. There is no mysterious entity apart from these decisions. If the judges in any case come to a "wrong" result and give forth a decision which is discordant with their own or any one else's rules, their decision is none the less law. The "law of a great nation" means the decisions of a handful of old gentlemen, and whatever they refuse to decide is not law. Of course those old gentlemen in deciding cases do not follow their own whims, but derive their views from many sources. And among those sources are not only statutes, precedents, customs and the like, but the rules which other courts have announced when deciding cases. Those rules are no more law than statutes are law. For, after all, rules are merely words and those words can get into action only through decisions; it is for the courts in deciding any case to say what the rules mean, whether those rules are embodied in a statute or in the opinion of some other court. The shape in which rules are imposed on the community is those rules as translated into concrete decisions. Your bad man doesn't care what the rules may be if the decisions are in his favor. He is not concerned with any mysterious entity such as the Law of Massachusetts which consists of the rules usually applied by the courts; he regards only what a very definite court decides in the very definite case which he is involved. . . .

Often when a judge decides a case he simultaneously publishes an essay, called an opinion, explaining that he used an old rule or invented a new rule to justify his judgment. But no matter what he says, it is his decision which fixes the legal positions of the litigants. If Judge Brilliant decides that Mr. Evasion must pay the federal government $50,000 for back taxes or that Mrs. Goneril is entitled to nothing under the will of her father, Mr. Lear, the contents of the judge's literary effusion makes not one iota of practical difference to Mr. Evasion or Mrs. Goneril. Opinion or no opinion, opinion-with-a-new-rule-announced or opinion-with-old-rules-proclaimed—it is all one to the parties whose contentions he adjudicated.

To be sure, this opinion may affect Judge Conformity who is later called on to decide the case of Rex vs. Humpty Dumpty. If Judge Brilliant in

Mr. Evasion's case describes a new legal doctrine, his innovations may be *one* of the factors which actuates Judge Conformity to decide for Humpty Dumpty, if Judge Conformity thinks the facts in Humpty Dumpty's case are like those in Mr. Evasion's case. But—need it be reiterated?—the new doctrine will be but one of the factors actuating Judge Conformity.

The business of the judges is to decide particular cases. They, or some third person viewing their handiwork, may choose to generalize from these decisions, may claim to find common elements in the decisions in the cases of Fox vs. Grapes and Hee vs. Haw and describe the common elements as "rules." But those descriptions of alleged common elements are, at best, some aid to lawyers in guessing or bringing about future judicial conduct or some help to judges in settling other disputes. The rules will not directly decide any other cases in any given way, nor authoritatively compel the judges to decide those other cases in any given way; nor make it possible for lawyers to bring it about that the judges will decide any other cases in any given way, nor infallibly to predict how the judges will decide any other cases. Rules . . . are not law.

REVIEW AND DISCUSSION QUESTIONS

1. Describe the "conventional view" of law that Frank attacks.

2. Why does he think precedents are "illusory"?

3. If legal rules and principles do not usually decide particular cases, how then *should* a responsible judge make a decision, according to the realist?

4. Describe the distinction between "sources" of law and "law" according to Frank.

5. What, finally, is law according to realists?

6. What Frank calls the "conventional view" is really the "legal formalism" of Langdell and Beale. Discuss this statement.

7. Frank was an appeals court judge, not an ordinary criminal or civil judge hearing day-to-day cases. How might this fact have influenced his thinking?

Interpretation as Formal

Tony Honoré

Interpretation, as Tony Honoré points out, is of great importance to the law. But what, precisely, is interpretation? Beginning with brief remarks about how we interpret one another's meaning in ordinary life, Honoré goes on to discuss the formal nature of legal interpretation and the strengths of different approaches to interpretation. He provides an example of interpretation involving drinking and driving, and he explains why it is the case that "words cannot mean just anything." He then discusses the role of legislative intention in interpretation. Tony Honoré was professor of philosophy at Oxford.

Interpretation is one of the main concerns of lawyers.

Originally, lawyers were people who specialized in drafting and interpreting documents, rather than arguing cases in court or judging disputes. A person drafting a document must try to see in advance how the law, treaty, contract or will he is drafting will be interpreted, so that his text covers the areas he wants it to cover. Arguments in court are often about the interpretation of a text, and judges have to decide what the right interpretation is. So, one way and another, interpretation is a key part of legal practice.

How documents should be interpreted is disputed. Suppose a by-law forbids vehicles in a park. Does this apply to bicycles, motorcycles or powered lawn-mowers? More important, how do you set about deciding? Do you go by the dictionary meaning of the word 'vehicle'? Do you ask what purpose banning vehicles from the park is meant to serve? Do you ask what hardship to the public would be caused if, for example, bicycles or baby-carriages were included in the ban? Or how inconvenient it would be if powered lawn-mowers were excluded?

Some lawyers give priority to the letter of the text, others to its spirit or purpose, others again to the likely result of interpreting it this way or that. This chapter is mainly concerned with the clash between these different approaches.

WHAT IS INTERPRETATION?

First of all, what is interpretation? To interpret what someone says is to attach a meaning to their remarks. When the meaning is at once clear the remark does not have to be interpreted, but if it is not clear, or not immediately clear, it does. The interpreter then has to choose between two or more possible ways of understanding what was said.

Wanting to travel to Manchester, you ask me to get you a time-table. I am not sure whether you meant a coach time-table or a railway time-table. I may be able to ask you which you meant. But if I cannot, I have to make up my mind, perhaps on the basis of how you usually travel, or what the easiest way of getting to Manchester is.

Interpreting a request of this sort is not just interpreting the words 'please get me a time-table', which are straightforward enough, but interpreting them in the context of a purpose, a wish to travel to Manchester. Interpreting texts, which is so central a part of a lawyer's work, is in some ways similar. A lawyer interprets a text as part of a statute, contract, will, treaty, regulation or whatever. But there are differences. When I have to interpret your request for a time-table I am free to go about it in any way I choose. A lawyer's interpretation of a text is a more formal process.

LEGAL INTERPRETATION IS FORMAL

It is formal, first, because the texts a lawyer interprets are in writing. Not only are they in writing but they have authority. If they are statutes they are part of state law. If they are contracts or treaties they bind the parties to the contract or treaty. If they are wills they bind whoever is dealing with the property of the person who has died. The interpretation chosen will make a difference to someone's rights and duties.

There is another way in which the interpretation of a legal text is formal. When it is disputed, there is such a thing as an official interpretation of the text. Judges provide this when they try cases or hear appeals. Ministers and civil servants, for example tax officials, also issue official interpretations of statutes, though their interpretations have in the end to give way to those of judges if there is a difference of opinion between the two.

Another way in which the interpretation of legal texts is unlike interpreting a request from a friend is that the evidence on which the interpreter of legal texts has to come to a decision is limited. If I am not sure what my friend meant by his request my best move is to ask him. But the interpreter of a legal text cannot solve the problem by going back to the author of the text and asking what he meant. For one thing, legal texts often have no single author. They are enacted by legislators, hundreds in number, or agreed by the parties to a contract or treaty, of whom there may be many.

Legislators do not have time to explain what they meant by the statutes they have passed. Even if they did, and all agreed, it might not be a good idea to ask them, because they would be tempted to explain the law with the benefit of hindsight. They would be tempted to put themselves in a better light by saying that it meant something that they would not have said it meant at the time it was passed. This would not be fair to those who have to obey the law. They are entitled to be judged by what in the view of an impartial person the law meant at the time they had to obey it.

The interpreter of a will obviously cannot consult the testator about what it meant, as he is dead. It might seem that the interpreter of a contract or treaty could consult the parties to the treaty or contract. But if a dispute has arisen it is often because the parties disagree about how it should be interpreted. A neutral interpretation is called for. So to ask the parties is not a real option. In general, problems of interpreting legal texts cannot be solved by going back to the authors of the text.

Another way in which the evidence available to the interpreter of a text is limited is that the text has to speak for itself. Earlier drafts of a statute, will, contract or treaty are superseded by the final version. The authors of the text are committed to the final version, and this replaces whatever discussions or negotiations went on beforehand. Even what the authors said they meant at the time the text was agreed is treated with reserve. For instance, some systems of law do not accept that in interpreting the text of a statute the interpreter can go by what the Minister said it meant when he spoke in the legislature.

How far one presses the idea that a text should speak for itself is a matter of dispute, but at its core there lies a sound idea. This is that a person who agrees that a certain form of words is to be binding should be willing for the words to be taken in their ordinary sense. Otherwise he should have insisted on a different form of words or said at the time that he attached a special meaning to them, not the ordinary meaning.

Attaching a special meaning is in fact quite a common practice. Statutes and contracts often have clauses that lay down the meaning to be given to the words they use. For instance they may say that 'owner' includes the occupier of a house. In that case a tenant who does not own the house is treated for purposes of the statute (but not otherwise) as if he did. Behind this practice lies the view that in legal texts the words should be taken in their ordinary sense unless the author of the text lays down a different sense.

WHAT IS THE BEST APPROACH TO INTERPRETATION?

THE TEXTUAL APPROACH

The idea that a text must speak for itself embodies one approach to interpretation, which I shall call the textual approach. It holds that a text must be understood in its ordinary sense. If vehicles are excluded from the park that means that what are ordinarily spoken of as vehicles (cars, coaches, trucks) are excluded. This may be inconvenient if it means, for example, that some disabled people cannot use the park because they can only get there by a motorized vehicle. But that has to be accepted.

Sometimes of course a word or phrase has no ordinary sense, because it is not one used by ordinary people. When technical terms, legal or scientific, are used, what corresponds to the ordinary meaning of the term is its technical meaning. The technical meaning is what it ordinarily means to legal or scientific experts.

But those who favour the textual approach admit that there are exceptional cases where it is unsatisfactory. When it would produce an absurd result to read the words in their ordinary sense, they can be interpreted in a different sense, one that does not produce an absurd result.

What amounts to an absurd result is of course debatable; what is absurd to one judge is merely unusual to another. Would it be absurd if the meaning given to 'vehicle' resulted in excluding some disabled people from the park? A text that is self-contradictory or unworkable in practice is clearly absurd, but how far one should treat a meaning that some people think unreasonable as absurd is not clear.

However we understand absurdity, the textual approach gives priority to the language used in the text in its ordinary sense over other evidence of the author's intention. The textual approach is sometimes attacked by critics, who call it 'literalism', going by the letter. But what is the point of putting a statute, contract, treaty, or will into words unless those words are to be treated as binding?

THE PURPOSIVE APPROACH

A different approach to interpreting texts is the purposive approach. According to this, priority in interpreting texts should be given to the purpose of the statute, contract, treaty, will, or regulation. Account should also be taken of the general aims of the legal system, such as justice, security, and efficiency. This is specially important in interpreting statutes. A law (say the law forbidding vehicles in the park) can have special purposes of its own (say to ensure peace and quiet for those who use the park). But more general purposes have also to be taken into account (for instance that public places should be kept tidy, which may require powered lawn-mowers to be admitted even if they make a noise).

If these special or general purposes point to an interpretation different from the ordinary meaning of the words, supporters of the purposive approach say that the 'purposive' meaning should be adopted in preference to the ordinary meaning.

In looking for the purpose of a document there are, however, some limits on how far afield one can range. Legal systems vary a bit in the limits they set. When a statute is interpreted the interpreter can certainly look at the whole statute and any earlier laws on the subject. He can take account of what the previous state of the law was and what were thought to be its defects. Supporters of the purposive approach go further, and say that the interpreter should be able to take account of reports and proposals of official commissions and other materials prepared with a view to passing a law or making a treaty. Many systems of law do in fact allow these materials to be considered.

A 'Drinking and Driving' Example

Which approach is better, the textual or the purposive approach? I take an example (altering it a bit) from a law in Britain that has since been replaced. Suppose a statute lays down that a policeman may require someone who is driving a vehicle to take a blood test. If the blood test shows that he has more than a certain amount of alcohol in the blood, he may be charged with the offence of drinking and driving.

What does 'driving' mean in this statute? Like most words, 'driving' has a range of meanings. But in its ordinary meaning, many people would say, a person is driving a vehicle when he is at the controls and the vehicle is moving. When the vehicle stops he stops driving. But if we interpret driving in this way, we make the statute absurd. How could a policeman tell a driver to take a blood test while the vehicle was moving?

So, even on the textual approach, we ought to ask if 'driving' can be understood in another way. If the statute is to have some point, the driver must still be driving after he has stopped the vehicle because the policeman has told him to. Can driving be understood in this wider sense? It probably can, since from one point of view the driver of a vehicle is driving from the moment he sets off until he gets to his destination, even if he stops on the way for a meal. If asked during the meal what he was doing he would say he was 'driving to Manchester'. So does 'driving' in the statute mean simply that the driver is still on the way to his destination?

From the words alone this is a possible interpretation. But ought not the purpose of the law to be taken into account when we interpret 'driving'? The point of the law is surely to make the person driving liable to take a blood test; and the purpose of this is to reduce the danger that the motorist will drive with more than a certain amount of alcohol in his blood. Would it fit that purpose to give a blood test to someone having a meal who has not been driving for the last half-hour and may not set off again for some time? Would it be fair to him?

Perhaps, taking the purpose of the law into account, a driver is 'driving' only if he has already started and means to go on with the journey the moment he can. It is only then that, if the alcohol in his blood is over the limit, he will be a danger on the road. In that case he may be driving though he is temporarily at a halt in a traffic jam, or because a policeman has stopped him. If the driver has stopped for a meal he is not driving for the purpose of the blood test, but the driver who has got out of his car in a traffic jam to buy a paper is still driving.

On the textual approach the ordinary meaning of 'driving' (that the vehicle must be in motion) leads to an absurdity, so that other ways of understanding 'driving' can be considered. On the purposive approach the ordinary meaning of 'driving' has no special priority and a motorist can be said to be driving when it would promote the purpose of the drinking and driving law to give him a blood test. This might suggest a very wide interpretation of driving, one that would include the stage when he is having a meal on the way.

But the purpose of reducing drinking and driving is not the only purpose that the interpreter has to take into account. There are also general aims of the legal system. One of these is to be fair to people who may be charged with a crime. They should be able to know roughly when they are in danger of being tested and prosecuted. This brings us back by a roundabout route to the ordinary meaning of 'driving'. When a statute uses a term that is part of ordinary language, those affected by it are likely to understand it in its ordinary sense. So the purposes of the legal system itself require close attention to be paid to the words used in the text.

WORDS CANNOT MEAN JUST ANYTHING

Though words have a range of meanings, they cannot mean just anything. For instance, there are some things that 'driving' could not mean. A driver whose vehicle is in the garage and who has not yet set off, though he intends to leave shortly, and who is in the meantime having a few drinks, is not driving. It is true that, if he were held to be driving, the purpose of the law against drinking and driving would be satisfied. But this cannot justify the interpreter in stretching the meaning of driving to cover the driver whose vehicle is still in the garage.

It is very rare for a judge to decide that a text means something that it could not mean in ordinary or technical language. On the few occasions when a judge does this, he does it because he thinks that an obvious mistake has been made by the author of the text, and that he has a duty to correct it.

There is little doubt that 'or' cannot mean 'and'. Elephants and hyenas means both species, but elephants or hyenas means one of the two. So if a statute lays down that no one may hunt elephants and hyenas without a licence, the draftsman has probably made a mistake. As it stands, the law seems to say that one may hunt either elephants or hyenas without a licence but not both. It is unlikely that this is what the legislators meant. Most hunters will be hunting one or the other, not both, and the prohibition will then have very little effect.

So if a judge had to interpret this statute he would probably interpret 'and' as 'or', and say that 'elephants and hyenas' should read as if it said 'elephants or hyenas'. That seems to go against the textual approach, by taking a word to mean what it cannot mean. It seems as if the judge is opting for the purposive approach, in order to make the statute workable. A different way of putting it, more consistent with the textual approach, is that the judge has the power to correct an obvious mistake by substituting 'or' for 'and'. In that case he is not interpreting the text but correcting it, something that can obviously be allowed only within very narrow limits.

INTENTION

The textual approach and the purposive approach are often put forward as different ways of getting at the intention of the author of the text. That is not quite right, because the textual approach opts for what the words ordinarily mean, and the author of the text may not have meant to use the actual words he did (take the elephants and hyenas example).

But assuming the author of the text did mean to use the words he used, there is sometimes a contrast between what he meant by the words used and what he meant to achieve by using them. These are two different things, though they can both be called his 'intention'. Does it help to think of interpretation as a search for the intention of the legislators, the parties to the contract etc.?

Individuals have both sorts of intention, and bodies like legislatures and associations can have both too. But often the members of these bodies do not study the texts that are produced in their name at all carefully. They can say roughly what they want to achieve by passing a law. They may for example be against drinking and driving and in favour of animal conservation. But they probably have not thought about what is meant by 'driving' in the blood testing statute or 'elephants and hyenas' in the hunting statute.

All the same there is good reason, I think, to say that the interpreter should try to discover the intention of the legislature or the parties to a contract or treaty. A statute, contract or treaty is a compromise between different views. Perhaps no member of the legislature, and no party to the contract or treaty, would themselves have chosen the text that was finally agreed, if it depended on them alone. The point of speaking of the intention of the legislature or the contracting parties is not that any particular person's views should govern the interpretation of the text. It is rather that the interpreter should treat the text as if it represented the views of a single individual, and make it as coherent as the words permit.

This is a fiction, but it expresses a sound policy. The interpreter should not treat the views of individual members of a large body as if they were the views of the whole body. There may have been no agreed view about what the text meant. In the same way, the views of one party to a contract about what the contract means should be not be treated as if they were the views of both parties. The interpreter should aim at a neutral, impartial reading of the text and its purposes.

Whether the textual or the purposive approach to interpretation is preferred, every text has to be seen against the background of the society and the legal system of which it forms part.

REVIEW AND DISCUSSION QUESTIONS

1. In what senses does Honoré think that legal interpretation is more "formal" than the interpretation of a railroad time-table?

2. Describe the textual and the purposive approaches to interpretation.

3. Using the statute involving drinking and driving, discuss Honoré's position on the advantages of the different approaches to interpretation.

4. Why does Honoré think using intentions to interpret is a "fiction"? Why does he nonetheless think it is a useful fiction?

5. How would a legal realist respond to Honoré? Discuss whether or not that response is adequate. Who is closer to the truth, a realist or a formalist?

7

THE CONTEMPORARY DEBATE: HART VERSUS DWORKIN

H. L. A. Hart is widely regarded as the most important recent defender of legal positivism. His 1961 book *The Concept of Law* did much to reinvigorate philosophical discussion of law and legal obligation, including the claim of natural law that some sort of essential connection exists between law on one hand and justice or morality on the other. But Hart was far from just a defender of Austinian positivism; indeed, he finds much to criticize in Austin's writings despite sharing his broadly positivistic conclusions. Ronald Dworkin was Hart's student at Oxford and eventually succeeded him as professor of jurisprudence there. Dworkin's criticisms of Hart and of positivism generally have also been widely discussed, along with his fascinating defense of natural law (shorn of Aquinas's religious assumptions) and his insightful analysis of legal interpretation.

Positivism and the Separation of Law and Morals

H. L. A. Hart

Perhaps more than any single philosopher, H. L. A. Hart is responsible for the upsurge of interest in jurisprudence and philosophy of law during the past few decades. Hart's criticisms of Austin and his brilliant defense of his own theory have provoked much debate and interest in the subject. Beginning with an account of the historical importance of positivism, he weighs in this essay various criticisms of

147

different aspects of the theory, including its insistence on the separation of law and morals, and Austin's claim that laws are the commands of the sovereign. He then examines the "distinctly American criticism" leveled by legal realists. Hart was professor of jurisprudence at Oxford University.

In this article I shall discuss and attempt to defend a view which Mr. Justice Holmes, among others, held and for which he and they have been much criticized. . . . Contemporary voices tell us we must recognize something obscured by the legal "positivists" whose day is now over: that there is a "point of intersection between law and morals," or that what *is* and what *ought* to be are somehow indissolubly fused or inseparable, though the positivists denied it. What do these phrases mean? Or rather which of the many things that they *could* mean, *do* they mean? Which of them do "positivists" deny and why is it wrong to do so?

1

I shall present the subject as part of the history of an idea. At the close of the eighteenth century and the beginning of the nineteenth the most earnest thinkers in England about legal and social problems and the architects of great reforms were the great utilitarians. Two of them, Bentham and Austin, constantly insisted on the need to distinguish, firmly and with the maximum of clarity, law as it is from law as it ought to be. This theme haunts their work, and they condemned the natural-law thinkers precisely because they had blurred this apparently simple but vital distinction. By contrast, at the present time in this country and to a lesser extent in England, this separation between law and morals is held to be superficial and wrong. Some critics have thought that it blinds men to the true nature of law and its roots in social life. Others have thought it not only intellectually misleading but corrupting in practice, at its worst apt to weaken resistance to state tyranny or absolutism, and at its best apt to bring law into disrepect. The nonpejorative name "legal positivism," like most terms which are used as missiles in intellectual battles, has come to stand for a baffling multitude of different sins. One of them is

the sin, real or alleged, of insisting, as Austin and Bentham did, on the separation of law as it is and law as it ought to be.

How then has this reversal of the wheel come about? What are the theoretical errors in this distinction? Have the practical consequences of stressing the distinction as Bentham and Austin did been bad? . . .

Bentham and Austin were not dry analysts fiddling with verbal distinctions while cities burned, but were the vanguard of a movement which laboured with passionate intensity and much success to bring about a better society and better laws. Why then did they insist on the separation of law as it is and law as it ought to be? What did they mean? Let us first see what they said. Austin formulated the doctrine:

> The existence of law is one thing; its merit or demerit is another. Whether it be or be not is one enquiry; whether it be or be not conformable to an assumed standard, is a different enquiry. A law, which actually exists, is a law, though we happen to dislike it, or though it vary from the text, by which we regulate our approbation and disapprobation. This truth, when formally announced as an abstract proposition, is so simple and glaring that it seems idle to insist upon it. But simple and glaring as it is, when enunciated in abstract expressions the enumeration of the instances in which it has been forgotten would fill a volume.
>
> Sir William Blackstone, for example, says in his "Commentaries," that the laws of God are superior in obligation to all other laws; that no human laws should be suffered to contradict them; that human laws are of no validity if contrary to them; and that all valid laws derive their force from that Divine original.
>
> Now, he *may* mean that all human laws ought to conform to the Divine laws. If this be his meaning, I assent to it without hesitation. . . . Perhaps, again, he means that human lawgivers are themselves obliged by the Divine laws to fashion the laws which they impose by that ultimate standard, because if they do not, God will punish them. To this also I entirely assent. . . .

But the meaning of this passage of Blackstone, if it has a meaning, seems rather to be this: that no human law which conflicts with the Divine law is obligatory or binding; in other words, that no human law which conflicts with the Divine law *is a law. . . .*

Austin's protest against blurring the distinction between what law is and what it ought to be is quite general: it is a mistake, whatever our standard of what ought to be, whatever "the text by which we regulate our approbation or disapprobation." His examples, however, are always a confusion between law as it is and law as morality would require it to be. For him, it must be remembered, the fundamental principles of morality were God's commands, to which utility was an "index": besides this there was the actual accepted morality of a social group or "positive" morality. . . .

In view of later criticisms it is also important to distinguish several things that the utilitarians did not mean by insisting on their separation of law and morals. They certainly accepted many of the things that might be called "the intersection of law and morals." First, they never denied that, as a matter of historical fact, the development of legal systems had been powerfully influenced by moral opinion, and, conversely, that moral standards had been profoundly influenced by law, so that the content of many legal rules mirrored moral rules or principles. . . .

Secondly, neither Bentham nor his followers denied that by explicit legal provisions moral principles might at different points be brought into a legal system and form part of its rules, or that courts might be legally bound to decide in accordance with what they thought just or best. . . .

What both Bentham and Austin were anxious to assert were the following two simple things: first, in the absence of an expressed constitutional or legal provision, it could not follow from the mere fact that a rule violated standards of morality that it was not a rule of law; and, conversely, it could not follow from the mere fact that a rule was morally desirable that it was a rule of law. . . .

2

So much for the doctrine in the heyday of its success. Let us turn now to some of the criticisms.

. . . We must remember that the utilitarians combined with their insistence on the separation of law and morals two other equally famous but distinct doctrines. One was the important truth that a purely analytical study of legal concepts, a study of the meaning of the distinctive vocabulary of the law, was as vital to our understanding of the nature of law as historical or sociological studies, though of course it could not supplant them. The other doctrine was the famous imperative theory of law—that law is essentially a command.

These three doctrines constitute the utilitarian tradition in jurisprudence; yet they are distinct doctrines. It is possible to endorse the separation between law and morals and to value analytical inquiries into the meaning of legal concepts and yet think it wrong to conceive of law as essentially a command. One source of great confusion in the criticism of the separation of law and morals was the belief that the falsity of any one of these three doctrines in the utilitarian tradition showed the other two to be false; what was worse was the failure to see that there were three quite separate doctrines in this tradition. . . . [Some] critics . . . have thought that the inadequacies of the command theory which gradually came to light were sufficient to demonstrate the falsity of the separation of law and morals.

This was a mistake, but a natural one. To see how natural it was we must look a little more closely at the command idea. The famous theory that law is a command was a part of a wider and more ambitious claim. Austin said that the notion of a command was "the *key* to the sciences of jurisprudence and morals," and contemporary attempts to elucidate moral judgments in terms of "imperative" or "prescriptive" utterances echo this ambitious claim. But the command theory, viewed as an effort to identify even the quintessence of law, let alone the quintessence of morals, seems breathtaking in its simplicity and quite inadequate. There is much, even in the simplest legal system, that is distorted if presented as a command. Yet the utilitarians thought that the essence of a legal system could be conveyed if the notion of a command were supplemented by that of a habit of obedience. The simple scheme was this: What is a command? It is simply an expression by one person of the desire that another person should do or abstain from some action, accompanied by a threat of punishment which is likely to follow disobedience. Commands are laws if two conditions are satisfied: First, they must be general; second, they must be commanded by what (as both Bentham and Austin claimed) exists in every political society whatever its constitutional form, namely, a person or a group of persons who are in receipt of habitual obedience from most of the society but pay no such obedience to others. These persons are its sovereign. Thus law is the command of the uncommanded commanders of society—the creation of the legally untrammelled will of the sovereign who is by definition outside the law.

It is easy to see that this account of a legal system is threadbare. One can also see why it might seem that its inadequacy is due to the omission of some essential connection with morality. The situation which the simple trilogy of command, sanction, and sovereign avails to describe, if you take these notions at all precisely, is like that of a gunman saying to his victim, "Give me your money or your life." The only difference is that in the case of a legal system the gunman says it to a large number of people who are accustomed to the racket and habitually surrender to it. Law surely is not the gunman situation writ large, and legal order is surely not to be thus simply identified with compulsion.

This scheme, despite the points of obvious analogy between a statute and a command, omits some of the most characteristic elements of law. Let me cite a few. It is wrong to think of a legislature (and a fortiori an electorate) with a changing membership, as a group of persons habitually obeyed: this simple idea is suited only to a monarch sufficiently long-lived for a "habit" to grow up. Even if we waive this point, nothing which legislators do makes law unless they comply with fundamental accepted rules specifying the essential lawmaking procedures. This is true

even in a system having a simple unitary constitution like the British. These fundamental accepted rules specifying what the legislature must do to legislate are not commands habitually obeyed, nor can they be expressed as habits of obedience to persons. They lie at the root of a legal system, and what is most missing in the utilitarian scheme is an analysis of what it is for a social group and its officials to accept such rules. This notion, not that of a command as Austin claimed, is the "key to the science of jurisprudence," or at least one of the keys.

Again, Austin, in the case of a democracy, looked past the legislators to the electorate as "the sovereign" (or in England as part of it). He thought that in the United States the mass of the electors to the state and federal legislatures were the sovereign whose commands, given by their "agents" in the legislatures, were law. But on this footing the whole notion of the sovereign outside the law being "habitually obeyed" by the "bulk" of the population must go: for in this case the "bulk" obeys the bulk, that is, it obeys itself. Plainly the general acceptance of the authority of a lawmaking procedure, irrespective of the changing individuals who operate it from time to time, can be only distorted by an analysis in terms of mass habitual obedience to certain persons who are by definition outside the law, just as the cognate but much simpler phenomenon of the general social acceptance of a rule, say of taking off the hat when entering a church, would be distorted if represented as habitual obedience by the mass to specific persons.

Other critics dimly sensed a further and more important defect in the command theory, yet blurred the edge of an important criticism by assuming that the defect was due to the failure to insist upon some important connection between law and morals. This more radical defect is as follows. The picture that the command theory draws of life under law is essentially a simple relationship of the commander to the commanded, of superior to inferior, of top to bottom; the relationship is vertical between the commanders or authors of the law conceived of as essentially outside the law and those who are commanded and subject to the law. In this picture no place, or only an accidental or subordinate place, is afforded for a distinction between types of legal rules which are in fact radically different. Some laws require men to act in certain ways or to abstain from acting whether they wish to or not. The criminal law consists largely of rules of this sort: like commands they are simply "obeyed" or "disobeyed." But other legal rules are presented to society in quite different ways and have quite different functions. They provide facilities more or less elaborate for individuals to create structures of rights and duties for the conduct of life within the coercive framework of the law. Such are the rules enabling individuals to make contracts, wills, and trusts, and generally to mould their legal relations with others. Such rules, unlike the criminal law, are not factors designed to obstruct wishes and choices of an antisocial sort. On the contrary, these rules provide facilities for the realization of wishes and choices. They do not say (like commands) "do this whether you wish it or not," but rather "if you wish to do this, here is the way to do it." Under these rules we exercise powers, make claims, and assert rights. These phrases mark off characteristic features of laws that confer rights and powers; they are laws which are, so to speak, put at the disposition of individuals in a way in which the criminal law is not.

. . . Rules that confer rights, though distinct from commands, need not be moral rules or coincide with them. Rights, after all, exist under the rules of ceremonies, games, and in many other spheres regulated by rules which are irrelevant to the question of justice or what the law ought to be. Nor need rules which confer rights be just or morally good rules. The rights of a master over his slaves show us that. "Their merit or demerit," as Austin termed it, depends on how rights are distributed in society and over whom or what they are exercised. These critics indeed revealed the inadequacy of the simple notions of command and habit for the analysis of law; at many points it is apparent that the social acceptance of a rule or standard of authority (even if it is motivated only by fear or superstition or rests on inertia) must be brought into the analysis and cannot itself be reduced to the two simple terms. Yet nothing in this showed the utilitarian insistence on the distinction between the existence of law and its "merits" to be wrong.

3

I now turn to a distinctively American criticism of the separation of the law that is from the law that ought to be. It emerged from the critical study of the judicial process with which American jurisprudence has been on the whole so beneficially occupied. The most skeptical of these critics—the loosely named "Realists" of the 1930s—perhaps too naïvely accepted the conceptual framework of the natural sciences as adequate for the characterization of law and for the analysis of rule-guided action of which a living system of law at least partly consists. But they opened men's eyes to what actually goes on when courts decide cases, and the contrast they drew between the actual facts of judicial decision and the traditional terminology for describing it as if it were a wholly logical operation was usually illuminating; for in spite of some exaggeration the "Realists" made us acutely conscious of one cardinal feature of human language and human thought, emphasis on which is vital not only for the understanding of law but in areas of philosophy far beyond the confines of jurisprudence. The insight of this school may be presented in the following example. A legal rule forbids you to take a vehicle into the public park. Plainly this forbids an automobile, but what about bicycles, roller skates, toy automobiles? What about airplanes? Are these, as we say, to be called "vehicles" for the purpose of the rule or not? If we are to communicate with each other at all, and if, as in the most elementary form of law, we are to express our intentions that a certain type of behavior be regulated by rules, then the general words we use—like "vehicle" in the case I consider—must have some standard instance in which no doubts are felt about its application. There must be a core of settled meaning, but there will be, as well, a penumbra of debatable cases in which words are neither obviously applicable nor obviously ruled out. These cases will each have some features in common with the standard case; they will lack others or be accompanied by features not present in the standard case. Human invention and natural processes continually throw up such variants on the familiar, and if we are to say that these ranges of facts do or do not fall under existing rules, then the classifier must make a decision which is not dictated to him, for the facts and phenomena to which we fit our words and apply our rules are as it were *dumb*. The toy automobile cannot speak up and say, "I am a vehicle for the purpose of this legal rule," nor can the roller skates chorus, "We are not a vehicle." Fact situations do not await us neatly labeled, creased, and folded, nor is their legal classification written on them to be simply read off by the judge. Instead, in applying legal rules, someone must take the responsibility of deciding that words do or do not cover some case in hand with all the practical consequences involved in this decision.

We may call the problems which arise outside the hard core of standard instances or settled meaning "problems of the penumbra"; they are always with us whether in relation to such trivial things as the regulation of the use of the public park or in relation to the multidimensional generalities of a constitution. If a penumbra of uncertainty must surround all legal rules, then their application to specific cases in the penumbral area cannot be a matter of logical deduction, and so deductive reasoning, which for generations has been cherished as the very perfection of human reasoning, cannot serve as a model for what judges, or indeed anyone, should do in bringing particular cases under general rules. In this area men cannot live by deduction alone. And it follows that if legal arguments and legal decisions of penumbral questions are to be rational, their rationality must lie in something other than a logical relation to premises. So if it is rational or "sound" to argue and to decide that for the purposes of this rule an airplane is not a vehicle, this argument must be sound or rational without being logically conclusive. What is it then that makes such decisions correct or at least better than alternative decisions? Again, it seems true to say that the criterion which makes a decision sound in such cases is some concept of what the law ought to be; it is easy to slide from that into saying that it must be a moral judgment about what law ought to be. So here we touch upon a point of necessary "intersection between law and morals" which demonstrates the falsity or, at any rate, the misleading character of the utilitarians' emphatic insistence on the separation of law as it is and ought to be. Surely, Bentham and Austin could only have written as they did because they misunderstood or neglected this aspect of the judicial process, because they ignored the problems of the penumbra.

The misconception of the judicial process which ignores the problems of the penumbra and which views the process as consisting preeminently in deductive reasoning is often stigmatized as the error of "formalism" or "literalism." My question now is, how and to what extent does the demonstration of this error show the utilitarian distinction to be wrong or misleading? Here there are many issues which have been confused, but I can only disentangle some. The charge of formalism has been leveled both at the "positivist" legal theorist and at the courts, but of course it must be a very different charge in each case. Leveled at the legal theorist, the charge means that he has made a theoretical mistake about the character of legal decision; he has thought of the reasoning involved as consisting in deduction from premises in which the judges' practical choices or decision play no part. It would be easy to show that Austin was guiltless of this error; only an entire misconception of what analytical jurisprudence is and why he thought it important has led to the view that he, or any other analyst, believed that the law was a closed logical system in which judges deduced their decisions from premises. On the contrary, he was very much alive to the character of language, to its vagueness or open character; he thought that in the penumbral situation judges must necessarily legislate, and, in accents that sometimes recall those of the late Judge Jerome Frank, he berated the common-law judges for legislating feebly and timidly and for blindly relying on real or fancied analogies with past cases instead of adapting their decisions to the growing needs of society as revealed by the moral standard of utility. The villains of this piece, responsible for the conception of the judge as an automaton, are not the utilitarian thinkers. The responsibility, if it is to be laid at the door of any theorist, is with . . . Blackstone's "childish fiction" (as Austin termed it) that judges only "find," never "make," law.

But we are concerned with "formalism" as a vice not of jurists but of judges. What precisely is it for a judge to commit this error, to be a "formalist," "automatic," a "slot machine"? . . . It is clear that the essence of his error is to give some general term an interpretation which is blind to social values and consequences (or which is in some other way stupid or perhaps merely disliked by critics). But logic does not prescribe interpretation of terms; it dictates neither the stupid nor intelligent interpretation of any expression. Logic only tells you hypothetically that *if* you give a certain term a certain interpretation then a certain conclusion follows. Logic is silent on how to classify particulars—and this is the heart of a judicial decision. So this reference to logic and to logical extremes is a misnomer for something else, which must be this. A judge has to apply a rule to a concrete case—perhaps the rule that one may not take a stolen "vehicle" across state lines, and in this case an airplane has been taken. He either does not see or pretends not to see that the general terms of this rule are susceptible of different interpretations and that he has a choice left open uncontrolled by linguistic conventions. He ignores, or is blind to, the fact that he is in the area of the penumbra and is not dealing with a standard case. Instead of choosing in the light of social aims, the judge fixes the meaning in a different way. He either takes the meaning that the word most obviously suggests in its ordinary nonlegal context to ordinary men, or one which the word has been given in some other legal context, or, still worse, he thinks of a standard case and then arbitrarily identifies certain features in it—for example, in the case of a vehicle, (1) normally used on land, (2) capable of carrying a human person, (3) capable of being self-propelled—and treats these three as always necessary and always sufficient conditions for the use in all contexts of the word "vehicle," irrespective of the social consequences of giving it this interpretation. This choice, not "logic," would force the judge to include a toy motor car (if electrically propelled) and to exclude bicycles and the airplane. In all this there is possibly great stupidity but not more "logic," and no less, than in cases in which the interpretation given to a general term and the consequent application of some general rule to a particular case is consciously controlled by some identified social aim.

Decisions made in a fashion as blind as this would scarcely deserve the name of decisions; we might as well toss a penny in applying a rule of law. But it is at least doubtful whether any judicial decisions (even in England) have been quite as automatic as this. Rather either the interpretations stigmatized as automatic have resulted from the conviction that it is fairer in a criminal statute to take a meaning which would jump to the mind of the ordinary man at the cost even of defeating other values, and this itself is a social policy (though possibly a bad one); or much more frequently, what is stigmatized as "mechanical" and "automatic" is a determined choice made indeed in the light of a social aim but of a conservative social aim. Certainly many of the Supreme Court decisions at the turn of the century which have been so stigmatized represent clear choices in the penumbral area to give effect to a policy of a conservative type. . . .

But how does the wrongness of deciding cases in an automatic and mechanical way and the rightness of deciding cases by reference to social purposes show that the utilitarian insistence on the distinction between what the law is and what it ought to be is wrong? I take it that no one who wished to use these vices of formalism as proof that the distinction between what is and what ought to be is mistaken would deny that the decisions stigmatized as automatic are law; nor would he deny that the system in which such automatic decisions are made is a legal system. Surely he would say that they are law, but they are bad law, they ought not to be law. But this would be to use the distinction, not to refute it; and of course both Bentham and Austin used it to attack judges for failing to decide penumbral cases in accordance with the growing needs of society.

Clearly, if the demonstration of the errors of formalism is to show the utilitarian distinction to be wrong, the point must be drastically restated.

The point must be not merely that a judicial decision to be rational must be made in the light of some conception of what ought to be, but that the aims, the social policies and purposes to which judges should appeal if their decisions are to be rational, are themselves to be considered as part of the law in some suitably wide sense of "law" which is held to be more illuminating than that used by the utilitarians. This restatement of the point would have the following consequence: Instead of saying that the recurrence of penumbral questions shows us that legal rules are essentially incomplete, and that, when they fail to determine decisions, judges must legislate and so exercise a creative choice between alternatives, we shall say that the social policies which guide the judges' choice are in a sense there for them to discover; the judges are only "drawing out" of the rule what, if it is properly understood, is "latent" within it. To call this judicial legislation is to obscure some essential continuity between the clear cases of the rule's application and the penumbral decisions. I shall question later whether this way of talking is salutory, but I wish at this time to point out something obvious, but likely, if not stated, to tangle the issues. It does not follow that, because the opposite of a decision reached blindly in the formalist or literalist manner is a decision intelligently reached by reference to some conception of what ought to be, we have a junction of law and morals. . . . The point here is that intelligent decisions which we oppose to mechanical or formal decisions are not necessarily identical with decisions defensible on moral grounds. We may say of many a decision: "Yes, that is right; that is as it ought to be," and we may mean only that some accepted purpose or policy has been thereby advanced; we may not mean to endorse the moral propriety of the policy or the decision. So the contrast between the mechanical decision and the intelligent one can be reproduced inside a system dedicated to the pursuit of the most evil aims. . . .

We can now return to the main point. It is true that the intelligent decision of penumbral questions is one made not mechanically but in the light of aims, purposes, and policies, though not necessarily in the light of anything we would call moral principles. But is it wise to express this important fact by saying that the firm utilitarian distinction between what the law is and what it ought to be should be dropped? Perhaps the claim that it is wise cannot be theoretically refuted for it is, in effect, an *invitation* to revise our conception of what a legal rule is. We are invited to include in the "rule" the various aims and policies in the light of which its penumbral cases are decided on the ground that these aims have, because of their importance, as much right to be called law as the core of legal rules whose meaning is settled. But though an invitation cannot be refuted, it may be refused and I would proffer two reasons for refusing this invitation. First, every thing we have learned about the judicial process can be expressed in other less mysterious ways. We can say laws are incurably incomplete and we must decide the penumbral cases rationally by reference to social aims. I think Holmes, who had such a vivid appreciation of the fact that "general propositions do not decide concrete cases," would have put it that way. Second, to insist on the utilitarian distinction is to emphasize that the hard core of settled meaning is law in some centrally important sense and that even if there are borderlines, there must first be lines. If this were not so the notion of rules controlling courts' decisions would be senseless as some of the "Realists"—in their most extreme moods, and, I think, on bad grounds—claimed.

By contrast, to soften the distinction, to assert myteriously that there is some fused identity between law as it is and as it ought to be, is to suggest that all legal questions are fundamentally like those of the penumbra. It is to assert that there is no central element of actual law to be seen in the core of central meaning which rules have, that there is nothing in the nature of a legal rule inconsistent with *all* questions being open to reconsideration in the light of social policy. Of course, it is good to be occupied with the penumbra. Its problems are rightly the daily diet of the law schools. But to be occupied with the penumbra is one thing, to be preoccupied with it another. And preoccupation with the penumbra is, if I may say so, as rich a source of confusion in the American legal tradition as formalism in the English. Of course we might abandon the notion that rules have authority; we might cease to attach force or even meaning to an argument that a case falls clearly within a rule and the scope of a precedent. We might call all such reasoning "automatic" or "mechanical," which is already the routine invective of the courts. But until we decide that this *is* what we want; we should not encourage it by obliterating the utilitarian distinction. . . .

4

The third criticism of the separation of law and morals is of a very different character: it certainly is less an intellectual argument against the utilitarian distinction than a passionate appeal supported not by detailed reasoning but by reminders of a terrible experience. For it consists of the testimony of those who have descended into Hell, and, like Ulysses or Dante, brought back a message for human beings. Only in this case the Hell was not beneath or beyond earth, but on it; it was a Hell created on earth by men for other men.

This appeal comes from those German thinkers who lived through the Nazi regime and reflected upon its evil manifestations in the legal system. One of these thinkers, Gustav Radbruch, had himself shared the "positivist" doctrine until the Nazi tyranny, but he was converted by this experience and so his appeal to other men to discard the doctrine of the separation of law and morals has the special poignancy of a recantation. What is important about this criticism is that it really does confront the particular point which Bentham and Austin had in mind in urging the separation of law as it is and as it ought to be. . . .

. . . Austin, it may be recalled, was emphatic in condemning those who said that if human laws conflicted with the fundamental principles of morality that they cease to be laws, as talking "stark nonsense."

The most pernicious laws, and therefore those which are most opposed to the will of God, have been and are continually enforced as laws by judicial tribunals. Suppose an act innocuous, or positively beneficial, be prohibited by the sovereign under the penalty of death; if I commit this act, I shall be tried and condemned, and if I object to the sentence, that it is contrary to the law of God . . . the court of justice will demonstrate the inconclusiveness of my reasoning by hanging me up, in pursuance of the law of which I have impugned the validity. An exception, demurrer, or plea, founded on the law of God was never heard in a Court of Justice, from the creation of the world down to the present moment.

These are strong, indeed brutal words, but we must remember that they went along—in the case of Austin and, of course, Bentham—with the conviction that if laws reached a certain degree of iniquity then there would be a plain moral obligation to resist them and to withhold obedience. We shall see, when we consider the alternatives, that this simple presentation of the human dilemma which may arise has much to be said for it. . . .

It is impossible to read without sympathy [the] passionate demand that the German legal conscience should be open to the demands of morality and [the] complaint that this has been too little the case in the German tradition. On the other hand there is an extraordinary naïveté in the view that insensitiveness to the demands of morality and subservience to state power in a people like the Germans should have arisen from the belief that law might be law though it failed to conform with the minimum requirements of morality. Rather this terrible history prompts inquiry into why emphasis on the slogan "law is law," and the distinction between law and morals, acquired a sinister character in Germany, but elsewhere, as with the utilitarians themselves, went along with the most enlightened liberal attitudes.

. . . If with the utilitarians we speak plainly, we say that laws may be law but too evil to be obeyed. This is a moral condemnation which everyone can understand and it makes an immediate and obvious claim to moral attention. If, on the other hand, we formulate our objection as an assertion that these evil things are not law, here is an assertion which many people do not believe, and if they are disposed to consider it at all, it would seem to raise a whole host of philosophical issues before it can be accepted. So perhaps the most important single lesson to be learned from this form of the denial of the utilitarian distinction is the one that the utilitarians were most concerned to teach: when we have the ample resources of plain speech we must not present the moral criticism of institutions as propositions of a disputable philosophy.

REVIEW AND DISCUSSION QUESTIONS

1. What are the key claims made by legal positivists ("utilitarians" as Hart sometimes calls them)?

2. Why does Hart reject Austin's "command" theory of law?

3. What is the distinction between the "core" and the "penumbra," and how is it relevant to the dispute between formalism and legal realism?

4. How does Hart answer those who suggest that legal positivism contributed to the Germans' willingness to accept Nazism?

5. How might Austin respond to Hart's criticisms?

Law as the Union of Primary and Secondary Rules

H. L. A. Hart

In the following selection taken from his influential book The Concept of Law, *Hart begins with a discussion of the nature of legal obligation. Using Austin's command theory as a backdrop, Hart first criticizes Austin and then develops his own account of legal obligation, which he thinks escapes the problems in Austin. Then in the second part of the selection, Hart presents his view of the nature of law, a theory that although still consistent with the basic tenets of positivism, nonetheless is not open to the objections raised against Austin. Hart begins by asking the reader to imagine the weaknesses of a society with only "primary" rules of obligation and then goes on to explain why in a developed system it is essential that "secondary" rules be added. Law, for Hart, is an affair of rules.*

It is, of course, possible to imagine a society without a legislature, courts or officials of any kind. Indeed, there are many studies of primitive communities which not only claim that this possibility is realized but depict in detail the life of a society where the only means of social control is that general attitude of the group towards its own standard modes of behaviour in terms of which we have characterized rules of obligation. A social structure of this kind is often referred to as one of "custom"; but we shall not use this term, because it often implies that the customary rules are very old and supported with less social pressure than other rules. To avoid these implications we shall refer to such a social structure as one of primary rules of obligation. If a society is to live by such primary rules alone, there are certain conditions which, granted a few of the most obvious truisms about human nature and the world we live in, must clearly be satisfied. The first of these conditions is that the rules must contain in some form restrictions on the free use of violence, theft, and deception to which human beings are tempted but which they must, in general, repress, if they are to co-exist in close proximity to each other. Such rules are in fact always found in the primitive societies of which we have knowledge, together with a variety of others imposing on individuals various positive duties to perform services or make contributions to the common life. Secondly, though such a society may exhibit the tension, already described, between those who accept the rules and those who reject the rules except where fear of social pressure induces them to conform, it is plain that the latter cannot be more than a minority, if so loosely organized a society of persons, approximately equal in physical strength, is to endure: for otherwise those who reject the rules would have too little social pressure to fear. This too is confirmed by what we know of primitive communities where, though there are dissidents and malefactors, the majority live by the rules seen from the internal point of view.

More important for our present purpose is the following consideration. It is plain that only a small community closely knit by ties of kinship, common sentiment, and belief, and placed in a stable environment, could live successfully by such a régime of unofficial rules. In any other conditions such a simple form of social control must prove defective and will require supplementation in different ways. In the first place, the rules by which the group lives will not form a system, but will simply be a set of separate standards, without any identifying or common mark, except of course that they are the rules which a particular group of human beings accepts. They will in this respect resemble our own rules of etiquette. Hence if doubts arise as to what the rules are or as to the precise scope of some given rule, there will be no procedure for settling this doubt, either by reference to an authoritative text or to an official whose declarations on this point are authoritative. For, plainly, such a procedure and the acknowledgment of either authoritative text or persons involve the existence of rules of a type different from the rules of obligation or duty which *ex hypothesi* are all that the group has. This defect in the simple social structure of primary rules we may call its *uncertainty*.

A second defect is the *static* character of the rules. The only mode of change in the rules known to such a society will be the slow process of growth, whereby courses of conduct once thought optional become first habitual or usual, and then obligatory, and the converse process of decay, when deviations, once severely dealt with, are first tolerated and then pass unnoticed. There will be no means, in such a society, of deliberately adapting the rules to changing circumstances, either by eliminating old rules or introducing new ones: for, again, the possibility of doing this presupposes the existence of rules of a different type from the primary rules of obligation by which alone the society lives. In an extreme case the rules may be static in a more drastic sense. This, though never perhaps fully realized in any actual community, is worth considering because the remedy for it is something very characteristic of law. In this extreme case, not only would there be no way of deliberately changing the general rules, but the obligations which arise under the rules in particular cases could not be varied or modified by the deliberate choice of any individual. Each individual would simply have fixed obligations or duties to do or abstain from doing certain things. It might indeed very often be the case that others would benefit from the performance of these obligations; yet if there are only primary rules of obligation they would have no power to release those bound from performance or to transfer to others the benefits which would accrue from performance. For such operations of release or transfer create changes in the initial positions of individuals under the primary rules of obligation, and for these operations to be possible there must be rules of a sort different from the primary rules

The third defect of this simple form of social life is the *inefficiency* of the diffuse social pressure by which the rules are maintained. Disputes as to whether an admitted rule has or has not been violated will always occur and will, in any but the smallest societies, continue interminably, if there is no agency specially empowered to ascertain finally, and authoritatively, the fact of violation. Lack of such final and authoritative determinations is to be distinguished from another weakness associated with it. This is the fact that punishments for violations of the rules, and other forms of social pressure involving physical effort or the use of force, are not administered by a special agency but are left to the individuals affected or to the group at large. It is obvious that the waste of time involved in the group's unorganized efforts to catch and punish offenders, and the smouldering vendettas which may result from self help in the absence of an official monopoly of "sanctions," may be serious. The history of law does, however, strongly suggest that the lack of official agencies to determine authoritatively the fact of violation of the rules is a much more serious defect; for many societies have remedies for this defect long before the other.

The remedy for each of these three main defects in this simplest form of social structure consists in supplementing the *primary* rules of obligation with *secondary* rules which are rules of a different kind. The introduction of the remedy for each defect might, in itself, be considered a step from the pre-legal into the legal world; since each remedy brings with it many elements that permeate law: certainly all three remedies together are enough to convert the régime of primary rules into what is indisputably a legal system. We shall consider in turn each of these remedies and show why law may most illuminatingly be characterized as a union of primary rules of obligation with such secondary rules. Before we do this, however, the following general points should be noted. Though the remedies consist in the introduction of rules which are certainly different from each other, as well as from the primary rules of obligation which they supplement, they have important features in common and are connected in various ways. Thus they may all be said to be on a different level from the primary rules, for they are all *about* such rules; in the sense that while primary rules are concerned with the actions that individuals must or must not do, these secondary rules are all concerned with the primary rules themselves. They specify the ways in which the primary rules may be conclusively ascertained, introduced, eliminated, varied, and the fact of their violation conclusively determined.

The simplest form of remedy for the *uncertainty* of the régime of primary rules is the introduction of what we shall call a "rule of recognition." This will specify some feature or features possession of which by a suggested rule is taken as a conclusive affirmative indication that it is a rule of the group to be supported by the social pressure it exerts. The existence of such a rule of recognition may take any of a huge variety of forms, simple or complex. It may, as in the early law of many societies, be no more than that an authoritative list or text of the rules is to be found in a written document or carved on some public monument. No doubt as a matter of history this step from the pre-legal to the legal may be accomplished in distinguishable stages, of which the first is the mere reduction to writing of hitherto unwritten rules. This is not itself the crucial step, though it is a very important one: what is crucial is the acknowledgement of reference to the writing or inscription as *authoritative*, i.e., as the *proper* way of disposing of doubts as to the existence of the rule. Where there is such an acknowledgement there is a very simple form of secondary rule: a rule for conclusive identification of the primary rules of obligation.

In a developed legal system the rules of recognition are of course more complex; instead of identifying rules exclusively by reference to a text or list they do so by reference to some general characteristic possessed by the primary rules. This may be the fact of their having been enacted by a specific body, or their long customary practice, or their relation to judicial decisions. Moreover, where more than one of such general characteristics are treated as identifying criteria, provision may be made for their possible conflict by their arrangement in an order of superiority, as by the common subordination of custom or precedent to statute, the latter being a "superior source" of law. Such complexity may make the rules of recognition in a modern legal system seem very different from the simple acceptance of an authoritative text: yet even in this simplest form, such a rule brings with it many elements distinctive of law. By providing an authoritative mark it introduces, although in embryonic form, the idea of a legal system: for the rules are now not just a discrete unconnected set but are, in a simple way, unified. Further, in the simple operation of identifying a given rule as possessing the required feature of being an item on an authoritative list of rules we have the germ of the idea of legal validity.

The remedy for the *static* quality of the régime of primary rules consists in the introduction of what we shall call "rules of change." The simplest form of such a rule is that which empowers an individual or body of persons to introduce new primary rules for the conduct of the life of the group, or of some class within it, and to eliminate old rules. As we have already argued . . . it is in terms of such a rule, and not in terms of orders backed by threats, that the ideas of legislative enactment and repeal are to be understood. Such rules of change may be very simple or very complex: the powers conferred may be unrestricted or limited in various ways: and the rules may, besides specifying the persons who are to legislate, define in more or less rigid terms the procedure to be followed in legislation. Plainly, there will be a very close connexion between the rules of change and the rules of recognition: for where the former exists the latter will necessarily incorporate a reference to legislation as an identifying feature of the rules, though it need not refer to all the details of procedure involved in legislation. Usually some official certificate or official copy will, under the rules of recognition, be taken as a sufficient proof of due enactment. Of course if there is a social structure so simple that the only "source of law" is legislation, the rule of recognition will simply specify enactment as the unique identifying mark or criterion of validity of the rules. This will be the case for example in the imaginary kingdom of Rex I . . . [where] the rule of recognition would simply be that whatever Rex I enacts is law.

We have already described in some detail the rules which confer on individuals power to vary their initial positions under the primary rules. Without such private power-conferring rules society would lack some of the chief amenities which law confers upon it. For the operations which these rules make possible are the making of wills, contracts, transfers of property, and many other voluntarily created structures of rights and duties which typify life under law, though of course an elementary form of

power-conferring rule also underlies the moral institution of a promise. The kinship of these rules with the rules of change involved in the notion of legislation is clear, and as recent theory such as Kelsen's has shown, many of the features which puzzle us in the institutions of contract or property are clarified by thinking of the operations of making a contract or transferring property as the exercise of limited legislative powers by individuals.

The third supplement to the simple régime of primary rules, intended to remedy the *inefficiency* of its diffused social pressure, consists of secondary rules empowering individuals to make authoritative determinations of the question whether, on a particular occasion, a primary rule has been broken. The minimal form of adjudication consists in such determinations, and we shall call the secondary rules which confer the power to make them "rules of adjudication." Besides identifying the individuals who are to adjudicate, such rules will also define the procedure to be followed. Like the other secondary rules these are on a different level from the primary rules: though they may be reinforced by further rules imposing duties on judges to adjudicate, they do not impose duties but confer judicial powers and a special status on judicial declarations about the breach of obligations. Again these rules, like the other secondary rules, define a group of important legal concepts: in this case the concepts of judge or court, jurisdiction and judgment. Besides these resemblances to the other secondary rules, rules of adjudication have intimate connexions with them. Indeed, a system which has rules of adjudication is necessarily also committed to a rule of recognition of an elementary and imperfect sort. This is so because, if courts are empowered to make authoritative determinations of the fact that a rule has been broken, these cannot avoid being taken as authoritative determinations of what the rules are. So the rule which confers jurisdiction will also be a rule of recognition, identifying the primary rules through the judgments of the courts and these judgments will become a "source" of law. It is true that this form of rule of recognition, inseparable from the minimum form of jurisdiction, will be very imperfect. Unlike an authoritative text or a statute book, judgments may not be couched in general terms and their use as authoritative guides to the rules depends on a somewhat shaky inference from particular decisions, and the reliability of this must fluctuate both with the skill of the interpreter and the consistency of the judges.

It need hardly be said that in few legal systems are judicial powers confined to authoritative determinations of the fact of violation of the primary rules. Most systems have, after some delay, seen the advantages of further centralization of social pressure; and have partially prohibited the use of physical punishments or violent self help by private individuals. Instead they have supplemented the primary rules of obligation by further secondary rules, specifying or at least limiting the penalties for violation, and have conferred upon judges, where they have ascertained the fact of violation, the exclusive power to direct the application of penalties by other officials. These secondary rules provide the centralized official "sanctions" of the system.

If we stand back and consider the structure which has resulted from the combination of primary rules of obligation with the secondary rules of recognition, change and adjudication, it is plain that we have here not only the heart of a legal system, but a most powerful tool for the analysis of much that has puzzled both the jurist and the political theorist.

[Editor's Note: Hart later compares the rule of recognition to the meter bar in Paris, which serves to define the measure of length we conventionally call a meter. Just as it is senseless to ask if that bar really is a meter long, so too is it senseless to ask if the rule of recognition is "valid" legally.]

REVIEW AND DISCUSSION QUESTIONS

1. What are the three defects of a system of primary rules?

2. How does Hart define a "secondary rule"?

3. How do secondary rules solve the three defects he describes?

4. Hart suggests here (and later in his book makes explicit) that the rule of recognition is neither valid nor invalid, but rather is the test for validity. Explain.

5. Even if the rule of recognition is neither valid nor invalid, it could still be criticized on other grounds. Describe some possible rules of recognition and indicate how each might be assessed.

6. What is the rule of recognition where you live? Describe it.

7. Is it important for Hart's theory that a constitution can include rules governing how it is to be amended? Explain.

The Model of Rules

Ronald Dworkin

In this essay Ronald Dworkin (who once studied philosophy of law under H. L. A. Hart and once held the same position Hart held at Oxford) offers a careful, detailed criticism of each of the key positivist claims. Beginning with a brief summary of how both Austin and Hart exemplify the positivist position, he goes on to attack positivism's three basic tenets: that law is a set of rules identifiable by their "pedigree," that the law is limited to those rules, and that to claim some people have a legal obligation means that their behavior falls under a valid legal rule. Along the way Dworkin distinguishes between principles and rules, discusses different types of discretion, and concludes with a discussion of the "rule of recognition" as a test that can be used to identify the law.

. . . Before we can decide that our concepts of law and of legal obligation are myths, we must decide what they are. We must be able to state, at least roughly, what it is we all believe that is wrong. But the nerve of our problem is that we have great difficulty in doing just that. Indeed, when we ask what law is and what legal obligations are, we are asking for a theory of how we use these concepts and of the conceptual commitments our use entails. We cannot conclude, before we have such a general theory, that our practices are stupid or superstitious.

Of course, the [realists] think they know how the rest of us use these concepts. They think that when we speak of "the law," we mean a set of timeless rules stocked in some conceptual warehouse awaiting discovery by judges, and that when we speak of legal obligation we mean the invisible chains these mysterious rules somehow drape around us. The theory that there are such rules and chains they call "mechanical jurisprudence," and they are right in ridiculing its practitioners. Their difficulty, however, lies in finding practitioners to ridicule. So far they have had little luck in caging and exhibiting mechanical jurisprudents (all specimens captured—even Blackstone and Joseph Beale—have had to be released after careful reading of their texts). . . .

Of course the suggestion that we stop talking about "the law" and "legal obligation" is mostly bluff. These concepts are too deeply cemented into the structure of our political practices—they cannot be given up like cigarettes or hats. Some of the [realists] have half-admitted this and said that the myths they condemn should be thought of as Platonic myths and retained to seduce the masses into order. This is perhaps not so cynical a suggestion as it seems; perhaps it is a covert hedging of a dubious bet.

. . . I want to examine the soundness of positivism, particularly in the powerful form that Professor H. L. A. Hart of Oxford has given to it. I choose to focus on his position, not only because of its clarity and elegance, but because here, as almost everywhere else in legal philosophy, constructive thought must start with a consideration of his views.

POSITIVISM

Positivism has a few central and organizing propositions as its skeleton, and though not every philosopher who is called a positivist would subscribe to these in the way I present them, they do define the general position I want to examine. These key tenets may be stated as follows:

A. The law of a community is a set of special rules used by the community directly or indirectly for the purpose of determining which behavior will be punished or coerced by the public power. These special rules can be identified and distinguished by specific criteria, by tests having to do not with their content but with their *pedigree* or the manner in which they were adopted or developed. These tests of pedigree can be used to distinguish valid legal rules from spurious legal rules (rules which lawyers and litigants wrongly argue are rules of law) and also from other sorts of social rules (generally lumped together as "moral rules") that the community follows but does not enforce through public power.

B. The set of these valid legal rules is exhaustive of "the law," so that if someone's case is not clearly covered by such a rule (because there is none that seems appropriate, or those that seem appropriate are vague, or for some other reason) then that case cannot be decided by "applying the law." It must be decided by some official, like a judge, "exercising his discretion," which means reaching beyond the law for some other sort of standard to guide him in manufacturing a fresh legal rule or supplementing an old one.

C. To say that someone has a "legal obligation" is to say that his case falls under a valid legal rule that requires him to do or to forbear from doing something. (To say he has a legal right, or has a legal power of some sort, or a legal privilege or immunity, is to assert, in a shorthand way, that others have actual or hypothetical legal obligations to act or not to act in certain ways touching him.) In the absence of such a valid legal rule there is no legal obligation; it follows that when the judge decides an issue by exercising his discretion, he is not enforcing a legal obligation as to that issue.

This is only the skeleton of positivism. The flesh is arranged differently by different positivists, and some even tinker with the bones. Different versions differ chiefly in their description of the fundamental test of pedigree a rule must meet to count as a rule of law.

Austin, for example, framed his version of the fundamental test as a series of interlocking definitions and distinctions. He defined having an obligation as lying under a rule, a rule as a general command, and a command as an expression of desire that others behave in a particular way, backed by the power and will to enforce that expression in the event of disobedience. He distinguished classes of rules (legal, moral or religious) according to which person or group is the author of the general command the rule represents. In each political community, he thought, one will find a sovereign—a person or a determinate group whom the rest obey habitually, but who is not in the habit of obeying anyone else. The legal rules of a community are the general commands its sovereign has deployed. Austin's definition of legal obligation followed from this definition of law. One has a legal obligation, he thought, if one is among the addressees of some general order of the sovereign, and is in danger of suffering a sanction unless he obeys that order.

Of course, the sovereign cannot provide for all contingencies through any scheme of orders, and some of his orders will inevitably be vague or have furry edges. Therefore (according to Austin) the sovereign grants those who enforce the law (judges) discretion to make fresh orders when novel or troublesome cases are presented. The judges then make new rules or adapt old rules, and the sovereign either overturns their creations, or tacitly confirms them by failing to do so.

Austin's model is quite beautiful in its simplicity. It asserts the first tenet of positivism, and the law is a set of rules specially selected to govern public order, and offers a simple factual test—what has the sovereign commanded?—as the sole criterion for identifying those special rules. In time, however, those who studied and tried to apply Austin's model found it too simple. Many objections were raised, among which were two that seemed fundamental. First, Austin's key assumption that in each community a determinate group or institution can be found, which is in ultimate control of all other groups,

seemed not to hold in a complex society. Political control in a modern nation is pluralistic and shifting, a matter of more or less, of compromise and cooperation and alliance, so that it is often impossible to say that any person or group has that dramatic control necessary to qualify as an Austinian sovereign. One wants to say, in the United States for example, that the "people" are sovereign. But this means almost nothing, and in itself provides no test for determining what the "people" have commanded, or distinguishing their legal from their social or moral commands.

Second, critics began to realize that Austin's analysis fails entirely to account for, even to recognize, certain striking facts about the attitudes we take toward "the law." We make an important distinction between law and even the general orders of a gangster. We feel that the law's strictures—and its sanctions—are different in that they are obligatory in a way that the outlaw's commands are not. Austin's analysis has no place for any such distinction, because it defines an obligation as subjection to the threat of force, and so founds the authority of law entirely on the sovereign's ability and will to harm those who disobey. Perhaps the distinction we make is illusory—perhaps our feelings of some special authority attaching to the law is based on religious hangover or another sort of mass self-deception. But Austin does not demonstrate this, and we are entitled to insist that an analysis of our concept of law either acknowledge and explain our attitudes, or show why they are mistaken.

H. L. A. Hart's version of positivism is more complex than Austin's, in two ways. First, he recognizes, as Austin did not, the rules are of different logical kinds (Hart distinguishes two kinds, which he calls "primary" and "secondary" rules). Second, he rejects Austin's theory that a rule is a kind of command, and substitutes a more elaborate general analysis of what rules are. We must pause over each of these points, and then note how they merge in Hart's concept of law.

Hart's distinction between primary and secondary rules is of great importance.[1] Primary rules are those that grant rights or impose obligations upon members of the community. The rules of the criminal law that forbid us to rob, murder or drive too fast are good examples of primary rules. Secondary rules are those that stipulate how, and by whom, such primary rules may be formed, recognized, modified or extinguished. The rules that stipulate how Congress is composed, and how it enacts legislation, are examples of secondary rules. Rules about forming contracts and executing wills are also secondary rules because they stipulate how very particular rules governing particular legal obligations (that is, the terms of a contract or the provisions of a will) come into existence and are changed.

His general analysis of rules is also of great importance. Austin had said that every rule is a general command, and that a person is obligated under a rule if he is liable to be hurt should he disobey it. Hart points out that this obliterates the distinction between being *obliged* to do something and being *obligated* to do it. If one is bound by a rule he is obligated, not merely obliged, to do what it provides, and therefore being bound by a rule must be different from being subject to an injury if one disobeys an order. A rule differs from an order, among other ways, by being *normative*, by setting a standard of behavior that has a call on its subject beyond the threat that may enforce it. A rule can never be binding just because some person with physical power wants it to be so. He must have *authority* to issue the rule or it is no rule, and such authority can only come from another rule which is already binding on those to whom he speaks. That is the difference between a valid law and the orders of a gunman.

So Hart offers a general theory of rules that does not make their authority depend upon the physical power of their authors. If we examine the way different rules come into being, he tells us, and attend to the distinction between primary and secondary rules, we see that there are two possible sources of a rule's authority.[2]

A. A rule may become binding upon a group of people because that group through its practices *accepts* the rule as a standard for its conduct. It is not enough that the group simply conforms to a pattern of behavior: even though most Englishmen may go to the movies on Saturday evening, they have not accepted a rule requiring that they do so. A practice constitutes the acceptance of a rule only when those who follow the practice regard the rule as binding, and recognize the rule as a reason or justification for their own behavior and as a reason for criticizing the behavior of others who do not obey it.

B. A rule may also become binding in quite a different way, namely by being enacted in conformity with some *secondary* rule that stipulates that rules so enacted shall be binding. If the constitution of a club stipulates, for example, that by-laws may be adopted by a majority of the members, then particular by-laws so voted are binding upon all the members, not because of any practice of acceptance of these particular by-laws, but because the constitution says so. We use the concept of *validity* in this connection: rules binding because they have been created in a manner stipulated by some secondary rule are called "valid" rules. Thus we can record Hart's fundamental distinction this way: a rule may be binding (a) because it is accepted or (b) because it is valid.

Hart's concept of law is a construction of these various distinctions. Primitive communities have only primary rules, and these are binding entirely because of practices of acceptance. Such communities cannot be said to have "law," because there is no way to distinguish a set of legal rules from amongst other social rules, as the first tenet of positivism requires. But when a particular community has developed a fundamental secondary rule that stipulates how legal rules are to be identified, the idea of a distinct set of legal rules, and thus of law, is born.

Hart calls such a fundamental secondary rule a "rule of recognition." The rule of recognition of a given community may be relatively simple ("What the king enacts is law") or it may be very complex (the United States Constitution, with all its difficulties of interpretation, may be considered a single rule of recognition). The demonstration that a particular rule is valid may therefore require tracing a complicated chain of validity back from that particular rule ultimately to the fundamental rule. Thus a parking ordinance of the city of New Haven is valid because it is adopted by a city council, pursuant to the procedures and within the competence specified by the municipal law adopted by the state of Connecticut, in conformity with the procedures and within the competence specified by the constitution of the state of Connecticut, which was in turn adopted consistently with the requirements of the United States Constitution.

Of course, a rule of recognition cannot itself be valid, because by hypothesis it is ultimate, and so cannot meet tests stipulated by a more fundamental rule. The rule of recognition is the sole rule in a legal system whose binding force depends upon its acceptance. If we wish to know what rule of recognition a particular community has adopted or follows, we must observe how its citizens, and particularly its officials, behave. We must observe what ultimate arguments they accept as showing the validity of a particular rule, and what ultimate arguments they use to criticize other officials or institutions. We can apply no mechanical test, but there is no danger of our confusing the rule of recognition of a community with its rules of morality. The rule of recognition is identified by the fact that its province is the operation of the governmental apparatus of legislatures, courts, agencies, policemen, and the rest.

In this way Hart rescues the fundamentals of positivism from Austin's mistakes. Hart agrees with Austin that valid rules of law may be created through the acts of officials and public institutions. But Austin thought that the authority of these institutions lay only in their monopoly of power. Hart finds their authority in the background of constitutional standards against which they act, constitutional standards that have been accepted, in the form of a fundamental rule of recognition, by the community which they govern. This background legitimates the decisions of government and gives them the cast and call of obligation that the naked commands of Austin's sovereign lacked. Hart's theory differs from Austin's also, in recognizing that different communities use different ultimate tests of law, and that some allow other means of creating law than the deliberate act of a legislative institution. Hart mentions "long customary practice" and "the relation [of a rule] to judicial decisions" as other criteria that are often used, though generally along with and subordinate to the test of legislation.

So Hart's version of positivism is more complex than Austin's, and his test for valid rules of law is more sophisticated. In one respect, however, the two models are very similar. Hart, like Austin, recognizes that legal rules have fuzzy edges (he speaks of them as having "open texture") and, again like Austin, he accounts for troublesome cases by saying that judges have had to exercise discretion to decide these cases by fresh legislation. (I shall later try to show why one who thinks of law as a special set of rules is almost inevitably drawn to account for difficult cases in terms of someone's exercise of discretion.)

RULES, PRINCIPLES, AND POLICIES

I want to make a general attack on positivism, and I shall use H. L. A. Hart's version as a target, when a particular target is needed. My strategy will be organized around the fact that when lawyers reason or dispute about legal rights and obligations, particularly in those hard cases when our problems with these concepts seem most acute, they make use of standards that do not function as rules, but operate differently as principles, policies, and other sorts of standards. Positivism, I shall argue, is a model of and for a system of rules, and its central notion of a single fundamental test for law forces us to miss the important roles of these standards that are not rules.

I just spoke of "principles, policies, and other sorts of standards." Most often I shall use the term "principle" generically, to refer to the whole set of these standards other than rules; occasionally, however, I shall be more precise, and distinguish between principles and policies. Although nothing in the present argument will turn on the distinction, I should state how I draw it. I call a "policy" that kind of standard that sets out a goal to be reached, generally an improvement in some economic, political, or social feature of the community (though some goals are negative, in that they stipulate that some present feature is to be protected from adverse change). I call a "principle" a standard that is to be observed, not because it will advance or secure an economic, political, or social situation deemed desirable, but because it is a requirement of justice or fairness or some other dimension of morality. Thus the standard that automobile accidents are to be decreased is a policy, and the standard that no man may profit by his own wrong a principle. The distinction can be collapsed by construing a principle as stating a social goal (that is, the goal of a society in which no man profits by his own wrong), or by construing a policy as stating a principle (that is, the principle that the goal the policy embraces is a worthy one) or by adopting the utilitarian thesis that principles of justice are disguised statements of goals (securing the greatest happiness of the greatest number). In some contexts the distinction has uses which are lost if it is thus collapsed.[3]

My immediate purpose, however, is to distinguish principles in the generic sense from rules, and I shall start by collecting some examples of the former. The examples I offer are chosen haphazardly; almost any case in a law school casebook would provide examples that would serve as well. In 1889 a New York court, in the famous case of *Riggs v. Palmer*[4] *[Reprinted above–Ed.]* had to decide whether an heir named in the will of his grandfather could inherit under that will, even though he had murdered his grandfather to do so. The court began its reasoning with this admission: "It is quite true that statutes regulating the making, proof and effect of wills, and the devolution of property, if literally construed, and if their force and effect can in no way and under no circumstances be controlled or modified, give this property to the murderer." But the court continued to note that "all laws as well as all contracts may be controlled in their operation and effect by general, fundamental maxims of the common law. No one shall be permitted to profit by his own fraud, or to take advantage of his own wrong, or to found any claim upon his own iniquity, or to acquire property by his own crime." The murderer did not receive his inheritance.

In 1960, a New Jersey court was faced, in *Henningsen v. Bloomfield Motors, Inc.*,[5] with the important question of whether (or how much)

an automobile manufacturer may limit his liability in case the automobile is defective. Henningsen had bought a car, and signed a contract which said that the manufacturer's liability for defects was limited to "making good" defective parts—"this warranty being expressly in lieu of all other warranties, obligations or liabilities." Henningsen argued that, at least in the circumstances of his case, the manufacturer ought not to be protected by this limitation, and ought to be liable for the medical and other expenses of persons injured in a crash. He was not able to point to any statute, or to any established rule of law, that prevented the manufacturer from standing on the contract. The court nevertheless agreed with Henningsen. At various points in the court's argument the following appeals to standards are made: (a) "[W]e must keep in mind the general principle that, in the absence of fraud, one who does not choose to read a contract before signing it cannot later relieve himself of its burdens." (b) "In applying that principle, the basic tenet of freedom of competent parties to contract is a factor of importance." (c) "Freedom of contract is not such an immutable doctrine as to admit of no qualification in the area in which we are concerned." (d) "In a society such as ours where the automobile is a common and necessary adjunct of daily life, and where its use is so fraught with danger to the driver, passengers and the public, the manufacturer is under a special obligation in connection with the construction, promotion and sale of his cars. Consequently, the courts must examine purchase agreements closely to see if consumer and public interests are treated fairly." (e) " '[I]s there any principle which is more familiar or more firmly embedded in the history of Anglo-American law than the basic doctrine that the courts will not permit themselves to be used as instruments of inequity and injustice?' "[6] (f) " 'More specifically, the courts generally refuse to lend themselves to the enforcement of a "bargain" in which one party has unjustly taken advantage of the economic necessities of [the] other. . . .' "[7]

The standards set out in these quotations are not the sort we think of as legal rules. They seem very different from propositions like "The maximum legal speed on the turnpike is sixty miles an hour" or "A will is invalid unless signed by three witnesses." They are different because they are legal principles rather than legal rules.

The difference between legal principles and legal rules is a logical distinction. Both sets of standards point to particular decisions about legal obligation in particular circumstances, but they differ in the character of the direction they give. Rules are applicable in an all-or-nothing fashion. If the facts a rule stipulates are given, then either the rule is valid, in which case the answer it supplies must be accepted, or it is not, in which case it contributes nothing to the decision.

This all-or-nothing is seen most plainly if we look at the way rules operate, not in law, but in some enterprise they dominate—a game, for example. In baseball a rule provides that if the batter has had three strikes, he is out. An official cannot consistently acknowledge that this is an accurate statement of a baseball rule, and decide that a batter who has had three strikes is not out. Of course, a rule may have exceptions (the batter who has taken three strikes is not out if the catcher drops the third strike). However, an accurate statement of the rule would take this exception into account, and any that did not would be incomplete. If the list of exceptions is very large, it would be too clumsy to repeat them each time the rule is cited; there is, however, no reason in theory why they could not all be added on, and the more that are, the more accurate is the statement of the rule.

If we take baseball rules as a model, we find that rules of law, like the rule that a will is invalid unless signed by three witnesses, fit the model well. If the requirement of three witnesses is a valid legal rule, then it cannot be that a will has been signed by only two witnesses and is valid. The rule might have exceptions, but if it does then it is inaccurate and incomplete to state the rule so simply, without enumerating the exceptions. In theory, at least, the exceptions could all be listed, and the more of them that are, the more complete is the statement of the rule.

But this is not the way the sample principles in the quotations operate. Even those which look most like rules do not set out legal consequences that follow automatically when the conditions provided are met. We say that our law respects the principle that no man may profit from his own wrong, but we do not mean that the law never permits a man to profit from wrongs he commits. In fact, people often profit, perfectly legally, from their legal wrongs. The most notorious case is adverse possession—if I trespass on your land long enough, some day I will gain a right to cross your land whenever I please. There are many less dramatic examples. If a man leaves one job, breaking a contract, to take a much higher paying job, he may have to pay damages to his first employer, but he is usually entitled to keep his new salary. If a man jumps bail and crosses state lines to make a brilliant investment in another state, he may be sent back to jail, but he will keep his profits.

We do not treat these—and countless other counter-instances that can easily be imagined—as showing that the principle about profiting from one's wrongs is not a principle of our legal system, or that it is incomplete and needs qualifying exceptions. We do not treat counter-instances as exceptions (at least not exceptions in the way in which a catcher's dropping the third strike is an exception) because we could not hope to capture these counter-instances simply by a more extended statement of the principle. They are not, even in theory, subject to enumeration, because we would have to include not only these cases (like adverse possession) in which some institution has already provided that profit can be gained through a wrong, but also those numberless imaginary cases in which we know in advance that the principle would not hold. Listing some of these might sharpen our sense of the principle's weight (I shall mention that dimension in a moment), but it would not make for a more accurate or complete statement of the principle.

A principle like "No man may profit from his own wrong" does not even purport to set out conditions that make its application necessary. Rather, it states a reason that argues in one direction, but does not necessitate a particular decision. If a man has or is about to receive something, as a direct result of something illegal he did to get it, then that is a reason which the law will taken into account in deciding whether he should keep it. There may be other principles or policies arguing in the other direction—a policy of securing title, for example, or a principle limiting punishment to what the legislature has stipulated. If so, our principle may not prevail, but that does not mean that it is not a principle of our legal system, because in the next case, when these contravening considerations are absent or less weighty, the principle may be decisive. All that is meant, when we say that a particular principle is a principle of our law, is that the principle is one which officials must take into account, if it is relevant, as a consideration inclining in one direction or another.

The logical distinction between rules and principles appears more clearly when we consider principles that do not even look like rules. Consider the proposition, set out under "(d)" in the excerpts from the *Henningsen* opinion, that "the manufacturer is under a special obligation in connection with the construction, promotion and sale of his cars." This does not even purport to define the specific duties such a special obligation entails, or to tell us what rights automobile consumers acquire as a result. It merely states—and this is an essential link in the *Henningsen* argument—that automobile manufacturers must be held to higher standards than other manufacturers, and are less entitled to rely on the competing principle of freedom of contract. It does not mean that they may never rely on that principle, or that courts may rewrite automobile purchase contracts at will; it means only that if a particular clause seems unfair or burdensome, courts have less reason to enforce the clause than if it were for the purchase of neckties. The "special obligation" counts in favor, but does not in itself necessitate, a decision refusing to enforce the terms of an automobile purchase contract.

This first difference between rules and principles entails another. Principles have a dimension that rules do not—the dimension of weight or importance. When principles intersect (the policy of protecting automobile consumers intersecting with principles of freedom of contract, for example), one who must resolve the conflict has to take into account the relative weight of each. This cannot be, of course, an exact measurement, and the judgment that a particular principle or policy is more important than another will often be a controversial one. Nevertheless, it is an integral part of the concept of a principle that it has this dimension, that it makes sense to ask how important or how weighty it is.

Rules do not have this dimension. We can speak of rules as being *functionally* important or unimportant (the baseball rule that three strikes are out is more important than the rule that runners may advance on a balk, because the game would be much more changed with the first rule altered than the second). In this sense, one legal rule may be more important than another because it has a greater or more important role in regulating behavior. But we cannot say that one rule is more important than another within the system of rules, so that when two rules conflict one supersedes the other by virtue of its greater weight. If two rules conflict, one of them cannot be a valid rule. The decision as to which is valid, and which must be abandoned or recast, must be made by appealing to considerations beyond the rules themselves. A legal system might regulate such conflicts by other rules, which prefer the rule enacted by the higher authority, or the rule enacted later, or the more specific rule, or something of that sort. A legal system may also prefer the rule supported by the more important principles. (Our own legal system uses both of these techniques.)

It is not always clear from the form of a standard whether it is a rule or a principle. "A will is invalid unless signed by three witnesses" is not very different in form from "A man may not profit from his own wrong," but one who knows something of American laws knows that he must take the first as stating a rule and the second as stating a principle. In many cases the distinction is difficult to make—it may not have been settled how the standard should operate, and this issue may itself be a focus of controversy. The First Amendment to the United States Constitution contains the provision that Congress shall not abridge freedom of speech. Is this a rule, so that if a particular law does abridge freedom of speech, it follows that it is unconstitutional?

Those who claim that the first amendment is "an absolute" say that it must be taken in this way, that is, as a rule. Or does it merely state a principle, so that when an abridgement of speech is discovered, it is unconstitutional unless the context presents some other policy or principle which in the circumstances is weighty enough to permit the abridgement? That is the position of those who argue for what is called the "clear and present danger" test or some other form of "balancing."

Sometimes a rule and a principle can play much the same role, and the difference between them is almost a matter of form alone. The first section of the Sherman Act states that every contract in restraint of trade shall be void. The Supreme Court had to make the decision whether this provision should be treated as a rule in its own terms (striking down every contract "which restrains trade," which almost any contract does) or as a principle, providing a reason for striking down a contract in the absence of effective contrary policies. The Court construed the provision as a rule, but treated that rule as containing the word "unreasonable," and as prohibiting only "unreasonable" restraints of trade.[8] This allowed the provision to function logically as a rule (whenever a court finds that the restraint is "unreasonable" it is bound to hold the contract invalid) and substantially as a principle (a court must take into account a variety of other principles and policies in determining whether a particular restraint in particular economic circumstances is "unreasonable").

Words like "reasonable," "negligent," "unjust," and "significant" often perform just this function. Each of these terms makes the application of the rule which contains it depend to some extent upon principles or policies lying beyond the rule, and in this way makes that rule itself more like a principle. But they do not quite turn the rule into a principle, because even the least confining of these terms restricts the *kind* of other principles and policies on which the rule depends. If we are bound by a rule that says that "unreasonable" contracts are void, or that grossly "unfair" contracts will not be enforced, much more judgment is required than if the quoted terms were omitted. But suppose a case in which some consideration of policy or principle suggests that a contract should be enforced even though its restraint is not reasonable, or even though it is grossly unfair. Enforcing these contracts would be forbidden by our rules, and thus permitted only if these rules were abandoned or modified. If we were dealing, however, not with a rule but with a policy against enforcing unreasonable contracts, or a principle that unfair contracts ought not to be enforced, the contracts could be enforced without alteration of the law. . . .

Once we identify legal principles as separate sorts of standards, different from legal rules, we are suddenly aware of them all around us. Law teachers teach them, lawbooks cite them, legal historians celebrate them. But they seem most energetically at work, carrying most weight, in difficult lawsuits like *Riggs* and *Henningsen*. In cases like these principles play an essential part in arguments supporting judgments about particular legal rights and obligations. . . .

THE RULE OF RECOGNITION

. . . If principles of the *Riggs* and *Henningsen* sort are to count as law, and we are nevertheless to preserve the notion of a master rule for law, then we must be able to deploy some test that all (and only) the principles that do count as law meet. Let us begin with the test Hart suggests for identifying valid *rules* of law, to see whether these can be made to work for principles as well.

Most rules of law, according to Hart, are valid because some competent institution enacted them. Some were created by a legislature, in the form of statutory enactments. Others were created by judges who formulated them to decide particular cases, and thus established them as precedents for the future. But this test of pedigree will not work for the *Riggs* and *Henningsen* principles. The origin of these as legal principles lies not in a particular decision of some legislature or court, but in a sense of appropriateness developed in the profession and the public over time. Their continued power depends upon this sense of appropriateness being sustained. If it no longer seemed unfair to allow people to profit by their wrongs, or fair to place special burdens upon oligopolies that manufacture potentially dangerous machines, these principles would no longer play much of a role in new cases, even if they had never been overruled or repealed. (Indeed, it hardly makes sense to speak of principles like these as being "overruled" or "repealed." When they decline they are eroded, not torpedoed.)

True, if we were challenged to back up our claim that some principle is a principle of law, we would mention any prior cases in which that principle was cited, or figured in the argument. We would also mention any statute that seemed to exemplify that principle (even better if the principle was cited in the preamble of the statute, or in the committee reports or other legislative documents that accompanied it). Unless we could find some such institutional support, we would probably fail to make out our case, and the more support we found, the more weight we could claim for the principle.

Yet we could not devise any formula for testing how much and what kind of institutional support is necessary to make a principle a legal principle, still less to fix its weight at a particular order of magnitude. We argue for a particular principle by grappling with a whole set of shifting, developing and interacting standards (themselves principles rather than rules) about institutional responsibility, statutory interpretation, the persuasive force of various sorts of precedent, the relation of all these to contemporary moral practices, and hosts of other such standards. We could not bolt all of these together into a single "rule," even a complex one, and if we could the result would bear little relation to Hart's picture of a rule of recognition, which is the picture of a fairly stable master rule specifying "some feature or features possession of which by a suggested rule is taken as a conclusive affirmative indicating that it is a rule. . . ."[9]

Moreover, the techniques we apply in arguing for another principle do not stand (as Hart's rule of recognition is designed to) on an entirely different level from the principles they support. Hart's sharp distinction between acceptance and validity does not hold. If we are arguing for the principle that a man should not profit from his own wrong, we could cite the acts of courts and legislatures that exemplify it, but this speaks as much to the principle's acceptance as its validity. (It seems odd to speak of a principle as being valid at all, perhaps because validity is an all-or-nothing concept, appropriate for rules, but inconsistent with a principle's dimension of weight.) If we are asked (as we might well be) to defend the particular doctrine of precedent, or the particular technique of statutory interpretation, that we used in this argument, we should certainly cite the practice of others in using that doctrine or technique. But we should also cite other general principles that we believe support that practice, and this introduces a note of validity into the chord of acceptance. We might argue, for example, that the use we make of earlier cases and statutes is supported by a particular analysis of the point of practice of legislation or the doctrine of precedent, or by the principles of democratic theory, or by a particular position on the proper division of authority between national and local institutions, or something else of that sort. Nor is this path of support a one-way street leading to some ultimate principle resting on acceptance alone. Our principles of legislation, precedent, democracy, or federalism might be challenged too; and if they were we should argue for them, not only in terms of practice, but in terms of each other and in terms of the implications of trends of judicial and legislative decisions, even though this last would involve appealing to those same doctrines of interpretation we justified through the principles we are now trying to support. At this level of abstraction, in other words, principles rather hang together than link together.

So even though principles draw support from the official acts of legal institutions, they do not have a simple or direct enough connection with these acts to frame that connection in terms of criteria specified by some ultimate master rule of recognition. . . .

NOTES

[1]*See* H. L. A. Hart, The Concept of Law 89–96 (1961).
[2]*Id.* at 97–107.

[3]*See* Dworkin, *Wasserstrom: The Judicial Decision*, 75 Ethics 47 (1964), reprinted as *Does Law Have a Function?*, 74 Yale L. J. 640 (1965).
[4]115 N.Y. 506, 22 N.E. 188 (1889).
[5]32 N.J. 358, 161 A.2d 69 (1960).
[6]*Id.* at 389, 161 A.2d at 86 (quoting Frankfurter, J., in *United States v. Bethlehem Steel*, 315 U.S. 289, 326 (1942).
[7]*Id.*
[8]*Standard Oil v. United States*, 221 U.S. 1, 60 (1911); *United States v. American Tobacco Co.*, 221 U.S. 106, 180 (1911).

REVIEW AND DISCUSSION QUESTIONS

1. What are the three key tenets of positivism, according to Dworkin?
2. Explain the role of principles in *Riggs v. Palmer*.
3. Principles in the general sense include two sorts of standards. What are the two?
4. How do principles differ from rules, according to Dworkin?
5. Why cannot Hart modify his view to include principles, according to Dworkin?

"Natural" Law Revisited

Ronald Dworkin

Ronald Dworkin begins this essay with a brief discussion of "naturalism," or natural law, indicating that the view he wishes to defend can best be understood to fall within that general camp. He goes on to explain his theory of law with the example of a "chain novel" in which each author is responsible for taking the chapters by previous writers and continuing the novel. With this he illustrates the two dimensions of legal or literary interpretation: fit and justification. He then explains how his theory of law, which began with questions of interpretation, belongs within the natural law tradition.

Everyone likes categories, and legal philosophers like them very much. So we spend a good deal of time, not all of it profitably, labeling ourselves and the theories of law we defend. One label, however, is particularly dreaded: no one wants to be called a natural lawyer. Natural law insists that what the law is depends in some way on what the law should be. This seems metaphysical or at least vaguely religious. In any case it seems plainly wrong. If some theory of law is shown to be a natural law theory, therefore, people can be excused if they do not attend to it much further.

. . . If the crude description of natural law I just gave is correct, that any theory which makes the content of law sometimes depend on the correct answer to some moral question is a natural law theory, then I am guilty of natural law. I am not now interested, I should add, in whether this crude characterization is historically correct, or whether it succeeds in distinguishing natural law from positivist theories of law. My present concern is rather this. Suppose this *is* natural law. What in the world is wrong with it?

A. NATURALISM

I shall start by giving the picture of adjudication I want to defend a name, and it is a name which accepts the crude characterization. I shall call this picture naturalism. According to naturalism, judges should decide hard cases by interpreting the political structure of their community in the following, perhaps special way: by trying to find the best *justification* they can find, in principles of political morality, for the structure as a whole, from the most profound constitutional rules and arrangements to the details of, for example, the private law of tort or contract. Suppose the question arises for the first time, for example, whether and in what circumstances careless drivers are liable, not only for physical injuries to those whom they run down, but also for any emotional damage suffered by relatives of the victim who are watching. According to naturalism, judges should then ask the following questions of the history (including the contemporary history) of their political structure. Does the best possible justification of that history suppose a principle according to which people who are injured emotionally in this way have a right to recover damages in court? If so, what, more precisely, is that principle? Does it entail, for example, that only immediate relatives of the person physically injured have that right? Or only relatives on the scene of the accident, who might themselves have suffered physical damage?

Of course a judge who is faced with these questions in an actual case cannot undertake anything like a full justification of all parts of the constitutional arrangement, statutory system and judicial precedents that make up his "law." I had to invent a mythical judge, called Hercules, with superhuman powers in order even to contemplate what a full justification of the entire system would be like.[1] Real judges can attempt only what we might call a partial justification of the law. They can try to justify, under some set of principles, those parts of the legal background which seem to them immediately relevant, like, for example, the prior judicial decisions about recovery for various sorts of damage in automobile accidents. Nevertheless it is useful to describe this as a partial justification—as a part of what Hercules himself would do—in order to emphasize that, according to this picture, a judge should regard the law he mines and studies as embedded in a much larger system, so that it is

always relevant for him to expand his investigation by asking whether the conclusions he reaches are consistent with what he would have discovered had his study been wider.

It is obvious why this theory of adjudication invites the charge of natural law. It makes each judge's decision about the burden of past law depend on his judgment about the best political justification of that law, and this is of course a matter of political morality. Before I consider whether this provides a fatal defect in the theory, however, I must try to show how the theory might work in practice. . . .

B. THE CHAIN NOVEL

Imagine, then, that a group of novelists is engaged for a particular project. They draw lots to determine the order of play. The lowest number writes the opening chapter of a novel, which he then sends to the next number who is given the following assignment. He must add a chapter to that novel, which he must write so as to make the novel being constructed the best novel it can be. When he completes his chapter, he then sends the two chapters to the next novelist, who has the same assignment, and so forth. Now every novelist but the first has the responsibility of interpreting what has gone before in the sense of interpretation I described for a naturalist judge. Each novelist must decide what the characters are "really" like; what motives in fact guide them; what the point or theme of the developing novel is; how far some literary device or figure consciously or unconsciously used can be said to contribute to these, and therefore should be extended, refined, trimmed or dropped. He must decide all this in order to send the novel further in one direction rather than another. But all these decisions must be made, in accordance with the directions given, by asking which decisions make the continuing novel better as a novel.

Some novels have in fact been written in this way (including the soft-core pornographic novel *Naked Came the Stranger*) though for a debunking purpose, and certain parlor games, for rainy weekends in English country houses, have something of the same structure. But in this case the novelists are expected to take their responsibilities seriously, and to recognize the duty to create, so far as they can, a single unified novel rather than, for example, a series of independent short stories with characters bearing the same names. Perhaps this is an impossible assignment; perhaps the project is doomed to produce, not simply an impossibly bad novel, but no novel at all, because the best theory of art requires a single creator, or if more than one, that each have some control over the whole. (But what about legends and jokes? What about the Old Testament, or, on some theories, the *Iliad?*) I need not push that question further, because I am interested only in the fact that the assignment makes sense, that each of the novelists in the chain can have some sense of what he or she is asked to do, whatever misgivings each might have about the value or character of what will then be produced.

The crucial question each must face is this. What is the difference between continuing the novel in the best possible way, by writing plot and development that can be seen to flow from what has gone before, and starting a fresh novel with characters having the same names? Suppose you are a novelist well down the chain, and are handed several chapters which are, in fact, the first sections of the Dickens short novel *A Christmas Carol*. You consider these two interpretations of the central character: that Scrooge is irredeemably, inherently evil, and so an example of the degradation of which human nature is intrinsically capable, or that Scrooge is inherently good, but progressively corrupted by the false values and perverse demands of high capitalist society. The interpretation you adopt will obviously make an enormous difference in the way you continue the story. You aim, in accordance with your instructions, to make the continuing novel the best novel it can be; but you must nevertheless choose an interpretation that makes the novel a single work of art. So you will have to respect the text you have been given, and not choose an interpretation that you believe the text rules out. The picture that text gives of Scrooge's early life, for example, might be incompatible with the claim that he is inherently wicked. In that case you have no choice. If, on the other hand, the text is equally consistent with both interpretations, then you do have

a choice. You will choose the interpretation that you believe makes the work more significant or otherwise better, and this will probably (though not inevitably) depend on whether you think people like Scrooge are in fact, in the real world, born bad or corrupted by capitalism.

Now consider a more complex case. Suppose the text does not absolutely rule out either interpretation, but is marginally less consistent with one, which is, however, the interpretation you would pick if they both fit equally well. Suppose you believe that the original sin interpretation (as we might call it) is much the more accurate depiction of human nature. But if you choose that interpretation you will have to regard certain incidents and attributions established in the text you were given as "mistakes." You must then ask yourself which interpretation makes the work of art better *on the whole*, recognizing, as you will, that a novel whose plot is inconsistent or otherwise lacks integrity is thereby flawed. You must ask whether the novel is still better as a novel, read as a study of original sin, even though it must now be regarded as containing some "mistakes" in plot, than it would be with fewer "mistakes" but a less revealing picture of human nature. You may never have reflected on that question before, but that is no reason why you may not do so now, and once you make up your mind you will believe that the correct interpretation of Scrooge's character is the interpretation that makes the novel better on the whole.

C. THE CHAIN OF LAW

Naturalism is a theory of adjudication not of the interpretation of novels. But naturalism supposes that common law adjudication is a chain enterprise sharing many of the features of the story we invented. According to naturalism, a judge should decide fresh cases in the spirit of a novelist in the chain writing a fresh chapter. The judge must make creative decisions, but must try to make these decisions "going on as before" rather than by starting in a new direction as if writing on a clean slate. He must read through (or have some good idea through his legal training and experience) what other judges in the past have written, not simply to discover what these other judges have said, or their state of mind when they said it, but to reach an opinion about what they have collectively *done*, in the way that each of our novelists formed an opinion about the collective novel so far written. Of course, the best interpretation of past judicial decisions is the interpretation that shows these in the best light, not aesthetically but politically, as coming as close to the correct ideals of a just legal system as possible. Judges in the chain of law share with the chain novelists the imperative of interpretation, but they bring different standards of success—political rather than aesthetic—to bear on that enterprise.

The analogy shows, I hope, how far naturalism allows a judge's beliefs about the personal and political rights people have "naturally"— that is, apart from the law—to enter his judgments about what the law requires. It does not instruct him to regard these beliefs as the only test of law. A judge's background and moral convictions will influence his decisions about what legal rights people have under the law. But the brute facts of legal history will nevertheless limit the role these convictions can play in those decisions. The same distinction we found in literary interpretation, between interpretation and ideal, holds here as well. An Agatha Christie mystery thriller cannot be interpreted as a philosophical novel about the meaning of death even by someone who believes that a successful philosophical novel would be a greater literary achievement than a successful mystery. It cannot be interpreted that way because, if it is, too much of the book must be seen as accidental, and too little as integrated, in plot, style and trope, with its alleged genre or point. Interpreted that way it becomes a shambles and so a failure rather than a success at anything at all. In the same way, a judge cannot plausibly discover, in a long and unbroken string of prior judicial decisions in favor of the manufacturers of defective products, any principle establishing strong consumers' rights. For that discovery would not show the history of judicial practice in a better light; on the contrary it would show it as the history of cynicism and inconsistency, perhaps of incoherence. A naturalist judge must

show the facts of history in the best light he can, and this means that he must not show that history as unprincipled chaos.

Of course this responsibility, for judges as well as novelists, may best be fulfilled by a dramatic reinterpretation that both unifies what has gone before and gives it new meaning or point. This explains why a naturalist decision, though it is in this way tied to the past, may yet seem radical. A naturalist judge might find, in some principle that has not yet been recognized in judicial argument, a brilliantly unifying account of past decisions that shows them in a better light than ever before. American legal education celebrates dozens of such events in our own history. In the most famous single common law decision in American jurisprudence, for example, Cardozo reinterpreted a variety of cases to find, in these cases, the principle on which the modern law of negligence was built.

Nevertheless the constraint, that a judge must continue the past and not invent a better past, will often have the consequence that a naturalist judge cannot reach decisions that he would otherwise, given his own political theory, want to reach. A judge who, as a matter of political conviction, believes in consumers' rights may nevertheless have to concede that the law of his jurisdiction has rejected this idea. It is in one way misleading to say, however, that he will be then forced to make decisions *at variance with* his political convictions. The principle that judges should decide consistently with principle, and that law should be coherent, is part of his convictions, and it is this principle that makes the decision he otherwise opposes necessary.

D. INTERPRETATION IN PRACTICE

In this section I shall try to show how a self-conscious naturalist judge might construct a working approach to adjudication, and the role his background moral and political convictions would play in that working approach. When we imagined you to be a novelist in the chain novel, several pages ago, we considered how you would continue the first few chapters of *A Christmas Carol*. We distinguished two dimensions of a successful interpretation. An interpretation must "fit" the data it interprets, in order not to show the novel as sloppy or incoherent, and it must also show that data in its best light, as serving as well as can be some proper ambition of novels. Just now, in noticing how a naturalist judge who believed in consumers' rights might nevertheless have to abandon the claim that consumers' rights are embedded in legal history, . . . the same distinction between these two dimensions was relied upon. A naturalist judge would be forced to reject a politically attractive interpretation, we supposed, simply because he did not believe it fit the record well enough. If fit is indeed an independent dimension of success in interpretation, then any judge's working approach would include some tacit conception of what "fit" is, and of how well a particular interpretation must fit the record of judicial and other legal decisions in order to count as acceptable.

This helps us to explain why two naturalist judges might reach different interpretations of past judicial decisions about accidents, for example. They might hold different conceptions of "fit" or "best fit," so that, for instance, one thinks that an interpretation provides an acceptable fit only if it is supported by the opinions of judges in prior cases, while the other thinks it is sufficient, to satisfy the dimension of fit, that an interpretation fit the actual decisions these judges reached even if it finds no echo in their opinions. This difference might be enough to explain, for example, why one judge could accept an "economic" interpretation of the accident cases—that the point of negligence law is to reduce the overall social costs of accidents—while another judge, who also found that interpretation politically congenial, would feel bound by his beliefs about the requirement of fit to reject it.

At some point, however, this explanation of differences between two judges' theories of the same body of law would become strained and artificial. Suppose Judge X believes, for example, that pedestrians ought to look out for themselves, and have no business walking in areas in which drivers are known normally to exceed the legal speed limit. He might rely on this opinion in deciding that "our law recognizes no general right to recover whenever someone is injured by a speeding driver while walking on a highway where most drivers speed." If Judge Y reaches a different judgment about what the law is, because he believes that pedestrians should be entitled to assume that people will obey the law even when there is good evidence that they will not, then it would strain language to explain this difference by saying that these judges disagree about the way or the degree in which an interpretation of the law must fit past decisions. We would do better to say that these judges interpret the law differently, in this instance, because they bring different background theories of political morality to their interpretations just as two art critics might disagree about the correct interpretation of impressionism because they bring different theories about the value of art to that exercise.

Any naturalist judge's working approach to interpretation will recognize this distinction between two "dimensions" of interpretations of the prior law, and so we might think of such a theory as falling into two parts. One part refines and develops the idea that an interpretation must fit the data it interprets. This part takes up positions on questions like the following. How many decisions (roughly) can an interpretation set aside as mistakes, and still count as an interpretation of the string of decisions that includes those "mistakes"? How far is an interpretation better if it is more consistent with later rather than earlier past decisions? How far and in what way must a good interpretation fit the opinions judges write as well as the decisions they make? How far must it take account of popular morality contemporary with the decisions it offers to interpret? A second part of any judge's tacit theory of interpretation, however, will be quite independent of these "formal" issues. It will contain the substantive ideals of political morality on which he relies in deciding whether any putative interpretation is to be preferred because it shows legal practice to be better as a matter of substantive justice. Of course, if any working approach to interpretation has these two parts, then it must also have principles that combine or adjudicate between them.

This account of the main structure of a working theory of interpretation has heuristic appeal. It provides judges, and others who interpret the law, with a model they might use in identifying the approach they have been using, and self-consciously to inspect and improve that model. A thoughtful judge might establish for himself, for example, a rough "threshold" of fit which any interpretation of data must meet in order to be "acceptable" on the dimension of fit, and then suppose that if more than one interpretation of some part of the law meets this threshold, the choice among these should be made, not through further and more precise comparisons between the two along that dimension, but by choosing the interpretation which is "substantively" better, that is, which better promotes the political ideals he thinks correct. Such a judge might say, for example, that since both the foreseeability and the area-of-physical-risk interpretations rise above the threshold of fit with the emotional damage cases I mentioned earlier, foreseeability is better *as an interpretation* because it better accords with the "natural" rights of people injured in accidents. . . .

. . . The idea of a threshold of fit, and therefore of a lexical ordering between the two dimensions, is simply a working hypothesis, valuable so far as the impressionistic characterization of fit on which it depends is adequate, but which must be abandoned in favor of a more sophisticated and piecemeal analysis when the occasion demands.

Of course the moment when more sophisticated analysis becomes necessary because the impressionistic distinction of the working theory no longer serves, is a moment of difficulty calling for fresh political judgments that may be hard to make. Suppose a judge faces, for the first time, the possibility of overruling a narrow rule followed for some time in his jurisdiction. Suppose, for example, that the courts have consistently held, since the issue was first raised, that lawyers may not be sued in negligence. Our judge believes that this rule is wrong and unjust, and that it is inconsistent in principle with the general rule allowing actions in negligence against other professional people like doctors and accountants. Suppose he can nevertheless find some putative principle, in which others find [merit] though he does not, which would justify the distinction the law has drawn. Like the principle, for example, that because lawyers owe obligations to the courts or to abstract justice it would be unfair to impose on them the legal obligation of due care to their clients. He must ask whether the best interpretation of the past includes *that* principle in spite of the fact that he himself would reject it.

Neither answer to this question will seem wholly attractive to him. If he holds that the law does include this putative principle, then this argument would present the law, including the past decisions about suits against lawyers as coherent; but he would then expose what he would believe to be a flaw in the substantive law. He would be supposing that the law includes a principle he believes is wrong, and therefore has no place in a just and wise system. If he decides that the law does not include the putative principle, on the other hand, then he can properly regard this entire line of cases about actions against lawyers as mistakes, and ignore or overrule them; but he then exposes a flaw in the record of a different sort, namely that past judges have acted in an unprincipled way, and a demerit in his own decision, that it treats the lawyer who loses the present case differently from how judges have treated other lawyers in the past. He must ask which is, in the end, the greater of these flaws; which way of reading the record shows it, in the last analysis, in the better and which in the worse light.

It would be absurd to suppose that all the lawyers and judges of any common law community share some set of convictions from which a single answer to that question could be deduced. Or even that many lawyers or judges would have ready at hand some convictions of their own which could supply an answer without further ado. But it is nevertheless possible for any judge to confront issues like these in a principled way, and this is what naturalism demands of him. He must accept that in deciding one way rather than another about the force of a line of precedents, for example, he is developing a working theory of legal interpretation in one rather than another direction, and this must seem to him the right direction as a matter of political principle, not simply an appealing direction for the moment because he likes the answer it recommends in the immediate case before him. Of course there is, in this counsel, much room for deception, including self-deception. But in most cases it will be possible for judges to recognize when they have submitted some issue to the discipline this description requires and also to recognize when some other judge has not.

Let me recapitulate. Interpretation is not a mechanical process. Nevertheless, judges can form working styles of interpretation, adequate for routine cases, and ready for refinement when cases are not routine. These working styles will include what I called formal features. They will set out, impressionistically, an account of fit, and may characterize a threshold of fit an interpretation must achieve in order to be eligible. But they will also contain a substantive part, formed from the judge's background political morality, or rather that part of his background morality which has become articulate in the course of his career. Sometimes this heuristic distinction between fit and substantive justice, as dimensions of a successful interpretation, will itself seem problematic, and a judge will be forced to elaborate that distinction by reflecting further on the full set of the substantive and procedural political rights of citizens a just legal system must respect and serve. In this way any truly hard case develops as well as engages a judge's style of adjudication.

NOTE

[1] R. Dworkin, *Taking Rights Seriously* 105–130 (1977).

REVIEW AND DISCUSSION QUESTIONS

1. How does Dworkin define "naturalism"?

2. What is the "chain novel"?

3. Describe the two dimensions of interpretation used in legal adjudication.

4. Discuss the example of lawyers' being exempt from negligence lawsuits, explaining how it illustrates Dworkin's theory of law.

5. In what sense is Dworkin a "natural lawyer"?

6. Explain whether Dworkin is more of a realist or a formalist.

7. How does Dworkin (as a naturalist) analyze the dilemma of an antislavery judge deciding whether to enforce the Fugitive Slave Law and return a runaway slave to his owner?

8. It is sometimes said that following Dworkin's recommendation would mean that judges have more discretion than they should have or than they in fact do have. Do you agree? How could Dworkin respond?

8

LAW AND ECONOMICS

The law and economics movement is one of the most important in contemporary legal theory. Its basic claim is that by applying the tools of economic analysis, we are able to interpret much of the law in a way that makes the law both coherent and sound. Central to this approach, as described by Judge Richard Posner—one of its most important defenders—is the goal of securing as much "wealth" for society as possible. "Wealth" is here defined as being both the monetary and nonmonetary satisfaction of people based on willingness to pay. Thus, if you refuse to purchase an inexpensive safety device and your machinery causes serious injury, you may have acted unreasonably (in the sense that you have reduced total satisfaction by not taking the most cost-effective measures). According to law and economics, the law should hold you liable since that would have the effect of encouraging others to act in a more economically rational way in the future. Following Posner's discussion of this approach is a more detailed discussion by Andrew Altman of the value and the limits of the law and economics legal theory.

The Economic Approach to Law

Richard A. Posner

Among the recent developments in legal thinking has been a resurgence of interest in the connections between economic theory and law. Richard Posner is among the most important figures of the law and economics movement. In this selection, taken from his recent book, Posner first sets out the major tenets of his approach including legislative bargains, the nature of wealth maximization, and the ca-

pacity of judges to promote efficiency. He shows that by viewing law as wealth maximizing rules, we can understand not only contract and property law, but tort and criminal law as well. Richard Posner is a federal judge and professor of law at the University of Chicago Law School.

The most ambitious and probably the most influential effort in recent years to elaborate an overarching concept of justice that will both explain judicial decision making and place it on an objective basis is that of scholars working in the interdisciplinary field of "law and economics," as economic analysis of law is usually called. . . .

The basic assumption of economics that guides the version of economic analysis of law that I shall be presenting is that people are rational maximizers of their satisfactions—*all* people (with the exception of small children and the profoundly retarded) in *all* of their activities (except when under the influence of psychosis or similarly deranged through drug or alcohol abuse) that involve choice. Because this definition embraces the criminal deciding whether to commit another crime, the litigant deciding whether to settle or litigate a case, the legislator deciding whether to vote for or against a bill, the judge deciding how to cast his vote in a case, the party to a contract deciding whether to break it, the driver deciding how fast to drive, and the pedestrian deciding how boldly to cross the street, as well as the usual economic actors, such as businessmen and consumers, it is apparent that most activities either regulated by or occurring within the legal system are grist for the economic analyst's mill. It should go without saying that nonmonetary as well as monetary satisfactions enter into the individual's calculus of maximizing (indeed, money for most people is a means rather than an end) and that decisions, to be rational, need not be well thought out at the conscious level—indeed, need not be conscious at all. Recall that "rational" denotes suiting means to ends, rather than mulling things over, and that much of our knowledge is tacit.

Since my interest is in legal doctrines and institutions, it will be best to begin at the legislative (including the constitutional) level. I assume that legislators are rational maximizers of their satisfactions just like everyone else. Thus nothing they do is motivated by the public interest as such. But they want to be elected and reelected, and they need money to wage an effective campaign. This money is more likely to be forthcoming from well-organized groups than from unorganized individuals. The rational individual knows that his contribution is unlikely to make a difference; for this reason and also because voters in most elections are voting for candidates rather than policies, which further weakens the link between casting one's vote and obtaining one's preferred policy, the rational individual will have little incentive to invest time and effort in deciding whom to vote for. Only an organized group of individuals (or firms or other organizations—but these are just conduits for individuals) will be able to overcome the informational and free-rider problems that plague collective action.[1] But such a group will not organize and act effectively unless its members have much to gain or much to lose from specific policies, as tobacco farmers, for example, have much to gain from federal subsidies for growing tobacco and much to lose from the withdrawal of those subsidies. The basic tactic of an interest group is to trade the votes of its members and its financial support to candidates in exchange for an implied promise of favorable legislation. Such legislation will normally take the form of a statute transferring wealth from unorganized taxpayers (for example, consumers) to the interest group. If the target were another interest group, the legislative transfer might be effectively opposed. The unorganized are unlikely to mount effective opposition, and it is their wealth, therefore, that typically is transferred to interest groups.

On this view, a statute is a deal. . . . But because of the costs of transactions within a multi-headed legislative body, and the costs of effective communication through time, legislation does not spring full-grown from the head of the legislature; it needs interpretation and application, and this is the role of the courts. They are agents of the legislature. But to impart credibility and durability to the deals the legislature strikes with interest groups, courts must be able to resist the wishes of current legislators who want to undo their predecessors' deals yet cannot do so through repeal because the costs of passing legislation (whether original or amended) are so high, and who might therefore look to the courts for a repealing "interpretation." The impediments to legislation actually facilitate rather than retard the striking of deals, by giving interest groups some assurance that a deal struck with the legislature will not promptly be undone by repeal. An independent judiciary is one of the impediments.

Judicial independence makes the judges imperfect agents of the legislature. This is tolerable not only for the reason just mentioned but also because an independent judiciary is necessary for the resolution of ordinary disputes in a way that will encourage trade, travel, freedom of action, and other highly valued activities or conditions and will minimize the expenditure of resources on influencing governmental action. Legislators might appear to have little to gain from these widely diffused rule-of-law virtues. But if the aggregate benefits from a particular social policy are very large and no interest group's ox is gored, legislators may find it in their own interest to support the policy. Voters understand in a rough way the benefits to them of national defense, crime control, dispute settlement, and the other elements of the night watchman state, and they will not vote for legislators who refuse to provide these basic public services. It is only when those services are in place, and when (usually later) effective means of taxation and redistribution develop, that the formation of narrow interest groups and the extraction by them of transfers from unorganized groups become feasible.

The judges thus have a dual role: to interpret the interest-group deals embodied in legislation and to provide the basic public service of authoritative dispute resolution. They perform the latter function not only by deciding cases in accordance with preexisting norms, but also—especially in the Anglo-American legal system—by elaborating those norms. They fashioned the common law out of customary practices, out of ideas borrowed from statutes and from other legal systems (for example, Roman law), and out of their own conceptions of public policy. The

law they created exhibits, according to the economic theory that I am expounding, a remarkable substantive consistency. It is as if the judges *wanted* to adopt the rules, procedures, and case outcomes that would maximize society's wealth.

I must pause to define "wealth maximization," a term often misunderstood. The "wealth" in "wealth maximization" refers to the sum of all tangible and intangible goods and services, weighted by prices of two sorts: offer prices (what people are willing to pay for goods they do not already own); and asking prices (what people demand to sell what they do own). If A would be willing to pay up to $100 for B's stamp collection, it is worth $100 to A. If B would be willing to sell the stamp collection for any price above $90, it is worth $90 to B. So if B sells the stamp collection to A (say for $100, but the analysis is qualitatively unaffected at any price between $90 and $100—and it is only in that range that a transaction will occur), the wealth of society will rise by $10. Before the transaction A had $100 in cash and B had a stamp collection worth $90 (a total of $190); After the transaction A has a stamp collection worth $100 and B has $100 in cash (a total of $200). The transaction will not raise measured wealth—gross national product, national income, or whatever—by $10; it will not raise it at all unless the transaction is recorded, and if it is recorded it is likely to raise measured wealth by the full $100 purchase price. But the real addition to social wealth consists of the $10 increment in *nonpecuniary* satisfaction that A derives from the purchase, compared with that of B. This shows that "wealth" in the economist's sense is not a simple monetary measure. . . .

[I]f I am given a choice between remaining in a job in which I work forty hours a week for $1,000 and switching to a job in which I would work thirty hours for $500, and I decide to make the switch, the extra ten hours of leisure must be worth at least $500 to me, yet GNP will fall when I reduce my hours of work. Suppose the extra hours of leisure are worth $600 to me, so that my full income rises from $1,000 to $1,100 when I reduce my hours. My former employer presumably is made worse off by my leaving (else why did he employ me?), but not more than

$100 worse off; for if he were, he would offer to pay me a shade over $1,100 a week to stay—and I would stay. (The example abstracts from income tax.)

Wealth is *related* to money, in that a desire not backed by ability to pay has no standing—such a desire is neither an offer price nor an asking price. I may desperately desire a BMW, but if I am unwilling or unable to pay its purchase price, society's wealth would not be increased by transferring the BMW from its present owner to me. Abandon this essential constraint (an important distinction, also, between wealth maximization and utilitarianism—for I might derive greater utility from the BMW than its present owner or anyone else to whom he might sell the car), and the way is open to tolerating the crimes committed by the passionate and the avaricious against the cold and the frugal.

The common law facilitates wealth-maximizing transactions in a variety of ways. It recognizes property rights, and these facilitate exchange. It also protects property rights, through tort and criminal law. (Although today criminal law is almost entirely statutory, the basic criminal protections—for example, those against murder, assault, rape, and theft—have, as one might expect, common law origins.) Through contract law it protects the process of exchange. And it establishes procedural rules for resolving disputes in these various fields as efficiently as possible.

The illustrations given thus far of wealth-maximizing transactions have been of transactions that are voluntary in the strict sense of making everyone affected by them better off, or at least no worse off. Every transaction has been assumed to affect just two parties, each of whom has been made better off by it. Such a transaction is said to be Pareto superior [i.e., at least one person is better off, and nobody is worse off], but Pareto superiority is not a necessary condition for a transaction to be wealth maximizing. Consider an accident that inflicts a cost of $100 with a probability of .01 and that would have cost $3 to avoid. The accident is a wealth-maximizing "transaction" . . . because the expected accident cost ($1) is less than the cost of avoidance. (I am assuming risk neutrality. Risk aversion would complicate the analysis but not

change it fundamentally.) It is wealth maximizing even if the victim is not compensated. The result is consistent with Learned Hand's formula, which defines negligence as the failure to take cost-justified precautions. If the only precaution that would have averted the accident is not cost-justified, the failure to take it is not negligent and the injurer will not have to compensate the victim for the costs of the accident.

If it seems artificial to speak of the accident as the transaction, consider instead the potential transaction that consists of purchasing the safety measure that would have avoided the accident. Since a potential victim would not pay $3 to avoid an expected accident cost of $1, his offer price will be less than the potential injurer's asking price and the transaction will not be wealth maximizing. But if these figures were reversed—if an expected accident cost of $3 could be averted at a cost of $1—the transaction would be wealth maximizing, and a liability rule administered in accordance with the Hand formula would give potential injurers an incentive to take the measures that potential victims would pay them to take if voluntary transactions were feasible. The law would be overcoming transaction-cost obstacles to wealth-maximizing transactions—a frequent office of liability rules.

The wealth-maximizing properties of common law rules have been elucidated at considerable length in the literature of the economic analysis of law. Such doctrines as conspiracy, general average (admiralty), contributory negligence, equitable servitudes, employment at will, the standard for granting preliminary injunctions, entrapment, the contract defense of impossibility, the collateral-benefits rule, the expectation measure of damages, assumption of risk, attempt, invasion of privacy, wrongful interference with contract rights, the availability of punitive damages in some cases but not others, privilege in the law of evidence, official immunity, and the doctrine of moral consideration have been found—at least by some contributors to this literature—to conform to the dictates of wealth maximization. . . . It has even been argued that the system of precedent itself has an economic equilibrium. Precedents are created as a by-product of litigation. The greater the number of recent precedents in an area, the lower the rate of litigation will be. In particular, cases involving disputes over legal as distinct from purely factual issues will be settled. The existence of abundant, highly informative (in part because recent) precedents will enable the parties to legal disputes to form more convergent estimates of the likely outcome of a trial, and . . . if both parties agree on the outcome of trial they will settle beforehand because a trial is more costly than a settlement. But with less litigation, fewer new precedents will be produced, and the existing precedents will obsolesce as changing circumstances render them less apt and informative. So the rate of litigation will rise, producing more precedents and thereby causing the rate of litigation again to fall.

This analysis does not explain what drives judges to decide common law cases in accordance with the dictates of wealth maximization. Prosperity, however, which wealth maximization measures more sensitively than purely monetary measures such as GNP, is a relatively uncontroversial policy, and most judges try to steer clear of controversy: their age, method of compensation, and relative weakness vis-à-vis the other branches of government make the avoidance of controversy attractive. It probably is no accident, therefore, that many common law doctrines assumed their modern form in the nineteenth century, when laissez-faire ideology, which resembles wealth maximization, had a strong hold on the Anglo-American judicial imagination. . . .

It may be objected that in assigning ideology as a cause of judicial behavior, the economist strays outside the boundaries of his discipline; but he need not rest on ideology. The economic analysis of legislation implies that fields of law left to the judges to elaborate, such as the common law fields, must be the ones in which interest-group pressures are too weak to deflect the legislature from pursuing goals that are in the general interest. Prosperity is one of these goals, and one that judges are especially well equipped to promote. The rules of the common law that they promulgate attach prices to socially undesirable conduct, whether free riding or imposing social costs

without corresponding benefits.[2] By doing this the rules create incentives to avoid such conduct, and these incentives foster prosperity. In contrast, judges can, despite appearances, do little to redistribute wealth. A rule that makes it easy for poor tenants to break leases with rich landlords, for example, will induce landlords to raise rents in order to offset the costs that such a rule imposes, and tenants will bear the brunt of these higher costs. Indeed, the principal redistribution accomplished by such a rule may be from the prudent, responsible tenant, who may derive little or no benefit from having additional legal rights to use against landlords—rights that enable a tenant to avoid or postpone eviction for nonpayment of rental—to the feckless tenant. That is a capricious redistribution. Legislatures, however, have by virtue of their taxing and spending powers powerful tools for redistributing wealth. So an efficient division of labor between the legislative and judicial branches has the legislative branch concentrate on catering to interest-group demands for wealth distribution and the judicial branch on meeting the broad-based social demand for efficient rules governing safety, property, and transactions. Although there are other possible goals of judicial action besides efficiency and redistribution, many of these (various conceptions of "fairness" and "justice") are labels for wealth maximization, or for redistribution in favor of powerful interest groups; or else they are too controversial in a heterogeneous society, too ad hoc, or insufficiently developed to provide judges who desire a reputation for objectivity and disinterest with adequate grounds for their decisions.

Finally, even if judges have little commitment to efficiency, their inefficient decisions will, by definition, impose greater social costs than their efficient ones will. As a result, losers of cases decided mistakenly from an economic standpoint will have a greater incentive, on average, to press for correction through appeal, new litigation, or legislative action than losers of cases decided soundly from an economic standpoint—so there will be a steady pressure for efficient results. Moreover, cases litigated under inefficient rules tend to involve larger stakes than cases litigated under efficient rules (for the inefficient rules, by definition, generate social waste), and the larger the stakes in a dispute the likelier it is to be litigated rather than settled; so judges will have a chance to reconsider the inefficient rule.

Thus we should not be surprised to see the common law tending to become efficient, although since the incentives of judges to perform well along any dimension are weak (this is a by-product of judicial independence), we cannot expect the law ever to achieve perfect efficiency. Since wealth maximization is not only a guide in fact to common law judging but also a genuine social value and the only one judges are in a good position to promote, it provides not only the key to an accurate description of what the judges are up to but also the right benchmark for criticism and reform. If judges are failing to maximize wealth, the economic analyst of law will urge them to alter practice or doctrine accordingly. In addition, the analyst will urge—on any legislator sufficiently free of interest-group pressures to be able to legislate in the public interest—a program of enacting only legislation that conforms to the dictates of wealth maximization.

Besides generating both predictions and prescriptions, the economic approach enables the common law to be reconceived in simple, coherent terms and to be applied more objectively than traditional lawyers would think possible. From the premise that the common law does and should seek to maximize society's wealth, the economic analyst can deduce in logical—if you will, formalist—fashion (economic theory is formulated nowadays largely in mathematical terms) the set of legal doctrines that will express and perfect the inner nature of the common law, and can compare these doctrines with the actual doctrines of common law. After translating from the economic vocabulary back into the legal one, the analyst will find that most of the actual doctrines are tolerable approximations to the implications of economic theory and so far formalistically valid. Where there are discrepancies, the path to reform is clear—yet the judge who takes the path cannot be accused of making rather than finding law, for he is merely contributing to the program of realizing the essential nature of the common law.

The project of reducing the common law—with its many separate fields, its thousands of separate doctrines, its hundreds of thousands of reported decisions—to a handful of mathematical formulas may seem quixotic, but the economic analyst can give reasons for doubting this assessment. Much of the doctrinal luxuriance of common law is seen to be superficial once the essentially economic nature of the common law is understood. A few principles, such as cost-benefit analysis, the prevention of free riding, decision under uncertainty, risk aversion, and the promotion of mutually beneficial exchanges, can explain most doctrines and decisions. Tort cases *[i.e., cases involving private harms, such as negligent driving, where the injured person sues for damages—Ed.]* can be translated into contract cases by recharacterizing the tort issue as finding the implied pre-accident contract that the parties would have chosen had transaction costs not been prohibitive, and contract cases can be translated into tort cases by asking what remedy if any would maximize the expected benefits of the contractual undertaking considered ex ante. The criminal's decision whether to commit a crime is no different in principle from the prosecutor's decision whether to prosecute; a plea bargain is a contract; crimes are in effect torts by insolvent defendants because if all criminals could pay the full social costs of their crimes, the task of deterring antisocial behavior could be left to tort law. Such examples suggest not only that the logic of the common law really is economics but also that the teaching of law could be simplified by exposing students to the clean and simple economic structure beneath the particolored garb of legal doctrine.

If all this seems reminiscent of Langdell, it differs fundamentally in being empirically verifiable. The ultimate test of a rule derived from economic theory is not the elegance or logicality of the derivation but the rule's effect on social wealth. . . .

NOTES

[1]A free rider is someone who derives a benefit without contributing to the cost of creating the benefit. For example,

even if A and B both favor the enactment of a statute, X, each will prefer the other to invest what is necessary in getting X enacted, since the benefit of X to A or to B will be the same whether or not he contributes to the cost of obtaining it. In Chapter 11 I gave national defense as an example of an activity that would encounter severe free rider problems if provided privately.

[2]Such imposition is well illustrated by acquisitive crimes: the time and money spent by the thief in trying to commit thefts and the property owner in trying to prevent them have no social product, for they are expended merely in order to bring about, or to prevent, a redistribution of wealth. Overall wealth decreases, as in the case of monopoly, discussed earlier.

REVIEW AND DISCUSSION QUESTIONS

1. Describe how Posner understands the role of the legislature, including its relationship with courts.

2. Using the example of the stamp collection, explain "wealth maximization."

3. Illustrate, using examples, how the law facilitates wealth maximization.

4. Why would a judge who made it easy for poor tenants to break leases with rich landlords not effectively benefit the poor, according to Posner?

5. Explain the formula used by Judge Learned Hand.

6. Is wealth, by itself, something of moral value? If not, does this pose a problem for Posner's theory?

7. Is Posner really a utilitarian, who uses wealth maximization as a stand-in for well-being or happiness of society? Explain.

Law and Economics:
An Analysis and Critique

Andrew Altman

In this reading, taken from his book Thinking About Law, *Andrew Altman first describes the basic approach taken by law and economics, including the idea of economic rationality and the different ways of understanding efficiency. He then describes how law and economics applies in three areas of law: negligence, contract, and property. In the final sections, he discusses the strengths and weaknesses of law and economics, focusing specifically on whether or not its goal of efficient legal rules is justified and on the debate between conservatives and liberals about the economic policies that should be adopted. Andrew Altman is professor of philosophy at George Washington University.*

THE ECONOMIC ANALYSIS OF LAW

Positive law is made and maintained by the decisions and actions of human beings. In light of that fact, it is reasonable to think that fields of study focusing on human behavior and institutions can contribute to the understanding of the law. Accordingly, it is unsurprising to find that such fields as sociology, psychology, and anthropology have made important contributions

to the study of law. Psychologists, for example, have studied how verdicts in criminal cases are affected by whether the prosecution or the defense goes last in giving its closing statement to the jury. And anthropologists have described and contrasted the distinct ways in which different cultures handle disputes that break out among their members. But in recent years, some thinkers have proposed that the principles of economics provide the best way to describe, explain, and evaluate the rules of any system of positive law.

These thinkers have established the "law and economics movement."

The law and economics movement is part of a trend that uses economic ideas, such as the concept of efficiency, to account for decisions and practices seemingly far removed from the impersonal transactions of the marketplace. For example, economic analyses have been given of dating, courtship and marriage. The underlying idea here is that the principles of economics do not apply merely to some narrowly restricted range of human behavior: they apply to human activities and practices across the board, including the law.

We should be careful to distinguish among three separate theses belonging to the law and economics approach: the descriptive, the explanatory, and the evaluative. The descriptive thesis holds that economic concepts and principles provide illuminating descriptions of legal rules. The explanatory thesis holds that economic concepts and principles help provide the best explanation for why society has the legal rules it has. And the evaluative thesis holds that economic concepts and principles provide sound criteria for evaluating legal rules and determining which ones society ought to have. . . .

The evaluative thesis of law and economics is made more specific by the claim that economic efficiency provides a criterion for evaluating the law: other things being equal, inefficient legal rules should be replaced by efficient ones, and efficient ones should be maintained. These evaluative claims about efficiency stand or fall, regardless of whether the law as a whole (or some area of it) is explained by its economic efficiency or is even efficient in the first place. The idea that the law should be efficient must be defended or criticized apart from the other claims of the law and economics movement about what the law is and why it is.

ECONOMIC RATIONALITY

In this section, we will focus on the economic concept of rationality. It is one of two concepts at the center of how the economic approach describes, explains, and evaluates human actions and institutions. The other concept is that of efficiency, which we will examine in the next main section.

RATIONAL ACTION

From the economic perspective, human action is essentially rational, and the rationality of an action is a function of its costs and benefits to the agent. *Costs* and *benefits* refer to the entire range of considerations that make something better or worse for an individual. Monetary considerations are included, but costs and benefits are not restricted to financial gains and losses. Suppose I receive an award for my work. Suppose that no money goes along with the award and that having it will not indirectly increase my income in any way (unlike, say, an Olympic gold medal). Still, the award would count as a benefit so long as it made me better off in some way, for example, by increasing my prestige among my colleagues or just by making me feel good.

According to the economic approach, each individual is the ultimate judge of what makes her better or worse off. In other words, each person's preferences determine what counts as a cost or benefit for her. Moreover, the economic approach assumes that all costs and benefits can be mathematically represented in terms of some common unit of measurement. In practice, monetary units (e.g., dollars) are used. Thus, gaining prestige among my colleagues is not itself monetary compensation, but its value to me can be represented in terms of dollars.

Rational decisions reflect the *net* benefits of the decision. In other words, they reflect the gains *minus* the losses. For economic analysts, the crucial gains and losses are the *marginal* ones. Marginal costs and benefits are the ones added to (or subtracted from) what one already has. By focusing on marginal costs and benefits, one can determine when one has maximized one's net benefits.

AN EXAMPLE: THE RATIONAL ATHLETE

Consider an athlete whose training involves sit-ups in order to increase the strength of her abdominal muscles. Suppose that we ignore all of her other aims in life and focus only on her task of strengthening her abdominal muscles. If she has done fifteen sit-ups at a certain training session, doing an extra, sixteenth sit-up will bring an added benefit. But the extra benefit will be less than the extra benefit of doing the tenth sit-up after having already done nine of them. The marginal benefit of the sixteenth sit-up is still positive, but it is not as high as the marginal benefit of the tenth.

In general, the marginal benefits of a beneficial activity decrease as the activity continues. Similarly, the marginal benefits of a good thing decrease as one obtains more of the thing: the added benefit of a loaf of bread is less to you if you already have ten loaves than if you only have one.

Benefits are maximized when one engages in a beneficial activity until the point at which its net marginal benefits drop to zero. After that point, further activity decreases one's overall benefits, while up to that point, further activity increases the benefits. Of course, even beneficial activities have costs that must be accounted for in determining their net marginal benefits, in particular, the opportunity cost of forgoing some other activity. Suppose that by doing sit-ups our athlete is forgoing another exercise, say, leg lifts, which provides the next best way of increasing the strength of her abdominal muscles. The cost of doing sit-ups is determined by how much benefit she forgoes by not doing the leg lifts. How many sit-ups would she do, assuming she is rational?

Suppose that the marginal benefit of the thirtieth sit-up is greater than that of the first leg lift, but the marginal benefit of the thirty-first sit-up is less than that of the first leg lift. She would maximize her net benefits by doing thirty sit-ups and then switching to leg lifts. How many leg lifts would she do? Assuming she is rational, she would perform each additional leg lift until the marginal benefits decrease so as to become equal to the marginal costs. Past that point, she would be detracting from her net benefits instead of maximizing them.

According to economic analysis, then, rational action maximizes one's net benefits, and maximizing one's net benefits entails acting to the point at which marginal benefits minus marginal costs becomes zero.

RATIONALITY AND UNCERTAINTY

In most situations in life, it is not certain what the gains and losses will be from any given choice or action. Rational choice under such conditions of uncertainty is handled using the idea of *expected* benefits (or losses). The expected benefit of a choice is simply the benefit multiplied by the probability of its occurrence. If there is a 10 percent chance (0.10) of my receiving $10, then my expected benefit is $1.

Economic analysts will concede that not all human conduct is rational in exactly the way they describe. But they will insist that their idea of rational action provides a very good approximation of much human conduct, applicable across the spectrum of human activities. Moreover, economic analysts will contend that their approach provides the most systematic and comprehensive approach to describing and explaining human conduct. It might be possible to come up with counterexamples, in which persons do not maximize their net (expected) benefits. But there is no alternative theory that does a better job than the economic approach. It may not be perfect, because humans are not always perfectly rational, but the economic approach is by far the best game in town. Or so the economic analysts of law argue.

ECONOMIC EFFICIENCY

The economic concept of efficiency concerns the costs and benefits of an action, rule, or institution to society as a whole rather than to a specific individual. The concept rests on the idea that society is simply the sum of the individuals who make it up. Accordingly, the costs and benefits to society as a whole is a function of the costs and benefits to each affected individual. But how are the costs and benefits to different individuals to be compared and weighed against one another?

UTILITARIANISM AND BEYOND

Economic thinkers developed their answer to this question by considering the problems with a utilitarian approach and formulating several alternatives to it. Let us examine the utilitarian approach and the problems it encounters.

In its classic formulation, the utilitarian approach holds that the total good to society of some act or rule is determined by the net balance of pleasure over pain produced by the act or rule. The net balance is calculated by summing up the pleasure produced for each individual (taking into account its intensity, duration, and so on) and subtracting the pain produced for each individual (also taking account of its intensity, duration, and so on). If we used this approach to define efficiency, we would say that an efficient act or rule is one that maximizes the net balance of pleasure over pain, summing up the pleasures and pain over all affected individuals.

The critical problem that economic thinkers see in this approach to defining efficiency is that it assumes one can compare the pleasures and pains of different persons and say how much more one person's pleasure (or pain) is than another's. The simple fact seems to be that there is no way to make such "interpersonal utility comparisons."

Jack may be able to say reliably that his pleasure in eating fried chicken outweighs his pain in having indigestion. Or that his pleasure in playing basketball is greater than his pleasure in playing cards. But how can anyone determine how much more (or less) Jack's pleasure in playing basketball is than Jill's pleasure in playing cards? It seems that there is no way to compare the subjective experiences of different individuals because that would demand the impossible task of getting inside their heads. Yet, if we want to know whether it is efficient for Jack and Jill to play basketball or to play cards, a utilitarian approach to efficiency demands that we make such comparisons between the pleasures of Jack and those of Jill.

PARETO'S CONCEPTS OF EFFICIENCY

Pareto, an economist, developed two concepts of efficiency that circumvented the problem of interpersonal utility comparisons. The two concepts are called "Pareto optimality" and "Pareto superiority." Both concepts enable one to measure the efficiency of different ways of allocating

society's resources, and both can be applied without getting inside the minds of the affected persons and comparing their subjective experiences. Let us examine their meanings.

Suppose that all of society's resources are in a box, waiting to be allocated to its members. Suppose that X represents one specific allocation of those resources. X is Pareto-optimal if and only if there is no way to change that allocation to make at least one person better off without making anyone worse off. Conversely, X would fail to be Pareto-optimal if and only if there were some way to change the allocation so as to make at least one person better off without making anyone else worse off.

Pareto superiority involves a comparison between any two ways of allocating the same set of resources. Let X represent one way of allocating the resources and Y another. X is Pareto-superior to Y if and only if at least one person is better off with X than with Y and no one is worse off with X than with Y. And if some persons are better off with X than with Y but others are worse off with X than Y, then we cannot say that either X or Y is Pareto-superior. X and Y are noncomparable.

Both Pareto optimality and Pareto superiority dispense with interpersonal utility comparisons in the determination of efficiency. For they only require us to determine for each affected individual whether he or she would better off, worse off, or the same under various, possible allocations. And according to the economic analysts who use these Pareto criteria, it is not necessary to get inside anyone's head in order to determine whether someone is made better off or not by some change in the allocation of resources. That is because a person's *behavior* will show whether he is made better off or not. If a person would voluntarily pay (i.e., give up some valuable resource of his) in order to move from what he has with allocation X to what he would have with Y, then that person is better off with Y than with X. And if the person would pay to avoid moving from what he has with X to what he would have with Y, then he is worse off with Y than with X.

For example, suppose that Jack and Jill are the only two people involved, X consists of Jack having a cow and Jill having a horse, and Y consists of Jill having a cow and Jack having a horse. Suppose further that X is the current allocation and that Jack and Jill can get together and strike a bargain without incurring costs such as hiring lawyers and paying postage and other "transaction costs" (i.e., the costs of negotiating and making an agreement).

If Jack is willing to give Jill his cow in order to gain her horse, then he would be better off under Y. If Jill is willing to trade her horse to get Jack's cow, she too would be better off under Y. Accordingly, they will voluntarily exchange their possessions and move from X to Y. That move will be a Pareto-superior move, because it will produce an allocation that is Pareto-superior to the allocation from which they started. Whether it is Pareto-optimal will depend on whether they are willing to undertake any other exchange. If not, Y will also be Pareto-optimal.

The concepts of Pareto optimality and Pareto superiority are thus understood by economists in terms of economic exchange: each voluntary exchange produces an outcome that is Pareto-superior to the starting point (assuming that no one is affected other than the parties to the exchange), and the point at which no further voluntary exchange takes place (assuming no transaction costs) represents a Pareto-optimal distribution.

The Pareto criteria thus circumvent the problem of interpersonal utility comparisons by making the economic behavior of a person the measure of his or her well-being. Yet, certain difficulties make the criteria almost worthless in evaluating legal rules and systems.

THE LIMITATIONS OF PARETO'S EFFICIENCY CONCEPTS

The first problem stems from the fact that economic exchanges typically have effects on third parties that can make them worse off. While a voluntary exchange makes the parties to the exchange better off—at least according to economic theory, it may make persons who are not parties to the exchange worse off. If I buy my groceries from Jill's store rather than Jack's, I might be making Jack worse off by increasing the profits of his competitor who could then use the extra profits to offer better services and take away more of Jack's business.

The Pareto criteria give us no way of comparing and evaluating the outcomes of such exchanges. As soon as even one person is made worse off by some transaction, the Pareto criteria are silent on whether the transaction produces an improvement or not. The starting point and outcome are noncomparable. Since most transactions have these third-party effects, the Pareto criteria are usually inapplicable.

Second, virtually any change in existing legal rules or social policies will produce some winners and some losers. It does not matter whether the change is a radical one (such as replacing a command economy with a market one) or a more modest one (such as lowering tax rates). In almost every case, a change in the status quo will make at least one person worse off. This means that the Pareto criteria are practically useless for judging proposed changes in legal rules and policies, for the criteria will again be silent on the question of which is better, society before the change or after.

KALDOR, HICKS, AND POSNER

The severe limitations of the Pareto criteria have led some economic analysts of law to develop and employ yet another standard of efficiency: the Kaldor-Hicks criterion. According to this standard, the move from one allocation, X, to another, Y, is an improvement in efficiency if and only if those who benefit from the move gain enough extra benefits so that they could fully compensate those who lose out from the move. Fully compensating a loser means giving her enough benefits so that she is as well off as she was before the move from X to Y. The Pareto demand that efficiency improvements help at least some and harm no one is replaced by the requirement that overall improvements outweigh overall harm. To that extent, the Kaldor-Hicks standard is similar to the principle of utility, which allows trade-offs between the gains of some and the losses of others.

In addition, a leading economic analyst of law, Richard Posner, has proposed a way of interpreting

Kaldor-Hicks that enables it to avoid the problem of interpersonal utility comparisons. He calls his version of Kaldor-Hicks "wealth maximization," and it appears to give us the best of both worlds. We can use it to weigh the gains of some against the losses of others but without doing any interpersonal utility comparisons.

According to Posner's wealth maximization criterion, the efficient allocation of society's resources is the allocation that puts each resource in the control of the person who values it the most. And efficient legal rules are ones that serve to bring about such an allocation. But the degree to which a person values a resource is not defined in terms of the pleasure or happiness or satisfaction she would receive from possessing it. Such a definition would throw us back into the intractable problem of getting inside the heads of others. Instead, the value that a person places on possessing something is determined by her economic behavior: how much she is willing and able to pay to obtain it, if she does not already have it, or how much she asks for in order to give it up, if she does already possess it.

Posner's wealth maximization standard is the most useful of the efficiency criteria that have been developed by economic analysts of law. Accordingly, when we discuss efficiency, the idea should henceforth be understood in terms of wealth maximization.

SCARCITY AND EFFICIENCY

On the economic view, efficiency is important for virtually every human society because humans generally live under conditions of scarcity. Scarcity means that the resources we need to satisfy our preferences are too few for everyone to get all that they would prefer to have.

The implication of scarcity is that some potential, preference-satisfying uses for a given resource must be denied when that resource is put to a different use. The efficient use of a resource by society means that the resource is allocated to the use(s) that has the highest value, as measured by how much people are willing to pay.

Does the law help society deal with scarcity by promoting efficiency? According to many economic analysts, the rules of common law do

so: they are efficient in that they generally ensure that resources wind up in the hands of those who put them to their highest-valued use. In the next section, we will examine the descriptive claim that the common law is efficient. . . .

THE EFFICIENCY OF THE COMMON LAW

The common law consists of the judge-made system of legal rules that govern property, contracts, and torts. Although much of it was originally inherited from England, the common law underwent modification and development at the hands of American judges. Economic analysts of law often claim that the rules of common law, on the whole, lead to an economically efficient allocation of resources.

CONTRACT LAW

Promoting Efficient Exchange. In order to promote efficiency, a system of legal rules must ensure that resources end up in the hands of those who place the most value on them. If you value my wheat more than I do and I value your corn more than you do, it is inefficient if I keep the wheat and you keep the corn. That is because the two resources, wheat and corn, are not in the hands of the people who value them the most. Economic analysts argue that market transactions are vital in promoting efficiency because the transactions help ensure that resources end up in the hands of those who value them the most.

Accordingly, an efficient system of law must have rules that enable persons voluntarily to exchange the resources they possess. In the common-law system, according to economic analysis, the rules of contract law help to ensure that resources get transferred to those who value them the most. The rules are especially important in those situations where the parties to a contract do not simultaneously exchange their respective goods.

For example, suppose that my wheat is ready for harvesting and delivery now but that your corn will not be ready until next month. We might enter a contract in which I deliver the wheat to you before you deliver the corn to me. When I deliver the wheat, though, I am in a vulnerable situation. Now that you have my wheat, you might be tempted to hold onto your corn. The rules of contract law aim to deter such inefficient behavior on your part and thus give me sufficient assurance to send you my wheat. Only in that way will the economically efficient transaction occur. Accordingly, the rules of contract law provide that you must pay damages to me in case you breach our contract.

Suppose, however, that someone else who values your corn even more than I do gets in contact with you after I have delivered my wheat to you but before you have delivered your corn to me. She makes you a better offer for the corn than I made. Thus, it would be more economically efficient for that person to get the corn than for me to do so: she values it more. Does the law allow that to happen? Yes, because contract law only requires you to pay me the cash value of the corn to me. If you get a better offer for the corn from someone else, then you can pay me that cash amount and still have some left over for yourself. Everyone ends up better off, and economic efficiency is promoted.

Certain kinds of contracts are legally unenforceable, for example, those made as a result of duress. If you coerce me into signing a contract with you at gunpoint, the law will refuse to enforce the contract. Economic analysts point out that the rule regarding duress is economically efficient. If I do not willingly enter into a contract with you for something I possess, economic analysis will conclude that you do not really value the item more than I do. If you did, then you would voluntarily pay me for it. For the economic analyst, a person's willingness to pay is the most reliable evidence of the value of something to that person.

According to economic analysis, it is not efficient for society's legal system to enforce every promise or agreement, even when we ignore the ones made under duress. Enforcement uses society's resources, and if it costs more to enforce a contract or promise than the net gain that accrues as a result of meeting its terms, society will have lost more than it gains. Economic analysis claims that contract law contains a doctrine that

helps society avoid the inefficient enforcement of such promises and contracts, the doctrine of consideration.

The Doctrine of Consideration. *Consideration* is defined by the law as something of value that is given or promised in exchange for something of value. If I offer to sell you my car and you promise to pay me $500, then your $500 and my car both count as consideration: in consideration of your money, I will give you my car, and in consideration of my car, you will give me your money. Consideration is the essence of the deal we make.

The doctrine of consideration says that in order for a promise or agreement to be legally binding, each party must give (or promise) consideration for what the other gives (or promises). This means that "gratuitous" promises are not legally binding. Thus, suppose I promise to give you $10 so you can buy a new compact disc, and I ask for nothing (and you offer nothing) in return. The promise is without consideration and so is gratuitous. It is not legally binding and so, in general, I may change my mind the next day without incurring legal liability.

Does the doctrine of consideration promote efficiency? Economic analysts say yes. They claim that it excludes from legal enforcement relatively trivial "social" promises whose enforcement would be economically inefficient. After all, it uses up society's resources when you take me to court in a dispute over my promise to give you $10 to buy a compact disc or when Joe takes Jane to court in order to settle a dispute about whether she promised to go out on a date with him. The valuable time of judges, lawyers, court employees could be more efficiently spent if such informal social promises were denied legal enforcement, which is what the doctrine of consideration does.

Economic analysts also argue that the doctrine excludes from enforcement those agreements that are so vague that the courts would, in effect, be required to define the terms. In order for there to be consideration, there must be a definite something—a sum of money or a specific item or a specific promise of such—that is given in the exchange. Where nothing definite is given or promised, the courts have no specific bargain to enforce. That means that the courts would have to set the terms of the bargain in order to enforce it. But that is largely inefficient because the parties themselves are in a much better position than the courts to say what contract terms make them better off. The parties know better what value they place on things and what it is worth to them to obtain the item that the other party is offering. As a general rule, efficiency demands that the parties to a contract set the terms themselves and that courts restrict themselves to enforcing the terms that the parties have set. Accordingly, the doctrine of consideration helps promote efficiency by telling potential contract partners, "You need to settle on the specific terms of the contract yourselves, and, if you fail to do so, we are not going to formulate the terms for you."

Contract law generally requires that there be consideration for a promise to be legally enforceable. But it also keeps courts out of the business of evaluating whether the consideration given for a particular promise is adequate. The law is concerned with the existence of consideration but not with its adequacy. In other words, the courts will not inquire into whether each of the parties to a contract is getting his or her money's worth.

Economic analysts argue that the law's refusal to consider adequacy is efficient. This is due to the fundamental economic principle that individuals are in the best position to say what something is worth to them. The principle helps explain why it is efficient for courts to insist on definite consideration before they will enforce a contract, but it also helps explain why it is efficient for them to avoid questions about the adequacy of consideration. If you are the one in the best position to say what something offered as part of a contract is worth to you, then the courts should not second-guess whether you are getting your money's worth.

NEGLIGENCE AND THE HAND FORMULA

The common law not only sets the rules for the enforceable bargains people make. One of its important functions is to enable those injured by another's negligence to gain compensation. The tort law sets the rules covering negligent behavior, including the criteria that determine what behavior counts as negligent.

Negligence is ordinarily explained as the failure to exercise reasonable care in one's activities. But what level of care is reasonable? Economic analysts claim that the idea of efficiency can help answer that question. Reasonable care, they say, is economically efficient care.

Suppose that unusually cold weather causes the underground water pipe that I installed to burst, causing damage to your property. Was I negligent in not putting the pipe deeper in the ground, where it would not have frozen and burst? The economic analyst will answer this question by comparing the cost of putting the pipe deeper to the *expected* cost of the burst pipe. The expected cost of the burst pipe is obtained by multiplying the probability that the pipe would burst by the harm done. Suppose that the probability of such a burst was 0.01 and that $1,000 worth of harm was caused. That means that the expected cost of the harm was $10. Suppose that it would have cost me an extra $20 to have put the pipe deep enough to avoid the bursting. Then it would *not* have been "cost justified" to have placed the pipe that deep: it would have cost more than its expected benefit of saving $10. Taking precautions that are not cost justified is not economically efficient.

Suppose, however, that it would have only cost me $8 to have placed the pipe deep enough to avoid the bursting. Then it *would* have been cost justified to place the pipe that deep, and for that reason it would have been economically efficient to do so. Thus, I was acting in an inefficient way by not placing the pipe that deep, and according to the economic interpretation of negligence, I was being negligent.

The economic interpretation of negligence was first proposed by the famous judge Learned Hand. Judge Hand ruled that a defendant was negligent if the cost of precautions that could have prevented the harm she caused was less than the expected harm. Thus, the so-called "Hand formula" for negligence is that a defendant is negligent if and only if B is less than PL, where B = the cost of preventative measures,

P = the probability of harm, and L = the harm caused. . . .

On the economic view, then, the common-law doctrine of negligence promotes efficiency by encouraging persons to take cost-justified measures to prevent harm to others. It holds them liable for carelessness if but only if they failed to invest resources in prevention up to the point where additional investment would cost as much or more than the expected marginal savings.

PROPERTY

In addition to negligence and contracts, an important part of the common law covers the ownership and use of property. Economic analysts claim that these common-law rules are efficient as well.

Consider the rule that a property owner owes no duty of care to a trespasser. If I own land that has hidden pits and crevices on it, the common law does not require me to post signs that would warn trespassers of the danger. Suppose you come onto my land without my consent and fall into a pit, injuring yourself. Under the common law, I am not liable for the harm, since you are a trespasser, regardless of whether I was negligent in failing to fill in the pit or take other precautionary measures.

The economic understanding for the rule is that it promotes efficiency because the trespasser can generally avoid the cost of injury more cheaply than the landowner can: he need only refrain from trespassing, which will usually cost less than my filling the pit, putting a fence around it or taking some similar precautionary measure. Requiring the trespasser to shoulder the costs of the injury creates an incentive for potential trespassers to refrain from that kind of illegal action. And since the potential trespasser can take measures to avoid the costs of trespassing injuries more cheaply than can landowners, efficiency is thereby promoted, according to economic analysts.

The trespassing example can be generalized to cases in which both parties are engaged in perfectly legitimate activities. In many types of disputes, the uses to which two people put their respective pieces of property end up causing harm to one of the properties. It is efficient for the harm to be avoided, but this can be accomplished only if one of the parties alters his use of his property. Economic analysis says that in such cases of "incompatible" property use, the common law typically assigns rights to the parties based on which one can take steps that avoid the harm more cheaply. The cheaper "cost avoider" is given the burden of altering his use of his property, while the other party is given the legal right to continue using his property as he has been.

Suppose a railroad emits sparks and that, once in a while, the sparks will cause a fire that burns down the crops on a farm adjacent to the railroad. The railroad could prevent the sparks by slowing its speed by 15 mph. But that slowdown will cost the railroad $100 in revenues. The farmer could prevent the fires by not planting on land within thirty feet of the tracks. But not planting on that land will cost the farmer $50 in revenues. The common law will, according to economic analysis, give the railroad the right to emit sparks and put the burden of avoiding fires on the farmer, the cheaper cost avoider. The farmer will have no choice but to refrain from planting crops within thirty feet of the tracks. . . .

THE EVALUATION OF LAW: SHOULD LAW MAXIMIZE WEALTH?

We now turn to the evaluative aspect of the law and economics movement: its claims about what the law should be. . . .

THE BIGGEST PIE?

A standard claim of the law and economics movement is that efficient legal rules create the "biggest economic pie." Various interest groups may fight one another over how the slices of the pie are to be distributed, but it is in every one's interests to have legal rules that create the biggest pie. After all, the more there is to fight over, the better off everyone seems to be. For that reason, economic analysts say that efficiency is a "neutral" value that all can endorse, whatever their differences about the just or fair distribution of resources. And for that reason, economic analysts claim that efficient legal rules are, insofar as they are efficient, good legal rules.

The claim that efficient legal rules create the biggest pie seems to be conflating the idea of efficiency as wealth maximization with a very different idea of efficiency. That different idea can be called "productive efficiency," which can be explained in terms of a simple example.

Imagine a society whose sole product is widgets. The society faces a choice between mutually exclusive legal rules A and B. Suppose that the choice of rule A will lead to a higher output of widgets per work hour. We can then say that A has greater productive efficiency than B.

Legal rules can promote productive efficiency in a number of distinct ways. For example, they may create incentives for society's laborers to work harder or faster in a given period of time. Or they may create incentives for persons to come up with technological innovations that increase the output of a given period of labor time. Or they may create incentives for persons to invest in available technology that increases the output of labor.

The idea of productive efficiency is logically distinct from that of wealth maximization. For a society to have the highest possible output per work hour is one thing; for it to allocate goods and services into the hands of those who value them the most, as measured by their willingness and ability to pay, is quite different. When economic analysts of law refer to the size of the pie, sometimes they are referring to productive efficiency and sometimes to wealth maximization, and it is not always clear which one.

Moreover, it would seem misleading to refer to wealth maximization as the creation of the biggest pie possible. For the concept of wealth maximization is about who gets what slice; it is not about the overall size of the pie. Strictly speaking, it would be more accurate to claim that wealth maximization ensures that each person gets the particular slice of pie for which he or she is willing and able to pay the most.

However, Posner would argue that there is an empirical connection between wealth maximization and productive efficiency. The connection stems from the fact that the slices of the pie are economic goods that can be used to make

other goods (used to "grow" the pie). The degree to which I value some good will depend, at least in part, on how productively I can use it. The more I can make with it, the more value it is to me. And when I obtain the good through market transactions, I have every incentive to use it as productively as I can, for such use maximizes its value to me.

OTHER VIRTUES OF WEALTH MAXIMIZATION?

In Posner's view, the wealth maximization standard has many other virtues in addition to promoting productive efficiency. Among the most important is that it provides a stronger support for individual rights than utilitarianism. Consider slavery. Slaves do not have any right to their own labor: they must work for the master and cannot decide to withhold their labor or to work for someone else who is offering a better deal. Our belief that no one should be a slave rests on the idea that everyone has a right to their own labor. But what is the basis of such a right? Utilitarianism bases the "right" on the claim that slavery fails to maximize the net balance of pleasure over pain. But Posner regards that as a weak basis: there could be circumstances in which the pleasure of the slave owners and their families outweighs the pain of the slaves. He suggests that maximizing wealth, as opposed to utility, provides a stronger basis for the right to one's own labor.

The value of a slave's labor is much greater to the slave than to the owner. After all, everything the slave produces goes to the owner, with nothing to the slave. This reality creates a powerful incentive for the slave to work very unproductively. In contrast, as a free person with a right to his own labor, the individual has a strong incentive to work as productively as possible. This means that a person's labor is of greatest value to himself, and so maximizing wealth requires that the right to such labor be given to the individual and not to anyone else.

This conclusion of Posner's may seem a bit bizarre in light of the fact that he insists that the value of something to a person is a function of how much they are willing and able to pay for it. If a slave has nothing to pay for his freedom, does it not have zero value to him, given Posner's criterion for measuring value?

Posner's answer is that the slave can borrow the amount of money that represents the value of his freedom to him. That amount would be more than the owner would be willing to pay to keep him a slave, and so wealth maximization requires that the right to a person's labor be assigned to the person himself rather than to someone else. The fact that a slave who is forced to borrow to buy his freedom would have a large debt is irrelevant in Posner's view. For wealth maximization tells us that we should assign to every person the right to freedom from the beginning. The borrowing scenario is simply a hypothetical device that helps us determine who values the slave's freedom more—the owner or the slave himself—and thus enables us to determine whether there should be a right to freedom or a right to own slaves.

WEALTH MAXIMIZATION AND THE POOR

Markets and the Work Ethic. Some critics of Posner charge that the wealth maximization standard is biased against the poor in society. They point out that a person's willingness and ability to pay for something is a function of his or her wealth. The wealthy are in a position to shell out more money for something than the indigent (or to borrow more, if they do not have enough cash on hand), and so they will end up getting much more of society's goods and services if Posner's wealth maximization standard is used. The fact that an indigent person may desire some good much more than a wealthy person or may derive much more pleasure from it is irrelevant according to Posner's standard.

Yet for Posner, one of the strengths of wealth maximization is that it does not allocate goods based simply on the intensity of a person's desire for it or the amount of pleasure she would receive from it. Such utilitarian bases for allocation flout an important moral intuition: people are not entitled to goods simply by virtue of wanting them or getting pleasure from them. Posner believes that people should have to work for what they get, and wealth maximization reinforces this work ethic. Wealth maximization

supports a market society (recall the efficiency of market transactions), and in such a society the wealth of persons is generally a reflection of their productive labor. At least that is Posner's view of the matter.

The claim that wealth maximization is biased against the poor is one aspect of a broader criticism of the evaluative side of the economic approach to law. According to that criticism, reliance on notions of economic efficiency for evaluating the law is biased in favor of a right-wing political agenda. Efficiency-based recommendations, it is charged, invariably favor the sorts of solutions to social problems that political conservatives advocate.

Efficiency and the Welfare State. Posner's claim about how the market rewards the work ethic is dubious: many thinkers, including conservatives, have pointed out how success in the market is often more a matter of luck than any work ethic. But even if we reject Posner's claim, the general charge that the economic analysis of law exhibits a political bias is mistaken in a number of key respects. First, it is simply not true that efficiency-based recommendations invariably favor conservative solutions over liberal ones. Consider, for example, the question of whether government should operate a welfare program to prevent the poorest from starving or suffering similar serious deprivation. Liberals have, of course, been strong advocates of such welfare policies. Conservatives tend to be skeptical or downright hostile toward them.

Yet, Posner quite plausibly points out that a welfare system could well be justified on the basis of economic efficiency. Private charity is likely to prove insufficient, and starving persons will not generally die quietly in the street. They will commit crimes in order to feed themselves and their children. It may well be more efficient economically to establish welfare programs to ensure that such persons are fed than to leave them no choice but to feed themselves through criminal activity. That is because crime creates very heavy social costs: people spend a great deal to avoid being crime victims (buying alarm systems, not going out at night, etc.), and society spends a great deal investigating and prosecuting crimes and in imprisoning offenders. Running a welfare system may not be cheap, but it may well be cheaper for society than paying the increased costs of crime that would ensue were there no welfare system.

Another efficiency reason for some kind of a welfare program is rooted in the altruistic desires of many citizens. These citizens have a preference that their fellow citizens not suffer from drastic deprivation. If enough people who are well off have such a preference, then a welfare program might be called for on efficiency grounds.

It may be asked why efficiency cannot be served by having altruistic citizens donate to private charity. What is the need for the liberal, government imposed solution? Posner points out that there is an efficiency-based justification for reliance on government in this context. Although a well-off person may really want to see all the poor fed, the donations to private charity of others may make her contribution unnecessary. And her contribution, by itself, will not determine whether there are enough total contributions so that all the poor can be fed. Thus, a rational incentive exists for the well-off person to hold back from giving to private charity—in the hopes that others will give and make her contribution unnecessary—so that she can be a "free rider." As a free rider, she would get what she wants—all the poor fed—but not have to pay for it. But since each well-off person would have a rational incentive to refrain from donating so she could be a free rider, the result is likely to be a lower level of actual charitable contributions than would be efficient. And as Posner points out, government action solves this free-rider problem by financing a welfare program out of taxes that the well-off person has no choice but to pay.

There are many social problems in which a free-rider analysis can lead to liberal solutions. Environmental problems are rife with free-rider considerations, and many proponents of law and economics argue that strict environmental laws of the sort typically favored by political liberals are needed to promote efficiency. This is not to say that there is unanimity among the proponents of law and economics on environmental issues or any other politically controversial topic. But that very point takes us to the nub of the problem with the claim that law and economics

has an inherent conservative bias: many proponents of law and economics use its ideas to advocate liberal solutions to policy issues.

POLITICAL DISAGREEMENT IN LAW AND ECONOMICS

WHAT KIND OF MARKET?

The views that economic analysts of law have on current issues span the political spectrum from liberal to conservative. There is general agreement among them that Kaldor-Hicks efficiency is a politically neutral value that society should take account of in developing its law. And the free market is virtually unanimously endorsed as the main engine of the economic system. But there are serious disagreements as well that lead to very different conclusions about what kinds of legal policies society should adopt.

Roughly, we can distinguish between a conservative and a liberal side to the law and economics movement. The two sides disagree over the extent to which the market should be left to operate free of legal interference and regulation. The liberal side advocates greater legal regulation and interference than does the conservative. The disagreement is rooted in conflicting conceptions of the efficiency and morality of unregulated market outcomes.

CONSERVATIVES VERSUS LIBERALS

Those on the conservative side of the law and economics movement tend to think that the market almost always produces efficient outcomes and so is only rarely in need of legal correction in order to achieve efficiency. They do not reject the existence of transaction costs and other factors that interfere to some extent with the efficiency of market operations. But they judge that such interferences are usually minimal and that legal efforts to alter market outcomes usually create more inefficiency than they correct.

In contrast, the liberal side sees a greater need for legal correction of the market. It holds that transaction costs, free-rider problems, and other factors that interfere with market efficiency are more extensive than the conservative side admits.

And it believes that legal regulation or circumvention of the market can effectively counteract such costs and problems and yield efficient outcomes for society.

In addition, those on the liberal side tend to subscribe to theories of justice that claim the priority of justice over efficiency and that require substantial redistribution from the outcomes produced by the market, even when the market is operating efficiently. For example, their theories of justice generally hold that government must provide significant assistance to the indigent and significantly reduce the disparities in wealth and income that result from the operation of market forces.

In contrast, those on the conservative side either deny that justice is a value that can take priority over efficiency or else hold a theory of justice according to which market outcomes are essentially just. Thus, the conservatives argue that, when transaction costs do interfere with the efficiency of market exchange, the law should generally "mimic the market." In other words, the law should produce the same outcome the market would have produced had transaction costs not interfered.

Conservatives who deny that justice takes priority over efficiency tend to be skeptical of all value judgments other than those about efficiency and to adopt a "deflationary" attitude toward such judgments. They regard judgments about justice and other moral values as no more than expressions of personal preference. Such subjective moral preferences can be incorporated along with all the other preferences people have in order to decide what is most efficient, that is, what maximizes the satisfaction of preferences. But these law and economics conservatives doubt that justice and other moral values can provide legitimate constraints on the pursuit of efficiency.

Notice that this deflationary attitude toward values other than efficiency sharply distinguishes these law-and-economics conservatives from many of the political groups in society that are regarded as conservative.

For example, consider fundamentalist religious groups that favor state-sponsored prayer in school, oppose homosexual rights, reject abortion, and otherwise argue that moral values must be enforced by the government. Such groups do not conceive of the moral values they advocate as personal preferences to be cranked into the efficiency equation along with the differing personal preferences of their political opponents. Rather, they think of their moral values as the true ones and as disqualifying from consideration any preferences that conflict with those values. Such persons might consistently adopt the other elements of conservative law and economics: the efficiency of markets and so on. But they would have to judge that, where market transactions would violate their moral values, the market must yield.

Some law-and-economics conservatives reject the deflationary account of justice and morality. They believe that justice is the primary value to which social institutions must conform. But they wind up with the same conclusion that the deflationary conservatives endorse: the free market should be largely left alone to operate without legal interference or regulation. This is because they hold to a theory of justice that says that market outcomes are largely just. Liberals, in turn, will counter with a view that questions the justice of market outcomes.

REVIEW AND DISCUSSION QUESTIONS

1. Explain what is meant by economic efficiency and by rational economic action.
2. Discuss the different ways of understanding economic efficiency, including the views of Pareto, Kaldor and Hicks, and Posner.
3. Explain the economic approach to negligence law.
4. Explain the economic approach to contract law.
5. Explain the economic approach to property law.
6. What are the advantages and disadvantages of using wealth maximization as a test for legal rules? How does Altman think these rules would apply to the poor?

9

CRITICAL LEGAL THEORY AND FEMINIST JURISPRUDENCE

Essays in this section also exemplify recent developments in the study of law and legal theory. Here, however, the focus is on critical legal theory and feminist jurisprudence, each of which questions traditional approaches to law and jurisprudence. Critical legal theory builds on the ideas of legal realists discussed in Section 6, while feminists emphasize the failure of philosophers to take adequate account of law's impact on women. Though the jury is still out on these developments, there is no question that the ideas being advanced are intellectually exciting, politically challenging, and philosophically important. The section concludes with an essay that defends critical legal theory against Dworkin's effort to provide a secure foundation for adjudication and with Dworkin's response to these criticisms.

Critical Legal Studies

Robert W. Gordon

Critical Legal Studies (CLS) is deeply controversial, as Robert Gordon explains. In this essay, Gordon describes the CLS perspective on legal "discourses," legal education, trashing, deconstruction, and history. He concludes by comparing how CLS and traditional lawyers might approach a free-speech case involving pickets in a shopping mall. Robert Gordon is professor of law at the University of Wisconsin.

In April 1987 Assistant Professor Clare Dalton was up for tenure at Harvard Law School. Uninformed outsiders would have rated her chances high. She had written a book on nineteenth-century tort law, accepted by Oxford Press and praised by all but one of the thirteen eminent outside reviewers asked to read it. Colleagues with weaker files than hers had received tenure earlier in the year. Her case, however, provoked passionate and bitter debate. After several meetings, she fell short of the two-thirds faculty vote she needed for tenure. . . .

While the episode has attracted a lot of press coverage, little is remarkable about it except that it happened at Harvard and so involved Lifestyles of the Rich and Famous. The story is depressingly familiar, although unpublicized elsewhere. Job troubles for CLS–affiliated teachers are common. One was denied tenure at Rutgers-Camden last year, for instance, four others were fired from New England Law School last fall, and refusals to hire Crits, however qualified, may now be more the custom than the exception. The dean of the Duke University Law School published a speech asserting that CLS adherents were "nihilists" who had no place in professional schools. The retiring dean of Case Western Law School suggested they were a menace comparable in gravity only to declining applications. As the president of the law teachers' association observed last fall, "[F]aculty members at self-proclaimed prestigious schools and more modest ones alike express determination that no Critical Legal Studies adherent will find a place on their faculty." (Susan Westerberg Prager, "President's Message: Collegial Diversity," Association of American Law Schools *Newsletter*, September 1986.)

But again, this is an old story. People with identified left-wing associations have always had trouble finding and holding on to jobs. In universities these days leftists can count on some protection from liberals who remember or have heard about the appalling costs of cowardice and silence in the 1950s and know that next time the bell may toll for them. . . . But the number of professors with impeccable liberal credentials who will vote against leftists because they are "ideologues" or "disruptive" or "bad colleagues" remains large, and the number who regularly finds that work outside the mainstream fails to meet scholarly "standards" is legion.

Still there's something fascinating about the CLS phenomenon. CLS *has* made headway in some law schools, despite many setbacks. And it has provoked enormous controversy—in the newspapers, the *New Yorker* and the *New Republic*, the lawyers' press and bar journals, in law school alumni meetings, and in academic law reviews. It has reduced its opponents to spluttering rants, generally incoherent ones. (Very few discussions of CLS outside its circle of members and sympathizers are aimed at understanding, much less engaging with, the substance of its ideas.) So it's worth asking: What are Critical Legal Studies and why do they make people so angry?

Critical Legal Studies began as a meeting in Madison, Wisconsin in 1977—a ragtag collection of friends and friends of friends in their thirties, who had been active in radical or left-liberal (civil rights and antiwar) politics in the 1960s and had gone on to law school and later into law teaching. This group wrote a number of books and law review articles that together made up an initial set of critiques of mainstream legal ideas—what they thought was wrong with their own legal education. They also organized a series of annual conferences and summer camps. Over the next ten years the movement spread well beyond the originating group. It has outposts of at least two or three adherents or sympathizers at several law schools—apart from Harvard. . . .

If the original CLS membership was hard to generalize about, the expanded new one is so exotically varied and internally divided as to defy characterization almost entirely. Some aspects of CLS work, however, generally distinguish it from the more traditional left-wing critiques of the legal system, such as those of the National Lawyers Guild, with whom the Critics have formed occasional if rather contentious alliances. Marxist lawyers usually take law to be an infernal machine for the projects of the ruling class, albeit one full of tricks and devices that can sometimes be turned back upon its makers.

More liberal lawyers think law contains many good rules and expresses noble purposes, but that its rules and procedures are constantly bent out of shape by the powerful. Oppositional lawyers can bend it back and use it to advance progressive causes or to soften oppression of the weak and dissident.

For the Crits, law is inherently neither a ruling-class game plan nor a repository of noble if perverted principles. It is a plastic medium of discourse that subtly conditions how we experience social life. Crits therefore tend to take the rhetoric of law very seriously and to examine its content carefully.

To get a picture of the way Crits think, consider all the habitual daily invocations of law in official and unofficial life—from the rhetoric of judicial opinions through advice lawyers give to clients, down to all the assertions and arguments about legal rights and wrongs in ordinary interactions between police and suspects, employers and workers, creditors and debtors, husbands, wives, and neighbors, or television characters portraying such people. Sometimes these ways of speaking about law (*legal discourses*, let's call them) appear as fancy technical arguments, sometimes as simple common sense. ("An employer has the right to control what happens on his own property, doesn't he?") In whatever form, they are among the discourses that help us to make sense of the world, that fabricate what we interpret as its reality. They construct roles for us like "Owner" and "Employee," and tell us how to behave in the roles. (The person cast as "Employee" is subordinate. Why? It just is that way, part of the role.) They wall us off from one another by constituting us as separate individuals given rights to protect our isolation, but then prescribe formal channels (such as contracts, partnerships, corporations) through which we can reconnect. They split up the world into categories that filter our experience—sorting out the harms we must accept as the hand of fate, or as our own fault, from the outrageous injustices we may resist as wrongfully forced upon us. Until recently, for instance, an employer's sexual advances didn't occupy any legal category. They were a kind of indignity that a woman had to interpret as something her own dress and manner had invited, or as an inevitable occupational risk, given natural male aggression (and the statistical frequency of creeps), one that could get her fired unless she gave in or had incredible tact. Now such advances have the legal name of "sexual harassment." This doesn't always improve the practical situation of the victims—since vindicating legal rights costs money, emotion, smooth working relations, the chance of promotion, and maybe even one's career—but for many men and women the feminist politics that forced the change in legal categories has completely changed how they interpret and feel about the behavior.

Some of the basic points the Critics want to make about legal discourses are as follows:

These are discourses of power. Law is not, of course, uniquely the tool of the powerful. Everyone invokes the authority of law in everyday interactions, and the content of laws registers many concessions to groups struggling for change from below, as well as to the wishes of the politically and economically dominant. But to be able to wield legal discourses with facility and authority or to pay others (lawyers, legislators, lobbyists, etc.) to wield them on your behalf is a large part of what it means to possess power in society. Legal discourses therefore tend to reflect the interests and the perspectives of the powerful people who make most use of them.

Whether actually being used by the powerful or the powerless, legal discourses are saturated with categories and images that for the most part rationalize and justify in myriad subtle ways the existing social order as natural, necessary, and just. A complaint about a legal wrong—let's say the claim that one is a "victim of discrimination"—must be framed as a complaint that there has been a momentary disturbance in a basically sound world, for which a quick fix is available within the conventional working of existing institutions. A black applicant to professional school, whose test scores are lower than those of a competing white applicant, asks for admission on grounds of "affirmative action." Everybody in that interaction (including the applicant) momentarily submits to the spell of the worldview promoted in that discourse, that the scores measure an "objective" merit (though nobody really has the foggiest idea *what* they measure besides standardized test-taking ability) that would have to be set aside to let him in. A middle-aged widow buys a cheap promotional package of lessons at a dance studio. The studio hooks her on flattery and attention, then gets her to sign a contract for 4,000 hours of dance instruction. To break her contract, she will have to struggle to make a case that her situation is grotesquely exceptional—the result of serious fraud, and, even if she wins, she and her lawyers will have participated in and reinforced the law's endorsement of "normal" marketplace relations as unproblematically voluntary, informed, non-coercive, and efficient.

Thus legal discourses—in conjunction with dozens of other nonlegal discourses—routinely help to create and maintain the ordinary inequities of everyday social life: the coercions, dominations, and dependencies of daily relations in the marketplace, the workplace, and the family; the ordering of access to privilege, authority, wealth, and power by hierarchies of class, race, gender, and "merit."

Yet legal discourses have the legitimating power they do because they sketch pictures of widely shared, wistful, inchoate visions of an ideal—a society of dealings between genuinely free and independent equals, one so ordered that we could cooperate with others without having to worry that they would hurt or enslave us, so structured as continually to open to question the legitimacy of its hierarchies. Thus law is always a source of images and ideals that challenge and urge us to revise current arrangements as well as justifying them. The problem is that, in the ordinary uses of law, the revisionary images are realized in scattered fragments and otherwise muted and repressed.

So the big premise of the CLS method, the *raison d'être* of its scholarship and local political tactics, is that the deployment of ordinary legal discourse is a form of political practice, and one

with *unnecessarily* conservative consequences. If we experience a sense of stasis and paralysis about the possibilities for social change, we owe our passivity in part to the character of these pervasive discourses. CLS people believe that when you take legal discourse apart and see how it works, you can start to reinterpret it and to gain the energy and motivation to engage in local political action that in turn can help to change the social context that the discourse has hardened. Since most of the Crits were academics in law schools, they first picked on the targets that were closest to them, the standard ways that other law teachers wrote, taught, and talked about, the first-year legal subjects, such as Torts, Contracts, and Property.

Their first problem was to figure out how legal training produces its mind-numbing paralysis—how even left-liberal students trained by left-liberal teachers end up drained of energy and hope for social change. One big reason, of course, is that graduates of the elite schools are lavishly rewarded in money and social status for going into large-firm corporate law practice and tend over time to adjust their ideals to their situations. Graduates of less elite schools think themselves lucky to get any legal job on any terms that are offered. But both types of lawyers tend to excuse their passivity with the gloomy thought that nothing can change anyway, and that conclusion—so the Crits speculate—they owe in part to the conservatizing elements in academic-legal discourse.

Those elements take a number of different forms. There is a traditional kind of law teaching, perfected around the 1950s and still probably the dominant one, that is very elusive because it never makes any of its premises or assumptions explicit. The teacher creates confusion by slashing up the reasoning of the judges who decide the cases assigned for classroom reading and also the reasoning of the students, but ends up suggesting that there's a delicate, complex balance-point, a moderate centrist position, that a smart, sensible, *professional* lawyer can settle on. Such a teacher presents a centrist politics as if it were a craft. There is now a fresh set of discourses urging the natural necessity of conservative or mildly reformed social arrangements; this is the economic analysis of law by scholars such as Guido Calabresi of Yale and Richard Posner of Chicago—far more intellectually formidable than the old style of legal theory and increasingly influential among policymakers and scholars. Legal economists assert that disputes about particular legal arrangements (e.g, decisions about whether polluters should have to pay homeowners to pollute the air, or homeowners pay polluters not to pollute) may be resolved through value-neutral comparisons of alternative solutions as more or less "efficient."

Fighting, as they saw it, fire with fire, the Crits responded to long articles in elite law journals with longer articles in elite law journals. Streetwise radical lawyers have always mocked the Crits for "footnote activism," using up political energy in pedantic swiping at mandarin doctrines, but from the CLS point of view, the strategy made sense: they were matching a local discourse of power and constraint—one that had some discernible impact on their own and their students' lives—with a discourse of resistance. It is a modest form of political action simply to try to reduce the authority of those people who control the local situation and thus to create a little extra space for your own projects, your counterinterpretations of the same discourses. Through this work, the Crits hoped to develop a set of critical insights and demolition rhetorics that they and others could pick up and use on all sorts of legal discourses, not just those of other scholars. (The success of the project has been mixed. Some of their students picked up and improved on this early work, and went on to teach it to others. Most radical or left-liberal lawyers probably found it too arcane, abstract, and not obviously enough connected to the goals of practice to be of immediate use. Some teaching has been done through conferences, summer camps, and more popular books, but not yet enough to make the ideas widely accessible.)

Here are some of the methods the Crits have deployed against mainstream legal discourses:

TRASHING

This sixties-evoking phrase covers a big miscellaneous grab bag of techniques designed to dent the complacent message embedded in legal discourse, that the system has figured out the arrangements that are going to make social life about as free, just, and efficient as it ever can be. The trasher tries to show how discourse has turned contingency into necessity and to reveal the repressed alternative interpretations that are perfectly consistent with the discourse's stated premises. Trashing techniques are used sometimes simply to attack the discourses on their own terms—to show their premises to be contradictory or incoherent and their conclusions to be arbitrary or based on dubious assumptions or hidden rhetorical tricks. The CLS critiques of legal economics, for instance, have borrowed from and added to the multidisciplinary critiques of the neoclassical economic model of human beings as rational self-interested maximizers of their satisfactions: critiques that the model is vacuous (it tells you that people "want" *everything* they get); that when the model is given concrete content, it is obviously wrong (people are often irrational or altruistic) and too narrow (people want self-worth and the esteem of others as well); that there are fatal ambiguities in the notion of choosing selves (personalities are divided in their desires, desires change over time, short-term desires are often destructive to long-term selves); that the individualism of the model is a culturally and historically specific image of human conduct (a product of certain modern market cultures) that the model falsely claims is universal; and so forth. Crits by no means reject economic analysis as valueless: they teach it and make regular use of it in their work (although the economists do not reciprocate). But by showing that the agile interpreter can justify as economically efficient virtually any imaginable scheme of social arrangements, the critique helps to deprive technocracy of its mystery; its pretense that science, magically substituting for agonizing political and ethical choices, dictates that if we want to remain prosperous we must endure all the miscellaneous injustices now in place and even invent new ones. The Critics' message is that the economic-efficiency analysis of legal practices isn't a science, it's just a very manipulable rhetoric, often a useful rhetoric which highlights problems and possible consequences that one wouldn't otherwise notice, but a myopic rhetoric, too, which systematically obscures from view—has no way even to *talk* about—the violence, coercion, irrationality, cultural variety, solidarity, and self-sacrifice of lived experience.

DECONSTRUCTION

The Crits do not believe, however, that their trashing reveals a random chaos or that what lies behind the seeming order of legal decisions is just pure power (or personal whim). There is a *patterned* chaos, and the aim of Critical scholarship is in part to uncover the patterns. Some of their best work is a familiar kind of left-wing scholarship, unmasking the often unconscious ideological bias behind legal structures and procedures, which regularly makes it easy for business groups to organize collectively to pursue their economic and political interests but which makes it much more difficult for labor, poor people, or civil rights groups to pursue theirs. Other work aims at laying bare "structures of contradiction" that underlie fields of law. Contract law in the Critics' view, for example, draws regularly for its inspiring assumptions upon two diametrically opposed visions of social life. One is a stark neo-Hobbesian world of lonely individuals, predatory and paranoid, who don't dare associate with each other except through formal contracts that strictly limit their obligations. The other is a world in which trustful cooperation is the norm and people assume indefinite open-ended responsibilities to others with whom they deal regularly and who have come to rely on them. Both sets of images, and the regimes of legal obligation they recommend, are potentially available in every legal decision about a contract. Yet the legal system persistently gives one of the regimes (the rule-bound, formal, individualistic one in this case) an arbitrarily privileged position and partially suppresses the other or reserves it for the deviant or exceptional case.

GENEALOGY

Still another way to heighten awareness of the transitory, problematic, and manipulable ways legal discourses divide the world is to write their history. The Crits have turned out a lot of history of legal categories. They have focused their attention, for instance, on the mid-nineteenth century moment, when the business corporation, once an entity created only to serve the "public" ends of the commonwealth, was reclassified as "private" and thus free as any individual to do what its managers pleased in the market, while the city corporation was reclassified as the "public" agent of the legislature and its managers' legal powers from then on were strictly confined. Crits also write social history revealing that even the most basic legal concepts, such as "private property," have never had any definite, agreed-upon content but have, on the contrary, always been fiercely struggled over, so that any conventional stability the concepts may now seem to possess represents nothing more than a temporary truce that could be unsettled at any moment.

Such techniques owe much to standard liberal and radical analyses. But in the hands of Critics they add up to a style and method of critique that is quite distinctive. Consider the case of picketers who want to demonstrate in a shopping mall and are kicked off the mall by the owner. Lawyers usually approach this situation as one involving a conflict between two opposing "rights," the property right of the owner to exclude unwanted visitors or behavior and the demonstrators' right to free speech. Judicial decisions suggest that the way to resolve the conflict is to ask whether the mall is "public" or "private" in character (the more "private" it is, the greater the right to exclude). The Crit begins by asking why labeling the mall as "property" should give the right to exclude picketers in the first place and goes through the standard justifications for property rights. The efficiency rationale says that owner control will yield the highest valued uses of the property. But it is not at all clear that the shoppers do not value diverse viewpoints at the mall, that they are only there to buy and not to converse and socialize, or that their decisions to shop at this mall or go elsewhere are likely to any important extent to depend on being free from picketers.

Anyway, the "taste" of owner and shoppers, if real, to be free from exposure to political speech may be one (like the "taste" for not serving or sitting next to blacks at lunch counters) that should not be entitled to recognition, rendering the whole "efficiency" calculus irrelevant. The privacy rationale for exclusion has much less appeal when the owner is a bodiless corporation that lets hordes of strangers swarm over "its" property daily. Crits examine the private versus public distinction, what it means, and why any of those meanings should be dispositive. How "private," for instance, is the owner's decision to exclude picketers, once he asks the cops and courts for injunctions, fines, and jails to back it up? History lends a hand here, pointing out that common law traditionally prescribed social obligations to property-holders (such as public access to inns and common carriers) in return for the protections of public force and the privileges of corporate status. Some argue that the picketers' right of access ought to turn on how "public" the property is in the sense of how many links it has to state agencies—zoning privileges, tax exemptions, police services—a bundle of attributes only arbitrarily related to the crucial issue of the appropriate sites of political debate.

This brief sketch of one Critical approach certainly does not demand the conclusion that the correct legal solution is to allow pickets, although all Crits probably would favor that result. One can examine just as skeptically the scope of "free speech" rights, which as currently interpreted would allow demonstrators no access at all even to platforms *intended* for public political discussion, such as newspapers, unless they first purchase a controlling shareholders' interest. All the approach is meant to do is to show that when legal discourse identifies the shopping mall as "private property," it sets up a powerful mystifying charm that sends the pickets scrambling to find a stronger countercharm— "free speech." When you pick the discourse apart, you may find that calling the mall "private property"—even if you completely accept all the standard justifications for private property—tells you virtually nothing about whether owners should be able to exclude pickets.

Trashing, deconstruction, and history have the very real utility of exposing the vulnerability of the routine justifications of power, of enabling people to spot the structural defects and to challenge many of the rationales they hear advanced for especially ugly legal practices. But nobody can be content just to trash, and in the second phase of CLS many Crits find themselves trying to do the intellectual spadework, and often some of the political organizing as well, for various concrete projects of reconstruction. Some of these, notably that of the Harvard theorist Roberto Mangabeira Unger, are on the grand scale—a thousand-page reimagination of democracy, with detailed architectural sketches of political, economic, and social life as it might become. Most are much less ambitious and take the form of activism regarding low-income housing policy, legal regulation of pornography and rape, immigration reform, welfare and social security policy, delivery of legal services, labor law and specifically university labor practices, and always, naturally, law school politics.

If one of the effects of law is to constrict our ability to imagine alternative social arrangements, then it should be possible to liberate social imagination by dredging up and then working to flesh out some of the alternatives that are already present but have been suppressed in legal discourse. Historians have recently been revising the "republican" view of the purpose of politics as that of facilitating self-development through participation in community self-governance—a periodic rival to the dominant liberal view that the end of politics is only to facilitate the individual pursuit of self-interest. Several Crits have begun to ask how republican ideology might influence the redesign of legal institutions—cities, corporations, workplaces, local administrative agencies. Others have followed what Unger calls the method of "doctrinal deviation," taking a set of practices that have been routinely applied in one social field and imaginatively transferring them to another. Economic democracy is one example. Another is William Simon's program of "downward professionalization." In detailed studies of welfare administration, Simon makes the case (backed up by the historical example of the New Deal–era social workers) for entrusting the kind of broad discretionary decision making habitually given by judges and corporate managers to street-level welfare workers, arguing that such a regime could be superior in terms of both efficiency and humanity than the current regime of mechanized administration. Still other Crits are making use of feminist theory and phenomenology to try to evoke richer and fuller descriptions of intersubjective experience than can be found in the abstract and impoverished categories of law and legal economics, to try to recapture the selves from which they claim legal discourses have alienated us, as well as exposing the techniques of alienation.

To return now to where I began: What is it about CLS that makes people so angry? As American critical movements in law go, it has stung the sharpest of any since the Legal Realism of the 1920s and 1930s, which CLS much resembles in its evident delight in showing up the manipulability, vacuity, and arbitrarily conservative conclusions of legal discourses. The other main challenge to mainstream legal thought has been the movement to study law in its social context, which has repeatedly shown how power politics and cultural variation prevent formal legal rules from being enforced and applied in real life the way legal theories and doctrines predict they will be. But lawyers who make their livings expounding formal legal doctrine have been mostly impervious to demonstrations of its limited relevance. It has taken rowdies invading the heart of their own citadel to make them sit up. Still, why such fury?

For one thing, for all the use it makes of conventional academic argument, CLS is a radical movement and of the left, and that's enough in itself to make some fellow lawyers see Red. The public attacks on CLS make up a fascinating collage of what Americans tend to think a left-wing movement must be about, with bits and pieces pulled from the French Revolution (Burke-Carlyle-Dickens version), vulgar Marxism, Soviet Stalinism, sixties anarchism. In these bizarre fantasies, Crits are Bolshevik saboteurs who will take over if you allow any in your faculty or firm, dangerous (in the Age of Reagan, yet), "nihilist" subverters of the "rule of law," infantile but basically harmless hippie/yippies—or all of these at once. The attackers automatically suppose—obviously without bothering to read any of their work—that Crits must believe law to be nothing more than the result of ruling-class domination or the personal and political whims of judges, and that the Crit program must be, after a violent seizure of the state, to "socialize the means of production."

But there are more sophisticated opponents, too. After all, the Crits really are out to reduce the legitimacy and authority of their elders in the intellectual legal establishment; and those elders, no fools, realize that and despise them for it, the more so because the Crits are not always kind or polite. Along with the academic trashing techniques I've described go ruder ones—satire, savage mockery, even sometimes scatology and a sort of juvenile thumb-nosing irreverence. Such trashing has a function. As the Norwegian philosopher Jon Elster puts it, in a society where authority is typically legitimized through control of the rational discourses, sometimes the most effective challenges to authority are those of "irony, eloquence, and propaganda," refusing to talk authority's language and aping its forms. Law in particular has lent a lot of its persuasive power by its manners: the pompous gravity of its hierophants, their arrogant certainty that the "smartness" certified by their success carries with it command over social truth. (At the same time, such rudeness, while helping to preserve the movement's edge and to save it from becoming normalized into just another academic school, has undoubtedly alienated a lot of potential supporters.)

Harder to forgive than rudeness is rejection—not only of the elders themselves but of their whole elaborate structure of deference to their own seniors, their system for picking successors, their canon of heroes and respected texts. Much of the Harvard bitterness derives from the Crits' insulting refusal to accept the long-approved criteria of "smartness" and "competence" for choosing colleagues—criteria, the Crits unkindly pointed out, that (besides yielding a faculty of look-alikes—people who wrote mostly the same kind of doctrinal scholarship, had views varying from the center–right to the center–left of the political spectrum, and included almost no women or minorities), were plainly deficient on their own terms, as evidenced by the fact that many teachers who met them burned out early and produced very little. Some CLS work is disrespectful not only of their elders' scholarship, but of the political achievements these men personally struggled for and are proudest of, such as the labor-relations policies of the New Deal and after. And CLS perversely sets up its own intellectual counterheroes, who include the disreputable Legal Realists, as well as weird foreign imports, such as Hegel, Sartre, and Foucault. (I have heard one eminent legal scholar denounce CLS as "un-American" and another disparage it as infected with "French and German" influences. Ah, the Continent—that dark breeding ground of dirty postcards and pestilential philosophic vapors!)

Among younger CLS opponents—not caught up in the generational struggle and often as critical in their own way of their elders' work and politics—are the true technocrats, committed to a positivist model of science that seeks, even from social knowledge, law-like regularities that can be used for prediction and control. The technocrats are naturally revolted by CLS's aggressive antiscientistic stance and furious at the reduction of social sciences to rhetorics. Their real quarrel, of course, isn't exclusively with CLS but with the entire "interpretive" strain of philosophy and social science that denies the possibility of objective knowledge. . . .

Some opponents see CLS as a threat to liberal freedoms, those maintained by the "rule of law." If every "right" is seen as contingent, up for grabs, capable of being flipped inside out through reinterpretation in the twinkling of an eye, what will we rely on to save us from the "fascists" or the "mob"? These are hard questions, too hard for this sort of space, but a brief Critical answer might run like this: Legal "rights" are shorthand symbols for social practices that we collectively maintain. We value the symbols because of the latent utopian promises they hold out to us—promises of a world where we could freely and safely choose our associations with others without fear of domination by arbitrary authority. Yet, in any actual version of the legal code and its application, such promises will be realized only partially, occasionally, in fragments. The pretense that legal rules have an objective fixed set of meanings, above and beyond political

choice, may sometimes help to keep monsters fenced in: If you live in Chile or Poland, or belong to a habitually trampled group in this country, you want to appeal as often as you can to rights and legal principles transcending those recognized by the dominant political forces. But the pretense of the objectivity of law also harmfully mystifies social life, encouraging people to think that the practices codified in law have fixed and frozen what they can hope to achieve, that so long as their rights are protected they can't complain, and discouraging them from political action aimed at transforming the content of rights so as to realize the emancipatory potential of law. A commitment to legalism can never substitute for a commitment to the ideals law distortedly symbolizes. As the Czech dissident Vaclav Havel writes in *The Power of the Powerless* (1985), after insisting at length on the importance of a politics of legalism aimed at embarrassing state authorities into giving some real content to the legal rituals that sustain their legitimacy:

> [E]ven in the most ideal of cases, the law is only one of several imperfect and more or less external ways of defending what is better in life against what is worse. . . . Establishing respect for the law does not automatically ensure a better life, for that, after all, is a job for people and not for laws and institutions. It is possible to imagine a society with good laws that are fully respected but in which it is impossible to live. Conversely one can imagine life being quite bearable even where the laws are imperfect and imperfectly applied. . . . Without keeping one's eyes open to the real dimensions of life's beauty and misery, and without a moral relationship to life, this struggle [for legality] will sooner or later come to grief on some self-justifying system of scholastics.

Possibly the most violent of all reactions to CLS have come from people who are (like most lawyers) neither technocratic prophets of a scientifically managed social order nor committed to a view of law as determinate neutral principles. After all, if what you're looking for is a picture of law as irrational, chaotic, arbitrary, idiotically administered, loaded in favor of the rich and well-connected, you don't go to CLS, but to a veteran practitioner. *Nobody* is more cynical about law than lawyers. The fiercest reactions seem to come from people who have made their own complex peace with the way things are, have labeled that compact maturity and realism, and, for the sake of their own peace, wish that others would as well. For them, CLS is a form of class treachery.

REVIEW AND DISCUSSION QUESTIONS

1. Explain the role of law in legitimizing power, according to CLS.
2. Explain "trashing."
3. Explain what Gordon means by "deconstruction" of law, using the example of contract law.

4. Compare and contrast CLS with legal realism.
5. What political program does CLS advocate?
6. Compare CLS and the views defended by Gabel and Harris in Section 1.

Toward a Theory of Law and Patriarchy

Janet Rifkin

Feminist jurisprudence is in some ways the continuation of CLS, though for Rifkin and other feminists, the key to understanding the law is the role it plays in legitimizing male dominance. Law is deeply ideological, she argues, and until its oft-unstated cultural assumptions about males and females are exposed, it will continue to reflect a traditional, patriarchal understanding of gender and serve to reinforce traditional patters of inequality.

I. IDEOLOGY, LAW AND POWER

The nature and meaning of patriarchal social order and of patriarchal culture has recently become the subject of intense scholarly questioning. Historians, literary scholars, political theorists, economists, anthropologists, sociologists, psychologists, and law teachers have been attempting through their respective disciplines, to understand the origin of patriarchy and the perpetuation of a patriarchal social order. By patriarchy, I mean any kind of group organization in which males hold dominant power and determine what part females shall and shall not play, and in which capabilities assigned to women are relegated generally to the mystical and aesthetic and excluded from the practical and political realms, these realms being regarded as separate and mutually exclusive.

Law plays a primarily and significant role in social order. The relationship between law and patriarchy, however, needs to be clarified and developed. I intend to suggest a theoretical framework in which the fundamental connections between culture, patriarchy and law can begin to become clearer. In this context, I will examine the cultural and anthropological origins of patriarchy: how law is a paradigm of maleness; how law and legal ideology under capitalism preserved, transformed and updated preexisting patriarchal forms to serve the interests of the emerging bourgeoisie; and finally, why legal change does not lead to social reordering. I want to emphasize that my efforts are directed primarily toward developing a theoretical base from which many of these issues can be more exhaustively reviewed and studied in the future.

Law is powerful as both a symbol and a vehicle of male authority. This power is based both on an ideology of law and an ideology of women which is supported by law. One function of ideology is to mystify social reality and to block social change.[1] Law functions as a form of hegemonic ideology.[2] Thus, a court could rule that

> civil law, as well as nature herself, has always recognized a wide difference in the respective spheres and destinies of man and woman. Man is, or should be, woman's protector and defender. The natural and proper timidity and delicacy which belongs to the female sex evidently unfits it for many of the occupations of civil life.[3]

By the acceptance of this as a statement of reality, law is reinforced as a powerful ideological force of social cohesion and stability.

The ideology of law is also tied to its manifestation as a written set of formulations, principles and regulation. "Freezing ideas and information in words makes it possible to assess more coolly and rigorously the validity of an argument, . . . thus, 'reinforcing a certain kind and measure of [increased] rationality.'"[4] The power of law as ideology is to mask or distort social reality in the name of tradition. Law, in relation to women, is seen as a measured and rational set of beliefs which at the same time asserts a mythological vision which is believed by many to present an accurate statement of the world.

A good example of this phenemonon is found in the suffragist movement of the early twentieth century. "Operating within the male-dominant paradigm, the form, language, and mode of Suffragist protest was set not so much by the objective conditions of female oppression as by their response to the idealizations and mystifications and legalities which rationalized continuance of the *status quo*."[5] Thus, the suffragist, in not challenging the ideology of law which supported an ideology of women, perpetuated mystifications which supported the status quo.

The power of legal ideology is so great that it often becomes hard to differentiate between legal principles and social customs. For example, American women have long worked outside the home in significant numbers. This fact of women's work in the labor market is constantly restricted by specific laws,[6] and is at odds with the basic legal ideology that females should be excluded from the public sphere of work. The legal ideology of these restrictions carries forward the basic message that women *are to be* at home. The legal ideology of women does not bend to accommodate the economic reality of working women.

In 1908, when a substantial number of American women were working,[7] the United States Supreme Court upheld a maximum hours law which applied to women only, reasoning that "her physical structure and a proper discharge of her maternal functions—having in view not merely her own health, but the well being of the race, justify legislation to protect her from the steed as well as the passion of man."[8] The ideological statement that women should be at home was couched in the context of the capitalist framework of competition for jobs. Economic competition between women and men was recognized, and in the name of protecting women, the hierarchical, male-dominated sex/gender system was reinforced. This reinforcement is supported by the ideological assertion that women are in need of greater protection than men.

The power of law as ideology continues into the present and may be examined in light of massive litigative efforts to change the status of women in contemporary society. The reliance on litigation reflects the belief in law as a source of social change, while ignoring the ideological power of law to mask social reality and block social change. Court battles about "women's issues" are waged and sometimes won with the result that a new body of rights is created and deployed in battle, but the basic sexual hierarchy is not changed. Although the hierarchy may be threatened in that each battle subjects the traditional law and legal ideology to examination and review, the litigation of "rights" never reaches the question of collective social organization.

In the area of the law of abortion, for instance, one sees that while the decisions relating to contraception and abortion have been thought of in terms of the expansion of a woman's right to privacy and reproductive freedom, a challenge asserting a competing claim surfaces after every expression of an apparently broadened claim. Thus, after the decision in *Roe v. Wade* recognizing a limited constitutional right to abortion, cases were brought alleging that the rights of fathers were violated, arguments were made that the rights of parents would be violated if minors had full rights to choose abortion and laws and restrictions threatened doctors who performed abortions.

Another significant example of this pattern is in the legal war over affirmative action, where there have been numerous lawsuits brought by individuals claiming that granting members of minority groups preference discriminates against members of the majority group. Here the struggle is articulated as a battle between individuals competing for jobs and education. This focus ignores and obscures the more fundamental social and political questions of power which generate these lawsuits.

The crucial point is that these legal battles reflect anger and dissatisfaction which, in reality, potentially threaten the patriarchal hierarchy. The power of law is that by framing the issues as questions of law, claims of right, precedents and problems of constitutional interpretation, the effect is to divert potential public consciousness from an awareness of the deeper roots of the expressed dissatisfaction and anger. The ideology of law serves to mask the real social and political questions underlying these problems of law. At the same time, the paradigm of law which historically has been and continues to be the symbol of male authority is not only unchallenged but reinforced as a legitimate mechanism for resolving social conflict. In the end, patriarchy as a form of power and social order will not be eliminated unless the male power paradigm of law is challenged and transformed. In order to challenge the male paradigm of law, the origin of law as a form of male authority and power must be discovered and examined more thoroughly.

Although the relationship between women and the law has been the subject of a number of recent books, law school courses, undergraduate programs, and law review articles, few of these efforts have helped to elucidate the complexity of the relationship between law and patriarchal power. Similarly, the practice of law now includes "women's" litigation and women litigators. Litigation has resulted in challenges to statutory restrictions and common law practices in areas such as marriage and parenting, abortion, pregnancy disabilities, and equal employment benefits and opportunities. Nonetheless, these litigation efforts have not challenged the fundamental patriarchal social order. Litigation and other forms of formal legal relief, however, cannot lead to social changes, because in upholding and relying on the paradigm of law, the paradigm of patriarchy is upheld and reinforced.

The fact that little exploration of the connection between law and patriarchy has been done can be largely attributed to the fact that the study of law takes place primarily in the context of law school where the focus is exclusively on legal principles and case study. The study of law in law school is confined to a narrow doctrinal analysis of law and largely excludes an approach which examines the connections between law and social theory. For the most part, law school does not provide students with a framework of ideas to aid them in formulating personal values to help them explore the relationship between social values and law. Because traditional legal education ignores the cultural, political and social foundations of law, it is not possible, in the law school context, to illuminate the relationship of patriarchy and law.

II. NATURE, CULTURE AND WOMEN

The efforts to find and explain the origins of patriarchy have led some scholars to examine mythology, fables and kinship bonds. . . .

In *The Elementary Structure of Kinship*,[9] Levi-Strauss, in analyzing the meaning of the universality of incest taboos, also analyzes the role of women in pre-state societies. He suggests that the concept of women as the property of men that is based in the universal notion of the exchange of women emerges as a fundamental tenet of culture. The origins of social order then are grounded on the conception of women as the property of men; the patriarchal social order is the basis of culture itself.

Levi-Strauss begins by asking where nature ends and culture begins. He suggests that the "absence of rules seems to provide the surest criterion for distinguishing a natural from a cultural process.[10] He finds that the incest taboo is a phenomenon which has the "distinctive characteristics both of nature and of its theoretical contradiction, culture. The prohibition of incest has the universality of bent and instinct and the coercive character of law and institution."[11] The rule against incest gives rise to rules of marriage, which although varying somewhat from group to group, are universally based on the taboo against incest. The rules of marriage also universally are based on the idea of exchange, and in particular, the exchange of women.[12] The exchange of women is a universal mode of culture, although not everywhere equally developed. Levi-Strauss asserts further that the incest taboo "is at once on the threshold of culture, in culture, and in one sense, . . . culture itself."[13] Since, as he shows, the exchange of women is integrally connected to the incest taboo, it can also be said that the exchange of women, as objects of male property, is also on the threshold of culture, in culture and is culture itself.

Levi-Strauss states that the role of exchange

in primitive society is essential because it embraces material objects, social values and women. But while in the case of merchandise this role has progressively diminished in importance in favour of other means of acquisition, as far as women are concerned, reciprocity has maintained its fundamental function, . . . because women are the most precious possession . . . [and] a natural stimulant.[14]

He asserts the universality of the exchange of women: "The inclusion of women in the number of reciprocal prestations from group to group and from tribe to tribe is such a general custom that a whole volume would not be sufficient to enumerate the instances of it."[15]

The notion of women as male property is then at the heart of cultural-social order. Matrimonial exchange is only a particular case of those forms of multiple exchanges embracing material goods, rights and persons:

The total relationship of exchange which constitutes marriage is not established between a man and a woman, . . . but between two groups of men, and the woman figures only as one of the objects in the exchange, not as one of the partners between whom the exchange takes place.[16]

Even where matrilinear descent is established, the woman is never more than the symbol of her lineage. And Levi-Strauss disposes of the myth of the "reign of women" which he says is "remembered only in mythology, [as] an age . . . when men had not resolved the antimony which is always likely to appear between their roles as takers of wives and givers of sisters, making them both the authors and victims of their exchanges."[17]

The origin of culture as reflected in kinship systems is universally based on the idea that women are the property of men to be exchanged between individuals or groups of males. Levi-Strauss sees a "masculinity of political authority"[18] when political power takes precedence over other forms of organization. Early political philosophy, as reflected by the writings of Aristotle, did not challenge this universal social fact. Aristotle, who developed a philosophy of politics and power, also saw political authority as masculine and saw women as nonparticipants in the political world.[19]

Aristotle radically bifurcates public (political) from private (apolitical) realms. . . . Fully realized moral goodness and reason are attainable only through participation in public life, and this involvement is reserved to free, adult males. Women *share* in goodness and rationality in the limited sense appropriate to their confinement in a lesser association, the household. . . . Indeed, it can be said with no exaggeration that women in Aristotle's schema are *idiots* in the Greek sense of the word, that is, persons who do not participate in the *polis*.[20]

The political analysis of Aristotle upholds a male-dominant power paradigm which "serves to perpetuate an arbitrary bifurcation between that which is politics and that which is not. . . .

Implicit within the paradigm is a concept of persons which admits into the privileges of full personhood . . . only those individuals who hold dual statuses as both public and private persons"—i.e., men.[21] The male-dominant paradigm of political power is also the paradigm of law. The historical image of maleness—objective, rational and public—is the dominant image of law.

Law, in mythology, in culture and in philosophy, is the ultimate symbol of masculine authority and patriarchal society. The form of law is different in varying social groups, ranging from kinship bonds, custom, and the tribal rules in pre-state societies; to written codes in modern society. The point, however, is that law in state and nonstate contexts is based on male authority and patriarchal social order.

III. PATRIARCHY, LAW AND CAPITALISM

In *Law and the Rise of Capitalism*, Michael Tigar and Madeline Levy show that the Thirteenth Century in England and in continental Europe "saw the creation and application of specific rules about contracts, property and procedure which strengthened the power of the rising bourgeoisie."[22] They show that these "rules were fashioned in the context of a legal ideology which identified freedom of action for businessmen with natural law and natural reason."[23]

In their study, however, Tigar and Levy do not examine the emerging law in relation to women. They do not discuss, for example, how the rise of capitalism profoundly changed the nature of work, the family, and the role of women. I maintain that law, which emerged "as a form of rationality appropriate to the social relations generated by the emergence of entrepreneurial capitalism,"[24] retained the pre-existing hierarchy of masculine authority and made more explicit the subordination of women to men by increasingly excluding women from working in trades and relegating them to the private world of the home, which itself also became more and more non-productive.

The feudal world, which was organized for war, was essentially a masculine world. Although laws and custom put wives under the power of their husbands, records indicate, nonetheless, participation by some noble women in social, political and legal activities. Women also demonstrated great productive capacity when society was organized on the basis of family and domestic industry. At the end of the Fourteenth Century, one-fourth of the cloth woven in York was produced by women. Laws, restrictive in some spheres, there encouraged women's economic participation. The Act of 1363, for example, declared that:

> [T]he intent of the king and of his council is that women, that is to say brewers, bakers, carders and spinners, and workers as well of wool as of linen-clothing . . . , and all other that do use and work all handiworks, may freely use and work as they have done before this time.[25]

This attitude began to change, however, during the next century as legal regulations promulgated by various guilds became increasingly restrictive of women's participation. Many of these laws reflected the blatant threat of competition to the male workers. In Bristol in 1461, it was complained that weavers employed their wives, daughters, and maidens "by the which many and divers of the king's liege people, likely men to do the king service in his wars and in the defence of this his land, and sufficiently learned in the said craft, goeth vagrant and unoccupied, and may not have their labour to their living."[26]

Sometimes a guild prohibited employment of women, though generally widows could work in their husband's craft. As late as 1726, the Baker's craft in Aberdeen which was distressed by the competition of women who used their own ovens and sold the produce themselves passed a law which mandated a severe fine to any freeman in the baking trade who allowed a woman to use his oven.[27] Other craft guilds were equally restrictive of women working in trades. Rachel Baxter, for example, was admitted to the tailor's craft provided "that she shall . . . have only the privilege of mantua-making, and no ways make stays, or import the same to sell from any other place . . . and it is hereby declared that thi [sic] presents to be no precedent to any woman in tyme coming."[28]

Thus, with the emergence of capitalism and through the power of legal regulation, women were affected in several fundamental ways: individual wages were substituted for family earnings, enabling men to organize themselves in the competition of the labor market without sharing with the women of their families all the benefits derived through their combination; the withdrawal of wage-earners from home life to work upon the premises of the masters and the prevention of the employment of the wage-earner's wife in her husband's occupation, and the rapid increase of wealth which allowed the upper class women to withdraw altogether from business.

Whereas the system of family industry united labor and capital in one person or family group, capitalism brought them into conflict and competition; men and women struggled with each other to secure work and wages. The keystone of the male journeymen's superior economic position in capitalism lay in their ability to restrict their own numbers by promulgating and enforcing laws which specifically limited numbers, imposed long apprenticeship programs and limited the number of apprentices.

The pre-existing patriarchal culture supported historically by kinship bonds and custom was transformed in capitalism through law in the service of new economic interest.

[C]ustomary and traditional modes of conceptualizing bonds of obligation and duty were of diminishing relevance in bourgeois society, where people experienced a growing and radical separation between public life and private life. . . . [F]amily, and personal dependence begin to dissolve and crumble under the corrosive impact of the single universalist principles of social solidarity underlying capitalist social relations— *exchange*.[29]

The role of law in early capitalism was to help create a climate in which production for exchange could thrive. To accomplish this, law, always a symbol of male authority, fostered competition between women and men and severely limited female participation in the world of market production. Law became a primary and powerful tool of the rising bourgeoisie. Legal regulations were enacted which symbolized a continuation of the male authority of the past and which transformed and updated patriarchal society to serve new capitalistic interests. Laws were used increasingly to restrict women from working in trades, relegating them to the private world of the home. Thus, legal rules helped to create a social order where women were excluded from the public world of production exchange. And these new laws, justified in the name of the natural order, were accepted as an accurate vision of the world.

CONCLUSION

This discussion has suggested that there are fundamental connections between culture, patriarchy and law. The origins of culture, according to Levi-Strauss, are grounded in the conception of women as the property of men and that patriarchal social order is the basis of culture itself. Law emerges as the symbol of patriarchal authority in varying ways. With the emergence of capitalist society, law became a crucial, substantial and ideological mechanism which updated a pre-existing patriarchal social order to meet the needs of emerging capitalist interests. Through law women were relegated to the private world of the home and family and excluded from the public world of monetary exchange.

Although the recent litigation efforts to change the role of women in society have resulted in alleviating some oppressive practices, the paradigm of law as a symbol of male authority has not been challenged. Indeed, the reliance on litigative and legislative strategies has reinforced the belief that the law-paradigm is a legitimate mechanism for resolving conflict and that it is a source of social change. As long as the male-dominant power paradigm of law remains unchallenged, the basic social hierarchy will not change. The struggle for sexual equality can be successful only if it challenges, rather than reifies, the male paradigm of law.

NOTES

[1]Kellner, *Ideology, Marxism, and Advanced Capitalism*, 42 SOCIALIST REV. 38 (1978).

[2]*Id.* at 49–50. "Ideology becomes hegemonic when it is widely accepted as describing 'the way things are,' inducing people to consent to their society and its way of life as natural, good, and just." *Id.*

[3]*Bradwell v. State*, 83 U.S. (16 Wall.) 130, 141 (Bradley, J., concurring).

[4]Kellner, *supra* note 10, at 45, quoting A. GOULDNER, THE DIALECTIC OF IDEOLOGY AND TECHNOLOGY 41 (1976).

[5]Elshtain, *Moral Woman and Immoral Man: A Consideration of the Public-Private Split and its Political Ramifications*, 4 POL. & SOC'Y 453, 469 (1974).

[6]*E.g., Muller v. Oregon*, 208 U.S. 412 (1908); Goesart v. Cleary, 335 U.S. 464 (1948).

[7]In 1900, 5,114,461 (20.4%) women aged fourteen years and over were gainfully employed out of a total female population in this age group of 25,024,415. By 1910, the number had increased to 7,788,826 out of 30,959,473 (25.2%). BUREAU OF THE CENSUS, UNITED STATES DEP'T OF COMMERCE, STATISTICAL ABSTRACT OF THE UNITED STATES 1944–45, at 134 (1945).

[8]*Muller v. Oregon*, 208 U.S. 412, 422 (1908).

[9]C. LEVI STRAUSS, THE ELEMENTARY STRUCTURES OF KINSHIP (2d ed. J. Bell & J. von Stariner trans. 1969).

[10]*Id.* at 8.

[11]*Id.* at 10.

[12]*Id.* at 62.

[13]*Id.* at 12.

[14]*Id.* at 62.

[15]*Id.* at 63.

[16]*Id.* at 115.

[17]*Id.* at 118.

[18]*Id.* at 116.

[19]Elshtain, *supra* note 5, at 453. *See* ARISTOTLE, POLITICS 1127–30, 1194–97, 1.2, 13. 1252a–1253a, 1259b–1260b (R. McKeon ed. 1941).

[20]*Id.* at 455 (emphasis in original).

[21]*Id.* at 472.

[22]M. TIGAR & M. LEVY, LAW AND THE BASE OF CAPITALISM 6 (1978).

[23]*Id.*

[24]Fraser, *The Legal Theory We Need Now*, 37 SOCIALIST REV. 147, 154 (1978).

[25]E. LIPSON, I THE ECONOMIC HISTORY OF ENGLAND 359 (7th ed. 1937), at 361.

[26]*Id.*

[27]E. BAIN, MERCHANT AND CRAFT GUILDS 228 (1887).

[28]*Id.* at 257.

[29]Fraser, *supra* note 33, at 15–55 (emphasis in original).

REVIEW AND DISCUSSION QUESTIONS

1. In what way does Rifkin think law is a "paradigm of maleness"?

2. Discuss how Rifkin understands the connections between law and hegemonic ideology.

3. What lesson does Rifkin draw from Levi-Strauss's work on culture?

4. Rifkin argues that the rise of capitalism had a substantial impact on women. Explain.

5. Compare Rifkin's view with that of CLS and legal realism.

6. How does feminist jurisprudence, as presented by Rifkin, compare with the earlier discussions of positivism and natural law? Is her position closer to one or the other of those viewpoints, or is her viewpoint entirely different?

Jurisprudence and Gender

Robin West

Western legal and political thought has been dominated by men. Robin West argues that this fact introduces a deep, pervasive bias into the debate: the fundamental experiences and stories men use to understand law are radically different from women's experiences and the stories they would have told had they influenced political theory and law.

West distinguishes what she terms liberal legalism—*a view she traces to Hobbes and Dworkin—from Critical Legal Studies. CLS emphasizes the role political ideology plays in law's development, particularly the ideological and political contradictions found in legal doctrine and theory. Legal debate cannot, claims CLS, be separated from political conflict. CLS is also critical of much traditional political theory, which it sees as overly individualistic at the expense of the values of community. West's focus is on the conflict between these two male approaches, liberal legalism and critical legal studies, on the one hand, and the two approaches to law taken by feminists, namely, cultural feminism and radical feminism, on the other. Robin West is professor of law at the University of Maryland School of Law.*

What is a human being? Legal theorists must, perforce, answer this question: jurisprudence, after all, is about human beings. The task has not proven to be divisive. In fact, virtually all modern American legal theorists, like most modern moral and political philosophers, either explicitly or implicitly embrace what I will call the "separation thesis" about what it means to be a human being: a "human being," whatever else he is, is physically separate from all other human beings. I am one human being and you are another, and that distinction between you and me is central to the meaning of the phrase "human being." . . . We are each physically "boundaried"—this is the trivially true meaning of the claim that we are all individuals. In Robert Nozick's telling phrase, the "root idea" of any acceptable moral or political philosophy is that "there are individuals with separate lives."[1] . . .

The first purpose of this essay is to put forward the global and critical claim that by virtue of their shared embrace of the separation thesis, all of our modern legal theory—by which I mean "liberal legalism" and "critical legal theory" collectively—is essentially and irretrievably masculine. My use of "I" above was inauthentic, just as the modern, increasing use of the female pronoun in liberal and critical legal theory,

although well-intended, is empirically and experientially false. For the cluster of claims that jointly constitute the "separation thesis"—the claim that human beings are, definitionally, distinct from one another, the claim that the referent of "I" is singular and unambiguous, the claim that the word "individual" has an uncontested biological meaning, namely that we are each physically individuated from every other, the claim that we are individuals "first," and the claim that what separates us is epistemologically and morally prior to what connects us—while "trivially true" of men, are patently untrue of women. Women are not essentially, necessarily, inevitably, invariably, always, and forever separate from other human beings: women, distinctively, are quite clearly "connected" to another human life when pregnant. In fact, women are in some sense "connected" to life and to other human beings during at least four recurrent and critical material experiences: the experience of pregnancy itself; the invasive and "connecting" experience of heterosexual penetration, which may lead to pregnancy; the monthly experience of menstruation, which represents the potential for pregnancy; and the post-pregnancy experience of breast-feeding. Indeed, perhaps the central insight of feminist theory of the last decade has been that women are "essentially connected," not "essentially separate," from the rest of human life, both materially, through pregnancy, intercourse, and breast-feeding, and existentially, through the moral and practical life. . . .

. . . First, masculine jurisprudence is presently divided into two camps: "liberal legalism" on the one hand, and "critical legal theory" on the other. While both liberal legal theorists and critical legal theorists subscribe to the "separation thesis" described above, each group presents radically divergent accounts of what I will call the "subjective experience" of the state of separation. Similarly, "feminist theory" is sharply divided between "cultural feminism" on the one hand and "radical feminism" on the other. And, in a parallel sense, while both cultural and radical feminists subscribe to the "connection thesis" described above, they present divergent accounts of the subjective experience of the state of connection. Therefore . . . this article will present what is ultimately a four-way contrast between the complex and possibly conflicted human being constructed by masculine jurisprudence on the one hand, and the complex and possibly conflicted woman constructed by feminist theory on the other. . . .

The by now very well publicized split in masculine jurisprudence between legal liberalism and critical legal theory can be described in any number of ways. The now standard way to describe the split is in terms of politics: "liberal legal theorists" align themselves with a liberal political philosophy which entails, among other things, allegiance to the Rule of Law and the Rule of Law virtues, while "critical legal theorists," typically left wing and radical, are skeptical of the Rule of Law and the split between law and politics which the Rule of Law purportedly delineates. Critical legal theorists are potentially far more sensitive to the political underpinnings of purportedly neutral legalistic constructs than are liberal legalists. . . .

An alternative description of the difference (surely not the only one) is that liberal legal theory and critical legal theory provide two radically divergent phenomenological descriptions of the paradigmatically male experience of the inevitability of separation of the self from the rest of the species, and indeed from the rest of the natural world. Both schools, as we shall see, accept the separation thesis: they both view human beings as materially (or physically) separate from each other, and both view this fact as fundamental to the origin of law. But their accounts of the subjective experience of physical separation from the other—an individual other, the natural world, and society—are in nearly diametrical opposition. Liberal legalists, in short, describe an inner life enlivened by freedom and autonomy from the separate other, and threatened by the danger of annihilation by him. Critical legal theorists, by contrast, tell a story of inner lives dominated by feelings of alienation and isolation from the separate other, and enlivened by the possibility of association and community with him. These differing accounts of the subjective experience of being separate from others, I believe, are at the root of at least some of the divisions between critical and liberal legal theorists. I want to review each of these experiential descriptions of separation in some detail, for I will ultimately argue that they are not as contradictory as they first appear. Each story, I will suggest, constitutes a legitimate and true part of the total subjective experience of masculinity.

. . . I will start with the liberal description of separation, because it is the most familiar, and surely the most dominant. According to liberal legalism, the inevitability of the individual's material separation from the "other," entails, first and foremost, an existential state of highly desirable and much valued freedom: because the individual is *separate* from the other, he is *free* of the other. Because I am separate from you, *my* ends, *my* life, *my* path, *my* goals are necessarily my own. Because I am separate, I am "autonomous." Because I am separate, I am existentially free (whether or not I am politically free). And, of course, this is true not just of me, but of everyone: it is the universal human condition. We are each separate and we are all separate, so we are each free and we are all free. We are, that is, equally free.

This existential condition of freedom in turn entails the liberal's conception of value. Because we are all free and we are each equally free, we should be treated by our government as free, and as equally free. The individual must be treated by his government (and by others) in a way that respects his equality and his freedom. The government must honor at the level of politics the existential claim made above: that my ends are *my* ends; that I cannot be forced to embrace your ends as my own. Our separation entails our freedom which in turn entails our right to establish and pursue our own concept of value, independent of the concept of value pursued or favored by others. Ronald Dworkin puts the point in this way:

> What does it mean for the government to treat its citizens as equals? *That is . . . the same question as the question of what it means for the government to treat all its citizens as free, or as independent,* or with equal dignity. . . . [To accord with this demand, a government must] be neutral on what might be called the question of the good life. . . . [P]olitical decisions must be, so far as is possible, independent of any particular conception of the good life, or of what gives value to life. Since the citizens of a society differ in their conceptions, the government does not treat them as equals if it prefers one conception to another, either because the officials believe that one is intrinsically superior, or because one is held by the more numerous or more powerful group.[2]

Because of the dominance of liberalism in this culture, we might think of autonomy as the "official" liberal value entailed by the physical, material condition of inevitable separation from the other: separation from the other entails my freedom from him, and that in turn entails my political right to autonomy. I can form my own conception of the good life, and pursue it. Indeed, any conception of the good which *I* form, will necessarily be *my* conception of the good life. That freedom must be respected. Because I am free, I value and have a right to autonomy. You must value it as well. The state must protect it. This in turn implies other (more contested) values, the most important of which is (or may be) equality. Dworkin continues:

> I now define a liberal as someone who holds . . . [a] liberal . . . theory of what equality requires. Suppose that a liberal is asked to found a new state.

He is required to dictate its constitution and fundamental institutions. He must propose a general theory of political distribution. . . . He will arrive initially at something like this principal of rough equality: resources and opportunities should be distributed, so far as possible, equally, so that roughly the same share of whatever is available is devoted to satisfying the ambitions of each. Any other general aim of distribution will assume either that the fate of some people should be of greater concern than that of others, or that the ambitions or talents of some are more worthy, and should be supported more generously on that account.[3]

Autonomy, freedom and equality collectively constitute what might be called the "up side" of the subjective experience of separation. Autonomy and freedom are both entailed by the separation thesis, and autonomy and freedom both feel very good. However, there's a "down side" to the subjective experience of separation as well. Physical separation from the other entails not just my freedom; it also entails my vulnerability. Every other discrete, separate individual—because he is the "other"—is a source of danger to me and a threat to my autonomy. I have reason to fear you solely by virtue of the fact that I am me and you are you. You are not me, so by definition *my* ends are not your ends. Our ends might conflict. You might try to frustrate my pursuit of my ends. In an extreme case, you might even try to kill me—you might cause my annihilation. . . .

Thus, according to liberal legalism, the subjective experience of physical separation from the other determines both what we value (autonomy) and what we fear (annihilation). We value, and seek societal protection of, our autonomy: the liberal insists on my right to define and pursue my own life, my own path, my own identity, and my own conception of the good life free of interference from others. Because I am me and you are you, I value what I value, and you value what you value. The only value we truly share, then, is our joint investment in autonomy from each other: we both value our right to pursue our lives relatively free of outside control. We can jointly insist that our government grant us this protection. We also share the same fears. I fear the possibility—indeed the likelihood—that our ends will conflict, and you will frustrate my ends and in an extreme case cause my annihilation, and you fear the same thing about me. I want the right and the power to pursue my own chosen ends free of the fear that you will try to prevent me from doing so. You, of course, want the same. . . .

Now, Critical Legal Theory diverges from liberal legalism on many points, but one striking contrast is this: critical theorists provide a starkly divergent phenomenological description of the subjective experience of separation. According to our critical legal theorists, what that material state of separation existentially entails is not a perpetual celebration of autonomy, but rather, a perpetual longing for community, or attachment, or unification, or *connection*. The separate individual strives to connect with the "other" from whom he is separate. The separate individual lives in a state of perpetual dread not of annihilation by the other, but of the alienation, loneliness, and existential isolation that his material separation from the other imposes upon him. The individual strives through love, work, and government to achieve a unification with the other, the natural world, and the society from which he was originally and continues to be existentially separated. The separate individual seeks *community*—not autonomy—and dreads isolation and alienation from the other—not annihilation by him. If we think of liberalism's depiction of the subjectivity of separation as the official story, then, we might think of this alternative description of the subjectivity of separation as the unofficial story. . . .

The longing for connection with the other, and the dread of alienation from him, according to the critical theorists, is in a state of constant "contradiction" with the official value and official harm that flow from separation—autonomy from the other and annihilation by him. Nevertheless, in spite of that tension, both the dread of alienation and the desire for connection are constantly *there*. The dominant culture insists we value autonomy from the other and fear annihilation by him. But subjectively, the individual lives with a more or less unrealized desire to connect with the other, and a constant

dread or fear, of becoming permanently alienated, isolated—lost—from the other. . . .

Let me now turn to feminist theory. . . . According to one group of feminists, sometimes called "cultural feminists," the important difference between men and women is that women raise children and men don't. According to a second group of feminists, now called "radical feminists," the important difference between men and women is that . . . "women," definitionally, are "those from whom sex is taken," just as workers, definitionally, are those from whom labor is taken. . . . Underlying both radical and cultural feminism is a conception of women's existential state that is grounded in women's potential for physical, material connection to human life, just as underlying both liberal and critical legalism is a conception of men's existential state that is grounded in the inevitability of men's physical separation from the species. I will call the shared conception of women's existential lives the "connection thesis." The divisions between radical and cultural feminism stem from the divergent accounts of the subjectivity of the potential for connection, just as what divides liberal from critical legal theory are divergent accounts of the subjectivity of the inevitability of separation.

The "connection thesis" is simply this: Women are actually or potentially materially connected to other human life. Men aren't. This material fact has existential consequences. While it may be true *for men* that the individual is "epistemologically and morally prior to the collectivity," it is not true for women. The potential for material connection with the other defines women's subjective, phenomenological and existential state, just as surely as the inevitability of material separation from the other defines men's existential state. Our potential for material connection engenders pleasures and pains, values and dangers, and attractions and fears, which are entirely different from those which follow, for men, from the necessity of separation. . . .

If both cultural and radical feminists hold some version of the connection thesis, then one way of understanding the issues that divide radical and cultural feminists, different from the standard account given above, is that while radical and cultural feminists agree that women's lives are distinctive in their potential for material connection to others, they provide sharply contrasting accounts of the subjective experience of the material and existential state of connection. According to cultural feminist accounts of women's subjectivity, women value intimacy, develop a capacity for nurturance, and an ethic of care for the "other" with which we are connected, just as we learn to dread and fear separation from the other. Radical feminists tell a very different story. According to radical feminism, women's connection with the "other" is above all else invasive and intrusive: women's potential for material "connection" invites invasion into the physical integrity of our bodies, and intrusion into the existential integrity of our lives. . . .

Why are men and women different in this essential way? The cultural feminist explanation for women's heightened sense of connection is that women are more "connected" to life than are men because it is women who are the primary caretakers of young children. A female child develops her sense of identity as "continuous" with her caretaker's, while a young boy develops a sense of identity that is distinguished from his caretaker's. Because of the gender alignment of mothers and female children, young girls "fuse" their growing sense of identity with a sense of sameness with and attachment to the other, while because of the gender distinction between mothers and male children, young boys "fuse" their growing sense of identity with a sense of difference and separation from the other. This turns out to have truly extraordinary and far reaching consequences, for both cognitive and moral development. Nancy Chodorow explains:

> [This means that] [g]irls emerge from this period with a basis for "empathy" built into their primary definition of self in a way that boys do not. . . . [G]irls come to experience themselves as less differentiated than boys, as more continuous with and related to the external object-world and as differently oriented to their inner object-world as well.[4]

Women are therefore capable of a degree of physical as well as psychic *intimacy* with the other which greatly exceeds men's capacity. . . .

The most significant aspect of our difference, though, is surely the moral difference. According to cultural feminism, women are more nurturant, caring, loving and responsible to others than are men. This capacity for nurturance and care dictates the moral terms in which women, distinctively, construct social relations: women view the morality of actions against a standard of responsibility to others, rather than against a standard of rights and autonomy from others. . . .

Cultural feminists, to their credit, have reidentified these differences as women's strengths, rather than women's weaknesses. Cultural feminism does not simply *identify* women's differences—patriarchy too insists on women's differences—it celebrates them. Women's art, women's craft, women's narrative capacity, women's critical eye, women's ways of knowing, and women's heart, are all, for the cultural feminist, redefined as things to celebrate. . . .

. . . Because women are fundamentally connected to other human life, women value and enjoy intimacy with others (just as because men are fundamentally separate from other human life men value and enjoy autonomy). Because women are connected with the rest of human life, intimacy with the "other" comes naturally. Caring, nurturance, and an ethic of love and responsibility for life is second nature. Autonomy, or freedom from the other constitutes a value for men because it reflects an existential state of being: separate. Intimacy is a value for women because it reflects an existentially connected state of being.

Intimacy, the capacity for nurturance and the ethic of care constitute what we might call the "up side" of the subjective experience of connection. It's all good. Intimacy feels good, nurturance is good, and caring for others morally is good. But there's a "down side" to the subjective experience of connection. There's danger, harm, and fear entailed by the state of connection as well as value. Whereas men fear annihilation from the separate other (and consequently have trouble achieving intimacy), women fear separation from the connected other (and consequently have trouble achieving independence). Gilligan makes the point succinctly: "Since masculinity is defined through separation while femininity is defined through attachment, male gender identity is threatened by intimacy while female gender identity is threatened by separation.[5] . . .

Now, while Gilligan is undoubtedly explaining a real experiential phenomenon—I don't know of any woman who hasn't recognized herself somewhere in this book—her material explanation of that phenomenon is incomplete. Which is not to say it isn't *true:* It seems quite plausible that women are more psychically connected to others in just the way Gilligan describes and for just the reason she expounds. Mothers raise children, and as a consequence girls, and not boys, think of themselves as continuous with, rather than separate from, that first all-important "other"—the mother. But this psychological and developmental explanation just raises—it does not answer—the background material question: Why do women, rather than men, raise, nurture, and cook for children? What is the cause of *this* difference?

Although Gilligan doesn't address the issue, other cultural feminists have, and their explanations converge, I believe, implicitly if not explicitly, on a material, or mixed material-cultural, and not just a cultural answer: women *raise* children—and hence raise girls who are more connected and nurturant, and therefore more likely to be nurturant caretakers themselves—because it is women who bear children. Women are not inclined to abandon an infant they've carried for nine months and then delivered. If so, then women are ultimately more "connected"—psychically, emotionally, and morally—to other human beings because women, as children, were raised by women, and women raise children because women, uniquely, are physically and materially "connected" to those human beings when the human beings are fetuses and then infants. Women are more empathic to the lives of others because women are physically tied to the lives of others in a way which men are not. Women's moral voice is one of responsibility, duty and care for others because women's material circumstance is one of responsibility, duty and care for those who are first physically attached, then physically dependent, and then emotionally interdependent. Women think in terms of the needs of others rather than the rights of others because women materially, and then physically, and then psychically, provide for the needs of others. Lastly, women fear separation from the other rather than annihilation by him, and "count" it as a harm, because women experience the "separating" pain of childbirth and more deeply feel the pain of the maturation and departure of adult children. . . .

Against the cultural feminist backdrop, the story that radical feminists tell of women's invaded, violated lives is "subterranean" in the same sense that, against the backdrop of liberal legalism, the story critical legal theorists tell of men's alienation and isolation from others is subterranean. According to radical feminism, women's connection to others is the source of women's misery, not a source of value worth celebrating. For cultural feminists, women's connectedness to the other (whether material or cultural) is the source, the heart, the root, and the cause of women's different morality, different voice, different "ways of knowing," different genius, different capacity for care, and different ability to nurture. For radical feminists, that same potential for connection—experienced materially in intercourse and pregnancy, but experienced existentially in all spheres of life—is the source of women's debasement, powerlessness, subjugation, and misery. It is the cause of our pain, and the reason for our stunted lives. Invasion and intrusion, rather than intimacy, nurturance and care, is the "unofficial" story of women's subjective experience of connection.

Thus, modern radical feminism is unified among other things by its insistence on the invasive, oppressive, destructive implications of women's material and existential connection to the other. So defined, radical feminism (of modern times) begins not with the eighties critique of heterosexuality, but rather in the late sixties, with Shulamith Firestone's angry and eloquent denunciation of the oppressive consequences for women of the physical condition of pregnancy. . . .

The radical feminist argument for reproductive freedom appears in legal argument only inadvertently or surreptitiously, but it does on occasion appear. It appeared most recently in the phenomenological descriptions of unwanted pregnancies collated in the *Thornburgh* amicus brief recently filed by the National Abortion Rights Action League ("NARAL").[6] The descriptions of pregnancy collated in that peculiarly non-legal legal document are filled with metaphors of invasion—metaphors, of course, because we lack the vocabulary to name these harms precisely. Those descriptions contrast sharply with the "joy" that cultural feminists celebrate in pregnancy, childbirth and childraising. The invasion of the self by the other emerges as a source of oppression, not a source of moral value.

"During my pregnancy," one woman explains, "I was treated *like a baby machine—an incubator without feelings.*"[7] "Then I got pregnant again," another woman writes,

> This one would be only 13 months younger than the third child. I was faced with the unpleasant fact that I could not stop the babies from coming no matter what I did. . . . *You cannot possibly know what it is like to be the helpless pawn of nature.* I am a 71 year old widow.[8]

"Almost exactly a decade ago," writes another, "I learned I was pregnant. . . . I was sick in my heart and I thought I would kill myself. *It was as if I had been told my body had been invaded with cancer.* It seemed that very wrong."[9] One woman speaks directly, without metaphor: "On the ride home from the clinic, the relief was enormous. I felt happy for the first time in weeks. I had a future again. *I had my body back.*"[10] According to these women's self-descriptions, when the unwanted baby arrives, the injury is again one of invasion, intrusion and limitation. The *harm* of an unwanted pregnancy is that the baby will elicit a *surrender* (not an end) of the mother's life. The *fear* of unwanted pregnancy is that one will lose control of one's individuated being (not that one will die). Thus, one woman writes, "I was like any other woman who had an unintended pregnancy, I was terrified and felt as though my life was out of my control."[11]

This danger, and the fear of it, is gender-specific. It is a fear which grips women, distinctively, and it is a fear about which men, apparently, know practically nothing. . . .

. . . From the point of view of the "connection thesis," what the radical feminists of the eighties find objectionable, invasive, and oppressive about heterosexual intercourse, is precisely what the radical feminists of the sixties found objectionable, invasive, and oppressive about pregnancy and motherhood. According to the eighties radical critique, intercourse, like pregnancy, blurs the physical boundary between self and other, and that blurring of boundaries between self and other constitutes a profound invasion of the self's physical integrity. That invasion—the "dissolving of boundaries"—is something to condemn, not celebrate. Andrea Dworkin explains:

> Sexual intercourse is not intrinsically banal, though pop-culture magazines like *Esquire* and *Cosmopolitan* would suggest that it is. It is intense, often desperate. The internal landscape is violent upheaval, a wild and ultimately cruel disregard of human individuality, . . . no respecter of boundaries. . . .
>
> Sometimes, the skin comes off in sex. *The people merge, skinless. The body loses its boundaries.* . . . There is no physical distance, no self-consciousness, nothing withdrawn or private or alienated, no existence outside physical touch. The skin collapses as a boundary—it has no meaning. . . . Instead, there is necessity, nothing else—being driven, physical immersion in "each other" but with no experience of "each other" as separate entities coming together. . . .
>
> The skin is a line of demarcation, a periphery, the fence, the form, the shape, the first clue to identity in a society . . . and, in purely physical terms, the formal precondition for being human. It is a thin veil of matter separating the outside from the inside. . . . The skin is separation, individuality, the basis for corporeal privacy. . . .[12]

Women, distinctively, lose this "formal precondition for being human" and they lose it in intercourse:

A human being has a body that is inviolate; and when it is violated, it is abused. A woman has a body that is penetrated in intercourse: permeable, its corporeal solidness a lie. The discourse of male truth—literature, science, philosophy, pornography—calls that penetration *violation*. This it does with some consistency and some confidence. *Violation* is a synonym for intercourse. At the same time, the penetration is taken to be a use, not an abuse; it is appropriate to enter her, to push into ("violate") the boundaries of her body. She is human, of course, but by a standard that does not include physical privacy. She is, in fact, human by a standard that precludes physical privacy, since to keep a man out altogether and for a lifetime is deviant in the extreme, a psychopathology, a repudiation of the way in which she is expected to manifest her humanity.[13]

Like pregnancy, then, intercourse is invasive, intrusive and violative, and like pregnancy it is therefore the cause of women's oppressed, invaded, intruded, violated, and debased lives. . . .

The material, sporadic violation of a woman's body occasioned by pregnancy and intercourse implies an existential and pervasive violation of her privacy, integrity and life projects. According to radical feminists, women's longings for individuation, physical privacy, and independence go well beyond the desire to avoid the dangers of rape or unwanted pregnancy. Women also long for liberation from the oppression of intimacy (and its attendant values) which both cultural feminism and most women officially, and wrongly, overvalue. Intimacy, in short, is *intrusive*, even when it isn't life threatening (perhaps *especially* when it isn't life threatening). An unwanted pregnancy is disastrous, but even a *wanted* pregnancy and motherhood are intrusive. The child *intrudes*, just as the fetus invades.

Similarly, while unwanted heterosexual intercourse is disastrous, even wanted heterosexual intercourse is intrusive. The penis occupies the body and "divides the woman" internally, to use Andrea Dworkin's language, in consensual intercourse no less than in rape. It preempts, challenges, negates, and *renders impossible* the maintenance of physical integrity and the formation of a unified self. The deepest unofficial story of radical feminism may be that intimacy—

the official value of cultural feminism—is itself oppressive. Women secretly, unofficially, and surreptitiously long for the very individuation that cultural feminism insists women fear: the freedom, the independence, the individuality, the sense of wholeness, the confidence, the self-esteem, and the security of identity which can only come from a life, a history, a path, a voice, a sexuality, a womb, and a body of one's own. Dworkin explains:

In the experience of intercourse, she loses the capacity for integrity because her body—the basis of privacy and freedom in the material world for all human beings—is entered and occupied; the boundaries of her physical body are—neutrally speaking—violated. What is taken from her in that act is not recoverable, and she spends her life—wanting, after all to have something—pretending that pleasure is in being reduced through intercourse to insignificance. . . . She learns to eroticize powerlessness and self-annihilation. The very boundaries of her own body become meaningless to her, and even worse, useless to her. The transgression of those boundaries comes to signify a sexually charged degradation into which she throws herself, having been told, convinced, that identity, for a female, is there—somewhere beyond privacy and self-respect.[14]

Radical feminism, then, is unified by a particular description of the subjectivity of the material state of connection. According to that description, women dread intrusion and invasion, and long for an independent, individualized, *separate* identity. While women may indeed "officially" value intimacy, what women unofficially crave is physical privacy, physical integrity, and sexual celibacy—in a word, physical exclusivity. In the moral realm, women officially value contextual, relational, caring, moral thinking, but secretly wish that everyone would get the hell out of our lives so that we could pursue our own projects—we loathe the intrusion that intimacy entails. In the epistemological and moral realms, while women officially value community, the web, the spinning wheel, and the weave, we privately crave solitude, self-regard, self-esteem, linear thinking, legal rights, and principled thought. . . .

	The Official Story (Liberal legalism and cultural feminism)		The Unofficial Story (Critical legalism and radical feminism)	
	Value	Harm	Longing	Dread
LEGAL THEORY (human beings)	Autonomy	Annihilation; Frustration	Attachment; Connection	Alienation
FEMINIST THEORY (women)	Intimacy	Separation	Individuation	Invasion; Intrusion

[In this way,] then, we can schematize the contrast between the description of the "human being" that emerges from modern legal theory, and the description of women that emerges from modern feminism [see diagram].

As the diagram reveals, the descriptions of the subjectivity of human existence told by feminist theory and legal theory contrast at every point. There is no overlap. First, and most obviously, the "official" descriptions of human beings' subjectivity and women's subjectivity contrast rather than compare. According to liberal theory, human beings respond aggressively to their natural state of relative physical equality. . . . The description of women's subjectivity told by cultural feminism is much the opposite. According to cultural feminism, women inhabit a realm of natural *inequality*. They are physically stronger than the fetus and the infant. Women respond to their natural inequality over the fetus and infant not with aggression, but with nurturance and care. . . .

The subterranean descriptions of subjectivity that emerge from the unofficial stories of radical feminism and critical legalism also contrast rather than compare. According to the critical legalists, human beings respond to their natural state of physical separateness not with aggression, fear and mutual suspicion, as liberalism holds, but with longing. Men suffer from a perpetual dread of isolation and alienation and a fear of rejection, and harbor a craving for community, connection, and association. Women, by contrast, according to radical feminism, respond to their natural state of material connection to the other with a craving for individuation and a loathing for invasion. Just as clearly, the subterranean dread men have of alienation (according to critical legalism) contrasts sharply with the subterranean dread that women have

of invasion and intrusion (according to radical feminism). . . .

Further, the potential for connection which women naturally have and which cultural feminism celebrates, is in a sense the *goal* of critical legalism's alienated hero. For that reason, perhaps, the critical description of subjectivity may be confusedly identified as feminist. Nevertheless, the identification is over-stated. . . .

[W]omen value love and intimacy because they express the unity of self and nature within our own selves. More generally, women do not struggle toward connection with others, against what turn out to be insurmountable obstacles. Intimacy is not something which women fight to become capable of. We just do it. It is ridiculously easy. It is also, I suspect, qualitatively beyond the pale of male effort. The difference might be put pictorially: the intimacy women value is a sharing of intersubjective territory that preexists the effort made to identify it. The connection that I suspect men strive for does not preexist the effort, and it is not a sharing of space; at best it is an adjacency. . . .

Similarly, the dread of alienation that (according to critical legal studies) permeates men's lives is not the same as the fear of isolation and separation from the other that characterizes women's lives. The fear of separation, for women, is fundamental, physical, economic, empathic, and psychological, as well as psychic. Separation from one's infant will kill the infant to whom the mother has been physically and then psychically connected, and therefore a part of the mother will die as well; separation from one's community may have similarly life threatening consequences. The alienation men dread is not the fear that oneself or the one with whom one is in symbiosis will be threatened. The alienation that men dread is not a sorrow over fundamental, basic, "first" existential state of being. The longing to overcome alienation is a socially constructed reaction against the natural fact of individuation. More bluntly—love, for men, is an acquired skill; separation (and therefore autonomy) is what comes naturally. The separation that endangers women, by contrast, is what is socially constructed—attachment is natural. Separation and the dread of it, is the response to the natural (and pleasant) state of connection.

Second, the description of women's subjective nature, aspirations, and fears drawn by radical feminism is not the same as the description of "human nature" employed by liberalism. It is not hard, however, to see the basis for this confusion. . . . From the radical feminist point of view, "liberal rights-talk," so disparaged by critical legalists, is just fine, and it would be even better if it protected women against the dangers that characterize their lives, as well as protecting men against the dangers that characterize their lives.

The structural similarity ends there, though. The *invasion* and *intrusion* that women dread from the penetrating and impregnating potential of the connected other is not the same as the annihilation and frustration by the separate other that men fear. Men's greatest fear is that of being wiped out—of being killed. The fear of sexual and fetal invasion and intrusion that permeates women's lives is not the fear of annihilation or frustration. The fear of sexual and fetal invasion is the fear of being occupied *from within*, not annihilated from without; of having one's self overcome, not ended; of having one's own physical and material life taken over by the pressing physical urgency of another, not ended by the conflicting interests of another; of being, in short, overtaken, occupied, displaced, and invaded, not killed. Furthermore, the intrusiveness of less damaging forms of intimacy—"wanted" intimacy—is not equivalent to the lesser form of annihilation liberalism recognizes: having one's ends frustrated by the conflicting ends of the other. I do not fear having my "ends" frustrated; I fear having my ends "displaced" before I even formulate them. I fear that I will be refused the right to be an "I" who fears. I fear that my ends will not be my own. I fear that the

phrase "my ends" will prove to be (or already is) oxymoronic. I fear I will never feel the freedom, or have the space, to become an ends-making creature.

Similarly, the individuation prized by radical feminism is not the same as the autonomy liberalism heralds, although it may be a precondition of it. The "autonomy" praised by liberalism is one's right to pursue one's own ends. "Individuation," as understood by radical feminism, is the right *to be* the sort of creature who might have and then pursue one's "own" ends. Women's longing for individuation is a longing for a transcendent state of individuated being against that which is internally contrary, given, fundamental, and first. Autonomy is something which is natural to men's existential state and which the state might protect. Individuation, by contrast, is the material precondition of autonomy. Individuation is what you need to be before you can even begin to think about what you need to be free.

These, then, are the differences between the "human beings" assumed by legal theory and women, as their lives are now being articulated by feminist theory. . . .

. . . Women often, and perhaps increasingly, experience heterosexual intercourse as freely chosen intimacy, not invasive bondage. A radicalism that flatly denies the reality of such a lived experience runs the risk of making itself unintelligible and irrelevant to all people, not to mention the audience that matters most: namely, those women for whom intercourse is not free, not chosen, and anything but intimate, and who have no idea that it either could be or should be both.

. . . I am not denying that heterosexuality is compulsory in this culture or that women as a consequence of that compulsion become alienated from their desire for freedom. It is indeed true that both heterosexuality and heterosexual intercourse are compulsory. But heterosexuality is compulsory because of the institutions that render it compulsory, not because of the nature of the act. The same is true of motherhood and pregnancy. Because they are compulsory, motherhood and heterosexuality are tremendously constraining, damaging, and oppressive. It is indeed true that the institutions which render them such need to be, ought to be, and will be destroyed. But it does not follow from any of this that either motherhood or intercourse themselves will be, need to be, or ought to be destroyed. . . .

Now, it is also true—emphatically true—that neither motherhood nor intercourse have been "released" from patriarchy. Until they are, there is no project more vital to our understanding of women's present oppression than the description of the subjective experience of motherhood, and of intercourse, within the patriarchal institutions that render those activities compulsory. . . .

. . . Even if it is true that women, like men, live within the parameters of a contradiction, women live within the parameters of this fundamental contradiction *within the oppressive conditions of patriarchy.* Men don't (although men do live within the parameters of the oppressive conditions of capitalism). Therefore, feminists need to develop not just an examination of the experience of the contradiction between invasion and intimacy to which our potential for connection gives rise, but also a description of how patriarchy affects, twists, perverts, and surely to some extent causes that contradiction. We also need, however, to imagine how the contradiction would be felt outside of patriarchy, and we need to reflect on our own experiences of nonpatriarchal mothering, intercourse, and intimacy to generate such imaginings. For while women's bodies may continue to be "materially connected" to others as long as they are women's bodies, they need not forever be *possessed* by others. Our connection to the other is a function of our material condition; our possession by the other, however, is a function of patriarchy. We need to imagine both having power over our bodies and power over our contradictory material state. We need to imagine how this fundamental contradiction would feel outside of the context of the dangers and fears that patriarchy requires. . . .

We need to ask these questions of intercourse as well. What would intercourse feel like, or *be,* in a world in which it was freely chosen? What would it mean to have intercourse in a world in which women's pleasures were honored, and

women's injuries were cared for, and women's labor was compensated? And finally we need to ask these questions of intimacy generally. How would the "contradiction" between invasion and intimacy feel in a world free of the fear of male sexual aggression? Would intimacy be entirely non-threatening where there was no reason to fear rape? Would individuation be as enticing where intercourse and motherhood were not mandatory? Would separation be as harmful where familial association was not the assumed form of women's lives? How would the contradiction between intimacy and intrusion feel, if we had no reason to fear the more life threatening forms of invasion? We need to ask these questions, but we also need to *answer* them.

We need to show what the exclusion of women from law's protection has meant to both women and law, and we need to show what it means for the Rule of Law to exclude women and women's values.

The way to do this—the only way to do this—is to tell true stories of women's lives. The Hobbesian "story" of deliverance from the state of nature to the Rule of Law, as both liberal and radical legal scholars are fond of pointing out, does not purport to be history. But that doesn't make it fantasy. The Hobbesian story of the state of nature (and the critical story of alienation as well) is a synthesis of umpteen thousands of personal, subjective, everyday, male experiences. *Images* are generated from that synthesis, and those images, sometimes articulate, sometimes not, of what it means to be a human being then become the starting point of legal theory. Thus, for example, the Hobbesian, liberal picture of the "human being" as someone who treasures autonomy and fears annihilation from the other comes from men's primary experiences, presumably, of school yard fights, armed combat, sports, games, work, big brothers, and fathers. Similarly, the critical picture of the human being as someone who longs for attachment and dreads alienation comes from the male child's memory of his mother, from rejection experiences painfully culled from his adolescence, and from the adult male's continuing inability to introspect, converse, or commune with the natural world, including the natural world of others.

NOTES

[1]Robert Nozick, *Anarchy, State, and Utopia* 33 (1974).
[2]Ronald Dworkin, *A Matter of Principle* 191 (1985) (capitalization omitted) (emphasis added).
[3]*Id.* at 192–3 (capitalization omitted).
[4]Nancy Chodorow, *The Reproduction of Mothering* 167 (1978).
[5]Carol Gilligan, *In a Different Voice* at 8 (1982).

[6]Amicus Brief for the National Abortion Rights Action League, et al., *Thornburgh v. American College of Obstetricians and Gynecologists*, Nos. 84–495 and 84–1379 ("NARAL Amicus Brief") (on file at The University of Chicago Law Review). For the Supreme Court opinion, see 476 U.S. 747 (1986).
[7]NARAL Amicus Brief at 13 (emphasis added).
[8]*Id.* at 19 (emphasis added).
[9]*Id.* at 28 (emphasis added).
[10]*Id.* at 29 (emphasis added).
[11]*Id.* at 29.
[12]Andrea Dworkin, *Intercourse* 21–22 (1987) (emphasis added).
[13]*Id.* at 122.
[14]*Id.* at 137–38.

REVIEW AND DISCUSSION QUESTIONS

1. What is the "separation thesis"? Why is it not true of women?
2. Describe the image of human nature and law offered by liberal legalism and critical legal studies.
3. Describe the image of human nature and law offered by cultural feminists and radical feminists.
4. "Though their views of community are similar, the cultural feminists and CLS also differ in an important respect." Explain.
5. Compare and contrast the harm or fear expressed by liberal legalism with that of radical feminists.
6. Does West's acknowledgment that these positions are not universally true of either men or women undermine her claim? Is the basis of the claim cultural or biological?
7. Describe West's recommendations regarding what women should now do to further their understanding of law and politics.
8. Women are in some sense separated from other people, including their children, just as men are in some sense connected. Does that matter for West's argument?

Legal Realism, Critical Legal Studies, and Dworkin

Andrew Altman

In this essay, Andrew Altman discusses the challenge posed by Critical Legal Studies to Dworkin's account of law and interpretation. Beginning with a description of the legal realists' position, Altman goes on to show how Dworkin might be thought to offer a response. But, argues Altman, the CLS arguments cannot be so easily met by Dworkin. Beginning with the claim that the law is a "patchwork quilt" of competing ideologies, CLS offers two challenges to Dworkin. The first questions Dworkin's claim that there is a single, best interpretation of the law; the other challenges the legitimacy of judicial authority within Dworkin's theory. Both arguments depend, finally, on the fact that there is room for significant disagreement among well-intentioned judges about both law and political morality.

A.

. . . Legal realists insist that the legal system contains competing rules which will be available for a judge to choose in almost any litigated case. . . .

This may seem to leave the realist open to one of the principal criticisms which Dworkinians have made of Hart: the law is more than just legal rules. It is also the ethical principles and ideals of which the rules are an (albeit imperfect) expression, and it is these principles and ideals which help to guide judges to a determinate outcome.[1] Indeed, the Dworkinian might try to use the realist indeterminacy analysis to his advantage: if the law were simply a collection of rules, as Hart thinks, it would be afflicted by exactly the kind of deep and pervasive indeterminacy which the realist posits. Yet, if the law were indeterminate to the degree suggested by the realist analysis, it would not be much more than a pious fraud: judges would be "legislating" not only in penumbral cases, but in all cases. Judges would always be creating law, in flagrant violation of their institutional duty to apply preexisting law. The Dworkinian may conclude that we face this choice: either include principles and ideals as part of the law in order to contain (and, perhaps, eliminate) the indeterminacy it would have were it simply a collection of rules or admit that common-law adjudication is a fraud. Although the latter choice is logically possible, assumptions shared by both Dworkin and his positivist critics make it an entirely implausible one from their point of view. The only plausible alternative may thus seem to be the acceptance of Dworkin's important idea that ethical principles be understood as part of the law even when they are not explicitly formulated in some authoritative legal text or clearly identifiable by the application of some noncontroversial, positivist rule for specifying authoritative legal norms in terms of their source. Thus, Dworkin argues that adjudication requires the invocation of principles which take judges "well past the point where it would be accurate to say that any 'test' of pedigree exists. . . ."[2] Moreover, such principals are, on Dworkin's view, binding on judges and so we must realize that "legal obligation . . . [is] . . . imposed by a constellation of principles as well as by an established rule."[3] Indeed, it is this constellation of principles which must guide the judge to a determinate outcome when the relevant legal rules are in competition with one another. For instance, the principles could indicate to the judge the proper scope of application of each of the competing rules and thus resolve any apparent conflict by showing that just one of the rules was properly applicable in the case at hand.

Yet, which principles are legally binding? Dworkin's answer is that they are those which belong to the "soundest theory of the settled law."[4] The settled law consists of those legal rules and doctrines which would be accepted as authoritative by the consensus of the legal community. The soundest theory is the most defensible ethical and political theory which coheres with and justifies those legal rules and doctrines. The coherence does not have to be perfect, for Dworkin allows that the soundest theory may characterize some rules and legal outcomes as mistakes, but coherence with most of the settled law is demanded. In principle, the soundest theory is to encompass every area of law: every branch of the common law, all statutes, the whole body of administrative law, and the entire range of constitutional law. Of course, Dworkin recognizes that no merely human judge could ever formulate and defend such a theory. But his character, Hercules, is intended to show us that, in principle, such a theory could be formulated and defended by a sufficiently great intelligence.[5] Even though the fictional, judicial Hercules has powers far beyond those of mortal judges, Dworkin tells us that mortal judges are committed both to the logical possibility of such a character and to the task of trying to arrive at the outcome he would arrive at were he to be hearing their cases. Mortal judges thus can and do appeal to principles in reaching determinate outcomes, and, in doing so, they are giving force to preexisting legal obligations, and not simply making a political choice among competing legal rules. . . .

In this section, I have raised the possibility that Dworkin's jurisprudential project succeeds where Hart failed in defeating the radical realist indeterminacy thesis. However, it would be premature to make a judgment regarding the success of Dworkin's project in this respect, for scholars in the Critical Legal Studies movement have picked up and elaborated realist ideas in a way that seriously threatens the foundations of Dworkinian jurisprudence. . . .

B.

CLS scholars accept the Dworkinian idea that legal rules are infused with ethical principles and ideals. Moreover, they take such principles as seriously as Dworkinians in that they conceive of the articulation and examination of such principles to be one of the major tasks of legal theory. Thus, Duncan Kennedy has analyzed the role in the form and content of legal doctrine of what he characterizes as "individualist" and "altruist" ethical conceptions. And Roberto Unger has examined the normative principles which he takes to be embodied in the common law of contracts.[6] Yet, one of the main themes of CLS work is that the incorporation of ethical principles and ideals into the law cuts against Dworkinian efforts to rescue legal determinacy. The operative claim in CLS analysis is that the law is infused with irresolvably opposed principles and ideals. Kennedy writes that the opposing ethical conceptions which inform legal doctrine "reflect a deeper level of contradiction. At this deeper level, we are divided, among ourselves and also within ourselves, between irreconcilable visions of humanity and society, and between radically different aspirations for our common future."[7] While the realists stress competing rules, CLSers stress competing, and indeed irreconcilable, principles and ideals. Yet, the basic theme is the same: the judge must make a choice which is not dictated by the law. In the CLS analysis, the choice is one of several competing principles or ideals to be used in guiding her to a decision. Different choices lead to different outcomes. Thus, from the CLS perspective, the jurisprudential invocation of principles only serves to push back to another stage the point at which legal indeterminacy enters and judicial choice takes place.

The Dworkinian response would be to deny that legal indeterminacy follows from the fact that the law contains principles which pull in opposing directions. One of Dworkin's major points in his account of principles is that they have differing weights. Thus, even if we have a case in which two competing principles appear applicable, for example, "A person should not be held liable unless she was at fault" versus "As between two innocents, the one who caused the harm should pay," Dworkin will argue that, in all likelihood, one of those principles will carry greater weight in the case at hand and it is that principle which determines the correct legal outcome. Dworkin does allow for the possibility that there may be a case in which the weights of all applicable principles are exactly equal, leaving the legal outcome truly indeterminate, but goes on to claim that such cases will be extremely rare in any developed legal system.

It must be noted here that Dworkin's conception of the soundest theory of the settled law assumes that there is some metalevel principle for determining the appropriate weights to be assigned to the different principles which may be applicable in a given case. This assumption becomes clear once we see that Dworkin's conception of the soundest theory rejects intuitionism, according to which relative weights are intuited in each case without there being any higher order standard in virtue of which each principle has its particular weight. Dworkin's position is that there is a legal fact of the matter regarding the weight of a given principle in a given case, and this fact is determined by the weight that principle receives according to the standards of the soundest theory of the settled law. Moreover, this rejection of intuitionism is firmly rooted in a commitment to the rule of law ideal. That ideal requires that legal decisions be the outcome of reasoning that can be reconstructed according to principles which can be articulated and understood. To use a term which has been popular among legal theorists, judicial decision must be "principled." This means that the judge cannot simply appeal to his inarticulate sense that a particular principle is weightier than some competing principle in the case before him. He must believe that there is some higher order principle which makes the one weightier than the other, and he must at least try to figure out and articulate what that higher order principle is.

Now, one line of CLS attack against Dworkin is to argue that there is no discoverable metaprinciple for assigning weights. Duncan Kennedy suggests this line in discussing the possibility of using moral theory to justify legal doctrine. Kennedy admits that, in the context of the fact situation of a particular case, opposing principles do not necessarily carry the same weight: "we are able to distinguish particular fact situations in which one side is more plausible than the other. The difficulty, the mystery, is that there are no available metaprinciples to explain just what it is about these particular situations that make them ripe for resolution."[8] Actually, Kennedy's point should be put in a less sweeping way: no one has come up with such metaprinciples, and it is implausible to think that it can be done. When put in these terms, the CLS position becomes an essentially reactive one which awaits Dworkinian efforts and then reacts against them: Dworkinians put forth their rational/ethical reconstructions of the law (or some portion of it), complete with metaprinciples for assigning weights to principles, and then CLSers and others attempt to show that the reconstruction is inadequate and incoherent. The burden of production thus seems to be on the Dworkinians. What have they produced?

The closest thing we have from them to a Dworkinian reconstruction of a portion of the settled law is Charles Fried's effort to reconstruct contract law on the basis of the principle that one ought to keep one's promises and related conceptions from a liberal individualist philosophy. . . .[9]

It is important to recognize here that I am not talking about the theory which Dworkin's Hercules would try to construct, one encompassing the entire body of the law. Rather, what is at issue is a theory for some connected but limited portion of the law, such as the law of contracts. Both CLS and I assume that Dworkinians are committed to the notion that such limited theories can be built by humans, not merely by gods. . . .

. . . CLSers would judge as totally implausible the belief that any coherent Dworkinian

theory, complete with metaprinciples, can be developed for any significant portion of the settled law. Yet, the CLS claims in this regard are unpersuasive, given the argument that has been adduced in their behalf to this point. Even if it is admitted that there are difficulties in the way of constructing a Dworkinian theory for any significant portion of the settled law because such a portion will invariably embody principles in tension with one another, surely no argument has yet been given that makes it implausible to believe that such a theory can be constructed. . . .

More fundamentally, the point is that these principles have their weight and scope of application in the settled law determined, not by some metalevel philosophical principle which imposes order and harmony, but by an ideological power struggle in which coherent theories become compromised and truncated as they fit themselves into the body of law. The settled law as a whole, and each field within it, represents the (temporary) outcome of such an ideological conflict. This is, to be sure, a causal claim about the genesis of legal doctrines and principles, rather than a logical one regarding the lack of amenability of such doctrines and principles to rational reconstruction. But the CLS positions can be interpreted as linking the logical claim to the causal one. The position is that it is implausible to believe that any system of norms generated by such a process of struggle and compromise will be capable of an ethically principled reconstruction. Unger summarizes the CLS view this way:

> . . . it would be strange if the results of a coherent, richly developed normative theory were to coincide with a major portion of any extended branch of law. The many conflicts of interest and vision that lawmaking involves, fought out by countless minds and wills working at cross purposes, would have to be the vehicle of an immanent moral rationality whose message could be articulated by a single cohesive theory. This daring and implausible sanctification of the actual is in fact undertaken by the dominant legal theories. . . .[10]

This idea that the law is a patchwork quilt, as it were, of irreconcilably opposed ideologies is tied to CLS's version of the repudiation of the distinction between law (adjudication) and politics. Sometimes CLS scholars suggest that the distinction unravels principally because of the fact that controversial normative and descriptive judgments are just as much an ineliminable part of adjudication as they are of politics. Yet, I think that there is a more important, though related, way in which the distinction is thought to unravel. The idea is this: all of those ideological controversies which play a significant part in the public debate of our political culture are replicated in the argument of judicial decision. In other words, the spectrum of ideological controversy in politics is reproduced in the law. Of course, CLS recognizes that in legal argument the controversies will often be masked or hidden by talk of the intent of the framers, the requirements of *stare decisis*, and so on. The point is that the same ideological debates which fragment political discourse are replicated in one form or another in a legal argument. As a patchwork quilt of irreconcilable ideologies, the law is a mirror which faithfully reflects the fragmentation of our political culture. Such, at least, is a principal CLS theme.

How is it possible to parlay these CLS ideas regarding the patchwork-quilt character of doctrine and the unraveling of the law/politics distinction into a cogent argument against Dworkinian jurisprudence? I think there are two principal lines of argument. The first seeks to show that it makes no sense to think there is any soundest theory of the settled law. The second seeks to show that the Dworkinian theory fails on its own terms to provide a satisfactory account of the legitimacy of judicial decision making. Let us explore each of these lines of argument in turn.

C.

One possible line of CLS argument is that legal doctrine is so internally inconsistent that it is implausible to believe that there is any single, coherent theory capable of justifying enough of it to satisfy the Dworkinian fit requirement. Consistently applying any of the theories embodied in some significant portion of the law across the entire body of doctrine would, the

argument goes, involve such substantial doctrinal reconstruction that it would violate the Dworkinian mandate that any theory invoked to decide cases fit or cohere with the bulk of the settled law. Thus, ethically principled reconstruction of any substantial portion of doctrine is ruled out by the law's internal contradictions, such contradictions being symptomatic of the law's conception in ideological compromise and struggle and of its tendency to reflect the range of political conflict present in the culture. This means that there simply is no soundest theory of the settled law, and so the Dworkinian efforts to rescue legal determinacy by appealing to such a notion fail. . . .

. . . This state of incoherence is due to the fact that modern ethical thought amounts to an amalgam of fragments of irreconcilable ethical views. Conventional philosophers not only fail to perceive the utter incoherence of modern ethical thought, but operate on the assumption that it is largely in good order. . . . In a very similar way, the debate between Dworkin and his conventional critics fails to join the issue with CLS. They assume a doctrinal coherence which CLS repudiates, and so the conventional debate takes place in terms which are largely irrelevant to the CLS position.

Duncan Kennedy makes the CLS position on doctrinal incoherence plain in his description of a private law field which he takes to be representative of doctrine in general:

> In contract law, for example, there are *two* principles: there is a reliance, solidarity, joint enterprise concept, and there is a hands-off, arms length, expectancy-oriented, "no flexibility and no excuses" orientation. They can be developed very coherently, but only if one accepts that they are inconsistent. There are fifteen or twenty contract doctrines about which there is a conflict. . . . That is the structure of contract doctrine, and it's typical. Doctrine is not consistent or coherent. The outcomes of these conflicts form a patchwork, rather than following straight lines.[11]

Given the terms in which the CLS position has been stated, it is clear what the Dworkinian reply must be in order to join the issue: that doctrine is not as internally contradictory as CLS claims. The main argument would have to be that any internal inconsistencies in legal doctrine are merely marginal, capable of characterization as "mistakes" without any substantial rupture to the fabric of doctrine. This argument would be supplemented, I think, by one to the effect that CLS exaggerates the degree to which theory must fit the settled law in order to be said to fit well enough. To make out these arguments would not be at all easy. CLS analyses have sought to exhibit the deep and pervasive incoherence of doctrine in such areas as constitutional law, labor law, contract law, administrative law, and criminal law, to name only a few. . . . Meanwhile, Dworkinians have done little to respond to these CLS analyses. Moreover, Dworkin's most recent efforts to clarify the character of the fit test provide little ammunition against the CLS argument. Let us briefly examine those efforts in order to see why this is so.

Dworkin's recent writing indicates that the fit test is more sophisticated than some of his critics have taken it to be. He tells us that the degree of fit is not just a matter of adding up the number of precedents and rules for which a given theory accounts. One must also take into consideration such factors as the trend of recent decisions. Two theories may account for the same number of precedents and rules, but, if one accounts for more of the recent decisions and the other for more of the older decisions, then the former has a better fit, according to Dworkin.

Dworkin does not indicate how much weight should be given to the capacity to account for recent trends. Nor does he explain why accounting for a trend in new decisions makes for a better fit than accounting for the pre-trend pattern of old ones. Moreover, he ignores the point that the question of what counts as a significant trend and what counts as an insignificant blip or anomaly is not a theory-neutral one. What counts as a trend from the perspective of one theory may count as an anomaly to be ignored from the perspective of another. It does no good to be told here that the soundest theory of the law determines what is a trend and what is an anomaly, since the fit test is supposed to help us figure out which theory is the soundest

one. But, more to the point for the doctrinal incoherence issue, the CLS contention is that the patchwork character of law is manifested within the body of recent decisions and not just between recent ones and old ones. There may be trends but there are countertrends as well. Some decisions may introduce or expand new lines of doctrine, but other recent decisions will continue the older lines. By characterizing the former as "trends" and giving their line of doctrine greater weight, Dworkin is merely picking out one line of doctrine for favored status from among several conflicting lines. . . .

. . . However, CLS analyses suggest that doctrinal incoherence is so deep and pervasive that, even if one grants that accounting for certain doctrinal lines (the trends) gives somewhat better fit than accounting for others (the countertrends), any coherent theory will prove incompatible with such a broad range of doctrine as to make implausible the notion that it has satisfied the threshold. These analyses do not conclusively establish the point, but they do raise a strong prima facie case to which there has been only the most meager response by conventional legal philosophers of any stripe, Dworkinian or otherwise.

It seems to me, then, that the patchwork quilt line of argument presents unmet and serious challenges to the viability of the Dworkinian jurisprudential project, as well as to other conventional legal philosophies. Even if this CLS argument is met by some cogent conventional response, however, there is an independent line of CLS argument against another key Dworkinian position. Let us now turn to that position.

D.

Dworkin is concerned to defend the legitimacy of judicial decision making that invokes controversial principles of ethical or political philosophy. The Dworkinian judge is licensed to rely on such principles because, as Dworkin well realizes, it is inevitable that a judge who, in a hard case, seeks to enunciate and invoke the principles embodied in the settled law will fail to find principles on which everyone can agree. If the judge is to guide her decision by the principles she thinks are embodied in the law, then the reliance of adjudication on controversial principles is inescapable, at least for many cases. In this sense, Dworkin is willing to acknowledge that adjudication is "political."[12] Yet, he thinks that such an acknowledgment does nothing to impugn the legitimacy of the adjudication.

Dworkin's arguments in favor of the legitimacy of such admittedly "political adjudication" are not entirely clear. Let me suggest the following as the principal Dworkinian argument on this point. The invocation of controversial ethical or political principles in adjudication is constrained by the judicial duty to decide a hard case according to the dictates of the soundest theory of the settled law. Thus, the "political" reasoning and choice of the judge take place within much narrower confines than if she were a legislator deciding what sort of legislative enactment was best. As Dworkin says in his discussion of a judge deciding an abortion case, it is one thing for her to decide whether political philosophy dictates that government should acknowledge a right to an abortion, and it is quite another for her to decide whether the settled law of our legal/political system is best accounted for by a theory incorporating a conception of dignity which entails such a right. The former decision is, of course, appropriate for a legislature, not a court. Yet, it is the latter decision, not the former, which the Dworkinian judge is under a duty to make, and it is a decision which is made within much narrower confines than the former. . . .

. . . What makes this CLS argument particularly interesting for current purposes is that it does not hinge on the adequacy of the patchwork-quilt argument examined in the preceding section. Indeed, it can be construed as granting, *arguendo*, that there is a unique soundest theory of the law which does dictate the correct legal outcomes in hard cases. . . .

The CLS claim that the range of ideological conflict in the political arena is replicated in legal doctrine and argument can be viewed in two ways. On the first, it is taken as reinforcing the patchwork-quilt argument against Dworkin. To the extent that one documents the claim, one lends support to the idea that doctrine is a patchwork quilt of inconsistent political ideologies of which no single, coherent political theory could ever capture very much. Take Kennedy's account of contract law. The CLS argument can be put this way: to the extent that we have no reason to believe that the political philosophy of a welfare-state liberal can be reconciled with that of a libertarian, we have no reason to think that the opposing doctrines of contract law can be logically reconciled with one another, for those doctrines are the legal embodiment of just those opposing political philosophies (or something close to them). The position is then generalized to cover all fields of law. This way of setting up the CLS argument is, at bottom, another effort to show that the law is too internally incoherent for there to be any soundest theory of it and thereby to discredit Dworkin's attempts to defend judicial legitimacy by invoking a judicial duty to decide according to the dictates of the soundest theory.

There is, however, another way to view the CLS claim about the range of ideological conflict embodied in legal doctrine. This alternate reading leads to a line of argument whose key contention is that, even if there were a Dworkinian soundest theory, it would impose no practical constraint on judges whose favored political ideology is in conflict with the one embodied in that theory. The theory would exert no effective pull or tug on the decisions of judges who fail to share its ideology. This is because judges who conscientiously attempt to carry out their Dworkinian duty to decide a hard case according to the soundest theory of the law will read their favored ideology into the settled law and see it as the soundest theory. This would happen, the argument goes, because the authoritative legal materials, in replicating the ideological conflicts of the political arena, contain a sufficient number of doctrines, rules, and arguments representing any politically significant ideology that a judge who conscientiously consults the materials would find his favored ideology in some substantial portion of the settled law and conclude that it was the soundest theory of the law.

Of course, no one expects that the true soundest theory of law will have the power to persuade all conscientious judges of its status. However, the Dworkinian argument for the legitimacy of adjudication in hard cases does presuppose that the theory imposes some practical constraint on judicial decision making by exerting a kind of gravitational pull on those judges who recognize their abstract duty to decide according to the soundest theory but who are in fact in ideological disagreement with the principles of the true theory. (Keep in mind that this judicial duty is abstract in the sense that the statement of the duty contains no specification of the particular theory which is the soundest one, and so recognition of the duty, by itself, does nothing to insure that a judge's decisions will be pulled in any particular direction.) The pull of the true soundest theory doesn't have to be an irresistible one, but, for the Dworkinian legitimacy argument to work, it must be substantial enough to make a difference to the decisions of conscientious judges who in fact hold to an ideology which conflicts with the soundest theory. Many of the decisions of these judges would have to be different from what they would be if there were no soundest theory, and the difference has to be explainable in terms of the pull of the theory. If the soundest theory were to lack any such pull, then the constraint imposed by the duty to decide according to the soundest theory would be illusory, and the Dworkinian defense of judicial legitimacy would fall apart. The CLS argument is that the constraint is an illusion. Judges holding to virtually any ideology which is of significance in the American political arena will simply read their favored ideology into the settled law as its soundest theory. This can be and is done, even by the most conscientious judge, because each view on the political spectrum is embodied in some substantial portion of the authoritative materials. . . .

CLS can agree with Dworkin's important point that judges do not leave the authoritative materials behind when they make a decision in a case where those materials fail to dictate unambiguously an answer to the case. It can also agree with Dworkin that in such cases judges look for the most convincing principles and theories embodied in the materials. The point of the present CLS argument is that, even though judges typically do decide in such Dworkinian fashion and even if there happens to be a soundest theory dictating the correct legal outcome, the existence of such a theory makes no practical difference because a judge will typically see her favored ideology as constituting that theory. The soundest theory is not some brooding omnipresence in the sky, but rather a brooding irrelevance in the sky (assuming it is anywhere at all).

There are two potential lines of response for the Dworkinian to this CLS argument. The first is to deny that the full spectrum of ideological controversy in politics is to be found in legal doctrine and decision and so to hold on to the idea that legal form, particularly the fit requirement, does screen out a significant range of political controversy. This line of response does not appear to me to be very promising. There are a host of CLS analyses of both private and public law, making quite persuasive its contention regarding the extent of ideological controversy within legal doctrine and argument.

A second line of response is to deny that the legitimacy of "political adjudication" in hard cases hinges on whether or not ideological controversy within the law is as wide as it is in the political arena. The idea is that Dworkin's defense of adjudication works, even if the law/politics distinction unravels in precisely the way CLS asserts. In fact, we can find in Dworkin's work two arguments which can be construed in this way. They concern the issue of whether courts have correctly held that there is a legal right to an abortion under our constitutional arrangements. Dworkin imagines the issue turning on the question of whether the concept of dignity implicit in our legal and political institutions implies the existence of such a right. He then examines the suggestion that legislatures, which reflect the will and ideas of the ordinary person, rather than courts, are the most appropriate forum in which to find the answer to such a question. In other words, the suggestion is the positivist one that in hard cases courts should act as legislatures would.

Dworkin claims that there are two arguments against such a suggestion and, by implication, in favor of the judge deciding the issue by what she thinks the (soundest theory of the) law dictates, and not by what (she thinks) the legislature thinks it ought to be. The first argument is that judges think more carefully about the meaning our institutions give to the idea of dignity when they decide cases than ordinary folks do when they cast their ballots (or politicians do when they vote on legislation). Judges are thus thought to have greater competence in handling such hard cases than legislatures do. The second argument is that a Dworkinian judge will legitimately refuse to defer to legislative judgment, even if she thinks that it does reflect the considered opinion of the ordinary person, when she thinks that the opinion is inconsistent with the soundest theory of the law. This is legitimate because such a judge believes that the law really does have a determinate answer to the hard case before her and that it is her duty to discover and announce it, whatever anyone else thinks. By doing so she is acting no differently from a positivist judge in an easy case, who would certainly refrain from a decision contrary to his legal judgment, no matter what the ordinary person/legislature may think.

Neither one of these arguments provides a convincing response to the CLS position. The first would justify the most far-reaching judicial usurpations on the grounds that judges have thought more carefully about the issue in question than did the electorate or their representatives. There is virtually no legislative enactment or policy which is safe from such reasoning. The second argument clearly begs the whole question of whether the law is determinate in hard cases. The Dworkinian judge may believe that it is, but, if that belief is incorrect or even unjustified, it can hardly be claimed that her refusal to defer to legislative judgment in a hard case is analogous to the positivist judge's refusal to do so in an easy case. Yet, even granting the law's determinacy, Dworkin's argument presumes that the soundest theory of the law does impose some effective constraints on judicial decision making. For otherwise there will be no practical difference between a legal regime in which judges have no duty to decide hard cases according to

the dictates of (the soundest theory of) the law but may decide such cases on the basis of their favored ideology, and one in which they do have such a duty. Dworkin's views commit him to the claim that there is not only a difference between the two regimes, but that the latter sort of regime alone can be legitimated in terms of the principles of liberal democracy. . . .

. . . From the CLS perspective, the positivist injunction to decide according to the will of the legislature leaves as much room for judges to make their favored ideology the basis of decision as does the Dworkinian injunction to decide according to the soundest theory. My principal point here, though, concerns Dworkinian jurisprudence. Dworkinians must show that the soundest theory of law is not only a logical possibility, given the tensions existing within doctrine, but that it can exert an effective practical constraint on judges who hold conflicting ideological views. CLS's law/politics argument raises serious doubts about whether the theory, even conceding its existence, would exert any such constraint, and thus far Dworkinians have done little to assuage such doubts.

In this article, I have not aimed at providing the last word on the points of contention between CLS and Dworkinian jurisprudence. I have tried to locate some of the more important issues within a frame that recognizes the influence of legal realism on contemporary legal thought. CLS has picked up and elaborated upon the realist contention that the law largely fails to determine the outcome in cases which are brought to litigation. Among the important advances of the CLS analysis over that of their realist forerunners are: the effort to take seriously and to analyze the conflicting ethical visions and principles which infuse legal doctrine; the painstaking attempts to display doctrinal inconsistencies and incoherencies; and the effort to show how debates in the political arena are replicated in unsuspected corners of private-law doctrine. I believe that these are substantial advances on the realist position and that they can be parlayed into powerful arguments which are thus far unmet by Dworkinians or indeed by conventional legal philosophers of any stripe. It is well past the time when legal philosophers can justifiably ignore the body of work associated with the Critical Legal Studies movement.

NOTES

[1]Dworkin, *Taking Rights Seriously*, pp. 25–26, 36, 44–45, 67–68, 71–80, 82–90, 96–97, 105ff.

[2]Ibid., p. 67.

[3]Ibid., p. 44.

[4]Ibid, p. 67–68, 79, 283, and 340.

[5]Ibid., pp. 105ff.

[6]Kennedy, "Form and Substance in Private Law Adjudication"; Unger, "Critical Legal Studies Movement," *Harvard Law Review* 96 (1983): 561, 616–46. Also see Kennedy, "The Structure of Blackstone's Commentaries," *Buffalo Law Review* 28 (1978): 205. Morton Horwitz, *The Transformation of American Law: 1780–1860* (Cambridge, MA: Harvard University Press, 1977); and Mark Kelman, "Interpretive Construction in the Substantive Criminal Law." *Stanford Law Review* 33 (1981): 591.

[7]Kennedy, "Form and Substance in Private Law Adjudication," p. 1685.

[8]Kennedy, "Form and Substance in Private Law Adjudication," p. 1724.

[9]Fried, *Contract as Promise*.

[10]Unger, "The Critical Legal Studies Movement," p. 571.

[11]Kennedy, "The Political Significance of the Structure of the Law School Curriculum." p. 15.

[12]Dworkin, *Taking Rights Seriously*, p. 127.

REVIEW AND DISCUSSION QUESTIONS

1. Describe the "patchwork quilt" thesis. What two arguments against Dworkin does it lead to?

2. The first CLS argument involves the extent to which law is internally contradictory. Why does that matter, according to Altman?

3. Altman suggests law places no "practical" constraints on judges. Explain why.

4. Altman thinks CLS arguments undermine Dworkin's position on political legitimacy and judicial power even if there is a single, soundest theory. Explain Altman's argument.

Skepticism, Objectivity, and Democracy

Ronald Dworkin

In this essay, Ronald Dworkin discusses two issues that have been raised against him and others by a variety of critics, including CLS proponents and feminists. The first is the skeptical claim that because law and legal interpretation demand that judges rely on their moral and political beliefs, the law is inherently subjective. In response, Dworkin distinguishes two forms of skepticism about moral objectivity or truth: external (which holds that moral claims cannot be proved scientifically and are not about the natural world) and internal (which is a moral position in competition with other moral views). Only global internal skepticism, Dworkin argues, is incompatible with the objectivity of moral and legal interpretation, and that form of skepticism is entirely implausible. The other, related charge is that when judges rely on political morality in their decisions, they undermine their own authority by making decisions that are more properly left to elected officials. But again, Dworkin disagrees, claiming that the alternative, positivist (or conventionalist, as he terms it) understanding of interpretation is subject to the same criticisms—all of which can be easily answered.

IS IT DELUSION?

INTERNAL AND EXTERNAL SCEPTICISM

I have been describing naturalism as a theory about how judges should decide cases. It is of course a further question whether American (or any other) judges actually do decide cases that way. I shall not pursue that further question now. Instead, I want to consider certain arguments that I expect will be made against naturalism simply as a recommendation. . . . I shall begin with what might be called the sceptical attack.

I put my description of naturalism in what might be called a subjective mode. I described the question which, according to naturalism, judges should put to themselves and answer from their own convictions. Someone is bound to object that, although each judge can answer these questions for himself, different judges will give different answers, and no single answer can be said to be *objectively* right. "There are as many different 'best' interpretations as there are interpreters," he will say, "because no one can offer any argument in favor of one interpretation over another, except that it strikes him as the best, and it will strike some other interpreter as the worst. No doubt judges (as well as many other people) would deny this. They think their opinions can have some objective standing, that they can be either true or false. But this is delusion merely."

What response can naturalism, as I have described it, make to this sceptical challenge? We must begin by asking what kind of scepticism is in play. I have in mind a distinction which, once again, might be easier to state if we return to a literary analogy. Suppose we are studying Hamlet and the question is put by some critic whether, before the play begins, Hamlet and Ophelia have been lovers. This is a question of interpretation, and two critics who disagree might present arguments trying to show why the play is, all things considered, more valuable as a work of art on one or the other understanding about Hamlet and Ophelia. But plainly a third position is possible. Someone might argue that it makes no difference to the importance or value of the play which of these assumptions is made about the lovers, because the play's importance lies in a humanistic vision of life and fate, not in any detail of plot or character whose reading would be affected by either assumption. This third position argues that the right answer to this particular question of interpretation is only that there is no right answer; that there is no "best" interpretation of the sexual relationship between Hamlet and Ophelia, only "different" interpretations, because neither interpretation would make the play more or less valuable as a work of art. This might strike you (it does me) as exactly the right position to take on this particular issue. It is, in a sense, a sceptical position, because it denies "truth" both to the proposition that Hamlet slept with Ophelia, and to the apparently contrary proposition that he did not. But if this is scepticism, it is what [we] might call *internal* scepticism. It does not challenge the idea that good arguments can in principle be found for one interpretation of Hamlet rather than another. On the contrary it *relies* on an interpretive argument—that the value of the play lies in a dimension that does not intersect the sexual question—in order to reach its "sceptical" position on that question.

Contrast the position of someone who says that no one interpretation of any work of art could ever succeed in showing it to be either really better or really worse, because there is not and cannot be any such thing as "value" in art at all. He means that there is something very wrong with the enterprise of interpretation (at least as I have described it) as a whole, not simply with particular issues or arguments within it. Of course he may have arguments for his position, or think he has; but these will not be arguments that, like the arguments of the internal sceptic, explicitly assume a positive theory of the value of art in general or of a particular work of art. They will be a priori, philosophical arguments attempting to show that the very idea of value in art is a deep mistake, that people who say they find a work of art "good" or "valuable" are not describing any objective property, but only expressing their own subjective reaction.

This is *external* scepticism about art, and about interpretation in art.

THE THREAT OF SCEPTICISM

If a lawyer says that no one interpretation of a legal record can be "objectively" the correct interpretation, he might have external scepticism in mind. He might mean that if two judges disagree about the "correct" interpretation of the emotional damages cases, because they hold different theories of what a just law of negligence would be like, their disagreement is for that reason alone merely "subjective," and neither side can be "objectively" right. I cannot consider, in this essay, the various arguments that philosophers have offered for external scepticism about political morality. The best of these arguments rely on a general thesis of philosophy that might be called the "demonstrability hypothesis." This holds that no proposition can be true unless the means exist, at least in principle, to demonstrate its truth through arguments to everyone who understands the language and is rational. If the demonstrability hypothesis is correct, then external scepticism is right about a great many human enterprises and activities; perhaps about all of them, including the activities we call scientific. I know of no good reason to accept the demonstrability hypothesis (it is at least an embarrassment that this hypothesis cannot itself be demonstrated in the sense it requires) and I am not myself an external sceptic. But rather than pursue the question of the demonstrability hypothesis, I shall change the subject.

Suppose you are an external sceptic about justice and other aspects of political morality. What follows about the question of how judges should decide cases? About whether naturalism is better than other (more conservative or more radical) theories of adjudication? You might think it follows that you should take no further interest in these questions at all. If so, I have some sympathy with your view. After all, you believe, on what you take to be impressive philosophical grounds, that no way of deciding cases at law can really be thought to be any better than any other, and that no way of interpreting legal practice can be preferred to any other on rational grounds. The "correct" theory of what judges should do is only a matter of what judges feel like doing, or of what they believe will advance political causes to which they happen to be drawn. The "correct" interpretation of legal practice is only a matter of reading legal history so that it appeals to you, or so that you can use it in your own political interests. If you are convinced of these externally sceptical propositions, you might well do better to take up the interesting questions raised by certain sociologists of law—questions about the connection between judges' economic class and the decisions they are likely to reach, for example. Or to take up the study of strategies for working your will on judges if you ever come to argue before them, or on other judges if you ever join the bench yourself. Your external scepticism might well persuade you to take up these "practical" questions and set aside the "theoretical" questions you have come to see as meaningless.

But it is worth noticing that philosophers who say they are external sceptics rarely draw that sort of practical conclusion for themselves. Most of them seem to take a rather different line, which I do not myself fully understand, but which can, I think, fairly be represented as follows. External scepticism is not a position within an enterprise, but about an enterprise. It does not tell us to stop making the kinds of arguments we are disposed to make and accept and act on within morality or politics, but only to change our beliefs about what we are doing when we act this way. Imagine that some chessplayers thought that chess was an "objective" battle between forces of light and darkness, so that when black won good had triumphed in some metaphysical sense. External sceptics about chess would reject this view, and think that chess was entertainment merely; but they would not thereupon cease playing chess or play it any differently from their deluded fellow players. So external sceptics about political morality will still have opinions and make arguments about justice; they will simply understand, in their philosophical moments, that when they do this they are not discovering timeless and objective truths.

If you are an external sceptic who takes this attitude, you will have driven a wedge between your external scepticism and any judgments you might make about how judges should decide cases, in general, or about what the best justification is of some part of the law, in particular. You will have your own opinions about these matters, which you will express in arguments or, if you are an academic lawyer, in law review articles or, if you are a judge, in your decisions. You may well come to believe that the best interpretation of the emotional [damage] cases shows them to be grounded in the principle of foreseeability, for example. When you retreat to your philosophical study, you will have a particular view about the opinions you expressed or exhibited while you were "playing the game." You will believe that your opinions about the best justification of the emotional damage cases were "merely" subjective opinions (whatever that means) with no basis in any "objective" reality. But this does not itself provide any argument in favor of *other* opinions about the best interpretation. In particular, it does not provide any argument in favor of the *internally* sceptical opinion that no interpretation of the accident cases is best.

Of course your external scepticism leaves you free to take up that internally sceptical position if you believe you have good internal arguments for it. Suppose you are trying to decide whether the best interpretation of the emotional damage cases lies in the principle that people in the area of physical risk may recover for emotional damage, or the broader principle that anyone whose emotional damage was foreseeable may recover. After the most diligent search and reflection asking yourself exactly the questions naturalism poses, you may find that the case for neither of these interpretations seems to you any stronger than the case for the other. I think this is very unlikely, but that is beside the present point, which is only that it is possible. You would be internally sceptical, in this way, about any uniquely "correct" interpretation of this group of cases; but you would have supplied an affirmative argument, beginning in your naturalistic theory, for that internally sceptical conclusion. It would not have mattered whether you were an external sceptic, who nevertheless "played the game" as a naturalist, or an external "believer"

who thought that naturalism was stitched into the fabric of the universe. You would have reached the same internally sceptical conclusion, on these assumed beliefs and facts, in either case.

What is, then, the threat that external scepticism poses to naturalism? It is potentially very threatening indeed, not only to naturalism, but to all its rival theories of adjudication as well. It may persuade you to try to have nothing to do with morality or legal theory at all, though I do not think you will succeed in giving up these immensely important human activities. If this very great threat fails (as it seems to have failed for almost all external sceptics) then no influence remains. For in whatever spirit you do enter any of these enterprises—however firmly your fingers may be crossed—the full range of positions within the enterprise is open to you on equal terms. If you end in some internally sceptical position of some sort, this will be because of the internal power of the arguments that drove you there, not because of your external sceptical credentials.

We must now consider another possibility. The sceptical attack upon naturalism may in fact consist, not in the external scepticism I have been discussing, but in some global form of internal scepticism. I just conceded the possibility that we might find reason for internal scepticism about the best interpretation of some particular body of law. Suppose we had reasons to be internally sceptical about the best interpretation of any and all parts of the law? It is hard to imagine the plausible arguments that would bring us to that conclusion, but not hard to imagine how someone with bizarre views might be brought to it. Suppose one holds that all morality rests on God's will, and had just decided that there is no God. Or he believes that only spontaneous and unreflective decisions can have moral value, and that no judicial decision can either be spontaneous or encourage spontaneity. These would be arguments not rejecting the idea or sense of morality, as in the case of external scepticism, but employing what the author takes to be the best conception of morality in service of a wholesale internally sceptical position. If this position were in fact the right view to take up about political morality, then it would always be wrong to suppose that one interpretation of past judicial decisions was better than another, at least in cases when both passed the threshold test of fit. Naturalism would therefore be a silly theory to recommend to judges. So the threat of [global internal] scepticism, it materializes, is in fact much greater than the threat of external scepticism. But (as the examples I chose may have suggested) I cannot think of any plausible arguments for global internal scepticism about political morality.

Of course, nothing in this short discussion disputes the claim, which is plainly true, that different judges hold different political moralities, and will therefore disagree about the best justification of the past. Or the claim, equally true, that there will be no way for any side in such disagreements to prove that it is right and its opponents wrong. The demonstrability thesis (as I said) argues from these undeniable facts to general external scepticism. But even if we reject that thesis, as I do, the bare fact of disagreement may be thought to support an independent challenge of naturalism, which does not depend on either external or internal scepticism. For it may be said that whether or not there is an objectively right answer to the question of justification, it is unfair that the answer of one judge be accepted as final when he has no way to prove, as against those who disagree, that his position is better. This is part of the argument from democracy to which we must now turn.

IS IT UNDEMOCRATIC?

So if we are to reject naturalism, in favor of some other positive theory of adjudication, this cannot be by virtue of any general appeal to external scepticism as a philosophical doctrine. We need arguments of substantive political morality showing why naturalism is unwise or unjust. . . . Of course arguments against naturalism must compare it, unfavorably, with some other theory, and arguments that might be effective in the context of one such comparison would be self-defeating in another. . . .

I shall consider, first, the arguments that might be made against naturalism from the standpoint of what I believe is a more positivist theory of adjudication, though nothing turns on whether this theory is properly called positivism. Someone might propose, as an alternative to naturalism, that judges should decide cases in the following way. First, they should identify the persons or institutions which are authorized to make law by the social conventions of their community. Next, they should check the record of history to see whether any such persons or institutions have laid down a rule of law whose language unambiguously covers the case at hand. If so, they should decide that case by applying that rule. If not—if history shows that no rule has been laid down deciding the case either way—then they should create the best rule for the future, and apply it retrospectively. The rule they thus create would then become, for later judges, part of the record endorsed by convention, so that later judges facing the same issue could then find, in that decision, language settling the matter for them. We might call this theory of adjudication "conventionalism."

Some people are drawn to conventionalism, over naturalism, because they think the former is more democratic. It argues that people only have the rights, in court, that legislators and judges, whom convention recognizes to have legislative power, have already decided to give them. Naturalism, on the other hand, assigns judges the power to draw from judicial history rights that no official institution has ever sanctioned before, and to do so on no stronger argument than that the past is seen in a better light, according to the convictions of the judges, if these rights are presupposed. This seems the antithesis of what democracy requires.

But this argument mistakes the cases in which a conventionalist and a naturalist are likely to disagree. Conventionalist judges can dispose of cases at the first stage, by copying the decisions already made by elected officials, only in those cases in which some statute exactly in point unambiguously dictates a particular result. Any conscientious naturalist is very likely to make exactly the same decisions in those "simple" cases, so conventionalism cannot be more democratic because it decides these differently. The two styles of adjudication will normally recommend different decisions only when some fresh judicial judgment is required which goes beyond what the legislature has unarguably said, either because the statute in play is open to different interpretations, or because no particular statute is in play at all. But in these "hard" cases the difference between the two theories of adjudication cannot be that one defers to the legislature's judgment while the other challenges that judgment. Because, by hypothesis, there is no legislative judgment that can be treated in either of these ways. Conventionalism argues that the judge must, in these "hard" cases, choose the rule of decision which best promotes the good society as he conceives it. It is hardly more democratic for judges to rely on their own convictions about the best design of the future than to rely instead on their convictions about the best interpretation of the past.

So the argument from democracy in favor of conventionalism over naturalism seems to come to nothing. But we should consider one possible counter-argument. I have been assuming that conventionalism and naturalism will designate the same cases as "easy," that is, as cases in which no fresh judgment is required by the judge. . . .

. . . Nothing in the design of naturalism insures that a judge with silly or mad opinions will not be appointed; but nothing in the design of conventionalism insures that either, and conventionalism will not prevent him from reaching preposterous decisions once appointed. A conventionalist judge needs a concept of convention. He must decide, for example, whether it is a convention of our society that the Constitution should be followed, and nothing in the structure of conventionalism can insure that a judge will in fact reach the correct answer to that question. No theory of adjudication can guarantee that only sensible decisions will be reached by judges who embrace that theory. We can protect ourselves from madness or gross stupidity only by independent procedures governing how judges are to be appointed, how their decisions may be appealed and reversed, and how they may be removed from office if this should appear necessary.

But it may now be said that naturalism would encourage anti-democratic decisions from judges who hold, not mad, but plausible and even attractive political convictions, and who deploy perfectly sensible theories about how much of the past an interpretation must fit. For naturalism leaves no doctrine or practice immune from re-examination. We may use an earlier example as an illustration. Suppose a firm line of cases has rejected the idea that clients may sue lawyers who are negligent. Conventionalism is then committed (so it might be said) to continuing that doctrine until it is reversed by legislation, which seems the democratic solution. But naturalism encourages judges to put this line of cases in a wider context, and ask whether the rule refusing recovery against negligent lawyers would not itself be rejected by the best justification of the rest of the law, which allows recovery for negligent injury of almost every other kind. So a naturalist might be led to overrule these cases, which a conventionalist would leave for the legislature to review.

Indeed there is nothing in the theory of naturalism, as I described it, which would prevent an intelligent and sensible naturalist from taking the same line with certain statutes. Suppose an old statute makes blasphemy a crime and, though it has not been enforced in centuries, it is suddenly revived by a public prosecutor anxious to make a splash. A naturalist judge might well develop a theory of obsolescence, even though this had never been recognized in the jurisdiction before. He might say that the best interpretation of judicial practice as a whole yields the following qualification to the rule that statutes are always to be enforced. "Old statutes quite at variance with the spirit of the present time, which would not be enacted by the present legislature, and which have not been employed since ancient times, are unavailable as grounds of criminal prosecution." If prosecutors have not tried to revive old statutes in the fairly recent past, this qualification would be consistent with judicial practice, and it might plausibly be thought to show that practice in a better light, as both more rational and more closely tying what counts as valid legislation to the will of the people.

So both in the case of precedent and legislation a competent naturalist judge might find certain cases hard, and amenable to the command of imaginative reinterpretation, which a conventionalist must concede to be easy even when the obvious answer is unattractive. So perhaps naturalism would sometimes produce "novel" decisions by sensible judges that conventionalism would discourage. But is it right to say that naturalism is for this reason less "democratic"? A minimally competent naturalist judge would begin his argument by recognizing, indeed, insisting, that our political system is a democracy; he would continue by arguing that democracy, properly understood, is best served by a coherent rather than an unprincipled private law of negligence, and by an institution of legislation that is sensitive rather than obdurate to changes in popular morality. So the disagreement between naturalism and conventionalism about which cases are really "easy" is not a disagreement between those who oppose and those who respect democracy; it is rather the more familiar disagreement about what democracy really is. When the disagreement is seen in this light, it is far from apparent that the naturalist has the worst of the argument. . . .

REVIEW AND DISCUSSION QUESTIONS

1. Explain the distinction between external skepticism and internal skepticism about the truth of moral claims.

2. What is global internal skepticism? Why does Dworkin think it, alone, constitutes a challenge to legal interpretation? How does he answer the challenge?

3. In what way does Dworkin think that naturalism might be said to be incompatible with democratic values?

4. How does Dworkin respond to those who suggest that naturalism is antidemocratic?

PART III

PHILOSOPHICAL ISSUES IN CRIMINAL LAW

❖

10

PUNISHMENT: THEORY AND PRACTICE

Punishment involves inflicting harm on a person; that is, it involves doing something to someone that would normally be wrong to do to another person (such as taking away his or her property or freedom). Because of this, the practice of punishment requires moral justification. Punishment is often defended because of its usefulness: it deters potential criminals and protects society by rehabilitating the offenders or by removing them from society. Some contend that punishment cannot be morally justified on the basis of social utility but only on the ground that the criminal *deserves* to be punished as a result of his or her wrongdoing. The essays and cases of this section explore these and other conflicting approaches to punishment.

The Case of the Dog "Provetie" is unusual because it involves punishing a dog for murder. It poses the philosophically important issue of who should be punished and why. *Gregg v. Georgia* airs the arguments for and against the death penalty, thus probing the moral justification for punishment in a very real and important context. In their essays, Richard B. Brandt and Herbert Morris present, respectively, the utilitarian and retributivist approaches to punishment. Alternatively, Randy Barnett defends restitution as an alternative to punishment. The section concludes with two important Supreme Court cases, one concerned with the legal implications of racial disparities in capital punishment cases, the other with whether, in some cases, recidivist or "three strikes and you're out" statutes impose a punishment that is unconstitutional because it is "cruel and unusual."

Who Should Be Punished?

The Case of the Dog Provetie

In this case from 1595, a dog named Provetie was accused of biting a child in the hand, a wound that led to the child's death. The court finds Provetie guilty, condemning him to be hung on the gallows like other murderers. Although from a modern perspective the case seems bizarre, trials of animals were recorded throughout the Middle Ages. They raise a basic philosophical question, who should be punished and why?

Lot Huygens Gael, Schout of the Town of Leiden, prosecutor on behalf of his lordship [the Count of Holland] in criminal matters, accuses in the open Court of the Schepenes of the Town of Leiden the dog of Jan Jansse van der Poel, named Provetie, or by whatsoever other name he may be called, now a prisoner, and says that he, the said Provetie, did not scruple on Sunday last, being the 5th of May, 1595, to bite the child of Jan Jacobsz van der Poel, which child was then playing at his uncle's house and had a piece of meat in his hand, and the said Provetie snapping at it did bite the said child and thus inflicted a wound in the second finger of the right hand, going through the skin to the flesh in such manner that the blood flowed therefrom, and the child a few days after died in consequence of fright, for which cause the prosecutor apprehended the said Provetie, all of which appears from the prisoner's own confession, made by him without torture or being put in irons. . . .

Sentence: The Schepenen of Leiden, having seen the claim and conclusion made and taken by Lot Huygens Gael, Schout of this town, against and to the charge of the dog of Jan Jansse van der Poel, named Provetie, or by whatsoever other name or surname he may be known, the prisoner being present, having seen, moreover, the information obtained by the prosecutor for the purpose, besides the prisoner's own confession made without torture or being placed in irons, doing justice in the name of, etc., have condemned and hereby do condemn him to be led and taken to the plain of Gravesteijn in this town, where evildoers are customarily punished, and that he be there hanged by the executioner to the gallows with a rope until death ensues, that further his dead body be dragged on a hurdle to the gallows-field, and that he there remain hanging to the gallows, to the deterring of other dogs and to all as an example; moreover, they declare all his goods, should he have any, to be confiscated and forfeited for the benefit of the countship.

This done in the open court, all schepenen being present, the 15th May, 1595.

REVIEW AND DISCUSSION QUESTIONS

1. Owners of dogs frequently discipline their pets for bad behavior, and many believe that their pets know when they have misbehaved. If so, then why do we find it odd for this court to have punished a dog?

2. Did Provetie deserve to die? Did he deserve to be punished in some other way for biting the child's hand? Was Provetie responsible for his actions? Are we responsible for ours?

3. The court orders Provetie's dead body to be displayed "to the deterring of other dogs and to all as an example." Can dogs be deterred from bad behavior by the punishing of other dogs? Can human beings be deterred by punishing dogs?

4. Could one justify executing Provetie on grounds of social protection? What would a utilitarian say about punishing dogs?

5. When the court refers to "the prisoner's own confession," what could it have had in mind?

6. What exactly is it about human beings that makes us believe that punishing people for their conduct is sometimes appropriate or justified, whereas punishing dogs is inappropriate?

Capital Punishment

Gregg v. Georgia

Gregg v. Georgia *gives the issue of punishment a very specific and important focus: namely, the justifiability of the death penalty.* Gregg *is one of the United States Supreme Court's most important decisions concerning capital punishment, and, as is apparent from the dissenting opinions, few of its cases involve deeper legal, moral, and philosophical division than those concerning execution.*

Mr. Justice Stewart, with Justices Powell and Stevens concurring:

We address initially the basic contention that the punishment of death for the crime of murder is, under all circumstances, "cruel and unusual" in violation of the Eighth and Fourteenth Amendments of the Constitution. [Later in] this opinion, we will consider the sentence of death imposed under the Georgia statutes at issue in this case.

The Court on a number of occasions has both assumed and asserted the constitutionality of capital punishment. . . . But until *Furman v. Georgia*, 408 U.S. 238 (1972), the Court never confronted squarely the fundamental claim that the punishment of death always, regardless of the enormity of the offense or the procedure followed in imposing the sentence, is cruel and unusual punishment in violation of the Constitution. Although this issue was presented and addressed in *Furman*, it was not resolved by the Court. Four Justices would have held that capital punishment is not unconstitutional *per se;* two Justices would have reached the opposite conclusion; and three Justices, while agreeing that the statutes then before the Court were invalid as applied, left open the question whether such punishment may ever be imposed. We now hold that the punishment of death does not invariably violate the Constitution. . . .

The substantive limits imposed by the Eighth Amendment on what can be made criminal and punished were discussed in *Robinson v. California*, 370 U.S. 660 (1962). The Court

found unconstitutional a state statute that made the status of being addicted to a narcotic drug a criminal offense. It held, in effect, that it is "cruel and unusual" to impose any punishment at all for the mere status of addiction. The cruelty in the abstract of the actual sentence imposed was irrelevant: "Even one day in prison would be a cruel and unusual punishment for the 'crime' of having a common cold." Most recently, in *Furman v. Georgia, supra,* three Justices in separate concurring opinions found the Eighth Amendment applicable to procedures employed to select convicted defendants for the sentence of death.

It is clear from the foregoing precedents that the Eighth Amendment has not been regarded as a static concept. As Mr. Chief Justice Warren said, in an oft-quoted phrase, "[t]he Amendment must draw its meaning from the evolving standards of decency that mark the progress of a maturing society." . . . Thus, an assessment of contemporary values concerning the infliction of a challenged sanction is relevant to the application of the Eighth Amendment. As we develop below more fully, . . . this assessment does not call for a subjective judgment. It requires, rather, that we look to objective indicia that reflect the public attitude toward a given sanction.

But our cases also make clear that public perceptions of standards of decency with respect to criminal sanctions are not conclusive. A penalty also must accord with "the dignity of man," which is the "basic concept underlying the Eighth Amendment." *Trop v. Dulles.* . . . This means, at least, that the punishment not be "excessive." When a form of punishment in the abstract (in this case, whether capital punishment may ever be imposed as a sanction for murder)

---

428 U.S. 153 (1976). Some footnotes and citations omitted.

rather than in the particular (the propriety of death as a penalty to be applied to a specific defendant for a specific crime) is under consideration, the inquiry into "excessiveness" has two aspects. First, the punishment must not involve the unnecessary and wanton infliction of pain. . . . Second, the punishment must not be grossly out of proportion to the severity of the crime. . . .

The imposition of the death penalty for the crime of murder has a long history of acceptance both in the United States and in England. The common-law rule imposed a mandatory death sentence on all convicted murderers. . . . And the penalty continued to be used into the 20th century by most American States, although the breadth of the common-law rule was diminished, initially by narrowing the class of murders to be punished by death and subsequently by widespread adoption of laws expressly granting juries the discretion to recommend mercy. . . .

It is apparent from the text of the Constitution itself that the existence of capital punishment was accepted by the Framers. At the time the Eighth Amendment was ratified, capital punishment was a common sanction in every State. Indeed, the First Congress of the United States enacted legislation providing death as the penalty for specified crimes. . . .

Four years ago, the petitioners in *Furman* and its companion cases [predicated] their argument primarily upon the asserted proposition that standards of decency had evolved to the point where capital punishment no longer could be tolerated. The petitioners in those cases said, in effect, that the evolutionary process had come to an end, and that standards of decency required that the Eighth Amendment be construed finally as prohibiting capital punishment for any crime regardless of its depravity and impact on society. This view was accepted by two Justices. Three other Justices were unwilling to go so far; focusing on the procedures by which convicted defendants were selected for the death penalty rather than on the actual punishment inflicted, they joined in the conclusion that the statutes before the Court were constitutionally invalid.

The petitioners in the capital cases before the Court today renew the "standards of decency" argument, but developments during the four years since *Furman* have undercut substantially the assumptions upon which their argument rested. Despite the continuing debate, dating back to the 19th century, over the morality and utility of capital punishment, it is now evident that a large proportion of American society continues to regard it as an appropriate and necessary criminal sanction.

The most marked indication of society's endorsement of the death penalty for murder is the legislative response to *Furman*. The legislatures of at least 35 States have enacted new statutes that provide for the death penalty for at least some crimes that result in the death of another person. And the Congress of the United States, in 1974, enacted a statute providing the death penalty for aircraft piracy that results in death. These recently adopted statutes have attempted to address the concerns expressed by the Court in *Furman* primarily (i) by specifying the factors to be weighed and the procedures to be followed in deciding when to impose a capital sentence, or (ii) by making the death penalty mandatory for specified crimes.

. . . [H]owever, the Eighth Amendment demands more than that a challenged punishment be acceptable to contemporary society. The Court also must ask whether it comports with the basic concept of human dignity at the core of the Amendment. . . . Although we cannot "invalidate a category of penalties because we deem less severe penalties adequate to serve the ends of penology," *Furman v. Georgia, supra*, at 451 (Powell, J., dissenting), the sanction imposed cannot be so totally without penological justification that it results in the gratuitous infliction of suffering. . . .

The death penalty is said to serve two principal social purposes: retribution and deterrence of capital crimes by prospective offenders.[1]

In part, capital punishment is an expression of society's moral outrage at particularly offensive conduct. This function may be unappealing to many, but it is essential in an ordered society that asks its citizens to rely on legal processes rather than self-help to vindicate their wrongs.

The instinct for retribution is part of the nature of man, and channeling that instinct in the administration of criminal justice serves an important purpose in promoting the stability of a society governed by law. When people begin to believe that organized society is unwilling or unable to impose upon criminal offenders the punishment they "deserve," then there are sown the seeds of anarchy—of self-help, vigilante justice, and lynch law. *Furman v. Georgia, supra,* at 308 (Stewart, J., concurring).

"Retribution is no longer the dominant objective of the criminal law," *Williams v. New York*, 337 U.S. 241, 248 (1949), but neither is it a forbidden objective nor one inconsistent with our respect for the dignity of men. . . . Indeed, the decision that capital punishment may be the appropriate sanction in extreme cases is an expression of the community's belief that certain crimes are themselves so grievous an affront to humanity that the only adequate response may be the penalty of death.

Statistical attempts to evaluate the worth of the death penalty as a deterrent to crimes by potential offenders have occasioned a great deal of debate. The results simply have been inconclusive. . . .

Although some of the studies suggest that the death penalty may not function as a significantly greater deterrent than lesser penalties, there is no convincing empirical evidence either supporting or refuting this view. We may nevertheless assume safely that there are murderers, such as those who act in passion, for whom the threat of death has little or no deterrent effect. But for many others, the death penalty undoubtedly is a significant deterrent. There are carefully contemplated murders, such as murders for hire, where the possible penalty of death may well enter into the cold calculus that precedes the decision to act.[2] And there are some categories of murder, such as murder by a life prisoner, where other sanctions may not be adequate.

The value of capital punishment as a deterrent of crime is a complex factual issue the resolution of which properly rests with the legislatures, which can evaluate the results of statistical studies in terms of their own local conditions and with a flexibility of approach that is not available to the courts. . . . Indeed, many of the post-*Furman* statutes reflect just such a responsible effort to define those crimes and

those criminals for which capital punishment is most probably an effective deterrent.

In sum, we cannot say that the judgment of the Georgia Legislature that capital punishment may be necessary in some cases is clearly wrong. Considerations of federalism, as well as respect for the ability of a legislature to evaluate, in terms of its particular State, the moral consensus concerning the death penalty and its social utility as a sanction, require us to conclude, in the absence of more convincing evidence, that the infliction of death as a punishment for murder is not without justification and thus is not unconstitutionally severe.

Finally, we must consider whether the punishment of death is disproportionate in relation to the crime for which it is imposed. There is no question that death as a punishment is unique in its severity and irrevocability. . . . When a defendant's life is at stake, the Court has been particularly sensitive to insure that every safeguard is observed. . . . But we are concerned here only with the imposition of capital punishment for the crime of murder, and when a life has been taken deliberately by the offender, we cannot say that the punishment is invariably disproportionate to the crime. It is an extreme sanction, suitable to the most extreme of crimes.

We hold that the death penalty is not a form of punishment that may never be imposed, regardless of the circumstances of the offense, regardless of the character of the offender, and regardless of the procedure followed in reaching the decision to impose it.

We now consider whether Georgia may impose the death penalty on the petitioner in this case.

While *Furman* did not hold that the infliction of the death penalty *per se* violates the Constitution's ban on cruel and unusual punishments, it did recognize that the penalty of death is different in kind from any other punishment imposed under our system of criminal justice. Because of the uniqueness of the death penalty, *Furman* held that it could not be imposed under sentencing procedures that created a substantial risk that it would be inflicted in an arbitrary and capricious manner. Mr. Justice White concluded that "the death penalty is exacted with great infrequency even for the most atrocious crimes and . . . there is no meaningful basis for distinguishing the few cases in which it is imposed from the many cases in which it is not." 408 U.S., at 313 (concurring). Indeed, the death sentences examined by the Court in *Furman* were "cruel and unusual in the same way that being struck by lightning is cruel and unusual. For, of all the people convicted of [capital crimes], many just as reprehensible as these, the petitioners [in *Furman* were] among a capriciously selected random handful upon whom the sentence of death has in fact been imposed. . . . [T]he Eighth and Fourteenth Amendments cannot tolerate the infliction of a sentence of death under legal systems that permit this unique penalty to be so wantonly and so freakishly imposed." *Id.*, at 309–310 (Stewart, J., concurring).

Furman mandates that where discretion is afforded a sentencing body on a matter so grave as the determination of whether a human life should be taken or spared, that discretion must be suitably directed and limited so as to minimize the risk of wholly arbitrary and capricious action. . . .

In summary, the concerns expressed in *Furman* that the penalty of death not be imposed in an arbitrary or capricious manner can be met by a carefully drafted statute that ensures that the sentencing authority is given adequate information and guidance. As a general proposition these concerns are best met by a system that provides for a bifurcated proceeding at which the sentencing authority is apprised of the information relevant to the imposition of sentence and provided with standards to guide its use of the information. . . .

The basic concern of *Furman* centered on those defendants who were being condemned to death capriciously and arbitrarily. Under the procedures before the Court in that case, sentencing authorities were not directed to give attention to the nature or circumstances of the crime committed or to the character or record of the defendant. Left unguided, juries imposed the death sentence in a way that could only be called freakish. The new Georgia sentencing procedures, by contrast, focus the jury's attention on the particularized nature of the crime and the particularized characteristics of the individual defendant. While the jury is permitted to consider any aggravating or mitigating circumstances, it must find and identify at least one statutory aggravating factor before it may impose a penalty of death. In this way the jury's discretion is channeled. No longer can a jury wantonly and freakishly impose the death sentence; it is always circumscribed by the legislative guidelines. In addition, the review function of the Supreme Court of Georgia affords additional assurance that the concerns that prompted our decision in *Furman* are not present to any significant degree in the Georgia procedure applied here.

For the reasons expressed in this opinion, we hold that the statutory system under which Gregg was sentenced to death does not violate the Constitution. Accordingly, the judgment of the Georgia Supreme Court is affirmed.

It is so ordered.

Mr. Justice Brennan, dissenting:

The Cruel and Unusual Punishments Clause "must draw its meaning from the evolving standards of decency that mark the progress of a maturing society."[3] The opinions of Mr. Justice Stewart, Mr. Justice Powell, and Mr. Justice Stevens today hold that "evolving standards of decency" require focus not on the essence of the death penalty itself but primarily upon the procedures employed by the State to single out persons to suffer the penalty of death. Those opinions hold further that, so viewed, the Clause invalidates the mandatory infliction of the death penalty but not its infliction under sentencing procedures that Mr. Justice Stewart, Mr. Justice Powell, and Mr. Justice Stevens conclude adequately safeguard against the risk that the death penalty was imposed in an arbitrary and capricious manner.

In *Furman v. Georgia*, . . . I read "evolving standards of decency" as requiring focus upon the essence of the death penalty itself and not primarily or solely upon the procedures under which the determination to inflict the penalty upon a particular person was made. I there said:

From the beginning of our Nation, the punishment of death has stirred acute public controversy.

Although pragmatic arguments for and against the punishment have been frequently advanced, this longstanding and heated controversy cannot be explained solely as the result of differences over the practical wisdom of a particular government policy. At bottom, the battle has been waged on moral grounds. The country has debated whether a society for which the dignity of the individual is the supreme value can, without a fundamental inconsistency, follow the practice of deliberately putting some of its members to death. In the United States, as in other nations of the western world, "the struggle about this punishment has been one between ancient and deeply rooted beliefs in retribution, atonement or vengeance on the one hand, and, on the other, beliefs in the personal value and dignity of the common man that were born of the democratic movement of the eighteenth century, as well as beliefs in the scientific approach to an understanding of the motive forces of human conduct, which are the result of the growth of the sciences of behavior during the nineteenth and twentieth centuries." It is this essentially moral conflict that forms the backdrop for the past changes in and the present operation of our system of imposing death as a punishment for crime. *Id.*, at 296.[4]

That continues to be my view. For the Clause forbidding cruel and unusual punishments under our constitutional system of government embodies in unique degree moral principles restraining the punishments that our civilized society may impose on those persons who transgress its laws. Thus, I too say: "For myself, I do not hesitate to assert the proposition that the only way the law has progressed from the days of the rack, the screw and the wheel is the development of moral concepts, or, as stated by the Supreme Court . . . the application of 'evolving standards of decency.' . . ."[5]

This Court inescapably has the duty, as the ultimate arbiter of the meaning of our Constitution, to say whether, when individuals condemned to death stand before our Bar, "moral concepts" require us to hold that the law has progressed to the point where we should declare that the punishment of death, like punishments on the rack, the screw, and the wheel, is no longer morally tolerable in our civilized society. . . . I emphasize only that foremost among

the "moral concepts" recognized in our cases and inherent in the Clause is the primary moral principle that the State, even as it punishes, must treat its citizens in a manner consistent with their intrinsic worth as human beings—a punishment must not be so severe as to be degrading to human dignity. A judicial determination whether the punishment of death comports with human dignity is therefore not only permitted but compelled by the Clause. . . .

The fatal constitutional infirmity in the punishment of death is that it treats "members of the human race as nonhumans, as objects to be toyed with and discarded. [It is] thus inconsistent with the fundamental premise of the Clause that even the vilest criminal remains a human being possessed of common human dignity." *Id.*, at 273. As such it is a penalty that "subjects the individual to a fate forbidden by the principle of civilized treatment guaranteed by the [clause]." I therefore would hold, on that ground alone, that death is today a cruel and unusual punishment prohibited by the Clause. "Justice of this kind is obviously no less shocking than the crime itself, and the new 'official' murder, far from offering redress for the offense committed against society, adds instead a second defilement to the first."[6]

Mr. Justice Marshall, dissenting:

In *Furman* I concluded that the death penalty is constitutionally invalid for two reasons. First, the death penalty is excessive. And second, the American people, fully informed as to the purposes of the death penalty and its liabilities, would in my view reject it as morally unacceptable.

Since the decision in *Furman*, the legislatures of 35 States have enacted new statutes authorizing the imposition of the death sentence for certain crimes, and Congress has enacted a law providing the death penalty for air piracy resulting in death. . . . I would be less than candid if I did not acknowledge that these developments have a significant bearing on a realistic assessment of the moral acceptability of the death penalty to the American people. But if the constitutionality of the death penalty turns, as I have urged, on the opinion of an *informed* citizenry, then even the enactment of new death statutes cannot be viewed as conclusive. In *Furman*, I observed that the American people are largely unaware of the information critical to a judgment on the morality of the death penalty, and concluded that if they were better informed they would consider it shocking, unjust, and unacceptable. A recent study, conducted after the enactment of the post-*Furman* statutes, has confirmed that the American people know little about the death penalty, and that the opinions of an informed public would differ significantly from those of a public unaware of the consequences and effects of the death penalty.[7]

Even assuming, however, that the post-*Furman* enactment of statutes authorizing the death penalty renders the prediction of the views of an informed citizenry an uncertain basis for a constitutional decision, the enactment of those statutes has no bearing whatsoever on the conclusion that the death penalty is unconstitutional because it is excessive. An excessive penalty is invalid under the Cruel and Unusual Punishments Clause "even though popular sentiment may favor" it. . . . The inquiry here, then, is simply whether the death penalty is necessary to accomplish the legitimate legislative purposes in punishment, or whether a less severe penalty—life imprisonment—would do as well. . . .

The two purposes that sustain the death penalty as nonexcessive in the Court's view are general deterrence and retribution. In *Furman*, I canvassed the relevant data on the deterrent effect of capital punishment. . . . The state of knowledge at that point, after literally centuries of debate, was summarized as follows by a United Nations Committee:

> It is generally agreed between the retentionists and abolitionists, whatever their opinions about the validity of comparative studies of deterrence, that the data which now exist show no correlation between the existence of capital punishment and lower rates of capital crime.[8]

The available evidence, I concluded in *Furman*, was convincing that "capital punishment is not necessary as a deterrent to crime in our society." . . .

The other principal purpose said to be served by the death penalty is retribution. . . . It is this notion that I find to be the most disturbing aspect of today's unfortunate decisions.

The concept of retribution is a multifaceted one, and any discussion of its role in the criminal law must be undertaken with caution. On one level, it can be said that the notion of retribution or reprobation is the basis of our insistence that only those who have broken the law be punished, and in this sense the notion is quite obviously central to a just system of criminal sanctions. But our recognition that retribution plays a crucial role in determining who may be punished by no means requires approval of retribution as a general justification for punishment.[9] It is the question whether retribution can provide a moral justification for punishment—in particular, capital punishment—that we must consider.

My Brothers Stewart, Powell, and Stevens offer the following explanation of the retributive justification for capital punishment:

> "The instinct for retribution is part of the nature of man, and channeling that instinct in the administration of criminal justice serves an important purpose in promoting the stability of a society governed by law. When people begin to believe that organized society is unwilling or unable to impose upon criminal offenders the punishment they 'deserve,' then there are sown the seeds of anarchy—of self-help, vigilante justice, and lynch law."

This statement is wholly inadequate to justify the death penalty. As my Brother Brennan stated in *Furman*, "[t]here is no evidence whatever that utilization of imprisonment rather than death encourages private blood feuds and other disorders." It simply defies belief to suggest that the death penalty is necessary to prevent the American people from taking the law into their own hands.

In a related vein, it may be suggested that the expression of moral outrage through the imposition of the death penalty serves to reinforce basic moral values—that it marks some crimes as particularly offensive and therefore to be avoided. The argument is akin to a deterrence argument, but differs in that it contemplates the individual's shrinking from antisocial conduct, not because he fears punishment, but because he has been told in the strongest possible way that the conduct is wrong. This contention, like the previous one, provides no support for the death penalty. It is inconceivable that any individual concerned about conforming his conduct to what society says is "right" would fail to realize that murder is "wrong" if the penalty were simply life imprisonment.

The foregoing contentions—that society's expression of moral outrage through the imposition of the death penalty pre-empts the citizenry from taking the law into its own hands and reinforces moral values—are not retributive in the purest sense. They are essentially utilitarian in that they portray the death penalty as valuable because of its beneficial results. These justifications for the death penalty are inadequate because the penalty is, quite clearly I think, not necessary to the accomplishment of those results.

There remains for consideration, however, what might be termed the purely retributive justification for the death penalty—that the death penalty is appropriate, not because of its beneficial effect on society, but because the taking of the murderer's life is itself morally good. Some of the language of the opinion of my Brothers Stewart, Powell, and Stevens in No. 74–6257 appears positively to embrace this notion of retribution for its own sake as a justification for capital punishment. They state:

[T]he decision that capital punishment may be the appropriate sanction in extreme cases is an expression of the community's belief that certain crimes are themselves so grievous an affront to humanity that the only adequate response may be the penalty of death.

They then quote with approval from Lord Justice Denning's remarks before the British Royal Commission on Capital Punishment:

"The truth is that some crimes are so outrageous that society insists on adequate punishment, because the wrong-doer deserves it, irrespective of whether it is a deterrent or not."

Of course, it may be that these statements are intended as no more than observations as to the popular demands that it is thought must be responded to in order to prevent anarchy. But the implication of the statements appears to me to be quite different—namely, that society's judgment that the murderer "deserves" death must be respected not simply because the preservation of order requires it, but because it is appropriate that society make the judgment and carry it out. It is this latter notion, in particular, that I consider to be fundamentally at odds with the Eighth Amendment. . . . The mere fact that the community demands the murderer's life in return for the evil he has done cannot sustain the death penalty, for as Justices Stewart, Powell, and Stevens remind us, "the Eighth Amendment demands more than that a challenged punishment be acceptable to contemporary society." . . . To be sustained under the Eighth Amendment, the death penalty must "compor[t] with the basic concept of human dignity at the core of the Amendment," ibid.; the objective in imposing it must be "[consistent] with our respect for the dignity of [other] men." . . . Under these standards, the taking of life "because the wrongdoer deserves it" surely must fall, for such a punishment has as its very basis the total denial of the wrongdoer's dignity and worth.

The death penalty, unnecessary to promote the goal of deterrence or to further any legitimate notion of retribution, is an excessive penalty forbidden by the Eighth and Fourteenth Amendments. I respectfully dissent from the Court's judgment upholding the sentences of death imposed upon the petitioners in these cases.

NOTES

[1]Another purpose that has been discussed is the incapacitation of dangerous criminals and the consequent prevention of crimes that they may otherwise commit in the future.

[2]Other types of calculated murders, apparently occurring with increasing frequency, include the use of bombs or other means of indiscriminate killings, the extortion murder of hostages or kidnap victims, and the execution-style killing of witnesses to a crime.

[3]*Trop v. Dulles*, 356 U.S. 86, 101 (1958) (plurality opinion of Warren, C. J.).

[4]Quoting T. Sellin, *The Death Penalty, A Report for the Model Penal Code Project of the American Law Institute* 15 (1959).

[5]*Novak v. Beto*, 453 F. 2d 661, 672 (CA5 1971) (Tuttle, J., concurring in part and dissenting in part).

[6]A. Camus, *Reflections on the Guillotine*, 5–6 (Fridtjof-Karla Pub. 1960).

[7]Sarat & Vidmar, "Public Opinion, The Death Penalty, and the Eighth Amendment: Testing the Marshall Hypothesis." 1976 *Wis. L. Rev.* 171.

[8]United Nations, Department of Economic and Social Affairs, *Capital Punishment*, pt. II, ¶ 159, p. 123 (1968).

[9]See, *e.g.*, H. Hart, *Punishment and Responsibility*, 8–10, 71–83 (1968); H. Packer, *Limits of the Criminal Sanction* 38–39, 66 (1968).

REVIEW AND DISCUSSION QUESTIONS

1. According to the Court the Eighth Amendment rules out "excessive" punishment. What two issues does the question of excessiveness raise? In your view, is capital punishment excessive in either respect?

2. The Court states that the death penalty serves two main social purposes. What are they? Can execution be morally justified either way?

3. What is the basic position of the Court, and how does its decision in this case compare with its earlier decision in the *Furman* case? On what terms is the Court now willing to permit executions?

4. What is Justice Brennan's view of the constitutionality of capital punishment? Is his reasoning persuasive?

5. Does Justice Marshall successfully rebut the argument of the majority concerning deterrence? Retribution? Whose position is more convincing—the majority's or the dissenters'?

The Utilitarian Theory of Criminal Punishment

Richard B. Brandt

Utilitarianism maintains that actions, institutions, and social policies are morally justified insofar as they promote more net social good (or happiness or well-being) than any alternative action, institution, or policy. Beginning with the views of Jeremy Bentham, one of the founders of utilitarianism, Richard B. Brandt, professor of philosophy at the University of Michigan, explains the utilitarian approach to criminal justice and defends it against several common criticisms. He concludes by raising some difficulties for nonutilitarian or retributive theories of punishment.

What is meant by an "examination of the ethical foundations of the institution and principles of criminal justice"? The job of such an examination is *not* to provide a moral blessing for the status quo, for the system of criminal justice as it actually is in the United States. . . . Rather, it is to identify the more important valid ethical principles that are relevant to the institution of criminal justice and to furnish a model of their use in criticism or justification of important features of this institution.

The broad questions to be kept in the forefront of discussion are the following: (1) What justifies anyone in inflicting pain or loss on an individual on account of his past acts? (2) Is there a valid general principle about the punishments proper for various acts? (Possibly there should be no close connection between offense and penalty; perhaps punishment should be suited to the individual needs of the criminal, and not to his crime.) (3) What kinds of defense should excuse from punishment? An answer to these questions would comprise prescriptions for the broad outlines of an ideal system of criminal justice.

In our [earlier] discussion of "distributive justice," we decided that "to act unjustly" means the same as "to treat unequally, in some matter that involves the distribution of things that are good or bad, except as the inequality is required by moral considerations (principles) with substantial weight in the circumstances." If this definition of "act unjustly" is correct, then there are two distinct ways in which there can be injustice in the treatment of criminals. First, criminals are *punished* whereas noncriminals are not. Punishment, however, is *unequal* treatment, in a matter that involves distribution of things good or bad. Therefore, if punishment is to be just, it must be shown that the unequal treatment is required by moral principles of weight. Thus, one thing that must be done in order to show that the practice of punishing criminals is not unjust, is to show that there are moral principles that require it. But second, the *procedures of applying* the principles directing unequal treatment for criminals may themselves operate unequally. One man gets a "fair" trial and another does not. There can be inequality in the chances given people to escape the application of legal sanctions in their case. Part of treating people "justly," then, is providing legal devices so that everyone has an equal hearing: scrupulous adherence to the rules of evidence, opportunity for appeal to higher courts for remedy of deviation from standard rules in the lower courts, and so on. We shall not here consider details about how legal institutions should be devised in order to secure equal application of the law; that is a specialized inquiry that departs too far from the main problems of ethical principle. It is a part of "justice," however. Indeed, we may view "criminal justice" as having two main aspects: just laws for the punishment of offenders and procedures insuring just application of these laws by the courts and other judicial machinery.

The existence of just laws directing certain punishments for certain offenses, then, is not the whole of justice for the criminal, but we shall concentrate on identifying such laws. . . .

1. THE UTILITARIAN THEORY

Historically there has been a cleavage of opinion about the kind of general ethical principles required for coherence with our concrete justified beliefs about criminal justice. Many writers have thought that a utilitarian principle is adequate. Others have thought that some nonutilitarian principle, or more than one, is necessary. Most of the latter writers (formalists) have espoused some form of *retributive* principle—that is, a principle roughly to the effect that a wrongdoer should be punished approximately in correspondence with either the moral reprehensibility of his offense or with the magnitude of his breach or of the public harm he commits.

It is convenient to begin with the utilitarian theory. . . . The essence of the rule-utilitarian theory, we recall, is that our actions, whether legislative or otherwise, should be guided by a set of prescriptions, the conscientious following of which by all would have maximum net expectable utility. As a result, the utilitarian is not, just as such, committed to any particular view about how anti-social behavior should be treated by society—or even to the view that society should do anything at all about immoral conduct. It is only the utilitarian principle *combined* with statements about the kind of laws and practices which will maximize expectable utility that has such consequences. Therefore, utilitarians are free to differ from one another about the character of an ideal system of criminal justice; some utilitarians think that the system prevalent in Great Britain and the United States essentially corresponds to the ideal, but others think that the only system that can be justified is markedly different from the actual systems in these Western countries. We shall concentrate our discussion, however, on the more traditional line of utilitarian thought which holds that roughly the actual system of criminal law, say in the United States, is morally justifiable, and we shall follow roughly the classic exposition of the reasoning given by Jeremy Bentham[1]—but modifying this freely when we feel amendment is called for. At the end of the chapter we shall look briefly at a different view.

Traditional utilitarian thinking about criminal justice has found the rationale of the practice, in the United States, for example, in three main facts. (Those who disagree think the first two of these "facts" happen not to be the case.) (1) People who are tempted to misbehave, to trample on the rights of others, to sacrifice public welfare for personal gain, can usually be deterred from misconduct by fear of punishment, such as death, imprisonment, or fine. (2) Imprisonment or fine will teach malefactors a lesson; their characters may be improved, and at any rate a personal experience of punishment will make them less likely to misbehave again. (3) Imprisonment will certainly have the result of physically preventing past malefactors from misbehaving, during the period of their incarceration.

In view of these suppositions, traditional utilitarian thinking has concluded that having laws forbidding certain kinds of behavior on pain of punishment, and having machinery for the fair enforcement of these laws, is justified by the fact that it maximizes expectable utility. Misconduct is not to be punished just for its own sake; malefactors must be punished for their past acts, according to law, as a way of maximizing expectable utility.

The utilitarian principle, of course, has implications for decisions about the severity of punishment to be administered. Punishment is itself an evil, and hence should be avoided where this is consistent with the public good. Punishment should have precisely such a degree of severity (not more or less) that the probable disutility of greater severity just balances the probable gain in utility (less crime because of the more serious threat). The cost, in other words, should be counted along with the value of what is bought; and we should buy protection up to the point where the cost is greater than the protection is worth. How severe will such punishment be? Jeremy Bentham had many sensible things to say about this. Punishment, he said, must be severe enough so that it is to no one's advantage to commit an offense even if he receives the punishment; a fine of $10 for bank robbery would give no security at all. Further, since many criminals will be undetected, we must make the penalty heavy enough in comparison with the prospective gain from crime, that a prospective criminal will consider the risk

hardly worth it, even considering that it is not certain he will be punished at all. Again, the more serious offenses should carry the heavier penalties, not only because the greater disutility justifies the use of heavier penalties in order to prevent them, but also because criminals should be motivated to commit a less serious rather than a more serious offense. Bentham thought the prescribed penalties should allow for some variation at the discretion of the judge, so that the actual suffering caused should roughly be the same in all cases; thus, a heavier fine will be imposed on a rich man than on a poor man.

Bentham also argued that the goal of maximum utility requires that certain facts should *excuse* from culpability, for the reason that punishment in such cases "must be inefficacious." He listed as such (1) the fact that the relevant law was passed only after the act of the accused, (2) that the law had not been made public, (3) that the criminal was an infant, insane, or was intoxicated, (4) that the crime was done under physical compulsion, (5) that the agent was ignorant of the probable consequences of his act or was acting on the basis of an innocent misapprehension of the facts, such that the act the agent thought he was performing was a lawful one, and (6) that the motivation to commit the offense was so strong that no threat of law could prevent the crime. Bentham also thought that punishment should be remitted if the crime was a collective one and the number of the guilty so large that great suffering would be caused by its imposition, or if the offender held an important post and his services were important for the public, or if the public or foreign powers would be offended by the punishment; but we shall ignore this part of his view.

Bentham's account of the logic of legal "defenses" needs amendment. What he should have argued is that *not* punishing in certain types of cases (cases where such defenses as those just indicated can be offered) reduces the amount of suffering imposed by law and the insecurity of everybody, and that failure to impose punishment in these types of cases will cause only a negligible increase in the incidence of crime.

How satisfactory is this theory of criminal justice? Does it have any implications that are far from being acceptable when compared with concrete justified convictions about what practices are morally right?[2]

Many criminologists would argue that Bentham was mistaken in his facts: The deterrence value of threat of punishment, they say, is much less than he imagined, and criminals are seldom reformed by spending time in prison. If these contentions are correct, then the ideal rules for society's treatment of malefactors are very different from what Bentham thought, and from what actual practice is today in the United States. To say all this, however, is not to show that the utilitarian *principle* is incorrect. . . . Utilitarian theory might still be correct, but its implications would be different from what Bentham thought. . . .

The whole utilitarian approach, however, has been criticized on the grounds that it ought not in consistency to approve of *any* excuses from criminal liability.[3] Or at least, it should do so only after careful empirical inquiries. It is not obvious, it is argued, that we increase net expectable utility by permitting such defenses. At the least, the utilitarian is committed to defend the concept of "strict liability." Why? Because we could get a more strongly deterrent effect if everyone knew that *all behavior* of a certain sort would be punished, irrespective of mistaken supposals of fact, compulsion, and so on. The critics admit that knowledge that all behavior of a certain sort will be punished will hardly deter from crime the insane, persons acting under compulsion, persons acting under erroneous beliefs about facts, and others, but, as Professor Hart points out, it does not follow from this that general knowledge that certain acts will always be punished will not be salutary.

The utilitarian, however, has a solid defense against charges of this sort. We must bear in mind (as the critics do not) that the utilitarian principle, *taken by itself, implies nothing whatever* about whether a system of law should excuse persons on the basis of certain defenses. What the utilitarian does say is that, when we *combine* the principle of utilitarianism with *true* propositions about a certain thing or situation, then we shall come out with true statements about obligations. . . . Moreover, in fact the utilitarian

can properly claim that we do have excellent reason for believing that the general public would be no better motivated to avoid criminal offenses than it now is, if the insane and others were also punished along with intentional wrongdoers. Indeed, he may reasonably claim that the example of punishment of these individuals could only have a hardening effect—like public executions. Furthermore, the utilitarian can point out that abolition of the standard exculpating excuses would lead to serious insecurity. Imagine the pleasure of driving an automobile if one knew one could be executed for running down a child whom it was absolutely impossible to avoid striking! One certainly does not maximize expectable utility by eliminating the traditional excuses. In general, then, the utilitarian theory is not threatened by its implications about exculpating excuses.

It might also be objected against utilitarianism that it cannot recognize the validity of *mitigating* excuses. Would not consequences be better if the distinction between premeditated and impulsive acts were abolished? The utilitarian can reply that people who commit impulsive crimes, in the heat of anger, do not give thought to legal penalties; they would not be deterred by a stricter law. Moreover, such a person is unlikely to repeat his crime, so that a mild sentence saves an essentially good man for society.[4]

Sometimes it is objected to utilitarianism that it must view imprisonment for crime as morally no different from quarantine. This, it is said, shows that the utilitarian theory must be mistaken, since actually there is a vast moral difference between being quarantined and being imprisoned for crime. *Why* is it supposed utilitarian theory must view imprisonment as a kind of quarantine? The answer is that utilitarianism looks to the future; the treatment it prescribes for individuals is treatment with an eye to maximizing net expectable utility. The leper is quarantined because otherwise he will expose others to disease. The criminal is imprisoned because otherwise he, or others who are not deterred by the threat of punishment, will expose the public to crime. Both the convicted criminal and the leper are making contributions to the public good. So, quarantine and imprisonment are essentially personal sacrifices for the public welfare, if we think of punishment as the utilitarian does. But in fact, the argument goes on, we feel there is a vast difference. The public is obligated to do what is possible to make the leper comfortable, to make his necessary sacrifice as easy for him and his family as possible. But we feel no obligation to make imprisonment as comfortable as possible.

Again the utilitarian has a reply. He can say that people cannot help contracting leprosy, but they can avoid committing crimes—and the very discomforts and harshness of prison life are deterring factors. If prison life were made attractive, there might be more criminals—not to mention the indolent who would commit a crime in order to enjoy the benefits of public support. Furthermore, the utilitarian can say, why should we feel that we "ought to make it up to" a quarantined leper? At least partly because it is useful to encourage willingness to make such sacrifices. But we do not at all wish to encourage the criminal to make his "sacrifice"; rather, we wish him not to commit his crimes. There is all the difference between the kind of treatment justified on utilitarian grounds for a person who may have to make a sacrifice for the public welfare through no fault of his own, and for a person who is required to make a sacrifice because he has selfishly and deliberately trampled on the rights of others, in clear view of the fact that if he is apprehended society must make an example of him. There are all sorts of utilitarian reasons for being kindly to persons of the former type, and stern with people of the latter type.

Another popular objection to the utilitarian theory is that the utilitarian must approve of prosecutors or judges occasionally withholding evidence known to them, for the sake of convicting an innocent man, if the public welfare really is served by so doing. Critics of the theory would not deny that there *can* be circumstances where the dangers are so severe that such action is called for; they only say that utilitarianism calls for it all too frequently. Is this criticism justified? Clearly, the utilitarian is not committed to advocating that a provision should be written into the *law* so as to permit punishment of

persons for crimes they did not commit if to do so would serve the public good. Any such provision would be a shattering blow to public confidence and security. The question is only whether there should be an informal moral rule to the same effect, for the guidance of judges and prosecutors. Will the rule-utilitarian necessarily be committed to far too sweeping a moral rule on this point? We must recall that he is not in the position of the act-utilitarian, who must say that an innocent man must be punished if in *his particular case* the public welfare would be served by his punishment. The rule-utilitarian rather asserts only that an innocent man should be punished if he falls within a class of cases such that net expectable utility is maximized if *all* members of the class are punished, taking into account the possible disastrous effects on public confidence if it is generally known that judges and prosecutors are guided by such a rule. . . . When we take these considerations into account, it is *not* obvious that the rule-utilitarian is committed to action that we are justifiably convinced is immoral.[5]. . .

Everything considered, the utilitarian theory seems to be in much less dire distress, in respect of its implications for criminal justice, than has sometimes been supposed. It does not seem possible to show that in any important way its implications are clearly in conflict with our valid convictions about what is right. The worst that can be said is that utilitarian theory does not in a clear-cut way definitely require us to espouse some practices we are inclined to espouse. But to this the utilitarian may make two replies. First, that there is reason to think our ordinary convictions about punishment for crime ought to be thoroughly re-examined in important respects. Second, the utilitarian may reply that if we consider our convictions about the punishments we should administer *as a parent*—and this is the point where our moral opinions are least likely to be affected by the sheer weight of tradition—we shall find that we think according to the principles of rule-utilitarianism. Parents do regard their punishment of their children as justified only in view of the future good of the child, and in order to make life in the home tolerable and in order to distribute jobs and sacrifices equally.

2. THE RETRIBUTIVE THEORY OF CRIMINAL JUSTICE

. . . [The] "retributive theory" . . . asserts that it is a basic principle of ethics roughly that pain or loss should be caused to persons who have done wrong, with a severity corresponding with the moral gravity of their deed—and of course the "gravity" of the deed not being defined to accord exactly with the utilitarian theory about how severely wrongdoers should be made to suffer. In saying that such a principle is a "basic" principle of ethics, proponents of the retributive theory deny the possibility of deriving this principle from any principle directing to do good, that is, from any kind of utilitarian principle. . . .

The traditional retributive principle is perhaps best stated today in a way suggested by Ross' formalist system, somewhat as follows: "It is prima facie obligatory for society to cause pain or loss to every person who commits a morally objectionable act to an extent corresponding with the moral gravity of his offense." We can assume that other considerations, such as the obligation to avoid general insecurity, will require that punishment be imposed only for infractions of properly publicized laws, by specially authorized persons, and after a trial according to procedures selected in order to guarantee a fair application of the law.

Should we accept the retributive principle as a basic "axiom" about moral obligation (or else the assertion that it is intrinsically better for offenders to be punished than to go unpunished)? Various considerations suggest that we should answer this question *negatively.*

1. Our ethical theory is *simpler* without this principle, and therefore it should be rejected unless it enables us to deduce, as theorems (when we combine it with true factual premises), ethical principles which are valid, and which cannot be deduced without it. But since our discussion of the rule-utilitarian theory of punishment has not disclosed any major objection to that theory, there is no reason to complicate our theory by adding a retributive principle.

2. The retributive principle asserts in effect that a principle aim of the law is to punish moral guilt. But if so, then it ought to punish merely *attempted* crimes as severely as successful crimes, and since an attempt is a case of setting oneself to commit a crime, it is as much a deliberate deviation from subjective obligation as the successful commission of a crime. Assuming that this implication is incorrect, clearly the retributive principle alone will not do as a principle guiding legislative practice.

3. According to retributivism, laws should be so framed that no one will be punished, no matter what he does, if he is morally blameless. This is objectionable. It is of great importance that the law be able to set up standards of conduct, and require all to conform, whether or not they are convinced of the desirability of the standards. The law must be in a position to demand certain conduct from individuals, say in the Defense Department, whose conscientious deliberations might lead them to betray secrets essential to the national defense. Again, the law must be in a position to ban some practice like polygamy, irrespective of the value judgments of any persons. Therefore, we must again say that the retributive principle cannot be the only principle guiding the framing of law and judicial practice.

NOTES

[1]In *Principles of Morals and Legislation.*
[2]Act-utilitarians face some special problems. For instance, if I am an act-utilitarian and serve on a jury, I shall work to get a verdict that will do the most good, irrespective of the charges of the judge, and of any oath I may have taken to give a reasonable answer to certain questions on the basis of the evidence presented—unless I think my doing so will have indirect effects on the institution of the jury, public confidence in it, and so on. This is certainly not what we think a juror should do. Of course, neither a juror nor a judge can escape his prima facie obligation to do what good he can; this obligation is present in some form in every theory. The act-utilitarian, however, makes this the whole of one's responsibility.
[3]See H. L. A. Hart, "Legal Responsibility and Excuses," in Sidney Hook (ed.), *Determinism and Freedom* (New York: New York University Press, 1958), pp. 81–104; and David Braybrooke, "Professor Stevenson, Voltaire, and the Case of Admiral Byng," *Journal of Philosophy*, LIII (1956), 787–96.
[4]The utilitarian must admit that the same thing is true for many deliberate murders and probably he should also admit that some people who commit a crime in the heat of anger

would have found time to think had they known that a grave penalty awaited them.

[5]In any case, a tenable theory of punishment must approve of punishing persons who are *morally* blameless. Suppose someone commits treason for moral reasons. We may have to say that his deed is not reprehensible at all, and might even (considering the risk he took for his principles) be morally admirable. Yet we think such persons must be punished no matter what their motives; people cannot be permitted to take the law into their own hands.

REVIEW AND DISCUSSION QUESTIONS

1. What are the two distinct ways in which there can be injustice in the treatment of criminals?

2. From a utilitarian perspective, what reasons are there for punishment? What are the implications of the utilitarian approach for the severity of punishment? For permitting exculpatory or mitigating excuses?

3. How satisfactory is Brandt's response to the criticism that utilitarianism must approve of prosecutors or judges occasionally convicting innocent people, if the public welfare would be served by doing so?

4. Assess Brandt's three reasons for rejecting the retributivist principle.

5. Are there possible objections to the utilitarian theory of punishment that Brandt has overlooked or failed to deal with adequately?

6. Assess capital punishment from a utilitarian viewpoint. What considerations can be raised for and against it? When, if ever, and for what crimes and under what circumstances would a utilitarian favor the death penalty?

Persons and Punishment

Herbert Morris

Some retributivists have held not only that criminals deserve to be punished but also that they have a right to be punished. In this essay, professor of law Herbert Morris upholds the strange-sounding idea that we have a right to punishment. He does this by contrasting two systems of social control. The first is a system of just punishment. Where the rules are designed to benefit everyone, punishment prevents those who violate the rules from gaining an unfair advantage over those who adhere to them, and the offender can be seen as owing a debt to society. The second system is one that views criminal behavior as a kind of disease and sees the criminal as in need of therapeutic treatment. Because Morris finds such a therapy system morally objectionable, he concludes that we have not just a right to a system of punishment (rather than therapy) but, once such a system is in existence, a right to be punished.

They acted and looked . . . at us, and around in our house, in a way that had about it the feeling—at least for me—that we were not people. In their eyesight we were just things, that was all.

—Malcolm X

We have no right to treat a man like a dog.

—Governor Maddox of Georgia

Alfredo Traps in Dürrenmatt's tale discovers that he has brought off, all by himself, a murder involving considerable ingenuity. The mock prosecutor in the tale demands the death penalty "as reward for a crime that merits admiration, astonishment, and respect." Traps is deeply moved; indeed, he is exhilarated, and the whole of his life becomes more heroic, and, ironically, more precious. His defense attorney proceeds to argue that Traps was not only innocent but incapable of guilt, "a victim of the age." This defense Traps disavows with indignation and anger. He makes claim to the murder as his and demands the prescribed punishment—death.

The themes to be found in this macabre tale do not often find their way into philosophical discussions of punishment. These discussions deal with large and significant questions of whether or not we ever have the right to punish, and if we do, under what conditions, to what degree, and in what manner. There is a tradition, of course, not notable for its present vitality, that is closely linked with motifs in Dürrenmatt's tale of crime and punishment. Its adherents have urged that justice requires a person be punished if he is guilty. Sometimes—though rarely—these philosophers have expressed themselves in terms of the criminals's *right to be punished*. Reaction to the claim that there is such a right has been astonishment combined, perhaps, with a touch of contempt for the perversity of the suggestion. A strange right that no one would ever wish to claim! With that flourish the subject is buried and the right disposed of. In this paper the subject is resurrected.

My aim is to argue . . . that we have a right to punishment. . . .

When someone claims that there is a right to be free, we can easily imagine situations in which the right is infringed and easily imagine situations in which there is a point to asserting or claiming the right. With the right to be punished, matters are otherwise. The immediate reaction to the claim that there is such a right is puzzlement. And the reasons for this are apparent. People do not normally value pain and suffering. Punishment is associated with pain and suffering. When we think about punishment we naturally think of the strong desire most persons have to avoid it, to accept, for example, acquittal of a criminal charge with relief and eagerly, if convicted, to hope for pardon or probation. Adding, of course, to the paradoxical character of the claim of such a right is difficulty in imagining circumstances in which it would be denied one. When would one rightly demand punishment and meet with any threat of the claim being denied?

So our first task is to see when the claim of such a right would have a point. I want to approach this task by setting out two complex types of institutions both of which are designed to maintain some degree of social control. In the one a central concept is punishment for wrongdoing and in the other the central concepts are control of dangerous individuals and treatment of disease.

Let us first turn attention to the institutions in which punishment is involved. The institutions I describe will resemble those we ordinarily think of as institutions of punishment; they will have, however, additional features we associate with a system of just punishment.

Let us suppose that men are constituted roughly as they now are, with a rough equivalence in strength and abilities, a capacity to be injured by each other and to make judgments that such injury is undesirable, a limited strength of will, and a capacity to reason and to conform conduct to rules. Applying to the conduct of these men are a group of rules, ones I shall label "primary," which closely resemble the core rules of our criminal law, rules that prohibit violence and deception and compliance with which provides benefits for all persons. These benefits consist in noninterference by others with what each person values, such matters as continuance of life and bodily security. The rules define a sphere for each person, then, which is immune from interference by others. Making possible this mutual benefit is the assumption by individuals of a burden. The burden consists in the exercise of self-restraint by individuals over inclinations that would, if satisfied, directly interfere or create a substantial risk of interference with others in proscribed ways. If a person fails to exercise self-restraint even though he might have and gives in to such inclinations, he renounces a burden which others have voluntarily assumed and thus gains an advantage which others, who have restrained themselves, do not possess. This system, then, is one in which the rules establish a mutuality of benefit and burden and in which the benefits of noninterference are conditional upon the assumption of burdens.

Connecting punishment with the violation of these primary rules, and making public the provision for punishment, is both reasonable and just. First, it is only reasonable that those who voluntarily comply with the rules be provided some assurance that they will not be assuming burdens which others are unprepared to assume. Their disposition to comply voluntarily will diminish as they learn that others are with impunity renouncing burdens they are assuming. Second, fairness dictates that a system in which benefits and burdens are equally distributed have a mechanism designed to prevent a maldistribution in the benefits and burdens. Thus, sanctions are attached to noncompliance with the primary rules so as to induce compliance with the primary rules among those who may be disinclined to obey. In this way the likelihood of an unfair distribution is diminished.

Third, it is just to punish those who have violated the rules and caused the unfair distribution of benefits and burdens. A person who violates the rules has something others have— the benefits of the system—but by renouncing what others have assumed, the burdens of self-restraint, he has acquired an unfair advantage. Matters are not even until this advantage is in some way erased. Another way of putting it is that he owes something to others, for he has something that does not rightfully belong to him. Justice—that is punishing such individuals—restores the equilibrium of benefits and burdens by taking from the individual what he owes, that is, exacting the debt. It is important to see that the equilibrium may be restored in another way. Forgiveness—with its legal analogue of a pardon—while not the righting of an unfair distribution by making one pay his debt is, nevertheless, a restoring of the equilibrium by forgiving the debt. Forgiveness may be viewed, at least in some types of cases, as a gift after the fact, erasing a debt, which had the gift been given before the fact, would not have created a debt. But the practice of pardoning has to proceed sensitively, for it may endanger in a way the practice of justice does not, the maintenance of an equilibrium of benefits and burdens. If all are indiscriminately pardoned less incentive is provided individuals to restrain their inclinations, thus increasing the incidence of persons taking what they do not deserve.

There are also in this system we are considering a variety of operative principles compliance with which provides some guarantee that the system of punishment does not itself promote an unfair distribution of benefits and burdens. For one thing, provision is made for a variety of defenses, each one of which can be said to have as its object diminishing the chances of forcibly depriving a person of benefits others have if that person has not derived an unfair advantage. A person has not derived an unfair advantage if he could not have restrained himself or if it is unreasonable to expect him to behave otherwise than he did. Sometimes the rules preclude punishment of classes of persons such as children. Sometimes they provide a defense if on a particular occasion a person lacked the capacity to conform his conduct to the rules. Thus, someone who in an epileptic seizure strikes another is excused. Punishment in these cases would be punishment of the innocent, punishment of those who do not voluntarily renounce a burden others have assumed. Punishment in such cases, then, would not equalize but rather cause an unfair distribution in benefits and burdens.

Along with principles providing defenses there are requirements that the rules be prospective and relatively clear so that persons have a fair opportunity to comply with the rules. There are, also, rules governing, among other matters, the burden of proof, who shall bear it and what it shall be, the prohibition on double jeopardy, and the privilege against self-incrimination. Justice requires conviction of the guilty, and requires their punishment, but in setting out to fulfill the demands of justice we may, of course, because we are not omniscient, cause injustice by convicting and punishing the innocent. The resolution arrived at in the system I am describing consists in weighing as the greater evil the punishment of the innocent. The primary function of the system of rules was to provide individuals with a sphere of interest immune from interference. Given this goal, it is determined to be a greater evil for society to interfere unjustifiably with an individual by depriving him of good than for the society to fail to punish those that have unjustifiably interfered.

Finally, because the primary rules are designed to benefit all and because the punishments prescribed for their violation are publicized and the defenses respected, there is some plausibility in the exaggerated claim that in choosing to do an act violative of the rules an individual has chosen to be punished. This way of putting matters brings to our attention the extent to which, when the system is as I have described it, the criminal "has brought the punishment upon himself" in contrast to those cases where it would be misleading to say "he has brought it upon himself," cases, for example, where one does not know the rules or is punished in the absence of fault.

To summarize, then: first, there is a group of rules guiding the behavior of individuals in the community which establish spheres of interest immune from interference by others; second, provision is made for what is generally regarded as a deprivation of something of value if the rules are violated; third, the deprivations visited upon any person are justified by that person's having violated the rules; fourth, the deprivation, in this just system of punishment, is linked to rules that fairly distribute benefits and burdens and to procedures that strike some balance between not punishing the guilty and punishing the innocent, a class defined as those who have not voluntarily done acts violative of the law, in which it is evident that the evil of punishing the innocent is regarded as greater than the nonpunishment of the guilty.

At the core of many actual legal systems one finds, of course, rules and procedures of the kind I have sketched. It is obvious, though, that any ongoing legal system differs in significant respects from what I have presented here, containing "pockets of injustice."

I want now to sketch an extreme version of a set of institutions of a fundamentally different kind, institutions proceeding on a conception of man which appears to be basically at odds with that operative within a system of punishment.

Rules are promulgated in this system that prohibit certain types of injuries and harms.

In this world we are now to imagine when an individual harms another his conduct is to be regarded as a symptom of some pathological condition in the way a running nose is a symptom of a cold. Actions diverging from some conception of the normal are viewed as manifestations of a disease in the way in which we might today regard the arm and leg movements of an epileptic during a seizure. Actions conforming to what is normal are assimilated to the normal and healthy functioning of bodily organs. What a person does, then, is assimilated, on this conception, to what we believe today, or at least most of us believe today, a person undergoes. We draw a distinction between the operation of the kidney and raising an arm on request. This distinction between mere events or happenings and human actions is erased in our imagined system.[1] . . .

Let us elaborate on this assimilation of conduct of a certain kind to symptoms of a disease. First, there is something abnormal in both the case of conduct, such as killing another, and a symptom of a disease such as an irregular heart beat. Second, there are causes for this abnormality in action such that once we know of them we can explain the abnormality as we now can explain the symptoms of many physical diseases. The abnormality is looked upon as a happening with a causal explanation rather than an action for which there were reasons. Third, the causes that account for the abnormality interfere with the normal functioning of the body, or, in the case of killing with what is regarded as a normal functioning of an individual. . . .

With this view of man the institutions of social control respond, not with punishment, but with either preventive detention, in case of "carriers," or therapy in the case of those manifesting pathological symptoms. The logic of sickness implies the logic of therapy. . . . I am concerned now . . . with what the implications would be were the world indeed one of therapy . . . for I want to suggest tendencies of thought that arise when one is immersed in the ideology of disease and therapy.

First, punishment is the imposition upon a person who is believed to be at fault of something commonly believed to be a deprivation where that deprivation is justified by the person's guilty behavior. It is associated with resentment, for the guilty are those who have done what they had no right to do by failing to exercise restraint when they might have and where others have. Therapy is not a response to a person who is at fault. We respond to an individual, not because of what he has done, but because of some condition from which he is suffering. If he is no longer suffering from the condition, treatment no longer has a point. Punishment, then, focuses on the past; therapy on the present. Therapy is normally associated with compassion for what one undergoes, not resentment for what one has illegitimately done.

Second, with therapy, unlike punishment, we do not seek to deprive the person of something acknowledged as a good, but seek rather to help and to benefit the individual who is suffering by ministering to his illness in the hope that the person can be cured. The good we attempt to do is not a reward for desert. The individual suffering has not merited by his disease the good we seek to bestow upon him but has, because he is a creature that has the capacity to feel pain, a claim upon our sympathies and help.

Third, we saw with punishment that its justification was related to maintaining and restoring a fair distribution of benefits and burdens. Infliction of the prescribed punishment carries the implication, then, that one has 'paid one's debt' to society, for the punishment is the taking from the person of something commonly recognized as valuable. It is this conception of 'a debt owed' that may permit, as I suggested earlier, under certain conditions, the nonpunishment of the guilty, for operative within a system of punishment may be a concept analogous to forgiveness, namely pardoning. . . . What is clear is that the conceptions of "paying a debt" or "having a debt forgiven" or pardoning have no place in a system of therapy.

Fourth, with punishment there is an attempt at some equivalence between the advantage gained by the wrongdoer—partly based upon the seriousness of the interest invaded, partly on the state of mind with which the wrongful act was performed—and the punishment meted out. Thus, we can understand a prohibition on "cruel and unusual punishments" so that disproportionate pain and suffering are avoided.

With therapy attempts at proportionality make no sense. It is perfectly plausible giving someone who kills a pill and treating for a lifetime within an institution one who has broken a dish and manifested accident proneness. We have the concept of "painful treatment." We do not have the concept of "cruel treatment." Because treatment is regarded as a benefit, though it may involve pain, it is natural that less restraint is exercised in bestowing it, than in inflicting punishment. Further, protests with respect to treatment are likely to be assimilated to the complaints of one whose leg must be amputated in order for him to live, and, thus, largely disregarded. To be sure, there is operative in the therapy world some conception of the "cure being worse than the disease," but if the disease is manifested in conduct harmful to others, and if being a normal operating human being is valued highly, there will naturally be considerable pressure to find the cure acceptable.

Fifth, the rules in our system of punishment governing conduct of individuals were rules violation of which involved either direct interference with others or the creation of a substantial risk of such interference. . . . Though we are interested in diminishing violations of the primary rules, we are not prepared to punish too many individuals who would never have violated the rules in order to achieve this aim. In a system motivated solely by a preventive and curative ideology there would be less reason to wait until symptoms manifest themselves in socially harmful conduct. It is understandable that we should wish at the earliest possible stage to arrest the development of the disease. In the punishment system, because we are dealing with deprivations, it is understandable that we should forbear from imposing them until we are quite sure of guilt. In the therapy system, dealing as it does with benefits, there is less reason for forbearance from treatment at an early stage.

Sixth, a variety of procedural safeguards we associate with punishment have less significance in a therapy system. To the degree objections to double jeopardy and self-incrimination are based on a wish to decrease the chances of the innocent being convicted and punished, a therapy system, unconcerned with this problem, would disregard such safeguards. When one is out to help people there is also little sense in urging that the burden of proof be on those providing the help. And there is less point to imposing the burden of proving that the conduct was pathological beyond a reasonable doubt. Further, a jury system which, within a system of justice, serves to make accommodations to the individual situation and to introduce a human element, would play no role or a minor one in a world where expertise is required in making determinations of disease and treatment.

In our system of punishment an attempt was made to maximize each individual's freedom of choice by first of all delimiting by rules certain spheres of conduct immune from interference by others. The punishment associated with these primary rules paid deference to an individual's free choice by connecting punishment to a freely chosen act violative of the rules, thus giving some plausibility to the claim, as we saw, that what a person received by way of punishment he himself had chosen. With the world of disease and therapy all this changes and the individual's free choice ceases to be a determinative factor in how others respond to him. All those principles of our own legal system that minimize the chances of punishment of those who have not chosen to do acts violative of the rules tend to lose their point in the therapy system, for how we respond in a therapy system to a person is not conditioned upon what he has chosen but rather on what symptoms he has manifested or may manifest and what the best therapy for the disease is that is suggested by the symptoms.

Now, it is clear I think, that were we confronted with the alternatives I have sketched, between a system of just punishment and a thoroughgoing system of treatment, a system, that is, that did not reintroduce concepts appropriate to punishment, we could see the point in claiming that a person has a right to be punished, meaning by this that a person had a right to all those institutions and practices linked to punishment. For these would provide him with, among other things, a far greater ability to predict what would happen to him on the occurrence of certain events than the therapy system. There is the inestimable value to each of us of

having the responses of others to us determined over a wide range of our lives by what we choose rather than what they choose. A person has a right to institutions that respect his choices. Our punishment system does; our therapy system does not.

Apart from those aspects of our therapy model which would relate to serious limitations on personal liberty, there are clearly objections of a more profound kind to the mode of thinking I have associated with the therapy model.

First, human beings pride themselves in having capacities that animals do not. A common way, for example, of arousing shame in a child is to compare the child's conduct to that of an animal. In a system where all actions are assimilated to happenings we are assimilated to creatures—indeed, it is more extreme than this—whom we have always thought possessed of less than we. Fundamental to our practice of praise and order of attainment is that one who can do more—one who is capable of more and one who does more is more worthy of respect and admiration. And we have thought of ourselves as capable where animals are not of making, of creating, among other things, ourselves. The conception of man I have outlined would provide us with a status that today, when our conduct is assimilated to it in moral criticism, we consider properly evocative of shame.

Second, if all human conduct is viewed as something men undergo, thrown into question would be the appropriateness of that extensive range of peculiarly human satisfactions that derive from a sense of achievement. For these satisfactions we shall have to substitute those mild satisfactions attendant upon a healthy well-functioning body. Contentment is our lot if we are fortunate; intense satisfaction at achievement is entirely inappropriate.

Third, in the therapy world nothing is earned and what we receive comes to us through compassion, or through a desire to control us. Resentment is out of place. We can take credit for nothing but must always regard ourselves—if there are selves left to regard once actions disappear—as fortunate recipients of benefits or unfortunate carriers of disease who must be controlled. We know that within our own world human beings who have been so regarded and who come to accept this view of themselves come to look upon themselves as worthless. When what we do is met with resentment, we are indirectly paid something of a compliment.

Fourth, attention should also be drawn to a peculiar evil that may be attendant upon regarding a man's actions as symptoms of disease. The logic of cure will push us toward forms of therapy that inevitably involve changes in the person made against his will. The evil in this would be most apparent in those cases where the agent, whose action is determined to be a manifestation of some disease, does not regard his action in this way. He believes that what he has done is, in fact, "right" but his conception of "normality" is not the therapeutically accepted one. When we treat an illness we normally treat a condition that the person is not responsible for. He is "suffering" from some disease and we treat the condition, relieving the person of something preventing his normal functioning. When we begin treating persons for actions that have been chosen, we do not lift from the person something that is interfering with his normal functioning but we change the person so that he functions in a way regarded as normal by the current therapeutic community. We have to change him and his judgments of value. In doing this we display a lack of respect for the moral status of individuals, that is, a lack of respect for the reasoning and choices of individuals. They are but animals who must be conditioned. I think we can understand and, indeed, sympathize with a man's preferring death to being forcibly turned into what he is not.

Finally, perhaps most frightening of all would be the derogation in status of all protests to treatment. If someone believes that he has done something right, and if he protests being treated and changed, the protest will itself be regarded as a sign of some pathological condition, for who would not wish to be cured of an affliction? What this leads to are questions of an important kind about the effect of this conception of man upon what we now understand by reasoning. Here what a person takes to be a reasoned defense of an act is treated, as the action was, on the model of a happening of a pathological kind.

Not just a person's acts are taken from him but also his attempt at a reasoned justification for the acts. In a system of punishment a person who has committed a crime may argue that what he did was right. We make him pay the price and we respect his right to retain the judgment he has made. A conception of pathology precludes this form of respect. . . .

I want also to make clear in concluding this section that I have argued, though very indirectly, not just for a right to a system of punishment, but for a right to be punished once there is in existence such a system. Thus, a man has the right to be punished rather than treated if he is guilty of some offense. And, indeed, one can imagine a case in which, even in the face of an offer of a pardon, a man claims and ought to have acknowledged his right to be punished.

NOTE

[1]"When a man is suffering from an infectious disease, he is a danger to the community, and it is necessary to restrict his liberty of movement. But no one associates any idea of guilt with such a situation. On the contrary, he is an object of commiseration to his friends. Such steps as science recommends are taken to cure him of his disease, and he submits as a rule without reluctance to the curtailment of liberty involved meanwhile. The same method in spirit ought to be shown in the treatment of what is called 'crime.'"
Bertrand Russell, *Roads to Freedom* (London: George Allen and Unwin Ltd., 1918), p. 135.

"We do not hold people responsible for their reflexes—for example, for coughing in church. We hold them responsible for their operant behavior—for example, for whispering in church or remaining in church while coughing. But there are variables which are responsible for whispering as well as coughing, and these may be just as inexorable. When we recognize this, we are likely to drop the notion of responsibility altogether and with it the doctrine of free will as an inner causal agent."
B. F. Skinner, *Science and Human Behavior* (1953), pp. 115–6.

"Basically, criminality is but a symptom of insanity, using the term in its widest generic sense to express unacceptable social behavior based on unconscious motivation flowing from a disturbed instinctive and emotional life, whether this appears in frank psychoses, or in less obvious form in neuroses and unrecognized psychoses. . . . If criminals are products of early environmental influences in the same sense that psychotics and neurotics are, then it should be possible to reach them psychotherapeutically."
Benjamin Karpman, "Criminal Psychodynamics," *Journal of Criminal Law and Criminology*, 47 (1956), p. 9.

"We, the agents of society, must move to end the game of tit-for-tat and blow-for-blow in which the offender has foolishly and futilely engaged himself and us. We are not driven, as he is, to wild and impulsive actions. With knowledge comes power, and with power there is no need for the frightened vengeance of the old penology. In its place should go a quiet, dignified, therapeutic program for the rehabilitation of the disorganized one, if possible, the protection of society during the treatment period, and his guided return to useful citizenship, as soon as this can be effected."

Karl Menninger, "Therapy, Not Punishment," *Harper's Magazine* (August 1959), pp. 63–64.

REVIEW AND DISCUSSION QUESTIONS

1. What are the basic features of a just system of punishment as Morris describes it? To what extent does our criminal justice system approximate Morris's idealized model?

2. Should Morris be considered a retributivist or a utilitarian?

3. What are the basic features of the disease-and-therapy model? What evidence do you see of the model in contemporary thinking about criminal justice? How representative are the authors quoted in Morris's footnote?

4. How do the two models differ in the way they view human beings? What difference is there between the two models in practice? Do you agree with Morris that, philosophically, there is something deeply objectionable about the therapy model? How might a proponent of that model respond to Morris?

Restitution: A New Paradigm of Criminal Justice

Randy E. Barnett

Utilitarianism and retributivism usually occupy center stage in philosophical discussions of punishment. By contrast, Randy E. Barnett, professor of law at the Chicago-Kent College of Law, proposes thinking about criminal justice in terms of restitution. The idea of restitution focuses on the crime as an offense not against society but against an individual. In a restitutional system, the criminal's debt is to the victim, not to society, and the victim's right to restitution determines the nature and extent of criminal liability.[1]

OUTLINE OF A NEW PARADIGM

The idea of restitution is actually quite simple. It views crime as an offense by one individual against the rights of another. The victim has suffered a loss. Justice consists of the culpable offender making good the loss he has caused. It calls for a complete refocusing of our image of crime. Kuhn would call it a "shift of worldview." Where we once saw an offense against society, we now see an offense against an individual victim. In a way, it is a common sense view of crime. *The armed robber did not rob society, he robbed the victim.* His debt, therefore, is not to society; it is to the victim. . . .

"Recompense or restitution is scarcely a punishment as long as it is merely a matter of returning stolen goods or money. . . . The point is not that the offender deserves to suffer; it is rather that the offended party desires compensation."[2] This represents the complete overthrow of the paradigm of punishment. No longer would the deterrence, reformation, disablement, or rehabilitation of the criminal be the guiding principle of the judicial system. The attainment of these goals would be incidental to, and as a result of, reparations paid to the victim. No longer would the criminal deliberately be made to suffer for his mistake. Making good that mistake is all that would be required. What follows is a possible scenario of such a system.

When a crime occurred and a suspect was apprehended, a trial court would attempt to determine his guilt or innocence. If found guilty, the criminal would be sentenced to make restitution to the victim. If a criminal is able to make restitution immediately, he may do so. This would discharge his liability. If he were unable to make restitution, but were found by the court to be trustworthy, he would be permitted to remain at his job (or find a new one) while paying restitution out of his future wages. This would entail a legal claim against future wages. Failure to pay could result in garnishment or a new type of confinement.

If it is found that the criminal is not trustworthy, or that he is unable to gain employment, he would be confined to an employment project. This would be an industrial enterprise, preferably run by a private concern, which would produce actual goods or services. The level of security at each employment project would vary according to the behavior of the offenders. Since the costs would be lower, inmates at a lower-security project would receive higher wages. There is no reason why many workers could not be permitted to live with their families inside or outside the facility, depending, again, on the trustworthiness of the offender. Room and board would be deducted from the wages first, then a certain amount for restitution. Anything over that amount the worker could keep or apply toward further restitution, thus hastening his release. If a worker refused to work, he would be unable to pay for his maintenance, and therefore would not in principle be entitled to it. If he did not make restitution he could not be released. The exact arrangement which would best provide for high productivity, minimal security, and maximum incentive to work and repay the victim cannot be determined in advance. Experience is bound to yield some plans superior to others. In fact, the experimentation has already begun.

While this might be the basic system, all sorts of refinements are conceivable, and certainly many more will be invented as needs arise. A few examples might be illuminating. With such a system of repayment, victim *crime insurance* would be more economically feasible than at present and highly desirable. The cost of awards would be offset by the insurance company's right to restitution in place of the victim (right of subrogation). The insurance company would be better suited to supervise the offender and mark his progress than would the victim. To obtain an earlier recovery, it could be expected to innovate so as to enable the worker to repay more quickly (and, as a result, be released that much sooner). The insurance companies might even underwrite the employment projects themselves as well as related industries which would employ the skilled worker after his release. Any successful effort on their part to reduce crime and recidivism would result in fewer claims and lower premiums. The benefit of this insurance scheme for the victim is immediate compensation, conditional on the victim's continued cooperation with the authorities for the arrest and conviction of the suspect. In addition, the centralization of victim claims would, arguably, lead to efficiencies which would permit the pooling of small claims against a common offender.

Another highly useful refinement would be *direct arbitration* between victim and criminal. This would serve as a sort of healthy substitute for plea bargaining. By allowing the guilty criminal to negotiate a reduced payment in return for a guilty plea, the victim (or his insurance company) would be saved the risk of an adverse finding at trial and any possible additional expense that might result. This would also allow an indigent criminal to substitute personal services for monetary payments if all parties agreed. . . .

Something analogous to the medieval Irish system of *sureties* might be employed as well.[3] Such a system would allow a concerned person, group, or company to make restitution (provided the offender agrees to this). The worker might then be released in the custody of the surety. If the surety had made restitution, the offender would owe restitution to the surety who might enforce the whole claim or show mercy. Of course, the more violent and unreliable the offender, the more serious and costly the offense, the less likely it would be that anyone would take the risk. But for first offenders, good workers, or others that charitable interests found deserving (or perhaps unjustly convicted) this would provide an avenue of respite.

RESTITUTION AND RIGHTS

These three possible refinements clearly illustrate the flexibility of a restitutional system. It may be less apparent that this flexibility is *inherent* to the restitutional paradigm. Restitution recognizes rights in the victim, and this is a principal source of its strength. The nature and limit of the victim's right to restitution at the same time defines the nature and limit of the criminal liability. In this way, the aggressive action of the criminal creates a *debt* to the victim. The recognition of rights and obligations make possible many innovative arrangements. Subrogation, arbitration, and suretyship are three examples mentioned above. They are possible because this right to compensation[4] is considered the property of the victim and can therefore be delegated, assigned, inherited, or bestowed. One could determine in advance who would acquire the right to any restitution which he himself might be unable to collect.

The natural owner of an unenforced death claim would be an insurance company that had insured the deceased. The suggestion has been made that a person might thus increase his personal safety by insuring with a company well known for tracking down those who injure its policy holders. In fact, the partial purpose of some insurance schemes might be to provide the funds with which to track down the malefactor. The insurance company, having paid the beneficiaries would "stand in their shoes." It would remain possible, of course, to simply assign or devise the right directly to the beneficiaries, but this would put the burden of enforcement on persons likely to be unsuited to the task.

If one accepts the Lockean trichotomy of property ownership,[5] that is, acquiring property via exchange, gifts, and *homesteading* (mixing one's labor with previously unowned land or objects), the possibility arises that upon a person's

wrongful death, in the absence of any heirs or assignees, his right to compensation becomes unowned property. The right could then be claimed (homesteaded) by anyone willing to go to the trouble of catching and prosecuting the criminal. Firms might specialize in this sort of activity, or large insurance companies might make the effort as a kind of "loss leader" for public relations purposes.

This does, however, lead to a potentially serious problem with the restitutional paradigm: what exactly constitutes "restitution"? What is the *standard* by which compensation is to be made? Earlier we asserted that any such problem facing the restitutional paradigm faces civil damage suits as well. The method by which this problem is dealt with in civil cases could be applied to restitution cases. But while this is certainly true, it may be that this problem has not been adequately handled in civil damage suits either.

Restitution in cases of crimes against property is a manageable problem. Modern contract and tort doctrines of restitution are adequate. The difficulty lies in cases of personal injury or death. How can you put a price on life or limb, pain or suffering? Is not any attempt to do so of necessity arbitrary? It must be admitted that a fully satisfactory solution to this problem is lacking, but it should also be stressed that this dilemma, though serious, has little impact on the bulk of our case in favor of a restitutional paradigm. It is possible that no paradigm of criminal justice can solve every problem, yet the restitutional approach remains far superior to the paradigm of punishment or any other conceivable rival.

This difficulty arises because certain property is unique and irreplaceable. As a result, it is impossible to approximate a "market" or "exchange" value expressed in monetary terms. Just as there is no rational relationship between a wrongfully taken life and ten years in prison, there is little relationship between that same life and $20,000. Still, the nature of this possibly insoluble puzzle reveals a restitutional approach theoretically superior to punishment. For it must be acknowledged that a real, tangible loss *has* occurred. The problem is only one of incommensurability. Restitution provides *some* tangible, albeit inadequate, compensation for personal injury. Punishment provides none at all.[6] . . .

ADVANTAGES OF A RESTITUTIONAL SYSTEM

1. The first and most obvious advantage is the assistance provided to victims of crime. They may have suffered an emotional, physical, or financial loss. Restitution would not change the fact that a possibly traumatic crime has occurred (just as the award of damages does not undo tortious conduct). Restitution, however, would make the resulting loss easier to bear for both victims and their families. At the same time, restitution would avoid a major pitfall of victim compensation/welfare plans: Since it is the criminal who must pay, the possibility of collusion between victim and criminal to collect "damages" from the state would be all but eliminated.

2. The possibility of receiving compensation would encourage victims to report crimes and to appear at trial. This is particularly true if there were a crime insurance scheme which contractually committed the policyholder to testify as a condition for payment, thus rendering unnecessary oppressive and potentially tyrannical subpoenas and contempt citations. Even the actual reporting of the crime to police is likely to be a prerequisite for compensation. Such a requirement in auto theft insurance policies has made car thefts the most fully reported crime in the United States. Furthermore, insurance companies which paid the claim would have a strong incentive to see that the criminal was apprehended and convicted. Their pressure and assistance would make the proper functioning of law enforcement officials all the more likely.

3. Psychologist Albert Eglash has long argued that restitution would aid in the rehabilitation of criminals. "Restitution is something an inmate does, not something done for or to him. . . . Being reparative, restitution can alleviate guilt and anxiety, which can otherwise precipitate further offenses."[7] Restitution, says Eglash, is an active effortful role on the part of the offender. It is socially constructive, thereby contributing to the offender's self-esteem. It is related to the offense and may thereby redirect the thoughts which motivated the offense. It is reparative, restorative, and may actually leave the situation better than it was before the crime, both for the criminal and victim.

4. This is a genuinely "self-determinative" sentence. The worker would know that the length of his confinement was in his own hands. The harder he worked, the faster he would make restitution. He would be the master of his fate and would have to face that responsibility. This would encourage useful, productive activity and instill a conception of reward for good behavior and hard work. Compare this with the current probationary system and "indeterminate sentencing" where the decision for release is made by the prison bureaucracy, based only (if fairly administered) on "good behavior"; that is, passive acquiescence to prison discipline. Also, the fact that the worker would be acquiring *marketable* skills rather than more skillful methods of crime should help to reduce the shocking rate of recidivism.

5. The savings to taxpayers would be enormous. No longer would the innocent taxpayer pay for the apprehension and internment of the guilty. The cost of arrest, trial, and internment would be borne by the criminal himself. In addition, since now-idle inmates would become productive workers (able, perhaps, to support their families), the entire economy would benefit from the increase in overall production.

6. Crime would no longer pay. Criminals, particularly shrewd white-collar criminals, would know that they could not dispose of the proceeds of their crime and, if caught, simply serve time. They would have to make full restitution plus enforcement and legal costs, thereby greatly increasing the incentive to prosecute. While this would not eliminate such crime it would make it rougher on certain types of criminals, like bank and corporation officials, who harm many by their acts with a virtual assurance of lenient legal sanctions. It might also encourage such criminals to keep the money around for a while so that, if caught, they could repay more easily. This would make a full recovery more likely.

A restitutional system of justice would benefit the victim, the criminal, and the taxpayer. The humanitarian goals of proportionate punishment, rehabilitation, and victim compensation are dealt with on a *fundamental* level making their achievement more likely. In short, the paradigm of restitution would benefit all but the entrenched penal bureaucracy and enhance justice at the same time. What then is there to stop us from overthrowing the paradigm of punishment and its penal system and putting in its place this more efficient, more humane, and more just system? The proponents of punishment and others have a few powerful counterarguments. It is to these we now turn.

OBJECTIONS TO RESTITUTION

1. Practical criticisms of restitution. It might be objected that "crimes disturb and offend not only those who are directly their victim, but also the whole social order."[8] Because of this, society, that is, individuals other than the victim, deserves some satisfaction from the offender. Restitution, it is argued, will not satisfy the lust for revenge felt by the victim or the "community's sense of justice." This criticism appears to be overdrawn. Today most members of the community are mere spectators of the criminal justice system, and this is largely true even of the victim. One major reform being urged presently is more victim involvement in the criminal justice process. The restitution proposal would necessitate this involvement. And while the public generally takes the view that officials should be tougher on criminals, with "tougher" taken by nearly everyone to mean more severe in punishing, one must view this "social fact" in light of the lack of a known alternative. The real test of public sympathies would be to see which sanction people would choose: incarceration of the criminal for a given number of years or the criminal's being compelled to make restitution to the victim: While the public's choice is not clearly predictable, nei-

ther can it be assumed that it would reject restitution. There is some evidence to the contrary.

This brings us to a second practical objection: that monetary sanctions are insufficient deterrents to crime. Again, this is something to be discovered, not something to be assumed. There are a number of reasons to believe that our *current* system of punishment does not adequately deter. . . . In fact, many have argued that the deterrent value of sanctions has less to do with *severity* than with *certainty*, and the preceding considerations indicate that law enforcement would be more certain under a restitutional system. In the final analysis, however, it is irrelevant to argue that more crimes may be committed if our proposal leaves the victim better off. It must be remembered: *Our goal is not the suppression of crime; it is doing justice to victims.*

A practical consideration which merits considerable future attention is the feasibility of the employment project proposal. A number of questions can be raised. At first blush, it seems naively optimistic to suppose that offenders will be able or willing to work at all, much less earn their keep and pay reparations as well. On the contrary, this argument continues, individuals turn to crime precisely because they lack the skills which the restitutional plan assumes they have. Even if these workers have the skills, but refuse to work, what could be done? Would not the use of force to compel compliance be tantamount to slavery?

. . . [O]ne can advance several responses. First, the problem as usually posed assumes the offender to be highly irrational and possibly mentally unbalanced. There is no denying that some segment of the criminal population fits the former description. What this approach neglects, however, is the possibility that many criminals are making rational choices within an irrational and unjust political system. Specifically I refer to the myriad laws and regulations which make it difficult for the unskilled or persons of transitory outlook to find legal employment. I refer also to the laws which deny legality to the types of services which are in particular demand in economically impoverished communities. Is it "irrational" to choose to steal or rob when one is virtually foreclosed from the legal opportunity to do otherwise? Another possibility is that the criminal chooses crime not because of foreclosure, but because he enjoys and obtains satisfaction from a criminal way of life. Though morally repugnant, this is hardly irrational.

Furthermore, it no longer can be denied that contact with the current criminal justice system is itself especially damaging among juveniles. The offenders who are hopelessly committed to criminal behavior are not usually the newcomers to crime but those who have had repeated exposure to the penal system. In Kuhn's words, "Existing institutions have ceased to meet the problems posed by an environment *they have in part created.*" While a restitutionary system might not change these hard-core offenders, it could, by the early implementation of sanctions perceived by the criminal to be just, break the vicious circle which in large part accounts for their existence.

Finally, if offenders could not or would not make restitution, then the logical and just result of their refusal would be confinement until they could or would. Such an outcome would be entirely in their hands. While this "solution" does not suggest who should justly pay for this confinement, the problem is not unique to a restitutionary system. In this and other areas of possible difficulty we must seek guidance from existing pilot programs as well as from the burgeoning research in this area and in victimology in general.

2. Distributionary criticisms of restitution. There remains one criticism of restitution which is the most obvious and the most difficult with which to deal. Simply stated, it takes the following form: "Doesn't this mean that rich people will be able to commit crimes with impunity if they can afford it? Isn't this unfair?" The *practical* aspect of this objection is that whatever deterrent effect restitution payments may have, they will be less for those most able to pay. The *moral* aspect is that whatever retributive or penal effect restitution payments may have they will be less for those who are well off. Some concept of equality of justice underlies both considerations.

Critics of restitution fail to realize that the "cost" of crime will be quite high. In addition to compensation for pain and suffering, the criminal must pay for the cost of his apprehension, the cost of the trial, and the legal expenditures of *both* sides. This should make even an unscrupulous wealthy person think twice about committing a crime. The response to this is that we cannot have it both ways. If the fines would be high enough to bother the rich, then they would be so high that a project worker would have no chance of earning that much and would, therefore, have no incentive to work at all. If, on the other hand, you lower the price of crime by ignoring all its costs, you fail to deter the rich or fully compensate the victim.

This is where the option of arbitration and victim crime insurance becomes of practical importance. If the victim is uninsured, he is unlikely to recover for all costs of a very severe crime from a poor, unskilled criminal, since even in an employment project the criminal might be unable to earn enough. If he had no hope of earning his release, he would have little incentive to work very hard beyond paying for his own maintenance. The victim would end up with less than if he had "settled" the case for the lesser amount which a project worker could reasonably be expected to earn. If, however, the victim had full-coverage criminal insurance, he would recover his damages in full, and the insurance company would absorb any disparity between full compensation and maximal employment project worker's output. This cost would be reflected in premium prices, enabling the insurance company which settled cases at an amount which increased the recovery from the criminal to offer the lowest rates. Eventually a "maximum" feasible fine for project workers would be determined based on these considerations. The "rich," on the other hand, would naturally have to pay in full. This arrangement would solve the practical problem, but it should not be thought of as an imperative of the restitutional paradigm.

The same procedure of varying the payments according to ability to pay would answer the moral considerations as well (that the rich are not hurt enough) and this is the prime motive behind *punitive* restitution proposals. However, we reject the moral consideration outright. The paradigm of restitution calls not for the (equal) hurting of criminals, but for restitution to victims. Any appeal to "inadequate suffering" is a reversion to the paradigm of punishment, and by varying the sanction for crimes of the same magnitude according to the economic status of the offender it reveals its own inequity. *Equality of justice means equal treatment of victims.* It should not matter to the victim if his attacker was rich or poor. His plight is the same regardless. Any reduction of criminal liability because of reduced earning power would be for practical, not moral, reasons.

Equality of justice derives from the fact that the rights of men should be equally enforced and respected. Restitution recognizes a victim's right to compensation for damages from the party responsible. Equality of justice, therefore, calls for equal enforcement of each victim's right to restitution. *Even if necessary or expedient, any lessening of payment to the victim because of the qualities of the criminal is a violation of that victim's rights and an inequality of justice.* Any such expedient settlement is only a recognition that an imperfect world may make possible only imperfect justice. As a practical matter, a restitutional standard gives victims an enormous incentive to pursue wealthy criminals since they can afford quick, full compensation. Contrast this with the present system where the preference given the wealthy is so prevalent that most victims simply assume that nothing will be done.

The paradigm of restitution, to reiterate, is neither a panacea for crime nor a blueprint for utopia. Panaceas and utopias are not for humankind. We must live in a less than perfect world with less than perfect people. Restitution opens the possibility of an improved and more just society. The old paradigm of punishment, even reformed, simply cannot offer this promise.

NOTES

[1] For further discussion of this proposal, *see* Randy E. Barnett, "The Justice of Restitution," 25 *American Journal of Jurisprudence* 117 (1980); Randy E. Barnett, "Pursuing Justice in a Free Society: Part One—Power vs. Liberty," *Criminal Justice Ethics*, Summer/Fall 1985, at 50; Randy E. Barnett, "Pursuing Justice in a Free Society: Part Two—Crime Prevention and the Legal Order," *Criminal Justice Ethics*, Winter/Spring 1986, at 30.

[2] Kaufmann, p. 55.

[3] For a description of the Irish system, see Joseph R. Peden, "Property Rights in Medieval Ireland: Celtic Law versus Church and State" (paper presented at the Symposium on the Origins and Development of Property Rights, University of San Francisco, January 1973); for a theoretical discussion of a similar proposal, see Spencer, pp. 182–86.

[4] Or, perhaps more accurately, the compensation itself.

[5] For a brief explanation of this concept and several of its possible applications, see Murray N. Rothbard, "Justice and Property Rights" in *Property in a Humane Economy*, ed. Samuel L. Blumenfeld (La Salle, Ill.: Open Court Publishing Co., 1974), pp. 101–22.

[6] That the "spiritual" satisfaction which punishment may or may not provide is to be recognized as a legitimate form of "compensation" is a claim retributionists must defend.

[7] Albert Eglash, "Creative Restitution: Some Suggestions for Prison Rehabilitation Programs," *American Journal of Correction* 40 (November–December 1958): 20.

[8] Del Vecchio, p. 198.

REVIEW AND DISCUSSION QUESTIONS

1. What is the difference between restitution and punishment?

2. With reference to Barnett's discussion of insurance, arbitration, and sureties, what sort of a system of restitution would be most feasible? In practice, how could we determine the exact compensation owed to a victim?

3. Assess the six advantages that Barnett claims for a restitutional system.

4. What do you see as the most important objections to a restitutional system? How would Brandt and Morris respond to Barnett's proposal? Whose approach to punishment and criminal justice do you find the most attractive?

Racial Bias in Sentencing

McCleskey v. Kemp

Some studies contend that blacks are more likely to receive the death penalty than whites who commit the same crime. Other studies challenge this conclusion. But there is no dispute about figures involving the impact of the race of the victim: people who kill whites are more likely to be executed than people who kill blacks. The Supreme Court considered the legal implications of this fact in the McCleskey case. A jury of eleven whites and one black convicted Warren McCleskey, who is black, of murdering a white man. McCleskey appealed his conviction, relying on a detailed study of Georgia's sentencing patterns conducted by David Baldus and others. The Baldus study indicated that anybody, black or white, who kills a white is 4.3 times more likely to receive the death penalty than someone who kills a black. McCleskey's lawyers used this and other figures to argue that Georgia's criminal justice system is racially biased and that, therefore, it denied McCleskey equal protection of the laws.

Justice Powell delivered the opinion of the Court:

Out analysis begins with the basic principle that a defendant who alleges an equal protection violation has the burden of proving "the existence of purposeful discrimination." . . . McCleskey must prove that the decisionmakers in *his* case acted with discriminatory purpose. He offers no evidence specific to his own case that would support an inference that racial considerations played a part in his sentence. Instead, he relies solely on the Baldus study. . . .

Each jury is unique in its composition, and the Constitution requires that its decision rest on consideration of innumerable factors that vary according to the characteristics of the individual defendant and the facts of the particular capital offense. . . .

Implementation of laws necessarily requires discretionary judgments. Because discretion is essential to the criminal justice process, we would demand exceptionally clear proof before we would infer that the discretion has been abused. . . .

McCleskey also suggests that the Baldus study proves that the State as a whole has acted with a discriminatory purpose. . . . [In *Furman*] this Court found that the Georgia capital sentencing system could operate in a fair and neutral

---

107 S. Ct. 1756 (1987). Footnotes omitted.

manner. There was no evidence then, and there is none now, that the Georgia Legislature enacted the capital punishment statute to further a racially discriminatory purpose. . . .

[McCleskey] contends that the Georgia capital punishment system is arbitrary and capricious in a *application*, and therefore this sentence is excessive, because racial considerations may influence capital sentencing decisions in Georgia. . . .

The capital sentencing decision requires the individual jurors to focus their collective judgment on the unique characteristics of a particular criminal defendant. It is not surprising that such collective judgments often are difficult to explain. But the inherent lack of predictability of jury decisions does not justify their condemnation. On the contrary, it is the jury's function to make the difficult and uniquely human judgments that defy codification and that "buil[d] discretion, equity, and flexibility into a legal system." . . .

Even Professor Baldus does not contend that his statistics *prove* that race enters into any capital sentencing decisions or that race was a factor in McCleskey's particular case. Statistics at most may show only a likelihood that a particular factor entered into some decisions. There is, of course, some risk of racial prejudice influencing a jury's decision in a criminal case. . . . The question is at what point that risk becomes constitutionally unacceptable. At most, the Baldus study indicates a discrepancy that appears to correlate with race. Apparent disparities in sentencing are an inevitable part of our criminal justice system. . . . As this Court has recognized, any mode for determining guilt or punishment "has its weaknesses and the potential for misuse." . . .

Where the discretion that is fundamental to our criminal process is involved, we decline to assume that what is unexplained is invidious. In light of the safeguards designed to minimize racial bias in the process, the fundamental value of jury trial in our criminal justice system, and the benefits that discretion provides to criminal defendants, we hold that the Baldus study does not demonstrate a constitutionally significant risk of racial bias affecting the Georgia capital-sentencing process.

Justice Brennan, dissenting:

At some point in this case, Warren McCleskey doubtless asked his lawyer whether a jury was likely to sentence him to die. A candid reply to this question would have been disturbing. First, counsel would have to tell McCleskey that few of the details of the crime or of McCleskey's past criminal conduct were more important than the fact that his victim was white. Furthermore, counsel would feel bound to tell McCleskey that defendants charged with killing white victims in Georgia are 4.3 times as likely to be sentenced to death as defendants charged with killing blacks. In addition, frankness would compel the disclosure that it was more likely than not that the race of McCleskey's victim would determine whether he received a death sentence: 6 of every 11 defendants convicted of killing a white person would not have received the death penalty if their victims had been black, while, among defendants with aggravating and mitigating factors comparable to McCleskey, 20 of every 34 would not have been sentenced to die if their victims had been black. Finally, the assessment would not be complete without the information that cases involving black defendants and white victims are more likely to result in a death sentence than cases featuring any other racial combination of defendant and victim. The story could be told in a variety of ways, but McCleskey could not fail to grasp its essential narrative line: there was a significant chance that race would play a prominent role in determining if he lived or died.

The Court today holds that Warren McCleskey's sentence was constitutionally imposed. It finds no fault in a system in which lawyers must tell their clients that race casts a large shadow on the capital sentencing process. The Court arrives at this conclusion by stating that the Baldus Study cannot "*prove* that race enters into any capital sentencing decisions or that race was a factor in McCleskey's particular case." According to Professor Baldus, . . . we can identify only "a likelihood that a particular factor entered into some decisions," and "a discrepancy that appears to correlate with race." This "likelihood" and "discrepancy," holds the Court, is insufficient to establish a constitutional violation. . . .

The Baldus study indicates that, after taking into account some 230 nonracial factors that might legitimately influence a sentencer, the jury *more likely than not* would have spared McCleskey's life had his victim been black. . . . Data unadjusted for the mitigating or aggravating effect of other factors show an even more pronounced disparity by race. The capital sentencing rate for all white-victim cases was almost *11 times* greater than the rate for black-victim cases. Furthermore, blacks who kill whites are sentenced to death at nearly *22 times* the rate of blacks who kill blacks, and more than *7 times* the rate of whites who kill blacks. In addition, prosecutors seek the death penalty for 70% of black defendants with white victims, but for only 15% of black defendants with black victims, and only 19% of white defendants with black victims. . . .

Georgia's legacy of a race-conscious criminal justice system, as well as this Court's own recognition of the persistent danger that racial attitudes may affect criminal proceedings, indicate that McCleskey's claim is not a fanciful product of mere statistical artifice. . . .

For many years, Georgia operated openly and formally precisely the type of dual system the evidence shows is still effectively in place. The criminal law expressly differentiated between crimes committed by and against blacks and whites, distinctions whose lineage traced back to the time of slavery. . . .

This Court has invalidated portions of the Georgia capital sentencing system 3 times over the past 15 years. The specter of race discrimination was acknowledged by the Court in striking down the Georgia death-penalty statute in *Furman*. . . .

Formal dual criminal laws may no longer be in effect, and intentional discrimination may no longer be prominent. Nonetheless, "subtle, less consciously held racial attitudes" continue to be of concern, and the Georgia system gives such attitudes considerable room to operates. . . . The determination of the significance of his evidence is at its core an exercise in human moral judgment, not a mechanical statistical analysis. . . . It is true that every nuance of decision cannot be statistically captured, nor can any individual judgment be plumbed with absolute certainty. Yet the fact that we must always act without the illumination of complete knowledge cannot induce paralysis when we confront what is literally an issue of life and death.

REVIEW AND DISCUSSION QUESTIONS

1. Why does the Court reject the statistical argument of McCleskey's lawyers? What would McCleskey have to establish to show that he had been denied equal protection? For what reasons does Brennan dissent?

2. McCleskey's claim was not that there was prejudice against him. Rather, racial bias is alleged to operate at one remove: that is, he probably would not have been sentenced to death if his *victim* had been black. Has McCleskey therefore been treated unfairly? Under what circumstances, if any, can an individual sentence be just if the criminal justice system as a whole is infected by racism?

3. Defenders of capital punishment argue that those who murder blacks are getting off too easily while those who murder whites are simply getting what they (and all murderers) deserve. The real racial discrimination, they contend, is not against criminals like McCleskey but against their black victims, whose murderers get off too easily. Assess this argument.

4. Can capital punishment be morally or legally justified if it is administered in an arbitrary or racially biased way? Can any punishment?

Cruel and Unusual Punishment

Rummel v. Estelle

In 1964 William James Rummel was convicted of fraudulent use of a credit card, in 1969 of forging a check, and again in 1973 of obtaining money by false pretenses. The sums involved were $80, $28.36, and $120.75, respectively. Like some other states, Texas has a recidivist or "three-time-loser" statute, which directs that a criminal convicted of a third felony be sentenced to life imprisonment. In this case the Supreme Court examines the question of whether putting Rummel in prison for life violates the Eighth Amendment's ban on "cruel and unusual" punishments.

Mr. Justice Rehnquist delivered the opinion of the Court:

Petitioner William James Rummel is presently serving a life sentence imposed by the State of Texas in 1973 under its "recidivist

---

445 U.S. 263 (1980). Some notes and citations omitted.

statute," . . . which provided that "[w]hoever shall have been three times convicted of a felony less than capital shall on such third conviction be imprisoned for life in the penitentiary." On January 19, 1976, Rummel sought a writ of habeas corpus in the United States District Court for the Western District of Texas, arguing that life imprisonment was "grossly disproportionate" to the three felonies that formed the predicate for his sentence and that therefore the sentence violated the ban on cruel and unusual punishments of the Eighth and Fourteenth Amendments. The District Court and the United States Court of Appeals for the Fifth Circuit rejected Rummel's claim, finding no unconstitutional disproportionality. We granted certiorari . . . and now affirm.

In 1964 the State of Texas charged Rummel with fraudulent use of a credit card to obtain $80 worth of goods or services. Because the amount in question was greater than $50, the charged offense was a felony punishable by a minimum of 2 years and a maximum of 10 years in the Texas Department of Corrections. Rummel eventually pleaded guilty to the charge and was sentenced to three years' confinement in a state penitentiary.

In 1969 the State of Texas charged Rummel with passing a forged check in the amount of $28.36, a crime punishable by imprisonment in a penitentiary for not less than two nor more than five years. Rummel pleaded guilty to this offense and was sentenced to four years' imprisonment.

In 1973 Rummel was charged with obtaining $120.75 by false pretenses. Because the amount obtained was greater than $50, the charged offense was designated "felony theft," which, by itself, was punishable by confinement in a penitentiary for not less than 2 nor more than 10 years. The prosecution chose, however, to proceed against Rummel under Texas'[s] recidivist statute, and cited in the indictment his 1964 and 1969 convictions as requiring imposition of a life sentence if Rummel were convicted of the charged offense. A jury convicted Rummel of felony theft and also found as true the allegation that he had been convicted of two prior felonies. As a result, on April 26, 1973, the trial court imposed upon Rummel the life sentence mandated by Art. 63 [of the Texas Penal Code]. . . .

This Court has on occasion stated that the Eighth Amendment prohibits imposition of a sentence that is grossly disproportionate to the severity of the crime. In recent years this proposition has appeared most frequently in opinions dealing with the death penalty. . . .

Because a sentence of death differs in kind from any sentence of imprisonment, no matter how long, our decisions applying the prohibition of cruel and unusual punishments to capital cases are of limited assistance in deciding the constitutionality of the punishment meted out to Rummel.

Outside the context of capital punishment, successful challenges to the proportionality of particular sentences have been exceedingly rare. In Weems v. United States [217 U.S. 349 (1910)], a case coming to this Court from the Supreme Court of the Philippine Islands, petitioner successfully attacked the imposition of a punishment known as "cadena temporal" for the crime of falsifying a public record. . . . The mandatory "remedy" for this offense was *cadena temporal*, a punishment described graphically by the Court:

> Its minimum degree is confinement in a penal institution for twelve years and one day, a chain at the ankle and wrist of the offender, hard and painful labor, no assistance from friend or relative, no marital authority or parental rights or rights of property, no participation even in the family council. These parts of his penalty endure for the term of imprisonment. From other parts there is no intermission. His prison bars and chains are removed, it is true, after twelve years, but he goes from them to a perpetual limitation of his liberty. He is forever kept under the shadow of his crime, forever kept within voice and view of the criminal magistrate, not being able to change his domicil without giving notice to the "authority immediately in charge of his surveillance," and without permission in writing. . . .

Although Rummel argues that the length of Weems's imprisonment was, by itself, a basis for the Court's decision, the Court's opinion does not support such a simple conclusion. The opinion consistently referred jointly to the length of imprisonment and its "accessories" or "accompaniments." . . .

In an attempt to provide us with objective criteria against which we might measure the proportionality of his life sentence, Rummel points to certain characteristics of his offenses that allegedly render them "petty." He cites, for example, the absence of violence in his crimes. But the presence or absence of violence does not always affect the strength of society's interest in deterring a particular crime or in punishing a particular criminal. A high official in a large corporation can commit undeniably serious crimes in the area of antitrust, bribery, or clean air or water standards without coming close to engaging in any "violent" or short-term "life-threatening" behavior. Additionally, Rummel cites the "small" amount of money taken in each of his crimes. But to recognize that the State of Texas could have imprisoned Rummel for life if he had stolen $5,000, $50,000, or $500,000, rather than the $120.75 that a jury convicted him of stealing, is virtually to concede that the lines to be drawn are indeed "subjective," and therefore properly within the province of legislatures, not courts. Moreover, if Rummel had attempted to defraud his victim of $50,000, but had failed, no money whatsoever would have changed hands; yet Rummel would be no less blameworthy, only less skillful, than if he had succeeded.

In this case, however, we need not decide whether Texas could impose a life sentence upon Rummel merely for obtaining $120.75 by false pretenses. Had Rummel only committed that crime, under the law enacted by the Texas Legislature he could have been imprisoned for no more than 10 years. In fact, at the time that he obtained the $120.75 by false pretenses, he already had committed and had been imprisoned for two other felonies, crimes that Texas and other States felt were serious enough to warrant significant terms of imprisonment even in the absence of prior offenses. Thus the interest of the State of Texas here is not simply that of making criminal the unlawful acquisition of another person's property; it is in addition the interest, expressed in all recidivist statutes, in dealing in a harsher manner with those who by repeated criminal acts have shown that they are simply incapable of conforming to the norms of society as established by its criminal law. By conceding the validity of recidivist statutes generally, Rummel himself concedes that the State of Texas, or any other State, has a valid interest in so dealing with that class of persons.

. . . Thus, under Art. 63, a three-time felon receives a mandatory life sentence, with possibility of parole, only if commission and conviction of each succeeding felony followed conviction for the preceding one, and only if each prior conviction was followed by actual imprisonment. Given this necessary sequence, a recidivist must twice demonstrate that conviction and actual imprisonment do not deter him from returning to crime once he is released. One in Rummel's position has been both graphically informed of the consequences of lawlessness and given an opportunity to reform, all to no avail. Article 63 thus is nothing more than a societal decision that when such a person commits yet another felony, he should be subjected to the admittedly serious penalty of incarceration for life, subject only to the State's judgment as to whether to grant him parole.[1]

Mr. Justice Powell, with whom Mr. Justice Brennan, Mr. Justice Marshall, and Mr. Justice Stevens join, dissenting:

The scope of the Cruel and Unusual Punishments Clause extends not only to barbarous methods of punishment, but also to punishments that are grossly disproportionate. Disproportionality analysis measures the relationship between the nature and number of offenses committed and the severity of the punishment inflicted upon the offender. The inquiry focuses on whether a person deserves such punishment, not simply on whether punishment would serve a utilitarian goal. A statute that levied a mandatory life sentence for overtime parking might well deter vehicular lawlessness, but it would offend our felt sense of justice. The Court concedes today that the principle of disproportionality plays a role in the review of sentences imposing the death penalty, but suggests that the principle may be less applicable when a noncapital sentence is challenged. Such a limitation finds no support in the history of Eighth Amendment jurisprudence.

The principle of disproportionality is rooted deeply in English constitutional law. The Magna Carta of 1215 insured that "[a] free man shall not be [fined] for a trivial offence, except in accordance with the degree of the offence; and for a serious offence he shall be [fined] according to its gravity." By 1400, the English common law had embraced the principle, not always followed in practice, that punishment should not be excessive either in severity or length. . . .

In sum, a few basic principles emerge from the history of the Eighth Amendment. Both barbarous forms of punishment and grossly excessive punishments are cruel and unusual. A sentence may be excessive if it serves no acceptable social purpose, or is grossly disproportionate to the seriousness of the crime. The principle of disproportionality has been acknowledged to apply to both capital and noncapital sentences. . . .

Examination of the objective factors traditionally employed by the Court to assess the proportionality of a sentence demonstrates that petitioner suffers a cruel and unusual punishment. Petitioner has been sentenced to the penultimate criminal penalty because he committed three offenses defrauding others of about $230. The nature of the crimes does not suggest that petitioner ever engaged in conduct that threatened another's person, involved a trespass, or endangered in any way the peace of society. A comparison of the sentence petitioner received with the sentences provided by habitual offender statutes of other American jurisdictions demonstrates that only two other States authorize the same punishment. A comparison of petitioner to other criminals sentenced in Texas shows that he has been punished for three property-related offenses with a harsher sentence than that given first-time offenders or two-time offenders convicted of far more serious offenses. The Texas system assumes that all three-time offenders deserve the same punishment whether they commit three murders or cash three fraudulent checks.

The petitioner has committed criminal acts for which he may be punished. He has been given a sentence that is not inherently barbarous. But the relationship between the criminal acts and the sentence is grossly disproportionate. For having defrauded others of about $230, the State of Texas has deprived petitioner of his freedom for the rest of his life. The State has not attempted to justify the sentence as necessary either to deter other persons or to isolate a potentially violent individual. Not has petitioner's status as a habitual offender been shown to justify a mandatory life sentence. My view, informed by examination of the "objective indicia that reflect the public attitude toward a given sanction," is that this punishment violates the principle of proportionality contained within the Cruel and Unusual Punishments Clause.

NOTE

[1]Thus, it is not true that, as the dissent claims, the Texas scheme subjects a person to life imprisonment "merely because he is a three-time felon." On the contrary, Art. 63 mandates such a sentence only after shorter terms of actual imprisonment have proved ineffective.

REVIEW AND DISCUSSION QUESTIONS

1. On what basis does the Court reject the claim that Rummel's sentence was grossly disproportionate to the severity of his crime? What are the dissenters' arguments to the contrary? With whom do you agree and why? Do you think Rummel's sentence was unconstitutional?

2. In your view, were Rummel's offenses "petty"? Do you think the Texas legislature had criminals like Rummel in mind when it drafted its recidivist statute?

3. Constitutionality aside, are such statutes wise social policy? Would a utilitarian reject them, defend them, or modify them in some way? Because one clearly does not deserve life imprisonment merely for obtaining $120 on false pretenses, is there any way a retributivist could justify sentencing Rummel to life in prison?

4. Could recidivist statutes be defended, not as punishment but rather as a way of incapacitating an individual who has shown himself or herself to be dangerous to society?

5. Are recidivist statutes fair? If two people commit the same crime (or even commit a crime together), would one of them deserve a stiffer sentence simply because he or she is a previous offender?

11

PROBLEMS OF CRIMINAL LIABILITY

Even if we assume that punishment is morally justifiable, many intriguing and philosophically important issues are raised by the law's effort to specify the exact extent of one's liability to criminal prosecution. In particular, when should conduct that is normally illegal or wrongful be excused or its punishment mitigated?

The Queen v. Dudley and Stephens poses this issue in a very dramatic context, namely, when killing another person appears to be the only way to save one's own life. In "The Principles of Criminal Law," Richard B. Brandt explains the legal elements of a crime and distinguishes different kinds of legal justifications and excuses, while H. L. A. Hart probes the important role of intention in criminal law. *United States v. Ovieda* and *People v. Dlugash* concern criminal liability for crimes that were impossible for the accused person to have committed. Susan Estrich pursues these issues in cases of rape, examining how American law's neglect of *mens rea* has worked to the disadvantage of rape victims. The following essay discusses a related question: the claim that women who have been abused over an extended period of time should be allowed to plead self-defense even when their act of killing was not done in response to an immediate face-to-face threat. The next two essays deal with the insanity defense. R. J. Gerber proposes restructuring the legal treatment of insanity, and Joel Feinberg explores the moral significance of mental illness with respect to blame and punishment. The concluding essay looks at another defense that has been raised against criminal charges, in which defendants ask that they not be punished on grounds that their cultures and values differ from those informing U.S. law.

Survival on a Lifeboat

The Queen v. Dudley and Stephens

Life-and-death decisions in extreme circumstances make for hard cases, morally and legally. This famous English case concerns four sailors adrift in a lifeboat. After twenty days with little food or water, two of them—Dudley and Stephens—killed the youngest member of their party, a boy seventeen or eighteen years old, and ate him. Four days later, the sailors were rescued. It is unlikely that they would have survived otherwise, and it is probable that the boy would have died before them.

Indictment for the murder of Richard Parker on the high seas within the jurisdiction of the Admiralty.

At the trial before Huddleston, B., at the Devon and Cornwall Winter Assizes, November 7, 1884, the jury, at the suggestion of the learned judge, found the facts of the case in a special verdict which stated "that on July 5, 1884, the prisoners, Thomas Dudley and Edward Stephens, with one Brooks, all ablebodied English seamen, and the deceased also an English boy, between seventeen and eighteen years of age, the crew of an English yacht, a registered English vessel, were cast away in a storm on the high seas 1600 miles from the Cape of Good Hope, and were compelled to put into an open boat belonging to the said yacht. That in this boat they had no supply of water and no supply of food, except two 1 lb. tins of turnips, and for three days they had nothing else to subsist upon. That on the fourth day they caught a small turtle, upon which they subsisted for a few days, and this was the only food they had up to the twentieth day when the act now in question was committed. That on the twelfth day the remains of the turtle were entirely consumed, and for the next eight days they had nothing to eat. That they had no fresh water, except such rain as they from time to time caught in their oilskin capes. That the boat was drifting on the ocean, and was probably more than 1000 miles away from land. That on the eighteenth day, when they had been seven days without food and five without water, the prisoners spoke to Brooks as to what should be done if no succour came, and suggested that some one should be sacrificed to save the rest, but Brooks dissented, and the boy, to whom they were understood to refer, was not consulted. That on the 24th of July, the day before the act now in question, the prisoner Dudley proposed to Stephens and Brooks that lots should be cast who should be put to death to save the rest, but Brooks refused to consent, and it was not put to the boy, and in point of fact there was no drawing of lots. That on that day the prisoners spoke of their having families, and suggested it would be better to kill the boy that their lives should be saved, and Dudley proposed that if there was no vessel in sight by the morrow morning the boy should be killed. That next day, the 25th of July, no vessel appearing, Dudley told Brooks that he had better go and have a sleep, and made signs to Stephens and Brooks that the boy had better be killed. The prisoner Stephens agreed to the act, but Brooks dissented from it. That the boy was then lying at the bottom of the boat quite helpless, and extremely weakened by famine and by drinking sea water, and unable to make any resistance, nor did he ever assent to his being killed. The prisoner Dudley offered a prayer asking forgiveness for them all if either of them should be tempted to commit a rash act, and that their souls might be saved. That Dudley, with the assent of Stephens, went to the boy, and telling him that his time was come, put a knife into his throat and killed him then and there; that the three men fed upon the body and blood of the boy for four days; that on the fourth day after the act had been committed the boat was picked up by a passing vessel, and the prisoners were rescued, still alive, but in the lowest state of prostration. That they were carried to the port of Falmouth, and committed for trial at Exeter. That if the men had not fed upon the body of the boy they would probably not have survived to be so picked up and rescued, but would within the four days have died of famine. That the boy, being in a much weaker condition, was likely to have died before them. That at the time of the act in question there was no sail in sight, nor any reasonable prospect of relief. That under these circumstances there appeared to the prisoners every probability that unless they then fed or very soon fed upon the boy or one of themselves they would die of starvation. That there was no appreciable chance of saving life except by killing some one for the others to eat. That assuming any necessity to kill anybody, there was no greater necessity for killing the boy than any of the other three men. But whether upon the whole matter by the jurors found the killing of Richard Parker by Dudley and Stephens be felony and murder the jurors are ignorant, and pray the advice of the Court thereupon, and if upon the whole matter the Court shall be of opinion that the killing of Richard Parker be felony and murder, then the jurors say that Dudley and Stephens were each guilty of felony and murder as alleged in the indictment.

The learned judge then adjourned the assizes until the 25th of November at the Royal Courts of Justice. On the application of the Crown they were again adjourned to the 4th of December, and the case ordered to be argued before a Court consisting of five judges.

Dec. 4. *Sir H. James, A.G.* . . . appeared for the Crown and *A. Collins,* . . . *Q.C.* for the prisoners. . . . *Sir H. James, A.G.,* for the Crown:

. . . With regard to the substantial question in the case—whether the prisoners in killing Parker were guilty of murder—the law is that where a private person acting upon his own judgment takes the life of a fellow creature, his act can only be justified on the ground of self-defence—self-defence against the acts of the person whose life is taken. This principle has been extended to include the case of a man killing another to prevent him from committing some great crime upon a third person. But the principle has no application to this case, for the prisoners were not protecting themselves against any act of Parker. If he had had food in his possession and they had taken it from him, they would have been guilty of theft; and if they killed him to obtain this food, they would have been guilty of murder. . . .

***A. Collins, Q.C.,* for the prisoners:**

The facts found on the special verdict shew that the prisoners were not guilty of murder, at the time when they killed Parker, but killed him under the pressure of necessity. Necessity will excuse an act which would otherwise be a crime. Stephen, *Digest of Criminal Law*, art. 32, Necessity. The law as to compulsion by necessity is further explained in Stephen's *History of the Criminal Law*, vol. ii., p. 108, and an opinion is expressed that in the case often put by casuists, of two drowning men on a plank large enough to support one only, and one thrusting the other off, the survivor could not be subjected to legal punishment. In the American case of *The United States v. Holmes*, the proposition that a passenger on board a vessel may be thrown overboard to save the others is sanctioned. The law as to inevitable necessity is fully considered in *Russell on Crimes*, vol. i. p. 847. . . . Lord Bacon . . . gives the instance of two shipwrecked persons clinging to the same plank and one of them thrusting the other from it, finding that it will not support both, and says that this homicide is excusable through unavoidable necessity and upon the great universal principle of self-preservation, which prompts every man to save his own life in preference to that of another, where one of them must inevitably perish. It is true that Hale's *Pleas of the Crown*, p. 54, states distinctly that hunger is no excuse for theft, but that is on the ground that there can be no such extreme necessity in this country. In the present case the prisoners were in circumstances where no assistance could be given. The essence of the crime of murder is intention, and here the intention of the prisoners was only to preserve their lives. . . .

Dec. 9. The judgment of the Court . . . was delivered by Lord Coleridge, C.J.:

The two prisoners, Thomas Dudley and Edwin Stephens, were indicted for the murder of Richard Parker on the high seas on the 25th of July in the present year. They were tried before my Brother Huddleston at Exeter on the 6th of November, and, under the direction of my learned Brother, the jury returned a special verdict, the legal effect of which has been argued before us, and on which we are now to pronounce judgment.

The special verdict as, after certain objections by Mr. Collins to which the Attorney General yielded, it is finally settled before us is as follows. [His Lordship read the special verdict as above set out.] From these facts, stated with the cold precision of a special verdict, it appears sufficiently that the prisoners were subject to terrible temptation, to sufferings which might break down the bodily power of the strongest man, and try the conscience of the best. Other details yet more harrowing, facts still more loathsome and appalling, were presented to the jury, and are to be found recorded in my learned Brother's notes. But nevertheless this is clear, that the prisoners put to death a weak and unoffending boy upon the chance of preserving their own lives by feeding upon his flesh and blood after he was killed, and with the certainty of depriving *him* of any possible chance of survival. The verdict finds in terms that "if the men had not fed upon the body of the boy they would *probably* not have survived," and that "the boy being in a much weaker condition was *likely* to have died before them." They might possibly have been picked up next day by a passing ship; they might possibly not have been picked up at all; in either case it is obvious that the killing of the boy would have been an unnecessary and profitless act. It is found by the verdict that the boy was incapable of resistance, and, in fact, made none; and it is not even suggested that his death was due to any violence on his part attempted against, or even so much as feared by, those who killed him. Under these circumstances the jury say that they are ignorant whether those who killed him were guilty of murder, and have referred it to this Court to determine what is the legal consequence which follows from the facts which they have found. . . .

There remains to be considered the real question in the case—whether killing under the circumstances set forth in the verdict be or be not murder. The contention that it could be anything else was, to the minds of us all, both new and strange, and we stopped the Attorney General in his negative argument in order that we might hear what could be said in support of a proposition which appeared to us to be at once dangerous, immoral, and opposed to all legal principle and analogy. All, no doubt, that can be said has been urged before us, and we are now to consider and determine what it amounts to. First it is said that it follows from various definitions of murder in books of authority, which definitions imply, if they do not state, the doctrine, that in order to save your own life you may lawfully take away the life of another, when that other is neither attempting nor threatening yours, nor is guilty of any illegal act whatever towards you or any one else. But if these definitions be looked at they will not be found to sustain this contention. . . .

Is there, then, any authority for the proposition which has been presented to us? Decided cases there are none. . . . The American case cited by my Brother Stephen in his *Digest*, from *Wharton on Homicide*, in which it was decided, correctly indeed, that sailors had no right to throw passengers overboard to save themselves, but on the somewhat strange ground that the proper mode of determining who was to be sacrificed was to vote upon the subject by ballot, can hardly, as my Brother Stephen says, be an authority satisfactory to [this court]. . . .

The one real authority of former time is Lord Bacon, who . . . lays down the law as follows:— "Necessity carrieth a privilege in itself. Necessity is of three sorts—necessity of conservation of life, necessity of obedience, and necessity of the act of God or of a stranger. First of conservation of life; if a man steal viands to satisfy his present hunger, this is no felony nor larceny. So if divers be in danger of drowning by the casting away of some boat or barge, and one of them get to some plank, or on the boat's side to keep himself above water, and another to save his life thrust him from it, whereby he is drowned, this is neither se defendendo nor by misadventure, but justifiable." On this it is to be observed that Lord Bacon's proposition that stealing to satisfy hunger is no larceny is hardly supported by Staundforde, whom he cites for it, and is expressly contradicted by Lord Hale. . . . And for the proposition as to the plank or boat, it is said to be derived from the canonists. At any rate he cites no authority for it, and it must stand upon his own. Lord Bacon was great even as a lawyer; but it is permissible to much smaller men, relying upon principle and on the authority of others, the equals and even the superiors of Lord Bacon as lawyers, to question the soundness of his dictum. There are many conceivable states of things in which it might possibly be true, but if Lord Bacon meant to lay down the broad proposition that a man may save his life by killing, if necessary, an innocent and unoffending neighbour, it certainly is not law at the present day.

There remains the authority of my Brother Stephen, who, both in his *Digest* and in his *History of the Criminal Law*, uses language perhaps wide enough to cover this case. The language is somewhat vague in both places, but it does not in either place cover this case of necessity, and we have the best authority for saying that it was not meant to cover it.

. . . We are dealing with a case of private homicide, not one imposed upon men in the service of their Sovereign and in the defence of their country. Now it is admitted that the deliberate killing of this unoffending and unresisting boy was clearly murder, unless the killing can be justified by some well-recognised excuse admitted by the law. It is further admitted that there was in this case no such excuse, unless the killing was justified by what has been called "necessity." But the temptation to the act which existed here was not what the law has ever called necessity. Nor is this to be regretted. Though law and morality are not the same, and many things may be immoral which are not necessarily illegal, yet the absolute divorce of law from morality would be of fatal consequence; and such divorce would follow if the temptation to murder in this case were to be held by law an absolute defence of it. It is not so. To preserve one's life is generally speaking a duty, but it may be the plainest and the highest duty to sacrifice it. War is full of instances in which it is a man's duty not to live, but to die. The duty, in case of shipwreck, of a captain to his crew, of the crew to the passengers, of soldiers to women and children, as in the noble case of the *Birkenhead;* these duties impose on men the moral necessity, not of the preservation, but of the sacrifice of their lives for others, from which in no country, least of all, it is to be hoped, in England, will men ever shrink, as indeed, they have not shrunk. It is not correct, therefore, to say that there is any absolute or unqualified necessity to preserve one's life. . . . It is not needful to point out the awful danger of admitting the principle which has been contended for. Who is to be the judge of this sort of necessity? By what measure is the comparative value of lives to be measured? Is it to be strength, or intellect, or what? It is plain that the principle leaves to him who is to profit by it to determine the necessity which will justify him in deliberately taking another's life to save his own. In this case the weakest, the youngest, the most unresisting, was chosen. Was it more necessary to kill him than one of the grown men? The answer must be "No." . . . [I]t is quite plain that such a principle once admitted might be made the legal cloak for unbridled passion and atrocious crime. There is no safe path for judges to tread but to ascertain the law to the best of their ability and to declare it according to their judgment; and if in any case the law appears to be too severe on individuals, to leave it to the Sovereign to exercise that prerogative of mercy which the Constitution has intrusted to the hands fittest to dispense it.

It must not be supposed that in refusing to admit temptation to be an excuse for crime it is forgotten how terrible the temptation was; how awful the suffering; how hard in such trials to keep the judgment straight and the conduct pure. We are often compelled to set up standards we cannot reach ourselves, and to lay down rules which we could not ourselves satisfy. But a man has no right to declare temptation to be an excuse, though he might himself have yielded to it, nor allow compassion for the criminal to change or weaken in any manner the legal definition of the crime. It is therefore our duty to declare that the prisoners' act in this case was wilful murder, that the facts as stated in the verdict are no legal justification of the homicide; and to say that in our unanimous opinion the prisoners are upon this special verdict guilty of murder.[1]

> *The Court then proceeded to pass sentence of death upon the prisoners.*[2]

NOTES

[1] My brother Grove has furnished me with the following suggestion, too late to be embodied in the judgment but well worth preserving: "If the two accused men were justified in killing Parker, then if not rescued in time, two of the three survivors would be justified in killing the third, and of the two who remained the stronger would be justified in killing the weaker, so that three men might be justifiably killed to give the fourth a chance of surviving." [Note by Lord Coleridge.]

[2] This sentence was afterwards commuted by the Crown to six months' imprisonment.

REVIEW AND DISCUSSION QUESTIONS

1. Counsel for the Crown (i.e., the prosecutor) says that only self-defense can justify the taking of a life. The defense lawyer says that necessity can excuse a crime. What is the difference between justifying an action and excusing it?

2. Does "necessity" excuse, either morally or legally, an action that would otherwise be a crime, as the lawyer for Dudley and Stephens claims? If not, why not? If so, what constitutes "necessity," and when, if ever, can necessity excuse the killing of a human being? How would a utilitarian assess the defense of necessity?

3. In finding Dudley and Stephens guilty of murder, the Court says that there was "temptation" but not "necessity" and, moreover, that there is no "absolute or unqualified necessity to preserve one's life." Do you agree?

4. Assess the Court's contention that to excuse Dudley and Stephens would set a dangerous precedent.

5. Dudley and Stephens were sentenced to death for murder, but their sentence was later commuted to six months of imprisonment. This strikes many people as just. But if they were really guilty of murder, should they have been imprisoned for only six months? And if they were not guilty, why should they be imprisoned at all?

6. What verdict would you have given if you were judge? What would you have done if you were in the lifeboat?

7. Is it reasonable to apply standard moral and legal principles to a case like this, or are morality and law inapplicable in such extreme circumstances?

The Principles of Criminal Law

Richard B. Brandt

In this selection Richard Brandt reviews the main concepts and principles of criminal law, thus providing the legal and theoretical backdrop to the issues discussed in this section. After comparing moral and legal obligation, he carefully distinguishes different kinds of legal justifications and excuses and goes on to explore the ways in which legal guilt and moral reprehensibility can diverge.

Let us review the main concepts and principles of criminal law. Unfortunately there is controversy among judges and professors of law about what these concepts and principles are, and about whether they should be changed; our brief survey must necessarily ignore such differences of opinion and other subtleties, in large part.

The central feature of the system of criminal justice in the United States is the existence of laws, statutory or common, requiring that persons be caused pain or loss by the state if a judicial process has found them guilty of a crime. It is difficult to explain in general what constitutes a crime, but we can, for a start, say that criminal action always includes overt behavior which causes or threatens a "public harm," that is, some effects considered to be harmful to the community as a whole. The law provides different penalties for different offenses, the more severe ones attaching to those crimes considered in some sense more serious. For most offenses the law does not specify an exact penalty for a particular type of offense, but only a range of permitted penalties; the judge must then select some penalty within the permitted range which strikes him as appropriate, everything considered. The executive department of the government, however, has the power to reduce a sentence or pardon a criminal altogether for any reasons which strike it as proper; but it does not have the power to increase the penalty set by the judge. Various boards established by the executive department may pardon or parole, or make recommendations for such actions. Theoretically juries decide only a factual question: whether the accused acted in a way defined by the law as criminal; but practically they often refuse to convict, when they regard the penalty prescribed by law for a certain offense as markedly out of line with the moral merits of the case. In some instances juries may make recommendations about the severity of sentences.

In order to get a deeper understanding of what it is to commit a certain crime, it is helpful to draw an analogy between legal and moral concepts. Let us recall the relations between prima facie obligation, over-all obligation, and blameworthiness. In general we incline to think that, for instance, if a person has promised to do something, he has a prima facie obligation to do that thing. Sometimes, however, he will not have an over-all obligation to do this, on account of the weight of conflicting obligations, such as obligation to avoid serious injury to other persons, or to give important assistance in case of need. A prima facie obligation to keep a promise, then, does not imply an over-all obligation to keep it. Moreover, failure to keep a promise, even if one is over all obligated to keep it, does not necessarily imply moral blameworthiness. . . .

Corresponding roughly to objective prima facie obligations are the law's prohibitions of certain kinds of conduct. The law aims to prevent certain kinds of overt behavior, and sometimes the law states, in a preamble preceding clauses prescribing punishment, what kind of conduct it is aiming to prevent. For instance, it may say that "No company shall sell, . . . or offer for sale . . . any security of its own issue until it shall have . . . secured . . . a permit authorizing it so to do." (California Corporate Securities Act, Cal. Stats. 1917, p. 673.) But the law recognizes that conduct of the sort it aims to prevent in general may sometimes be justified; and therefore it permits, as defense against a criminal charge, a showing that the accused's action was justified (that in the special circumstances the agent did what the law does not really want to prevent). For instance, the law forbids killing another person; but it is prepared to accept the defense that the killing was in self-defense. Roughly, a defense of justification is analogous to a showing, in morals, that although one had a prima facie obligation not to do so-and-so, in the total circumstances doing this was the right thing. Moreover, just as infraction of overall obligation does not imply blameworthiness in morals, so the commission of some act the law intends to prevent is not necessarily criminally culpable, even if it cannot be justified in the foregoing sense. Just as there may be excuses in morals for doing what one ought not, so there are excuses in law. It is useful to distinguish three kinds of excuses in law: (a) excuses which completely exculpate, wholly free from taint of crime, (b) excuses which mitigate in the sense of reducing the crime to one of the types which the law regards as less serious (e.g., reducing from murder in the first degree to involuntary manslaughter), and (c) considerations which are properly viewed by the judge as calling for the selection of a lower penalty from among those permitted by law.

We can now see more clearly what it is to have committed some specific crime, for instance, murder in the first degree. It is (1) to have behaved in some overt way which the law aims to prevent, here to have caused the death of someone, (2) to be unable to show a legally acceptable justification of one's act, and (3) to be unable to offer an excuse of the above types (a) or (b). In a carefully written penal code, the crime of murder in the first degree will be carefully described so that one will not have committed it unless all these conditions are satisfied. To commit a certain crime, then, is to behave in a certain way, and be unable to offer one of these defenses.

It will illuminate the relation between legal liability to punishment and moral excuses and blameworthiness, to review the major types of defense. We begin with the major *justifications*. (1) An act, otherwise subject to punishment, is not a crime if done in reasonable self-defense against unlawful attack, by a soldier in execution of lawful orders, in order to prevent treason or a felony (at least one done with violence), or in the service of public welfare (as destruction of property in order to prevent flood damage or to bring a forest fire under control). (2) An act, otherwise subject to punishment, is not a crime if performed because someone threatened the agent with loss of life or personal injury, in such circumstances as would intimidate a person of ordinary firmness. This justification, however, is ordinarily not accepted for homicide. (3) One may perform a forbidden act with impunity if, in case one does not, the result one causes and worse will in all probability happen anyway. For instance, one judge has indicated that a seaman is not liable for putting persons out of an overcrowded lifeboat in a storm if otherwise the boat would sink, provided the selection of the unfortunates is made in a reasonable manner. (For a contrary opinion, see *Regina v. Dudley and Stephens*.) This is one sense in which "necessity knows no law."

Let us now survey the *excuses which exculpate*. (4) A person is usually exculpated if he causes a harm the law seeks to prevent, by accident, for instance, if he causes the death of someone, but unforeseeably, despite all reasonable precautions. However, such accidental harm is some-times punished; in many situations in which the defendant is committing an unlawful act when the accident happens, he is treated as if he intended to cause the accident. (5) A man is exculpated if because of an innocent mistake in belief about facts he performs an unlawful act which would have been lawful had the facts been as he thought they were. For instance, it is lawful to shoot a person who has broken into one's house at night for the purpose of theft; and if a person shoots his wife or servant on account of a genuine and innocent supposition that the person fired at is a burglar, he is exonerated.[1] (6) If a person is physically compelled to perform an unlawful act, e.g., if the hands of a stronger person held and guided his dagger, he is thought not to have performed that act at all, and will not be prosecuted. (7) The law excuses a man for doing what it is impossible not to do. It may forbid a car standing in a certain place, but if a car stands there because traffic is jammed and the car cannot be moved, the act is not subject to punishment. (8) A person under seven years of age cannot commit a crime; and he is not guilty of a crime if under fourteen unless malicious intent is established—although he may be subject to treatment under rules for juveniles. (9) A person is excused if he performed an otherwise unlawful act while walking in his sleep. Insanity is also an excuse if the defendant's mental disease or defect is such that he did "not know the nature and quality of the act he was doing; or, if he did know it, that he did not know he was doing what was wrong." (*The Queen v. M'Naghten.*)[2] (10) Theoretically a person is excused from guilt if he performs an unlawful act because of involuntary intoxication—even though in practice courts are often reluctant to admit that intoxication is "involuntary."

There are also *mitigating* excuses, which reduce the seriousness of the crime. (11) In the case of homicide, a showing that the act was done impulsively often affects the degree of guilt. Premeditation is commonly necessary for first degree murder. If one kills in the heat of passion, without forethought, he is guilty only of second degree murder. Furthermore, if such heat of passion is brought about by legally recognized provocation—such as finding one's wife in the act of adultery—the defendant may be guilty only of manslaughter. (12) Voluntary intoxication may reduce the degree of crime, but it will not exculpate, on the ground that intoxication is itself an immoral act which cannot be used as a shield for wrong conduct.

Finally, judges regularly take into account various considerations as grounds for reducing the severity of a sentence: such as severe temptation, neurotic constitution, previous lack of opportunities in life, evidence indicating that the culprit is not a menace to society, the convicted person's state of health, probable serious affects of a harsh sentence on his family. Judges sometimes make a sentence *more* severe when they think the outrage of the community requires it—if the law would be brought disrespect by a mild sentence.

The excuses (nos. four to twelve) are of interest because they give practical content to the "mental element" or "guilty mind" (*mens rea*) which the law holds must be present in order for a person to be guilty of a crime on account of his overt behavior. In view of these excuses, is there any general statement possible about the identity of this mental element? There are several things we can say. (1) It must have been possible for the accused to have behaved, as a result of different decisions or volitions, in a way that was lawful (a requirement of excuses nos. six and seven). (2) The agent must have been aware to some degree that the events which the law proscribes would flow from his bodily behavior—or at any rate that they might, that his behavior was *risking* such consequences. (3) The agent must have been aware that it is wrong to produce such consequences, *or* that it is unlawful, *or* at least that society generally regards the production of such consequences as wrong. In general, all these three conditions are required. There are two major exceptions: the so-called "public welfare" or "strict liability" offenses, where *intent* in the sense of (2) is not required at all; and the rule which imputes intent to commit offenses which in fact were accidental, to persons engaged in committing some other wrong intentionally. These exceptions are regarded by many as simply illogical elements in the law, which are without justification.

These conditions required for legal guilt are not exactly identical with those required for moral reprehensibility, the latter requiring that an act show *defect of character.* Moral guilt usually goes with legal guilt, but not necessarily. In practice, imputation of legal guilt is likely to be even more closely conformed to imputation of moral guilt than theory allows; for an unlawful act which is clearly consistent with moral character may not be prosecuted, or if prosecuted the jury may refuse to bring in a verdict of guilty.

How nearly is there a parallel between degree of moral reprehensibility of an act and seriousness of the act as a crime? We must expect some divergencies. The law, for instance, cannot concern itself with minor matters. Again, the law must be drawn in terms of relatively precise general rules, so that its administration does not place an intolerable burden of discretion on the officials charged with its application. Further, the law must be so phrased that available evidence can answer questions about its applicability; it is unfortunate if application of the law must turn on decisions about fact which are necessarily speculative.

At some points moral reprehensibility is more severe than the law. The law condemns only for overt behavior (including attempts) which is in some way publicly undesirable; it never condemns a man for his motives alone, or for his thoughts or feelings. Again, there are morally indefensible injuries of other persons (for instance, refusal to repay borrowed money) which, although they are actionable in civil suits, are not crimes and not punishable in criminal law. Again, there are many minor offenses that are morally wrong but legally are not prohibited. Further, the law automatically excuses offenses in persons under a certain age; moral judgments are more flexible and individual.

At other points, however, the law is more severe. (1) For instance, it is an axiom of the law that "ignorance of the law excuses nobody." And, we can add, it is no excuse to believe that it is morally right to do what the law forbids. Now, to some extent the same principles obtain in moral judgments: we would think it odd if anyone tried to excuse murder or rape on the ground that he did not believe the act to be wrong. Nevertheless, within a certain range, absence of belief that an act is wrong (or positive belief that it is a duty) serves as an excuse in morals; we hardly condemn a Mormon for practising polygamy, and we partly if not wholly excuse a Christian Scientist who refuses to take an ill child to the hospital. The law, however, does not regard the absence of belief that an act was unlawful as an excuse. Part of the reason for this is that the law in major part is enforcing moral rules that are well known and that are respected as right by the vast majority. (This class of cases, however, does not include many regulations that a moral person could hardly be expected to observe as a part of moral behavior, for example, peculiar traffic regulations in a small town. It is not clear that there is any moral justification for the law's refusing to accept ignorance as an excuse, in these cases where law fails to coincide with morals and where a man of character could hardly be expected to know the law.) There is also reason for not permitting conscientious objection to the law as an excuse: the law cannot permit a man to set up his own conscience as the law of the land, since if it did law enforcement could probably not proceed at all, or at least only under great handicaps. So, both the Mormon and the Christian Scientist may go to jail on serious charges.

An even more striking difference (2) between law and moral judgment is the existence of "strict liability." There is a class of infractions of law that are *not excused by demonstrable lack of intent*; any infraction of these laws is liable to punishment even if it was unforeseeable, inadvertent, and practically impossible to prevent. Thus, a butcher who sells diseased meat innocently and without any negligence, and even on the advice of experts about the quality of his meat, may incur a prison sentence. In general, a highly conscientious and law-abiding man might, through no moral fault whatever, infringe one of these laws and be subject to serious penalty. Moral condemnation certainly does not follow the law at this point.

Finally (3) some excuses that exculpate in morals only mitigate in law. In morals, whenever the circumstances are such that a man of character might be expected to do what the defendant did, he is exonerated. This is not so in law. Suppose a person imbibes a cocktail for

the first time, not knowing that one drink will affect him so much that he will thoughtlessly accept another, and then be drunk. Suppose as a result of the first drink (and the second), he becomes drunk. Suppose further that this man has no reason to think that, even if he became drunk, he would be belligerent—beyond the vague awareness that some people do become belligerent when drunk. And suppose that, after becoming drunk, this person actually attacks a man and kills him. In law this can be a very serious offense; but in morals it is difficult to believe that the act is not blameless, as far as the homicide is concerned. The man *will* be morally to blame if, knowing what he did, he permits himself to become drunk again. But his drunken action was not rationally foreseeable. (It is a different matter if a man drinks, knowing that he is going to drive a car immediately after doing so.) Similarly, the rule that homicide is automatically manslaughter if the agent was committing a misdemeanor, or murder in the first degree if he was committing a felony, is by no means followed by moral judgment; perhaps in most cases the assumption of intent is reasonable, but it is not necessarily so in all cases.[3]

It is often said that the law takes no account of *motives*, but only of the *intent* to perform a specific act. We have already noted that in practice this is not quite true. But we should also notice that, if we have a clear idea of what a *motive* is (namely, that for a person to have a certain motive is for him to be inclined or disinclined to perform a certain act by his belief that doing so will have a certain property or consequence), we can construe "intent" and *mens rea* as facts about a person's motives. Clearly, if a person intentionally performs a prohibited act, he thereby shows that he was *not motivated sufficiently* to avoid that act, and this fact is as much a fact about his motives as any other. What is true is that the law takes this fact about one's motives as very decisive for the legal culpability of one's act. But other motives also play an important role. One can, if one likes, construe justifying exculpations as based on a consideration of motives: for instance, one might say that the law recognizes the fact that the motive of saving oneself or one's children from death, or saving many from the destruction of a forest fire, is a good and sufficient justification for performing an unlawful act. Moreover, a showing of good motives or strong temptations may, although not exculpating from legal liability, result in a suspended or very light sentence (and, of course, may induce a jury not to convict at all—witness cases in which juries have refused to convict persons who practiced euthanasia under circumstances approved by the jury but against the law).

One might inquire whether any examination of the "ethical foundations" of the law can show that we are obligated to support and maintain the law at those points where it diverges from judgments of moral culpability. The answer is that it can, on matters where the law is less severe than morals (except for some of the artificial distinctions between crimes and torts—damages actionable in civil suits). It can because there is no alternative for law which is not excessively expensive and burdensome, or which would not introduce objectionably speculative elements into legal procedure. But, on some matters where the law is more severe than moral judgment, it cannot be shown that we ought to support the maintenance of present legal principles. It is quite

true that (except for matters like traffic regulations where legal restrictions do not correspond with accepted judgments of moral obligation) it is impossible to accept ignorance of the law, or conscientious disagreement with the law, as an excuse. The law cannot cease to protect what it sets out to protect because some do not agree or are unaware. But the other practices of the law that morals cannot follow appear to be morally unjustified, and there is no obligation to defend them; on the contrary, there is an obligation to do what one can to get them changed.

NOTES

[1]The supposition must be "innocent" in the sense that it is one a "reasonable" man might make in the circumstances. A person who supposes something negligently is not excused, except in some types of case.

[2]The question of what should constitute legal insanity is the most vigorously discussed issue in criminal law today. For an important alternative view (in *Durham v. United States*) and discussion, see L. Hall and S. Glueck, *Cases on Criminal Law and Its Enforcement* (St. Paul, Minn.: West Publishing Co., 1958), pp. 298–325.

[3]For a full discussion of some of these moral difficulties in legal practice, see Jerome Hall, *General Principles of Criminal Law* (Indianapolis: Bobbs-Merrill Co., Inc., 1947), chaps. 10, 11, and 13.

REVIEW AND DISCUSSION QUESTIONS

1. Give an example of a defense of justification. What is the difference between that and an excuse? How do exculpatory excuses, mitigating excuses, and considerations that lead judges to lower penalties differ?

2. Apply the distinctions that Brandt draws to the *Dudley and Stephens* case.

3. What is a "strict liability" offense, and how is it an exception to the general principles of criminal law?

4. In what ways might legal guilt and moral reprehensibility differ? At what points is morality

severer than the law, and at what points is the law severer?

5. Explain what Brandt means when he writes that the common saying that the law takes no account of motive, but only of intent, is not quite true.

6. Are we obligated to support the law at those points where it diverges from judgments of moral culpability?

7. How does Brandt define *mens rea*?

Intention

H. L. A. Hart

Intention is the most prominent and in many ways the most important element of mens rea, *and in this essay Professor Hart examines the place of intention in the criminal law—with respect to both liability for punishment and severity of punishment. After describing three aspects of intention and the difference between oblique and direct intention, Hart discusses the role of intention in the law concerning attempted crimes and criminal negligence.*

1

In this essay I shall [focus] attention on the place which the criminal law of most countries allocates to the idea of intention, as one of the principal determinants both of liability to punishment and of its severity. All civilized penal systems make liability to punishment for at any rate serious crime dependent not merely on the fact that the person to be punished has done the outward act of a crime, but on his having done it in a certain state or frame of mind or will. These mental or intellectual elements are many and various and are collected together in the terminology of English jurists under the simple sounding description of *mens rea*, a guilty mind. But the most prominent, of these mental elements, and in many ways the most important, is a man's intention, and in English law and in most other legal systems intention, *or something like it,* is relevant at two different points. It is relevant first at the stage before conviction when the question is "Can this man be convicted of this crime?"—even if, in fact, he will not actually be punished. At this stage, so far as *mens rea* is concerned, it is normally, though not quite always, sufficient, and normally, though not quite always, necessary that the accused did the particular act forbidden by law, and did it intentionally or with something like intention. It is true that it is not always sufficient, because sometimes duress or provocation or certain forms of mental abnormality may become relevant, and in such cases the accused may not be convicted for a particular crime even if he intended to do the act forbidden by law. But the scope of these matters is small indeed; provocation, for example, is in English law limited to

homicide, and duress does not extend to it. So intention, or something like it, is usually, though not quite always, *sufficient* so far as murder is concerned, for conviction of a man who has killed another. Intention to do the act forbidden by law, or something like it, is also generally *necessary* for serious crime, though there are exceptions. Gross unthinking negligence may be enough, e.g. in certain cases of manslaughter, as is carelessness in certain motoring offences, and there are also certain forms of strict liability when a man may be liable for punishment even though he did not intend to do what the law forbids, and was not even guilty of negligence. In regard to murder, the law, in certain types of case has applied doctrines of "constructive" murder and "objective" tests of liability so as to render the question of the accused's actual intention largely irrelevant. But these are exceptions, and there is no doubt of the central importance of intention or something like it when the question is, "Is the accused liable for punishment?"

Intention is also relevant when the stage of conviction is past, and the question is, "How severely is the accused to be punished?" This is the stage of sentencing, as distinguished from conviction. Sometimes the legislature will mark off a greater maximum penalty for things done with a certain intention than for the same thing done without that intention. So wounding with intention to kill, (even though the victim is not killed) or wounding with intention to resist arrest, is punishable with the maximum penalty of life imprisonment,[1] and thus much more severely than the simple offence of "unlawfully and maliciously wounding" a man, for which the maximum penalty is five years.[2] Sometimes, however, the greater severity of punishment is settled not by the legislature, but is a matter for the judge to settle within the exercise of his discretion, and in doing this he may often allow the question of intention to weigh. However, too much importance should not be attached to these varying maximum penalties in the case of statutory crimes, since many different features may account for the variation. No philosophical principles, presumably, are needed or competent to account for the fact that, whereas maliciously damaging a work of art is punishable with a maximum of six months imprisonment, maliciously damaging textiles is punishable with imprisonment for life.[3]

2

The law's concern with intention at these two different stages (conviction and sentence) generates a number of problems, some of which I consider here. But there is first an analytical question to be faced before we reach these problems. What, after all, is a man's intention? This is a question which, quite apart from the law, philosophers have found both intriguing and enormously difficult to answer in any simple terms, and there is an additional difficulty in the case of the law. For though jurists or expositors of the criminal law will certainly speak as I have done up to now, and say that the notion of a man's intention is relevant to his criminal responsibility at many important points, what they refer to is the use by the law of a concept which, though it corresponds at many points to what is ordinarily meant in nonlegal use by intention, cannot be said to be identical with it. . . .

What in the law corresponds to intention can . . . be made clear in the following way. Intention is to be divided into three related parts, to which I shall give what I hope are three self-explanatory names. The first I shall call "intentionally doing something"; the second "doing something with a further intention," and the third "bare intention" because it is the case of intending to do something in the future without doing anything to execute this intention now. The following are simple legal examples of these three aspects of intention. Suppose first that a man has done something which fits the definition of a crime so far as concerns the outward movements of his body which he has made and the harmful consequences; he has, for example, fired a gun at and thereby wounded or killed another man. On these facts the question then arises, "Did he wound (or kill) him intentionally?" Though these facts may, in the absence of further evidence, entitle others to conclude (both in and out of the law) that the answer to this question is "Yes," further evidence may show that he wounded or killed the other accidentally owing to a mistaken belief that the gun was unloaded, and so did it unintentionally. With such cases contrast those illustrating the second aspect of intention: doing something with a further intention. A man gets into a dwelling house at night and the question is not, or not merely, "Did he do that intentionally?" but "Did he do that with the further intention, or (as lawyers like to say,) 'with the intent,' of stealing something?" If so he is guilty of burglary, even if in fact he did not steal anything. Many statutory crimes are framed in terms of such further intent, including the crime already mentioned of wounding with intent to kill, or with an intent to resist arrest, as contrasted with a simple "malicious" wounding which, subject to the considerations mentioned below, is equivalent merely to intentionally wounding. The third aspect of intention, bare intention, or just intending to do something in the future without taking any present steps towards its execution, is not, for reasons which I shall mention later, of central importance in the criminal law, though it is important in the civil law. Indeed, a landlord's right to eject a tenant on the termination of a lease may depend on the question whether he intended before its expiration to reconstruct the premises. Of these three notions the first, intentionally doing something, is for legal purposes the most important, and I shall begin my discussion of problems by pointing to the divergence between the legal use of this notion and common usage. This shows itself in the following way. . . .

. . . Consider . . . the facts of a famous Victorian case, *R. v. Desmond, Barrett and Others.*[4] In 1868 there lay in jail two Irish Fenians, whom the accused attempted to liberate. For the purpose, one of them, Barrett, dynamited the prison wall outside the area where he mistakenly believed they would be at exercise. Though the plot failed, the explosion killed some persons living nearby. In this case we can distinguish Barrett's movements made in igniting the fuse from the harmful upshot or consequences in the death of the victims. Given such facts, we may ask outside the law, "Did he kill those men intentionally?" Inside the law the cognate question is "Did he kill them with such malice aforethought as is required to constitute murder?" Generally speaking, so far as any question like that of intentionally harming is concerned, the law, though it may also be content with less, is content to hold a man guilty if the harmful consequence, e.g. death, was foreseen by the accused in the sense that he believed that it would come about as a result of some voluntary action on his part. Whether he thought this would be certain or only likely to ensue may . . . determine the choice between the words "intentionally" or "recklessly" for the description of the case, but will not affect the accused's liability. But the point to be observed here is that, for the law, a foreseen outcome is enough, even if it was unwanted by the agent, even if he thought of it as an undesirable by-product of his activities, and in Desmond's case this is what the death of those killed by the explosion was. It was no part of Barrett's purpose or aim to kill or injure anyone; the victims' deaths were not a means to his end, to bring them about was not his reason or part of his reason for igniting the fuse, but he was convicted on the ground that he foresaw their death or serious injury. As Lord Coleridge said in Desmond's case, it is murder "if a man did [an] act not with the purpose of taking life but with the knowledge or belief that life was likely to be sacrificed by it."

The law therefore does not require in such cases that the outcome should have been something intended in the sense that the accused set out to achieve it, either as a means or an end, and here the law diverges from what is ordinarily meant by expressions like "he intentionally killed those men." For outside the law a merely foreseen, though unwanted, outcome is not usually considered as intended, and this is so in big matters as well as small. The neighbour who for the pleasure of the music plays her gramophone at 6 A.M., well knowing from my frequent complaints that it will wake me from sleep, as it does, would not normally be said to have intentionally woken me up or woken me up intentionally, any more than Barrett in ordinary parlance would have been said to have killed the victims of the explosion intentionally. . . . Some legal theorists, Bentham among them, have recorded this divergence by distinguishing (as "*oblique* intention"), mere foresight of consequences from "*direct* intention" where the consequences must have been contemplated by the accused not merely as a foreseen outcome but as an end which he set out to achieve, or as a means to an end, and constituted at least part of his reason for doing what he did. . . .

It is perhaps easy to understand why when a man is accused of killing and the question is "Is he to be convicted and so liable to punishment for this?," as distinguished from "How severely shall we punish him?," the law should neglect the difference between oblique and direct intention, and why lawyers should come as they have in England to use the beautifully ambiguous expression, "He contemplated this outcome," to cover both. The reason is, I suggest, that both the case of direct intention and that of oblique intention share one feature which any system of assigning responsibility for conduct must always regard as of crucial importance. This can be seen if we compare the actual facts of the Desmond case with a case of direct intention. Suppose Barrett shot the prison guard in order to obtain from them the keys to release the prisoners. Both in the actual Desmond case and in this imaginary variant, so far as Barrett had control over the alternative between the victims' dying or living, his choice tipped the balance; in both cases he had control over and may be considered to have chosen the outcome, since he consciously opted for the course leading to the victims' deaths. Whether he sought to achieve this as an end or a means to his end, or merely foresaw it as an unwelcome consequence of his intervention, is irrelevant at the stage of conviction where the question of control is crucial. However, when it comes to the question of sentence and the determination of the severity of punishment it may be (though I am not at all sure that this is in fact the case) that on both a retributive and a utilitarian theory of punishment the distinction between direct and oblique intention is relevant. . . .

3

. . . The law courts do apparently recognize this distinction between oblique and direct intention when they are confronted with that second aspect of intention which I have called further intention: that is, when the offence is defined as doing one thing with the intention that something else shall occur or be done, like wounding with intent to kill, or doing an act likely to assist the enemy with the intention of assisting the enemy. Here it seems that it is not enough that the accused believed that there would be a certain outcome; for conviction on such a charge it must be shown that he contemplated that outcome as an end or as a means to some end. The case most frequently cited in support of this view of the law is *R. v. Steane*.[5] The facts of this case were that Steane, who was resident in Germany on the outbreak of war, was threatened by the Gestapo that he and his wife would be beaten up unless he broadcast enemy propaganda in English. To save them, he did broadcast, and after the war was charged with the offence of doing an act likely to assist the enemy with the intention of assisting the enemy. He was, in fact, acquitted on the ground that unless it was shown that he broadcast in order to assist the enemy the charge was not made out, and his mere knowledge that it was likely to assist the enemy was not enough. The decision seems to me to be based on a correct interpretation of the statutory language; but the moral or policy justification for acquitting Steane on this ground [rather than duress] has seemed far from clear to many critics. . . .

I shall leave the topic of direct and oblique intention to consider the more general problems generated by the law relating to attempts. As everyone knows, a bare intention to commit a crime is not punishable by English law. This has been often repeated from the Bench since Lord Mansfield in 1784 said: "So long as an act rests in bare intention alone it is not punishable by our law." The reasons for this are perhaps not far to seek. Not only would it be a matter of extreme difficulty to ferret out those who were guilty of harbouring, but not executing, mere intentions to commit crimes, but the effort to do so would involve vast incursions into individual privacy and liberty. The Victorian judge, James Fitzjames Stephen, said that to punish bare intention "would be utterly intolerable: all mankind would be criminals, and most of their lives would be passed in trying and punishing each other for offences which could never be proved."[6] But the law, though it does not punish bare intention, does punish as an attempt the doing of something quite harmless in itself, if it is done with the further intention of committing a crime and if the relationship between the act done and the crime is sufficiently "proximate" or close. So the would-be thief who puts his hand into a pocket which contrary to his expectations proves empty, or who writes a letter to obtain money by false pretences which fails to deceive his intended victim, or the would-be murderer who puts poison into the cup which is emptied before the intended victim can drink out of it, are all guilty of attempts to commit crimes.

It is not obvious, however, at least on some versions of utilitarian theory of punishment, why attempts should be punishable, as they are, in most legal systems. On a retributive view perhaps the answer is easy. The criminal had gone so far as to do his best to execute a wicked intention, and the difficulties of proof and so on are removed by his overt act. But on what is generally known as a deterrent theory the case for punishing attempts has seemed, even to some of its supporters, unclear. Thus it has been argued that if we think of the law, as the deterrent theory requires us to think of it, as threatening punishment to those persons who are tempted to commit offenses, there can be no need to attach any punishment to the unsuccessful attempt, because those who set about crime intend to succeed and the law's threat has all the deterrent force it can have if it is attached to the crime; no additional effect is given to it if unsuccessful attempts are also punished. . . . [But] there seems a clear case for the use of punishment as an individual deterrent in the cases of unsuccessful attempts to commit crimes; for the accused has manifested a dangerous disposition to do all he can to commit a crime, and the experience of punishment may check him in the future, since it may cause him to attach more weight to the law's threats. From this point of view the punishment of a man who has attempted but failed seems as well justified on deterrent grounds as the punishment of a man who has succeeded in committing a crime, although I shall consider later the usual practice of punishing the attempt less severely. But even from the point of view of the general deterrent, the skeptical argument which suggested that there is no case for punishing an attempt is, after all, mistaken. It is perfectly true that those who commit crimes intend to succeed, but this does not show that punishing a man for an unsuccessful attempt will not increase the efficacy of the law's threats, or that failure to punish him would not often diminish their efficacy. This is so for two reasons: first, there must be many who are not completely confident that they will succeed in their criminal objective, but will be prepared to run the risk of punishment if they can be assured that they have to pay nothing for attempts which fail; whereas if unsuccessful attempts were also punished the price might appear to them to be too high. Again, there must be many cases where men might with good or bad reason believe that if they succeed in committing some crime they will escape, but if they fail they may be caught. Treason is only the most obvious of such cases, and unless attempts were punished, there would, in such cases, be no deterrent force in the law's threat attached to the main crime.

A more difficult question concerns the almost universal practice of legal systems of fixing a more severe punishment for the completed crime than for the mere attempt. How is this to be justified? Here a retributive theory in which severity of punishment is proportioned to the allegedly evil intentions of the criminal is in grave difficulty; for there seems to be no difference in wickedness, though there may be in skill, between the successful and the unsuccessful attempt

in this respect. Very often an unsuccessful attempt is merely the accidental failure to commit the crime because somebody unexpectedly intervenes and frustrates the attempt. As far as I can see a deterrent theory, except in relation to a very specialized class of crimes, is in similar difficulties. . . . There seems no reason on any form of deterrent theory, whether we consider the general deterrent or the individual deterrent, for punishing the unsuccessful attempt less severely than the completed crime. The individual who has tried but failed to carry out the planned crime may need just as much punishment to keep him straight in the future as the successful criminal. He may be as much disposed to repeat his crime.

The almost universal tendency in punishing to discriminate between attempts and completed crimes rests, I think, on a version of the retributive theory which has permeated certain branches of English law, and yet has on occasion been stigmatized even by English judges as illogical. This is the simple theory that it is a perfectly legitimate ground to grade punishments according to the amount of harm actually done, whether this was intended or not; "if he has done the harm he must pay for it, but if he has not done it he should pay less." To many people such a theory of punishment seems to confuse punishment with compensation, the amount of which should indeed be fixed in relation to harm done. Even if punishment and compensation were not distinguished in primitive law, many think that this is no excuse for confusing them now. Why should the accidental fact that an intended harmful outcome has not occurred be a ground for punishing less a criminal who may be equally dangerous and equally wicked? I may be wrong in thinking that there is so little to be said for this form of retributive theory. It is certainly popular, and the nearest to a rational defense that I know of it is the following. It is pointed out that in some cases the successful completion of a crime may be a source of gratification, and, in the case of theft, of actual gain, and in such cases to punish the successful criminal more severely may be one way of depriving him of these illicit satisfactions which the unsuccessful have never had. This argument, which certainly has some attraction where the successful criminal has hidden loot to enjoy on emerging from prison, would be an interesting addition to theories of punishment of the principle that the wicked should not be allowed to profit by their crimes.

My own belief is that this form of retributive theory appeals to something with deeper instinctive roots than the last mentioned principle. Certainly the resentment felt by a victim actually injured is normally much greater than that felt by the intended victim who has escaped harm because an attempted crime has failed. Bishop Butler, in his sermon on resentment explains on this ground the distinction men draw between "an injury done" and one "which, though designed, was prevented, in cases where the guilt is perhaps the same." But again the question arises, if this form of retributive theory depends on the connexion between blame and resentment, whether the law should give effect to such a theory. Can we not control resentment, however natural, in the interests of some deliberate forward-looking policy, much as we control our natural fears in the interest of forward-looking prudential aims? And if we can do this, should we not do so? And might not this require us in some cases to punish attempts as severely as the completed offence?

Now to my last topic. I have said that the intention, as the law understands it (that is either oblique or direct intention), is generally, though not always sufficient and generally necessary for criminal liability. But it is not always so, and in conclusion I shall consider certain cases where a man may be punished for a crime, although he had no intention, oblique or direct, to do the act forbidden by law. Here too, we shall be forced in the end, if we are to fit any theories of punishment to the facts, to ask what we mean precisely by the idea of retribution or deterrence, and to refine these ideas in further new directions.

There are two main types of case where no form of intention is required for criminal liability. The first type consists of those crimes known as crimes of strict liability, where it is no defence to prove that you did not intend to do the act forbidden, did not know that you were doing it, and indeed took every care to avoid doing it. Strict liability of this sort is usually thought odious by academic writers, even though most of the offences in question are punished with fairly minor penalties. They include such things as selling liquor to an intoxicated person, or selling adulterated milk, or driving a car without insurance; though they also include more serious offences. The second type of case on which I shall spend a little time are cases of negligence, and I shall concentrate on this, since some useful lessons can be learnt from it.

English law is rather sparing in its punishment of negligence in the sense of unintentional neglect to take reasonable precautions against harm to others, and apart from a few isolated situations, it can be said that negligence is only punishable as a crime if it results in death (where it constitutes one species of manslaughter) or if it is shown in driving motor vehicles on the road: not only is there the offence of driving without due care and attention but there is also the more severely punished offence of causing death by dangerous driving. There are no doubt some general historical reasons why the law should be slow to punish a man who is negligent in the sense of not realizing, though he ought to have realized, that his actions or omissions might occasion a serious harm; but in addition to these historical grounds it is the case that many lawyers feel uncomfortable in accepting negligence as a basis of criminal liability, though, in fact, in our ordinary life it is not usually held to be a good excuse to say "I didn't mean to do it" or "I just didn't stop to think." Certain jurists draw a very dramatic line between the cases where a man intended or foresaw that his actions would be harmful, and those where he was grossly careless, but, as they say, "inadvertent." To such lawyers it appears that the "state of mind" of the merely careless man is not in any way wicked, and presents nothing on which a retributive theory can, as it were, bite. But what is more extraordinary is that very many utilitarian-minded jurists think that there is no intelligible case for punishing gross inadvertent negligence as a deterrent. This seems to conflict very much with the common-sense belief that in some cases we may make people more careful by blaming or punishing them for carelessness. . . .

[But] threats may not only guide your deliberations—your practical thinking—but may cause you to think. A man drives a car with one arm round his girl friend's neck and gazes into her eyes instead of at the road, and is subsequently punished for careless driving in spite of his protestations that he "just didn't think" of the possibilities of the harmful outcome to others on the road. Surely it is not absurd to hope that, as a result, next time he drives he may approach his car, and perhaps his girl friend, in a very different spirit. Recollection of the punishment and the knowledge that others are punished may make a driver think; and if he thinks (since he has no intention to drive badly) he may say to himself "this time I must attend to my driving," and the effect may well be that he drives with due care and attention. No doubt the connexion between the threat of punishment and subsequent good behaviour is not of the rationalistic kind pictured in the guiding-type of case. The threat of punishment is something which causes him to exert his faculties, rather than something which enters as a reason for conforming to the law when he is deliberating whether to break it or not. It is perhaps more like a goad than a guide. But there seems to me to be nothing disreputable in allowing the law to function in this way, and it is arguable that it functions in this way rather than in the rationalistic way more frequently than is generally allowed. At any rate, consideration of the punishment of negligence (and also punishment in the strict liability cases) brings out the need to refine in this way the idea of deterrence by threat.

The punishment of negligence has in England, and I suspect in most legal systems, some further curious features, for here the severity of punishment is often determined by the seriousness of the outcome, and the explanation of this involves recourse again to that sense of retribution which I have already mentioned in explaining the lighter punishments normally accorded to unsuccessful attempts to commit crimes. In 1956, when the offence known as "causing death by dangerous driving" was created, there was an illuminating debate in the House of Lords, where Lord Hailsham pointed out how absurd it was that, where two people were equally careless in driving on the roads, one of them should be liable to be punished with the severe sentence of five years' imprisonment if the bad driving resulted in someone's death, whereas if it resulted only in the victim being crippled, or if no one was harmed he would be liable only for the maximum penalty of two years. Of course, a similar "illogicality" as Lord Hailsham called it, is to be seen in the very existence of one species of manslaughter where the accused's grossly negligent act is punishable if it causes the victim's death. The then Lord Chancellor (Lord Kilmuir) recognized the "illogicality" of this mode of determining the relevant severity of punishment by reference to the harm done, but said in the debate, "Such doubts have of course affected every penal thinker and penal reformer. But no one has been able to translate these doubts into a workable system. Results must be taken into account if the penalties are going to have the effects which it is desirable they should have." I have never understood that answer in defence of this form of retributive theory. Does it merely state obscurely what Stephen stated with great clarity seventy years earlier, "It gratifies a natural public feeling to choose out for punishment the one who actually has caused great harm."?[7]

NOTES

[1] Offences against the Person Act. 1861, s. 18.

[2] Ibid., s. 20.

[3] Malicious Damage Act. 1861, ss. 39 and 14.

[4] *The Times,* 28 April 1868 (hereinafter referred to as "Desmond's case").

[5] (1947) K.B. 997.

[6] Stephen, *A History of the Criminal Law of England,* Vol. II, p. 78.

[7] Stephen, op. cit., Vol. III, p. 311.

REVIEW AND DISCUSSION QUESTIONS

1. What are the two different stages at which the law is concerned with a defendant's intention?

2. Explain the three aspects of intention that Hart distinguishes.

3. What principle does the *Desmond* case illustrate?

4. What is the difference between oblique and direct intention? Why does Hart believe that in

cases of killing the distinction is relevant to the severity of punishment but not to the question of liability to punishment?

5. What did the Court decide in *R. v. Steane?* Was the decision a sensible one?

6. Should attempts be punished less severely than successful crimes? Why or why not?

7. When, if ever, should negligence be criminally punished? Explain your answer. Is the seriousness of the outcome relevant to sentencing? Why or why not?

Attempting the Impossible

United States v. Oviedo and *People v. Dlugash*

Although criminal liability for attempting to commit a crime is relatively recent, it is now well established in the criminal law and for good reasons, both retributivist and utilitarian. But difficult questions arise in cases in which it is literally impossible for a person to have committed successfully the crime he or she is accused of attempting, and in the following cases two courts wrestle with these questions. The first case concerns Oviedo's conviction for attempted distribution of heroin on the basis of having sold procaine hydrochloride, a legal substance that looks like heroin, to an undercover agent attempting to purchase narcotics. In the second case, Dlugash was convicted of murder for shooting a man who was most likely already dead or who, at least, would have been dead in a very short time anyway. On appeal, the Appellate Division Court (1) reversed the conviction for murder and (2) ruled that the judgment could not be modified to a conviction for attempted murder. In the case reprinted here, the Court of Appeals of New York upheld the decision of the appellate division court with respect to Dlugash's murder conviction but ruled that he was guilty of attempted murder.

United States v. Oviedo

Dyer, Circuit Judge:

Oviedo appeals from a judgment of conviction for the attempted distribution of heroin.

Oviedo was contacted by an undercover agent, who desired to purchase narcotics. Arrangements were made for the sale of one pound of heroin. The agent met Oviedo at the appointed time and place. Oviedo transferred the substance to the agent, and asked for his money in return. However, the agent informed Oviedo that he would first have to test the substance. A field test was performed with a positive result. Oviedo was placed under arrest.

Subsequent to the arrest, a search warrant was issued for Oviedo's residence. When the search was executed, two pounds of a similar substance was found hidden in a television set. Up to this point, the case appeared unexceptional.

A chemical analysis was performed upon the substances seized, revealing that the substances were not in fact heroin, but rather procaine hydrochloride, an uncontrolled substance. Since any attempt to prosecute for distribution of heroin would have been futile, the defendant was charged with an attempt to distribute heroin.

At trial, Oviedo took the stand and stated that he knew the substance was not heroin, and that he, upon suggestion of his cohorts, was merely attempting to "rip off" the agent. It was, in his view, an easy way to pocket a few thousand dollars.

525 F.2d 881 (1976) and N.E.2d 1155 (1977), respectively. Some citations and notes omitted.

The court instructed the jury that they could find Oviedo guilty of attempted distribution if he delivered the substance thinking it to be heroin. The jury rejected Oviedo's claimed knowledge of the true nature of the substance, and returned a verdict of guilty. Although Oviedo argues on appeal that there was insufficient evidence to establish that he thought the substance was heroin, this contention is without merit. We thus take as fact Oviedo's belief that the substance was heroin.

The facts before us are therefore simple—Oviedo sold a substance he thought to be heroin, which in reality was an uncontrolled substance. The legal question before us is likewise simple—are these combined acts and intent cognizable as a criminal attempt. The answer, however, is not so simple.

Oviedo and the government both agree the resolution of this case rests in an analysis of the doctrines of legal and factual impossibility as defenses to a criminal attempt. Legal impossibility occurs when the actions which the defendant performs or sets in motion, even if fully carried out as he desires, would not constitute a crime. Factual impossibility occurs when the objective of the defendant is proscribed by the criminal law but a circumstance unknown to the actor prevents him from bringing about that objective. The traditional analysis recognizes legal impossibility as a valid defense, but refuses to so recognize factual impossibility.

These definitions are not particularly helpful here, for they do nothing more than provide a different focus for the analysis. In one sense, the impossibility involved here might be deemed legal, for those *acts* which Oviedo set in motion, the transfer of the substance in his possession, were not a crime. In another sense, the impossibility is factual, for the *objective* of Oviedo, the sale of heroin, was proscribed by law, and failed only because of a circumstance unknown to Oviedo.

Although this issue has been the subject of numerous legal commentaries, federal cases reaching this question are few, and no consensus can be found.

In *Roman*, the defendants were transporting a suitcase containing heroin. Through the aid of an informer and unknown to the defendants, the contents of the suitcase were replaced with soap powder. The defendants were arrested when they attempted to sell the contents of the suitcase, and were subsequently charged with *attempted* possession with intent to distribute. The court rejected defendant's contention that they could not be charged with attempted possession, since it was impossible for them to possess heroin. Recognizing the difficulty in distinguishing between legal and factual impossibility, the court never so categorized the case. Nevertheless, the court concluded that since the objective of the defendants was criminal, impossibility would not be recognized as a defense.

The defendants in *Berrigan* were charged with attempting to violate 18 U.S.C.A. §1791, prohibiting the smuggling of objects into or out of a federal correctional institution. Since the evidence established that the warden had knowledge of the smuggling plan, and since lack of knowledge was a necessary element of the offense, the defendants could not be found guilty of violating the statute. The court held that such knowledge by the warden would also preclude conviction for the attempt, since "attempting to do that which is not a crime is not attempting to commit a crime."

The *Berrigan* court rested its determination on a strict view of legal impossibility. According to the court, such impossibility exists when there is an intention to perform a physical act, the intended physical act is performed, but the consequence resulting from the intended act does not amount to a crime. In this analysis, the intent to perform a physical act is to be distinguished from the motive, desire or expectation to violate the law.

The application of the principles underlying these cases leads to no clearer result than the application of our previous definitions of legal and factual impossibility. Applying *Roman*, we would not concern ourselves with any theoretical distinction between legal and factual impossibility, but would affirm the conviction, since the objective of Oviedo was criminal. Applying *Berrigan*, we would look solely to the physical act which Oviedo "intended," the transfer of the procaine in his possession, and we would conclude that since the transfer of procaine is not criminal, no offense is stated. The choice is between punishing criminal intent without regard to objective acts, and punishing objective acts, regarding intent as immaterial.

In our view, both *Roman* and *Berrigan* miss the mark, but in opposite directions. A strict application of the *Berrigan* approach would eliminate any distinction between factual and legal impossibility, and such impossibility would *always* be a valid defense, since the "intended" physical acts are never criminal. The *Roman* approach turns the attempt statute into a new substantive criminal statute where the critical element to be proved is *mens rea simpliciter*. It would allow us to punish one's thoughts, desires, or motives, through indirect evidence, without reference to any objective fact. The danger is evident.

We reject the notion of *Roman*, adopted by the district court, that the conviction in the present case can be sustained since there is sufficient proof of intent, not because of any doubt as to the sufficiency of the evidence in that regard, but because of the inherent dangers such a precedent would pose in the future.

When the question before the court is whether certain conduct constitutes mere preparation which is not punishable, or an attempt which is, the possibility of error is mitigated by the requirement that the objective acts of the defendant evidence commitment to the criminal venture and corroborate the *mens rea*. To the extent that this requirement is preserved it prevents the conviction of persons engaged in innocent acts on the basis of a *mens rea* proved through speculative inferences, unreliable forms of testimony, and past criminal conduct.

Courts could have approached the preparation–attempt determination in another fashion, eliminating any notion of particular objective facts, and simply could have asked whether the evidence at hand was sufficient to prove the necessary intent. But this approach has been rejected for precisely the reasons set out above, for conviction upon proof of mere intent provides too great a possibility of speculation and abuse.

In urging us to follow *Roman*, which found determinative the criminal intent of the defendants, the government at least implicitly argues that we should reject any requirement demanding the same objective evidentiary facts required in the preparation–attempt determination. We refuse to follow that suggestion.

When the defendant sells a substance which is actually heroin, it is reasonable to infer that he knew the physical nature of the substance, and to place on him the burden of dispelling the inference. However, if we convict the defendant of attempting to sell heroin for the sale of a nonnarcotic substance, we eliminate an objective element that has major evidentiary significance and we increase the risk of mistaken conclusions that the defendant believed the goods were narcotics.

Thus, we demand that in order for a defendant to be guilty of a criminal attempt, the objective acts performed, without any reliance on the accompanying *mens rea*, mark the defendant's conduct as criminal in nature. The acts should be unique rather than so commonplace that they are engaged in by persons not in violation of the law.

Here we have only two objective facts. First, Oviedo told the agent that the substance he was selling was heroin, and second, portions of the substance were concealed in a television set. If another objective fact were present, if the substance were heroin, we would have a strong objective basis for the determination of criminal intent and conduct consistent and supportive of that intent. The test set out above would be met, and, absent a delivery, the criminal attempt would be established. But when this objective basis for the determination of intent is removed, when the substance is not heroin, the conduct becomes ambivalent, and we are left with a sufficiency-of-the-evidence determination of intent rejected in the preparation–attempt dichotomy. We cannot conclude that the objective acts of Oviedo apart from any direct evidence of intent mark his conduct as criminal in nature. Rather, those acts are consistent with a noncriminal enterprise. Therefore, we will not allow the jury's determination of Oviedo's intent to form the sole basis of a criminal offense.

The government also argues that *United States v. Mandujano*, although involving a preparation–attempt determination, compels a contrary result. In *Mandujano*, the defendant negotiated a sale of heroin with an undercover agent. After taking the agent's money, the defendant set about to find his source. He was unsuccessful, and returned a few hours later with the money and without the heroin. We found the evidence sufficient to take the case beyond preparation, and to support his conviction for attempted distribution.

In making that determination, we recognized that in order to be guilty of an attempt, the objective conduct of the defendant must strongly corroborate the firmness of the defendant's criminal intent. The objective acts must not be equivocal in nature. In that case, we had as objective facts defendant's act of taking money and his personal statements that he would purchase heroin with that money. Importantly, there were no objective facts which made these acts equivocal.

The situation in *Mandujano* is distinguishable from that now before us. Just as it is reasonable to infer a person's knowledge and criminal intent from the possession of a substance which is in fact narcotics, it is also reasonable to infer that same knowledge and intent from an individual's statement of future intention. However, just as it is impossible to infer that intent when the substance possessed is not in fact narcotics, it is also impossible to infer that intent when objective facts indicate that the person did not carry out his self-proclaimed intention.

Thus, when Mandujano stated that he would purchase heroin, we could infer that he intended to purchase heroin since there were no objective facts to the contrary. But here, Oviedo stated he would sell heroin and then sold procaine. Based on these objective facts, we cannot infer that he intended to do that which he said he was going to do, because he in fact did something else.

Reversed.

People v. Dlugash

Jasen, Judge:

The criminal law is of ancient origin, but criminal liability for attempt to commit a crime is comparatively recent. At the root of the concept of attempt liability are the very aims and purposes of penal law. The ultimate issue is whether an individual's intentions and actions, though failing to achieve a manifest and malevolent criminal purpose, constitute a danger to organized society of sufficient magnitude to warrant the imposition of criminal sanctions. Difficulties in theoretical analysis and concomitant debate over very pragmatic questions of blameworthiness appear dramatically in reference to situations where the criminal attempt failed to achieve its purpose solely because the factual or legal context in which the individual acted was not as the actor supposed them to be. Phrased somewhat differently, the concern centers on whether an individual should be liable for an attempt to commit a crime when, unknown to him, it was impossible to successfully complete the crime attempted. . . . The 1967 revision of the Penal law approached the impossibility of defense to the inchoate crime of attempt in a novel fashion. The statute provides that, if a person engages in conduct which would otherwise constitute an attempt to commit a crime, "it is no defense to a prosecution for such attempt that the crime charged to have been attempted was, under the attendant circumstances, factually or legally impossible of commission, if such crime could have been committed had the attendant circumstances been as such person believed them to be." (Penal Law, §110.10.) This appeal presents to us, for the first time, a case involving the application of the modern statute. We hold that, under the proof presented by the People at trial, defendant Melvin Dlugash may be held for attempted murder, though the target of the attempt may have already been slain, by the hand of another, when Dlugash made his felonious attempt.

On December 22, 1973, Michael Geller, 25 years old, was found shot to death in the bedroom of his Brooklyn apartment. The body, which had literally been riddled by bullets, was found lying face up on the floor. An autopsy revealed that the victim had been shot in the face and head no less than seven times. Powder burns on the face indicated that the shots had been fired from within one foot of the victim. Four small caliber bullets were recovered from the victim's skull. The victim had also been critically wounded in the chest. One heavy caliber bullet passed through the left lung, penetrated the heart chamber, pierced the left ventricle of the heart upon entrance and again upon exit, and lodged in the victim's torso. Although a second bullet was damaged beyond identification, the bullet tracks indicated that these wounds were also inflicted by a bullet of heavy caliber. A tenth bullet, of unknown caliber, passed through the thumb of the victim's left hand. The autopsy report listed the cause of death as "[m]ultiple bullet wounds of head and chest with brain injury and massive bilateral hemothorax with penetration of [the] heart." Subsequent ballistics examination established that the four bullets recovered from the victim's head were .25 caliber bullets and that the heart piercing bullet was of .38 caliber.

Detective Joseph Carrasquillo of the New York City Police Department was assigned to investigate the homicide. On December 27, 1973, five days after the discovery of the body, Detective Carrasquillo and a fellow officer went to the defendant's residence in an effort to locate him. The officers arrived at approximately 6:00 P.M. The defendant answered the door and, when informed that the officers were investigating the death of Michael Geller, a friend of his, defendant invited the officers into the house. Detective Carrasquillo informed defendant that the officers desired any information defendant might have regarding the death of Geller and, since defendant was regarded as a suspect, administered the standard preinterrogation warnings. The defendant told the officers that he and another friend, Joe Bush, had just returned from a four- or five-day trip "upstate someplace" and learned of Geller's death only upon his return. Since Bush was also a suspect in the case and defendant admitted knowing Bush, defendant agreed to accompany the officers to the station house for the purposes of identifying photographs of Bush and of lending assistance to the investigation. Upon arrival at the police station, Detective Carrasquillo and the defendant went directly into an interview room. Carrasquillo advised the defendant that he had witnesses and information to the effect that as late as 7:00 P.M. on the day before the body was found, defendant had been observed carrying a .25 caliber pistol. Once again, Carras-

quillo administered the standard preinterrogation statement of rights. The defendant then proceeded to relate his version of the events which culminated in the death of Geller. Defendant stated that, on the night of December 21, 1973, he, Bush and Geller had been out drinking. Bush had been staying at Geller's apartment and, during the course of the evening, Geller several times demanded that Bush pay $100 towards the rent on the apartment. According to defendant, Bush rejected these demands, telling Geller that "you better shut up or you're going to get a bullet." All three returned to Geller's apartment at approximately midnight, took seats in the bedroom, and continued to drink until sometime between 3:00 and 3:30 in the morning. When Geller again pressed his demand for rent money, Bush drew his .38 caliber pistol, aimed it at Geller and fired three times. Geller fell to the floor. After the passage of a few minutes, perhaps two, perhaps as much as five, defendant walked over to the fallen Geller, drew his .25 caliber pistol, and fired approximately five shots in the victim's head and face. Defendant contended that, by the time he fired the shots, "it looked like Mike Geller was already dead." After the shots were fired, defendant and Bush walked to the apartment of a female acquaintance. Bush removed his shirt, wrapped the two guns and a knife in it, and left the apartment, telling Dlugash that he intended to dispose of the weapons. Bush returned 10 or 15 minutes later and stated that he had thrown the weapons down a sewer two or three blocks away.

After Carrasquillo had taken the bulk of the statement, he asked the defendant why he would do such a thing. According to Carrasquillo, the defendant said, "gee, I really don't know." Carrasquillo repeated the question 10 minutes later, but received the same response. After a while, Carrasquillo asked the question for a third time and defendant replied, "well, gee, I guess it must have been because I was afraid of Joe Bush."

At approximately 9:00 P.M., the defendant repeated the substance of his statement to an Assistant District Attorney. Defendant added that at the time he shot at Geller, Geller was not moving and his eyes were closed. While he did not check for a pulse, defendant stated the Geller had not been doing anything to him at the time he shot because "Mike was dead."

Defendant was indicted by the Grand Jury of Kings County on a single count of murder in that, acting in concert with another person actually present, he intentionally caused the death of Michael Geller. At the trial, there were four principal prosecution witnesses: Detective Carrasquillo, the Assistant District Attorney who took the second admission, and two physicians from the office of the New York City Chief Medical Examiner. For proof of defendant's culpability, the prosecution relied upon defendant's own admissions as related by the detective and the prosecutor. From the physicians, the prosecution sought to establish that Geller was still alive at the time defendant shot at him. Both physicians testified that each of the two chest wounds, for which defendant alleged Bush to be responsible, would have caused death without prompt medical attention. Moreover, the victim would have remained alive until such time as his chest cavity became fully filled with blood. Depending on the circumstances, it might take 5 to 10 minutes for the chest cavity to fill. Neither prosecution witness could state, with medical certainty, that the victim was still alive when, perhaps five minutes after the initial chest wounds were inflicted, the defendant fired at the victim's head. The defense produced but a single witness, the former Chief Medical Examiner of New York City. This expert stated that, in his view, Geller might have died of the chest wounds "very rapidly" since, in addition to the bleeding, a large bullet going through a lung and the heart would have other adverse medical effects. "Those wounds can be almost immediately or rapidly fatal or they may be delayed in there, in the time it would take for death to occur. But I would say that wounds like that which are described here as having gone through the lungs and the heart would be fatal wounds and in most cases they're rapidly fatal."

The jury found the defendant guilty of murder. The defendant then moved to set the verdict aside. He submitted an affidavit in which he contended that he "was absolutely, unequivocally and positively certain that Michael Geller was dead before [he] shot him." This motion was denied.

On appeal, the Appellate Division reversed the judgment of conviction on the law and dismissed the indictment. The court ruled that "the People failed to prove beyond a reasonable doubt that Geller had been alive at the time he was shot by defendant; defendant's conviction of murder thus cannot stand." Further, the court held that the judgment could not be modified to reflect a conviction for attempted murder because "the uncontradicted evidence is that the defendant, at the time that he fired the five shots into the body of the decedent, believed him to be dead, and . . . there is not a scintilla of evidence to contradict his assertion in that regard."

While the defendant admitted firing five shots at the victim approximately two to five minutes after Bush had fired three times, all three medical expert witnesses testified that they could not, with any degree of medical certainty, state whether the victim had been alive at the time the latter shots were fired by the defendant. Thus, the People failed to prove beyond a reasonable doubt that the victim had been alive at the time he was shot by the defendant. Whatever else it may be, it is not murder to shoot a dead body.

The distinction between "factual" and "legal" impossibility is a nice one indeed and the courts tend to place a greater value on legal form than on any substantive danger the defendant's actions pose for society. The approach of the draftsmen of the Model Penal Code was to eliminate the defense of impossibility in virtually all situations. Under the code provision, to constitute an attempt, it is still necessary that the result intended or desired by the actor constitute a crime. However, the code suggested a fundamental change to shift the locus of analysis to the actor's mental frame of reference and away from undue dependence upon external considerations. The basic premise of the code provision is that what was in the actor's own mind should be the standard for determining his dangerousness to society and, hence, his liability for attempted criminal conduct.

In the belief that neither of the two branches of the traditional impossibility arguments detracts from the offender's moral culpability, the Legislature substantially carried the code's treatment of impossibility into the 1967 revision of the Penal Law. Thus, a person is guilty of an attempt when, with intent to commit a crime, he engages in conduct which tends to effect the commission of such crime. (Penal Law, §110.10.) Thus, if defendant believed the victim to be alive at the time of the shooting, it is no defense to the charge of attempted murder that the victim may have been dead.

Turning to the facts of the case before us, we believe that there is sufficient evidence in the record from which the jury could conclude that the defendant believed Geller to be alive at the time defendant fired shots into Geller's head. Defendant admitted firing five shots at a most vital part of the victim's anatomy from virtually point blank range. Although defendant contended that the victim had already been grievously wounded by another, from the defendant's admitted actions, the jury could conclude that the defendant's purpose and intention was to administer the coup de grace.

Defendant argues that the jury was bound to accept, at face value, the indications in his admissions that he believed Geller dead. Certainly, it is true that the defendant was entitled to have the entirety of the admissions, both the inculpatory and the exculpatory portions, placed in evidence before the trier of facts.

However, the jury was not required to automatically credit the exculpatory portions of the admissions. The general rule is, of course, that the credibility of witnesses is a question of fact and the jury may choose to believe some, but not all, of a witness' testimony.

In this case, there is ample other evidence to contradict the defendant's assertion that he believed Geller dead. There were five bullet wounds inflicted with stunning accuracy in a vital part of the victim's anatomy. The medical testimony indicated that Geller may have been alive at the time defendant fired at him. The defendant voluntarily left the jurisdiction immediately after the crime with his coperpetrator. Defendant did not report the crime to the police when left on his own by Bush. Instead, he attempted to conceal his and Bush's involvement with the homicide. In addition, the other portions of defendant's admissions make his contended belief that Geller was dead extremely improbable. Defendant, without a word of instruction from Bush, voluntarily got up from his seat after the passage of just a few minutes and fired five times point blank into the victim's face, snuffing out any remaining chance of life that Geller possessed. Certainly, this alone indicates a callous indifference to the taking of a human life. His admissions are barren of any claim of duress and reflect, instead, an unstinting co-operation in efforts to dispose of vital incriminating evidence. Indeed, defendant maintained a false version of the occurrence until such time as the police informed him that they had evidence that he lately possessed a gun of the same caliber as one of the weapons involved in the shooting. From all of this, the jury was certainly warranted in concluding that the defendant acted in the belief that Geller was yet alive when shot by defendant.

The jury convicted the defendant of murder. Necessarily, they found that defendant intended to kill a live human being. Subsumed within this finding is the conclusion that defendant acted in the belief that Geller was alive. Thus, there is no need for additional fact findings by a jury. Although it was not established beyond a reasonable doubt that Geller was, in fact, alive, such is no defense to attempted murder since a murder would have been committed "had the attendant circumstances been as [defendant] believed them to be." (Penal Law, §110.10.) The jury necessarily found that defendant believed Geller to be alive when defendant shot at him.

The Appellate Division erred in not modifying the judgment to reflect a conviction for the lesser included offense of attempted murder. An attempt to commit a murder is a lesser included offense of murder and the Appellate Division has the authority, where the trial evidence is not legally sufficient to establish the offense of which the defendant was convicted, to modify the judgment to one of conviction for a lesser included offense which is legally established by the evidence.

1. Why does the court in *Oviedo* find the distinction between legal and factual impossibility unhelpful?

2. How do the principles underlying the rulings in the *Roman* and *Berrigan* cases differ, and what would be the conflicting implications of those principles given the facts of *Oviedo*?

3. What did the court decide in *Oviedo* and why? Is its reasoning sound?

4. Suppose that it was highly probable but not beyond a reasonable doubt that Michael Geller was still alive when Dlugash shot him. Should Dlugash have been found guilty of murder? What if it were certain that Geller was alive but that he would die within five minutes no matter what happened?

5. Should Dlugash have been found guilty of attempted murder? The Court of Appeals appears to believe that he should be if he shot Geller believing him alive, even if Geller was in fact quite dead. Is this a reasonable legal principle?

6. Are the verdicts in these two cases consistent?

Rape

Susan Estrich

The criminal law's handling of rape has long been rife with sexism, with the law appearing to be more concerned to protect men from unfair convictions than to do justice to rape victims. In this essay, Susan Estrich, professor of law at the University of Southern California, explores the ways in which male standards and traditional conceptions of sex roles have shaped the crime of rape. Unlike their British counterparts, American courts have tended to omit mens rea *from the definition of rape— thus treating what the man knew or should have known about the victim's consent as irrelevant. But the results of this have not been favorable to women. Instead, by making force or threat of force central to rape and by requiring that the victim prove lack of consent by her resistance, the courts have made the burden of proving rape unacceptably high.*

THE DEFINITION OF RAPE

The traditional way of defining a crime is by describing the prohibited act (*actus reus*) committed by the defendant and the prohibited mental state (*mens rea*) with which he must have done it. We ask: What did the defendant do? What did he know or intend when he did it?

The definition of rape stands in striking contrast to this tradition, because courts, in defining the crime, have focused almost incidentally on the defendant—and almost entirely on the victim. It has often been noted that, traditionally at least, the rules associated with the proof of a rape charge—the corroboration requirement, the requirement of cautionary instructions, and the fresh complaint rule—as well as the evidentiary rules relating to prior sexual conduct by the victim, placed the victim as much on trial as the defendant. Such a reversal also occurs in the course of defining the elements of the crime. *Mens rea*, where it might matter, is all but eliminated; prohibited force tends to be defined according to the response of the victim; and nonconsent—the *sine qua non* of the offense— turns entirely on the victim's response.

But while the focus is on the female victim, the judgment of her actions is entirely male. If the issue were what the defendant knew, thought, or intended as to key elements of the offense, this perspective might be understandable; yet the issue has instead been the appropriateness of the woman's behavior, according to male standards of appropriate female behavior.

To some extent, this evaluation is but a modern response to the longstanding suspicion of rape victims. As Matthew Hale put it three centuries ago: "Rape is . . . an accusation easily to be made and hard to be proved, and harder to be defended by the party accused, tho never so innocent."[1]

But the problem is more fundamental than that. Apart from the woman's conduct, the law provides no clear, working definition of rape. This rather conspicuous gap in the law of rape presents substantial questions of fair warning for men, which the law not so handily resolves by imposing the burden of warning them on women.

At its simplest, the dilemma lies in this: If nonconsent is essential to rape (and no amount of force or physical struggle is inherently inconsistent with lawful sex), and if no sometimes means yes, and if men are supposed to be aggressive in any event, how is a man to know when he has crossed the line? And how are we to avoid unjust convictions?

This dilemma is hardly inevitable. Partly, it is a product of the way society (or at least a powerful part of it) views sex. Partly, it is a product of the lengths to which the law has gone to enforce and legitimize those views. We could prohibit the use of force and threats and coercion in sex, regardless of "consent." We could define consent in a way that respected the autonomy of women. Having chosen neither course, however, we have created a problem of fair warning, and force and consent have been defined in an effort to resolve this problem.

Usually, any discussion of rape begins (and ends) with consent. I begin instead with *mens rea*, because if unjust punishment of the blameless man is our fear (as it was Hale's), then *mens rea* would seem an appropriate place to start addressing it. At least a requirement of *mens rea* would avoid unjust convictions without adjudicating the "guilt" of the victim. It could also be the first step in expanding liability beyond the most traditional rape. . . .

MENS REA

It is difficult to imagine any man engaging in intercourse accidentally or mistakenly. It is just as difficult to imagine an accidental or mistaken use of force, at least as force is conventionally defined. But it is not at all difficult to imagine cases in which a man might claim that he did not realize that the woman was not consenting to sex. He may have been mistaken in assuming that no meant yes. He may not have bothered to inquire. He may have ignored signs that would have told him that the woman did not welcome his forceful penetration.

In doctrinal terms, such a man could argue that his mistake of fact should exculpate him because he lacked the requisite intent or *mens rea* as to the woman's required nonconsent.[2] American courts have altogether eschewed the *mens rea* or mistake inquiry as to consent, opting instead for a definition of the crime of rape that is so limited that it leaves little room for men to be mistaken, reasonably or unreasonably, as to consent. The House of Lords, by contrast, has confronted the question explicitly and, in its leading case, has formally restricted the crime of rape to men who act recklessly, a state of mind defined to allow even the unreasonably mistaken man to avoid conviction.

This Section argues that the American courts' refusal to confront the *mens rea* problem works to the detriment of the victim. In order to protect men from unfair convictions, American courts end up defining rape with undue restrictiveness. . . .

In defining the crime of rape, most American courts have omitted *mens rea* altogether. In Maine, for example, the Supreme Judicial Court has held that there is no *mens rea* requirement at all for rape. In Pennsylvania, the Superior Court held in 1982 that even a reasonable belief as to the victim's consent would not exculpate a defendant charged with rape. In 1982 the Supreme Judicial Court of Massachusetts left open the question whether it would recognize a defense of reasonable mistake of fact as to consent, but it rejected the defendant's suggestion that any mistake, reasonable or unreasonable, would be sufficient to negate the required intent to rape; such a claim was treated by the court as bordering on the ridiculous. The following year the court went on to hold that a specific intent that intercourse be without consent was not an element of the crime of rape; that decision has since been construed to mean that there is no intent requirement at all as to consent in rape cases.

To treat what the defendant intended or knew or even should have known about the victim's consent as irrelevant to his liability sounds like a result favorable to both prosecution and women as victims. But experience makes all too clear that it is not. To refuse to inquire into *mens rea* leaves two possibilities: turning rape into a strict liability offense where, in the absence of consent, the man is guilty of rape regardless of whether he (or anyone) would have recognized nonconsent in the circumstances; or defining the crime of rape in a fashion that is so limited that it would be virtually impossible for any man to be convicted where he was truly unaware or mistaken as to nonconsent. In fact, it is the latter approach which has characterized all of the older, and many of the newer, American cases. In practice, abandoning *mens rea* produces the worst of all possible worlds: The trial emerges not as an inquiry into the guilt of the defendant (is he a rapist?) but of the victim (was she really raped? did she consent?). The perspective that governs is therefore not that of the woman, nor even of the particular man, but of a judicial system intent upon protecting against unjust conviction, regardless of the dangers of injustice to the woman in the particular case.

The requirement that sexual intercourse be accompanied by force or threat of force to constitute rape provides a man with some protection against mistakes as to consent. A man who uses a gun or knife against his victim is not likely to be in serious doubt as to her lack of consent, and the more narrowly force is defined, the more implausible the claim that he was unaware of nonconsent.

But the law's protection of men is not limited to a requirement of force. Rather than inquire whether the man believed (reasonably or unreasonably) that his victim was consenting, the courts have demanded that the victim demonstrate her nonconsent by engaging in resistance that will leave no doubt as to nonconsent. The definition of nonconsent as resistance—in the older cases, as utmost resistance, while in some more recent ones, as "reasonable" physical resistance—functions as a substitute for *mens rea* to ensure that the man has notice of the woman's nonconsent.

The choice between focusing on the man's intent or focusing on the woman's is not simply a doctrinal flip of the coin.

First, the inquiry into the victim's nonconsent puts the woman, not the man, on trial. Her intent, not his, is disputed; and because her state of mind is key, her sexual history may be considered relevant (even though utterly unknown to the man). Considering consent from *his* perspective, by contrast, substantially undermines the relevance of the woman's sexual history where it was unknown to the man.

Second, the issue for determination shifts from whether the man is a rapist to whether the woman was raped. A verdict of acquittal thus does more than signal that the prosecution has failed to prove the defendant guilty beyond a reasonable doubt; it signals that the prosecution has failed to prove the woman's sexual violation—her innocence—beyond a reasonable doubt. Thus, as one dissenter put it in disagreeing with the affirmance of a conviction of rape: "The majority today . . . declares the innocence of an at best distraught young woman."[3] Presumably, the dissenter thought the young woman guilty.

Third, the resistance requirement is not only ill conceived as a definition of nonconsent, but is an overboard substitute for *mens rea* in any event. Both the resistance requirement and the *mens rea* requirement can be used to enforce a male perspective on the crime, but while *mens rea* might be justified as protecting the individual defendant who has not made a blameworthy choice, the resistance standard requires women to risk injury to themselves in cases where there may be no doubt as to the man's intent or blameworthiness. The application of the resistance requirement has not been limited to cases in which there was uncertainty as to what the man thought, knew or intended; it has been fully applied in cases where there can be no question that the man knew that intercourse was without consent. Indeed, most of the cases that have dismissed claims that *mens rea* ought to be required have been cases where both force and resistance were present, and where there was no danger of any unfairness.

Finally, by ignoring *mens rea*, American courts and legislators have imposed limits on the fair expansion of our understanding of rape. As long as the law holds that *mens rea* is not required, and that no instructions on intent need by given, pressure will exist to retain some form of resistance requirement and to insist on force as conventionally defined in order to protect men against conviction for "sex." Using resistance as a substitute for *mens rea* unnecessarily and unfairly immunizes those men whose victims are afraid enough, or intimidated enough, or, frankly, smart enough, not to take the risk of resisting physically. In doing so, the resistance test may declare the blameworthy man innocent and the raped woman guilty. . . .

In situations where a "reasonable man" would have known that the woman was not consenting, most defendants will face great difficulty in arguing that they were honestly mistaken or inadvertent as to consent. . . .

My view is that such a "negligent rapist" should be punished, albeit—as in murder—less severely than the man who acts with purpose or knowledge, or even knowledge of the risk. First, he is sufficiently blameworthy for it to be just to punish him. Second, the injury he inflicts is sufficiently grave to deserve the law's prohibition. . . .

In holding a man to such a standard of reasonableness, the law signifies that it considers a woman's consent to sex to be significant enough to merit a man's reasoned attention. In effect, the law imposes a duty on men to open their eyes and use their heads before engaging in sex—not to read a woman's mind, but to give her credit for knowing her own mind when she speaks it. The man who has the inherent capacity to act reasonably, but fails to do so, has made the blameworthy choice to violate this duty. . . .

FORCE AND THREATS

This Section examines two views of force in human relations. The first understands force as most schoolboys do on the playground: Force is when he hits me; resistance is when I hit back. That is the definition of force traditionally enforced in rape cases. A second understanding of force, not acknowledged in the law of rape, recognizes that bodily integrity means more than freedom from the force of fists, that power can

be exercised without violence, and that coercion is not limited to what boys do in schoolyards.

Virtually every jurisdiction has traditionally made "force" or "threat of force" an element of the crime of rape. Where a defendant threatens his victim with a deadly weapon, beats her, or threatens to hurt her, and then proceeds immediately to have sex, few courts have difficulty finding that force is present. These facts fit the schoolboy definition of force. But when some time elapses between the force and intercourse, when the force is more of the variety considered "incidental" to sex, or when the situation is threatening but no explicit threat of harm is communicated, "force" as defined and required by the criminal law may not be present at all. In such cases, the law fails to recognize, let alone protect, a woman's interest in bodily integrity. . . .

The requirement of force is not unique to the law of rape. But rape is different in two critical respects. First, unlike theft, if "force" is not inherent in noncriminal sex, at least physical contact is. Certainly, if a person stripped his victim, flattened that victim on the floor, lay down on top, and took the other person's wallet or jewelry, few would pause before the conclusion of a forcible robbery. Second, rape does not involve "one person" and "another person." It involves, in practice if not everywhere by definition, a male person using "force" against a female person. The question of whose definition of "force" should apply, whose understanding should govern, is therefore critical.

The distinction between the "force" incidental to the act of intercourse and the "force" required to convict a man of rape is one commonly drawn by courts. Once drawn, however, the distinction would seem to require the courts to define what additional acts are needed to constitute prohibited rather than incidental force. This is where the problems arise. For many courts and jurisdictions, "force" triggers an inquiry identical to that which informs the understanding of consent. Both serve as substitutes for a *mens rea* requirement. Force is required to constitute rape, but force—even force that goes far beyond the physical contact necessary to accomplish penetration—is not itself prohibited. Rather, what is required, and prohibited, is force used to overcome female nonconsent. The prohibition is defined in terms of a woman's resistance. Thus, "forcible compulsion" becomes the force necessary to overcome reasonable resistance. When the woman does not physically resist, the question becomes then whether the force was sufficient to overcome a reasonable woman's will to resist. Prohibited force turns on the judge's evaluation of a reasonable woman's response.

In *State v. Alston*,[4] Mr. Alston and the victim had been involved in a "consensual" relationship for six months. That relationship admittedly involved "some violence" by the defendant and some passivity by the victim. The defendant would strike the victim when she refused to give him money or refused to do what he wanted. As for sex, the court noted that "she often had sex with the defendant just to accommodate him. On those occasions, she would stand still and remain entirely passive while the defendant undressed her and had intercourse with her." This was their "consensual" relationship. It ended when, after being struck by the defendant, the victim left him and moved in with her mother.

A month later, the defendant came to the school which the victim attended, blocked her path, demanded to know where she was living and, when she refused to tell him, grabbed her arm and stated that she was coming with him. The victim told the defendant she would walk with him if he released her arm. They then walked around the school and talked about their relationship. At one point, the defendant told the victim he was going to "fix" her face; when told that their relationship was over, the defendant stated that he had a "right" to have sex with her again. The two went to the house of a friend. The defendant asked her if she was "ready," and the victim told him she did not want to have sexual relations. The defendant pulled her up from the chair, undressed her, pushed her legs apart, and penetrated her. She cried.

The defendant was convicted of rape, and his conviction was affirmed by the intermediate court of appeals. On appeal, the North Carolina Supreme Court agreed that the victim was not required to resist physically to establish nonconsent: The victim's testimony that she did not consent was "unequivocal" and her testimony provided substantial evidence that the act of sexual intercourse was against her will.

But the North Carolina Supreme Court nonetheless reversed on the ground that, even viewing the evidence in the light most favorable to the state, the element of force had not been established by substantial evidence. The victim did not "resist"—physically, at least. And her failure to resist, in the court's evaluation, was not a result of what the defendant did before penetration. Therefore, there was no "force."

The force used outside the school, and the threats made on the walk, "although they may have induced fear," were considered to be "unrelated to the act of sexual intercourse." Indeed, the court emphasized that the victim testified that it was not what the defendant said that day, but her experience with him in the past, that made her afraid. Such past experience was deemed irrelevant. . . .

Later in 1984, the North Carolina Court of Appeals applied *Alston* to another case where the defendant and the victim knew each other and had had previous sexual relations. In this case, however, the parties were not "boyfriend" and "girlfriend." They were a father and his 15-year-old daughter.

The defendant in *State v. Lester*[5] was the father of three daughters and a son. Prior to the parents' divorce, the defendant frequently beat the children's mother in their presence. He also beat his girlfriend and his son. He had a gun and on one occasion pointed it at his children. He engaged in sexual activity with all three of his daughters. He first had sexual relations with the daughter whose rape was at issue when she was 11 years old. Her mother found out and confronted the defendant. He swore never to touch her again, and then threatened to kill both mother and daughter if they told anyone of his actions. On both of the occasions in question, the victim initially refused her father's demand to take her clothes off and "do it." In both cases, she complied when the demand was repeated and she sensed that her father was becoming angry. The court held that the defendant could be convicted of incest, but not of rape.

. . . In each case [*Lester* and *Alston*], the court says and this is explicit, not implicit—that sex was without the woman's consent. It also says that there was no force. In other words, the woman was not forced to engage in sex, but the sex she engaged in was against her will.

Such a paradox is almost inevitable if one adopts, and then enforces, the most traditional male notion of a fight as the working definition of "force." In a fight, you hit your assailant with your fists or your elbows or your knees. In a fight, the one attacked fights back. In these terms, there was no fight in *Alston*. Therefore, there was no force.

I am not at all sure how the judges who decided *Alston* would explain the victim's simultaneous refusal to consent and failure to resist. For myself, it is not at all difficult to understand that a woman who had been repeatedly beaten, who had been a passive victim of both violence and sex during the "consensual" relationship, who had sought to escape from the man, who is confronted and threatened by him, who summons the courage to tell him their relationship is over only to be answered by his assertion of a "right" to sex—a woman in such a position would not fight. She wouldn't fight; she might cry. Hers is the reaction of "sissies" in playground fights. Hers is the reaction of people who have already been beaten, or who never had the power to fight in the first instance. Hers is, from my reading, the most common reaction of women to rape. It certainly was mine. . . .

Unable to understand force as the power one need not use (at least physically), courts are left . . . to look for threats of force. Technically, these threats of force may be implicit as well as explicit. But implicit to whom? That a woman feels genuinely afraid, that a man has created the situation that she finds frightening, even that he had done it intentionally in order to secure sexual satisfaction, may not be enough to constitute the necessary force or even implicit threat of force which earns bodily integrity any protection under the law of rape. . . .

The simplest approach would be to ask whether this woman's will to resist was in fact overcome by this defendant's actions. Is she lying, or did she submit because she was truly frightened? If she is not lying—and none of the courts suggested that any of the women in these cases

were actually lying—then affirm the conviction. But what about the poor man who didn't realize that the woman was overcome by fear of him, rather than desire for him? Properly regarded, such a man lacks *mens rea* as to force or consent.

A second approach resolves that problem without relying explicitly on *mens rea*. It asks instead: Were the defendant's acts and behavior intended to overcome this woman's will to resist? Under such a standard, . . . Mr. Lester [and] Mr. Alston . . . will have a hard time claiming that they didn't mean to succeed, and that success was not defined as creating a situation that would frighten the woman into submission.

A third approach probes whether the defendant's acts and statements were calculated to overcome the will of a reasonable woman. This standard . . . obviously allows men greater freedom than the second approach. It tolerates their exploitation of naive and gullible women by claiming that, in their "reasonableness calculation," the tactics should not have been threatening enough. Even at its best, the "reasonably calculated" standard creates something of a paradox: If most women have a different understanding of force than most men, then the reasonable calculation standard is one that asks how a reasonable man understands the mind of a reasonable woman. But at least it focuses primarily on the defendant's actions and thoughts and makes his guilt or innocence the center of the trial.

The final approach doesn't even do that. It judges the woman, not the man. It asks—as did the court in each of these cases—whether the will of the reasonable woman would have been overcome given the circumstances. The focus is on women generally, and on the victim as she compares (poorly) to the court's assessment of the reasonable woman. The court then proceeds to conclude that a reasonable woman's will would not have been overcome in those circumstances, because there is no "force" as men understand it.

Such an approach accomplishes two things. First, it ensures broad male freedom to "seduce" women who feel powerless, vulnerable, and afraid; the force standard guarantees men freedom to intimidate women and exploit their weaknesses, as long as they don't "fight" with them. Second, it makes clear that the responsibility and blame for such seductions belong with the woman. Because the will of a reasonable woman by definition would not have been overcome, a particular woman's submission can only mean that she is sub-par as women go or that she was complicitous in the intercourse. . . .

It is almost certainly impossible to expect that the law could address all of the techniques of power and coercion which men use against women in sexual relations. I am not suggesting that we try. Rather, I am suggesting that we do something that is actually quite easy—prohibit fraud to secure sex to the same extent we prohibit fraud to secure money, and prohibit extortion to secure sex to the same extent we prohibit extortion to secure money. . . .

CONSENT

This Section will examine what has long been viewed as the most important concept in rape law—the notion of female consent. Nonconsent has traditionally been a required element in the definition of a number of crimes, including theft, assault and battery. Thus rape may be the most serious crime to encompass a consent defense, but it is certainly not the only one. . . .

The justification for the central role of consent in the law of rape is that it protects women's choice and women's autonomy in sexual relations. Or, as one leading commentator put it: "In all cases the law of rape protects the woman's discretion by proscribing coitus contrary to her wishes." Not exactly. As discussed in the preceding Section, the law does not protect the woman from "coitus contrary to her wishes" when there is no "force." Secondly, the definition of nonconsent requires victims of rape, unlike victims of any other crime, to demonstrate their "wishes" through physical resistance. . . .

The 1981 case of *State v. Lima*[6] is . . . an example of the sort of rape case that is causing concern and division in the appeals courts today. . . .

Lima . . . involved an alleged rape in an open field involving no weapons and two individuals who knew each other. In *Lima*, the defendant had agreed to give his wife's 14-year-old cousin a ride home, and stopped at a park on the way.

Once there, he pinned her shoulder to the ground with his left hand and moved his right hand inside of her blouse to her breast. When she told him to remove his hand, he told her to "shut up" and began to unbutton her shorts. She protested, "Willy, why are you doing this to me, you're my cousin," and began to cry.

Both the court of appeals and the supreme court viewed the key issue in *Lima* as whether, on these facts, the prosecution had established the "earnest resistance" of the victim required by Hawaii law. The court of appeals answered the question in the negative, because the "only resistance shown by the record are the victim's pleas to appellant to stop and an attempt to push appellant off of her." In reversing, the Supreme Court of Hawaii made much of this "push" in its interpretation of nonconsent. . . . The court affirmed the conviction on the ground that the victim "did not simply lie supine and unresisting while the respondent had his way with her." Thus, it could not be said, as a matter of law, that "the complainant here did not exhibit a 'genuine physical effort' to resist."[7] Presumably, in Hawaii, to say no, cry, and then "simply lie supine and unresisting while [a man] ha[s] his way" is to consent to sex.

Hawaii is not unique in holding that a victim must do more than say no, at least in the absence of deadly force. In *Goldberg v. State*,[8] where the defendant brought a would-be modeling prospect to his fictitious and deserted "temporary studio," his conviction of rape was reversed both on the ground that the force used was insufficient and on the ground that the victim had failed to offer "real resistance." On the latter point, the court drew a bright line between verbal and physical resistance: "It is true that she *told* the appellant she 'didn't want to do that [stuff].' But the resistance that must be shown involves not merely verbal but *physical* resistance 'to the extent of her ability at the time.'"

No similar effort is required of victims of other crimes for which consent is a defense. In trespass, for example, the posting of a sign or the offering of verbal warnings generally suffices to meet the victim's burden of nonconsent. . . .

[T]he law puts a special burden on the rape victim to prove through her actions her nonconsent (or at least to account for why her actions did not demonstrate "nonconsent"), while imposing no similar burden on the victim of trespass, battery, or robbery. . . .

Were the purpose of the consent requirement really to afford autonomy to women, there is no reason why a simple but clearly stated "no" would not suffice to signify nonconsent. Viewing women as autonomous human beings would mean treating them as persons who know what they want and mean what they say. A woman who wanted sex would say yes; a woman who did not would say no, and those verbal signals would be respected.

From a woman's point of view, the danger in this position is that many women who say "yes" are not in fact choosing freely, but are submitting because they feel a lack of power to say "no." From some men's point of view, the problem is that some women who say "no" would be willing to say "yes," or at least to "go along," if properly pressured. The "no means yes" philosophy, from this perspective, affords sexual enjoyment to those women who desire it but will not say so—at the cost of violating the integrity of all those women who say "no" and mean it.

A system of law that has traditionally celebrated female chastity and frowned upon sex outside of marriage might be expected to err on the side of less sex and to presume nonconsent in the absence of evidence to the contrary. But if ours has now become a society in which women have been "liberated" to say yes, that provides all the more reason—if more were needed—to respect a no. If the stigma attached to saying yes has been eliminated, then so have the grounds for claiming that no means yes. . . .

The consent standard, like the force standard, thus emerges as another means to protect men against unfair convictions by giving them full and fair warning that their (forceful) advances constitute an unwelcome rape rather than a welcome, or at least accepted, seduction. An alternative approach to this fair warning problem would be to spell out the crime or crimes of "rape" in detail, without regard to the response of the woman. In fact, most courts recognize the use of deadly weapons or a threat of imminent death as criminal without the need for too much

reliance on the woman's response, at least most of the time. But to go further and prohibit all forms of physical force would inject the criminal law into what many conceive as private and appropriate choices: It is one thing to ban guns and deadly weapons, or even fraud and extortion, but quite another to say that "love bites" or vigorous thrashing or pushing is criminal regardless of consent.

Our inability or unwillingness to detail the sexual practices that we as a society will not tolerate, regardless of consent, creates the law's heavy reliance on the behavior of the woman. Because the law has provided that if the woman "consents"—regardless of the amount of force used—intercourse is not rape, men have a right to a fair warning as to consent. But the consent standard does not necessarily lead to the denial of autonomy to women, or to the "no means yes" philosophy. Quite the contrary, the consent standard could be viewed as a means to afford women their deserved freedom to engage in sex however they choose. . . . Indeed, a consent standard that allowed the individual woman to say "yes" as well as "no," to define all of the limits of permissible sex for herself and then to have that definition incorporated and respected in law, would be a means of empowering women. It could also expand liability for criminal sex to any man who refuses to respect those limits. . . .

The refusal of the law (and the society it reflects) either to limit the scope of seduction regardless of consent or to empower women through the consent standard creates the fair warning problem that demands a resistance standard as its answer. We could seek to prohibit certain forms of seduction. We could seek to empower women, at least when they say no. Both alternatives would mean less freedom for men to coerce submission and secure sexual access. Both would eliminate the need for women to resist physically. Having chosen neither, we have created a fair warning problem whose only solution, at least to many courts and commentators, is to interpret force and consent in ways that punish women for "complicity" in sex, making their conduct the determinant of liability and the subject of our verdicts. There is nothing inevitable about either the problem or the solution.

NOTES

[1]M. Hale, *The History of the Pleas of the Crown* 635 (1778). This statement is the usual basis for the "cautionary" instructions traditionally given in rape cases.

[2]Mistakes of fact which are unrelated to elements of the offense are irrelevant to guilt or innocence; those which exculpate do so precisely because they negate the required *mens rea* as to an element of the offense. Thus, it matters not at all if the defendant believed—reasonably or unreasonably—that his victim was a professional model (the example is suggested by one case in which the defendant's stated intent was to have intercourse with a model; the victim was a clerical employee of a modeling agency); it should matter if he believes she is consenting, however, because nonconsent is an element of the crime. In order for the prohibited act to be criminal, it should not be significant, for these purposes, whether nonconsent is considered to be part of the definition of the *actus reus* prohibited by rape law, or a required "circumstance." In either case, the prosecution should be held to prove that the defendant in fact had the requisite mental state, whether it is . . . purpose, knowledge, recklessness or even negligence, as to nonconsent. See G. Williams, *Criminal Law* 137 (1953) ("It is impossible to assert that a crime requiring intention or recklessness can be committed although the accused labored under a mistake that negatived the requisite intention or recklessness. Such an assertion carries its own refutation.") . . .

[3]*State v. Rush*, 289 Md. 230, 256, 424 A.2d 720, 733 (1981) (Cole, J., dissenting).

[4]310 N.C. 399, 312 S.E.2d 470 (1984).

[5]*State v. Lester*, 70 N.C. App. 757, 321 S.E.2d 166 (1984), aff'd, 313 N.C. 595, 330 S.E.2d 205 (1985).

[6]2 Hawaii App. 18, 624 P.2d 1374 (1981), rev'd., 64 Hawaii 470, 643 P.2d 536 (1982).

[7]643 P.2d at 541. . . .

[8]41 Md. App. 58, 395, A.2d 1212 (1979). . . .

REVIEW AND DISCUSSION QUESTIONS

1. Explain what Estrich sees as the basic dilemma of rape law. In what way does this dilemma reflect our society's view of sex?

2. American courts dealing with rape pay little attention to *mens rea*. Why have the results of this not been favorable to prosecutors and victims?

3. Assess the four reasons Estrich gives for her view that nonconsent as resistance is not a satisfactory substitute for *mens rea*.

4. Should a man who sincerely but falsely believes that a woman is consenting to sex be found guilty of rape? Does it make a difference whether his false belief is reasonable or unreasonable?

5. What is the "schoolboy" understanding of force, and how is it evident in the law of rape? What sort of force in necessary to constitute the crime of rape?

6. Explain the decisions in the *Alston* and *Lester* cases. What do they reveal about rape law? What, if anything, is deficient about the courts' understanding of force in these cases? According to Estrich, what four approaches might be used to determine whether sex in threatening situations constitutes rape? What are the two implications of the approach actually adopted by the courts in these cases?

7. Nonconsent is a required element of some other crimes besides rape. What is different about the role of consent in rape? What point do the *Lima* and *Goldberg* cases illustrate?

8. Should the law of rape be reformed? If so, how?

The Battered Woman's Defense

Cathryn Jo Rosen

Self-defense usually occurs when a person who is immediately threatened with death or serious harm attacks another in the name of self-protection. Normally such actions are treated as justified, rather than excused, since the law does not regard killing another in these circumstances as wrong. But as Cathryn Jo Rosen points out, it has become increasingly common for women to claim self-defense in circumstances other than the standard, face-to-face threats that law envisions. How, then, should law treat abused women who kill? Should society approve such "self-help" or should it hold such women criminally liable? Rosen discusses these questions, along with the justification of killing in self-defense more generally and whether the battered woman's defense should be seen more as an excuse of insanity than a justification based on self-defense.

Defining the battered woman's defense is not an easy task. The literature is full of claims that the defense is misconceived. Yet, even those authors who bemoan the misconceptions have difficulty arriving at a cogent definition of the term. Indeed, use of the term at all is widely disparaged. A number of writers repeatedly emphasize that the theory should be denominated "women's self-defense," perhaps to dispel the notion that there is a special exception to the normal rules of self-defense for battered women. Nonetheless, courts and the media relentlessly choose to adhere to the battered woman's defense phraseology.

One explanation for some of the confusion between "self-defense," "women's self-defense," and "battered woman's defense" may lie in the defense's historical development. The best descriptions of the battered woman's defense are by feminist lawyers who based their strategy on lessons learned while representing women who defended themselves against male aggression under circumstances that fell outside the setting of traditional self-defense. Self-defense rules were developed to acquit a man who kills to protect himself or his family against a threatened attack from a man of similar size and strength with whom the defender usually has had only a single encounter. Rules requiring like force, imminency of the threatened harm, consideration of only the circumstances surrounding the single encounter, and use of an objective reasonable man standard are more than adequate in such circumstances. Women, however, usually use deadly force to protect themselves under very different circumstances. Usually their male victims are larger and stronger and are not strangers. The woman's fear of the man will be influenced by her knowledge of his character and reputation for violence. Rules requiring like force, imminency, consideration of only the circumstances immediately surrounding the killing, and use of an objective reasonable man standard necessarily defeat the woman's claim.

The first successes for the notion of women's self-defense were not battered women's cases. In the early 1970s, feminists rallied to support the defense of Joan Little, a prisoner in a North Carolina jail who stabbed and killed a male guard. Little claimed that she stabbed the unarmed guard because he threatened to rape her. Ms. Little was acquitted on the theory of self-defense despite the arguable absence of equal force.

Two years later, Inez Garcia was acquitted by a jury after her second trial on homicide charges. She claimed a self-defense. Garcia was physically and sexually assaulted by two male acquaintances. Before leaving the scene, the men threatened to return and rape Garcia again. She took her shotgun and went to search for her assailants. Several hours later she found one of the men on a street and shot and killed him. Judged by an objective standard of reasonableness, Garcia's motive appeared to be vengeance rather than self-defense. The jury, however, was permitted to consider the defendant's ethnic background, her rape, and the men's threat to repeat their attack when determining whether she reasonably believed that the use of deadly force was necessary to avoid an imminent threat of serious bodily harm.

Soon acquittals of women, including battered women, who pleaded self-defense became common in many jurisdictions. The most important appellate victory for the feminist advocates of women's self-defense was in a case that did not involve a battered woman. In 1977, the Washington Supreme Court reversed Yvonne Wanrow's second degree murder conviction in a decision holding that use of the reasonable man objective standard of self-defense violated Wanrow's right to equal protection of the law. Wanrow shot an intoxicated, unarmed man whom she knew had a reputation for violence when he approached her in a threatening manner. At the time, Wanrow, who was five-foot-four, had a broken leg and was using a crutch. Recognizing that Wanrow's fear and perception of danger was affected by her status as a woman, the court held that use of the reasonable man standard in the jury instruction was improper because it deprived Wanrow of the right to have the jury consider her conduct in light of her own perceptions. The court directed that the jury on retrial should be instructed to apply a subjective, sex-specific standard of reasonableness.

Little, Garcia, and *Wanrow* involved situations in which an objectively reasonable observer of the confrontation would not have perceived that the aggressor threatened imminent death or serious bodily harm to the defendant nor have believed that defensive use of deadly force was the only alternative available. Application of traditional rules of self-defense inevitably would lead to a murder conviction. Defense counsel were able to persuade the courts that their mistaken beliefs that the circumstances justified self-help were subjectively reasonable given the particular experiences and perceptions of the defendants.

The same problems occur in battered women's cases, often in more extreme forms. In the late 1970s, feminist lawyers began to outline a defense strategy for battered women who kill their abusers. They combined the women's self-defense theory developed in cases like *Little, Garcia,* and *Wanrow* with the use of expert testimony on the psychological impact of an abusive relationship on battered women. The feminists assumed from the start that homicides committed by women are equally reasonable as homicides committed by men. The defense strategy is to persuade the judge and jury that a variety of social factors cause women to perceive imminent, lethal danger in situations where men would not. Although stemming from unique factors, women's perceptions of danger demand equal recourse to deadly force. This argument is necessary because traditional self-defense, permeated as it is by male experience, does not acknowledge that a woman's response to a set of circumstances could be reasonable even though it was different than a man's response to the same set of circumstances. Rather than requesting that battered women receive special treatment from the law, the creators of the defense hoped to encourage application of the law of self-defense in a sex-neutral, individualized manner to all women, including those who kill their abusers.

The feminists proposed to obtain equality under the law by removing stereotypical myths and misconceptions about battered women from the trial process. Yet their self-defense theory for battered women who kill depends upon persuading the judge and the jury to accept an alternate set of factual generalizations about women in general, battered women in particular, the efficacy of the criminal justice system, and society. These assumptions, which serve to remedy the failure of battered women who kill to prove the traditional elements of self-defense, include the following:

1. Women find it necessary to resort to self-help because the courts and police do not provide them with adequate protection from their abusers. Therefore, even in the absence of an imminent or immediate threat of harm, their belief that self-defense is necessary may be reasonable.

2. A woman's perception of danger will be affected by her smaller size, socialization regarding passive attributes of femininity, and poor physical training. Therefore, it is perfectly reasonable for a woman to believe an unarmed man may be able to kill her.

3. A woman may reasonably feel the need to use a weapon to protect herself from an unarmed assailant.

4. Consideration of surrounding circumstances should not be limited to the time immediately preceding the killing. Prior conduct of the victim toward defendant will influence her perception of the dangerous nature of his behavior at the time of the homicide. Prior specific acts of violence should be admissible as well as the victim's general reputation for violence.

5. Defendant's rage and desire for revenge is not inconsistent with self-defense.

These assumptions widen the scope of relevant testimony and constitute the framework for the argument that the defendant's belief that self-defense was necessary was subjectively reasonable. Borrowing from Fletcher's writings, the feminists argued that the reasonableness of the woman's act of self-help should be adjudged in a sex-neutral, individualized manner in which the individual defendant's characteristics and culpability are relevant. The jurors should be instructed to place themselves in defendant's shoes and determine under all the circumstances, including defendant's history as a battered woman, the reasonableness of defendant's belief that use of deadly force was necessary.

Among the trial tactics the creators of the battered woman's defense recommend is the careful and strategic use of lay and expert testimony to neutralize stereotypical prejudices and ideas that may interfere with the jury's ability to perceive the defendant's conduct as a reasonable act of self-defense. Although the expert testimony may take numerous forms, many defense attorneys have used expert psychiatrist or psychological testimony. Often it consists primarily of a description of Dr. Lenore E. Walker's cycle of violence and learned helplessness theories which together constitute the battered woman syndrome. The expert will describe the battered woman syndrome in general terms after which she may be permitted to testify that the defendant suffers from battered woman syndrome.

Expert testimony is used to show why, under the particular circumstances of the case, the defendant's conduct was reasonable and, therefore, justified. Theoretically, the woman's defensive action will be proved necessary and proportionate to showing how the defendant could perceive a threat of imminent danger in verbal threats alone, in nondeadly attack from an unarmed spouse, or from a sleeping man. The testimony explains why the woman stayed with her spouse despite the abusive relationship and why, on the occasion in question she may not have run away or sought assistance from friends, relatives, or the police despite an apparent opportunity to do so. Finally, the testimony explains why the woman cannot be faulted for becoming involved in an abusive relationship. Rather she is a victim of her social reality, responding to circumstances in accordance with the values of femininity and life-long marriage to which she was acculturated.

The problem is that such an inquiry is inconsistent with the theory of justification which assumes that anyone who does the same act under the same external circumstances has done the right thing. By including a certain psychological trait of the individual in the circumstances, we have moved closer to the theory of

excuse than to justification. Nonetheless, the feminist theory is based on the premise that explanation of the reasonableness of defendant's belief that use of deadly force was proportionate and necessary will establish that the woman's act was justified rather than excused. Feminists argue that recognition of the woman's act as justified rather than excused is crucial.

> [E]xcusable self-defense would imply that her response was typically and idiosyncratically emotional. The doctrine would perpetuate the views that the woman could not have been rational in assessing the danger and that the legal system must compensate for her mental and physical weaknesses. . . .
>
> Justification, on the other hand, would assume that society values a woman's and a man's lives equally, and thus considers women's lives worthy of self-defense. It would recognize that a woman has the capacity to correctly and reasonably perceive that the act is warranted, legitimate, and justified. Justification would encourage, indeed would compel, a legal recognition that a woman's capacity for reasonable judgment—comparable to that of a man's—can be the basis for engaging in the "correct behavior" of self-defense.[1]

This doctrinaire insistence on treatment of the battered woman's defense as a justification is unnecessary and may be fatal to widespread and successful use of the battered woman's defense. Most battered woman's defense cases involve situations in which the defendant was not, in fact, in imminent danger of death or serious bodily harm at her victim's hands. The defense relies on persuading the jury that the defendant suffered from an identifiable psychological syndrome that caused her to assess the dangerousness of the situation in a different manner than an average, ordinary person—including a woman who does not suffer from battered woman syndrome. In other words, acquittal is dependent upon proving that defendant had . . . a disability that caused a mistaken, but reasonable, belief in the existence of circumstances that would justify self-defense. It is a theory of excuse rather than of justification. Because defendant responded to internal and external coercive pressures, for which she was not responsible but which were created by her social reality as a battered woman, she is not to blame for her conduct. A person who did not suffer from battered woman syndrome, however, would be culpable under identical external circumstances. Indeed, successful use of the battered woman's defense theory depends in part on defense counsel's ability to persuade the court and jury that a person who did not suffer from battered woman syndrome would not be justified under identical objectively identifiable circumstances. This, however, is inherently inconsistent with the concept of justification.

Efforts to characterize artificially the battered woman's defense as a justification must ultimately lead to some of the current misapprehensions as to its nature and the fears that its adoption will ultimately lead to justification of all killings that the defendant subjectively believed were necessary and proportionate. Conversely, it may explain, in part, the tendency to incorrectly view battered women as bearing a special right to self-defense based on their victimized status alone. Recognition that the defense is categorized properly as an excuse rather than a justification may enhance the ability of battered women who kill to win acquittals. To present a complete defense, a defendant would still have to show that her belief that justificatory circumstances existed was subjectively reasonable. Because the defendant is excused rather than justified, however, there would be no chance that the conduct will be encouraged.

The fact that the battered woman's defense is more consistent with excuse theory does not answer the feminist concern that excusing battered women who kill, in circumstances they believe create a right of self-defense, may perpetuate undesirable views that women are by nature irrational and that their lives are unworthy of self-defense against a man. First, however, these concerns are overblown. Treatment of the battered woman's defense as an excuse does not preclude justifying women who kill men under objectively identifiable circumstances more akin to traditional self-defense. Second, for the same reasons that battered women should be excused for killing their spouses, men who kill under mistaken beliefs as to justifying circumstances should also be excused. Third, even if treatment

of the battered woman's defense as an excuse does lead to perpetuation of sex discrimination under the current law, it may be that the problem should be cured in a different manner than the feminists recommend. All self-defense should be treated as excused rather than justified conduct. Indeed, the difficulties that the courts and commentators have encountered with the battered woman's defense vividly illustrate the need for such a reconceptualization of the defense. Excused self-defense would better meet the needs of battered women, of the criminal justice system, and of society in general. . . .

Today, most American jurisdictions classify self-defense as a justification even though it traditionally developed as an excuse. As a result, principles of excuse have become merged with principles of justification in the law of self-defense. Consequently, results in some cases are illogical and inconsistent with basic principles of criminal law. The problem is particularly apt to arise when demands are made to justify self-help behavior that is harmful to society in instances where the actor cannot fairly be held blameworthy because of circumstances particular to that individual. Battered women who kill their abusers present the paradigm example of such cases. Although the defendant's conduct is understandable, and absolving her from moral blame is not difficult, we are hesitant to proclaim that the act was justified and therefore to be encouraged. Even in traditional cases, self-defense is, at most, permissible and tolerated. Treatment of all self-defense as an excuse would further the criminal justice system's interest in discouraging self help, promote society's interest in preserving the sanctity of human life, and fulfill the feminist goal of absolving battered women who kill of guilt without proclaiming that such women are inferior to men.

Justification requires that the actor chose to violate the criminal law only because it was the lesser of a necessary choice of evils. Classification of self-defense as a justification, therefore, requires that the defender's interest in life be regarded as superior to that of the unlawful aggressor's. The act is accordingly one that is encouraged because it was beneficial to society or at least created no harm. The qualitative balancing act required to justify killings in self-defense, however, is not easy to perform.

The law's prohibition against intentional killing coincides with contemporary society's emphasis on the importance of human life as the most valuable interest protected by the criminal law. Clearly, however, there are also circumstances when intentional killing is justified because of the benefit it confers upon society as a whole. The intentional killings originally justified by the criminal law illustrate such situations. For example, one who kills a military enemy in battle is justified, as is the officer who kills to prevent an act of terrorism or to apprehend a person who has taken others hostage. Similarly, if we assume for the moment that capital punishment is acceptable, the executioner's act of killing the condemned is certainly justified. In all of these circumstances (the list is not exclusive), one life is taken to save many lives and to enhance the power of the rule of law. And, except in the instance of war, arguably the person whose life has been taken already has been shown to be dangerous and a threat to society as a whole.

A classic self-defense case involves a situation in which the actor takes the life of another to save the actor's life. One life has been chosen over one other life and the choice has been made in contravention of the legal rule generally prohibiting intentional killings. In the best of cases, it is difficult to identify any benefit that might accrue to society in general as a result of the killing. Moreover, the common law has always had great difficulty making judgments that one human life is more valuable than another. The result is the rule that a person can only defend against unlawful force. Yet, even this rule, the basis of which is uncertain, does not entirely solve the problem. First, modern criminal codes, for the most part, classify at least those cases in which the mistake was reasonable as justified self-defense. The closer the law moves toward a subjective standard of reasonableness, the greater the threat to the attacker's basic human rights. The extent of the attacker's rights would be defined solely by the victim's judgment of what was the right response under the circumstances. Indeed, cases involving mistake regarding the perception that the victim was threatening unlawful deadly force could result in the taking of an entirely innocent life. The killing of an innocent victim cannot be justified rationally. Society has been harmed by the taking of an innocent life and the actor can only be acquitted under an excuse theory. Second, even an unlawful aggressor is not necessarily a threat to all society. The attacker may only be a threat to one other person, the defender. Therefore, self-defense can only be the lesser evil if the interests of the defender that the aggressor threatens are greater than the aggressor's interest in life.

A variety of theories have been suggested to support the relative devaluation of the unlawful aggressor's life. Robinson[2] postulates that, although the relative physical harms to be suffered by the defender and the aggressor are equal, the defender also has an interest in bodily integrity. When the right to bodily integrity is added to the defender's right to be free from physical injury, the aggressor's interest in freedom from physical injury is outweighed. This view, however, is problematic because it blithely ignores the fact that the aggressor must also have a right to bodily integrity.

Essentially, Robinson's theory is a forfeiture theory. The idea behind the moral forfeiture theory that self-defense is correctly classified as a justification is that by virtue of his act of aggression, the aggressor forfeits some interest or right he would otherwise have had—such as the right to bodily integrity, his interest in life, or his right to freedom from aggression. The forfeiture theories cannot withstand a number of difficulties. If the defender is mistaken as to the unlawfulness of the aggression, his act will still be justified. Yet, it is difficult to say that one whose aggression was not unlawful has waived any rights. Even when the aggressor's conduct is actually unlawful there are difficulties. The criminal law generally does not permit express consent to one's own death. Yet, any forfeiture theory presumes that the victim's act of aggression constitutes implied consent to the use of defensive force.

Ultimately, there probably is no acceptable calculus to support treatment of self-defense as a justification. Its modern classification as such is likely the product of historical accident. If the law were to recognize that even traditional self-defense is properly considered an excuse, the nonculpable defensive acts of many more people could be excepted from punishment without the threat of escalating societal violence.

The difficulty in devaluing the life of the aggressor is particularly acute in some battered women's cases. Many men who abuse their spouses never display aggressive or violent behavior outside the confines of their homes. Certainly, perpetrators of domestic violence are not nice people. Yet, it is doubtful that anyone seriously could argue that ridding society of people merely because they are not nice benefits all. Feminists assert that the abuser's intent to kill or seriously injure his wife makes his death nonharmful rather than his character as a wife-beater. A victim of battered woman syndrome, however, may be mistaken as to the true nature of her spouse's threats on a particular occasion. Even if the mistake is reasonable or if there is no mistake, the difficulty with the calculus remains. Proponents of the battered woman's defense sympathize so much with the defendant that they have a tendency to focus exclusively on the psychological and physical harm suffered by the woman while forgetting the abuser. His right to life, though, is equally important as the woman's.

One of the most difficult problems confronted by legal theorists is the question of whether killing a legally insane aggressor in self-defense can be justified. Forfeiture theories of self-defense that rely on devaluing the aggressor's interest in life, freedom from aggression, or bodily integrity because of his wrongful conduct disintegrate in cases where the aggressor is not culpable. This problem is particularly acute in battered woman's defense cases. If we sympathize with the women as being victims of their social reality, we must sympathize with the batterers as well. Abusers are not entirely morally reprehensible. According to psychological and sociological literature, they also are victims of "disease" or of their social reality. This makes it even more difficult for the legal system to determine that the abuser's life is less valuable than his victim's.

The most that can be said in battered woman's defense cases, as in all self-defense cases, is that society is neutral with respect to the killing. By treating such cases as instances of excuse rather than justification, the difficulties created by weighing qualitative values of human lives and according a lesser interest to a potentially "innocent" person can be avoided. An excuse analysis would lead to identical results—acquittal—but do so by focusing on the pressure confronted by the defendant and the lack of available options.

It is difficult to identify a positive benefit that accrues to anyone other than the killer from the taking of an aggressor's life in self-defense. Thus, there is no reason for the law affirmatively to encourage such conduct. To the contrary, classification of self-defense as a justification may be detrimental to society. The early common law failed to recognize self-defense as either a justification or an excuse because self-help was inimical to the goal of creating respect for the rule of law and, in turn, for governmental authority. Although lack of respect for properly constituted legal authority is not generally a problem today, the law still serves a vital function of discouraging self-help.

There are a number of reasons why self-help is contrary to the interests of modern society. Reliance on self-help tends to diminish respect for the rule of law. Self-help in the form of self-defense carries the additional problem of increasing the quantum of violence in an already violent society. More troublesome is the possibility that the more widespread resort to self-help becomes, the more often innocent people may be killed erroneously.

It is troublesome even when a person who is guilty of a crime becomes the victim of proper self-help. The constant decline in the number of capital crimes throughout American history attests to the general view that only the most vicious of intentional killers deserve to die for their deeds. We cling to the hope that criminals can be reformed, or at least deterred, if only they are subjected to incarceration, institutionalization, or community corrections. Most persons killed in self-defense would not have been eligible for capital punishment if duly convicted of their threatened crimes. This is particularly true of many of the abusive husbands in battered woman's defense cases.

The proportionate force, necessity, and imminence prerequisites for self-defense are designed to quiet the law's uneasiness about encouraging self-help. The requirement that deadly force only be used to counter deadly force is geared to ensure that the aggressor, in fact, will commit an intentional homicide if not met with defensive force. One must suffer nondeadly harm if use of deadly force would be the only way to avoid it. The necessity rule seeks to limit the use of self-help to circumstances in which there is absolutely no other alternative to striking back against the aggressor. It is intended to encourage the defendant to seek, in the first instance nonviolent or nondeadly defensive means. By requiring strict necessity, it is hoped that use of deadly force in self-defense will be considered only as a last resort. Finally, the imminence requirement is meant to restrict self-defense to those situations where there is no time to turn to actors in the criminal justice system to do their designated job and save the defendant from the need to resort to self-defense. Relaxation of any of these strict, narrow requirements raises the specter of justifying, and thus encouraging, self-help—conduct that the law and society prefer to discourage.

The battered woman's defense requires relaxation of all of these requirements. Rather than limiting the determination of whether these elements of the defense have been met to very limited, objectively ascertainable circumstances, defenders of battered women ask the courts to consider circumstances that would be unknown to the casual observer. Factors such as relative strength, the defendant's physical training, and the defendant's prior experiences with and knowledge about her victim are neither external nor objectively identifiable. Consideration of such circumstances is not compatible with the notion of self-defense as behavior that is justified and should be encouraged.

Even more worrisome, however, is the assumption underlying the battered woman's defense that self-defense is necessary in some situations—even when the threatened attack is not imminent—because the criminal justice system has not adequately protected women. This assertion supports the feminist demand that the concepts of imminence and necessity be broadened. Yet, it is exactly this notion that the law must suppress. For the logical corollary is that any person who believes reasonably or unreasonably, that the criminal justice system does not offer adequate protection can resort to self-help even though there may have been sufficient time to summon the aid of lawful authority. Even when we understand the actor's unusual need to resort to self-help, the actor's behavior may still be dangerous to society. If self-defense is a justification and if justified conduct is conduct we consistently encourage because it benefits society whenever similar circumstances arise, the defense cannot rationally be expanded to encompass the battered woman's defense. Indeed, it may be that if those who suffer from battered woman syndrome or other psychological trauma induced by their social reality are more likely to kill in self-help, the criminal law should be doing even more than it currently does to prevent them from doing so. Domestic abuse is a serious societal problem but promotion of vigilantism is certainly not the solution. Treatment of self-defense as an excuse allows the judge to make a determination that it would be unjust to convict the defendant while at the same time avoiding a determination that the defendant did the right and just thing and the consequent risk of increasing the quantum of violence in an all too violent society.

Just as the early common law's difficulty with condoning self-help has survived into late twentieth century America, the conflicting recognition that an individual whose life is threatened cannot be expected to die meekly also has survived. When self-defense is categorized as an excuse, it reflects the community's understanding that, under all circumstances, the defendant understandably believed that she had no option but to kill or be killed. Although self-help should not be affirmatively encouraged, the pressure to resort to self-help can be understood. A person who submits to these pressures is not culpable and should not be convicted of any crime. . . .

Battered women who kill their abusers in perceived self-defense present a special challenge to the criminal justice system, especially to the evolution of the law of self-defense. Although self-defense first appeared in the common law as an excuse, in the twentieth century it has been classified as a justification. Justified conduct is otherwise criminal conduct that under particular external, objectively identifiable circumstances did not harm society. Under these circumstances it was the exact opposite of a discouraged criminal act; it was an encouraged desirable course of conduct. Few cases in which self-defense is claimed, however, fit the model of a justification. The problem is that self-defense constitutes self-help, and self-help is inimical to the rule of law.

Battered woman's defense cases are illustrative of this policy conflict. Often battered women use deadly force in self-defense under external circumstances where their act is not objectively reasonable. The woman's status as a battered woman makes her resort to deadly force understandable; it is subjectively reasonable. It is, therefore, easy to conclude that the woman is not to be blamed for her actions and should not be convicted of homicide. To hold that she acted in self-defense, however, is a determination that her act was justified. To justify such conduct may result in the encouragement of self-help as the preferred solution to domestic abuse. On the other hand, to convict or to excuse women who act in self-defense is to treat women as inferior to men whose defensive acts are justified.

The solution to this dilemma is to return self-defense to its original theoretical basis as an excuse in all cases. Excuse recognizes that, even though self-help may not be desirable and may harm society, such conduct often results from a person's understandable inability to choose an alternative course of action due to overwhelming external or internal pressures. Treatment of self-defense as an excuse accommodates the defensive needs of battered women and other individuals who act in subjectively reasonable fear given their social reality. It allows the fact-finder to consider the defender's subjective beliefs without risking the possibility that all bona fide defensive acts, no matter how objectively unreasonable, will be condoned by the criminal law. Concomitantly, it furthers the criminal law's goals of preserving life and discouraging self-help.

NOTES

[1]Crocker, "The Meaning of Equality for Battered Women Who Kill Men in Self-Defense," 8 *Harvard Women's Law Journal* 121 (1985), no. 20 at 131 (footnotes omitted).

[2]Paul Robinson, "Criminal Law Defenses: A Systematic Analysis," 82 *Columbia Law Review* (1982): 199–291.

REVIEW AND DISCUSSION QUESTIONS

1. Describe the three legal cases Rosen discusses.
2. What are the assumptions that Rosen thinks feminists are urging the law to accept about women when they argue for the battered woman's defense?
3. Why does Rosen think it is preferable to understand these cases as raising questions about excuses rather than about justifications?
4. Explain the "subjective" standard of reasonableness. Why does Rosen question whether it should be used?

5. Describe the three prerequisites that the law demands before accepting self-defense as a justification.
6. Explain what Rosen concludes about the battered woman's defense.
7. Compare Rosen's argument with the position of Gabel and Harris on the *Inez Garcia* case as discussed in the Section 1 reading "Building Power and Breaking Images: Critical Legal Theory and the Practice of Law."

Is the Insanity Test Insane?

R. J. Gerber

The insanity defense is a source of continuing controversy. In this essay, R. J. Gerber critically reviews the main tests of insanity that the courts have devised: the M'Naghten test, the irresistible impulse test, the Durham test, and the Brawner test. All are unsatisfactory. After contending that insanity is not really a mens rea *issue at all, Gerber argues that the* mens rea *requirement in criminal law should not be eliminated and puts forward a proposal for restructuring the legal treatment of insanity that would avoid the problems with the preceding tests of insanity.*

[N]othing so preoccupies the arena of criminal law today as the fate of the insanity defense. Crime-conscious reactionaries . . . propose to inter the defense forever to curb its "unconscionable abuse." Liberal-minded reformers want to enlarge the categories of mental illness to avoid results such as *State v. Everett* where severe emotional trauma was of no avail in the sanity determination of a person who could only intellectually perceive right from wrong. Finally, some neoreactionaries of a radically liberal bent strive to abolish the defense completely as the first step toward the entire abolition of *mens rea* from criminal law. . . .

At the heart of the debate lurk two central issues: should the defense be modified or abolished? and secondly, what is the impact of altering the defense on the supposition of free will presumably at the cornerstone of criminal law itself? An approach to these major issues involves an investigation of the origin and history of the insanity defense, its various formulations, and the conflict between a "free will" vs. therapeutic concept of criminal responsibility. Of particular importance is an assessment of the advantages and disadvantages of the various existing tests, as well as the respective merits involved in the extremes of abolishing or widening the defense.

1. M'NAGHTEN AND HIS SICK MIND

The modern insanity defense derives from a bizarre English trial in 1843. Daniel M'Naghten, a wood turner in Glasgow, suffered the delusion that Sir Robert Peel, the British prime minister, as well as the Jesuits and the Pope, were all conspiring against him. He couldn't get at the Pope or the Jesuits, so he determined that Peel must die. M'Naghten went to London with his gun, and on January 20, 1843, in a garden next to the prime minister's house, he shot and killed Peel's secretary, Edward Drummond, believing him the prime minister.

His trial developed into a battle between medical knowledge and ancient legal authority. In anticipation of the insanity defense, the prosecutor opened with a detailed discussion of the background of criminal insanity. The origins of that defense deserve detailed review here as a prelude to understanding the eventual decision in M'Naghten's trial.

2. ORIGINS OF INSANITY DEFENSE

. . . Initially, insanity was not a trial defense but a tool for pardon. The English Crown used complete insanity as a reason to grant arbitrary pardons to convicted murderers. Madmen then were not persons but "akin to beasts" because they lacked reasoning powers. This notion bred the infamous "wild brute" or "wild beast" test of insanity. By Edward I's reign (1272–1307) the concept of insanity as "the King's grace" entered the trial process, where it functioned to mitigate punishment but not guilt.

By the time of Elizabeth I (c. 1581), a legal rationale existed for excluding certain groups from criminal responsibility. Infants and the insane were "non persons" for their supposed lack of moral capacity. They were exempted from punishment since they did not comprehend the morality of their acts. . . .

Between 1812 and 1840, three major cases framed the "wild beast" formula for insanity by requiring a total absence of criminal awareness at the time of the act. In these cases defendants, charged with murder, pleaded insanity. They all suffered from severe and actual mental disorders. On the total insanity test, one of the defendants was found guilty and executed; the other two were acquitted. . . .

From this historical record, the following conclusions emerge: first, the defense of insanity has never resulted in total freedom for the acquitted defendant. Kings and courts assumed that a defendant acquitted by reason of insanity should be restrained, not released.

Secondly, one notes the overwhelming correlation between insanity tests and free will: . . . Recurring analogies to children and "wild beasts" reflect the insane's deprivation of free will stemming from the disease of the will's counterpart, the intellect. . . . Little if any thought was given to defects in the will alone which might impair conduct.

Finally, throughout this historical excursus, one cannot escape the common law's hesitancy over partial vs. total insanity. Lying at the heart of this honest confusion as to which should exonerate are at least two important if ill-defined insights: first, sanity may be not an absolute, fixed state but a degree on a continuum with insanity—a conclusion implied by the fact that "wild beasts" and children *do* usually know rudimentary, moral differences and do intend their immoral acts. Secondly, one notes the suggestion, crystallized perhaps best for a time in the thirteenth century, that insanity should be a factor in the determination not of guilt but of pardon. These two clues are important pieces in the modern insanity jigsaw puzzle.

3. THE M'NAGHTEN TEST

At M'Naghten's trial in 1843, nine medical witnesses testified that M'Naghten was totally insane. Dr. Isaac Ray's book on forensic psychiatry was quoted to the court to attack Lord Hale's

more restricted test of criminal insanity and the English cases resting on it. The testimony was so convincing that Chief Justice Tindal nearly directed a verdict of insanity, surprisingly commenting to the jury: ". . . I cannot help remarking . . . that the whole of the medical evidence is on one side, and that there is no part of it which leaves any doubt in the mind." Instead he committed the case to the jurors who found the defendant not guilty on the ground of insanity. M'Naghten was committed to Broadmoor, a mental institution, where he later died.

After M'Naghten's trial, both Houses of Parliament and Queen Victoria debated whether M'Naghten's acquittal presaged a dangerously liberalized state of affairs. The fifteen common law judges were required to respond to five parliamentary questions. Their answers constitute the famous M'Naghten test of insanity. . . .

> To establish a defence on the ground of insanity, it must be clearly proved, that, at the time of the committing of the act, the party accused was labouring under such a defect of reason, from disease of the mind, as not to know the nature and quality of the act he was doing, or if he did know it, that he did not know he was doing what was wrong.

. . . M'Naghten's unequivocal recognition of the "right and wrong" standard as an established rule and the national attention it attracted at the time make it a case of special significance. With its sharp focus on the offender's ability to know right from wrong with respect to the particular act charged, M'Naghten clarified and brought order out of existing but confusing precedent and produced a distinct, workable rule from which the more modern tests for insanity have evolved. It is the formula used in the clear majority of the states. . . . It is a formula filled with paradox, not the least of which is that its own moral and cognitional criteria should have convicted rather than acquitted its namesake.

4. ANALYSIS OF THE M'NAGHTEN TEST

Under the M'Naghten Rule, the accused is not criminally responsible if a mental disease at the time of the act prevented him from knowing

(a) the nature and quality of the act or (b) that it was wrong. The basic postulate of the test is capacity to follow the right course once one is able to perceive it. Its emphasis is on the cognitive capacity to understand the moral nature of acts. The assumption is that when cognition is defective the personality as a whole is so impaired that the accused cannot "know" the wrongfulness of his actions. . . .

Above all, two phrases of the M'Naghten test cause major trouble: "disease of the mind" and "know." Courts have not precisely defined "disease of the mind," but this phrase clearly is not equivalent to all the various medical classifications of mental diseases. It takes its meaning instead from the rest of the test and thus becomes limited by the word "know." Noncognitive mental disorders are therefore not "diseases of the mind." . . . In effect, to qualify as a "disease of the mind," a malady must touch an accused's reflective powers so severely that he is deprived of knowledge of the nature and quality of his act, so that he did not know what he was doing was wrong.

The word "know" may become ambiguous for persons suffering from serious mental illness not directly cognitional. A sick person's knowledge is often divorced from all affect, somewhat like the knowledge that children have of propositions they can recite but cannot understand. The knowledge crucial for criminal responsibility ought to be an appreciation or awareness of legal and moral consequences, not an abstract philosophical assent to a proposition. . . . Mental illness usually does not destroy the minimal moral awareness required by the test; it may, however, destroy the capacity to use such knowledge to control behavior.

The M'Naghten test literally calls for total impairment; the accused must not know at all. Thus the traditional English hallmark of "total" insanity enshrined in the test continues to require a near impossibility. Few if any persons are "total" madmen; insanity is rather a matter of degree and context. . . .

5. THE IRRESISTIBLE IMPULSE TEST

Other tests have sought to remedy M'Naghten's defects. One of these, the infrequent "Irresistible Impulse" test, is well put by New Mexico's Supreme Court, which typically joins it to the M'Naghten test:

> Assuming defendant's knowledge of the nature and quality of his act and his knowledge that the act is wrong, if, by reason of disease of the mind, defendant has been deprived of or has lost the power of his will which would enable him to prevent himself from doing the act, he can not be found guilty.

The test represents the first wholesale amendment of M'Naghten. Text writers have misnamed this the "irresistible impulse" test; it is really a control test. Goldstein has found so many differing formulations of the test that "there is no monolith called the 'irresistible impulse' test." Their central idea, however, is loss of control, and their universal motivation is to remedy M'Naghten's omission of noncognitive control data.

Weighty objections, however, cut against a narrowly formulated control test that connotes the idea of sudden, impulsive or irresistible loss of control. Just as an intellectual interpretation of the M'Naghten knowledge requirement ignores emotional factors, a "sudden impulse" interpretation of the control test may restrict evidence and jury deliberations solely to immediacy, thus keeping from the jury the durational nature of an accused's mental condition. The "impulse" connotation fails to account for cases where loss of volition takes place not suddenly but gradually, as in cases of melancholia and paranoia. . . . It gives no consideration to the defendant whose mental disease is characterized by brooding, introspection and reflection. The connotation ascribed to "control" means that an individual with sufficient powers temporarily to control or forestall his impulses is legally sane even though he ultimately surrendered completely to these impulses. . . .

6. THE DURHAM TEST

In 1954, in Washington, D.C., the United States Court of Appeals for the District of Columbia Circuit reversed the conviction of a Monte Durham for housebreaking and petit larceny. The court held that Durham had presented enough evidence on the question of his insanity to raise an issue for decision under the District of Columbia's version of the M'Naghten test for criminal responsibility. In the course of an extensive opinion, however, the court rejected the M'Naghten rule in all its formulations and held that "a broader test" should be adopted for the District of Columbia: "[A]n accused is not criminally responsible if his unlawful act was the product of a mental disease or mental defect." . . .

Widely hailed by both jurists and psychiatrists, *Durham* seemingly represented a scientific advance in criminal jurisprudence. Clearly, it represents the psychiatrization of the criminal law, an attempt to transform into legal terms the notion that there are two modes of existence—one sane, and the other insane. The *Durham* standard views mental functioning as essentially unitary but multifaced. No single mental faculty determines the existence or nonexistence of sanity, just as no single faculty is responsible for the control of human behavior. Impaired control may result from a wide variety of causes in the psyche, not all of which are cognitional.

Yet ambiguities lingered with *Durham*. While the approach permitted the psychiatrist to testify on the full range of rational, emotional, and volitional elements influencing an individual's psyche, this test drew a single line on one side of which a defendant was held criminally responsible for his actions and on the other side of which he was completely exculpated. The test does not account for the psychic reality of a continuous graduated scale of responsibility. . . .

Defining "mental disease" became another acute problem. Early experience under *Durham* was that "mental disease" was synonymous with psychosis, with the apparent agreement of all the participants in the trial process. Psychiatrists believed that they were using a legal term with an understood legal meaning; lawyers believed they were using a medical term with a standard medical content. The problem burst into the open in 1957, when the staff of Saint Elizabeth's Hospital decided that nonpsychotic diagnosis—particularly, the diagnosis of "sociopathic personality disturbances"—would be explicitly recorded in reports of mental examinations, thus opening the insanity defense to a larger number of defendants. . . .

Ultimately at least [several] intertwined problems arose with the vague "mental disease" concept in *Durham*. In the first place, *Durham* failed to define the parameters of mental disease clearly enough to determine whether sociopathy would count. Durham himself was diagnosed a sociopath and held sane. Shortly thereafter one Blocker, on trial for murdering his wife, pled insanity, was diagnosed a sociopath, and also found guilty. One month later, however, when the St. Elizabeth's staff broadened its forensic concept of mental disease to include sociopathy, Blocker appealed and was granted a new trial. This sudden reversal of psychiatric opinion on the legal process provoked judicial tempers. . . .

The first problem brought a second: the domination of the courtroom by psychiatrists. Whereas Judge Bazelon [who wrote the *Durham* opinion] merely wanted to open the door to liberal psychiatric testimony, he in fact opened the floodgates to medical conjecture frequently inscrutable and just as frequently overbearing for judges and jurors. Particularly onerous to the jury's role was the tendency by psychiatrists to make unfounded statements regarding the vexing issue of just which psychic conditions did or did not cause the criminal act, thus permitting psychiatrists to determine criminal responsibility. . . .

7. BRAWNER: A NEW TEST

. . . In the *Brawner* case, the defendant's jaw had been broken in a fight. He returned half an hour later with a gun, fired five shots through a closed apartment door, and killed one of the occupants. Four expert witnesses agreed that Brawner was suffering from a psychiatric or neurological abnormality, variously described as "epileptic personality disorder," "personality disorder associated with epilepsy." The prosecution witnesses apparently regarded Brawner's actions as a normal response in the circumstances, a more or less legitimate response. He had been severely injured in a fight and was very vindictive. As one of the doctors testified, "I think I would, too, under the same circumstances, want to get even with somebody who broke my jaw."

Determined to abandon *Durham*, the *Brawner* court turned to the ALI's proposed rule of criminal responsibility:

1. A person is not responsible for criminal conduct if at the time of such conduct as a result of mental disease or defect he lacks substantial capacity either to appreciate the criminality [wrongfulness] of his conduct or to conform his conduct to the requirements of law.

2. As used in this Article, the terms "mental disease or defect" do not include an abnormality manifested only by repeated criminal or otherwise antisocial conduct.

. . . Critical reading of *Brawner in toto* reveals serious inconsistencies touching the insanity defense relative to *mens rea*. The court's jury instruction on insanity provides: "You are not to consider this defense unless you have first found that the government has proved beyond a reasonable doubt each essential element of the offense." This instruction obviously means that insanity becomes an issue only after a prior finding that the defendant (1) did the criminal act (2) with its defining mental element, viz., intentionally, knowingly, etc. The defense comes alive then only for defendants already inculpated in crime. As a separate issue from *mens rea*, the defense is not an evidentiary standard for weighing intent or free will at all but an escape valve for persons whose mental state, while criminal, is disturbed beyond the range of full responsibility.

Having established this commendable distinction between *mens rea* and the insanity defense, the court next erases that distinction completely in saying it refuses to abolish the insanity defense because its abolition would eliminate free will from the criminal law. The court could reach this conclusion only by confusing the proposal to abolish the insanity defense with the quite broader proposal to abolish *mens rea*. It further mistakenly assumes that the abolition of insanity would inaugurate strict liability crimes, i.e., criminality apart from criminal intent, when in fact that result follows only from the abolition of *mens rea*. These assumptions are inconsistent with the court's own suggested jury instruction. They contribute nothing toward clarifying the role of insanity relative to *mens rea*. . . .

In hopes of clearing the air for a possible solution, *Brawner* generates the need to analyze the following propositions anew: (1) insanity is not a *mens rea* issue; (2) *mens rea* should not be abolished, and (3) the insanity defense needs to be restructured.

8. INSANITY IS NOT A *MENS REA* ISSUE

Ennui over the proliferation of tests has spawned the proposal to abolish the insanity defense completely. Some critics have gone considerably further to urge the abolition of the defense not merely for its own sake but as a first step toward abolishing *mens rea* from criminal law. Before the ultimate merits of either proposal can be considered, it is imperative to realize that insanity is not properly a *mens rea* question, but a unique issue distinct from criminal intent.

Mens rea means criminal intent. It refers to the mental element which, together with a physical act, constitutes a crime. These mental elements, as defined by the Model Penal Code and most revised state codes, basically can appear in any one of three forms: (1) "Intentionally," (2) "Knowingly," or (3) "Recklessly, i.e., with disregard of known risks." Intentionally means acting toward a conscious criminal goal. Knowingly refers to acting with the awareness of the circumstances of the act. Recklessly means acting with the awareness that certain dangerous results are likely to occur. Any one of the three mental states constitutes *mens rea*.

Absence of criminal intent means that no crime has been committed, in effect, that a bodily movement occurred independently of the mind's acquiescence. The absence of *mens rea* thus establishes an innocence claim. This claim is not a defense but a denial that any crime occurred at all.

Insanity is a wholly separate matter. It is not an innocence claim denying a crime, but an excuse to an established crime. Insanity asserts that although a crime has occurred, some sort of irrationality colored the guilty criminal intent. It acts as a second wind, as a second string in the bow of an already guilty defendant. As *Brawner* confusedly perceived, insanity is not really a negation of intent or knowledge or disregard of risk but a psychic distortion coloring these guilty and quite compatible mental states. Like the similar excuses of infancy and necessity, insanity tacitly admits both the act and the guilty criminal intent but asserts the need for some exception from the punitive consequences of guilt.

The foregoing analysis supports two conclusions: the first is that the fates of *mens rea* and insanity are separate. Altering the defense does not entail the abolition of *mens rea* or of the free will postulate upholding *mens rea*. Hence the disutility of the widespread bellowing that the insanity defense is necessary in order to retain the entire concept of free will at the heart of the criminal law system.

The second conclusion is more psychiatric and factual: as any defense lawyer knows, the vast majority if not all insane criminals do actually intend or know or recklessly risk their criminal acts. To take one example which stands for all, M'Naghten himself quite obviously intended the death of the prime minister. He knew what he was doing, wanted its result, and knew that it was frowned upon by his peers. The same can be said for every or nearly every insane defendant. It is simply not the case that the insane are incapable of intention, deliberation, moral understanding etc.; rather, like "wild beasts" and children, their mental operations occur within an unusually restricted context of a certain few misinterpreted objects, the context of which prevents the usual inhibitions from arresting the criminal plan. One may say, of course, that the insane defendant didn't "fully" or "really" know what he was doing; but such an interpretation cannot cloud the fact that the insane's knowledge and intention nonetheless are notably at work in the planning of the criminal act, often to the point of being overbearing. In a word, insanity rarely if ever precludes a criminal *mens rea*.

If the insane do in fact intend and know their criminal acts, such evidence properly touches on a finding of *mens rea*, not of insanity. Hence, their fate on the guilt-innocence issue should be dependent upon the much debated fate of *mens rea*, not on the role of insanity.

9. *MENS REA* CANNOT BE ABOLISHED

The criminological positivists in the early 1900s first proposed to eliminate from the criminal law the entire *mens rea* requirement. While complex, their motivation was one of social defense which placed the security of society above the fate of the individual. In more recent years this proposal has taken a therapeutic pallor. Lady Wootten argues that *mens rea* must go because we cannot get inside a person's mind to really see intent at work.[1] Karl Menninger feels that all crime is really sickness, so there is no point in showing a sick mind in a criminal trial.[2] Kittrie urges the abolition of *mens rea* as the essential step toward a *"parens patriae* therapeutic state."[3] Their proposals are not directed precisely at insanity; they seek to eliminate *all* evidence of mental state from the criminal law so as to replace the concepts of guilt, blame, free will, and responsibility with the simpler concept of social danger.

Packer suggests several of the likely assumptions that underlie this therapeutic system of criminal law:

1. Free will is an illusion because human conduct is determined by forces that lie beyond the power of the individual to modify.

2. Moral responsibility, accordingly, is an illusion because blame cannot be ascribed for behavior that is ineluctably conditioned.

3. Human conduct, being causally determined, can and should be scientifically studied and controlled.

4. The function of the criminal law should be purely and simply to bring into play processes for modifying the personality, and hence the behavior of people who commit them in the future; or, if all else fails, to restrain them from committing offenses by the use of external compulsion (e.g., confinement).

5. We have . . . real knowledge about how to rehabilitate people.

6. We know how to predict those who exhibit traits that are dangerous.[4]

The advocates of this streamlined criminal law see it as more scientific, manageable, and forward-looking than the existing punishment-oriented free will system rooted in the moral concept of *mens rea*.

There are, however, any number of cogent reasons why *mens rea* cannot be abolished. At the phenomenological level, *mens rea* is simply a legalistic way of enshrining (perhaps confusing) certain patent nonlegal concepts that operate effectively in everyday noncriminal contexts. *Mens rea* is a crystallization of a pervasive but elusive rationale of responsibility based on assessment of purpose. In the everyday world, people intend goals, direct means to ends, and anticipate consequences of their acts. When a person is shoved in a crowd, for example, the "shovee's" response to the "shover" depends entirely upon whether the shove is interpreted as deliberate or accidental.

Similarly, punishment and administrative consequences differ for a person who causes an automobile accident through recklessness as opposed to a person whose automobile causes the same kind of accident through some non-controllable mechanical defect. Within the criminal law, *mens rea* adopts these everyday assumptions of intent for evaluating persons charged with crime. *Mens rea* thus is rooted not so much in legal history as in human history, in the everyday working predication of merit and blame on those who are deserving because they intend their acts. A public trial is a public morality play that serves to underscore these everyday concepts of intentionality and knowledge as valid criteria for evaluating behavior. *Mens rea* is actually an assertion that human society is a society of persons who do not view themselves as mere bodies moving as harmful vectors; persons

interpret the movements of other people as manifestations of intention and choice. We can and do read the intentionality of persons in and through their words and deeds. Abolition of *mens rea* from the law would not abolish it from the everyday world.

To this phenomenological analysis must be added a further, more psychological objection: abolition of *mens rea* makes for strict liability for all crimes, with the crimes themselves reduced to merely bodily acts. Manslaughter becomes undistinguishable from homicide, tax fraud no different than an error in arithmetic (and, of course, vice versa). Inchoate crimes like attempt and conspiracy become eliminated or, more likely, overextended. Many crimes would merge with torts; assault, battery, false imprisonment would be undistinguishable as crimes or torts, with the curious result that criminals might be subject to dollar damages and ordinary tort-feasors or accident-prone persons subject to prison or other criminal terms. Wootten's strict liability coalesces exactly with Skinner's notion that it is not the person but the environment which needs the blame—and the change. Crime is in the woodwork, not in the criminal. Every error becomes a crime.

To this Clockwork Orange scenario are two further, obvious objections: the emotional one is that such a degrading picture of human responsibility will never appeal to more than mad academics. The second is that the public experiences the "free will myth" in certain central acts like long-range planning and resistance to negative conditioning. This experience, valid or not, supports the assurance of free will resting at the heart of *mens rea*. Even if this is illusion, it is an illusion that all persons experience and which the criminal law necessarily reinforces.

The Wootten-Skinner-Menninger-Kittrie proposal to abolish *mens rea* is impractical for a final reason. It substitutes for "bad" and "mad" the nebulous concept of social deviancy, which would subject to state control not only the bad and the mad but all tort-feasors, idealist reformers and eccentrics—in a word, all nonconformists. This kind of law encroaches on all, for once guilt is abolished, so too is innocence. The trouble with a criminal policy based on social defense is that the individual has no defense against an infallible, static society. Such people as Martin Luther King, Daniel Berrigan, William Sloan Coffin and Henry David Thoreau need "treatments," if at all, differing in degree and in kind from that imposed on the violent armed robber and rapist. With the abolition of *mens rea*, criminal law loses any discriminating index of culpability and hence of disposition. Despite Wootten's deterministic assumption that crime is a unilateral bodily concept, the fact is that a mental chasm separates a genetic compulsion to crime (such as the XYY chromosome) from deliberate, prolonged defiance to a detested law (as in the instance of war protestors or civil rights activists). And neither of these *mens rea* covers a third, more commonplace situation where crime reflects a spontaneous attempt to capitalize on an immediate opportunity (as in most burglaries and auto thefts). The point is that mental state varies for varying crimes and its variation dictates varying degrees of culpability. If mental state becomes either a unilateral or a nonexistent concept in defining criminality, neither the severity of the crime nor the propriety of treatment can be determined.

10. INSANITY NEEDS RESTRUCTURING

Retaining *mens rea* need not blind one, as it did the *Brawner* court, to the problems involved in retaining any or all of the insanity tests. Regardless of form, each test has at least five lingering problems: (1) exclusion of certain evidence, (2) domination of the lay jurors by medical experts; (3) discrediting psychiatric testimony in the adversary process; (4) the conception of sanity in absolute rather than relative terms of degree on a continuum; and (5) the eventual inconsistency of detaining a person found not guilty by reason of insanity.

To solve these . . . problems . . . [we should] consider seriously the propriety of a two-phase court procedure in cases where sanity is at issue. Phase one would be a conventional criminal trial to determine two precise things: (1) whether the defendant did the act, and (2) whether he did it with its defining mental state. Affirmative findings on both of these by judge or jury would result in a guilty verdict. The only other alternative would be outright acquittal. . . . [I]nsanity evidence would be admissible only to the extent that it negates the precise *mens rea* defining the crime, which in modernized codes strictly means only to the extent it negates intentionality, knowledge, or consciousness of risk (or whatever other precise mental state is defined in the description of the offense). In practice, this means that very few insane defendants could successfully introject evidence of insanity in this trial. Certainly, M'Naghten himself could not, nor could Jack Ruby nor Lee Harvey Oswald, nor most truly insane defendants, since insanity is quite compatible with intent, moral awareness, and awareness of risk. Furthermore, where *mens rea* is really at issue, the kind of evidence adduced is not likely to be medical diagnoses but circumstantial, factual data touching on lack of planning, scheme, design, lack of awareness, etc. Except for the rare case where insanity may negate the required mental state, psychiatric jargon would not be introduced into evidence before a jury.

Following a guilty verdict, a second procedure would become available at the option of the defense: a court-ordered psychiatric test of the defendant by appropriate psychiatrists followed by a sanity hearing—a nonadversary procedure before a judge, not a jury. The narrow purpose of this hearing would be for evaluating evidence of reduced responsibility, including perhaps not only insanity but diminished responsibility or voluntariness generally. Unlike the trial, this hearing would determine if defendant's sanity is or was reduced to such a degree that it would be unjust to imprison him when other remedies are more likely to protect society and to assure his beneficial return to it. In practice, the dispositional alternatives would be not only prison but also hospitals and medical or community-related therapy programs. Most importantly, at the termination of this hearing, the judge would make a finding on the defendant's degree of sanity. . . . If the court found the defendant insane, the judge thereupon would amend the original jury verdict of guilt to "guilty of the act but insane." This amended verdict would be his mandate for committing the defendant to a treatment program rather than to prison. . . .

The advantages of such a proposal are obvious. In the first place, insanity and guilt would be retained as major factors in criminal law. Insanity would operate, however, not in the context of disputes over the wording of ambiguous medical tests, not in the context of the adversary guilt-innocence issue, but rather in the early common law tradition as a mitigating factor decisive in pardon and disposition. Precise insanity tests would be unnecessary at both the trial and the sanity hearing. . . . Criminal trials would speed up. Jurors would decide guilt but not medically mitigating factors. Prosecutors would not be encumbered with insanity defenses threatening loss of their cases. Defendants would possess, at their option, a second exculpatory string in their bows to mitigate guilt and to receive medical care. The truly insane would receive neither guilt nor punishment in the conventional sense. Such a procedure would remedy the absolutism of present insanity tests, which now envision insanity-sanity in all-or-nothing terms, when in fact sanity is a matter of fluctuating degree. Finally, this procedure would extend the use of insanity evidence to a far broader class than the predominantly serious felons who now invoke it, with the expectation that insane car thieves and burglars might get, at their option, psychiatric rather than purely penal attention, without having to confuse a reluctant jury to do so.

NOTES

[1]Wootten, *Crime and the Criminal Law* (1963).

[2]Menninger, "Medico-Legal Proposals of the American Psychiatric Association," *J. Crim. L. C. and P. S.*, 19 (1928), p. 367, 373. Lately Menninger has tempered his view to the confusing point where he now says crime "is not an illness, although I think it should be," in *The Crime of Punishment* (1968), p. 254.

[3]Kittrie's views are expressed best in "The Therapeutic State," *Wayne L. R.* 19 (1975), p. 871.

[4]Packer, *The Limits of The Criminal Sanction* (1969). Cf. also his "Enemies of Progress," *New York Review of Books*, Oct. 23, 1969, p. 17.

REVIEW AND DISCUSSION QUESTIONS

1. What is the M'Naghten test, and what are the problems with it?

2. Assess the strong and weak points of the irresistible impulse, Durham, and Brawner tests. Which is the soundest?

3. On what grounds does Gerber contend that insanity is not a *mens rea* issue? Do you agree? Compare Gerber's understanding of *mens rea* with that of Brandt.

4. What reasons can be given for abolishing *mens rea*? Do you agree with Gerber that it should not be abolished?

5. Assess Gerber's proposal for restructuring the legal treatment of insanity. Do you see any difficulties with it? Is the issue of insanity sometimes relevant to guilt? Does Gerber's proposal avoid the problems he has raised for the courts' various tests of insanity?

6. "Gerber's proposal would allow criminals to avoid punishment." Assess this statement, explaining why you agree or disagree with it.

What Is So Special About Mental Illness?

Joel Feinberg

Most legal writers argue that mental illness is not itself an independent basis of legal exculpation; at most it is evidence that one of the traditional excuses—compulsion or ignorance—applies. After explaining this view and why it is plausible, Joel Feinberg, professor of philosophy at the University of Arizona, raises some doubts about it. In particular, the standard view does not do full justice to the moral significance of mental illness as it bears on blame and punishment. At the heart of criminal behavior that is both voluntary and sick, Feinberg argues, is the irrationality of the criminal's motives. While punishment in such case may be justified to deter others, it does not seem to be an appropriate way of dealing with the offender himself.

Professor Dershowitz has [argued that] . . . mental illness should not itself be an independent ground of exculpation, but only a sign that one of the traditional standard grounds—compulsion, ignorance of fact, or excusable ignorance of law—may apply.[1] Mental illness, then, while often relevant to questions of responsibility, is no more significant—and significant in no different way—than other sources of compulsion and misapprehension.

Now although I am almost completely convinced that this is the correct account of the matter, I am nevertheless going to air my few lingering doubts as if they were potent objections, just to see what will happen to them. I shall suggest, then, in what follows, that mental illness has an independent significance for questions of responsibility not fully accounted for by reference to its power to deprive one of the capacity to be law-abiding.

1

At the outset we must distinguish two questions about the relation of mental illness to criminal punishment. . . .

1. How are mentally sick persons to be distinguished from normal persons?

2. When should we accept mental illness as an excuse?

The first appears to be a medical question that requires the expertise of the psychiatrist to answer; the second appears to be an essentially controversial question of public policy that cannot be answered by referring to the special expertise of any particular group.

Some psychiatrists may wish to deny this rigid separation between the two questions. They might hold it self-evident that sick people are not to be treated as responsible people; hence the criteria of illness are themselves criteria of nonresponsibility. But, obviously, this won't do. First of all, the fact of illness itself, even greatly incapacitating illness, does not automatically lead us to withhold ascription of responsibility, or else we would treat *physical* illness as an automatic excuse. But in fact we would not change our judgments of Bonnie and Clyde one jot if we discovered that they both had had 103-degree fevers during one of their bank robberies, or of Al Capone if we learned that he had ordered one of his gangland assassinations while suffering from an advanced case of chicken pox. Secondly, there are various crimes that can be committed by persons suffering from mental illness that can have no relevant bearing on their motivation. We may take exhibitionism to be an excuse for indecent exposure, or pedophilia for child molestation, but neither would be a plausible defense to the charge of income-tax evasion or price-fixing conspiracy. These examples show, I think, that the mere fact of mental illness, no more than the mere fact of physical illness, automatically excuses. We need some further criterion, then, for distinguishing cases of mental illness that do excuse from those that do not, and this further question is not an exclusively psychiatric one. What we want to know is this: what is it about mental illness that makes it an excuse when it is an excuse?

So much, I think, is clear. But now there are two types of moves open to us. The first is preferred by most legal writers, and it is the one about which I intend to raise some doubts. According to this view, there is nothing very special about mental disease as such. Mental illness is only one of numerous possible causes of *incapacity*, and it is incapacity—or, more precisely, the incapability to conform to law—that is incompatible with responsibility. Ultimately, there is only one kind of consideration that should lead us to exempt a person from responsibility for his wrongful deeds, and that is that he *couldn't help it*. Sometimes a mental illness compels a man to do wrong, or at least makes it unreasonably difficult for him to abstain. . . . But in other cases, as we have seen, mental illness no more compels a given wrongful act than the chicken pox does, or may be totally irrelevant to the explanation of the wrongdoing. . . . What counts, then, for questions of responsibility is whether the accused could have helped himself, not whether he was mentally well or ill.

Aristotle put much the same point in somewhat different but equally familiar language. A man is responsible, said Aristotle, for all and only those of his actions that were voluntary; to whatever extent we think a given action less than voluntary, to that extent we are inclined to exempt the actor from responsibility for it. There are, according to Aristotle, two primary ways in which an action can fail to be voluntary: it can be the result of *compulsion*, or it can be done in *ignorance*. Thus if a hurricane wind blows you twenty yards across a street, you cannot be said to have crossed the street voluntarily, since you were compelled to do it and given no choice at all in the matter. And if you put arsenic in your wife's coffee honestly but mistakenly believing it to be sugar, you cannot be said to have poisoned her voluntarily, since you acted in genuine ignorance of what you were doing.

Now if we take just a few slight liberties with Aristotle, we can interpret most of the traditionally recognized legal excuses in terms of his categories. Acting under duress or necessity, or in self-defense, or defense of others, or defense of property, and so on, can all be treated as cases of acting under compulsion, whereas ignorance or mistake of fact, ignorance or mistake of law, and perhaps even what used to be called "moral idiocy" or ignorance of the "difference between right and wrong" can all be treated as cases of acting in responsibility-cancelling ignorance. On the view I am considering . . . the mental illness of an actor is not still a third way in which his actions might fail to be voluntary; rather, it is a factor which may or may not compel him to act in certain ways, or which may or may not delude, or mislead, or misinform him in ways that would lead him to act in ignorance. Indeed, on this view, mental illness ought not even to be an independent category of exculpation on a level with, say, self-defense or mistake of fact. Self-defense and relevant blameless mistakes of fact always excuse, whereas mental illness excuses only when it compels or deludes. . . .

The nineteenth-century judges who formulated the famous McNaghten Rules were presumably quite sympathetic with the view I have been describing, that there really is nothing very special about mental illness. These rules are not at all concerned with neurotically compulsive behavior—a category which simply was not before their minds at the time. Rather, they were concerned with those dramatic and conspicuous disorders that involve what we call today "paranoid delusions" and "psychotic hallucinations." The interesting thing about the rules is that they treat these aberrations precisely the same as any other innocent "mistakes of fact"; in effect the main point of this part of the McNaghten Rules is to acknowledge that mistakes of fact resulting from "disease of the mind" really are genuine and innocent and, therefore, have the same exculpatory force as more commonplace errors and false beliefs. The rules state that, "when a man acts under an insane delusion, then he is excused only when it is the case that *if* the facts were as he supposed them his act would be innocent. . . ." Thus if a man suffers the insane delusion that a passerby on the street is an enemy agent about to launch a mortal attack on him and kills him in what he thinks is "self-defense," he is excused, since if the facts were as he falsely supposed them to be, his act would have been innocent. But if . . . he shoots his wife because, in his insane delusion, he thinks her hair has turned gray, that would not have been an allowable defense. Note that the mental disease that leads to the insane delusion in these instances is given no special significance except insofar as it mediates the application of another kind of defense that can be used by mentally healthy as well as mentally ill defendants. . . .

To summarize the view I have been considering: a mere finding of mental illness is not itself a sufficient ground for exempting a person from responsibility for a given action; nor is it a sufficient ground for finding him not to be a responsible or competent person generally, with the loss of civil rights such a finding necessarily entails. At most, in criminal proceedings mental illness may be evidence that one of the traditional grounds for moral exculpation—compulsion or ignorance—applies to the case at hand, and in civil commitment hearings it may be evidence of dangerousness or of cognitive impairment. But it has no independent moral or legal significance in itself either as an excuse or as a ground for commitment.

2

. . . But . . . I have a lingering doubt that the above account does full justice to the moral significance of mental illness as it bears on blame and punishment. I shall devote the remainder of my remarks to a statement of that doubt.

Let me turn immediately to the kind of case that troubles me. I have in mind cases of criminal conduct which appear to be both voluntary (by the usual Aristotelian tests) and sick. Let me give some examples and then contrast them with normal voluntary criminal acts.

First consider a nonviolent child molester. He is sexually attracted to five- and six-year-old boys and girls. His rational faculties are perfectly normal. He knows that sexual contacts with children are forbidden by the criminal law, and he takes no unnecessary risks of detection. For the most part, he manages to do without sex altogether. When he does molest a child he characteristically feels guilt, if not remorse, afterward. He has no understanding of his own motivation and often regrets that his tastes are so odd.

Next in our rogues' gallery is a repetitive exhibitionist. He has been arrested numerous times for exposing his genitalia in public. He does this not to solicit or threaten, but simply to derive satisfaction from the act itself: exposure for exposure's sake. For some reason he cannot understand, he finds such exposure immensely gratifying. Still, he knows that it is offensive to others, that it is in a way publicly humiliating, that it is prohibited by law, and that the chances of being caught and punished are always very great. These things trouble him much, and they often, but not always, lead him to restrain himself when the impulse to self-exposure arises.

My third example is drawn from a landmark case in the criminal law, one of the first in which kleptomania was accepted as an excuse: *State v. McCullough*, 114 Iowa 532 (1901). The defendant, a high school student, was charged with stealing a school book worth seventy-five cents. It was discovered that stolen property in his possession included "14 silverine watches, 2 old brass watches, 2 old clocks, 24 razors, 21 pairs of cuff buttons, 15 watch chains, 6 pistols, 7 combs, 34 jack knives, 9 bicycle wrenches, 4 padlocks, 7 pair of clippers, 3 bicycle saddles, 1 box of old keys, 4 pairs of scissors, 5 pocket mirrors, 6 mouth organs, rulers, bolts, calipers, oil cans, washers, punches, pulleys, spoons, penholders, ramrods, violin strings, etc." ["etc."!]. One can barely imagine the great price in anxiety this boy must have paid for his vast accumulation of worthless junk.

Finally, consider a well-off man who shoplifts only one kind of item, women's brassieres. He could easily afford to pay for these items and, indeed, often does when there is no other way of getting them, or when he is in danger of being caught. He does not enjoy stealing them and suffers great anxiety in worrying about being found out. Yet his storerooms are overflowing with brassieres. He burgles homes only to steal them; he assaults women only to rip off their brassieres and flee. And if you ask him for an explanation of his bizarre conduct, he will confess himself as puzzled by it as any observer.

Now, for contrast, consider some typical voluntary normal crimes. A respectable middle-aged bank teller, after weighing the risks carefully, embezzles bank funds and runs off to Mexico with his expensive lady friend. A home-owner in desperate need of cash sets his own house on fire to defraud an insurance company. A teenager steals a parked car and drives to a nearby city for a thrill. An angry man consumed with jealousy, or indignation, or vengefulness, or spite, commits criminal battery on a person he hates. A revolutionary throws a bomb at the king's carriage during an insurrection. These criminals act from a great variety of unmysterious motives—avarice, gain, lust, hate, ideological zeal; they are all rationally capable of calculating risks; they all act voluntarily.

How do the "sick" criminals in my earlier list differ from these normal ones? We might be tempted to answer that the pedophiliac, the exhibitionist, the kleptomaniac, and the fetishist are all "compulsives" and that their criminal conduct is therefore not entirely voluntary after all; but I believe it is important to understand that this answer is unsatisfactory. There is no *a priori* reason why the desires, impulses, and motives that lead a person to do bizarre things need necessarily be more powerful or compulsive than the desires that lead normal men to do perfectly ordinary things. It is by no means self-evident, for example, that the sex drives of a pedophiliac, an exhibitionist, or a homosexual must always be stronger than the sexual desires normal men and women feel for one another.

There is much obscurity in the notion of the "strength of a desire," but I think several points are clear and relevant to our purposes. The first is that, strictly speaking, no impulse is "irresistible." For every case of giving in to a desire, I would argue, it will be true that, if the person had tried harder, he would have resisted it successfully. The psychological situation is never—or hardly ever—like that of the man who hangs from a windowsill by his fingernails until the sheer physical force of gravity rips his nails off and sends him plummeting to the ground, or like that of the man who dives from a sinking ship in the middle of the ocean and swims until he is exhausted and then drowns. Human endurance puts a severe limit on how long one can stay afloat in an ocean; but there is no comparable limit to our ability to resist temptation. Nevertheless, it does make sense to say that some desires are stronger than others and that some have an intensity and power that are felt as overwhelming. Some desires, in fact, may be so difficult to resist for a given person in a given state at a given time that it would be unreasonable to expect him to resist. A dieting man with a strong sweet tooth may find it difficult to resist eating an ice cream sundae for dessert; but a man who has not eaten for a week will have a much harder time still resisting the desire to eat a loaf of bread, which just happens to belong to his neighbor. Any person in a weakened condition, whether the cause be hunger or depression, fatigue or gripping emotion, will be less able to resist any given antisocial impulse than a person in a normal condition. But, again, there is no reason to suppose that bizarre appetites and odd tastes are always connected with a "weakened condition," so that they are necessarily more difficult to resist than ordinary desires. And thus there is no reason to suppose that so-called sick desires must always be compulsive or unreasonably difficult to resist.

It might seem to follow that there is *no* morally significant difference between normal and mentally ill offenders, that the one class is just as responsible as the other, provided only that their criminal actions are voluntary in the usual sense. But if this is the proper conclusion, then I am at a loss to see what difference there can be between mental illness and plain wickedness. As an ordinary citizen, before I begin to get confused by philosophy, I sometimes permit myself to feel anger and outrage at normal criminals, whereas I cannot help feeling some pity (mixed, perhaps, with repugnance) toward those whose conduct appears bizarre and unnatural. But unless I can find some morally telling difference between the two classes of criminals, then these natural attitudes must be radically reshaped, so that the fetish thief, for example, be thought as wicked as the professional burglar.

There do seem to be some striking differences between the two classes, however, and perhaps some of these can rescue my prephilosophical attitudes. Most of them have to do not with the criminal's intentions, but with his underlying motivation—the basis of the appeal in his immediate goals or objectives. The first such difference is that the sick criminal's motives appear quite *unintelligible* to us. We sometimes express our puzzlement by saying that his crimes have no apparent motive at all. We cannot see any better than the criminal himself "what he gets out of it," and it overburdens our imaginative faculties to put ourselves in his shoes. We understand the avaricious, irascible, or jealous man's motives all too well, and we resent him for them. But where crimes resist explanation in terms of ordinary motives, we hardly know what to resent. Here the old maxim "to understand all is to forgive all" seems to be turned on its ear. It is closer to the truth to say of mentally ill wrongdoers that to forgive is to despair of understanding.

Yet mere unintelligibility of motive is not likely to advance our search for the moral significance of mental illness very far, especially if we take the criterion of unintelligibility in turn to be the frustration of our "imaginative capacities" to put ourselves in the criminal's shoes and understand what he gets out of his crimes. This test of imaginability is far too elastic and variable. On the one hand, it seems too loose, since it permits the classification as unintelligible (or even sick) of *any* particular passion or taste, provided only that it is sufficiently different from those of the person making the judgment. Some nonsmokers cannot understand what smokers get out of their noxious habit, and males can hardly understand what it is like to enjoy bearing children. On the other hand, once we begin tightening up the test of imaginability, there is likely to be no stopping place short of the point at which *all* motives become intelligible to anyone with a moderately good imagination and sense of analogy. The important thing is not that the sick criminal's motives may seem unintelligible, but rather that they are unintelligible in a certain respect or for a certain reason.

We get closer to the heart of the matter, I think, if we say that the mentally ill criminal's motives are unintelligible because they are irrational—not just unreasonable, but *irrational*. All voluntary wrongdoing, of course, is unreasonable. It is always unreasonable conduct to promote one's own good at another's expense, to be cruel, deceitful, or unfair. But in a proper sense of "rational," made familiar by economists and lawyers, wrongdoing, though unreasonable, can be perfectly rational. A wrongdoer might well calculate his own interests, and gains and risks thereto, and decide to advance them at another's expense, without making a single intellectual mistake. A rational motive, in the present sense, is simply a *self-interested* motive, or perhaps an intelligently self-interested one. The motives of mentally ill criminals are not usually very self-interested. The Supreme Court of Iowa, in overturning the conviction of young McCullough, held that the question of the jury should have been: did the accused steal because of a mental disease driving him by "an insane and irresistible impulse" to steal, or did he commit said acts "through excessive greed or avarice?" The Court's alternatives are not exhaustive. Very likely McCullough's impulses were neither irresistible nor "greedy and avaricious." Greed and avarice are forms of selfishness, excessive desires for material goods and riches for oneself. As motives they are preeminently self-interested and "rational." McCullough's sick desires, however, were not for his own good, material or otherwise. He stole objects that could do him no good at all and assumed irrational risks in the process. The desire to steal and hoard these useless trinkets was a genuine enough desire, and it was *his* desire; but it does not follow that it was a desire to promote his own good.

This point too, however, can be overstated. It may well be true that none of the mentally ill crimes we are considering is done from a self-interested motive, but this feature hardly distinguishes them (yet) from a wide variety of voluntary crimes of great blameworthiness committed by perfectly normal criminals. By no means all voluntary crimes by normal criminals are done from the motive of gain. Some are done to advance or retard a cause, to help a loved one, or to hurt an enemy, often at great cost to the criminal's self-interest. What distinguishes the sick crimes we have been considering is not that they are unself-interested, but rather that they are *not interested at all*. They do not further *any* of the actor's interests, self *or* other-regarding, benevolent or malevolent. The fetishist's shoplifting is not rational and self-serving; he attains no economic objective by it. But neither does it hurt anyone he hates nor help anyone he loves; it neither gains him good will and prestige, nor satisfies his conscience, nor fulfills his ideals. It is, in short, not interested behavior.

But even this distinction does not quite get to the very core of the matter. The fetishist's behavior not only fails to be interested; it fails even to appear interested to him. To be sure, it is designed to fulfill the desire which is its immediate motive; but fulfillment of desire is not necessarily the same thing as abiding satisfaction. He may be gratified or relieved for an instant, but this kind of fulfillment of desire leaves only the taste of ashes in one's mouth. The important point is that his behavior tends to be *contrary to interest*, as *senseless* almost as the repetitive beating of one's head against an unyielding stone wall. . . .

Not only are the motives of some mentally ill but noncompulsive wrongdoers *senseless*, they are senseless in the special way that permits us to speak of them as *incoherent*. Their motives do not fit together and make a coherent whole because one kind of desire, conspicuous as a sore thumb, keeps getting in the way. These desires serve ill the rest of their important interests, including their overriding interest in personal integration and internal harmony. They "gum up the works," as we would say of machinery, and throw the person out of "proper working order." The reason they do is that, insofar as these desires are fulfilled, barriers are put in the paths of the others. They are inconsistent with the others in that it is impossible for all to be jointly satisfied, even though it is possible that the others could, in principle, be satisfied together. Moreover, the "senseless" desires, because they do not cohere, are likely to seem alien, not fully expressive of their owner's essential character.[2] When a person acts to satisfy them, it is as if he were acting on somebody else's desires. And, indeed, the alien desires may have a distinct kind of unifying character of their own, as if a new person were grafted on to the old one.

The final and perhaps most important feature common to the examples of voluntary crimes by mentally ill persons is the actor's *lack of insight into his own motive*. The normal person, in rehearsing the possibilities open to him, finds some prospects appealing and others repugnant, and he usually (but not always) knows what it is about a given prospect that makes it appealing or repugnant. If robbing a bank appeals to him, the reason may be that the excitement, the romance, or (far more likely) the money attracts him; and if having more money appeals to him, he usually knows *why* it does too. Normal persons, to be sure, can be mistaken. A criminal may think it is the adventure that is attracting him, instead of the money, or vice versa. It is easy enough to be confused about these things. Often enough we can test our understanding of our own motives by experimental methods. I may think that prospect X, which has characteristics a, b, and c, appeals to me solely because of a; but then, to my surprise, prospect Y, which has characteristics a and b, but not c, *repels* me. Hence I conclude that it was not simply the a-ness of X after all that attracted me. Moreover, even a person who is a model of mental health will be often ignorant or mistaken about the *ultimate* basis of appeal in the things that appeal to him.

The mentally ill person, however, will be radically and fundamentally benighted about the source of the appeal in his immediate objectives, and the truth will be hid from his view by an internal iron curtain. He may think that he is constructed in such a way that little children arouse him sexually, and that is the end of the matter, hardly suspecting that it is the playful, exploratory, irresponsible, and nonthreatening character of his recollected childhood experiences that moves him; or he may think that "exposure for exposure's sake" is what appeals to him in the idea of public undress, whereas really what appeals to him is the public "affirmation of masculinity, a cry of 'Look, here is proof I am a man.'"[3] The true basis of appeal in the criminal's motivation may be, or become, obvious to an outsider, but his illness keeps him blind to it, often, I think, because this blindness is a necessary condition of the appeal itself. At any rate, his lack of self-awareness is no merely contingent thing, like the ignorance that can be charged to absentmindedness, unperceptiveness, objective ambiguities, or the garden varieties of self-deception. The ignorance is the necessary consequence, perhaps even a constituent, of the mental illness, which, taken as a collection of interconnected symptoms, is an alien condition involuntarily suffered.

3

We come back to our original question, then, in a new guise: why should the incoherent and self-concealed character of the mentally ill man's motives be a ground for special consideration when he has voluntarily committed a crime? Perhaps we should enlarge our conception of *compulsion* so that senseless, misunderstood motives automatically count as compulsive. If Jones's chronic desire to do something harmful is as powerful as, but no more powerful than, normal people's desires to do socially acceptable things, then we might think of Jones's desire as a kind of unfair burden. It is no harder for him to restrain on individual occasions, but he must be restraining it *always;* one slip and he is undone. He is really quite unlucky to have this greater burden and danger. The ordinary person is excused when he is made to do what he does not want to do; but the mentally ill man, the argument might go, is excused because of the compulsive weight of his profitless *wants* themselves.

There may be some justice in this argument, but there is little logic. When we begin to tamper this profoundly with the concept of compulsion, it is likely to come completely apart. If men can be said to be compelled by their own quite resistible desires, then what is there left to contrast compulsion with?

A more plausible move is to enlarge our conception of what it is to act "in ignorance"—the other category in the Aristotelian formula. The

kleptomaniac and the fetishist have no conception of what it is that impels them to their bizarre actions. As we have seen, their conduct may well seem as puzzling to themselves as to any observer. So there is a sense in which they do not know, or realize, what it is they are really doing, and perhaps we should make this ignorance a ground for exculpation; but if we do, we shall be in danger of providing a defense for almost all criminals, normal and ill alike. The bank robber, who is deceived into thinking that it is the adventure that appeals to him when it really is the money, has this excuse available to him, as well as the bully who thinks he inflicts beatings in self-defense when it really is the sight of blood that appeals to him. Lack of insight by itself, then, can hardly be a workable extension of the ignorance defense in courts of law.

It is plain, I think, why the penal law requires rather strict interpretations of compulsion and ignorance. One of its major aims is to deter wrongdoers by providing them with a motive, namely, fear of punishment, which they would not otherwise have for refraining from crime. In close cases involving competent calculators, this new motive might be sufficient to tip the motivational scales toward self-restraint. Mentally ill but rationally competent offenders of the sort I have been discussing, provided only that they *can* restrain themselves, are eminently suited for responsibility because the fear of punishment might make some difference in their behavior. But if they truly cannot help what they do, then the fear of punishment is totally useless and might as well not be induced in them in the first place.

Thus, from the point of view of what punishment can achieve for others, it is a perfectly appropriate mode of treatment for rationally competent, noncompulsive, mentally ill persons. But from the point of view of what can be achieved for the offender himself, I still think it is altogether inappropriate. Some of the aims of an enlightened criminal law, after all, do concern the offender himself. Sometimes punishment is supposed to "reform" him by intimidation. This no doubt works once in a while for normally prudent and self-interested offenders. For others, greater claims still are made for punishment, which is expected to achieve not merely effective intimidation but also moral regeneration of the offender. But if we treat the mentally ill criminal in precisely the same way as we treat the normal one, we can only bring him to the point of hopeless despair. The prisoner, still devoid of insight into his own motives, will naturally come to wonder how his so-called illness differs from plain wickedness. His bizarre desires will be taken as simply "given," as evil impulses with no point and no reward, simply "there," an integral and irreducible part of himself; and there is no one more pitiably incorrigible than the man convinced of his own intrinsic wickedness and simply resigned to it.

NOTES

[1]Alan M. Dershowitz, "The Psychiatrist's Power in Civil Commitment: A Knife that Cuts Both Ways." An abridged version of this talk was published in *Psychology Today*, 2/9 (Feb. 1969), 43–47.

[2]Hence the point of the ancient metaphor of "possession."

[3]Paul H. Gebhard et al., *Report on Sex Offenders* (New York: Harper & Row, and Paul B. Hoeber, 1965), 399.

REVIEW AND DISCUSSION QUESTIONS

1. Why does mental illness not automatically excuse an agent? What legal view of mental illness do Dershowitz and other writers defend?

2. How do the M'Naghten Rules fit with the preceding viewpoint?

3. How do "sick" criminals differ from ordinary ones? What difference is there between mental illness and plain wickedness?

4. Why does Feinberg reject the claim that mental illness is a form of compulsion?

5. According to Feinberg, what are the key features common to voluntary crimes by mentally ill persons? How do these features call into question the idea that insanity is not itself a defense?

6. Is punishment an appropriate response to crimes committed by rationally competent, noncompulsive, mentally ill persons? Explain why or why not.

7. How does Gerber's position in the previous essay compare with Feinberg's position and the position Feinberg criticizes?

The Cultural Defense in the Criminal Law

Editors, Harvard Law Review

How should the criminal law treat foreign nationals or recently arrived immigrants who commit crimes in the United States that reflect the cultural norms of the societies from which they have come? In this essay, which is an unsigned note written by editors of the Harvard Law Review, the case is made for the law taking account of different cultural values in deciding whether or not to punish. Resting the case on the American justice system's commitment to individualized justice and on the value of diversity, the editors argue that it is often unfair to people raised in other cultures to hold them to the same criminal standards as born or assimilated Americans. Nor, argue the editors, would recognizing this defense lead to a reduction in the level of deterrence. The essay concludes by considering the extent to which this defense should be allowed in American courts.

The values of individuals who are raised in minority cultures may at times conflict with the values of the majority culture. To the extent that the values of the majority are embodied in the criminal law, these individuals may face the dilemma of having to violate either their cultural values or the criminal law. Two recent cases in the United States illustrate this conflict and the difficult issues it raises for American jurisprudence. In People v. Kimura,[1] a Japanese-American woman's children died when she attempted to commit oyakoshinju—parent-child suicide—after learning of her husband's extramarital affair. According to the defense attorney and members of the Japanese community, in traditional Japanese culture, the death ritual was an accepted means for a woman to rid herself of the shame resulting from her husband's infidelity.[2] A second example of cultural conflict arose in a case in which a member of the Hmong tribe from the mountains of Laos living in the United States exercised his right under Hmong culture to execute his adulterous wife.[3] In both of these cases, the defendants were confronted with charges of felony homicide. Should cases like these proceed to trial, the defendants may attempt to raise an affirmative defense based on their cultural backgrounds—a 'cultural defense.'

This Note explores the possibility of developing a *'cultural defense'* in the criminal law. . . .

I. THE CURRENT ROLE OF CULTURAL FACTORS IN THE CRIMINAL LAW

Both American and British courts have been largely unwilling to allow variations between a defendant's culture and her society's majority culture to constitute an independent, substantive defense in criminal trials. Cultural factors, however, may be relevant insofar as they establish a case for one or more traditional criminal law defenses. Further, they may be important during the charging and sentencing phases of the criminal process when the prosecutor and judge can exercise discretion.

The role of cultural factors in establishing traditional criminal defenses is limited by their admissibility as evidence of the defendant's state of mind at the time of the crime. First, it may be possible in some cases to introduce cultural factors into court under the rubric of the insanity defense. The defendant might argue, for example, that his cultural values were so different

from the majoritarian values reflected in the criminal law that 'he lack[ed] substantial capacity either to appreciate the criminality [wrongfulness] of his conduct or to conform his conduct to the requirements of law.' Second, under existing legal doctrine, cultural factors may be relevant insofar as they negate the intent required to satisfy the definition of a crime. Thus, the defendant's cultural background could entitle her to recognized defenses that go to the question of intent; cultural factors could, for example, help establish a defense of mistake of fact or diminished capacity.

The American legal system also provides discretionary procedures that permit prosecutors and judges to take account of cultural variations. The prosecutor may consider extenuating circumstances when charging the defendant with a crime or when plea bargaining with the defense attorney. In Kimura, for example, the prosecutor allowed the defendant to plead guilty to voluntary manslaughter, even though the prosecutor believed that the deliberate, premeditated killing satisfied the technical definition of first-degree murder. The sentencing process also allows extenuating cultural variables to be considered. Sentencing statutes commonly give judges considerable latitude in fixing appropriate sentences. Courts have used this discretion in recognizing culture as a factor to be considered before imposing sentence. Cultural factors, in this context, serve not to exculpate the defendant, but to mitigate her punishment. Thus, even when the substantive law does not acknowledge the role of cultural factors, these alternative mechanisms may allow the legal system to consider such factors in determining the ultimate sanction to be applied.

II. THE RATIONALE FOR THE CULTURAL DEFENSE

. . . In most cases in which a cultural defense could be raised, there is little question that the defendant actually intended to commit the act for which she is being tried. For example, in State v. Butler,[4] members of an American Indian tribe deliberately killed an intruder who had desecrated their tribe's sacred burial grounds. Even if it could be shown that the defendants' cultural values differed significantly from those of the majority, it would be difficult to argue that the defendants did not intend to kill a human being. But if the trial court were willing to recognize an independent cultural defense, and if the defendants could demonstrate that under their tribal law the killing was considered condign punishment for an act of desecration and that they were entitled to inflict that punishment, then the defendants would have a defense to a crime that would otherwise qualify as murder. . . .

The American criminal justice system is committed to securing justice for the individual defendant. In the context of the criminal law, the ultimate aim of this principle of individualized justice is to tailor punishment to fit the degree of the defendant's personal culpability. The American legal system recognizes that, because of mitigating circumstances, it may be unjust to punish a particular defendant to the limits of the law. Consistent with the principle of individualized justice, courts have recently recognized new criminal defenses. The battered spouse defense, for example, was created in response to situations in which convicting the defendant would be unfair, but traditional defenses of self-defense and insanity would not be entirely appropriate.

Similarly, the principle of individualized justice militates in favor of the cultural defense. There are two situations in which strict application of the law might be unfair to a person raised in a foreign culture. First, such a person may have committed a criminal act solely because she was ignorant of the applicable law. Although ignorance of the law is generally no excuse in a criminal prosecution, fairness to the individual defendant suggests that ignorance of the law ought to be a defense for persons who were raised in a foreign culture. Treating persons raised in a foreign culture differently should not be viewed as an exercise in favoritism, but rather as a vindication of the principles of fairness and equality that underlie a system of individualized justice. It may be fair to impute knowledge of American law to persons raised in this country: various socializing institutions such as the family, school, and place of worship can reasonably be expected to have instructed these persons about the norms upon which society's laws are based. A new immigrant, however, has not been given the same opportunity to absorb—through exposure to important socializing institutions—the norms underlying this nation's criminal laws. The principle of individualized justice demands that the law take this factor into account.

Second, an ordinarily law-abiding person raised in a foreign culture may have committed a criminal act solely because the values of her native culture compelled her to do so. Mere awareness that her act is contrary to the law may not be enough to override her adherence to fundamental cultural values. Laws are more effective in commanding obedience when individuals internalize the underlying norms to the point where they believe that the law embodies morally correct values. A society's socializing institutions not only make its members aware of its norms, but also instill in its people a sense that they are morally obligated to abide by their culture's norms. Thus, persons raised in other cultures, who are subject to influences that inculcated in them a different set of norms, will likely feel morally obligated to follow those norms. Once norms have acquired this moral dimension, conformity with conflicting laws becomes more difficult. For this reason, a person's cultural background represents a relevant individual factor that a just legal system should take into account.

Through its commitment to individualized justice, the legal system advances a second principle that favors the recognition of a cultural defense: cultural pluralism. By judging each person according to the standards of her native culture, the principle of individualized justice preserves the values of that culture, and thus maintains a culturally diverse society. The United States should remain committed to cultural pluralism for several reasons. First, pluralism maintains a society's vigor. John Stuart Mill believed that 'what the improvement of mankind and of all their works most imperatively demands is variety, not uniformity.'[5] By absorbing cultural elements from a broad spectrum of ethnic groups, American culture has remained dynamic and creative, continually evolving as it weaves threads of various immigrant cultures into its fabric. Second, cultural pluralism emanates from the principle of equality underlying the American system of justice. Equality among different ethnic groups ultimately requires that each group respect other groups' right to be different and that the majority not penalize a minority group simply because it is different.

A third justification for encouraging cultural pluralism is that the amount of diversity in the United States measures, in part, the value that the majority places on liberty. Cultural pluralism is an inevitable product of this nation's commitment to liberty. In a nation with members drawn from diverse backgrounds, allowing people the freedom to live by their values will lead to a culturally pluralistic society. By quashing cultural values that diverge from mainstream norms, the majority foists upon all others a single orthodoxy—a result repugnant to the American political paragon. Finally, cultural pluralism not only reflects American ideals of liberty, but also may stand as a bulwark against despotism.

The cultural defense is integral to the United States' commitment to pluralism: it helps maintain a diversity of cultural identities by preserving important ethnic values. The cultural values that conflict with criminal laws are often among the most fundamental, involving questions of life, death, and morality. In traditional Lebanese Muslim communities, for example, the ideology of honor is a fundamental precept to which people look for guidance and around which they structure their social relations. Blanket repudiation of a cultural defense in a case in which a person's attempt to uphold that honor collides with the criminal law might be perceived as an official indictment of the principle of honor, rather than as a denunciation of the particular means of vindicating that ideal. If the United States wishes to remain a culturally diverse nation, it must be alert to this danger of overkill: in the zeal to quash certain undesirable values or manifestations of those values, the majority may inadvertently destroy desirable values as well. More disturbing perhaps than the risk of overkill is the possibility that repudiation of a cultural defense may send out a broader message that an ethnic group must trade in its cultural values for that of the mainstream if it is to be accepted as an equal by the majority. It is hard to imagine a system more likely to convince a person that the majority regards her culture as inferior than one that punishes her for following the dictates of her culture.

Individualized justice and cultural pluralism, however, are not the only ideals that are fundamental to society. Any commitment to these ideals must be constrained by a conflicting objective in the law: the desire to lay down a set of common values that society considers important for everyone to share. Perhaps the principal reason for imposing a set of common values is to maintain social order. Societies usually regard the preservation of social order—societal self-protection—as a primary aim. To maintain this order, it has been argued, societies must lay down a body of positive law that compels the obedience of all regardless of individual notions of morality: if each person were required to adhere to the law only to the extent that it was consistent with her own values, societies would tend toward anarchy. Legal systems attempt to compel this obedience by imposing punitive sanctions in order to deter people from breaking the law.

Deterrence can be divided into specific (or particular) and general deterrence. Specific deterrence is achieved when punishing the defendant discourages her from engaging in similar conduct in the future. General deterrence is accomplished when punishing the defendant dissuades others from emulating her conduct. Courts may oppose the cultural defense because they feel that it would undermine the specific deterrent effects of the law. A person punished for breaking a law would normally be less likely to misbehave again than one who received no punishment. Courts may also resist a cultural defense because they suspect that the defense would detract from the law's general deterrent effects. According to some observers, general deterrence is most effective when punishment for committing a proscribed act is certain. Thus, members of immigrant groups might be less deterred by the law if their transgressions could be excused by their cultural values.

In many cases, however, it is questionable whether recognition of the cultural defense would significantly impair the deterrent capacity of the law. Specific deterrence will often be needless in cases of culturally motivated crimes. In situations in which the defendant's conduct was triggered by extraordinary circumstances that are unlikely to recur, specific deterrence is unnecessary. More important, because these criminal acts often stem solely from ignorance of the existing laws—and not from any malevolent motive—punishment is unnecessary to deter similar conduct in the future: the mere invocation of the criminal process is likely to have a normative effect on the accused such that she will not commit similar violations in the future. Particularly if the defendant is informed that her ignorance will excuse her only once, then much of the specific deterrent effect of the law will be preserved. The defendant will know that she faces the regular punishment should she repeat her actions.

Punishing the defendant in cultural defense cases will serve as an effective general deterrent in only one of the two categories of culturally related crimes. In the first category—in which members of an ethnic culture commit crimes out of ignorance of the law—punishing the defendant may serve to instruct other members of her culture of the law, and thus may advance the goal of general deterrence. In such cases, however, punishment may not be necessary to accomplish this educational function. Efforts of local government agencies targeted at informing recent immigrant communities of the laws and other social norms would be a more far-reaching method of deterrence than punishing those few individuals who come in contact with the law. Moreover, such programs would avoid the unnecessary practice of making examples of the first few members of an immigrant community who violate the law. Such needless exemplary punishment conflicts with the moral principle of not deliberately causing human suffering where it can possibly be avoided.

In the other category of culturally related crimes—those motivated by a sense of moral and social compulsion—punishing the defendant may only marginally deter others in her culture whose actions are similarly motivated. Further, to the extent that extreme acts induced by adherence to cultural mores, such as oyako-shinju, are relatively rare, the threat to social order, and thus the need for deterrence, becomes less pressing. Although these extreme cases are highly publicized when they occur, it seems unlikely that many American women of Japanese origin will commit oyakoshinju upon learning of their husbands' infidelity or that many Hmong tribesmen living in America will actually exercise their cultural right to execute an adulterous wife.

An argument that might be raised against the cultural defense is that it would have a counter-deterrent effect, thus encouraging crime by its implicit guarantee of an excuse. As contended above, however, the threat of punishment may have only a marginal deterrent effect in many cases of culturally motivated crimes. Therefore, any loss in deterrence from a cultural defense would be, at most, minimal. Moreover, this argument about the counter-deterrent impact of the cultural defense could be leveled against every existing defense. The criminal law has been able to maintain social order despite the availability of defenses such as insanity and diminished capacity. In recent years, concern over deterrence has not prevented courts from recognizing several new defenses, including the battered spouse defense and the Vietnam veterans' defense. Experience with these and other defenses reveals that their acceptance by the judiciary has not undermined the ability of the criminal law to protect society.

Indeed, the protection of cultural beliefs through a cultural defense may actually further the goal of maintaining social order. A stable, respected order requires a system of internal norms that reinforce the law's external dictates. The American legal system must rely on moral restraints to guide behavior in the interstices where the criminal law is vague, ambiguous, or altogether silent. Cultural values provide norms of conduct to fill the gaps in the criminal codes: such values serve independently from legal sanctions as a check on undesirable behavior.

Recognition of a cultural defense is one way of preserving this nucleus of values that, although leading to undesirable behavior in some contexts, is conducive to law-abiding conduct in many others. For example, the emphasis that traditional Japanese culture places on living according to a principle of honor may create occasional tragedies in exceptional cases like Kimura, but it often serves to encourage desirable conduct. In addition, denial of a cultural defense may be perceived as evidence of disdain for an ethnic minority's cultural values. When an ethnic group's cultural values are ignored by the mainstream society, the group is likely to become alienated from the majority culture. Alienation could, in turn, engender hostility and intergroup conflict that disrupt social order.

However important societal self-protection may be as a reason for members of a society to share values, having a set of common values may also serve a more transcendent purpose. Common values may help to create a broad sense of community and common purpose among a society's people. Cultural pluralism run rampant may destroy any possibility of forging these bonds among a nation's cultural subgroups. Further, some argue that certain values represent a standard of morality to which all persons, regardless of upbringing, should aspire. The values that the criminal law seeks to impose on all ethnic groups may reflect fundamental aspects of a society's dominant moral code. Suicide rites involving children and rituals of marriage-by-capture, for example, may so shock moral sensibilities as to make the majority insist that the defendant's culture immediately abandon such practices regardless of how little impact isolated incidents of such acts have on social order. To the extent that a cultural defense preserves the cultural values of immigrant groups, the defense can be seen as inimical to any attempt to establish a set of common norms.

But insofar as society desires that ethnic communities accept a set of common norms, this objective may be hampered by disregarding a cultural group's fundamental values. Ethnic groups may adjust more readily to the majority culture when the majority respects their ways and when the majority recognizes that their cultures have something to offer. Given time, this approach will result in the acceptance of fundamental American values, but without the social costs that are incurred whenever the majority attempts to impose its values all at once on other cultures.

The desire to establish common values must also be constrained by America's commitment to cultural pluralism, which entails a belief that acceptance of all mainstream values is undesirable. The very meaning of cultural pluralism is that each ethnic group is entitled to retain certain cultural values, thereby maintaining its own identity. Although society would ideally reap only the benefits of diversity, avoiding the dark consequences seen in cases like Kimura, it may prove difficult to carve out of a culture particular values deemed 'undesirable,' or acts motivated by such values, without destroying other values that society should not disrupt through the criminal law. In order to maintain pluralism within the context of a society united by common values, immigrant groups must be given time to assimilate those common values. The cultural defense, meanwhile, would function as a buffer, protecting those ethnic values implicated by the criminal law.

America's commitment to the ideals of individualized justice and cultural pluralism justifies the recognition of the cultural defense. Although society has countervailing interests in imposing common values on all of its members, including the preservation of social order and the forging of common bonds, an appropriately defined cultural defense is consistent with the objectives behind these interests. The following Part attempts to define parameters that will make an accommodation of these competing objectives possible.

III. DEFINING THE SCOPE OF THE CULTURAL DEFENSE

Judicial rejection of a cultural defense may rest on the concern that once the defense is introduced, it will be impossible to define its proper scope. Thus, before courts recognize the defense, they must first identify factors that delineate its boundaries. These factors must determine in a principled way under what circumstances and to what extent a cultural defense should apply. Some of these factors can be derived from the principles of individualized justice and cultural pluralism. Other factors follow readily from the interests, such as societal self-protection and sense of community, that are promoted by common values. The crucial objective in defining the scope of the defense is to advance the goals of individualized justice and cultural pluralism while recognizing the concerns reflected in the desire for common values. The factors proposed below are each intimately tied to one or more of these three principles. The task of the courts would be to balance these factors in each case in order to arrive at the appropriate scope of the cultural defense.

The interest in societal self-protection directs courts to evaluate factors such as the probability of recurrence and severity of the crime in determining whether and to what extent to recognize a cultural defense in a particular case. Judicial receptiveness to a cultural defense should vary inversely with both the likelihood of recurrence and the severity of the crime. The greater the likelihood of recurrence of the proscribed conduct, the greater is the need to deter such conduct if social order is to be maintained; consequently, courts should be less receptive to a cultural defense. With respect to the question of severity, at least three variables are relevant. First, courts should consider whether the crime is victimless. Prohibition of self-regarding acts cannot readily be justified by considerations of societal self-protection. Second, if there is a victim, courts should inquire whether the crime is confined to voluntary participants within the defendant's culture. A cultural defense should more readily be admitted when the crime is limited to persons capable of meaningful consent who belong to that culture and subscribe to its tenets. Third, when there is a victim, courts should ask whether serious bodily or emotional harm was inflicted.

The desire for social order further demands that courts consider factors such as the identifiability, degree of self-containment, and size of the defendant's cultural group. Identifiability is important because membership in the exempted group would otherwise be difficult to ascertain, thus complicating the task of applying the defense. Self-containment is important because it tends both to insulate the rest of society from harm and to minimize the loss of general deterrence that may accompany a judicial decision excusing a particular forbidden act. Finally, the size of the exempted group is significant because exempting a large percentage of the population from a law would itself impose significant costs and would also send a conspicuous signal to the remaining population that the proscribed conduct is acceptable. When recognizing the cultural defense is likely to create any of these dangers, courts will understandably be loath to do so.

Consistent with the goals of individualizing justice and fostering cultural pluralism are factors that direct an inquiry into the influence of the defendant's culture on her behavior. Courts might, for example, measure the degree of the defendant's assimilation into the mainstream culture. The less assimilated the accused, the more compelling are justice-based arguments that it is unfair to punish her for not complying with the law. Moreover, the less assimilated the accused, the more a cultural defense will encourage pluralism by maintaining a spectrum of widely divergent values.

A desire to maintain pluralism should further lead courts to assess the importance of the cultural value that impelled the prohibited act. Because a cultural defense confers a partial 'exemption' from an otherwise legitimate law, only values of sufficient importance to the defendant's culture should be protected. Honor, for example, is considered a fundamental principle in the Japanese and Lebanese Muslim cultures. Thus, individuals in these cultures who are motivated by honor to commit prohibited acts may well be entitled to a cultural defense—subject, of course, to appropriate regard for social order and the desire to build a sense of community among all members of society.

By considering these factors, courts will be able to determine when and to what extent a cultural defense should apply. The precise way in which courts will balance these factors will, of course, vary from case to case. But as long as the evolutionary process of identifying and refining relevant factors is based on an accommodation of society's several interests in establishing a set of common values with the ideals of individualizing justice and maintaining cultural pluralism, courts can minimize interference with society's diverse cultures while preserving the stability of community life.

IV. CONCLUSION

Neither the current law nor discretionary procedures within the criminal justice system are adequate vehicles for dealing with cultural factors: what is needed is a formal cultural defense within the substantive law. It is often all too tempting for a society to betray its underlying values when confronted with overstated fears of violence and anarchy. In the case of American society, blanket repudiation of the cultural defense sacrifices two very important values—individualized justice and cultural pluralism. Perhaps more telling, the American legal system's rejection of the cultural defense reveals an underlying fear of beliefs that are different from ours. Immolating one's own children for the sake of honor, executing an adulterous wife, and lashing out at someone in order to break a voodoo spell may seem very bizarre—indeed barbaric and disturbing—to the majority. But this is no reason to attempt immediately to quash the values of foreign cultures. American society has thrived on tolerance, curiosity toward the unknown, and experimentation with new ideas. The legal system, however, recognizes that if tolerance, curiosity, and experimentation are carried too far, social disorder and disintegration of common values may result. The cultural defense would give courts an opportunity to strike the necessary balance among these competing interests.

NOTES

[1] No. A-091133 (Los Angeles Cty. Super. Ct. filed Apr. 24, 1985), cited in Sherman, Legal Clash of Cultures, Nat'l L. J., Aug. 5, 1985, at 1.

[2] See id. at 1, 26.

[3] See Cultural Defense Fails to Mitigate Wife-Slayer's Sentence, L. A. Daily J., Nov. 29, 1985, at 15, col. 1.

[4] No. 44496 (Lincoln Cty. Cir. Ct. filed Mar. 11, 1981), cited in Sherman, supra note 1, at 27.

[5] J. Mill, Endowments, in Essays on Economics and Society 617 (J. Robson ed. 1967).

REVIEW AND DISCUSSION QUESTIONS

1. Explain the values that lead toward recognizing the cultural defense.

2. How do the authors respond to the claim that the defense would undermine the law's ability to deter future criminal activity by these or other people?

3. What are the limits of the defense that the authors suggest? How should judges decide whether or not to accept a cultural defense?

4. The authors claim that American law should show respect for different cultural "values." What do they mean by that? Is accepting the cultural defense in the cases that are described a reasonable way to respect such values?

5. Do the authors of this article assume that "values" are relative to cultures? Explain.

6. How would Cathryn Jo Rosen respond to this defense, given her views on the battered woman's defense?

7. Should a commitment to pluralism require the encouragement of cultures that are oppressive or discriminatory? Explain.

12

THE RIGHTS OF DEFENDANTS

Among our most important legal rights as citizens are those that protect us from arbitrary police conduct and from unjust treatment by the criminal justice system. Many people, however, view skeptically the rights of criminal defendants because they believe that those whom the police arrest are usually guilty as charged. In "Convicting the Innocent," James McCloskey challenges this belief, arguing that at least 10 percent of those convicted of serious crimes are completely innocent.

The Fourth Amendment protects us from unreasonable searches and seizures, requiring that the police have probable cause before a warrant is issued. To enforce this right, the Supreme Court has held that illegally obtained evidence should be excluded from criminal trials. This is called the exclusionary rule, and in their essays, Malcolm Richard Wilkey and Stephen H. Sachs debate its wisdom. The Fifth Amendment provides that no one "shall be compelled in any criminal case to be a witness against himself," and the Sixth Amendment affords us the right to counsel, but specifying the exact nature and limits of these rights in real life situations is not always easy. In the controversial *Miranda, Williams,* and *Innis* cases, the Supreme Court has tried to spell out the exact procedural safeguards that the police must follow to respect these constitutional protections.

The vast majority of criminal cases are settled by plea bargains. Because trials are expensive and time consuming, without plea bargaining our criminal justice system would probably grind to a halt. Kenneth Kipnis argues, however, that plea bargains may violate one's right not to incriminate oneself and that they rarely produce a just outcome.

Some prosecutors have violated the rights of criminal defendants by making racial appeals in court, but how are we to assess defense lawyers who "play the race card" in favor of black defendants? And what are we to make of the argument that since white America has long oppressed African Americans, black jurors should now refrain from convicting black defendants even if they are guilty? Randall Kennedy takes up these issues in the final essay of this section.

Convicting the Innocent

James McCloskey

Most people assume that it is very rare for an innocent person to be convicted of a crime and that such a miscarriage of justice would be an isolated aberration in an otherwise sound system. James McCloskey of Centurion Ministries in Princeton, New Jersey, argues to the contrary. He estimates that at least 10 percent of those convicted of serious and violent crimes are completely innocent, and in this essay he examines seven major causes of wrongful convictions.

On most occasions when it has been discovered that the wrong person was convicted for another's crime, the local law enforcement community, if it has commented at all, has assured the public that such instances are indeed rare and isolated aberrations of a criminal justice system that bats nearly 1,000 percent in convicting the guilty and acquitting the innocent. And this view is shared, I think, not only by the vast majority of the public but also by almost all of the professionals (lawyers and judges) whose work comes together to produce the results.

I realize that I am a voice crying in the wilderness, but I believe that the innocent are convicted far more frequently than the public cares to believe, and far more frequently than those who operate the system dare to believe. An innocent person in prison, in my view, is about as rare as a pigeon in the park. The primary purpose of this article is to delineate why and how I have come to believe that this phenomenon of the "convicted innocent" is so alarmingly widespread in the United States. Although no one has any real idea of what proportion it has reached, it is my perception that at least 10 percent of those convicted of serious and violent crimes are completely innocent. Those whose business it is to convict or to defend would more than likely concede to such mistakes occurring in only 1 percent of cases, if that. Regardless of where the reader places his estimate, these percentages, when converted into absolute numbers, tell us that thousands and even tens of thousands of innocent people languish in prisons across the nation.

Allow me to outline briefly the ground of experience on which I stand and speak. For the past eight years I have been working full time on behalf of the innocent in prison. To date, the nonprofit organization I founded to do this work has freed and vindicated three innocent lifers in New Jersey. Another, on Texas's death row, has been declared "innocent" by a specially appointed evidentiary hearing judge, who has recommended a new trial to Texas's highest court. Currently we are working on ten cases across the country (New Jersey, Pennsylvania, Virginia, Louisiana, Texas, and California). We have received well over 1,000 requests for assistance and have developed extensive files on more than 500 of these requests, which come to us daily from every state of the nation from those who have been convicted, or from their advocates, proclaiming their innocence. We serve as active advisors on many of those cases.

Besides being innocent and serving life or death sentences, our beneficiaries have lost their legal appeals. Their freedom can be secured only by developing new evidence sufficient to earn a retrial. This new evidence must materially demonstrate either that the person is not guilty or that the key state witnesses lied in critical areas of their testimony. We are not lawyers. We are concerned only with whether the person is in fact completely not guilty in that he or she had nothing whatsoever to do with the crime. When we enter the case it is usually five to fifteen years after the conviction. Our sole focus is to reexamine the factual foundation of the conviction—to conduct an exhaustive investigation of the cast of characters and the circumstances in the case, however long that might take. . . .

APPELLATE RELIEF
FOR THE CONVICTED INNOCENT

As all lawyers and jurists know, but most lay people do not, innocence or guilt is irrelevant when seeking redress in the appellate courts. As the noted attorney F. Lee Bailey observed, "Appellate courts have only one function, and that is to correct legal mistakes of a serious nature made by a judge at a lower level. Should a jury have erred by believing a lying witness, or by drawing an attractive but misleading inference, there is nothing to appeal." So, if the imprisoned innocent person is unable to persuade the appellate judges of any legal errors at trial, and generally he cannot, even though he suffered the ultimate trial error, he has no recourse. Nothing can be done legally to free him unless new evidence somehow surfaces that impeaches the validity of the conviction. Commonly, the incarcerated innocent are rubber-stamped into oblivion throughout the appeals process, both at the state and at the federal level. . . .

Once he is convicted, no one in whose hands his life is placed (his lawyer and the appellate judges) either believes him or is concerned about his innocence or guilt. It is no longer an issue of relevance. The only question remaining that is important or material is whether he "legally" received a fair trial, not whether the trial yielded a result that was factually accurate. Appellate attorneys are not expected to, nor do they have the time, inclination, and resources to, initiate an investigation designed to unearth new evidence that goes to the question of a false conviction. Such an effort is simply beyond the scope of their thinking and beyond the realm of their professional responsibility. It is a rare attorney indeed who would dare go before any American appellate court and attempt to win a retrial for his client based on his innocence. That's like asking an actor in a Shakespearian tragedy to go on stage and pretend it's a comedy. It is simply not done.

CAUSES OF WRONGFUL
CONVICTION

But enough of this post-conviction appellate talk. That's putting the cart before the horse. Let's return to the trial and discuss those elements that commonly combine to convict the innocent. Let me state at the outset that each of these ingredients is systemic and not peculiar to one part of the country or one type of case. We see these elements as constant themes or patterns informing the cases that cross our desks. They are the seeds that sow wrongful convictions. After one has reflected on them individually and as a whole, it becomes readily apparent, I think, how easy it is and how real the potential is in every courthouse in America for wrongful convictions to take place.

(A) PRESUMPTION OF GUILT

The first factor I would like to consider is the "presumption-of-innocence" principle. Although we would all like to believe that a defendant is truly considered innocent by those who represent and judge him, this is just not so. Once accusations have matured through the system to the point at which the accused is actually brought to trial, is it not the tendency of human nature to suspect deep down or even believe that the defendant probably did it? Most people are inclined to believe that where there is smoke, there is fire. This applies to professional and lay people alike albeit for different reasons perhaps.

The innate inclinations of the average American law-abiding citizen whose jury experience is that person's first exposure to the criminal justice system is to think that law enforcement people have earnestly investigated the case and surely would not bring someone to trial unless they had bonafide evidence against the person. That is a strong barrier and a heavy burden for the defense to overcome. And how about judges and defense lawyers? These professionals, like members of any profession, have a natural tendency to become somewhat cynical and callous with time. After all, isn't it true that the great majority of the defendants who have paraded before them in the past have been guilty? Why should this case be any different? As far as defense attorneys are concerned, if they really believe in their clients' innocence, why is that in so many instances they are quick to urge them to take a plea for a lesser sentence than they would get with a trial conviction? So, by the time a person is in the trial docket, the system (including the media) has already tarnished him with its multitude of prejudices, which of course, would all be denied by those who entertain such prejudices.

(B) PERJURY BY POLICE

Another reason for widespread perversions of justice is the pervasiveness of perjury. The recent District Attorney of Philadelphia once said, "In almost any factual hearing or trial, someone is committing perjury; and if we investigate all of those things, literally we would be doing nothing but prosecuting perjury cases." If he is guilty, the defendant and his supporters would lie to save his skin and keep him from going to prison. That is assumed and even expected by the jury and the judge. But what would surprise and even shock most jury members is the extent to which police officers lie on the stand to reinforce the prosecution and not jeopardize their own standing within their own particular law enforcement community. The words of one twenty-five-year veteran senior officer of a northern New Jersey police force still ring in my ears: "They [the defense] lie, so we [police] lie. I don't know one of my fellow officers who hasn't lied under oath." Not too long ago a prominent New York judge, when asked if perjury by police was a problem, responded, "Oh, sure, cops often lie on the stand."

(C) FALSE WITNESSES FOR THE PROSECUTION

What is more, not only do law officers frequently lie, but the primary witnesses for the prosecution often commit perjury for the state, and do so under the subtle guidance of the prosecutor. Inveterately, common criminals who are in deep trouble themselves with the same prosecutor's office or local police authority are employed as star state witnesses. In exchange for their false testimony, their own charges are dismissed, or they are given non-custodial or greatly reduced prison sentences. In other words a secret deal is struck whereby the witness is paid for his fabricated testimony with that most precious of all commodities—freedom!

Such witnesses are usually brought forward by the state to say either that the defendant confessed the crime to them or that they saw the defendant near the crime scene shortly before it happened, or they saw him flee the scene of the

crime as it was occurring. If I have seen one, I have seen a hundred "jailhouse confessions" spring open the prison doors for the witness who will tell a jury on behalf of the state that the defendant confessed the crime to him while they shared the same cell or tier. When the state needs important help, it goes to its bullpen, the local county jail, and brings in one of the many ace relievers housed there to put out the fire. As several of these "jailhouse priests" have told me, "It's a matter of survival: either I go away or he [the defendant] goes away, and I'm not goin'." Jailhouse confessions are a total perversion of the truthseeking process. Amazingly enough, they are a highly effective prosecutorial means to a conviction. Part and parcel of a jailhouse confession is the witness lying to the jury when he assures them that he expects nothing in return for his testimony, that he is willing to swallow whatever pill he must for his own crimes.

(D) PROSECUTORIAL MISCONDUCT

The right decision by a jury depends largely on prosecutorial integrity and proper use of prosecutorial power. If law enforcement officers, in their zeal to win and convict, manipulate or intimidate witnesses into false testimony, or suppress evidence that impeaches the prosecution's own witnesses or even goes to the defendant's innocence, then the chances of an accurate jury verdict are greatly diminished. Sadly, we see this far too often. It is frightening how easily people respond to pressure or threats of trouble by the authorities of the law. Our insecurities and fears as well as our desires to please those who can punish us allow all of us to be far more malleable than we like to think.

Few of us have the inner strength we think we have to resist such overreaching by the law. This applies to mainline citizenry as well as to those living on the margins. However, the underclasses are particularly vulnerable and susceptible to police pressure because they are powerless; and both they and the police know it. A few examples will illustrate.

In 1981 three white high school janitors were threatened by the Texas Rangers into testifying that they had seen Clarence Brandley, their black custodial supervisor, walking into the restroom area of the high school where the victim had entered only minutes before she had disappeared. Brandley was convicted and sentenced to death based on the inferential testimony that since he was the last person seen near her, then he must have killed her. Eight years later Brandley was exonerated by the judge who conducted his evidentiary hearing when one of these janitors came forward and told how they had lied in implicating Brandley because of coercion by the investigating law officer.

On the eve of the Rene Santana trial in Newark, New Jersey, which was a year and a half after the crime, the prosecutors produced a surprise "eyewitness" who said he saw Mr. Santana flee the scene of the crime. A decade later that same witness visited Mr. Santana at New Jersey's Rahway State Prison and asked for his forgiveness after admitting to him that he had concocted the "eyewitness" testimony in response to intense pressure from the prosecutor's investigator. Since this "eyewitness" was from Trujillo's Dominican Republic police state, his innate fear of the police made him vulnerable to such police coercion.

Or how about the Wingo case in white, rural northwestern Louisiana? Wingo's common-law wife came forward on the eve of his execution and admitted that she had lied at his trial five years earlier because the deputy sheriff had threatened to put her in jail and forever separate her from her children unless she regurgitated at trial what he wanted her to say.

And in the Terry McCracken case in the suburbs of Philadelphia, a fellow high school student of the caucasian McCracken testified that he saw McCracken flee the convenience store moments after a customer was shot to death during the course of a robbery. The teenager was induced to manufacture this false eyewitness account after three visits to the police station. Among the evidence that vindicates McCracken are the confessions by the real robber/killers. So, you see, it not only can happen anywhere, it does happen everywhere; and it does happen to all different people, regardless of race and background.

Another common trait of wrongful convictions is the prosecutor's habit of suppressing or withholding evidence which he is obliged to provide to the defendant in the interests of justice and fairness. Clarence Darrow was right when he said, "A courtroom is not a place where truth and innocence inevitably triumph; it is only an arena where contending lawyers fight not for justice but to win." And so many times this hidden information is not only "favorable" to the defendant but it clears him. In Philadelphia's Miguel Rivera case the district attorney withheld the fact that two shopkeepers had seen the defendant outside their shop when the art museum murder was actually in progress. And in the Gordon Marsh case near Baltimore, Maryland, the state failed to tell the defendant that its main witness against him was in jail when she said she saw him running from the murder scene. One has to wonder what the primary objective of prosecutors is. Is it to convict, regardless of the factual truth, or is it to pursue justice?

The prosecution is the "house" in the criminal justice system's game of poker. The cards are his, and he deals them. He decides whom and what to charge for crimes, and if there will be a trial or whether a plea is acceptable. He dominates. Unfortunately, his power is virtually unchecked because he is practically immune from punishment for offenses, no matter how flagrant or miscreant. According to many state and federal courts, prosecutorial misbehavior occurs with "disturbing frequency." When the "house" cheats, the innocent lose. . . .

It is human nature to resist any information that indicates that we have made a grievous mistake. This is particularly true of prosecutors when presented with new evidence that impeaches a conviction and goes to the innocence of a person convicted by their office at a prior time, whether it occurred four months or forty years before. Not only are they coldly unresponsive to such indications but they quickly act to suppress or stamp them out. New evidence usually comes in the form of a state witness who, plagued with a guilty conscience, admits that he lied at the trial; or from a person completely new to the case who comes forward with his exculpatory knowledge. Without exception, in my experience, the prosecutor's office will treat that person with total contempt in its usually successful attempt to force the person to retreat into silence. If that doesn't work, it will dismiss such testimony as somehow undeserving of any credibility and blithely ignore it. This prosecutorial impishness reminds me of a little boy holding his hands to his ears on hearing an unpleasant sound.

The Joyce Ann Brown case is a poignant illustration of this kind of prosecutorial posturing. One year after Joyce's 1980 conviction for being one of two black women who had robbed a Dallas, Texas furrier and killed one of the proprietors, the admitted shooter was captured and pleaded guilty while accepting a life sentence. She also told her attorney that the district attorney had convicted the wrong woman (Joyce Brown) as her partner in the crime. She had never known or even heard of that Joyce Brown. With the district attorney fighting her with all of his might, Joyce sits in prison to this day trying to win a retrial as we try to develop new evidence on her behalf.

(E) Shoddy Police Work

The police work of investigating crimes, when done correctly and thoroughly, is indeed a noble profession. Law and order are essential to a cohesive and just society. Because police work is fraught with so many different kinds of pressures, it is rather easy for an investigation to go awry. The high volume of violent crime plagues every urban police department. Skilled detectives are few, and their caseloads are overwhelming. The "burnout" syndrome is a well-documented reality within police ranks. Interdepartmental politics and the bureaucracy stifle initiative and energy. The pressure to "solve" a case is intensely felt by the line detective and comes both from his superiors and the community and from his own ambitious need for recognition and advancement. If today's climate of "burn or bury" them puts more pressure on the detective to resolve, it also gives him more license to do so by whatever means.

Too often, as a result of the above factors, police officers take the easy way out. Once they come to suspect someone as the culprit, and this often occurs early within the investigation and is based on rather flimsy circumstantial information, then the investigation blindly focuses in on that

adopted "target." Crucial pieces of evidence are overlooked and disregarded. Some witnesses are not interviewed who should be, while others are seduced or coerced into telling the police what they want to hear. Evidence or information that does not fit the suspect or the prevailing theory of the crime is dismissed as not material or is changed to implicate the suspect. Good old-fashioned legwork is replaced by expediency and shortcuts. Coercive confessions are extracted and solid leads are ignored.

Before too long, momentum has gathered, and the "project" now is to put it on the suspect. Any information that points to the suspect, no matter how spuriously secured, is somehow obtained; and anything that points away from him is ridiculed and twisted into nothingness. The task is made much easier if the suspect has a police record because he should be "taken off the streets" anyhow. That kind of person is not only a prime suspect but also a prime scapegoat. An example of this is Clarence Brandley, who was mentioned earlier. He was arrested in late August four days after the crime and on the weekend before school was to begin. The high school where the rape and murder took place was flooded with telephone calls by scared parents who refused to send their children to school until the murderer was caught. The arrest of Brandley calmed the community, and school started as scheduled. It was after Brandley's arrest that the investigation then spent five hundred hours building the case against him.

(F) Incompetent Defense Counsel

The wrongly convicted invariably find themselves between the rock of police/prosecutorial misconduct and the hard place of an incompetent and irresponsible defense attorney. While the correct decision by a jury hinges on a fair prosecution, it also depends on dedicated and skilled defendant lawyering. And there is such a paucity of the latter. Not only are there very few highly competent defense lawyers but there are very few criminal defense lawyers, period. They are rapidly becoming an extinct species.

The current Attorney General of New Jersey not too long ago told the New Jersey State Bar

Association that finding quality private defense attorneys "may be the most crying need that we have." He also told this same assemblage that unless there is an adequate number of well-trained private defense lawyers, there will be little hope for justice. Of the 30,000 lawyers in New Jersey, the number of those doing primarily criminal defense work is only in the hundreds. At this same conference the First Assistant Attorney General pointed out that 85 percent of New Jersey's criminal cases are handled by the public defender system; and he wondered if there would be a private defense bar by the year 2000.

This means, of course, that 85 percent of those charged with a crime cannot afford an attorney, so they are forced to use the public defender system. As competent as New Jersey's full-time salaried public defenders generally are, their resources (budget and people) are vastly inadequate and are dwarfed by those of their adversaries (the local prosecutor's office). Moreover, they are so overwhelmed by the sheer volume of caseload that no defender can give quality attention to any one of his cases, let alone all of them. So, in response to this shortage, public defender cases are farmed out to "pooled" attorneys, who are paid a pittance relative to what they earn from other clients who retain them privately.

The experience of these pooled attorneys in criminal matters is often limited and scanty. In addition, they do not bring to their new-found indigent client the desired level of heart and enthusiasm for their cases. All of these conditions leave the defendant with an attorney somewhat lacking in will, effort, resources, and experience. Thus, the defendant goes to trial with two strikes against him.

What we have discovered as a common theme among those whose cases we have studied from all over the country is that their trial attorney, whether from the public domain or privately retained, undertakes his work with an appalling lack of assiduity. Communication with the defendant is almost nonexistent. When it does take place, it is carried on in a hurried, callous, and dismissive manner. Attempts at discovery are made perfunctorily. Prosecutors are not pressed for this material. Investigation is

shallow and narrow, if conducted at all. Preparation meets minimal standards. And advocacy at trial is weak. Cross-examination is superficial and tentative.

Physical evidence is left untested, and forensic experts are not called to rebut whatever scientific evidence the state introduces through its criminalists. I cannot help thinking of the Nate Walker case, where, at Nate's 1976 trial for rape and kidnapping, the doctor who examined the victim the night of her ordeal testified that he found semen in her vaginal cavity. Walker's privately retained attorney had no questions for the doctor when it came time for cross-examination, nor did he even ask anyone to test the vaginal semen for blood type. Twelve years later, that test was performed at our request, and Walker was exonerated and immediately freed. . . .

(G) NATURE OF CONVICTING EVIDENCE

The unschooled public largely and erroneously believes that convictions are mostly obtained through the use of one form of tangible evidence or another. This naive impression is shaped by watching too many TV shows like Perry Mason or Matlock. The reality is that in most criminal trials the verdict more often than not hinges on whose witnesses—the state's or defendant's—the jury chooses to believe. It boils down to a matter of credibility. There is no "smoking gun" scientific evidence that clearly points to the defendant. This puts an extremely heavy burden on the jury. It must somehow ferret out and piece together the truth from substantially inconsistent and contradictory testimony between and within each side. The jury is forced to make one subjective call after another in deciding whom to believe and what inferences to draw from conflicting statements.

For example, how can a jury accept a victim's positive identification at trial of the defendant as her assailant when she had previously described her attacker in physical terms that were very different from the actual physical characteristics of the defendant, or when the defense has presented documented information that precludes the defendant from being the assaulter? Several cases come to mind. Boy was convicted of robbing a convenience store in Georgia. The clerk initially told the police that since she was 5 feet 3 inches, was standing on a 3-inch platform, and had direct eye contact with the robber, he must have been about 5 feet 6 inches tall. Boy is 6 feet 5 inches tall. Four teenage girls identified Russell Burton as their rapist on a particular day in Arkansas. Burton introduced evidence that on that day his penis was badly blistered from an operation two days before for removal of a wart. And a Virginia woman was certain that Edward Honaker was her rapist even though her rapist had left semen within her, and Honaker had had a vasectomy well in advance of the assault.

Criminal prosecutions that primarily or exclusively depend on the victim's identification of the defendant as the perpetrator must be viewed with some skepticism unless solid corroborating evidence is also introduced. Traumatized by a crime as it occurs, the victim frequently is looking but not seeing. Victims are extremely vulnerable and can easily be led by the police, through unduly suggestive techniques, into identifying a particular person. The victim in Nate Walker's case, for example, was with her abductor/rapist for two and a half hours with ample opportunity to clearly view him. She told the jury without hesitation eighteen months later that "he's the man." Nate had an ironclad alibi. The jury struggled for several days but in the end came in with a guilty verdict. As mentioned earlier, he was scientifically vindicated twelve years later.

When juries are confronted with a choice between a victim's ringing declaration that "that's the man" and solid evidence that "it couldn't be him," they usually cast their lot with the victim. I suggest that this can be a very dangerous tendency and practice. And this is particularly so when identification crosses racial lines, that is, when a white victim says it was that black person. Future jurors should be aware that identifications can be very unreliable forms of evidence.

Another type of evidence that can be misleading and even confusing to jurors is that offered by laboratory scientists. Results of laboratory tests that are presented by the forensic scientists are not always what they appear to be, although they strongly influence jury decisions. A recent New York Times article pointed out that there is a "growing concern about the professionalism and impartiality of the laboratory scientists whose testimony in court can often mean conviction or acquittal." This article went on to say that the work of forensic technicians in police crime laboratories is plagued by uneven training and questionable objectivity.

We share this mounting concern because we see instance after instance where the prosecutor's crime laboratory experts cross the line from science to advocacy. They exaggerate the results of their analysis of hairs, fibers, blood, or semen in such a manner that it is absolutely devastating to the defendant. To put the defendants at a further disadvantage, the defense attorneys do not educate themselves in the forensic science in question, and therefore conduct a weak cross-examination. Also, in many cases, the defense does not call in its own forensic experts, whose testimony in numerous instances could severely damage the state's scientific analysis.

One case profoundly reflects this common cause of numerous unjust convictions. Roger Coleman sits on Virginia's death row today primarily because the Commonwealth's Bureau of Forensic Science expert testified that the two foreign pubic hairs found on the murdered victim were "consistent" with Mr. Coleman's, and that it was "unlikely" that these hairs came from someone other than Mr. Coleman. The defense offered nothing in rebuttal, so this testimony stood unchallenged. In a post conviction hearing Mr. Coleman's new lawyer introduced the testimony of a forensic hair specialist who had twenty-five years of experience with the F.B.I. He testified that "it is improper to conclude that it is likely that hairs came from a particular person simply because they are consistent with that person's hair because hairs belonging to different people are often consistent with each other, especially pubic hairs."

Another problem that we continually observe within the realm of forensic evidence is the phenomenon of lost and untested physical evidence. Often, especially in cases up to the early 1980s, the specimens that have the potential to exclude the defendant have not been tested and eventually get misplaced. At best this is gross negligence on the part of both the police technician and the defense attorney in not ensuring that the tests be done.

CONCLUSION

. . . My contention is that at least 10 percent of those convicted for serious, violent crimes are incorrectly convicted because some combina-tion of the trial infirmities described in this ar-ticle results in mistaken jury determinations.

Everyone will agree that the system is not perfect, but the real question is this: To what extent do its imperfections prevail? I contend that for all the reasons detailed above the sys-tem is a far leakier cistern than any among us has ever imagined. Untold numbers of inno-cents have tumbled into the dark pit of prison. Some of them have eventually gained their free-dom, but a majority remain buried in prison, completely forsaken and forgotten by the out-side world.

REVIEW AND DISCUSSION QUESTIONS

1. What leads McCloskey to say that "inno-cence or guilt is irrelevant when seeking redress in the appellate courts"?

2. McCloskey identifies the following as causes of wrongful convictions: presumption of guilt, perjury by police, false witnesses for the prosecution, prosecu-torial misconduct, shoddy police work, incompetent defense counsel, and the nature of conflicting evi-dence. Assess what he has to say about each of these factors. Which do you think are the most important?

3. Are you persuaded by McCloskey that many innocent people are wrongfully convicted? If he is right, why is the contrary so widely believed?

4. What can be done to reduce or eliminate wrongful convictions? Which of the causes identi-fied by McCloskey could be most easily corrected? Which would be the most difficult to remedy?

5. Assume that McCloskey is correct about the number of wrongful convictions. What implications does this have for our adversary system? Is that sys-tem one of the causes of wrongful convictions, or is it part of the solution to that problem?

A Debate on the Exclusionary Rule

Malcolm Richard Wilkey and Stephen H. Sachs

The Fourth Amendment protects us from unreasonable searches and seizures, and it requires that po-lice warrants be issued only for probable cause. The important case of Mapp v. Ohio *provides a good example of an unconstitutional search and seizure. Here is how the Supreme Court described the events leading to the arrest of a certain Miss Mapp for having obscene material in her possession.*

On May 23, 1957, three Cleveland police officers arrived at appellant's residence in that city pursuant to information that "a person [was] hiding out in the home, who was wanted for questioning in connection with a recent bombing, and that there was a large amount of policy paraphernalia being hidden in the home." Miss Mapp and her daughter by a former marriage lived on the top floor of the two-family dwelling. Upon their arrival at that house, the officers knocked on the door and demanded entrance but appellant, after telephoning her attorney, refused to admit them without a search warrant. They advised their headquarters of the situation and undertook a surveillance of the house.

The officers again sought entrance some three hours later when four or more additional officers arrived on the scene. When Miss Mapp did not come to the door immediately, at least one of the several doors to the house was forcibly opened and the policemen gained admittance. Meanwhile Miss Mapp's attorney arrived, but the officers, having secured their own entry, and continuing in their defiance of the law, would permit him neither to see Miss Mapp nor to enter the house. It appears that Miss Mapp was halfway down the stairs from the upper floor to the front door when the officers, in this highhanded manner, broke into the hall. She demanded to see the search warrant. A paper, claimed to be a warrant, was held up by one of the officers. She grabbed the "warrant" and placed it in her bosom. A struggle ensued in which the officers recovered the piece of paper and as a result of which they handcuffed appellant because she had been "belligerent" in resisting their official rescue of the "warrant" from her person. Running roughshod over appellant, a policeman "grabbed" her, "twisted [her] hand," and she "yelled [and] pleaded with him" because "it was hurting." Appellant, in handcuffs, was then forcibly taken upstairs to her bedroom where the officers searched a dresser, a chest of drawers, a closet and some suitcases. They also looked into a photo album and through personal papers belonging to the appellant. The search spread to the rest of the second floor including the child's bedroom, the living room, the kitchen and a dinette. The basement of the building and a trunk found therein were also searched. The obscene materials for possession of which she was ultimately convicted were discovered in the course of that widespread search.[1]

To uphold the Fourth Amendment and deter the police from violating it, the Supreme Court has held in Mapp *and other cases that illegally obtained evidence should be excluded from criminal trial; that is, it should not be heard by the jury. This is called the exclusionary rule, and violation of it is grounds for an appellate court to overturn a conviction. Sometimes, of course, the excluded evidence may not only be reliable but may also be necessary to convict an undeniably guilty defendant such as Miss Mapp. Preventing the jury from hearing such evidence results in a guilty person going free. For this and other reasons, Malcolm Richard Wilkey, an appellate court judge, argues that the rule is irrational and should be replaced by a system that enforces the Fourth Amendment without letting guilty people off. Stephen H. Sachs, a Maryland prosecutor, contends, to the contrary, that the rule results in relatively few criminals being set free and that it is the only effective means of deterring the police and prosecutors from violating our constitutional rights.*

Wilkey: A Critique of the Exclusionary Rule

WHAT I PROPOSE

The time has come to abolish the exclusionary rule. This judicial creation has failed. Its alleged value has always hinged on the assumption, still unproven after seventy years, that it will deter police illegality. This doubtful gain is overwhelmed by the rule's horrible side effects, which are so destructive of the efficiency and integrity of our criminal justice system and whose costs are undeniable. Fourth Amendment suppression motions arise so frequently that, whether granted or not, they constitute the single issue most burdensome to the courts in criminal trials. And when a motion is granted the result is a manifest injustice—the exclusion of reliable evidence which may be essential to convicting the undeniably guilty. Moreover, the exclusionary rule perversely insures that the wrongdoer, the police officer who conducted the illegal search, escapes punishment as well. Under the rule's logic, two wrongs apparently make a right.

Abolition of the rule does not mean abolition of our constitutional rights. The exclusionary rule is not the Fourth Amendment, and it is not a constitutional necessity. It is clear from the way the rule originated in *Weeks v. United States* in 1914 that the Court was simply choosing a method of enforcing the Fourth Amendment. The search and seizure opinions of the Supreme Court for the last twenty years exhibit a reiteration by one Justice after another that this is *a* method of enforcing a constitutional protection, not necessarily *the* precise method commanded by the Constitution but instead one chosen by the High Court. . . . The Constitution prohibits unreasonable searches and seizures: It may mandate *a* remedy to enforce that prohibition, but nowhere does the Constitution mandate the exclusion of all other possible remedies.

Three workable legislative alternatives are available: an independent review board in the executive branch; a civil tort action against the government; and a mini-trial separate from the main criminal trial. One alternative which should *not* be adopted is the "good faith" exception advocated by the Attorney General's Task Force on Violent Crime. Although appealing to the extent that it reduces the number of guilty criminals who go free, the good faith proposal perpetuates all the other evils of the exclusionary rule and adds new additional costs.

Of all the civilized countries in the world, only the United States applies this demonstrably illogical exclusionary remedy to illegal searches and seizures of material evidence. The Congress should act decisively to repudiate the absurd notion that the United States alone is incapable of using its executive, administrative, and judicial processes *directly* to control the conduct of its law enforcement officials.

COSTS OF THE PRESENT IRRATIONALITY

In my monograph on the Fourth Amendment I have described at some length twelve costs of the exclusionary rule. Without going into a detailed description of each, well known to students of the exclusionary rule, let me enumerate these twelve undeniable costs for reference:

Cost 1: "The criminal is to go free because the constable has blundered."

Cost 2: Only the undeniably guilty benefit from the exclusionary rule, while innocent victims of illegal searches have neither protection nor remedy.

Cost 3: The exclusionary rule in any form vitiates all internal disciplinary efforts by law enforcement agencies.

Cost 4: The disposition of exclusionary rule issues constitutes an unnecessary and intolerable burden on the court system.

Cost 5: The exclusionary rule forces the judiciary to perform the executive branch's job of disciplining its employees.

Cost 6: The misplaced burden on the judiciary deprives innocent defendants of due process.

Cost 7: The exclusionary rule encourages perjury by the police.

Cost 8: The exclusionary remedy makes hypocrites out of judges.

Cost 9: The high cost of applying the exclusionary rule causes the courts to expand the scope of search and seizure for all citizens.

Cost 10: The exclusionary remedy is applied with no sense of proportion to the crime of the accused.

Cost 11: The exclusionary remedy is applied with no sense of proportion to the misconduct of the officer.

Cost 12: All of the above costs result inevitably in greatly diminished respect for the judicial process among lawyers and laymen alike.[2]

The astounding fact about all twelve costs is that they are undenied and undeniable. . . . The proponents of preserving the exclusionary remedy are forced to admit the existence of these high costs in our criminal justice system, yet they blithely assume that the only purported rationale of the rule outweighs these admitted costs.

IMPACT ON THE COURTS

While the most dramatic cost of the exclusionary remedy has been that "the criminal is to go free because the constable has blundered," this should not overshadow the tremendous impact that the rule has on the sheer work load of the courts. A recent General Accounting Office (GAO) study, though focusing on the intake of cases in selected United States Attorneys' offices, reveals the enormous burden that the exclusionary rule has placed on the trial and appellate courts. According to the GAO data, Fourth Amendment suppression motions are far and away the most common issue in the trial of criminal cases. As was stated on the first page of the GAO report, "*thirty-three percent* of the defendants who went to trial filed Fourth Amendment suppression motions." . . .

The Fourth Amendment suppression motion is the most important and frequent single issue arising in criminal trials. The GAO study illustrates this: 60.1 percent of all motions filed involved the Fourth Amendment. The next most numerous type of motion—dealing with confessions—amounted to only 23.2 percent: hence there is no single legal issue which even comes close to Fourth Amendment search and seizure motions for importance in the trial of criminal cases. Irrespective of whether the evidence is excluded or not, the burden on the trial court is undeniable. . . .

RATIONALE FOR IRRATIONALITY

The sole rationale for preserving the rule is now, and has been at least since *Linkletter v. Walker,* that it deters police misconduct. Efforts to resurrect other rationales, long since discarded by the Supreme Court, are a very revealing admission by even the rule's most ardent supporters that deterrence has *not* been proved by seventy years of experience, and such efforts arouse a sneaking suspicion that the supporters know deterrence is impossible to prove. . . .

[A]s Justice Blackmun remarked in *United States v. Janis* in 1976, "No empirical researcher, proponent or opponent of the rule, has yet been able to establish with any assurance whether the rule has a deterrent effect even in situations in which it is now applied." On this same point, Chief Justice Burger in *Bivens* described the current situation:

I do not question the need for some remedy to give meaning and teeth to the constitutional guarantees against unlawful conduct by government officials. . . . But the hope that this objective could be accomplished by the exclusion of reliable evidence from criminal trials was hardly more than a wistful dream. . . . There is no empirical evidence to support the claim that the rule actually deters illegal conduct of law enforcement officials. . . . We

should view the suppression doctrine as one of the experimental steps in the great tradition of the common law and acknowledge its shortcomings. But in the same spirit we should be prepared to discontinue what the experience of over half a century has shown neither deters errant officers nor affords a remedy to the totally innocent victim of official misconduct.

It is highly significant that, in nearly seventy years of Supreme Court decisions on the exclusionary rule, the High Court itself has never cited empirical data to support its faith that the rule actually deters. Indeed, the fragmented nature itself of law enforcement and the pressures generated by the exclusionary rule may make it logically impossible for it to have any appreciable deterrent effect.

And even if there were shown to be *some* deterrent effect, supporters of the rule have never addressed what would seem to be a primary question: How much deterrence is necessary to outweigh the admitted cost of the rule? . . .

BURDEN OF PROOF

. . . Nowhere else in our system of proof do we bar valid, probative, irrefutable, relevant, material evidence on some unproven nebulous theory of overall gain in the system. Those who want to bar this evidence never seem to realize that the *burden of proving* that some greater good will be gained is on them.

Evidentiary privileges, it must be conceded, constitute another exception to the general rule of law that valid probative evidence of unquestioned truth is to be admitted at trial. However, a careful analysis of these privileges reveals that they are grounded in a rationale which cannot be used to sustain the exclusionary rule.

The overriding policy underlying the basic evidentiary privileges is the preservation of confidentiality. Many of the privileges exist to preserve confidential interpersonal relationships—for example, husband-wife, lawyer-client, doctor-patient. The other privileges are aimed at preventing the release of information, for various and obvious policy reasons. Thus we have privileges for the identity of a police informer, for the political votes cast by a person, for trade secrets, and for state secrets and other official information.

In each of these cases, the legal system makes the rational evaluation that the preservation of confidentiality is of greater public interest than the availability of the evidence thereby excluded. The crucial fact about making this determination in any of these situations is that *there is no alternative.* If the evidence or testimony is required in open court, the underlying confidentiality interest vanishes. Thus there is a stark choice between disclosure or a privilege. Whatever the decision, there will be a gain and a cost, and we can hope only that we can achieve a net benefit.

The case of the exclusionary rule is exactly the opposite. If the evidence is admitted, the Fourth Amendment interest at stake is not inherently and irretrievably forsaken. *Alternatives do exist.* The police officer may be disciplined, and the victim of illegal search may recover damages. Moreover, when we recognize an evidentiary privilege, the benefit gained is clear and tangible: The confidential information is protected. But with the exclusionary rule we are asked to put our faith behind the assumption that if we throw out enough solid evidence and let enough guilty criminals go free, we ultimately will achieve a greater protection of Fourth Amendment rights. The dubious nature of this reasoning, when combined with a recognition of the available alternatives for *directly* vindicating the Fourth Amendment interests at stake, makes clear that we are throwing away important and irrefutable evidence for no good reason. . . .

NO RESTORATION OF PRESEARCH SITUATION

One of the most astonishing assertions by the contemporary supporters of the exclusionary rule is that the remedy simply restores the situation between the government and the target of the illegal search to precisely what it was before the violation of the Fourth Amendment took place, that is, that matters are returned to how they would have been had the constable not blundered. This assertion is simply divorced

from the reality of what goes on in a Fourth Amendment search and seizure case. The exclusionary rule never restores the parties to where they were before the search.

In at least 75 to 80 percent of the search and seizure cases coming into the federal court, the objects of the search are contraband items: narcotics, smuggled goods, illegal weapons, gambling paraphernalia, or stolen property. These are *never* returned to the possessor from whom they were taken at the time of the illegal search, so this party is hardly in the same situation as before. On the other hand not only does the government lose the prosecution based on the unquestioned material evidence which is secured, the government may also be precluded by the doctrine of "the fruit of the poisonous tree" from prosecuting a defendant on the basis of other evidence which it could have obtained validly. So the exclusionary rule never restores the prior status of either party.

The fact that the situation is *not* restored to its pristine condition points up another illogicality of the exclusionary rule. If the government can take away an unlicensed pistol from a person on the street and confiscate it, and yet not strike a damaging blow to the integrity of justice, why should it be demeaning and unworthy of the government to prosecute the man who carried the pistol? If the government seizes, legally or illegally, a million dollars worth of cocaine, it has the right and statutory duty to destroy that cocaine, not to restore it to its original owner. If this is not an affront to our concept of justice, why would it be an affront to the integrity of the judicial system to prosecute the smuggler of the cocaine? . . .

ABSENCE OF THE RULE IN OTHER CIVILIZED COUNTRIES

To my mind, one of the most damning indictments of the exclusionary rule has been the fact that, while we have had it for nearly seventy years, no other civilized country has adopted our mandatory rule of the exclusion of probative material evidence because of police misconduct. . . .

This failure to follow our example has not been mere happenstance. Law reform commissions in England, Canada, Israel, and other countries have studied the application and the impact of our exclusionary rule and have not adopted it. . . . These countries do discipline their police, they do protect their citizens from illegal searches and seizures and from police harassment, and they do this by methods other than the irrational exclusion of evidence. The obvious existence of other civilized methods of protecting the citizenry against illegal police action totally refutes the idea that there are no viable alternatives to the exclusionary rule. . . .

ALTERNATIVES

. . . [T]here are several alternative choices for enforcing the Fourth Amendment protection against unreasonable searches and seizures. Each of these I have discussed at some length in my monograph.[3] To enumerate: The first and most logical alternative would be to adopt a system under which the executive branch disciplines itself. While the judiciary may ultimately have the responsibility for implementing all constitutional protections, this does not mean that the judiciary must intervene in every single instance of an alleged violation, as happens now when the exclusionary rule functions as the sole method of enforcing the Fourth Amendment. While individual law enforcement agencies may be too close to their own people to discipline them effectively all the time, this does not preclude the setting up of an overall disciplinary board or agency in the executive branch, where the alleged misdeeds of enforcement officials can be investigated, tried, and punished appropriately without any impact on the trial of the accused for his or her crime.

Second, surely a civil tort remedy can be created, under the Federal Tort Claims Act or elsewhere, which would give victims of searches and seizures a claim remedy against erring police officers. Under the present exclusionary rule, no one is compensated in any way for a constitutional violation unless he or she is actually guilty of possessing incriminating material objects and is successful in having them suppressed. If the search turns up nothing incriminating, no matter how outrageous the violation, the victim of the search has no remedy whatsoever.

The above two remedies, in general outline, are the remedies usually relied upon in other countries in the world with judicial systems similar to ours—in England, Israel, and the British Commonwealth nations—to discipline their law enforcement personnel and to protect the citizenry against illegal searches and seizures. There is no reason why similar remedies could not work in the United States of America. . . .

I have suggested a third method of enforcement which, even in the absence of any congressional legislation on the matter, could be implemented by our judicial system to enforce the Fourth Amendment in a much more logical fashion. There could be a mini-trial of the alleged offending officer after the trial of the accused for his substantive crime. If a motion charging the officer with an illegal search were made, the trial judge would reserve judgment on that extraneous matter until the guilt or innocence of the accused had been established. The evidence seized would come in, for the officer's conduct would be totally irrelevant to the question of whether the narcotics, the unlicensed gun, or the contraband had been found in the possession of the accused, that is, the conduct would be irrelevant to the guilt of the defendant. The material evidence would be admitted, though, only on condition that the conduct of the officer be appraised later. After subsequent judicial inquiry into the officer's conduct, if the officer overstepped legal bounds, the trial judge would then inform the agency that the conviction of the accused would stand only if proportional disciplinary measures were taken against the officer and if a report of these was provided to the court within a given time. But if the agency did not discipline the officer sufficiently to act as a deterrent—not only to his, but his colleagues', future misconduct of this type—then the motion of the defense to exclude the seized evidence would be granted under the present exclusionary rule. The result in the usual case would be insufficient evidence to sustain the conviction. Of course, if the trial judge found that the officer's conduct was well within Fourth Amendment standards, then there would be no exclusion of the evidence and no required punishment of the officer.

This, I submit, would form an effective and rational deterrent to law enforcement officials' violations of the Fourth Amendment. It would result in freeing the criminal only if the law enforcement agency were recalcitrant and refused to punish its erring officer. Assuming that the law enforcement agency took disciplinary action, this method would not free the guilty, but instead would result in the proportionate punishment of the erring officer while the obviously guilty also received his or her just deserts. It is my belief that if a United States district court inaugurated a system of required investigation and punishment of alleged Fourth Amendment violators—separate and distinct from the trial and conviction or acquittal of the accused—the Supreme Court ultimately would sustain this as a far more effective and logical method of enforcing the Fourth Amendment.

Sachs: A Defense of the Exclusionary Rule

Like most law enforcement officials, I share our citizens' alarm and anger at the dreadful impact of crime in our society and want to strengthen law enforcement's capabilities. I agree with many of the recommendations made to Attorney General Smith by his Task Force on Violent Crime, including those which facilitate pretrial detention of some demonstrably dangerous criminals and curb collateral review of state convictions by federal courts. Furthermore, I deplore the hypertechnical excess with which some courts have interpreted the *substance* of the Fourth Amendment's guarantees against unreasonable searches and seizures. . . .

What I also believe, however, is that the exclusionary rule, the *remedy* for a Fourth Amendment violation which suppresses its fruits and denies government the benefit of its unconstitutional conduct, is sound in theory and effective in practice.

The rule is also very fragile, especially in today's atmosphere of understandable public outrage at crime and at our perceived inability to do much about it. It is vulnerable to attack because its values are abstract while its costs are tangible. It frequently excludes hard evidence—the truth—from trial. It appears to reward the undeserving criminal, whom it sometimes frees because "the constable blundered." It seems to give aid and comfort only to the enemy in the war on crime. It makes almost no sense to citizens fed up with crime and impatient with legal "technicalities" who want to believe that crime would disappear if only courts would stop coddling criminals. That is why the rule, although it has plenty of responsible critics, has become a favorite whipping boy of anticrime rhetoricians.

My purpose in this essay is to bear witness to what my own experience and study have taught me:

1. the rule is of constitutional origin and beyond the reach of Congress;

2. it results in freeing guilty criminals in a relatively small proportion of cases;

3. it definitely deters police and prosecutor violations of constitutional rights to privacy;

4. it manifests our refusal to stoop to conquer, to convict lawbreakers by relying on official lawlessness, a vital demonstration of our commitment to the rule of law. . . .

THE CONSTITUTIONAL STATUS OF THE EXCLUSIONARY RULE

I believe that the exclusionary rule is a rule of constitutional origin which only the Supreme Court, as part of its process of constitutional adjudication, can alter. The rule was first announced in *Weeks v. United States*, where Justice Day focused on the *constitutional necessity* of effectively enforcing the Fourth Amendment:

The effect of the Fourth Amendment is to put the courts of the United States and Federal officials in the exercise of their power and authority, under limitations and restraints as to the exercise of such power and authority. . . . This protection reaches all alike, whether accused of crime or not, and the duty of giving to it force and effect is obligatory upon all intrusted under our Federal system with the enforcement of the laws. The tendency of those who execute the criminal laws of the country to obtain conviction by means of unlawful seizures and enforced confessions, the latter often obtained after subjecting accused persons to unwarranted practices destructive of rights secured by the Federal Constitution, *should find no sanction in the judgments of the courts*, which are charged at all times with the support of the Constitution, and to which people of all conditions have a right to appeal for the maintenance of such fundamental rights. [Emphasis added by Sachs.]

The Supreme Court emphatically established the exclusionary rule's constitutional roots when it made the rule applicable to the states in *Mapp v. Ohio*:

We hold that all evidence obtained by searches and seizures in violation of the Constitution is, *by that same authority*, inadmissable in a state court. . . . Moreover, our holding that *the exclusionary rule is an essential part of both the Fourth and Fourteenth Amendments* is not only the logical dictate of prior cases, but it also makes very good sense. [Emphasis added by Sachs.] . . .

While the Court has occasionally limited the reach of the rule, it has not retreated from its constitutional base. The rule may be a "judicially created remedy," but it has clear constitutional underpinnings.

EXAGGERATED CLAIMS ABOUT THE CONSEQUENCES OF THE EXCLUSIONARY RULE

The most severe indictment of the rule and, in the present climate of fear about crime the most damaging one, is that it releases hordes of dangerous and demonstrably guilty criminals to prey upon society.

I believe that such claims are greatly exaggerated. In cases where unconstitutionally seized evidence is indispensable to conviction, convictions will of course be lost. Police and prosecutors will be frustrated. In the occasional celebrated case, the public will be angry. But a recent study by the Comptroller General of the

United States proves that the rule operates to free federal criminal suspects in only a tiny percentage of cases. The Comptroller General studied the rule's operation in 2,804 cases in 38 representative United States Attorneys Offices throughout the country during the period July 1 through August 31, 1978. Of all the cases presented to those federal prosecutors for prosecution, *only 0.4 percent* were declined by the prosecutors because of Fourth Amendment search and seizure problems. Evidence was excluded at trial as a result of Fourth Amendment motions in *only 1.3 percent* of the cases. And over 50 percent of the few defendants whose suppression motions were granted in whole or in part were nonetheless convicted. This data is powerful proof that at least in federal prosecutions—the only cases, it should be remembered, to which proposed federal legislation would apply—the specter of muggers, rapists, and dope pushers set loose by the rule is the product of rhetoric that is not in touch with reality.

To my knowledge, no comparable study of state and local experience has been conducted. Based on my personal observation and my contacts with other Maryland prosecutors, however, I would expect the impact of the rule on state prosecutions to be somewhat greater, but still fall far short of justifying the claims of the alarmists. I believe a fair summary of the Maryland experience to be that the rule has small effect on either declinations by prosecutors or loss at trial in almost all categories of crime, including violent crime, although it should be added that a higher percentage of suppression motions is granted in drug possession cases resulting from spontaneous street encounters than in other types of cases. As Professor LaFave has written in his treatise on search and seizure: "There is reason to believe that the 'cost' of the exclusionary rule, in terms of acquittals or dismissed cases, is much lower than is commonly assumed."[4]

There is an even more fundamental response to the claim that the exclusionary rule frees criminals. As pointed out by Yale Kamisar, we tend to examine the legality of a search only after it has occurred—and after incriminating evidence has been discovered—and therefore lose sight of the fact that if the police had obeyed the

Fourth Amendment they would not have the evidence at all. Thus, it is the guarantee of the Fourth Amendment, a cornerstone of our personal liberty, which constricts the police. The rule serves only to put the police in the same position they would have been in had they done what the Constitution commanded. As Kamisar asks: "If the government could not have gained a conviction had it obeyed the Constitution, why should it be permitted to prevail because it has violated the Constitution?"[5]

AN EFFECTIVE DETERRENT

A fundamental assumption underlying creation of the rule was the judicial belief that it deters official lawlessness and "compel[s] respect for the constitutional guaranty in the only effectively available way—by removing the incentive to disregard it." Critics charge that the rule fails in this primary purpose and point to various empirical studies which, they argue, demonstrate that the rule is ineffective as a deterrent. The studies have been thoroughly dissected elsewhere. I have read most of them and agree with Justice Powell's conclusion that they are "inconclusive."

I can't offer statistical studies on the deterrent effect of the rule. What I can offer, however, is my testimony that I have watched the rule deter, routinely, throughout my years as a prosecutor. When an Assistant United States Attorney, for example, advises an FBI agent that he lacks probable cause to search for bank loot in a parked automobile unless he gets a better "make" on the car; or that the agent has a "staleness" problem with the probable cause to believe that the ski masks used in the robbery are still in the suspect's friend's apartment; or that he should apply for a search warrant from a magistrate and not rely on the "consent" of the suspect's sister to search his home—the rule is working. The principal, perhaps the only, reason those conversations occur is that the assistant and the agent want the search to stand up in court.

Episodes like these are commonplace. They are part of the routine of every federal prosecutor with whom I have worked. Although my present office has more limited criminal jurisdiction, such police-prosecutor consultation is customary in all of our cases when Fourth Amendment concerns arise. I strongly suspect that scenes like these are repeated daily throughout federal law enforcement and on homicide, narcotics, and gambling squads in cities throughout the country. In at least three Maryland jurisdictions, for example, prosecutors are on twenty-four hour call to field search and seizure questions presented by police officers.

These contracts do not occur because of some self-limiting controls in the police and prosecutors themselves. I hope and trust that most of us in law enforcement are principled enough to avoid violating the clear constitutional rights of suspects. But in the heat of the chase, and in the absence of effective sanction, I believe that we would define those rights somewhat narrowly. Questions of adequate identification, "staleness" of information, and the need for a warrant will be answered differently by unchecked law enforcers than by judges. We are, after all, hunters stalking crime. It is simply too much to ask for objectivity in the midst of the hunt, especially when the quarry is in sight. This is precisely what the warrant requirement of the Fourth Amendment is about. As Justice Jackson once put it:

> The point of the Fourth Amendment, which often is not grasped by zealous officers, is not that it denies law enforcement support of the usual inferences which reasonable men draw from evidence. Its protection consists in requiring that those inferences be drawn by a neutral and detached magistrate instead of being judged by the officer engaged in the often competitive enterprise of ferreting out crime.

Exclusion from evidence is almost certainly the only effective deterrent in the vast majority of unconstitutional intrusions. Even critics of the rule are quick to acknowledge the severe limitations of police self-discipline or court damage actions as deterrents when crime-fighting police officers are in the dock. In rare cases involving especially gross misconduct, a police disciplinary board or a court or jury in a damage action might impose sanctions, at least if the victim of the trespass is innocent and the police misconduct truly outrageous.

But most of the suppression cases do not deal with such outrageous conduct. They deal with undramatic Fourth Amendment concerns—the sufficiency of "probable cause" in a given case, whether "exigent circumstances" excuse the necessity of a warrant, whether there is sufficient corroboration of the tip of an anonymous informer to justify intrusion into a suspect's apartment. These requirements are not the stuff to move police disciplinary boards, or judges and juries accustomed to awarding damages on the basis of "fault." But they are our constitutional rules of the road and only the suppression sanction, the exclusionary rule, will force prosecutors and police to obey them.

There are many who would object to these requirements as unnecessary impediments in the path of aggressive law enforcement. I disagree. These requirements are the way we attempt to reach a balance between the claims of public safety and the claims of personal freedom in a nation that believes that government, including police, should not have limitless power. And only by demonstrating that our courts will not permit their violation can we underscore their importance or enforce them at all.

My views about the deterrence inherent in the close police-prosecution contacts with which I am most familiar are subject to the criticism that they do not describe the rule's impact on the uniformed officer on patrol or the agent on the street who is called upon to make split-second arrest and search decisions and who measures his success by arrests made, not convictions won.

There is force to this criticism. I don't doubt that the rule works less well in street encounters. But here, too, the rule is at work because of the enormous increase in police training and education about constitutional rights directly attributable to the exclusion sanction.

Federal agencies, subjected to the exclusionary rule since 1914, have traditionally devoted substantial time to such training. . . .

In my state, *Mapp* has been responsible for a virtual explosion in the amount and quantity of police training in the last twenty years. . . .

AN ASSESSMENT OF TWO PROPOSED MODIFICATIONS

THE GOOD FAITH EXCEPTION

Critics of the rule frequently complain that courts exclude illegally seized evidence even though the officers who seized it believed in good faith that their conduct was lawful. . . . The Task Force proposes that "in general, evidence should not be excluded from a criminal proceeding if it has been obtained by an officer acting in the reasonable, good faith belief that it was in conformity to the Fourth Amendment to the Constitution." Proposed legislation reflects this point of view, although it seems to admit illegally seized evidence that even the "reasonable, good faith" rule would bar.

As several commentators have pointed out, the "good faith" test puts a premium on "police ignorance."[6] If the "good faith" loophole is established, pretrial hearings in every Fourth Amendment case will test the "reasonableness" of the police officer's ignorance of the Fourth Amendment's commands. Often (*very* often, given the antipathy of some judges toward the rule and public pressure to jettison it) the officer's ignorance will be found to have been "reasonable." And each time unconstitutional behavior is thus excused, the benchmarks of Fourth Amendment compliance will drop another notch. It is worth asking what impact such an exemption will have on the courses and classroom hours police will devote to the constitutional limitations on their profession if, in fact, it pays to be ignorant. Introduction of the "reasonable good faith" test would, I fear, depress Fourth Amendment compliance to the level of our tolerance for the lowest standards of the least informed officer. And there would be no incentive to do better. . . .

Advocates of the good faith [exception] . . . sometimes forget that the Fourth Amendment proscribes only "unreasonable" searches and seizures. Probable cause is supposed to turn on "the factual and practical considerations of everyday life on which reasonable and prudent men, not legal technicians, act." Scores of Supreme Court pronouncements make it clear that practical, common sense standards, including appreciation of the alternatives available to officers at the scene of crimes, are the guideposts for interpreting the Fourth Amendment's standard of reasonableness.

When courts fail to honor these standards of reasonableness, application of the exclusionary rule works to keep out evidence that should have been admitted. But once a violation of the constitutional commands of the Fourth Amendment is found, it would do serious violence to the deterrent purposes and societal values of the rule to say that, on the one hand, the police conduct is unconstitutional but that, on the other hand, the evidence it produced should be admitted anyway. The cure for such wrong interpretations of the Fourth Amendment is a better, sounder, and more practical judiciary. One does not have to agree with every court that ever found a search unconstitutional under the Fourth Amendment in order to believe, as I do, that the exclusionary rule is a sound remedy.

A TORT REMEDY AS SUBSTITUTE FOR THE EXCLUSIONARY RULE

[The proposal] which abolishes the exclusionary rule and replaces it with an exclusive tort remedy against the United States for damages resulting from a search conducted in violation of the Fourth Amendment is an open invitation to official lawlessness. If it were law, a federal officer could engage in essentially risk-free violations of the Constitution. If he engaged in an unconstitutional search, the risk of personal liability would not increase no matter how offensive the search might be. . . .

[Such a law might] even prompt agencies to encourage constitutional shortcuts by their employees. An agency that now may be required to spend time and money to put together a lawful case, including probable cause to search for incriminating evidence, might well seek to economize by accepting the fixed risk of a . . . "fine" assuming suit is even brought. . . . The agency might well conclude that the cost of doing business would be cheap at twice the price. Thus important constitutional protections are demeaned and budget cutting is brought to unaccustomed lengths.

Supplementing the deterrent effect of the exclusionary rule in federal court by a tort remedy against the United States makes sense. It would open an avenue of compensation for innocent victims of government misconduct not afforded by the suppression remedy. But to abolish the exclusionary rule and to replace it with a system that would fund unconstitutional conduct is to stand the Fourth Amendment on its head.

THE IMPERATIVE OF JUDICIAL INTEGRITY

It is sometimes said that the exclusionary rule breeds disrespect for the law because it suppresses the truth and permits crime to go unpunished. I believe that abolition of the rule would be far more destructive of respect for law. When an American court admits evidence obtained in violation of the Constitution, it is not merely permitting the truth to be heard. It is inescapably condoning, validating, even welcoming, the illegality that produced it. It becomes part of that illegality. It paints a portrait of hypocrisy in a nation that professes to believe in the rule of law and whose courts, in the words of Madison, are to be the great "bulwarks" and "guardians" of our liberties. And the admission of such evidence is dangerous. As Justice Brandeis put it:

> In a government of laws, existence of the government will be imperilled if it fails to observe the law scrupulously. Our Government is the potent, the omnipresent teacher. For good or for ill, it reaches the whole people by its example. Crime is contagious. If the Government becomes a lawbreaker, it breeds contempt for law; it invites every man to become a law unto himself; it invites anarchy. To declare that in the administration of the criminal law the end justifies the means—to declare that the government may commit crimes in order to secure the conviction of a private criminal—would bring terrible retribution.

Law enforcement, in particular, needs public trust and respect for its authority in order to do its job effectively and safely. Official lawlessness destroys that trust, poisons police relations with the citizenry, and thus adds immeasurably to law enforcement's burdens.

It is easy to salute the liberties of the Bill of Rights in the abstract. But these freedoms have a price. It is difficult to remember, but we must never forget, that we cannot apply them selectively. Only insofar as we permit their effective exercise by the guilty will they remain strong protection for the innocent. Rights atrophy with disuse. They must be used not only in times of calm but in times of passion and fear as well.

In the play *A Man for All Seasons*, an account of the martyrdom of Saint Thomas More, More warns a zealot against "cut[ting] a great road through the law to get after the Devil."

"When the last law was down, and the Devil turned round on you, where would you hide," he asks, "the laws all being flat?" "Yes," More

adds, "I'd give the Devil benefit of law, for my own safety's sake."

In this time of great passion about crime we should be extremely careful, for our own safety's sake, not to let our zeal to "get after the Devil" lead us to cut a great road through the Bill of Rights.

NOTES

[1]*Mapp v. Ohio*, 367 U.S. 643 (1961).
[2]Malcolm Wilkey, *Enforcing the Fourth Amendment by Alternatives to the Exclusionary Rule* (Washington, D.C.: National Legal Center for the Public Interest, March 1982).
[3]Wilkey, *Enforcing the Fourth Amendment*.
[4]Wayne LaFave, *Search and Seizure: 1981 Supplement* (St. Paul, Minn.: West Publishing Co., 1981), 1.2 n.9
[5]Yale Kamisar, "Defense of the Exclusionary Rule," *Crim. L. Bull.* 15 (1979): 13.
[6]Ibid., p. 35, n.

REVIEW AND DISCUSSION QUESTIONS

1. Wilkey enumerates twelve costs of the exclusionary rule. Assess each of these. Which are the most important? Do any of them seem exaggerated?

2. What do you see as the strongest argument against the exclusionary rule? As the strongest argument for the exclusionary rule?

3. What three alternatives to the exclusionary rule does Wilkey propose? Are these likely to be as effective? How persuasive is Sachs's critique of the "good faith" exception and tort remedies?

4. Wilkey and Sachs disagree about the effectiveness of the exclusionary rule as a deterrent to police illegality and about whether some alternative method might protect our Fourth Amendment rights equally well but at a lower cost. Whose position do you find the most convincing and why?

Interrogation and the Right to Counsel

Miranda v. Arizona; Brewer v. Williams; and Rhode Island v. Innis

These three cases are among the Supreme Court's most important deliberations on criminal procedure and the rights of defendants. In Miranda, *the Court held that procedural safeguards must be employed to respect the constitutional privilege against self-incrimination and, in particular, to inform accused persons of their right to remain silent—the now famous "Miranda warning." In* Brewer, *the Court debated the related issue of a defendant's right to counsel. Although three justices dissented from the decision, the majority determined that Robert Williams's conviction for murder was based on evidence obtained in violation of his constitutional right to the assistance of counsel. In the* Innis *case, the Court undertook to define and delimit the meaning of "interrogation." Although the Supreme Court of Rhode Island had relied on the U.S. Supreme Court's* Miranda *and* Brewer *decisions to overturn Innis's conviction, the U.S. Supreme Court, despite a vigorous dissent by Justice Stevens, decided that Innis had not been illegally interrogated.*

Miranda v. Arizona

[Editors' Note: The facts of this case were summarized in Justice Harlan's dissent from the majority opinion, as follows:]

[I]t may make the analysis more graphic to consider the actual facts of one of the four cases reversed by the Court. *Miranda v. Arizona* serves best, being neither the hardest nor easiest of the four under the Court's standards.

On March 3, 1963, an 18-year-old girl was kidnapped and forcibly raped near Phoenix, Arizona. Ten days later, on the morning of March 13, petitioner Miranda was arrested and taken to the police station. At this time Miranda was 23 years old, indigent, and educated to the extent of completing half the ninth grade. He had 'an emotional illness' of the schizophrenic type, according to the doctor who eventually examined him; the doctor's report also stated that Miranda was 'alert and oriented as to time, place, and person,' intelligent within normal limits, competent to stand trial, and sane within the legal definition. At the

police station, the victim picked Miranda out of a line-up, and two officers then took him into a separate room to interrogate him, starting about 11:30 A.M. Though at first denying his guilt, within a short time Miranda gave a detailed oral confession and then wrote out in his own hand and signed a brief statement admitting and describing the crime. All this was accomplished in two hours or less without any force, threats or promises and—I will assume this though the record is uncertain. . . without any effective warnings at all.

Mr. Chief Justice Warren delivered the opinion of the court:

The cases before us raise questions which go to the roots of our concepts of American criminal jurisprudence: the restraints society must observe consistent with the Federal Constitution in prosecuting individuals for crime. More specifically, we deal with the admissibility of statements obtained from an individual who is subjected to custodial police interrogation and the necessity for procedures which assure that the individual is accorded his privilege under the Fifth Amendment to the Constitution not to be compelled to incriminate himself. . . .

384 U.S. 436 (1966); 430 U.S. 378 (1976); and 446 U.S. 291 (1979), respectively. Some footnotes and citations omitted.

Our holding will be spelled out with some specificity in the pages which follow but briefly stated it is this: the prosecution may not use statements, whether exculpatory or inculpatory, stemming from custodial interrogation of the defendant unless it demonstrates the use of procedural safeguards effective to secure the privilege against self-incrimination. By custodial interrogation, we mean questioning initiated by law enforcement officers after a person has been taken into custody or otherwise deprived of his freedom of action in any significant way. As for the procedural safeguards to be employed, unless other fully effective means are devised to inform accused persons of their right of silence and to assure a continuous opportunity to exercise it, the following measures are required. Prior to any questioning, the person must be warned that he has a right to remain silent, that any statement he does make may be used as evidence against him, and that he has a right to the presence of an attorney, either retained or appointed. The defendant may waive effectuation of these rights, provided the waiver is made voluntarily, knowingly and intelligently. If, however, he indicates in any manner and at any stage of the process that he wishes to consult with an attorney before speaking there can be no questioning. Likewise, if the individual is alone and indicates in any manner that he does not wish to be interrogated, the police may not question him. The mere fact that he may have answered some questions or volunteered some statements on his own does not deprive him of the right to refrain from answering any further inquiries until he has consulted with an attorney and thereafter consents to be questioned.

1

The constitutional issue we decide in each of these cases is the admissibility of statements obtained from a defendant questioned while in custody or otherwise deprived of his freedom of action in any significant way. In each, the defendant was questioned by police officers, detectives, or a prosecuting attorney in a room in which he was cut off from the outside world. In none of these cases was the defendant given a full and effective warning of his rights at the outset of the interrogation process. In all the cases, the questioning elicited oral admissions, and in three of them, signed statements as well which were admitted at their trials. They all thus share salient features—incommunicado interrogation of individuals in a police-dominated atmosphere, resulting in self-incriminating statements without full warnings of constitutional rights.

An understanding of the nature and setting of this in-custody interrogation is essential to our decisions today. The difficulty in depicting what transpires at such interrogations stems from the fact that in this country they have largely taken place incommunicado. From extensive factual studies undertaken in the early 1930s, including the famous Wickersham Report to Congress by a Presidential Commission, it is clear that police violence and the "third degree" flourished at that time. In a series of cases decided by this Court long after these studies, the police resorted to physical brutality—beating, hanging, whipping—and to sustained and protracted questioning incommunicado in order to extort confessions. The Commission on Civil Rights in 1961 found much evidence to indicate that "some policemen still resort to physical force to obtain confessions," 1961 Comm'n on Civil Rights Rep., Justice, pt. 5, 17. The use of physical brutality and violence is not, unfortunately, relegated to the past or to any part of the country. Only recently in Kings County, New York, the police brutally beat, kicked and placed lighted cigarette butts on the back of a potential witness under interrogation for the purpose of securing a statement incriminating a third party.[1]

The examples given above are undoubtedly the exception now, but they are sufficiently widespread to be the object of concern. Unless a proper limitation upon custodial interrogation is achieved—such as these decisions will advance—there can be no assurance that practices of this nature will be eradicated in the foreseeable future. The conclusion of the Wickersham Commission Report, made over 30 years ago, is still pertinent:

To the contention that the third degree is necessary to get the facts, the reporters aptly reply in the language of the present Lord Chancellor of England (Lord Sankey): "It is not admissible to do a great right by doing a little wrong. . . . It is not sufficient to do justice by obtaining a proper result by irregular or improper means." Not only does the use of the third degree involve a flagrant violation of law by the officers of the law, but it involves also the dangers of false confessions, and it tends to make police and prosecutors less zealous in the search for objective evidence. As the New York prosecutor quoted in the report said, "It is a short cut and makes the police lazy and unenterprising." Or, as another official quoted remarked: "If you use your fists, you are not so likely to use your wits." We agree with the conclusion expressed in the report, that "The third degree brutalizes the police, hardens the prisoner against society, and lowers the esteem in which the administration of justice is held by the public." IV National Commission on Law Observance and Enforcement, Report on Lawlessness in Law Enforcement 5 (1931)

Again we stress that the modern practice of in-custody interrogation is psychologically rather than physically oriented. . . . Interrogation still takes place in privacy. Privacy results in secrecy and this in turn results in a gap in our knowledge as to what in fact goes on in the interrogation rooms. A valuable source of information about present police practices, however, may be found in various police manuals and texts which document procedures employed with success in the past, and which recommend various other effective tactics.[2] . . .

The officers are told by the manuals that the "principal psychological factor contributing to a successful interrogation is *privacy*—being alone with the person under interrogation."[3] The efficacy of this tactic has been explained as follows:

If at all practicable, the interrogation should take place in the investigator's office or at least in a room of his own choice. The subject should be deprived of every psychological advantage. In his own home he may be confident, indignant, or recalcitrant. He is more keenly aware of his rights and more reluctant to tell of his indiscretions or criminal behavior within the walls of his home. Moreover his family and other friends are nearby, their presence lending moral support. In his own office, the investigator possesses all the advantages. The atmosphere suggests the invincibility of the forces of the law.[4]

To highlight the isolation and unfamiliar surroundings, the manuals instruct the police to display an air of confidence in the suspect's guilt and from outward appearance to maintain only an interest in confirming certain details. The guilt of the subject is to be posited as a fact. The interrogator should direct his comments toward the reasons why the subject committed the act, rather than court failure by asking the subject whether he did it. Like other men, perhaps the subject has had a bad family life, had an unhappy childhood, had too much to drink, had an unrequited desire for women. The officers are instructed to minimize the moral seriousness of the offense, to cast blame on the victim or on society. These tactics are designed to put the subject in a psychological state where his story is but an elaboration of what the police purport to know already—that he is guilty. Explanations to the contrary are dismissed and discouraged.

The texts thus stress that the major qualities an interrogator should possess are patience and perseverance. One writer describes the efficacy of these characteristics in this manner:

In the preceding paragraphs emphasis has been placed on kindness and strategems. The investigator will, however, encounter many situations where the sheer weight of his personality will be the deciding factor. Where emotional appeals and tricks are employed to no avail, he must rely on an oppressive atmosphere of dogged persistence. He must interrogate steadily and without relent, leaving the subject no prospect of surcease. He must dominate his subject and overwhelm him with his inexorable will to obtain the truth. He should interrogate for a spell of several hours pausing only for the subject's necessities in acknowledgment of the need to avoid a charge of duress that can be technically substantiated. In a serious case, the interrogation may continue for days, with the required intervals for food and sleep, but with no respite from the atmosphere of domination. It is possible in this way to induce the subject to talk without resorting to duress or coercion. The method should be used only when the guilt of the subject appears highly probable.[5]

. . . The interrogators sometimes are instructed to induce a confession out of trickery. The technique here is quite effective in crimes which require identification or which run in series. In the identification situation, the interrogator may take a break in his questioning to place the subject among a group of men in a line-up. "The witness or complainant (previously coached, if necessary) studies the line-up and confidently points out the subject as the guilty party."[6] Then the questioning resumes "as though there were now no doubt about the guilt of the subject." A variation on this technique is called the "reverse line-up":

The accused is placed in a line-up, but this time he is identified by several fictitious witnesses or victims who associated him with different offenses. It is expected that the subject will become desperate and confess to the offense under investigation in order to escape from the false accusations.[7]

. . . In the event that the subject wishes to speak to a relative or an attorney, the following advice is tendered:

[T]he interrogator should respond by suggesting that the subject first tell the truth to the interrogator himself rather than get anyone else involved in the matter. If the request is for an attorney, the interrogator may suggest that the subject save himself or his family the expense of any such professional service, particularly if he is innocent of the offense under investigation. The interrogator may also add, "Joe, I'm only looking for the truth, and if you're telling the truth, that's it. You can handle this by yourself."[8]

From these representative samples of interrogation techniques, the setting prescribed by the manuals and observed in practice becomes clear. In essence, it is this: To be alone with the subject is essential to prevent distraction and to deprive him of any outside support. The aura of confidence in his guilt undermines his will to resist. He merely confirms the preconceived story the police seek to have him describe. Patience and persistence, at times relentless questioning, are employed. To obtain a confession, the interrogator must "patiently maneuver himself or his quarry into a position from which the desired objective may be attained."[9] When normal procedures fail to produce the needed result, the police may resort to deceptive stratagems such as giving false legal advice. It is important to keep the subject off balance, for example, by trading on his insecurity about himself or his surroundings. The police then persuade, trick, or cajole him out of exercising his constitutional rights.

Even without employing brutality, the "third degree" or the specific stratagems described above, the very fact of custodial interrogation exacts a heavy toll on individual liberty and trades on the weakness of individuals. . . .

2

. . . Those who framed our Constitution and the Bill of Rights were ever aware of subtle encroachments on individual liberty. They knew that "illegitimate and unconstitutional practices get their first footing . . . by silent approaches and slight deviations from legal modes of procedure." *Boyd v. United States*, 116 U.S. 616, 635 (1886).

. . . We may view the historical development of the privilege [against self-incrimination] as one which groped for the proper scope of governmental power over the citizen. As a "noble principle often transcends its origins," the privilege has come rightfully to be recognized in part as an individual's substantive right, a "right to a private enclave where he may lead a private life. That right is the hallmark of our democracy." *United States v. Grunewald*, 233 F.2d. . . . [The] constitutional foundation underlying the privilege is the respect a government—state or federal—must accord to the dignity and integrity of its citizens. To maintain a "fair state-individual balance," to require the government "to shoulder the entire load," . . . to respect the inviolability of the human personality, our accusatory system of criminal justice demands that the government seeking to punish an individual produce the evidence against him by its own independent labors, rather than by the cruel, simple expedient of compelling it from his own mouth. . . . In sum, the privilege is fulfilled only when the person is guaranteed the right "to remain silent unless he chooses to speak in the unfettered exercise of his own will." *Malloy v. Hogan*, 378 U.S. 1, 8 (1964).

. . . We are satisfied that all the principles embodied in the privilege apply to informal compulsion exerted by law-enforcement officers during in-custody questioning. An individual swept from familiar surroundings into police custody, surrounded by antagonistic forces, and subjected to the techniques of persuasion described above cannot be otherwise than under compulsion to speak. As a practical matter, the compulsion to speak in the isolated setting of the police station may well be greater than in courts or other official investigations, where there are often impartial observers to guard against intimidation or trickery. . . .

3

Today, then, there can be no doubt that the Fifth Amendment privilege is available outside of criminal court proceedings and serves to protect persons in all settings in which their freedom of action is curtailed in any significant way from being compelled to incriminate themselves. We have concluded that without proper safeguards the process of in-custody interrogation of persons suspected or accused of crime contains inherently compelling pressures which work to undermine the individual's will to resist and to compel him to speak where he would not otherwise do so freely. In order to combat these pressures and to permit a full opportunity to exercise the privilege against self-incrimination, the accused must be adequately and effectively apprised of his rights and the exercise of those rights must be fully honored. . . .

The principles announced today deal with the protection which must be given to the privilege against self-incrimination when the individual is first subjected to police interrogation while in custody at the station or otherwise deprived of his freedom of action in any significant way. It is at this point that our adversary system of criminal proceedings commences, distinguishing itself at the outset from the inquisitorial system recognized in some countries. Under the system of warnings we delineate today or under any other system which may be devised and found effective, the safeguards to be erected about the privilege must come into play at this point.

Our decision is not intended to hamper the traditional function of police officers in investigating crime. . . . When an individual is in custody on probable cause, the police may, of course, seek out evidence in the field to be used at trial against him. Such investigation may include inquiry of persons not under restraint. General on-the-scene questioning as to facts surrounding a crime or other general questioning of citizens in the fact-finding process is not affected by our holding. It is an act of responsible citizenship for individuals to give whatever information they may have to aid in law enforcement. In such situations the compelling atmosphere inherent in the process of in-custody interrogation is not necessarily present.

In dealing with statements obtained through interrogation, we do not purport to find all confessions inadmissible. Confessions remain a proper element in law enforcement. Any statement given freely and voluntarily without any compelling influences is, of course, admissible in evidence. The fundamental import of the privilege while an individual is in custody is not whether he is allowed to talk to the police without the benefit of warnings and counsel, but whether he can be interrogated. There is no requirement that police stop a person who enters a police station and states that he wishes to confess to a crime, or a person who calls the police to offer a confession or any other statement he desires to make. Volunteered statements of any kind are not barred by the Fifth Amendment and their admissibility is not affected by our holding today. . . .

To summarize, we hold that when an individual is taken into custody or otherwise deprived of his freedom by the authorities in any significant way and is subjected to questioning, the privilege against self-incrimination is jeopardized. Procedural safeguards must be employed to protect the privilege, and unless other fully effective means are adopted to notify the person of his right of silence and to assure that the exercise of the right will be scrupulously honored, the following measures are required. He must be warned prior to any questioning that he has the right to remain silent, that anything he says can be used against him in a court of law, that he has the right to the presence of an attorney, and that if he cannot afford an attorney one will be appointed for him prior to any questioning if he so desires. Opportunity to exercise these rights must be afforded to him throughout the interrogation. After such warnings have been given, and such opportunity afforded him, the individual may knowingly and intelligently waive these rights and agree to answer questions or make a statement. But unless and until such warnings and waiver are demonstrated by the prosecution at trial, no evidence obtained as a result of interrogation can be used against him.

NOTES

[1]In addition, see *People v. Wakat* . . . (defendant suffering from broken bones, multiple bruises and injuries sufficiently serious to require eight months' medical treatment after being manhandled by five policemen); *Kier v. State* . . . (police doctor told accused, who was strapped to a chair completely nude, that he proposed to take hair and skin scrapings from anything that looked like blood or sperm from various parts of his body); *Bruner v. People* . . . (defendant held in custody over two months, deprived of food for 15 hours, forced to submit to a lie detector test when he wanted to go to the toilet); *People v. Matlock* . . . (defendant questioned incessantly over an evening's time, made to lie on cold board and to answer questions whenever it appeared he was getting sleepy).

[2]The manuals quoted in the text following are the most recent and representative of the texts currently available.

[3]Inbau and Reid, Criminal Interrogation and Confessions (1962), at 1.

[4]O'Hara, Fundamentals of Criminal Investigation (1956), at 99.

[5]O'Hara, *supra*, at 112.

[6]O'Hara, *supra*, at 105–106.

[7]*Id.*, at 106.

[8]Inbau and Reid, *supra*, at 112.

[9]Inbau and Reid, Lie Detection and Criminal Interrogation 185 (3d ed. 1953).

Brewer v. Williams

Mr. Justice Stewart delivered the opinion of the court:

An Iowa trial jury found the respondent, Robert Williams, guilty of murder. The judgment of conviction was affirmed in the Iowa Supreme Court by a closely divided vote. In a subsequent habeas corpus proceeding a Federal District Court ruled that under the United States Constitution Williams is entitled to a new trial, and a divided Court of Appeals for the Eighth Circuit agreed. The question before us is whether the District Court and the Court of Appeals were wrong.

1

On the afternoon of December 24, 1968, a 10-year-old girl named Pamela Powers went with her family to the YMCA in Des Moines, Iowa, to watch a wrestling tournament in which her brother was participating. When she failed to return from a trip to the washroom, a search for her began. The search was unsuccessful.

Robert Williams, who had recently escaped from a mental hospital, was a resident of the YMCA. Soon after the girl's disappearance Williams was seen in the YMCA lobby carrying some clothing and a large bundle wrapped in a blanket. He obtained help from a 14-year-old boy in opening the street door of the YMCA and the door to his automobile parked outside. When Williams placed the bundle in the front seat of his car the boy "saw two legs in it and they were skinny and white." Before anyone could see what was in the bundle Williams drove away. His abandoned car was found the following day in Davenport, Iowa, roughly 160 miles east of Des Moines. A warrant was then issued in Des Moines for his arrest on a charge of abduction.

On the morning of December 26, a Des Moines lawyer named Henry McKnight went to the Des Moines police station and informed the officers present that he had just received a long-distance call from Williams, and that he had advised Williams to turn himself in to the Davenport police. Williams did surrender that morning to the police in Davenport, and they booked him on the charge specified in the arrest warrant and gave him the warnings required by *Miranda v. Arizona*, 384 U.S. 436. The Davenport police then telephoned their counterparts in Des Moines to inform them that Williams had surrendered. McKnight, the lawyer, was still at the Des Moines police headquarters, and Williams conversed with McKnight on the telephone. In the presence of the Des Moines chief of police and a police detective named Leaming, McKnight advised Williams that Des Moines police officers would be driving to Davenport to pick him up, that the officers would not interrogate him or mistreat him, and that Williams was not to talk to the officers about Pamela Powers until after consulting with McKnight upon his return to Des Moines. As a result of these conversations, it was agreed between McKnight and the Des Moines police officials that Detective Leaming and a fellow officer would drive to Davenport to pick up Williams, that they would bring him directly back to Des Moines, and that they would not question him during the trip.

In the meantime Williams was arraigned before a judge in Davenport on the outstanding arrest warrant. The judge advised him of his *Miranda* rights and committed him to jail. Before leaving the courtroom, Williams conferred with a lawyer named Kelly, who advised him not to make any statements until consulting with McKnight back in Des Moines.

Detective Leaming and his fellow officer arrived in Davenport about noon to pick up Williams and return him to Des Moines. Soon after their arrival they met with Williams and Kelly, who, they understood, was acting as Williams' lawyer. Detective Learning repeated the *Miranda* warnings, and told Williams:

[W]e both know that you're being represented here by Mr. Kelly and you're being represented by Mr. McKnight in Des Moines, and . . . I want

you to remember this because we'll be visiting between here and Des Moines.

Williams then conferred again with Kelly alone, and after this conference Kelly reiterated to Detective Leaming that Williams was not to be questioned about the disappearance of Pamela Powers until after he had consulted with McKnight back in Des Moines. When Leaming expressed some reservations, Kelly firmly stated that the agreement with McKnight was to be carried out—that there was to be no interrogation of Williams during the automobile journey to Des Moines. Kelly was denied permission to ride in the police car back to Des Moines with Williams and the two officers.

The two detectives, with Williams in their charge, then set out on the 160-mile drive. At no time during the trip did Williams express a willingness to be interrogated in the absence of an attorney. Instead, he stated several times that "[w]hen I get to Des Moines and see Mr. McKnight, I am going to tell you the whole story." Detective Leaming knew that Williams was a former mental patient, and knew also that he was deeply religious.

The detective and his prisoner soon embarked on a wide-ranging conversation covering a variety of topics, including the subject of religion. Then, not long after leaving Davenport and reaching the interstate highway, Detective Leaming delivered what has been referred to in the briefs and oral arguments as the "Christian burial speech." Addressing Williams as "Reverend," the detective said:

I want to give you something to think about while we're traveling down the road. . . . Number one, I want you to observe the weather conditions, it's raining, it's sleeting, it's freezing, driving is very treacherous, visibility is poor, it's going to be dark early this evening. They are predicting several inches of snow for tonight, and I feel that you yourself are the only person that knows where this little girl's body is, that you yourself have only been there once, and if you get a snow on top of it you yourself may be unable to find it. And, since we will be going right past the area on the way into Des Moines, I feel that we could stop and locate the body, that the parents of this little girl should be entitled to a Christian burial for the little girl who was snatched away from them on Christmas [E]ve and murdered. And I feel we should stop and locate it on the way in rather than waiting until morning and trying to come back out after a snow storm and possibly not being able to find it at all.

Williams asked Detective Leaming why he thought their route to Des Moines would be taking them past the girl's body, and Leaming responded that he knew the body was in the area of Mitchellville   a town they would be passing on the way to Des Moines.[1] Leaming then stated: "I do not want you to answer me. I don't want to discuss it any further. Just think about it as we're riding down the road."

. . . The car continued towards Des Moines and as it approached Mitchellville, Williams said that he would show the officers where the body was. He then directed the police to the body of Pamela Powers.

Williams was indicted for first-degree murder. . . .

The evidence in question was introduced over counsel's continuing objection at the subsequent trial. The jury found Williams guilty of murder. . . .

2

. . . [T]here is no need to review in this case the doctrine of *Miranda v. Arizona*, a doctrine designed to secure the constitutional privilege against compulsory self-incrimination. . . . For it is clear that the judgment before us must in any event be affirmed upon the ground that Williams was deprived of a different constitutional right— the right to the assistance of counsel.

This right, guaranteed by the Sixth and Fourteenth Amendments, is indispensable to the fair administration of our adversary system of criminal justice.

. . . Whatever else it may mean, the right to counsel granted by the Sixth and Fourteenth Amendments means at least that a person is entitled to the help of a lawyer at or after the time that judicial proceedings have been initiated against him—"whether by way of formal charge, preliminary hearing, indictment, information, or arraignment." . . .

There can be no doubt in the present case that judicial proceedings had been initiated against Williams before the start of the automobile ride from Davenport to Des Moines. A warrant had been issued for his arrest, he had been arraigned on that warrant before a judge in a Davenport courtroom, and he had been committed by the court to confinement in jail. The State does not contend otherwise.

There can be no serious doubt, either, that Detective Leaming deliberately and designedly set out to elicit information from Williams just as surely as—and perhaps more effectively than—if he had formally interrogated him. Detective Leaming was fully aware before departing for Des Moines that Williams was being represented in Davenport by Kelly and in Des Moines by McKnight. Yet he purposely sought during Williams' isolation from his lawyers to obtain as much incriminating information as possible. Indeed, Detective Leaming conceded as much when he testified at Williams' trial:

Q: In fact, Captain, whether he was a mental patient or not, you were trying to get all the information you could before he got to his lawyer, weren't you?

A: I was sure hoping to find out where that little girl was, yes, sir. . . .

Q: Well, I'll put it this way: You was [sic] hoping to get all the information you could before Williams got back to McKnight, weren't you?

A: Yes, sir.

The state courts clearly proceeded upon the hypothesis that Detective Leaming's "Christian burial speech" had been tantamount to interrogation. Both courts recognized that Williams had been entitled to the assistance of counsel at the time he made the incriminating statements. Yet no such constitutional protection would have come into play if there had been no interrogation. . . .

3

The Iowa courts . . . held . . . that he had waived that right during the course of the automobile trip from Davenport to Des Moines. The state trial court explained its determination of waiver as follows:

> The time element involved on the trip, the general circumstances of it, and more importantly the absence on the Defendant's part of any assertion of his right or desire not to give information absent the presence of his attorney, are the main foundations for the Court's conclusion that he voluntarily waived such right.

. . . After carefully reviewing the evidence, the District Court concluded:

> [U]nder the proper standards for determining waiver, there simply is no evidence to support a waiver. . . . [T]here is no affirmative indication . . . that [Williams] did waive his rights. . . . [T]he state courts' emphasis on the absence of a demand for counsel was not only legally inappropriate, but factually unsupportable as well, since Detective Leaming himself testified that [Williams], on several occasions during the trip, indicated that he would talk *after* he saw Mr. McKnight. . . . Moreover, the statements were obtained only after Detective Leaming's use of psychology on a person whom he knew to be deeply religious and an escapee from a mental hospital—with the specific intent to elicit incriminating statements. In the face of this evidence, the State has produced no affirmative evidence whatsoever to support its claim of waiver, and, a fortiori, it cannot be said that the State has met its "heavy burden" of showing a knowing and intelligent waiver of . . . Sixth Amendment rights. *Id.*, at 182–183.

The Court of Appeals approved the reasoning of the District Court. . . .

The District Court and the Court of Appeals were . . . correct in their understanding of the proper standard to be applied in determining the question of waiver as a matter of federal constitutional law—that it was incumbent upon the State to prove "an intentional relinquishment or abandonment of a known right or privilege." *Johnson v. Zerbst*, 304 U.S., at 464. That standard has been reiterated in many cases. We have

said that the right to counsel does not depend upon a request by the defendant, *Miranda v. Arizona*, 384 U.S., at 471, and that courts indulge in every reasonable presumption against waiver. . . .

[Williams's] statements while in the car that he would tell the whole story *after* seeing McKnight in Des Moines were the clearest expressions by Williams himself that he desired the presence of an attorney before an interrogation took place. But even before making these statements, Williams had effectively asserted his right to counsel by having secured attorneys at both ends of the automobile trip, both of whom, acting as his agents, had made clear to the police that no interrogation was to occur during the journey. Williams knew of that agreement and, particularly in view of his consistent reliance on counsel, there is no basis for concluding that he disavowed it.

Despite Williams' express and implicit assertions of his right to counsel, Detective Leaming proceeded to elicit incriminating statements from Williams. Leaming did not preface this effort by telling Williams that he had a right to the presence of a lawyer, and made no effort at all to ascertain whether Williams wished to relinquish that right. The circumstances of record in this case thus provide no reasonable basis for finding that Williams waived his right to the assistance of counsel.

The Court of Appeals did not hold, nor do we, that under the circumstances of this case Williams *could not*, without notice to counsel, have waived his rights under the Sixth and Fourteenth Amendments. It only held, as do we, that he did not.

4

The crime of which Williams was convicted was senseless and brutal, calling for swift and energetic action by the police to apprehend the perpetrator and gather evidence with which he could be convicted. No mission of law enforcement officials is more important. Yet "[d]isinterested zeal for the public good does not assure either wisdom or right in the methods it pursues." *Haley v. Ohio* . . . Although we do not lightly affirm the issuance of a writ of habeas corpus in this case, so clear a violation of the Sixth and Fourteenth Amendments as here occurred cannot be condoned. The pressures on state executive and judicial officers charged with the administration of the criminal law are great, especially when the crime is murder and the victim a small child. But it is precisely the predictability of those pressures that makes imperative a resolute loyalty to the guarantees that the Constitution extends to us all.

The judgment of the Court of Appeals is affirmed.

It is so ordered.

Mr. Chief Justice Burger, dissenting:

The result in this case ought to be intolerable in any society which purports to call itself an organized society. It continues the Court—by the narrowest margin—on the much-criticized course of punishing the public for the mistakes and misdeeds of law enforcement officers, instead of punishing the officer directly, if in fact he is guilty of wrongdoing. It mechanically and blindly keeps reliable evidence from juries whether the claimed constitutional violation involves gross police misconduct or honest human error.

Williams is guilty of the savage murder of a small child; no member of the Court contends he is not. While in custody, and after no fewer than *five* warnings of his rights to silence and to counsel, he led police to the concealed body of his victim. The Court concedes Williams was not threatened or coerced and that he spoke and acted voluntarily and with full awareness of his constitutional rights. In the face of all this, the Court now holds that because Williams was prompted by the detective's statement—not interrogation but a statement—the jury must not be told how the police found the body.

Today's holding fulfills Judge (later Mr. Justice) Cardozo's grim prophecy that someday some court might carry the exclusionary rule to the absurd extent that its operative effect would exclude evidence relating to the body of a murder victim because of the means by which it was found. In so ruling the Court regresses to playing a grisly game of "hide and seek," once more exalting the sporting theory of criminal justice which has been experiencing a decline in our jurisprudence. With Justices White, Blackmun, and Rehnquist, I categorically reject the remarkable notion that the police in this case were guilty of unconstitutional misconduct, or any conduct justifying the bizarre result reached by the Court.

Mr. Justice White, with whom Mr. Justice Blackmun and Mr. Justice Rehnquist join, dissenting:

. . . The majority simply finds that no waiver was *proved* in this case. I disagree. That respondent knew of his right not to say anything to the officers without advice and presence of counsel is established on this record to a moral certainty. He was advised of the right by three officials of the State—telling at least one that he understood the right—and by two lawyers. Finally, he further demonstrated his knowledge of the right by informing the police that he would tell them the story in the presence of McKnight when they arrived in Des Moines. The issue in this case, then, is whether respondent relinquished that right intentionally.

Respondent relinquished his right not to talk to the police about his crime when the car approached the place where he had hidden the victim's clothes. Men usually intend to do what they do, and there is nothing in the record to support the proposition that respondent's decision to talk was anything but an exercise of his own free will. Apparently, without any prodding from the officers, respondent—who had earlier said that he would tell the whole story when he arrived in Des Moines—spontaneously changed his mind about the timing of his disclosures when the car approached the places where he had hidden the evidence. However, even if his statements were influenced by Detective Leaming's above-quoted statement, respondent's decision to talk in the absence of counsel can hardly be viewed as the product of an overborne will. The statement by Leaming was not coercive; it was accompanied by a request that respondent not respond to it; and it was delivered hours before respondent decided to make any statement. Respondent's waiver was thus knowing and intentional.

The majority's contrary conclusion seems to rest on the fact that respondent "asserted" his right to counsel by retaining and consulting with one lawyer and by consulting with another. How this supports the conclusion that respondent's later relinquishment of his right not to talk in the absence of counsel was unintentional is a mystery. The fact that respondent consulted with counsel on the question whether he should talk to the police in counsel's absence makes his later decision to talk in counsel's absence *better* informed and, if anything, more intelligent.

. . . Waiver is shown whenever the facts establish that an accused knew of a right and intended to relinquish it. Such waiver, even if not express, was plainly shown here. The only other conceivable basis for the majority's holding is the implicit suggestion . . . that the right . . . involved in *Miranda v. Arizona* . . . is a right not to be *asked* any questions in counsel's absence rather than a right not to *answer* any questions in counsel's absence, and that the right not to be *asked* questions must be waived *before* the questions are asked. Such wafer-thin distinctions cannot determine whether a guilty murderer should go free. The only conceivable purpose for the presence of counsel during questioning is to protect an accused from making incriminating *answers*. Questions, unanswered, have no significance at all.

NOTE

[1]The fact of the matter, of course, was that Detective Leaming possessed no such knowledge.

Rhode Island v. Innis

Mr. Justice Stewart delivered the opinion of the court:

In *Miranda v. Arizona* the Court held that, once a defendant in custody asks to speak with a lawyer, all interrogation must cease until a lawyer is present. The issue in this case is whether the respondent was "interrogated" in violation of the standards promulgated in the *Miranda* opinion.

1

On the night of January 12, 1975, John Mulvaney, a Providence, R.I., taxicab driver, disappeared after being dispatched to pick up a customer. His body was discovered four days later buried in a shallow grave in Coventry, R.I. He had died from a shotgun blast aimed at the back of his head.

On January 17, 1975, shortly after midnight, the Providence police received a telephone call from Gerald Aubin, also a taxicab driver, who reported that he had just been robbed by a man wielding a sawed-off shotgun. . . . Aubin identified a picture of the same person. That person was the respondent. Shortly thereafter, the Providence police began a search of the Mount Pleasant area.

At approximately 4:30 A.M. on the same date, Patrolman Lovell, while cruising the streets of Mount Pleasant in a patrol car, spotted the respondent standing in the street facing him. When Patrolman Lovell stopped his car, the respondent walked towards it. Patrolman Lovell then arrested the respondent, who was unarmed, and advised him of his so-called *Miranda* rights. While the two men waited in the patrol car for other police officers to arrive, Patrolman Lovell did not converse with the respondent other than to respond to the latter's request for a cigarette.

Within minutes, Sergeant Sears arrived at the scene of the arrest, and he also gave the respondent the *Miranda* warnings. Immediately thereafter, Captain Leyden and other police officers arrived. Captain Leyden advised the respondent of his *Miranda* rights. The respondent stated that he understood those rights and wanted to speak with a lawyer. Captain Leyden then directed that the respondent be placed in a "caged wagon," a four-door police car with a wire screen mesh between the front and rear seats, and be driven to the central police station. Three officers, Patrolmen Gleckman, Williams, and McKenna, were assigned to accompany the respondent to the central station. . . .

While en route to the central station, Patrolman Gleckman initiated a conversation with Patrolman McKenna concerning the missing shotgun. As Patrolman Gleckman later testified:

A. At this point, I was talking back and forth with Patrolman McKenna stating that I frequent this area while on patrol and [that because a school for handicapped children is located nearby,] there's a lot of handicapped children running around in this area, and God forbid one of them might find a weapon with shells and they might hurt themselves. App. 43–44.

Patrolman McKenna apparently shared his fellow officer's concern:

A. I more or less concurred with him [Gleckman] that it was a safety factor and that we should, you know, continue to search for the weapon and try to find it. Id., at 53.

While Patrolman Williams said nothing, he overheard the conversation between the two officers:

A. He [Gleckman] said it would be too bad if the little—I believe he said a girl—would pick up the gun, maybe kill herself. Id., at 59.

The respondent then interrupted the conversation, stating that the officers should turn the car around so he could show them where the gun was located. At this point, Patrolman McKenna radioed back to Captain Leyden that they were returning to the scene of the arrest, and that the respondent would inform them of the location of the gun. At the time the respondent indicated that the officers should turn back, they had traveled no more than a mile, a trip encompassing only a few minutes.

The police vehicle then returned to the scene of the arrest where a search for the shotgun was in progress. There, Captain Leyden again advised the respondent of his *Miranda* rights. The respondent replied that he understood those rights but that he "wanted to get the gun out of the way because of the kids in the area in the school." The respondent then led the police to a nearby field, where he pointed out the shotgun under some rocks by the side of the road.

On March 20, 1975, a grand jury returned an indictment charging the respondent with the kidnaping, robbery, and murder of John Mulvaney. Before trial, the respondent moved to suppress the shotgun and the statements he had made to the police regarding it. After an evidentiary hearing at which the respondent elected not to testify, the trial judge found that the respondent had been "repeatedly and completely advised of his *Miranda* rights." He further found that it was "entirely understandable that [the officers in the police vehicle] would voice their concern [for the safety of the handicapped children] to each other." The judge then concluded that the respondent's decision to inform the police of the location of the shotgun was "a waiver, clearly, and on the basis of the evidence that I have heard, and [sic] intelligent waiver, of his [*Miranda*] right to remain silent." Thus, without passing on whether the police officers had in fact "interrogated" the respondent, the trial court sustained the admissibility of the shotgun and testimony related to its discovery. That evidence was later introduced at the respondent's trial, and the jury returned a verdict of guilty on all counts.

On appeal, the Rhode Island Supreme Court, in a 3–2 decision, set aside the respondent's conviction. . . . Relying at least in part on this Court's decision in *Brewer v. Williams,* the court concluded that the respondent had invoked his *Miranda* right to counsel and that, contrary to *Miranda*'s mandate that, in the absence of counsel, all custodial interrogation then cease, the police officers in the vehicle had "interrogated" the respondent without a valid waiver of his right to counsel. It was the view of the state appellate court that, even though the police officers may have been genuinely concerned about the public safety and even though the respondent had not been addressed personally by the police officers, the respondent nonetheless had been subjected to "subtle coercion" that was the equivalent of "interrogation" within the meaning of the *Miranda* opinion. Moreover, contrary to the holding of the trial court, the appellate court concluded that the evidence was insufficient to support a finding of waiver. Having concluded that both the shotgun and testimony relating to its discovery were obtained in violation of the *Miranda* standards and therefore should not have been admitted into evidence, the Rhode Island Supreme Court held that the respondent was entitled to a new trial.

We granted certiorari to address for the first time the meaning of "interrogation" under *Miranda v. Arizona*.

2

. . . The starting point for defining "interrogation" in this context is, of course, the Court's *Miranda* opinion. There the Court observed that "[b]y custodial interrogation, we mean *questioning* initiated by law enforcement officers after a person has been taken into custody or otherwise deprived of his freedom of action in any significant way." This passage and other references throughout the opinion to "questioning" might suggest that the *Miranda* rules were to apply only to those police interrogation practices that involve express questioning of a defendant while in custody.

We do not, however, construe the *Miranda* opinion so narrowly. The concern of the Court in *Miranda* was that the "interrogation environment" created by the interplay of interrogation and custody would "subjugate the individual to the will of his examiner" and thereby undermine the privilege against compulsory self-incrimination. The police practices that evoked this concern included several that did not involve express questioning. For example, one of the practices discussed in *Miranda* was the use of line-ups in which a coached witness would pick the defendant as the perpetrator. This was designed to establish that the defendant was in fact guilty as a predicate for further interrogation. A variation on this theme discussed in *Miranda* was the so-called "reverse lineup" in which a defendant would be identified by coached witnesses as the perpetrator of a fictitious crime, with the object of inducing him

to confess to the actual crime of which he was suspected in order to escape the false prosecution. The Court in *Miranda* also included in its survey of interrogation practices the use of psychological ploys, such as to "posi[t]" "the guilt of the subject," to "minimize the moral seriousness of the offense," and "to cast blame on the victim or on society." It is clear that these techniques of persuasion, no less than express questioning, were thought, in a custodial setting, to amount to interrogation. . . .

We conclude that the *Miranda* safeguards come into play whenever a person in custody is subjected to either express questioning or its functional equivalent. That is to say, the term "interrogation" under *Miranda* refers not only to express questioning, but also to any words or actions on the part of the police (other than those normally attendant to arrest and custody) that the police should know are reasonably likely to elicit an incriminating response from the suspect. The latter portion of this definition focuses primarily upon the perceptions of the suspect, rather than the intent of the police. This focus reflects the fact that the *Miranda* safeguards were designed to vest a suspect in custody with an added measure of protection against coercive police practices, without regard to objective proof of the underlying intent of the police. A practice that the police should know is reasonably likely to evoke an incriminating response from a suspect thus amounts to interrogation. But, since the police surely cannot be held accountable for the unforeseeable results of their words or actions, the definition of interrogation can extend only to words or actions on the part of police officers that they *should have known* were reasonably likely to elicit an incriminating response.[1]

Turning to the facts of the present case, we conclude that the respondent was not "interrogated" with the meaning of *Miranda*. It is undisputed that the first prong of the definition of "interrogation" was not satisfied, for the conversation between Patrolmen Gleckman and McKenna included no express questioning of the respondent. Rather, that conversation was, at least in form, nothing more than a dialogue between the two officers to which no response from the respondent was invited.

Moreover, it cannot be fairly concluded that the respondent was subjected to the "functional equivalent" of questioning. It cannot be said, in short, that Patrolmen Gleckman and McKenna should have known that their conversation was reasonably likely to elicit an incriminating response from the respondent. There is nothing in the record to suggest that the officers were aware that the respondent was peculiarly susceptible to an appeal to his conscience concerning the safety of handicapped children. Nor is there anything in the record to suggest that the police knew that the respondent was unusually disoriented or upset at the time of his arrest.[2]

The case thus boils down to whether, in the context of a brief conversation, the officers should have known that the respondent would suddenly be moved to make a self-incriminating response. Given the fact that the entire conversation appears to have consisted of no more than a few offhand remarks, we cannot say that the officers should have known that it was reasonably likely that Innis would so respond. This is not a case where the police carried on a lengthy harangue in the presence of the suspect. Nor does the record support the respondent's contention that, under the circumstances, the officers' comments were particularly "evocative." It is our view, therefore, that the respondent was not subjected by the police to words or actions that the police should have known were reasonably likely to elicit an incriminating response from him.

The Rhode Island Supreme Court erred, in short, in equating "subtle compulsion" with interrogation. That the officers' comments struck a responsive chord is readily apparent. Thus, it may be said, as the Rhode Island Supreme Court did say, that the respondent was subjected to "subtle compulsion." But that is not the end of the inquiry. It must also be established that a suspect's incriminating response was the product of words or actions on the part of the police that they should have known were reasonably likely to elicit an incriminating response. This was not established in the present case.

Mr. Justice Stevens, dissenting:

1

. . . As the Court recognizes, *Miranda v. Arizona* makes it clear that, once respondent requested an attorney, he had an absolute right to have any type of interrogation cease until an attorney was present. As it also recognizes, *Miranda* requires that the term "interrogation" be broadly construed to include "either express questioning or its functional equivalent." In my view any statement that would normally be understood by the average listener as calling for a response is the functional equivalent of a direct question, whether or not it is punctuated by a question mark. The Court, however, takes a much narrower view. It holds that police conduct is not the "functional equivalent" of direct questioning unless the police should have known that what they were saying or doing was likely to elicit an incriminating response from the suspect.[3] This holding represents a plain departure from the principles set forth in *Miranda*.

In *Miranda* the Court required the now-familiar warnings to be given to suspects prior to custodial interrogation in order to dispel the atmosphere of coercion that necessarily accompanies such interrogations. In order to perform that function effectively, the warnings must be viewed by both the police and the suspect as a correct and binding statement of their respective rights. Thus, if after being told that he has a right to have an attorney present during interrogation, a suspect chooses to cut off questioning until counsel can be obtained, his choice must be "scrupulously honored" by the police. . . . At the least this must mean that the police are prohibited from making deliberate attempts to elicit statements from the suspect. Yet the Court is unwilling to characterize all such attempts as "interrogation," noting only that "where a police practice is designed to elicit an incriminating response from the accused, it is unlikely that the practice will not also be one which the police should have known was reasonably likely to have that effect."

From the suspect's point of view, the effectiveness of the warnings depends on whether it appears that the police are scrupulously honoring his rights. Apparent attempts to elicit information from a suspect after he has invoked his right to cut off questioning necessarily demean that right and tend to reinstate the imbalance between police and suspect that the *Miranda* warnings are designed to correct. Thus, if the rationale for requiring those warnings in the first place is to be respected, any police conduct or statements that would appear to a reasonable person in the suspect's position to call for a response must be considered "interrogation."

In short, in order to give full protection to a suspect's right to be free from any interrogation at all, the definition of "interrogation" must include any police statement or conduct that has the same purpose or effect as a direct question. Statements that appear to call for a response from the suspect, as well as those that are designed to do so, should be considered interrogation. By prohibiting only those relatively few statements or actions that a police officer should know are likely to elicit an incriminating response, the Court today accords a suspect considerably less protection. Indeed, since I suppose most suspects are unlikely to incriminate themselves even when questioned directly, this new definition will almost certainly exclude every statement that is not punctuated with a question mark from the concept of "interrogation."

The difference between the approach required by a faithful adherence to *Miranda* and the stinted test applied by the Court today can be illustrated by comparing three different ways in which Officer Gleckman could have communicated his fears about the possible dangers posed by the shotgun to handicapped children. He could have:

1. directly asked Innis: Will you please tell me where the shotgun is so we can protect handicapped schoolchildren from danger?

2. announced to the other officers in the wagon: If the man sitting in the back seat with me should decide to tell us where the gun is, we can protect handicapped children from danger, or

3. stated to the other officers: It would be too bad if a little handicapped girl would pick up the gun that this man left in the area and maybe kill herself.

In my opinion, all three of these statements should be considered interrogation because all three appear to be designed to elicit a response from anyone who in fact knew where the gun was located. Under the Court's test, on the other hand, the form of the statements would be critical. The third statement would not be interrogation because in the Court's view there was no reason for Officer Gleckman to believe that Innis was susceptible to this type of an implied appeal; therefore, the statement would not be reasonably likely to elicit an incriminating response. Assuming that this is true, . . . then it seems to me that the first two statements, which would be just as unlikely to elicit such a response, should also not be considered interrogation. But, because the first statement is clearly an express question, it *would* be considered interrogation under the Court's test. The second statement, although just as clearly a deliberate appeal to Innis to reveal the location of the gun, would presumably not be interrogation because (a) it was not in form a direct question and (b) it does not fit within the "reasonably likely to elicit an incriminating response" category that applies to indirect interrogation.

As this example illustrates, the Court's test creates an incentive for police to ignore a suspect's invocation of his rights in order to make continued attempts to extract information from him. If a suspect does not appear to be susceptible to a particular type of psychological pressure, the police are apparently free to exert that pressure on him despite his request for counsel, so long as they are careful not to punctuate their statements with question marks. And if, contrary to all reasonable expectations, the suspect makes an incriminating statement, that statement can be used against him at trial. The Court thus turns *Miranda*'s unequivocal rule against any interrogation at all into a trap in which unwary suspects may be caught by police deception.

2

. . . In any event, I think the Court is clearly wrong in holding, as a matter of law, that Officer Gleckman should not have realized that his statement was likely to elicit an incriminating response. The Court implicitly assumes that, at least in the absence of a lengthy harangue, a criminal suspect will not be likely to respond to indirect appeals to his humanitarian impulses. It then goes on to state that the officers in this case had no reason to believe that respondent would be unusually susceptible to such appeals. . . . Finally, although the significance of the officer's intentions is not clear under its objective test, the Court states in a footnote that the record "in no way suggests" that Officer Gleckman's remarks were designed to elicit a response. . . .

The Court's assumption that criminal suspects are not susceptible to appeals to conscience is directly contrary to the teachings of police interrogation manuals, which recommend appealing to a suspect's sense of morality as a standard and often successful interrogation technique. Surely the practical experience embodied in such manuals should not be ignored in a case such as this in which the record is devoid of any evidence—one way or the other—as to the susceptibility of suspects in general or of Innis in particular.

NOTES

[1] Any knowledge the police may have had concerning the unusual susceptibility of a defendant to a particular form of persuasion might be an important factor in determining whether the police should have known that their words or actions were reasonably likely to elicit an incriminating response from the suspect.

[2] The record in no way suggests that the officers' remarks were *designed* to elicit a response. . . . It is significant that the trial judge, after hearing the officers' testimony, concluded that it was "entirely understandable that [the officers] would voice their concern [for the safety of the handicapped children] to each other."

[3] In limiting its test to police statements "likely to elicit an incriminating response," the Court confuses the scope of the exclusionary rule with the definition of "interrogation." Of course, any incriminating statement as defined in *Miranda* . . . must be excluded from evidence if it is the product of impermissible interrogation. But I fail to see how this rule helps in deciding whether a particular statement or tactic constitutes "interrogation." After all, *Miranda* protects a suspect in Innis' position not simply from interrogation that is likely to be successful, but from any interrogation at all.

REVIEW AND DISCUSSION QUESTIONS

1. The Fifth Amendment states that no one "shall be compelled in any criminal case to be a witness against himself." What possible moral or political justification is there for a right against self-incrimination? What, if anything, would be morally objectionable about a judicial system that required accused persons to testify?

2. In *Miranda* the Court describes various interrogation techniques that involve trickery and psychological manipulation. What, if anything, is morally objectionable about such techniques? The Court states that its "decision is not intended to hamper the traditional function of police officers in investigating a crime," but is effective police work possible without the use of such techniques? Do the Court's examples support McCloskey's reasons for believing that many innocent people are wrongfully convicted?

3. Why is the issue in *Brewer* one of the right to counsel rather than self-incrimination?

4. Did the "Christian burial speech" violate Williams's right to counsel? Who is right about this—the majority or the dissenters? Explain.

5. In *Innis,* the Court states that "the *Miranda* safeguards come into play whenever a person in custody is subjected to either express questioning or its functional equivalent." Was the Court justified in deciding that Innis had not been subject to interrogation in either sense? Why or why not? What factors need to be considered in determining whether a suspect like Innis was or was not interrogated?

6. Consider the three statements distinguished by Stevens in his dissent. Is he correct that all three should be considered interrogation? Would you agree with Stevens that the Court's decision creates "an incentive for police to ignore a suspect's invocation of his rights in order to make continued attempts to extract information from him"?

Criminal Justice and the Negotiated Plea

Kenneth Kipnis

Most criminal cases are settled by negotiated pleas ("plea bargains"). In fact, our criminal justice system today depends on most defendants agreeing not to go to trial. Kenneth Kipnis, professor of philosophy at the University of Hawaii–Manoa, criticizes the institution of plea bargaining on the ground that it involves something comparable to duress and thus erodes our right to be free from compelled self-incrimination. Furthermore, innocent people may be forced to "cop a plea," and because even guilty individuals are not given the punishment they deserve, plea bargaining rarely, if ever, produces a just outcome.

In recent years it has become apparent to many that, in practice, the criminal justice system in the United States does not operate as we thought it did. The conviction secured through jury trial, so familiar in countless novels, films, and television programs, is beginning to be seen as the aberration it has become. What has replaced the jury's verdict is the negotiated plea. In these "plea bargains" the defendant agrees to plead guilty in exchange for discretionary consideration on the part of the state. Generally, this consideration amounts to some kind of assurance of a minimal sentence. . . . It is at present a commonplace that plea bargaining could not be eliminated without substantial alterations in our criminal justice system.

Plea bargaining involves negotiations between the defendant (through an attorney in the standard case) and the prosecutor as to the conditions under which the defendant will enter a guilty plea. Both sides have bargaining power in these negotiations. The prosecutor is ordinarily burdened with cases and does not have the wherewithal to bring more than a fraction of them to trial. Often there is not sufficient evidence to ensure a jury's conviction. Most important, the prosecutor is typically under administrative and political pressure to dispose of cases and to secure convictions as efficiently as possible. If the defendant exercises the constitutional right to a jury trial, the prosecutor must decide whether to drop the charges entirely or to expend scarce resources to bring the case to trial. Since neither prospect is attractive, prosecutors typically exercise their broad discretion to induce defendants to waive trial and to plead guilty.

From the defendant's point of view, such prosecutorial discretion has two aspects: it darkens the prospect of going to trial as it brightens the prospect of pleading guilty. Before negotiating, a prosecutor may improve his bargaining position by "overcharging" defendants or by developing a reputation for severity in the sentences he recommends to judges. Such steps greatly increase the punishment that the defendant must expect if convicted at trial. On the other hand, the state may offer to reduce or to drop some charges, or to recommend leniency to the judge if the defendant agrees to plead guilty. These steps minimize the punishment that will result from a guilty plea. Though the exercise of prosecutorial discretion to secure pleas of guilty may differ somewhat in certain jurisdictions and in particular cases, the broad outlines are as described.

Of course a defendant can always reject any offer of concessions and challenge the state to prove its case. A skilled defense attorney can do much to force the prosecutor to expend resources in bringing a case to trial. But the trial route is rarely taken by defendants. Apart from prosecutorial pressure, other factors may contribute to a defendant's willingness to plead guilty: feelings of guilt which may or may not be connected with the charged crime; the discomforts of the pretrial lockup as against the comparatively better facilities of a penitentiary; the costs of going to trial as against the often cheaper option of consenting to a plea; a willingness or unwillingness to lie; and the delays which are almost always present in awaiting trial, delays which the defendant may sit out in jail in a kind of preconviction imprisonment which may not be credited to a postconviction sentence. It is not surprising that the right to a trial by jury is rarely exercised. . . .

No deliberative body ever decided that we would have a system in which the disposition of criminal cases is typically the result of negotiations between the prosecutor and the defendant's attorney on the conditions under which the defendant would waive trial and plead guilty to a mutually acceptable charge. No legislature ever voted to adopt a procedure in which defendants who are convicted after trial typically receive sentences far greater than those received by defendants charged with similar offenses but pleading guilty. The practice of plea bargaining has evolved in the unregulated interstices of our criminal justice system. Its development has not gone unnoticed. There is now a substantial literature on the legality and propriety of plea bargaining. But though philosophers do not often treat issues arising in the area of criminal procedure, there are problems here that cry for our attention. In the preceding pages I have been concerned to sketch the institution of plea bargaining. In what follows I will raise some serious questions about it that should concern us. I will first discuss generally the intrinsic fairness of plea bargains and then, in the final section, I will examine critically the place of such bargains in the criminal justice system.

1

As one goes through the literature on plea bargaining one gets the impression that market forces are at work in this unlikely context. The terms "bargain" and "negotiation" suggest this. One can see the law of supply and demand operating in that, other things being equal, if there are too many defendants who want to go to trial, prosecutors will have to concede more in order to get the guilty pleas that they need to clear their case load. And if the number of prosecutors and courts goes up, prosecutors will be able to

concede less. Against this background it is not surprising to find one commentator noting: "In some places a 'going rate' is established under which a given charge will automatically be broken down to a given lesser offense with the recommendation of a given lesser sentence." Prosecutors, like retailers before them, have begun to appreciate the efficiency of the fixed-price approach.

The plea bargain in the economy of criminal justice has many of the important features of the contract in commercial transactions. In both institutions offers are made and accepted, entitlements are given up and obtained, and the notion of an exchange, ideally a fair one, is present to both parties. Indeed one detects something of the color of consumer protection law in a few of the decisions on plea bargaining. In *Bailey v. MacDougal* the court held that "a guilty plea cannot be accepted unless the defendant understands its consequences." And in *Santo Bello v. New York* the court secured a defendant's entitlement to a prosecutorial concession when a second prosecutor replaced the one who had made the promise. . . . Though plea bargains may not be seen as contracts by the parties, agreements like them are the stuff of contract case law. While I will not argue that plea bargains are contracts (or even that they should be treated as such), I do think it proper to look to contract law for help in evaluating the justice of such agreements.

The law of contracts serves to give legal effect to certain bargain-promises. In particular, it specifies conditions that must be satisfied by bargain-promises before the law will recognize and enforce them as contracts. As an example, we could look at that part of the law of contracts which treats duress. Where one party wrongfully compels another to consent to the terms of an agreement the resulting bargain has no legal effect. Dan B. Dobbs, a commentator on the law in this area, describes the elements of duress as follows: "The defendant's act must be wrongful in some attenuated sense; it must operate coercively upon the will of the plaintiff, judged subjectively, and the plaintiff must have no adequate remedy to avoid the coercion except to give in. . . . The earlier requirement that the coercion must have been the kind that would coerce a reasonable man, or even a brave one, is now generally dispensed with, and it is enough if it in fact coerced a spineless plaintiff." Coercion is not the same as fraud, nor is it confined to cases in which a defendant is physically compelled to assent. In Dobbs' words: "The victim of duress knows the facts but is forced by hard choices to act against his will." The paradigm case of duress is the agreement made at gunpoint. Facing a mortal threat, one readily agrees to hand over the cash. But despite such consent, the rules of duress work to void the effects of such agreements. There is no legal obligation to hand over the cash and, having given it over, entitlement to the money is not lost. The gunman has no legal right to retain possession even if he adheres to his end of the bargain and scraps his murderous plans.

Judges have long been required to see to it that guilty pleas are entered voluntarily. And one would expect that, if duress is present in the plea-bargaining situation, then, just as the handing over of cash to the gunman is void of legal effect (as far as entitlement to the money is concerned), so no legal consequences should flow from the plea of guilty which is the product of duress. However, Rule 11 of the Federal Rules of Criminal Procedure requires the court to insure that a plea of guilty (or nolo contendere) is voluntary by "addressing the defendant personally in open court, determining that the plea is voluntary and not the result of force or promises *apart from a plea agreement*" (emphasis added). In two important cases (*North Carolina v. Alford* and *Brady v. United States*) defendants agreed to plead guilty in order to avoid probable death sentences. Both accepted very long prison sentences. In both cases the Supreme Court decided that guilty pleas so entered were voluntary (though Brennan, Douglas, and Marshall dissented). In his dissent in *Alford*, Brennan writes: ". . . the facts set out in the majority opinion demonstrate that Alford was 'so gripped by fear of the death penalty' that his decision to plead guilty was not voluntary but was that product of duress as much so as choice reflecting physical constraint.'" In footnote 2 of the *Alford* opinion, the Court sets out the defendant's testimony given at the time of the entry of his plea of guilty

before the trial court. That testimony deserves examination: "I pleaded guilty on second degree murder because they said there is too much evidence, but I ain't shot no man, but I take the fault for the other man. We never had an argument in our life and I just pleaded guilty because they said if I didn't they would gas me for it, and that is all." The rule to be followed in such cases is set out in *Brady:* "A plea of guilty entered by one fully aware of the direct consequences, including the actual value of any commitments made to him by the court, prosecutor or his own counsel, must stand unless induced by threats (or promises to discontinue improper harassment), misrepresentation (including unfilled or unfillable promises), or perhaps by promises that are by their very nature improper as having no proper relationship to the prosecutor's business (e.g. bribes)." Case law and the Federal Rules both hold that the standard exercise of prosecutorial discretion in order to secure a plea of guilty cannot be used to prove that such a plea is [in]voluntary. Even where the defendant enters a guilty plea in order to avert his death at the hands of the state, as in *Alford*, the Court has not seen involuntariness. Nevertheless, it may be true that some guilty pleas are involuntary in virtue of prosecutorial inducement considered proper by the Supreme Court.

Regarding the elements of duress, let us compare the gunman situation with an example of plea bargaining in order to examine the voluntariness of the latter. Albert W. Alschuler, author of one of the most thorough studies of plea bargaining, describes an actual case:

San Francisco defense attorney Benjamin M. Davis recently represented a man charged with kidnapping and forcible rape. The defendant was innocent, Davis says, and after investigating the case Davis was confident of an acquittal. The prosecutor, who seems to have shared the defense attorney's opinion on this point, offered to permit a guilty plea to simple battery. Conviction on this charge would not have led to a greater sentence than thirty days' imprisonment, and there was every likelihood that the defendant would be granted probation. When Davis informed his client of this offer, he emphasized that conviction at trial seemed highly improbable.

The defendant's reply was simple: "I can't take the chance."

Both the gunman and the prosecutor require persons to make hard choices between a very certain smaller imposition and an uncertain greater imposition. In the gunman situation I must choose between the very certain loss of money and the difficult-to-assess probability that my assailant is willing and able to kill me if I resist. As a defendant I am forced to choose between a very certain smaller punishment and a substantially greater punishment with a difficult-to-assess probability. As the size of the certain smaller imposition comes down and as the magnitude and probability of the larger imposition increases, it becomes more and more reasonable to choose the former. This is what seems to be occurring in Alschuler's example: "Davis reports that he is uncomfortable when he permits innocent defendants to plead guilty; but in this case it would have been playing God to stand in the defendant's way. The attorney's assessment of the outcome at trial can always be wrong, and it is hard to tell a defendant that 'professional ethics' require a course that may ruin his life." Davis's client must decide whether to accept a very certain, very minor punishment or to chance a ruined life. Of course the gunman's victim can try to overpower his assailant and the defendant can attempt to clear himself at trial. But the same considerations that will drive reasonable people to give in to the gunman compel one to accept the prosecutor's offer. Applying the second and third elements of duress, one can see that, like the gunman's acts, the acts of the prosecutor can "operate coercively upon the will of the plaintiff, judged subjectively," and both the gunman's victim and the defendant may "have no adequate remedy to avoid the coercion except to give in." In both cases reasonable persons might well conclude (after considering the gunman's lethal weapon or the gas chamber) "I can't take the chance." A spineless person would not need to deliberate. . . .

One might argue that not all "hard choices" are examples of duress. A doctor could offer to sell vital treatment for a large sum. After the patient has been cured it will hardly do for her to claim that she has been the victim of duress. The doctor may have forced the patient to choose between a certain financial loss and the risk of death. But surely doctors are not like gunmen.

Two important points need to be made in response to this objection. First, the doctor is not, one assumes, responsible for the diseased condition of the patient. The patient would be facing death even if she had never met the doctor. But this is not true in the case of the gunman, where both impositions are his work. And in this respect the prosecutor offering a plea bargain in a criminal case is like the gunman rather than like the doctor. For the state forces a choice between adverse consequences that it imposes. And, of course, one cannot say that in the defendant's wrongoing he has brought his dreadful dilemma upon himself. To do so would be to ignore the good reasons there are for the presumption of innocence in dispositive criminal proceedings.

Second, our laws do not prohibit doctors from applying their healing skills to maximize their own wealth. They are free to contract to perform services in return for a fee. But our laws do severely restrict the state in its prosecution of criminal defendants. Those who framed our constitution were well aware of the great potential for abuse that the criminal law affords. Much of the Constitution (especially the Bill of Rights) checks the activity of the state in this area. In particular, the Fifth Amendment provides that no person "shall be compelled in any criminal case to be a witness against himself." If I am right in judging that defendants like Alford and Davis's client do not act freely in pleading guilty to the facts of their cases, that the forced choice of the prosecutor may be as coercive as the forced choice of the gunman, that a defendant may be compelled to speak against himself (or herself) by a prosecutor's discretion inducing him to plead guilty, then given the apparent constitutional prohibition of such compulsion, the prosecutor acts wrongfully in compelling such pleas. And in this manner it may be that the last element of duress, wrongfulness, can be established. But it is not my purpose here to establish the unconstitutionality of plea bargaining, for it is not necessary to reach to unconstitutionality to grasp the wrongfulness of that institution. One need only reflect upon what justice amounts to in our system of criminal law. This is the task I will take up in the final section of this paper.

2

Not too long ago plea bargaining was an officially prohibited practice. Court procedures were followed to ensure that no concessions had been given to defendants in exchange for guilty pleas. But gradually it became widely known that these procedures had become charades of perjury, shysterism, and bad faith involving judges, prosecutors, defense attorneys and defendants. This was scandalous. But rather than cleaning up the practice in order to square it with the rules, the rules were changed in order to bring them in line with the practice. . . .

Without going deeply into detail, I believe that it can be asserted without controversy that the liberal-democratic approach to criminal justice—and in particular the American criminal justice system—is an institutionalization of two principles. The first principle refers to the intrinsic point of systems of criminal justice.

A. Those (and only those) individuals who are clearly guilty of certain serious specified wrongdoings deserve an officially administered punishment which is proportional to their wrongdoing. In the United States it is possible to see this principle underlying the activities of legislators specifying and grading wrongdoings which are serious enough to warrant criminalization and, further, determining the range of punishment appropriate to each offense; the activities of policemen and prosecutors bringing to trial those who are suspected of having committed such wrongdoings; the activities of jurors determining if defendants are guilty beyond a reasonable doubt; the activities of defense attorneys insuring that relevant facts in defendants' favor are brought out at trial; the activities of judges seeing to it that proceedings are fair and that those who are convicted receive the punishment they deserve; and the activities of probation officers, parole officers, and prison personnel executing the sentences of the courts. All of these people play a part in bringing the guilty to justice.

But in liberal-democratic societies not everything is done to accomplish this end. A second principle makes reference to the limits placed upon the power of the state to identify and punish the guilty.

B. Certain basic liberties shall not be violated in bringing the guilty to justice. This second principle can be seen to underlie the constellation of constitutional checks on the activities of virtually every person playing a role in the administration of the criminal justice system.

Each of these principles is related to a distinctive type of injustice that can occur in the context of criminal law. An injustice can occur in the outcome of the criminal justice procedure. That is, an innocent defendant may be convicted and punished, or a guilty defendant may be acquitted or, if convicted, he or she may receive more or less punishment than is deserved. Because these injustices occur in the meting out of punishment to defendants who are being processed by the system, we can refer to them as internal injustices. They are violations of the first principle. On the other hand, there is a type of injustice which occurs when basic liberties are violated in the operation of the criminal justice system. It may be true that Star Chamber proceedings, torture, hostages, bills of attainder, dragnet arrests, unchecked searches, *ex post facto* laws, unlimited invasions of privacy, and an arsenal of other measures could be employed to bring more of the guilty to justice. But these steps lead to a dystopia where our most terrifying nightmares can come true. However we limit the activity of the criminal justice system in the interest of basic liberty, that limit can be overstepped. We can call such infringements upon basic liberties external injustices. They are violations of the second principle. If, for example, what I have suggested in the previous section is correct, then plea bargaining can bring about an external injustice with respect to a basic liberty secured by the Fifth Amendment. The remainder of this section will be concerned with internal injustice or violations of the first principle.

It is necessary to draw a further distinction between aberrational and systemic injustice. It may very well be that in the best criminal justice system that we are capable of devising human limitations will result in some aberrational injustice. Judges, jurors, lawyers, and legislators with the best of intentions may make errors in judgment that result in mistakes in the administration of punishment. But despite the knowledge that an unknown percentage of all dispositions of criminal cases are, to some extent, miscarriages of justice, it may still be reasonable to believe that a certain system of criminal justice is well calculated to avoid such results within the limits referred to by the second principle. We can refer to these incorrect outcomes of a sound system of criminal justice as instances of aberrational injustice. In contrast, instances of systemic injustice are those that result from structural flaws in the criminal justice system itself. Here incorrect outcomes in the operations of the system are not the result of human error. Rather, the system itself is not well calculated to avoid injustice. What would be instances of aberrational injustice in a sound system are not aberrations in an unsound system: they are a standard result.

. . . [S]ystemic injustice in the context of criminal law is a much more serious matter than aberrational injustice. It should not be forgotten that the criminal sanction is the most severe imposition that the state can visit upon one of its citizens. While it is possible to tolerate occasional error in a sound system, systematic carelessness in the administration of punishment is negligence of the highest order.

With this framework in mind, let us look at a particular instance of plea bargaining recently described by a legal aid defense attorney. Ted Alston has been charged with armed robbery. Let us assume that persons who have committed armed robbery (in the way Alston is accused of having committed it) deserve five to seven years of prison. Alston's attorney sets out the options for him: "I told Alston it was possible, perhaps even probable, that if he went to trial he would be convicted and get a prison term of perhaps five to seven years. On the other hand, if he agreed to plead guilty to a low-grade felony, he

would get a probationary sentence and not go to prison. The choice was his." Let us assume that Alston accepts the terms of the bargain and pleads guilty to a lesser offense. If Alston did commit the armed robbery, there is a violation of the first principle in that he receives far less punishment than he deserves. On the other hand, if Alston did not commit the armed robbery, there is still a violation of the first principle in that he is both convicted of and punished for a crime that he did not commit, a crime that no one seriously believes to be his distinctive wrongdoing. It is of course possible that while Alston did not commit the armed robbery, he did commit the lesser offense. But though justice would be done here, it would be an accident. Such a serendipitous result is a certain sign that what we have here is systemic injustice.

If we assume that legislatures approximate the correct range of punishment for each offense, that judges fairly sentence those who are convicted by juries, and that prosecutors reasonably charge defendants, then, barring accidents, justice will *never* be the outcome of the plea-bargaining procedure: the defendant who "cops a plea" will never receive the punishment which is deserved. Of course legislatures can set punishments too high, judges can oversentence those who are convicted by juries, and prosecutors can overcharge defendants. In these cases the guilty can receive the punishment they deserve through plea bargaining. But in these cases we compensate for one injustice by introducing others that unfairly jeopardize the innocent and those that demand trials.

In contrast to plea bargaining, the disposition of criminal cases by jury trial seems well calculated to avoid internal injustices even if these may sometimes occur. Where participants take their responsibilities seriously we have good reason to believe that the outcome is just, even when this may not be so. In contrast, with plea bargaining we have no reason to believe that the outcome is just even when it is.

I think that the appeal that plea bargaining has is rooted in our attitude toward bargains in general. Where both parties are satisfied with the terms of an agreement, it is improper to interfere. Generally speaking, prosecutors and defendants are pleased with the advantages they gain by negotiating a plea. And courts, which gain as well, are reluctant to vacate negotiated pleas where only "proper" inducements have been applied and where promises have been understood and kept. Such judicial neutrality may be commendable where entitlements are being exchanged. But the criminal justice system is not such a context. Rather it is one in which persons are justly given, not what they have bargained for, but what they deserve, irrespective of their bargaining position.

To appreciate this, let us consider another context in which desert plays a familiar role; the assignment of grades in an academic setting. Imagine a "grade bargain" negotiated between a grade-conscious student and a harried instructor. A term paper has been submitted and, after glancing at the first page, the instructor says that if he were to read the paper carefully, applying his usually rigid standards, he would probably decide to give the paper a grade of D. But if the student were to waive his right to a careful reading and conscientious critique, the instructor would agree to a grade of B. The grade-point average being more important to him than either education or justice in grading, the student happily accepts the B, and the instructor enjoys a reduced workload.

One strains to imagine legislators and administrators commending the practice of grade bargaining because it permits more students to be processed by fewer instructors. Teachers can be freed from the burden of having to read and to criticize every paper. One struggles to envision academicians arguing for grade bargaining, suggesting that a quick assignment of a grade is a more effective influence on the behavior of students, urging that grade bargaining is necessary to the efficient functioning of the schools. There can be no doubt that students who have negotiated a grade are more likely to accept and to understand the verdict of the instructor. Moreover, in recognition of a student's help to the school (by waiving both the reading and the critique), it is proper for the instructor to be lenient. Finally, a quickly assigned grade enables the guidance personnel and the registrar to respond rapidly and appropriately to the student's situation.

What makes all of this laughable is what makes plea bargaining outrageous. For grades, like punishments, should be deserved. Justice in retribution, like justice in grading, does not require that the end result be acceptable to the parties. To reason that because the parties are satisfied the bargain should stand is to be seriously confused. For bargains are out of place in contexts where persons are to receive what they deserve. And the American courtroom, like the American classroom, should be such a context.

In this section, until now I have been attempting to show that plea bargaining is not well calculated to insure that those guilty of wrongdoing will receive the punishment they deserve. But a further point needs to be made. While the conviction of the innocent would be a problem in any system we might devise, it appears to be a greater problem under plea bargaining. With the jury system the guilt of the defendant must be established in an adversary proceeding and it must be established beyond a reasonable doubt to each of twelve jurors. This is very staunch protection against an aberrational conviction. But under plea bargaining the foundation for conviction need only include a factual basis for the plea (in the opinion of the judge) and the guilty plea itself. Considering the coercive nature of the circumstances surrounding the plea, it would be a mistake to attach much reliability to it. Indeed, as we have seen in *Alford*, guilty pleas are acceptable even when accompanied by a denial of guilt. . . . Now it is one thing to show to a judge that there are facts which support a plea of guilty and quite another to prove to twelve jurors in an adversary proceeding guilt beyond a reasonable doubt. Plea bargaining substantially erodes the standards for guilt and it is reasonable to assume that the sloppier we are in establishing guilt, the more likely it is that innocent persons will be convicted. So apart from having no reason whatever to believe that the guilty are receiving the punishment they deserve, we have far less reason to believe that the convicted are guilty in the first place than we would after a trial.

In its coercion of criminal defendants, in its abandonment of desert as the measure of punishment, and in its relaxation of the standards for conviction, plea bargaining falls short of the justice we expect of our legal system. I have no doubt that substantial changes will have to be made if the institution of plea bargaining is to be obliterated or even removed from its central position in the criminal justice system. No doubt we need more courts and more prosecutors. Perhaps ways can be found to streamline the jury trial procedure without sacrificing its virtues. Certainly it would help to decriminalize the host of victimless crimes—drunkenness and other drug offenses, illicit sex, gambling, and so on—

in order to free resources for dealing with more serious wrongdoings. And perhaps crime itself can be reduced if we begin to attack seriously those social and economic injustices that have for too long sent their victims to our prisons in disproportionate numbers. In any case, if we are to expect our citizenry to respect the law, we must take care to insure that our legal institutions are worthy of that respect. I have tried to show that plea bargaining is not worthy, that we must seek a better way. Bargain justice does not become us.

REVIEW AND DISCUSSION QUESTIONS

1. Is it fair that defendants who plead guilty are given more lenient sentences than those who are found guilty by trial?

2. Do prosecutor and defendant have equal bargaining weight in plea negotiations? Does plea bargaining involve duress or just a "hard choice"? If duress, is there something unfair about this duress? Is Kipnis's analogy between plea bargaining and a gunman demanding one's wallet an accurate comparison? Or is plea bargaining more like a doctor offering to sell a vital treatment or an auto mechanic offering to assist a stranded motorist for a large sum?

3. What two principles does our criminal justice system institutionalize, and how is each related to a distinctive type of injustice? What is the difference between aberrational and systemic injustice? On what grounds does Kipnis argue that plea bargaining involves systemic injustice? Do you agree?

4. Should plea bargaining be abolished, restricted, or reformed in some way? What alternatives, if any, are there to the present system? Could we feasibly eliminate plea bargaining altogether in favor of trials?

The Race Card and Jury Nullification

Randall Kennedy

American legal history is filled with examples of unfair treatment of racial minorities. Among other things, prosecutors have sometimes appealed to the racial prejudice of white jurors in order to convict black defendants. These days, however, the courts are more conscious of our racist heritage and generally endeavor to ensure fairness and to respect the rights of black defendants by preventing prosecutors from making racially biased statements or utilizing racially inflammatory tactics. The controversial O. J. Simpson case, however, raised the prospect of lawyers playing the "race card" in defense of black defendants. In this selection from his book Race, Crime, and the Law, *Randall Kennedy, an African American professor of law at Harvard Law School, critically examines Johnny Cochran's tactics in the Simpson case and Judge Ito's response to them. Kennedy goes on to rebut those who would encourage African American jurors to engage in "jury nullification" by refusing to convict black defendants even if they are guilty.*

DID JOHNNIE COCHRAN USE THE "RACE CARD"? PROBLEMS OF INTERPRETATION

In the summer of 1994, prosecutors accused O. J. Simpson, a famous (now notorious) African-American athlete and entertainer, of murdering two white people: his former wife (Nicole Brown Simpson) and an acquaintance of hers (Ronald Goldman). Police allegedly found incriminating evidence at the murder site and at Simpson's residence, including a bloody glove presumably worn by the murderer. Simpson's attorneys maintained that the bloody glove had been planted by the police officer who claimed to have found it. That officer, Mark Fuhrman, was later shown to be prejudiced against blacks. On October 4, 1995, Simpson was acquitted by a jury composed of seven black women, two white women, one Hispanic man, and one black man. After Simpson's acquittal, one of his attorneys, Robert Shapiro, complained, remarkably, that his co-counsel, Johnnie L. Cochran, Jr., had not only played the race card but "dealt it from the bottom of the deck." Many observers concur with this appraisal (although many who do refuse to permit Shapiro to distance himself from Cochran). Still others, however, contend that Cochran responded appropriately to circumstances that required a detailed examination of the racial views of a bigoted police officer.

Although racial issues were present to some degree throughout the O. J. Simpson trial, on three occasions they completely dominated the proceedings. The first was when the prosecution requested Judge Lance Ito to prevent the defense from questioning Detective Fuhrman regarding his alleged use of the epithet "nigger." The prosecution made a motion *in limine*, which is, essentially, a request by a party asking a judge for a protective order that prohibits the other party from voicing specified statements or questions that the moving party believes will be prejudicial. Motions *in limine* are typically made before trial in order to prevent the matters objected to from being brought to the attention of the jury.

The prosecution argued that the judge should prevent the defense from examining Fuhrman about his alleged use of racial epithets on the ground that the information sought was irrelevant to the case and that, even if relevant, the information was more prejudicial than informative. Pleading for the judge to exclude inquiry into the history of the detective's use of the N-word, prosecutor Christopher Darden declared:

> If we really want the jury's attention focused on the evidence and on the legal and factual issues . . . we shouldn't let them hear this word, because if they hear this word they are going to focus their attention on the issue of race. They are going to be more concerned with whether Mark Fuhrman is a racist than they are with whether there was any way, any possibility . . . that Mark Fuhrman planted evidence. . . . That is what Mr. Cochran wants the jury to do. Skip the evidence.

Darden asserted that permitting inquiry into the record of Fuhrman's use of the N-word would prejudice the state's case against Simpson because that word "is the filthiest, dirtiest, nastiest word in the English language" and would mainly accomplish one thing:

> It will upset the black jurors. It will issue a test . . . and the test will be: Whose side are you on? The side of the white prosecutors and the white policemen or on the side of the black defendant and his very prominent and black lawyer? That is what it is going to do. Either you are with the man or you are with the brothers. That is what it does.

Summarizing the state's position, Darden told Judge Ito:

> If you allow Mr. Cochran to use this word and to play this race card, not only does the direction and the focus of the case change, but the entire complexion of the cases changes. It is a race case then. It is white versus black, African American versus Caucasian, us versus them, us versus the system.

The defense, of course, objected and responded with a dual argument. First, the defense contended that evidence relating to Fuhrman's racial views was relevant to its theory that, out of racial animus, he planted evidence suggestive of Simpson's guilt. Second, the defense contended that the evidence it sought would be more enlightening than confusing to the jury. Addressing himself directly to Darden's assertions regarding the blinding effect that the N-word would have on the black jurors, Cochran said that it was "demeaning" to suggest that "African Americans who have lived under oppression for 200 plus years in this country," who have lived with "offensive words, offensive looks, [and] offensive treatment every day," would be unable to deliberate fairly just because they heard the offensive N-word.

The judge ultimately decided to permit the defense to ask Fuhrman whether, during the preceding ten years, he had used the N-word. Fuhrman denied that he had, a denial which, instead of ending the matter, set the stage for the second occasion on which racial conflict became the overwhelming consideration in the case.

Several months after Fuhrman's denial, audiotapes were unearthed in which he was heard to use the N-word liberally and with obvious relish. On the taped conversations, Fuhrman offered his interlocutor (an aspiring screenwriter) opinions and anecdotes that were not only laden with contempt for blacks but also laced with boasts that he had destroyed or otherwise tampered with evidence related to false charges he had lodged against blacks, particularly black men accompanying white women. The defense, of course, sought to introduce the tapes into evidence in order to impeach Fuhrman's previous testimony. The prosecution sought to minimize, if not prevent, the jury's exposure to the tapes, arguing again that the issue of Fuhrman's racial attitudes was collateral to the central issue of the case and would serve more to confuse than to enlighten the jury.

The judge compromised. He permitted the jury to hear Fuhrman say the N-word twice and also permitted the defense to elicit from the person with whom Fuhrman had spoken the fact that over the course of their taped discussions Fuhrman had used the word "nigger" approximately forty-one times. Furthermore, Judge Ito permitted larger portions of the tape to be played in court, albeit outside the presence of the jury. This decision was important because it increased the possibility that members of the jury would be informed by relatives or spouses of the contents of the tape notwithstanding the judge's order that jurors refrain from exchanging information about the case with anyone. On the other hand, Judge Ito did not permit the defense to play the tape in its entirety to the jury. Moreover, in selecting what the jury would be permitted to hear, the judge excluded those portions of the tape that dealt with Fuhrman's boasts that, in dealing with blacks whom he disliked, he had previously tampered with evidence.

The third time that race became the dominant focus of the trial was when defense counsel Johnnie Cochran presented a closing argument that, according to some observers, violated the rules of advocacy. Two aspects of the closing will likely remain an important part of the folklore of this remarkable case. One was his demonizing characterization of Mark Fuhrman and another police officer as the "twin devils of deception." The other was his plea to the jury suggesting that there were considerations other than evidence relating to the defendant's conduct that the jurors should take into account in determining their verdict. Referring to Fuhrman, Cochran stated, "This man could've been off the force long ago if [the authorities] had done their job, but they didn't . . . they did not have the courage. . . . That is what I am asking you to do. Stop this cover-up. . . . If you don't stop it, then who?" Later, Cochran declared, "And when you go back to the jury room, some of you may want to say, well, gee, you know, boys will be boys. . . . That is not acceptable as the conscience of this community. . . . You are empowered to say we are not going to take that anymore." Returning to the same theme, Cochran stated:

> Who then polices the police? You police the police. You police them by your verdict. You are the ones to send a message. Nobody else is going to do it in our society . . . nobody has the courage. . . . Maybe you are the right people at the right time at the right place to say: No more. We are not going to have this.

Did the legal system (in the person of Judge Ito) respond appropriately to these controversies? The record is mixed. Ito ruled wrongly in initially permitting the defense to examine Fuhrman on his use of the N-word. The applicable rules of evidence permitted questions going to Fuhrman's credibility. Whether or not he used the N-word was irrelevant, however, at least initially, to the question of credibility. Asking Fuhrman whether in the past he had falsely testified or fabricated evidence would have related to credibility,* but asking him whether he was in the habit of referring to blacks as "niggers" did not. There is a sense, felt by many, that, in any event, it was relevant whether Fuhrman had referred to blacks as "niggers." This sense stems from the intuition that if Fuhrman used the N-word, it was a bit more probable that he was a bigot, and that if he was a bigot, it was a bit more probable that he might have planted evidence as the defense alleged. This chain of "ifs," however, highlights the initial tenuousness of the N-word inquiry. Properly applied, the law of evidence, which manifests considerable distrust of jurors' abilities to resist diversions, would have excluded the inquiry that Judge Ito permitted, especially in light of the impact that merely asking about the N-word would foreseeably have on at least some jurors.

Ironically, once Fuhrman denied using the N-word, the history of his racial language did become relevant to his credibility. Thus, Judge Ito rightly permitted the defense to requestion Fuhrman for purposes of impeachment and to play for the jury portions of the utterly discrediting audiotape.†

---

*The defense was precluded from asking this question because, at the outset of the trial, it had no evidentiary basis for doing so.

†Judge Ito was wrong, however, in two other respects. First, he was wrong in excluding from the jury's attention Fuhrman's boasts about planting or destroying evidence. To quote Ito's most unforgiving critic, Vincent Bugliosi: "How in Ito's mind, could Fuhrman's mere use of the work 'nigger' in the past suggest he was more apt to have framed Simpson than if he claimed to have set up other criminal defendants in the past?" Vincent Bugliosi, *Outrage*, 73 (1996). Even worse was Ito's decision to play in open court portions of the tapes he excluded from the jury's consideration. The judge said that he did not want to be accused of suppressing information of vital public interest. If this was his concern, though, he could have addressed it by releasing the tapes *after* a verdict. What should have been his primary, overarching concern was not the public's thirst for information but rather the need for a fair trial. Judge Ito reversed those priorities, putting the fairness of the trial at risk for the sake of serving immediately mere curiosity. "In so far as the Fuhrman affair was concerned, Ito didn't know whether he was coming or going." Ibid.

What about Johnnie Cochran's famous summation?

Some maintain that it was an improper call for jury nullification. Others maintain that it was a proper call for jurors to weigh heavily evidence suggesting that improper police behavior, including dishonesty, had deeply infected the prosecution's case. Both observations grasp a piece of a complicated reality. On the one hand, Cochran expressly denied that his client committed murder and challenged the factual basis of the prosecution's allegations. He did not adopt the stance of an advocate who conceded his client's guilt but pleaded for an acquittal nonetheless. On the other hand, it is possible to understand Cochran as saying that, even if jurors believed Simpson to be guilty beyond a reasonable doubt based on the evidence presented at trial, there was yet another reason to vote to acquit: the supposed need to "send a message" about police mendacity and racism, a need brought about by the inability or unwillingness of other authorities to "police the police." . . .

BLACK POWER IN THE JURY BOX?

Whatever message Johnnie Cochran intended to send with his famous summation, the fact is that a small but appreciable number of Americans believe that it is proper for them to engage in jury nullification. Jury nullification means voting to acquit a defendant despite a belief beyond reasonable doubt that, based on proper evidence, the defendant is guilty of the crime with which he is charged. Nullification occurs when guilt is established but the jury decides to acquit based on its own sense of fairness, propriety, prejudice, or any other sentiment or concern. Race-conscious jury nullification has historically been exercised predominantly by whites. The focus of this discussion will be race-conscious nullification exercised by blacks, particularly the provocative encouragement of it voiced by Professor Paul Butler.

In "Racially Based Jury Nullification: Black Power in the Criminal Justice System," Professor Butler urges black jurors to refuse to vote to convict black defendants charged with certain crimes regardless of the evidence arrayed against them.

He proposes this course of action because "the black community is better off when some nonviolent lawbreakers remain in the community rather than go to prison." More specifically, Butler argues that, absent special circumstances, black jurors should nullify convictions of guilty black defendants charged with what he describes as "nonviolent, *malum prohibitum* offenses, including victimless crimes like narcotics offenses."[1]

Butler does not argue in favor of nullification in all cases. He asserts that black jurors should vote to convict black defendants guilty of *violent* crimes like murder, rape, and assault. For an intermediate level of nonviolent crime, for example, theft or perjury, Butler contends that "nullification is an option that the [black] juror should consider, although there should be no presumption in favor of it." In this middle tier of cases, a black juror might appropriately vote for acquittal when a poor black woman steals from Tiffany's, but not when the same woman steals from her next-door neighbor. "The decision as to what kind of conduct by African Americans ought to be punished is better made by African Americans themselves," Butler writes, "based on the costs and benefits to their community, than by the traditional criminal justice process, which is controlled by white lawmakers and white law enforcers." It is "the moral responsibility of black jurors," Butler concludes, "to emancipate some guilty black outlaws."

Butler's proposal rests on three main points. One is that a juror's power to vote to acquit a defendant who has been shown to be guilty is a power that may be put to laudable uses. He cites the refusal of a jury in *Bushnell's Case* to convict a group of Quakers for unlawful assembly and disturbance of the peace, a landmark instance of resistance to governmental religious oppression. He cites the acquittal of Peter Zenger, who was accused of seditious libel for criticizing British colonial rule in North America, a landmark in the growth of freedom of expression. English law authorized the judge exclusively to determine whether statements made by the defendant were libelous. Yet, at trial, Zenger's attorney told the jury that it should ignore the judge's instructions and "make use of their own consciences and understandings, in judging of the

lives, liberties, or estates of their fellow subjects." Butler also cites *United States v. Morris* and other cases in which juries, prompted by defense attorneys, acquitted guilty defendants accused of violating the federal Fugitive Slave Act, which helped owners to recapture runaway slaves.

Butler's second point is that a total breach of America's constitutional promises absolves blacks of a moral duty to obey the society's rules. "'Democracy' as practiced in the United States," he writes, "has betrayed African Americans far more than they could ever betray it." According to Butler, the American power structure remains a pigmentocracy that condemns blacks to an inferior place in the social order and then punishes them harshly for antisocial conduct largely caused by the circumstances into which they have been thrown. Butler's third point overlaps with the second. It is that white racism is the cause of much of the criminal conduct engaged in by blacks. "But for the (racist) environment," he writes, "the African-American criminal would not be a criminal. . . . Racism creates and sustains the criminal breeding ground which produces the black criminal. Thus, when many African Americans are locked up, it is because of a situation that white supremacy created." . . .

Professor Butler's essay brings into the open a clearly articulated version of a belief that had been known about previously only through furtive, vague, unnamed sources. Over the past few years, reports have surfaced of cases in which the evidence against black defendants being tried before predominantly black juries appeared to be so overwhelming that some observers speculated that jury nullification must account for acquittals or hung juries. One example is the prosecution of Marion Barry, the mayor of Washington, D.C. After viewing a Federal Bureau of Investigation videotape that showed Barry smoking cocaine, and after listening to strong incriminating evidence from other sources, a predominantly black jury nonetheless declined to convict him of the most serious charges he faced. Further evidence that black jurors engage in race-conscious nullification is provided by anonymous admissions of such conduct. In the District of Columbia, for instance, a person wrote an anonymous letter to court officials in which she identified herself as a juror who had recently declined to vote to convict a defendant charged with first degree murder. The letter writer stated that she and other members of the jury believed that the prosecution had proven the defendant's guilt but that they had voted to acquit anyway in deference to members of the jury who "didn't want to send any more Young Black Men to jail."

The trial of O. J. Simpson, the most publicized criminal proceeding in American history, tremendously enlarged the specter (or hope) of race-conscious nullification by black jurors. Early on some commentators suggested that, in light of the intense anger felt by many blacks over racially discriminatory mistreatment by law enforcement officials, some black jurors might decline to vote to convict Simpson as a form of protest, regardless of the evidence in that particular case. Those speculations were magnified when Johnnie Cochran focused jurors' attention on the infamous Mark Fuhrman. Anxieties were heightened even more when, following Simpson's acquittal, some people celebrated in a fashion which suggested that they perceived the trial as a racial show of strength. Stating that he was happy with the acquittal even if Simpson did commit the murder, a black man in Boston ascribed his satisfaction to his perception that "we [blacks] never win *anything*." "A black man was charged with killing a white woman—a blond white woman at that," this man mused. "And the court said he didn't do it. Hell, that's worth celebrating." . . .

Butler's proposal rests on a seriously flawed assessment of the state of race relations within the administration of criminal law. According to Butler's portrayal, white racism is almost wholly triumphant in the criminal law system. He sees black–white race relations as a narrative completely dominated by the continuity of African-American subordination, as opposed to a narrative marked by significant discontinuity—the leap from slavery to freedom, and from caste-like stigmatization to an increasingly respected place in all aspects of American life. That explains why he feels justified in calling for subversion. He perceives blacks as occupying a place

in the mind, soul, politics, and law of America that is essentially the same as that occupied by their enslaved or segregated forebears. . . .

Racial wrongdoing, however, is *all* that Butler sees. His portrayal of the criminal law system wholly omits any facts, developments, or tendencies that contradict, or even merely complicate, his preferred narrative. He portrays a static, one-dimensional system that is totally at odds with what black Americans need and want, a system that unequivocally represents and unrelentingly imposes "the white man's law." To illustrate his argument, Butler provides a long list of examples that document "racism in criminal justice." . . .

Butler's account withholds completely any recognition that restrictions on state power that define much of the constitutional law of criminal procedure are limits that emerged largely from struggles against racism. Similarly, his account neglects to credit the significant presence of African Americans in law enforcement, including those blacks in major urban areas who exercise power at the highest circles of executive police authority. . . .

Another major failing of Butler's analysis is his failure to recognize that jury nullification is an exceedingly poor means for advancing the goal of a racially fair administration of criminal law. . . . There is no reason to believe that a campaign of jury nullification will succeed in bringing about the broad social reforms that Butler demands. Jury nullification as typically implemented is a low-visibility, highly ambiguous protest unlikely to focus the attention of the public clearly on social problems in need of reform. . . . To publicize their aims, nullificationists would have to publicize their subversion of the criminal justice system, a route few have chosen to take.

That jury nullification is widely perceived as illegitimate under present circumstances suggests another reason for doubting the efficacy of Butler's proposal. . . . If a large number of blacks clearly engage in "guerrilla warfare" as jurors, their action might call into question the right of blacks to be selected for jury service on precisely the same terms as others. Widespread adoption of Butler's proposal would likely give rise to measures designed to exclude prospective nullifiers from juries, measures that would result almost certainly in the disproportionate exclusion of blacks. Moreover, if adherents to the Butler program proved to be especially clever and relentless in their subversion, one can imagine (with horror) the emergence of demands that black prospective jurors show a special sign of allegiance to the legal system in return for the opportunity to be considered for jury service or, worse yet, demands that blacks be excused from jury service altogether during the pendency of the nullification crisis. . . .

There are additional reasons to object to Butler's scheme and the reasoning and sensibility that it embodies. Butler suggests that black criminals should be exempt from *punishment* on the grounds that "but for the [racist] environment, the African-American criminal would not be a criminal." Butler urges the conviction and incarceration of black *violent* criminals, but he claims to do so only for purposes of deterrence and incapacitation, not for purposes of retribution. Butler hints that he rejects retribution in general as a basis for coercive action. However, as with every other significant aspect of his analysis, Butler develops a racial critique of retribution as applied to *black* criminals, maintaining that it is unfair to punish people for "negative" reactions to racist, oppressive conditions. . . .

There is good reason to scrutinize closely all of the abuse excuses that have been advanced recently to absolve persons of criminal responsibility for acts typically viewed as criminal. Some appear to be of dubious merit. The racial oppression excuse that Butler offers is particularly ill-founded.* Unlike other abuse excuses, Butler's is untethered to particular events or individuals. Rather, it refers to all of American

history and embraces an entire race, *all* African Americans, from Colin Powell on down.

The implications of Butler's theory for American race relations are staggering. If it were believed and acted upon, his conception of the irresponsibility of blacks would impose upon African Americans a disability from which they were free even during the era of slavery: the disability of being perceived as people wholly devoid of moral choice and thus blameless for purposes of retribution, the same way that infants, the insane, and animals are typically viewed as morally blameless. The slave codes were based in part on a racially demeaning perception of blacks. As bad as those codes were, though, they all conceded that blacks were sufficiently human, moral, and responsible to be held accountable for their actions. . . .

Butler exudes keen sympathy for nonviolent drug offenders and similar criminals. By contrast, Butler is inattentive to the aspirations, frustrations, and fears of law-abiding people compelled by circumstances to live in close proximity to the criminals for whom he is willing to urge subversion of the legal system. Butler simply overlooks the sector of the black law-abiding population that desires *more* rather than *less* prosecution and punishment for *all* types of criminals. According to data collected by a 1993 Gallup Poll, 82 percent of the blacks surveyed believed that the courts in their area do not treat criminals harshly enough; 75 percent favored putting more police on the streets to combat crime; and 68 percent favored building more prisons so that longer sentences could be given. One would never know from Butler's analysis that a large number of ordinary, grass-roots blacks embrace such views. . . .

The most fundamental reason to oppose Professor Butler's call for racially selective jury nullification is that it is based on a sentiment that is regrettably widespread in American culture: an ultimately destructive sentiment of racial kinship that prompts individuals of a given race to care more about "their own" than people of another race. He expresses this sentiment throughout his essay by explicitly erecting racial boundaries around his conception of

---

*Butler, of course, is not alone in pursuing this path. After Colin Ferguson shot twenty-five people on the Long Island Railroad on December 7, 1993, his attorneys announced that they would mount a black rage defense based on the idea that American racism had pushed their already unstable client into insanity. Ferguson fired his attorneys before they could present their theory. He represented himself, was convicted, and was sentenced to imprisonment for life. . . .

responsibility, community, and empathy.* Because of that sentiment, he assumes that it is proper for prospective black jurors to care more about black communities than white communities, that it is proper for black jurors to be more concerned with the fate of black defendants than white defendants, and that it is proper for the black juror to be more protective of the property (and perhaps the lives?) of black people than white people. Along that road lies moral and political disaster. The disaster includes not only increasing but, worse, *legitimizing* the tendency of people to privilege in racial terms "their own."[†] Some will say that this racial privileging has already happened and is, in any event, inevitable. The situation can and will get worse, however, if Butler's plan and the thinking behind it gain adherents. His program, although animated by a desire to challenge racial injustice, would demolish the moral framework upon which an effective, attractive, and compelling alternative can and must be built.

NOTE

[1] 105 *Yale Law Journal* 677, 679, 715 (1995).

REVIEW AND DISCUSSION QUESTIONS

1. Kennedy writes that on three occasions, racial issues completely dominated the O. J. Simpson trial. What were they? Did Simpson's lawyers act appropriately on those occasions? Were his lawyers simply upholding Simpson's rights as a defendant or were they guilty of abusing the legal system? Did Judge Ito handle these issues fairly and wisely? What would you have done in his place?

2. Why were Americans so fascinated by the O. J. Simpson trial, and what, if anything, did that trial reveal about the role of, and attitudes toward, race in the United States?

3. Butler makes three points in support of African Americans' engaging in jury nullification. Critically assess each point.

4. On what grounds does Kennedy object to Butler's proposal? How strong are his arguments against Butler? Are there considerations in favor of Butler's position that Kennedy neglects or to which he gives insufficient attention?

5. Is jury nullification ever justified? If so, under what circumstances? Given our history of slavery, segregation, and racial discrimination, should the legal system treat black defendants more leniently than it does now?

---

*He writes, for instance, that "African-American jurors should . . . exercise their power in the best interests of the black community." Butler, "Racially-Based Jury Nullification," 715. If that is so, should white jurors exercise their power in the best interests of the white community? Some white jurors, judges, and legislators do exercise their power in what they perceive to be the best interest of the white community. They are wrong, however, to the extent that they do so on a racial basis. That correct sense of wrong is the basis upon which a moral critique of their actions must rest.

---

†One of the black members of the jury that acquitted O. J. Simpson reportedly stated after the verdict, "We've got to protect our own." See Jeffrey Toobin, *The Run of His Life: The People v. O. J. Simpson*, 431 (1996). One should be careful with this report; the author reporting it does not offer a specific source that permits an assessment of reliability. For my purposes, though, it is enough to note that the juror's alleged statement is wholly plausible because of the widespread existence of the racial sentiments I criticize.

PART IV

PHILOSOPHICAL ISSUES IN CIVIL LAW

❖

13

COMPENSATION FOR PRIVATE HARMS: THE LAW OF TORTS

A *tort* is a civil wrong or harm, other than a breach of contract, for which the injured party is entitled to compensation. By contrast with the sanctions and penalties of criminal law, tort law provides for civil redress of the damage that one individual suffers at the hands of another. Alongside contract law and property law, tort law is one of the main branches of civil law. It concerns the standards of conduct and rules of liability that govern civil suits between individuals over harms resulting from such things as libel, battery, trespass, nuisance, defective products, automobile accidents, and a wide range of other untoward conduct.

One very important tort is negligence. In the first selection of this section, William Prosser explains its main elements. Among other things, to be liable for negligence one must have exposed others to an unreasonable risk of harm, a risk that the agent of the harm should have foreseen. A plaintiff who has been injured cannot successfully sue a defendant for negligence if the injury resulted from a risk that was too unlikely for the defendant to have anticipated. When is a risk foreseeable? That issue is at the heart of *Stone v. Bolton*. To be liable for negligence the defendant's conduct must have fallen below the standard of care owed by law to the plaintiff. But when X's negligent conduct toward Y freakishly results in injury to Z, hard questions about tort liability surface. These are taken up in the famous *Palsgraf* case. In "Tort Liability and Corrective Justice," Jeffrie G. Murphy and Jules L. Coleman examine further some of the philosophical issues that underlie tort liability—in particular, the notion of fault and the requirements of corrective justice—in the context of proposals for no-fault automobile insurance systems.

This section concludes with four sets of cases that illustrate different aspects of tort law. *Carroll Towing* represents a cost-benefit approach to tort liability. *Summers v. Tice* is well known because it permitted a defendant to be sued for negligence even though his actions could not be shown to have caused the harm suffered by the plaintiff. *Yania v. Bigan* and its companion cases address the issue of whether and when one has a duty to rescue another. If a defendant is to be held liable for his negligence, he or she must have harmed the plaintiff through negligence in some way. Can life itself be a harm? The final case, *Berman v. Allan,* takes up this issue.

Negligence

William Prosser

Torts are private legal actions claiming compensation for damages. Some torts concern intentional injuries—for example, punching someone in the face or spreading lies about him or her. Negligence as a tort, however, concerns unintentional injuries—for example, accidentally running over a sunbather with your dune buggy. Although it was not distinguished as a separate and distinct ground of legal liability until the early nineteenth century, today negligence is probably the most important and certainly the most frequently litigated category of torts. William Prosser, one of the foremost authorities on the law of torts, in the following essay spells out the main elements of the tort of negligence: that is, the circumstances under which one can be held legally liable for negligent conduct. He explains what the law means by negligence and explicates such crucial concepts as that of unreasonable risk and the standard of the "reasonable man."

About the year 1825, negligence began to be recognized as a separate and independent basis of tort liability. Its rise coincided in a marked degree with the Industrial Revolution; and it very probably was stimulated by the rapid increase in the number of accidents caused by industrial machinery, and in particular by the invention of railways. . . .

Intentional injuries, whether direct or indirect, began to be grouped as a distinct field of liability, and negligence remained as the main basis for unintended torts. Today it is not at all disputed that separate problems and principles, as well as distinct questions of policy, arise in negligence cases.

ELEMENTS OF CAUSE OF ACTION

Negligence, as we shall see, is simply one kind of conduct. But a cause of action founded upon negligence, from which liability will follow, requires more than conduct. The traditional formula for the elements necessary to such a cause of action may be stated briefly as follows:

1. A duty, or obligation, recognized by the law, requiring the actor to conform to a certain standard of conduct, for the protection of others against unreasonable risks.

2. A failure on his part to conform to the standard required. These two elements go to make up what the courts usually have called negligence; but the term quite frequently is applied to the second alone. Thus it may be said that the defendant was negligent, but is not liable because he was under no duty to the plaintiff not to be.

3. A reasonably close causal connection between the conduct and the resulting injury. This is what is commonly known as "legal cause," or "proximate cause."

4. Actual loss or damage resulting to the interests of another. Since the action for negligence developed chiefly out of the old form of action on the case, it retained the rule of that action, that proof of damage was an essential part of the plaintiff's case. Nominal damages, to vindicate a technical right, cannot be recovered in a negligence action, where no actual loss has occurred. The threat of future harm, not yet realized, is not enough. Negligent conduct in itself is not such an interference with the interests of the world at large that there is any right to complain of it, or to be free from it, except in the case of some individual whose interests have suffered.

Such a statement must, however, be qualified to the extent that, as in the case of other torts, where irreparable injury is threatened, a court of equity may act by injunction to prevent the harm before it occurs. Even here the damage, even though only potential, is the basis for granting relief. . . .

Negligence is a matter of risk—that is to say, of recognizable danger of injury. It has been defined as "conduct which involves an unreasonably great risk of causing damage," or, more fully, conduct "which falls below the standard established by law for the protection of others against unreasonably great risk of harm." "Negligence is conduct, and not a state of mind." In most instances, it is caused by heedlessness or carelessness, which makes the negligent party unaware of the results which may follow from his act. But it may also exist where he has considered the possible consequences carefully, and has exercised his own best judgment. The standard imposed by society is an external one, which is not necessarily based upon any moral fault of the individual; and a failure to conform to it is negligence, even though it may be due to stupidity, forgetfulness, an excitable temperament, or even sheer ignorance. The almost universal use of the phrase "due care" to describe conduct which is not negligent, should not be permitted to obscure the fact that the real basis of negligence is not carelessness, but behavior which should be recognized as involving unreasonable danger to others.

Previous reference has been made to the distinction between negligence and intent. In negligence, the actor does not desire to bring about the consequences which follow, nor does he know that they are substantially certain to occur, or believe that they will. There is merely a risk of such consequences, sufficiently great to lead a reasonable man in his position to anticipate them, and to guard against them. If an automobile driver runs down a man in the street before him, with the desire to hit him, or with the belief that he is certain to do so, it is an intentional battery; but if he has no such desire or belief, but merely acts unreasonably in failing to guard against a risk which he should appreciate, it is negligence. As the probability of injury to another, apparent from the facts within his knowledge, becomes greater, his conduct takes on more of the attributes of intent, until it reaches that substantial certainty of harm which juries, and sometimes courts, may find inseparable from intent itself. Such intermediate mental states, based upon a recognizable great probability of harm, may still properly be classed as "negligence," but are commonly called "reckless," "wanton," or even "wilful." They are dealt with, in many respects, as if the harm were intended, so that they become in effect a hybrid between intent and negligence, occupying a sort of penumbra between the two. They will be dealt with in a later section.

Negligence already has been defined as conduct which falls below a standard established by the law for the protection of others against unreasonable risk of harm. The idea of risk necessarily involves a recognizable danger, based upon some knowledge of the existing facts, and some reasonable belief that harm may follow. A risk is a danger which is apparent, or should be apparent, to one in the position of the actor. The culpability of the actor's conduct must be judged in the light of the possibilities apparent to him at the time, and not by looking backward "with the wisdom born of the event." The standard must be one of conduct, rather than of consequences. It is not enough that everyone can see now that the risk was great, if it was not apparent when the conduct occurred. The court must put itself in the actor's place. At the same time, the standard imposed must be an external one, based upon what society demands of the individual, rather than upon his own notions of what is proper. An honest blunder, or a mistaken belief that no damage will result, may absolve him from moral blame, but the harm to others is still as great, and the actor's individual standards must give way to those of the public. In other words, society may require of him not to be a fool.

In the light of the recognizable risk, the conduct, to be negligent, must be unreasonable. Nearly all human acts, of course, carry some recognizable but remote possibility of harm to another. No man so much as rides a horse without some chance of a runaway, or drives a car without the risk of a broken steering gear or a heart attack. But these are not unreasonable risks. Those against which the actor is required to take precautions are those which society, in general, considers sufficiently great to demand them. No man can be expected to guard against harm from events which are not reasonably to be anticipated at all, or are so unlikely to occur that the risk, although recognizable, would commonly be disregarded. An unprecedented frost or flood, an automobile thrown unexpectedly against a pillar on the corner, a child picking up a plank with a nail in it and dropping it on his foot, a pedestrian slipping on a small bit of gravel in the highway, the ricochet of a bullet at an almost impossible angle—all of these things have happened, and will occur again; but they are not so likely to do so on any particular occasion as to make it necessary to burden the freedom of human action with precautions against them. Such events are regarded as "unavoidable accidents," for which there is no liability.

On the other hand, if the risk is an appreciable one, and the possible consequences are serious, the question is not one of mathematical probability alone. The odds may be a thousand to one that no train will arrive at the very moment that an automobile is crossing a railway track, but the risk of death is nevertheless sufficiently serious to require the driver to look for the train. It may be highly improbable that lightning will strike at any given place or time; but the possibility is there, and it requires precautions for the protection of inflammables. As the gravity of the possible harm increases, the apparent likelihood of its occurrence need be correspondingly less.

Against this probability, and gravity, of the risk, must be balanced in every case the utility of the type of conduct in question. The problem is whether "the game is worth the candle." Many risks may reasonably be run, with the full approval of the community. Chief among the factors which must be considered is the social value of the interest which the actor is seeking to advance. A man may be justified in dashing into the path of a train to save the life of a child, where it would be arrant folly to save his hat. A railway will be permitted, or even required, to blow a whistle to warn travelers at a crossing, although it is likely to frighten horses on the highway; it may be negligence to blow the same whistle without the same occasion for warning. The public interest will justify the use of dangerous machinery, so long as the benefits outweigh the risk, and a railroad may reasonably be constructed near a highway, even at the expense of some danger to those who use it. . . .

Consideration must also be given to any alternative course open to the actor. Whether it is reasonable to travel a dangerous road may depend upon the disadvantages of another route; and while mere inconvenience or cost may not in themselves be sufficient to justify proceeding in the face of great danger, they may justify taking other risks which are not too extreme. A county will not be required, at ruinous expense, to build a bridge which will be safe against any accident that might be anticipated; but the converse is also true, and where it can cheaply and easily post a warning, it may be required to do so. A railroad need not do without a turntable because there is some chance that children will play on it and be hurt; but it is quite another matter to keep it locked.

The alternative dangers to the actor himself and to others must be thrown into the scale, and a balance struck in which all of these elements are weighed.

It is fundamental that the standard of conduct which is the basis of the law of negligence is determined by balancing the risk, in the light of the social value of the interest threatened, and the probability and extent of the harm, against the value of the interest which the actor is seeking to protect, and the expedience of the course pursued. For this reason, it is seldom possible to reduce negligence to any definite rules; it is "relative to the need and the occasion," and conduct which would be proper under some circumstances becomes negligence under others.

THE REASONABLE MAN

The whole theory of negligence presupposes some uniform standard of behavior. Yet the infinite variety of situations which may arise makes it impossible to fix definite rules in advance for all conceivable human conduct. The utmost that can be done is to devise something in the nature of a formula, the application of which in each particular case must be left to the jury, or to the court. The standard of conduct which the community demands must be an external and objective one, rather than the individual judgment, good or bad, of the particular actor; and it must be, so far as possible, the same for all persons, since the law can have no favorites. At the same time, it must make proper allowance for the risk apparent to the actor, for his capacity to meet it, and for the circumstances under which he must act.

The courts have dealt with this very difficult problem by creating a fictitious person, who never has existed on land or sea: the "reasonable man of ordinary prudence." Sometimes he is described as a reasonable man, or a prudent man, or a man of average prudence, or a man of ordinary sense using ordinary care and skill. It is evident that all such phrases are intended to mean very much the same thing. The actor is required to do what such an ideal individual would be supposed to do in his place. A model of all proper qualities, with only those human shortcomings and weaknesses which the community will tolerate on the occasion, "this excellent but odious character stands like a monument in our Courts of Justice, vainly appealing to his fellow-citizens to order their lives after his own example."

The courts have gone to unusual pains to emphasize the abstract and hypothetical character of this mythical person. He is not to be identified with any ordinary individual, who might occasionally do unreasonable things; he is a prudent and careful man, who is always up to standard. Nor is it proper to identify him even with any member of the very jury who are

to apply the standard; he is rather a personification of a community ideal of reasonable behavior, determined by the jury's social judgment. It is sometimes difficult to escape the conviction that the refinements which have been developed in instructing the jury, in the effort to avoid any personal standard which one of them might be tempted to apply, are artificial and unreal, and quite beyond the comprehension of the average man in the box. Their only possible justification lies in a basis of experience justifying considerable uneasiness about what any jury may conceivably do, which has led to an excess of precaution in the effort to give them proper guidance.

PHYSICAL ATTRIBUTES

The conduct of the reasonable man will vary with the situation with which he is confronted. The jury must therefore be instructed to take the circumstances into account; negligence is a failure to do what the reasonable man would do "under the same or similar circumstances." Under the latitude of this phrase, the courts have made allowance not only for the external facts, but for many of the characteristics of the actor himself, and have applied, in many respects, a more or less subjective standard. "It would appear that there is no standardized man; that there is only in part an objective test; that there is no such thing as reasonable or unreasonable conduct except as viewed with reference to certain qualities of the actor—his physical attributes, his intellectual powers, probably, if superior, his knowledge and the knowledge he would have acquired had he exercised standard moral and at least average mental qualities at the time of action or at some connected time."

As to his physical characteristics, the reasonable man may be said to be identical with the actor. The man who is blind or deaf, or lame, or is otherwise physically disabled, is entitled to live in the world and to have allowance made by others for his disability, and he cannot be required to do the impossible by conforming to physical standards which he cannot meet. Similar allowance has been made for the weaknesses of age and sex. At the same time, the conduct of the handicapped individual must be reasonable in the light of his knowledge of his infirmity, which is treated merely as one of the circumstances under which he acts. A blind man may be negligent in going into a place of known danger, just as one who knows that he is subject to epileptic fits, or is about to fall asleep, may be negligent in driving a car. It is sometimes said that a blind man must use a greater degree of care than one who can see; but it is now generally agreed that as a fixed rule this is inaccurate, and that the correct statement is merely that he must take the precautions, be they more or less, which the ordinary reasonable man would take if he were blind. In theory the standard remains the same, but it is sufficiently flexible to take his physical defects into account.

MENTAL CAPACITY

As to the mental attributes of the actor, the standard remains of necessity an external one. "The law," says Mr. Justice Holmes in a much quoted passage, "takes no account of the infinite varieties of temperament, intellect, and education which make the internal character of a given act so different in different men. It does not attempt to see men as God sees them, for more than one sufficient reason." The fact that the individual is a congenital fool, cursed with inbuilt bad judgment, or that in the particular instance he "did not stop to think," or that he is merely a stupid ox, or of an excitable temperament which causes him to lose his head and get "rattled," obviously cannot be allowed to protect him from liability. Apart from the very obvious difficulties of proof as to what went on in his head, it may be no bad policy to hold a fool according to his folly. The harm to his neighbors is quite as great, and may be greater, than if he had a modicum of brains; and if he is to live in the community, he must learn to conform to its standards or pay for what he breaks. As to all such mental deficiency, no allowance is made; the standard of reasonable conduct is applied, and "it is not enough that the defendant did the best he knew how."

Obviously, however, an extreme is reached at which the mental deficiency has prevented the individual from comprehending the danger, or from taking action to avoid it; and the question then becomes, how can we find the tort of negligence at all? Can a complete imbecile, for example, be negligent? It is a rather mysterious fact that no case can be found involving such a condition on the part of a defendant. There are, however, quite a few cases dealing with contributory negligence of plaintiffs; and in all of them except one, it has been held that the jury could find that there was no negligence. . . .

In cases in which the mental aberration has reached the point of actual insanity, the tendency has been to carry over the standard of the reasonable man, and to apply it even to the negligence of those who are definitely insane. This has not gone without criticism, and there has been much argument that the exception should be made when mental deficiency reaches such an extreme. There are a handful of contributory negligence cases in which the mental state has prevented the individual from comprehending or avoiding the danger, and the jury has been permitted to find that there is no negligence. There are two decisions in Wisconsin and Ontario which have come to the same conclusion as to insane defendants. It seems rather probable that the cases as to lunatics will follow the line of mental deficiency in general.

On the other hand a transitory unconsciousness, or delirium due to illness, commonly is regarded as a "circumstance" depriving the actor of control over his conduct, which will relieve him of liability.

Whether intoxication is to be regarded as a physical or a mental disability is probably of no importance at all to anyone. On either basis, it is common enough; and it is uniformly held that voluntary or negligent intoxication cannot serve as excuse or absolution for acts done in that condition which would otherwise be negligent. One good reason is that such an excuse would be far too common and too easy to assert; another is that drunkenness is so anti-social that one who indulges in it ought to be held to the consequences. It is sometimes said that such intoxication is negligence in itself; but this is scarcely correct, since a drunken man may still behave in a perfectly reasonable manner. The proper statement would seem to be that one who intentionally or negligently becomes intoxicated is held thereafter to the same standard of conduct as if he were sober. . . .

KNOWLEDGE

One of the most difficult questions in connection with negligence is that of what the actor may be required to know. . . . So far as perception is concerned, it seems clear that, unless his attention is legitimately distracted, the actor must give to his surroundings the attention which a standard reasonable man would consider necessary under the circumstances, and that he must use such senses as he has to discover what is readily apparent. He may be negligent in failing to look, or in failing to observe what is visible when he does look. As to memory, he is required to fix in his mind those matters which would make such an impression upon the standard man, and, unless he is startled, or his attention is distracted for some sufficient reason, to bear them in mind, at least for a reasonable length of time.

The real difficulty lies with the question of experience. The late Henry T. Terry came to the conclusion that "there are no facts whatever which every person in the community is absolutely bound at his peril to know." It seems clear, however, that there are certain things which every adult with a minimum of intelligence must necessarily have learned: the law of gravity, the fact that fire burns and water will drown, that inflammable objects will catch fire, that a loose board will tip when it is trod on, the ordinary features of the weather to which he is accustomed, and similar phenomena of nature. He must know in addition a few elementary facts about himself: the amount of space he occupies, the principles of balance and leverage as applied to his own body, and, to the extent that it is reasonable to demand it of him, the limits of his own strength, as well as some elementary rules of health.

But beyond this, it seems clear that any individual who has led a normal existence will have learned much more: the traits of common animals, the normal habits, capacities and reactions of other human beings, including their propensities toward negligence and crime, the danger involved in explosives, inflammable liquids, electricity, moving machinery, slippery surfaces and firearms, the fact that an automobile is not easy to control in deep sand, that worn tires will blow out, and many other things. Such an individual will not be credited or excused when he denies knowledge of the risk; and to this extent, at least, there is a minimum standard of knowledge, based upon what is common to the community.

The few cases which have considered the question have held that when an abnormal individual who lacks the experience common to the particular community comes into it, as in the case of the old lady from the city who comes to the farm without ever having learned that a bull is a dangerous beast, the standard of knowledge will still be applied, and it is the individual who must conform to the community, rather than vice versa.

Above this minimum, once it is determined, the individual will not be held to knowledge of risks which are not known or apparent to him. He may, however, know enough to be conscious of his own ignorance, and of possible danger into which it may lead him; and if that is the case, as where a layman attempts to give medical treatment, or one enters a strange dark passage, or an automobile driver proceeds with a mysterious wobble in his front wheels, or traverses a strange town without an attempt to discover the meaning of unfamiliar purple traffic lights which suddenly confront him, he will be found negligent in proceeding in the face of known ignorance. He may, furthermore, be engaged in an activity, or stand in a relation to others, which imposes upon him an obligation to investigate and find out, so that he becomes liable not so much for being ignorant as for remaining ignorant; and this obligation may require him to know at least enough to conduct an intelligent inquiry as to what he does not know. The occupier of premises who invites business visitors to enter, the landlord who installs a gas heater in a bathroom used by his tenants, the telephone company which erects wires in the street, the manufacturer of goods to be sold to the public, the carrier who undertakes to transport passengers, all are charged with the duty of the affirmative action which would be taken by a reasonable man in their position, to discover dangers of which they may not be informed. As scientific knowledge advances, and more and more effective tests become available, what was excusable ignorance yesterday becomes negligent ignorance today.

SUPERIOR KNOWLEDGE, SKILL AND INTELLIGENCE

Thus far the question has been one of a minimum standard, below which the individual will not be permitted to fall. But if he has in fact knowledge, skill, or even intelligence superior to that of the ordinary man, the law will demand of him conduct consistent with it. The vendor of fur coats who has learned from experience that some few persons are especially susceptible to dermatitis caused by a particular dye must take precautions which might not be required if he had remained in ignorance. Upon the same basis, a physician who is possessed of unusual skill or knowledge must use care which is reasonable in the light of his special ability and information, and may be negligent where an ordinary doctor would not.

Professional men in general, and those who undertake any work calling for special skill, are required not only to exercise reasonable care in what they do, but also to possess a standard minimum of special knowledge and ability. Most of the decided cases have dealt with physicians and surgeons, but the same is undoubtedly true of dentists, pharmacists, psychiatrists, attorneys, architects and engineers, accountants, abstracters of title, and many other professions and even skilled trades. Since, allowing for the inevitable differences in the work done, the principles applied to all of these appear to be quite identical, and since the medical cases are by far the most numerous, it will be convenient to talk only of physicians and surgeons.

A physician may, although he seldom does, contract to cure his patient, or to accomplish a particular result, in which case he may be liable for breach of contract when he does not succeed. In the absence of such an express agreement, he does not warrant or insure the outcome of his treatment, and he will not be liable for an honest mistake of judgement, where the proper course is open to reasonable doubt. But by undertaking to render medical services, even though gratuitously, he will ordinarily be understood to hold himself out as having standard professional skill and knowledge. The formula under which this usually is put to the jury is that he must have the skill and learning commonly possessed by members of the profession in good standing; and he will be liable if harm results because he does not have them. Sometimes this is called the skill of the "average" member of the profession; but this is clearly misleading, since only those in good professional standing are to be considered; and of these it is not the middle but the minimum common skill which is to be looked to. If the defendant represents himself as having greater skill than this, as for example where he holds himself out as a specialist, or as having less, and the patient accepts treatment with that understanding, the standard is modified accordingly.

The courts have been compelled to recognize that there are areas in which even experts will disagree. Where there are different schools of medical thought, it is held that the dispute cannot be settled by the law, and the doctor is entitled to be judged according to the tenets of the school he professes to follow. This does not mean, however, that any quack, charlatan or crackpot can set himself up as a "school," and so apply his individual ideas without liability. A "school" must be a recognized one with definite principles, and it must be the line of thought of at least a respectable minority of the profession. In addition, there are minimum requirements of skill and knowledge as to both diagnosis and treatment, particularly in the light of modern licensing statutes, which anyone who holds himself out as competent to treat human ailments is required to have, regardless of his personal views on medical subjects. Furthermore the physician is required to exercise reasonable care in ascertaining the operational facts upon which his diagnosis is based, and will be liable if he fails to do so.

REVIEW AND DISCUSSION QUESTIONS

1. What four basic elements are necessary to establish negligence as a legal cause of action? Give examples of conduct that is not negligent because one of these elements is missing.

2. Why is it difficult to reduce negligence to a specific set of rules?

3. Who or what is the "reasonable man"? How do the courts use the concept? What physical and mental characteristics does the "reasonable man" have? How does the reasonable man standard apply to the conduct of a blind or handicapped person? A stupid or hotheaded person? What difficulties or limitations, if any, do you see in the standard?

4. How does the law treat those such as physicians who have superior knowledge or skill?

5. Do you see any ways in which the law's treatment of negligence differs from common sense or our ordinary ideas of fault and responsibility?

Foreseeability of Risk

Stone v. Bolton

Negligence, as William Prosser explained in the previous essay, is conduct that falls below a standard established by the law for the protection of others against unreasonable risk of harm. The idea of risk, as he says, necessarily involves a recognizable danger: "A risk is a danger which is apparent, or should be apparent, to one in the position of the actor." But "the culpability of the actor's conduct must be judged in the light of the possibilities apparent to him at the time, and not by looking backward 'with wisdom born of the event.'" At issue in the English case of Stone v. Bolton *is what exactly constitutes a reasonably foreseeable risk.*

[The plaintiff, Miss Bessie Stone, lived on Beckenham Road, a side street next to a cricket ground. One day, as she had just passed outside the gate in front of her house, she was struck on the head by a cricket ball that had been hit from the grounds. The ball was hit by a player on the visiting team, and by all accounts, was one of the longest balls—travelling about 100 yards before it struck the plaintiff—that had ever been hit at the grounds during the last 40 years. The cricket ground was found at trial to be "quite large enough for all practical purposes," even after it was remodeled in 1910 or 1911 to allow for construction of Beckenham Road. The field itself was surrounded by a twelve-foot-high fence or hoarding which, owing to a rise in the ground, was about seventeen feet above the street on the Beckenham Road side. The southern wicket from which the ball was struck was about 78 yards from Beckenham Road fence. Witnesses testified that over a 30-year period about six to ten balls had been hit onto Beckenham Road, and that several others had landed in the garden of one Mr. Brownson, whose house was the closest to the cricket grounds of all the houses in the neighborhood. The plaintiff did not sue the batsman or his club; but she did sue the home cricket club and all of its members, alleging first that the grounds constituted a public nuisance. A second and separate count was based on common law negligence. The particulars of negligence were that the defendants had placed the cricket pitch too close to Beckenham Road, that they

Stone v. Bolton, 1 K.B. 201 (C.A. 1950); *Bolton v. Stone*, A. C. 850 (1951).

failed to erect a fence of sufficient height to prevent balls from being hit onto the road, and that they otherwise failed to insure that cricket balls would not be hit into said road. At trial, Oliver, J., gave judgment to the defendants on both the public nuisance and negligence counts. That judgment was reversed by a two-to-one vote in the Court of Appeal, which held for the plaintiff on the negligence question.]

Jenkins, L. J. [for the Court of Appeal]:

The case as regards negligence, therefore, seems to me to resolve itself into the question whether, with the wickets sited as they were, and the fence at the Beckenham Road end as it was, on August 9, 1947, the hitting into Beckenham Road of the ball which struck and injured the plaintiff was the realization of a reasonably foreseeable risk, or was in the nature of an unprecedented occurrence which the defendants could not reasonably have foreseen.

On the evidence this question seems to me to admit of only one answer. Balls had been hit into Beckenham Road before. It is true this had happened only at rare intervals, perhaps no more than six times in thirty seasons. But it was known from practical experience to be an actual possibility in the conditions in which matches were customarily played on the ground from about 1910 onwards, that is to say, with the wickets sited substantially as they were, and the fence at the Beckenham Road end, I gather, exactly as it was as regards height and position on August 9, 1947. What had happened several times before could, as it seems to me, reasonably be expected to happen again sooner or later. It was not likely to happen often, but it was certainly likely to happen again in time. When or how often it would happen again no one could tell, as this would depend on the strength of the batsmen playing on the ground (including visitors about whose capacity the defendants might know nothing) and the efficiency or otherwise of the bowlers. In my opinion, therefore, the hitting out of the ground of the ball which struck and injured the plaintiff was a realization of a reasonably foreseeable risk, which because it could reasonably be foreseen, the defendants were under a duty to prevent.

The defendants had, in fact, done nothing since the rearrangement of the ground on the making of Beckenham Road in or about 1910, whether by heightening the fence (e.g., by means of a screen of wire netting on poles) or by altering the position of the pitch, to guard against the known possibility of balls being hit into Beckenham Road. It follows that, if I have rightly defined the extent of the defendants' duty in this matter, the hitting out of the ground of the ball which injured the plaintiff did involve a breach of that duty for the consequences of which the defendants must be held liable to the plaintiff in damages. . . .

It was also, I think, suggested that no possible precaution would have arrested the flight of this particular ball, so high did it pass over the fence. This seems to me an irrelevant consideration. If cricket cannot be played on a given ground without foreseeable risk of injury to persons outside it, then it is always possible in the last resort to stop using that ground for cricket. The plaintiff in this case might, I apprehend, quite possibly have been killed. I ask myself whether in that event the defendants would have claimed the right to go on as before, because such a thing was unlikely to happen again for several years, though it might happen again on any day on which one of the teams in the match included a strong hitter. No doubt as a practical matter the defendants might decide that the double chance of a ball being hit into the road and finding a human target there was so remote that, rather than go to expense in the way of a wire screen or the like, or worse still abandon the ground, they would run the risk of such an occurrence and meet any ensuing claim for damages if and when it arose. But I fail to see on what principle they can be entitled to require people in Beckenham Road to accept the risk, and, if hit by a ball, put up with the possibly very serious harm done to them as damnum sine injuria, unless able to identify, trace, and successfully sue the particular batsman who made the hit.

[After judgment went against the defendants in the Court of Appeal, they took the case to the House of Lords, which unanimously decided the case in favor of the defendants.]

Lord Reid:

This case, therefore raises sharply the question what is the nature and extent of the duty of a person who promotes on his land operations which may cause damage to persons on an adjoining highway. Is it that he must not carry out or permit an operation which he knows or ought to know clearly can cause such damage, however improbable that result may be, or is it that he is only bound to take into account the possibility of such damage if such damage is a likely or probable consequence of what he does or permits, or if the risk of damage is such that a reasonable man, careful of the safety of his neighbor, would regard that risk as material? . . .

Counsel for the respondent in this case had to put his case so high as to say that, at least as soon as one ball had been driven into the road in the ordinary course of a match, the appellants could and should have realized that that might happen again and that, if it did, someone might be injured; and that that was enough to put on the appellants a duty to take steps to prevent such an occurrence. If the true test is foreseeability alone I think that must be so. Once a ball has been driven on to a road without there being anything extraordinary to account for the fact, there is clearly a risk that another will follow, and if it does there is clearly a chance, small though it may be, that someone may be injured. On the theory that it is foreseeability alone that matters it would be irrelevant to consider how often a ball might be expected to land in the road and it would not matter whether the road was the busiest street, or the quietest country lane; the only difference between these cases is in the degree of risk.

It would take a good deal to make me believe that the law has departed so far from the standards which guide ordinary careful people in ordinary life. In the crowded conditions of modern life even the most careful person cannot avoid creating some risks and accepting others. What a man must not do, and what I think a careful man tries not to do, is to create a risk which is substantial. Of course there are numerous cases where special circumstances require that a higher standard shall be observed and where that is recognized by the law. But I do not think that this case comes within any such special category. . . . In my judgment the test to be applied here is whether the risk of damage to a person on the road was so small that a reasonable man in the position of the appellants, considering the matter from the point of view of safety, would have thought it right to refrain from taking steps to prevent the danger.

In considering that matter I think that it would be right to take into account not only how remote is the chance that a person might be struck but also how serious the consequences are likely to be if a person is struck; but I do not think that it would be right to take into account the difficulty of remedial measures. If cricket cannot be played on a ground without creating a substantial risk, then it should not be played there *at all*. I think that this is in substance the test which Oliver, J., applied in this case. He considered whether the appellants' ground was large enough to be safe for all practical purposes and held that it was. This is a question not of law but of fact and degree. It is not an easy question and it is one on which opinions may well differ. I can only say that having given the whole matter repeated and anxious consideration I find myself unable to decide this question in favour of the respondent. But I think that this case is not far from the borderline. If this appeal is allowed, that does not in my judgment mean that in every case where cricket has been played on a ground for a number of years without accident or complaint those who organize matches there are safe to go on in reliance on past immunity. I would have reached a different conclusion if I had thought that the risk here had been other than extremely small, because I do not think that a reasonable man considering the matter from the point of view of safety would or should disregard any risk unless it is extremely small.

REVIEW AND DISCUSSION QUESTIONS

1. Why does appellate judge Jenkins hold that Miss Stone's injury was a "reasonably foreseeable risk," rather than "an unprecedented occurrence which the defendants could not reasonably have foreseen"? Do you agree? What facts are the most relevant and important for answering this question?

2. How does Justice Jenkins respond to the claim that no possible precaution could have stopped this particular ball? If this claim is true, should the cricket grounds be closed?

3. In reversing the appellate court's decision, what factors does Lord Reid consider besides the foreseeability of risk?

4. Lord Reid argues that the appellate court's decision departs "from the standards which guide ordinary people in ordinary life." Do you agree? What would the reasonable man test tell us in this case?

5. If Lord Reid is correct, then Miss Stone apparently has no legal redress for the injury she has suffered. Is this fair?

Negligence and Due Care

Palsgraf v. Long Island Railroad Co.

In this very famous and closely reasoned case, the New York Court of Appeals debates the nature and limits of negligence as a tort. Justice Benjamin Cardozo, one of the most distinguished jurists of the twentieth century and later a Supreme Court justice, contends that the negligence of the defendant's guards was not a wrong in relation to Mrs. Palsgraf, even though it resulted in her being injured. In his dissent Judge Andrews rejects the idea that negligence must involve the breach of a duty owed to a particular person. He argues, rather, that one is liable for all the "proximate" consequences of actions that threaten the safety of others.

Chief Justice Cardozo:

Plaintiff was standing on a platform of defendant's railroad after buying a ticket to go to Rockaway Beach. A train stopped at the station, bound for another place. Two men ran forward to catch it. One of the men reached the platform of the car without mishap, though the train was already moving. The other man, carrying a package, jumped aboard the car, but seemed unsteady as if about to fall. A guard on the car, who had held the door open, reached forward to help him in, and another guard on the platform pushed him from behind. In this act, the package was dislodged, and fell upon the rails. It was a package of small size, about fifteen inches long, and was covered by a newspaper. In fact it con-

tained fireworks, but there was nothing in its appearance to give notice of its contents. The fireworks when they fell exploded. The shock of the explosion threw down some scales at the other end of the platform, many feet away. The scales struck the plaintiff, causing injuries for which she sues.

The conduct of the defendant's guard, if a wrong in its relation to the holder of the package, was not a wrong in its relation to the plaintiff, standing far away. Relatively to her it was not negligence at all. Nothing in the situation gave notice that the falling package had in it the potency of peril to persons thus removed. Negligence is not actionable unless it involves the invasion of a legally protected interest, the violation of a right. "Proof of negligence in the air, so to speak, will not do." "Negligence is the absence of care, according to the circumstances." The

248 N.Y. 339 (1928). Some citations omitted.

plaintiff as she stood upon the platform of the station might claim to be protected against intentional invasion of her bodily security. Such invasion is not charged. She might claim to be protected against unintentional invasion by conduct involving in the thought of reasonable men an unreasonable hazard that such invasion would ensue. These, from the point of view of the law, were the bounds of her immunity, with perhaps some rare exceptions, survivals for the most part of ancient forms of liability, where conduct is held to be at the peril of the actor. . . . If no hazard was apparent to the eye of ordinary vigilance, an act innocent and harmless, at least to outward seeming, with reference to her, did not take to itself the quality of a tort because it happened to be a wrong, though apparently not one involving the risk of bodily insecurity, with reference to some one else. "In every instance, before negligence can be predicated of a given act, back of the act must be sought and found a duty to the individual complaining, the observance of which would have averted or avoided the injury." "The ideas of negligence and duty are strictly correlative." (Bowen, L. J., in *Thomas v. Quartermaine*, 18 Q. B. D. 685, 694). The plaintiff sues in her own right for a wrong personal to her, and not as the vicarious beneficiary of a breach of duty to another.

A different conclusion will involve us, and swiftly too, in a maze of contradictions. A guard stumbles over a package which has been left upon a platform. It seems to be a bundle of newspapers. It turns out to be a can of dynamite. To the eye of ordinary vigilance, the bundle is abandoned waste, which may be kicked or trod on with impunity. Is a passenger at the other end of the platform protected by the law against the unsuspected hazard concealed beneath the waste? If not, is the result to be any different, so far as the distant passenger is concerned, when the guard stumbles over a valise which a truckman or a porter has left upon the walk? The passenger far away, if the victim of a wrong at all, has a cause of action, not derivative, but original and primary. His claim to be protected against invasion of his bodily security is neither greater nor less because the act resulting in the invasion is a wrong to another far removed. In this case,

the rights that are said to have been violated, the interests said to have been invaded, are not even of the same order. The man was not injured in his person nor even put in danger. The purpose of the act, as well as its effect, was to make his person safe. If there was a wrong to him at all, which may very well be doubted, it was a wrong to a property interest only, the safety of his package. Out of this wrong to property, which threatened injury to nothing else, there has passed, we are told, to the plaintiff by derivation or succession a right of action for the invasion of an interest of another order, the right to bodily security. The diversity of interests emphasizes the futility of the effort to build the plaintiff's right upon the basis of a wrong to some one else. The gain is one of emphasis, for a like result would follow if the interests were the same. Even then, the orbit of the danger as disclosed to the eye of reasonable vigilance would be the orbit of the duty. One who jostles one's neighbor in a crowd does not invade the rights of others standing at the outer fringe when the unintended contact casts a bomb upon the ground. The wrongdoer, as to them is the man who carries the bomb, not the one who explodes it without suspicion of the danger. Life will have to be made over, and human nature transformed, before prevision so extravagant can be accepted as the norm of conduct, the customary standard to which behavior must conform.

The argument for the plaintiff is built upon the shifting meanings of such words as "wrong" and "wrongful," and shares their instability. What the plaintiff must show is "a wrong" to herself, *i.e.*, a violation of her own right, and not merely a wrong to some one else, nor conduct "wrongful" because unsocial, but not "a wrong" to any one. We are told that one who drives at reckless speed through a crowded city street is guilty of a negligent act and, therefore, of a wrongful one irrespective of the consequences. Negligent the act is, and wrongful in the sense that it is unsocial, but wrongful and unsocial in relation to other travelers, only because the eye of vigilance perceives the risk of damage. If the same act were to be committed on a speedway or a race course, it would lose its wrongful quality. The risk reasonably to be perceived defines the duty to be obeyed, and risk imports relation; it is risk to another or to others within the range of apprehension. . . . This does not mean, of course, that one who launches a destructive force is always relieved of liability if the force, though known to be destructive, pursues an unexpected path. It was not necessary that the defendant should have had notice of the particular method in which an accident would occur, if the possibility of an accident was clear to the ordinarily prudent eye. . . . Some acts, such as shooting, are so imminently dangerous to any one who may come within reach of the missile, however unexpectedly, as to impose a duty of prevision not far from that of an insurer. Even today, and much oftener in earlier stages of the law, one acts sometimes at one's peril. Under this head, it may be, fall certain cases of what is known as transferred intent, an act willfully dangerous to A resulting by misadventure in injury to B. These cases aside, wrong is defined in terms of the natural or probable, at least when unintentional. The range of reasonable apprehension is at times a question for the court, and at times, if varying inferences are possible, a question for the jury. Here, by concession, there was nothing in the situation to suggest to the most cautious mind that the parcel wrapped in newspaper would spread wreckage through the station. If the guard had thrown it down knowingly and willfully, he would not have threatened the plaintiff's safety, so far as appearances could warn him. His conduct would not have involved, even then, an unreasonable probability of invasion of her bodily security. Liability can be no greater where the act is inadvertent.

Negligence, like risk, is thus a term of relation. Negligence in the abstract, apart from things related, is surely not a tort, if indeed it is understandable at all. Negligence is not a tort unless it results in the commission of a wrong, and the commission of a wrong imports the violation of a right, in this case, we are told, the right to be protected against interference with one's bodily security. But bodily security is protected, not against all forms of interference or aggression, but only against some. One who seeks redress at law does not make out a cause of action by showing without more that there

has been damage to his person. If the harm was not willful, he must show that the act as to him had possibilities of danger so many and apparent as to entitle him to be protected against the doing of it though the harm was unintended. Affront to personality is still the keynote of the wrong. Confirmation of this view will be found in the history and development of the action on the case. Negligence as a basis of civil liability was unknown to mediaeval law. For damage to the person, the sole remedy was trespass, and trespass did not lie in the absence of aggression, and that direct and personal. Liability for other damage, as where a servant without orders from the master does or omits something to the damage of another, is a plant of later growth. When it emerged out of the legal soil, it was thought of as a variant of trespass, an offshoot of the parent stock. This appears in the form of action, which was known as trespass on the case. The victim does not sue derivatively, or by right of subrogation, to vindicate an interest invaded in the person of another. Thus to view his cause of action is to ignore the fundamental difference between tort and crime. He sues for breach of a duty owing to himself.

The law of causation, remote or proximate, is thus foreign to the case before us. The question of liability is always anterior to the question of the measure of the consequences that go with liability. If there is no tort to be redressed, there is no occasion to consider what damage might be recovered if there were a finding of a tort. We may assume, without deciding, that negligence, not at large or in the abstract, but in relation to the plaintiff, would entail liability for any and all consequences, however novel or extraordinary. There is room for argument that a distinction is to be drawn according to the diversity of interests invaded by the act, as where conduct negligent in that it threatens an insignificant invasion of an interest in property results in an unforeseeable invasion of an interest of another order, as *e.g.*, one of bodily security. Perhaps other distinctions may be necessary. We do not go into the question now. The consequences to be followed must first be rooted in a wrong.

The judgment of the Appellate Division and that of the Trial Term should be reversed, and the complaint dismissed, with costs in all courts.

Andrews, J. (dissenting):

Assisting a passenger to board a train, the defendant's servant negligently knocked a package from his arms. It fell between the platform and the cars. Of its contents the servant knew and could know nothing. A violent explosion followed. The concussion broke some scales standing a considerable distance away. In falling they injured the plaintiff, an intending passenger.

Upon these facts may she recover the damages she has suffered in an action brought against the master? The result we shall reach depends upon our theory as to the nature of negligence. Is it a relative concept—the breach of some duty owing to a particular person or to particular persons? Or where there is an act which unreasonably threatens the safety of others, is the doer liable for all its proximate consequences, even where they result in injury to one who would generally be thought to be outside the radius of danger? This is not a mere dispute as to words. We might not believe that to the average mind the dropping of the bundle would seem to involve the probability of harm to the plaintiff standing many feet away whatever might be the case as to the owner or to one so near as to be likely struck by its fall. If, however, we adopt the second hypothesis we have to inquire only as to the relation between cause and effect. We deal in terms of proximate cause, not of negligence.

Negligence may be defined roughly as an act or omission which unreasonably does or may affect the rights of others, or which unreasonably fails to protect oneself from the dangers resulting from such acts. Here I confine myself to the first branch of the definition. Nor do I comment on the word "unreasonable." For present purposes it sufficiently describes that average of conduct that society requires of its members.

There must be both the act or the omission, and the right. It is the act itself, not the intent of the actor, that is important. In criminal law both the intent and the result are to be considered. Intent again is material in tort actions, where punitive damages are sought, dependent on actual malice—not on merely reckless conduct. But here neither insanity nor infancy lessens responsibility.

As has been said, except in cases of contributory negligence, there must be rights which are or may be affected. Often though injury has occurred, no rights of him who suffers have been touched. A licensee or trespasser upon my land has no claim to affirmative care on my part that the land be made safe. Where a railroad is required to fence its tracks against cattle, no man's rights are injured should he wander upon the road because such fence is absent. An unborn child may not demand immunity from personal harm.

But we are told that "there is no negligence unless there is in the particular case a legal duty to take care, and this duty must be one which is owed to the plaintiff himself and not merely to others." This, I think too narrow a conception. Where there is the unreasonable act, and some right that may be affected there is negligence whether damage does or does not result. That is immaterial. Should we drive down Broadway at a reckless speed, we are negligent whether we strike an approaching car or miss it by an inch. The act itself is wrongful. It is a wrong not only to those who happen to be within the radius of danger but to all who might have been there—a wrong to the public at large. Such is the language of the street. Such is the language of the courts when speaking of contributory negligence. Such again and again their language in speaking of the duty of some defendant and discussing proximate cause in cases where such a discussion is wholly irrelevant on any other theory. As was said by Mr. Justice Holmes many years ago, "the measure of the defendant's duty in determining whether a wrong has been committed is one thing, the measure of liability when a wrong has been committed is another." Due care is a duty imposed on each one of us to protect society from unnecessary danger, not to protect A, B or C alone.

It may well be that there is no such thing as negligence in the abstract. "Proof of negligence in the air, so to speak, will not do." In an empty world negligence would not exist. It does involve a relationship between man and his fellows. But not merely a relationship between man and those whom he might reasonably expect his act would injure. Rather, a relationship between him and those whom he does in fact injure. If his act has a tendency to harm some one, it harms him a mile away as surely as it does those on the scene. We now permit children to recover for the negligent killing of the father. It was never prevented on the theory that no duty was owing to them. A husband may be compensated for the loss of his wife's services. To say that the wrong-doer was negligent as to the husband as well as to the wife is merely an attempt to fit facts to theory. An insurance company paying a fire loss recovers its payment of the negligent incendiary. We speak of subrogation—of suing in the right of the insured. Behind the cloud of words is the fact they hide, that the act, wrongful as to the insured, has also injured the company. Even if it be true that the fault of father, wife or insured will prevent recovery, it is because we consider the original negligence not the proximate cause of the injury.

In the well-known *Polemis Case* (1921, 3 K. B. 560), Scrutton, L. J., said that the dropping of a plank was negligent for it might injure "workman or cargo or ship." Because of either possibility the owner of the vessel was to be made good for his loss. The act being wrongful the doer was liable for its proximate results. Criticized and explained as this statement may have been, I think it states the law as it should be and as it is.

The proposition is this. Every one owes to the world at large the duty of refraining from those acts that may unreasonably threaten the safety of others. Such an act occurs. Not only is he wronged to whom harm might reasonably be expected to result, but he also who is in fact injured, even if he be outside what would generally be thought the danger zone. There needs be duty due the one complaining but this is not a duty to a particular individual because as to him harm might be expected. Harm to some one being the natural result of the act, not only that one alone, but all those in fact injured may complain. We have never, I think, held otherwise. Indeed in the *Di Caprio* case we said that a breach

of a general ordinance defining the degree of care to be exercised in one's calling is evidence of negligence as to every one. We did not limit this statement to those who might be expected to be exposed to danger. Unreasonable risk being taken, its consequences are not confined to those who might probably be hurt.

If this be so, we do not have a plaintiff suing by "derivation or succession." Her action is original and primary. Her claim is for a breach of duty to herself—not that she is subrogated to any right of action of the owner of the parcel or of a passenger standing at the scene of the explosion.

The right to recover damages rests on additional considerations. The plaintiff's rights must be injured, and this injury must be caused by the negligence. We build a dam, but are negligent as to its foundations. Breaking, it injures property down stream. We are not liable if all this happened because of some reason other than the insecure foundation. But when injuries do result from our unlawful act we are liable for the consequences. It does not matter that they are unusual, unexpected, unforeseen and unforeseeable. But there is one limitation. The damages must be so connected with the negligence that the latter may be said to be the proximate cause of the former.

These two words have never been given an inclusive definition. What is a cause in a legal sense, still more what is a proximate cause, depend in each case upon many considerations, as does the existence of negligence itself. Any philosophical doctrine of causation does not help us. A boy throws a stone into a pond. The ripples spread. The water level rises. The history of that pond is altered to all eternity. It will be altered by other causes also. Yet it will be forever the resultant of all causes combined. Each one will have an influence. How great only omniscience can say. You may speak of a chain, or if you please, a net. An analogy is of little aid. Each cause brings about future events. Without each the future would not be the same. Each is proximate in the sense it is essential. But that is not what we mean by the word. Nor on the other hand do we mean sole cause. There is no such thing.

Should analogy be thought helpful, however, I prefer that of a stream. The spring, starting on its journey, is joined by tributary after tributary. The river, reaching the ocean, comes from a hundred sources. No man may say whence any drop of water is derived. Yet for a time distinction may be possible. Into the clear creek, brown swamp water flows from the left. Later, from the right comes water stained by its clay bed. The three may remain for a space, sharply divided. But at last, inevitably no trace of separation remains. They are so commingled that all distinction is lost.

As we have said, we cannot trace the effect of an act to the end, if end there is. Again, however, we may trace it part of the way. A murder at Sarajevo may be the necessary antecedent to an assassination in London twenty years hence. An overturned lantern may burn all Chicago. We may follow the fire from the shed to the last building. We rightly say the fire started by the lantern caused its destruction.

A cause, but not the proximate cause. What we do mean by the word "proximate" is, that because of convenience, of public policy, of a rough sense of justice, the law arbitrarily declines to trace a series of events beyond a certain point. This is not logic, it is practical politics. Take our rule as to fires. Sparks from my burning haystack set on fire my house and my neighbor's. I may recover from a negligent railroad. He may not. Yet the wrongful act as directly harmed the one as the other. We may regret that the line was drawn just where it was, but drawn somewhere it had to be. We said the act of the railroad was not the proximate cause of our neighbor's fire. Cause it surely was. The words we used were simply indicative of our notions of public policy. Other courts think differently. But somewhere they reach the point where they cannot say the stream comes from any one source.

Take the illustration given in an unpublished manuscript by a distinguished and helpful writer on the law of torts. A chauffeur negligently collides with another car which is filled with dynamite, although he could not know it. An explosion follows. A, walking on the sidewalk nearby, is killed. B, sitting in a window of a building opposite, is cut by flying glass. C, likewise sitting in a window a block away, is similarly injured. And a further illustration. A

nursemaid, ten blocks away, startled by the noise, involuntarily drops a baby from her arms to the walk. We are told that C may not recover while A may. As to B it is a question for court or jury. We will all agree that the baby might not. Because, we are again told, the chauffeur had no reason to believe his conduct involved any risk of injuring either C or the baby. As to them he was not negligent.

But the chauffeur, being negligent in risking the collision, his belief that the scope of the harm he might do would be limited is immaterial. His act unreasonably jeopardized the safety of any one who might be affected by it. C's injury and that of the baby were directly traceable to the collision. Without that, the injury would not have happened. C had the right to sit in his office, secure from such dangers. The baby was entitled to use the sidewalk with reasonable safety.

The true theory is, it seems to me, that the injury to C, if in truth he is to be denied recovery, and the injury to the baby is that their several injuries were not the proximate result of the negligence. And here not what the chauffeur had reason to believe would be the result of his conduct, but what the prudent would foresee, may have a bearing. May have some bearing, for the problem of proximate cause is not to be solved by any one consideration.

It is all a question of expediency. There are no fixed rules to govern our judgment. There are simply matters of which we may take account. We have in a somewhat different connection spoken of "the stream of events." We have asked whether that stream was deflected—whether it was forced into new and unexpected channels. This is rather rhetoric than law. There is in truth little to guide us other than common sense.

There are some hints that may help us. The proximate cause, involved as it may be with many other causes, must be, at the least, something without which the event would not happen. The court must ask itself whether there was a natural and continuous sequence between cause and effect. Was the one a substantial factor in producing the other? Was there a direct connection between them, without too many intervening causes? Is the effect of cause on result not too attenuated? Is the cause likely, in the usual judgment of mankind, to produce the result? Or by the exercise of prudent foresight could the result be foreseen? Is the result too remote from the cause, and here we consider remoteness in time and space, where we passed upon the construction of a contract—but something was also said on this subject. Clearly we must so consider, for the greater the distance either in time or space, the more surely do other causes intervene to affect the result. When a lantern is overturned the firing of a shed is a fairly direct consequence. Many things contribute to the spread of the conflagration—the force of the wind, the direction and width of the streets, the character of intervening structures, other factors. We draw an uncertain and wavering line, but draw it we must as best we can.

Once again, it is all a question of fair judgment, always keeping in mind the fact that we endeavor to make a rule in each case that will be practical and in keeping with the general understanding of mankind.

Here another question must be answered. In the case supposed it is said, and said correctly, that the chauffeur is liable for the direct effect of the explosion although he had no reason to suppose it would follow a collision. "The fact that the injury occurred in a different manner than that which might have been expected does not prevent the chauffeur's negligence from being in law the cause of the injury." But the natural results of a negligent act—the results which a prudent man would or should foresee—do have a bearing upon the decision as to proximate cause. We have said so repeatedly. What should be foreseen? No human foresight would suggest that a collision itself might injure one a block away. On the contrary, given an explosion, such a possibility might be reasonably expected. I think the direct connection, the foresight of which the courts speak, assumes prevision of the explosion, for the immediate results of which, at least, the chauffeur is responsible.

It may be said this is unjust. Why? In fairness he should make good every injury flowing from his negligence. Not because of tenderness toward him we say he need not answer for all that follows his wrong. We look back to the catastrophe, the fire kindled by the spark, or the explosion. We trace the consequences—not indefinitely, but to a certain point. And to aid us in fixing that point we ask what might ordinarily be expected to follow the fire or the explosion.

This last suggestion is the factor which must determine the case before us. The act upon which defendant's liability rests is knocking an apparently harmless package onto the platform. The act was negligent. For its proximate consequences the defendant is liable. If its contents were broken, to the owner; if it fell upon and crushed a passenger's foot, then to him. If it exploded and injured one in the immediate vicinity, to him also as to A in the illustration. Mrs. Palsgraf was standing some distance away. How far cannot be told from the record—apparently twenty-five or thirty feet. Perhaps less. Except for the explosion, she would not have been injured. We are told by the appellant in his brief "it cannot be denied that the explosion was the direct cause of the plaintiff's injuries." So it was a substantial factor in producing the result—there was here a natural and continuous sequence—direct connection. The only intervening cause was that instead of blowing her to the ground the concussion smashed the weighing machine which in turn fell upon her. There was no remoteness in time, little in space. And surely, given such an explosion as here it needed no great foresight to predict that the natural result would be to injure one on the platform at no greater distance from its scene than was the plaintiff. Just how no one might be able to predict. Whether by flying fragments, by broken glass, by wreckage of machines or structures no one could say. But injury in some form was most probable.

Under these circumstances I cannot say as a matter of law that the plaintiff's injuries were not the proximate result of the negligence. That is all we have before us. The court refused to so charge. No request was made to submit the matter to the jury as a question of fact, even would that have been proper upon the record before us.

The judgment appealed from should be affirmed, with costs.

Judgment reversed, etc.

REVIEW AND DISCUSSION QUESTIONS

1. What are the facts of the case and in what way are they unusual? Do you think the Long Island Railroad Company should have been held liable for Mrs. Palsgraf's injury? Did the defendant's employees cause her injury?

2. Explain Cardozo's position. What does he mean by the statement, "Proof of negligence in the air, so to speak, will not do"? Why does he think no wrong has been done to Mrs. Palsgraf?

3. Why does Cardozo maintain that deciding in favor of Mrs. Palsgraf would involve us in a "maze of contradictions"? Do you agree?

4. Cardozo contends that "the law of causation, remote or proximate, is thus foreign to the case before us." Is it true that Cardozo's decision ignores the issue of causation altogether?

5. According to Andrews, what is "proximate" cause, and how is it different from the factual issue of what caused the injury? How is proximate cause to be determined?

6. What is Judge Andrews's position, and how does it compare with that of Cardozo? Who has the better argument, and why?

Tort Liability and Corrective Justice

Jeffrie G. Murphy and Jules L. Coleman

When a person is injured, the initial legal presumption is that the victim should bear the losses himself. As Jeffrie G. Murphy and Jules L. Coleman explain, the rules of tort liability spell out when a victim's losses can be shifted to another party. Sometimes the rule of fault liability applies, at other times, the rule of strict liability. Reasons can be advanced for either fault or strict liability, and reflecting on these leads to questions about the whole nature of tort liability. Murphy and Coleman pursue these questions in the context of the debate over no-fault automobile insurance plans, which entail abandoning the tort system in accident cases. Whereas no-fault accident systems are defended on grounds of social utility, the fault system is generally upheld by appeals to retributive justice and compensatory or corrective justice. The authors argue, however, that when a tort is not intentional, neither retributive justice nor corrective justice require compensation to be based on fault. Jeffrie Murphy teaches philosophy at Arizona State University, and Jules Coleman teaches law and philosophy at Yale University.

THE RULES OF TORT LIABILITY

Often when an individual is injured by the doings of another, he suffers measurable damages. The law of torts provides the victim with a possible source of recovery. Were there no remedy, the victim would have to shoulder the costs occasioned by the conduct of others. In torts, we capture this by the expression that *initially* losses shall lie where they have fallen. In short, we begin with the presumption that victims should bear their losses. This is a presumption that can be overridden. Specifying the conditions under which the presumption can be overridden make up the body of tort law.

One reason we might have for our initial presumption that the victims should bear their losses is that it is costly to shift them to others. If there is no good reason for shifting a loss, why incur unnecessary costs? By letting the loss lie where it falls, in effect we hold the victim liable for the costs of harms he suffers, unless he or she is prepared to take steps to have us consider shifting the loss to another—usually but not always, his injurer. The victim has the burden of coming forward and initiating litigation and the additional burden of persuading a jury that his loss ought to be borne by another.

The courts recognize only some reasons as good ones for shifting losses or, in other words, for overriding the presumption that the victim should bear his own costs. These reasons are captured in *liability rules*. Liability rules set forth the conditions a victim must meet in order to have his losses borne by another. Usually these rules are not conclusive. If the conditions set out by a liability rule are satisfied, the burden is shifted from the victim to the defendant. The plaintiff-victim has met his burden; he has given the court good reason for thinking that he ought not bear his losses, and for thinking that the defendant should. Now the defendant has available to her the opportunity to present an argument to the effect that she ought not shoulder the victim's costs. Not every reason she might offer is a good one. The good ones are captured under the rules of *positive defense*.

We can illustrate the mechanisms involved [with an example]. . . . The home owner whose kitchen your car has entered will bear the costs your recklessness caused unless he can convince a jury that you should. In an effort to convince someone that the responsibility for these costs lies with you, he initiates litigation. He goes to court and establishes that you were reckless in your driving and that your recklessness caused his damages. He has met the initial burden by showing that you were at fault and that your fault caused the harm. His costs will be your responsibility unless you have a compelling reason why they should not be. Suppose it turns out that you drove haphazardly because earlier that night at a party the victim without your knowledge had slipped you severely intoxicating beverages. Moreover, the effects of the beverages would be delayed so that you would experience intoxication long after you started driving. The net effect is that you would be unable to reason clearly about what you ought to do in your intoxicated state. All would be beyond your control. In that case, you would have shown that the victim's very own mischief was responsible for the damage he suffered. In doing so, you have offered a positive defense sufficient to shift the burden back to him. Not every

defense you might have tried would have been so successful. Had you argued that you were drunk because you are an alcoholic, you might have received some sympathy from the court, but you could hardly have expected to be freed of the burden of recompense.

In this section, we will focus on liability rules rather than on the rules of positive defense. In other words, we will be concerned with the conditions that must be satisfied in order for a victim to overcome the initial presumption that the losses that have befallen him should remain his responsibility. In general, a distinction is drawn between two kinds of liability rules; these are the rules of fault and of strict liability. If a case is covered by a rule of strict liability, the victim must establish that:

1. The defendant acted.
2. He, the victim, suffered a compensable loss.
3. The defendant's action caused the loss.

Under a rule of fault liability, the plaintiff-victim must establish that each of these three conditions has been satisfied and that the following condition has been satisfied as well.

4. The defendant's conduct was at fault.

Under the rule of strict liability, it is enough that the plaintiff show that the injurer caused the harm for which he seeks recompense. Under the rule of fault liability, he must show both that the injurer is at fault and that his fault is causally responsible for the victim's loss.[1] Certain cases that come before a court are decided on a strict liability basis, others on a fault basis. One question in tort theory is which sorts of cases should be adjudicated under which sort of rule. This question presupposes that we have already determined the relative advantages of each sort of liability rule, and what we are trying to do is to fit the rules to their most appropriate applications. The philosopher of law wants to look more closely at what the traditional analysis takes for granted; he or she wants to know what reasons can be advanced on behalf of either strict or fault liability. The legal philosopher wants to know, in other words, what the relative virtues of the rules are. Does fault liability, for example, promote justice, and strict liability, utility? Or is it the other way around? Indeed, the legal philosopher is troubled by an even more basic question: why rectify gains and losses according to the traditions, customs, and rules developed over the history of tort law? Maybe the whole system of liability rules and positive defence fails to achieve either justice or utility—or maybe it is less successful at promoting justice or utility than alternatives to it might be.

In the law of torts, individuals bring their claims to court on a case-by-case basis. But, theoretically, we could deal with their claims in other ways, for example, by lumping together the costs of certain kinds of harms as they accumulate among victims over a period of time, and then compensate the victims as a class through the tax coffers. I don't want to claim that such a plan is preferable to the tort system, but I do want to suggest that we cannot determine if it is unless we first determine what goals we think the law of torts ought to pursue. Only when we have an idea of what it is we want the law of torts to accomplish, will we be able to determine if all cases should be adjudicated on a case-by-case basis. Only then will we be able to determine the relative advantages of the rules of strict and fault liability in securing them.

I want now to explore these questions in the context of a particular issue within the law of torts: namely, the debate over no-fault automobile insurance. No fault presents a good focal point for this discussion because under a no-fault system, cases are not, in fact, adjudicated individually; indeed, in theory they are not to be adjudicated at all. No-fault, in short, involves abandoning the tort law system as we know it. The costs of accidents under a no-fault scheme are not distributed according to the rule of fault liability, and this seems initially troubling to those who think that justice requires imposing the costs of accidents upon those whose fault occasions them. The intuitive view is that the fault liability rule promotes justice, and that the rule of strict liability abandons justice to promote utility. Abandoning the tort system in general and the rule of fault liability in particular as instruments for rectifying wrongful losses that result from negligent motoring seems to conflict with our ideals of just law, and in what follows I want to see if this initial impression stands up under scrutiny.

JUSTICE AND THE COSTS OF AUTOMOBILE ACCIDENTS

. . . Interestingly enough, if justice were to require that fault-related burdens be distributed exclusively according to the criterion of fault, it would be very hard to imagine how such demands could be met by the fault system, at least as we know it. In the first place, all traditional forms of insurance would be ruled out since they would allocate burdens in part among individuals whose records have been (and may remain) spotless, as well as among past and present wrongdoers. The burdens of the faultless would not reflect their desert and would be objectionable on those grounds. In the absence of insurance, the costs of particular accidents would fall either on individual victims or injurers, with victims being ruled out on the same grounds as the faultless: no fault, no penalty. But if the costs of accidents were to fall entirely on individual wrongdoers, they would often prove disproportionate to the wrongdoing involved—slight errors can result in costly accidents—and this would be objectionable on the grounds that the burden would not reflect the degree of fault. . . .

. . . [D]efenders of the fault system [believe] that distributing losses in this way—by having them fall initially on individual injurers—secures the goal of justice, a legitimate aim of accident law, by penalizing the wrongdoing of those at fault. The fault system, by penalizing the wrongful conduct, is therefore required by principles of retributive justice. On related grounds, prohibitions against no-fault are supported by principles of compensatory justice, which are said to require that recompense for losses must originate with those at fault. I want to consider both of these arguments in turn.

According to the standard conception of retributive justice, wrongdoing deserves its comeuppance: a measure of pain, suffering, or deprivation should be exacted from wrongdoers, and the deprivation should reflect the nature and magnitude of the wrongdoing. In its most prevalent and, I believe, least acceptable form the retributivist principle is a moral position in a very strong sense that in order for penalization to be deserved, the defective conduct must be morally defective, and the author of it morally at fault. Thus legal fault, insofar as it is based on the moral fault of the actor, ought to be penalized.

One of the most prevalent defenses of a fault system rests on the claim that this principle of retributive justice requires it. The argument usually takes the following form. If an actor's defective conduct is a substantial contributory factor in bringing about harm, we impute the harm to him as his fault. He has, in the legal jargon, satisfied the fault requirement. The fault system, by making those at fault in causing accidents liable for their costs, guarantees that culpable motoring gets its comeuppance and is therefore required by the retributivist principle.

This argument in favor of the fault system does not purport to establish that every time an actor is at fault he is morally blameworthy. It establishes only that he is blameworthy in some sense of the term. And although some faulty driving is morally defective, for example, drunken, reckless driving, most driving faults are not moral shortcomings. If the retributivist principle were to support penalties only for moral wrongdoing, the fault system would justify too much. However, we need not interpret the retributivist principle this narrowly. Perhaps we should understand it as endorsing penalties for nonmoral as well as for moral shortcomings. H. L. A. Hart, for one, has argued persuasively that it is permissible morally to penalize wrongdoing that is an actor's fault—to his genuine discredit—whether or not the flaw in his conduct is a moral one.[2] If Hart is correct, then there exists a moral license to impose penalties on drivers who fail to satisfy the legal standard of due care, provided that failure can be charged against their personal records, that is, is something for which they are to blame. Hart's position does not amount to an endorsement of retributivism since he claims only that genuine wrongdoing may be penalized, while retributivists claim that such penalties are not merely permissible but a matter of right action.

Being at fault, morally or otherwise, has two essential ingredients. One element in fault judgments relates to the character of the act and its relationship to the appropriate standard of conduct, while the other relates to the actor's "state of mind." Most fault judgments are true just in case both the act-regarding and the actor-regarding requirements are satisfied. The essence of these requirements is perhaps best illustrated by the defenses alleged wrongdoers offer to defeat accusations of fault—that is, justifications and excuses. When an actor has a justification for what he has done, he denies that the act, all things considered, fails to satisfy the appropriate norm, or he argues that his conduct is an exception to the rule usually governing that type of conduct, or that it is an exception to the rule that such conduct is wrong. Should he have an excuse for what he has done, he would not be denying that his conduct was substandard, only that it was his fault. The "subjective" or mental element necessary to charge the act against his record, he thus argues, is missing.

If an actor has an excuse for his actions, he is not at fault in the sense appropriate to justify imposing penalties against him on the grounds of retributive justice. That is because retributivism licenses penalties for *genuine* wrongdoing only. Insofar as excuses evidence the nonvoluntary character of the conduct, failure to measure up under excusing conditions cannot be considered something for which the actor is to blame. Though the retributivist principle would not endorse penalties for what would ordinarily count as excusable departures from the standard of due care, the system of awarding liability for accident costs on the basis of fault often penalizes those who in Hart's words "could not help doing what they did."

This feature of the fault system is well known among lawyers and has led some legal theorists to question if the courts should apply subjective (internal) or objective (external) standards of fault to determine liability in accident law. In other words, should the law require no more of each member of the community than he is capable of (the subjective test of fault) or should it require each to live up to a standard that may exceed the capacities of some (the objective test).

The most famous and perhaps still the most compelling defense of the objective test is articulated in Oliver Wendell Holmes:

> If, for instance, a man is borne hasty and awkward, is always having accidents and hurting himself or his neighbors, no doubt his congenital defects will be allowed for in the courts of Heaven, but his slips are no less troublesome to his neighbors than if they sprang from guilty neglect. His neighbors, accordingly require him, at his proper peril, to come up to their standard, and the courts which they establish decline to take his personal equation into account.[3]

Ascriptions of fault that are verified by applying objective criteria of conduct are not defeasible by excuses. That is their distinctive feature. Thus, if an injurer genuinely could do no better than he did—if, in other words, his conduct was, in a suitably narrow sense, nonvoluntary—this would *not* suffice to free him from the burdens of recompense under the present system of accident law, though the nonvoluntary character of his actions would normally constitute excusing conditions and free him from blame.

We could of course amend the fault system to obviate this sort of difficulty by requiring that it apply only subjective criteria of fault. In this way, the fault system would penalize only those whose failure to exercise due care is to their personal discredit. But even if we recommend the application of the subjective test, the fault system would fail to satisfy the retributivist principle. That is because, in the fault system, only accident-causing wrongful driving receives its due—where the penalty is liability for accident costs—leaving unpenalized the class of dangerous and unnecessarily risky, but not harm-causing, wrongful motoring. From the retributivist point of view, this is unacceptable, since suitably culpable conduct without harmful causal upshots falls within its ambit. Thus, in the criminal law, so-called wrongful attempts are punishable, for example, attempted murder, attempted rape, and so on. From the retributivist point of view, the punishment of wrongful attempts is mandatory. The rough civil law analogue of criminal attempts is conduct that is "at fault," that is, unreasonably risky, harm-threatening, or dangerous. If securing the goal of

retributive justice were the only goal of accident law, and if the penalty of liability for accident costs were the only sort of penalty befitting wrongful conduct of this sort, securing that goal would require that liability be spread among those at fault, not merely among those at fault in causing injuries. But even in this system driving faults are rendered market, not moral, values.

Moreover, the retributivist principle requires only that a fitting penalty be administered to wrongdoers. Nothing in the principle specifies that the penalty be liability for accident costs. Indeed, we have seen some of the difficulties inherent in trying to "fit" the penalty of civil liability to driving faults. An accident law in which liability for accident costs is the penalty for wrongful driving conflates two distinguishable issues: those of retribution and recompense. The fault system may be characterized by the fact that it joins these two issues, since in that system, the retribution for wrongdoing is recompense for injuries that are one's fault. The distinguishing feature of no-fault is the separation of these two concerns. By referring to accident law as a no-fault system, we do not mean to imply that there exist no purposes for which conduct should be examined for fault. Indeed, the criterion of fault is perfectly relevant to contriving penal fines or other penalties themselves suggested by the retributivist principle: penalties more fitting than civil liability in the sense that they are not subject to market fluctuations.[4] All we mean to imply by the label "no-fault" is that the criterion of fault is irrelevant to the issue of recompense. That goal is to be satisfied by ensuring that the traffic victim receives the compensation to which he is entitled. Our notions of retributive justice therefore do not require that compensation, in order to be just, originate with those at fault. Whether or not our notions of corrective justice do is what I now want to consider.

There are a number of statements or ways of characterizing the requirements of corrective justice. I want to begin with the following conception of corrective justice. On this view, corrective or rectificatory justice is concerned with wrongful gains and losses. Rectification is, on this view, a matter of justice when it is necessary to protect a distribution of holdings (or entitlements) from distortions that arise from unjust enrichments or wrongful losses. The principle of corrective justice requires the annulment of both wrongful gains and losses.

In order to invoke the principle of corrective justice to support eliminating or rectifying a distortion in a distribution of holdings or entitlements, the distribution need not itself be just. Corrective justice is a matter of justice on this view *not* because it promotes justice in the distribution of holdings, but rather because it remedies unjust departures from the prevailing distribution of holdings. However, following the requirements of corrective justice is necessary to maintain a just distribution of holdings. Therefore, any theory of distributive justice must make provisions for a theory of corrective justice. Corrective justice is an independent principle of justice precisely because it may be legitimately invoked to protect or reinstate distributions of holdings that would themselves fail the test of distributive justice.

Under the principle of corrective or compensatory justice, the victim of another's fault may have a right to recompense. The principle of corrective justice does not establish the right of victims to recompense for "faultlessly" caused injuries, and though an insurance scheme that protected policy holders against errorless as well as faultily caused injuries might be preferable, the protection such a scheme could offer would extend beyond what injured parties could claim as their *right*.

If compensation for wrongfully inflicted harms is one's right, against whom does the right bearer hold it? Upon whom does the corresponding obligation fall? In an insurance scheme, the injured party's right to recompense may be against his insurance company or against the insurance company of his injurer. That depends on whether the insurance coverage is a "first" or "third" party plan; that is, whether individuals insure themselves against personal loss owing to the conduct of others (or themselves)—first party—or against liability for the injuries they may cause others—third party. According to the most extensive form of no-fault coverage, the victim's right to recompense is a valid claim he holds against his own insurance company: that

right being derived from contract. The underlying moral issue is whether or not such contracts and their corresponding rights and obligations are consistent with principles of corrective justice. Is compensation for accidental harms to be analyzed broadly to require only that victims receive the compensation to which they are entitled, or narrowly to require that recompense for victims must originate with respective injurers.

Suppose now that two individuals, X and Y, were involved in an accident that is Y's fault. X's right to compensation creates a corresponding duty to provide recompense that seems to fall on Y, his injurer. It seems, moreover, that justice would require that Y compensate X. If this is so, it suggests the general conclusion that, in order to be just, compensation must come from those at fault.

Why is it that justice requires that Y bear X's costs? Perhaps, if Y does not compensate X, X will go without compensation. One consequence of this would be that X's conduct would be penalized. Certainly that would be unjust. But that justice is avoidable by guaranteeing that X does not have to bear his own costs. That goal is accomplished when anyone other than X, including, but not necessarily, Y shoulders them. Perhaps by Y not bearing X's costs, Y's wrongdoing would go unpenalized. That would presumably constitute a retributive injustice. But the retributive principle requires only that Y's wrongdoing be penalized, and that goal is accomplished not only when Y is made to compensate X, but also when Y is penalized in some other way, for example, through penal channels.

Both compensation and punishment are concerned with wrongdoing—wrongful gain, advantage, or benefit. But where punishment involves wrongdoers incurring some evil—usually the loss of assorted legal rights—for their wrongfully obtained (or sought) gains or advantages, compensation aims at annulling, rectifying, or eliminating these undeserved or otherwise unjustifiable gains. Where punishment is concerned with victims only secondarily, the overriding concern of compensation is the nullification of the victim's losses; the reordering of his affairs to make him whole again. James Nickel has simply but insightfully captured this feature of compensatory justice as the elimination of unjustifiable *gains and losses* owing to human action—what he aptly terms "distortions."[5]

If compensation involves the elimination of distortions, surely we must acknowledge that not every means of securing that goal would be endorsed by principles of compensatory justice. However seductive the myth of Robin Hood may be, there is little evidence to suggest that such a method for nullifying unwarranted gains and losses would satisfy the demands of compensatory justice. What further distinguishes compensatory from other principles of justice is that, in order to secure the elimination of distortions, it supports a system of correlative rights and duties between respective victims and wrongdoers. In the typical case of compensation, finding for the plaintiff amounts to a recognition of his or her (legal) rights to recompense; a right that imposes a correlative duty upon the defendant to provide compensation. In the typical instance of punishment, a verdict of guilty confers upon the state a right to impose some penalty against the defendant. But this right is a moral license, and unlike a claim-right, it does not give rise to a correlative duty; in this case, an obligation on the defendant to be punished or to allow himself to be punished.

But if a distinguishing feature of compensatory justice is this structure of correlative rights and duties, wouldn't principles of compensatory justice therefore prohibit contractual relations that supersede this structure by imposing duties of recompense on the *victim's* insurance company—contractual relations that require the victim's insurance company to discharge what are, in fact, the duties of wrongdoers? Compensation is a kind of repayment, and it is therefore with the category of obligations to repay that we are concerned. In the case of obligations to repay debts or loans, justice does not as a rule require that the repayment originate with the party obligated to repay. Thus, when someone borrows money from the local bank, few protests of injustice are heard above clicking safe locks, provided the money is returned in sufficient quantities and at appropriate intervals, regardless of exactly who is forwarding the payments on whose behalf. My obligation to repay a debt of, say, $100 to you is discharged when my wealthy patron approaches you with that sum, and you accept it as repayment, even if I know nothing of this transaction. Of course some obligations to repay may be described so determinately that they could not justly be discharged by another. Here the requirement that the repayment originate with the obligated party is built into the description of the obligation, and the fact that it cannot justly be discharged by another is a function of the determinacy of the obligation, not of justice.

Though it is a misleading way of talking, we sometimes describe punishment as a kind of repayment. We talk, for example, about criminals as owing "debts to society," which are presumably repaid through incarceration. If there is any merit in viewing punishment as a debt of repayment, then surely it is the sort of debt that in order to be just must be repaid by the "obligated" party, that is, the wrongdoer.[6] Now, is the obligation to provide compensation for accidental torts something that can justly be discharged by intervening parties—in this case, insurance companies—and therefore like obligations to repay debts in this respect, or is it something that can be discharged justly only by wrongdoers—like the purported obligation criminals have to pay back society? If compensation is, in this regard, like punishment, in order to be just, recompense for accidental torts must therefore originate with those at fault.

Unlike the obligation to repay debts, the obligation to compensate traffic victims is not derived from contractual relation or promise. It is derived from wrongdoing. But wrongdoing plays significantly different roles in punishment and in compensation. In compensation, unlike punishment, wrongdoing is not viewed as something in itself worthy of penalty. Instead compensation is concerned with wrongdoing only insofar as it either involves wrongful gain or benefit at another's expense, or it is evidence of the unjustifiable character of the victim's loss. In the absence of wrongful gain, proof of wrongdoing supports the victim's assertion that his losses have been wrongfully absorbed, and therefore justifies his demanding compensation as a matter of right, rather than requesting it as a matter of benevolence, utility, or welfare.

The distinguishing feature of automobile accidents and of accidental torts generally is that the injurer does not, as a rule, gain from his wrong, nor is it plausible to interpret his conduct as directed at securing some temporary or long-term advantage. It is, after all, the nature of the beast; accidents are unintentional. One does not plan an accident. On the contrary, intentional torts such as fraud are undertaken to secure wrongful advantage at another's expense. A no-fault allocation of losses owing to intentional torts involving gain would not nullify the wrongdoer's gain and would be objectionable on those grounds. Nor would punishing him under the criminal law eliminate the gain, since the penal statute requires only that he suffer some evil for his wrong; nothing in it requires that he forfeit his gain. But in the case of accidental torts there is, in general, no gain on the wrongdoer's behalf that needs to be eliminated. That his conduct is wrongful supports the right of the victim to recompense, nothing more. Of course, his conduct may exhibit sufficient fault to merit penalty, but that is a concern of retributive justice and may best be dealt with by penal fine. Thus, it is my contention that principles of compensatory justice would not support a no-fault allocation of losses owing to certain intentional torts—i.e., because of the element of wrongful gain—but would not prohibit no-fault accident law precisely because of the absence of wrongful gain.[7]

This conclusion should be especially comforting to legal reformers such as Guido Calabresi and Jeffrey O'Connell, both of whom have recently urged the separation of accident law from the main body of tort law. Such proposals suggest that accident law govern recompense for harms owing primarily to negligence and defective products, and that they do so on a no-fault, no-defect basis. They are usually recommended to us by dint of their cost-saving features. The arguments I have been considering in this section on compensatory justice suggest still further support for their position. It is hoped that support from these quarters will surprise only those who are wedded to the view that justice and utility cannot be achieved except at one another's expense.

NOTES

[1]A person is at fault in torts if his conduct is either negligent, reckless, or is the result of a wrongful intent to injure. A negligent person is one who simply fails to exercise the care of a reasonable man or woman of ordinary prudence.

[2]Cf. H. L. A. Hart, "Legal Responsibility and Excuses," in *Punishment and Responsibility* (New York: Oxford, 1968), 39.

[3]O. W. Holmes, *The Common Law* (Boston: Little, Brown and Company, 1963), 86.

[4]Though such penalties are not affected by market values, they may be subject to considerations other than moral fault, e.g., deterrent value.

[5]James Nickel, "What Is Compensatory Justice?" *William and Mary Law Review*, Vol. 3.

[6]Imagine the effects on our notions of responsibility of an insurance scheme for criminal liability!

[7]What I want to claim here is not that we can't imagine any situations in which accidents are beneficial to wrongdoers, but only that accidents in general are not beneficial to them, and, moreover, that accidents in general do not discriminate between victims and injurers in terms of likelihood of harm or gain. In other words, a priori, there is no reason to think that injurers more than victims will gain from accidents, just as there is no reason to assume that victims more than injurers will lose from them.

REVIEW AND DISCUSSION QUESTIONS

1. What is the difference between fault liability and strict liability? What is no-fault automobile insurance, and why would such a system involve "abandoning the tort law system as we know it"?

2. Fault has two essential ingredients. What are they, and how do they relate to justification and excuse? How does the contrast between subjective (internal) and objective (external) standards of fault apply to automobile accident cases?

3. Assess the argument that retributive justice requires the fault system in automobile accident cases.

4. What is corrective justice? Are Murphy and Coleman right that it does not require the fault system? Explain.

Efficiency and the Law

United States v. Carroll Towing Company

A tugboat owned by Carroll Towing was moving a line of barges when one barge (the Anna C*) owned by Conners Company broke away and crashed into another ship. The* Anna C *leaked oil, and the U.S. government, the owner of the oil, sued Carroll Towing (owner of the tug who pulled* Anna C*) for the oil. The issue in this case is whether the* Anna C*'s owners (Connors Co.) were partly negligent for the lost oil in the barge because they did not have anybody on board who could prevent the* Anna C *from crashing into another ship.*

L. Hand, C. J.:

It appears from the foregoing review that there is no general rule to determine when the absence of a bargee or other attendant will make the owner of the barge liable for injuries to other vessels if she breaks away from her moorings. However, in any cases where he would be so liable for injuries to others, obviously he must reduce his damages proportionately, if the injury is to his own barge. It becomes apparent why there can be no such general rule, when we consider the grounds for such a liability. Since there are occasions when every vessel will break from her moorings, and since, if she does, she becomes a menace to those about her, the owner's duty, as in other similar situations, to provide against resulting injuries is a function of three variables: (1) The probability that she will break away; (2) the gravity of the resulting injury, if she does; (3) the burden of adequate precautions. Possibly it serves to bring this notion into relief to state it in algebraic terms: if the probability be called P; the injury, I; and the burden, B; liability depends upon whether B is less than I, multiplied by P: i.e., whether $B < PI$. Applied to the situation at bar, the likelihood that a barge will break from her fasts and the damage she will do, vary with the place and time; for example, if a storm threatens, the danger is greater; so it is, if she is in a crowded harbor where moored barges are constantly being shifted about. On the other hand, the barge must not be the bargee's prison, even though he lives aboard; he must go ashore at times. We need not say whether, even in such crowded waters as New York Harbor a bargee must be aboard at night at all; it may be that the custom is otherwise, as Ward, J., supposed in *The Kathryn B. Guinan*, 176 F.2d 301; and that, if so, the situation is one where custom should control. We leave that question open; but we hold that it is not in all cases a sufficient answer to a bargee's absence without excuse, during working hours, that he has properly made fast his barge to a pier, when he leaves her. In the case at bar the bargee left at five o'clock in the afternoon of January 3rd, and the flotilla broke away at about two o'clock in the afternoon of the following day, twenty-one hours afterwards. The bargee had been away all the time, and we hold that his fabricated story was affirmative evidence that he had no excuse for his absence. At the locus in quo—especially during the short January days and in the full tide of war activity—barges were being constantly "drilled" in and out. Certainly it was not beyond reasonable expectation, that with the inevitable haste and bustle, the work might not be done with adequate care. In such circumstances we hold—and it is all that we do hold—that it was a fair requirement that the Conners Company should have a bargee aboard (unless he had some excuse for his absence), during the working hours of daylight.

159 F.2d 169 (2d Cir. 1947).

REVIEW AND DISCUSSION QUESTIONS

1. Describe the facts in this case, along with the legal issue that Judge Hand is weighing.

2. Explain the importance of the formula $B < Pl$. Does it suffice to determine whether it is fair to hold a particular defendant liable?

3. This case is often described as one that illustrates the "economic" approach to law. Why might somebody say that?

4. Hand does not hold that a bargee must always be on board. Why not?

Liability Without Causation?

Summers v. Tice

The plaintiff Charles Summers went quail hunting with Harold Tice and Ernest Simonson. When a quail was flushed, Tice and Simonson fired negligently in Summers's direction, and he was wounded in the face. Because Tice and Simonson fired similar pellets from similar guns, however, it could not be proved which of them, or which gun, had actually injured Summers. Although a basic element of negligence as a tort is that the defendant's conduct must be the cause of the plaintiff's injury, in this case the California Supreme Court upheld Summers's suit.

Actions by Charles A. Summers against Harold W. Tice and against Ernest Simonson for negligently shooting plaintiff while hunting. From judgments for plaintiff, defendants appeal. . . .

Justice Carter delivered the opinion of the Court:

Each of the two defendants appeals from a judgment against them in an action for personal injuries. Pursuant to stipulation the appeals have been consolidated.

Plaintiff's action was against both defendants for an injury to his right eye and face as the result of being struck by bird shot discharged from a shotgun. The case was tried by the court without a jury and the court found that on November 20, 1945, plaintiff and the two defendants were hunting quail on the open range. Each of the defendants was armed with a 12 gauge shotgun loaded with shells containing 7½ size shot. Prior to going hunting plaintiff discussed the

hunting procedure with defendants, indicating that they were to exercise care when shooting and to "keep in line." In the course of hunting, plaintiff proceeded up a hill, thus placing the hunters at the points of a triangle. The view of defendants with reference to plaintiff was unobstructed and they knew his location. Defendant Tice flushed a quail which rose in flight to a ten foot elevation and flew between plaintiff and defendants. Both defendants shot at the quail, shooting in plaintiff's direction. At that time defendants were 75 yards from plaintiff. One shot struck plaintiff in his eye and another in his upper lip. Finally it was found by the court that as the direct result of the shooting by defendants the shots struck plaintiff as above mentioned and that defendants were negligent in so shooting and plaintiff was not contributorily negligent.

. . . First, on the subject of negligence, defendant Simonson contends that the evidence is insufficient to sustain the finding on that score, but he does not point out wherein it is lacking. There is evidence that both defendants, at about the same time or one immediately after the other, shot at a quail and in so doing shot toward

199 P.2d (1948).

plaintiff who was uphill from them, and that they knew his location. That is sufficient from which the trial court could conclude that they acted with respect to plaintiff other than as persons of ordinary prudence. . . .

Defendant Tice states in his opening brief, "we have decided not to argue the insufficiency of negligence on the part of defendant Tice." It is true he states in his answer to plaintiff's petition for a hearing in this court that he did not concede this point but he does not argue it. Nothing more need be said on the subject.

. . . Defendant Simonson urges that plaintiff was guilty of contributory negligence and assumed the risk as a matter of law. He cites no authority for the proposition that by going on a hunting party the various hunters assume the risk of negligence on the part of their companions. Such a tenet is not reasonable. It is true that plaintiff suggested that they all "stay in line," presumably abreast, while hunting, and he went uphill at somewhat of a right angle to the hunting line, but he also cautioned that they use care, and defendants knew plaintiff's position. We hold, therefore, that the trial court was justified in finding that he did not assume the risk or act other than as a person of ordinary prudence under the circumstances. . . .

The problem presented in this case is whether the judgment against both defendants may stand. It is argued by defendants that they are not joint tort feasors, and thus jointly and severally liable, as they were not acting in concert, and that there is not sufficient evidence to show which defendant was guilty of the negligence which caused the injuries—the shooting by Tice or that by Simonson. Tice argues that there is evidence to show that the shot which struck plaintiff came from Simonson's gun because of admissions allegedly made by him to third persons and no evidence that they came from his gun. Further in connection with the latter contention, the court failed to find on plaintiff's allegation in his complaint that he did not know which one was at fault—did not find which defendant was guilty of the negligence which caused the injuries to plaintiff.

. . . Considering the last argument first, we believe it is clear that the court sufficiently found

on the issue that defendants were jointly liable and that thus the negligence of both was the cause of the injury or to that legal effect. It found that both defendants were negligent and "That as a direct and proximate result of the shots fired by *defendants, and each of them,* a birdshot pellet was caused to and did lodge in plaintiff's right eye and that another birdshot pellet was caused to and did lodge in plaintiff's upper lip." In so doing the court evidently did not give credence to the admissions of Simonson to third persons that he fired the shots, which it was justified in doing. It thus determined that the negligence of both defendants was the legal cause of the injury—or that both were responsible. Implicit in such finding is the assumption that the court was unable to ascertain whether the shots were from the gun of one defendant or the other or one shot from each of them. The one shot that entered plaintiff's eye was the major factor in assessing damages and that shot could not have come from the gun of both defendants. It was from one or the other only.

It has been held that where a group of persons are on a hunting party, or otherwise engaged in the use of firearms, and two of them are negligent in firing in the direction of a third person who is injured thereby, both of those so firing are liable for the injury suffered by the third person, although the negligence of only one of them could have caused the injury. . . . Oliver v. Miles, Miss., 110 So. 666, 50 A.L.R. 357. . . . The same rule has been applied in criminal cases . . . and both drivers have been held liable for the negligence of one where they engaged in a racing contest causing an injury to a third person. . . . These cases speak of the action of defendants as being in concert as the ground of decision, yet it would seem they are straining that concept and the more reasonable basis appears in Oliver v. Miles, supra. There two persons were hunting together. Both shot at some partridges and in so doing shot across the highway injuring plaintiff who was traveling on it. The court stated that they were acting in concert and thus both were liable. The court then stated . . . : "We think that . . . each is liable for the resulting injury to the boy, although no one can say definitely who actually shot him.

To hold otherwise would be to exonerate both from liability, although each was negligent, and the injury resulted from such negligence." ...

... When we consider the relative position of the parties and the results that would flow if plaintiff was required to pin the injury on one of the defendants only, a requirement that the burden of proof on that subject be shifted to defendants becomes manifest. They are both wrongdoers—both negligent toward plaintiff. They brought about a situation where the negligence of one of them injured the plaintiff, hence it should rest with them each to absolve himself if he can. The injured party has been placed by defendants in the unfair position of pointing to which defendant caused the harm. If one can escape the other may also and plaintiff is remediless. Ordinarily defendants are in a far better position to offer evidence to determine which one caused the injury. This reasoning has recently found favor in this Court. In a quite analogous situation this Court held that a patient injured while unconscious on an operating table in a hospital could hold all or any of the persons who had any connection with the operation even though he could not select the particular acts by the particular person which led to his disability. Ybarra v. Spangard ... 154 P.2d 687.... There the Court was considering whether the patient could avail himself of res ipsa loquitur, rather than where the burden of proof lay, yet the effect of the decision is that plaintiff has made out a case when he has produced evidence which gives rise to an inference of negligence which was the proximate cause of the injury. It is up to defendants to explain the cause of the injury....

The foregoing discussion disposes of the authorities cited by defendants ... , stating the general rule that one defendant is not liable for the independent tort of the other defendant, or that ordinarily the plaintiff must show a causal connection between the negligence and the injury. There was an entire lack of such connection in the Hernandez case and there were not several negligent defendants, one of whom must have caused the injury....

Cases are cited for the proposition that where two or more tort feasors acting independently of each other cause an injury to plaintiff, they are not joint tort feasors and plaintiff must establish the portion of the damage caused by each, even though it is impossible to prove the portion of the injury caused by each....

... In view of the foregoing discussion it is apparent that defendants in cases like the present one may be treated as liable on the same basis as joint tort feasors, and hence the last cited cases are distinguishable inasmuch as they involve independent tort feasors.

... In addition to that, however, it should be pointed out that the same reasons of policy and justice shift the burden to each of [the] defendants to absolve himself if he can—relieving the wronged person of the duty of apportioning the injury to a particular defendant, apply here where we are concerned with whether plaintiff is required to supply evidence for the apportionment of damages. If defendants are independent tort feasors and thus each liable for the damage caused by him alone, and, at least, where the matter of apportionment is incapable of proof, the innocent wronged party should not be deprived of his right to redress. The wrongdoers should be left to work out between themselves any apportionment.... Some of the cited cases refer to the difficulty of apportioning the burden of damages between the independent tort feasors, and say that where factually a correct division cannot be made, the trier of fact may make it the best it can, which would be more or less a guess, stressing the factor that the wrongdoers are not in a position to complain of uncertainty....

... It is urged that plaintiff now has changed the theory of his case in claiming a concert of action; that he did not plead or prove such concert. From what has been said it is clear that there has been no change in theory. The joint liability, as well as the lack of knowledge as to which defendant was liable, was pleaded and the proof developed the case under either theory. We have seen that for the reasons of policy discussed herein, the case is based upon the legal proposition that, under the circumstances here presented, each defendant is liable for the whole damage whether they are deemed to be acting in concert or independently.

The judgment is affirmed.

REVIEW AND DISCUSSION QUESTIONS

1. What is the court's reasoning in upholding Summers's suit against Tice? Do you agree that Tice and Simonson were jointly liable?

2. Would it have been unfair to Summers to deny him compensation because he could not prove who shot him? The Court explicitly places the burden of proof on Tice to show that he was not the cause of Summers's injury, rather than on Summers to show that he was injured by Tice. Is this reasonable and fair?

3. One defendant—either Tice or Simonson—caused Summers no harm whatsoever. Is it just that this defendant be required to compensate Summers for an injury for which he (the defendant) is not responsible?

4. In this case, both Tice and Simonson shot in Summers's direction. Suppose only one of them had done so, but it could not be proved which one. Should Summers still win his suit?

5. When is it fair, and when is it unfair, to impose tort liability without proof of causation?

A Duty to Rescue?

Yania v. Bigan; Farwell v. Keaton; and *McFall v. Shimp*

The Bible holds up the Good Samaritan as a moral exemplar, but it is an ancient, if often criticized, principle of the common law that one has no affirmative legal duty to save the life of another person, if one is not responsible for his or her plight and if one has no prior legal responsibility for that person. In the following cases, the Supreme Court of Pennsylvania, the Supreme Court of Michigan, and a lower Pennsylvania court concern themselves with defendants who have been sued, in differing circumstances, for failing to save the life of another person. The answers they reach differ.

Yania v. Bigan

Justice Benjamin R. Jones:

A bizarre and most unusual circumstance provides the background of this appeal.

On September 25, 1957 John F. Bigan was engaged in a coal strip-mining operation in Shade Township, Somerset County. On the property being stripped were large cuts or trenches created by Bigan when he removed the earthen overburden for the purpose of removing the coal underneath. One cut contained water 8 to 10 feet in depth with side walls or embankments 16 to 18 feet in height; at this cut Bigan had installed a pump to remove the water.

At approximately 4 P.M. on that date, Joseph F. Yania, the operator of another coal strip-mining operation, and one Boyd M. Ross went upon Bigan's property for the purpose of discussing a business matter with Bigan, and, while there, were asked by Bigan to aid him in starting the pump. Ross and Bigan entered the cut and stood at the point where the pump was located. Yania stood at the top of one of the cut's side walls and then jumped from the side wall—a height of 16 to 18 feet—into the water and was drowned.

Yania's widow, in her own right and on behalf of her three children, instituted wrongful death and survival actions against Bigan contending Bigan was responsible for Yania's death.

---

155 A. 2d 343 (1959); 240 N.W. 2d 217 (1976); No. 78-177711 (1978) 10th Penn. District, Allegheny County, respectively.

. . . Summarized, Bigan stands charged with threefold negligence: (1) by urging, enticing, taunting and inveigling Yania to jump into the water; (2) by failing to warn Yania of a dangerous condition on the land, i.e., the cut wherein lay 8 to 10 feet of water; (3) by failing to go to Yania's rescue after he had jumped into the water.[1]

. . . Appellant initially contends that Yania's descent from the high embankment into the water and the resulting death were caused "entirely" by the spoken words and blandishments of Bigan delivered at a distance from Yania. The complaint does not allege that Yania slipped or that he was pushed or that Bigan made any *physical* impact upon Yania. On the contrary, the only inference deducible from the facts alleged in the complaint is that Bigan, by the employment of cajolery and inveiglement, caused such a *mental* impact on Yania that the latter was deprived of his volition and freedom of choice and placed under a compulsion to jump into the water. Had Yania been a child of tender years or a person mentally deficient then it is conceivable that taunting and enticement could constitute actionable negligence if it resulted in harm. However, to contend that such conduct directed to an adult in full possession of all his mental faculties constitutes actionable negligence is not only without precedent but completely without merit.

. . . Appellant next urges that Bigan, as the possessor of the land, violated a duty owed to Yania in that his land contained a dangerous condition, i.e., the water-filled cut or trench, and he failed to warn Yania of such condition. Yania was a business invitee in that he entered upon the land for a common business purpose for the mutual benefit of Bigan and himself. . . .

The *only* condition on Bigan's land which could possibly have contributed in any manner to Yania's death was the water-filled cut with its high embankment. Of this condition there was neither concealment nor failure to warn, but, on the contrary, the complaint specifically avers that Bigan not only requested Yania and Boyd to assist him in starting the pump to remove the water from the cut but "led" them to the cut itself. If this cut possessed any potentiality of danger, such

a condition was as obvious and apparent to Yania as to Bigan, both coal strip-mine operators. Under the circumstances herein depicted Bigan could not be held liable in this respect.

. . . Lastly, it is urged that Bigan failed to take the necessary steps to rescue Yania from the water. The mere fact that Bigan saw Yania in a position of peril in the water imposed upon him no legal, although a moral, obligation or duty to go to his rescue unless Bigan was legally responsible, in whole or in part, for placing Yania in the perilous position. . . . The language of this Court in *Brown v. French*, 104 Pa. 604, 607, 608, is apt: "If it appeared that the deceased, by his own carelessness, contributed in any degree to the accident which caused the loss of his life, the defendants ought not to have been held to answer for the consequences resulting from that accident. . . . He voluntarily placed himself in the way of danger, and his death was the result of his own act. . . . That his undertaking was an exceedingly reckless and dangerous one, the event proves, but there was no one to blame for it but himself. He had the right to try the experiment, obviously dangerous as it was, but then also upon him rested the consequences of that experiment, and upon no one else; he may have been, and probably was, ignorant of the risk which he was taking upon himself, or knowing it, and trusting to his own skill, he may have regarded it as easily superable. But in either case, the result of his ignorance, or of his mistake, must rest with himself—and cannot be charged to the defendants." The complaint does not aver any facts which impose upon Bigan legal responsibility for placing Yania in the dangerous position in the water and, absent such legal responsibility, the law imposes on Bigan no duty of rescue.

Recognizing that the deceased Yania is entitled to the benefit of the presumption that he was exercising due care and extending to appellant the benefit of every well pleaded fact in this complaint and the fair inferences arising therefrom, yet we can reach but one conclusion: that Yania, a reasonable and prudent adult in full possession of all his mental faculties, undertook to perform an act which he knew or should have known was attended with more or less peril and it was the performance of that act and not any conduct upon Bigan's part which caused his unfortunate death.

Order affirmed.

NOTE

[1] So far as the record is concerned we must treat the 33 year old Yania as in full possession of his mental faculties at the time he jumped.

Farwell v. Keaton

Justice Levin:

On the evening of August 26, 1966, Siegrist and Farwell drove to a trailer lot to return an automobile which Siegrist had borrowed from a friend who worked there. While waiting for the friend to finish work, Siegrist and Farwell consumed some beer.

Two girls walked by the entrance to the lot. Siegrist and Farwell attempted to engage them in conversation; they left Farwell's car and followed the girls to a drive-in restaurant down the street.

The girls complained to their friends in the restaurant that they were being followed. Six boys chased Siegrist and Farwell back to the lot. Siegrist escaped unharmed, but Farwell was severely beaten. Siegrist found Farwell underneath his automobile in the lot. Ice was applied to Farwell's head. Siegrist then drove Farwell around for approximately two hours, stopping at a number of drive-in restaurants. Farwell went to sleep in the back seat of his car. Around midnight Siegrist drove the car to the home of Farwell's grandparents, parked it in the driveway, unsuccessfully attempted to rouse Farwell and left. Farwell's grandparents discovered him in the car the next morning and took him to the hospital. He died three days later of an epidural hematoma.

At trial, plaintiff contended that had Siegrist taken Farwell to the hospital, or had he notified someone of Farwell's condition and whereabouts, Farwell would not have died. A neurosurgeon testified that if a person in Farwell's condition is taken to a doctor before, or within half an hour after, consciousness is lost, there is an 85 to 88 percent chance of survival. Plaintiff testified that Siegrist told him that he knew Farwell was badly injured and that he should have done something.

The jury returned a verdict for plaintiff and awarded $15,000 in damages. The Court of Appeals reversed, finding that Siegrist had not assumed the duty of obtaining aid for Farwell and that he neither knew nor should have known of the need for medical treatment. . . .

Siegrist contends that he is not liable for failure to obtain medical assistance for Farwell because he had no duty to do so.

Courts have been slow to recognize a duty to render aid to a person in peril. Where such a duty has been found, it has been predicated upon the existence of a special relationship between the parties; in such a case, if defendant knew or should have known of the other person's peril, he is required to render reasonable care under all the circumstances. . . .

Farwell and Siegrist were companions on a social venture. Implicit in such a common undertaking is the understanding that one will render assistance to the other when he is in peril if he can do so without endangering himself. Siegrist knew or should have known when he left Farwell, who was badly beaten and unconscious, in the back seat of his car that no one would find him before morning. Under these circumstances, to say that Siegrist had no duty to obtain medical assistance or at least to notify someone of Farwell's condition and whereabouts would be "shocking to humanitarian considerations" and fly in the face of "the commonly accepted code of social conduct." "[C]ourts will find a duty where, in general, reasonable men would recognize it and agree that it exists."

Farwell and Siegrist were companions engaged in a common undertaking; there was a special relationship between the parties. Because Siegrist knew or should have known of the peril Farwell was in and could render assistance without endangering himself he had an affirmative duty to come to Farwell's aid.

Justice Fitzgerald (dissenting):

The unfortunate death of Richard Farwell prompted this wrongful death action brought by his father against the defendant, David Siegrist, a friend who had accompanied Farwell during the evening in which the decedent received injuries which ultimately caused his death three days later. The question before us is whether the defendant, considering his relationship with the decedent and the activity they jointly experienced on the evening of August 26–27, 1966, by his conduct voluntarily or otherwise assumed, or should have assumed, the duty of rendering medical or other assistance to the deceased. We find that defendant had no obligation to assume, nor did he assume, such a duty. . . .

Defendant did not voluntarily assume the duty of caring for the decedent's safety. Nor did the circumstances which existed on the evening of August 26, 1966, impose such a duty. Testimony revealed that only a qualified physician would have reason to suspect that Farwell had suffered an injury which required immediate medical attention. The decedent never complained of pain and, in fact, had expressed a desire to retaliate against his attackers. Defendant's inability to arouse the decedent upon arriving at his grandparents' home does not permit us to infer, as does plaintiff, that defendant knew or should have known that the deceased was seriously injured. While it might have been more prudent for the defendant to insure that the decedent was safely in the house prior to leaving, we cannot say that defendant acted unreasonably in permitting Farwell to spend the night asleep in the back seat of his car.

The close relationship between defendant and the decedent is said to establish a legal duty upon defendant to obtain assistance for the decedent. No authority is cited for this proposition other than the public policy observation that the interest of society would be benefited if its members were required to assist one another. This is not the appropriate case to establish a standard of conduct requiring one to legally assume the duty of insuring the safety of another. Recognizing that legal commentaries have expressed moral outrage at those decisions which permit one to refuse aid to another whose life may be in peril, we cannot say that, considering the relationship between these two parties and the existing circumstances, defendant acted in an unreasonable manner.

Plaintiff believes that a legal duty to aid others should exist where such assistance greatly benefits society and only a reasonable burden is imposed upon those in a position to help. He contends further that the determination of the existence of a duty must rest with the jury where questions of foreseeability and the relationship of the parties are primary considerations.

It is clear that defendant's nonfeasance, or the "passive inaction or a failure to take steps to protect [the decedent] from harm" is urged as being the proximate cause of Farwell's death. We must reject plaintiff's proposition which elevates a moral obligation to the level of a legal duty where, as here, the facts within defendant's knowledge in no way indicated that immediate medical attention was necessary and the relationship between the parties imposes no affirmative duty to render assistance. . . . The posture of this case does not permit us to create a legal duty upon one to render assistance to another injured or imperiled party where the initial injury was not caused by the person upon whom the duty is sought to be imposed.

McFall v. Shimp

Judge Flaherty:

The Plaintiff, Robert McFall, suffers from a rare bone marrow disease and the prognosis for his survival is very dim, unless he receives a bone marrow transplant from a compatible donor. Finding a compatible donor is a very difficult task, and limited to a selection among close relatives. After a search and certain tests, it has been determined that only the Defendant is suitable as a donor. The defendant refuses to submit to the necessary transplant, and before the Court is a request for a preliminary injunction which seeks to compel the defendant to

---

78-177711 (1978) 10th Penn. District.

submit to further tests, and, eventually, the bone marrow transplant.

Although a diligent search has produced no authority, the Plaintiff cites the ancient statute of King Edward I, St. Westminster 2, 13 Ed. I, c 24, pointing out, as is the case, that this Court is a successor to the English courts of Chancery and derives power from this statute, almost 700 years old. The question posed by the Plaintiff is that, in order to save the life of one of its members by the only means available, may society infringe upon one's absolute right to his "bodily security"?

The common law has consistently held to a rule which provides that one human being is under no legal compulsion to give aid or to take action to save that human being or to rescue. A great deal has been written regarding this rule which, on the surface, appears to be revolting in a moral sense. Introspection, however, will demonstrate that the rule is founded upon the very essence of our free society. It is noteworthy that counsel for the Plaintiff has cited authority which has developed in other societies in support of the Plaintiff's request in this instance. Our society, contrary to many others, has as its first principle, the respect for the individual, and that society and government exist to protect the individual from being invaded and hurt by another. Many societies adopt a contrary view which has the individual existing to serve the society as a whole. In preserving such a society as we have it is bound to happen that great moral conflicts will arise and will appear harsh in a given instance. In this case, the chancellor is being asked to force one member of society to undergo a medical procedure which would provide that part of that individual's body would be removed from him and given to another so that the other could live. Morally, this decision rests with the Defendant, and, in the view of the Court, the refusal of the Defendant is morally indefensible. For our law to *compel* the Defendant to submit to an intrusion of his body would change the very concept and principle upon which our society is founded. To do so would defeat the sanctity of the individual, and would impose a rule which would know no limits, and one could not imagine where the line would be drawn. This request is not to be compared with an action at law for damages, but rather is an action in equity before a Chancellor, which, in the ultimate, if granted, would require the [forcible] submission to the medical procedure. For a society, which respects the rights of *one* individual, to sink its teeth into the jugular vein or neck of one of its members and suck from it sustenance for *another* member, is revolting to our hardwrought concepts of jurisprudence. [Forcible] extraction of living body tissue causes revulsion to the judicial mind. Such would raise the spectre of the swastika and the inquisition, reminiscent of the horrors this portends.

This court makes no comment on the law regarding the Plaintiff's right in an action at law for damages, but has no alternative but to deny the requested equitable relief. An Order will be entered denying the request for a preliminary injunction.

REVIEW AND DISCUSSION QUESTIONS

1. Did Bigan cause Yania's death? Was he morally responsible for it? Should he be held legally liable for it?

2. According to the court, why did Bigan have no legal duty to rescue Yania? In your view, should he have such a duty?

3. On what grounds does the court hold David Siegrist responsible for not saving Richard Farwell's life? Is it possible to make Justice Levin's decision consistent with the verdict in *Yania v. Bigan?*

4. On what grounds does Justice Fitzgerald dissent in the *Farwell* case? What decision would you have reached?

5. Why does Judge Flaherty refuse to compel Shimp to submit to a bone marrow transplant? Does Shimp have a moral duty to do so? Legality aside, would compelling Shimp to do so be morally right? Does it make a difference that McFall and Shimp are related?

6. Is the *McFall* decision consistent with the *Farwell* case? Suppose a different court held Bigan liable for Yania's death but did not compel Shimp to undergo the operation. Would this be consistent?

7. How ought the law to handle these three cases? Should people be legally obligated to be Good Samaritans?

Wrongful Life and Wrongful Birth

Berman v. Allan

A basic element of negligence or any other tort is that the plaintiff suffered some wrong, harm, or injury. But can life itself be a harm? That question is addressed in this case, in which suit was brought, in part, on behalf of an infant suffering from Down's syndrome against her mother's doctor. The doctor was not responsible for the infant's affliction, but he was negligent in failing to tell the mother, Shirley Berman, about amniocentesis, a procedure that would have indicated this birth defect early enough in Mrs. Berman's pregnancy to have enabled her to have terminated it. On appeal, the Supreme Court of New Jersey rejected the idea that "wrongful life" can be a valid cause of legal action. But it also broke with precedent and held that the parents could claim damages in their own right for "wrongful birth." In his partially dissenting opinion, Justice Handler argues that the child herself has suffered an injury that calls for compensation.

The opinion of the court was delivered by Pashman, J.:

1

In *Gleitman v. Cosgrove*, decided 12 years ago, this Court refused to recognize as valid causes of action either a claim for "wrongful life" asserted on behalf of a physically deformed infant or a claim for "wrongful birth" put forth by the infant's parents. Both prayers for relief were premised upon the allegation that had the physician treating Mrs. Gleitman during her pregnancy followed standard medical practice, an abortion would have been procured and the child would never have come into existence. In this case, we are called upon to assess the continued validity of both of our holdings in *Gleitman*.

On September 11, 1975, Paul and Shirley Berman, suing both in their own names and as Guardians *ad litem* for their infant daughter Sharon, instituted the present malpractice action against Ronald Allan and Michael Attardi, medical doctors licensed by the State of New Jersey. . . . At the time of her pregnancy, Mrs. Berman was 38 years of age. On November 3, Sharon was born afflicted with Down's Syn-

drome—a genetic defect commonly referred to as mongolism.

Plaintiffs allege that defendants deviated from accepted medical standards by failing to inform Mrs. Berman during her pregnancy of the existence of a procedure known as amniocentesis. This procedure involves the insertion of a long needle into a mother's uterus and the removal therefrom of a sample of amniotic fluid containing living fetal cells. Through "karyotype analysis"—a procedure in which the number and structure of the cells' chromosomes are examined—the sex of the fetus as well as the presence of gross chromosomal defects can be detected. . . .

Due to Mrs. Berman's age at the time of her conception, plaintiffs contend that the risk that her child, if born, would be afflicted with Down's Syndrome was sufficiently great that sound medical practice at the time of pregnancy required defendants to inform her both of this risk and the availability of amniocentesis as a method of determining whether in her particular case that risk would come to fruition. Had defendants so informed Mrs. Berman, the complaint continues, she would have submitted to the amniocentesis procedure, discovered that the child, if born, would suffer from Down's Syndrome, and had the fetus aborted.

As a result of defendants' alleged negligence, the infant Sharon, through her Guardian *ad litem*, seeks compensation for the physical and emotional pain and suffering which she will

From 404 A.2d 8 (1979). Some citations omitted.

endure throughout life because of her mongoloid condition. Mr. and Mrs. Berman, the child's parents, request damages in their own right both for the emotional anguish which they have experienced and will continue to experience on account of Sharon's birth defect, and the medical and other costs which they will incur in order to properly raise, educate and supervise the child.

On November 4, 1977, the trial judge granted summary judgment in favor of defendants on the ground that plaintiffs had failed to state any actionable claim for relief. . . .

2

The claim for damages asserted on behalf of the infant Sharon has aptly been labeled a cause of action grounded upon "wrongful life." Sharon does not contend that absent defendants' negligence she would have come into the world in a normal and healthy state. There is no suggestion in either the pleadings below or the medical literature which we have scrutinized that any therapy could have been prescribed which would have decreased the risk that, upon birth, Sharon would suffer from Down's Syndrome. Rather, the gist of the infant's complaint is that had defendants informed her mother of the availability of amniocentesis, Sharon would never have come into existence.

As such, this case presents issues different from those involved in malpractice actions where a plaintiff asserts that a defendant's deviation from sound medical practices *increased* the probability that an infant would be born with defects. . . . Nor are we here confronted with a situation in which an individual's negligence while a child was in gestation caused what otherwise would have been a normal and healthy child to come into the world in an impaired condition. . . . Here, defendants' alleged negligence neither caused the mongoloid condition nor increased the risk that such a condition would occur. In the words of the *Gleitman* majority, "the infant plantiff [asserts]. . . . not that [she] should have been born without defects but [rather] that [she] should not have been born at

all." . . . In essence, Sharon claims that her very life is "wrongful."

The *Gleitman* majority refused to recognize as valid a cause of action predicated upon wrongful life. Its main reason for so holding was that damages would be impossible to ascertain. . . .

The primary purpose of tort law is that of compensating plaintiffs for the injuries they have suffered wrongfully at the hands of others. As such, damages are ordinarily computed by "comparing the condition plaintiff would have been in, had the defendants not been negligent, with plaintiff's impaired condition as a result of the negligence." . . . In the case of a claim predicated upon wrongful life, such a computation would require the trier of fact to measure the difference in value between life in an impaired condition and the "utter void of nonexistence." . . . Such an endeavor, however, is literally impossible. As Chief Justice Weintraub noted, man, "who knows nothing of death or nothingness," simply cannot affix a price tag to non-life. . . .

Nevertheless, although relevant to our determination, we would be extremely reluctant today to deny the validity of Sharon's complaint solely because damages are difficult to ascertain. The courts of this and other jurisdictions have long held that where a wrong itself is of such a nature as to preclude the computation of damages with precise exactitude, it would be a "perversion of fundamental principles of justice to deny all relief to the injured [party], and thereby relieve the wrongdoer from making any amend for his acts." . . . To be sure, damages may not be determined by mere speculation or guess and, as defendants emphasize, placing a value upon non-life is not simply difficult—it is humanly impossible. Nonetheless, were the *measure* of damages our sole concern, it is possible that some judicial remedy could be fashioned which would redress plaintiff, if only in part, for injuries suffered. . . .

Difficulty in the *measure* of damages is not, however, our sole or even primary concern. Although we conclude, as did the *Gleitman* majority, that Sharon has failed to state an actionable claim for relief, we base our result upon a different premise—that Sharon has not suffered any damage cognizable at law by being brought into existence. . . .

One of the most deeply held beliefs of our society is that life—whether experienced with or without a major physical handicap—is more precious than non-life. . . . Concrete manifestations of this belief are not difficult to discover. The documents which set forth the principles upon which our society is founded are replete with references to the sanctity of life. The federal constitution characterizes life as one of three fundamental rights of which no man can be deprived without due process of law. *U.S. Const.*, Amends V and XIV. Our own state constitution proclaims that the "enjoying and defending [of] life" is a natural right. . . . The Declaration of Independence states that the primacy of man's "unalienable" right to life is a "self-evident truth." Nowhere in these documents is there to be found an indication that the lives of persons suffering from physical handicaps are to be less cherished than those of non-handicapped human beings.

State legislatures—and thus the people as a whole—have universally reserved the most severe criminal penalties for individuals who have unjustifiably deprived others of life. Indeed, so valued is this commodity that even one who has committed first degree murder cannot be sentenced to death unless he is accorded special procedural protections in addition to those given all criminal defendants. . . . Moreover, it appears that execution is constitutionally impermissible unless the crime which a defendant has perpetrated was one which involved the taking of another's life. . . . Again, these procedural protections and penalties do not vary according to the presence or absence of physical deformities in the victim or defendant. It is life itself that is jealously safeguarded, not life in a perfect state.

Finally, we would be remiss if we did not take judicial notice of the high esteem which our society accords to those involved in the medical profession. The reason for this is clear. Physicians are the preservers of life.

No man is perfect. Each of us suffers from some ailments or defects, whether major or minor, which make impossible participation in all the activities the world has to offer. But our lives are not thereby rendered less precious than those of others whose defects are less pervasive or less severe.

We recognize that as a mongoloid child, Sharon's abilities will be more circumscribed than those of normal, healthy children and that she, unlike them, will experience a great deal of physical and emotional pain and anguish. We sympathize with her plight. We cannot, however, say that she would have been better off had she never been brought into the world. Notwithstanding her affliction with Down's Syndrome, Sharon, by virtue of her birth, will be able to love and be loved and to experience happiness and pleasure—emotions which are truly the essence of life and which are far more valuable than the suffering she may endure. To rule otherwise would require us to disavow the basic assumption upon which our society is based. This we cannot do.

Accordingly, we hold that Sharon has failed to state a valid cause of action founded upon "wrongful life."

3

The validity of the parents' claim for relief calls into play considerations different from those involved in the infant's complaint. As in the case of the infant, Mr. and Mrs. Berman do not assert that defendants increased the risk that Sharon, if born, would be afflicted with Down's Syndrome. Rather, at bottom, they allege that they were tortiously injured because Mrs. Berman was deprived of the option of making a meaningful decision as to whether to abort the fetus. . . . They thus claim that Sharon's "birth"— as opposed to her "life"—was wrongful.

Two items of damage are requested in order to redress this allegedly tortious injury: (1) the medical and other costs that will be incurred in order to properly raise, supervise and educate the child; and (2) compensation for the emotional anguish that has been and will continue to be experienced on account of Sharon's condition.

The *Gleitman* majority refused to recognize as valid a cause of action grounded upon wrongful birth. Two reasons underlay its determination.

The first related to measure of damages should such a claim be allowed. In this view,

> In order to determine [the parents'] compensatory damages a court would have to evaluate the denial to them of the intangible, unmeasurable, and complex human benefits of motherhood and fatherhood and weigh these against the alleged emotional and money injuries. Such a proposed weighing is . . . impossible to perform. . . .

Second, even though the Court's opinion was premised upon the assumption that Mrs. Gleitman could have legally secured an abortion, the majority concluded that "substantial [public] policy reasons" precluded the judicial allowance of tort damages "for the denial of the opportunity to take an embryonic life." . . .

In light of changes in the law which have occurred in the 12 years since *Gleitman* was decided, the second ground relied upon by the *Gleitman* majority can no longer stand in the way of judicial recognition of a cause of action founded upon wrongful birth. The Supreme Court's ruling in *Roe v. Wade* . . . clearly establishes that a woman possesses a constitutional right to decide whether her fetus should be aborted, at least during the first trimester of pregnancy. Public policy now supports, rather than militates against, the proposition that she not be impermissibly denied a meaningful opportunity to make that decision.

As in all other cases of tortious injury, a physician whose negligence has deprived a mother of this opportunity should be required to make amends for the damage which he has proximately caused. Any other ruling would in effect immunize from liability those in the medical field providing inadequate guidance to persons who would choose to exercise their constitutional right to abort fetuses which, if born, would suffer from genetic defects. . . . Accordingly, we hold that a cause of action founded upon wrongful birth is a legally cognizable claim.

Troublesome, however, is the measure of damages. As noted earlier, the first item sought to be recompensed is the medical and other expenses that will be incurred in order to properly raise, educate and supervise the child. Although these costs were "caused" by defendants' negligence in the sense that but for the failure to inform, the child would not have come into existence, we conclude that this item of damage should not be recoverable. In essence, Mr. and Mrs. Berman desire to retain all the benefits inhering in the birth of the child—i.e., the love and joy they will experience as parents—while saddling defendants with the enormous expenses attendant upon her rearing. Under the facts and circumstances here alleged, we find that such an award would be wholly disproportionate to the culpability involved, and that allowance of such a recovery would both constitute a windfall to the parents and place too unreasonable a financial burden upon physicians. . . .

The parents' claim for emotional damages stands upon a different footing. In failing to inform Mrs. Berman of the availability of amniocentesis, defendants directly deprived her—and, derivatively, her husband—of the option to accept or reject a parental relationship with the child and thus caused them to experience mental and emotional anguish upon their realization that they had given birth to a child afflicted with Down's Syndrome. . . .

Unlike the *Gleitman* majority, we do not feel that placing a monetary value upon the emotional suffering that Mr. and Mrs. Berman have and will continue to experience is an impossible task for the trier of fact. In the 12 years that have elapsed since *Gleitman* was decided, courts have come to recognize that mental and emotional distress is just as "real" as physical pain, and that its valuation is no more difficult. Consequently, damages for such distress have been ruled allowable in an increasing number of contexts. . . . Moreover, . . . to deny Mr. and Mrs. Berman redress for their injuries merely because damages cannot be measured with precise exactitude would constitute a perversion of fundamental principles of justice. . . .

Consequently, we hold that Mr. and Mrs. Berman have stated actionable claims for relief. Should their allegations be proven at trial, they are entitled to be recompensed for the mental and emotional anguish they have suffered and will continue to suffer on account of Sharon's condition.

Accordingly, the judgment of the trial court is affirmed in part and reversed in part, and this case remanded for a plenary trial.

Handler, J., concurring in part and dissenting in part:

1

. . . The Court now recognizes that the parents of the impaired child have a cause of action for the doctors' breach of duty to render competent medical advice and services and that they are entitled to compensation for their mental and emotional suffering over the birth of their damaged child. I agree with this. However, I hold to a somewhat broader view of mental and emotional injury in these circumstances and would also include as an element of these damages impaired parenthood or parental capacity.

The Court does not, in its opinion, recognize as sustainable a cause of action on behalf of the child. On this, I differ. The child, in my view, was owed directly, during its gestation, a duty of reasonable care from the same physicians who undertook to care for its mother—then expectant—and that duty, to render complete and competent medical advice, was seriously breached. The child, concededly, did not become defective because of the physicians' dereliction; nevertheless, it suffered a form of injury or loss in having been born of parents whose parental capacity may have been substantially diminished by the negligence of their doctors. This is a loss to the child which should be recompensed. For these reasons I concur in part and dissent in part from the opinion of the Court.

2

It is important to have a clear picture of the claims which are asserted on behalf of the respective plaintiffs. . . .

Without doubt, expectant parents, kept in ignorance of severe and permanent defects affecting their unborn child, suffer greatly when the awful truth dawns upon them with the birth of the child. Human experience has told each of us, personally or vicariously, something of this anguish. Parents of such a child experience a welter of negative feelings—bewilderment, guilt, remorse and anguish—as well as anger, depression and despair. . . . When such a tragedy comes without warning these terrible emotions are bound to be felt even more deeply. "Novelty shock" may well exacerbate the suffering. . . . This, I believe, is the crux of the wrong done in this case. Through the failure of the doctors to advise an expectant mother, and father, of the likelihood or certainty of the birth of a mongoloid child, the parents were given no opportunity to cushion the blow, mute the hurt, or prepare themselves as parents for the birth of their seriously impaired child. Their injury is real and palpable. . . .

Because of the unique nature of the tort, involving as it does the denial of the opportunity to decide whether to become the parents of a handicapped child, the suffering of the parents assumes another, important dimension. There should be recognized in the stressful setting of this case the reality of moral injury. Such injury may be thought of as the deprivation of moral initiative and ethical choice. . . . Persons, confronted with the awesome decision of whether or not to allow the birth of a defective child, face a moral dilemma of enormous consequence. They deal with a profound moral problem. . . . To be denied the opportunity—indeed, the right—to apply one's own moral values in reaching that decision is a serious, irreversible wrong. . . . Shorn of ethical choice in bringing into the world a defective human being, some individuals will be torn by moral conflict. Moral suffering in this sense may be felt keenly by a person who, as a matter of personal conscience, would choose not to allow the birth of such a child. . . . The moral affront, however, is not diminished because the parents, if given the choice, would have permitted the birth of the child. The crucial moral decision, which was theirs to make, was denied them.

A full perception of the mental, emotional—and, I add, moral—suffering of parents in this situation reveals another aspect of their loss.

Mental, emotional and moral suffering can involve diminished parental capacity. Such incapacity of the mother and father *qua* parents is brought about by the wrongful denial of a reasonable opportunity to learn of and anticipate the birth of a child with permanent defects, and to prepare for the heavy obligations entailed in rearing so unfortunate an individual. Such parents may experience great difficulty adjusting to their fate and accepting the child's impairment as nature's verdict. . . . While some individuals confronted by tragedy respond magnificently and become exemplary parents, others do not. . . . Individuals suffering this form of parental incapacity or dysfunction are denied to a great extent the fuller joys, satisfaction and pride which comes with successful and effective parenting. This may endure for some time during the early developmental years of the child. . . . Impaired parenthood, so understood, constitutes another dimension of the injury and loss suffered by plaintiffs in this case. In this sense, impaired parenthood, together with mental and emotional and moral suffering, should be recognized and compensated as elements of damages.

3

The Court in this case, as in *Gleitman* before it, fails to accord a cause of action to the afflicted infant plaintiff. This denial, I most respectfully urge, is wrong. . . .

An adequate comprehension of the infant's claims under these circumstances starts with the realization that the infant has come into this world and is here, encumbered by an injury attributable to the malpractice of the doctors. That injury does not consist of the child's afflicted condition; her affliction was not the doctor's doing. Rather, the injury consists of a diminished childhood in being born of parents kept ignorant of her defective state while unborn and who, in that account, were less fit to accept and assume their parental responsibilities. The frightful weight of the child's natural handicap has been made more burdensome by defendants' negligence because her parents' ca-

pacity has been impaired; they are less able to cope with the extraheavy parental obligations uniquely involved in providing a child so afflicted with the unfaltering love, constant devotion and extraordinary care such a child specially requires.

There has been some judicial appreciation of the notion that a diminished childhood may be the consequence of impaired parental capacity. In *Berger v. Weber* . . . the Court recognized a cause of action in a suit brought by a mentally retarded child to recover damages for the loss of society, companionship, love and affection of her mother as a result of injuries sustained by the mother in an auto accident. The mother had sustained both physical and psychological injuries and could no longer continue to administer to the peculiar needs of her retarded daughter. The Court upheld a cause of action for such losses when a parent is "severely" injured. It recognized that the loss of parental guidance and training can have a severe impact on a child's development and personality and found the reasons for denying a cause of action, such as lack of precedent, uncertainty of damages, possibility of double recovery and potential for a multiplicity of suits, unpersuasive. The Court also thought it anomalous to say that a child suffers a compensable loss in a wrongful death action when the parent is killed but not when a parent is injured so severely that he or she cannot perform the parental function. It concluded that the magnitude of the child's loss outweighs the factors which would militate against allowing recovery. . . .

Plausibly, the child's injury and loss in the form of diminished childhood can be viewed as a derivative claim based solely on the parents' injury. The great majority of jurisdictions which have considered a child's cause of action for damages as derivative from injuries negligently inflicted on a parent have generally rejected such claims. This, in fact, was the unanimous holding of the Court in *Russell v. Salem Transportation Co., Inc.* . . . The reasons for denying recognition of such a cause of action in *Russell* were several. The Court felt that the damages to the child were remote and speculative and feared a substantial accretion of liability against a tortfeasor from a single transaction, a possibility of a double recovery in that consequential damages to children from a parent's accident are frequently already compensated in jury awards and conflicts within families in relation to the apportionment of settlement offers. . . . According to W. Prosser, *Law of Torts* (4th ed. 1971) §125, pp. 898–899 (fns. omit.):

> It is not easy to understand and appreciate this reluctance to compensate the child who has been deprived of the care, companionship and education of his mother, or for that matter his father, through the defendant's negligence. This is surely a genuine injury, and a serious one, which has received a great deal more sympathy from the legal writers than from the judges. There is of course the . . . problem of preventing double compensation . . . , since the child will to some extent benefit by any sum recovered by the injured parent; but it is quite evident that this will not and cannot recompense him for all that he has lost. The obstacles in the way of satisfactory limitation of recovery are no greater than in the case of the wife

[suing for loss of consortium]. As has been said even by one court which considered itself forced to deny recovery, it is difficult "on the basis of natural justice to reach the conclusion that this type of action will not lie." It is particularly difficult when recovery is permitted to the wife, but denied to the child.

Solution to this legal conundrum—whether and how to protect the infant's interests—should not turn on labels or definitions. It is to be emphasized in this case that the doctors' medical malpractice encompasses the child. . . . Their negligence consists of the failure to render proper advice to Mrs. Berman as an *expectant* mother. Indisputably in this relationship the doctors were caring for the unborn child as well as the mother; the duty they owed to Mrs. Berman enveloped a duty to the unborn child. The breach of that duty affects both. "The risk created by a negligent act of one who stands in a physician-patient relationship is of enormous consequence to mother and child."

REVIEW AND DISCUSSION QUESTIONS

1. Why does the court reject the "wrongful life" portion of the suit? Do you agree with Justice Pashman's argument?

2. Can someone's life and future prospects be so terrible that he or she would be better off not having been born? Do you think this was true in Sharon Berman's case?

3. The earlier *Gleitman* case refused to recognize "wrongful birth" as a cause of action for two reasons. How does the court now respond to those two considerations? Do you agree that parents can be wronged by not being given medical information that would have led them to obtain an abortion?

4. What does Justice Handler mean by "impaired parenthood or parental capacity"? Were the Bermans damaged in this way? Should such impairment, if it exists, be the basis for compensation?

5. According to Justice Handler, what exactly is the injury that young Sharon Berman has suffered? How persuasive do you find his reasoning?

14

PRIVATE OWNERSHIP: THE LAW OF PROPERTY

Property law is a large part of the law simply because private property is such a fundamental feature of our socioeconomic system. Inevitably, philosophical disagreements over the nature and justification of private property constitute the backdrop to legal debates over the adjudication of particular cases and the interpretation of property law in general. One philosophical tradition maintains that private property is a natural right and that the only legitimate role of positive property law is to uphold and safeguard that fundamental right. This perspective is represented by the selection from John Locke's *Second Treatise of Government*. A rival philosophical tradition rejects the notion of an unbridled natural right to property in favor of a more social perspective on property and a more utilitarian attitude toward it. This tradition emphasizes that property is a socioeconomic institution, with different societies having different systems of property, that is, different rules for determining what constitutes property and for governing its acquisition and transfer. In this view, the courts should interpret and shape property law so as to benefit society. This philosophical perspective is represented here by the selection from Morris Cohen. Although he accepts the idea of natural rights, Cohen maintains that the state can be justified in regulating and even in confiscating private property.

One's assessment of Locke's and Cohen's positions will influence one's view of the cases that follow. *Haslem v. Lockwood* deals with the initial acquisition of private property, that is, the circumstances in which a previously unowned item becomes property. The famous *Penn Central* case addresses the constitutional legitimacy of government-imposed restrictions on the use of private property, an issue that divides the two schools of thought distinguished earlier.

Property

John Locke

Few, if any, political theorists have had as much influence on the thinking of the framers of the American legal and constitutional order as John Locke did. Locke believed that legitimate government derives its powers from the consent of the governed and that such consent is best understood by first imagining people in a prepolitical "state of nature." There, Locke thought, people would accept certain restrictions on their natural rights in order to gain the protection and other benefits of government.

In the following excerpt from his Second Treatise of Government, *Locke argues that, even though God gave the world to humanity in common, in the state of nature people have a natural right to property based on their labor. This right to acquire property, though, is subject to certain limitations: "enough and as good" must be left for others, and we have no title to what we do not use or allow to spoil. The introduction of money, however, enables us to overcome these limitations and permits people legitimately to heap up wealth beyond what they can immediately use. In this way, Locke squares inequalities of wealth and possession with the initial equality of the state of nature.*

OF THE STATE OF NATURE

To understand political power aright, and derive it from its original, we must consider what state all men are naturally in, and that is a state of perfect freedom to order their actions and dispose of their possessions and persons as they think fit, within the bounds of the law of nature, without asking leave, or depending upon the will of any other man.

A state also of equality, wherein all the power and jurisdiction is reciprocal, no one having more than another; there being nothing more evident than that creatures of the same species and rank, promiscuously born to all the same advantages of nature, and the use of the same faculties, should also be equal one amongst another without subordination or subjection, unless the Lord and Master of them all should by any manifest declaration of His will set one above another, and confer on him by an evident and clear appointment an undoubted right to domination and sovereignty.

But though this be a state of liberty, yet it is not a state of license; though man in that state have an uncontrollable liberty to dispose of his person or possessions, yet he has not liberty to destroy himself, or so much as any creature in his possession, but where some nobler use than its bare preservation calls for it. The state of nature has a law of nature to govern it, which obliges everyone; and reason, which is that law, teaches all mankind who will but consult it, that, being all equal and independent, no one ought to harm another in his life, health, liberty, or possessions. For men being all the workmanship of one omnipotent and infinitely wise Maker—all the servants of one sovereign Master, sent into the world by His order, and about His business—they are His property, whose workmanship they are, made to last during His, not one another's pleasure; and being furnished with like faculties, sharing all in one community of nature, there cannot be supposed any such subordination among us, that may authorize us to destroy one another, as if we were made for one another's uses, as the inferior ranks of creatures are for ours. Everyone, as he is bound to preserve himself, and not to quit his station willfully, so, by the like reason, when his own preservation comes not in competition, ought he, as much as he can, to preserve the rest of mankind, and not, unless it be to do justice on an offender, take away or impair the life, or what tends to the preservation of the life, the liberty, health, limb, or goods of another.

And that all men may be restrained from invading others' rights, and from doing hurt to one another, and the law of nature be observed, which willeth the peace and preservation of all mankind, the execution of the law of nature is in that state put into every man's hand, whereby everyone has a right to punish the transgressors of that law to such a degree as may hinder its violation. For the law of nature would, as all other laws that concern men in this world, be in vain if there were nobody that, in the state of nature, had a power to execute that law, and thereby preserve the innocent and restrain offenders. And if anyone in the state of nature may punish another for any evil he has done, everyone may do so. For in that state of perfect equality, where naturally there is no superiority or jurisdiction of one over another, what any may do in prosecution of that law, everyone must needs have a right to do.

And thus in the state of nature one man comes by a power over another; but yet no absolute or arbitrary power, to use a criminal, when he has got him in his hands, according to the passionate heats or boundless extravagance of his own will; but only to retribute to him so far as calm reason and conscience dictate what is proportionate to his transgression, which is so much as may serve for reparation and restraint. For these two are the only reasons why one man may lawfully do harm to another, which is that we call punishment. In transgressing the law of nature, the offender declares himself to live by another rule than that of common reason and equity, which is that measure God has set to the actions of men, for their mutual security; and so he becomes dangerous to mankind, the tie which is to secure them from injury and violence being slighted and broken by him. Which, being a trespass against the whole species, and the peace and safety of it, provided for by the law of nature, every man upon this score, by the right he hath to preserve mankind in general, may restrain, or, where it is necessary, destroy things noxious to them, and so may bring such evil on anyone who hath transgressed that law, as may make him repent the doing of it, and thereby deter him, and by his example others, from doing the like mischief. And in this case, and upon this ground, every man hath a right to punish the offender, and be executioner of the law of nature. . . .

Besides the crime which consists in violating the law, and varying from the right rule of reason, whereby a man so far becomes degenerate, and declares himself to quit the principles of human nature, and to be a noxious creature, there is commonly injury done, and some person or other, some other man receives damage by his transgression, in which case he who hath received any damage, has, besides the right of punishment common to him with other men, a particular right to seek reparation from him that has done it. And any other person who finds it just, may also join with him that is injured, and assist him in recovering from the offender so much as may make satisfaction for the harm he has suffered.

. . . The magistrate, who by being magistrate hath the common right of punishing put into his hands, can often, where the public good demands not the execution of the law, remit the punishment of criminal offenses by his own authority, but yet cannot remit the satisfaction due to any private man for the damage he has received. That he who has suffered the damage has a right to demand in his own name, and he alone can remit. The damnified person has this power of appropriating to himself the goods or service of the offender, by right of self-preservation, as every man has a power to punish the crime, to prevent its being committed again, by the right he has of preserving all mankind, and doing all reasonable things he can in order to that end. And thus it is that every man in the state of nature has a power to kill a murderer, both to deter others from doing the like injury, which no reparation can compensate, by the example of the punishment that attends it from everybody, and also to secure men from the attempts of a criminal who having renounced reason, the common rule and measure God hath given to mankind, hath by the unjust violence and slaughter he hath committed upon one, declared war against all mankind, and therefore may be destroyed as a lion or a tiger, one of those wild savage beasts with whom men can have no society nor security. . . .

To this strange doctrine—viz., that in the state of nature everyone has the executive power of the law of nature—I doubt not but it will be objected that it is unreasonable for men to be judges in their own cases, that self-love will make men partial to themselves and their friends. And on the other side, that ill-nature, passion, and revenge will carry them too far in punishing others; and hence nothing but confusion and disorder will follow; and that therefore God hath certainly appointed government to restrain the partiality and violence of men. I easily grant that civil government is the proper remedy for the inconveniences of the state of nature, which must certainly be great where men may be judges in their own case, since 'tis easy to be imagined that he who was so unjust as to do his brother an injury, will scarce be so just as to condemn himself for it. But I shall desire those who make this objection, to remember that absolute monarchs are but men, and if government is to be the remedy of those evils which necessarily follow from men's being judges in their own cases, and the state of nature is therefore not to be endured, I desire to know what kind of government that is, and how much better it is than the state of nature, where one man commanding a multitude, has the liberty to be judge in his own case, and may do to all his subjects whatever he pleases, without the least question or control of those who execute his pleasure; and in whatsoever he doth, whether led by reason, mistake, or passion, must be submitted to, which men in the state of nature are not bound to do one to another? And if he that judges, judges amiss in his own or any other case, he is answerable for it to the rest of mankind.

'Tis often asked as a mighty objection, Where are, or ever were there, any men in such a state of nature? To which it may suffice as an answer at present: That since all princes and rulers of independent governments all through the world are in a state of nature, 'tis plain the world never was, nor ever will be, without numbers of men in that state. I have named all governors of independent communities, whether they are or are not in league with others. For 'tis not every compact that puts an end to the state of nature between men, but only this one of agreeing together mutually to enter into one community, and make one body politic; other promises and compacts men may make one with another, and yet still be in the state of nature. The promises and bargains for truck, etc., between the two men in Soldania, in or between a Swiss and an Indian, in the woods of America, are binding to them, though they are perfectly in a state of nature in reference to one another. For truth and keeping of faith belong to men as men, and not as members of society. . . .

OF PROPERTY

Whether we consider natural reason, which tells us that men being once born have a right to their preservation, and consequently to meat and drink and such other things as nature affords for their subsistence; or revelation, which give us an account of those grants God made of the world to Adam, and to Noah and his sons, 'tis very clear that God, as King David says, Psalm cxv. 16, "has given the earth to the children of men," given it to mankind in common. But this being supposed, it seems to some a very great difficulty how anyone should ever come to have a property in anything. I will not content myself to answer that if it be difficult to make out property upon a supposition that God gave the world to Adam and his posterity in common, it is impossible that any man but one universal monarch should have any property upon a supposition that God gave the world to Adam and his heirs in succession, exclusive of all the rest of his posterity. But I shall endeavor to show how men might come to have a property in several parts of that which God gave to mankind in common, and that without any express compact of all the commoners.

God, who hath given the world to men in common, hath also given them reason to make use of it to the best advantage of life and convenience. The earth and all that is therein is given to men for the support and comfort of their being. And though all the fruits it naturally produces, and beasts it feeds, belong to mankind in common, as they are produced by the spontaneous hand of nature; and nobody has originally a private dominion exclusive of the rest of mankind in any of them as they are thus in their natural state; yet being given for the use of men, there must of necessity be a means to appropriate them some way or other before they can be of any use or at all beneficial to any particular man. The fruit or venison which nourishes the wild Indian, who knows no enclosure, and is still a tenant in common, must be his, and so his, i.e., a part of him, that another can no longer have any right to it, before it can do any good for the support of his life.

Though the earth and all inferior creatures be common to all men, yet every man has a property in his own person; this nobody has any right to but himself. The labor of his body and the work of his hands we may say are properly his. Whatsoever, then, he removes out of the state that nature hath provided and left it in, he hath mixed his labor with, and joined to it something that is his own, and thereby makes it his property. It being by him removed from the common state nature placed it in, it hath by this labor something annexed to it that excludes the common right of other men. For this labor being the unquestionable property of the laborer, no man but he can have a right to what that is once joined to, at least where there is enough, and as good left in common for others.

He that is nourished by the acorns he picked up under an oak, or the apples he gathered from the trees in the wood, has certainly appropriated them to himself. Nobody can deny but the nourishment is his. I ask, then, When did they begin to be his—when he digested, or when he ate, or when he boiled, or when he brought them home, or when he picked them up? And 'tis plain if the first gathering made them not his, nothing else could. That labor put a distinction between them and common; that added something to them more than nature, the common mother of all, had done, and so they became his private right. And will anyone say he had no right to those acorns or apples he thus appropriated, because he had not the consent of all mankind to make them his? Was it robbery thus to assume to himself what belonged to all in common? If such a consent as that was necessary, man had starved, notwithstanding the plenty God had given him. We see in commons which remain so by compact that 'tis the taking any part of what is common and removing it out of the state nature leaves it in, which begins the property; without which the common is of no use. And the taking of this or that part does not depend on the express consent of all the commoners. Thus the grass my horse has bit, the turfs my servant has cut, and the ore I have dug in any place where I have a right to them in common with others, become my property without the assignation or consent of anybody. The labor that was mine removing them out of that common state they were in, hath fixed my property in them. . . .

It will perhaps be objected to this, that if gathering the acorns, or other fruits of the earth, etc., makes a right to them, then anyone may engross as much as he will. To which I answer, Not so. The same law of nature that does by this means give us property, does also bound that property too. "God has given us all things richly" (1 Tim. vi. 17), is the voice of reason confirmed by inspiration. But how far has He given it us? To enjoy. As much as anyone can make use of to any advantage of life before it spoils, so much he may by his labor fix a property in; whatever is beyond this, is more than his share, and belongs to others. Nothing was made by God for man to spoil or destroy. And thus considering the plenty of natural provisions there was a long time in the world and the few spenders, and to how small a part of that provision the industry of one man could extend itself, and engross it to the prejudice of others—especially keeping within the bounds, set by reason, or what might serve for his use—there could be then little room for quarrels or contentions about property so established.

But the chief matter of property being now not the fruits of the earth, and the beasts that subsist on it, but the earth itself, as that which takes in and carries with it all the rest. I think it is plain that property in that, too, is acquired as the former. As much land as a man tills, plants, improves, cultivates, and can use the product of, so much is his property. He by his labor does as it were enclose it from the common. Nor will it invalidate his right to say, everybody else has an equal title to it; and therefore he cannot appropriate, he cannot enclose, without the consent of all his fellow-commoners, all mankind. God, when He gave the world in common to all mankind, commanded man also to labor, and the penury of his condition required it of him. God and his reason commanded him to subdue the earth, i.e., improve it for the benefit of life, and therein lay out something upon it that was his own, his labor. He that, in obedience to this command of God, subdued, tilled, and sowed any part of it, thereby annexed to it something that was his property, which another had no title to, nor could without injury take from him.

Nor was this appropriation of any parcel of land, by improving it, any prejudice to any other man, since there was still enough and as good left; and more than the yet unprovided could use. So that in effect there was never the less left for others because of his enclosure for himself. For he that leaves as much as another can make use of, does as good as take nothing at all. Nobody could think himself injured by the drinking of another man, though he took a good draught, who had a whole river of the same water left him to quench his thirst; and the case of land and water, where there is enough of both, is perfectly the same. . . .

Before the appropriation of land, he who gathered as much of the wild fruit, killed, caught, or tamed as many of the beasts as he could; he that so employed his pains about any of the spontaneous products of nature as any way to alter them from the state which nature put them in, by placing any of his labor on them, did thereby acquire a propriety in them. But if they perished in his possession without their due use; if the fruits rotted, or the venison putrefied before he could spend it, he offended against the common law of nature, and was liable to be punished; he invaded his neighbor's share, for he had no right further than his use called for any of them and they might serve to afford him conveniences of life.

The same measures governed the possessions of land, too. Whatsoever he tilled and reaped, laid up, and made use of before it spoiled, that was his peculiar right; whatsoever he enclosed and could feed and make use of, the cattle and product was also his. But if either the grass of his enclosure rotted on the ground, or the fruit of his planting perished without gathering and laying up, this part of the earth, notwithstanding his enclosure, was still to be looked on as waste, and might be the possession of any other. . . .

The greatest part of things really useful to the life of man, and such as the necessity of subsisting made the first commoners of the world look after, as it doth the Americans now, are generally things of short duration, such as, if they are not consumed by use, will decay and perish of themselves: gold, silver, and diamonds are things that fancy or agreement have put the value on more than real use and the necessary support of life. Now, of those good things which nature hath provided in common, everyone hath a right, as hath been said, to as much as he could use, and had a property in all he could effect with his labor—all that his industry could extend to, to alter from the state nature had put it in, was his. He that gathered a hundred bushels of acorns or apples had thereby a property in them; they were his goods as soon as gathered. He was only to look that he used them before they spoiled, else he took more than his share, and robbed others; and, indeed, it was a foolish thing, as well as dishonest, to hoard up more than he could make use of. If he gave away a part to anybody else, so that it perished not uselessly in his possession, these he also made use of; and if he also bartered away plums that would have rotted in a week, for nuts that would last good for his eating a whole year, he did no injury; he wasted not the common stock, destroyed no part of the portion of goods that belonged to others, so long as nothing perished uselessly in his hands. Again, if he would give his nuts for a piece of metal, pleased with its color, or exchange his sheep for shells, or wool for a sparkling pebble or a diamond, and keep those by him all his life, he invaded not the right of others; he might heap up as much of these durable things as he pleased, the exceeding of the bounds of his just property not lying in the largeness of his possessions, but the perishing of anything uselessly in it.

And thus came in the use of money—some lasting thing that men might keep without spoiling, and that, by mutual consent, men would take in exchange for the truly useful but perishable supports of life.

And as different degrees of industry were apt to give men possessions in different proportions, so this invention of money gave them the opportunity to continue and enlarge them; for supposing an island, separate from all possible commerce with the rest of the world, wherein there were but a hundred families—but there were sheep, horses, and cows, with other useful animals, wholesome fruits, and land enough for corn for a hundred thousand times as many, but nothing in the island, either because of its commonness or perishableness, fit to supply the place of money—what reason could anyone have there to enlarge his possessions beyond the use of his family and a plentiful supply to its consumption, either in what their own industry produced, or they could barter for like perishable useful commodities with others? Where there is not something both lasting and scarce, and so valuable to be hoarded up, there men will not be apt to enlarge their possessions of land, were it never so rich, never so free for them to take; for I ask, what would a man value ten thousand or a hundred thousand acres of excellent land, ready cultivated, and well stocked too with cattle, in the middle of the inland parts of America, where he had no hopes of commerce with other parts of the world, to draw money to him by the sale of the product? It would not be worth the enclosing, and we should see him give up again to the wild common of nature whatever was more than would supply the conveniences of life to be had there for him and his family. . . .

But since gold and silver, being little useful to the life of man in proportion to food, raiment, and carriage, has its value only from the consent of men, whereof labor yet makes, in great part, the measure, it is plain that the consent of men have agreed to a disproportionate and unequal possession of the earth—I mean out of the bounds of society and compact; for in governments the laws regulate it; they having, by consent, found out and agreed in a way how a man may rightfully and without injury possess more than he himself can make use of by receiving gold and silver, which may continue long in a man's possession, without decaying for the overplus, and agreeing those metals should have a value.

And thus, I think, it is very easy to conceive without any difficulty how labor could at first begin a title of property in the common things of nature, and how the spending it upon our uses bounded it; so that there could then be no reason of quarrelling about title, nor any doubt about the largeness of possession it gave. Right and conveniency went together; for as a man had a right to all he could employ his labor upon, so he had no temptation to labor for more than he could make use of. This left no room for controversy about the title, nor for encroachment on the right of others; what portion a man carved to himself was easily seen, and it was useless, as well as dishonest, to carve himself too much, or take more than he needed.

REVIEW AND DISCUSSION QUESTIONS

1. Describe the "state of nature" as envisioned by Locke. How is this a state of equality? What does Locke mean when he writes that it is a state of liberty but not of license? What do you think Locke means by the "law of nature"?

2. If the world is given to human beings in common, how can we be justified in appropriating anything for ourselves?

3. Locke states that "every man has a property in his own person." What are the implications of this for Locke?

4. What restrictions does Locke place on the acquisition of resources? Why?

5. What is the origin of money? How does its introduction change things?

6. Has Locke succeeded in justifying private property and inequalities of wealth and possession? Explain why or why not.

Property and Sovereignty

Morris Raphael Cohen

Morris Cohen was one of the leading legal philosophers of the twentieth century. In this essay, he critically examines four justifications of private property: the occupation theory, the labor theory, personal self-assertion, and the economic theory. Although each points to an important value or interest that the legal order needs to protect, private property is only one among other human interests: it is not sacrosanct, and state interference with private property—even the confiscation or abolition of certain types of it—may be justified.

THE JUSTIFICATION OF PROPERTY

1. THE OCCUPATION THEORY

The oldest and up to recently the most influential defense of private property was based on the assumed right of the original discoverer and occupant to dispose of that which thus became his. This view dominated the thought of Roman jurists and of modern philosophers—from Grotius to Kant—so much so that the right of the laborer to the produce of his work was sometimes defended on the ground that the laborer "occupied" the material which he fashioned into the finished product.

It is rather easy to find fatal flaws in this view. Few accumulations of great wealth were ever simply found. Rather were they acquired by the labor of many, by conquest, by business manipulation, and by other means. It is obvious that today at any rate few economic goods can be acquired by discovery and first occupancy.[1] Even in the few cases when they are, as in fishing and trapping, we are apt rather to think of the labor involved as the proper basis of the property acquired. Indeed, there seems nothing ethically self-evident in the motto that "findings is keepings." There seems nothing wrong in a law that a treasure trove shall belong to the king or the state rather than to the finder. Shall the finder of a river be entitled to all the water in it?

Moreover, even if we were to grant that the original finder or occupier should have possession as against anyone else, it by no means follows that he may use it arbitrarily or that his rule shall prevail indefinitely after his death. The right of others to acquire the property from him by bargain, by inheritance, or by testamentary disposition, is not determined by the principle of occupation.

Despite all these objections, however, there is a kernel of positive value in this principle. Protecting the discoverer or first occupant, is really part of the more general principle that possession as such should be protected. There is real human economy in doing so until somebody shows a better claim than the possessor. It makes for certainty and security of transaction as well as for public peace—provided the law is ready to set aside possession acquired in ways that are inimical to public order. Various principles of justice may determine the distribution of goods and the retribution to be made for acts of injustice. But the law must not ignore the principle of inertia in human affairs. Continued possession creates expectations in the possessor and in others and only a very poor morality would ignore the hardship of frustrating these expectations and rendering human relations insecure, even to correct some old flaws in the original acquisition. Suppose some remote ancestor of yours did acquire your property by fraud, robbery or conquest, *e.g.* in the days of William of Normandy. Would it be just to take it away from you and your dependents who have held it in good faith? Reflection on the general insecurity that would result from such procedure leads us to see that as habit is the basis of individual life, continued practice must be the basis of social procedure. Any form of property which exists has therefore a claim to continue until it can be shown that the effort to change it is worth while. Continual changes in property laws would certainly discourage enterprise.

Nevertheless, it would be as absurd to argue that the distribution of property must never be modified by law as it would be to argue that the distribution of political power must never be changed. No less a philosopher than Aristotle argued against changing even bad laws, lest the habit of obedience be thereby impaired. There is something to be said for this, but only so long as we are in the realm of merely mechanical obedience. When we introduce the notion of free or rational obedience, Aristotle's argument loses its force in the political realm; and similar considerations apply to any property system that can claim the respect of rational beings.

2. THE LABOR THEORY

That everyone is entitled to the full produce of his labor is assumed as self-evident by both socialists and conservatives who believe that capital is the result of the savings of labor. However, as economic goods are never the result of any one man's unaided labor, our maxim is altogether inapplicable. How shall we determine what part of the value of a table should belong to the carpenter, to the lumberman, to the transport worker, to the policeman who guarded the peace while the work was being done, and to the indefinitely large numbers of others whose cooperation was necessary? Moreover, even if we could tell what any one individual has produced—let us imagine a Robinson Crusoe growing up all alone on an island and in no way indebted to any community—it would still be highly questionable whether he has a right to keep the full produce of his labor when some shipwrecked mariner needs his surplus food to keep from starving.

In actual society no one ever thinks it unjust that a wealthy old bachelor should have part of his presumably just earnings taken away in the form of a tax for the benefit of other people's

children, or that one immune to certain diseases, should be taxed to support hospitals, etc. We do not think there is any injustice involved in such cases because social interdependence is so intimate that no man can justly say: "This wealth is entirely and absolutely mine as the result of my own unaided effort."

The degree of social solidarity varies, of course; and it is easy to conceive of a sparsely settled community, such as Missouri at the beginning of the 19th century, where a family of hunters or isolated cultivators of the soil might regard everything which it acquired as the product of its own labor. Generally, however, human beings start with a stock of tools or information acquired from others and they are more or less dependent upon some government for protection against foreign aggression, etc.

Yet despite these and other criticisms, the labor theory contains too much substantial truth to be brushed aside. The essential truth is that labor has to be encouraged and that property must be distributed in such a way as to encourage ever greater efforts at productivity.

As not all things produced are ultimately good, as even good things may be produced at an unjustified expense in human life and worth, it is obvious that other principles besides that of labor or productivity are needed for an adequate basis or justification of any system of property law. We can only say dialectically that all other things being equal, property should be distributed with due regard to the productive needs of the community. We must, however, recognize that a good deal of property accrues to those who are not productive, and a good deal of productivity does not and perhaps should not receive its reward in property. Nor should we leave this theme without recalling the Hebrew-Christian view—and for that matter, the specifically religious view—that the first claim on property is by the man who needs it rather than the man who has created it. Indeed, the only way of justifying the principle of distribution of property according to labor is to show that it serves the larger social need.

The occupation theory has shown us the necessity for security of possession and the labor theory the need for encouraging enterprise. These two needs are mutually dependent. Anything which discourages enterprise makes our possessions less valuable, and it is obvious that it is not worth while engaging in economic enterprise if there is no prospect of securely possessing the fruit of it. Yet there is also a conflict between these two needs. The owners of land, wishing to secure the continued possession by the family, oppose laws which make it subject to free financial transactions or make it possible that land should be taken away from one's heirs by a judgment creditor for personal debts. In an agricultural economy security of possession demands that the owner of a horse should be able to reclaim it no matter into whose hands it has fallen. But in order that markets should be possible, it becomes necessary that the innocent purchaser should have a good title. This conflict between static and dynamic security has been treated most suggestively by Demogue and I need only refer you to his masterly book, "*Les Notions fondementales du Droit privé.*"

3. Property and Personality

Hegel, Ahrens, Lorimer, and other idealists have tried to deduce the right of property from the individual's right to act as a free personality. To be free one must have a sphere of self-assertion in the external world. One's private property provides such an opportunity.

Waiving all traditional difficulties in applying the metaphysical idea of freedom to empirical legal acts, we may still object that the notion of personality is too vague to enable us to deduce definite legal consequences by means of it. How, for example, can the principle of personality help us to decide to what extent there shall be private rather than public property in railroads, mines, gas-works, and other public necessities?

Not the extremest communist would deny that in the interest of privacy certain personal belongings such as are typified by the toothbrush, must be under the dominion of the individual owner, to the absolute exclusion of everyone else. This, however, will not carry us far if we recall that the major effect of property

in land, in the machinery of production, in capital goods, etc., is to enable the owner to exclude others from *their necessities*, and thus to compel them to serve him. Ahrens, one of the chief expounders of the personality theory, argues "It is undoubtedly contrary to the right of personality to have persons dependent on others on account of material goods."[3] But if this is so, the primary effect of property on a large scale is to limit freedom, since the one thing that private property law does not do is to guarantee a minimum of subsistence or the necessary tools of freedom to everyone. So far as a regime of private property fails to do the latter it rather compels people to part with their freedom.

It may well be argued in reply that just as restraining traffic rules in the end give us greater freedom of motion, so, by giving control over things to individual property owners, greater economic freedom is in the end assured to all. This is a strong argument, as can be seen by comparing the different degrees of economic freedom that prevail in lawless and in law abiding communities. It is, however, an argument for legal order rather than any particular form of government or private property. It argues for a regime where every one has a definite sphere of rights and duties, but it does not tell us where these lines should be drawn. The principle of freedom of personality certainly cannot justify a legal order wherein a few can, by virtue of their legal monopoly over necessities, compel others to work under degrading and brutalizing conditions. A government which limits the right of large land-holders limits the rights of property and yet may promote real freedom. Property owners, like other individuals, are members of a community and must subordinate their ambition to the larger whole of which they are a part. They may find their compensation in spiritually identifying their good with that of the larger life.

4. The Economic Theory

The economic justification of private property is that by means of it a maximum of productivity is promoted. The classical economic argument may be put thus: The successful business man, the one who makes the greatest profit, is the one who has the greatest power to foresee effective demand. If he has not that power his enterprise fails. He is therefore, in fact, the best director of economic activities.

There can be little doubt that if we take the whole history of agriculture and industry, or compare the economic output in countries like Russia with that in the United States, there is a strong *prima facie* case for the contention that more intensive cultivation of the soil and greater productiveness of industry prevail under individual ownership. Many *a priori* psychologic and economic reasons can also be brought to explain why this must be so, why the individual cultivator will take greater care not to exhaust the soil, etc. All this, however, is so familiar that we may take it for granted and look at the other side of the case, at the considerations which show that there is a difference between socially desirable productivity and the desire for individual profits.

In the first place let us note that of many things the supply is not increased by making them private property. This is obviously true of land in cities and of other monopoly or limited goods. Private ownership of land does not increase the amount of rainfall, and irrigation works to make the land more fruitful have been carried through by government more than by private initiative. Nor was the productivity of French or Irish lands reduced when the property of their landlords in rent charges and other incidents of seigniorage was reduced or even abolished. In our own days, we frequently see tobacco, cotton or wheat farmers in distress because they have succeeded in raising too plentiful crops; and manufacturers who are well informed know when greater profit is to be made by a decreased output. Patents for processes which would cheapen the product are often bought up by manufacturers and never used. Durable goods which are more economic to the consumer are very frequently crowded out of the market by shoddier goods which are more profitable to produce because of the larger turnover. Advertising campaigns often persuade people to buy the less economical goods and to pay the cost of the uneconomic advice.

In the second place, there are inherent sources of waste in a regime of private enterprise and free competition. If the biologic analogy of the struggle for existence were taken seriously, we should see that the natural survival of the economically fittest is attended, as in the biologic field, with frightful wastefulness. The elimination of the unsuccessful competitor may be a gain to the survivor but all business failures are losses to the community.

Finally, a regime of private ownership in industry is too apt to sacrifice social interests to immediate monetary profits. This shows itself in speeding up industry to such a pitch that men are exhausted in a relatively few years whereas a slower expenditure of their energy would prolong their useful years. It shows itself in the way in which private ownership enterprise has wasted a good deal of the natural resources of the United States to obtain immediate profits. Even when the directors of a modern industrial enterprise see the uneconomic consequences of immediate profits, the demand of shareholders of immediate dividends,[4] and the ease with which men can desert a business and leave it to others to stand the coming losses, all tend to encourage ultimately wasteful and uneconomic activity. Possibly the best illustration of this is child labor, which by lowering wages increases immediate profits, but in the end is really wasteful of the most precious wealth of the country, its future manhood and womanhood.

Surveying our arguments thus far: We have seen the roots of property in custom and in the need for economic productivity, in individual needs of privacy and in the need for social utility. But we have also noted that property, being only one among other human interests, cannot be pursued absolutely without detriment to human life. Hence we can no longer maintain Montesquieu's view that private property is sacrosanct and that the general government must in no way interfere with or retrench its domain. The issue before thoughtful people is therefore not the maintenance or abolition of private property, but the determination of the precise lines along which private enterprise must be given free scope and where it must be restricted in the interests of the common good.

LIMITATIONS OF PROPERTY RIGHTS

The traditional theory of rights, and the one that still prevails in this country, was molded by the struggle in the 17th and 18th centuries against restrictions on individual enterprise. These restrictions in the interest of special privilege were fortified by the divine (and therefore absolute) rights of kings. As is natural in all revolts, absolute claims on one side were met with absolute denials on the other. Hence the theory of the natural rights of the individual took not only an absolute but a negative form; men have *in*alienable rights, the state must never interfere with private property, etc. The state, however, must interfere in order that individual rights should become effective and not degenerate into public nuisances. To permit anyone to do absolutely what he likes with his property in creating noise, smells, or danger of fire, would be to make property in general valueless. To be really effective, therefore, the right of property must be supported by restrictions or positive duties on the part of owners, enforced by the state as much as the right to exclude others which is the essence of property. Unfortunately, however, whether because of the general decline of juristic philosophy after Hegel or because law has become more interested in defending property against attacks by socialists, the doctrine of natural rights has remained in the negative state and has never developed into a doctrine of the positive contents of rights.[5] . . .

As a believer in natural rights, I believe that the state can, and unfortunately often does enact unjust laws. But I think it is a sheer fallacy based on verbal illusion to think that the rights of the community against an individual owner are no better than the rights of a neighbor. Indeed, no one has in fact had the courage of this confusion to argue that the state has no right to deprive an individual of property to which he is so attached that he refuses any money for it. Though no neighbor has such a right the public interest often justly demands that a proprietor shall part with his ancestral home to which he may be attached by all the roots of his being.

When taking away a man's property, is the state always bound to pay a direct compensation? I submit that while this is generally advisable in order not to disturb the general feeling of security, no absolute principle of justice requires it. I have alluded before to the fact that there is no injustice in taxing an old bachelor to educate the children of others, or to tax one immune to typhoid for the construction of sewers or other sanitary measures. We may go farther and say that the whole business of the state depends upon its rightful power to take away the property of some (in the form of taxation) and use it to support others, such as the needy, those invalided in the service of the state in war or peace, and those who are not yet able to produce but in whom the hope of humanity is embodied. Doubtless, taxation and confiscation may be actuated by malice and may impose needless and cruel hardship on some individuals or classes. But this is not to deny that taxation and confiscation are within the just powers of the state. A number of examples may make this clearer.

A. Slavery. When slavery is abolished by law, the owners have their property taken away. Is the state ethically bound to pay them the full market value of their slaves? It is doubtless a grievous shock to a community to have a large number of slave owners whose wealth often makes them leaders of culture, suddenly deprived of their income. It may also be conceded that it is not always desirable for the slave himself to be suddenly taken away from his master and cut adrift on the sea of freedom. But when one reads of the horrible ways in which some of those slaves were violently torn from their homes in Africa and shamelessly deprived of their human rights, one is inclined to agree with Emerson that compensation should first be paid to the slaves. This compensation need not be in the form of a direct bounty to them. It may be more effectively paid in the form of rehabilitation and education for freedom; and such a charge may take precedence over the claims of the former owners. After all, the latter claims are no greater than those of a protected industry when the tariff is removed. If the state should decide that certain import duties, *e.g.* those on scientific instruments, or hospital supplies, are unjustified and proceed to abolish them, many manufacturers may suffer. Are they entitled to compensation by the state?

It is undoubtedly for the general good to obviate as much as possible the effect of economic shock to a large number of people. The routine of life prospers on security. But when that security contains a large element of injustice the shock of an economic operation by law may be necessary and ethically justified.

This will enable us to deal with other types of confiscation.

B. Financial loss through the abolition of public office. It is only in very recent times that we have got into the habit of ignoring the fact that public office is and always has been regarded as a source of revenue like any other occupation. When, therefore, certain public offices are abolished for the sake of good government, a number of people are deprived of their expected income. In the older law and often in popular judgment of today this does not seem fair. But reflection shows that the state is not obligated to pay anyone when it finds that particular services of his are unnecessary. At best, it should help him to find a new occupation.

Part of the prerogative of the English or Scotch landlord was the right to nominate the priest for the parish on his land. To abolish this right of advowson is undoubtedly a confiscation of a definite property right. But while I cannot agree with my friend Mr. Laski that the courts were wrong to refuse to disobey the law which subordinated the religious scruples of a church to the property rights of an individual, I do not see that there could have been any sound ethical objection to the legislature changing the law without compensating the landlord.

C. In our own day, we have seen the confiscation of many millions of dollars of property through prohibition. Were the distillers and brewers entitled to compensation for their losses? We have seen that property on a large scale is power and the loss of it, while evil to those who are accustomed to exercise it, may not be an evil to the community. In point of fact, the shock to the distillers and brewers was not as serious as to others, *e.g.* saloon keepers and bartenders who did not lose any legal property since they were only employees, but who found it difficult late in life to enter new employments.

History is full of examples of valuable property privileges abolished without any compensation, *e.g.* the immunity of nobles from taxation, their rights to hunt over other people's lands, etc. It would be absurd to claim that such legislation was unjust.

These and other examples of justifiable confiscation without compensation are inconsistent with the absolute theory of private property. An adequate theory of private property, however, should enable us to draw the line between justifiable and unjustifiable cases of confiscation. Such a theory I cannot undertake to elaborate on this occasion, though the doctrine of security of possession and avoidance of unnecessary shock seem to me suggestive. I wish however to urge that if the large property owner is viewed, as he ought to be, as a wielder of power over the lives of his fellow citizens, the law should not hesitate to develop a doctrine as to his positive duties in the public interest. The owner of a tenement house in a modern city is in fact a public official and has all sorts of positive duties. He must keep the halls lighted, he must see that the roof does not leak, that there are fire-escape facilities, he must remove tenants guilty of certain public immoralities, etc., and he is compensated by the fees of his tenants which the law is beginning to regulate. Similar is the case of a factory owner. He must install all sorts of safety appliances, hygienic conveniences, see that the workmen are provided with a certain amount of light, air, etc.

In general, there is no reason for the law insisting that people should make the most economic use of their property. They have a motive in doing so themselves and the cost of the enforcing machinery may be a mischievous waste. Yet there may be times, such as occurred during the late war, when the state may insist that man shall cultivate the soil intensively and be otherwise engaged in socially productive work.

With considerations such as these in mind, it becomes clear that there is no unjustifiable taking away of property when railroads are prohibited from posting notice that they will discharge their employees if the latter join trade unions, and that there is no property taken away without due or just process of law when an industry is compelled to pay its laborers a minimum of subsistence instead of having it done by private or public charity or else systematically starving its workers.

NOTES

[1]In granting patents, copyrights, etc., the principle of reward for useful work or to encourage productivity seems so much more relevant that the principle of discovery and first occupancy seems to have little force.

[2]Economists often claim that the unearned increment is the greatest source of wealth. See Bull. of Am. Econ. Ass'n (4th ser., No. 2) 542 ff.

[3]*Il Cours de Droit Naturel* (6th ed.) 108.

[4]Thus the leading brewers doubtless foresaw the coming of prohibition and could have saved millions in losses by separating their interests from that of the saloon. But the large temporary loss involved in such an operation was something that stockholders could never have agreed to.

[5]Thus our courts are reluctant to admit that rules against unfair competition may be in the interest of the general public and not merely for those whose immediate property interests are directly affected. . . .

REVIEW AND DISCUSSION QUESTIONS

1. Restate each of the four justifications of property discussed by Cohen. What does he see as the strong and weak points of each? Do you agree? What do you see as the most compelling argument for private property?

2. Would Cohen agree with Locke that we have a natural, prepolitical right to property?

3. According to Cohen, does the state have the right to deprive an individual of property? Must it pay compensation? Explain.

Property Acquisition

Haslem v. Lockwood

What constitutes property and under what conditions can one acquire it through labor or possession? These and related questions are addressed in this case. The Court of Common Pleas for Fairfield County, Connecticut, ruled that the plaintiff in this case had not established a sufficient interest in, or right of possession to, the manure he had collected alongside a public road, which the defendant found the next morning and took for himself. On appeal, Connecticut's Supreme Court of Errors overturned this judgment and ordered a new trial.

---

37 Conn. 500 (1871). Citations and notes omitted.

Trover [a suit for return of property], for a quantity of manure; brought before a justice of the peace and appealed by the defendant to the Court of Common Pleas for the county of Fairfield, and tried in that court, on the general issue closed to the court, before Brewster, J.:

On the trial it was proved that the plaintiff employed two men to gather into heaps, on the evening of April 6, 1869, some manure that lay scattered along the side of a public highway, for several rods, in the borough of Stamford, intending to remove the same to his own land the next evening. The men began to scrape the manure into heaps at six o'clock in the evening, and after gathering eighteen heaps, or about six cart-loads, left the same at eight o'clock in the evening in the street. The heaps consisted chiefly of manure made by horses hitched to the railing of the public park in, and belonging to, the borough of Stamford, and was all gathered between the center of the highway and the park; the rest of the heaps consisting of dirt, straw and the ordinary scrapings of highways. The defendant on the next morning, seeing the heaps, endeavored without success to ascertain who had made them, and inquired of the warden of the borough if he had given permission to any one to remove them, and ascertained from him that he had not. He thereupon, before noon on that day, removed the heaps and also the rest of the manure scattered along the side of the highway adjacent to the park, to his own land.

The plaintiff and defendant both claimed to have received authority from the warden to remove the manure before the 6th of April, but in fact neither had any legal authority from the warden, or from any officer of the borough or of the town. The borough of Stamford was the sole adjoining proprietor of the land on which the manure lay scattered before it was gathered by the plaintiff. No notice was left on the heaps or near by, by the plaintiff or his workmen, to indicate who had gathered them, nor had the plaintiff or his workmen any actual possession of the heaps after eight o'clock in the evening on the 6th of April.

Neither the plaintiff while gathering, nor the defendant while removing the heaps, was interfered with or opposed by any one. The removal of the manure and scrapings was calculated to improve the appearance and health of the borough. The six loads were worth one dollar per load. The plaintiff, on ascertaining that the defendant had removed the manure, demanded payment for the same, which the defendant refused. Neither the plaintiff nor the defendant owned any land adjacent to the place where the manure lay. The highway was kept in repair by the town of Stamford. . . .

The court ruled adversely to the claims of the plaintiff and held that on the facts proved the plaintiff had not made out a sufficient interest in, or right of possession to, the subject matter in dispute, to authorize a recovery in the suit, and rendered judgment for the defendant.

The plaintiff moved for a new trial for error in this ruling of the court.

Curtis and Joyt [Counsel for the plaintiff-appellant], in support of the motion:

1. The manure in question was personal property abandoned by its owners.

2. It never became a part of the real estate on which it was abandoned.

3. It being personal property abandoned by its owners, and lying upon the highway, and neither the owners of the fee nor the proper authorities of the town and borough having by any act of theirs shown any intention to appropriate the same, it became lawful for the plaintiff to gather it up and remove it from the highway, providing he did not commit a trespass, and removed it without objection from the owners of the land. And no trespass was in fact committed. No person interfered with the plaintiff or made any objection. This court cannot presume a trespass to have been committed.

4. But if the manure had become a part of the real estate, yet when it was gathered into heaps by the plaintiff it was severed from the realty and became personal estate. And being gathered without molestation from any person owning or claiming to own the land, it is to be considered as having been taken by the tacit consent of such owner.

5. The plaintiff therefore acquired not only a valid legal possession, but a title by occupancy, and by having expended labor and money upon the property. Such a title is a good legal title against every person but the true owner.

6. If the plaintiff had a legal title then he had the constructive possession. If he had legal possession, and only left the property for a short time intending to return and take it away, then he might maintain an action against a wrongdoer for taking it away. The leaving of property for a short time, intending to return, does not constitute an abandonment. The property is still to be considered as in the possession of the plaintiff.

Olmstead [Counsel for the defendant-respondent], contra:

1. The manure mixed with the dirt and ordinary scrapings of the highway, being spread out over the surface of the highway, was a part of the *real estate*, and belonged to the owner of the fee, subject to the public easement.

2. The scraping up of the manure and dirt into piles, if the same was a part of the real estate, did not change its nature to that of *personal property*, unless there was a severance of it from the realty by removal, (which there was not), whether the plaintiff had the consent of the owner of the fee or not, which consent it is conceded the plaintiff did not have.

3. Unless the scraping up of the heaps made their substance *personal property*, the plaintiff could not maintain his action either for trespass or trespass on the case.

4. In trespass *de bonis asportatis*, or Trover, the plaintiff must have had the *actual possession*, or a right to the immediate possession, in order to recover.

5. If the manure was always personal estate, it being spread upon the surface of the earth, it was in possession of the owner of the fee, who was not the plaintiff. The scraping of it into heaps, unless it was removed, would not change the *possession* from the owner of the fee to the plaintiff. The plaintiff therefore never had the *possession*.

6. If the heaps were personal property the plaintiff never had any right in the property, but only *mere possession*, if anything, which he abandoned by leaving the same upon the public highway from 8 o'clock in the evening until 12 o'clock the next day, without leaving any notice on or about the property, or any one to exercise control over the same in his behalf.

Judge Park:

We think the manure scattered upon the ground, under the circumstances of this case, was personal property. The cases referred to by the defendant to show that it was real estate are not in point. The principle of those cases is, that manure made in the usual course of husbandry upon a farm is so attached to and connected with the realty that, in the absence of any express stipulation to the contrary, it becomes appurtenant to it. The principle was established for the benefit of agriculture. It found its origin in the fact that it is essential to the successful cultivation of a farm that the manure, produced from the droppings of cattle and swine fed upon the products of the farm, and composted with earth and vegetable matter taken from the land, should be used to supply the drain made upon the soil in the production of crops, which otherwise would become impoverished and barren; and in the fact that manure so produced is generally regarded by farmers in this country as a part of the realty and has been so treated by landlords and tenants from time immemorial.

But this principle does not apply to the droppings of animals driven by travelers upon the highway. The highway is not used, and cannot be used, for the purpose of agriculture. The manure is of no benefit whatsoever to it, but on the contrary is a detriment; and in cities and large villages it becomes a nuisance, and is removed by public officers at public expense. The finding in this case is, "that the removal of the manure and scrapings was calculated to improve the appearance and health of the borough." It is therefore evident that the cases relied upon by the defendant have no application to the case.

But it is said that if the manure was personal property, it was in the possession of the owner of the fee, and the scraping it into heaps by the plaintiff did not change the possession, but it continued as before, and that therefore the plaintiff cannot recover, for he neither had the possession nor the right to the immediate possession.

The manure originally belonged to the travelers whose animals dropped it, but it being worthless to them was immediately abandoned; and whether it then became the property of the borough of Stamford which owned the fee of the land on which the manure lay, it is unnecessary to determine; for, if it did, the case finds that the removal of the filth would be an improvement to the borough, and no objection was made by any one to the use that the plaintiff attempted to make of it. Considering the character of such accumulations upon highways in cities and villages, and the light in which they are everywhere regarded in closely settled communities, we cannot believe that the borough in this instance would have had any objection to the act of the plaintiff in removing a nuisance that affected the public health and the appearance of the streets. At all events, we think the facts of the case show a significant right in the plaintiff to the immediate possession of the property as against a mere wrongdoer.

The defendant appears before the court in no enviable light. He does not pretend that he had a right to the manure, even when scattered upon the highway, superior to that of the plaintiff; but after the plaintiff had changed its original condition and greatly enhanced its value by his labor, he seized and appropriated to his own use the fruits of the plaintiff's outlay, and now seeks immunity from responsibility on the ground that the plaintiff was a wrong doer as well as himself. The conduct of the defendant is in keeping with his claim, and neither commends itself to the favorable consideration of the court. The plaintiff had the peaceable and quiet possession of the property; and we deem this sufficient until the borough of Stamford shall make complaint.

It is further claimed that if the plaintiff had a right to the property by virtue of occupancy, he lost the right when he ceased to retain the actual possession of the manure after scraping it into heaps.

We do not question the general doctrine, that where the right by occupancy exists, it exists no longer than the party retains the actual possession of the property, or till he appropriates it to his own use by removing it to some other place. If he leaves the property at the place where it was discovered, and does nothing whatsoever to enhance its value or change its nature, his right by occupancy is unquestionably gone. But the question is, if a party finds property comparatively worthless, as the plaintiff found the property in question, owing to its scattered condition upon the highway, and greatly increases its value by his labor and expense, does he lose his right if he leaves it a reasonable time to procure the means to take it away, when such means are necessary for its removal?

Suppose a teamster with a load of grain, while traveling the highway, discovers a rent in one of his bags, and finds that his grain is scattered upon the road for the distance of a mile. He considers the labor of collecting his corn of more value than the property itself, and he therefore abandons it, and pursues his way. *A* afterwards finds the grain in this condition and gathers it kernel by kernel into heaps by the side of the road, and leaves it a reasonable time to procure the means necessary for its removal. While he is gone for his bag, *B* discovers the grain thus conveniently collected in heaps and appropriates it to his own use. Has *A* any remedy? If he has not, the law in this instance is open to just reproach. We think under such circumstances, *A* would have a reasonable time to remove the property, and during such reasonable time his right to it would be protected. If this is so, then the principle applies to the case under consideration.

A reasonable time for the removal of this manure had not elapsed when the defendant seized and converted it to his own use. The statute regulating the rights of parties in the gathering of sea-weed, gives the party who heaps it upon a public beach twenty-four hours in which to remove it, and that length of time for the removal of the property we think would not be unreasonable in most cases like the present one.

We therefore advise the Court of Common Pleas to grant a new trial.

In this opinion the other judges concurred.

REVIEW AND DISCUSSION QUESTIONS

1. What are the main arguments presented by each of the lawyers on behalf of their clients?

2. Do you agree with the conclusion of the court? Was Judge Park correct to reverse the decision of the trial court? How would you have decided this case?

3. Was the manure private property before being collected by the plaintiff? If so, whose was it? If not, did it become the plaintiff's private property upon being collected? If so, was it still his property when the defendant happened upon it the next day? Why or why not?

Taking Without Compensation

Penn Central Transportation Co. v. New York City

As part of its commitment to preserving historic landmarks, New York City, like several other municipalities, protects buildings designated as historic structures from destruction and restricts what their owners can do to them. When New York turned down Penn Central's request to build a multistory office building atop Grand Central Terminal, which had been designated a landmark, because this would impair the aesthetic quality of one of New York's most famous buildings, the dispute was pursued in court and eventually reached the United States Supreme Court. At issue is the correct interpretation of the Fifth Amendment, which stipulates that "private property [shall not] be taken for public use, without just compensation."

Mr. Justice Brennan delivered the opinion of the Court:

Over the past 50 years, all 50 States and over 500 municipalities have enacted laws to encourage or require the preservation of buildings and areas with historic or aesthetic importance. These nationwide legislative efforts have been precipitated by two concerns. The first is recognition that, in recent years, large numbers of historic structures, landmarks, and areas have been destroyed without adequate consideration of either the values represented therein or the possibility of preserving the destroyed properties for use in economically productive ways. The second is a widely shared belief that structures with special historic, cultural, or architectural significance enhance the quality of life for all. Not only do these buildings and their workmanship represent the lessons of the past and

embody precious features of our heritage, they serve as examples of quality for today. . . .

The New York City law is typical of many urban landmark laws in that its primary method of achieving its goals is not by acquisitions of historical properties, but rather by involving public entities in land-use decisions affecting these properties and providing services, standards, controls, and incentives that will encourage preservation by private owners and users. While the law does place special restrictions on landmark properties as a necessary feature to the attainment of its larger objectives, the major theme of the law is to ensure the owners of any such properties both a "reasonable return" on their investments and maximum latitude to use their parcels for purposes not inconsistent with the preservation goals. . . .

[Final] designation as a landmark results in restrictions upon the property owner's options concerning use of the landmark site. First, the law imposes a duty upon the owner to keep the

438 U.S. 104 (1978).

exterior features of the building "in good repair" to assure that the law's objectives not be defeated by the landmark's falling into a state of irremediable disrepair. [Second,] the Commission must approve in advance any proposal to alter the exterior architectural features of the landmark or to construct any exterior improvement on the landmark site, thus ensuring that decisions concerning construction on the landmark site are made with due consideration of both the public interest in the maintenance of the structure and the landowner's interest in use of the property. . . .

In the event an owner wishes to alter a landmark site, [procedures] are available through which administrative approval may be obtained. . . .

Although the designation of a landmark and landmark site restricts the owner's control over the parcel, designation also enhances the economic position of the landmark owner in one significant respect. Under New York City's zoning laws, owners of real property who have not developed their property to the full extent permitted by the applicable zoning laws are allowed to transfer development rights to contiguous parcels on the same city block. . . .

This case involves the application of New York City's Landmarks Preservation Law to Grand Central Terminal (Terminal).

[The Court noted that the terminal is one of New York City's most famous buildings and that it had been designated as occupying a landmark site. Penn Central submitted two plans to the Commission for construction of an office building atop the terminal. One plan called for a fifty-five-story office building; another called for tearing down some of its facade and constructing a fifty-three-story office building. The Commission denied permission to go forward with the plans. With respect to the second plan, the Commission observed, "To protect a Landmark, one does not tear it down." With respect to the first plan, the Commission referred primarily to the adverse effect of the proposed tower on the dramatic view of the terminal from Park Avenue South. "To balance a 55-story office tower above a flamboyant Beaux-Arts facade seems nothing more than an aesthetic joke. Quite simply, the tower would overwhelm the Terminal by its sheer mass."]

The [issue is whether] the restrictions imposed by New York City's law upon appellants' exploitation of the Terminal site effect a "taking" of appellants' property for a public use within the meaning of the Fifth Amendment. [The] question of what constitutes a "taking" for purposes of the Fifth Amendment has proved to be a problem of considerable difficulty. While this Court has recognized that the "Fifth Amendment's guarantee . . . [is] designed to bar Government from forcing some people alone to bear public burdens which, in all fairness and justice, should be borne by the public as a whole," *Armstrong v. United States*, 364 U.S. 40, 49 (1960), this Court, quite simply, has been unable to develop any "set formula" for determining when "justice and fairness" require that economic injuries caused by public action be compensated by the government, rather than remain disproportionately concentrated on a few persons. [Indeed,] we have frequently observed that whether a particular restriction will be rendered invalid by the government's failure to pay for any losses proximately caused by it depends largely "upon the particular circumstances [in that] case." *United States v. Central Eureka Mining Co.*, 357 U.S. 155, 168 (1958). . . .

In engaging in these essentially ad hoc, factual inquiries, the Court's decisions have identified several factors that have particular significance. The economic impact of the regulation on the claimant and, particularly, the extent to which the regulation has interfered with distinct investment-backed expectations are, of course, relevant considerations. [So,] too, is the character of the governmental action. A "taking" may more readily be found when the interference with property can be characterized as a physical invasion by government, see, e.g., *United States v. Causby*, 328 U.S. 256 (1946), than when interference arises from some public program adjusting the benefits and burdens of economic life to promote the common good.

"Government hardly could go on if to some extent values incident to property could not be diminished without paying for every such change in the general law," [*Mahon*], and this Court has accordingly recognized, in a wide variety of contexts, that government may execute laws or programs that adversely affect recognized economic values. Exercises of the taxing power are one obvious example. A second are the decisions in which this Court has dismissed "taking" challenges on the ground that, while the challenged government action caused economic harm, it did not interfere with interests that were sufficiently bound up with the reasonable expectations of the claimant to constitute "property" for Fifth Amendment purposes. . . .

More importantly for the present case, in instances in which a state tribunal reasonably concluded that "the health, safety, morals, or general welfare" would be promoted by prohibiting particular contemplated uses of land, this Court has upheld land-use regulations that destroyed or adversely affected recognized real property interests. [Zoning] laws are, of course, the classic example, see *Euclid v. Ambler Realty Co.*, 272 U.S. 365 (1926) (prohibition of industrial use). . . .

Zoning laws generally do not affect existing uses of real property, but "taking" challenges have also been held to be without merit in a wide variety of situations when the challenged governmental actions prohibited a beneficial use to which individual parcels had previously been devoted and thus caused substantial individualized harm. . . .

In contending that the New York City law has "taken" their property in violation of the Fifth and Fourteenth Amendments, appellants make a series of arguments, which [urge] that any substantial restriction imposed pursuant to a landmark law must be accompanied by just compensation if it is to be constitutional. Before considering these, we emphasize what is not in dispute. . . .

[The] submission that appellants may establish a "taking" simply by showing that they have been denied the ability to exploit a property interest that they heretofore had believed was available for development is quite simply untenable. ["Taking"] jurisprudence does not divide a single parcel into discrete segments and attempt to determine whether rights in a particular segment have been entirely abrogated. In deciding whether a particular governmental action has effected a taking, this Court focuses rather both on the character of the action and on

the nature and extent of the interference with rights in the parcel as a whole—here, the city tax block designated as the "landmark site."

Secondly, appellants [argue] that [the law] effects a "taking" because its operation has significantly diminished the value of the Terminal site. Appellants concede that the decisions sustaining other land-use regulations [reject] the proposition that diminution in property value, standing alone, can establish a "taking," [and] that the "taking" issue in these contexts is revolved by focusing on the uses the regulations permit. [Appellants,] moreover, also do not dispute that a showing of diminution in property value would not establish a "taking" if the restriction had been imposed as a result of historic-district legislation. [But] appellants argue that New York City's regulation of individual landmarks is fundamentally different from zoning or from historic-district legislation because the controls imposed by New York City's law apply only to individuals who own selected properties.

Stated baldly, appellants' position appears to be that the only means of ensuring that selected owners are not singled out to endure financial hardship for no reason is to hold that any restriction imposed on individual landmarks pursuant to the New York City scheme is a "taking" requiring the payment of "just compensation." Agreement with this argument would, of course, invalidate not just New York City's law, but all comparable landmark legislation in the Nation. . . .

[Contrary] to appellants' suggestions, landmark laws are not like discriminatory [zoning:] that is, a land-use decision which arbitrarily singles out a particular parcel for different, less favorable treatment than the neighboring ones. [In] contrast to discriminatory zoning, [the] New York City law embodies a comprehensive plan to preserve structures of historic or aesthetic interest wherever they might be found in the city, and [over] 400 landmarks and 31 historic districts have been designated pursuant to this plan.

Equally without merit is the related argument that the decision to designate a structure as a landmark "is inevitably arbitrary or at least subjective, because it is basically a matter of taste," [thus] unavoidably singling out individual landowners for disparate and unfair treatment.

. . . It is, of course, true that the Landmarks Law has a more severe impact on some landowners than on others, but that in itself does not mean that the law effects a "taking." Legislation designed to promote the general welfare commonly burdens some more than others.

. . . [The] New York City law does not interfere in any way with the present uses of the Terminal. Its designation as a landmark [contemplates] that appellants may continue to use the property precisely as it has been used for the past 65 years; as a railroad terminal containing office space and concessions. So the law does not interfere with what must be regarded as Penn Central's primary expectation concerning the use of the parcel [or its ability] to obtain a "reasonable return" on its investment. . . .

On this record, we conclude that the application of New York City's Landmarks Law has not effected a "taking" of appellants' property. The restrictions imposed are substantially related to the promotion of the general welfare and not only permit reasonable beneficial use of the landmark site but also afford appellants opportunities further to enhance not only the Terminal site proper but also other properties.

Affirmed.

Mr. Justice Rehnquist, with whom The Chief Justice and Mr. Justice Stevens join, dissenting:

Only in the most superficial sense of the word can this case be said to involve "zoning." Typical zoning restrictions may, it is true, so limit the prospective uses of a piece of property as to diminish the value of that property in the abstract because it may not be used for the forbidden purposes. But any such abstract decrease in value will more than likely be at least partially offset by an increase in value which flows from similar restrictions as to use on neighboring properties. All property owners in a designated area are placed under the same restrictions, not only for the benefit of the municipality as a whole but also for the common benefit of one another. In the words of Mr. Justice Holmes,

speaking for the Court in [*Mahon,*] there is "an average reciprocity of advantage."

Where a relatively few individual buildings, all separated from one another, are singled out and treated differently from surrounding buildings, no such reciprocity exists. [And] the cost associated with landmark legislation is likely to be of a completely different order of magnitude than that which results from the imposition of normal zoning restrictions. [Under] the historic-landmark preservation scheme adopted by New York, the property owner is under an affirmative duty to *preserve* his property as a *landmark* at his own expense. To suggest that because traditional zoning results in some limitation of use of the property zoned, the New York City landmark preservation scheme should likewise be upheld, represents the ultimate in treating as alike things which are different. The rubric of "zoning" has not yet sufficed to avoid the well-established proposition that the Fifth Amendment bars the "Government from forcing some people alone to be public burdens which, in all fairness and justice, should be borne by the public as a whole." . . .

[Before] the city of New York declared Grand Central Terminal to be a landmark, Penn Central could have used its "air rights" over the Terminal to build a multistory office building, at an apparent value of several million dollars per year. Today, the Terminal cannot be modified in *any* form, including the erection of additional stories, without the permission of the Landmark Preservation Commission, a permission which appellants, despite good-faith attempts, have so far been unable to obtain. . . .

Appellees do not dispute that valuable property rights have been destroyed. [While] the term "taken" might have been narrowly interpreted to include only physical seizures of property rights, "the construction of the phrase has not been so narrow. The courts have held that the deprivation of the former owner rather than the accretion of a right or interest to the sovereign constitutes the taking." . . .

[As] early as 1887, the Court recognized that the government can prevent a property owner from using his property to injure others without having to compensate the owner for the value of the forbidden use. [Thus,] there is no "taking" where a city prohibits the operation of a brickyard within a residential area, [or] forbids excavation for sand and gravel below the water line, *see Goldblatt v. Hempstead,* 369 U.S. 590 (1962). Nor is it relevant, where the government is merely prohibiting a noxious use of property, that the government would seem to be singling out a particular property owner. . . .

The nuisance exception to the taking guarantee is not coterminous with the police power itself. The question is whether the forbidden use is dangerous to the safety, health, or welfare of others. . . .

Appellees are not prohibiting a nuisance. The record is clear that the proposed addition to the Grand Central Terminal would be in full compliance with zoning, height limitations, and other health and safety requirements. Instead, appellees are seeking to preserve what they believe to be an outstanding example of beaux arts architecture. [The] city of New York, because of its unadorned admiration for the design, has decided that the owners of the building must preserve it unchanged for the benefit of sightseeing New Yorkers and tourists.

Unlike land-use regulations, appellees' action do not merely *prohibit* Penn Central from using its property in a narrow set of noxious ways. Instead, appellees have placed an *affirmative* duty on Penn Central to maintain the Terminal in its present state and in "good repair." . . .

Even where the government prohibits a noninjurious use, the Court has ruled that a taking does not take place if the prohibition applies over a broad cross section of land and thereby "secure[s] an average reciprocity of advantage." [*Mahon.*] [While] zoning at times reduces *individual* property values, the burden is shared relatively evenly and it is reasonable to conclude that on the whole an individual who is harmed by one aspect of the zoning will be benefited by another.

Here, however, a multimillion dollar loss has been imposed on appellants; it is uniquely felt and is not offset by any benefits flowing from the preservation of some 400 other "landmarks" in New York City. Appellees have imposed a substantial cost on less than one one-tenth of one percent of the buildings in New York City for the general benefit of all its people. It is exactly this imposition of general costs on a few individuals at which the "taking" protection is directed. . . .

As Mr. Justice Holmes pointed out in [*Mahon,*] "the question at bottom" in an eminent domain case "is upon whom the loss of the changes desired should fall." The benefits that appellees believe will flow from preservation of the Grand Central Terminal will accrue to all the citizens of New York City. There is no reason to believe that appellants will enjoy a substantially greater share of these benefits. If the cost of preserving Grand Central Terminal were spread evenly across the entire population of the city of New York, the burden per person would be in cents per year—a minor cost appellees would surely concede for the benefit accrued. Instead, however, appellees would impose the entire cost of several million dollars per year on Penn Central. But it is precisely this sort of discrimination that the Fifth Amendment prohibits.

REVIEW AND DISCUSSION QUESTIONS

1. According to the Court, the restrictions on Penn Central's development of Grand Central Station are not a "taking" within the meaning of the Fifth Amendment. Explain why. On what grounds do Justices Rehnquist and his colleagues dissent? Who is right about this and why?

2. Zoning restrictions, typically, do not violate the Fifth Amendment, although they limit what one may do with one's property. Why is this? Are the restrictions on Penn Central's development plans analogous to zoning restrictions?

3. Has Penn Central, in your view, been treated unfairly? When and under what circumstances should government restrictions on property development involve compensation for the owners?

4. Are municipal efforts to protect historic buildings a legitimate interference with private property? What arguments can be given for and against statutes mandating the preservation of historic buildings?

15

PRIVATE AGREEMENTS: THE LAW OF CONTRACT

In any socioeconomic system based on private property and market exchange, agreements between private parties will play an extensive and important role. It is not surprising, then, that contract law is a main branch of the civil law. Whereas tort law concerns violations of various legally recognized duties, in contracts the parties themselves, in large measure, determine through mutual agreement what their obligations toward one another will be. By contrast with the criminal law, contractual obligations are not only self-imposed but also privately enforced: litigation begins only when one party to the contract believes that the other has failed to live up to the terms of the agreement.

As with property law, philosophical disagreements over the moral basis of contract, and the nature of the obligation that contracts create, pervade legal debates over the adjudication of particular cases and the interpretation of contract law in general. These disagreements are reflected in the readings that follow. Morris Cohen explains the historical context of contract law and emphasizes its institutional aspects. Although contracts are private agreements, they have broader ramifications and grow into social and legal institutions. Society, therefore, has a legitimate interest in imposing certain standards and shaping contracts in ways that meet its goals. Charles Fried stands in an opposed tradition. He sees contractual obligation as rooted in promise. In his view, it is the moral force of promising—not social utility—that is the basis of contract law and that should guide the way the courts adjudicate contract disputes.

This contrast of perspectives plays out in the cases that follow. The *Baby M* case concerns the legality of surrogacy contracts. Although no one doubts that both parties to this case intentionally entered into a formal compact, the question remains whether the law should recognize and uphold their consensual agreement as a binding contract. The famous *Lochner* case, and the cases that accompany it, deal with the right of the government to impose limits and restrictions on employment contracts into which private parties have entered.

The Basis of Contract

Morris Raphael Cohen

Contract law is complicated, and its details concern the conditions that must be met for a contract to be valid and legally enforceable as well as, of course, the various remedies available to those damaged by a breach of contract. In this essay, however, Morris Raphael Cohen discusses the nature of contract as a legal and social institution from a broader historical and philosophical perspective. After examining the social and historical roots of contract and assessing the political and economic arguments for what he calls contractualism, Cohen emphasizes the extent to which contract law can be seen as a branch of public law. Because the law must have regard for the general and institutional effects of classes of transactions, it must, when settling disputes, be prepared to go beyond the original intention of the contracting parties.

The nature of contract has been much discussed by lawyers interested in specific technical doctrines, and by moralists, economists, and political theorists interested in general social philosophy. There is still need for some effort to combine these points of view. The bearings of general philosophy become more definite through its applications, and the meaning of a technical doctrine receives illumination when we see it in the light of those wider ideas of which it is the logical outcome.

This large and important task is obviously beyond the limits of a short paper. But a few suggestions may indicate something of the scope of the problem.

1. THE SOCIAL ROOTS OF CONTRACT

One of the most influential of modern saws is Maine's famous dictum that the progress of the law has been from status to contract. It has generally been understood as stating not only a historical generalization but also a judgment of sound policy—that a legal system wherein rights and duties are determined by the agreement of the parties is preferable to a system wherein they are determined by "status."

. . . That Maine's generalization is not a universal and necessary law, he himself recognized in his treatment of feudal land tenure. The rights and duties of sovereign and subject, of homage or fealty and protecting lordship, were contractual in the early Middle Ages, and gradually ceased to be so as they became customary and were later replaced by the legislation of the modern national states. It is also true . . . that the modern state has, in all civilized countries, been steadily increasing the scope of its functions, so that men now do things by virtue of their status as citizens and taxpayers which formerly they did by voluntary agreement. One only needs to mention the fields of charity and education to make this obvious. Moreover, in many relations in which men are more or less free to enter into contracts, such as that between insurer and insured, landlord and tenant, employer and employee, shipper and carrier, the terms of the agreement are more and more being fixed by law, so that the entering into these relations has something analogous to the entering into the relation of marriage, trusteeship, or public office. The specific rights and duties are not fixed by agreement, though the assumption of the relations is more or less voluntary.

Nevertheless there is enough truth in Maine's observation to warrant a more discriminating attitude to it than that of complete acceptance or complete rejection.

Looking at the matter macroscopically rather than microscopically, there can be little doubt that legally binding agreements or promises play a smaller part in the earlier history of all known peoples. The development of contract is largely an incident of commercial and industrial enterprises that involve a greater anticipation of the future than is necessary in a simpler or more primitive economy. In the latter the solidarity of relatively self-sufficient family groups and the fear of departing from accustomed ways limit individual initiative as well as the scope and importance of what can be achieved by deliberate agreements or bargains. In some respects, however, less developed societies resort more than we do to contracts or compacts and enforce promises that we no longer enforce. Thus they preserve peace not by organized police or standing armies, but by agreements like our present treaties of peace between nations; and promises to the gods, which are now matters of individual conscience, used to be enforced by the community as a whole because it feared the undiscriminating effects of divine wrath. . . .

2. THE POLITICAL THEORY OF CONTRACTUALISM

Contractualism in the law, that is, the view that in an ideally desirable system of law all obligation would arise only out of the will of the individual contracting freely, rests not only on the will theory of contract but also on the political doctrine that all restraint is evil and that the government is best which governs least. This in turn is connected with the classical economic optimism that there is a sort of preëstablished harmony between the good of all and the pursuit by each of his own selfish economic gain. . . .

The argument that a régime of free contract assures the greatest amount of liberty for all is characteristic of the eighteenth century philosophy of the Enlightenment and is still essential to the faith of Jeffersonian democracy behind our bills of rights. The older Calvinistic argument for government rested on the need of restraining the wickedness of man (due to the corruption of the flesh) by rules and magistrates deriving their power from God. Against this the deistic and bourgeois Enlightenment developed the contrary view, that men are inherently good and that their dark deeds have been due to the corruption and superstition brought about by tyrants and priests. As we get rid of the latter, the original, benevolent nature of man asserts itself and history indeed shows a gradual but steady progress in the direction of freedom. It was natural for the representatives of the growing commercial and industrial interests to view the state, controlled as it had been by landed barons and prelates (lords temporal and spiritual), as exclusively an instrument of oppression, and necessarily evil. But their argument overshot its mark. They forgot that not only industry but also the whole life of civilization depends on the feeling of security that the protection of the government or organized community affords. . . .

Since what we want generally seems to us good, freedom, as the removal of obstacles to achievement, is a necessary part or condition of this good. But mere freedom as absence of restraint, without positive power to achieve what we deem good, is empty and of no real value. The freedom to make a million dollars is not worth a cent to one who is out of work. Nor is the freedom to starve, or to work for wages less than the minimum of subsistence, one that any rational being can prize—whatever learned courts may say to the contrary.

The tragic fallacy of supposing that mere absence of restraint or of other temporary evil can be an absolute good is poignantly illustrated when men, chafing at oppressive work or company, suppose that mere release will make them for-ever happy. When this release comes we may find ourselves abjectly miserable, not knowing what to do with ourselves. We then look for some other work that will absorb our attention or other company to fill our interests. So all rev-olutionists complaining against the oppression of government must as soon as they are suc-cessful—indeed, even to attain such success—set up a new government. The new work, the new company, or the new government must prove more congenial or beneficent if we are to escape or mitigate the human inclination to re-gret the struggle and the pain that brought about the change. . . .

In the United States, the Jeffersonian dem-ocrats fought against the power of the govern-ment both in the nation and in their states. They feared that the merchants and the large landowners of the seaboard, who had controlled the older states, would control the central gov-ernment. To limit the power of government by a system of checks and balances was therefore the way to assure liberty from oppression. So long as the country was sparsely settled and our people remained for the most part a nation of independent freeholders, this was a workable theory. It never, however, was carried out con-sistently. For the temptation to use the govern-ment for positive ends, such as education or the safeguarding of our commercial interests in the West and on the seas, could not be resisted even by Jefferson himself. In the last forty or fifty years the representatives of large industry have invoked this theory of the bills of rights to limit legislative power to regulate industry in the in-terests not only of the workers but also of the future manhood and womanhood of the nation. The same group, however, that protests against a child labor law, or against any minimum wage law intended to insure a minimum standard of decent living, is constantly urging the gov-ernment to protect industry by tariffs. Clearly, the theory of *laissez faire*, of complete non-interference of the government in business, is not really held consistently by those who so fre-quently invoke it. A government so limited in its powers that it could do no harm would be useless, since it could do no good. . . .

THE ECONOMIC ARGUMENT FOR CONTRACTUALISM

When the political argument is closely pressed, it is found to rest on the economic one that a regime in which contracts are freely made and generally enforced gives greater scope to indi-vidual initiative and thus promotes the greatest wealth of a nation. . . .

The clearest and most convincing statement of the case for the classical theory of free com-petition is that of Mr. Justice Holmes. Let us, he urges, get behind the fact of ownership, and look at the processes of production and con-sumption of goods. The men who achieve great private fortunes do not consume very much of this social wealth. Their fortunes denote rather power to control the flow of goods. And who is better fitted to command this process of pro-duction and distribution than the man who wins it in the competition of the market? The as-sumption behind this is that the man who suc-ceeds in winning a fortune (not, it should be noted, the man who receives it by inheritance) has succeeded because he has been able to an-ticipate the largest effective demand for goods and to organize the most economical way of pro-ducing them.

One weakness of this argument is that it ig-nores the frightful waste involved in competi-tion. The community as a whole ultimately pays the cost, in labor and capital goods (including their extensive sales and advertising forces), of all the economic enterprises that are allowed to compete and fail. Moreover, the greatest profits do not always come with the greatest produc-tivity. There are monopoly profits, like the un-earned increment of land value, that clearly do not arise from productivity of the owners, and there are monopoly profits that are swelled by reducing the output, so that fishermen, wheat and cotton growers, and other producers are often advised to do this. Neither can free com-petition prevent the paradoxical situation that our economic crises repeatedly show, namely, an overstocked food market and general destitu-tion from inability to buy. The latter is certainly in part due to the fact that, under unrestrained competition, wages and the return for the labor of the farmer are not sufficient to enable the vast majority of the people to buy enough of what they have produced. Thus, some of the supposedly greater efficiency of private over public business, to the extent that it involves lower real wages, is detrimental to the general welfare. The latter depends not only on the mass of production, but also on the kind of goods produced, on the conditions under which men work, and on the ways in which the product is distributed.

For these reasons it is rare nowadays to find any advocates of a régime of free competition except among certain lawyers and judges who use it to oppose regulation of the "labor contract" by the state. The general consensus among business men has demanded the organization of our Interstate Commerce Commission and Federal Trade Commission, our state railway and public service commissions, our state insurance and industrial commissions, and other administrative bodies that limit and regulate certain essential business contracts. Also the great captains of industry are everywhere trying to eliminate free competition. And those who talk about "keeping the government out of business" are the last to desire that the government shall not help or protect, by proper rules, the business in which they are involved. The differences that divide men in this respect concern the questions of what interests should be protected and who should control the government. . . .

EXCESSES OF CONTRACTUALISM

As the result of the various forces that have thus supported the cult of contractualism there has been developed in all modern European countries (and in those which derive from them) a tendency to include within the categories of contract transactions in which there is no negotiation, bargain, or genuinely voluntary agreement. Let us consider a few typical situations.

A citizen going to work boards a street car and drops a coin in the conductor's or motorman's box. This, or the buying of a ticket, is treated as a contract, and courts and jurists speak of its "terms" and of the rights and duties under it. No one claims that there is any actual "meeting of minds" of the passenger and the street railway corporation. There is no actual offer or acceptance—certainly no bargaining between the two parties. The rights and duties of both are prescribed by law and are the same no matter what, if anything, goes on in the passenger's mind, or in the corporation's, if it has any mind. Moreover, the liabilities of the railway corporation to the passenger are in many circumstances exactly the same even if he does not buy any ticket. Obviously, therefore, we have here a situation in which the law regulates the relation between different parties and it is pure fiction to speak of it as growing out of any agreement of the wills of the parties.

A more serious confusion of fact and fiction occurs when we speak of the "labor contract." There is, in fact, no real bargaining between the modern large employer (say the United States Steel Corporation) and its individual employees. The workingman has no real power to negotiate or confer with the corporation as to the terms under which he will agree to work. He either decides to work under the conditions and schedule of wages fixed by the employer or else he is out of a job. If he is asked to sign any paper he does so generally without any knowledge of what it contains and without any real freedom to refuse. For we cannot freely change our crafts, and if a man is a weaver or shoe laster, he is dependent on the local carpet or shoe factory for his livelihood, especially so if he has a family, which is not as mobile as money. The greater economic power of the employer exercises a compulsion as real *in fact* as any now recognized by law as duress. The extreme form of such duress, the highwayman's pistol, still leaves us with the freedom to accept the terms offered or else take the consequences. But such choice is surely the very opposite of what men value as freedom.

Clearly, then, the element of consent on the part of the employee may be a minor one in the relation of employment—a relation much more aptly and realistically described by the old law as that between master and servant. Down to the end of the eighteenth century this relation was in fact regulated by the government. Wages used to be regularly fixed by justices of the peace under the authority of parliamentary enactments, and even the beer that the master was to serve to the servant with his bread had its strength regulated by law. Any demand by workmen for higher wages or any accession to such demands on the part of masters was a violation of the law. Yet courts now speak as if the effort on the part of the state to regulate wages were an unheard of interference with the eternal laws of nature. . . . [But] only after the Civil War [was] the doctrine [invented] that the "right *to* contract" [is a constitutionally protected property right]. . . .

The spread of contractualistic notions shows itself in the tendency to speak of marriage as itself a contract. Now there are, usually, solemn promises exchanged when the marriage ceremony is performed and there may be agreements as to dowry and other property rights. But the specific legal relations of husband and wife are by no means determined thereby. These relations are entirely fixed by law and the parties to it cannot vary its terms, just as they cannot vary the terms of their obligations to any children they may bring into the world. If there is no sense in speaking of the rights and duties between parents and minor children as contractual, neither is there in speaking of the relations of husband and wife as contractual. The fact that an act is more or less voluntary does not make its legal consequences contractual.

The extreme of contractualistic thought was reached when European publicists of the eighteenth century and American judges of the nineteenth century spoke of the social compact or contract as the basis of society and of all law.

I do not want to add to the many (in fact, too many) refutations of the social-contract theory. . . . The tradition of Hebrew history and Greek philosophy that bases government and law upon covenant or agreement has had a salutary influence in challenging all law to justify itself at the bar of reason. It is good to ask of any law whether it is such as rational beings would adopt if they wanted to establish a society. Nevertheless, there are obviously insuperable difficulties in trying to derive all legal obligations from contract. Children have certain obligations to their parents that are not contractual. Indeed, we may well ask, "Why should we obey laws that our ancestors and not we agreed to?" We may even go

further and ask, "Why *should* we keep agreements that we made some time ago when we were younger and less experienced or wise than we are now?" If there is any rational answer to either of these queries, it must take the form of indicating some social good or necessity that is served by our keeping our promises. But if so, why may not the same social good or necessity be served by making children obey and at times support their parents, or by making those who hold property pay for sewage, education, and other communal necessities, even if they do not agree? The merits of the issue are not really affected by introducing a fictional contract.

These attempts to stretch the category of contract err in failing to recognize a certain necessary social solidarity, especially that of any generation with its ancestors, as not the outcome but the very basis of contract itself. . . .

3. CONTRACT AND SOVEREIGNTY

. . . This task of formulating a comprehensive theory of contract, that shall do justice to its many sources and various phases, is one that I shall not undertake here. But I wish to emphasize certain considerations that supplement the theories discussed so far.

The cardinal error of the traditional individualistic theories of contract is their way of speaking as if the law does nothing but put into effect what the contracting parties originally agreed on. The best that can be said for this is that it may sometimes be true. But even if that were more generally the case, we should still have to attach more importance to the factor of enforcement than the prevailing theories do. The fact that two people agree to do something not prohibited by the public criminal law and carry out their agreement, or fail to do so, does not of itself bring the law of contract into being. A large number of important agreements, even in business, as in social, political, and religious matters, are left to be directly regulated by other agencies, such as the prevailing sense of honor, individual conscience, or the like. It is an error then to speak of the law of contract as if it merely allows people to do things. The absence of criminal prohibition will do that much. The law of contract plays a more positive role in social life, and this is seen when the organized force of the state is brought into play to compel the loser of a suit to pay or to do something. Doubtless most people live up to their promises or agreements either through force of custom or because it is in the long run more advantageous to do so. But there can be no doubt that the possibility of the law's being invoked against us if we fail to do so is an actual factor in the situation. Even if the transactions that come to be litigated are atypical, their judicial determination is still influential in molding the legal custom. For the ruling in a case that departs from the mode supports or opposes some direction of variation and thus fixes the direction of growth of what becomes customary. The fact, then, that in the general run of transactions people do not resort to actual litigation, is certainly in part due to the fact that they know in a general way what will be the outcome of that process. . . .

From this point of view the law of contract may be viewed as a subsidiary branch of public law, as a body of rules according to which the sovereign power of the state will be exercised as between the parties to a more or less voluntary transaction.

The first rules of public law, generally called constitutional law, regulate the conduct of the chief state officials by indicating the scope of their powers. Within this scope legislatures use their discretion or wisdom to enact certain statutes; and judges, by following precedents, elaborate certain rules as to when and how the power of the state shall be exercised. Among these rules we have the laws of partnership, leases, agreements for services, contracts of surety or insurances, and the like. Now, just as the rules of constitutional law are general and leave blanks to be filled in by the legislature, courts, and administrative officials (whose rules and habitual practices are law to those over whom they have authority), so do the rules of contracts allow men to formulate for themselves, within the prescribed limits, certain rights and duties governing certain transactions between them; and when the parties have thus formulated their agreements, the latter become

a part of the law of the land, just as much as do treaties between our nation and others, compacts between states, contracts between a state or division thereof and a private corporation, or the grant of a pension to the widow of a former president. When a state or a municipality makes a contract with a public service corporation for gas or transportation at a given price to the consumer, no one doubts that such an agreement is part of the legal order. But so are private agreements that the law sanctions. Thus, when a trade union makes an agreement with an association of employers, or even with a single employer, the result is law not only for those "represented" at the signing of the papers but for all those who wish to enter the industry at any time that the agreement is in force. This is in general true of all more or less permanently organized partnerships, companies, corporations, or other groups; and enforceable agreements between individuals, no matter on how limited a scale, are similarly part of the law by virtue of the general rules of state action that apply to them.

If, then, the law of contract confers sovereignty on one party over another (by putting the state's forces at the disposal of the former), the question naturally arises: For what purposes and under what circumstances shall that power be conferred? Adherents of the classical theory have recognized that legal enforcement serves to protect and encourage transactions that require credit or reliance on the promises of others. But we also need care that the power of the state be not used for unconscionable purposes, such as helping those who exploit the dire need or weaknesses of their fellows. Usury laws have recognized that he who is under economic necessity is not really free. To put no restrictions on the freedom to contract would logically lead not to a maximum of individual liberty but to contracts of slavery, into which, experience shows, men will "voluntarily" enter under economic pressure—a pressure that is largely conditioned by the laws of property. Regulations, therefore, involving some restrictions on the freedom to contract are as necessary to real liberty as traffic restrictions are necessary to assure real freedom in the general use of our highways.

From this point of view, the movement to standardize the forms of contract—even to the extent of prohibiting variations or the right to "contract out"—is not to be viewed as a reaction to, but rather as the logical outcome of, a régime of real liberty of contract. It is a utilization of the lessons of experience to strengthen those forms which best serve as channels through which the life of the community can flow most freely. . . .

The function of the law of contract in promoting the standardization of transactions is at all times an important one. And the more developed and complicated transactions become, the more there is need for eliminating as much uncertainty as possible by standardization. This is certainly true today. Consider the case of a man who wants to publish a book, to buy an insurance policy or a letter of credit, to ship his goods or to store them in a warehouse, to lease an apartment, to have gas or electricity or telephone service supplied to him, to mortgage his house, or to obtain a surety bond—in all these and in many other relations his freedom to contract is facilitated by standard forms molded by past law and custom. Naturally, standardized contracts, like other laws, serve the interests of some better than those of others; and the question of justice thus raised demands the attention not only of legislatures but also of courts that have to interpret these standard forms and of administrative bodies that have to supervise their enforcement. In a changing social order these standards or forms must grow or become modified; and to make them function more serviceably it is not sufficient to wait until trouble develops and is brought before the courts for adjudication. The need of intelligent anticipation that can be effected by initiating inquiries cannot be met by our traditional court procedure, and this has compelled the joining of administrative with judicial power in the hands of bodies like the Interstate Commerce Commission and our various state public service commissions.

A realization of the growth of standard forms suggests the introduction of a point of view in the study of contract similar to what has been called the institutional approach in the study of economics. . . . A similar change of approach in the study of the law of contract means beginning not with the bargaining between the two parties, but with the legal form or way of doing things, with the established institution within which negotiation is possible.

. . . Contracts are voluntary, fixed, and temporary, while institutions are socially hereditary, grow, and last longer. Yet . . . contracts, especially collective ones, grow into institutions. The marriage relation shows the passage from one to the other. . . . [We should reject] the absolute separation of freedom of contract from government regulation, the former conceived as purely negative and the latter as purely arbitrary. In actual life real freedom to do anything, in art as in politics, depends upon acceptance of the rules of our enterprise. As has been remarked elsewhere, the rules of the sonnet do not hamper real poets but rather help weak ones. Real or positive freedom depends upon opportunities supplied by institutions that involve legal regulation. Our legislative forces may be narrowly partisan and the rules may be poor ones. But this can be remedied not by the abrogation of all rules but by the institution of better ones.

For this reason the notion that government rests on contract—a notion that runs through both our Hebrew and Greek heritage, and largely conforms to our peculiar American experience—contains a partial truth that should not be utterly disregarded because of some poor arguments in its behalf. If we discard the notion that *all* organized society began in a voluntary contract—a proposition that few have advanced as a literal truth—we may yet recognize that as men become more enlightened they can treat government as if it were a contractual affair, that is, judge the services of governmental rules by the price we pay for them. The great men who founded the rationalistic legal and political tradition of the Enlightenment, Althusius, Grotius, Leibniz, and Locke, may have underestimated the force of tradition, but in treating governmental rights and duties under the categories of contract, they helped to liberalize and humanize our international and our criminal law, as well as the law of private and commercial transactions.

There is no inherent reason for rejecting the view that the roots of the law of contract are many rather than one. Agreements and promises are enforced to enable people to rely on them as a rule and thus make the path of enterprise more secure; but in this connection the law must also go beyond the original intention of the parties to settle controversies as to the distribution of gains and losses that the parties did not anticipate in the same way. Some recognition must always be given to the will or intention of those who made the contract, but the law must always have regard for the *general* effects of classes of transactions, and it cannot free men from the necessity of acting at their peril when they do not know the consequences that the law will attach to their acts—and this needs to be emphasized in any attempt to formulate a rational theory. The law is a going concern and like all social institutions is governed by habit. It therefore will continue to enforce promises and agreements, for no better reason than that they have been enforced and there is no sufficient countervailing consideration to force or justify a break with the established habit that has become the basis of social expectancies. Legal and other habits are not always deliberately formed to serve a definite purpose. Certain forms or ceremonies arise under special circumstances but continue to appeal to us through the principle of economy of effort: it is generally easier to use the existing forms than to break with them and adopt new ones. Of course old forms may become inconvenient or positive hindrances. They are then whittled away by pious fiction or violently changed by revolutionary legislation. In general, however, the ancient truth that men are creatures of habit will put us on guard against the vain assumption that we can get rid of formalism in the law of contract or anywhere else. We may flatter ourselves on getting rid of seal or other ancient binding ceremony. But we must remember that these forms seemed as naturally obligatory to our fathers as the signing of papers or the administering of oaths seem to us today.

In arguing for their indispensability we may recognize that not all forms are perfectly congenial or responsive to the need of the life that pulses through them. And as men become more enlightened they become more ready to discard, as well as employ, diverse instruments or vessels. Wisdom is not attained either by blind acceptance or blind rejection. We need a discriminating evaluation of what exists and what is possible.

REVIEW AND DISCUSSION QUESTIONS

1. Cohen refers to Maine's thesis that there has been an evolution in the law from status to contract. What does this mean, and to what extent is it true?

2. What is the political theory of contractualism? What is the economic argument for contractualism? What reservations does Cohen have about both of them? More generally, what does he see as the "excesses" of contractualism? Can more be said on behalf of contractualism than Cohen says?

3. What does Cohen mean when he writes that "the law of contract may be viewed as a subsidiary branch of public law"? What are the implications of this? What would an "institutional" approach to the study of contract involve?

4. What is important about the standardization of contracts? How can standardization and, more generally, the acceptance of rules promote freedom?

Contract as Promise

Charles Fried

Many writers emphasize the social and institutional aspects of contract law. As noted earlier, contracts are private agreements that have broad ramifications and evolve into social institutions. Society, therefore, needs to try to impose standards and shape contracts to meet its goals. The conclusion these writers draw is that the law, rather than simply and neutrally upholding private agreements freely arrived at by the contracting parties, imposes on them legal obligations based on society's own needs.

In this selection from his book Contract as Promise, *Charles Fried, professor of law at Harvard University and former U.S. solicitor general, upholds a different view of contract, which sees contractual obligation as based on the moral force of promise rather than social or institutional utility. He analyzes the nature of promise and promissory obligation and defends his view of contract as promise against various objections.*

INTRODUCTION: THE LIFE OF CONTRACT

The promise principle, which in this book I argue is the moral basis of contract law, is that principle by which persons may impose on themselves obligations where none existed before.

Security of the person, stability of property, and the obligation of contract were for David Hume the bases of a civilized society. Hume expressed the liberal, individualistic temper of his time and place in treating respect for person, property, and contract as the self-evident foundations of law and justice. Through the greater part of our history, our constitutional law and politics have proceeded on these same premises. In private law particularly these premises have taken root and ramified in the countless particulars necessary to give them substance. The law of property defines the boundaries of our rightful possessions, while the law of torts seeks to make us whole against violations of those boundaries, as well as against violations of the natural boundaries of our physical person. Contract law ratifies and enforces our joint ventures beyond those boundaries. Thus the law of torts and the law of property recognize our rights as individuals in our persons, in our labor, and in some definite portion of the external world, while the law of contracts facilitates our disposing of these rights on terms that seem best to us. The regime of contract law, which respects the dispositions individuals make of their rights, carries to its natural conclusion the liberal premise that individuals have rights. And the will theory of contract, which sees contractual obligations as essentially self-imposed, is a fair implication of liberal individualism.

This conception of contractual obligation as essentially self-imposed has been under increasing pressure over the last fifty years. One essentially historicist line of attack points out that until the eighteenth century communal controls, whether of families, guilds, local communities, or of the general government, hardly conceded enough discretion to individuals over their labor or property to give the liberal conception much to work on. And beginning in the last century and proceeding apace since, the state, unions, corporations, and other intermediate institutions have again withdrawn large areas of concern from individual control and thus from the scope of purely contractual arrangements. That there has been such an ebb and flow of collective control seems fairly clear. But from the fact that contract emerged only in modern times as a principal form of social organization, it does not follow that therefore the concept of contract as promise (which is indeed a centerpiece of nineteenth-century economic liberalism) was itself the invention of the industrial revolution; whatever the accepted scope for contract, the principle of fidelity to one's word is an ancient one. Still less does it follow that the validity, the rightness of the promise principle, of self-imposed obligation, depended on its acceptance in that earlier period, or that now, as the acceptance is in doubt, the validity of the principle is under a cloud. The validity of a moral, like that of a mathematical truth, does not depend on fashion or favor.

A more insidious set of criticisms denies the coherence or the independent viability of the promise principle. Legal obligation can be imposed only by the community, and so in imposing it the community must be pursuing its goals and imposing its standards, rather than neutrally endorsing those of the contracting parties. These lines of attack—found recently in the writings of legal scholars such as Patrick Atiyah, Lawrence Friedman, Grant Gilmore, Morton Horwitz, Duncan Kennedy, Anthony Kronman, and Ian Macneil, as well as in philosophical writings—will provide the foil for much of my affirmative argument. Here I shall just set out their main thrust so that my readers may be clear what I am reacting against.

Not all promises are legally enforced, and of those which are, different categories receive differing degrees of legal recognition: some only if in writing, others between certain kinds of parties, still others only to the extent that they have been relied on and that reliance has caused measurable injury. And some arrangements that are not promissory at all—preliminary negotiations, words mistakenly understood as promises, schemes of cooperation—are assimilated to the contractual regime. Finally, even among legally binding arrangements that are initiated by agreement, certain ones are singled out and made subject to a set of rules that often have little to do with that agreement. Marriage is the most obvious example, but contracts of employment, insurance, or carriage exhibit these features as well. Thus the conception of the will binding itself—the conception at the heart of the promise principle—is neither necessary nor sufficient to contractual obligation. Indeed it is a point of some of these critics (for example, Friedman, Gilmore, Macneil) that the search for a central or unifying principle of contract is a will-o'-the-wisp, an illusion typical of the ill-defined but much excoriated vice of conceptualism. These critics hold that the law fashions contractual obligation as a way to do justice between, and impose social policy through, parties who have come into a variety of relations with each other. Only some of these relations start in an explicit agreement, and even if they do, the governing considerations of justice and policy are not bound by the terms or implications of that agreement. . . .

CONTRACT AS PROMISE

It is a first principle of liberal political morality that we be secure in what is ours—so that our persons and property not be open to exploitation by others, and that from a sure foundation we may express our will and expend our powers in the world. By these powers we may create good things or low, useful articles or luxuries, things extraordinary or banal, and we will be judged accordingly—as saintly or mean, skillful or ordinary, industrious and fortunate or debased, friendly and kind or cold and inhuman. But whatever we accomplish and however that accomplishment is judged, morality requires that we respect the person and property of others, leaving them free to make their lives as we are left free to make ours. This is the liberal ideal.

. . . [W]hen we forbear to bend some external object to our use because of its natural preciousness we use it still, for it is to our judgment of its value that we respond, our own conception of the good that we pursue. Only other persons are not available to us in this way—they alone share our self-consciousness, our power of self-determination; thus to use them as if they were merely part of external nature is to poison the source of the moral power we enjoy. But others *are* part of the external world, and by denying ourselves access to their persons and powers, we drastically shrink the scope of our efficacy. So it was a crucial moral discovery that free men may yet freely serve each others' purposes: the discovery that beyond the fear of reprisal or the hope of reciprocal favor, morality itself might be enlisted to assure not only that you respect me and mine but that you actively serve my purposes. When my confidence in your assistance derives from my conviction that you will do what is right (not just what is prudent), then I trust you, and trust becomes a powerful tool for our working our mutual wills in the world. So remarkable a tool is trust that in the end we pursue it for its own sake; we prefer doing things cooperatively when we might have relied on fear or interest or worked alone.

The device that gives trust its sharpest, most palpable form is promise. By promising we put in another man's hands a new power to accomplish his will, though only a moral power: What he sought to do alone he may now expect to do with our promised help, and to give him this new facility was our very purpose in promising. By promising we transform a choice that was morally neutral into one that is morally compelled. Morality, which must be permanent and beyond our particular will if the grounds for our willing are to be secure, is itself invoked, molded to allow us better to work that particular will. Morality then serves modest, humdrum ends: We make appointments, buy and sell, harnessing this loftiest of all forces.

What is a promise, that by my words I should make wrong what before was morally indifferent? A promise is a communication—usually verbal; it says something. But how can my saying something put a moral charge on a choice that before was morally neutral? Well, by my misleading you, or by lying. Is lying not the very paradigm of doing wrong by speaking? But this won't do, for a promise puts the moral charge on a *potential* act—the wrong is done later, when the promise is not kept—while a lie is a wrong committed at the time of its utterance. Both wrongs abuse trust, but in different ways. When I speak I commit myself to the truth of my utterance, but when I promise I commit myself to *act*, later. Though these two wrongs are thus quite distinct there has been a persistent tendency to run them together by treating a promise as a lie after all, but a particular kind of lie: a lie about one's intentions. Consider this case:

1. I sell you a house, retaining an adjacent vacant lot. At the time of our negotiations, I state that I intend to build a home for myself on that lot. What if several years later I sell the lot to a person who builds a gas station on it? What if I sell it only one month later? What if I am already negotiating for its sale as a gas station at the time I sell the house to you?

If I was already negotiating to sell the lot for a gas station at the time of my statement to you, I have wronged you. I have lied to you about the state of my intentions, and this is as much a lie as a lie about the state of the plumbing. If, however, I sell the lot many years later, I do you no wrong. There are no grounds for saying I lied about my intentions; I have just changed my mind. Now if I had *promised* to use the lot only as a residence, the situation would be different. Promising is more than just truthfully reporting my present intentions, for I may be free to change my mind, as I am not free to break my promise.

Let us take it as given here that lying is wrong and so that it is wrong to obtain benefits or cause harm by lying (including lying about one's intentions). It does not at all follow that to obtain a benefit or cause harm by breaking a promise is also wrong. That my act procures me a benefit or causes harm all by itself proves nothing. If I open a restaurant near your hotel and prosper as I draw your guests away from the standard hotel fare you offer, this benefit I draw from you places me under no obligation to you. I should make restitution only if I benefit *unjustly*, which I do if I deceive you—as when I lie to you about my intentions in example 1. But where is the injustice if I honestly intend to keep my promise at the time of making it, and later change my mind? . . .

Perhaps the statement of intention in promising is binding because we not only foresee reliance, we invite it: We intend the promisee to rely on the promise. Yet even this will not do. If I invite reliance on my stated intention, then that is all I invite. Certainly I may hope and intend, in example 1, that you buy my house on the basis of what I have told you, but why does that hope bind me to do more than state my intention honestly? And that intention and invitation are quite compatible with my later changing my mind. In every case, of course, I should weigh the harm I will do if I do change my mind. If I am a doctor and I know you will rely on me to be part of an outing on which someone may fall ill, I should certainly weigh the harm that may come about if that reliance is disappointed. Indeed I should weigh that harm even if you do not rely on me, but are foolish enough not to have made a provision for a doctor. Yet in none of these instances am I bound as I would be had I promised.

A promise invokes trust in my future actions, not merely in my present sincerity. We need to isolate an additional element, over and above benefit, reliance, and the communication of intention. That additional element must *commit* me, and commit me to more than the truth of some statement. That additional element has so far eluded our analysis.

It has eluded us, I believe, because there is a real puzzle about how we can commit ourselves to a course of conduct that absent our commitment is morally neutral. . . . The way out of the puzzle is to recognize the bootstrap quality of the argument: To have force in *a particular case* promises must be assumed to have force generally. Once that general assumption is made, the effects we intentionally produce by a particular promise may be morally attributed to us. This recognition is not as paradoxical as its abstract statement here may make it seem. It lies, after all, behind every conventional structure: games, institutions and practices, and most important, language.

Let us put to one side the question of how a convention comes into being, or of when and why we are morally bound to comply with its terms, while we look briefly at what a convention is and how it does its work. Take the classical example of a game. What the players do is defined by a system of rules—sometimes quite vague and informal, sometimes elaborate and codified. These rules apply only to the players—that is, to persons who invoke them. These rules are a human invention, and their consequences (castling, striking out, winning, losing) can be understood only in terms of the rules. The players may have a variety of motives for playing (profit, fun, maybe even duty to fellow players who need participants). A variety of judgments

are applicable to the players—they may be deemed skillful, imaginative, bold, honest, or dishonest—but these judgments and motives too can be understood only in the context of the game. For instance, you can cheat only by breaking rules to which you pretend to conform. . . .

Promising too is a very general convention—though less general than language, of course, since promising is itself a use of language. The convention of promising (like that of language) has a very general purpose under which we may bring an infinite set of particular purposes. In order that I be as free as possible, that my will have the greatest possible range consistent with the similar will of others, it is necessary that there be a way in which I may commit myself. It is necessary that I be able to make nonoptional a course of conduct that would otherwise be optional for me. By doing this I can facilitate the projects of others, because I can make it possible for those others to count on my future conduct, and thus those others can pursue more intricate, more far-reaching projects. If it is my purpose, my will that others be able to count on me in the pursuit of their endeavor, it is essential that I be able to deliver myself into their hands more firmly than where they simply predict my future course. Thus the possibility of commitment permits an act of generosity on my part, permits me to pursue a project whose content is that *you* be permitted to pursue *your* project. But of course this purely altruistic motive is not the only motive worth facilitating. More central to our concern is the situation where we facilitate each other's projects, where the gain is reciprocal. Schematically the situation looks like this:

You want to accomplish purpose *A* and I want to accomplish purpose *B*. Neither of us can succeed without the cooperation of the other. Thus I want to be able to commit myself to help you achieve *A* so that you will commit yourself to help me achieve *B*.

Now if *A* and *B* are objects or actions that can be transferred simultaneously there is no need for commitment. As I hand over *A* you hand over *B*, and we are both satisfied. But very few things are like that. We need a device to permit a trade over time: to allow me to do *A* for you when you need it, in the confident belief that you will do *B* for me when I need it. Your commitment puts your future performance into my hands in the present just as my commitment puts my future performance into your hands. A future exchange is transformed into a present exchange. And in order to accomplish this all we need is a conventional device which we both invoke, which you know I am invoking when I invoke it, which I know that you know I am invoking, and so on.

The only mystery about this is the mystery that surrounds increasing autonomy by providing means for restricting it. But really this is a pseudomystery. The restrictions involved in promising are restrictions undertaken just in order to increase one's options in the long run, and thus are perfectly consistent with the principle of autonomy—consistent with a respect for one's own autonomy and the autonomy of others. . . .

THE MORAL OBLIGATION OF PROMISE

Once I have invoked the institution of promising, why exactly is it wrong for me then to break my promise? . . .

The obligation to keep a promise is grounded not in arguments of utility but in respect for individual autonomy and in trust. . . . An individual is morally bound to keep his promises because he has intentionally invoked a convention whose function it is to give grounds—moral grounds—for another to expect the promised performance. To renege is to abuse a confidence he was free to invite or not, and which he intentionally did invite. To abuse that confidence now is like (but only *like*) lying: the abuse of a shared social institution that is intended to invoke the bonds of trust. A liar and a promise-breaker each *use* another person. In both speech and promising there is an invitation to the other to trust, to make himself vulnerable; the liar and the promise-breaker then abuse that trust. The obligation to keep a promise is thus similar to

but more constraining than the obligation to tell the truth. To avoid lying you need only believe in the truth of what you say when you say it, but a promise binds into the future, well past the moment when the promise is made. There will, of course, be great social utility to a general regime of trust and confidence in promise and truthfulness. But this just shows that a regime of mutual respect allows men and women to accomplish what in a jungle of unrestrained self-interest could not be accomplished. If this advantage is to be firmly established, there must exist a ground for mutual confidence deeper than and independent of the social utility it permits.

The utilitarian counting the advantages affirms the general importance of enforcing *contracts*. The moralist of duty, however, sees *promising* as a device that free, moral individuals have fashioned on the premise of mutual trust, and which gathers its moral force from that premise. The moralist of duty thus posits a general obligation to keep promises, of which the obligation of contract will be only a special case—that special case in which certain promises have attained legal as well as moral force. But since a contract is first of all a promise, the contract must be kept because a promise must be kept.

To summarize: There exists a convention that defines the practice of promising and its entailments. This convention provides a way that a person may create expectations in others. By virtue of the basic Kantian principles of trust and respect, it is wrong to invoke that convention in order to make a promise, and then to break it.

WHAT A PROMISE IS WORTH

If I make a promise to you, I should do as I promise; and if I fail to keep my promise, it is fair that I should be made to hand over the equivalent of the promised performance. In contract doctrine this proposition appears as the expectation measure of damages for breach. The expectation standard gives the victim of a breach no more or less than he would have had had there been no breach—in other words, he gets the benefit of his bargain. Two alternative measures of damage, reliance and restitution, express the different notions that if a person has relied on a promise and been hurt, that hurt must be made good; and that if a contract-breaker has obtained goods or services, he must be made to pay a fair (just?) price for them. Consider three cases:

2-A. I enter your antique shop on a quiet afternoon and agree in writing to buy an expensive chest I see there, the price being about three times what you paid for it a short time ago. When I get home I repent of my decision, and within half an hour of my visit—before any other customer has come to your store—I telephone to say I no longer want the chest.

2-B. Same as above, except in the meantime you have waxed and polished the chest and had your delivery van bring it to my door.

2-C. Same as above, except I have the use of the chest for six months, while your shop is closed for renovations.

To require me to pay for the chest in case 2-A (or, if you resell it, to pay any profit you lost, including lost business volume) is to give you your expectation, the benefit of your bargain. In 2-B if all I must compensate is your effort I am reimbursing your reliance, and in 2-C to force me to pay a fair price for the use I have had of the chest is to focus on making me pay for, restore, an actual benefit I have received.

The assault on the classical conception of contract, the concept I call contract as promise, has centered on the connection—taken as canonical for some hundred years—between contract law and expectation damages. To focus the attack on this connection is indeed strategic. As the critics recognize and as I have just stated, to the extent that contract is grounded in promise, it seems natural to measure relief by the expectation, that is, by the promise itself. If that link can be threatened, then contract itself may be grounded elsewhere than in promise, elsewhere than in the will of the parties. In his recent comprehensive treatise, *The Rise and Fall of Freedom of Contract*, Patrick Atiyah makes the connection between the recourse to expectation damages and the emerging enforceability of executory contracts—that is, contracts enforced, though no detriment has been suffered in reliance and no benefit has been conferred. (Case 2-A is an example of an executory contract.) Before the nineteenth century, he argues, a contractual relation referred generally to one of a number of particular, community-sanctioned relations between persons who in the course of their dealings (as carriers, innkeepers, surgeons, merchants) relied on each other to their detriment or conferred benefits on each other. It was these detriments and benefits that had to be reimbursed, and an explicit promise—if there happened to be one—was important primarily to establish the reliance or to show that the benefit had been conferred in expectation of payment, not officiously or as a gift. All this, Atiyah writes, turned inside out when the promise itself came to be seen as the basis of obligation, so that neither benefit nor reliance any longer seemed necessary and the proper measure of the obligation was the promise itself, that is, the expectation. The promise principle was embraced as an expression of the principle of liberty—the will binding itself, to use Kantian language, rather than being bound by the norms of the collectivity—and the award of expectation damages followed as a natural concomitant of the promise principle.

The insistence on reliance or benefit is related to disputes about the nature of promising. As I have argued, reliance on a promise cannot alone explain its force: There is reliance because a promise is binding, and not the other way around. But if a person is bound by his promise and not by the harm the promisee may have suffered in reliance on it, then what he is bound to is just its performance. Put simply, I am bound to do what I promised you I would do—or I am bound to put you in as good a position as if I had done so. To bind me to do no more than to reimburse your reliance is to excuse me to that extent from the obligation I undertook. If your reliance is less than your expectation (in case 2-A there is no reliance), then to that extent a reliance standard excuses me from the very obligation I undertook and so weakens the force of an obligation I chose to assume. Since by hypothesis I chose to assume the obligation in its stronger form (that is, to render the performance promised), the reliance rule indeed precludes me from incurring the very obligation I chose to undertake at the time of promising. The most compelling of the arguments for resisting this conclusion and for urging that we settle for reliance is the sense that it is sometimes harsh and ungenerous to insist on the full measure of expectancy. (This is part of Atiyah's thrust when he designates the expectation standard as an aspect of the rigid Victorian promissory morality.) The harshness comes about because in the event the promisor finds the obligation he assumed too burdensome.

This distress may be analyzed into three forms: (1) The promisor regrets having to pay for what he has bought (which may only have been the satisfaction of promising a gift or the thrill of buying a lottery ticket or stock option), though he would readily do the same thing again. I take it that this kind of regret merits no sympathy at all. Indeed if we gave in to it we would frustrate the promisor's ability to engage in his own continuing projects and so the promisor's plea is, strictly speaking, self-contradictory. (2) The promisor regrets his promise because he was mistaken about the nature of the burdens he was assuming—the purchaser in case 2-A thought he would find the money for the antique but in fact his savings are depleted, or perhaps the chest is not as old nor as valuable as he had imagined, or his house has burned down and he no longer needs it. All of these regrets are based on mistaken assumptions about the facts as they are or as they turn out to be. As we shall see . . . , the doctrines of mistake, frustration, and impossibility provide grounds for mitigating the effect of the promise principle without at all undermining it.

Finally there is the most troublesome ground of regret: (3) The promisor made no mistake about the facts or probabilities at all, but now that it has come time to perform he no longer values the promise as highly as when he made it. He regrets the promise because he regrets the value judgment that led him to make it. He concludes that the purchase of an expensive antique is an extravagance. Compassion may lead a promisee to release an obligation in such a case, but he releases as an act of generosity, not as a duty, and certainly not because the promisor's repentance destroys the force of the original obligation. The intuitive reason for holding fast is that such repentance should be the promisor's own responsibility, not one he can shift onto others. It seems too easy a way of getting out of one's obligations. Yet our intuition does not depend on suspicions of insincerity alone. Rather we feel that holding people to their obligations is a way of taking them seriously and thus of giving the concept of sincerity itself serious content. Taking this intuition to a more abstract level, I would say that respect for others as free and rational requires taking seriously their capacity to determine their own values. I invoke again the distinction between the right and the good. The right defines the concept of the self as choosing its own conception of the good. Others must respect our capacity as free and rational persons to choose our own good, and that respect means allowing persons to take responsibility for the good they choose. And, of course, that choosing self is not an instantaneous self but one extended in time, so that to respect those determinations of the self is to respect their persistence over time. If we decline to take seriously the assumption of an obligation because we do not take seriously the promisor's prior conception of the good that led him to assume it, to that extent we do not take him seriously as a person. We infantilize him, as we do quite properly when we release the very young from the consequences of their choices. . . .

REMEDIES IN AND AROUND THE PROMISE

Those who have an interest in assimilating contract to the more communitarian [and utilitarian] standards of tort law have been able to obscure the link between contract and promise because in certain cases the natural thing to do *is* to give damages for the harm that has been suffered, rather than to give the money value of the promised expectation. But it does not follow from these cases that expectation is not a normal and natural measure for contract damages. First, these are situations in which the harm suffered is the measure of damages because it is hard to find the monetary value of the expectation. A leading case, *Security Stove & Mfg. Co. v. American Railway Express Co.*, illustrates the type. The plaintiff stove manufacturer had arranged to have a new kind of stove shipped by the defendant express company to a trade convention, at which the plaintiff hoped to interest prospective buyers in his improved product. The president and his workmen went to the convention, but the defendant failed to deliver a crucial part of the exhibit in time, and they had nothing to show. Plaintiff brought suit to recover the cost of renting the booth, the freight charges, and the time and expenses lost as a result of the fruitless trip to the convention. The recovery of these items of damages, which (with the possible exception of the prepaid booth rental) seem typical examples of reliance losses, is generally agreed to have been appropriate. There was no way of knowing what results the plaintiff would have obtained had he succeeded in exhibiting his product at the convention. There was no way of knowing what his expectancy was, and so the court gave him his loss through reliance. But this illustrates only that where expectancy cannot be calculated, reliance may be a reasonable surrogate. It is reasonable to suppose that the plaintiff's expectation in *Security Stove* was at least as great as the monies he put out to exhibit his goods—after all, he was a businessman and is assumed to have been exhibiting his goods to make an eventual profit. If it could somehow be shown that the exhibit would have been a failure and the plaintiff would have suffered a net loss, the case for recovery would be undermined, and most authorities would then deny recovery.

Second are the cases in which the amount needed to undo the harm caused by reliance is itself the fairest measure of expectation.

3-A. Buyer approaches manufacturer with the specifications of a small, inexpensive part—say a bolt—for a machine buyer is building. Manufacturer selects the part and sells it to buyer. The bolt is badly made, shears, and damages the machine.

The value of the thing promised, a well-made bolt, is negligible, but to give buyer his money back and no more would be a grave injustice. Here it does seem more natural to say that the manufacturer induced buyer's reasonable reliance and should compensate the resulting harm. But it is equally the case that it is a fair implication of the simple-seeming original transaction that manufacturer not only delivered and promised to transfer good title to the bolt, but promised at the same time that the bolt would do the job it was meant to do. . . .

Third, there are cases in which wrongs are committed and loss is suffered in and around the attempt to make an agreement. In these cases too reliance is the best measure of compensation. A striking example is *Hoffman v. Red Owl Stores:* A prospective Red Owl supermarket franchisee sold his previously owned business and made other expenditures on the assumption that his negotiations to obtain a Red Owl franchise would shortly be concluded. The award of reliance damages was not a case of enforcement of a promise at all, since the parties had not reached the stage where clearly determined promises had been made. Reliance damages were awarded because Red Owl had not dealt fairly with Hoffman. It had allowed him to incur expenses based on hopes that Red Owl knew or should have known were imprudent and that Red Owl was not prepared to permit him to realize. Red Owl was held liable not in order to force it to perform a promise, which it had never made, but rather to compensate Hoffman for losses he had suffered through Red Owl's inconsiderate and temporizing assurances. There is nothing at all in my conception of contract as promise that precludes persons who behave badly and cause unnecessary harm from being forced to make fair compensation. Promissory obligation is not the only basis for liability; principles of tort are sufficient to provide that people who give vague assurances that cause foreseeable harm to others should make compensation. Cases like *Hoffman* are seen to undermine the conception of contract as promise: If contract is really discrete and if it is really based in promise, then whenever there has been a promise in the picture (even only a potential promise) contractual principles must govern the whole relation. To state the argument is to reveal it as a non sequitur. It is a logical fallacy of which the classical exponents of contract as promise were themselves supremely guilty in their reluctance to grant relief for fraud or for mistakes that prevented a real agreement from coming into being. Modern critics of contractual freedom have taken the classics at their word. Justice often requires relief and adjustment in cases of accidents in and around the contracting process, and the critics have seen in this a refutation of the classics' major premise. . . . Here it is sufficient to introduce the notion that contract as promise has a distinct but neither exclusive nor necessarily dominant place among legal and moral principles.

REVIEW AND DISCUSSION QUESTIONS

1. What is the view of contract that Fried opposes? To what extent can Cohen be seen as representing that perspective?

2. Fried points out that promising is a convention and argues that a particular promise has moral force only because promises in general have force. Explain what he means. Is this consistent with his claim that the obligation to keep a promise is grounded not in utility but "in respect for individual autonomy and in trust"?

3. In your view, what moral force do promises have, and why are they morally binding? What is important about the institution of promising?

4. With reference to the three versions of the antique chest story, explain the differences among expectation, reliance, and restitution as measures of damages for breach of contract. Why does Fried's view of contract lead one to the expectation measure? How do the two alternative measures of damage support a different view of the nature of contract?

5. What do you see as the pros and cons of these three measures of damages? How does Fried respond to the argument that the expectation measure is harsh and ungenerous?

6. What difficulties for Fried's view are raised by the *Security Stove* and *Hoffman* cases, and how does he respond to them?

7. Compare Fried's position on punishment to that of Cohen.

Surrogate Mother Contracts

In the Matter of Baby M

In this famous case, the Supreme Court of New Jersey ruled on the legality of surrogacy contracts: contracts, that is, in which a woman agrees, in exchange for money, to be artificially inseminated with the sperm of a stranger, to carry his child to term, and after its birth to surrender the child to the biological father. In this case, the details of which are given in the Court's opinion, William Stern sued Mary Beth Whitehead for breach of contract when she refused to turn over the infant girl—called Sara by her, Melissa by the Sterns, and "Baby M" by the courts—who had been conceived with Stern's sperm. A New Jersey judge in a lower court had awarded the child to Stern and his wife, a decision later upheld by a three-judge panel. But on appeal, the New Jersey Supreme Court ruled surrogate mother contracts "illegal, perhaps criminal, and potentially degrading to women."

---

537 A.2d 1227 (1988). Citations and some notes omitted.

Chief Justice Robert Wilentz:

In this matter the Court is asked to determine the validity of a contract that purports to provide a new way of bringing children into a family. For a fee of $10,000, a woman agrees to be artificially inseminated with the semen of another woman's husband; she is to conceive a child, carry it to term, and after its birth surrender it to the natural father and his wife. The intent of the contract is that the child's natural mother will thereafter be forever separated from her child. The wife is to adopt the child, and she and the natural father are to be regarded as its parents for all purposes. The contract providing for this is called a "surrogacy contract," the natural mother inappropriately called the "surrogate mother."

We invalidate the surrogacy contract because it conflicts with the law and public policy of this State. While we recognize the depth of the yearning of infertile couples to have their own children, we find the payment of money to a "surrogate" mother illegal, perhaps criminal, and potentially degrading to women. Although in this case we grant custody to the natural father, the evidence having clearly proved such custody to be in the best interests of the infant, we void both the termination of the surrogate mother's parental rights and the adoption of the child by the wife/stepparent. We thus restore the "surrogate" as the mother of the child. . . .

We find no offense to our present laws where a woman voluntarily and without payment agrees to act as a "surrogate" mother, provided that she is not subject to a binding agreement to surrender her child. Moreover, our holding today does not preclude the Legislature from altering the current statutory scheme, within constitutional limits, so as to permit surrogacy contracts. Under current law, however, the surrogacy agreement before us is illegal and invalid.

1. FACTS

In February 1985, William Stern and Mary Beth Whitehead entered into a surrogacy contract. It recited that Stern's wife, Elizabeth, was infertile, that they wanted a child, and that Mrs. Whitehead was willing to provide that child as the mother with Mr. Stern as the father.

The contract provided that through artificial insemination using Mr. Stern's sperm, Mrs. Whitehead would become pregnant, carry the child to term, bear it, deliver it to the Sterns, and thereafter do whatever was necessary to terminate her maternal rights so that Mrs. Stern could thereafter adopt the child. Mrs. Whitehead's husband, Richard,[1] was also a party to the contract; Mrs. Stern was not. . . .

Mr. Stern, on his part, agreed to attempt the artificial insemination and to pay Mrs. Whitehead $10,000 after the child's birth, on its delivery to him. In a separate contract, Mr. Stern agreed to pay $7,500 to the Infertility Center of New York ("ICNY"). The Center's advertising campaigns solicit surrogate mothers and encourage infertile couples to consider surrogacy. ICNY arranged for the surrogacy contract by bringing the parties together, explaining the process to them, furnishing the contractual form, and providing legal counsel.

The history of the parties' involvement in this arrangement suggests their good faith. William and Elizabeth Stern were married in July 1974, having met at the University of Michigan, where both were Ph.D. candidates. Due to financial considerations and Mrs. Stern's pursuit of a medical degree and residency, they decided to defer starting a family until 1981. Before then, however, Mrs. Stern learned that she might have multiple sclerosis and that the disease in some cases renders pregnancy a serious health risk. Her anxiety appears to have exceeded the actual risk, which current medical authorities assess as minimal. Nonetheless that anxiety was evidently quite real, Mrs. Stern fearing that pregnancy might precipitate blindness, paraplegia, or other forms of debilitation. Based on the perceived risk, the Sterns decided to forego having their own children. The decision had a special significance for Mr. Stern. Most of his family had been destroyed in the Holocaust. As the family's only survivor, he very much wanted to continue his bloodline. . . .

On February 6, 1985, Mr. Stern and Mr. and Mrs. Whitehead executed the surrogate parenting agreement. After several artificial inseminations over a period of months, Mrs. Whitehead became pregnant. The pregnancy was uneventful and on March 27, 1986, Baby M was born.

Not wishing anyone at the hospital to be aware of the surrogacy arrangement, Mr. and Mrs. Whitehead appeared to all as the proud parents of a healthy female child. Her birth certificate indicated her name to be Sara Elizabeth Whitehead and her father to be Richard Whitehead. In accordance with Mrs. Whitehead's request, the Sterns visited the hospital unobtrusively to see the newborn child.

Mrs. Whitehead realized, almost from the moment of birth, that she could not part with this child. She had felt a bond with it even during pregnancy. Some indication of the attachment was conveyed to the Sterns at the hospital when they told Mrs. Whitehead what they were going to name the baby. She apparently broke into tears and indicated that she did not know if she could give up the child. She talked about how the baby looked like her other daughter, and made it clear that she was experiencing great difficulty with the decision.

Nonetheless, Mrs. Whitehead was, for the moment, true to her word. Despite powerful inclinations to the contrary, she turned her child over to the Sterns on March 30 at the Whitehead's home. . . .

Later in the evening of March 30, Mrs. Whitehead became deeply disturbed, disconsolate, stricken with unbearable sadness. She had to have her child. She could not eat, sleep, or concentrate on anything other than her need for her baby. The next day she went to the Sterns' home and told them how much she was suffering.

The depth of Mrs. Whitehead's despair surprised and frightened the Sterns. She told them that she could not live without her baby, that she must have her, even if only for one week, that thereafter she would surrender her child. The Sterns, concerned that Mrs. Whitehead might indeed commit suicide, not wanting under any circumstances to risk that, and in any event believing that Mrs. Whitehead would keep her word, turned the child over to her. It was not until four months later, after a series of attempts to regain possession of the child, that

Melissa was returned to the Sterns, having been forcibly removed from the home where she was then living with Mr. and Mrs. Whitehead, the home in Florida owned by Mary Beth Whitehead's parents.

The struggle over Baby M began when it became apparent that Mrs. Whitehead could not return the child to Mr. Stern. Due to Mrs. Whitehead's refusal to relinquish the baby, Mr. Stern filed a complaint seeking enforcement of the surrogacy contract. He alleged, accurately, that Mrs. Whitehead had not only refused to comply with the surrogacy contract but had threatened to flee from New Jersey with the child in order to avoid even the possibility of his obtaining custody. The court papers asserted that if Mrs. Whitehead were to be given notice of the application for an order requiring her to relinquish custody, she would, prior to the hearing, leave the state with the baby. And that is precisely what she did. After the order was entered, *ex parte*, the process server, aided by the police, in the presence of the Sterns, entered Mrs. Whitehead's home to execute the order. Mr. Whitehead fled with the child, who had been handed to him through a window while those who came to enforce the order were thrown off balance by a dispute over the child's current name.

The Whiteheads immediately fled to Florida with Baby M. They stayed initially with Mrs. Whitehead's parents, where one of Mrs. Whitehead's children had been living. For the next three months, the Whiteheads and Melissa lived at roughly twenty different hotels, motels, and homes in order to avoid apprehension. From time to time Mrs. Whitehead would call Mr. Stern to discuss the matter; the conversations, recorded by Mr. Stern on advice of counsel, show an escalating dispute about rights, morality, and power, accompanied by threats of Mrs. Whitehead to kill herself, to kill the child, and falsely to accuse Mr. Stern of sexually molesting Mrs. Whitehead's other daughter.

Eventually the Sterns discovered where the Whiteheads were staying, commenced supplementary proceedings in Florida, and obtained an order requiring the Whiteheads to turn over the child. Police in Florida enforced the order, forcibly removing the child from her grandparents' home. She was soon thereafter brought to New Jersey and turned over to the Sterns. . . .

The trial took thirty-two days over a period of more than two months. It included numerous interlocutory appeals and attempted interlocutory appeals. There were twenty-three witnesses to the facts recited above and fifteen expert witnesses, eleven testifying on the issue of custody and four on the subject of Mrs. Stern's multiple sclerosis; the bulk of the testimony was devoted to determining the parenting arrangement most compatible with the child's best interests. Soon after the conclusion of the trial, the trial court announced its opinion from the bench. It held that the surrogacy contract was valid; ordered that Mrs. Whitehead's parental rights be terminated and that sole custody of the child be granted to Mr. Stern; and, after hearing brief testimony from Mrs. Stern, immediately entered an order allowing the adoption of Melissa by Mrs. Stern, all in accordance with the surrogacy contract. Pending the outcome of the appeal, we granted a continuation of visitation to Mrs. Whitehead, although slightly more limited than the visitation allowed during the trial. . . .

Mrs. Whitehead appealed. . . .

Mrs. Whitehead contends that the surrogacy contract, for a variety of reasons, is invalid. She contends that it conflicts with public policy since it guarantees that the child will not have the nurturing of both natural parents—presumably New Jersey's goal for families. She further argues that it deprives the mother of her constitutional right to the companionship of her child, and that it conflicts with statutes concerning termination of parental rights and adoption. With the contract thus void, Mrs. Whitehead claims primary custody (with visitation rights in Mr. Stern) both on a best interests basis (stressing the "tender years" doctrine) as well as the policy basis of discouraging surrogacy contracts. She maintains that even if custody would ordinarily go to Mr. Stern, here it should be awarded to Mrs. Whitehead to deter future surrogacy arrangements. . . .

2. INVALIDITY AND UNENFORCEABILITY OF SURROGACY CONTRACT

We have concluded that this surrogacy contract is invalid. Our conclusion has two bases: direct conflict with existing statutes and conflict with the public policies of this State, as expressed in its statutory and decisional law.

One of the surrogacy contract's basic purposes, to achieve the adoption of a child through private placement, though permitted in New Jersey "is very much disfavored." *Sees v. Baber*, 74 N.J. 201, 217, 377 A.2d 628 (1977). Its use of money for this purpose—and we have no doubt whatsoever that the money is being paid to obtain an adoption and not, as the Sterns argue, for the personal services of Mary Beth Whitehead—is illegal and perhaps criminal. In addition to the inducement of money, there is the coercion of contract: the natural mother's irrevocable agreement, prior to birth, even prior to conception, to surrender the child to the adoptive couple. Such an agreement is totally unenforceable in private placement adoption. Even where the adoption is through an approved agency, the formal agreement to surrender occurs only *after* birth (as we read N.J.S.A. 9:2–16 and 17, and similar statutes), and then, by regulation, only after the birth mother has been counseled. . . .

A. Conflict with Statutory Provisions

The surrogacy contract conflicts with: . . . laws prohibiting the use of money in connection with adoptions . . . [and] laws that make surrender of custody and consent to adoption revocable in private placement adoptions.

Our law prohibits paying or accepting money in connection with any placement of a child for adoption. Violation is a high misdemeanor. Excepted are fees of an approved agency (which must be a non-profit entity) and certain expenses in connection with childbirth.

Considerable care was taken in this case to structure the surrogacy arrangement so as not to violate this prohibition. The arrangement was structured as follows: the adopting parent, Mrs. Stern, was not a party to the surrogacy contract; the money paid to Mrs. Whitehead was stated to be for her services—not for the adoption; the sole purpose of the contract was stated as being that "of giving a child to William Stern, its natural and biological father"; the money was purported to be "compensation for services and expenses and in no way . . . a fee for termination of parental rights or a payment in exchange for consent to surrender a child for adoption"; the fee to the Infertility Center ($7,500) was stated to be for legal representation, advice, administrative work, and other "services." Nevertheless, it seems clear that the money was paid and accepted in connection with an adoption. . . .

Mr. Stern knew he was paying for the adoption of a child; Mrs. Whitehead knew she was accepting money so that a child might be adopted; the Infertility Center knew that it was being paid for assisting in the adoption of a child. The actions of all three worked to frustrate the goals of the statute. It strains credulity to claim that these arrangements, touted by those in the surrogacy business as an attractive alternative to the usual route leading to an adoption, really amount to something other than a private placement adoption for money.

The prohibition of our statute is strong. Violation constitutes a high misdemeanor, a third-degree crime, carrying a penalty of three to five years imprisonment. The evils inherent in baby bartering are loathsome for a myriad of reasons. The child is sold without regard for whether the purchasers will be suitable parents. N. Baker, *Baby Selling: The Scandal of Black Market Adoption* (1978). The natural mother does not receive the benefit of counseling and guidance to assist her in making a decision that may affect her for a lifetime. In fact, the monetary incentive to sell her child may, depending on her financial circumstances, make her decision less voluntary. Furthermore, the adoptive parents may not be fully informed of the natural parents' medical history.

Baby-selling potentially results in the exploitation of all parties involved. Conversely, adoption statutes seek to further humanitarian goals, foremost among them the best interests of the child. H. Witmer, E. Herzog, E. Weinstein, & M. Sullivan, *Independent Adoptions: A Follow-Up Study* 32 (1967). The negative consequences of baby buying are potentially present in the surrogacy context, especially the potential for placing and adopting a child without regard to the interest of the child or the natural mother. . . .

The provision in the surrogacy contract stating that Mary Beth Whitehead agrees to "surrender custody . . . and terminate all parental rights" contains no clause giving her a right to rescind. It is intended to be an irrevocable consent to surrender the child for adoption—in other words, an irrevocable commitment by Mrs. Whitehead to turn Baby M over to the Sterns and thereafter to allow termination of her parental rights. The trial court required a "best interests" showing as a condition to granting specific performance of the surrogacy contract. Having decided the "best interests" issue in favor of the Sterns, that court's order included, among other things, specific performance of this agreement to surrender custody and terminate all parental rights.

Mrs. Whitehead, shortly after the child's birth, had attempted to revoke her consent and surrender by refusing, after the Sterns had allowed her to have the child "just for one week," to return Baby M to them. The trial court's award of specific performance therefore reflects its view that the consent to surrender the child was irrevocable. We accept the trial court's construction of the contract; indeed it appears quite clear that this was the parties' intent. Such a provision, however, making irrevocable the natural mother's consent to surrender custody of her child in a private placement adoption, clearly conflicts with New Jersey law.

Our analysis commences with the statute providing for surrender of custody to an approved agency and termination of parental rights on the suit of that agency. The two basic provisions of the statute are N.J.S.A. 9:2–14 and 9:2–16. The former provides explicitly that:

Except as otherwise provided by law or by order or judgment of a court of competent jurisdiction or by testamentary disposition, no surrender of the custody of a child shall be valid in this state unless made to an approved agency pursuant to the provisions of this act. . . .

. . . Requirements for a voluntary surrender to an approved agency was set forth in N.J.S.A. 9:2–16. This section allows an approved agency to take a voluntary surrender of custody from the parent of a child but provides stringent requirements as a condition to its validity.

. . . These strict prerequisites to irrevocability constitute a recognition of the most serious consequences that flow from such consents: termination of parental rights, the permanent separation of parent from child, and the ultimate adoption of the child. Because of those consequences, the Legislature severely limited the circumstances under which such consent would be irrevocable. The legislative goal is furthered by regulations requiring approved agencies, prior to accepting irrevocable consents, to provide advice and counseling to women, making it more likely that they fully understand and appreciate the consequences of their acts.

Contractual surrender of parental rights is not provided for in our statutes as now written. . . . There is no doubt that a contractual provision purporting to constitute an irrevocable agreement to surrender custody of a child for adoption is invalid. . . .

B. PUBLIC POLICY CONSIDERATIONS

The surrogacy contract's invalidity, resulting from its direct conflict with the above statutory provisions, is further underlined when its goals and means are measured against New Jersey's public policy. The contract's basic premise, that the natural parents can decide in advance of birth which one is to have custody of the child, bears no relationship to the settled law that the child's best interests shall determine custody. . . .

The surrogacy contract guarantees permanent separation of the child from one of its natural parents. Our policy, however, has long been that to the extent possible, children should remain with and be brought up by both of their natural parents. . . . This is not simply some theoretical ideal that in practice has no meaning. The impact of failure to follow that policy is nowhere better shown than in the results of this surrogacy contract. A child, instead of starting off its life with as much peace and security as possible, finds itself immediately in a tug-of-war between contending mother and father.

The surrogacy contract violates the policy of this State that the rights of natural parents are equal concerning their child, the father's right no greater than the mother's. "The parent and child relationship extends equally to every child and to every parent, regardless of the marital status of the parents." . . . The whole purpose and effect of the surrogacy contract was to give the father the exclusive right to the child by destroying the rights of the mother.

The policies expressed in our comprehensive laws governing consent to the surrender of a child, stand in stark contrast to the surrogacy contract and what it implies. Here there is no counseling, independent or otherwise, of the natural mother, no evaluation, no warning.

The only legal advice Mary Beth Whitehead received regarding the surrogacy contract was provided in connection with the contract that she previously entered into with another couple. Mrs. Whitehead's lawyer was referred to her by the Infertility Center, with which he had an agreement to act as counsel for surrogate candidates. His services consisted of spending one hour going through the contract with the Whiteheads, section by section, and answering their questions. Mrs. Whitehead received no further legal advice prior to signing the contract with the Sterns.

Mrs. Whitehead was examined and psychologically evaluated, but if it was for her benefit, the record does not disclose that fact. The Sterns regarded the evaluation as important, particularly in connection with the question of whether she would change her mind. Yet they never asked to see it, and were content with the assumption that the Infertility Center had made an evaluation and had concluded that there was no danger that the surrogate mother would change her mind. From Mrs. Whitehead's point of view, all that she learned from the evaluation was that "she had passed." It is apparent that the profit motive got the better of the Infertility Center. Although the evaluation was made, it was not put to any use, and understandably so, for the psychologist warned that Mrs. White-head demonstrated certain traits that might make surrender of the child difficult and that there should be further inquiry into this issue in connection with her surrogacy. To inquire further, however, might have jeopardized the Infertility Center's fee. The record indicates that neither Mrs. Whitehead nor the Sterns were ever told of this fact, a fact that might have ended their surrogacy arrangement.

Under the contract, the natural mother is irrevocably committed before she knows the strength of her bond with her child. She never makes a totally voluntary, informed decision, for quite clearly any decision prior to the baby's birth is, in the most important sense, uninformed, and any decision after that, compelled by a pre-existing contractual commitment, the threat of a lawsuit, and the inducement of a $10,000 payment, is less than totally voluntary. Her interests are of little concern to those who controlled this transaction.

Although the interest of the natural father and adoptive mother is certainly the predominant interest, realistically the *only* interest served, even they are left with less than what public policy requires. They know little about the natural mother, her genetic makeup, and her psychological and medical history. Moreover, not even a superficial attempt is made to determine their awareness of their responsibilities as parents.

Worst of all, however, is the contract's total disregard of the best interests of the child. There is not the slightest suggestion that any inquiry will be made at any time to determine the fitness of the Sterns as custodial parents, of Mrs. Stern as an adoptive parent, their superiority to Mrs. Whitehead, or the effect on the child of not living with her natural mother.

This is the sale of a child, or, at the very least, the sale of a mother's right to her child, the only mitigating factor being that one of the purchasers is the father. Almost every evil that prompted the prohibition of the payment of money in connection with adoptions exists here.

The differences between an adoption and a surrogacy contract should be noted, since it is asserted that the use of money in connection with surrogacy does not pose the risks found where money buys an adoption.

First, and perhaps most important, all parties concede that it is unlikely that surrogacy will survive without money. Despite the alleged selfless motivation of surrogate mothers, if there is no payment, there will be no surrogates, or very few. That conclusion contrasts with adoption; for obvious reasons, there remains a steady supply, albeit insufficient, despite the prohibitions against payment. The adoption itself, relieving the natural mother of the financial burden of supporting an infant, is the equivalent of payment.

Second, the use of money in adoptions does not *produce* the problem—conception occurs, and usually the birth itself, before illicit funds are offered. With surrogacy, the "problem," if one views it as such, consisting of the purchase of a woman's procreative capacity, at the risk of her life, is caused by and originates with the offer of money.

Third, with the law prohibiting the use of money in connection with adoptions, the built-in financial pressure of the unwanted pregnancy and the consequent support obligation do not lead the mother to the highest paying, ill-suited, adoptive parents. She is just as well off surrendering the child to an approved agency. In surrogacy, the highest bidders will presumably become the adoptive parents regardless of suitability, so long as payment of money is permitted.

Fourth, the mother's consent to surrender her child in adoptions is revocable, even after surrender of the child, unless it be to an approved agency, where by regulation there are protections against an ill-advised surrender. In surrogacy, consent occurs so early that no amount of advice would satisfy the potential mother's need, yet the consent is irrevocable.

The main difference, that the plight of the unwanted pregnancy is unintended while the situation of the surrogate mother is voluntary and intended, is really not significant. Initially, it produces stronger reactions of sympathy for the mother whose pregnancy was unwanted than for the surrogate mother, who "went into this with her eyes wide open." On reflection, however, it appears that the essential evil is the same, taking advantage of a woman's circumstances (the unwanted pregnancy or the need for money) in order to take away her child, the difference being one of degree. . . .

Intimated, but disputed, is the assertion that surrogacy will be used for the benefit of the rich at the expense of the poor. In response it is noted that the Sterns are not rich and the Whiteheads not poor. Nevertheless, it is clear to us that it is unlikely that surrogate mothers will be as proportionately numerous among those women in the top twenty percent income bracket as among those in the bottom twenty percent. Put differently, we doubt that infertile couples in the low-income bracket will find upper income surrogates.

In any event, even in this case one should not pretend that disparate wealth does not play a part simply because the contrast is not the dramatic "rich versus poor." At the time of trial, the Whiteheads' net assets were probably negative—Mrs. Whitehead's own sister was foreclosing on a second mortgage. Their income derived from Mr. Whitehead's labors. Mrs. Whitehead is a homemaker, having previously held part-time jobs. The Sterns are both professionals, she a medical doctor, he a biochemist. Their combined income when both were working was about $89,500 a year and their assets sufficient to pay for the surrogacy contract arrangements.

The point is made that Mrs. Whitehead *agreed* to the surrogacy arrangement, supposedly fully understanding the consequences. Putting aside the issue of how compelling her need for money may have been, and how significant her understanding of the consequences, we suggest that her consent is irrelevant. There are, in a civilized society, some things that money cannot buy. In America, we decided long ago that merely because conduct purchased by money was "voluntary" did not mean that it was good or beyond regulation and prohibition. Employers can no longer buy labor at the lowest price they can bargain for, even though that labor is "voluntary," or buy women's labor for less money than paid to men for the same job, or purchase the agreement of children to perform oppressive labor, or purchase the agreement of workers to subject themselves to unsafe or unhealthy working conditions (Occupational Health and Safety Act of 1970). There are, in short, values that society deems more important than granting to wealth whatever it can buy, be it labor, love, or life. Whether this principle recommends prohibition of surrogacy, which presumably sometimes results in great satisfaction to all of the parties, is not for us to say. We note here only that, under existing law, the fact that Mrs. Whitehead "agreed" to the arrangement is not dispositive.

The long-term effects of surrogacy contracts are not known, but feared—the impact on the child who learns her life was bought, that she is the offspring of someone who gave birth to her only to obtain money; the impact on the natural mother as the full weight of her isolation is felt along with the full reality of the sale of her body and her child; the impact on the natural father and adoptive mother once they realize the consequences of their conduct. Literature in related areas suggests these are substantial considerations, although, given the newness of surrogacy, there is little information.

The surrogacy contract creates, it is based upon, principles that are directly contrary to the objectives of our laws. It guarantees the separation of a child from its mother; it looks to adoption regardless of suitability; it totally ignores the child; it takes the child from the mother regardless of her wishes and her maternal fitness; and it does all of this, it accomplishes all of its goals, through the use of money.

Beyond that is the potential degradation of some women that may result from this arrangement. In many cases, of course, surrogacy may bring satisfaction, not only to the infertile couple, but to the surrogate mother herself. The fact, however, that many women may not perceive surrogacy negatively but rather see it as an opportunity does not diminish its potential for devastation to other women.

In sum, the harmful consequences of this surrogacy arrangement appear to us all too palpable. In New Jersey the surrogate mother's agreement to sell her child is void. Its irrevocability infects the entire contract, as does the money that purports to buy it. . . .

CONCLUSION

This case affords some insight into a new reproductive arrangement: the artificial insemination of a surrogate mother. The unfortunate events that have unfolded illustrate that its unregulated use can bring suffering to all involved. Potential victims include the surrogate mother and her family, the natural father and his wife, and most importantly, the child. Although surrogacy has apparently provided positive results for some infertile couples, it can also, as this case demonstrates, cause suffering to participants, here essentially innocent and well intended.

We have found that our present laws do not permit the surrogacy contract used in this case. Nowhere, however, do we find any legal prohibition against surrogacy when the surrogate mother volunteers, without any payment, to act as a surrogate and is given the right to change her mind and to assert her parental rights. Moreover, the Legislature remains free to deal with this most sensitive issue as it sees fit, subject only to constitutional constraints.

If the Legislature decides to address surrogacy, consideration of this case will highlight many of its potential harms. We do not underestimate the difficulties of legislating on this subject. In addition to the inevitable confrontation with the ethical and moral issues involved, there is the question of the wisdom and effectiveness of regulating a matter so private, yet of such public interest. Legislative consideration of surrogacy may also provide the opportunity to begin to focus on the overall implications of the new reproductive biotechnology—*in vitro* fertilization, preservation of sperm and eggs, embryo implantation and the like. The problem is how to enjoy the benefits of the technology—especially for infertile couples—while minimizing the risk of abuse. The problem can be addressed only when society decides what its values and objectives are in this troubling, yet promising, area.

The judgment is affirmed in part, reversed in part, and remanded for further proceedings consistent with this opinion.

NOTE

[1]Subsequent to the trial court proceedings, Mr. and Mrs. Whitehead were divorced, and soon thereafter Mrs. Whitehead remarried. Nevertheless, in the course of this opinion we will make reference almost exclusively to the facts as they existed at the time of trial, the facts on which the decision we now review was reached. We note moreover that Mr. Whitehead remains a party to this dispute. For these reasons, we continue to refer to appellants as Mr. and Mrs. Whitehead.

REVIEW AND DISCUSSION QUESTIONS

1. Justice Wilentz contends that surrogacy contracts conflict with New Jersey statute. Why? Do you think Wilentz would have ruled that there was a conflict if he had approved of such contracts?

2. Is the Baby M case a case of "baby selling," as Justice Wilentz implies, or are surrogate agencies correct to claim that they are simply selling a woman's services? Under either description, is there anything morally questionable about surrogate mother agreements?

3. What public policy considerations does Justice Wilentz raise against surrogacy contracts? What public policy considerations might be raised in their favor? Did Justice Wilentz make the correct decision?

4. Assess this case from Fried's theory of contract as promise. Does Wilentz's releasing Mary Beth Whitehead from her contract with Stern "infantilize" her (in Fried's words) and fail to take her "seriously as a person"? Or are such contracts, as Wilentz suggests, degrading to women? Do you think Justice Wilentz's view of contract law is closer to Cohen's or to Fried's?

5. Could surrogacy contracts be modified or regulated in some way that gets around the objections that Justice Wilentz and other critics have of them?

Employment Contracts

Lochner v. New York, Muller v. Oregon, Coppage v. Kansas, and West Coast Hotel Co. v. Parrish

Although common law establishes the general right of individuals to make employment contracts on any mutually agreeable terms, the courts have long permitted the government to restrict certain sorts of contracts when necessary to promote the safety, health, morals, or general welfare of the public. In the famous Lochner *case of 1905, however, the U.S. Supreme Court struck down a New York labor law that prevented bakers from working more than sixty hours a week on the ground that the statute unreasonably interfered with the right of contract between employer and employees. Three years later, though, it upheld an Oregon statute that prevented women from working more than ten hours a day in factories and laundries. In 1915, in the* Coppage *case, the Court reaffirmed its* Lochner *position by invalidating a Kansas law that forbade "yellow dog" contracts, that is, contracts in which employers require, as a condition of employment, that employees not belong to a labor union. In the early 1930s, the Supreme Court's resistance to government interference with employment contracts brought it into collision with President Franklin D. Roosevelt, who threatened to add new members to the Court who would uphold his progressive labor legislation. Thereafter, the Court backed away from its position in* Lochner *and* Coppage. *In* West Coast Hotel Co. v. Parrish, *the Supreme Court reversed its own position in an earlier case, explicitly upholding a minimum-wage law and implicitly removing any constitutional barriers to the regulation of labor contracts.*

Lochner v. New York

Mr. Justice Peckham delivered the opinion of the Court:

The indictment, it will be seen, charges that the plaintiff in error violated the 110th section of article 8, chapter 415, of the Laws of 1897, known as the labor law of the state of New York, in that he wrongfully and unlawfully required and permitted an employee working for him to work more than sixty hours in one week. . . .

It is not an act merely fixing the number of hours which shall constitute a legal day's work, but an absolute prohibition upon the employer permitting, under any circumstances, more than ten hours' work to be done in his establishment. The employee may desire to earn the extra money which would arise from his working more than the prescribed time, but this statute forbids the employer from permitting the employee to earn it.

The statute necessarily interferes with the right of contract between the employer and employees, concerning the number of hours in which the latter may labor in the bakery of the employer. The general right to make a contract in relation to his business is part of the liberty of the individual protected by the 14th Amendment of the Federal Constitution. Allgeyer v. Louisiana, 165 U.S. 578. Under that provision no state can deprive any person of life, liberty, or property without due process of law. The right to purchase or to sell labor is part of the liberty protected by this amendment, unless there are circumstances which exclude the right. There are, however, certain powers, existing in the sovereignty of each state in the Union, somewhat vaguely termed police powers, the exact description and limitation of which have not been attempted by the courts. Those powers, broadly

---

198 U.S. 45 (1905), 208 U.S. 412 (1908), 236 U.S. 1 (1915), and 300 U.S. 379 (1937).

stated, and without, at present, any attempt at a more specific limitation, relate to the safety, health, morals, and general welfare of the public. Both property and liberty are held on such reasonable conditions as may be imposed by the governing power of the state in the exercise of those powers, and with such conditions the 14th Amendment was not designed to interfere. Mugler v. Kansas, 123 U.S. 623. . . .

Therefore, when the state, by its legislature, in the assumed exercise of its police powers, has passed an act which seriously limits the right to labor or the right of contract in regard to their means of livelihood between persons who are *sui juris* (both employer and employee), it becomes of great importance to determine which shall prevail,—the right of the individual to labor for such time as he may choose, or the right of the state to prevent the individual from laboring, or from entering into any contract to labor, beyond a certain time prescribed by the state.

This court has recognized the existence and upheld the exercise of the police powers of the states in many cases which might fairly be considered as border ones, and it has, in the course of its determination of questions regarding the asserted invalidity of such statutes, on the ground of their violation of the rights secured by the Federal Constitution, been guided by rules of a very liberal nature, the application of which has resulted, in numerous instances, in upholding the validity of state statutes thus assailed. Among the later cases where the state law has been upheld by this court is that of Holden v. Hardy, 169 U.S. 366. A provision in the act of the legislature of Utah was there under consideration, the act limiting the employment of workmen in all underground mines or workings, to eight hours per day, "except in cases of emergency, where life or property is in imminent danger." It also limited the hours of labor in smelting and other institutions for the reduction or refining of ores or metals to eight hours per day, except in like cases of emergency. The act was held to be a valid exercise of the police powers of the state. . . .

It must, of course, be conceded that there is a limit to the valid exercise of the police power by the state. . . .

In every case that comes before this court, therefore, where legislation of this character is concerned, and where the protection of the Federal Constitution is sought, the question necessarily arises: Is this a fair, reasonable, and appropriate exercise of the police power of the state, or is it an unreasonable, unnecessary, and arbitrary interference with the right of the individual to his personal liberty, or to enter into those contracts in relation to labor which may seem to him appropriate or necessary for the support of himself and his family? Of course the liberty of contract relating to labor includes both parties to it. The one has as much right to purchase as the other to sell labor.

This is not a question of substituting the judgment of the court for that of the legislature. If the act be within the power of the state it is valid, although the judgment of the court might be totally opposed to the enactment of such a law. But the question would still remain: Is it within the police power of the state? and that question must be answered by the court.

The question whether this act is valid as a labor law, pure and simple, may be dismissed in a few words. There is no reasonable ground for interfering with the liberty of persons or the right of free contract by determining the hours of labor, in the occupation of a baker. . . . Viewed in the light of a purely labor law with no reference whatever to the question of health, we think that a law like the one before us involves neither the safety, the morals, nor the welfare of the public, and that the interest of the public is not in the slightest degree affected by such an act. The law must be upheld, if at all, as a law pertaining to the health of the individual engaged in the occupation of a baker. . . .

We think the limit of the police power has been reached and passed in this case. There is, in our judgment, no reasonable foundation for holding this to be necessary or appropriate as a health law to safeguard the public health, or the health of the individuals who are following the trade of a baker. . . .

It is also urged, pursuing the same line of argument, that it is to the interest of the state that its population should be strong and robust, and therefore any legislation which may be said to tend to make people healthy must be valid as health laws, enacted under the police power. If this be a valid argument and a justification for this kind of legislation, it follows that the protection of the Federal Constitution from undue interference with liberty of person and freedom of contract is visionary, wherever the law is sought to be justified as a valid exercise of the police power. Scarcely any law but might find shelter under such assumptions, and conduct, properly so called, as well as contract, would come under the restrictive sway of the legislature. Not only the hours of employees, but the hours of employers, could be regulated, and doctors, lawyers, scientists, all professional men, as well as athletes and artisans, could be forbidden to fatigue their brains and bodies by prolonged hours of exercise, lest the fighting strength of the state be impaired. We mention these extreme cases because the contention is extreme. We do not believe in the soundness of the views which uphold this law. . . .

Statutes of the nature of that under review, limiting the hours in which grown and intelligent men may labor to earn their living, are mere meddlesome interferences with the rights of the individual, and they are not saved from condemnation by the claim that they are passed in the exercise of the police power and upon the subject of the health of the individual whose rights are interfered with, unless there be some fair ground, reasonable in and of itself, to say that there is material danger to the public health, or to the health of the employees, if the hours of labor are not curtailed. . . .

It is impossible, for us to shut our eyes to the fact that many of the laws of this character, while passed under what is claimed to be the police power for the purpose of protecting the public health or welfare, are, in reality, passed from other motives. We are justified in saying so when, from the character of the law and the subject upon which it legislates, it is apparent that the public health or welfare bears but the most remote relation to the law. The purpose of a statute must be determined from the natural and legal effect of the language employed; and whether it is or is not repugnant to the Constitution of the United States must be determined from the natural effect of such statutes when put into operation, and not from their proclaimed purpose. . . .

It is manifest to us that the limitation of the hours of labor as provided for in this section of the statute under which the indictment was found, and the plaintiff in error convicted, has no such direct relation to, and no such substantial effect upon, the health of the employee, as to justify us in regarding the section as really a health law. It seems to us that the real object and purpose were simply to regulate the hours of labor between the master and his employees (all being men, *sui juris*), in a private business, not dangerous in any degree to morals, or in any real and substantial degree to the health of the employees. Under such circumstances the freedom of master and employee to contract with each other in relation to their employment, and in defining the same, cannot be prohibited or interfered with, without violating the Federal Constitution.

The judgment of the Court of Appeals of New York, as well as that of the Supreme Court and of the County Court of Oneida County, must be reversed and the case remanded to the County Court for further proceedings not inconsistent with this opinion.

Reversed.

Mr. Justice Holmes dissenting:

I regret sincerely that I am unable to agree with the judgment in this case, and that I think it my duty to express my dissent.

This case is decided upon an economic theory which a large part of the country does not entertain. If it were a question whether I agreed with that theory, I should desire to study it further and long before making up my mind. But I do not conceive that to be my duty, because I strongly believe that my agreement or disagreement has nothing to do with the right of a majority to embody their opinions in law. It is settled by various decisions of this court that state constitutions and state laws may regulate life in many ways which we as legislators might think as injudicious, or if you like as tyrannical, as this, and which, equally with this, interfere with the liberty to contract. Sunday laws and usury laws are ancient examples. A more modern one is the prohibition of lotteries. The liberty of the citizen to do as he likes so long as he does not interfere with the liberty of others to do the same which has been a shibboleth for some well-known writers, is interfered with by school laws, by the Postoffice, by every state or municipal institution which takes his money for purposes though desirable, whether he likes it or not. The 14th Amendment does not enact Mr. Herbert Spencer's Social Statics. The other day we sustained the Massachusetts vaccination law. Jacobson v. Massachusetts, 197 U.S. 11. United States and state statutes and decisions cutting down the liberty to contract by way of combination are familiar to this court. Northern Securities Co. v. United States, 193 U.S. 197. Two years ago we upheld the prohibition of sales of stock on margins, or for future delivery, in the Constitution of California. Otis v. Parker, 187 U.S. 606. The decision sustaining an eight-hour law for miners is still recent. Holden v. Hardy, 169 U.S. 366. Some of these laws embody convictions or prejudices which judges are likely to share. Some may not. But a Constitution is not intended to embody a particular economic theory, whether of paternalism and the organic relation of the citizen to the state or of *laissez faire*. It is made for people of fundamentally differing views, and the accident of our finding certain opinions natural and familiar, or novel, and even shocking, ought not to conclude our judgment upon the question whether statutes embodying them conflict with the Constitution of the United States.

General propositions do not decide concrete cases. The decision will depend on a judgment or intuition more subtle than any articulate major premise. But I think that the proposition just stated, if it is accepted, will carry us far toward the end. Every opinion tends to become a law. I think that the word "liberty," in the 14th Amendment, is perverted when it is held to prevent the natural outcome of a dominant opinion, unless it can be said that a rational and fair man necessarily would admit that the statute proposed would infringe fundamental principles as they have been understood by the traditions of our people and our law. It does not need research to show that no such sweeping condemnation can be passed upon the statute before us. A reasonable man might think it a proper measure on the score of health. Men whom I certainly could not pronounce unreasonable would uphold it as a first instalment of a general regulation of the hours of work. Whether in the latter aspect it would be open to the charge of inequality I think it unnecessary to discuss.

MR. JUSTICE HARLAN (with whom MR. JUSTICE WHITE and MR. JUSTICE DAY concurred) also dissented.

Muller v. Oregon

In this case, the Court upheld an Oregon statute that prevented women from working in factories or laundries for more than ten hours a day. In doing so, it relied on a brief by Louis Brandeis that distinguished the present case from the Lochner *precedent on the grounds that women are physically different from men. Thus, the Court interpreted the Oregon statue as health regulation properly within the police power of the state.*

In patent cases counsel are apt to open the argument with a discussion of the state of the art. It may not be amiss, in the present case, before examining the constitutional question, to notice the course of legislation as well as expressions of opinion from other than judicial sources. In the brief filed by Mr. Louis D. Brandeis, for the defendant in error, is a very copious collection of all these matters, an epitome of which is found in the margin. . . .

The legislation and opinions referred to in the margin may not be, technically speaking, authorities, and in them is little or no discussion of the constitutional question presented to us for determination, yet they are significant of a widespread belief that woman's physical structure, and the functions she performs in consequence thereof, justify special legislation restricting or qualifying the conditions under which she should be permitted to toil. Constitutional questions, it is true, are not settled by even a consensus of present public opinion, for it is the peculiar value of a written constitution that it places in unchanging form limitations upon legislative action, and thus gives a permanence and stability to popular government which otherwise would be lacking. At the same time, when a question of fact is debated and debatable, and the extent to which a special constitutional limitation goes is affected by the truth in respect to that fact, a widespread and long continued belief concerning it is worthy of consideration. We take judicial cognizance of all matters of general knowledge.

Coppage v. Kansas

Striking down legislation that outlawed so-called "yellow dog" contracts, the Court said:

An interference with this liberty so serious as that now under consideration, and so disturbing of equality of right, must be deemed to be arbitrary, unless it be supportable as a reasonable exercise of the police power of the State. But, notwithstanding the strong general presumption in favor of the validity of state laws, we do not think the statute in question, as construed and applied in this case, can be sustained as a legitimate exercise of that power. . . .

As to the interest of the employed, it is said by the Kansas Supreme Court (87 Kansas Rep., p. 759) to be a matter of common knowledge that "employees, as a rule, are not financially able to be as independent in making contracts for the sale of their labor as are employers in making contracts of purchase thereof." No doubt, wherever the right of private property exists, there must and will be inequalities of fortune; and thus it naturally happens that parties negotiating about a contract are not equally unhampered by circumstances. This applies to all contracts and not merely to that between employer and employee. Indeed a little reflection will show that wherever the right of private property and the right of free contract coexist each party when contracting is inevitably more or less influenced by the question whether he has much property, or little, or none; for the contract is made to the very end that each may gain something that he needs or desires more urgently than that which he proposes to give in exchange. And, since it is self-evident that, unless all things are held in common, some persons must have more property than others, it is from the nature of things impossible to uphold freedom of contract and the right of private property without at the same time recognizing as legitimate those inequalities of fortune that are the necessary result of the exercise of those rights. But the Fourteenth Amendment, in declaring that a State shall not "deprive any person of life, liberty or property without due process of law," gives to each of these an equal sanction; it recognizes "liberty" and "property" as coexistent human rights, and debars the States from any unwarranted interference with either.

And since a State may not strike them down directly it is clear that it may not do so indirectly, as by declaring in effect that the public good requires the removal of those inequalities that are but the normal and inevitable result of their exercise, and then invoking the police power in order to remove the inequalities, without other object in view. The police power is broad, and not easily defined, but it cannot be given the wide scope that is here asserted for it, without in effect nullifying the constitutional guaranty.

West Coast Hotel Co. v. Parrish

Mr. Chief Justice Hughes delivered the opinion of the Court:

This case presents the question of the constitutional validity of the minimum wage law of the State of Washington.

The Act . . . authorizes the fixing of minimum wages for women and minors. . . .

The appellant conducts a hotel. The appellee Elsie Parrish was employed as a chambermaid and (with her husband) brought this suit to recover the difference between the wages paid her and the minimum wage fixed pursuant to the state law . . . The Supreme Court of the State . . . sustained the statute. . . .

[The violation of the due process clause alleged by the appellant] is deprivation of freedom of contract. What is this freedom? The Constitution does not speak of freedom of contract. It speaks of liberty and prohibits the deprivation of liberty without due process of law. . . . But the liberty safeguarded is liberty in a social organization which requires the protection of law against the evils which menace the health, safety, morals and welfare of the people. Liberty under the Constitution is thus necessarily subject to the restraints of due process, and regulation which is reasonable in relation to its subject and is adopted in the interests of the community is due process.

This essential limitation of liberty in general governs freedom of contract in particular. . . .

We think . . . that the decision in the *Adkins* case [*which in 1923 struck down congressional legislation setting minimum wages for women and children in the District of Columbia*—Ed.] was a departure from the true application of the principles governing the regulation by the state of the relation of employer and employed. . . .

With full recognition of the earnestness and vigor which characterize the prevailing opinion in the *Adkins* case we find it impossible to reconcile that ruling with these well-considered declarations. What can be closer to the public interest than the health of women and their protection from unscrupulous and overreaching employers? And if the protection of women is a legitimate end of the exercise of state power, how can it be said that the requirement of the payment of a minimum wage fairly fixed in order to meet the very necessities of existence is not an admissible means to that end? . . .

There is an additional and compelling consideration which recent economic experience has brought into a strong light. The exploitation of a class of workers who are in an unequal position with respect to bargaining power and are thus relatively defenseless against the denial of a living wage is not only detrimental to their health and well being, but casts a direct burden for their support upon the community. What these workers lose in wages the taxpayers are called upon to pay. The bare cost of living must be met. We may take judicial notice of the unparalleled demands for relief which arose during the recent period of depression and still continue to an alarming extent despite the degree of economic recovery which has been achieved. It is unnecessary to cite official statistics to establish what is of common knowledge through the length and breadth of the land. While in the instant case no factual brief has been presented, there is no reason to doubt that the state of Washington has encountered the same social problem that is present elsewhere. . . .

Our conclusion is that the case of *Adkins v. Children's Hospital* . . . should be, and it is, overruled.

JUSTICES SUTHERLAND, VAN DEVANTER, MCREYNOLDS and BUTLER dissented.

REVIEW AND DISCUSSION QUESTIONS

1. In the *Lochner* case, the Court states it is sometimes permissible for government to interfere with employment contracts. Why did the Court not permit New York to do so in this case?

2. On what grounds does Holmes dissent from the majority's ruling in *Lochner?* Whose reasoning—Holmes's or the majority's—do you find more persuasive, and why?

3. Is the decision in *Muller v. Oregon* progressive because it protects employees from exploitation, or is it regressive because it holds that women deserve special protection not afforded to men?

4. In *Coppage v. Kansas,* the Court acknowledges that because employees have fewer material resources than do their employers, they are in a weaker bargaining position. Given this fact, one might question how free the contract between employee and employer really is. Nevertheless, the Court struck down legislation preventing employers from requiring, as a term of employment, that employees not belong to a labor union. What was the Court's reasoning?

5. What is the Supreme Court's position in *West Coast Hotel v. Parrish,* and how does it contrast with the positions upheld in the previous cases? On what grounds does it overrule the *Adkins* case?

6. Assess these cases from the points of view of Cohen and of Fried.

PART V

PHILOSOPHICAL ISSUES IN CONSTITUTIONAL LAW

❖

16

CONSTITUTIONAL GOVERNMENT AND THE PROBLEM OF INTERPRETATION

No field of law is philosophically richer than constitutional law. The readings in Part V begin with an essay by Ulrich Preuss, a German philosopher and judge. After looking at the nature and value of constitutionalism in general, Preuss then compares the French, British, and American ways of understanding and realizing the ideal of constitutional government. Next, the discussion turns to the historic debates between the opponents and defenders of the proposed Constitution for the United States in the 1780s. It includes the critical comments of Robert Yates, who presented the antifederalist case, as well as a letter from Thomas Jefferson to the Constitution's chief defender, James Madison, expressing Jefferson's concerns about constitutional government. Madison and Hamilton responded to these and other objections in the *Federalist Papers,* three of which are also included here. Other essays in this section explore two related issues. The first issue is the nature of judicial review: why should the majority, through its elected officials, be bound by a centuries-old Constitution that they did not choose and that requires huge majorities to amend? The second issue is how the U.S. Constitution, once in place, should be interpreted by judges when they are deciding whether or not a law, enacted by elected officials, violates the Constitution's protection of individual rights. In the background of these debates is what has been called the "countermajoritarian" difficulty—the fact that judges who strike down legislation are themselves unelected, yet their interpretations are often controversial and have the effect of law.

The Political Meaning of Constitutionalism: British, French, and American Perspectives

Ulrich K. Preuss

Constitutionalism, according to Ulrich Preuss, is an almost universally respected ideal. Yet despite its popularity, it is unclear just what constitutionalism involves. In the first part of this essay, Preuss describes both the nature and the importance of the ideal. Then in the second half of the essay, Preuss discusses three different forms of constitutionalism by comparing the constitutional traditions of Britain, France, and the United States. Ulrich Preuss is professor of constitutional and administrative law at the University of Bremen, Germany, and a member of the Constitutional Court in Bremen.

CONSTITUTIONALISM— A THRIVING CONCEPT

Constitutionalism is one of the few political ideas which have apparently escaped the general suspicion cast upon most of the other prominent 'isms' in the last decade. Perhaps one may even say that constitutionalism has risen to the status of the only contemporary political idea that enjoys almost universal acceptance. In the last 20 years, a considerable number of countries in different geographical regions with extremely diverse conditions have concurrently chosen the path to constitutionalism in order to find a way out of their respective quandaries: be it Argentina, Brazil, Paraguay and Uruguay in Latin America; Portugal, Spain and Greece at the Southern rim of Europe; South Africa; or Russia and the post-communist countries of Eastern and Central Europe—all of them (and several others) have regarded constitutionalism as the basic objective which sets the framework for their further economic, social, cultural, and political development. No less important is the envisioned role of constitutionalism for the project of European integration. There is a broadening consensus among the citizens of the EU Member States that a common market and more or less remote European institutions in Bruxelles, Strasbourg and Luxembourg will no longer suffice to sustain the aspiration of a European Union. Not accidentally, the idea of a European Polity—for some people a threat, for others a promise—has been associated with the

quest for a European constitution. For in Europe the concept of a polity has been intimately linked with the idea of constitutionalism since the end of the 18th century.

All this conveys strong indications of the vitality of the idea of constitutionalism. It may even be justified to credit constitutionalism with certain economic achievements. A comparative view of the present political world system reveals that constitutional democracies enjoy relatively robust economies and have been relatively successful in the domestication of class cleavages and in coping with other social conflicts. Moreover, despite the tendency of the industrial societies to overuse scarce natural resources and to pursue relentlessly the principle of efficient resource allocation, the average standard of environmental protection is higher in traditional constitutional states than in countries with authoritarian political systems. To be sure, these are correlations, not necessarily causal explanations, and there are exceptions. On the one hand, we know of constitutional states which suffer from serious economic difficulties, great social inequalities and severe religious and ethnic cleavages and yet have firmly resisted the temptation to lapse into authoritarianism. India is certainly the most prominent example. On the other hand, countries like Taiwan, South Korea, Singapore and nowadays also China take pride in the rapid economic development which they achieved in frameworks of government which have maintained, to say the least, large distances from the essentials of constitutionalism.

Whatever the causal linkages between the constitutional form of government and economic performance, there is one experience which merits our attention. Amartya Sen (1994, pp. 10–[1]7) has pointed to the striking fact that no substantial famine has ever occurred in a country with a democratic form of government. One of the reasons for that may be, as Sen hypothesises, the existence of a free press and its function both to publish information about impending disasters and to create and sustain a framework of public accountability of the ruling authorities. This hypothesis, however verifiable or not it may be, leads to the core problem of the concept of constitution and of constitutionalism.

When we speak of constitutionalism, we refer to the set of ideas and principles which form the common basis of the rich variety of constitutions which we find in many countries of the world. Roughly speaking, constitutionalism includes the key tenets of a polity which is based on the idea that the ruled are not merely passive objects of the rulers' willpower but have the status of active members of the political community. This relation entails certain bonds of mutuality between the rulers and the ruled which form the constitution. Thus, constitutionalism encompasses institutional devices and procedures which determine the formation, structure and orderly functioning of government, and it embodies the basic ideas, principles, and values of a polity which aspires to give its members a share in the government. This basket of ideas is fairly impressive and would certainly do the most excellent political philosophers much credit. However, it does not grasp the distinctiveness of constitutionalism. This is not to be found in certain ideas or institutional devices, ingenious as they may be, like, for example, the idea of the separation of powers, or the conception of the accountability of the rulers *vis-à-vis* the ruled; the essence of constitutionalism which has prompted both the admiration and the constant reasoning of the most spirited political philosophers of many centuries is the mystery of its binding force.

Several political philosophers have developed ideas about how to conceive of a good polity in which the rulers are benevolent and work for the best interests of the ruled, or in which the rulers have certain duties *vis-à-vis* their subjects. Moreover, long before the age of modern constitutionalism, we find many examples of compacts in which a ruler enters into binding promises and guarantees *vis-à-vis* his or her subjects. This is not constitutional government in the modern sense of the term. Constitutionalism in this sense is the response to two conditions of modernity: first, the emergence of a monistic sovereign state power after the downfall of the balance between secular and ecclesiastic authority characteristic of mediaeval society; and, second, the idea of the natural freedom of the individual who creates his or her obligations by virtue of his or her interests. Constitutionalism is the answer to the erosion of the inherently obligating forces of the Christian–feudal order and its transformation into an order based on the subjectivity of individuals' interests. In the evolving modern world of the 16th and 17th centuries, one torn by religious cleavages and civil wars, sovereign power became the guarantor of peace and order. At the same time, only the power which could be derived from the natural freedom of the individual was legitimate. Constitutionalism is the conception of a polity in which sovereign power and natural individual freedom coexist and create a political order which cannot resort to antecedent bonds of mutual obligation but must produce its very own mechanisms of obligations. Constitutionalism is, in other words, the answer to the horrifying experience that worldly rule has become immanent; that is, that naturally free individuals have to create a good order by their own limited means. The main problem of this difficult task is the construction of a device in which the sovereign and unlimited power of the united individuals is subjected to the restraining force of legally binding rules. In fact, the legal form of government which rejects the idea of any kind of pre-legal power is the main feature and the great achievement of modern constitutionalism.

THE CONSTITUTION AS A LAW

When I speak of the quality of the constitution as a law I refer to two characteristics. The first is the positivity of modern law. Positive law is the term for that kind of law which owes its authority and binding force not to its religious, philosophical or otherwise sacred content, nor to its tradition, but to its origin from a legitimate lawgiver (see Weber, 1978, Ch. VIII, Sect. VII, pp. 866ff). The law has become a function of the lawgiver's power and will, and in order to motivate the obedience of the ruled it need not refer to its immanent qualities and teleology, but relies on its formal–procedural quality as the result of a more or less arbitrary enactment. This is the essence of Thomas Hobbes' (1841, p. 202) famous statement that not the inherent truth, but the authority of the author provides the binding force of the law—'auctoritas, non veritas facit legem'. It is also the hallmark of positivity.

The second property of modern law consists in the separation of morality from legality. This means the institutionalisation of obedience without the invocation of any moral grounds on which the law may, or may not, be based. Modern law encompasses and obligates all members of society, irrespective of their moral, religious, or political convictions. This makes it possible to bind them together under a common law even if, which is likely to be the case, they do not share the same religious beliefs, philosophical values or historical traditions.

These two properties of modern law allow for the enactment and change of law on mere grounds of expediency according to changing circumstances. Since in modern societies circumstances change rapidly it is justified to say that the positivist and demoralised character of modern law implies the institutionalisation of legal changes and, by virtue of this, the abstraction from social relations which are integrated by commonly shared values (Luhmann, 1972, pp. 209 and *infra*). As Polanyi stated for the market, so we can speak of a high degree of disembeddedness of modern law in relation to other institutions of society.

What is the implication of the legal form of the constitution? What does it mean to say that the legitimation, limitation and regulation of political power assumes the form of legality, i.e., that the obligatory character of the rules which authorise, bind, limit and make political power accountable does not emanate from the inherent dignity of the values and principles which 'govern the governor', but instead from its enactment by a legitimate lawgiver? Does this presuppose a lawgiving authority superior to the ruler which itself has to be bound? This assumption would be self-contradictory. Constitutionalism does not cast out the devil by means of Beelzebub: it does not limit the sovereign power of the lawmaking authority by superimposing a super-sovereign power on it. Only God could rightfully claim this place, but it was the erosion of the undisputed authority of His commands that engendered the secularisation of the concept of supreme power in the first place. Obviously the idea of a super-sovereign would not be the solution of the problem, but its mere displacement.

How then to solve the problem of binding the absolutist sovereign power by means of law without relapsing into the idea of a transcendent power to which could be attributed the capacity of imposing its commands on the secular power? How could one possibly conceive of a source of authority which issued laws that were able to bind the sovereign ruler without transforming this authority into a super-sovereign ruler which now in its turn had to be bound? Does not this question lead us unfailingly into a logical impasse? The answer which shifts the problem onto a new theoretical level is the famous demand: for the 'rule of laws and not of men'. From an analytical perspective, the development proceeded in two steps.

The first developmental step towards the constitutional concept of the rule of law meant: the arbitrary and discretionary will power of the ruling person is substituted by the requirement that the government rule *through* laws (Gaus, 1994, p. 329). Acts of domination must acquire the form of the law. Obviously this principle makes sense only if the law has qualities which distinguish it from the mere will of the sovereign. This was the claim of the anti-absolutists. Just as the laws of nature reflected the inherent rationality, predictability and immutability of the world—laws which even the Deists' God Himself could not manipulate at will—so a law which imposed its binding force on individuals and which they had the moral duty to obey had to have similar qualities. A law must be a rule, i.e., it must be general (as opposed to an individual order of the sovereign), and it must be immutable in order to be immune from the arbitrariness and vacillations of the power holder. The law is the institutional expression of the continuity, calculability and predictability of the social world; it is the embodiment of reason which checks the passions of the ruler (Jellinek, 1919, pp. 43ff).

The underlying idea of the requirement that a law be abstract and general was the claim that what was binding for all should be the embodiment of universally valid truths and at the same time reflect the spirit of the whole polity, not just of particular segments or individual persons. The form of the law domesticates the will power of the sovereign ruler and thus forces it to exercise its power in a reasonable manner. Essentially, the law is not will, but reason; not *voluntas*, but *ratio*. This is the first step towards the conclusion that the law-giving authority must be vested in a body which is qualified for issuing general rules, i.e., which in some way represents the spirit of the whole body politic.

However, this first step did not yet mean the full attainment of constitutionalism. While the requirements of the rule *through* law forced the absolutist monarch to employ the form of the law for all acts which applied to all his or her subjects, it is not at all clear how this requirement could itself acquire the binding force of a law. The difficulty was succinctly stated by Madison (1961, p. 322):

If angels were to govern men, neither external nor internal controls on government would be necessary. In framing a government which is to be administered by men over men, the great difficulty lies in this: you must first enable the government to control the governed; and in the next place oblige it to control itself.

The full elaboration of this idea is nothing less than the invention of the concept of constitutionalism.

As I stated, the rule of law in the variant of the rule *through* law contains no inherent guarantee that the law's rationalising potential will unfold.

Only if the obligation of the ruler to employ the form of the law for his or her acts of rule is itself an obligation of the law can we speak of a constitutional rule. Hence, the rule of law has a twofold meaning: rule *through* law and rule *by* law (Gaus, 1994, p. 329): acts of domination must acquire the form of the law (government *through* law), and the government itself subjects its will power to the constraints of the law (rule *by* law). This latter element originates in the last analysis in what the famous English mediaeval jurist Henry de Bracton had already stated in the 13th century with great clarity: the king does not make the law, the law makes the king—not 'rex facit legem, lex facit regem' (de Bracton, 1968, pp. 33, 306, quoted in Bridge, 1995). In Britain, where absolutism was defeated in its early stages, the 'law-makes-the-king' doctrine gave rise to the constitutional theory that the power to make laws rested in the polity as a whole, not in any single part of it, and that the binding force of the laws followed from the consensus of all of its parts. As Richard Hooker (Jellinek, 1919, p. 48) put it, a legislative power of the king which was not authorised by the constitution but exercised in his own right was tantamount to tyranny.

From a jurist's conceptual perspective, one of the main questions of constitutionalism is how to establish a legal obligation of the lawmaker him- or herself without violating sound principles of jurisprudential reasoning. At first glance, the legalisation of lawmaking—i.e., the subjection of the lawgiver and his or her actions to the rules of the law—seems to presuppose a legal hierarchy: one is led to assume that the law which stipulates the requirements for the enactment of a law must have a higher authority than the enacted law itself. However, this would force us to surmise a hierarchy of lawgiving authorities, with the truly supreme authority of the ruler who makes the rules about lawmaking at the top, and the derived authority of the lawmaker proper who is bound by the rules of the supreme power below. This hierarchical concept of law forces us to find a source of law which is superior to the sovereign law giver, and even this 'super-sovereign' must be ruled by a super-super-sovereign because, according to this hierarchical logic, his or her right to make rules for the sovereign must in turn be based on a superior law. This drives us into an infinite regression. In fact, the creative invention of constitutionalism is different.

From a sociological perspective, the legalisation of lawmaking is but one example of a more general social practice which Luhmann (1972, 1974, pp. 32ff, 213ff) has termed 'reflexive mechanisms'. We speak of reflexivity when a particular process is applied to itself: the learning of learning, the research on research, the talking over talk, or the making of rules for rule making are examples for reflexive mechanisms. (Evidently H. L. A. Hart's secondary rules—rules about the making, unmaking and the validity of legal rules—are the result of reflexive mechanisms.) Two particularities of reflexivity are of special interest for our topic: first, it increases the range of options which are available in a society in that it allows for selection from among the huge bulk of possible actions. If I learn how to learn I do not have to learn everything that might be important—I gain the freedom to select what I need to learn in the different situations of life. Likewise, if a society makes rules over rule making it increases its capacity for rule making in that it creates and maintains the—more and more professionalised—knowledge about how, when and to what degree a matter should be regulated by law, and thus enhances the power to select among several possibilities.

The second property of reflexivity in our field of law is the surprising instance that in order to establish rules about rule making it is not necessary to establish a hierarchy of legal norms such that rules about how to enact rules and how to establish their validity etc. are superior to the laws which regulate substantive matters. This would finally amount to the idea of a government of angels over people, whereas the problem is the government of people over people whereby 'all men are created equal'. Rousseau (1968, Bk. 2, Ch. 7, p. 84) had analysed the problem in a manner very similar to that of the Federalists: In order to find the best rules of society,

there would need to exist a superior intelligence, who could understand the passions of men without

feeling any of them, who had no affinity with our nature but knew it to the full, whose happiness was independent of ours, but who would nevertheless make our happiness his concern. . . .

Rather than establishing an ultimate source of authority which controls the ruler by virtue of its superior power and authority, constitutionalism imagines a non-hierarchical order in which the single one and undivided state authority is divided into different functions which in turn are distributed among institutionalised branches of state authority. The separation of powers, which Article 16 of the French Declaration declared an indispensable element of any constitution, is indeed essential for constitutionalism, in that it establishes a rule which 'governs the governor' without resorting to the obvious idea of a monistic supreme authority which controls the governor and which therefore operates as the ultimate guarantor of an orderly political rule. The characteristic of constitutionalism is a horizontal order of state authority, in which a system of careful coordination of the functionally specified powers produces a web of mutual and almost circular dependence whereby either one state power can only act on the antecedent action of another or it is subject to subsequent scrutiny and, if need be, censure.

Although the essential property of constitutionalism is the quality of constitutions as a law, this does not mean that the source of legal authority is alike for all constitutions. In fact, I contend that the typologies and distinctions which have been offered in the long history of constitutional reasoning originate in the final analysis in different conceptions about the source of the legally binding force of the respective constitutions. Be it the distinction between written and unwritten constitutions; between rigid and flexible; between those which are more fundamental than ordinary laws (whatever this may mean) and those which have the status of ordinary law; between constitutions which can be amended by the ordinary legislature and those whose revision requires an exclusive amending authority, or the distinction between juridically and politically enforceable constitutions—all these distinctions aim at the clarification of the source and legitimation of the authority of the constitution in its quality as a law. Needless to say, probably the most debated questions of constitutionalism—the questions of who are the authoritative interpreters of the constitution and which methods have to be employed (Murphy, 1993, pp. 3–25)—lie at the core of this basic problem.

PATTERNS OF CONSTITUTIONAL AUTHORITY

In the third part of this lecture I want to give a brief account of three patterns of constitutional authority representing different versions of constitutionalism. Incidentally, they have also proven to be the most influential concepts in the last 300 years.

THE BRITISH CONSTITUTIONAL TRADITION

The British concept of constitutionalism is clearly the most traditional one and at the same time the one whose particular solution of the problem of the authority of the constitution is least transferable to other societies. At first glance it seems paradoxical to understand the doctrine of parliamentary sovereignty as the embodiment of the British concept of constitutionalism—after all, is not the negation of an unbound sovereign power the essence of constitutionalism? Does not constitutionalism require that the sovereign power, whoever may be its holder, be subject to the constitution? The British version of constitutionalism's answer to this question is rather complex. It rearranges the vertical problem of a hierarchical order, i.e., of supremacy and subordination, into a horizontal problem of coordinating and balancing different parts of the sovereign power: the Parliament consists of three elements; it is, strictly speaking, the Queen in Parliament, including the monarch, the House of Commons and the House of Lords. They are sovereign only through common action, and being bound to each other by mutual rights and duties, the concept of sovereignty acquires a meaning entirely inconsistent with that developed by Bodin (1962) or Hobbes (1991): while they conceived of it as an absolute, undivided and unbound power, in the concept of British constitutionalism it is instituted in a web of cooperative relations of the three constituents of Parliament. They can exercise their sovereign power only in joint action, and this gives rise to the complementary element of British constitutionalism, namely the doctrine of the rule of law.

Rule of law does *not* mean the supremacy of abstract legal principles over the sovereign—this would raise the logically and practically unsolvable problem of a sovereign superior to the sovereign; as I stated earlier, it signifies that the Parliament (always to be understood in its three constituents) can exercise its sovereign power only *through* law. For British subjects the 'rule of law' means the absence of 'arbitrariness, of prerogative, or even of wide discretionary authority on the part of the government' (Dicey, 1915, p. 120). Moreover, when the British invoke the 'rule of law' they do not think of abstract principles or of an enumeration of individual rights insured to them by some supreme power, but of the existence of remedies and courts which protect their freedoms—*ubi jus ibi remedium* (Dicey, 1915, p. 118). The law exists, as it were, in the operation of the courts which protect the citizens against any kind of wrongdoings which he or she might suffer from the government or a private person. In other words, the authority of the law which binds the government—that is, the 'law of the constitution'—does not derive from a supreme power, least of all from the sovereignty of Parliament, but from the operation of those institutions which secure the exercise of the individuals' freedoms. Note that this idea presupposes that 'there is an area of freedom into which the law should not intervene other than to ensure that the freedom is guaranteed' (Bridge, 1995, p. 1). The rights to individual freedom are not created by the law, i.e., derived from principles of the law, but, as Dicey put it, they are 'inherent in the ordinary law of the land' in that they flow from the remedies which the British are granted by the Courts. Thus, in Britain, 'the law of the constitution is little else than a generalisation of the rights which the Courts secure to individuals', or, put conversely, the rights of individuals are part of the constitution because they are inherent elements of the ordinary course of the law of the land (Dicey, 1915, p. 119). From this it follows that Dicey is quite right to state that, due to the embeddedness of individual rights in the institutional web of the law of the land, 'the right is one which can hardly be destroyed without a thorough revolution in the institutions and manners of the nation' (Dicey, 1915, p. 120). If this still holds true in our day it would mean that in order to suspend or do away with certain rights it would seem necessary to destroy entire entrenched institutions, which in the end may do more harm to the country than the cancellation of a single right by way of a revision of a written constitution. Or, to put it in a more pointed manner, in order to change the constitution the British must make a revolution, because the binding authority of their constitution is not freely disposable to an identifiable single actor, and its alteration is not subject to legally defined procedures. Thus, the constitution of Britain is very much the result of its political culture and not the emanation of one single authoritative source. Its legal quality is derived from the ordinary course of the law of the land, quite the opposite of the continental concepts of constitutionalism which teach that the validity and authority of the law is derived from the constitution. Not surprisingly, in Britain the idea of the constitution as embodied in one written document has never gained a foothold.

THE AMERICAN CONSTITUTIONAL TRADITION

As we know, in sharp contrast to Britain, the character of the constitution as a written text has become one of the hallmarks of the American concept of constitutionalism. Its other distinctive feature is the constitution's status as a supreme law. Of course, the written form is by no means a mere formality. In fact, it is as essential to the authority and validity of the constitution as is the textual embodiment of God's spirit and word in Holy Scripture (Grey, 1984). The written text is the solemn expression of the mutual promises and obligations of the citizens who by this very act constitute a polity among themselves—it is,

as Hannah Arendt (1973, pp. 169–73) put it, the result of a horizontal social contract which creates mutually binding legal obligations. The written form is the almost sacred affirmation of these promises. As Thomas Paine (1979, p. 209) wrote about the constitutions of the states which they had enacted before forming the United States of America, in each state that constitution served, 'not only as an authority, but as a law of control to the government. It was the political bible of the state'.

Evidently the authority derived from its legally binding character and that emanating from its quasi-biblical scriptural form merge and support the other feature of the US constitution, namely its character as a supreme law. Supreme law means that all branches of government, including the legislature itself are the creatures of the constitution. This constitution is, as Thomas Paine (1979, pp. 210, 213) put it, 'a thing antecedent to the government', originating from a compact 'of the people with each other, to produce and constitute a government'. More striking than the priority of the constitution over the government is its priority over the will of the people itself—the US constitution is clearly supposed to restrain and even to thwart the will of the majority. This is why time and again constitutionalism and democracy have been regarded as opposites, the term constitutional democracy verging on an oxymoron (see, e.g., Holmes, 1988).

I do not want to pursue this matter but, rather, to deal with the slightly different question of how the constitution can acquire the status of a law which is able to impose its superior authority on its own creator, the people. An obvious answer is the theory of self-binding, the so-called Ulysses strategy—the people protect themselves against their own potential myopia, passions, ignorance etc. This is a functional explanation which gives no reason how it is possible that the constitution is the supreme law and can bind not only the government, but even its own creator.

The answer is somewhat surprising. When we look for a justification of the supremacy of the constitution we are inclined to reason within a hierarchical framework, e.g., in Kelsen's theory of a hierarchy of the legal order. But despite the rhetoric of 'supreme law', which indeed suggests a hierarchical order, the supremacy of the constitution derives from neither of the sources which we have dealt with thus far, i.e., neither from an authority which claims superiority over the people—this is an obvious impossibility—nor from its 'immanent and teleological qualities' (Weber, 1978, p. 867), nor from its merely traditional character as originating in venerable old times which might convey to the constitution its superiority over all other laws. Rather, its quasi-sacred character emanates from its feature as a mutual promise of individuals who enter into a compact with each other by which they transform themselves into a nation; which means that they pledge to each other to stay together in a common polity in good and in bad times (Murphy, 1993, p. 9). It is the sanctity of the *founding act* by which the polity has been created which imputes to the constitution the authority of the supreme law. The supremacy of its authority over all other laws flows from the inherent significance and uniqueness of the act of nation building. The essential constitutional question which arises is how to preserve the legacy of the founding act, i.e., how to keep the polity alive. Is it more appropriate (and more loyal to the ideas of the founders) to stick to the letter of their sacred scripture in which their original intentions are best determined, or does the sanctity of the founding act require an adjustment of the founders' inspirations to the conditions of the contemporary world? The locus of this debate is the field of constitutional interpretation. Is the *text* of the constitution, the written embodiment of the founders' intentions, the supreme authority, or is it the contemporary *context* which gives the text its particular and, depending on circumstances, changing meaning, so that the constitution is the object of an ever changing struggle about its appropriate interpretation and implementation?

Whatever the right answer may be, the supremacy of the constitution is, in any case, presupposed not only over all branches of government, but also over the people themselves. This is the genuinely American spirit of constitutionalism: the making of the constitution is the act of founding the nation, and whatever purposes, aspirations, hopes, fears, achievements, disappointments, traumas and tragedies of the nation through its eventful history may have occurred or may arise in the future, it is the constitution from which the people will try to extract the right answers to their questions. That is the ultimate reason for the almost obsessive passion of American scholars, lawyers, politicians and great parts of the general public for questions of constitutional interpretation. Incidentally, the other obsession is with rights. Charles Taylor (1992, p. 429) has drawn our attention to the slightly aggressive character of American political life and its 'culture of rights', which underscores the 'value on energetic, direct defence of rights' (cf. Lacey and Haakonssen, 1992). Not surprisingly, in this culture the main guarantor of individuals' rights are the courts. The people living under a constitution whose Bill of Rights starts with the prohibition 'Congress shall make no law . . .' would certainly sense it as a mere perversity if they should regard the legislature as the defender of their rights rather than as the main source of their endangerment.

THE FRENCH CONSTITUTIONAL TRADITION

This rights-protecting and -engendering role of parliament is, in fact, one of the characteristics of the French model of constitutional authority. It is neither based on the rootedness of the law in the institutions which protect individuals against arbitrary rule nor on the sacredness of a founding act of nation building which is embodied in a written document. The French concept of constitutionalism is deeply rooted in the idea of the sovereignty of the constituent power and its logical priority over the constituted powers. This opposition explains the striking feature of French constitutional history and theory: that despite the importance which the idea of the constitution has gained during the Great French Revolution, the concept of an eternal, paramount, or supreme law never arose.

The legal authority of French constitutions has been considerably lower than that of the US since their revolutionary origination in 1789 and 1791 respectively (Henkin, 1989). The idea that the constitution is the supreme law to which all branches of government, including the Parliament and the President, are subordinated never gained a foothold in France. Until our day the French concept of constitutionalism has not embraced the institution of judicial review, i.e., the control of the constitutionality of an enacted law through the judiciary.[1] The arbiter in disputes over the interpretation of the constitution between the different branches of government is neither a Court nor the Constitutional Council, but the popularly elected President of the Republic who symbolises the unity and integrity of the Nation. Most surprisingly, the constitution of the homeland of the famous and globally influential and venerated Declaration of the Rights of Man and Citizen does not even include an explicit bill of rights. Its preamble contains a solemn proclamation of 'attachment' to the Rights of Man as they were defined in the Declaration of 1789, but this does not mean its legally binding incorporation into the constitution. To the contrary, Article 34 of the constitution explicitly states that the civil rights of the citizens and the guarantees for the exercise of their political freedoms will be taken care of by *law*.

In other words, when the French look for a guardian of their rights and their political freedom, they point to the parliament, not to the courts. The parliament is not viewed, as in the US, as a potential threat to individuals' rights against which the courts must be invoked, but as the guarantor of their realisation. In the French constitutional tradition the idea of political freedom has been inherently connected with the concept of the general will, which in the last analysis refers to the idea of collective redemption and to the belief in the inherent equality of all people before God. Evidently this basically Catholic doctrine stands in stark contrast to Protestant individualism. Consequently, French constitutional doctrine has always been much more concerned with the integrity of the collective will of the nation than about the rights of the individual.

What, then, is the political meaning of constitutionalism in the French tradition? On what does the authority of the constitution rest, and how can its binding force be explained? The answers are not easily found, but a few hypotheses offer themselves. First, the genuine spirit of constitutionalism and its binding force is not encapsulated in the *constitution* but in the *constituent power* of the nation. The constituent power is the creator of all constituted powers and cannot itself be bound by the constitution. The constitution is neither the source of political freedom nor of political integration, much less of political inspiration. All these purposes are embodied in the idea of the nation rather than in the notion of constitutionalism. Unlike the United States, the creation of the constitution has not been the founding act for the French nation—rather, the constitution is one of the emanations of the nation. The nation is antecedent to the constitution. True, there is also in the French version of constitutionalism a mythical founding act, but this is the act of founding the *nation*, i.e., of creating the constituent power which subsequently produces a constitution. This constitution cannot and must not bind its creator, that is, the nation itself. In the words of Emmanuel Joseph Sieyès (1963, pp. 124, 126–28): 'The nation is prior to everything. It is the source of everything. Its will is always legal; indeed, it is the law itself'. Therefore the nation cannot be subject to the constitution.

The essence of this concept of constitutionalism, then, is not embodied in the constitution itself; it is incarnated in the power of the nation to make and unmake a constitution at will and at any time. Constitutionalism, that is, consists of what one might call, 'constitution-creativity'; the potential of the nation to constitute and reconstitute its sovereign power and give it its appropriate institutional shape at will. This dynamic idea of constitutionalism accounts for many of the particularities which we encounter in the French tradition, for example, the comparatively large number of French constitutions in the last two centuries, or the relatively weak differentiation between ordinary laws and the constitution in terms of their legally binding force. As in the US, the idea of supremacy is there; but, unlike in the US, it is not associated with the idea of the constitution, but with the pre-constitutional notion of the constituent power of the nation. In fact, the constitution is the embodiment of an inferior rather than of a superior political and legal authority.

SOME PRELIMINARY CONCLUSIONS

This sketchy account of the three main traditions of constitutionalism (which are of course by no means exhaustive) shows the difficulty of conceiving a clear cut, unambiguous and undisputed idea of constitutionalism. This is, of course, not very surprising, since the concept is supposed to deliver the answer to one of the most intricate problems of political philosophy, namely the 'governance of the government'. Neither Plato's idea of the rule of the philosophers, nor pre-modern conceptions of the ruler as the worldly proxy of a Deity, or as the Vicar of Christ, can any longer, if they ever could, provide a solution to this problem in a world of immanence in which the normatively binding force of (moral or legal) obligations can only be established by inner-worldly mechanisms. When, in the 16th and 17th centuries, the traditional conceptions of the good and the right had been eroded and become radically pluralised, the idea of authority and governance had to be reformulated in as radical a manner. Not only the modern monistic concept of sovereignty, but its conceptual and normative foundation in the subjectivity of the governed required, but at the same time also facilitated, the conception of a political authority with which the rulers were entrusted and hence did not possess in their own right. The legal codification of this relation between the governors and the governed, who are conceived as parts of an overarching common polity, is the basic idea of constitutionalism. The quality of constitutions as laws, i.e., as generating the *legal* obligations of the governors, is essential. Only if the bond between the governors and the governed obligates the ruler, irrespective of his or her personal qualities, religious beliefs or else normative convictions, and if it cannot be revoked unilaterally by the ruler, is it possible to form a reliable institutional structure of government in which the governed are recognised as the ultimate source of political authority.

These are the common traits of any concept of constitutionalism. However, the answers to the question of how this authority is institutionalised and rendered a permanent element of the polity so that the government is effectively bound are quite different: while the British concept relies very much on the operation of deeply entrenched institutions which permeate through the social texture (the three elements of Parliament, its rule through and by law, and the remedy-engendering operation of the Courts), both the American and the French notions presuppose one single locus in which the source of the authority of the constitution is embodied. In the case of the US it is the charisma of the founding act which is to be preserved over history in the text of the constitution and which makes this document a legacy, sometimes perhaps a burdensome legacy of the past which imposes itself on future generations. Knowing that this original compact of the Founding Fathers cannot be repeated, all its solemnity and pathos is 'invested' into the text of the constitution. Not accidentally, an American author uses the image of a 'marriage consummated through the pledging partners' positive, active consent' when speaking of the founding generation, whereas for later generations the constitution 'may operate more as an arranged marriage in which consent is passive' (Murphy, 1993, p. 9). If we may apply this somewhat frivolous comparison to the French case it is obvious that the French, rather than passively accommodating to the routine and triteness of a long marriage, prefer to start afresh if they feel that the previous bond no longer fits their needs. The constitution is no less important for them, but their underlying idea is that it should not embody the spirit of a past venerable event which should be inscribed into the collective memory of the nation, but rather should become the historically changing incarnation of the essence of the French nation, namely its supreme power, creativity and authority to freely and independently pursue its historical mission. In other words, while the Americans find their self-assurance as a nation in the preservation of the solemn founding act as authenticated in their constitution, for the French the existence of their nation is a matter of course which is not embodied in the constitution, but in the general will of its constituent power—and this is not a sacred incident of the past, but an essential and hence eternal attribute.

Thus, in the last analysis constitutionalism involves much deeper issues than the idea of limited government, important as this undoubtedly is. At the heart of the concept of constitutionalism lies the question of how to find a way of civilising the unfathomable charisma of politics without destroying liberty. Europe was the continent where this question emerged for the first time in the history of humanity. Meanwhile, since the downfall of the bipolar world and the end of communism, the search for the right answers has become almost universal. Paradoxically, this coincides with a similarly unique step which Europe is about to make, namely the search for a constitution for a supranational political community. Will the multifaceted concept of constitutionalism as developed in the last 300 years provide us with the wisdom that is required for the solution of this new problem? Evidently this is a quite new issue which patently displays that no discussion of constitutionalism whatsoever will ever be concluded. This, then, is my provisional conclusion.

NOTE

[1]The present constitution establishes the Constitutional Council, which is more a council of elder statespeople and experienced politicians than of jurists. It has to check the constitutionality of organic laws *before* their enactment, whereas the compatibility of ordinary laws with the constitution *can* be scrutinised *before* their promulgation upon request of the President of the Republic, the Prime Minister of the Presidents of the two chambers of the Parliament.

REFERENCES

Arendt, H. (1973), *On Revolution*, Harmondsworth: Penguin.

Bodin, J. (1962), *The Six Bookes of a Commonweale*, first published 1576, trans. R. Knolles, McRae, K. D. (ed.), Harvard University Press: Cambridge, Mass.

Bridge, J. (1995), 'The Rule of Law and the Individual in the United Kingdom and in a Federal Europe', paper presented to the conference on *Constitutional History and the Rule of Law*, Bangalore, 16–18 February.

de Bracton, H. (1968), *De Legibus et Consuetudinibus Angliae*, trans. Samuel E. Thorne, Harvard University Press: Cambridge, Mass.

Dicey, A. V. (1982), *Introduction to the Study of the Law of the Constitution*, reprint of the eighth edition of 1915, Liberty Classics: Indianapolis.

Gaus, F. F. (1994), 'Public Reason and the Rule of Law' in Shapiro, I. (ed.), *The Rule of Law*, (Nomos XXXVI), New York University Press: New York/London.

Grey, T. (1984), 'The Constitution as Scripture', *Stanford Law Review*, 37, 1–25.

Hobbes, T. (1841), *Leviathan: the Latin Version, Opera philosophica quae Latine scripsit omnia*, Vol. 3, J. Bohn: London.

Hobbes, T. (1991), *Leviathan*, first published 1651, Tuck, R. (ed.), Cambridge University Press: Cambridge.

Henkin, L. (1989), 'Revolutions and Constitutions', *Louisiana Law Review*, Vol. 49, pp.1023–56.

Holmes, S. (1988), 'Precommitment and the paradox of democracy' in Elster, J. and Slagstad, R. (eds.), *Constitutionalism and Democracy*, Cambridge University Press: Cambridge/New York.

Jellinek, G. (1919), *Gesetz und Verordnung*, (v. 1887), Neudruck d. Ausg.: Tübingen.

Lacey, M. J. and Haakonssen, K. (eds.) (1992), *A Culture of Rights: The Bill of Rights in philosophy, politics, and law—1791 and 1991*, Cambridge University Press: Cambridge.

Luhmann, N. (1974), 'Reflexive Mechanismen', *Soziologische Aufklärung*, Aufl. Opladen, pp.92–112.

Luhmann, N. (1972), *Rechtssoziologie*, Rowohlt: Beinbek b. Hamburg.

Madison, J. (1961), *The Federalist Papers*, No. 51, Rossiter, C. (ed.), New American Library: New York/London.

Murphy, W. F. (1993), 'Constitutions, Constitutionalism, and Democracy' in Greenberg, D., Katz, S. N. et al. (eds.), *Constitutionalism and Democracy. Transitions in the Contemporary World*, Oxford University Press: New York/Oxford.

Paine, T. (1979), *Rights of Man*, Collins, H. (ed.), Penguin: Harmondsworth.

Rousseau, J.-J. (1968), *The Social Contract*, trans. Cranston, M. (ed.), Penguin: Harmondsworth.

Sen, A. (1994), 'Freedoms and Needs', *New Republic*, Vol. 31, January, pp. 10–[1]7.

Sieyès, E .J. (1963), *What is the Third Estate?*, first published 1789, trans. and introduced by Finer, S. E. and Blondel, M. (eds.), Pall Mall Press: London.

Taylor, C. (1992), 'Can Canada Survive the Charter?', *Alberta Law Review*, Vol. XXX, pp. 427–47.

Weber, M. (1978), *Economy and Society*, Roth, G. and Wittich, C. (eds.), University of California at Berkeley Press: Berkeley/Los Angeles/London.

REVIEW AND DISCUSSION QUESTIONS

1. One aspect of constitutionalism is mutuality. What does Preuss mean by that?

2. Constitutionalism is a response to two conditions of modernity, according to Preuss. Explain the two.

3. In claiming that a modern constitution has the character of law, Preuss argues that constitutions not only govern *through* law but also govern *by* law. Explain what he means.

4. Explain briefly the differences between the British, French, and American forms of constitutionalism.

Debating Ratification of the U.S. Constitution

Robert Yates, Thomas Jefferson, James Madison, and Alexander Hamilton

Article VII of the U.S. Constitution calls for it to be ratified by the states, and at the close of the Constitutional Convention there followed a period of intense debate over the proposed new U.S. Constitution. Best known of the works that appeared during that period are the Federalist Papers, *written by James Madison, Alexander Hamilton, and John Jay. The papers began appearing in a New York newspaper a few weeks after the convention adjourned, and they set forth in detail the significance of the various provisions of the document and presented the case for its adoption. Many, however, were initially skeptical, including Thomas Jefferson, who had not attended the convention. Although he was eventually convinced to support adoption, others remained opposed. Prominent among these antifederalist authors was a New York lawyer and delegate to the convention named Robert Yates. Writing under the name of Brutus, he published a series of essays in the* The New York Journal, *which appeared at the same time as the* Federalist Papers. *Jefferson and Yates raised a variety of political and philosophical objections to the Constitution, objecting particularly to its evident distrust of popular democracy and its emphasis on minority rights. One outcome of this antifederalist resistance was the inclusion as part of the Constitution of the Bill of Rights, which limited the national government, and which many states demanded as a condition of ratification.*

ROBERT YATES (BRUTUS): AN ANTIFEDERALIST CRITIQUE OF THE CONSTITUTION

Let us now proceed to enquire whether it is best the thirteen United States should be reduced to one republic, or not. . . .

If respect is to be paid to the opinion of the greatest and wisest men who have ever thought or wrote on the science of government, we shall be constrained to conclude, that a free republic cannot succeed over a country of such immense extent, containing such a number of inhabitants, and these encreasing in such rapid progression as that of the whole United States. Among the many illustrous authorities which might be produced to this point, quoting only two. The one is the baron de Montesquieu, spirit of laws, chap. xvi. vol. I [book VIII]. "It is natural to a republic to have only a small territory, otherwise it cannot long subsist. In a large republic there are men of large fortunes, and consequently of less moderation; there are trusts too great to be placed in any single subject; he has interest of his own; he soon begins to think that he may be happy, great and glorious, by oppressing his fellow citizens; and that he may raise himself to grandeur on the ruins of his country. In a large republic, the public good is sacrificed to a thousand views; it is subordinate to exceptions, and depends on accidents. In a small one, the interest of the public is easier perceived, better understood, and more within the reach of every citizen; abuses are of less extent, and of course are less protected."

History furnishes no example of a free republic, any thing like the extent of the United States. The Grecian republics were of small extent; so also was that of the Romans. Both of these, it is true, in process of time, extended their conquests over large territories of country; and the consequence was, that their governments were changed from that of free governments to those of the most tyrannical that ever existed in the world.

Not only the opinion of the greatest men, and the experience of mankind, are against the idea of an extensive republic, but a variety of reasons may be drawn from the reason and the nature of things, against it. In every government, the will of the sovereign is the law. In despotic governments, the supreme authority being lodged in one, his will is law, and can be as easily expressed to a large extensive territory as to a small one. In a pure democracy the people are the sovereign, and their will is declared by themselves; for this purpose they must all come together to deliberate, and decide. This kind of government cannot be exercised, therefore, over a country of any considerable extent: it must be confined to a single city, or at least limited to such bounds as that the people can conveniently assemble, be able to debate, understand the subject submitted to them, and declare their opinion concerning it.

In a free republic, although all laws are derived from the consent of the people, yet the people do not declare their consent by themselves in person, but by representatives, chosen by them, who are supposed to know the minds of their constituents, and to be possessed of integrity to declare this mind.

In every free government, the people must give their assent to the laws by which they are governed. This is the true criterion between a free government and an arbitrary one. The former are ruled by the will of the whole, expressed in any manner they may agree upon; the latter by the will of one, or a few. If the people are to give their assent to the laws, by persons chosen and appointed by them, the manner of the choice and the number chosen, must be such, as to possess, be disposed, and consequently qualified to declare the sentiments of the people; for if they do not know, or are not disposed to speak the sentiments of the people, the people do not govern, but the sovereignty is in a few. Now, in a large extended country, it is impossible to have a representation, possessing the sentiments, and of integrity, to declare the minds of the people, without having it so numerous and unwieldly, as to be subject in great measure to the inconveniency of a democratic government.

The territory of the United States is of vast extent; it now contains near three millions of souls, and is capable of containing much more than ten times that number. Is it practicable for a country, so large and so numerous as they will soon become, to elect a representation, that will speak their sentiments, without their becoming so numerous as to be incapable of transacting public business? It certainly is not.

In a republic, the manners, sentiments, and interests of the people should be similar. If this be not the case, there will be a constant clashing of opinions; and the representatives of one part will be continually striving against those of the other. This will retard the operations of government, and prevent such conclusions as will promote the public good. If we apply this remark to the condition of the United States, we shall be convinced that it forbids that we should be one government. The United States includes a variety of climates. The productions of the different parts of the union are very variant, and their interests, of consequence, diverse. Their manners and habits differ as much as their climates and productions; and their sentiments are by no means coincident. The laws and customs of the several states are, in many respects, very diverse, and in some opposite; each would be in favor of its own interests and customs, and, of consequence, a legislature, formed of representatives from the respective parts, would not only be too numerous to act with any care or decision, but would be composed of such heterogenous and discordant principles, as would constantly be contending with each other. . . .

The confidence which the people have in their rulers, in a free republic, arises from their knowing them, from their being responsible to them for their conduct, and from the power they have of displacing them when they misbehave; but in a republic of the extent of this continent, the people in general would be acquainted with very few of their rulers; the people at large would know little of their proceedings, and it would be extremely difficult to change them. The people in Georgia and New Hampshire would not know one another's mind, and therefore could not act in concert to enable them to effect a general change of representatives. The different parts of so extensive a country could not possibly be made acquainted with the conduct of their representatives, nor be informed of the reasons upon which measures were founded. The consequence will be, they will have no confidence in their legislature, suspect them of ambitious views, be jealous of every measure they adopt, and will not support the laws they pass. Hence the government will be nerveless and inefficient, and no way will be left to render it otherwise, but by establishing an armed force to execute the laws at the point of the bayonet—a government of all others the most to be dreaded.

In a republic of such vast extent as the United States, the legislature cannot attend to the various concerns and wants of its different parts. It cannot be sufficiently numerous to be acquainted with the local condition and wants of the different districts, and if it could, it is impossible it should have sufficient time to attend to and provide for all the variety of cases of this nature, that would be continually arising.

In so extensive a republic, the great officers of government would soon become above the control of the people, and abuse their power to the purpose of aggrandizing themselves, and oppressing them. The trust committed to the executive offices, in a country of the extent of the United States, must be various and of magnitude. The command of all the troops and navy of the republic, the appointment of officers, the power of pardoning offences, the collecting of all the public revenues, and the power of expending them, with a number of other powers, must be lodged and exercised in every state, in the hands of a few. When these are attended with great honor and emolument, as they always will be in large states, so as greatly to interest men to pursue them, and to be proper objects for ambitious and designing men, such men will be ever restless in their pursuit after them. They will use the power, when they have acquired it, to the purposes of gratifying their own interest and ambition, and it is scarcely possible, in a very large republic, to call them to account for their misconduct, or to prevent their abuse of power.

These are some of the reasons by which it appears, that a free republic cannot long subsist over a country of the great extent of these states. If then this new constitution is calculated to consolidate the thirteen states into one, as it evidently is, it ought not to be adopted. . . .

The constitution proposed to your acceptance, is designed not for yourselves alone, but for generations yet unborn. The principles, therefore, upon which the social compact is founded, ought to have been clearly and precisely stated, and the most express and full declaration of rights to have been made—But on this subject there is almost an entire silence.

If we may collect the sentiments of the people of America, from their own most solemn declarations, they hold this truth as self evident, that all men are by nature free. No one man, therefore, or any class of men, have a right, by the law of nature, or of God, to assume or exercise authority over their fellows. The origin of society then is to be sought, not in any natural right which one man has to exercise authority over another, but in the united consent of those who associate. The mutual wants of men, at first dictated the propriety of forming societies; and when they were established, protection and defence pointed out the necessity of instituting government. In a state of nature every individual pursues his own interest; in this pursuit it frequently happened, that the possessions or enjoyments of one were sacrificed to the views and designs of another; thus the weak were a prey to the strong, the simple and unwary were subject to imposition from those who were more crafty and designing. In this state of things, every individual was insecure; common interest therefore directed, that government should be established, in which the force of the whole community should be collected, and under such directions, as to protect and defend every one who composed it. The common good, therefore, is the end of civil government, and common consent, the foundation on which it was established. To effect this end, it was necessary that a certain portion of natural liberty should be surrendered, in order, that what remained should be preserved; how great a proportion of natural freedom is necessary to be yielded by individuals, when they submit to government, I shall not now enquire. So much, however, must be given up, as will be sufficient to enable those, to whom the administration of the government is committed, to establish laws for the promoting the happiness of the community, and to carry those laws into effect. But it is not necessary, for this purpose, that individuals should relinquish all their natural rights. Some are of such a nature that they cannot be surrendered. Of this kind are the rights of conscience, the right of enjoying and defending life, etc. Others are not necessary to be resigned, in order to attain the end for which government is instituted, these therefore ought not to be given up. To surrender them, would counteract the very end of government, to wit, the common good. . . .

I presume, to an American, then, that this principle is a fundamental one, in all the constitutions of our own states; there is not one of them but what is either founded on a declaration or bill of rights, or has certain express reservation of rights interwoven in the body of them. From this it appears, that at a time when the pulse of liberty beat high and when an appeal was made to the people to form constitutions for the government of themselves, it was their universal sense, that such declarations should make a part of their frames of government. It is therefore the more astonishing, that this grand security, to the rights of the people, is not to be found in this constitution. . . .

The very term, representative, implies, that the person or body chosen for this purpose, should resemble those who appoint them—a representation of the people of America, if it be a true one, must be like the people. It ought to be so constituted, that a person, who is a stranger to the country, might be able to form a just idea of their character, by knowing that of their representatives. They are the sign—the people are the thing signified. It is absurd to speak of one thing being the representative of another, upon any other principle. The ground and reason of representation, in a free government, implies the same thing. Society instituted government to promote the happiness of the whole, and this is the great end always in view in the delegation of powers. It must then have been intended, that those who are placed instead of the people, should possess their sentiments and feelings, and be governed by their interests, or, in other words, should bear the strongest resemblance of those in whose room they are substituted. It is obvious, that for an assembly to be a true likeness of the people of any country, they must be considerably numerous.—One man, or a few men, cannot possibly represent the feelings, opinions, and characters of a great multitude. In this respect, the new constitution is radically defective.—The house of assembly, which is intended as a representation of the people of America, will not, nor cannot, in the nature of things, be a proper one—sixty-five men cannot be found in the United States, who hold the sentiments, possess the feelings, or are acqainted with the wants and interests of this vast country. This extensive continent is made up of a number of different classes of people; and to have a proper representation of them, each class ought to have an opportunity of choosing their best informed men for the purpose; but this cannot possibly be the case in so small a number. According to the common course of human affairs, the natural aristocracy of the country will be elected. Wealth always creates influence, and this is generally much increased by large family connections; this class in society will for ever have a great number of dependents; besides, they will always favour each other—it is their interest to combine—they will therefore constantly unite their efforts to procure men of their own rank to be elected—they will concenter all their force in every part of the state into one point, and by acting together, will most generally carry their election. . . . The great body of the yeomen of the country cannot expect any of their order in this assembly—the station will be too elevated for them to aspire to—the distance between the people and their representatives, will be so very great, that there is no probability that a farmer, however respectable, will be chosen—the mechanicks of every branch, must expect to be excluded from a seat in this Body—It will and must be esteemed a station too high and exalted to be filled by any but the first men in the state, in point of fortune; so that in reality there will be no part of the people represented, but the rich, even in that branch of the legislature, which is called the democratic.—The well born, and highest orders in life, as they term themselves, will be ignorant of the sentiments of the midling class of citizens, strangers to their ability, wants, and difficulties, and void of sympathy, and fellow feeling. This government is a complete system, not only for making, but for executing laws. And the courts of law, which will be constituted by it, are not only to decide upon the constitution and the laws made in pursuance of it, but by officers subordinate to them to execute all their decisions. The real effect of this system of government, will therefore be brought home to the feelings of the people, through the medium of the judicial power. It is, moreover, of great importance, to examine with care the nature and extent of the judicial power, because those who are to be vested with it, are to be placed in a situation altogether unprecedented in a free country. They are to be rendered totally independent, both of the people and the legislature, both with respect to their offices and salaries. No errors they may commit can be corrected by any power above them, if any such power there be, nor can they be removed from office for making ever so many erroneous adjudications.

The only causes for which they can be displaced, is, conviction of treason, bribery, and high crimes and misdemeanors. . . .

The judicial are not only to decide questions arising upon the meaning of the constitution in law, but also in equity.

By this they are empowered, to explain the constitution according to the reasoning spirit of it, without being confined to the words or letter. . . .

They will give the sense of every article of the constitution, that may from time to time come before them. And in their decisions they will not confine themselves to any fixed or established rules, but will determine, according to what appears to them, the reason and spirit of the constitution. The opinions of the supreme court, whatever they may be, will have the force of law; because there is no power provided in the constitution, that can correct their errors, or controul their adjudications. From this court there is no appeal. And I conceive the legislature themselves, cannot set aside a judgment of this court, because they are authorised by the constitution to decide in the last resort. The legislature must be controuled by the constitution, and not the constitution by them. They have therefore no more right to set aside any judgment pronounced upon the construction of the constitution, than they have to take from the president, the chief command of the army and navy, and commit it to some other person. The reason is plain; the judicial and executive derive their authority from the same source, that the legislature do theirs; and therefore in all cases, where the constitution does not make the one responsible to, or controulable by the other, they are altogether independent of each other.

The judicial power will operate to effect, in the most certain, but yet silent and imperceptible manner, what is evidently the tendency of the constitution:—I mean, an entire subversion of the legislative, executive and judicial powers of the individual states. Every adjudication of the supreme court, on any question that may arise upon the nature and extent of the general government, will affect the limits of the state jurisdiction. In proportion as the former enlarge the exercise of their powers, will that of the latter be restricted. . . .

THOMAS JEFFERSON: A LETTER TO JAMES MADISON

PARIS, SEPTEMBER 6, 1789.

DEAR SIR,—I sit down to write to you without knowing by what occasion I shall send my letter. I do it because a subject comes into my head which I would wish to develope a little more than is practicable in the hurry of the moment of making up general despatches.

The question: Whether one generation of man has a right to bind another, seems never to have been started either on this or our side of the water. Yet it is a question of such consequences as not only to merit decision, but place also, among the fundamental principles of every government. The course of reflection in which we are immersed here on the elementary principles of society has presented this question to my mind; and that no such obligation can be transmitted I think very capable of proof. I set out on this ground which I suppose to be self-evident, *"that the earth belongs in usufruct to the living"*; that the dead have neither powers nor rights over it. The portion occupied by any individual ceases to be his when himself ceases to be, and reverts to the society. If the society has formed no rules for the appropriation of its lands in severalty, it will be taken by the first occupants. These will generally be the wife and children of the decedent. If they have formed rules of appropriation, those rules may give it to the wife and children, or to some one of them, or to the legatee of the deceased. So they may give it to his creditor. But the child, the legatee or creditor takes it, not by any natural right, but by a law of society of which they are members, and to which they are subject. Then no man can by *natural right* oblige the lands he occupied, or the persons who succeed him in that occupation, to the paiment of debts contracted by him. For if he could, he might during his own life, eat up

the usufruct of the lands for several generations to come, and then the lands would belong to the dead, and not to the living, which would be reverse of our principle. What is true of every member of the society individually, is true of them all collectively, since the rights of the whole can be no more than the sum of the rights of individuals. . . .

What is true of a generation all arriving to self-government on the same day, and dying all on the same day, is true of those on a constant course of decay and renewal, with this only difference. A generation coming in and going out entire, as in the first case, would have a right in the 1st year of their self dominion to contract a debt for 33. years, in the 10th. for 24. in the 20th. for 14. in the 30th. for 4. whereas generations changing daily, by daily deaths and births, have one constant term beginning at the date of their contract, and ending when a majority of those of full age at that date shall be dead. The length of that term may be estimated from the tables of mortality, corrected by the circumstances of climate, occupation &c. peculiar to the country of the contractors. . . .

I suppose that the received opinion, that the public debts of one generation devolve on the next, has been suggested by our seeing habitually in private life that he who succeeds to lands is required to pay the debts of his ancestor or testator, without considering that this requisition is municipal only, not moral, flowing from the will of the society which has found it convenient to appropriate the lands become vacant by the death of their occupant on the condition of a payment of his debts; but that between society and society, or generation and generation there is no municipal obligation, no umpire but the law of nature. We seem not to have perceived that, by the law of nature, one generation is to another as one independant nation to another. . . .

On similar ground it may be proved that no society can make a perpetual constitution, or even a perpetual law. The earth belongs always to the living generation. They may manage it then, and what proceeds from it, as they please, during their usufruct. They are masters too of their own persons, and consequently may govern them as they please. But persons and property make the sum of the objects of government. The constitution and the laws of their predecessors extinguish them, in their natural course, with those whose will gave them being. This could preserve that being till it ceased to be itself, and no longer. Every constitution, then, and every law, naturally expires at the end of 19 years [because half of the voters will be dead in 19 years]. If it be enforced longer, it is an act of force and not of right.

It may be said that the succeeding generation exercising in fact the power of repeal, this leaves them free as if the constitution or law had been expressly limited to 19. years only. In the first place, this objection admits the right, in proposing an equivalent. But the power of repeal is not an equivalent. It might be indeed if every form of government were so perfectly contrived that the will of the majority could always be obtained fairly and without impediment. But this is true of no form. The people cannot assemble themselves; their representation is unequal and vicious. Various checks are opposed to every legislative proposition. Factions get possession of the public councils. Bribery corrupts them. Personal interests lead them astray from the general interests of their constituents; and other impediments arise so as to prove to every practical man that a law of limited duration is much more manageable than one which needs a repeal. . . .

Turn this subject in your mind, my Dear Sir, . . . and develope it with that perspicuity and cogent logic which is so peculiarly yours. Your station in the councils of our country gives you an opportunity of producing it to public consideration, of forcing it into discussion. At first blush it may be rallied as a theoretical speculation; but examination will prove it to be solid and salutary. It would furnish matter for a fine preamble to our first law for appropriating the public revenue; and it will exclude, at the threshold of our new government the contagious and ruinous errors of this quarter of the globe, which have armed despots with means not sanctioned by nature for binding in chains their fellow-men. . . .

FEDERALIST—NUMBER 10

James Madison

Among the numerous advantages promised by a well constructed Union, none deserves to be more accurately developed than its tendency to break and control the violence of faction. The friend of popular governments, never finds himself so much alarmed for their character and fate, as when he contemplates their propensity to this dangerous vice. . . .

By a faction I understand a number of citizens, whether amounting to a majority or minority of the whole, who are united and actuated by some common impulse of passion, or of interest, adverse to the rights of other citizens, or to the permanent and aggregate interests of the community.

There are two methods of curing the mischiefs of faction: the one, by removing its causes; the other, by controlling its effects.

There are again two methods of removing the causes of faction: the one by destroying the liberty which is essential to its existence; the other, by giving to every citizen the same opinions, the same passions, and the same interests.

It could never be more truly said than of the first remedy, that it is worse than the disease. Liberty is to faction, what air is to fire, an aliment without which it instantly expires. But it could not be a less folly to abolish liberty, which is essential to political life, because it nourishes faction, than it would be to wish the annihilation of air, which is essential to animal life, because it imparts to fire its destructive agency.

The second expedient is as impracticable, as the first would be unwise. As long as the reason of man continues fallible, and he is at liberty to exercise it, different opinions will be formed. As long as the connection subsists between his reason and his self-love, his opinions and his passions will have a reciprocal influence on each other; and the former will be objects to which the latter will attach themselves. The diversity in the faculties of men from which the rights of property originate, is not less an insuperable obstacle to the uniformity of interests.

The protection of these faculties is the first object of Government. From the protection of different and unequal faculties of acquiring property, the possession of different degrees and kinds of property immediately results: and from the influence of these on the sentiments and views of the respective proprietors, ensues a division of the society into different interests and parties.

The latent causes of faction are thus sown in the nature of man; and we see them everywhere brought into different degrees of activity, according to the different circumstances of civil society. A zeal for different opinions concerning religion, concerning Government and many other points, as well of speculation as of practice; an attachment to different leaders ambitiously contending for pre-eminence and power; or to persons of other descriptions whose fortunes have been interesting to the human passions, have in turn divided mankind into parties, inflamed them with mutual animosity, and rendered them much more disposed to vex and oppress each other, than to co-operate for their common good. So strong is this propensity of mankind to fall into mutual animosities, that where no substantial occasion presents itself, the most frivolous and fanciful distinctions have been sufficient to kindle their unfriendly passions, and excite their most violent conflicts. But the most common and durable source of factions, has been the various and unequal distribution of property. Those who hold, and those who are without property, have ever formed distinct interests in society. Those who are creditors, and those who are debtors, fall under a like discrimination. A landed interest, a manufacturing interest, a mercantile interest, a monied interest, with many lesser interests, grow up of necessity in civilized nations, and divide them into different classes, actuated by different sentiments and views. The regulation of these various and interfering interests forms the principal task of modern Legislation, and involves the spirit of party and faction in the necessary and ordinary operations of Government.

No man is allowed to be a judge of his own cause; because his interest would certainly bias his judgment, and, not improbably, corrupt his integrity. With equal, nay with greater reason, a body of men, are unfit to be both judges and parties, at the same time; yet, what are many of the most important acts of legislation, but so many judicial determinations, not indeed concerning the rights of single persons, but concerning the rights of large bodies of citizens; and what are the different classes of legislators, but advocates and parties to the causes which they determine? Is a law proposed concerning private debts? It is a question to which the creditors are parties on one side, and the debtors on the other. Justice ought to hold the balance between them. Yet the parties are and must be themselves the judges; and the most numerous party, or, in other words, the most powerful faction must be expected to prevail. Shall domestic manufactures be encouraged, and in what degree, by restrictions on foreign manufactures? are questions which would be differently decided by the landed and the manufacturing classes; and probably by neither, with a sole regard to justice and the public good. The apportionment of taxes on the various descriptions of property, is an act which seems to require the most exact impartiality; yet, there is perhaps no legislative act in which greater opportunity and temptation are given to a predominant party, to trample on the rules of justice. Every shilling with which they over-burden the inferior number, is a shilling saved to their own pockets.

It is in vain to say, that enlightened statesmen will be able to adjust these clashing interests, and render them all subservient to the public good. Enlightened statesmen will not always be at the helm: Nor in many cases, can such an adjustment be made at all, without taking into view indirect and remote considerations, which will rarely prevail over the immediate interest which one party may find in disregarding the rights of another, or the good of the whole.

The inference to which we are brought, is, that the *causes* of faction cannot be removed; and that relief is only to be sought in the means of controlling its *effects*.

If a faction consists of less than a majority, relief is supplied by the republican principle, which enables the majority to defeat its sinister views by regular vote: It may clog the administration, it may convulse the society; but it will be unable to execute and mask its violence under the forms of the Constitution. When a majority is included in a faction, the form of popular government on the other hand enables it to sacrifice to its ruling passion or interest, both the public good and the rights of other citizens. To secure the public good, and private rights, against the danger of such a faction, and at the same time to preserve the spirit and the form of popular government, is then the great object to which our enquiries are directed: Let me add that it is the great desideratum, by which alone this form of government can be rescued from the opprobrium under which it has so long labored, and be recommended to the esteem and adoption of mankind.

By what means is this object attainable? Evidently by one of two only. Either the existence of the same passion or interest in a majority at the same time, must be prevented; or the majority, having such co-existent passion or interest, must be rendered, by their number and local situation, unable to concert and carry into effect schemes of oppression. If the impulse and the opportunity be suffered to coincide, we well know that neither moral nor religious motives can be relied on as an adequate control. They are not found to be such on the injustice and violence of individuals, and lose their efficacy in proportion to the number combined together; that is, in proportion as their efficacy becomes needful.

From this view of the subject, it may be concluded, that a pure Democracy, by which I mean, a Society, consisting of a small number of citizens, who assemble and administer the Government in person, can admit of no cure for the mischiefs of faction. A common passion or interest will, in almost every case, be felt by a majority of the whole; a communication and concert results from the form of Government itself; and there is nothing to check the inducements to sacrifice the weaker party, or an obnoxious individual. Hence it is, that such Democracies have ever been spectacles of turbulence and contention; have ever been found incompatible with personal security, or the rights of property; and have in general been as short in their lives, as they have been violent in their deaths. Theoretic politicians, who have patronized this species of Government, have erroneously supposed, that by reducing mankind to a perfect equality in their political rights, they would, at the same time, be perfectly equalized and assimilated in their possessions, their opinions, and their passions.

A Republic, by which I mean a Government in which the scheme of representation takes place, opens a different prospect, and promises the cure for which we are seeking. Let us examine the points in which it varies from pure Democracy, and we shall comprehend both the nature of the cure, and the efficacy which it must derive from the Union.

The two great points of difference between a Democracy and a Republic are, first, the delegation of the Government, in the latter, to a small number of citizens elected by the rest: secondly, the greater number of citizens, and greater sphere of country, over which the latter may be extended.

The effect of the first difference is, on the one hand to refine and enlarge the public views, by passing them through the medium of a chosen body of citizens, whose wisdom may best discern the true interest of their country, and whose patriotism and love of justice, will be least likely to sacrifice it to temporary or partial considerations. Under such a regulation, it may well happen that the public voice pronounced by the representatives of the people, will be more consonant to the public good, than if pronounced by the people themselves convened for the purpose. On the other hand, the effect may be inverted. Men of factious tempers, of local prejudices, or of sinister designs, may by intrigue, by corruption or by other means, first obtain the suffrages, and then betray the interests of the people. The question resulting is, whether small or extensive Republics are most favorable to the election of proper guardians of the public weal: and it is clearly decided in favor of the latter by two obvious considerations.

In the first place it is to be remarked that however small the Republic may be, the Representatives must be raised to a certain number, in order to guard against the cabals of a few; and that however large it may be, they must be limited to a certain number, in order to guard against the confusion of a multitude. Hence the number of Representatives in the two cases, not being in proportion to that of the Constituents, and being proportionally greatest in the small Republic, it follows, that if the proportion of fit characters, be not less, in the large than in the small Republic, the former will present a greater option, and consequently a greater probability of a fit choice.

In the next place, as each Representative will be chosen by a greater number of citizens in the large than in the small Republic, it will be more difficult for unworthy candidates to practise with success the vicious arts, by which elections are too often carried; and the suffrages of the people being more free, will be more likely to centre on men who possess the most attractive merit, and the most diffusive and established characters.

It must be confessed, that in this, as in most other cases, there is a mean, on both sides of which inconveniences will be found to lie. By enlarging too much the number of electors, you render the representative too little acquainted with all their local circumstances and lesser interests; as by reducing it too much, you render him unduly attached to these, and too little fit to comprehend and pursue great and national objects. The Federal Constitution forms a happy combination in this respect; the great and aggregate interests being referred to the national, the local and particular, to the state legislatures.

The other point of difference is, the greater number of citizens and extent of territory which may be brought within the compass of Republican, than of Democratic Government; and it is this circumstance principally which renders factious combinations less to be dreaded in the former, than in the latter. The smaller the society, the fewer probably will be the distinct parties and interests composing it; the fewer the distinct parties and interests, the more frequently will a majority be found of the same party; and the smaller the number of individuals composing a majority, and the smaller the compass within which they are placed, the more easily will they concert and execute their plans of oppression. Extend the sphere, and you take in a greater variety of parties and interests; you make it less probable that a majority of the whole will have a common motive to invade the rights of other citizens; or if such a common motive exists, it will be more difficult for all who feel it to discover their own strength, and to act in unison with each other. Besides other impediments, it may be remarked, that where there is a consciousness of unjust or dishonorable purposes, communication is always checked by distrust, in proportion to the number whose concurrence is necessary.

Hence it clearly appears, that the same advantage, which a Republic has over a Democracy, in controlling the effects of a faction, is enjoyed by a large over a small Republic—is enjoyed by the Union over the States composing it. Does this advantage consist in the substitution of Representatives, whose enlightened views and virtuous sentiments render them superior to local prejudices, and to schemes of injustice? It will not be denied, that the Representation of the Union will be most likely to possess these requisite endowments. Does it consist in the greater security afforded by a greater variety of parties, against the event of any one party being able to outnumber and oppress the rest? In an equal degree does the increased variety of parties, comprised within the Union, increase this security. Does it, in fine, consist in the greater obstacles opposed to the concert and accomplishment of the secret wishes of an unjust and interested majority? Here, again, the extent of the Union gives it the most palpable advantage.

The influence of factious leaders may kindle a flame within their particular States, but will be unable to spread a general conflagration through the other States: a religious sect, may degenerate into a political faction in a part of the Confederacy; but the variety of sects dispersed over the entire face of it, must secure the national Councils against any danger from that source: a rage for paper money, for an abolition of debts, for an equal division of property, or for any other improper or wicked project, will be less apt to pervade the whole body of the Union, than a particular member of it; in the same proportion as such a malady is more likely to taint a particular county or district, than an entire State.

In the extent and proper structure of the Union, therefore, we behold a Republican remedy for the diseases most incident to Republican Government. And according to the degree of pleasure and pride, we feel in being Republicans, ought to be our zeal in cherishing the spirit, and supporting the character of Federalists.

FEDERALIST—NUMBER 51

JAMES MADISON

To what expedient then shall we finally resort for maintaining in practice the necessary partition of power among the several departments, as laid down in the Constitution? The only answer that can be given is, that as all these exterior provisions are found to be inadequate, the defect must be supplied, by so contriving the interior structure of the government, as that its several constituent parts may, by their mutual relations, be the means of keeping each other in their proper places. Without presuming to undertake a full development of this important idea, I will hazard a few general observations, which may perhaps place it in a clearer light, and enable us to form a more correct judgment of the principles and structure of the government planned by the convention.

In order to lay a due foundation for that separate and distinct exercise of the different powers of government, which to a certain extent, is admitted on all hands to be essential to the preservation of liberty, it is evident that each department should have a will of its own; and consequently should be so constituted, that the members of each should have as little agency as possible in the appointment of the members of the others. . . .

But the great security against a gradual concentration of the several powers in the same department, consists in giving to those who administer each department, the necessary constitutional means, and personal motives, to resist encroachments of the others. The provision for defence must in this, as in all other cases, be made commensurate to the danger of attack. Ambition must be made to counteract ambition.

The interest of the man must be connected with the constitutional rights of the place. It may be a reflection on human nature, that such devices should be necessary to control the abuses of government. But what is government itself but the greatest of all reflections on human nature? If men were angels, no government would be necessary. If angels were to govern men, neither external nor internal controls on government would be necessary. In framing a government which is to be administered by men over men, the great difficulty lies in this: You must first enable the government to control the governed; and in the next place, oblige it to control itself. A dependence on the people is no doubt the primary control on the government; but experience has taught mankind the necessity of auxiliary precautions.

This policy of supplying by opposite and rival interests, the defect of better motives, might be traced through the whole system of human affairs, private as well as public. We see it particularly displayed in all the subordinate distributions of power; where the constant aim is to divide and arrange the several offices in such a manner as that each may be a check on the other; that the private interest of every individual, may be a sentinel over the public rights. These inventions of prudence cannot be less requisite in the distribution of the supreme powers of the state.

But it is not possible to give to each department an equal power of self defence. In republican government the legislative authority, necessarily, predominates. The remedy for this inconveniency is, to divide the legislature into different branches; and to render them by different modes of election, and different principles of action, as little connected with each other, as the nature of their common functions, and their common dependence on the society, will admit. . . .

There are moreover two considerations particularly applicable to the federal system of America, which place that system in a very interesting point of view.

First. In a single republic, all the power surrendered by the people, is submitted to the administration of a single government; and usurpations are guarded against by a division of the government into distinct and separate departments. In the compound republic of America, the power surrendered by the people, is first divided between two distinct governments, and then the portion allotted to each, subdivided among distinct and separate departments. Hence a double security arises to the rights of the people. The different governments will control each other; at the same time that each will be controlled by itself.

Second. It is of great importance in a republic, not only to guard the society against the oppression of its rulers; but to guard one part of the society against the injustice of the other part. Different interests necessarily exist in different classes of citizens. If a majority be united by a common interest, the rights of the minority will be insecure. There are but two methods of providing against this evil: The one by creating a will in the community independent of the majority, that is, of the society itself; the other by comprehending in the society so many separate descriptions of citizens, as will render an unjust combination of a majority of the whole, very improbable, if not impracticable. The first method prevails in all governments possessing an hereditary or self appointed authority. This at best is but a precarious security; because a power independent of the society may as well espouse the unjust views of the major, as the rightful interests, of the minor party, and may possibly be turned against both parties. The second method will be exemplified in the federal republic of the United States. Whilst all authority in it will be derived from and dependent on the society, the society itself will be broken into so many parts, interests and classes of citizens, that the rights of individuals or of the minority, will be in little danger from interested combinations of the majority. In a free government, the security for civil rights must be the same as for religious rights. It consists in the one case in the multiplicity of interests, and in the other, in the multiplicity of sects. The degree of security in both cases will depend on the number of interests and sects; and this may be presumed to depend on the extent of country and number of people comprehended under the same government. . . .

FEDERALIST—NUMBER 78

ALEXANDER HAMILTON

. . . Whoever attentively considers the different departments of power must perceive that, in a government in which they are separated from each other, the judiciary, from the nature of its functions, will always be the least dangerous to the political rights of the Constitution; because it will be least in capacity to annoy or injure them. The Executive not only dispenses honors, but holds the sword of the community. The legislature not only commands the purse, but prescribes the rules by which the duties and rights of every citizen are to be regulated. The judiciary, on the contrary, has no influence over either the sword or the purse; no direction either of the strength or of the wealth of the society; and can take no active resolution whatever. It may truly be said to have neither FORCE nor WILL, but merely judgment; and must ultimately depend upon the aid of the executive arm even for the efficacy of its judgment. . . .

Some perplexity respecting the rights of the courts to pronounce legislative acts void, because contrary to the Constitution, has arisen from an imagination that the doctrine would imply a superiority of the judiciary to the legislative power. . . . It is far more rational to suppose, that the courts were designed to be an intermediate body between the people and the legislature, in order, among other things, to keep the latter within the limits assigned to their authority. The interpretation of the laws is the proper and peculiar province of the courts. A constitution is, in fact, and must be regarded by the judges, as a fundamental law. It therefore belongs to them to ascertain its meaning, as well as the meaning of any particular act proceeding from the legislative body. If there should happen to be an irreconcilable variance between the two, that which has the superior obligation and validity ought, of course, to be preferred; or, in other words, the Constitution ought to be preferred to the statute, the intention of the people to the intention of their agents.

Nor does this conclusion by any means suppose a superiority of the judicial to the legislative power. It only supposes that the power of the people is superior to both; and that where the will of the legislature, declared in its statutes, stands in opposition to that of the people, declared in the Constitution, the judges ought to be governed by the latter rather than the former. They ought to regulate their decisions by the fundamental laws, rather than by those which are not fundamental. . . .

It can be of no weight to say that the courts, on the pretence of a repugnancy, may substitute their own pleasure to the constitutional intentions of the legislature. This might as well happen in the case of two contradictory statutes; or it might as well happen in every adjudication upon any single statute. The courts must declare the sense of the law; and if they should be disposed to exercise WILL instead of JUDGMENT, the consequence would equally be the substitution of their pleasure to that of the legislative body. The observation, if it prove any thing, would prove that there ought to be no judges distinct from that body.

If, then, the courts of justice are to be considered as the bulwarks of a limited constitution against legislative encroachments, this consideration will afford a strong argument for the permanent tenure of judicial offices, since nothing will contribute so much as this to that independent spirit in the judges which must be essential to the faithful performance of so arduous a duty.

This independence of the judges is equally requisite to guard the Constitution and the rights of individuals from the effects of those ill humors, which the arts of designing men, or the influence of particular conjunctures, sometimes disseminate among the people themselves, and which, though they speedily give place to better information, and more deliberate reflection, have a tendency, in the meantime, to occasion dangerous innovations in the government, and serious oppressions of the minor party in the community. . . . Until the people have, by some solemn and authoritative act, annulled or changed the established form, it is binding upon themselves collectively, as well as individually; and no presumption, or even knowledge, of their sentiments, can warrant their representatives in a departure from it, prior to such an act. But it is easy to see, that it would require an uncommon portion of fortitude in the judges to do their duty as faithful guardians of the Constitution, where legislative invasions of it had been instigated by the major voice of the community. . . .

REVIEW AND DISCUSSION QUESTIONS

1. Summarize the position of Yates on adopting the Constitution. What are his major objections to it?

2. Jefferson argues that there is ground to doubt the legitimacy of any constitution. Explain briefly the grounds for his conclusion.

3. According to Madison, what is a faction? What is the problem that Madison sees in constructing a government, given the existence of factions?

4. How does Madison propose to solve the problem of factions?

5. Explain Hamilton's theory of the role of judicial review in the Constitution.

6. In his response to Jefferson's letter, Madison said, in essence, that even though he agrees with Jefferson in theory, his suggestions would lead to insuperable practical and political problems for anyone constructing a workable government. What practical problems do you imagine Madison raised? Are they sufficient to answer Jefferson's concerns?

7. Did the *Federalist Papers* provide an adequate answer to the objections raised by Yates and Jefferson? Explain.

The Notion of a Living Constitution

William H. Rehnquist

William Rehnquist wrote this while serving as Associate Justice of the Supreme Court, before he was elevated to his current position of Chief Justice. In the essay, which was originally delivered as a lecture, he contends that judicial review has an inherently antidemocratic character and, accordingly, the use of it to overturn legislative enactments should be sharply limited. Building on John Marshall's defense of judicial review in Marbury v. Madison *(1803), Justice Rehnquist defends original intent against those who claim that judges may replace the Constitution's original meaning with their own sense of what its words should mean.*

At least one of the more than half-dozen persons nominated during the past decade to be an Associate Justice of the Supreme Court of the United States has been asked by the Senate Judiciary Committee at his confirmation hearings whether he believed in a living Constitution. It is not an easy question to answer; the phrase "living Constitution" has about it a teasing imprecision that makes it a coat of many colors. . . . The phrase is really a shorthand expression that is susceptible of at least two quite different meanings.

The first meaning was expressed over a half-century ago by Mr. Justice Holmes in *Missouri v. Holland*[1] with his customary felicity when he said:

> . . . When we are dealing with words that also are a constituent act, like the Constitution of the United States, we must realize that they have called into life a being the development of which could not have been foreseen completely by the most gifted of its begetters. It was enough for them to realize or to hope that they had created an organism; it has taken a century and has cost their successors much sweat and blood to prove that they created a nation.[2]

I shall refer to this interpretation of the phrase "living Constitution," with which scarcely anyone would disagree, as the Holmes version.

The framers of the Constitution wisely spoke in general language and left to succeeding generations the task of applying that language to the unceasingly changing environment in which they would live. Those who framed, adopted, and ratified the Civil War amendments to the Constitution likewise used what have been aptly described as "majesty generalities" in composing the fourteenth amendment. Merely because a particular activity may not have existed when the Constitution was adopted, or because the framers could not have conceived of a particular method of transacting affairs, cannot mean that general language in the Constitution may not be applied to such a course of conduct. Where the framers of the Constitution have used general language, they have given latitude to those who would later interpret the instrument to make that language applicable to cases that the framers might not have foreseen.

In my reading and travels I have sensed a second connotation of the phrase "living Constitution," however, one quite different from what I have described as the Holmes version, but which certainly has gained acceptance among some parts of the legal profession. Embodied in its most naked form, it recently came to my attention in some language from a brief that had been filed in a United States District Court on behalf of state prisoners asserting that the conditions of their confinement offended the United States Constitution. The brief urged:

> We are asking a great deal of the Court because other branches of government have abdicated their responsibility. . . . Prisoners are like other "discrete and insular" minorities for whom the Court must spread its protective umbrella because no other branch of government will do so. . . . This Court, as the voice and conscience of contemporary society, as the measure of the modern conception of human dignity, must declare that the [named prison] and all it represents

offends the Constitution of the United States and will not be tolerated.

Here we have a living Constitution with a vengeance. Although the substitution of some other set of values for those which may be derived from the language and intent of the framers is not urged in so many words, that is surely the thrust of the message. Under this brief writer's version of the living Constitution, non-elected members of the federal judiciary may address themselves to a social problem simply because other branches of government have failed or refused to do so. These same judges, responsible to no constituency whatever, are nonetheless acclaimed as "the voice and conscience of contemporary society."

. . . [J]udicial review has basically anti-democratic and antimajoritarian facets that require some justification in this Nation, which prides itself on being a self-governing representative democracy.

All who have studied law, and many who have not, are familiar with John Marshall's classic defense of judicial review in his opinion for the Court in *Marbury v. Madison.*[3] I will summarize very briefly the thrust of that answer, with which I fully agree, because while it supports the Holmes version of the phrase "living Constitution," it also suggests some outer limits for the brief writer's version.

The ultimate source of authority in this Nation, Marshall said, is not Congress, not the states, not for that matter the Supreme Court of the United States. The people are the ultimate source of authority; they have parceled out the authority that originally resided entirely with them by adopting the original Constitution and by later amending it. They have granted some authority to the federal government and have reserved authority not granted it to the states or to the people individually. As between the branches of the federal government, the people have given certain authority to the President, certain authority to Congress, and certain authority to the federal judiciary. In the Bill of Rights they have erected protections for specified individual rights against the actions of the federal government. From today's perspective we might add that they

have placed restrictions on the authority of the state governments in the thirteenth, fourteenth, and fifteenth amendments.

In addition, Marshall said that if the popular branches of government—state legislatures, the Congress, and the Presidency—are operating within the authority granted to them by the Constitution, their judgment and not that of the Court must obviously prevail. When these branches overstep the authority given them by the Constitution, in the case of the President and the Congress, or invade protected individual rights, and a constitutional challenge to their action is raised in a lawsuit brought in federal court, the Court must prefer the Constitution to the government acts.

John Marshall's justification for judicial review makes the provision for an independent federal judiciary not only understandable but also thoroughly desirable. Since the judges will be merely interpreting an instrument framed by the people, they should be detached and objective. A mere change in public opinion since the adoption of the Constitution, unaccompanied by a constitutional amendment, should not change the meaning of the Constitution. A merely temporary majoritarian groundswell should not abrogate some individual liberty truly protected by the Constitution.

Clearly Marshall's explanation contains certain elements of either ingenuousness or ingeniousness, which tend to grow larger as our constitutional history extends over a longer period of time. The Constitution is in many of its parts obviously not a specifically worded document but one couched in general phraseology. There is obviously wide room for honest difference of opinion over the meaning of general phrases in the Constitution; any particular Justice's decision when a question arises under one of these general phrases will depend to some extent on his own philosophy of constitutional law. One may nevertheless concede all of these problems that inhere in Marshall's justification of judicial review, yet feel that his justification for nonelected judges exercising the power of judicial review is the only one consistent with democratic philosophy of representative government. . . .

One senses no . . . connection with a popularly adopted constituent act in what I have referred to as the brief writer's version of the living Constitution. The brief writer's version seems instead to be based upon the proposition that federal judges, perhaps judges as a whole, have a role of their own, quite independent of popular will, to play in solving society's problems. Once we have abandoned the idea that the authority of the courts to declare laws unconstitutional is somehow tied to the language of the Constitution that the people adopted, a judiciary exercising the power of judicial review appears in a quite different light. Judges then are no longer the keepers of the covenant: instead they are a small group of fortunately situated people with a roving commission to second-guess Congress, state legislatures, and state and federal administrative officers concerning what is best for the country. Surely there is no justification for a third legislative branch in the federal government, and there is even less justification for a federal legislative branch's reviewing on a policy basis the laws enacted by the legislatures of the fifty states. Even if one were to disagree with me on this point, the members of a third branch of the federal legislature at least ought to be elected by and responsible to constituencies, just as in the case of the other two branches of Congress. If there is going to be a council of revision, it ought to have at least some connection with popular feeling. Its members either ought to stand for reelection on occasion, or their terms should expire and they should be allowed to continue serving only if reappointed by a popularly elected Chief Executive and confirmed by a popularly elected Senate.

The brief writer's version of the living Constitution is seldom presented in its most naked form, but is instead usually dressed in more attractive garb. The argument in favor of this approach generally begins with a sophisticated wink—why pretend that there is any ascertainable content to the general phrases of the Constitution as they are written since, after all, judges constantly disagree about their meaning? We are all familiar with Chief Justice Hughes' famous aphorism that "We are under a Constitution, but the Constitution is what the judges say it is."[4] We all know the basis of Marshall's justification for judicial review, the argument runs, but it is necessary only to keep the window dressing in place. Any sophisticated student of the subject knows that judges need not limit themselves to the intent of the framers, which is very difficult to determine in any event. Because of the general language used in the Constitution, judges should not hesitate to use their authority to make the Constitution relevant and useful in solving the problems of modern society. The brief writer's version of the living Constitution envisions all of the above conclusions.

At least three serious difficulties flaw the brief writer's version of the living Constitution. First, it misconceives the nature of the Constitution, which was designed to enable the popularly elected branches of government, not the judicial branch, to keep the country abreast of the times. Second, the brief writer's version ignores the Supreme Court's disastrous experiences when in the past it embraced contemporary, fashionable notions of what a living Constitution should contain. Third, however socially desirable the goals sought to be advanced by the brief writer's version, advancing them through a freewheeling, nonelected judiciary is quite unacceptable in a democratic society.

It seems to me that it is almost impossible, after reading the record of the Founding Fathers' debates in Philadelphia, to conclude that they intended the Constitution itself to suggest answers to the manifold problems that they knew would confront succeeding generations. The Constitution that they drafted was indeed intended to endure indefinitely, but the reason for this very well-founded hope was the general language by which national authority was granted to Congress and the Presidency. These two branches were to furnish the motive power within the federal system, which was in turn to coexist with the state governments; the elements of government having a popular constituency were looked to for the solution of the numerous and varied problems that the future would bring. Limitations were indeed placed upon both federal and state governments in the form of both a division of powers and express protection for individual rights. These limitations, however, were not themselves designed to solve the problems of the future, but were instead designed to make certain that the constituent branches, when *they* attempted to solve those problems, should not transgress these fundamental limitations.

Although the Civil War Amendments were designed more as broad limitations on the authority of state governments, they too were enacted in response to practices that the lately seceded states engaged in to discriminate against and mistreat the newly emancipated freed men. To the extent that the language of these amendments is general, the courts are of course warranted in giving them an application coextensive with their language. Nevertheless, I greatly doubt that even men like Thad Stevens and John Bingham, leaders of the radical Republicans in Congress, would have thought any portion of the Civil War Amendments, except section five of the fourteenth amendment,[5] was designed to solve problems that society might confront a century later. I think they would have said that those amendments were designed to prevent from ever recurring abuses in which the states had engaged prior to that time.

The brief writer's version of the living Constitution, however, suggests that if the states' legislatures and governors, or Congress and the President, have not solved a particular social problem, then the federal court may act. I do not believe that this argument will withstand rational analysis. Even in the face of a conceded social evil, a reasonably competent and reasonably representative legislature may decide to do nothing. It may decide that the evil is not of sufficient magnitude to warrant any governmental intervention. It may decide that the financial cost of eliminating the evil is not worth the benefit which would result from its elimination. It may decide that the evils which might ensue from the proposed solution are worse than the evils which the solution would eliminate.

Surely the Constitution does not put either the legislative branch or the executive branch in the position of a television quiz show contestant so that when a given period of time has elapsed and a problem remains unsolved by them, the federal judiciary may press a buzzer and take its turn at fashioning a solution.

The second difficulty with the brief writer's version of the living Constitution lies in its inattention to or rejection of the Supreme Court's historical experience gleaned from similar forays into problem solving.

Although the phrase "living Constitution" may not have been used during the nineteenth century and the first half of this century, the idea represented by the brief writer's version was very much in evidence during both periods. The apogee of the living Constitution doctrine during the nineteenth century was the Supreme Court's decision in *Dred Scott v. Sanford.*[6] ... The Court, speaking through Chief Justice Taney, held that Congress was without power to legislate upon the issue of slavery even in a territory governed by it, and that therefore Dred Scott had never become free. Congress, the Court held, was virtually powerless to check or limit the spread of the institution of slavery....

The frustration of the citizenry, who had thought themselves charged with the responsibility for making such decisions, is well expressed in Abraham Lincoln's First Inaugural Address:

> [T]he candid citizen must confess that if the policy of the government, upon vital questions affecting the whole people, is to be irrevocably fixed by decisions of the Supreme Court, the instant they are made, in ordinary litigation between parties in personal actions, the people will have ceased to be their own rulers, having to that extent practically resigned their government into the hands of that eminent tribunal.

The *Dred Scott* decision, of course, was repealed in fact as a result of the Civil War and in law by the Civil War amendments. The injury to the reputation of the Supreme Court that resulted from the *Dred Scott* decision, however, took more than a generation to heal. Indeed, newspaper accounts long after the *Dred Scott* decision bristled with attacks on the Court, and particularly on Chief Justice Taney, unequalled in their bitterness even to this day.

The brief writer's version of the living Constitution made its next appearance, almost as dramatically as its first, shortly after the turn of the century in *Lochner v. New York*.[7] The name of the case is a household word to those who have studied constitutional law, and it is one of the handful of cases in which a dissenting opinion has been overwhelmingly vindicated by the passage of time. In *Lochner* a New York law that limited to ten the maximum number of hours per day that could be worked by bakery employees was assailed on the ground that it deprived the bakery employer of liberty without due process of law. A majority of the Court held the New York maximum hour law unconstitutional, saying, "Statutes of the nature of that under review, limiting the hours in which grown and intelligent men may labor to earn their living, are mere meddlesome interferences with the rights of the individual. . . ."[8] . . .

One reads the history of these episodes in the Supreme Court to little purpose if he does not conclude that prior experimentation with the brief writer's expansive notion of a living Constitution has done the Court little credit. There remain today those, such as wrote the brief from which I quoted, who appear to cleave nevertheless to the view that the experiments of the Taney Court before the Civil War, and of the Fuller and Taft Courts in the first part of this century, ended in failure not because they sought to bring into the Constitution a principle that the great majority of objective scholars would have to conclude was not there but because they sought to bring into the Constitution the *wrong* extraconstitutional principle. . . . To the extent that one must go beyond even a generously fair reading of the language and intent of that document in order to subsume these principles, it seems to me that they are not really distinguishable from those espoused in *Dred Scott* and *Lochner*.

The third difficulty with the brief writer's notion of the living Constitution is that it seems to ignore totally the nature of political value judgments in a democratic society. If such a society adopts a constitution and incorporates in that constitution safeguards for individual liberty, these safeguards indeed do take on a generalized moral rightness or goodness. They assume a general social acceptance neither because of any intrinsic worth nor because of any unique origins in someone's idea of natural justice but instead simply because they have been incorporated in a constitution by the people. Within the limits of our Constitution, the representatives of the people in the executive branches of the state and national governments enact laws. The laws that emerge after a typical political struggle in which various individual value judgments are debated likewise take on a form of moral goodness because they have been enacted into positive law. It is the fact of their enactment that gives them whatever moral claim they have upon us as a society, however, and not any independent virtue they may have in any particular citizen's own scale of values.

Beyond the Constitution and the laws in our society, there simply is no basis other than the individual conscience of the citizen that may serve as a platform for the launching of moral judgments. There is no conceivable way in which I can logically demonstrate to you that the judgments of my conscience are superior to the judgments of your conscience, and vice versa. Many of us necessarily feel strongly and deeply about our own moral judgments, but they remain only personal moral judgments until in some way given the sanction of law. . . .

Should a person fail to persuade the legislature, or should he feel that a legislative victory would be insufficient because of its potential for future reversal, he may seek to run the more difficult gauntlet of amending the Constitution to embody the view that he espouses. Success in amending the Constitution would, of course, preclude succeeding transient majorities in the legislature from tampering with the principle formerly added to the Constitution.

I know of no other method compatible with political theory basic to democratic society by which one's own conscientious belief may be translated into positive law and thereby obtain the only general moral imprimatur permissible in a pluralistic, democratic society. It is always time consuming, frequently difficult, and not infrequently impossible to run successfully the legislative gauntlet and have enacted some facet of one's own deeply felt value judgments. It is even more difficult for either a single individual or indeed for a large group of individuals to succeed in having such a value judgment embodied in the Constitution. All of these burdens and difficulties are entirely consistent with the notion of a democratic society. It should not be easy for any one individual or group of individuals to impose by law their value judgments upon fellow citizens who may disagree with those judgments. Indeed, it should not be easier just because the individual in question is a judge. We all have a propensity to want to do it, but there are very good reasons for making it difficult to do. The great English political philosopher John Stuart Mill observed:

The disposition of mankind, whether as rulers or as fellow-citizens, to impose their own opinions and inclinations as a rule of conduct on others, is so energetically supported by some of the best and by some of the worst feeling incident to human nature, that it is hardly ever kept under restraint by anything but want of power. . . .[9]

The brief writer's version of the living Constitution, in the last analysis, is a formula for an end run around popular government. To the extent that it makes possible an individual's persuading one or more appointed federal judges to impose on other individuals a rule of conduct that the popularly elected branches of government would not have enacted and the voters have not and would not have embodied in the Constitution, the brief writer's version of the living Constitution is genuinely corrosive of the fundamental values of our democratic society.

NOTES

[1] 252 U.S. 416 (1920).
[2] *Id.* at 433.
[3] 5 U.S. (1 Cranch) 137 (1803).
[4] C. Hughes, Addresses 139 (1908).
[5] "The Congress shall have power to enforce, by appropriate legislation, the provisions of this article." U.S. Const. amend. XIV, § 5.
[6] 60 U.S. (19 How.) 393 (1857).
[7] 198 U.S. 45 (1905).
[8] *Id.* at 61.
[9] J. S. Mill, *On Liberty*, in *43 Great Books of the Western World* 273 (R. Hutchins ed. 1952).

REVIEW AND DISCUSSION QUESTIONS

1. Explain the position that Justice Rehnquist refers to as the brief writer's notion of a "living constitution."

2. What are the three objections he raises to this view?

3. What approach does Justice Rehnquist suggest to someone responsible for interpreting the Constitution's general concepts such as free speech, equal protection, and cruel and unusual punishment?

4. What role does the notion of a "covenant" play in Rehnquist's thinking?

5. Of what significance, if any, for Justice Rehnquist's theory are the following:

a. At the time of ratification only white men could vote, and even then it was sometimes necessary they own property, with the result that only about 20 percent of those we would now think eligible actually voted for ratification.

b. Among the people who drafted the Constitution and later amendments there was wide disagreement over the meaning.

c. The original constitutional convention kept no official records.

d. The original convention was not authorized to do anything more than amend the Articles of Confederation; such amendments required unanimous agreement of states, whereas the Constitution required only nine of the thirteen states to accept it for adoption.

e. The Fourteenth Amendment was adopted by the Thirty-ninth Congress, which did not allow southern delegates to be seated and vote.

6. Compare how Justice Rehnquist describes *Dred Scott* (*Scott v. Sanford*) and *Lochner v. New York* with the opinions themselves.

Constitutional Cases

Ronald Dworkin

In the following essay, Ronald Dworkin defends judicial activism against those who argue that judges should allow the decisions of other branches of government to stand whenever there is controversy about a law's constitutionality. The latter view, which he terms judicial restraint, *could be defended on one of two grounds: skepticism about the existence of moral rights and deference to democratic political institutions. Dworkin considers and rejects each of these defenses of judicial restraint.*

1

When Richard Nixon was running for President he promised that he would appoint to the Supreme Court men who represented his own legal philosophy, that is, who were what he called "strict constructionists." . . .

Nixon claimed that his opposition to the Warren Court's desegregation decisions, and to other decisions it took, were not based simply on a personal or political distaste for the results. He argued that the decisions violated the standards of adjudication that the Court should follow. The Court was usurping, in his views, powers that rightly belong to other institutions, including the legislatures of the various states whose school systems the Court sought to reform. . . .

Nixon is no longer president, and his crimes were so grave that no one is likely to worry very much any more about the details of his own legal philosophy. Nevertheless in what follows I shall use the name "Nixon" to refer, not to Nixon, but to any politician holding the set of attitudes about the Supreme Court that he made explicit in his political campaigns. There was, fortunately, only one real Nixon, but there are, in the special sense in which I use the name, many Nixons.

What can be the basis of this composite Nixon's opposition to the controversial decisions of the Warren Court? He cannot object to these decisions simply because they went beyond prior law, or say that the Supreme Court must never change its mind. Indeed the Burger Court itself seems intent on limiting the liberal decisions of the Warren Court, like *Miranda*.

The Constitution's guarantee of "equal protection of the laws," it is true, does not in plain words determine that "separate but equal" school facilities are unconstitutional, or that segregation was so unjust that heroic measures are required to undo its effects. But neither does it provide that as a matter of constitutional law the Court would be wrong to reach these conclusions. It leaves these issues to the Court's judgment. . . .

2

The constitutional theory on which our government rests is not a simple majoritarian theory. The Constitution, and particularly the Bill of Rights, is designed to protect individual citizens and groups against certain decisions that a majority of citizens might want to make, even when that majority acts in what it takes to be the general or common interest. Some of these constitutional restraints take the form of fairly precise rules, like the rule that requires a jury trial in federal criminal proceedings or, perhaps, the rule that forbids the national Congress to abridge freedom of speech. But other constraints take the form of what are often called "vague" standards, for example, the provision that the government shall not deny men due process of law, or equal protection of the laws.

This interference with democratic practice requires a justification. The draftsmen of the Constitution assumed that these restraints could be justified by appeal to moral rights which individuals possess against the majority, and which the constitutional provisions, both "vague" and precise, might be said to recognize and protect.

The "vague" standards were chosen deliberately, by the men who drafted and adopted them, in place of the more specific and limited rules that they might have enacted. But their decision to use the language they did has caused a great deal of legal and political controversy, because even reasonable men of good will differ when they try to elaborate, for example, the moral rights that the due process clause or the equal protection clause brings into the law. They also differ when they try to apply these rights, however defined, to complex matters of political administration, like the educational practices that were the subject of the segregation cases.

The practice has developed of referring to a "strict" and a "liberal" side to these controversies, so that the Supreme Court might be said to have taken the "liberal" side in the segregation cases and its critics the "strict" side. Nixon has this distinction in mind when he calls himself a "strict constructionist." But the distinction is in fact confusing, because it runs together two different issues that must be separated. Any case that arises under the "vague" constitutional guarantees can be seen as posing two questions: (1) Which decision is required by strict, that is to say faithful, adherence to the text of the Constitution or to the intention of those who adopted that text? (2) Which decision is required by a political philosophy that takes a strict, that is to say narrow, view of the moral rights that individuals have against society? Once these questions are distinguished, it is plain that they may have different answers. The text of the First Amendment, for example, says that Congress shall make *no* law abridging the freedom of speech, but a narrow view of individual rights would permit many such laws, ranging from libel and obscenity laws to the Smith Act.

In the case of the "vague" provisions, however, like the due process and equal protection clauses, lawyers have run the two questions together because they have relied, largely without recognizing it, on a theory of meaning that might be put this way: If the framers of the Constitution used vague language, as they did when they condemned violations of "due process of law," then what they "said" or "meant" is limited to the instances of official action that they had in mind as violations, or, at least, to those instances that they would have thought were violations if they had had them in mind. If those who were responsible for adding the due process clause to the Constitution believed that it was fundamentally unjust to provide separate education for different races, or had detailed views about justice that entailed that conclusion, then the segregation decisions might be defended as an application of the principle they had laid down. Otherwise, they could not be defended in this way, but instead would show that the judges had substituted their own ideas of justice for those the constitutional drafters meant to lay down.

This theory makes a strict interpretation of the text yield a narrow view of constitutional rights, because it limits such rights to those recognized by a limited group of people at a fixed date of history. It forces those who favor a more liberal set of rights to concede that they are departing from strict legal authority, a departure they must then seek to justify by appealing only to the desirability of the results they reach.

But the theory of meaning on which this argument depends is far too crude; it ignores a distinction that philosophers have made but lawyers have not yet appreciated. Suppose I tell my children simply that I expect them not to treat others unfairly. I no doubt have in mind examples of the conduct I mean to discourage, but I would not accept that my "meaning" was limited to these examples, for two reasons. First, I would expect my children to apply my instructions to situations I had not and could not have thought about. Second, I stand ready to admit that some particular act I had thought was fair when I spoke was in fact unfair, or vice versa, if one of my children is able to convince me of that later; in that case I should want to say that my instructions covered the case he cited, not that I had changed my instructions. I might say that I meant the family to be guided by the *concept* of fairness, not by any specific *conceptions* of fairness I might have had in mind.

This is a crucial distinction which it is worth pausing to explore. Suppose a group believes in common that acts may suffer from a special moral defect which they call unfairness, and which consists in a wrongful division of benefits and burdens, or a wrongful attribution of praise or blame. Suppose also that they agree on a great number of standard cases of unfairness and use these as benchmarks against which to test other, more controversial cases. In that case, the group has a concept of unfairness, and its members may appeal to that concept in moral instruction or argument. But members of that group may nevertheless differ over a large number of these controversial cases, in a way that suggests that each either has or acts on a different theory of *why* the standard cases are acts of unfairness. They may differ, that is, on which more fundamental principles must be relied upon to show that a particular division or attribution is unfair. In that case, the members have different conceptions of fairness.

If so, then members of this community who give instructions or set standards in the name of fairness may be doing two different things. First they may be appealing to the concept of fairness, simply by instructing others to act fairly; in this case they charge those whom they instruct with the responsibility of developing and applying their own conception of fairness as controversial cases arise. That is not the same thing, of course, as granting them a discretion to act as they like; it sets a standard which they must try—and may fail—to meet, because it assumes that one conception is superior to another. The man who appeals to the concept in this way may have his own conception, as I did when I told my children to act fairly; but he holds this conception only as his own theory of how the standard he set must be met, so that when he changes his theory he has not changed that standard.

On the other hand, the members may be laying down a particular conception of fairness; I would have done this, for example, if I had listed my wishes with respect to controversial examples or if, even less likely, I had specified some controversial and explicit theory of fairness, as if I had said to decide hard cases by applying the utilitarian ethics of Jeremy Bentham. The difference is a difference not just in the *detail* of the instructions given but in the *kind* of instructions given. When I appeal to the concept of fairness I appeal to what fairness means, and I give my views on that issue no special standing. When I lay down a conception of fairness, I lay down what I mean by fairness, and my view is therefore the heart of the matter. When I appeal to fairness I pose a moral issue; when I lay down my conception of fairness I try to answer it.

Once this distinction is made it seems obvious that we must take what I have been calling "vague" constitutional clauses as representing appeals to the concepts they employ, like legality, equality, and cruelty. The Supreme Court may soon decide, for example, whether capital punishment is "cruel" within the meaning of the constitutional clause that prohibits "cruel and unusual punishment." It would be a mistake for the Court to be much influenced by the fact that when the clause was adopted capital punishment was standard and unquestioned. That would be decisive if the framers of the clause had meant to lay down a particular conception of cruelty, because it would show that the conception did not extend so far. But it is not decisive of the different question the Court now faces, which is this: Can the Court, responding to the framers' appeal to the concept of cruelty, now defend a conception that does not make death cruel?

Those who ignore the distinction between concepts and conceptions, but who believe that the Court ought to make a fresh determination of whether the death penalty is cruel, are forced to argue in a vulnerable way. They say that ideas of cruelty change over time, and that the Court must be free to reject out-of-date conceptions; this suggests that the Court must change what the Constitution enacted. But in fact the Court can enforce what the Constitution says only by making up its own mind about what is cruel, just as my children, in my example, can do what I said only by making up their own minds about what is fair. If those who enacted the broad clauses had meant to lay down particular conceptions, they would have found the sort of language conventionally used to do this, that is, they would have offered particular theories of the concepts in question.

Indeed the very practice of calling these clauses "vague," in which I have joined, can now be seen to involve a mistake. The clauses are vague only if we take them to be botched or incomplete or schematic attempts to lay down particular conceptions. If we take them as appeals to moral concepts they could not be made more precise by being more detailed.[1]

The confusion I mentioned between the two senses of "strict" construction is therefore very misleading indeed. If courts try to be faithful to the text of the Constitution, they will for that very reason be forced to decide between competing conceptions of political morality. So it is wrong to attack the Warren Court, for example, on the ground that it failed to treat the Constitution as a binding text. On the contrary, if we wish to treat fidelity to that text as an overriding requirement of constitutional interpretation, then it is the conservative critics of the Warren Court who are at fault, because their philosophy ignores the direction to face issues of moral principle that the logic of the text demands.

I put the matter in a guarded way because we may *not* want to accept fidelity to the spirit of the text as an overriding principle of constitutional adjudication. It may be more important for courts to decide constitutional cases in a manner that respects that judgments of other institutions of government, for example. Or it may be more important for courts to protect established legal doctrines, so that citizens and the government can have confidence that the courts will hold to what they have said before. But it is crucial to recognize that these other policies compete with the principle that the Constitution is the fundamental and imperative source of constitutional law. They are not, as the "strict constructionists" suppose, simply consequences of that principle.

3

Once the matter is put in this light, moreover, we are able to assess these competing claims of policy, free from the confusion imposed by the popular notion of "strict construction." For this purpose I want now to compare and contrast two very general philosophies of how the courts should decide difficult or controversial constitutional issues. I shall call these two philosophies by the names they are given in the legal literature—the programs of "judicial activism" and "judicial restraint"—though it will be plain that these names are in certain ways misleading.

The program of judicial activism holds that courts should accept the directions of the so-called vague constitutional provisions in the spirit I described, in spite of competing reasons of the sort I mentioned. They should work out principles of legality, equality, and the rest, revise these principles from time to time in the light of what seems to the Court fresh moral insight, and judge the acts of Congress, the states, and the President accordingly. (This puts the program in its strongest form; in fact its supporters generally qualify it in ways I shall ignore for the present.)

The program of judicial restraint, on the contrary, argues that courts should allow the decisions of other branches of government to stand, even when they offend the judges' own sense of the principles required by the broad constitutional doctrines, except when these decisions are so offensive to political morality that they would violate the provisions on any plausible interpretation, or, perhaps, when a contrary decision is required by clear precedent. (Again, this puts the program in a stark form; those who profess the policy qualify it in different ways.) . . .

We must now . . . notice a distinction between two forms of judicial restraint, for there are two different, and indeed incompatible, grounds on which that policy might be based.

The first is a theory of political *skepticism* that might be described in this way. The policy of judicial activism presupposes a certain objectivity of moral principle; in particular it presupposes that citizens do have certain moral rights against the state, like a moral right to equality of public education or to fair treatment by the police. Only if such moral rights exist in some sense can activism be justified as a program based on something beyond the judge's personal preferences. The skeptical theory attacks activism at its roots; it argues that in fact individuals have no such moral rights against the state. They have only such *legal* rights as the Constitution grants them, and these are limited to the plain and uncontroversial violations or public morality that the framers must have had actually in mind, or that have since been established in a line of precedent.

The alternative ground of a program of restraint is a theory of judicial *deference*. Contrary to the skeptical theory, this assumes that citizens do have moral rights against the state beyond what the law expressly grants them, but it points out that the character and strength of these rights are debatable and argues that political institutions other than courts are responsible for deciding which rights are to be recognized.

This is an important distinction, even though the literature of constitutional law does not draw it with any clarity. The skeptical theory and the theory of deference differ dramatically in the kind of justification they assume, and in their implications for the more general moral theories of the men who profess to hold them. These theories are so different that most American politicians can consistently accept the second, but not the first.

A skeptic takes the view, as I have said, that men have no moral rights against the state and only such legal rights as the law expressly provides. But what does this mean, and what sort of argument might the skeptic make for his view? There is, of course, a very lively dispute in moral philosophy about the nature and standing of moral rights, and considerable disagreement about what they are, if they are anything at all. I shall rely, in trying to answer these questions, on a low key theory of moral rights against the state. . . . Under that theory, a man has a moral right against the state if for some reason the state would do wrong to treat him in a certain way, even though it would be in the general interest to do so. So a black child has a moral right to an equal education, for example, if it is wrong for the state not to provide that education, even if the community as a whole suffers thereby.

I want to say a word about the virtues of this way of looking at moral rights against the state. A great many lawyers are wary of talking about moral rights, even though they find it easy to talk about what is right or wrong for government to do, because they suppose that rights, if they exist at all, are spooky sorts of things that men and women have in much the same way as

they have nonspooky things like tonsils. But the sense of rights I propose to use does not make ontological assumptions of that sort; it simply shows a claim of right to be a special, in the sense of a restricted, sort of judgment about what is right or wrong for governments to do.

Moreover, this way of looking at rights avoids some of the notorious puzzles associated with the concept. It allows us to say, with no sense of strangeness, that rights may vary in strength and character from case to case, and from point to point in history. If we think of rights as things, these metamorphoses seem strange, but we are used to the idea that moral judgments about what it is right or wrong to do are complex and are affected by considerations that are relative and that change.

The skeptic who wants to argue against the very possibility of rights against the state of this sort has a difficult brief. He must rely, I think, on one of three general positions: (a) He might display a more pervasive moral skepticism, which holds that even to speak of an act being morally right or wrong makes no sense. If no act is morally wrong, then the government of North Carolina cannot be wrong to refuse to bus school children. (b) He might hold a stark form of utilitarianism, which assumes that the only reason we ever have for regarding an act as right or wrong is its impact on the general interest. Under that theory, to say that busing may be morally required even though it does not benefit the community generally would be inconsistent. (c) He might accept some form of totalitarian theory, which merges the interests of the individual in the good of the general community, and so denies that the two can conflict.

Very few American politicians would be able to accept any of these three grounds. Nixon, for example, could not, because he presents himself as a moral fundamentalist who knows in his heart that pornography is wicked and that some of the people of South Vietnam have rights of self-determination in the name of which they and we may properly kill many others.

I do not want to suggest, however, that no one would in fact argue for judicial restraint on grounds of skepticism; on the contrary, some of the best known advocates of restraint have pitched their arguments entirely on skeptical grounds. In 1957, for example, the great judge Learned Hand delivered the Oliver Wendell Holmes lectures at Harvard. Hand was a student of Santayana and a disciple of Holmes, and skepticism in morals was his only religion. He argued for judicial restraint, and said that the Supreme Court had done wrong to declare school segregation illegal in the *Brown* case. It is wrong to suppose, he said, that claims about moral rights express anything more than the speakers' preferences. If the Supreme Court justifies its decisions by making such claims, rather than by relying on positive law, it is usurping the place of the legislature, for the job of the legislature, representing the majority, is to decide whose preferences shall govern.

This simple appeal to democracy is successful if one accepts the skeptical premise. Of course, if men have no rights against the majority, if political decision is simply a matter of whose preferences shall prevail, then democracy does provide a good reason for leaving that decision to more democratic institutions than courts, even when these institutions make choices that the judges themselves hate. But a very different, and much more vulnerable, argument from democracy is needed to support judicial restraint if it is based not on skepticism but on deference, as I shall try to show.

4

If Nixon holds a coherent constitutional theory, it is a theory of restraint based not on skepticism but on deference. He believes that courts ought not to decide controversial issues of political morality because they ought to leave such decisions to other departments of government. . . .

There is one very popular argument in favor of the policy of deference, which might be called the argument from democracy. It is at least debatable, according to this argument, whether a sound conception of equality forbids segregated education or requires measures like busing to break it down. Who ought to decide these debatable issues of moral and political theory? Should it be a majority of a court in Washington, whose members are appointed for life and are not politically responsible to the public whose lives will be affected by the decision? Or should it be the elected and responsible state or national legislators? A democrat, so this argument supposes, can accept only the second answer.

But the argument from democracy is weaker than it might first appear. . . .

The argument assumes that in a democracy all unsettled issues, including issues of moral and political principle, must be resolved only by institutions that are politically responsible in the way courts are not. Why should we accept that view of democracy? To say that that is what democracy means does no good, because it is wrong to suppose that the word, as a word, has anything like so precise a meaning. Even if it did, we should then have to rephrase our question to ask why we should have democracy, if we assume that is what it means. Nor is it better to say that that view of democracy is established in the American Constitution, or so entrenched in our political tradition that we are committed to it. We cannot argue that the Constitution, which provides no rule limiting juridical review to clear cases, establishes a theory of democracy that excludes wider review, nor can we say that our courts have in fact consistently accepted such a restriction. The burden of Nixon's argument is that they have.

So the argument from democracy is not an argument to which we are committed either by our words or our past. We must accept it, if at all, on the strength of its own logic. In order to examine the arguments more closely, however, we must make a further distinction. The argument as I have set it out might be continued in two different ways; one might argue that judicial deference is required because democratic institutions, like legislatures, are in fact likely to make *sounder* decisions than courts about the underlying issues that constitutional cases raise, that is, about the nature of an individual's moral rights against the state.

Or one might argue that it is for some reason *fairer* that a democratic institution rather than a court should decide such issues, even though there is no reason to believe that the institution will reach a sounder decision. The distinction between these two arguments would make no sense to a skeptic, who would not admit that someone could do a better or worse job at identifying moral rights against the state, any more than someone could do a better or worse job of identifying ghosts. But a lawyer who believes in judicial deference rather than skepticism must acknowledge the distinction, though he can argue both sides if he wishes.

I shall start with the second argument that legislatures and other democratic institutions have some special title to make constitutional decisions, apart from their ability to make better decisions. One might say that the nature of this title is obvious, because it is always fairer to allow a majority to decide any issue than a minority. But that, as has often been pointed out, ignores the fact that decisions about rights against the majority are not issues that in fairness ought to be left to the majority. Constitutionalism—the theory that the majority must be restrained to protect individual rights—may be a good or bad political theory, but the United States has adopted that theory, and to make the majority judge in its own cause seems inconsistent and unjust. So principles of fairness seem to speak against, not for, the argument from democracy.

Chief Justice Marshall recognized this in his decision in *Marbury v. Madison*, the famous case in which the Supreme Court first claimed the power to review legislative decisions against constitutional standards. He argued that since the Constitution provides that the Constitution shall be the supreme law of the land, the courts in general, and the Supreme Court in the end, must have power to declare statutes void that offend that Constitution. Many legal scholars regard his argument as a *non sequitur*, because, they say, although constitutional constraints are part of the law, the courts, rather than the legislature itself, have not necessarily been given authority to decide whether in particular cases that law has been violated.[2] But the argument is not a *non sequitur* if we take the principle that no man should be judge in his own cause to be so fundamental a part of the idea of legality that Marshall would have been entitled to disregard it only if the Constitution had expressly denied judicial review.

Some might object that it is simple-minded to say that a policy of deference leaves the majority to judge its own cause. Political decisions are made, in the United States, not by one stable majority but by many different political institutions each representing a different constituency which itself changes its composition over time. The decision of one branch of government may well be reviewed by another branch that is also politically responsible, but to a larger or different constituency. The acts of the Arizona police which the Court held unconstitutional in *Miranda*, for example, were in fact subject to review by various executive boards and municipal and state legislatures of Arizona, as well as by the national Congress. It would be naïve to suppose that all of these political institutions are dedicated to the same policies and interests, so it is wrong to suppose that if the Court had not intervened the Arizona police would have been free to judge themselves.

But this objection is itself too glib, because it ignores the special character of disputes about individual moral rights as distinct from other kinds of political disputes. Different institutions do have different constituencies when, for example, labor or trade or welfare issues are involved, and the nation often divides sectionally on such issues. But this is not generally the case when individual constitutional rights, like the rights of accused criminals, are at issue. It has been typical of these disputes that the interests of those in political control of the various institutions of the government have been both homogeneous and hostile. Indeed that is why political theorists have conceived of constitutional rights as rights against the "state" or the "majority" as such, rather than against any particular body or branch of government. . . .

It does seem fair to say, therefore, that the argument from democracy asks that those in political power be invited to be the sole judge of their own decisions, to see whether they have the right to do what they have decided they want to do. That is not a final proof that a policy of judicial activism is superior to a program of deference. Judicial activism involves risks of tyranny; certainly in the stark and simple form I set out. It might even be shown that these risks override the unfairness of asking the majority to be judge in its own cause. But the point does undermine the argument that the majority, in fairness, must be allowed to decide the limits of its own power.

We must therefore turn to the other continuation of the argument from democracy, which holds that democratic institutions, like legislatures, are likely to reach *sounder* results about the moral rights of individuals than would courts. In 1969 the late Professor Alexander Bickel of the Yale Law School delivered his Holmes Lectures at Harvard and argued for the program of judicial restraint in a novel and ingenious way. He allowed himself to suppose, for purposes of argument, that the Warren Court's program of activism could be justified if in fact it produced desirable results.[3] He appeared, therefore, to be testing the policy of activism on its own grounds, because he took activism to be precisely the claim that the courts have the moral right to improve the future, whatever legal theory may say. Learned Hand and other opponents of activism had challenged that claim. Bickel accepted it, at least provisionally, but he argued that activism fails its own test. . . .

What are we to make of Bickel's argument? . . .

. . . His theory is novel because it appears to concede an issue of principle to judicial activism, namely, that the Court is entitled to intervene if its intervention produces socially desirable results. But the concession is an illusion, because his sense of what is socially desirable is inconsistent with the presupposition of activism that individuals have moral rights against the state. In fact, Bickel's argument cannot succeed, even if we grant his facts and his view of history, except on a basis of a skepticism about rights as profound as Learned Hand's. . . .

On this view, the rights of blacks, suspects, and atheists will emerge through the process of political institutions responding to political pressures in the normal way. If a claim of right cannot succeed in this way, then for that reason it is, or in any event it is likely to be, an improper claim of right. But this bizarre proposition is only a disguised form of the skeptical point that there are in fact no rights against the state.

Perhaps, as Burke and his modern followers argue, a society will produce the institutions that best suit it only by evolution and never by radical reform. But rights against the state are claims that, if accepted, require society to settle for institutions that may not suit it so comfortably. The nerve of a claim of right, even on the demythologized analysis of rights I am using, is that an individual is entitled to protection against the majority even at the cost of the general interest. Of course the comfort of the majority will require some accommodation for minorities but only to the extent necessary to preserve order; and that is usually an accommodation that falls short of recognizing their rights.

Indeed the suggestion that rights can be demonstrated by a process of history rather than by an appeal to principle shows either a confusion or no real concern about what rights are. A claim of right presupposes a moral argument and can be established in no other way. Bickel paints the judicial activists (and even some of the heroes of judicial restraint, like Brandeis and Frankfurter, who had their lapses) as eighteenth-century philosophers who appeal to principle because they hold the optimistic view that a blueprint may be cut for progress. But this picture confuses two grounds for the appeal to principle and reform, and two senses of progress.

It is one thing to appeal to moral principle in the silly faith that ethics as well as economics moves by an invisible hand, so that individual rights and the general good will coalesce, and law based on principle will move the nation to a frictionless utopia where everyone is better off than he was before. Bickel attacks that vision by his appeal to history, and by his other arguments against government by principle. But it is quite another matter to appeal to principle *as* principle, to show, for example, that it is unjust to force black children to take their public education in black schools, even if a great many people *will* be worse off if the state adopts the measures needed to prevent this.

This is a different version of progress. It is moral progress, and though history may show how difficult it is to decide where moral progress lies, and how difficult to persuade others once one has decided, it cannot follow from this that those who govern us have no responsibility to face that decision or to attempt that persuasion.

5

This has been a complex argument, and I want to summarize it. Our constitutional system rests on a particular moral theory, namely, that men have moral rights against the state. The difficult clauses of the Bill of Rights, like the due process and equal protection clauses, must be understood as appealing to moral concepts rather than laying down particular conceptions; therefore a court that undertakes the burden of applying these clauses fully as law must be an activist court, in the sense that it must be prepared to frame and answer questions of political morality. . . .

If we give the decisions of principle that the Constitution requires to the judges, instead of to the people, we act in the spirit of legality, so far as our institutions permit. But we run a risk that the judges may make the wrong decisions. Every lawyer thinks that the Supreme Court has gone wrong, even violently wrong, at some point in its career. If he does not hate the conservative decisions of the early 1930s, which threatened to block the New Deal, he is likely to hate the liberal decisions of the last decade.

We must not exaggerate the danger. Truly unpopular decisions will be eroded because public compliances will be grudging, as it has been in the case of public school prayers, and because old judges will die or retire and be replaced by new judges appointed because they agree with a President who has been elected by the people. The decisions against the New Deal did not stand, and the more daring decisions of recent years are now at the mercy of the Nixon Court. Nor does the danger of wrong decisions lie entirely on the side of excess; the failure of the Court to act in the McCarthy period, epitomized by its shameful decision upholding the legality of the Smith Act in the *Dennis* case, may be thought to have done more harm to the nation than did the Court's conservative bias in the early Roosevelt period. . . .

Constitutional law can make no genuine advance until it isolates the problem of rights against the state and makes that problem part of its own agenda. That argues for a fusion of constitutional law and moral theory, a connection that, incredibly, has yet to take place. It is perfectly understandable that lawyers dread contamination with moral philosophy, and particularly with those philosophers who talk about rights, because the spooky overtones of that concept threaten the graveyard of reason. But better philosophy is now available than the lawyers may remember. Professor Rawls of Harvard, for example, has published an abstract and complex book about justice which no constitutional lawyer will be able to ignore.[4] There is no need for lawyers to play a passive role in the development of a theory of moral rights against the state, however, any more than they have been passive in the development of legal sociology and legal economics. They must recognize that law is no more independent from philosophy than it is from these other disciplines. . . .

NOTES

[1] It is less misleading to say that the broad clauses of the Constitution "delegate" power to the Court to enforce its own conceptions of political morality. But even this is inaccurate if it suggests that the Court need not justify its conception by arguments showing the connections between its conception and standard cases, as described in the text. If the Court finds that the death penalty is cruel, it must do so on the basis of some principles or groups of principles that unite the death penalty with the thumbscrew and the rack.

[2] I distinguish this objection to Marshall's argument from the different objection, not here relevant, that the Constitution should be interpreted to impose a legal *duty* on Congress not, for example, to pass laws abridging freedom of speech, but it should not be interpreted to detract from the legal *power* of Congress to make such a law valid if it breaks its duty. In this view, Congress is in the legal position of a thief who has a legal duty not to sell stolen goods, but retains legal power to make a valid transfer if he does. This interpretation has little to recommend it since Congress, unlike the thief, cannot be disciplined except by denying validity to its wrongful acts, at least in a way that will offer protection to the individuals the Constitution is designed to protect.

[3] Professor Bickel also argued, with his usual very great skill, that many of the Warren Court's major decisions could not even be justified on conventional grounds, that is, by the arguments the Court advanced in its opinions. His criticism of these opinions is often persuasive, but the Court's failures of craftsmanship do not affect the argument I consider in the text. (His Holmes lectures were amplified in his book *The Supreme Court and the Ideal of Progress*, 1970.)

[4] *A Theory of Justice*, 1972. . . .

REVIEW AND DISCUSSION QUESTIONS

1. Dworkin distinguishes two senses of "strict constructionism" but accepts only one of them. What are the two?

2. Describe the distinction between a concept and a conception, according to Dworkin.

3. How does Dworkin describe judicial activism and judicial restraint?

4. Describe the argument for judicial restraint based on skepticism. Why does Dworkin reject that argument?

5. Describe the argument for judicial restraint based on deference. Why does Dworkin reject that argument?

6. Dworkin has been criticized on the ground that his position leaves too much discretion to judges. How is what he said about constitutional interpretation in his essay "On Not Prosecuting Civil Disobedience" relevant to that charge?

7. Has Dworkin responded adequately to Justice Rehnquist's arguments against those who believe in a "living constitution"?

Precommitment and Disagreement

Jeremy Waldron

Beginning with a distinction between popular sovereignty (a constitution chosen by the people) and democracy (a government that is itself democratic), Jeremy Waldron discusses the legitimacy of judicial review. Specifically, his concern is with those who defend limits on democratically elected officials on grounds that people have "precommitted" to limiting themselves through a bill of rights. Thus, it might be argued that while judicial review by unelected judges may seem antidemocratic, in fact, it protects the autonomy of the people, where that is understood to refer to their settled, clear intentions or desires. Waldron rejects that defense of judicial review, however, arguing that while it may work for certain sorts of individual decisions, it is not a good analogy for a political system. Jeremy Waldron is professor of law and philosophy at Columbia University.

I. DEMOCRACY AND POPULAR SOVEREIGNTY

The British are contemplating constitutional reform. Among the changes under consideration is the enactment of a bill of rights enforced, if necessary, by the judicial review of legislation, along lines well established in the United States.[1] The radical change in British law that this would involve provides us with an opportunity to reflect more expansively than American constitutional scholars often do on the nature and purpose of constitutional constraints and their relation to the democratic principles often taken to be embodied in the "sovereignty" of a Westminster-style legislature. The conclusions of such reflection will be relevant to the debate in the United Kingdom of course, but they will be relevant not only there. They may be helpful to us too, for we can often learn about our own constitution by comparing it with other constitutions,[2] and we often learn how to understand the characteristics of our own constitution by imagining them abroad as serious objects of political choice, rather than as features we were taught to revere in elementary school. Certainly to the extent that the political dramatics of judicial review are bound up with the self-image and self-importance of American lawyers and law professors, it may be easier to persuade them to consider the institution carefully, critically, and impartially when what is at stake are the role and image of lawyers and judges somewhere else.

On the other hand, the debate in other countries may be responsive to features that are not present in the American case. It is arguable, for example, that in the United Kingdom the institution of a bill of rights with judicial review will not be subject to the "counter-majoritarian difficulty" often associated with the American version.[3] For if these changes take place, they will not have been undemocratically imposed upon the British people; nor will they be something the British have inherited because they seemed like a good idea to a bunch of slave-owning revolutionaries living on the edge of an undeveloped continent at the end of the eighteenth century. If a bill of rights is incorporated into British law in the next few years, it will be because Parliament or perhaps the British people in a referendum have voted for incorporation on the understanding that they will be changing the British constitution by establishing a practice of judicial review. Indeed, far from posing a countermajoritarian difficulty, this will be one of the first opportunities the British people have had to control major aspects of their constitution by explicit majority decision.

Ronald Dworkin once argued that this alone is sufficient to dispose of the objection that the institution of such constraints is contrary to the spirit of democracy. On his view, the democratic objection to a bill of rights with judicial review is self-defeating because polls reveal that more than 71 percent of people believe that British democracy would be improved, not undermined, by the incorporation of a bill of rights.[4]

The objection cannot be disposed of quite so easily. The fact that there is popular support, even overwhelming popular support, for an alteration in the constitution does not show that such an alteration would make things more democratic. Certainly, a radical democrat is committed to saying that if the people want a regime of constitutional rights with judicial review, that is what they should have; that is what democratic principles require, as far as constitutional change is concerned. But we must not confuse the reason for carrying out a proposal with the character of the proposal itself. If the people voted to experiment with dictatorship, principles of

democracy might give us a reason to allow them to do so. But it would not follow that dictatorship is democratic. (This is just another way of saying that it is not conceptually impossible for a democracy to vote itself out of existence.)

Let me put the matter more theoretically. There is a distinction between democracy and popular sovereignty. The principle of popular sovereignty—basic to liberal thought—requires that the people should have whatever constitution, whatever form of government they want. But popular sovereignty does not remove or blur the differences that exist among the various forms of government on the menu from which the people are supposed to choose. John Locke and Thomas Hobbes both believed in popular sovereignty. They argued that the people—acting by majority decision—had the right to vest legislative authority in a single individual or small group of individuals (thus constituting a monarchy or an aristocracy) or alternatively in an assembly comprising the whole people or in a large representative institution (thus constituting a direct or an indirect democracy).[5] But although this decision was to be popular and majoritarian, and in that sense democratic, it was at the same time a significant choice between democratic and undemocratic options. Hobbes believed that the people would be making a mistake if they vested sovereignty in a democratic assembly.[6] Locke, on the other hand, credited the people with thinking that they "could never be safe . . . till the Legislature was placed in collective bodies of Men, call them Senate, Parliament, or what you please" and he thought it important for that collective body to be the "Supream Power" of the commonwealth.[7] Neither of them thought a constitution became more democratic simply by being the upshot of popular choice.

There may be a connection the other way. It may be easier to establish that a polity is based on popular sovereignty if it is in fact democratically organized. We can see this if we reflect a little on the artificiality of the Hobbes–Locke model. The distinction between a democratic method of constitutional choice and the democratic character of the constitution that is chosen is clearest when we can point to a founding moment in the life of a political society (a moment of constitutional choice) and distinguish between the decision procedures used at that moment and the decision procedures which, at that moment, it was decided to employ in all subsequent political decision-making. But in the real world, the formation of a new political order is seldom so tidy.

Often the decisions that determine the shape of a society's constitution are entangled with or woven into the fabric of ordinary political life.[8] As they occur they may be indistinguishable—in time, solemnity, or any other respect—from the ordinary run of political decision-making. Often, for example, we will not know whether a different way of doing things (in some run-of-the-mill case or even in some crisis that is not evidently or on its face a *constitutional* crisis) is going to "stick"—that is, whether it is going to become established as a rule or practice governing the conduct of political life, or whether it will turn out to be just an aberration, consigned to the minutiae of history. Even in the United States, where there is a full written constitution and an established tradition of interpreting it, an event that has fundamental significance for the basis on which political life is conducted may not advertise itself as "constitutional."[9] Certainly in the United Kingdom and elsewhere, understanding the formation and growth of the constitution is often a matter of studying apparently routine political events, to discern which of them have and which of them have not acquired normative significance as far as the conduct and organization of other political events are concerned.[10]

An attribution of popular sovereignty to a political system is therefore a matter of theoretical judgment. It requires us to figure out which decisions count as constitutive of the political system in question and to venture a certain explanatory hypothesis to account for the constitutional significance of those decisions—a hypothesis to the effect that they "stuck" or became established as constitutional practices because they were acceptable as such to most of the ordinary members of the society. Obviously this will be easiest to justify in a society whose ordinary workings are democratic, because the

events we adjudge "constitutional" will be part of that ordinary working.

The argument is not cast-iron, however. It is one thing for a particular decision to be made democratically; it is another thing for it to sustain the same popular support under the description that it is setting a constitutional precedent. The people may support the ratification of an important treaty in a referendum, but some of them might have voted no if they had thought their support was going to be regarded as effecting a change in the rule requiring that treaties be ratified by a vote in the Senate, not by a vote among the people.[11] Thus, the events that amount over time to a change in the constitution may be democratic events without its being proper to describe that constitutional change as democratic.

II. PRECOMMITMENT

Still, suppose that a bill of rights together with American style judicial review is chosen by the British people and supported by a majority in full awareness that this amounts to a reform of the constitution. Then, it may be said, even if we cannot infer that judicial review is democratic, we have surely nevertheless answered the democratic objection. The existence of written constitutional constraints and the courts' power to interpret and apply them—these would not be products of judicial usurpation. Rather they would be mechanisms of restraint that the British people have deliberately and for good reasons chosen to impose upon themselves.

Why would they do this? What makes this sort of self-restraint intelligible? The answer is that everyone knows that majoritarian legislation can be unjust; everyone knows that popular majorities can sometimes be driven by panic to pass measures that harm or discriminate against minorities who are powerless politically to resist them. Elsewhere I have argued that respect for individual rights is not compatible with a purely predatory image of legislative majorities, for majorities are made up of individual rights bearers and part of what we respect in individuals is their ability as rights bearers to figure out responsibly what they owe to others.[12] But of course this argument does not require us to think that rights bearers are always angels or to deny that, acting individually or en masse, they are sometimes capable of rights violations. It requires us to say, rather, that although rights bearers may on occasion be rights violators, they are not always themselves indifferent or partial to that possibility. To the extent that they foresee it, they have as rights bearers the moral capacity to condemn it in advance and take precautions against the temptations that may trigger it. Constitutional constraints and mechanisms of judicial review may be viewed, then, as precautions that responsible rights bearers have taken against their own imperfections. It follows that such precautions do not involve any fundamental disrespect for the people, individually or collectively, or for their capacities of self-government; on the contrary, taking such precautions represents the epitome of the exercise of those capacities in a troubled and complicated world.

I shall call this the "precommitment" view of constitutional constraints and much of the rest of this essay will be devoted to a critique of it. For the moment, however, let us consider it in the best possible light. In the words of one of its most persuasive proponents, the view presents the constitutional arrangements we have been discussing as "a kind of rational and shared precommitment among free and equal sovereign citizens at the level of constitutional choice."[13] Its effect can be summed up as follows:

> By the exercise of their rights of equal participation [the people] agree to a safeguard that prevents them, in the future exercise of their equal political rights, from later changing their minds and deviating from their agreement and commitment to a just constitution. . . . By granting to a non-legislative body that is not electorally accountable the power to review democratically enacted legislation, citizens provide themselves with a means for protecting their sovereignty and independence from the unreasonable exercise of their political rights in legislative processes. . . . By agreeing to judicial review, they in effect tie themselves into their unanimous agreement on the

equal basic rights that specify their sovereignty. Judicial review is then one way to protect their status as equal citizens.[14]

As I said, the precommitment view is an attractive one. We are familiar with it in personal ethics: An individual may have reason to impose on himself certain constraints as far as his future decision-making is concerned. Ulysses decided that he should be bound to the mast in order to resist the charms of the Sirens, and he instructed his crew that "if I beg you to release me, you must tighten and add to my bonds."[15] A smoker trying to quit may hide his own cigarettes, a chronic oversleeper with a weakness for the "snooze" button may place his alarm clock out of reach on the other side of the bedroom, and a heavy drinker may give his car keys to a friend at the beginning of a party with strict instructions not to return them when they are requested at midnight.

These arrangements strike us not as derogations from individual freedom, but as the epitome of self-government. Freedom, after all, is not just moving hither and yon with the play of one's appetites. It is a matter of *taking control* of the basis on which one acts; it is a matter of the self being in charge of its desires and not vice versa.[16] The idea is sometimes explicated in terms of the related concept of *autonomy:* "Autonomy of the will is the property that the will has of being a law to itself."[17] Aware now of a way in which it might be determined by various forces in the future, the autonomous will seeks to limit such determination by responding to certain considerations of principle in advance.

So, similarly, it may be said, an electorate may decide collectively to bind itself in advance to resist the siren charms of rights violations. Aware, as much as the smoker or the drinker, of the temptations of wrong or irrational action, the people as a whole in a lucid moment may put themselves under certain constitutional disabilities—disabilities that serve the same function in relation to democratic values as are served by strategies like hiding the cigarettes or handing the car keys to a friend in relation to the smoker's or the drinker's autonomy. The smoker really desires to stop smoking; the drinker does not really want to drive under the influence. The mechanisms they adopt, therefore, enable them to secure the good that they really want and avoid the evil that, occasionally despite themselves, they really want to avoid. Similarly, the people really do not want to discriminate on grounds of race, to restrict free speech, or to allow the police to search people's homes without a warrant. They are aware, however, that on occasion they may be driven by panic into doing these things. And so they have taken precautions, instituting legal constraints as safeguards to prevent them from doing in a moment of panic what in their more thoughtful moments they are sure they do not want to do. As Stephen Holmes states the view (though this is not quite Holmes's *own* account of constitutional precommitment):

> A constitution is Peter sober while the electorate is Peter drunk. Citizens need a constitution, just as Ulysses needed to be bound to his mast. If voters were allowed to get what they wanted, they would inevitably shipwreck themselves. By binding themselves to rigid rules, they can better achieve their solid and long-term collective aims.[18]

Constitutional constraint, in other words, is a means by which the will of the people secures its own responsible exercise.

III. CAUSAL MECHANISMS VERSUS EXTERNAL JUDGMENT

In a seminal study of precommitment, Jon Elster has suggested that a decision at t_1 counts as a way of "binding oneself" vis-à-vis some decision at t_2 only if "[t]he effect of carrying out the decision at t_1 [is] to set up some *causal* process in the external world."[19] He means to exclude purely internal strategies like deciding to decide: "[O]ur intuitive notion of what it is to bind oneself seems to require that we temporarily deposit our will in some external structure."[20]

In the political case, we may want to ask: What counts as an *external* structure? Elster himself has doubts about the application of his analysis to constitutional constraints:

> [T]he analogy between individual and political self-binding is severely limited. An individual can bind himself to certain actions, or at least make deviations from them more costly and hence less likely, by having recourse to a legal framework that is external to and independent of himself. *But nothing is external to society.* With the exception of a few special cases, like the abdication of powers to the International Monetary Fund, societies cannot deposit their will in structures outside their control; they can always undo their ties should they want to.[21]

His point is well taken as far as popular sovereignty is concerned: What the people can do, constitutionally, they can always *in some sense* undo.[22] Yet there is a sense nevertheless that constitutional provisions can be binding, a sense that has to do with the institutional articulation *within* the framework controlled overall by "the people" as popular sovereign. Even though the constraints are not external to that framework, they are in the relevant sense external to the particular agencies in which "the will of the people" is embodied for purposes of ordinary political decision. I shall return to these issues toward the end of the essay.

A separate set of issues is raised by Elster's reference to causal mechanisms. A decision at t_1 counts, he said, as a precommitment only if its effect is "to set up some causal process in the external world."[23] Does this include or exclude strategies like the drinker giving his car keys to a friend? The friend's possession of the car keys is not really a *causal* mechanism ensuring or increasing the probability that the drinker will not drive home at midnight. Instead, it operates by virtue of the friend's undertaking at t_1 not to give him back the car keys at t_2, together of course with the friend's willingness at t_2 to actually honor that undertaking. My point is not that the friend may prove unreliable, for so may a causal mechanism. It is rather that the precommitment operates via the friend's judgment and decision, and to that extent its operation at t_2 is not entirely under the drinker's ex ante control at t_1.

An advantage of using a noncausal mechanism such as the judgment of a friend is that it enables the agent to bind himself to a principle that does not operate deontologically or rigidly. Most people who condemn drunk driving (in themselves and others) do so without considering that there may be circumstances in which driving with an elevated blood alcohol level is the right thing to do. Suppose I design a mechanism that prevents me from ever starting my car when my blood alcohol level exceeds 0.05 percent. Then I may be dismayed to find that I cannot drive my baby to the hospital if the child becomes desperately ill while I am hosting a cocktail party at my home (and no one else has a car, and no one else can drive, etc., etc.). I discover, in other words, the need for exceptions to the rule. Now if the exceptions are clear-cut, then perhaps a sophisticated mechanism can embody them as well: I install a device that also measures the body temperature of my baby and allows me to drive drunk whenever that temperature exceeds 102 degrees Fahrenheit. But if the exceptions are at all complicated or if delicate judgment is required in order to establish whether exceptional conditions obtain, then of course it will be better to abandon causal mechanisms altogether and instead entrust the car keys to a friend, hoping that the friend will make what is in the circumstances an ethically appropriate decision.

Clearly, if constitutional constraints are regarded as forms of democratic precommitment, then they operate more on the model of the friend's judgment than on the model of a causal mechanism. Except in rare cases (like "dual key" controls of nuclear weapons), constitutional constraints do not operate mechanically, but work instead by vesting a power of decision in some person or body of persons (a court) whose job it is to determine *as a matter of judgment* whether conduct that is contemplated (say, by the legislature) at t_2 violates a constraint written down at t_1.

As I said, the advantage of such forms of constraint is that they do not operate rigidly, but instead leave some room for judgment. The disadvantage is that they then become capable of operating in ways that do not represent the intentions of the agent who instituted them at t_1. Provided that one's intention is sufficiently simpleminded, a causal mechanism can embody it perfectly: The physical rigidity of the mechanism represents, as it were, the strength and single-mindedness of the agent's resolve. Though the machine is a mindless thing, its operation may for that very reason enhance rather than undermine the agent's autonomy, because it works to bind him to exactly the decision *he* intended. But if Agent A has vested a power of decision in someone else, B, with room for the exercise of judgment by B, then one may wonder whether this is really an instance of autonomous precommitment by A. Binding oneself to do at t_2 exactly what one intends at t_1 to do at t_2 is one thing; delivering one's power of decision as to what to do at t_2 over to the judgment of another person is something quite different. Person A may have good reason to do that of course (i.e., surrender his judgment to B)—and *in a sense* that would be a form of precommitment. That is, the *act* of precommitment may be autonomous, but its operation may be something less than a consummation of the agent's autonomy inasmuch as it is subject to the judgment of another. In other words, it would not be a form of precommitment that enabled one to rebut an objection based on the importance of A's hanging on to his autonomy or, in the case of constitutional constraints, an objection on democratic grounds. It would be more like the vote to vest power in a dictator that we discussed in Section I: When the people vote for dictatorship, maybe dictatorship is what they need, and maybe dictatorship is what they should have, but let us not kid ourselves that dictatorship is therefore a form of democracy.

I believe this point is *not* rebutted by showing that an independent power of judgment is indispensable to the sort of constraint that the agent (or the people) want to set up. In a recent book Ronald Dworkin has presented an attractive picture of the United States Constitution in which many of the provisions of the Bill of Rights are taken to embody abstract moral principles.[24] Dworkin argues that an accurate historical understanding of the equal protection clause, for example, precludes any interpretation that does not represent it as a moral principle framed at a very high level of generality.[25] Since it is obvious (and was obvious in 1868) that abstract moral principles cannot be interpreted and applied without the exercise of human judgment, Dworkin believes that the framers of the Fourteenth Amendment evidently intended members of the judiciary to employ their powers of moral judgment to determine how exactly the actions of state legislatures should be constrained in the name of equal protection. Since this is what the states voted for when the amendment was ratified, the arrangement amounts to a deliberate decision by various agents, not to constrain themselves by mechanical means as in Ulysses' case, but to have themselves constrained by others' judgment.

Furthermore, in cases like this, the necessity for judgment cannot be understood except on the assumption that it will sometimes be exercised—and exercised properly—in ways that were not foreseen by those who set up the constraint. After all, if its proper exercise could always be foreseen, then no exercise of judgment would ever really be required; constitutional jurisprudence would become, as we say, "mechanical." Dworkin is quite right to insist, therefore, that once one accepts the abstract-principle interpretation of the Bill of Rights and the analytic connection between abstraction and judgment, it is a mistake to accuse modern judges of violating the framers' intentions simply because the framers did not contemplate or would have been surprised by some particular modern application of their principle.

But there is yet another point about the link between abstraction and judgment that *does* pose difficulties for the precommitment idea. Not only should we not expect particular applications of the principles embodied in the Bill of Rights to be ex ante foreseeable and unsurprising; we should also not expect them to be uncontroversial. The inference of particular applications from a complex principle is something on which people are likely to disagree, particularly if—as Dworkin rightly argues—the inference in every case should be from the whole

array of abstract principles embodied in the constitution, not just the principle embodied in the particular provision appealed to. Again, if we value judgment in relation to our constitutional commitments, we should not flinch at this conclusion. But it does eat away at any claim that precommitment is a form of self-government— that is, government not only of the people but *by* the people—or that it preserves the democratic or self-governing character of a regime. The argument to that effect goes as follows.

Early in our tradition, political theorists developed a taxonomy of various forms of constitution, of which the most familiar is the Aristotelian distinction between government by one man, government by a few men, and government by the many. The distinction was not necessarily a matter of whose *will* was to prevail in a society. According to Aristotle, the distinction was needed even in a society ruled by law, since the application of law required judgment and there was a question about who should apply the laws. Judgment foreshadows disagreement, and in politics the question is always how disagreements among the citizens are to be resolved. It is, I think, important to remember that this includes disagreements about rights and justice, and thus disagreements about the things covered by the abstract moral principles to which the people have committed themselves in their constitution. Different forms of government amount to different answers to the question: Whose judgment is to prevail when citizens disagree in their judgments about matters as important as this?

Now there may be good reasons for the people to offer as their answer: "Not us, or our representatives, but the judiciary." If so, that amounts pro tanto to a refusal of self-government. It amounts to the people's embrace of what Aristotle would call "aristocracy"—the rule of the few best.

Of course, it is not wholly aristocratic, for the few best are to exercise their judgment on the interpretation and application of principles that, initially at any rate and in their most general form, are chosen by the people. The fact that authority is accorded to the people's choice as to which abstract principles are to be adopted for interpretation by the judges makes this a mixed constitution.

But the aristocratic nature of the arrangement is not diminished by the mere fact that the aristocrats exercise judgment rather than will. For in our best understanding, politics is *always* a matter of judgment, even at the most abstract level: Even the framing of a provision like the Fourteenth Amendment is an act of judgment—by the people—as to what a good republic now requires (in light of its history, etc.). The democratic claim has always been that the people are entitled to govern themselves by their own judgments. So, to the extent that they invest the judiciary with an overriding power of judgment as to how something as basic as equal protection is to be understood, allowing that judgment to override the judgment of the people or their representatives on this very issue, it is undeniable that in terms of the Aristotelian taxonomy, they have set up what would traditionally be described as a nondemocratic arrangement.

Under these circumstances then—and there is no reason to believe that the problem will be any different with a British bill of rights—the constitutional arrangements we have been discussing cannot really be regarded as a form of precommitment by Agent A at time t_1 to a decision (for time t_2) that A himself has chosen. Instead, they involve a form of submission by A at t_1 to whatever judgment is made at t_2 by another agent, B, in the application of very general principles that A has instructed B to take into account.

One final observation to clarify the point I am making. It is sometimes said that what justifies judicial review is that it would be inappropriate for the representatives of the people (acting by majority decision) to be "judge in their own case," in determining whether a piece of legislation violates the rights of a minority. But if a constitutional provision (protecting minority rights) is really a precommitment of the people or their representatives, then there is in principle nothing whatever inappropriate about asking them: Was this the precommitment you intended? If a dispute arises among the crew as to whether Ulysses wanted to be blindfolded as well as bound to the mast, there is nothing to

do but *ask Ulysses*. To refrain from doing so on the ground that this would make him judge in his own case would be absurd—absurd, that is, if the name of the game really is precommitment. Precommitment cannot preserve the aura of autonomy (or democracy in the constitutional case) unless the person bound really is the judge of the point and extent of his being bound. Ulysses, of course, may not be able to give us a rational answer if we do not get around to asking him until he is already under the influence of the Sirens' song. Then there is nothing we can do but make our *own* decision about whether or not to blindfold him. At that stage we should stop justifying *our* decision by calling it a consummation of Ulysses' autonomy; the best we can now say on autonomy grounds is that we are acting, paternalistically, as Ulysses *would have acted* had he been lucid and in possession of full information, not that we are acting in the way he clearly wanted us to act in defense of his autonomy. So, similarly, if we follow the logic of precommitment in the political case, the people are presumably authorities—not judges in their own cause, but *authorities*—on what they have precommitted themselves to. If that authority is challenged—for example, because the people are now thought to be in the very state (of panic or anger, etc.) that they wanted their precommitment to counteract—then all we can say is that the notion of precommitment is now no longer useful in relation to the controversy. Once it becomes unclear or controversial what the people have committed themselves to, there is no longer any basis in the idea of precommitment for defending a particular interpretation against democratic objections.

IV. DISAGREEMENTS OR WEAKNESS OF WILL?

We have concentrated for a while on the implementation of a precommitment: Is it a causal mechanism, or does it consist rather in entrusting a decision to somebody else's judgment? There are also things to be said about what motivates precommitment in the first place.

In cases of individual precommitment, the agent is imagined to be quite certain, in his lucid moments, about the actions he wants to avoid, the reasons for their undesirability, and the basis on which he might be tempted nevertheless to perform them. The smoker knows that smoking is damaging his health, and he can furnish an explanation in terms of the pathology of nicotine addiction of why he craves a cigarette notwithstanding his possession of that knowledge. The drinker knows the statistics about drunk driving and he knows too how intoxication works. He knows at the beginning of the evening that at midnight both his ability to drive safely and his judgment about his ability to drive safely will be seriously impaired. . . . A constitutional "precommitment" in these circumstances is not the triumph of preemptive rationality that it appears to be in the cases of Ulysses and the smoker and the drinker. It is rather the artificially sustained ascendancy of one view in the polity over other views while the complex moral issues between them remain unresolved. To impose the template of precommitment on this situation would smack more of Procrustes than Ulysses.

A better individual analogy—better, that is, than the case of Ulysses or the drinker or the smoker—might be the following. Imagine a person—call her Bridget—who is torn between competing conceptions of religious belief. One day she opts decisively for fundamentalist faith in a personal God. She commits herself utterly to that view and abjures forever the private library of theological books in her house that, in the past, had excited and sustained her uncertainty. Though she is no book burner, she locks the door of her library and gives the keys to a friend, with strict instructions never to return them, not even on demand.

But new issues and old doubts start to creep into Bridget's mind after a while ("Maybe Tillich was right after all . . ."), and a few months later she asks for the keys. Should the friend return them? Clearly, this case is quite different from (say) withholding car keys from the drinker at midnight. Both involve forms of precommitment. But in Bridget's case, for the friend to sustain the precommitment would be for the friend to take sides, as it were, in a dispute between two or more conflicting selves or two or more conflicting aspects of the same self within Bridget, each with a claim to rational authority. It would be to take sides in a way that is simply not determined by any recognizable criteria of pathology or other mental aberration. To uphold the precommitment would be to sustain the temporary ascendancy of one aspect of the self at the time the library keys were given away and to neglect the fact that the self that demands them back has an equal claim to respect for *its* way of dealing with the vicissitudes of theological uncertainty.

Upholding another's precommitment may be regarded as a way of respecting that person's autonomy only if a clear line can be drawn between the aberrant mental phenomena the precommitment was supposed to override, on the one hand, and genuine uncertainty, changes of mind, conversions, and so on, on the other. In Ulysses' case and in the case of the potential drunk driver, we can draw such a line. In Bridget's case, we have much more difficulty, and that is why respecting the precommitment seems more like taking sides in an internal dispute between two factions warring on roughly equal terms.

As if that weren't bad enough, if we were really looking for an analogy to the judicial review example, we would imagine the theological case with this difference—that Bridget hands the keys of the library to a *group* of friends, who then decide by majority voting when it is appropriate to return them to her. They find they have to decide by majority voting, since they disagree about the issue along the very lines of the uncertainty that is torturing Bridget herself.

Clearly there are dangers in any simplistic analogy between the rational autonomy of individuals and the democratic governance of a community. The idea of a society binding itself against certain legislative acts in the future is problematic in cases where members disagree with one another about the need for such bonds or, if they agree abstractly about the need, disagree about their content or character. It is particularly problematic when such disagreements can be expected to persist and to develop and change in unpredictable ways. And it becomes ludicrously problematic in cases where the form of precommitment is to assign the decision procedurally to another body, whose members are just as torn and conflicted about the issues as the members of the first body were.

If, moreover, the best explanation of these persisting disagreements is that the issues the society is addressing are themselves very difficult, then we have no justification whatever for regarding the temporary ascendancy of one or other party to the disagreement as an instance of full and rational precommitment on the part of the entire society. In these circumstances the logic of precommitment must simply be put aside, and we must leave the members of the society to work out their differences and to change their minds in collective decision-making over time, the best way they can. . . .

NOTES

This is a slightly modified version of chapter 12 of Jeremy Waldron, *Law and Disagreement* (Oxford University Press, 1999).

[1]What this will involve is probably the incorporation into British law of the European Convention on Human Rights, conferring on British courts the powers of interpretation and enforcement presently vested in the European Court of Human Rights at Strasbourg.

[2]It is remarkable how rarely books and articles on American constitutional law refer to constitutional arrangements in other countries. It is as though "Constitution" were a proper name rather than the name of a kind of thing whose nature could best be understood by examining and comparing a variety of instances. For a critique of American parochialism in this regard, see Mary Ann Glendon, *Rights Talk: The Impoverishment of Political Discourse* (New York: Free Press, 1991), 153–70.

[3]See Alexander Bickel, *The Least Dangerous Branch: The Supreme Court at the Bar of Politics* (New Haven, Conn.: Yale University Press, 1962), 16.

[4]Ronald Dworkin, *A Bill of Rights for Britain* (London: Chatto & Windus, 1990), 36–7.

[5]Thomas Hobbes, *Leviathan*, ed. Richard Tuck (Cambridge University Press, 1991), 129–38; John Locke, *Two Treatises of Government*, ed. Peter Laslett (Cambridge University Press, 1988), II, para. 132, p. 354.

[6]Thomas Hobbes, *De Cive: The English Version*, ed. Howard Warrender (Oxford: Clarendon Press, 1983), 129–40.

[7]Locke, *Two Treatises*, II, para. 94, pp. 329–30 and para 149, pp. 366–7. I have discussed this view of Locke's at some

length in "Locke's Legislature," in *The Dignity of Legislation* (the 1996 Seeley Lectures) (Cambridge University Press, forthcoming), ch. 5.

[8]See Paul Brest, "Further Beyond the Republican Revival: Toward Radical Republicanism," *Yale Law Journal* 97 (1988): 1204–63.

[9]See C. G. Tiedeman, *The Unwritten Constitution of the United States* (New York: Putnam's, 1890).

[10]See Geoffrey Marshall, *Constitutional Conventions: The Rules and Forms of Political Accountability* (Oxford: Clarendon Press, 1984). There is also an accessible account of this aspect of the British constitution in Jeremy Waldron, *The Law* (London: Routledge, 1990), 56–87.

[11]This example is adapted from Bruce Ackerman and David Golove, "Is NAFTA Constitutional?" *Harvard Law Review* 108 (1995): 799–929.

[12]See Jeremy Waldron, "A Right-Based Critique of Constitutional Rights," *Oxford Journal of Legal Studies* 13 (1993): 18–51, at 27.

[13]Samuel Freeman, "Constitutional Democracy and the Legitimacy of Judicial Review," *Law and Philosophy* 9 (1990): 353. See also Jeremy Waldron. "Freeman's Defense of Judicial Review," *Law and Philosophy* 13 (1994): 27–41.

[14]Freeman, "Constitutional Democracy," 353–4.

[15]Quoted in Jon Elster, *Ulysses and the Sirens: Studies in Rationality and Irrationality* (Cambridge University Press, 1984), 36.

[16]See also the discussion of strong evaluation and second-order desires in Harry Frankfurt, "Freedom of the Will and the Concept of a Person" *Journal of Philosophy* 68 (1971): 55–81 and Charles Taylor, "What Is Human Agency?" in his collection *Human Agency and Language: Philosophical Papers* (Cambridge University Press, 1985), vol. 1.

[17]Immanuel Kant, *Grounding for the Metaphysics of Morals*, trans. J. Ellington (Indianapolis: Hackett, 1981), 44 (p. 440 of vol. 4 of the Prussian Academy edition of Kant's Works).

[18]Stephen Holmes, *Passions and Constraint: On the Theory of Liberal Democracy* (Chicago: University of Chicago Press, 1995), 135.

[19]Elster, *Ulysses*, 42.

[20]Ibid., 43 (my emphasis). In general, Elster says, decisions to decide have very little impact: "I decide that I shall decide that *p*" has the same ritual and redundant sound as "if someone were to buy several copies of the morning paper to assure himself that what it said was true." (Quoting Ludwig Wittgenstein, *Philosophical Investigations*, para. 265.)

[21]Jon Elster, *Solomonic Judgments: Studies in the Limits of Rationality* (Cambridge University Press, 1989), 196 (emphasis in original).

[22]See John Rawls, *Political Liberalism* (New York: Columbia University Press, 1993), 234–5.

[23]Elster, *Ulysses*, 42.

[24]Ronald Dworkin, *Freedom's Law* (Cambridge, Mass.: Harvard University Press, 1996), ch. 1. See also Ronald Dworkin, *A Matter of Principle* (Cambridge, Mass.: Harvard University Press, 1985), 69–71.

[25]Dworkin, *Freedom's Law*, 8–10.

REVIEW AND DISCUSSION QUESTIONS

1. Explain the distinction between popular sovereignty and democracy.

2. What is autonomy, and how is it relevant to Waldron's discussion of precommitment?

3. Why are external, causal processes, rather than internal strategies, essential for precommitment?

4. Where judgment is necessary, argues Waldron, the analogy of self-binding fails. Explain his reasoning.

5. Why does he think Bridget, a person torn between two conceptions of religious faith, is a better analogy than Ulysses for constitutional precommitment? Does that analogy help those who defend judicial review on grounds of precommitment? Explain.

Democracy, Judicial Review, and the Special Competency of Judges

John Arthur

Democratic government often seems incompatible with judicial review, since it allows judges to reject popular legislation passed by an elected legislature. But that claim, while oft-heard, is less clearly true than is usually supposed, according to John Arthur. In this essay, Arthur begins with a discussion of the nature of democratic government, arguing that instead of limiting democracy, judicial review often serves to promote it. He then considers another argument that also seeks to show how judicial review can be made compatible with self-government: self-incapacitation. Such an argument, he states, cannot rest merely on the claim that people hope to protect minority rights but instead depends on the fact that judges are better situated, institutionally, to make sound judgments. John Arthur is professor of philosophy and director of the Program in Philosophy, Politics, and Law at Binghamton University, State University of New York.

The United States[1] is famous for its practice of judicial review, in which judges are empowered to enforce constitutional limits on legislative power. But why should today's popularly elected officials be bound by a 200-year-old document, interpreted by unelected judges? Having a constitution, even a written one, is one thing; but it's quite another to give judges the power to interpret it. Why not let the people's representatives decide which laws are consistent with the Constitution and then if the electorate disagrees with their interpretation that opinion can be expressed at the next election? Surely that would be a far more democratic and therefore sounder basis on which to proceed. Or so, at any rate, it is often said.

That familiar line of thought poses an important challenge to the practice of judicial review—a challenge that I propose to take up in stages. First, I shall provide a few brief historical comments on the origins of the practice of judicial review in the United States. Next, I shall consider the claim that judicial review is undemocratic, first by asking what, exactly, is meant by the claim. How, I shall ask, ought we to understand the meaning of 'democratic' in this context? That will lead, in turn, to further reflections on some of the ways that judicial review may be said to be anti-democratic and, finally, to a discussion of the special competence of judges to serve as final arbiters over the Constitution's meaning.

BACKGROUND

Neither the Bill of Rights nor judicial review was explicitly included in the original US Constitution. Many states, fearful of the power of the new national government and the possibility that it might infringe on their own sovereignty, decided to press for a series of amendments designed to limit the powers of the newly formed Congress and protect individual rights against the national government. The result was that the first Congress passed and sent to the states for ratification what we now know as the Bill of Rights, which are the first ten amendments to the Constitution.

Nor, second, did the original Constitution explicitly call for judicial review as the mechanism by which to enforce those rights, or to enforce any of the other constitutional limits imposed on both the national and state governments, for that matter. 'Federalist Number 78', written by Alexander Hamilton (1787) to urge the adoption of the Constitution, is widely regarded as the canonical account of the role of the judiciary and the meaning of its powers under Article III of the Constitution. 'The interpretation of laws,' Hamilton (1787, p. 467) wrote, 'is the proper and peculiar province of the courts. The Constitution is and must be regarded as fundamental law. It therefore belongs to them (judges) to ascertain its meaning.' Hamilton went on to explain the sense in which the Constitution is regarded as fundamental law: 'If there should happen to be any irreconcilable variance between the law and the will of the people, that which has the superior obligation and validity ought, of course, to be preferred to the statute, the intention of the people to the intention of their agents' (Hamilton, 1787, p. 467). Hamilton's suggestion is that elected officials are not in fact the holders of sovereign power, but instead are bound by the document enacted by the people as a fundamental charter. In that way, it is the people rather than the elected officials who are sovereign and, further, it is on the people that the explanation and justification of judicial review ultimately depends.

It is far from clear, however, that this suggestion makes sense. In explaining it, we will first consider why people might limit the power of elected lawmakers whom, after all, they chose themselves. While such a practice seems contrary to the values on which democratic government rests, I shall argue that this familiar claim is mistaken and can be seen to be so when we reflect on the nature of those democratic values appealed to by judicial review's critics. First, then, we must ask what, exactly, is involved in the claim that a government 'respects democratic values'?

DEMOCRATIC VALUES AND JUDICIAL REVIEW

Democratic government is not achieved merely with the introduction of elections: Brezhnev and Stalin were regularly elected by large majorities. What, exactly, kept the old Soviet Union's system from embodying genuine democratic values?

Two points need to be made.[2] First, any genuinely democratic government must be open, in the sense that all those who are entitled to participate are, in fact, allowed to do so. If a government is to embody the ideals inherent in the democratic ideal, neither the vote nor the opportunity to run for office can be arbitrarily and unreasonably denied. Just which people are, in fact, entitled to participate can of course be controversial. In the US we have seen much disagreement about voting age, for example, as well as whether people who neither have children nor own property should be allowed to elect the officials governing school districts, which are financed by property taxes.[3] My point is not that these are simple issues, for plainly they are not; rather it is that inherent in the democratic ideal is the thought that governments must not arbitrarily or unfairly deny members of any group (women and racial minorities come to mind here) the opportunity to participate in the political process, either as candidates or as voters.

The second democratic value, in addition to openness, is fairness: democratic governments must not only allow open participation, but that participation must be on fair terms. By that I mean that political influence and power must be distributed *correctly* among all the participants; giving some people extra votes, for instance, would not be compatible with the democratic value of fairness. As with openness, there is also room to dispute just what fairness requires; not all cases will be as clear as plural voting.[4]

My concern here, however, is not to explore these issues but to point out their constitutional implications. If we assume fairness and openness are (among) the virtues of any democratic system, then the judiciary may be thought to play an important role in promoting democracy. Indeed, not only is judicial review compatible with democracy, but it may in fact be required by it.[5] I will assume that elected officials are sometimes tempted to act in ways that are incompatible with democratic values of openness and fairness since, having won an election, they often hope to stay in office. One of the roadblocks to winning the next election, of course, can be a democratic system's openness and fairness.

Thus, during the 1960s and 1970s, judicial review often served to make the political process both more open and more fair. Openness was encouraged as the Court, relying on the Constitutional guarantee of 'equal protection' of the law for all citizens and its requirement that every state maintain a 'republican form of government', abolished laws imposing literacy requirements on voters[6] and college students,[7] and rejected residency requirements for members of the military who wished to vote.[8] Each of these decisions was opposed by democratically-elected officials, yet each enhanced rather than reduced democratic values.

The Supreme Court also exercised its power of judicial review in order to enhance democratic fairness. One method it used involved re-apportioning districts set up to elect congressional representatives. Population shifts, usually from rural to urban areas, had taken place over the previous years to the point that in Georgia, for example, 50 per cent of the state's population was limited to electing only 10 per cent of its representatives to Congress. Relying on the Constitutional requirement that members of the US Congress must be chosen 'by the people', the Court overturned such districting schemes, stating that 'one man's vote . . . is to be worth as much as another's'.[9] The Court then went on to attack unfair districting patterns at both the state and local government levels. Relying on the equal protections clause, the Court held that it is a violation of the Constitution for a citizen's voting power to be diluted as compared with others. Again, then, we see an unelected judiciary overruling decisions made by elected officials, but doing so in a way that enhances democratic values.

In addition to imposing unequal voting influence, legislators can also undermine democratic fairness by limiting those who would criticise government officials or their actions. Those in power can thus help assure their re-election by preventing opponents from challenging their legislative records, policies and personal suitability for office. Here again, however, the US Supreme Court, under Chief Justice Warren, prevented these legislative abuses of democratic values by seeking to limit government censorship across a wide front. Unless political speech is 'directed to producing immanent lawless action and is likely to produce such action,' the Court said, government can not invoke police power against a critic.[10] In another important case, public officials seeking civil damages for libel and slander were required under the First Amendment's free speech and free press provisions to prove not only that what was said was false but also that it was uttered either with knowledge of its falsity or with reckless disregard of whether it was the truth.[11]

So besides equalising voting power, judicial review can also promote democratic fairness by protecting the rights of critics of government to criticise officials and their policies. Far from working against democratic values of openness and fairness, in these circumstances judicial review can, and has, served to enhance them. Other forms of judicial review, however, seem not to be able so easily to be dealt with from the perspective of democratic values, and it is to those cases that I now turn.

DEMOCRATIC SELF-INCAPACITATION

The US Constitution includes many provisions that seem to have little to do with either the fairness or openness of democratic government. It imposes limits on elected officials by banning practices such as 'cruel and unusual punishment', for example, as well as by requiring legislators not to deny citizens life, liberty or property without 'due process of law', to allow the 'free exercise of religion' and to prevent 'unreasonable searches and seizures', among many others. The Supreme Court has often made controversial and sometimes deeply unpopular decisions as it interprets provisions such as these. Because these are substantive rights, not ones required by democratic procedures, the Court's enforcement of its own interpretation of them against popularly-elected lawmakers may therefore seem incompatible with democratic values. Thus the earlier question arises once again: why should courts in a country committed to democratic values be allowed to give the final, definitive meaning of the constitutional limitations imposed on government?

One answer, familiar from the earlier comments by Alexander Hamilton, involves what might be termed 'self-incapacitating rules'. What I mean is this: We are all sometimes tempted to do things that we will at a future time regret. Thus, for example, I tend to turn my alarm clock off and go back to sleep. I might therefore put the alarm clock across the room before I go to sleep, knowing that in the morning I shall have to get out of bed in order to turn it off. By making it more difficult to violate the rule I have set for myself to arise early, I seek to avoid what my 'better self' knows would be a mistake; I incapacitate myself.

Such self-incapacitating rules might be thought to make political sense in various ways. Elected officials, under pressure from constituents, sometimes act in haste, without adequate information, or else out of anger and frustration with events; other decisions may reflect prejudice toward religious or racial minorities that, on further reflection, we would know to be wrong. Because of these tendencies, it might make sense for people to seek to provide constitutional guarantees that serve, in effect, to incapacitate themselves (or, in this case, their elected officials).

Due process guarantees for people accused of crimes fit neatly into this picture, since it is often tempting to respond to temporary increases in crime or to particularly violent acts by passing legislation under strong political pressure and without due consideration of its consequences. Similarly, we might also think that because there is a dangerous tendency for us to ignore the rights and interests of unpopular religious or ethnic minorities, it might also be reasonable to make it more difficult than normal to enact legislation which harms such groups.

The Supreme Court has in fact read the US Constitution to require such 'self-incapacitation'. Basic constitutional doctrine insists that laws disadvantaging minorities or infringing basic rights be subjected to 'strict scrutiny', which means that legislation must be shown to serve an important purpose that cannot reasonably be achieved by any other means. 'Strict scrutiny' fits easily within the model of self-incapacitating rules designed to require that the legislature has given due consideration to the possibility that its actions may be inconsistent with the ideals of equality and individual rights to which the society is committed. In that sense, as Hamilton observed, the Constitution—as representative of the people's will—is superior to the legislature.

Like Ulysses, who ordered himself tied to the mast, judicial review represents an attempt to insure that the political system is constrained from passing laws that express prejudice or violate rights. Viewed that way, the exercise of judicial review in the name of protecting basic rights and resisting legislative prejudice seems less anti-democratic. Though such limits cannot be defended as a means to enhance the democratic procedural values of openness and fairness, they are nonetheless compatible with the settled, deepest commitments of citizens to protect rights and reject prejudice as well as secure democratic fairness and openness.

It may seem on further reflection, however, that this picture is in fact quite confused. It depends on imagining that 'the people' who adopted the Constitution provide sufficient authority for the Supreme Court to uphold the right to get an abortion and to find that school prayer is unconstitutional. The US Supreme Court has taken just these positions in recent years, in each case against the strong opposition of elected officials and large numbers of citizens. Where, then, is the mythical political 'self', independent of the legislature, that made these unpopular self-incapacitating decisions?[12] Indeed, citizens are often unaware of the Court's decisions; or, if they are aware of them, they may strongly disagree with the Court's interpretation. It is therefore far from clear how judicial review can be understood in terms of 'self-incapacitating' rules.

CONSTITUTIONAL INTERPRETATION AND ORIGINAL INTENT

One familiar defence of the self-incapacitating model shifts the discussion away from the purposes of judicial review to the debate over constitutional interpretation. It is sometimes argued, in the spirit of self-incapacitation, that the only proper method of constitutional interpretation is for judges to set aside their own values and political principles and defer instead to the specific intentions of the document's framers.[13] Following this line, dissenters in *Roc v. Wade* argued that because the original framers did not think abortion rights were protected under the Constitution the case was wrongly decided.[14] Similarly, defenders of original intent point out, the framers had a fairly narrow understanding of the meaning of 'cruel and unusual punishment', believing it compatible with a variety of practices, including executions, and for that reason, they claim, capital punishment is not unconstitutional. By following the intentions of the framers, it is claimed, judges protect the legitimacy of their authority by enforcing only those self-incapacitating rules that 'the people' themselves originally intended. Judges are not free to inject their own understanding of what would have been reasonable self-incapacitating rules

for the people in place of the historical framers of the Constitution, any more than the legislature is free to ignore the limits on *it* that are imposed by the Constitution.

There are many problems with original intent, however, including the problem of identifying who the 'framers' actually were and the fact that many of the framers disagreed among themselves about how best to interpret the document.[15] Even setting those problems aside, it is not clear that original intent can undergird the self-incapacitation approach: why should the current generation be bound by the intentions of long-dead framers? *Their* choice of self-incapacitating rules is a dictatorship by framers that seems no more democratic than one by contemporary Supreme Court justices.[16] Given that, however, the anti-democratic nature of judicial review emerges once again. If original intent cannot save the self-incapacitating model, then how can it be defended against the point that the Supreme Court often overturns laws with wide popular support and strong legislative backing?

Recall first that the framers deliberately chose to include in the Constitution broad concepts like 'due process of law', 'cruel and unusual punishment' and 'free exercise of religion' even though they could have chosen not to do so. Why, we need to ask, might they have done that? One answer is suggested by the historical situation of the framers: as Enlightenment figures, we would expect them to believe in the power of reason to reach sound moral and political judgments, if only it can be brought to bear on problems.[17] Given that commitment, it would make sense for the framers to think that, however much they might believe they had the best account of these general concepts, they might nonetheless be mistaken. Instead of tying later generations to their specific understanding, they would have reasoned, it would be much better to leave them free to pursue the ideals of freedom, equality and due process as they see fit, in light of their own experience and understanding. To do otherwise would run the danger of sacrificing moral progress to the limited, historically-situated understanding of the framers, which is incompatible with the ideals of moral progress and faith in the capacity of reason and experience to enlighten moral reflection.

Having said that, however, the notion of the Supreme Court's enforcing self-incapacitating rules seems all the more troublesome. Granted that the Court's actions are often controversial, and contrary to both the original intent of the framing generation as well as to the wishes of the current majority, are we not led back to the thought that judicial review is antithetical to democratic values? In one sense, judicial review and the Bill of Rights *do* constitute a compromise with democratic values. If it is assumed that all decisions should be made by elected officials chosen in a free and open political process and unconstrained by anything but the fear of electoral defeat, then the US practice of judicial review should be rejected except insofar as it promotes those or other democratic values. [A contrary approach] relies on the idea that people might reasonably reject this absolutist vision of democratic power. Suppose that, like a person employing self-incapacitating rules, the polity in some sense or at some level in fact *wishes* to compromise democratic values, at least to a degree. This desire might, for example, be based on the feeling that majority rule does not provide adequate protection of individual rights and the hope that by limiting democratic processes the right balance between democracy and other values can be achieved. Why would such an electorate not then simply enact a written Bill of Rights and leave it to elected officials rather than judges to decide how best to interpret it, subject only to defeat at the next election? The answer to that important question depends on whether judges are better situated than elected officials to make such judgments, a subject to which I now turn.

THE ROLE OF THE JUDICIARY AND THE SPECIAL COMPETENCY OF JUDGES

Two types of argument are available to defenders of constitutional review by judges.[18] The first is a legal argument, and depends on appreciating the nature of the dispute in question. The legislature, we suppose, has passed a law that it believes is compatible with the limits imposed on it under the Constitution; it is not, in the opinion of the majority of the legislators, incompatible with basic constitutional rights. A citizen, however, disagrees and challenges the legislators on constitutional grounds. Perhaps, to take an actual example, the citizen has burned a flag in an act of political protest and has now been charged with violating a state law criminalising 'flag desecration'.[19] Arguing that the First Amendment protects citizens' right to freedom of speech, the citizen disagrees with the legislature's opinion that the Constitution permits such legislation. But now the question arises which branch of government, the legislative or the judicial, should resolve this dispute. The natural answer, Chief Justice John Marshall argued in *Marbury v. Madison*,[20] must be the judiciary; for to allow Congress to decide in this situation constitutes a breach of the ideal of the rule of law. Members of the legislature are a party to the dispute; they, like the citizen, occupy one of the two positions that is at issue in the case. To allow either party to decide the case thus seems contrary to basic principles of the rule of law.

Not only are judges better situated *legally* to make the decision, they are also *politically* better suited for it, for two reasons. First, federal judges are given life tenure, which insulates them from electoral politics and the need for reelection.[21] As a result, they are better positioned to decide cases on whatever they take to be the merits, independent of political pressure.[22]

Another important political consideration is of greater philosophical interest, as well as more controversial. Though it is important not to overstate the point, it does seem that there is an important difference in the roles of judges and elected lawmakers, which grows out of their diverging political and institutional responsibilities and different roles in the political system. Judicial interpretation and argument demand consideration of justice and morality in ways that legislative activities do not—or at least not to the same extent. Much of what goes on in the

US Congress involves hammering out political compromises between competing interests, while debate among judges on the bench involves different sorts of disputes. Edward H. Levi (1964, p. 266) puts the point nicely.

> [M]oral judgement is frequently involved in the conclusions reached by the judge. Moreover . . . the integrity of the process in which the judge is engaged depends not only on distinctions that he may make reasonably, but also on his own belief in the legitimacy and decisiveness of these distinctions. Thus there is an astonishing combination of compulsions on the Anglo-American judge: the duty of representing many voices, of justifying the new application in terms of a prior rule and the equality of other cases, the assumption that reason is a sufficient and necessary guide, the responsibility of moral judgement, and the importance of sincerity—all these tend to give uniqueness to the institution of judicial reasoning in our system and in our society.

Levi makes two important, related points here. First, he points out, legal analysis and interpretation stress the importance of precedent and therefore of consistency, which in turn reflects the ideal of treating similar cases similarly. Distinctions among citizens that a judge makes must, in his terms, be 'reasonable'. Furthermore, says Levi, judicial decisions and the reasoning on which they are based must reflect the judge's 'moral judgement'. This means, as I understand him, that judges aspire to rule in ways that protect the moral and political 'legitimacy' of government. Levi is therefore suggesting that both of these ideals—first, precedent and consistency (expressed as the requirement of justice that similar cases be treated similarly) and second, substantive moral soundness—are central to legal interpretation.[23]

Legislators, of course, should not completely ignore those ideals, but in a democratic system lawmakers are pulled in another direction as well: they must represent the needs and interests of their constituents. Often, therefore, we would expect legislators to feel a conflict between the needs of those who elected them (in the awareness that other legislators are working to protect *their* constituents) on the one hand, and the need to vote for what they take to be consistent with minority rights or the common good on the other. That dilemma is not a minor feature of governments; rather, it is built into any representative democracy. Elected officials must both represent their constituents *and* serve the greater good. Legislators therefore face a pair of dilemmas. Sometimes they confront the choice between doing what will get them elected and acting in accord with moral principle, but they also must sometimes choose between two principles governing their role: doing what is in their constituents' interests and doing what would serve the greater good.[24]

In the case of judges, however, the situation is different. Here we do not expect, or even tolerate, such compromises in principle. Were a judge to admit to voting in a case not on principle and in accord with what the law requires but instead because it was in the interests of an economic, racial or other 'constituency', we would think the judge did not live up to the expectations of the office.[25] Names for such behaviour, such as 'result oriented' and 'biased', carry a stigma for judges that would not be present when applied to a legislator who succeeds in winning a defence contract for her district or increased farm supports for her constituents.

CONCLUSION

I have argued in this paper that the familiar charge made against judicial review—that it is incompatible with democratic values—can be answered in a variety of ways. Once we are clear on the nature of democratic values we can see that judicial review can, and often does, promote both the openness and the fairness of democratic processes. I next argued that even in cases where the court is not promoting procedural democratic values, judicial review may nonetheless still be compatible with democratic principles. That is because, in protecting individual rights against majority tyranny, judicial review can reasonably be seen to reflect a deeper, more abstract commitment of the people to incapacitate themselves and their democratic representatives. That does not require judges to enforce the specific meaning the framers attached to the Bill of Rights and other guarantees of the Constitution. Nor should judges decide based on what they believe the majority would themselves understand to be the meaning of Constitutional protections designed to give substance to individual rights. Rather, the idea is that judicial review constitutes a sort of 'second-order' commitment of the people to a system that they hope, over time, will lead to decisions that respect individual rights and minimise the corrosive effects of racial, religious and sexual prejudice. There is no *guarantee*, of course, that judges' particular interpretations of basic constitutional ideals like free speech, free exercise of religion and equal protection of the laws will be correct, or even that they will be better than what the people's representatives would have chosen. I have argued, however, that there are important legal and political reasons for thinking that their judgment should be trusted over that of elected legislators. It is therefore possible that, despite disagreements over particular judicial decisions, reasonable citizens might nonetheless remain committed to judicial review and to protecting individual rights against the wishes of elected officials— and, indeed, even against their own wishes.

NOTES

[1]In the federal system of government used in the US, parallel issues arise at both the national and state levels. Each state of the US has a state constitution that limits and defines the governmental power of the state. As I discuss here, the federal constitution prohibits the *federal* government from taking specific actions that violate the rights of citizens or powers of state governments. After the US Civil War, the federal constitution was amended to allow the national government to prevent state governments from violating certain rights of their own citizens—much as citizens of countries in the European Union may now go to the Commission of European Communities to challenge statutes enacted by their own governments as being contrary to rights guaranteed by the Treaty on European Union. This paper considers the federal power of judicial review under the US Constitution only, although substantially similar issues arise when citizens ask state courts to rule whether acts of state legislatures pass muster under state constitutions.

[2]For a more extended discussion of these issues, see Arthur (1995, Ch. 2).

[3]In *Kramer v. Union Free School District*, 395 US 621 (1969) the US Supreme Court held unconstitutional a New York law requiring voters in school districts either to own property or to have children in school.

[4]For instance, as I discuss shortly, the US Supreme Court has ruled that electoral districts must be reapportioned to give each vote equal weight. But what about the US Senate, in which each state, no matter what its population, has two senators?

[5]This view, that judicial review can serve to 'perfect' the democratic process, is discussed by Ely (1980).

[6]*Lassiter v. Northhampton County Board of Election*, 360 US 621 (1969).

[7]*Dunn v. Blumstein*, 405 US 330 (1972).

[8]*Carrington v. Rash*, 380 US 89 (1965).

[9]*Wesberry v. Sanders*, 376 US 1 (1964) at 17.

[10]*Brandenburg v. Ohio*, 395 US 444 (1969).

[11]*New York Times v. Sullivan*, 376 US 254 (1964).

[12]Martin Hollis stressed this point in the question period following delivery of this paper at the UEA Conference. I am thankful to him for impressing on me the importance of this question.

[13]Robert Bork defends this view, as does Chief Justice William Rehnquist. See, for example, Bork (1971) and Rehnquist (1976).

[14]*Roe v. Wade*, 410 US 113 (1973).

[15]Among the many discussions of the problems with original intent, see Brest (1980), Dworkin (1985, Ch. 2), Bassham (1992) and Arthur (1995, Ch. 2).

[16]One possibility, which I have discussed elsewhere, is that the current generation has 'tacitly' consented to the framers' original understanding of the Constitution's self-incapacitating rules. See Arthur (1995, pp. 26–32).

[17]See in this regard Madison's (1787) famous account of the political theory behind the Constitution, 'Federalist Number 10', in which he argues that government's most important challenge is to control 'factions', by which he means groups of people committed to using political power contrary to the common good and in violation of individual rights.

[18]One further objection to judicial review that I have encountered in Britain, though it is rare in the US, is that judges tend to reflect particular, generally conservative, political views, and for that reason should not be given the power of judicial review. Assuming it is true that judges in the UK are overwhelmingly conservative, then the question is, what follows? Two responses are possible: that judicial review should be rejected, or that judges (and lawyers) should be more broadly representative. I can easily imagine someone's arguing that until judges are drawn more broadly from different political camps, US style judicial review should be rejected. If the facts are as described, that may be the correct reply.

[19]In *Texas v. Johnson*, 109 S. Ct. 2533 (1989), the Supreme Court held that burning a US flag is a constitutionally-protected expression of free speech under the First Amendment.

[20]*Marbury v. Madison*, 5 US 137 (1803).

[21]In contrast, in many states, state judges are popularly elected. Devices are often used to reduce political pressure, for instance term limits may be long. In other states judges are initially appointed and then the question put to the voters is simply whether the particular judge should be returned to office.

[22]That is not to say, however, that they are free from other pressures. Federal judges in the US South who enforced desegregation rulings by the Supreme Court came in for heavy social and personal criticism that sometimes included ostracism and threats of violence. That many of them could not have won election as judges, had it been necessary, goes without saying.

[23]For an more detailed discussion of the nature of law and legal interpretation that extends these points, see Dworkin (1977 and 1986).

[24]I do not mean to suggest that the former, as well as the latter, is not itself sometimes a moral dilemma. An unpopular vote may also be the wrong one in the long run since it can mean that in the future a far less responsible legislator has the seat.

[25]That is not to say, of course, that judges will not be affected in their thinking by their experiences as members of a particular class, race, gender, or religious group. Awareness of that is an important part of the argument for having more minorities and women on the bench. But appreciation of the role of perspective and moral outlook in judicial decision making is not to be confused with the further, mistaken, thought that judges are on the bench to represent the interests of their class, religion, race or gender.

REVIEW AND DISCUSSION QUESTIONS

1. What does Arthur mean in claiming that openness and fairness are the two values at the core of democratic government?

2. Explain how judicial review can serve rather than thwart democratic values.

3. Describe the idea of democratic self-incapacitation, indicating why it has seemed to many to make judicial review compatible with democracy.

4. How does Arthur think the Constitution should be interpreted, given his understanding of the limits of self-incapacitation?

5. How does Arthur respond to those who think that because there is no agreement about the meaning of controversial rights, self-incapacitation cannot be the ground of judicial review?

6. Is judicial review entirely compatible with democracy? Explain.

Precedent, Legitimacy, and Judicial Review

Planned Parenthood v. Casey

Many people expected that after the appointment of Supreme Court Justices O'Connor, Kennedy, and Souter—all of whom were thought to oppose the Roe v. Wade *decision protecting a woman's right to an abortion—the Court's position would soon change and* Roe *would be overturned. To the surprise of many, however, the three did not reject* Roe *when the opportunity arose but instead wrote a joint opinion explaining that while they may disagree with the decision on the merits, it would nonetheless be a mistake to overturn it twenty years later. Justice Scalia wrote a vigorous dissent.*

112 S.Ct. 2791 (1992).

Justices O'Connor, Kennedy and Souter:

While we appreciate the weight of the arguments made on behalf of the State in the case before us, arguments which in their ultimate formulation conclude that Roe should be overruled, the reservations any of us may have in reaffirming the central holding of Roe are outweighed by the explication of individual liberty we have given combined with the force of stare decisis. We turn now to that doctrine.

. . . With Cardozo, we recognize that no judicial system could do society's work if it eyed each issue afresh in every case that raised it. *The Nature of the Judicial Process* 149 (1921). Indeed, the very concept of the rule of law [requires] such continuity over time that a respect for precedent is, by definition, indispensable. At the other extreme, a different necessity would make itself felt if a prior judicial ruling should come to be seen so clearly as error that its enforcement was for that very reason doomed.

Even when the decision to overrule a prior case is not [virtually] foreordained, [the] rule of stare decisis is not an "inexorable command," and certainly it is not such in every constitutional case. . . . Rather, when this Court reexamines a prior holding, its judgment is customarily informed by a series of prudential and pragmatic considerations designed to test the consistency of overruling a prior decision with the ideal of the rule of law, and to gauge the respective costs of reaffirming and overruling a prior case. . . .

So in this case we may inquire whether Roe's central rule has been found unworkable; whether the rule's limitation on state power could be removed without serious inequity to those who have relied upon it or significant damage to the stability of the society governed by the rule in question; whether the law's growth in the intervening years has left Roe's central rule a doctrinal anachronism discounted by society; and whether Roe's premises of fact have so far changed in the ensuing two decades as to render its central holding somehow irrelevant or unjustifiable in dealing with the issue it addressed.

1. Although Roe has engendered opposition, it has in no sense proven "unworkable," representing as it does a simple limitation beyond which a state law is unenforceable. While Roe has [required] judicial assessment of [laws] affecting the exercise of the choice guaranteed against government infringement, and although the need for such review will remain as a consequence of today's decision, [these] determinations fall within judicial competence.

2. The inquiry into reliance counts the cost of a rule's repudiation as it would fall on those who have relied reasonably on the rule's continued application. . . . For two decades of economic and social developments, people have organized intimate relationships and made choices that define their views of themselves and their places in society, in reliance on the availability of abortion in the event that contraception should fail. The ability of women to participate equally in the economic and social life of the Nation has been facilitated by their ability to control their reproductive lives. [While] the effect of reliance on Roe cannot be exactly measured, neither can the certain cost of overruling Roe for people who have ordered their thinking and living around that case be dismissed.

3. No evolution of legal principle has left Roe's doctrinal footings weaker than they were in 1973. . . . Roe, however, may be seen not only as an exemplar of Griswold liberty but as a rule (whether or not mistaken) of personal autonomy and bodily integrity, with doctrinal affinity to cases recognizing limits on governmental power to mandate medical treatment or to bar its rejection. If so, our cases since Roe accord with Roe's view that a State's interest in the protection of life falls short of justifying any plenary override of individual liberty claims.

. . . Even on the assumption that the central holding of Roe was in error, that error would go only to the strength of the state interest in fetal protection, not to the recognition afforded woman's liberty. . . . If indeed the woman's interest in deciding whether to bear and beget a child had not been recognized as in Roe, the State might as readily restrict a woman's right to choose to carry a pregnancy to term as to terminate it, to further asserted state interests in population control, or eugenics, for example. Yet Roe has been sensibly relied upon to counter any such suggestions.

4. [Time] has overtaken some of Roe's factual assumptions: advances in maternal health care allow for abortions safe to the mother later in pregnancy than was true in 1973, and advances in neonatal care have advanced viability to a point somewhat earlier. But these facts . . . have no bearing on the central holding that viability marks the earliest point at which the State's interest in fetal life is constitutionally adequate to justify a legislative ban on nontherapeutic abortions. The soundness or unsoundness of that constitutional judgment in no sense turns on whether viability occurs at approximately 28 weeks, as was usual at the time of Roe; at 25 to 24 weeks, as it sometimes does today. . . . Whenever it may occur, the attainment of viability may continue to serve as the critical fact, just as it has done since Roe; [no] change in Roe's factual underpinning has left its central holding obsolete, and none supports an argument for overruling it.

5. The sum of the precedential inquiry to this point shows Roe's underpinnings unweakened in any way affecting its central holding. While it has engendered disapproval, it has not been unworkable. An entire generation has come of age free to assume Roe's concept of liberty in defining the capacity of women to act in society, and to make reproductive decisions; no erosion of principle going to liberty or personal autonomy has left Roe's central holding a doctrinal remnant; Roe portends no developments at odds with other precedent for the analysis of personal liberty; and no changes of fact have rendered viability more or less appropriate as the point at which the balance of interests tips. Within the bounds of normal stare decisis analysis, [the] stronger argument is for affirming Roe's central holding, with whatever degree of personal reluctance any of us may have, not for overruling it. . . .

. . . [As] Americans of each succeeding generation are rightly told, the Court cannot buy support for its decisions by spending money and, except to a minor degree, it cannot independently coerce obedience to its decrees. The Court's power lies, rather, in its legitimacy, a product of substance and perception that shows itself in the people's acceptance of the Judiciary as fit to determine what the Nation's law means and to declare what it demands. . . . Because not every conscientious claim of principled justification will be accepted as such, the justification claimed must be beyond dispute. The Court must take care to speak and act in ways that allow people to accept its decisions on the terms the Court claims for them, as grounded truly in principle, not as compromises with social and political pressures having, as such, no bearing on the principled choices that the Court is obliged to make. Thus, the Court's legitimacy depends on making legally principled decisions under circumstances in which their principled character is sufficiently plausible to be accepted by the Nation.

. . . In two circumstances, however, the Court would almost certainly fail to receive the benefit of the doubt in overruling prior cases. There is, first, a point beyond which frequent overruling would overtax the country's belief in the Court's good faith. . . . There is a limit to the amount of error that can plausibly be imputed to prior courts. If that limit should be exceeded, disturbance of prior rulings would be taken as evidence that justifiable reexamination of principle had given way to drives for particular results in the short term. The legitimacy of the Court would fade with the frequency of its vacillation.

That first circumstance can be described as hypothetical; the second is to the point here and now. Where, in the performance of its judicial duties, the Court decides a case in such a way as to resolve the sort of intensely divisive controversy reflected in Roe and those rare, comparable cases, its decision has a dimension that the resolution of the normal case does not carry. . . . So to overrule under fire in the absence of the most compelling reason to reexamine a watershed decision would subvert the Court's legitimacy beyond any serious question. . . . An extra price will be paid by those who themselves disapprove of the decision's results when viewed outside of constitutional terms, but who nevertheless struggle to accept it, because they respect the rule of law. To all those who will be so tested by following, the Court implicitly undertakes to remain steadfast, lest in the end a price be paid for nothing. The promise of constancy, once given, binds its maker for as long as the power to stand by the decision survives and the understanding of the issue has not changed so fundamentally as to render the commitment obsolete.

[Like] the character of an individual, the legitimacy of the Court must be earned over time. So, indeed, must be the character of a Nation of people who aspire to live according to the rule of law. Their belief in themselves as such a people is not readily separable from their understanding of the Court invested with the authority to decide their constitutional cases and speak before all others for their constitutional ideals. If the Court's legitimacy should be undermined, then, so would the country be in its very ability to see itself through its constitutional ideals. The Court's concern with legitimacy is not for the sake of the Court but for the sake of the Nation.

. . . Whether or not a new social consensus is developing on that issue, its divisiveness is no less today than in 1973, and pressure to overrule the decision, like pressure to retain it, has grown only more intense. A decision to overrule Roe's essential holding under the existing circumstances would address error, if error there was, at the cost of [profound] and unnecessary damage to the Court's legitimacy, and to the Nation's commitment to the rule of law. It is therefore imperative to adhere to the essence of Roe's original decision, and we do so today. . . .

Justice Scalia [dissenting]:

. . . I would uphold the Pennsylvania statute in its entirety. . . . Assuming that the question before us is to be resolved at such a level of philosophical abstraction, in such isolation from the traditions of American society, as by simply applying "reasoned judgment," I do not see how that could possibly have produced the answer the Court arrived at in Roe. Today's opinion describes the methodology of Roe, quite accurately, as weighing against the woman's interest the State's "important and legitimate interest in protecting the potentiality of human life." But

"reasoned judgment" does not begin by begging the question, as Roe unquestionably did by assuming that what the State is protecting is the mere "potentiality of human life." The whole argument of abortion opponents is that what the Court calls the fetus and what others call the unborn child is a human life. Thus, whatever answer Roe came up with after conducting its "balancing" is bound to be wrong, unless it is correct that the human fetus is in some critical sense merely potentially human. There is of course no way to determine that as a legal matter; it is in fact a value judgment. Some societies have considered newborn children not yet human, or the incompetent elderly no longer so.

The authors of the joint opinion [do] not squarely contend that Roe was a correct application of "reasoned judgment"; merely that it must be followed, because of stare decisis. But in their exhaustive discussion of all the factors that go into the determination of when stare decisis should be observed and when disregarded, they never mention "how wrong was the decision on its face?" Surely, if "the Court's power lies . . . in its legitimacy, a product of substance and perception," the "substance" part of the equation demands that plain error be acknowledged and eliminated. Roe was plainly wrong—even on the Court's methodology of "reasoned judgment," and even more so (of course) if the proper criteria of text and tradition are applied. The emptiness of the "reasoned judgment" that produced Roe is displayed in plain view by the fact that, after more than 19 years of effort by some of the brightest (and most determined) legal minds in the country, after more than 10 cases upholding abortion rights in this Court, and after dozens upon dozens of amicus briefs submitted in this and other cases, the best the Court can do to explain how it is that the word "liberty" must be thought to include the right to destroy human fetuses is to rattle off a collection of adjectives that simply decorate a value judgment and conceal a political choice. The right to abort, we are told, inheres in "liberty" because it is among "a person's most basic decisions"; it involves a "most intimate and personal choic[e]"; it is "central to personal dignity and autonomy"; it "originate[s] within the zone of conscience and belief"; it is "too intimate and personal" for state interference; it reflects "intimate views" of a "deep, personal character"; it involves "intimate relationships," and notions of "personal autonomy and bodily integrity"; and it concerns a particularly "important decision." But it is obvious to anyone applying "reasoned judgment" that the same adjectives can be applied to many forms of conduct that this Court has held are not entitled to constitutional protection—because, like abortion, they are forms of conduct that have long been criminalized in American society. Those adjectives might be applied, for example, to homosexual sodomy, polygamy, adult incest, and suicide, all of which are equally "intimate" and "deeply personal" decisions involving "personal autonomy and bodily integrity," and all of which can constitutionally be proscribed because it is our unquestionable constitutional tradition that they are proscribable. It is not reasoned judgment that supports the Court's decision; only personal predilection. . . . It is particularly difficult, in the circumstances of the present decision, to sit still for the Court's lengthy lecture upon the virtues of "constancy," of "remaining steadfast," of adhering to "principle." Among the five Justices who purportedly adhere to Roe, at most three agree upon the principle that constitutes adherence (the joint opinion's "undue burden" standard)—and that principle is inconsistent with Roe. To make matters worse, two of the three, in order thus to remain steadfast, had to abandon previously stated positions. It is beyond me how the Court expects these accommodations to be accepted "as grounded truly in principle, not as compromises with social and political pressures having, as such, no bearing on the principled choices that the Court is obliged to make." The only principle the Court "adheres" to, it seems to me, is the principle that the Court must be seen as standing by Roe. That is not a principle of law (which is what I thought the Court was talking about), but a principle of Realpolitik—and a wrong one at that.

I cannot agree with, indeed I am appalled by, the Court's suggestion that the decision whether to stand by an erroneous constitutional decision must be strongly influenced—against overruling, no less—by the substantial and continuing public opposition the decision has generated. The Court's judgment that any other course would "subvert the Court's legitimacy" must be another consequence of reading the error-filled history book that described the deeply divided country brought together by Roe. . . .

But whether it would "subvert the Court's legitimacy" or not, the notion that we would decide a case differently from the way we otherwise would have in order to show that we can stand firm against public disapproval is frightening. It is a bad enough idea, even in the head of someone like me, who believes that the text of the Constitution, and our traditions, say what they say and there is no fiddling with them. But when it is in the mind of a Court that believes the Constitution has an evolving meaning . . . and that the function of this Court is to "speak before all others for [the people's] constitutional ideals" unrestrained by meaningful text or tradition—then the notion that the court must adhere to a decision for as long as the decision faces "great opposition" and the Court is "under fire" acquires a character of almost czarist arrogance. . . .

In truth, I am as distressed as the Court is—and expressed my distress several years ago . . . —about the "political pressure" directed to the Court: the marches, the mail, the protests aimed at inducing us to change our opinions. How upsetting it is, that so many of our citizens (good people, not lawless ones, on both sides of this abortion issue, and on various sides of other issues as well) think that we Justices should properly take into account their views, as though we were engaged not in ascertaining an objective law but in determining some kind of social consensus. The Court would profit, I think, from giving less attention to the fact of this distressing phenomenon, and more attention to the cause of it. That cause permeates today's opinion: a new mode of constitutional adjudication that relies not upon text and traditional practice to determine the law, but upon what the Court calls "reasoned judgment," which turns out to be nothing but philosophical predilection and moral intuition. All manner of "liberties," the Court tells us, inhere in the Constitution and are enforceable by this Court—not just those mentioned in the text or established in the traditions of our society. . . .

What makes all this relevant to the bothersome application of "political pressure" against the Court are the twin facts that the American people love democracy and the American people are not fools. As long as this Court thought (and the people thought) that we Justices were doing essentially lawyers' work up here—reading text and discerning our society's traditional understanding of that text—the public pretty much left us alone. Texts and traditions are facts to study, not convictions to demonstrate about. But if in reality our process of constitutional adjudication consists primarily of making value judgments; if we can ignore a long and clear tradition clarifying an ambiguous text, [if our] pronouncement of constitutional law rests primarily on value judgments, then a free and intelligent people's attitude towards us can be expected to be (ought to be) quite different. The people know that their value judgments are quite as good as those taught in any law school—maybe better. If [the] "liberties" protected by the Constitution are [undefined] and unbounded, then the people should demonstrate, to protest that we do not implement their values instead of ours. Not only that, but confirmation hearings for new Justices should deteriorate into question-and-answer sessions in which Senators go through a list of their constituents' most favored and most disfavored alleged constitutional rights, and seek the nominee's commitment to support or oppose them. Value judgments, after all, should be voted on, not dictated; and if our Constitution has somehow accidentally committed them to the Supreme Court, at least we can have a sort of plebiscite each time a new nominee to that body is put forward.

REVIEW AND DISCUSSION QUESTIONS

1. Explain the reasons why the three justices decided not to overturn *Roe v. Wade.*

2. Justice Scalia argues that a mistake of the past should be corrected, and that the arguments of the three justices will have the opposite effect, perpetuating a mistaken law. Explain his reasoning.

3. Situating your discussion in the context of material you have read on precedent, legal reasoning and the rule of law, discuss whether or not you think this case was correctly decided. Suppose you believed strongly that *Roe* was a mistake at the time; would that affect your conclusion? Explain.

17

FREEDOM OF RELIGION, FREE SPEECH, AND PRIVACY

Protecting basic rights was important to the framers of the Constitution, as the *Federalist Papers* clearly reveal. But what are the justifications and the limits of individual rights? One view, familiar to the Framers, is that of the social contract, expressed here by John Locke in his *Letter Concerning Religious Toleration*. In it, Locke argues that there is a sharp boundary between matters of legitimate concern to the governmental "magistrate" and matters of conscience. We then include three cases involving religious freedoms, including the constitutionality of school prayer, the right of the Amish to keep their children out of public schools, and the right of the citizens that schools not teach evolution and "secular humanism."

A different defense of liberty is found in John Stuart Mill's classic essay *On Liberty*. Beginning with his important defense of freedom of conscience and speech, Mill goes on to argue that society may not justifiably compel an individual to do (or not do) something solely because the action would be in the individual's own interest, or because doing so would be morally better. Instead, Mill argues, society may interfere with an individual's actions only to prevent that person from harming others.

Turning to specific cases, the section first looks at freedom of speech, which is among our most cherished political and constitutional values, but it has also posed important challenges to the courts, embroiling them in political controversy. Legal battles over advocacy of illegal or violent acts, membership in dangerous political parties, hate speech, advocacy of Nazism, campus speech codes, and obscenity are all presented in legal opinions of the Supreme Court. Closely related to Mill's liberty principle is the right to privacy, and debates over the exact nature and extent of a constitutional right to privacy have loomed large in recent Supreme Court cases. Finally, nothing has been more controversial than cases involving private, consensual sexual conduct, the subject of the last essay in this section.

A Letter Concerning Toleration

John Locke

Few, if any, philosophers had as much influence on the thinking of the American framers as John Locke. Although today we focus more on his Second Treatise on Government, A Letter Concerning Toleration *was much more influential at the time. In his* Letter, *Locke begins with a brief indication of his general theory of the powers of government. Legitimate government, he thinks, derives its powers from the consent of the governed, but such consent can best be understood by first imagining people in a pre-political "state of nature." There, Locke thinks, people would give up their natural right to life and property in order to gain greater protection of those rights by the state. The powers of the state, however, are limited by the original reasons that would motivate people to join and accept its authority. With this as background, Locke considers freedom of religion and conscience, an issue of central importance to the American framers as well. No government, he argues, should exercise force to promote or prohibit religious beliefs and practices.*

Honored sir, . . . I esteem it above all things necessary to distinguish exactly the business of civil government from that of religion, and to settle the just bound that lie between the one and the other. If this be not done, there can be no end put to the controversies that will be always arising between those that have, or at least pretend to have, on the one side, a concernment for the interest of men's souls, and, on the other side, a care of the commonwealth.

The commonwealth seems to me to be a society of men constituted only for the procuring, preserving, and advancing their own civil interests.

Civil interests I call life, liberty, health, and indolency of body; and the possession of outward things, such as money, lands, houses, furniture, and the like.

It is the duty of the civil magistrate, by the impartial execution of equal laws, to secure unto all the people in general, and to every one of his subjects in particular, the just possession of these things belonging to this life. If any one presume to violate the laws of public justice and equity, established for the preservation of those things, his presumption is to be checked by the fear of punishment, consisting of the deprivation or diminution of those civil interests, or goods, which otherwise he might and ought to enjoy. But seeing no man does willingly suffer himself to be punished by the deprivation of any part of his goods, and much less of his liberty or life, therefore is the magistrate armed with the force and strength of all his subjects, in order to the punishment of those that violate any other man's rights.

Now that the whole jurisdiction of the magistrate reaches only to these civil concernments, and that all civil power, right, and dominion, is bounded and confined to the only care of promoting these things; and that it neither can nor ought in any manner to be extended to the salvation of souls, these following considerations seem unto me abundantly to demonstrate.

First, because the care of souls is not committed to the civil magistrate, any more than to other men. It is not committed unto him, I say, by God: because it appears not that God has ever given any such authority to one man over another, as to compel any one to his religion. Nor can any such power be vested in the magistrate by the consent of the people, because no man can so far abandon the care of his own salvation as blindly to leave to the choice of any other, whether prince or subject, to prescribe to him what faith or worship he shall embrace. For no man can, if he would, conform his faith to the dictates of another. All the life and power of true religion consist in the inward and full persuasion of the mind; and faith is not faith without believing. Whatever profession we make, to whatever outward worship we conform, if we are not fully satisfied in our own mind that the one is true, and the other well pleasing unto God, such profession and such practice, far from being any furtherance, are indeed great obstacles to our salvation. For in this manner, instead of expiating other sins by the exercise of religion, I say, in offering thus unto God Almighty such a worship as we esteem to be displeasing unto him, we add unto the number of our other sins those also of hypocrisy, and contempt of his Divine Majesty.

In the second place, the care of souls cannot belong to the civil magistrate, because his power consists only in outward force; but true and saving religion consists in the inward persuasion of the mind, without which nothing can be acceptable to God. And such is the nature of the understanding, that it cannot be compelled to the belief of anything by outward force. Confiscation of estate, imprisonment, torments, nothing of that nature can have any such efficacy as to make men change the inward judgment that they have framed of things.

It may indeed be alleged that the magistrate may make use of arguments, and thereby draw the heterodox into the way of truth, and procure their salvation. I grant it; but this is common to him with other men. In teaching, instructing, and redressing the erroneous by reason, he may certainly do what becomes any good man to do. Magistracy does not oblige him to put off either humanity or Christianity; but it is one thing to persuade, another to command; one thing to press with arguments, another with penalties. This civil power alone has a right to do; to the other good-will is authority enough. Every man has commission to admonish, exhort, convince another of error, and, by reasoning, to draw him into truth; but to give laws, receive obedience, and compel with the sword, belongs to none but the magistrate. And upon this ground, I affirm that the magistrate's power extends not to the establishing of any articles of faith, or forms of worship, by the force of his laws. For laws are of no force at all without penalties, and penalties in this case are absolutely impertinent, because they are not proper to convince the mind. Neither the profession of any articles of faith, nor the conformity to any outward form of worship (as has been already said), can be available to the salvation of souls, unless the truth of the one, and the acceptableness of the other unto God, be thoroughly believed by those that so profess and practise. But penalties are no way capable to produce such belief. It is only light and evidence that can work a change in men's opinions; which light can in no manner proceed from corporal sufferings, or any other outward penalties.

In the third place, the care of the salvation of men's souls cannot belong to the magistrate; because, though the rigour of laws and the force of penalties were capable to convince and change men's minds, yet would not that help at all to the salvation of their souls. For there being but one truth, one way to heaven, what hope is there that more men would be led into it if they had no rule but the religion of the court, and were put under the necessity to quit the light of their own reason, and oppose the dictates of their own consciences, and blindly to resign themselves up to the will of their governors, and to the religion which either ignorance, ambition, or superstition had chanced to establish in the countries where they were born? In the variety and contradiction of opinions in religion, wherein the princes of the world are as much divided as in their secular interests, the narrow way would be much straitened; one country alone would be in the right, and all the rest of the world put under an obligation of following their princes in the ways that lead to destruction; and that which heightens the absurdity, and very ill suits the notion of a Deity, men would owe their eternal happiness or misery to the places of their nativity.

These considerations, to omit many others that might have been urged to the same purpose, seem unto me sufficient to conclude that all the power of civil government relates only to men's civil interests, is confined to the care of the things of this world, and hath nothing to do with the world to come.

Let us now consider what a church is. A church, then, I take to be a voluntary society of men, joining themselves together of their own accord in order to the public worshipping of God in such manner as they judge acceptable to him, and effectual to the salvation of their souls.

I say it is a free and voluntary society. Nobody is born a member of any church; otherwise the religion of parents would descend unto children by the same right of inheritance as their temporal estates, and every one would hold his faith by the same tenure he does his lands, than which nothing can be imagined more absurd. Thus, therefore, that matter stands. No man by nature is bound unto any particular church or sect, but every one joins himself voluntarily to that society in which he believes he has found that profession and worship which is truly acceptable to God. The hope of salvation, as it was the only cause of his entrance into that communion, so it can be the only reason of his stay there. For if afterwards he discover anything either erroneous in the doctrine or incongruous in the worship of that society to which he has joined himself, why should it not be as free for him to go out as it was to enter? No member of a religious society can be tied with any other bonds but what proceed from the certain expectation of eternal life. A church, then, is a society of members voluntarily uniting to that end.

It follows now that we consider what is the power of this church, and unto what laws it is subject.

Forasmuch as no society, how free soever, or upon whatsoever slight occasion instituted, whether of philosophers for learning, of merchants for commerce, or of men of leisure for mutual conversation and discourse, no church or company, I say, can in the least subsist and hold together, but will presently dissolve and break in pieces, unless it be regulated by some laws, and the members all consent to observe some order. Place and time of meeting must be agreed on; rules for admitting and excluding members must be established; distinction of officers, and putting things into a regular course, and such-like, cannot be omitted. But since the joining together of several members into this church-society, as has already been demonstrated, is absolutely free and spontaneous, it necessarily follows that the right of making its

laws can belong to none but the society itself; or, at least (which is the same thing), to those whom the society by common consent has authorised thereunto. . . .

The end of a religious society (as has already been said) is the public worship of God, and, by means thereof, the acquisition of eternal life. All discipline ought therefore to tend to that end, and all ecclesiastical laws to be thereunto confined. Nothing ought nor can be transacted in this society relating to the possession of civil and worldly goods. No force is here to be made use of upon any occasion whatsoever. For force belongs wholly to the civil magistrate, and the possession of all outward goods is subject to his jurisdiction.

But, it may be asked, by what means then shall ecclesiastical laws be established, if they must be thus destitute of all compulsive power? I answer: They must be established by means suitable to the nature of such things, whereof the external profession and observation—if not proceeding from a thorough conviction and approbation of the mind—is altogether useless and unprofitable. The arms by which the members of this society are to be kept within their duty are exhortations, admonitions, and advices. If by these means the offenders will not be reclaimed, and the erroneous convinced, there remains nothing further to be done but that such stubborn and obstinate persons, who give no ground to hope for their reformation, should be cast out and separated from the society. This is the last and utmost force of ecclesiastical authority. No other punishment can thereby be inflicted than that, the relation ceasing between the body and the member which is cut off. The person so condemned ceases to be a part of that church.

These things being thus determined, let us inquire, in the next place: How far the duty of toleration extends, and what is required from every one by it?

And, first, I hold that no church is bound, by the duty of toleration, to retain any such person in her bosom as, after admonition, continues obstinately to offend against the laws of the society. For these being the condition of communion and the bond of the society, if the breach of them were permitted without any animadversion the society would immediately be thereby dissolved. . . .

Secondly, no private person has any right in any manner to prejudice another person in his civil enjoyments because he is of another church or religion. All the rights and franchises that belong to him as a man, or as a denizen, are inviolably to be preserved to him. These are not the business of religion. No violence nor injury is to be offered him, whether he be Christian or Pagan. Nay, we must not content ourselves with the narrow measures of bare justice; charity, bounty, and liberality must be added to it. This the Gospel enjoins, this reason directs, and this that natural fellowship we are born into requires of us. If any man err from the right way, it is his own misfortune, no injury to thee; nor therefore art thou to punish him in the things of this life because thou supposest he will be miserable in that which is to come.

What I say concerning the mutual toleration of private persons differing from one another in religion, I understand also of particular churches which stand, as it were, in the same relation to each other as private persons among themselves: nor has any one of them any manner of jurisdiction over any other; no, not even when the civil magistrate (as it sometimes happens) comes to be of this or the other communion. For the civil government can give no new right to the church, nor the church to the civil government. So that whether the magistrate join himself to any church, or separate from it, the church remains always as it was before—a free and voluntary society. It neither requires the power of the sword by the magistrate's coming to it, nor does it lose the right of instruction and excommunication by his going from it. This is the fundamental and immutable right of a spontaneous society—that it has power to remove any of its members who transgress the rules of its institution; but it cannot, by the accession of any new members, acquire any right of jurisdiction over those that are not joined with it. And therefore peace, equity, and friendship are always mutually to be observed by particular churches, in the same manner as by private persons, without any pretence of superiority or jurisdiction over one another.

. . . No peace and security, no, not so much as common friendship, can ever be established or preserved amongst men so long as this opinion prevails, that dominion is founded in grace and that religion is to be propagated by force of arms. . . .

REVIEW AND DISCUSSION QUESTIONS

1. What is the justification of the use of governmental power, according to Locke?

2. What are the three reasons why Locke thinks that the state must leave religious matters to the individual?

3. How does Locke understand religion, and how is that relevant to his discussion?

4. Do you agree with Locke's claim that "nobody is born a member of a church"? What do you think he means by it?

School Prayer

Engel v. Vitale

The Constitution's First Amendment has two separate religion clauses: one protecting the right of citizens to free exercise of their religion, the other preventing government from establishing a religion. Both clauses have led courts into difficult, controversial issues. Indeed, even today, nearly a half-century after school prayer was held unconstitutional, some still argue that this case was wrongly decided.

Black, J.:

. . . The respondent Board of Education of Union Free School District No. 9, New Hyde Park, New York, acting in its official capacity under state law, directed the School District's principal to cause the following prayer to be said aloud by each class in the presence of a teacher at the beginning of each school day:

> Almighty God, we acknowledge our dependence upon Thee, and we beg Thy blessings upon us, our parents, our teachers and our Country.

This daily procedure was adopted on the recommendation of the State Board of Regents, a governmental agency created by the State Constitution to which the New York Legislature has granted broad supervisory, executive, and legislative powers over the State's public school system. These state officials composed the prayer which they recommended and published as a part of their "Statement on Moral and Spiritual Training in the Schools," saying: "We believe that this Statement will be subscribed to by all men and women of good will, and we call upon all of them to aid in giving life to our program."

Shortly after the practice of reciting the Regent's prayer was adopted by the School District, the parents of ten pupils brought this action in a New York State Court insisting that use of this official prayer in the public schools was contrary to the beliefs, religions, or religious practices of both themselves and their children. Among other things, these parents challenged the constitutionality of both the state

law authorizing the School District to direct use of prayer in public schools and the School District's regulation ordering the recitation of this particular prayer on the ground that these actions of official governmental agencies violate . . . the First Amendment of the Federal Constitution . . .—a command which was "made applicable to the State of New York by the Fourteenth Amendment of the said Constitution." . . .

The petitioners contend among other things that the state laws requiring or permitting use of the Regents' prayer must be struck down as a violation of the Establishment Clause because that prayer was composed by governmental officials as a part of a governmental program to further religious beliefs. For this reason, petitioners argue, the State's use of the Regents' prayer in its public school system breaches the constitutional wall of separation between Church and State. We agree with the contention since we think that the constitutional prohibition against laws respecting an establishment of religion must at least mean that in this country it is no part of the business of government to compose official prayers for any group of the American people to recite as a part of a religious program carried on by government.

It is a matter of history that this very practice of establishing governmentally composed prayers for religious services was one of the reasons which caused many of our early colonists to leave England and seek religious freedom in America. The Book of Common Prayer, which was created under governmental direction and which was approved by Acts of Parliament in 1548 and 1549, set out in minute detail the accepted form and content of prayer and other religious ceremonies to be used in the established,

---

370 U.S. 421 (1962).

tax-supported Church of England. The controversies over the Book and what should be its content repeatedly threatened to disrupt the peace of that country as the accepted forms of prayer in the established church changed with the views of the particular ruler that happened to be in control at the time. Powerful groups representing some of the varying religious views of the people struggled among themselves to impress their particular views upon the Government and obtain amendments of the Book more suitable to their respective notions of how religious services should be conducted in order that the official religious establishment would advance their particular religious beliefs. Other groups, lacking the necessary political power to influence the government on the matter, decided to leave England and its established church and seek freedom in America from England's governmentally ordained and supported religion.

It is an unfortunate fact of history that when some of the very groups which had most strenuously opposed the established church of England found themselves sufficiently in control of colonial governments in this country to write their own prayers into law, they passed laws making their own religion the official religion of their respective colonies. Indeed, as late as the time of the Revolutionary War, there were established churches in at least eight of the thirteen former colonies and established religions in at least four of the other five. But the successful Revolution against the English political domination was shortly followed by intense opposition to the practice of establishing religion by law. This opposition crystallized rapidly into an effective political force in Virginia where the minority religious groups such as Presbyterians, Lutherans, Quakers and Baptists had gained such strength that the adherents to the established Episcopal Church were actually a minority themselves. In 1785–1786, those opposed to the established Church, led by James Madison and Thomas Jefferson, who, though themselves not members of any of these dissenting religious groups, opposed all religious establishments by law on grounds of principle, obtained the enactment of the famous "Virginia Bill for Religious Liberty" by which all religious groups were placed on an equal footing so far as the State was concerned. Similar though less far-reaching legislation was being considered and passed in other States.

By the time of the adoption of our Constitution, our history shows that there was a widespread awareness among many Americans of the dangers of a union of Church and State. These people knew, some of them from bitter personal experience, that one of the greatest dangers to the freedom of the individual to worship in his own way lay in the Government's placing its official stamp of approval upon one particular kind of prayer or one particular form of religious services. They knew the anguish, hardship and bitter strife that could come when zealous religious groups struggled with one another to obtain the Government's stamp of approval from each King, Queen, or Protector that came to temporary power. The Constitution was intended to avert a part of this danger by leaving the government of this country in the hands of the people rather than the hands of any monarch. But this safeguard was not enough. Our Founders were no more willing to let the content of their prayers and their privilege of praying whenever they pleased be influenced by the ballot box than they were to let these vital matters of personal conscience depend upon the succession of monarchs. The First Amendment was added to the Constitution to stand as a guarantee that neither the power nor the prestige of the Federal Government would be used to control, support or influence the kinds of prayer the American people can say—that the people's religions must not be subjected to the pressures of government for change each time a new political administration is elected to office. Under that amendment's prohibition against governmental establishment of religion, as reinforced by the provisions of the Fourteenth Amendment, government in this country, be it state or federal, is without power to prescribe by law any particular form of prayer which is to be used as an official prayer in carrying on any program of governmentally sponsored religious activity.

There can be no doubt that New York's State prayer program officially establishes the religious beliefs embodied in the Regents' prayer. The respondents' argument to the contrary, which is largely based upon the contention that the Regents' prayer is "non-denominational" and the fact that the program, as modified and approved by state courts, does not require all pupils to recite the prayer but permits those who wish to do so to remain silent or be excused from the room, ignores the essential nature of the program's constitutional defects. Neither the fact that the prayer may be denominationally neutral nor the fact that its observance on the part of students is voluntary can serve to free it from the limitations of the Establishment Clause, as it might from the Free Exercise Clause, of the First Amendment, both of which are operative against the States by virtue of the Fourteenth Amendment. Although these two clauses may in certain instances overlap, they forbid two quite different kinds of governmental encroachment upon religious freedom. The Establishment Clause, unlike the Free Exercise Clause, does not depend upon any showing of direct governmental compulsion and is violated by the enactment of laws which establish an official religion whether those laws operate directly to coerce nonobserving individuals or not. This is not to say, of course, that laws officially prescribing a particular form of religious worship do not involve coercion of such individuals. When the power, prestige, and financial support of government is placed behind a particular religious belief, the indirect coercive pressure upon religious minorities to conform to the prevailing officially approved religion is plain. But the purposes underlying the Establishment Clause go much further than that. Its first and most immediate purpose rested on the belief that a union of government and religion tends to destroy government and to degrade religion. The history of governmentally established religion, both in England and in this country, showed that whenever government had allied itself with one particular religion, the inevitable result had been it had incurred the hatred, disrespect and even contempt of those who held contrary beliefs. That same history showed that many people had lost their respect for any religion that had relied upon the support of government to spread its faith. The Establishment Clause thus stands as an expression of principle on the part of the Founders of our Constitution that religion is too personal, too sacred, too holy, to permit its "unhallowed perversion" by a civil magistrate. Another purpose of the Establishment Clause rested upon an awareness of the historical fact that governmentally established religions and religious persecutions go hand in hand. . . . It was in large part to get completely away from this sort of systematic religious persecution that the Founders brought into being our Nation, our Constitution, and our Bill of Rights with its prohibition against any governmental establishment of religion. The New York laws officially prescribing the Regents' prayer are inconsistent both with the purposes of the Establishment Clause and with the Establishment Clause itself.

It has been argued that to apply the Constitution in such a way as to prohibit state laws respecting an establishment of religious services in public schools is to indicate a hostility toward religion or toward prayer. Nothing, of course, could be more wrong. . . . It is neither sacrilegious nor antireligious to say that each separate government in this country should stay out of the business of writing or sanctioning official prayers and leave that purely religious function to the people themselves and to those the people choose to look for religious guidance.

. . . To those who may subscribe to the view that because the Regents' official prayer is so brief and general there can be no danger to religious freedom in its governmental establishment, however, it may be appropriate to say in the words of James Madison, the author of the First Amendment:

> [I]t is proper to take alarm at the first experiment on our liberties. . . . Who does not see that the same authority which can establish Christianity, in exclusion of all other religions, may establish with the same ease any particular sect of Christians, in exclusion of all other Sects? That the same authority which can force a citizen to contribute three pence only of his property for the support of any one establishment, may force him to conform to any other establishment in all cases whatsoever?

The judgment of the Court of Appeals of New York is reversed and the cause remanded for further proceedings not inconsistent with this opinion.

Stewart, J. (dissenting):

. . . With all respect, I think that the Court has misapplied a great constitutional principle. I cannot see how an "official religion" is established by letting those who want to say a prayer say it . . .

The Court's historical review of the quarrels over the Book of Common Prayer in England throws no light for me on the issue before us. England had then and has now an established church. Equally unenlightening, I think, is the history of the early establishment and later rejection of an official church in our own States. For we deal here not with the establishment of a state church, which would, of course, be constitutionally impermissible, but with whether school children who want to begin their day by joining in prayer must be prohibited from doing so. Moreover, I think that the Court's task . . . is not responsibly aided by the uncritical invocation of metaphors like the "wall of separation," a phrase nowhere to be found in the Constitution. What is relevant to the issue here is not the history of the established church in sixteenth century England or eighteenth century America, but the history of the religious traditions of our people, reflected in countless practices of the institutions and officials of our government.

At the opening of each day's session of this Court we stand, while one of our officials invokes the protection of God. Since the days of John Marshall our Crier has said, "God save the United States and this Honorable Court." Both the Senate and House of Representatives open their daily sessions with prayer. Each of our Presidents, from George Washington to John F. Kennedy, has upon assuming this Office asked the protection and help of God.

The Court today says that the state and federal governments are without constitutional power to prescribe any particular form of words to be recited by any group of the American people on any subject touching religion. One of the stanzas of "The Star Stangled Banner," made our National Anthem by Act of Congress in 1931, contains these verses:

> Blest with victory and peace, may the heav'n rescued land
> Praise the Pow'r that hath made and preserved us a nation!
> Then conquer we must, when our cause it is just
> And this be our motto "In God is our Trust."

In 1954 Congress added a phrase to the Pledge of Allegiance to the Flag so that it now contains the words "one Nation *under God*, indivisible, with liberty and justice for all." In 1952 Congress enacted legislation calling upon the President each year to proclaim a National Day of Prayer. Since 1865 the words "IN GOD WE TRUST" have been impressed on our coins.

Countless similar examples could be listed, but there is no need to belabor the obvious. It was all summed up by this court just ten years ago in a single sentence: "We are a religious people whose institutions presuppose a Supreme Being." *Zorach v. Clausen* (1952)

I do not believe that this Court, or the Congress, or the President has by the actions and practices I have mentioned established an "official religion" in violation of the Constitution. And I do not believe the State of New York has done so in this case. What each has done has been to recognize and to follow the deeply entrenched and highly cherished spiritual traditions of our Nation—traditions which come down to us from those who almost two hundred years ago avowed their "firm Reliance on the Protection of divine Providence" when they proclaimed the freedom and independence of this brave new world.

REVIEW AND DISCUSSION QUESTIONS

1. What reasons does Justice Black give for holding the New York school prayer unconstitutional?

2. Why does Justice Stewart reject Justice Black's argument?

3. Is the historical record described by Justice Black relevant or irrelevant to the argument?

4. How do you think Locke would have written this opinion?

Religious Freedom and Public Education

Wisconsin v. Yoder

This well-known case arose in response to a Wisconsin law requiring all children to be sent to school until the age of sixteen. The Amish parents of two children, ages fourteen and fifteen, refused to comply, arguing that compulsory school attendance beyond eighth grade violated their constitutional right of "free exercise" of religion protected by the First Amendment to the U.S. Constitution. The case went all the way to the Supreme Court, and the Court overturned the law, upholding the right of the Amish parents to guide the religious future and education of their children. In his dissenting opinion, Justice Douglas discusses problems associated with allowing parents to impose their religious notions on children as well as the possible effects of the Court's ruling on the children's educational development.

Mr. Chief Justice Burger:

On complaint of the school district administrator for the public schools, respondents [Mr. and Mrs. Yoder] were charged, tried, and convicted of violating the compulsory-attendance law in Green County Court and were fined the sum of $5 each. Respondents defended on the ground that the application of the compulsory-attendance law violated their rights under the First and Fourteenth Amendments. The trial testimony showed that respondents believed, in accordance with the tenets of Old Order Amish communities generally, that their children's attendance at high school, public or private, was contrary to the Amish religion and way of life. . . . The State stipulated that respondents' religious beliefs were sincere.

In support of their position, respondents presented as expert witnesses scholars on religion and education whose testimony is uncontradicted. They expressed their opinions on the relationship of the Amish belief concerning school attendance to the more general tenets of their religion, and described the impact that compulsory high school attendance could have on the continued survival of Amish communities as they exist in the United States today. . . .

Amish beliefs require members of the community to make their living by farming or closely related activities. Broadly speaking, the Old Order Amish religion pervades and determines the entire mode of life of its adherents. . . .

Amish objection to formal education beyond the eighth grade is firmly grounded in these central religious concepts. They object to the high school, and higher education generally, because the values they teach are in marked variance with Amish values and the Amish way of life; they view secondary school education as an impermissible exposure of their children to a "worldly" influence in conflict with their beliefs. The high school tends to emphasize intellectual and scientific accomplishments, self-distinction, competitiveness, worldly success, and social life with other students. Amish society emphasizes informal learning-through-doing; a life of "goodness," rather than a life of intellect; wisdom, rather than technical knowledge; community welfare, rather than competition; and separation from, rather than integration with, contemporary worldly society.

Formal high school education takes [Amish children] away from their community, physically and emotionally, during the crucial and formative adolescent period of life. During this period, the children must acquire Amish attitudes favoring manual work and self-reliance and the specific skills needed to perform the adult role of an Amish farmer or housewife. They must learn to enjoy physical labor. . . . And, at this time in life, the Amish child must also grow in his faith and his relationship to the Amish community if he is to be prepared to accept the heavy obligations imposed by adult baptism. . . .

406 U.S. 205 (1972).

The Amish do not object to elementary education through the first eight grades as a general proposition because they agree that their children must have basic skills in the "three Rs" in order to read the Bible, to be good farmers and citizens, and to be able to deal with non-Amish people when necessary in the course of daily affairs. They view such a basic education as acceptable because it does not significantly expose their children to worldly values or interfere with their development in the Amish community during the crucial adolescent period. . . .

On the basis of such considerations, [an expert] testified that compulsory high school attendance could not only result in great psychological harm to Amish children, because of the conflicts it would produce, but would also, in his opinion, ultimately result in the destruction of the Old Order Amish church community as it exists in the United States today. . . .

In order for Wisconsin to compel school attendance beyond the eighth grade against a claim that such attendance interferes with the practice of a legitimate religious belief, it must appear either that the State does not deny the free exercise of religious belief by its requirement, or that there is a state interest of sufficient magnitude to override the interest claiming protection under the Free Exercise Clause. . . .

A way of life, however virtuous and admirable, may not be interposed as a barrier to reasonable state regulation of education if it is based on purely secular considerations; to have the protection of the Religion Clauses, the claims must be rooted in religious belief. Although a determination of what is a "religious" belief or practice entitled to constitutional protection may present a most delicate question, the very concept of ordered liberty precludes allowing every person to make his own standards on matters of conduct in which society as a whole has important interests. Thus, if the Amish asserted their claims because of their subjective evaluation and rejection of the contemporary secular values accepted by the majority, much as Thoreau rejected the social values of his time and isolated himself at Walden Pond, their claims would not rest on a religious basis. Thoreau's choice was philosophical and personal rather than religious, and such belief does not rise to the demands of the Religion Clauses.

Giving no weight to such secular considerations, however, we see that the record in this case abundantly supports the claim that the traditional way of life of the Amish is not merely a matter of personal preference, but one of deep religious conviction, shared by an organized group, and intimately related to daily living. That the Old Order Amish daily life and religious practice stem from their faith is shown by the fact that it is in response to their literal interpretation of the Biblical injunction from the Epistle of Paul to the Romans, "be not conformed to this world. . . ."

Their way of life in a church-oriented community, separated from the outside world and "worldly" influences, their attachment to nature and the soil, is a way inherently simple and uncomplicated, albeit difficult to preserve against the pressure to conform. Their rejection of telephones, automobiles, radios, and television, their mode of dress, of speech, their habits of manual work do indeed set them apart from much of contemporary society; these customs are both symbolic and practical. . . .

The State advances two primary arguments in support of its system of compulsory education. It notes, as Thomas Jefferson pointed out early in our history, that some degree of education is necessary to prepare citizens to participate effectively and intelligently in our open political system if we are to preserve freedom and independence. Further, education prepares individuals to be self-reliant and self-sufficient participants in society. We accept these propositions.

However, the evidence adduced by the Amish in this case is persuasively to the effect that an additional one or two years of formal high school for Amish children in place of their long-established program of informal vocational education would do little to serve those interests. . . . It is one thing to say that compulsory education for a year or two beyond the eighth grade may be necessary when its goal is the preparation of the child for life in modern society as the majority live, but it is quite another if the goal of education be viewed as the preparation of the child for life in the separated agrarian community that is the keystone of the Amish faith. . . .

Whatever their idiosyncrasies as seen by the majority, the Amish community has been a highly successful social unit within our society, even if apart from the conventional "mainstream." Its members are productive and very law-abiding members of society; they reject public welfare in any of its usual modern forms. . . .

This case involves the fundamental interest of parents, as contrasted with that of the State, to guide the religious future and education of their children. The history and culture of Western civilization reflect a strong tradition of parental concern for the nurture and upbringing of their children. This primary role of the parents in the upbringing of their children is now established beyond debate as an enduring American tradition. . . .

To be sure, the power of the parent, even when linked to a free exercise claim, may be subject to limitation if it appears that parental decisions will jeopardize the health or safety of the child, or have a potential for significant social burdens. But in this case, the Amish have introduced persuasive evidence undermining the arguments the State has advanced to support its claims in terms of the welfare of the child and society as a whole.

Mr. Justice Douglas, Dissenting in Part:

The Court's analysis assumes that the only interests at stake in the case are those of the Amish parents on the one hand, and those of the State on the other. The difficulty with this approach is that, despite the Court's claim, the parents are seeking to vindicate not only their own free exercise claims, but also those of their high-school-age children. . . .

No analysis of religious-liberty claims can take place in a vacuum. If the parents in this case are allowed a religious exemption, the inevitable effect is to impose the parents' notions of religious duty upon their children. Where the child is mature enough to express potentially conflicting desires, it would be an invasion of the child's rights to permit such an imposition without canvassing his views. . . . As the child has no

other effective forum, it is in this litigation that his rights should be considered. And, if an Amish child desires to attend high school, and is mature enough to have that desire respected, the State may well be able to override the parents' religiously motivated objections.

This issue has never been squarely presented before today. Our opinions are full of talk about the power of the parents over the child's education. . . . And we have in the past analyzed similar conflicts between parent and State with little regard for the views of the child. . . . Recent cases, however, have clearly held that the children themselves have constitutionally protectible interests.

These children are "persons" within the meaning of the Bill of Rights. . . . While the parents, absent dissent, normally speak for the entire family, the education of the child is a matter on which the child will often have decided views. He may want to be a pianist or an astronaut or an oceanographer. To do so he will have to break from the Amish tradition. . . .

If a parent keeps his child out of school beyond the grade school, then the child will be forever barred from entry into the new and amazing world of diversity that we have today. . . .

[In the cases in which the Court held antipolygamy laws constitutional,] action which the Court deemed to be antisocial could be punished even though it was grounded on deeply held and sincere religious convictions. What we do today, at least in this respect, opens the way to give organized religion a broader base than it has ever enjoyed.

In another way, however, the Court retreats when in reference to Henry Thoreau it says his "choice was philosophical and personal rather than religious, and such belief does not rise to the demands of the Religion Clauses." That is contrary to what we held in *United States v. Seeger*, where we were concerned with the meaning of the words "religious training and belief" in the Selective Service Act, which were the basis of many conscientious objector claims. We said: "Within that phrase would come all sincere religious beliefs which are based upon a power or being, or upon a faith, to which all else is subordinate or upon which all else is ultimately dependent. The test might be stated in these words: A sincere and meaningful belief which occupies in the life of its possessor a place parallel to that filled by the God of those admittedly qualifying for the exemption comes within the statutory definition. This construction avoids imputing to Congress an intent to classify different religious beliefs, exempting some and excluding others, and is in accord with the well-established congressional policy of equal treatment for those whose opposition to service is grounded in their religious tenets."

REVIEW AND DISCUSSION QUESTIONS

1. Describe the legal issue in this case.

2. Does Justice Burger seem to rely more on religious freedom or the rights of parents over children? Explain.

3. On what basis does Justice Douglas dissent?

4. Does Justice Burger think the Constitution should be "neutral" among different religions?

Explain.

5. Children will eventually have the right to make decisions for themselves in many areas, independent of what government or others may think. Can parents sometimes damage their children's future right to self-determination? Explain, giving examples.

Secular Humanism and Religious Establishment

Smith v. Board of Education of Mobile

The First Amendment guarantees citizens the right to exercise their religion and prevents government from "establishing" an official religion. But if religion is defined broadly enough, then it is possible to argue that by teaching "secular humanism" schools establish secular humanism as a religion. U.S. District Court Judge Brevard Hand makes that argument in the following case, Smith v. Board of Education of Mobile. *The impetus for the case came in 1982 when the Supreme Court overruled an earlier decision by Judge Hand in which he had argued that a one-minute period of silent prayer in schools was not a violation of the establishment clause. Having lost that argument, Judge Hand did not let the issue die, suggesting in his opinion that should he be overruled (as he later was), he would then be willing to consider arguments that the school board had established another religion—secular humanism—in violation of the establishment clause. A group of religious conservatives took up the judge's offer and filed this case,* Smith v. Board of Education of Mobile. *After the trial, which included many expert witnesses on both sides, Judge Hand wrote a lengthy opinion contending that secular humanism is a religion and that the Mobile school board "established" it by requiring students to read certain textbooks. Although this decision was later overturned as well, Judge Hand's opinion in* Smith *raises important and difficult issues concerning the extent to which school texts that have the effect of undermining the values and religious beliefs of a community can be required.*

---

655 F. Supp. 939 (S.D. Ala. 1987).

I. A FIRST AMENDMENT DEFINITION OF RELIGION

The Supreme Court has never stated an absolute definition of religion under the first amendment. . . .

The application of these principles to the question of what constitutes a religion under the first amendment indicates that the state may not decide the question by reference to the validity of the beliefs or practices involved. . . . The state must instead look to factors common to all religious movements to decide how to distinguish those ideologies worthy of the protection of the religious clauses from those which must seek refuge under other constitutional provisions.

Any definition of religion must not be limited, therefore, to traditional religions, but must encompass systems of belief that are equivalent to them for the believer. . . . The Supreme Court has focused on such factors as a person's "ultimate concern," organization and social structure, and on equivalency to belief in a Supreme Deity. All of these are evidence of the type of belief a person holds. But all religious beliefs may be classified by the questions they raise and issues they address. Some of these matters overlap with nonreligious governmental concerns. A religion, however, approaches them on the basis of certain fundamental assumptions with which governments are unconcerned. These assumptions may be grouped as about: (1) the existence of supernatural and/or transcendent reality; (2) the nature of man; (3) the ultimate end, or goal or purpose of man's existence, both individually and collectively; (4) the purpose and nature of the universe. . . .

Whenever a belief system deals with fundamental questions of the nature of reality and man's relationship to reality, it deals with essentially religious questions. A religion need not posit a belief *in* a deity, or a belief *in* supernatural existence. A religious person adheres to some position on whether supernatural and/or transcendent reality exists at all, and if so, how, and if not, why. A mere "comprehensive world-view" or "way of life" is not by itself enough to identify a belief system as religious. A world-view may be merely economic, or so-ciological, and a person might choose to follow a "way of life" that ignores ultimate issues addressed by religions. . . .

There are also a number of characteristics exhibited by most known religious groups to which courts can look when trying to determine if a set of theories or system of ideas is religious in nature. First would be the sincerity of the adherents' claims. . . . Another factor is group organization and hierarchial structure, which evidence the social characteristics of a movement, and show that the adherents sincerely follow a theory of human relationship. Literary manifestations of a movement may also be important, particularly if they take the form of an authoritative text. Ritual and worship also would be significant because they would be evidence of the religion's belief about supernatural or transcendent reality. . . .

II. HUMANISM A RELIGION?

In the present case, the plaintiffs contend that a particular belief system fits within the first amendment definition of religion. . . . All of the experts, and the class representatives, agreed that this belief system [humanism] is a religion which: "makes a statement about supernatural existence a central pillar of its logic; defines the nature of man; and sets forth a goal or purpose for individual and collective human existence; and defines the nature of the universe, and thereby delimits its purpose."

It purports to establish a closed definition of reality; not closed in that adherents know everything, but in that everything is knowable: can be recognized by human intellect aided only by the devices of that intellect's own creation or discovery. The most important belief of this religion is its denial of the transcendent and/or supernatural: there is no God, no creator, no divinity. By force of logic the universe is thus self-existing, completely physical and hence, essentially knowable. Man is the product of evolutionary, physical forces. He is purely biological and has no supernatural or transcendent spiritual component or quality. Man's individual purpose is to seek and obtain personal fulfillment by freely developing every talent and ability, especially his rational intellect, to the highest level. Man's collective purpose is to seek the good life by the increase of every person's freedom and potential for personal development.

In addition, humanism, as a belief system, erects a moral code and identifies the source of morality. This source is claimed to exist in humans and the social relationships of humans. Again, there is no spiritual or supernatural origin for morals: man is merely physical, and morals, the rules governing his private and social conduct, are founded only on man's actions, situation and environment. In addition to a moral code, certain attitudes and conduct are proscribed since they interfere with personal freedom and fulfillment. In particular any belief in a deity or adherence to a religious system that is theistic in any way is discouraged.

Secular humanism, or humanism in the sense of a religious belief system, (as opposed to humanism as just an interest in the humanities), has organizational characteristics. . . .

These organizations publish magazines, newsletters and other periodicals, including *Free Inquiry, The Humanist and Progressive World.* The entire body of thought has three key documents that furnish the text upon which the belief system rests as on a platform: *Humanist Manifesto I, Humanist Manifesto II,* and the *Secular Humanist Declaration.* . . .

To say that science is only concerned with data collected by the five senses as enhanced by technological devices of man's creation is to define science's limits. These are the parameters within which scientists function. However, to claim that there is nothing real beyond observable data is to make an assumption based not on science, but on faith, faith that observable data is all that is real. A statement that there is no transcendent or supernatural reality is a *religious* statement. . . .

This Court is holding that the promotion and advancement of a religious system occurs when one faith-theory is taught to the exclusion of others and this is prohibited by the first amendment religion clauses.

For purposes of the first amendment, secular humanism is a religious belief system, entitled to the protections of, and subject to the prohibitions of, the religion clauses. It is not a mere scientific methodology that may be promoted and advanced in the public schools.

III. RELIGIOUS PROMOTION IN TEXTBOOKS?

. . . [T]he Supreme Court has declared that teaching religious tenets in such a way as to promote or encourage a religion violates the religion clauses. This prohibition is not implicated by mere coincidence of ideas with religious tenets. Rather, there must be systematic, whether explicit or implicit, promotion of a belief system as a whole. The facts showed that the State of Alabama has on its state textbook list certain volumes that are being used by school systems in this state, which engage in such promotion. . . .

The virtually unanimous conclusion of the numerous witnesses, both expert and lay, party and non-party, was that textbooks in the fields examined were poor from an educational perspective. Mere rotten and inadequate textbooks, however, have not yet been determined to violate any constitutional provision, much less the religion clauses. . . . Their expert opinion was that religion was so deliberately underemphasized and ignored that theistic religions were effectively discriminated against and made to seem irrelevant and unimportant within the context of American history. . . . The religious influence on the abolitionist, woman's suffrage, temperance, modern civil rights and peace movements is ignored or diminished to insignificance. The role of religion in the lives of immigrants and minorities, especially southern blacks, is rarely mentioned. After the Civil War, religion is given almost no play. . . .

In addition to omitting particular historical events with religious significance, these books uniformly ignore the religious aspect of most American culture. The vast majority of Americans, for most of our history, have lived in a society in which religion was a part of daily life. . . . For many people, religion is still this important. One would never know it by reading these books. Religion, where treated at all, is generally represented as a private matter, only influencing American public life at some extraordinary moments. This view of religion is one humanists have been seeking to instill for fifty years. These books assist that effort by perpetuating an inaccurate historical picture. . . .

According to humanistic psychology, as with humanism generally, man is the center of the universe and all existence. Morals are a matter of taste, dependent upon whether the consequences of actions satisfy human "needs." These needs are always defined as purely temporal and non-supernatural. . . .

The [social studies] books do not state that this is a *theory* of the way humans make choices, they teach the student that things *are* this way. . . . The books teach that the student must determine right and wrong based only on his own experience, feelings and "values." These "values" are described as originating from within. A description of the origin of morals must be based on a faith assumption: a religious dogma. The books are not simply claiming that a moral rule must be internally accepted before it becomes meaningful, because this is true of *all* facts *and* beliefs. . . . The books repeat, over and over, that the decision is "yours alone," or is "purely personal" or that "only you can decide."

The emphasis and overall approach implies, and would cause any reasonable, thinking student to infer, that the book is teaching that moral choices are just a matter of preference, because, as the books say, "you are the most important person in your life." . . . This faith assumes that self-actualization is the goal of every human being, that man has no supernatural attributes or component, that there are only temporal and physical consequences for man's actions, and that these results, alone, determine the morality of an action. This belief strikes at the heart of many theistic religions' beliefs that certain actions are in and of themselves immoral, *whatever the consequences*, and that, in addition, actions will have extratemporal consequences. The Court is not holding that high school . . . books must not discuss various theories of human psychology. But it must not present faith based systems to the exclusion of other faith based systems, it must not present one as true and the other as false, and it *must* use a comparative approach to withstand constitutional scrutiny. . . .

With these [history and social studies] books, the State of Alabama has overstepped its mark, and must withdraw to perform its proper non-religious functions. . . . The Court will enter an order to prohibit further use of the books.

REVIEW AND DISCUSSION QUESTIONS

1. Describe the legal issue that is before the court in this case.

2. How does Judge Hand understand the legal definition of *religion?*

3. Why does he think humanism is a religion?

4. What does Judge Hand find in the textbooks that leads him to believe that they "establish" a religion?

5. The court of appeals overturned Judge Hand's decision, and the Supreme Court agreed with the appeals court. Is Judge Hand's opinion consistent with the Supreme Court's ruling in *Wisconsin v. Yoder?* Explain.

6. In another, related case, the Supreme Court ruled that schools can teach evolutionary theory despite the fact that it is incompatible with some students' religious views. How would you decide such a case? Explain.

On Liberty

John Stuart Mill

John Stuart Mill (1806–73) had an unusual life by almost any account. His father, James Mill, who was a friend of the economist David Ricardo and legal theorist John Austin, was among the most devoted followers of Jeremy Bentham, the utilitarian philosopher. Like Bentham, the senior Mill held that human behavior is best understood in terms of self-interest and that government serves the common good by promoting the happiness of its citizens.

James resolved to raise his son John Stuart according to sound utilitarian principles. With Bentham's help, he developed a plan that included a rigorous tutoring program and keeping the boy away from other children. Young John Stuart was a brilliant student. By the age of three, he had begun learning Greek. At eight he learned Latin and pursued mathematics and history. By the age of twelve, he was studying logic and political economy, and at fifteen he studied law at University College, London, with John Austin. At twenty-four Mill began a lifelong friendship and intellectual collaboration with Harriet Taylor. Although they were close companions, Harriet Taylor remained married for two decades. When John Taylor died, John Stuart Mill and she were married. After their marriage the two withdrew from "insipid society" and the gossip they had endured for years; they lived happily for seven years until her death. Mill served briefly as a member of Parliament and died in France (where he had bought a house near the cemetery in which Harriet was buried).

Mill's influence has been tremendous; he wrote important books in logic, philosophy of science, and economics as well as ethics and political philosophy. One of his works, Utilitarianism, *remains a classic statement of that important theory. None of his books has had a greater impact than* On Liberty. *In fact,* On Liberty *should be thought of as a joint work authored by both Mill and Harriet Taylor. Mill had tremendous respect for her intellectual ability and wrote in a letter that there is not a sentence in the book that the two did not go over together many times. Harriet Taylor also had a major role in other works, including* On the Subjection of Women.

In On Liberty *Mill examines a fundamental question of political philosophy: What are the limits of society's power over the individual? Mill's answer is that society may interfere with an individual's speech or actions only on the grounds of self-protection. Accordingly, Mill first discusses briefly the history of the fight of the individual against tyrannical government. He next turns to the realm of freedom of thought, vigorously upholding freedom of opinion regardless of whether the belief is true or false. Indeed, he argues, it is essential that all opinions, including false ones, be freely expressed. Finally, he considers his famous "harm principle": that government is justified in interfering with a citizen's liberty only if the action involves a threat of harm to others.*

INTRODUCTORY

The subject of this essay is . . . civil, or social liberty: the nature and limits of power which can be legitimately exercised by society over the individual.

. . . [In] old times this contest was between subjects, or some classes of subjects, and the government. By liberty, was meant protection against the tyranny of the political rulers. The rulers were conceived (except in some of the popular governments of Greece) as in a necessarily antagonistic position to the people whom they ruled. . . .

A time, however, came, in the progress of human affairs, when men ceased to think it a necessity of nature that their governors should be an independent power, opposed in interest to themselves. It appeared to them much better that the various magistrates of the State should be their tenants or delegates, revocable at their pleasure. In that way alone, it seemed, could they have complete security that the powers of government would never be abused to their disadvantage. . . . What was now wanted was, that the rulers should be identified with the people; that their interest and will should be the interest and will of the nation. The nation did not need to be protected against its own will. There was no fear of its tyrannizing over itself. Let the rulers be effectually responsible to it, promptly removably by it, and it could afford to trust them with power of which it could itself dictate the use to be made. Their power was but the nation's own power, concentrated, and in a form convenient for exercise. . . .

But in political and philosophical theories, as well as in persons, success discloses faults and infirmities which failure might have concealed from observation. . . . It was now perceived that such phrases as "self-government," and "the power of the people over themselves," do not express the true state of the case. The "people" who exercise the power are not always the same people with those over whom it is exercised; and the "self-government" spoken of is not the government of each by himself, but of each by all the rest. The will of the people, moreover, practically means the will of the most numerous or the most active *part* of the people—the majority, or those who succeed in making themselves accepted as the majority; the people, consequently, *may* desire to oppress a part of their number, and precautions are as much needed against this as against any other abuse of power. The limitation, therefore, of the power of government over individuals loses none of its importance when the holders of power are regularly accountable to the community, that is, to the strongest party therein. . . .

The object of this essay is to assert one very simple principle, as entitled to govern absolutely the dealings of society with the individual in the way of compulsion and control, whether the means used by physical force in the form of legal penalties or the moral coercion of public opinion. That principle is, that the sole end for which mankind are warranted, individually or collectively, in interfering with the liberty of action of any of their number, is self-protection. That the only purpose for which power can be rightfully exercised over any member of a civilized community, against his will, is to prevent harm to others. His own good, either physical or moral, is not a sufficient warrant. He cannot rightfully be compelled to do or forbear because it will be better for him to do so, because it will make him happier, because, in the opinions of others, to do so would be wise or even right. These are good reasons for remonstrating with him, or reasoning with him, or persuading him, or entreating him, but not for compelling him or visiting him with any evil in case he do otherwise. To justify that, the conduct from which it is desired to deter him must be calculated to produce evil to someone else. The only part of the conduct of anyone, for which he is amenable to society, is that which concerns others. In the part which merely concerns himself, his independence is, of right, absolute. Over himself, over his own body and mind, the individual is sovereign.

It is, perhaps, hardly necessary to say that this doctrine is meant to apply only to human beings in the maturity of their faculties. We are not speaking of children, or of young persons below the age which the law may fix as that of manhood or womanhood. Those who are still in a state to require being taken care of by others, must be protected against their own actions as well as against external injury. For the same reason, we may leave out of consideration those backward states of society in which the race itself may be considered as in its nonage. The early difficulties in the way of spontaneous progress are so great, and there is seldom any choice of means for overcoming them; and a ruler full of the spirit of improvement is warranted in the use of any expedients that will attain an end, perhaps otherwise unattainable. Despotism is a legitimate mode of government in dealing with barbarians, provided the end be their improvement, and the means justified by actually effecting that end. Liberty, as a principle, has no application to any state of things anterior to the time when mankind have become capable of being improved by free and equal discussion. Until then, there is nothing for them but implicit obedience to an Akbar or a Charlemagne, if they are so fortunate as to find one. But as soon as mankind have attained the capacity of being guided to their own improvement by conviction or persuasion (a period long since reached in all nations with whom we need here concern ourselves), compulsion, either in the direct form or in that of pains and penalties for noncompliance, is no longer admissible as a means to their own good, and justifiable only for the security of others.

It is proper to state that I forego any advantage which could be derived to my argument from the idea of abstract right, as a thing independent of utility. I regard utility as the ultimate appeal on all ethical questions; but it must be utility in the largest sense, grounded on the permanent interests of a man as a progressive being. These interests, I contend, authorized the subjection of individual spontaneity to external control, only in respect to those actions of each which concern the interest of other people. If anyone does an act hurtful to others, there is a *prima facie* case for punishing him, by law, or, where legal penalties are not safely applicable, by general disapprobation. There are also many positive acts for the benefit of others, which he may rightfully be compelled to perform: such as to give evidence in a court of justice; to bear his fair share in the common defense, or in any other joint work necessary to the interest of the society of which he enjoys the protection; and to perform certain acts of individual beneficence, such as saving a fellow-creature's life, or interposing to protect the defenseless against ill-usage, things which whenever it is obviously a man's duty to do, he may rightfully be made responsible to society for not doing. A person may cause evil to others not only by his actions but by his inaction, and in either case he is justly accountable to them for the injury. The latter case, it is true, requires a much more cautious exercise of compulsion than the former. . . .

. . . This, then is the appropriate region of human liberty. It comprises, *first*, the inward domain of consciousness; demanding liberty of conscience in the most comprehensive sense; liberty of thought and feeling; absolute freedom of opinion and sentiment on all subjects, practical or speculative, scientific, moral or theological. The liberty of expressing and publishing opinions may seem to fall under a different principle, since it belongs to that part of the conduct of an individual which concerns other people; but, being almost of as much importance as the liberty of thought itself, and resting in great part on the same reasons, is practically inseparable from it. *Secondly*, the principle requires liberty of tastes and pursuits; of framing the plan of our life to suit our own character; of doing as we like, subject to such consequences as may follow: without impediment from our fellow-creatures, so long as what we do does not harm them, even though they should think our conduct foolish, perverse, to wrong. *Thirdly*, from this liberty of each individual, follows the liberty, within the same limits, of combinations among individuals; freedom to unite, for any purpose not involving harm to others: the persons combining being supposed to be of full age, and not forced or deceived.

No society in which these liberties are not, on the whole, respected, is free, whatever may be its form of government; and none is completely free in which they do not exist absolute and unqualified. The only freedom which deserves the name, is that of pursuing our own good in our own way, as long as we do not attempt to deprive others of theirs, or impede their efforts to obtain it. Each is the proper guardian of his own health, whether bodily, or mental and spiritual. Mankind are greater gainers by suffering each other to live as seems good to themselves, than by compelling each to live as seems good to the rest. . . .

OF THE LIBERTY OF THOUGHT AND DISCUSSION

The time, it is to be hoped, is gone by, when any defense would be necessary of the "liberty of the press" as one of the securities against corrupt or tyrannical government. No argument, we may suppose, can now be needed against permitting a legislature or an executive, not identified in interest with the people, to prescribe opinions to them, and determine what doctrines or what arguments they shall be allowed to hear. . . . Let us suppose . . . that government is entirely at one with the people, and never thinks of exerting any power of coercion unless in agreement with what it conceives to be their voice. But I deny the right of the people to exercise such coercion, either by themselves or by their government. The power itself is illegitimate. The best government has no more title to it than the worst. It is as noxious, or more noxious, when exerted in accordance with public opinion than when in opposition to it. If all mankind minus one were of one opinion, mankind would be no more justified in silencing that one person than he, if he had the power, would be justified in silencing mankind. Were an opinion a personal possession of no value except to the owner, if to be obstructed in the enjoyment of it were simply a private injury, it would make some difference whether the injury was inflicted only on a few persons or on many. But the peculiar evil of silencing the expression of an opinion is that it is robbing the human race, posterity as well as the existing generation—those who dissent from the opinion, still more than those who hold it. If the opinion is right, they are deprived of the opportunity of exchanging error for truth; if wrong, they lose, what is almost as great a benefit, the clearer perception and livelier impression of truth produced by its collision with error.

It is necessary to consider separately these two hypotheses, each of which has a distinct branch of the argument corresponding to it. We can never be sure that the opinion we are endeavoring to stifle is a false opinion; and if we were sure, stifling it would be an evil still.

First, the opinion which it is attempted to suppress by authority may possibly be true. Those who desire to suppress it, of course, deny its truth; but they are not infallible. They have no authority to decide the question for all mankind and exclude every other person from the means of judging. To refuse a hearing to an opinion because they are sure that it is false to assume that *their* certainty is the same thing as *absolute* certainty. All silencing of discussion is an assumption of infallibility. Its condemnation may be allowed to rest on this common argument, not the worse for being common.

Unfortunately for the good sense of mankind, the fact of their fallibility is far from carrying the weight in their practical judgment which is always allowed to it in theory; for while everyone well knows himself to be fallible, few think it necessary to take any precautions against their own fallibility, or admit the supposition that any opinion of which they feel very certain may be one of the examples of the error to which they acknowledge themselves to be liable. . . .

The objection likely to be made to this argument would probably take some such form as the following. There is no greater assumption of infallibility in forbidding the propagation of error than in any other thing which is done by public authority on its own judgment and responsibility. . . . It is the duty of governments, and of individuals, to form the truest opinions they can; to form them carefully, and never impose them upon others unless they are quite sure of being right. But when they are sure (such reasoners may say), it is not conscientiousness but cowardice to shrink from acting on their opinions and allow doctrines which they honestly think dangerous to the welfare of mankind, either in this life or in another, to be scattered abroad without restraint, because other people, in less enlightened times, have persecuted opinions now believed to be true. . . . There is no such thing as absolute certainty, but there is assurance sufficient for the purposes of human life. We may, and must, assume our opinion to be true for the guidance of our own conduct; and it is assuming no more when we forbid bad men to pervert society by the propagation of opinions which we regard as false and pernicious.

I answer, that it is assuming very much more. There is the greatest difference between presuming an opinion to be true because, with every opportunity for contesting it, it has not been refuted, and assuming its truth for the purpose of not permitting its refutation. Complete liberty of contradicting and disproving our opinion is the very condition which justifies us in assuming its truth for purposes of action; and on no other terms can a being with human faculties have any rational assurance of being right. . . .

In the present age—which has been described as "destitute of faith, but terrified at skepticism"—in which people feel sure, not so much that their opinions are true as that they should not know what to do without them—the claims of an opinion to be protected from public attack are rested not so much on its truth as on its importance to society. There are, it is alleged, certain beliefs so useful, not to say indispensable, to well-being that it is as much the duty of governments to uphold those beliefs as to protect any other of the interests of society. . . . The usefulness of an opinion is itself [a] matter of opinion—as disputable, as open to discussion, and requiring discussion as much as the opinion itself. There is the same need of an infallible judge of opinions to decide an opinion to be noxious as to decide it to be false, unless the opinion condemned has full opportunity of defending itself. And it will not do to say that the heretic may be allowed to maintain the utility or harmlessness of his opinion, though forbidden to maintain its truth. The truth of an opinion is part of its utility. If we would know whether or not it is desirable that a proposition should be believed, is it possible to exclude the consideration of whether or not it is true? In the opinion, not of bad men, but of the best men, no belief which is contrary to truth can be really useful. . . .

The dictum that truth always triumphs over persecution is one of those pleasant falsehoods which men repeat after one another till they pass into commonplaces, but which all experience refutes. History teems with instances of truth put down by persecution. If not suppressed forever, it may be thrown back for centuries. To speak only of religious opinions: the Reformation broke out at least twenty times before Luther, and was put down. . . Even after the era of Luther, wherever persecution was persisted in, it was successful. . . .

Let us now pass to the second division of the argument, and dismissing the supposition that any of the received opinions may be false, let us assume them to be true and examine into the worth of the manner in which they are likely to be held when their truth is not freely and openly canvassed. However unwillingly a person who has a strong opinion may admit the possibility that his opinion may be false, he ought to be moved by the consideration that, however true it may be, if it is not fully, frequently, and fearlessly discussed, it will be held as a dead dogma, not a living truth. . . .

If the cultivation of the understanding consists in one thing more than in another, it is surely in learning the grounds of one's own opinions. Whatever people believe, on subjects on which it is of the first importance to believe rightly, they ought to be able to defend against at least the common objections. . . . On every subject on which difference of opinion is possible, the truth depends on a balance to be struck between two sets of conflicting reasons. Even in natural philosophy, there is always some other explanation possible of the same facts; some geocentric theory instead of heliocentric, some phlogiston instead of oxygen; and it has to be shown why that other theory cannot be the true one; and until this is shown, and until we know how it is shown, we do not understand the grounds of our opinion. But when we turn to subjects infinitely more complicated, to morals, religion, politics, social relations, and the business of life, three-fourths of the arguments for every disputed opinion consist in dispelling the appearances which favor some opinion different from it. . . . Nor is it enough that he should hear the arguments of adversaries from his own teachers, presented as they state them, and accompanied by what they offer as refutations. That is not the way to do justice to the arguments or bring them into real contact with his own mind. He must be able to hear them from persons who actually believe them, who defend them in earnest and do their very utmost for them. He must know them in their most plausible and persuasive form; he must feel the whole force of the difficulty which the true view of the subject has to encounter and dispose of, else he will never really possess himself of the portion of truth which meets and removes that difficulty. . . .

The fact . . . is that not only the grounds of the opinion are forgotten in the absence of discussion, but too often the meaning of the opinion itself. The words which convey it cease to suggest ideas, or suggest only a small portion of those they were originally employed to communicate. Instead of a vivid conception and a living belief, there remain only a few phrases retained by rote; or, if any part, the shell and husk only of the meanings is retained, the finer essence being lost. The great chapter in human history which this fact occupies and fills cannot be too earnestly studied and meditated on.

It is illustrated in the experience of almost all ethical doctrines and religious creeds. They are all full of meaning and vitality to those who originate them, and to the direct disciples of the originators. Their meaning continues to be felt in undiminished strength, and is perhaps brought out into even fuller consciousness, so long as the struggle lasts to give the doctrine or creed an ascendancy over other creeds. . . .

We have hitherto considered only two possibilities: that the received opinion may be false, and some other opinion, consequently, true; or that, the received opinion being true, a conflict with the opposite error is essential to a clear apprehension and deep feeling of its truth. But there is a commoner case than either of these: when the conflicting doctrines, instead of being one true and the other false, shared the truth between them, and the nonconforming opinion is needed to supply the remainder of the truth of which the received doctrine embodies only a part. Popular opinions, on subjects not palpable to sense, are often true, but seldom or never the whole truth. They are a part of the truth, sometimes a greater, sometimes a smaller part, but exaggerated, distorted, and disjointed from the truths by which they ought to be accompanied and limited. Heretical opinions, on the other hand, are generally some of these suppressed and neglected truths, bursting the bonds which kept them down, and either seeking reconciliation with the truth contained in the common opinion, or fronting it as enemies, and setting themselves up, with similar exclusiveness, as the whole truth. The latter case is hitherto the most frequent, as, in the human mind, onesidedness has always been the rule, and many-sidedness the exception. Hence, even in revolutions of opinion, one part of the truth usually sets while another rises. Even progress, which ought to superadd, for the most part only substitutes one partial and incomplete truth for another; improvement consisting chiefly in this, that the new fragment of truth is more wanted, more adapted to the needs of the time than that which it displaces. Such being the partial character of prevailing opinions, even when resting on a true foundation, every opinion which embodies somewhat of the portion of truth which the common opinion omits ought to be considered precious, with whatever amount of error and confusion that truth may be blended. . . .

We have now recognized the necessity to the mental well-being of mankind (on which all their other well-being depends) of freedom of opinion, and freedom of the expression of opinion, on four distinct grounds, which we will now briefly recapitulate:

First, if any opinion is compelled to silence, that opinion may, for aught we can certainly know, be true. To deny this is to assume our own infallibility.

Secondly, although the silenced opinion be an error, it may, and very commonly does, contain a portion of truth; and since the general or prevailing opinion on any subjects is rarely or never the whole truth, it is only by the collision of adverse opinions that the remainder of the truth has any chance of being supplied.

Thirdly, even if the received opinion be not only true, but the whole truth; unless it is suffered to be, and actually is, vigorously and earnestly contested, it will, by most of those who receive it, be held in the manner of a prejudice, with little comprehension or feeling of its rational grounds. And not only this, but fourthly, the meaning of the doctrine itself will be in danger of being lost or enfeebled, and deprived of its vital effect on the character and conduct: the dogma becoming a mere formal profession, inefficacious for good, but cumbering the ground and preventing the growth of any real and heartfelt conviction from reason or personal experience. . . .

Before quitting the subject of freedom of opinion, it is fit to take some notice of those who say that the free expression of all opinions should be permitted on condition that the manner be temperate, and do not pass the bounds of fair discussion. Much might be said on the impossibility of fixing where these supposed bounds are to be placed; for if the test be offense to those whose opinions are attacked, I think experience testifies that this offense is given whenever the attack is telling and powerful, and that every opponent who pushes them hard, and whom they find it difficult to answer, appears to them, if he shows any strong feeling on the subject, an intemperate opponent. . . . With regard to what is commonly meant by intemperate discussion, namely invective, sarcasm, personality, and the like, the denunciation of these weapons would deserve more sympathy if it were ever proposed to interdict them equally to both sides; but it is only desired to restrain the employment of them against the prevailing opinion; against the unprevailing they may not only be used without general disapproval, but will be likely to obtain for him who uses them the praise of honest zeal and righteous indignation. Yet whatever mischief arises from their use is greatest when they are employed against the comparatively defenseless; and whatever unfair advantage can be derived by any opinion from this mode of asserting it accrues almost exclusively to received opinions. . . . In general, opinions contrary to these commonly received can only obtain a hearing by studied moderation of language, and the most cautious avoidance of unnecessary offense, from which they hardly ever deviate even in a slight degree without losing ground; while unmeasured vituperation employed on the side of the prevailing opinion really does deter people from professing contrary opinions, and from listening to those who profess them. For the interest, therefore, of truth and justice, it is far more important to restrain this employment of vituperative language than the other; and, for example, if it were necessary to choose, there would be much more need to discourage offensive attacks on infidelity than on religion. It is, however, obvious that law and authority have no business restraining either, while opinion ought, in every instance, to determine its verdict by the circumstances of the individual case; condemning everyone, on whichever side of the argument he places himself, in whose mode of advocacy either want of candor, or malignity, bigotry, or intolerance of feeling manifest themselves; but not inferring these vices from the side which a person takes, though it be the contrary side of the question of our own; and giving merited honor to everyone, whatever opinion he may hold, who has calmness to see the honesty to state what his opponents and their opinions really are, exaggerating nothing to their discredit, keeping nothing back which tells or can be supposed to tell, in their favor. This is the real morality of public discussion; and if often violated, I am happy to think that there are many controversialists who to a great extent observe it, and a still greater number who conscientiously strive towards it. . . .

OF THE LIMITS TO THE AUTHORITY OF SOCIETY OVER THE INDIVIDUAL

What, then, is the rightful limit to the sovereignty of the individual over himself? Where does the authority of society begin? How much of human life should be assigned to individuality, and how much to society?

Each will receive its proper share, if each has that which more particularly concerns it. To individuality should belong the part of life in which it is chiefly the individual that is interested; to society, the part which chiefly interests society.

Though society is not founded on a contract, and though no good purpose is answered by inventing a contract in order to deduce social obligations from it, everyone who receives the protection of society owes a return for the benefit, and the fact of living in society renders it indispensable that each should be bound to observe a certain line of conduct towards the rest. This conduct consists, *first*, in not injuring the interests of one another; or rather certain interests, which either by express legal provision or by tacit understanding, ought to be considered as rights; and *secondly*, in each person's bearing his share (to be fixed on some equitable principle) of the labors and sacrifices incurred for defending the society or its members from injury and molestation. These conditions society is justified in enforcing, at all costs to those who endeavor to withhold fulfillment. Nor is this all that society may do. The acts of an individual may be hurtful to others, or wanting in due consideration for their welfare, without going to the length of violating any of their constituted rights. The offender may then be justly punished by opinion, though not by law. As soon as any part of a person's conduct affects prejudicially the interests of others, society has jurisdiction over it, and the question whether the general welfare will or will not be promoted by interfering with it, becomes open to discussion. But there is no room for entertaining any such question when a person's conduct affects the interests of no persons besides himself, or need not affect them unless they like (all the persons concerned being of full age, and the ordinary amount of understanding). In all such cases, there should be perfect freedom, legal and social, to do the action and stand the consequences.

It would be a great misunderstanding of this doctrine to suppose that it is one of selfish indifference, which pretends that human beings have no business with each other's conduct in life, and that they should not concern themselves about the well-doing or well-being of one another, unless their own interest is involved. Instead of any diminution, there is need of a great increase of disinterested exertion to promote the good of others. But disinterested benevolence can find other instruments to persuade people to their good than whips and scourges, either of the literal or the metaphorical sort. I am the last person to undervalue the self-regarding virtues: they are only second in importance, if even second, to the social. It is equally the business of education to cultivate both. But even education works by conviction and persuasion as well as by compulsion, and it is by the former only that, when the period of education is passed, the self-regarding virtues should be inculcated. Human beings owe to each other help to distinguish the better from the worse, and encouragement to choose the former and avoid the latter. They should be forever stimulating each other to increased exercise of their higher faculties, and increased direction of their feelings and aims towards wise instead of foolish, elevating instead of degrading, objects and contemplations. But neither one person, nor any number of persons, is warranted in saying to another human creature of ripe years, that he shall not do with his life for his own benefit what he chooses to do with it. He is the person most interested in his own well-being: the interest which any other person, except in cases of strong personal attachment, can have in it, is trifling, compared with that which he himself has; the interest which society has in him individually (except as to conduct to others) is fractional, and altogether indirect; while with respect to his own feelings and circumstances, the most ordinary man or woman has means of knowledge immeasurably surpassing those that can be possessed by anyone else. The interference of society to overrule his judgment and purposes in what only regards himself must be grounded on general presumptions; which may be altogether wrong, and even if right, are as likely as not to be misapplied to individual cases, by person no better acquainted with the circumstances of such cases than those who look at them merely from without. In this department, therefore, of human affairs, individuality has its proper field of action. In the conduct of human beings towards one another it is necessary that general rules should for the most part be observed, in order that people may know what they have to expect; but in each person's own concerns his individual spontaneity is entitled to free exercise. Considerations to aid his judgment, exhortations to strengthen his will, may be offered to him, even obtruded on him, by others: but he himself is the final judge. All errors which he is likely to commit against advice and warning are far outweighed by the evil of allowing others to constrain him to what they deem his good. . . . .

Though doing no wrong to anyone, a person may so act as to compel us to judge him, and feel to him, as a fool, or as a being of an inferior order; and since this judgment and feeling are a fact which he would prefer to avoid, it is doing him a service to warn him of it beforehand, as of any other disagreeable consequence to which he exposes himself. . . . We have a right, also, in various ways, to act upon our unfavorable opinion of anyone, not to the oppression of his individuality, but in the exercise of ours. We are not bound, for example, to seek his society; we have a right to avoid it (though not to parade the avoidance), for we have a right to choose the society most acceptable to us. We have a right, and it may be our duty, to caution others against him, if we think his example or conversation likely to have a pernicious effect on those with whom he associates. We may give others a preference over him in optional good offices, except those which tend to his improvement. In these various modes a person may suffer very severe penalties at the hands of others for faults which directly concern only himself; but he suffers these penalties only in so far as they are the natural and, as it were, the spontaneous consequences of the faults themselves, not because they are purposely inflicted on him for the sake of punishment. . . .

What I contend for is, that the inconveniences which are strictly inseparable from the unfavorable judgment of others, are the only ones to which a person should ever be subjected for that portion of his conduct and character which concerns his own good, but which does not affect the interest of others in their relations with him. Acts injurious to others require a totally different treatment. Encroachment on their rights; infliction on them of any loss or damage not justified by his own rights; falsehood or duplicity in dealing with them; unfair or ungenerous use of advantages over them; even selfish abstinence from defending them against injury—these are fit objects of moral reprobation, and, in grave cases, of moral retribution and punishment. And not only these acts, but the dispositions which lead to them, are properly immoral, and fit subjects of disapprobation which may rise to abhorrence. . . .

The distinction here pointed out between the part of a person's life which concerns only himself, and that which concerns others, many persons will refuse to admit. How (it may be asked) can any part of the conduct of a member of society be a matter of indifference to the other members? No person is an entirely isolated being; it is impossible for a person to do anything seriously or permanently hurtful to himself, without mischief reaching at least to his near connections, and often far beyond them. If he injures his property, he does harm to those who directly or indirectly derived support from it, and usually diminishes, by a greater or less amount, the general resources of the community. If he deteriorates his bodily or mental faculties, he not only brings evil upon

all who depended on him for any portion of their happiness, but disqualifies himself for rendering the services which he owes to his fellow-creatures generally; perhaps becomes a burden on their affection or benevolence; and if such conduct were very frequent, hardly an offense that is committed would detract more from the general sum of good. Finally, if by his vices or follies a person does no direct harm to others, he is nevertheless (it may be said) injurious by his example; and ought to be compelled to control himself, for the sake of those whom the sight or knowledge of his conduct might corrupt or mislead.

And even (it will be added) if the consequences of misconduct could be confined to the vicious or thoughtless individual, ought society to abandon to their own guidance those who are manifestly unfit for it? If protection against themselves is confessedly due to children and persons under age, is not society equally bound to afford it to persons of mature years who are equally incapable of self-government? If gambling, or drunkenness, or incontinence, or idleness, or uncleanliness, are as injurious to happiness, and as great a hindrance to improvement, as many or most of the acts prohibited by law, why (it may be asked) should not law, so far as is consistent with practicability and social convenience, endeavor to repress these also? . . .

I fully admit that the mischief which a person does to himself may seriously affect, both through their sympathies and their interests, those nearly connected with him and, in a minor degree, society at large. When, by conduct of this sort, a person is led to violate a distinct and assignable obligation to any other person or persons, the case is taken out of the self-regarding class and becomes amenable to moral disapprobation in the proper sense of the term. If, for example, a man, through intemperance or extravagance, becomes unable to pay his debts, or, having undertaken the moral responsibility of a family, becomes from the same cause incapable of supporting or educating them, he is deservedly reprobated, and might be justly punished; but it is for the breach of duty to his family or creditors, not for the extravagance. . . . No person ought to be punished simply for being drunk; but a soldier or policeman should be punished for being drunk on duty. Whenever, in short, there is a definite damage, or a definite risk of damage, either to an individual or to the public, the case is taken out of the province of liberty and placed in that of morality or law.

But with regard to the merely contingent or, as it may be called, constructive injury which a person causes to society by conduct which neither violates any specific duty to the public, nor occasions perceptible hurt to any assignable individual except himself, the inconvenience is one which society can afford to bear, for the sake of the greater good of human freedom. If grown persons are to be punished for not taking proper care of themselves, I would rather it were for their own sake than under pretense of preventing them from impairing their capacity or rendering to society benefits which society does not pretend it has a right to exact. But I cannot consent to argue the point as if society had no means of bringing its weaker members up to its ordinary standard of rational conduct, except waiting till they do something irrational, and then punishing them, legally or morally, for it. Society has had absolute power over them during all the early portion of their existence; it has had the whole period of childhood and nonage in which to try whether it could make them capable of rational conduct in life. The existing generation is master both of the training and the entire circumstances of the generation to come; it cannot indeed make them perfectly wise and good, because it is itself so lamentably deficient in goodness and wisdom; and its best efforts are not always, in individual cases, its most successful ones; but it is perfectly well able to make the rising generation, as a whole, as good as, and a little better than, itself. If society lets any considerable number of its members grow up mere children, incapable of being acted on by rational consideration of distant motives, society has itself to blame for the consequences. Armed not only with all the powers of education, but with the ascendency which the authority of a received opinion always exercises over the minds who are least fitted to judge for themselves, and aided by the *natural* penalties which cannot be prevented from falling on those who incur the distaste or

the contempt of those who know them—let not society pretend that it needs, besides all this, the power to issue commands and enforce obedience in the personal concerns of individuals in which, on all principles of justice and policy, the decision ought to rest with those who are to abide the consequences. Nor is there anything which tends more to discredit and frustrate the better means of influencing conduct than a resort to the worse. If there be among those whom it is attempted to coerce into prudence or temperance any of the material of which vigorous and independent characters are made, they will infallibly rebel against the yoke. No such person will ever feel that others have a right to control him in his concerns, such as they have to prevent him from injuring them in theirs; and it easily comes to be considered a mark of spirit and courage to fly in the face of such usurped authority and do with ostentation the exact opposite of what it enjoins, as in the fashion of grossness which succeeded, in the time of Charles II, to the fanatical moral intolerance of the Puritans. With respect to what is said of the necessity of protecting society from the bad example set to others by the vicious or the self-indulgent, it is true that bad example may have a pernicious effect, especially the example of doing wrong to others with impunity to the wrongdoer. But we are now speaking of conduct which, while it does no wrong to others, is supposed to do great harm to the agent himself; and I do not see how those who believe this can think otherwise than that the example, on the whole, must be more salutary than hurtful since, if it displays the misconduct, it displays also the painful or degrading consequences which, if the conduct is justly censured, must be supposed to be in all or more cases attendant on it.

But the strongest of all the argument against the interference of the public with purely personal conduct is that, when it does interfere, the odds are that it interferes wrongly and in the wrong place. On questions of social morality, of duty to others, the opinion of the public, that is, of an overruling majority, though often wrong, is likely to be still oftener right, because on such questions they are only required to judge of their own interests, of the manner in which some mode of conduct, if allowed to be practiced, would affect themselves. But the opinion of a similar majority, imposed as a law on the minority, on questions of self-regarding conduct is quite as likely to be wrong as right, for in these cases public opinion means, at the best, some people's opinion of what is good or bad for other people, while very often it does not even mean that—the public, with the most perfect indifference, passing over the pleasure or convenience of those whose conduct they censure and considering only their own preference. There are many who consider as an injury to themselves any conduct which they have a distaste for, and resent it as an outrage to their feelings; as a religious bigot, when charged with disregarding the religious feelings of others, has been known to retort that they disregard his feelings by persisting in their abomitable worship or creed. But there is no parity between the feeling of a person for his own opinion and the feeling of another who is offended at his holding it, no more than between the desire of a thief to take a purse and the desire of the right owner to keep it. And a person's taste is as much his own peculiar concern as his opinion or his purse.

REVIEW AND DISCUSSION QUESTIONS

1. What values or purposes does Mill think are served by freedom of speech?

2. Why does Mill think even false speech should be tolerated or even encouraged?

3. Explain why Mill thinks those who would censor speech are assuming, falsely, they are "infallible."

4. How does Mill respond to those who say that "offensive" speech may be banned?

5. Suppose somebody defends censorship of Nazi speech based on the risk that they will eventually gain power, as occurred in post–World War I Germany. How could Mill respond to such an argument? Is that response sound?

6. Mill argues that the good life involves more than mere contentment. What else, specifically, does true well-being consist in?

7. How does Mill think most people make decisions about how they will live their lives?

8. Mill admits many acts may affect others but insists that unless they also "harm" them government may not intervene. How does Mill define "harm"?

9. Describe how Mill thinks society *may* try to influence people whose actions are harmless, yet either immoral or not in their true interest.

10. What reasons does Mill give to support his claim that harming others is necessary to justify punishment?

11. Sometimes, Mill says, society is wise not to interfere even though an act *is* harmful to another. Give an example of such an act, then explain why Mill thinks society should nevertheless not interfere.

Foundations of Free Speech

Schenck v. United States and Whitney v. California

In the following two opinions, Justices Oliver Wendell Holmes and Louis Brandeis set out what is known as the "clear and present danger test" and articulated the rationale behind the First Amendment's guarantees of freedom of speech and the press. The influence of these opinions can hardly be overstated; they constitute the philosophical and political basis of subsequent debate over the justification and limits of freedom of speech.

In this first case, Schenck was convicted of violating the 1917 Espionage Act by "causing or attempting to cause insubordination in the military" when he mailed fifteen thousand antiwar leaflets to potential draftees. Though Holmes wrote the opinion of the Court upholding the conviction, the principle he relied on—the clear and present danger test—became the basis of later debate over the meaning of the First Amendment.

Schenck v. United States

Justice Holmes delivered the opinion of the Court:

The document in question upon its first printed side recited the first section of the Thirteenth Amendment [forbidding slavery], said that the idea embodied in it was violated by the Conscription Act and that a conscript is little better than a convict. In impassioned language it intimated that conscription was despotism in its worst form and a monstrous wrong against humanity in the interest of Wall Street's chosen few. It said "Do not submit to intimidation," but in form at least confined itself to peaceful measures such as a petition for the repeal of the act. The other . . . side of the sheet was headed "Assert Your Rights." It stated reasons for alleging that any one violated the Constitution when he refused to recognize "your right to assert your opposition to the draft," and went on "If you do not assert and support your rights, you are helping to deny or disparage rights which it is the solemn duty of all citizens and residents of the United States to retain." It described the arguments on the other side as coming from cunning politicians and a mercenary capitalist law as helping to support an infamous conspiracy. It

denied the power to send our citizens away to foreign shores to shoot up the people of other lands, and added that words could not express the condemnation such cold-blooded ruthlessness deserves, &c., &c., winding up "You must do your share to maintain, support and uphold the rights of the people of this country." Of course the document would not have been sent unless it had been intended to have some effect, and we do not see what effect it could be expected to have upon persons subject to the draft except to influence them to obstruct the carrying of it out. The defendants do not deny that the jury might find against them on this point.

But it is said, suppose that was the tendency of this circular, it is protected by the First Amendment. . . . Two of the strongest expressions are said to be quoted respectively from well-known public men. It well may be that the prohibition of laws abridging the freedom of speech is not confined to previous restraints, although to prevent them may have been the main purpose. . . . We admit that in many places and in ordinary times the defendants in saying all that was said in the circular would have been within their constitutional rights. But the character of every act depends upon the circumstances in which it is done. The most stringent protection of free speech would not protect a

_____
249 U.S. 47 (1919). Citations omitted.

man in falsely shouting fire in a theatre and causing a panic. It does not even protect a man from an injunction against uttering words that may have all the effect of force. The question in every case is whether the words used are used in such circumstances and are of such a nature as to create a clear and present danger that they will bring about the substantive evils that Congress has a right to prevent. It is a question of proximity and degree. When a nation is at war many things that might be said in time of peace are such a hindrance to its effort that their utter-

ance will not be endured so long as men fight and that no Court could regard them as protected by any constitutional right. It seems to be admitted that if an actual obstruction of the recruiting service were proved, liability for words that produced that effect might be enforced. The statute of 1917 . . . punishes conspiracies to obstruct as well as actual obstruction. If the act, (speaking, or circulating a paper,) its tendency and the intent with which it is done are the same, we perceive no ground for saying that success alone warrants making the act a crime. . . .

REVIEW AND DISCUSSION QUESTIONS

1. Describe what the defendants did in this case to bring about criminal prosecution of them under the Espionage Act of 1917.

2. Does the defendant's act constitute a "clear and present danger" that a 'substantive evil' will occur? Explain.

Whitney v. California

Anita Whitney had attended a Communist Party convention in California, where she offered a motion that the party seek political change through peaceful means. Nevertheless, she was convicted under California's Criminal Syndicalism Act for membership in the Communist Party. Whitney refused to rely on the First Amendment at her trial, and the Court unanimously held that she had therefore not raised any federal issue. Though he concurred in the result in this case (because she had not raised free speech as a defense), Justice Brandeis wrote a separate opinion that eloquently outlines the First Amendment's central importance to the U.S. constitutional system.

Justice Brandeis, concurring:

This Court has not yet fixed the standard by which to determine when a danger shall be deemed clear; how remote the danger may be and yet be deemed present; and what degree of evil shall be deemed sufficiently substantial to justify resort to abridgment of free speech and assembly as the means of protection. To reach sound conclusions on these matters, we must bear in mind why a State is, ordinarily, denied the power to prohibit dissemination of social, economic and political doctrine which a vast

majority of its citizens believes to be false and fraught with evil consequence.

Those who won our independence believed that the final end of the State was to make men free to develop their faculties; and that in its government the deliberative forces should prevail over the arbitrary. They valued liberty both as an end and a means. They believed liberty to be the secret of happiness and courage to be the secret of liberty. They believed that freedom to think as you will and to speak as you think are means indispensable to the discovery and spread of political truth; that without free speech and assembly discussion would be futile; that with them, discussion affords ordinarily adequate protection against the dissemination of noxious

274 U.S. 357 (1929). Citations omitted.

doctrine; that the greatest menace to freedom is an inert people; that public discussion is a political duty; and that this should be a fundamental principle of the American government. They recognized the risks to which all human institutions are subject. But they knew that order cannot be secured merely through fear of punishment for its infraction; that it is hazardous to discourage thought, hope and imagination; that fear breeds repression; that repression breeds hate; that hate menaces stable government; that the path of safety lies in the opportunity to discuss freely supposed grievances and proposed remedies; and that the fitting remedy for evil counsels is good ones. Believing in the power of reason as applied through public discussion, they eschewed silence coerced by law—the argument of force in its worst form. Recognizing the occasional tyrannies of governing majorities, they amended the Constitution so that free speech and assembly should be guaranteed.

Fear of serious injury cannot alone justify suppression of free speech and assembly. Men feared witches and burnt women. It is the function of speech to free men from the bondage of irrational fears. To justify suppression of free speech there must be reasonable ground to fear that serious evil will result if free speech is practiced. There must be reasonable ground to believe that the danger apprehended is imminent. There must be reasonable ground to believe that the evil to be prevented is a serious one. Every denunciation of existing law tends in some measure to increase the probability that there will be violation of it. Condonation of a breach enhances the probability. Expressions of approval add to the probability. Propagation of the criminal state of mind by teaching syndicalism increases it. Advocacy of lawbreaking heightens it still further. But even advocacy of violation, however reprehensible morally, is not a justification for denying free speech where the advocacy falls short of incitement and there is nothing to indicate that the advocacy would be immediately acted on. The wide difference between advocacy and incitement, between preparation and attempt, between assembling and conspiracy, must be borne in mind. In order to support a finding of clear and present danger it must be shown either that immediate serious violence was to be expected or was advocated, or that the past conduct furnished reason to believe that such advocacy was then contemplated.

Those who won our independence by revolution were not cowards. They did not fear political change. They did not exalt order at the cost of liberty. To courageous, self-reliant men, with confidence in the power of free and fearless reasoning applied through the processes of popular government, no danger flowing from speech can be deemed clear and present, unless the incidence of the evil apprehended is so imminent that it may befall before there is opportunity for full discussion. If there be time to expose through discussion the falsehood and fallacies, to avert the evil by the processes of education, the remedy to be applied is more speech, not enforced silence. Only an emergency can justify repression. Such must be the rule if authority is to be reconciled with freedom. Such, in my opinion, is the command of the Constitution. It is therefore always open to Americans by showing that there was no emergency justifying it.

Moreover, even imminent danger cannot justify resort to prohibition of these functions essential to effective democracy, unless the evil apprehended is relatively serious. Prohibition of free speech and assembly is a measure so stringent that it would be inappropriate as the means for averting a relatively trivial harm to society. A police measure may be unconstitutional merely because the remedy, although effective as means of protection, is unduly harsh or oppressive. Thus, a State might, in the exercise of its police power, make any trespass upon the land of another a crime, regardless of the results or of the intent or purpose of the trespasser. It might, also, punish an attempt, a conspiracy, or an incitement to commit the trespass. But it is hardly conceivable that this Court would hold constitutional a statute which punished as a felony the mere voluntary assembly with a society formed to teach that pedestrians had the moral right to cross unenclosed, unposted, waste lands and to advocate their doing so, even if there was imminent danger that advocacy would lead to a trespass. The fact that speech is likely to result in some violence or in destruction of property is not enough to justify its suppression. There must be the probability of serious injury to the State. Among free men, the deterrents ordinarily to be applied to prevent crime are education and punishment for violations of the law, not abridgment of the rights of free speech and assembly.

REVIEW AND DISCUSSION QUESTIONS

1. What, exactly, was Whitney convicted of in this case? What had she done to warrant the prosecution?

2. Explain the goals and principles Justice Brandeis sees lying behind the First Amendment's free speech clause.

3. Compare Justice Brandeis's discussion of the purposes of speech in *Whitney* with the views Holmes articulated. Whose theory is sounder? Explain.

Flag Burning

Texas v. Johnson

After burning the U.S. flag as an act of political protest, Gregory Lee Johnson was convicted of desecrating a flag in violation of Texas law. The state of Texas, after losing in lower courts, appealed to the U.S. Supreme Court, which had to decide whether Johnson's conviction was consistent with the First Amendment's protection of freedom of speech. By a narrow 5-to-4 vote, the Court again held that the Texas law was unconstitutional. Delivering the opinion of the Court, Justice Brennan argues that the state cannot "prescribe what shall be orthodox" by punishing symbolic actions such as flag burning. The way to preserve the flag's special role in our national life, he argues, is not to punish those who feel differently about this symbol but to persuade them that they are wrong. In their separate dissents, Justice Rehnquist and Justice Stevens reject the idea that the flag is just another symbol, toward which it would be unconstitutional to require minimal respect.

Justice Brennan:

As in *Spence* [*v. Washington*, a 1974 case on expressive conduct], "[w]e are confronted with a case of prosecution for the expression of an idea through activity," and "[a]ccordingly, we must examine with particular care the interests advanced by [petitioner] to support its prosecution." . . . Johnson was not, we add, prosecuted

for the expression of just any idea; he was prosecuted for his expression of dissatisfaction with the policies of this country, expression situated at the core of our First Amendment values.

Moreover, Johnson was prosecuted because he knew that his politically charged expression would cause "serious offense." If he had burned the flag as a means of disposing of it because it was dirty or torn, he would not have been convicted of flag desecration under this Texas law: federal law designates burning as the preferred

57 L. W. 4770 (1989).

means of disposing of a flag "when it is in such condition that it is no longer a fitting emblem for display." . . .

If we are to hold that a state may forbid flag-burning wherever it is likely to endanger the flag's symbolic role, but allow it wherever burning a flag promotes that role—as where, for example, a person ceremoniously burns a dirty flag—we would be saying that when it comes to impairing the flag's physical integrity, the flag itself may be used as a symbol—as a substitute for the written or spoken word or a "short cut from mind to mind"—only in one direction. We would be permitting a state to "prescribe what shall be orthodox" by saying that one may burn the flag to convey one's attitude toward it and its referents only if one does not endanger the flag's representation of nationhood and national unity.

We never before have held that the government may ensure that a symbol be used to express only one view of that symbol or its referents. . . .

We are fortified in today's conclusion by our conviction that forbidding criminal punishment for conduct such as Johnson's will not endanger the special role played by our flag or the feelings it inspires. To paraphrase Justice [Oliver Wendell] Holmes, we submit that nobody can suppose that this one gesture of an unknown man will change our nation's attitude towards its flag. . . . Indeed, Texas's argument that the burning of an American flag " 'is an act having a high likelihood to cause a breach of peace,' " . . . and its statute's implicit assumption that physical mistreatment of the flag will lead to "serious offense," tend to confirm that the flag's special role is not in danger; if it were, no one would riot or take offense because a flag had been burned.

We are tempted to say, in fact, that the flag's deservedly cherished place in our community will be strengthened, not weakened, by our holding today. Our decision is a reaffirmation of the principles of freedom and inclusiveness that the flag best reflects, and of the conviction that our toleration of criticism such as Johnson's is a sign and source of our strength. Indeed, one of the proudest images of our flag,

the one immortalized in our own national anthem, is of the bombardment it survived at Fort McHenry. It is the nation's resilience, not its rigidity, that Texas sees reflected in the flag—and it is that resilience that we reassert today.

The way to preserve the flag's special role is not to punish those who feel differently about these matters. It is to persuade them that they are wrong. "To courageous, self-reliant men, with confidence in the power of free and fearless reasoning applied through the processes of popular government, no danger flowing from speech can be deemed clear and present, unless the incidence of the evil apprehended is so imminent that it may befall before there is opportunity for full discussion. If there be time to expose through discussion the falsehood and fallacies, to avert the evil by the processes of education, the remedy to be applied is more speech, not enforced silence." . . . And, precisely because it is our flag that is involved, one's response to the flag-burner may exploit the uniquely persuasive power of the flag itself. We can imagine no more appropriate response to burning a flag than waving one's own, no better way to counter a flag-burner's message than by saluting the flag that burns, no surer means of preserving the dignity even of the flag that burned than by—as one witness here did—according its remains a respectful burial. We do not consecrate the flag by punishing its desecration, for in doing so we dilute the freedom that this cherished emblem represents.

Johnson was convicted for engaging in expressive conduct. The state's interest in preventing breaches of the peace does not support his conviction because Johnson's conduct did not threaten to disturb the peace. Nor does the state's interest in preserving the flag as a symbol of nationhood and national unity justify his criminal conviction for engaging in political expression. The judgment of the Texas Court of Criminal Appeals is therefore affirmed.

Justice Rehnquist, Dissenting:

In holding this Texas statute unconstitutional, the court ignores Justice Holmes's familiar aphorism that "a page of history is worth a volume of logic." . . . For more than 200 years, the American flag has occupied a unique position as the symbol of our nation, a uniqueness that justifies a governmental prohibition against flag burning in the way respondent Johnson did here. . . .

In the First and Second World Wars, thousands of our countrymen died on foreign soil fighting for the American cause. At Iwo Jima in the Second World War, United States Marines fought hand-to-hand against thousands of Japanese. By the time the Marines reached the top of Mount Suribachi, they raised a piece of pipe upright and from one end fluttered a flag. That ascent had cost nearly 6,000 American lives. . . .

During the Korean War, the successful amphibious landing of American troops at Inchon was marked by the raising of an American flag within an hour of the event. . . .

The government is simply recognizing as a fact the profound regard for the American flag created by that history when it enacts statutes prohibiting the disrespectful public burning of the flag.

The court concludes its opinion with a regrettably patronizing civics lecture, presumably addressed to members of both houses of Congress, the members of the 48 state legislatures that enacted prohibitions against flag burning and the troops fighting under that flag in Vietnam who objected to its being burned: "The way to preserve the flag's special role is not to punish those who feel differently about these matters. It is to persuade them that they are wrong." . . .

The court's role as the final expositor of the Constitution is well established, but its role as a platonic guardian admonishing those responsible to public opinion as if they were truant school children has no similar place in our system of government. The cry of "no taxation without representation" animated those who revolted against the English crown to found our nation—the idea that those who submitted to government should have some say as to what kind of laws would be passed. Surely one of the high purposes of a democratic society is to legislate against conduct that is regarded as evil and profoundly offensive to the majority of people—whether it be murder, embezzlement, pollution or flag burning.

Our Constitution wisely places limits on powers of legislative majorities to act, but the declaration of such limits by this court "is, at all times, a question of much delicacy, which ought seldom, if ever, to be decided in the affirmative, in a doubtful case." . . . Uncritical extension of constitutional protection to the burning of the flag risks the frustration of the very purpose for which organized governments are instituted. The court decides that the American flag is just another symbol, about which not only must opinions pro and con be tolerated, but for which the most minimal public respect may not be enjoined. The government may conscript men into the armed forces where they must fight and perhaps die for the flag, but the government may not prohibit the public burning of the banner under which they fight. I would uphold the Texas statute as applied in this case.

Justice Stevens, Dissenting:

As the court analyzes this case, it presents the question whether the state of Texas, or indeed the federal government, has the power to prohibit the public desecration of the American flag. The question is unique. In my judgment, rules that apply to a host of other symbols, such as state flags, armbands or various privately promoted emblems of political or commercial identity, are not necessarily controlling. Even if flag burning could be considered just another species of symbolic speech under the logical application of the rules that the court has developed in its interpretation of the First Amendment in other contexts, this case has an intangible dimension that makes those rules inapplicable.

A country's flag is a symbol of more than "nationhood and national unity." . . . It also signifies the ideas that characterize the society that has chosen that emblem as well as the special history that has animated the growth and power of those ideas. The fleurs-de-lis and the tricolor both symbolized "nationhood and national unity," but they had vastly different meanings. The message conveyed by some flags—the swastika, for example—may survive long after it has outlived its usefulness as a symbol of regimented unity in a particular nation.

So it is with the American flag. It is more than a proud symbol of the courage, the determination and the gifts of nature that transformed 13 fledgling colonies into a world power. It is a symbol of freedom, of equal opportunity, of religious tolerance and of goodwill for other peoples who share our aspirations. The symbol carries its message to dissidents both at home and abroad who may have no interest at all in our national unity or survival.

The value of the flag as a symbol cannot be measured. Even so, I have no doubt that the interest in preserving that value for the future is both significant and legitimate. Conceivably that value will be enhanced by the court's conclusion that our national commitment to free expression is so strong that even the United States as ultimate guarantor of that freedom is without power to prohibit the desecration of its unique symbol. But I am unpersuaded. . . .

The case has nothing to do with "disagreeable ideas." . . . it involves disagreeable conduct that, in my opinion, diminishes the value of an important national asset.

The court is therefore quite wrong in blandly asserting that respondent "was prosecuted for his expression of dissatisfaction with the policies of this country, expression situated at the core of our First Amendment values." . . . Respondent was prosecuted because of the method he chose to express his dissatisfaction with those policies. Had he chosen to spray paint—or perhaps convey with a motion picture projector—his message of dissatisfaction on the facade of the Lincoln Memorial, there would be no question about the power of the government to prohibit his means of expression. The prohibition would be supported by the legitimate interest in preserving the quality of an important national asset. Though the asset at stake in this case is intangible, given its unique value, the same interest supports a prohibition on the desecration of the American flag.

The ideas of liberty and equality have been an irresistible force in motivating leaders like Patrick Henry, Susan B. Anthony and Abraham Lincoln, schoolteachers like Nathan Hale and Booker T. Washington, the Philippine Scouts who fought at Bataan, and the soldiers who scaled the bluff at Omaha Beach. If those ideas are worth fighting for—and our history demonstrates that they are—it cannot be true that the flag that uniquely symbolizes their power is not itself worthy of protection from unnecessary desecration.

I respectfully dissent.

REVIEW AND DISCUSSION QUESTIONS

1. What does Texas argue is the danger in allowing flag burning?

2. What is the "fixed star" in our constitutional system that Justice Brennan argues is at the heart of this issue?

3. Why, according to Justice Brennan, might allowing such political protests actually *increase* people's sense of patriotism?

4. Why does Justice Rehnquist think government is justified in prohibiting flag burning?

5. On what basis does Justice Stevens dissent?

6. How might it be argued that preventing flag burning is *not* tantamount to establishing political orthodoxy?

Nazi Marches

Village of Skokie v. National Socialist Party

Skokie, Illinois, was the home of more than forty thousand Jews and five to seven thousand survivors of Nazi concentration camps. When the National Socialist Party (the American Nazi Party) tried to march in Skokie, the village won an injunction preventing various forms of conduct. An appeals court modified that injunction but allowed the ban on displaying the swastika to stand. Here the Supreme Court of Illinois considers an appeal by the Nazi leader, Frank Collin, of the lower court's ban. (The U.S. Supreme Court later refused to reconsider this decision of the Illinois Supreme Court.)

Per Curiam:

[D]efendant Frank Collin, who testified that he was "party leader," stated that on or about March 20, 1977, he sent officials of the plaintiff village a letter stating that the party members and supporters would hold a peaceable, public assembly in the village on May 1, 1977, to protest the Skokie Park District's requirement that the party procure $350,000 of insurance prior to the party's use of the Skokie public parks for public assemblies. The demonstration was to begin at 3 P.M., last 20 to 30 minutes, and consist of 30 to 50 demonstrators marching in single file, back and forth, in front of the village hall. The marchers were to wear uniforms which include a swastika emblem or armband. They were to carry a party banner containing a swastika emblem and signs containing such statements as "White Free Speech," "Free Speech for the White Man," and "Free Speech for White America." The demonstrators would not distribute handbills, make any derogatory statements directed to any ethnic or religious group, or obstruct traffic. They would co-operate with any reasonable police instructions or requests.

At the hearing on plaintiff's motion for an "emergency injunction" a resident of Skokie testified that he was a survivor of the Nazi holocaust. He further testified that the Jewish community in and around Skokie feels the purpose of the march in the "heart of the Jewish population" is to remind the two million sur-

vivors "that we are not through with you" and to show "that the Nazi threat is not over, it can happen again." Another resident of Skokie testified that as the result of defendants' announced intention to march in Skokie, 15 to 18 Jewish organizations, within the village and surrounding area, were called and a counterdemonstration of an estimated 12,000 to 15,000 people was scheduled for the same day. There was opinion evidence that defendants' planned demonstration in Skokie would result in violence. . . .

In defining the constitutional rights of the parties who come before this court, we are, of course, bound by the pronouncements of the United States Supreme Court in its interpretation of the United States Constitution. The decisions of that court, particularly *Cohen v. California* . . . in our opinion compel us to permit the demonstration as proposed, including display of the swastika.

"It is firmly settled that under our Constitution the public expression of ideas may not be prohibited merely because the ideas are themselves offensive to some of their hearers" . . . and it is entirely clear that the wearing of distinctive clothing can be symbolic expression of a thought or philosophy. The symbolic expression of thought falls within the free speech clause of the first amendment . . . and the plaintiff village has the heavy burden of justifying the imposition of a prior restraint upon defendants' right to freedom of speech. . . . The village of Skokie seeks to meet this burden by application of the "fighting words" doctrine first enunciated in *Chaplinsky v. New Hampshire* (1942). . . . That doctrine was designed to

---

373 N.E. 2d 21 (Ill. 1978).

permit punishment of extremely hostile personal communication likely to cause immediate physical response, "no words being 'forbidden except such as have a direct tendency to cause acts of violence by the persons to whom, individually, the remark is addressed.'" . . . In *Cohen* the Supreme Court restated the description of fighting words as "those personally abusive epithets which, when addressed to the ordinary citizen, are, as a matter of common knowledge, inherently likely to provoke violent reaction," . . . Plaintiff urges, and the appellate court has held, that the exhibition of the Nazi symbol, the swastika, addresses to ordinary citizens a message which is tantamount to fighting words. Plaintiff further asks this court to extend *Chaplinsky*, which upheld a statute punishing the use of such words, and hold that the fighting-words doctrine permits a prior restraint on defendants' symbolic speech. In our judgment we are precluded from doing so.

In *Cohen*, defendant's conviction stemmed from wearing a jacket bearing the words "Fuck the Draft" in a Los Angeles County courthouse corridor. The Supreme Court for reasons we believe applicable here refused to find that the jacket inscription constituted fighting words. That court stated:

> The constitutional right of free expression is powerful medicine in a society as diverse and populous as ours. It is designed and intended to remove government restraints from the arena of public discussion, putting the decision as to what views shall be voiced largely into the hands of each of us, in the hope that use of such freedom will ultimately produce a more capable citizenry and more perfect polity and in the belief that no other approach would comport with the premise of individual dignity and choice upon which our political system rests. . . .
>
> To many, the immediate consequence of this freedom may often appear to be only verbal tumult, discord, and even offensive utterance. These are, however, within established limits, in truth necessary side effects of the broader enduring values which the process of open debate permits us to achieve. That the air may at times seem filled with verbal cacophony is, in this sense not a sign of weakness but of strength. We cannot lose sight of the fact that, in what otherwise might seem a trifling and annoying instance of individual distasteful abuse of a privilege, these fundamental societal values are truly implicated. . . . "[S]o long as the means are peaceful, the communication need not meet standards of acceptability." . . .

Against this perception of the constitutional policies involved, we discern certain more particularized considerations that peculiarly call for reversal of this conviction. First, the principle contended for by the State seems inherently boundless. How is one to distinguish this from any other offensive word [emblem]? Surely the State has no right to cleanse public debate to the point where it is grammatically palatable to the most squeamish among us. Yet no readily ascertainable general principle exists for stopping short of that result were we to affirm the judgment below. For, while the particular four letter word [emblem] being litigated here is perhaps more distasteful than most others of its genre, it is nevertheless often true that one man's vulgarity is another's lyric. Indeed, we think it is largely because governmental officials cannot make principled distinctions in this area that the Constitution leaves matters of taste and style so largely to the individual. . . .

Finally, and in the same vein, we cannot indulge the facile assumption that one can forbid particular words without also running a substantial risk of suppressing ideas in the process. Indeed, governments might soon seize upon the censorship of particular words [emblems] as a convenient guise for banning the expression of unpopular views. We have been able, as noted above, to discern little social benefit that might result from running the risk of opening the door to such grave results. . . .

The display of the swastika, as offensive to the principles of a free nation as the memories it recalls may be, is symbolic political speech intended to convey to the public the beliefs of those who display it. It does not, in our opinion, fall within the definition of "fighting words," and that doctrine cannot be used here to overcome the heavy presumption against the constitutional validity of a prior restraint.

Nor can we find that the swastika, while not representing fighting words, is nevertheless so offensive and peace threatening to the public that its display can be enjoined. We do not doubt that the sight of this symbol is abhorrent to the Jewish citizens of Skokie, and that the survivors of the Nazi persecutions, tormented by their recollections, may have strong feelings regarding its display. Yet it is entirely clear that this factor does not justify enjoining defendants' speech. The *Cohen* court spoke to this subject:

Finally, in arguments before this Court much has been made of the claim that Cohen's distasteful mode of expression was thrust upon unwilling or unsuspecting viewers, and that the State might therefore legitimately act as it did in order to protect the sensitive from otherwise unavoidable exposure to appellant's crude form of protest. Of course, the mere presumed presence of unwitting listeners or viewers does not serve automatically to justify curtailing all speech capable of giving offense. . . . While this Court has recognized that government may properly act in many situations to prohibit intrusion into the privacy of the home of unwelcome views and ideas which cannot be totally banned from the public dialogue, . . . we have at the same time consistently stressed that "we are often 'captives' outside the sanctuary of the home and subject to objectionable speech." . . . The ability of government, consonant with the Constitution, to shut off discourse solely to protect others from hearing it is, in other words, dependent upon a showing that substantial privacy interests are being invaded in an essentially intolerable manner. Any broader view of this authority would effectively empower a majority to silence dissidents simply as a matter of personal predilections." . . .

Rockwell v. Morris . . . also involved an American Nazi leader, George Lincoln Rockwell, who challenged a bar to his use of a New York City park to hold a public demonstration where anti-Semitic speeches would be made. Although approximately 2½ million Jewish New Yorkers were hostile to Rockwell's message, the court ordered that a permit to speak be granted, stating:

A community need not wait to be subverted by street riots and storm troopers; but, also, it cannot, by its policemen or commissioners, suppress a speaker, in prior restraint, on the basis of news reports, hysteria, or inference that what he did yesterday, he will do today. Thus, too, if the speaker incites others to immediate unlawful action he may be punished—in a proper case, stopped when disorder actually impends; but this is not to be confused with unlawful action from others who seek unlawfully to suppress or punish the speaker.

So, the unpopularity of views, their shocking quality, their obnoxiousness, and even their alarming impact is not enough. Otherwise, the preacher of any strange doctrine could be stopped; the antiracist himself could be suppressed, if he undertakes to speak in "restricted" areas; and one who asks that public schools be open indiscriminately to all ethnic groups could be lawfully suppressed, if only he choose to speak where persuasion is needed most. . . .

In summary, as we read the controlling Supreme Court opinions, use of the swastika is a symbolic form of free speech entitled to first amendment protections. Its display on uniforms or banners by those engaged in peaceful demonstrations cannot be totally precluded solely because that display may provoke a violent reaction by those who view it. Particularly is this true where, as here, there has been advance notice by the demonstrators of their plans so that they have become, as the complaint alleges, "common knowledge" and those to whom sight of the swastika banner or uniforms would be offense are forewarned and need not view them. A speaker who gives prior notice of his message has not compelled a confrontation with those who voluntarily listen.

As to those who happen to be in a position to be involuntarily confronted with the swastika, the following observations from *Erznoznik v. City of Jacksonville* . . . are appropriate:

The plain, if at times disquieting, truth is that in our pluralistic society, constantly proliferating new and ingenious forms of expression, "we are inescapably captive audiences for many purposes." . . . Much that we encounter offends our esthetic, if not our political and moral, sensibilities. Nevertheless, the Constitution does not permit government to decide which types of otherwise protected speech are sufficiently offensive to require protection for the unwilling listener or viewer. Rather, absent the narrow circumstances described above [home intrusion or captive audience], the burden normally falls upon the viewer to "avoid further bombardment of [his] sensibilities simply by averting [his] eyes."

REVIEW AND DISCUSSION QUESTIONS

1. Describe the factual background and legal issues in this case.

2. The Court relied on an earlier U.S. Supreme Court case, *Cohen v. California,* in deciding this one. What happened in *Cohen?* Why does the Court think it is relevant to *Skokie?*

3. What do you think the intention of the Nazis was in deciding to march in Skokie, if not to win political converts to their cause? Should the Court have considered their purposes?

4. Is the "clear and present danger test" rele-vant to this case? Explain.

5. How does the Court distinguish this case from *Chaplinsky* and the "fighting words" exception?

6. It is sometimes said that this case was rightly decided because for the Court to rule otherwise would put it on a slippery slope of trying to balance the offensiveness of speech against the First Amendment rights of the speaker, with the result that civil rights marches would have been jeopardized. Do you agree? Explain.

Obscenity

Paris Adult Theatre v. Slaton S&z

Defining obscenity has presented the Supreme Court with serious problems. This case accompanied another, Miller v. California *(1973), in which the justices offered a new definition. Revising the basic approach it had followed since its decision in* Roth v. United States *(1957), the Court said in* Miller *that there are three parts to the definition of obscenity:*

(a) whether the average person, applying contemporary community standards would find that the work, taken as a whole, appeals to the prurient interest; (b) whether the work depicts or describes, in a patently offensive way, sexual conduct specifically defined by the applicable state law; and (c) whether the work, taken as a whole, lacks serious literary, artistic, political, or scientific value.

The Court went on to say that "our nation is simply too big and too diverse" for a single standard to apply in all fifty states and therefore held that each jury should evaluate the material based on the individual "community" where the sale took place. Armed with its new definition, the Court went on in a companion case to explain the reasoning behind its unwillingness to extend constitutional protection to obscenity. That second case, Paris Adult Theatre v. Slaton, *arose when police prevented two Atlanta movie theaters from showing sexually explicit movies. No sexually explicit material was displayed outside the theater, and a sign at the entrance said "Adult Theatre—You must be 21 and able to prove it. If viewing the nude body offends you, Please Do Not Enter." The local district attorney tried to get two of the films declared obscene because of their graphic depiction of sexual acts. The lower court agreed that the films were obscene but also held that because there was "requisite notice" to the public of their nature and reasonable protection against admittance of minors, the showing of the films was constitutionally protected. The U.S. Supreme Court, however, disagreed.*

Chief Justice Burger, speaking for a majority of the justices, delivered the Supreme Court's verdict that the state is permitted to ban the public exhibition of obscene material to maintain a decent society. In a dissenting opinion, Justice Brennan argues that it is impossible to define "obscenity" satisfactorily.

---

413 U.S. 49 (1973).

Mr. Chief Justice Burger:

It should be clear from the outset that we do not undertake to tell the States what they must do, but rather to define the area in which they may chart their own course in dealing with obscene material. This Court has consistently held that obscene material is not protected by the First Amendment as a limitation on the state police power by virtue of the Fourteenth Amendment. . . .

We categorically disapprove the theory, apparently adopted by the trial judge, that obscene, pornographic films acquire constitutional immunity from state regulation simply because they are exhibited for consenting adults only. . . .

In particular, we hold that there are legitimate state interests at stake in stemming the tide of commercialized obscenity, even assuming it is feasible to enforce effective safeguards against exposure to juveniles and to passersby. Rights and interests "other than those of the advocates are involved." These include the interest of the public in the quality of life and the total community environment; the tone of commerce in the great city centers; and, possibly, the public safety itself. The Hill-Lind Minority Report of the Commission on Obscenity and Pornography indicates that there is at least an arguable correlation between obscene material and crime. Quite apart from sex crimes, however, there remains one problem of large proportions aptly described by Professor Bickel: "It concerns the tone of the society, the mode, or to use terms that have perhaps greater currency, the style and quality of life, now and in the future. A man may be entitled to read an obscene book in his room, or expose himself indecently there. . . . We should protect his privacy. But if he demands a right to obtain the books and pictures he wants in the market, and to foregather in public places—discreet, if you will, but accessible to all—with others who share his tastes, *then to grant him his right is to affect the world about the rest of us, and to impinge on other privacies.* Even supposing that each of us can, if he wishes, effectively avert the eye and stop the ear (which, in truth, we cannot), what is commonly read and seen and heard and done intrudes upon us all,

want it or not." 22 *The Public Interest* 25–26 (Winter 1971). (Emphasis added.)

As Mr. Chief Justice Warren stated, there is a "right of the Nation and of the States to maintain a decent society . . . ." *Jacobellis v. Ohio.*

But, it is argued, there are no scientific data which conclusively demonstrate that exposure to obscene material adversely affects men and women or their society. It is urged on behalf of the petitioners that, absent such a demonstration, any kind of state regulation is "impermissible." We reject this argument. It is not for us to resolve empirical uncertainties underlying state legislation, save in the exceptional case where that legislation plainly impinges upon rights protected by the Constitution itself. . . .

The sum of experience, including that of the past two decades, affords an ample basis for legislatures to conclude that a sensitive, key relationship of human existence, central to family life, community welfare, and the development of human personality, can be debased and distorted by crass commercial exploitation of sex. Nothing in the Constitution prohibits a State from reaching such a conclusion and acting on it legislatively. . . .

It is also argued that the State has no legitimate interest in "control [of] the moral content of a person's thoughts," and we need not quarrel with this. But we reject the claim that the State of Georgia is here attempting to control the minds or thoughts of those who patronize theaters. Preventing unlimited display or distribution of obscene material, which by definition lacks any serious literary, artistic, political, or scientific value as communication, is distinct from a control of reason and the intellect. . . . Where communication of ideas, protected by the First Amendment, is not involved, or the particular privacy of the home protected by *Stanley* or any of the other "areas or zones" of constitutionally protected privacy, the mere fact that, as a consequence, some human "utterances" or "thoughts" may be incidentally affected does not bar the State from acting to protect legitimate state interests. . . .

The issue in this context goes beyond whether someone, or even the majority, considers the conduct depicted as "wrong" or "sinful."

The States have the power to make a morally neutral judgment that public exhibition of obscene material, or commerce in such material, has a tendency to injure the community as a whole, to endanger the public safety, or to jeopardize, in Mr. Chief Justice Warren's words, the States' "right . . . to maintain a decent society." *Jacobellis v. Ohio.* . . .

Mr. Justice Brennan, dissenting:

. . . I am convinced that the approach initiated 16 years ago in *Roth v. United States*, 354 U.S. 476 (1957), and culminating in the Court's decision today, cannot bring stability to this area of the law without jeopardizing fundamental First Amendment values, and I have concluded that the time has come to make a significant departure from that approach. . . .

The essence of our problem in the obscenity area is that we have been unable to provide "sensitive tools" to separate obscenity from other sexually oriented but constitutionally protected speech, so that efforts to suppress the former do not spill over into the suppression of the latter. . . .

To be sure, five members of the Court did agree in *Roth* that obscenity could be determined by asking "whether to the average person, applying contemporary community standards, the dominant theme of the material taken as a whole appeals to prurient interest." 354 U.S., at 489. But agreement on that test—achieved in the abstract and without reference to the particular material before the Court—was, to say the least, short lived. . . .

Today a majority of the Court offers a slightly altered formulation of the basic *Roth* test, while leaving entirely unchanged the underlying approach.

Our experience with the *Roth* approach has certainly taught us that the outright suppression of obscenity cannot be reconciled with the fundamental principles of the First and Fourteenth Amendments. For we have failed to formulate a standard that sharply distinguishes protected from unprotected speech. . . . By disposing of cases through summary reversal or denial of certiorari we have deliberately and effectively obscured the rationale underlying the decisions. It comes as no surprise that judicial attempts to follow our lead conscientiously have often ended in hopeless confusion. . . .

The vagueness of the standards in the obscenity area produces a number of separate problems, and any improvement must rest on an understanding that the problems are to some extent distinct. First, a vague statute fails to provide adequate notice to persons who are engaged in the type of conduct that the statute could be thought to proscribe. The Due Process Clause of the Fourteenth Amendment requires that all criminal laws provide fair notice of "what the State commands or forbids." *Lanzetta v. New Jersey.* . . .

In addition to problems that arise when any criminal statute fails to afford fair notice of what it forbids, a vague statute in the areas of speech and press creates a second level of difficulty. . . .

[R]ecognizing the inherent vagueness of any definition of obscenity, we have held that the definition of obscenity must be drawn as narrowly as possible so as to minimize the interference with protected expression. . . .

The problems of fair notice and chilling protected speech are very grave standing alone. But it does not detract from their importance to recognize that a vague statute in this area creates a third, although admittedly more subtle, set of problems. These problems concern the institutional stress that inevitably results where the line separating protected from unprotected speech is excessively vague. In *Roth* we conceded that "there may be marginal cases in which it is difficult to determine the side of the line on which a particular fact situation falls. . . ." Our subsequent experience demonstrates that almost every case is "marginal." And since the "margin" marks the point of separation between protected and unprotected speech, we are left with a system in which almost every obscenity case presents a constitutional question of exceptional difficulty. . . .

Our experience since *Roth* requires us not only to abandon the effort to pick out obscene materials on a case-by-case basis, but also to reconsider a fundamental postulate of *Roth:* that there exists a definable class of sexually oriented expression that may be totally suppressed by the Federal and State Governments. Assuming that such a class of expression does in fact exist, I am forced to conclude that the concept of "obscenity" cannot be defined with sufficient specificity and clarity to provide fair notice to persons who create and distribute sexually oriented materials, to prevent substantial erosion of protected speech as a byproduct of the attempt to suppress unprotected speech, and to avoid very costly institutional harms.

REVIEW AND DISCUSSION QUESTIONS

1. Describe the three elements of the definition of obscenity outlined in the *Miller* case.
2. Explain the basis of Justice Burger's opinion upholding the Georgia law.

3. Why does Justice Brennan object to Burger's conclusions?
4. How would Mill analyze this case?

Pornography and Women

American Booksellers v. Hudnut

This case arose when the Indianapolis City Council passed an ordinance, advocated by Catharine MacKinnon, outlawing the production, sale, exhibition, and distribution of pornography. The ordinance defined pornography as any "graphic sexually explicit subordination of women" that also presented women as sexual objects "who enjoy rape, pain, or humiliation; enjoy being penetrated by objects or animals; in scenarios of degradation, injury, debasement, torture, shown as filthy or inferior; or presented as sexual objects for domination, conquest, violation, exploitation, possession, or use." The ordinance also allowed women who have been injured as a direct result of pornography to seek damages from the person who produced, sold, exhibited, or distributed it. The district court held the ordinance unconstitutional, and in the following selection, Judge Easterbrook, of the Court of Appeals, affirmed that decision.

Judge Easterbrook:

We do not try to balance the arguments for and against an ordinance such as this. The ordinance discriminates on the ground of the content of the speech. Speech treating women in the approved way—in sexual encounters "premised on equality" is lawful no matter how sexually explicit. Speech treating women in the disapproved way—as submissive in matters sexual or as enjoying humiliation—is unlawful no matter how

771 F.2nd 323 (1985).

significant the literary, artistic, or political qualities of the work taken as a whole. The state may not ordain preferred viewpoints in this way. The Constitution forbids the state to declare one perspective right and silence opponents. . . .

"If there is any fixed star in our constitutional constellation, it is that no official, high or petty, can prescribe what shall be orthodox in politics, nationalism, religion, or other matters of opinion or force citizens to confess by word or act their faith therein." *West Virginia State Board of Education v. Barnette*, 319 U.S. 624, 642 (1943). Under the First Amendment the government must leave to the people the evaluation of ideas. Bald or subtle, an idea is as powerful as the audience allows it to be. . . . A belief may be pernicious—the beliefs of Nazis led to the death of millions, those of the Klan to the repression of millions. A pernicious belief may prevail. Totalitarian governments today rule much of the planet, practicing suppression of billions and spreading dogma that may enslave others. One of the things that separates our society from theirs is our absolute right to propagate opinions that the government finds wrong or even hateful. . . .

Under the ordinance graphic sexually explicit speech is "pornography" or not depending on the perspective the author adopts. Speech that "subordinates" women and also, for example, presents women as enjoying pain, humiliation, or rape, or even simply presents women in "positions of servility or submission or display" is forbidden, no matter how great the literary or political value of the work taken as a whole. Speech that portrays women in positions of equality is lawful, no matter how graphic the sexual content. This is thought control. It establishes an "approved" view of women, of how they may react to sexual encounters, of how the sexes may relate to each other. Those who espouse the approved view may use sexual images; those who do not, may not.

Indianapolis justifies the ordinance on the ground that pornography affects thoughts. Men who see women depicted as subordinate are more likely to treat them so. Pornography is an aspect of dominance. It does not persuade people so much as change them. It works by socializing, by establishing the expected and the permissible. In this view pornography is not an idea; pornography is the injury.

There is much to this perspective. Beliefs are also facts. People often act in accordance with the images and patterns they find around them. People raised in a religion tend to accept the tenets of that religion, often without independent examination. People taught from birth that black people are fit only for slavery rarely rebelled against that creed; beliefs coupled with the self-interest of the masters established a social structure that inflicted great harm while

enduring for centuries. Words and images act at the level of the subconscious before they persuade at the level of the conscious. Even the truth has little chance unless a statement fits within the framework of beliefs that may never have been subjected to rational study.

Therefore we accept the premises of this legislation. Depictions of subordination tend to perpetuate subordination. The subordinate status of women in turn leads to affront and lower pay at work, insult and injury at home, battery and rape on the streets. . . .

Yet this simply demonstrates the power of pornography as speech. All of these unhappy effects depend on mental intermediation. Pornography affects how people see the world, their fellows, and social relations. If pornography is what pornography does, so is other speech. Hitler's orations affected how some Germans saw Jews. Communism is a world view, not simply a *Manifesto* by Marx and Engels or a set of speeches. Efforts to suppress communist speech in the United States were based on the belief that the public acceptability of such ideas would increase the likelihood of totalitarian government. Religions affect socialization in the most pervasive way. The opinion in *Wisconsin v. Yoder* shows how a religion can dominate an entire approach to life, governing much more than the relation between the sexes. . . .

Racial bigotry, anti-semitism, violence on television, reporters' biases—these and many more influence the culture and shape our socialization. None is directly answerable by more speech, unless that speech too finds its place in the popular culture. Yet all is protected as speech, however insidious. Any other answer leaves the government in control of all of the institutions of culture, the great censor and director of which thoughts are good for us.

Sexual responses often are unthinking responses, and the association of sexual arousal with the subordination of women therefore may have a substantial effect. But almost all cultural stimuli provoke unconscious responses. Religious ceremonies condition their participants. Teachers convey messages by selecting what not to cover; the implicit message about what is off limits or unthinkable may be more powerful than the messages for which they present rational argument. Television scripts contain unarticulated assumptions. People may be conditioned in subtle ways. If the fact that speech plays a role in a process of conditioning were enough to permit governmental regulation, that would be the end of freedom of speech. . . .

Much of Indianapolis's argument rests on the belief that when speech is "unanswerable," and the metaphor that there is a "marketplace of ideas" does not apply, the First Amendment does not apply either. The metaphor is honored; Milton's *Areopagitica* and John Stewart Mill's *On Liberty* defend freedom of speech on the ground that the truth will prevail, and many of the most important cases under the First Amendment recite this position. The Framers undoubtedly believed it. As a general matter it is true. But the Constitution does not make the dominance of truth a necessary condition of freedom of speech. To say that it does would be to confuse an outcome of free speech with a necessary condition for the application of the amendment.

A power to limit speech on the ground that truth has not yet prevailed and is not likely to prevail implies the power to declare truth. At some point the government must be able to say (as Indianapolis has said): "We know what the truth is, yet a free exchange of speech has not driven out falsity, so that we must now prohibit falsity." If the government may declare the truth, why wait for the failure of speech? Under the First Amendment, however, there is no such thing as a false idea. . . . The government may not restrict speech on the ground that in a free exchange truth is not yet dominant. . . .

We come, finally, to the argument that pornography is "low value" speech, that it is enough like obscenity that Indianapolis may prohibit it. Some cases hold that speech far removed from politics and other subjects at the core of the Framers' concerns may be subjected to special regulation. . . .

In *Pacifica* the FCC sought to keep vile language off the air during certain times. The Court held that it may; but the Court would not have sustained a regulation prohibiting scatological descriptions of Republicans but not scatological descriptions of Democrats, or any other form of selection among viewpoints. . . .

At all events, "pornography" is not low value speech within the meaning of these cases. . . . True, pornography and obscenity have sex in common. But Indianapolis left out of its definition any reference to literary, artistic, political, or scientific value.

REVIEW AND DISCUSSION QUESTIONS

1. Describe the Indianapolis ordinance's purpose. What sort of material, exactly, did it ban?

2. How was the ordinance to be enforced?

3. How does the ordinance differ from the Georgia statute upheld in *Paris Adult Theatre?*

4. Why did Judge Easterbrook reject the ordinance? Explain.

5. Suppose you were asked to appeal this decision to the Supreme Court. Explain how you would argue that case.

Privacy, Homosexuality, and the Constitution

John Arthur

In this essay John Arthur discusses one of the most controversial of the recent Supreme Court opinions: its 5-to-4 decision upholding a Georgia law criminalizing sodomy. He begins with a brief discussion of the evolution and meaning of the right to privacy itself, asking if it is best understood to involve only information, as some have suggested; or if the Court is correct in giving it a broader reading. He then goes on to consider the legal and philosophical issues raised by Bowers v. Hardwick, *in which the justices refused to hold that laws criminalizing sodomy implicate the right to privacy. He concludes with a brief discussion of the moral, political, and health issues surrounding this decision, focusing in particular on the brief filed by the state of Georgia in defense of its statute.*

In this essay I want to discuss in a general way some of the problems raised by the Supreme Court's so-called "privacy" decisions. These cases are of great interest not only because of the controversy surrounding one of them, the abortion decision of *Roe v. Wade* (1973), but also because of the deep disagreements over privacy itself—its parameters and even its existence have been the source of heated debate. Then after a brief account of the nature of the right, and a defense of the Court's approach against charges that it has simply confused privacy, which involves control over information, with liberty, I will look at a recent decision of the Court involving the rights of homosexuals.

The story begins with *Griswold v. Connecticut* (1965),[1] in which the Court struck down state laws banning contraceptives. Acknowledging that privacy is never mentioned explicitly in the Constitution, the Court nevertheless found that such a right is implicit in its various other provisions including the right against unreasonable searches and seizures, the right not to have troops quartered in any house during peacetime, the right against self-incrimination and freedom of association. That right to privacy, existing in the "penumbras" of other, explicitly stated rights, includes the right to use contraceptives, said Justice Douglas.

Although it provoked great interest among legal scholars, *Griswold* was largely ignored by the public. It was not until the Court confronted additional cases, sodomy and abortion in particular, that the public controversy surrounding

privacy became evident. An important step between *Griswold* and these later opinions, however, was *Eisenstadt v. Baird*[2] (1972), which involved the denial of access to contraceptives to unmarried people. In *Eisenstadt* the Court considered and rejected Harlan's narrow, marriage-based interpretation of *Griswold* in favor of Douglas's. Justice Brennan wrote for a 6-to-1 majority:

> Whatever the rights of the individual to access to contraceptives may be, the rights must be the same for unmarried and married alike. It is true that in *Griswold*, the right of privacy in question inhered in the marital relationship. Yet the marital couple is not an independent entity with a mind and heart of its own, but an association of two individuals each with a separate intellectual and emotional makeup. If the right of privacy means anything, it is the right of the *individual*, married or single, to be free from unwarranted governmental intrusion into matters so fundamentally affecting a person as the decision whether to bear or beget children.[3]

As we will see, there is room for considerable disagreement over just what privacy really means. One interpretation is that of Justice Brennan, who, perhaps echoing Brandeis's general idea of a right to be let alone, has characterized privacy as the right of the individual to be "free from unwarranted governmental intrusion." Marriage is one area of fundamental importance, to be sure, but the right to privacy on this view would concern far more than protecting and encouraging a particular institution. In *Eisenstadt* it appeared that the Court might be headed toward some more general principle of individual rights. There were many possibilities. One was for the Court to limit the right to privacy to contraception; another would be to extend protection to all areas of private sexual activity, including the choice of a partner and abortion; yet another even more expansive interpretation would allow the Court, still under the banner of privacy, to protect the right of individuals to do anything that does not harm others.

THE NATURE OF PRIVACY

The judicial protection of privacy prompted some of the most bitter criticism of the Court since the school desegregation and prayer cases. Some critics focused on the vagueness and lack of clear boundaries of the right to privacy; others have faulted the Court's logic. Former Supreme Court nominee Robert Bork put these points especially sharply. Yet the Court relied on *Griswold* to protect the rights of *unmarried* persons who wish to use contraceptives,[4] to overturn a Virginia statute prohibiting interracial marriage,[5] and eventually to reject a Texas statute prohibiting abortion. Some state courts have extended the right to privacy into still other areas. It was used to justify the right to die,[6] to use marijuana,[7] and to take laetrile to fight cancer.[8] All these privacy cases have their roots, says the Court, in earlier decisions protecting people's right to send children to private schools and to study the German language, as well as Fourth Amendment guarantees against unreasonable searches and seizures. How, then, should we understand "privacy"? Is it a single right of some sort, or should we interpret privacy as a family of rights that, though related in various respects, do not have a single feature in common?

It has seemed to many, including some who are sympathetic with the results of *Griswold* and its progeny, that the Court is confused when it uses the word *privacy* to describe those cases that actually involve liberty instead.[9] Contrary to the Court, *privacy*, according to this view, actually involves disclosure of personal *information* rather than restrictions on what we may *do*. Laws that prevent people from using contraceptives, sending children to private schools, or getting an abortion restrict *liberty* by denying them the opportunity to do what they want. The paradigm of a violation of privacy, in contrast, is publication of embarrassing information or eavesdropping on an intimate phone conversation, not limiting freedom of action. Imagine, for example, somebody who allows publication of her personal secrets. Clearly she has given up her privacy, although because she consented she has not had her liberty infringed. Nor is the issue one of control over information: although privacy was lost, control over the information was maintained. So it has seemed to many that liberty and privacy are different.

If privacy consists in not having personal information about ourselves become known to others, then what is the *right* to privacy? The answer cannot be that the right is violated whenever personal information is made public; remember the woman who consented. There are other disclosures of private information that also do not violate the right to privacy: a wiretap on the phone of a suspected criminal might reveal personal information but would not necessarily be a violation of either a legal or moral right. Nor, to take another example, would it seem to be a violation of the *right* to privacy when a public figure's drinking habits are made public (assuming that the official's ability to perform is hampered), although that would be a disclosure of private information. Whether the moral right to privacy is violated will therefore depend on whether the personal information was *wrongfully* disclosed. That judgment of the wrongfulness of the disclosure—will depend on many factors, including the importance of having the information made public, the way it was gathered, whether there was informed consent that it be made public, and what was done with the information after it was acquired. These will not make the acquisition of information any less an invasion of privacy; they can, however, make the invasion a legitimate one.

Are we then to conclude, coming back to the central issue, that the Court has simply confused liberty with privacy in *Griswold* and the other cases treating violations of liberty as if they were wrongful disclosures of information? I think not. For although the right to privacy clearly includes the right to prevent unjustified disclosure of personal information, it is not limited to that.

Suppose, for example, somebody repeatedly phoned you at your home despite requests to stop. Such an invasion of privacy, for surely it is that, could not be described as disclosure of personal information. Nonetheless, your privacy is violated: the caller has intruded into your personal, private life. She has violated your right to privacy. This example suggests that the Court is not off the mark when it includes certain liberties among the "right of privacy," especially ones that are associated with the home, family, and sexual intimacy. We do think of certain choices we want to make within the home as "private" ones with which others should not interfere in any way. It is not simply that others should not watch. Similarly, we often describe sexual and family decisions as private, again in the more inclusive sense that encompasses both freedom of action and lack of disclosure. The right to privacy thus has two aspects: one prevents unjustified disclosure of personal information, and the other protects certain types of liberty.

The two aspects are, however, connected. Notice, first, that not all disclosures of information about us could be an invasion of privacy. A photo of your car's left-rear tire, for example, would not qualify even if it appeared in the *New York Times*. Only if the information disclosed is personal would its disclosure constitute a violation of privacy. So both forms of privacy involve matters thought to be of a personal nature—sex, reproduction, family, and home, for example—and the Court has focused on just that feature in its privacy cases.

In fact, there is little suggestion in the opinions that the justices are confused about whether it is personal liberty or personal information that is being protected. In overturning laws preventing unmarried couples from using contraceptives, Justice Brennan wrote that the right to privacy prevents government from intruding into "matters so fundamentally affecting a person as the decision whether to bear or beget children." He was obviously aware that it is the *decision* to bear children that was at issue, not

information about the person's private life. The Court is thus quite clear about what it wants to protect: privacy, in its view, can be invaded either by publication of intimate details of a person's life or by infringing on the person's liberty to pursue certain personal aspects of that life. So the right to privacy that grew out of *Griswold*, having roots in the Fourth Amendment's guarantees against unreasonable searches, has come to encompass more than information; it includes the right to make certain decisions.

The link between these two aspects of privacy seems to be that unlike other, relatively trivial decisions we make, ones involving home, children, sex, and reproduction play a role in defining who we are and what we shall become. They are personal in a literal sense: they are close to the identity of the *person*. Limiting access to personal information is important for our emotional development and well-being. We often find that being on public display makes reflection and relaxation impossible, and we are frequently embarrassed to have others know personal details about our lives. Informational privacy is also important if we are to develop the bonds of friendship and love that are an essential ingredient in the identities of most people. If everybody knew everything about our most intimate feelings and actions, our personal relationships would lose much of what makes them personal rather than public, and thus much of their meaning for us. So the right to limit access to information is crucial if we are to have and enjoy those relationships that are most important in shaping our identities—relationships of loved one, parent, child, friend. In that way, the liberties identified under the heading of "private" (involving decisions about family, contraception, and so on) serve the same function as the right to limit dispersal of personal information. Limiting such information, using contraceptives, passing on our religion and language to our children, and deciding to get an abortion are important aspects of personal integrity and identity.

Limiting the spread of personal information and exercising freedom to make personal decisions have something else in common. Just as sometimes personal information may be divulged without violating anybody's right, so too some personal decisions may be restricted without violating *that* aspect of the right to privacy. The mere fact that some desired action falls within the realm of intimate, personal choices or that some information is personal does not show that the government cannot prevent the action or must not acquire the information. We do not have a right to sexually abuse children, although doing so would certainly qualify as a "personal" decision, any more than we have an absolute right that government or others never discover or disclose facts of our personal lives.

It is a mistake, therefore, to suppose that the Court is confused about what's at stake in privacy. The liberties it has identified are connected with each other as well as with our need to limit dissemination of personal information because they all involve people's interest in shaping their personal identity. Protecting intimate, personal choices involving family and parenthood are important in that process of self-definition, as is the ability to control dissemination of personal information.

SEXUAL PREFERENCE

Georgia law defines *sodomy* as submitting to or committing "any act involving the sex organs of one person and the anus or mouth of another." Sodomy is a criminal act in Georgia, whatever the sexes of the actors; violators are subject to prison terms of one to ten years. Michael Hardwick had been at a bar where police, in an effort to harass gays, had arrested him for displaying an open beer bottle. Unaware that Hardwick had paid the fine, an officer went to his house to collect. A friend of Hardwick let him in, and the officer observed Hardwick in the bedroom having sex with another man. After about a minute the officer arrested Hardwick and took him to jail, where he spent one night. When the jailer locked Michael Hardwick up, he told the others in the cell that they would enjoy themselves, because Hardwick had been arrested for sodomy. Although the prosecutor chose not to present the case to a grand jury, Hardwick nonetheless challenged the constitutionality of the statute.

A federal appeals court held that the Fourteenth Amendment protected privacy, including sexual freedom. The Court did not, however, demand that the statute be overturned; it merely held that the state of Georgia must demonstrate before a federal judge that the law served a compelling state interest. It was only that decision—that Georgia would be required to defend its sodomy law—which the Supreme Court reviewed.

Immediately after hearing the case, Justice Powell indicated that he would join four others in requiring review of the statute. But he later changed his mind, and in a 5-to-4 opinion the court upheld the Georgia law. (Powell said in speech three years later, however, that he had again changed his mind and would now vote to overturn the law.)

Writing for the majority, Justice White stated that:

> Respondent would have us announce, as the Court of Appeals did, a fundamental right to engage in homosexual sodomy. This we are quite unwilling to do. . . . In *Palko v. Connecticut*, it was said that fundamental liberties are "implicit in the concept of ordered liberty," such that "neither liberty nor justice would exist if [they] were sacrificed." A different description of fundamental liberties appeared in *Moore v. East Cleveland*, where they are characterized as those liberties that are "deeply rooted in this Nation's history and tradition." . . .
>
> Proscriptions against that conduct have ancient roots. Sodomy was a criminal offense at common law and was forbidden by the laws of the original thirteen States when they ratified the Bill of Rights. In 1868, when the Fourteenth Amendment was ratified, all but 5 of the 37 States in the Union had criminal sodomy laws. In fact, until 1961, all States outlawed sodomy, and today, 24 States and the District of Columbia continue to provide criminal penalties for sodomy performed in private and between consenting adults. Against this background, to claim that a right to engage in such conduct is "deeply rooted in this Nation's history and tradition" or "implicit in the concept of ordered liberty" is, at best, facetious. . . .
>
> Plainly enough, otherwise illegal conduct is not always immunized whenever it occurs in the home. Victimless crimes, such as the possession and use of illegal drugs do not escape the law where they are committed at home. . . . And if respondent's

submission is limited to the voluntary sexual conduct between consenting adults, it would be difficult, except by fiat, to limit the claimed right to homosexual conduct while leaving exposed to prosecution adultery, incest, and other sexual crimes even though they are committed in the home. We are unwilling to start down that road.[10]

Justice White argues that in previous cases the right to privacy revolved around marriage, family, and home, and that therefore homosexual sodomy does not fall within its scope. In short, Georgia's statute does not implicate any Fourteenth Amendment rights because only liberties that are fundamental or deeply rooted in our traditions are protected, and to make such a claim about sodomy is "at best facetious." Sodomy is not part of the traditional respect accorded the family, nor is it part of the basic liberties guaranteed by the Constitution.

Justice Blackmun, in dissent, argues that White has misunderstood the issue by focusing on the narrow question of sodomy instead of the principles that underlie the Court's earlier cases. In past privacy cases, he writes,

[T]he Court has proceeded along two somewhat distinct, albeit complementary, lines. First, it has recognized a privacy interest with reference to certain decisions that are properly for the individual to make. E.g., [Roe (right to abortion), Pierce (right to send children to private schools)]. Second, it has recognized a privacy interest with reference to certain places without regard for the particular activities in which the individuals who occupy them are engaged. The case before us implicates both the decisional and the spatial aspects of the right to privacy. . . .

[The] fact that individuals define themselves in a significant way through their intimate sexual relationships with others suggests, in a Nation as diverse as ours, that there may be many "right" ways of conducting those relationships, and that much of the richness of a relationship will come from the freedom an individual has to choose the form and nature of these intensely personal bonds. [The] Court claims that its decision today merely refuses to recognize a fundamental right to engage in homosexual sodomy; what the Court really has refused to recognize is the fundamental interest all individuals have in controlling the nature of their intimate associations with others.

The behavior for which Hardwick faces prosecution occurred in his own home, a place to which the Fourth Amendment attaches special significance. The Court's treatment of this aspect of the case is symptomatic of its overall refusal to consider the broad principles that have informed our treatment of privacy in specific cases. Just as the right to privacy is more than the mere aggregation of a number of entitlements to engage in specific behavior, so too, protecting the physical integrity of the home is more than merely a means of protecting specific activities that often take place there. . . .

I cannot agree that either the length of time a majority has held its convictions or the passions with which it defends them can withdraw legislation from the Court's scrutiny. [It] is precisely because the issue raised by this case touches the heart of what makes individuals what they are that we should be especially sensitive to the rights of those whose choices upset the majority. . . .

The mere knowledge that other individuals do not adhere to one's value system cannot be a legally cognizable interest, let alone an interest that can justify invading the houses, hearts, and minds of citizens who choose to live their lives differently.[11]

Justice Blackmun claims privacy has both a decisional and a spatial aspect. Some personal decisions are of such fundamental importance to the personal lives of individuals that they demand a compelling state interest before they can be restricted. The choice of a sexual partner is such a decision, Blackmun said, and is therefore included within the principles already enunciated by the Court. Privacy also has a spatial dimension: it matters where the law intrudes. Georgia's statute reaches into an area that the Constitution takes special care to shield from government: the home. *Bowers* therefore lies at the intersection of two important constitutional principles: protection of personal choices and protection of the sanctity of the home.

Justice Blackmun goes on to reject arguments advanced by Georgia to justify its restriction of Hardwick's liberty. There is no evidence, he says, that the public health is protected by the law, nor can the law be defended on grounds of society's right to protect moral decency. Hardwick's behavior took place in private, out of sight of people who find it offensive. In fact, he concludes, the statute is nothing more than an effort to dictate "private morality."

The disagreement between White and Blackmun turns in large measure on the same issues that divided Douglas and Harlan in *Griswold*. For White the majority is justified in enforcing its conception of the good life when, as in *Bowers*, it relies on the traditional values of family and marriage. Georgia's statute, however, does not present the conflict between tradition and the will of the legislature that Harlan saw in *Griswold*. Blackmun adopts the alternative view that government should aspire to neutrality and respect the rights of those who "choose to live their lives differently," especially when the issue involves sexual identity and personality to the extent that this does. Neither traditional disapproval of the practice nor legislative enactments, even if they reflect majority will, can justify intrusion into this private decision.

Blackmun would not say, however, that any conception of the good should be protected merely because it involves personal, sexual decisions. Rape, even if done in privacy, must be criminalized. How, then, are we to assess the risks to society that homosexuality may pose? In his brief, Georgia Attorney General Michael Bowers gave two arguments in support of the claim that the legislature acted reasonably in banning sodomy. The first argument goes to support the contention, adopted by White, that privacy protects traditional values of family and marriage and therefore does not provide protection to homosexual conduct. The attorney general wrote that traditionally the Court has

recognized the right of individuals to be free from governmental intrusion in decisions relating to marriage and family life, and used as a guide the teachings of history and the basic values of society to conclude that the Constitution protects the sanctity of the family, even the extended family, "precisely because the institution of the family is deeply rooted in this nation's history and tradition. It is through the family that we inculcate and pass down many of our most cherished values, moral and cultural" [*Moore v. East Cleveland* (1977)]. . . . The statute most certainly does not interfere with personal decisions concerning marriage or family life.[12]

Not only is homosexuality beyond the bounds of the family, but it poses a danger to that institution. Georgia's law, he wrote, reflects the view that

Homosexual sodomy is the anathema of the basic units of our society—marriage and the family. To decriminalize or artificially withdraw the public's expression of its disdain for this conduct does not uplift sodomy, but rather demotes these sacred institutions to merely other alternative lifestyles. If the legal distinctions between the intimacies of marriage and homosexual sodomy are lost, it is certainly possible to make the assumption, perhaps unprovable at this time, that the order of society, our way of life, could be changed in a harmful way. The states have a legitimate and, it is argued, compelling interest in the protection of the organization of society.[13]

On what grounds might a legislator or judge believe that decriminalizing homosexuality would endanger the family, our society, and "our way of life"? The American Psychological Association and the American Public Health Association filed an amicus curiae ("friend of the court") brief that argued against Georgia.[14] In that brief they pointed out that from 70 to 80 percent of gay men and lesbian women live as couples, despite the lack of social and legal encouragement. Equally important,

Couplehood, either as a reality or an aspiration, is as strong among gay people as it is among heterosexuals. Principal concerns for all types of couples include equity, loyalty, stability, intimacy, and love. The nontraditional couples also often make substantial commitments to each other and in many cases stay together for decades.[15]

Many heterosexual couples marry and maintain a "family" despite the absence of children; why, then, are homosexual couples who wish to do the same a threat to "the order of society, our way of life"? It is not clear that Georgia's law is consistent with the family values it purports to support. If the point of giving marriage special protection is to enable people to achieve bonds of love, intimacy, and commitment, then why should the fact that the partners are of different sexes be crucial? Oddly enough, Justice Powell, who provided the last-minute fifth vote in *Bowers*, had written an opinion just a few years earlier that indicated sympathy with people living in the "nontraditional" family. *Moore v. East Cleveland*[16] (1977) invalidated a Cleveland zoning law that limited occupancy within a dwelling to a single family. The ordinance defined "family" so narrowly that it prevented Mrs. Moore from living with her two grandsons. Powell wrote in *Moore:*

> Whether or not such a family is established because of personal tragedy, the choice of relatives in this degree of kinship to live together may not lightly be denied by the State. [*Pierce*] The Constitution prevents East Cleveland from standardizing its children—and its adults—by forcing all to live in certain narrowly defined family patterns.[17]

Justice White, who wrote the *Bowers* opinion, dissented in *Moore.* So although there is no evidence that they even considered the fact of homosexual families, those on the Court who believed that laws should promote family values should also have considered the real meaning behind that ideal. If the point is to facilitate intimacy, stability, and family life, they should oppose sodomy laws making such values harder for homosexuals to realize. In fact, as we have seen, the evidence indicates that homosexuals seek relationships that are for all intents and purposes familial; the underlying purpose is identical to that of heterosexuals, and often even includes raising children. So besides Blackmun's objection to the majority in *Bowers*, there is also a potentially powerful conservative attack on Georgia's law that sees the law as discouraging creation of stable families and undermining the same family values as Harlan invoked in *Griswold.*

Nor can it be maintained that homosexuality threatens the traditional family because it is contagious. Homosexuality is widely practiced in all societies, whether homosexuals are admired, ignored, or repressed.[18] And sexual preference, as opposed to sexual acts, is not something we choose. Estimates are that anywhere from 5 to 25 million Americans are homosexual in the sense that they are primarily or exclusively attracted to members of their own sex rather than of the opposite sex. Whether heterosexual or homosexual, we discover our sexual orientation rather as we discover that we are either right or left handed. Only a small fraction of those who find themselves attracted to people of the same sex could have their preference modified through therapy, perhaps no more than the percentage of heterosexuals whose preference would be changed.

The idea that sodomy laws protect heterosexual marriage is thus mistaken on two counts. Such laws do not reduce homosexual orientation of adults, and even if they did normal contact with homosexual adults does not affect the sexual orientation of others.[19] Homosexuals pose no threat to the institution of marriage and family; and allowing them to create families would arguably promote rather than hinder those values.

Georgia made two additional arguments in its brief: that sodomy is "immoral" and that it is a reasonable response to the public health dangers posed by acquired immune deficiency syndrome (AIDS). I will look at each in turn.

Homosexual sodomy, the state claimed, is "purely an unnatural means of satisfying an unnatural lust, which has been declared by Georgia to be morally wrong."[20] Again, however, both the medical and psychological evidence, as well as philosophical reflection, show this argument to be mistaken. Although the case was widely thought to involve only homosexuality, Georgia also criminalizes oral and anal intercourse between heterosexual couples. The law was passed at a time when such behavior was thought wrong regardless of the sex of those who do it. Today, however, sodomy is widely practiced among heterosexual as well as homosexual couples, and for exactly the same reasons. In a study cited in the American Psychological Association's brief, approximately 90 percent of heterosexual couples were found to engage in oral sex; another study found that 25 percent of all heterosexual married couples had engaged in anal intercourse within the past year.[21] Indeed, said the brief, such forms of intercourse are often recommended as a means to improve sexual function and health. Nor is there evidence that homosexuality causes mental illness or is associated with other emotional illnesses. Medical professionals are in wide agreement with the American Psychiatric Associations's 1977 finding that "homosexuality per se implies no impairment in judgment, stability, reliability or general social or vocational capabilities . . . homosexuality does not constitute any form of mental disease."[22]

In what sense, then, is sodomy "unnatural" and therefore morally wrong? Is it unnatural only when done by people of the same sex? Certainly it is not unnatural in the sense that it is uncommon, nor does the mere fact that it is not the most common form of sexual practice—if indeed it isn't—have anything to do with its being moral. Lying is far more common than viola playing, though that hardly makes the former moral and the latter not. Perhaps the real point is that homosexuality and sodomy are contrary to the "natural" purpose of sexual organs. If the true purpose of sex is reproduction, which can only occur through sexual intercourse between people of the opposite sex, then sodomy is contrary to nature and thus wrong. Much traditionally condoned sexual activity, however, also has nothing to do with reproduction: kissing, hugging, sex done with contraceptives, and sexual intercourse when either partner is infertile. And the other purposes that these activities serve, including expression of love or commitment, are achieved by homosexuals and heterosexuals alike. There's also the question of why it should matter that people use sex for purposes other than the one biology seems to prescribe. Besides hearing, people use ears to support eyeglasses and earrings, though it seems a bit harsh to condemn them for it. The claim that sodomy is immoral cannot withstand scrutiny. It is not uncommon, and even if it were that is no ground for condemnation. Nor is it unnatural in any morally relevant sense.

Georgia might also have based its criminalization of homosexuality on religion, claiming for example that it is condemned in the Bible. One problem with this, of course, is that the First Amendment guarantees religious freedom, promising that government will neither establish religion nor prevent its free exercise. The fact that homosexuality is condemned by one religion, or even all, would not, standing alone, justify its criminalization. Another argument would appeal simply to the disgust and homophobia that many Americans feel. Indeed, it seems impossible to explain the justices' decision in *Bowers* without appreciating the extent of homophobia in this culture. But that argument—that society can express its irrational dislike of minorities—would also find few supporters on the Court, at least until it were dressed up in more acceptable terms.

Public health, and especially the threat of AIDS, is another matter. Here, finally, is an argument that does not obviously rest on antiquated medicine, special psychology, or bad philosophy: AIDS is a major health problem. One of the two most common ways it is spread—anal intercourse—is a frequent practice of homosexual men. So perhaps Georgia's statute can be justified as a public health measure, though AIDS was clearly not what the legislature had in mind when the law was passed in 1816.

In fact, however, the evidence is overwhelming that sodomy laws not only are ineffective as a public health measure but are counterproductive. First, Georgia enforced its sodomy law only against homosexuals, making the statute doubly defective as a public health effort. It is too broad because it condemns oral sex, and there is no indication that people who practice oral sex, whatever the sexes of their partners are at an especially high risk of spreading AIDS. As it was actually enforced, the statute is also too narrow because it condemns anal intercourse only among homosexuals, despite the fact that the AIDS virus pays no attention to the sex of the person it infects. . . .

But even if it were meant as an attack on AIDS rather than homosexuals, health officials agree that criminalizing homosexuality makes the task of preventing the spread of AIDS much more difficult. There are many reasons for this. Antihomosexual statutes discourage accurate reporting and testing, requiring those who seek treatment to become prisoners. Sick people may not get treatment and are deterred from taking the tests that would tell them if they are likely to infect others.

Sodomy laws also frustrate researchers, making it more difficult for them to get the accurate information that is essential to fighting the disease effectively. Researchers initially found it difficult to explain why Haitians were a high-risk group, for example, because of the fears of those who were afflicted to report that they were either gay or intravenous drug users. Efforts at prevention are also hampered by sodomy laws. Condoms are extremely effective in limiting the spread of AIDS, yet government often finds it difficult to reconcile condemning sodomy through law with helping men practice it safely.

As a public health measure, Georgia's law is both badly drawn and counterproductive. This point is important because statutes limiting liberty must be closely tailored to meet their objectives. Even state laws that do not involve any fundamental right such as privacy must have at least a "rational basis" if the Supreme Court is to uphold them, although this test gives wide latitude to a legislature. Georgia's law not only fails the former test, of unduly infringing liberty, but is also arguably so irrational, counterproductive, and dangerous that it fails even the latter, "rational basis" test.

The *Bowers* decision did not meet with widespread approval, as the majority may have hoped. Many newspapers expressed surprise that the Court would allow Georgia to regulate consensual adult sexual activity in the bedroom. By ignoring the scientific and psychological evidence while adopting the state's homophobic moral arguments, the Court lost an opportunity to introduce a degree of thoughtful discussion to an important topic, contributed to the discrimination that homosexuals suffer, and added to the burdens facing responsible public health officials in trying to combat AIDS.

NOTES

[1] 381 U.S. 479 (1985).

[2] 405 U.S. 438 (1972).

[3] *Eisenstadt v. Baird*, 405 U.S. 438 (1972).

[4] *Eisenstadt v. Baird*, 405 U.S. 438 (1971).

[5] *Loving v. Virginia*, 388 U.S. 1 (1967).

[6] *The Matter of Quinlan*, 355 A. 2d. 647 (1976).

[7] *Ravin v. State*, 537 P.2d 494 (1975).

[8] *People v. Privitera*, 74 C.A. 3d. (1977). The California Supreme Court reversed this judgment, however, claiming that the right to privacy did not reach that broadly.

[9] See, for example, H. Gross, "Privacy and Autonomy," *Nomos XII: Privacy* (New York: Atherton, 1971).

[10] 106 S. Ct. 2846 (1986).

[11] Ibid.

[12] Brief of Attorney General Michael Bowers, in *Bowers v. Georgia* (1985), at 30, 32.

[13] *Bowers* Brief, at 37–38.

[14] Brief of Amici Curiae, American Psychological Association and American Public Health Association in Support of Respondents, *Bowers v. Hardwick* (1985), hereafter APA Brief.

[15] APA Brief (1985), at 14.

[16] 431 U.S. 494 (1977).

[17] *Moore v. East Cleveland*, 431 U.S. 494 (1977).

[18] APA Brief, at 7.

[19] APA Brief, at 28.

[20] *Bowers* Brief, at 27.

[21] APA Brief, at 6.

[22] Resolution of the American Psychiatric Association, December 15, 1973, quoted in APA Brief, at 9.

REVIEW AND DISCUSSION QUESTIONS

1. Why does Arthur think the Court is not confused when it treats the right to privacy as including certain liberties as well as the control of information?

2. How does the majority opinion in *Bowers v. Hardwick,* written by Justice White, understand the right to privacy? Why does Justice White think that sodomy is not included within the right to privacy?

3. According to Justice Blackmun, privacy has both a "decisional" and a "spatial" aspect. Explain what he means.

4. Summarize Justice Blackmun's argument against the majority's opinion.

5. Georgia claimed that antisodomy laws protect marriage. Why does Arthur reject that claim?

6. The state also claimed that sodomy is "unnatural." How does Arthur respond to that claim?

7. Discuss why Arthur thinks that the law is counterproductive as a public health measure to fight AIDS.

8. What is the best argument *for* the state's position that there is at least a "rational basis" for the law?

9. If privacy does not protect homosexual acts, yet does include the other rights discussed in the article, how would you explain the meaning of the right?

18

EQUALITY AND THE CONSTITUTION

The U.S. Constitution's Fourteenth Amendment demands that government respect the equality of citizens, stating that everyone must be provided "equal protection of the laws." It also might be argued that equality is implicit elsewhere in the Constitution, for instance in the requirements that government not infringe fundamental liberties, including the freedoms of religious practice and speech and the right to due process under the law. But what, precisely, is required of government if it is to respect equality? Beginning with essays that speak to this question by focusing on racial and gender equality, the readings and cases then weigh a range of topics, including affirmative action, gender discrimination, the internment of Japanese Americans during World War II, and the potential conflict between equality and the right of free speech.

Justice Engendered

Martha Minow

Impartiality is often thought central to the ideal of equality and equal treatment: to treat people unequally thus involves some sort of bias against them and their interests. Martha Minow discusses the problems surrounding the idea that people should be treated equally, given that there are evident differences among them—some of which may be thought to justify differential treatment. What she terms the "dilemma of difference" arises whenever courts must consider which differences between people should matter. This cannot be decided, she argues, without taking a particular vantage point or perspective, yet the objectivity of that perspective may be questioned, leading to charges that in either taking account of or ignoring differences a court is failing to be impartial. Illustrating this dilemma through a range of Supreme Court cases, Minow concludes with a description of two exercises that can be used to avoid false impartiality. Martha Minor is professor of law at Harvard Law School.

I. INTRODUCTION

A. WHAT'S THE DIFFERENCE?

The use of anesthesia in surgery spread quickly once discovered. Yet the nineteenth-century doctors who adopted anesthesia selected which patients needed it and which deserved it. Both the medical literature and actual medical practices distinguished people's need for pain-killers based on race, gender, ethnicity, age, temperament, personal habits, and economic class. Some people's pain was thought more serious than others; some people were thought to be hardy enough to withstand pain. Doctors believed that women, for example, needed painkillers more than men and that the rich and educated needed painkillers more than the poor and uneducated. How might we, today, evaluate these examples of discrimination? What differences between people should matter, and for what purposes?

The endless variety of our individualism means that we suffer different kinds of pain and may well experience pain differently. But when professionals use categories like gender, race, ethnicity, and class to presume real differences in people's pain and entitlement to help, I worry. I worry that unfairness will result under the guise of objectivity and neutrality. I worry that a difference assigned by someone with power over a more vulnerable person will become endowed with an apparent reality, despite powerful competing views. If no one can really know another's pain, who shall decide how to treat pain, and along what calculus? These are questions of justice, not science. These are questions of complexity, not justification for passivity, because failing to notice another's pain is an act with significance.

B. THE PROBLEM AND THE ARGUMENT

Each Term, the Supreme Court and the nation confront problems of difference in this heterogeneous society. The cases that present these problems attract heightened media attention and reenact continuing struggles over the meanings of sub-group identity in a nation committed to an idea called equality. The drama of these cases reveals the enduring grip of "difference" in the public imagination, and the genuine social and economic conflicts over what particular differences come to mean over time. During the 1986 Term, litigators framed for the Court issues about the permissible legal meanings of difference in the lives of individuals, minority groups, and majority groups in cases involving gender, race, ethnicity, religion and handicap.

Uniting these questions is the dilemma of difference. The dilemma of difference has three versions . . .

I believe these dilemmas arise out of powerful unstated assumptions about whose point of view matters, and about what is given and what is mutable in the world. "Difference" is only meaningful as a comparison. I am no more different from you than you are from me. A short person is different only in relation to a tall one. Legal treatment of difference tends to take for granted an assumed point of comparison: women are compared to the unstated norm of men, "minority" races to whites, handicapped persons to the ablebodied, and "minority" religions to "majorities." Such assumptions work in part through the very structure of our language, which embeds the unstated points of comparison inside categories that bury their perspective and wrongly imply a natural fit with the world. The term "working mother," modifies the general category "mother," revealing that the general term carries some unstated common meanings (that is, a woman who cares for her children full-time without pay), which, even if unintended, must expressly be modified. Legal treatment of difference thus tends to treat as unproblematic the point of view from which difference is seen, assigned, or ignored, rather than acknowledging that the problem of difference can be described and understood from multiple points of view.

Noticing the unstated point of comparison and point of view used in assessments of difference does not eliminate the dilemma of difference; instead, more importantly, it links problems

ive stance may appear partial from another
point of view. Furthermore, what initially appears to be a fixed and objective difference may
seem from another viewpoint like the subordination or exclusion of some people by others.
Regardless of which perspective ultimately seems
persuasive, the possibility of multiple viewpoints
challenges the assumption of objectivity and
shows how claims to knowledge bear the imprint
of those making the claims. . . .

. . . It is not only that justice is created by, and
defeated by, people who have genders, races, eth-
nicities, religions—people who are themselves
situated in relation to the differences they discuss. It is also the case that justice is made by
people who live in a world already made. Existing institutions and language already carve the
world and already express and recreate attitudes
about what counts as a difference, and who or
what is the relevant point of comparison. Once
we see that any point of view, including one's
own, *is* a point of view, we will realize that every
difference we see is seen in relation to something
already assumed as the starting point. Then we
can expose for debate what the starting points
should be. The task for judges is to identify vantage points, to learn how to adopt contrasting
vantage points, and to decide which vantage
points to embrace in given circumstances.

. . . Instead of a new solution, I urge struggles over descriptions of reality. Litigation in the
Supreme Court should be an opportunity to
endow rival vantage points with the reality that
power enables, to redescribe and remake the
meanings of difference in a world that has
treated only some vantage points on difference
as legitimate.

Far from being unmanageable, this approach
describes what happens already in the best practices of justice. Justice, in this view, is not abstract, universal, or neutral. Instead, justice is
the quality of human engagement with multiple
perspectives framed by, but not limited to, the
relationships of power in which they are formed.
Decisions, then, can and must be made. Despite
the distortions sometimes injected by a language
of objectivity and neutrality, the Supreme Court

has "engendered" justice in many cases. These
cases show the commitment in contemporary
statutory and constitutional law to give equality
meaning for people once thought to be "different" from those in charge. From the work of this
Term, . . . I hope to demonstrate how our common humanity wins when the Court struggles
with our differences.

II. A CASE OF DIFFERENCES

Arguments before the Supreme Court engage
all three versions of the difference dilemma and
cut across cases otherwise differentiated by doctrine and contexts. The dilemma arises in both
equality and religion cases, and in statutory and
constitutional contexts. This Section explicitly
draws connections across these seemingly disparate cases and explores the dilemma in cases
decided in the 1986 Term.

A. THE DILEMMA OF RECREATING DIFFERENCE BOTH BY IGNORING IT AND BY NOTICING IT

*California Federal Savings & Loan Association v.
Guerra (CalFed)* presented in classic form the
dilemma of recreating difference through both
noticing and ignoring it. Petitioners, a collection
of employers, argued that a California statute
mandating a qualified right to reinstatement following an unpaid pregnancy disability leave
amounted to special preferential treatment, in
violation of title VII's prohibition of discrimination on the basis of pregnancy. Writing an opinion announcing the judgment for the Court,
Justice Marshall transformed the question presented by the plaintiffs: instead of asking whether
the federal ban against discrimination on the
basis of pregnancy precluded a state's decision to
require special treatment for pregnancy, the majority asked whether the state could adopt a minimum protection for pregnant workers, while still
permitting employers to avoid treating pregnant
workers differently by extending similar benefits
to nonpregnant workers. Framing the problem
this way, the majority ruled that "Congress intended the PDA to be 'a floor beneath which
pregnancy disability benefits may not drop—not
a ceiling above which they may not rise.'" The

majority acknowledged the risk that recognizing the difference of pregnancy could recreate its stigmatizing effects, but noted that "a State could not mandate special treatment of pregnant workers based on stereotypes or generalizations about their needs and abilities." Thus, despite the federal antidiscrimination requirement, the majority found that states could direct employers to take the sheer physical disability of the pregnancy difference into account, but not any stereotyped views associated with that difference. The majority gave two responses to the problem of difference: first, accommodating pregnant workers would secure a workplace that would equally enable both female and male employees to work and have a family; second, the federal and state statutes should be construed as inviting employers to provide the same benefits to men and women in comparable situations of disability.

Writing for the dissenters, Justice White maintained that the California statute required disability leave policies for pregnant workers even in the absence of similar policies for men. It thus violated the PDA, which "leaves no room for preferential treatment of pregnant workers." In the face of this conflict, the federal statute must preempt the state law. The commands of nondiscrimination prohibit taking differences into account, Justice White argued, regardless of the impact of this neglect on people with the difference. Justice White acknowledged the majority's argument that preferential treatment would revive nineteenth-century protective legislation, perpetuating sex-role stereotypes and "imped[ing] women in their efforts to take their rightful place in the workplace." For Justice White, however, such arguments were irrelevant, because the Court's role was restricted to interpreting congressional intent and thus would not permit consideration of the arguments about stereotyping. Yet, to some extent, the issue of stereotypes was unavoidable: the dilemma in the case, from one point of view, was whether women could secure a benefit that would eliminate a burden connected with their gender, without at the same time reactivating negative meanings about their gender.

In two other cases in the 1986 Term, the Court confronted the dilemma of recreating difference in situations in which individuals claimed to be members of minority races in order to obtain special legal protections. By claiming an identity in order to secure some benefit from it, the individuals faced the dilemma that they might fuel negative meanings of that identity, meanings beyond their control. Although racial identification under federal civil rights statutes provides a means of legal redress, it also runs the risk of recreating stigmatizing associations, thereby stimulating prejudice.

In *Saint Francis College v. Al-Khazraji*, a man from Iraq who had failed to secure tenure from his employer, a private college, brought a claim of racial discrimination under 42 U.S.C. section 1981. His case foundered, however, when the lower courts rejected his claim that his Arab identity constituted racial membership of the sort protected by the federal statute.

In *Shaare Tefila Congregation v. Cobb*, members of a Jewish congregation whose synagogue was defaced by private individuals alleged violations of the federal guarantee against interference with property rights on racial grounds. The difference dilemma appeared on the face of the complaint: the petitioners argued that Jews are not a racially distinct group, and yet they claimed that Jews should be entitled to protection against racial discrimination because others treat them as though they were distinct. The petitioners thus demonstrated their reluctance to have a difference identified in a way that they themselves could not control, while simultaneously expressing their desire for protection against having that difference assigned to them by others. To gain this protection, the petitioners had to identify themselves through the very category they rejected as a definition of themselves. Both the district court and the court of appeals refused to allow the petitioners to be included in the protected group on the basis of the attitudes of others, without some proof of well-established traits internal to the group. . . . In contrast, one member of the appeals panel, dissenting on this point, argued: "Misperception lies at the heart of prejudice, and the animus formed of such ignorance sows malice and hatred wherever it operates without restriction." . . .

B. Neutrality and Non-neutrality: The Dilemma of Government Embroilment in Difference

The dilemma of difference appears especially acute for a government committed to acting neutrally. Neutral means might not produce neutral results, given historic practices and social arrangements that have not been neutral. For example, securing neutrality toward religious differences is the explicit goal of both the first amendment's ban against the establishment of religion and its protection of the free exercise of religion. Thus, to be truly neutral, the government must walk a narrow path between promoting or endorsing religion and failing to make room for religious exercise. Accommodation of religious practices may look non-neutral, but failure to accommodate may also seem non-neutral by burdening the religious minority whose needs were not built into the structure of mainstream institutions.

The "Creation Science" case, *Edwards v. Aguillard*, question of how the government, in the form of public schools, can respect religious differences while remaining neutral toward them. In *Edwards*, parents and students claimed that a Louisiana statute requiring public schools to teach creation science whenever they taught the theory of evolution violated the establishment clause. Community members subscribing to fundamentalist religious beliefs, however, have argued that public school instruction in evolution alone is not neutral, because it gives a persuasive advantage to views that undermine their own religious beliefs. Relying on similar arguments, the state avowed a neutral, nonreligious purpose for its statute.

The majority, in an opinion by Justice Brennan, concluded that the legislation was actually intended to "provide persuasive advantage to a particular religious doctrine that rejects the factual basis of evolution in its entirety." By contrast, the dissenting opinion by Justice Scalia, which was joined by Chief Justice Rehnquist, expressly tangled with the neutrality problem, noting the difficult tensions between anti-establishment and free exercise concerns, and between neutrality through indifference and neutrality through accommodation. In the end, the dissent was moved by the state's attempt to avoid undermining the different views of fundamentalist Christian students, while the majority was persuaded that the statute gave an illegal preference to a particular religious view. For both sides, however, the central difficulty was how to find a neutral position between these two risks. . . .

C. Discretion and Formality: The Dilemma of Using Power to Differentiate

The Court's commitment to the rule of law often leads it to specify, in formal terms, the rules that govern the decisions of others. This practice can secure adherence to the goals of equality and neutrality by assuring that differences are not taken into account except in the manner explicitly specified by the Court. . . .

This dilemma of discretion and formality most vividly occupied the Court in *McCleskey v. Kemp*, in which the Court evaluated charges of racial discrimination in the administration of the death penalty in Georgia's criminal justice system. A statistical study of over 2000 murder cases in Georgia during the 1970's submitted by the defendant and assumed by the Court to be valid, demonstrated that the likelihood of a defendant's receiving the death sentence was correlated with the victim's race and, to a lesser extent, the defendant's race. According to the study, black defendants convicted of killing white victims "have the greatest likelihood of receiving the death penalty." Should the Court treat a sentencing "discrepancy that appears to correlate with race" as a defect requiring judicial constraints on prosecutorial and jury discretion, or as an unavoidable consequence of such discretion? In making this choice, the majority and the dissenters each latched onto opposing sides of the dilemma about discretion and formality.

. . . In the majority's view, recognizing claims such as McCleskey's would open the door "to claims based on unexplained discrepancies that correlate to membership in other minority groups, and even to gender" or physical appearance. This argument, perhaps meant in part to trivialize the dissent's objections by linking physical appearance with race, sex, and ethnicity, implied that discrepancies in criminal sentences are random and too numerous to control. Furthermore, in the majority's view, any attempt to channel discretion runs the risk of undermining it altogether: "it is difficult to imagine guidelines that would produce the predictability sought by the dissent without sacrificing the discretion essential to a humane and fair system of criminal justice."

. . . To Justice Brennan, however, the statistical correlation between death sentences and the race of defendants and victims showed that participants in the state criminal justice system had, in fact, considered race and produced judgments "completely at odds with [the] concern that an individual be evaluated as a unique human being." Justice Brennan argued that "[d]iscretion is a means, not an end" and that, under the circumstances, the Court must monitor the discretion of others. Justice Brennan also responded to the majority's fear of widespread challenges to all aspects of criminal sentencing: "Taken on its face, such a statement seems to suggest a fear of too much justice. . . . The prospect that there may be more widespread abuse than McCleskey documents may be dismaying, but it does not justify complete abdication of our judicial role."

. . . The next Section argues that assumptions buried within the dilemmas make them seem more difficult than they need be. The task, then, is to articulate those assumptions and to evaluate the choices that remain for decisionmakers.

III. BEHIND AND BEYOND THE DILEMMA

The dilemma of difference appears unresolvable. The risk of non-neutrality—the risk of discrimination—accompanies efforts both to ignore and to recognize difference in equal treatment and special treatment; in color- or gender-blindness and in affirmative action; in governmental neutrality and in governmental preferences; and in decisionmakers' discretion and in formal constraints on discretion. Yet the dilemma is not as intractable as it seems. What makes it seem so difficult are unstated assumptions about the nature of difference. . . .

— First, we often assume that "differences" are intrinsic, rather than viewing them as expressions of comparisons between people. We are all different from one another in innumerable ways. Each of these differences is an implicit comparison we draw. And the comparisons themselves depend upon and reconfirm socially constructed meanings about what traits should matter for purposes of comparison.

— Second, typically we adopt an unstated point of reference when assessing others. From the point of reference of this norm, we determine who is different and who is normal. Women are different in relation to the unstated male norm. Blacks, Mormons, Jews, and Arabs are different in relation to the unstated white, Christian norm. Handicapped persons are different in relation to the unstated norm of able-bodiedness, or, as some have described it, the vantage point of the "Temporarily Able Persons." The unstated point of comparison is not neutral, but particular, and not inevitable, but only seemingly so when left unstated. A notion of equality that demands disregarding a "difference" calls for assimilation to an unstated norm. To strip away difference, then, often is to remove or ignore a feature distinguishing an individual from a presumed norm—like a white, able-bodied Christian man—but leaving that norm in place as the measure for equal treatment.

Third, we treat the perspective of the person doing the seeing or judging as objective, rather than as subjective. Although a person's perspective does not collapse into his or her demographic characteristics, no one is free from perspective, and no one can see fully from another's point of view.

Fourth, we assume that the perspectives of those being judged are either irrelevant or are already taken into account through the perspective of the judge. That is, we regard a person's self-conception or world view as unimportant to our treatment of that person.

Finally, there is an assumption that the existing social and economic arrangements are natural and neutral. We presume that individuals are free to form their own preferences and act upon them. In this view, any departure from the status quo risks non-neutrality and interference with free choice.

These related assumptions, once made explicit, must contend with some contrary ones. Consider these alternative starting points. Difference is relational, not intrinsic. Who or what should be taken as the point of reference for defining differences is debatable. There is no single, superior perspective for judging questions of difference. No perspective asserted to produce "the truth" is objective, but rather will obscure the power of the person attributing a difference while excluding important competing perspectives. Social arrangements can be changed: maintaining the status quo is not neutral and cannot be justified by the claim that everyone has freely chosen it. . . .

Discussion challenges the sheer power behind the usual practice of leaving [assumptions] unstated—the power that privileges unstated assumptions over alternative, competing views. Each of these assumptions bears the imprint of an historical association between power and the production of knowledge about the world. Thus, the characteristics and experiences of those people who have had power to construct legal rules and social arrangements also influence and reflect the dominant cultural expressions of what is different and what is normal.

IV. PERSPECTIVES
ON PERSPECTIVES

The difference dilemma seems paralyzing if framed by the unstated assumptions described in Part III. Those assumptions so entrench one point of view as natural and orderly that any conscious decision to notice or to ignore difference breaks the illusion of a legal world free of perspective. The assumptions make it seem that departures from unstated norms violate commitments to neutrality. Yet adhering to the unstated norms undermines commitments to neutrality—and to equality. Is it possible to proceed differently, putting these assumptions into question?

I will suggest that it is possible, even if difficult, to move beyond the constricting assumptions. . . . By asking how a member of a religious group might experience a seemingly neutral rule, or how a nonmember might experience the discretion of a religious group, Justices O'Connor, Brennan, and White made an effort in several cases to understand a different perspective. Justice Marshall and the majority in *CalFed* tried to assume the perspective of pregnant women by considering how treatment of pregnancy affects women's abilities to work outside the home while having a family. The dissenting Justices in *McCleskey* asked how defendants would react to the statistical disparity in capital sentencing by race, breaking out of the tendency to see the challenge only as a threat to the discretion and manageability of the criminal justice system. In *Saint Francis College* and *Shaare Tefila*, members of the Court struggled over whose perspective should count for purposes of defining a race and a handicap, reaching conclusions that refused to take the usual answers for granted. . . . Justice Harlan's dissent in *Plessy v. Ferguson* may have been assisted by Homer Plessy's attorney, who had urged the Justices to imagine themselves in the shoes of a black person:

Suppose a member of this court, nay, suppose every member of it, by some mysterious dispensation of providence should wake to-morrow with a black skin and curly hair . . . and in traveling through that portion of the country where the 'Jim Crow Car' abounds, should be ordered into it by the conductor. It is easy to imagine what would be the result. . . . What humiliation, what rage would then fill the judicial mind!

It may be ultimately impossible to take the perspective of another completely, but the effort to do so may help us recognize that our perspective is partial and that the status quo is not inevitable or ideal. After shaking free of these unstated assumptions and developing a sense of alternate perspectives, judges must then choose. The process of looking through other perspectives does not itself yield an answer but it may lead to an answer different from the one that the judge would otherwise have reached. Seen in this light, the dilemma is hard, but not impossible. . . .

V. ENGENDERING JUSTICE

The nineteenth-century American legal system recognized only three races: "white," "Negro," and "Indian." Californian authorities faced an influx of Chinese and Mexicans and were forced to confront the now complicated question of racial categorization. They solved the problem of categorizing Mexicans by defining them as "whites" and by according them the rights of free white persons. Chinese, however, were labeled "Indian" and denied the political and legal rights of white persons. Similarly, in 1922, a unanimous Supreme Court concluded that Japanese persons were not covered by a federal naturalization statute applicable to "free white persons," "aliens of African nativity," and "persons of African descent."

In retrospect, these results seem arbitrary. The legal authorities betrayed a striking inability to reshape their own categories for people who did not fit. Of course, it is impossible to know what might have happened if some piece of history had been otherwise. Still, it is tempting to wonder: what if the California legal authorities had changed their racial scheme, rather than forcing the Chinese and Mexican applicants into it? The officials then might have noticed that nationality, not race, distinguished these groups. What if these officials and the Justices in 1922 had tried to take the point of view of the people they were labeling? Perhaps, from this vantage point, the Justices would have realized the need for reasons—beyond racial classification—for granting or withholding legal rights and privileges. . . .

We think we know what is real, what differences are real, and what really matters, even though sometimes we realize that our perceptions and desires are influenced by others. Sometimes we realize that television, radio, classes we had in school, or the attitudes of people who matter to us affect our inclinations. Every time we wear an item of clothing that we

now think is fashionable, but used to think was ugly, we brush up against the outside influences on what we think inside. Yet we think that we think independently. We forget that widely held beliefs may be the ones most influenced from the outside.

The more powerful we are, the less we may be able to see that the world coincides with our view precisely because we shaped it in accordance with those views. . . .

If we want to preserve justice, we need to develop a practice for more knowing judgments about problems of difference. We must stop seeking to get close to the "truth" and instead seek to get close to other people's truths. The question is, how do we do this? . . .

A. IMPARTIALITY AND PARTIAL TRUTHS

It is a paradox. Only by admitting our partiality can we strive for impartiality. Impartiality is the guise partiality takes to seal bias against exposure. It looks neutral to apply a rule denying unemployment benefits to anyone who cannot fulfill the work schedule, but it is not neutral if the work schedule was devised with one religious Sabbath, and not another, in mind. The idea of impartiality implies human access to a view beyond human experience, a "God's eye" point of view. Not only do humans lack this inhuman perspective, but humans who claim it are untruthful, trying to exercise power to cut off conversation and debate.

. . . Whose partial view should resolve conflicts over how to treat assertions of difference, whether assigned or claimed? Preferring the standpoint of an historically denigrated group can reveal truths obscured by the dominant view, but it can also reconfirm the underlying conceptual scheme of the dominant view by focusing on it. Similarly, the perspective of those who are labeled "different" may offer an important challenge to the view of those who imposed the label, but it is a corrective lens, another partial view, not absolute truth. . . .

Instead of an impartial view, we should strive for the standpoint of someone who is committed to the moral relevance of contingent particulars. Put in personal terms, if I pretend to be impartial, I hide my partiality; however, if I embrace partiality, I risk ignoring you, your needs, and your alternate reality—or, conversely, embracing and appropriating your view into yet another rigid, partial view. I conclude that I must acknowledge and struggle against my partiality by making an effort to understand your reality and what it means for my own. I need to stop seeking certainty and acknowledge the complexity of our shared and colliding realities, as well as the tragic impossibility of all prevailing at once. It is this complexity that constitutes our reciprocal realities, and it is the conflict between our realities that constitutes us, whether we engage in it overtly or submerge it under a dominant view.

Moral action, then, takes place in a field of complexity, and we act ethically when we recognize what we give up as well as what we embrace. The solution is not to adopt and cling to some new standpoint, but instead to strive to become and remain open to perspectives and claims that challenge our own. . . .

Two exercises can help those who judge to glimpse the perspectives of others and to avoid a false impartiality. The first is to explore our own stereotypes, our own attitudes toward people we treat as different—and, indeed, our own categories for organizing the world. Audre Lorde put it powerfully: "I urge each one of us here to reach down into that deep place of knowledge inside herself and touch that terror and loathing of any difference that lives there. See whose face it wears. Then the personal as the political can begin to illuminate all our choices." . . . We must also examine and retool our methods of classification and consider how they save us from questioning our instincts, ourselves, and our existing social arrangements. Putting ourselves in the place of those who look different can push us to challenge our ignorance and fears and to investigate our usual categories for making sense of the world. This is an opportunity to enlarge judges' understanding and abilities to become better practitioners in the business of solving problems.

The second exercise is to search out differences and celebrate them, constructing new bases for connection. We can pursue the possibilities of difference behind seeming commonalities and seek out commonalities across difference, thereby confronting the ready association of sameness with equality and difference with inferiority. One route is to emphasize our common humanity, despite our different traits. Another tack is to disentangle difference from the allocation of benefits and burdens in society—a tack that may well require looking at difference to alter how people use it. The Court's effort to assure equality for women and men in the conjunction of work and family life in *CalFed* represents such an effort to disentangle institutional arrangements from the difference they create. A third approach is to cherish difference and welcome anomaly. Still another is to understand that which initially seems strange and to learn about sense and reason from this exercise—just as philosophers, anthropologists, and psychologists have urged us to take seriously the self-conceptions and perceptions of others. In the process of trying to understand how another person understands, we may even remake our categories of understanding. Other persons may not even define "self" the same way we do, and glimpsing their "self-concepts" thus challenges us to step beyond our operating assumptions. . . .

This exhortation—that we must take the perspective of another, while remembering that we cannot really know what another sees, and must put our own categories up for challenge, without ceding the definition of reality over to others—sounds quite complicated. What do we do with the sense of complexity?

B. COMPLEXITY, PASSIVITY, AND THE STATUS QUO: THE PROBLEM OF DEFERENCE

We are mistaken when we hold onto simple certainties. Yet complexity seems both overwhelming and incapacitating. By bearing into complexity rather than turning away from it, by listening to the variety of voices implicated in our problems, we may lose a sense of ready solutions and steady certainties. But clear answers have been false gods, paid homage to in the coinage of other people's opportunities, and also at cost to our own character. We harden ourselves when we treat our categories as though they were real, closing off responses to new facts and to challenges to how we live and think. Our certainties also leave unresolved conflicts among incompatible but deeply held values. In the face of complexity, "[t]he politics of difference can all too easily degenerate into the politics of 'mutual indifference. . . .'" If we care about justice, the biggest mistake would be to respond to complexity with passivity. That response is not impartial; it favors the status quo, those benefited by it, and the conception of reality it fosters.

1. Forms of Passivity.—Four forms of judicial passivity may be tempting in the face of complexity: deference, intent requirements, reliance on apparent choices or concessions of the parties, and reliance on doctrine. I will consider each in turn.

Respect for other institutions and persons is a critical part of judging, but there are particular risks when the Court, while acknowledging the complexity of a problem of difference, defers to other branches or levels of government, to private actors, or even to the parties before the Court. One risk is that the Court will pretend that it has no power over or responsibility for what results. When the Court defers to Congress, the executive, a state government, or a private actor, the Justices are saying, let's not make a decision, let's leave it to others, or let's endorse the freedom or respect the power of others. It is surely important for the Justices to understand their relationship with other people or institutions with interests in a matter, but such understanding is quite different from ceding responsibility for what ensues. . . .

Problems also arise when the Court takes on the second form of passivity: focusing on the intentions of the parties before it. When the Court demands evidence of intentional discrimination before upholding a plaintiff's charges, the Justices are deferring to and thereby entrenching the perspective of the defendant, thus rejecting the perspective of the plaintiff-victim. Asking only about the sincerity of the motive behind a statute whose effect is challenged is also an act that takes sides, defines which reality will govern, and avoids the real challenge of responding to the perspective of the plaintiff.

It is equally problematic for the Court, in a third form of passivity, to point to apparent choices made by plaintiffs, victims, or members of minority groups. . . . The Court may presume incorrectly that the choices are free and uncoerced, or the Court may wrongly attribute certain meanings to a choice. . . .

The fourth form of passivity is perhaps one of the most effective circumventions of responsibility: the Court's reliance on its own doctrinal boundaries and categories to resolve the cases before it. . . . Legal analogy is typically inseparable from precedential reasoning, telescoping the creative potential of a search for surprising similarities into a narrow focus on prior rulings that could "control" the instant case. The Court's practice vividly demonstrates how fabricated categories can assume the status of immutable reality. Of course, law would be overwhelming without doctrinal categories and separate lines of precedent. Yet by holding to rigid categories, the Court denies the existence of tensions and portrays a false simplicity amid a rabbit warren of complexity. The Court's strict segregation of doctrines also cloisters lines of thought and insights, thereby restricting the Court's ability to use larger frames of judgment.

2. Avoiding Passivity.—Besides resisting tempting forms of passivity—which do not lessen judicial responsibility—the Court can and should challenge rigid patterns of thought. . . .

Litigants and judges should search out unexpected analogies to scrape off barnacles of thought and to challenge views so settled that they are not thought to be views. This process may persuade particular judges, in particular cases, to see a different angle on a problem. It also holds promise as a method for finding surprising commonalities that can nudge us all to reassess well-established categories of thought.

The promise of reasoning by analogy is lost if it becomes an arid conceptualist enterprise.

Yet when immersed in the particulars of a problem, we sometimes are able to think up analogies that break out of ill-fitting conceptual schemes. . . . Similarly, dialogue in legal briefs and courtroom arguments can stretch the minds of listeners, especially if they are actively forming their own position and not simply picking between the ones before them.

The introduction of additional voices may enable adversary dialogue to expand beyond a stylized, either/or mode, prompting new and creative insights. . . . Seeking unusual perspectives enables justices to avail themselves of the "partial superiority" of other people's views and to reach for what is unfamiliar and perhaps suppressed under the dominant ways of seeing. Bringing in a wider variety of views can also make the so-called "counter-majoritarian" Court more "democratic."

Besides seeking out unfamiliar perspectives and analogies new to the law, all judges should also consider the human consequences of their decisions in difference cases, rather than insulating themselves in abstractions. . . . I petition all judges to open up to the chance that someone may move them—the experience will not tell them what to do, but it may give them a way outside of routinized categories to forge new approaches to the problem at hand.

This call to be open, to canvass personal experience, applies to all legal controversies, but it is especially important in the context of cases that present the dilemma of difference. Here the judicial mainstays of neutrality and distance prove most risky, for they blind judges to their own involvement in recreating the negative meanings of difference. Yet the dangers of making differences matter also argue against categorical solutions. By struggling to respond humanly to the dilemma in each particular context, the judge can supply the possibility of connection otherwise missing in the categorical treatments of difference.

. . . The struggle is not over the validity of principles and generalizations—it is over which ones should prevail in a given context. The choice from among principles, in turn, implicates choices about which differences, and which similarities, should matter. These are moral choices, choices about which voices should persuade those who judge.

Even when we understand them, some voices will lose. The fundamentalist Christians who supported the Balanced Treatment Act in Louisiana deserve respect and understanding: their view of the world may well be threatened by the curriculum taught to their children in the public schools. However, this is what the fight is about. Whose view of reality should prevail in public institutions? This deep conundrum involves the conflicts between the world view animating any rule for the entire society, and the world views of subgroups who will never share the dominant views. I am tempted to propose a seemingly "neutral" rule, such as a rule that judges interpreting the commitment to respect difference should make the choice that allows difference to flourish without imposing it on others. If exclusion of their world view from the biology curriculum creates an intolerable choice for the fundamentalists, they do and they must have the choice to establish their own educational institutions, and their own separate community. Yet this seemingly "neutral" position is a comfortable view for a nonfundamentalist like myself, who cannot appreciate the full impact of the evolution science curriculum as experienced by at least some fundamentalists. Rather than pretending to secure a permanent solution through a "neutral" rule, I must acknowledge the tragedy of non-neutrality—and admit that our very commitment to tolerance yields intolerance toward some views. If the fundamentalists lose in this case, they can continue to struggle to challenge the meaning of the commitment to separate church and state, and they may convince the rest of us in the next round. Although it may be little solace for the minority group, its challenge achieves something even when it loses, by reminding the nation of our commitment to diversity, and our inability, thus far, to achieve it fully.

Thus, choices from among competing commitments do not end after the Court announces its judgment. Continuing skepticism about the reality endorsed by the Court—or any source of governmental power—is the only guard against tyranny.

The continuing process of debate over deeply held but conflicting commitments is both the mechanism and the promise of our governmental system. Within that system, the Supreme Court's power depends upon persuasion. As Hannah Arendt wrote: "the thinking process which is active in judging something is not, like the thought process of pure reasoning, a dialogue between me and myself, but finds itself always and primarily, even if I am quite alone in making up my mind, in an anticipated communication with others with whom I know I must finally come to some agreement." The important question is, with whom must you come to agreement? In a society of diversity with legacies of discrimination, within a polity committed to self-governance, the judiciary becomes a critical arena for demands of inclusion. . . .

REVIEW AND DISCUSSION QUESTIONS

1. Explain what Minow means by the dilemma of difference.

2. Describe how she uses different legal decisions to illustrate the dilemma of difference.

3. What recommendations does Minow make that she thinks will bring about more equal treatment by judges in deciding cases?

Equality, Race, and Gender

Peter Singer

In this essay Peter Singer discusses various conceptions of equality, asking whether it is based on natural characteristics that people share. But if it is not based on shared characteristics, then what does equality mean, given that people differ so much emotionally, intellectually, and morally? After weighing the significance of "genetic diversity" for equality, Singer goes on to discuss the relevance of IQ and the differences between the sexes. He concludes with an argument that instead of equality of opportunity or treatment, the real basis of equality is equality of consideration. Peter Singer is professor of philosophy at Princeton University.

THE BASIS OF EQUALITY

The [twentieth] century has seen dramatic changes in moral attitudes. Most of these changes are still controversial. Abortion, almost everywhere prohibited thirty years ago, is now legal in many countries (though it is still opposed by substantial and respected sections of the population). The same is true of changes in attitudes to sex outside marriage, homosexuality, pornography, euthanasia, and suicide. Great as the changes have been, no new consensus has been reached. The issues remain controversial and it is possible to defend either side without jeopardising one's intellectual or social standing.

Equality seems to be different. The change in attitudes to inequality—especially racial inequality—has been no less sudden and dramatic than the change in attitudes to sex, but it has been more complete. Racist assumptions shared by most Europeans at the turn of the century are now totally unacceptable, at least in public life. A poet could not now write of 'lesser breeds without the law', and retain—indeed enhance—his reputation, as Rudyard Kipling did in 1897. This does not mean that there are no longer any racists, but only that they must disguise their racism if their views and policies are to have any chance of general acceptance. Even South Africa has abandoned apartheid. The principle that all humans are equal is now part of the prevailing political and ethical orthodoxy. But what, exactly, does it mean and why do we accept it?

Once we go beyond the agreement that blatant forms of racial discrimination are wrong, once we question the basis of the principle that all humans are equal and seek to apply this principle to particular cases, the consensus starts to weaken. One sign of this was the furor that occurred during the 1970s over the claims made by Arthur Jensen, professor of educational psychology at the University of California, Berkeley, and H. J. Eysenck, professor of psychology at the University of London, about genetically based variations in intelligence between different races. Many of the most forceful opponents of Jensen and Eysenck assume that these claims, if sound, would justify racial discrimination. Are they right? Similar questions can be asked about research into differences between males and females.

Another issue requiring us to think about the principle of equality is 'affirmative action'. Some philosophers and lawyers have argued that the principle of equality requires that when allocating jobs or university places we should favour members of disadvantaged minorities. Others have contended that the same principle of equality rules out any discrimination on racial grounds, whether for or against the worst-off members of society.

We can only answer these questions if we are clear about what it is we intend to say, and can justifiably say, when we assert that all humans are equal—hence the need for an inquiry into the ethical foundations of the principle of equality.

When we say that all humans are equal, irrespective of race or sex, what exactly are we claiming? Racists, sexists, and other opponents of equality have often pointed out that, by whatever test we choose, it simply is not true that all humans are equal. Some are tall, some are short; some are good at mathematics, others are poor at it; some can run 100 metres in ten seconds, some take fifteen or twenty; some would never intentionally hurt another being, others would

kill a stranger for $100 if they could get away with it; some have emotional lives that touch the heights of ecstasy and the depths of despair, while others live on a more even plane, relatively untouched by what goes on around them. And so we could go on. The plain fact is that humans differ, and the differences apply to so many characteristics that the search for a factual basis on which to erect the principle of equality seems hopeless.

John Rawls has suggested, in his influential book *A Theory of Justice,* that equality can be founded on the natural characteristics of human beings, provided we select what he calls a 'range property'. Suppose we draw a circle on a piece of paper. Then all points within the circle—this is the 'range'—have the property of being within the circle, and they have this property equally. Some points may be closer to the centre and others nearer the edge, but all are, equally, points inside the circle. Similarly, Rawls suggests, the property of 'moral personality' is a property that virtually all humans possess, and all humans who possess this property possess it equally. By 'moral personality' Rawls does not mean 'morally good personality'; he is using 'moral' in contrast to 'amoral'. A moral person, Rawls says, must have a sense of justice. More broadly, one might say that to be a moral person is to be the kind of person to whom one can make moral appeals, with some prospect that the appeal will be heeded.

Rawls maintains that moral personality is the basis of human equality, a view that derives from his 'contract' approach to justice. The contract tradition sees ethics as a kind of mutually beneficial agreement—roughly, 'Don't hit me and I won't hit you.' Hence only those capable of appreciating that they are not being hit, and of restraining their own hitting accordingly, are within the sphere of ethics.

There are problems with using moral personality as the basis of equality. One objection is that having a moral personality is a matter of degree. Some people are highly sensitive to issues of justice and ethics generally; others, for a variety of reasons, have only a limited awareness of such principles. The suggestion that being a moral person is the minimum necessary for coming within the scope of the principle of equality still leaves it open just where this minimal line is to be drawn. Nor is it intuitively obvious why, if moral personality is so important, we should not have grades of moral status, with rights and duties corresponding to the degree of refinement of one's sense of justice.

Still more serious is the objection that it is not true that all humans are moral persons, even in the most minimal sense. Infants and small children, along with some intellectually disabled humans, lack the required sense of justice. Shall we then say that all humans are equal, except for very young or intellectually disabled ones? This is certainly not what we ordinarily understand by the principle of equality. If this revised principle implies that we may disregard the interests of very young or intellectually disabled humans in ways that would be wrong if they were older or more intelligent, we would need far stronger arguments to induce us to accept it. (Rawls deals with infants and children by including *potential* moral persons along with actual ones within the scope of the principle of equality. But this is an ad hoc device, confessedly designed to square his theory with our ordinary moral intuitions, rather than something for which independent arguments can be produced. Moreover although Rawls admits that those with irreparable intellectual disabilities 'may present a difficulty' he offers no suggestions towards the solution of this difficulty.)

So the possession of 'moral personality' does not provide a satisfactory basis for the principle that all humans are equal. I doubt that any natural characteristic, whether a 'range property' or not, can fulfil this function, for I doubt that there is any morally significant property that all humans possess equally.

There is another possible line of defence for the belief that there is a factual basis for a principle of equality that prohibits racism and sexism. We can admit that humans differ as individuals, and yet insist that there are no morally significant differences between the races and sexes. Knowing that someone is of African or European descent, female or male, does not enable us to draw conclusions about her or his intelligence, sense of justice, depth of feelings, or

anything else that would entitle us to treat her or him as less than equal. The racist claim that people of European descent are superior to those of other races in these capacities is in this sense false. The differences between individuals in these respects are not captured by racial boundaries. The same is true of the sexist stereotype that sees women as emotionally deeper and more caring, but also less rational, less aggressive, and less enterprising than men. Obviously this is not true of women as a whole. Some women are emotionally shallower, less caring, and more rational, more aggressive, and more enterprising than some men.

The fact that humans differ as individuals, not as races or sexes, is important, and we shall return to it when we come to discuss the implications of the claims made by Jensen, Eysenck, and others; yet it provides neither a satisfactory principle of equality nor an adequate defence against a more sophisticated opponent of equality than the blatant racist or sexist. Suppose that someone proposes that people should be given intelligence tests and then classified into higher or lower status categories on the basis of the results. Perhaps those who scored above 125 would be a slave-owning class; those scoring between 100 and 125 would be free citizens but lack the right to own slaves; while those scoring below 100 would be made the slaves of those who had scored above 125. A hierarchical society of this sort seems as abhorrent as one based on race or sex; but if we base our support for equality on the factual claim that differences between individuals cut across racial and sexual boundaries, we have no grounds for opposing this kind of inegalitarianism. For this hierarchical society would be based on real differences between people.

We can reject this 'hierarchy of intelligence' and similar fantastic schemes only if we are clear that the claim to equality does not rest on the possession of intelligence, moral personality, rationality, or similar matters of fact. There is no logically compelling reason for assuming that a difference in ability between two people justifies any difference in the amount of consideration we give to their interests. Equality is a basic ethical principle, not an assertion of fact. We can see this if we return to our earlier discussion of the universal aspect of ethical judgments.

. . . When I make an ethical judgment I must go beyond a personal or sectional point of view and take into account the interests of all those affected. This means that we weigh up interests, considered simply as interests and not as my interests, or the interests of Australians, or of people of European descent. This provides us with a basic principle of equality: the principle of equal consideration of interests.

The essence of the principle of equal consideration of interests is that we give equal weight in our moral deliberations to the like interests of all those affected by our actions. This means that if only X and Y would be affected by a possible act, and if X stands to lose more than Y stands to gain, it is better not to do the act. We cannot, if we accept the principle of equal consideration of interests, say that doing the act is better, despite the facts described, because we are more concerned about Y than we are about X. What the principle really amounts to is this: an interest is an interest, whoever's interest it may be.

We can make this more concrete by considering a particular interest, say the interest we have in the relief of pain. Then the principle says that the ultimate moral reason for relieving pain is simply the undesirability of pain as such, and not the undesirability of X's pain, which might be different from the undesirability of Y's pain. Of course, X's pain might be more undesirable than Y's pain because it is more painful, and then the principle of equal consideration would give greater weight to the relief of X's pain. Again, even where the pains are equal, other factors might be relevant, especially if others are affected. If there has been an earthquake we might give priority to the relief of a doctor's pain so she can treat other victims. But the doctor's pain itself counts only once, and with no added weighting. The principle of equal consideration of interests acts like a pair of scales, weighing interests impartially. True scales favour the side where the interest is stronger or where several interests combine to outweigh a smaller number of similar interests; but they take no account of whose interests they are weighing.

From this point of view race is irrelevant to the consideration of interests; for all that counts are the interests themselves. To give less consideration to a specified amount of pain because that pain was experienced by a member of a particular race would be to make an arbitrary distinction. Why pick on race? Why not on whether a person was born in a leap year? Or whether there is more than one vowel in her surname? All these characteristics are equally irrelevant to the undesirability of pain from the universal point of view. Hence the principle of equal consideration of interests shows straightforwardly why the most blatant forms of racism, like that of the Nazis, are wrong. For the Nazis were concerned only for the welfare of members of the 'Aryan' race, and the sufferings of Jews, Gypsies, and Slavs were of no concern to them.

The principle of equal consideration of interests is sometimes thought to be a purely formal principle, lacking in substance and too weak to exclude any inegalitarian practice. We have already seen, however, that it does exclude racism and sexism, at least in their most blatant forms. If we look at the impact of the principle on the imaginary hierarchical society based on intelligence tests we can see that it is strong enough to provide a basis for rejecting this more sophisticated form of inegalitarianism, too.

The principle of equal consideration of interests prohibits making our readiness to consider the interests of others depend on their abilities or other characteristics, apart from the characteristic of having interests. It is true that we cannot know where equal consideration of interests will lead us until we know what interests people have, and this may vary according to their abilities or other characteristics. Consideration of the interests of mathematically gifted children may lead us to teach them advanced mathematics at an early age, which for different children might be entirely pointless or positively harmful. But the basic element, the taking into account of the person's interests, whatever they may be, must apply to everyone, irrespective of race, sex, or scores on an intelligence test. Enslaving those who score below a certain line on an intelligence test would not—barring extraordinary and implausible beliefs about human nature—be compatible with equal consideration. Intelligence has nothing to do with many important interests that humans have, like the interest in avoiding pain, in developing one's abilities, in satisfying basic needs for food and shelter, in enjoying friendly and loving relations with others, and in being free to pursue one's projects without unnecessary interference from others. Slavery prevents the slaves from satisfying these interests as they would want to; and the benefits it confers on the slave-owners are hardly comparable in importance to the harm it does to the slaves.

So the principle of equal consideration of interests is strong enough to rule out an intelligence-based slave society as well as cruder forms of racism and sexism. It also rules out discrimination on the grounds of disability, whether intellectual or physical, in so far as the disability is not relevant to the interests under consideration (as, for example, severe intellectual disability might be if we are considering a person's interest in voting in an election). The principle of equal consideration of interests therefore may be a defensible form of the principle that all humans are equal, a form that we can use in discussing more controversial issues about equality. Before we go on to these topics, however, it will be useful to say a little more about the nature of the principle.

Equal consideration of interests is a minimal principle of equality in the sense that it does not dictate equal treatment. Take a relatively straightforward example of an interest, the interest in having physical pain relieved. Imagine that after an earthquake I come across two victims, one with a crushed leg, in agony, and one with a gashed thigh, in slight pain. I have only two shots of morphine left. Equal treatment would suggest that I give one to each injured person, but one shot would not do much to relieve the pain of the person with the crushed leg. She would still be in much more pain than the other victim, and even after I have given her one shot, giving her the second shot would bring greater relief than giving a shot to the person in slight pain. Hence equal consideration of interests in this situation leads to what some may consider an inegalitarian result: two shots of morphine for one person, and none for the other.

There is a still more controversial inegalitarian implication of the principle of equal consideration of interests. In the case above, although equal consideration of interests leads to unequal treatment, this unequal treatment is an attempt to produce a more egalitarian result. By giving the double dose to the more seriously injured person, we bring about a situation in which there is less difference in the degree of suffering felt by the two victims than there would be if we gave one dose to each. Instead of ending up with one person in considerable pain and one in no pain, we end up with two people in slight pain. This is in line with the principle of declining marginal utility, a principle well-known to economists, which states that for a given individual, a set amount of something is more useful when people have little of it than when they have a lot. If I am struggling to survive on 200 grams of rice a day, and you provide me with an extra fifty grams per day, you have improved my position significantly; but if I already have a kilo of rice per day, I won't care much about the extra fifty grams. When marginal utility is taken into account the principle of equal consideration of interests inclines us towards an equal distribution of income, and to that extent the egalitarian will endorse its conclusions. What is likely to trouble the egalitarian about the principle of equal consideration of interests is that there are circumstances in which the principle of declining marginal utility does not hold or is overridden by countervailing factors.

We can vary the example of the earthquake victims to illustrate this point. Let us say, again, that there are two victims, one more severely injured than the other, but this time we shall say that the more severely injured victim, A, has lost a leg and is in danger of losing a toe from her remaining leg; while the less severely injured victim, B, has an injury to her leg, but the limb can be saved. We have medical supplies for only one person. If we use them on the more severely injured victim the most we can do is save her toe, whereas if we use them on the less severely injured victim we can save her leg. In other words, we assume that the situation is as follows: without medical treatment, A loses a leg and a toe, while B loses only a leg; if we give the treatment to A, A loses a leg and B loses a leg; if we give the treatment to B, A loses a leg and a toe, while B loses nothing.

Assuming that it is worse to lose a leg than it is to lose a toe (even when that toe is on one's sole remaining foot) the principle of declining marginal utility does not suffice to give us the right answer in this situation. We will do more to further the interests, impartially considered, of those affected by our actions if we use our limited resources on the less seriously injured victim than on the more seriously injured one. Therefore this is what the principle of equal consideration of interests leads us to do. Thus equal consideration of interests can, in special cases, widen rather than narrow the gap between two people at different levels of welfare. It is for this reason that the principle is a minimal principle of equality, rather than a thoroughgoing egalitarian principle. A more thoroughgoing form of egalitarianism would, however, be difficult to justify, both in general terms and in its application to special cases of the kind just described.

Minimal as it is, the principle of equal consideration of interests can seem too demanding in some cases. Can any of us really give equal consideration to the welfare of our family and the welfare of strangers? . . . [I]t does not force us to abandon the principle, although the principle may force us to abandon some other views we hold. Meanwhile we shall see how the principle assists us in discussing some of the controversial issues raised by demands for equality.

EQUALITY AND GENETIC DIVERSITY

In 1969 Arthur Jensen published a long article in the *Harvard Educational Review* entitled 'How Much Can We Boost IQ and Scholastic Achievement?' One short section of the article discussed the probable causes of the undisputed fact that—on average—African Americans do not score as well as most other Americans in standard IQ tests. Jensen summarised the upshot of this section as follows:

All we are left with are various lines of evidence, no one of which is definitive alone, but which, viewed altogether, make it a not unreasonable hypothesis that genetic factors are strongly implicated in the average negro–white intelligence difference. The preponderance of evidence is, in my opinion, less consistent with a strictly environmental hypothesis than with a genetic hypothesis, which, of course, does not exclude the influence of environment or its interaction with genetic factors.

This heavily qualified statement comes in the midst of a detailed review of a complex scientific subject, published in a scholarly journal. It would hardly have been surprising if it passed unnoticed by anyone but scientists working in the area of psychology or genetics. Instead it was widely reported in the popular press as an attempt to defend racism on scientific grounds. Jensen was accused of spreading racist propaganda and likened to Hitler. His lectures were shouted down and students demanded that he be dismissed from his university post. H. J. Eysenck, a British professor of psychology who supported Jensen's theories received similar treatment, in Britain and Australia as well as in the United States. Interestingly, Eysenck's argument did not suggest that those of European descent have the highest average intelligence among Americans; instead, he noted some evidence that Americans of Japanese and Chinese descent do better on tests of abstract reasoning (despite coming from backgrounds lower on the socioeconomic scale) than Americans of European descent.

The opposition to genetic explanations of alleged racial differences in intelligence is only one manifestation of a more general opposition to genetic explanations in other socially sensitive areas. It closely parallels, for instance, initial feminist hostility to the idea that there are biological factors behind male dominance. (The second wave of the feminist movement seems to be more willing to entertain the idea that biological differences between the sexes are influential in, for example, greater male aggression and stronger female caring behaviour.) The opposition to genetic explanations also has obvious links with the intensity of feeling aroused by sociobiological approaches to the study of human behaviour. The worry here is that if human social behaviour is seen as deriving from that of other social mammals, we shall come to think of hierarchy, male dominance, and inequality as part of our evolved nature, and as unchangeable. More recently, the commencement of the international scientific project that is designed to map the human genome—that is, to provide a detailed scientific description of the genetic code typical of human beings—has attracted protests because of apprehension over what such a map might reveal about genetic differences between humans, and the use to which such information might be put.

It would be inappropriate for me to attempt to assess the scientific merits of biological explanations of human behaviour in general, or of racial or sexual differences in particular. My concern is rather with the implications of these theories for the ideal of equality. For this purpose it is not necessary for us to establish whether the theories are right. All we have to ask is: suppose that one ethnic group does turn out to have a higher average IQ than another, and that part of this difference has a genetic basis. Would this mean that racism is defensible, and we have to reject the principle of equality? A similar question can be asked about the impact of theories of biological differences between the sexes. In neither case does the question assume that the theories are sound. It would be most unfortunate if our scepticism about such things led us to neglect these questions and then unexpected evidence turned up confirming the theories, with the result that a confused and unprepared public took the theories to have implications for the ideal of equality that they do not have.

I shall begin by considering the implications of the view that there is a difference in the average IQ of two different ethnic groups, and that genetic factors are responsible for at least a part of this difference. I shall then consider the impact of alleged differences in temperament and ability between the sexes.

RACIAL DIFFERENCES AND RACIAL EQUALITY

Let us suppose, just for the sake of exploring the consequences, that evidence accumulates supporting the hypothesis that there are differences in intelligence between the different ethnic groups of human beings. (We should not assume that this would mean that Europeans come out on top. As we have already seen, there is some evidence to the contrary.) What significance would this have for our views about racial equality?

First a word of caution. When people talk of differences in intelligence between ethnic groups, they are usually referring to differences in scores on standard IQ tests. Now 'IQ' stands for 'intelligence quotient' but this does not mean that an IQ test really measures what we mean by 'intelligence' in ordinary contexts. Obviously there is some correlation between the two: if schoolchildren regarded by their teachers as highly intelligent did not generally score better on IQ tests than schoolchildren regarded as below normal intelligence, the tests would have to be changed—as indeed they were changed in the past. But this does not show how close the correlation is, and since our ordinary concept of intelligence is vague, there is no way of telling. Some psychologists have attempted to overcome this difficulty by simply defining 'intelligence' as 'what intelligence tests measure', but this merely introduces a new concept of 'intelligence', which is easier to measure than our ordinary notion but may be quite different in meaning. Since 'intelligence' is a word in everyday use, to use the same word in a different sense is a sure path to confusion. What we should talk about, then, is differences in IQ, rather than differences in intelligence, since this is all that the available evidence could support.

The distinction between intelligence and scores on IQ tests has led some to conclude that IQ is of no importance; this is the opposite, but equally erroneous, extreme to the view that IQ is identical with intelligence. IQ is important in our society. One's IQ is a factor in one's prospects of improving one's occupational status, income, or social class. If there are genetic factors in racial differences in IQ, there will be genetic factors in racial differences in occupational status, income, and social class. So if we are interested in equality, we cannot ignore IQ.

When people of different racial origin are given IQ tests, there tend to be differences in the average scores they get. The existence of such differences is not seriously disputed, even by those who most vigorously opposed the views put forward by Jensen and Eysenck. What is hotly disputed is whether the differences are primarily to be explained by heredity or by environment—in other words, whether they reflect innate differences between different groups of human beings, or whether they are due to the different social and educational situations in which these groups find themselves. Almost everyone accepts that environmental factors do play a role in IQ differences between groups; the debate is over whether they can explain all or virtually all of the differences.

Let us suppose that the genetic hypothesis turns out to be correct (making this supposition, as I have said, not because we believe it is correct but in order to explore its implications); what would be the implications of genetically based differences in IQ between different races? I believe that the implications of this supposition are less drastic than they are often supposed to be and give no comfort to genuine racists. I have three reasons for this view.

First, the genetic hypothesis does not imply that we should reduce our efforts to overcome other causes of inequality between people, for example, in the quality of housing and schooling available to less well-off people. Admittedly, if the genetic hypothesis is correct, these efforts will not bring about a situation in which different racial groups have equal IQs. But this is no reason for accepting a situation in which any people are hindered by their environment from doing as well as they can. Perhaps we should put special efforts into helping those who start from a position of disadvantage, so that we end with a more egalitarian result.

Second, the fact that the average IQ of one racial group is a few points higher than that of another does not allow anyone to say that all members of the higher IQ group have higher IQs than all members of the lower IQ group—this is clearly false for any racial group   or that

any particular individual in the higher IQ group has a higher IQ than a particular individual in the lower IQ group—this will often be false. The point is that these figures are averages and say nothing about individuals. There will be a substantial overlap in IQ scores between the two groups. So whatever the cause of the difference in average IQs, it will provide no justification for racial segregation in education or any other field. It remains true that members of different racial groups must be treated as individuals, irrespective of their race.

The third reason why the genetic hypothesis gives no support for racism is the most fundamental of the three. It is simply that, as we saw earlier, the principle of equality is not based on any actual equality that all people share. I have argued that the only defensible basis for the principle of equality is equal consideration of interests, and I have also suggested that the most important human interests—such as the interest in avoiding pain, in developing one's abilities, in satisfying basic needs for food and shelter, in enjoying warm personal relationships, in being free to pursue one's projects without interference, and many others—are not affected by differences in intelligence. We can be even more confident that they are not affected by differences in IQ. Thomas Jefferson, who drafted the ringing assertion of equality with which the American Declaration of Independence begins, knew this. In reply to an author who had endeavoured to refute the then common view that Africans lack intelligence, he wrote:

> Be assured that no person living wishes more sincerely than I do, to see a complete refutation of the doubts I have myself entertained and expressed on the grade of understanding allotted to them by nature, and to find that they are on a par with ourselves . . . but whatever be their degree of talent, it is no measure of their rights. Because Sir Isaac Newton was superior to others in understanding, he was not therefore lord of the property or person of others.

Jefferson was right. Equal status does not depend on intelligence. Racists who maintain the contrary are in peril of being forced to kneel before the next genius they encounter.

These three reasons suffice to show that claims that for genetic reasons one racial group is not as good as another at IQ tests do not provide grounds for denying the moral principle that all humans are equal. The third reason, however, has further ramifications that we shall follow up after discussing differences between the sexes.

Sexual Differences and Sexual Equality

The debates over psychological differences between females and males are not about IQ in general. On general IQ tests there are no consistent differences in the average scores of females and males. But IQ tests measure a range of different abilities, and when we break the results down according to the type of ability measured, we do find significant differences between the sexes. There is some evidence suggesting that females have greater verbal ability than males. This involves being better able to understand complex pieces of writing and being more creative with words. Males, on the other hand, appear to have greater mathematical ability, and also do better on tests involving what is known as 'visual-spatial' ability. An example of a task requiring visual-spatial ability is one in which the subject is asked to find a shape, say a square, which is embedded or hidden in a more complex design.

We shall discuss the significance of these relatively minor differences in intellectual abilities shortly. The sexes also differ markedly in one major non-intellectual characteristic: aggression. Studies conducted on children in several different cultures have borne out what parents have long suspected: boys are more likely to play roughly, attack each other and fight back when attacked, than girls. Males are readier to hurt others than females; a tendency reflected in the fact that almost all violent criminals are male. It has been suggested that aggression is associated with competitiveness and the drive to dominate others and get to the top of whatever pyramid one is a part of. In contrast, females are readier to adopt a role that involves caring for others.

These are the major psychological differences that have repeatedly been observed in many studies of females and males. What is the origin of these differences? Once again the rival explanations are environmental versus biological, nurture versus nature. Although this question of origin is important in some special contexts, it was given too much weight by the first wave of feminists who assumed that the case for women's liberation rested on acceptance of the environmental side of the controversy. What is true of racial discrimination holds here, too: discrimination can be shown to be wrong whatever the origin of the known psychological differences. But first let us look briefly at the rival explanations.

Anyone who has had anything to do with children will know that in all sorts of ways children learn that the sexes have different roles. Boys get trucks or guns for their birthday presents; girls get dolls or brush and comb sets. Girls are put into dresses and told how nice they look; boys are dressed in jeans and praised for their strength and daring. Children's books almost invariably used to portray fathers going out to work while mothers clean the house and cook the dinner; some still do, although in many countries feminist criticisms of this type of literature have had some impact.

Social conditioning exists, certainly, but does it explain the differences between the sexes? It is, at best, an incomplete explanation. We still need to know *why* our society—and not just ours, but practically every human society—should shape children in this way. One popular answer is that in earlier, simpler societies, the sexes had different roles because women had to breast-feed their children during the long period before weaning. This meant that the women stayed closer to home while the men went out to hunt. As a result females evolved a more social and emotional character, while males became tougher and more aggressive. Because physical strength and aggression were the ultimate forms of power in these simple societies, males became dominant. The sex roles that exist today are, on this view, an inheritance from these simpler circumstances, an inheritance that became obsolete once technology made it possible for the weakest person to operate a crane that lifts fifty tons, or fire a missile that kills millions. Nor do women have to be tied to home and children in the way they used to be, since a woman can now combine motherhood and a career.

The alternative view is that while social conditioning plays some role in determining psychological differences between the sexes, biological factors are also at work. The evidence for this view is particularly strong in respect of aggression. In *The Psychology of Sex Differences*, Eleanor Emmons Maccoby and Carol Nagy Jacklin give four grounds for their belief that the greater aggression of males has a biological component:

1. Males are more aggressive than females in all human societies in which the difference has been studied.

2. Similar differences are found in humans and in apes and other closely related animals.

3. The differences are found in very young children, at an age when there is no evidence of any social conditioning in this direction (indeed Maccoby and Jacklin found some evidence that boys are more severely punished for showing aggression than girls).

4. Aggression has been shown to vary according to the level of sex hormones, and females become more aggressive if they receive male hormones.

The evidence for a biological basis of the differences in visual-spatial ability is a little more complicated, but it consists largely of genetic studies that suggest that this ability is influenced by a recessive sex-linked gene. As a result, it is estimated, approximately 50 percent of males have a genetic advantage in situations demanding visual-spatial ability, but only 25 percent of females have this advantage.

Evidence for and against a biological factor in the superior verbal ability of females and the superior mathematical ability of males is, at present, too weak to suggest a conclusion one way or the other.

Adopting the strategy we used before in discussing race and IQ, I shall not go further into the evidence for and against these biological explanations of differences between males and females. Instead I shall ask what the implications of the biological hypotheses would be.

The differences in the intellectual strengths and weaknesses of the sexes cannot explain more than a minute proportion of the difference in positions that males and females hold in our society. It might explain why, for example, there should be more males than females in professions like architecture and engineering, professions that may require visual-spatial ability; but even in these professions, the magnitude of the differences in numbers cannot be explained by the genetic theory of visual-spatial ability. This theory suggests that half as many females are as genetically advantaged in this area as males, which would account for the lower average scores of females in tests of visual-spatial ability, but cannot account for the fact that in most countries there are not merely twice as many males as females in architecture and engineering, but at least ten times as many. Moreover, if superior visual-spatial ability explains the male dominance of architecture and engineering, why isn't there a corresponding female advantage in professions requiring high verbal ability? It is true that there are more women journalists than engineers, and probably more women have achieved lasting fame as novelists than in any other area of life; yet female journalists and television commentators continue to be outnumbered by males, outside specifically 'women's subjects' such as cookery and child care. So even if one accepts biological explanations for the patterning of these abilities, one can still argue that women do not have the same opportunities as men to make the most of the abilities they have.

What of differences in aggression? One's first reaction might be that feminists should be delighted with the evidence on this point—what better way could there be of showing the superiority of females than by demonstrating their greater reluctance to hurt others? But the fact that most violent criminals are male may be only one side of greater male aggression. The other side could be greater male competitiveness, ambition, and drive to achieve power. This would have different, and for feminists less welcome, implications. Some years ago an American sociologist, Steven Goldberg, built a provocatively entitled book, *The Inevitability of Patriarchy*, around the thesis that the biological basis of greater male aggression will always make it impossible to bring about a society in which women have as much political power as men. From this claim it is easy to move to the view that women should accept their inferior position in society and not strive to compete with males, or to bring up their daughters to compete with males in these respects; instead women should return to their traditional sphere of looking after the home and children. This is just the kind of argument that has aroused the hostility of some feminists to biological explanations of male dominance.

As in the case of race and IQ, the moral conclusions alleged to follow from the biological theories do not really follow from them at all. Similar arguments apply.

First, whatever the origin of psychological differences between the sexes, social conditioning can emphasise or soften these differences. As Maccoby and Jacklin stress, the biological bias towards, say, male visual-spatial superiority is really a greater natural readiness to learn these skills. Where women are brought up to be independent, their visual-spatial ability is much higher than when they are kept at home and dependent on males. This is no doubt true of other differences as well. Hence feminists may well be right to attack the way in which we encourage girls and boys to develop in distinct directions, even if this encouragement is not itself responsible for creating psychological differences between the sexes, but only reinforces innate predispositions.

Second, whatever the origin of psychological differences between the sexes, they exist only when averages are taken, and some females are more aggressive and have better visual-spatial ability than some males. We have seen that the genetic hypothesis offered in explanation of male visual-spatial superiority itself suggests that a quarter of all females will have greater natural visual-spatial ability than half of all males. Our own observations should convince us that there are females who are also more aggressive than some males. So, biological explanations or not, we are never in a position to say: 'You're a woman, so you can't become an engineer', or 'Because you are female, you will not have the drive and ambition needed to succeed in politics.' Nor should we assume that no male can possibly have sufficient gentleness and warmth to stay at home with the children while their mother goes out to work. We must assess people as individuals, not merely lump them into 'female' and 'male' if we are to find out what they are really like; and we must keep the roles occupied by females and males flexible if people are to be able to do what they are best suited for.

The third reason is, like the previous two, parallel to the reasons I have given for believing that a biological explanation of racial differences in IQ would not justify racism. The most important human interests are no more affected by differences in aggression than they are by differences in intelligence. Less aggressive people have the same interest in avoiding pain, developing their abilities, having adequate food and shelter, enjoying good personal relationships, and so on, as more aggressive people. There is no reason why more aggressive people ought to be rewarded for their aggression with higher salaries and the ability to provide better for these interests.

Since aggression, unlike intelligence, is not generally regarded as a desirable trait, the male chauvinist is hardly likely to deny that greater aggression in itself provides no ethical justification of male supremacy. He may, however, offer it as an explanation, rather than a justification, of the fact that males hold most of the leading positions in politics, business, the universities and other areas in which people of both sexes compete for power and status. He may then go on to suggest that this shows that the present situation is merely the result of competition between males and females under conditions of equal opportunity. Hence, it is not, he may say, unfair. This suggestion raises the further ramifications of biological differences between people that, as I said at the close of our discussion of the race and IQ issue, need to be followed up in more depth.

FROM EQUALITY OF OPPORTUNITY TO EQUALITY OF CONSIDERATION

In most Western societies large differences in income and social status are commonly thought to be all right, as long as they were brought into being under conditions of equal opportunity. The idea is that there is no injustice in Jill earning

$200,000 and Jack earning $20,000, as long as Jack had his chance to be where Jill is today. Suppose that the difference in income is due to the fact that Jill is a doctor whereas Jack is a farm worker. This would be acceptable if Jack had the same opportunity as Jill to be a doctor, and this is taken to mean that Jack was not kept out of medical school because of his race, or religion, or a disability that was irrelevant to his ability to be a doctor, or something similar—in effect, if Jack's school results had been as good as Jill's, he would have been able to study medicine, become a doctor, and earn $200,000 a year. Life, on this view, is a kind of race in which it is fitting that the winners should get the prizes, as long as all get an equal start. The equal start represents equality of opportunity and this, some say, is as far as equality should go.

To say that Jack and Jill had equal opportunities to become a doctor, because Jack would have got into medical school if his results had been as good as Jill's, is to take a superficial view of equal opportunity that will not stand up to further probing. We need to ask why Jack's results were not as good as Jill's. Perhaps his education up to that point had been inferior—bigger classes, less qualified teachers, inadequate resources, and so on. If so, he was not competing on equal terms with Jill after all. Genuine equality of opportunity requires us to ensure that schools give the same advantages to everyone.

Making schools equal would be difficult enough, but it is the easiest of the tasks that await a thoroughgoing proponent of equal opportunity. Even if schools are the same, some children will be favoured by the kind of home they come from. A quiet room to study, plenty of books, and parents who encourage their child to do well at school could explain why Jill succeeds where Jack, forced to share a room with two younger brothers and put up with his father's complaints that he is wasting his time with books instead of getting out and earning his keep, does not. But how does one equalise a home? Or parents? Unless we are prepared to abandon the traditional family setting and bring up our children in communal nurseries, we can't.

This might be enough to show the inadequacy of equal opportunity as an ideal of equality, but the ultimate objection—the one that connects with our previous discussion of equality—is still to come. Even if we did rear our children communally, as on a kibbutz in Israel, they would inherit different abilities and character traits, including different levels of aggression and different IQs. Eliminating differences in the child's environment would not affect differences in genetic endowment. True, it might reduce the disparity between, say, IQ scores, since it is likely that, at present, social differences accentuate genetic differences; but the genetic differences would remain and on most estimates they are a major component of the existing differences in IQ. (Remember that we are now talking of *individuals*. We do not know if race affects IQ, but there is little doubt that differences in IQ between individuals of the same race are, in part, genetically determined.)

So equality of opportunity is not an attractive ideal. It rewards the lucky, who inherit those abilities that allow them to pursue interesting and lucrative careers. It penalises the unlucky, whose genes make it very hard for them to achieve similar success.

We can now fit our earlier discussion of race and sex differences into a broader picture. Whatever the facts about the social or genetic basis of racial differences in IQ, removing social disadvantages will not suffice to bring about an equal or a just distribution of income—not an equal distribution, because those who inherit the abilities associated with high IQ will continue to earn more than those who do not; and not a just distribution because distribution according to the abilities one inherits is based on an arbitrary form of selection that has nothing to do with what people deserve or need. The same is true of visual-spatial ability and aggression, if these do lead to higher incomes or status. If, as I have argued, the basis of equality is equal consideration of interests, and the most important human interests have little or nothing to do with these factors, there is something questionable about a society in which income and social status correlate to a significant degree with them.

When we pay people high salaries for programming computers and low salaries for cleaning offices, we are, in effect, paying people for having a high IQ, and this means that we are paying people for something determined in part before they are born and almost wholly determined before they reach an age at which they are responsible for their actions. From the point of view of justice and utility there is something wrong here. Both would be better served by a society that adopted the famous Marxist slogan: 'From each according to his ability, to each according to his needs.' If this could be achieved, the differences between the races and sexes would lose their social significance. Only then would we have a society truly based on the principle of equal consideration of interests.

Is it realistic to aim at a society that rewards people according to their needs rather than their IQ, aggression, or other inherited abilities? Don't we have to pay people more to be doctors or lawyers or university professors, to do the intellectually demanding work that is essential for our well-being?

There are difficulties in paying people according to their needs rather than their inherited abilities. If one country attempts to introduce such a scheme while others do not, the result is likely to be some kind of 'brain drain'. We have already seen this, on a small scale, in the number of scientists and doctors who have left Britain to work in the United States—not because Britain does pay people according to need rather than inherited abilities, but because these sections of the community, though relatively well-paid by British standards, were much better paid in the United States. If any one country were to make a serious attempt to equalise the salaries of doctors and manual workers, there can be no doubt that the number of doctors emigrating would greatly increase. This is part of the problem of 'socialism in one country'. Marx expected the socialist revolution to be a worldwide one. When the Russian Marxists found that their revolution had not sparked off the anticipated world revolution, they had to adapt Marxist ideas to this new situation. They did so by harshly restricting freedom, including the freedom to emigrate. Without these restrictions, during the communist period in the Soviet Union and other communist states, and despite the considerable pay differentials that still did exist in those nations when under communist rule, and that continue to exist in the remaining communist countries, there would have been a crippling outflow of skilled people to the capitalist nations, which rewarded skill more highly.[1] But if 'socialism in one country' requires making the country an armed camp, with border guards keeping watch on the citizens within as well as the enemy without, socialism may not be worth the price.

To allow these difficulties to lead us to the conclusion that we can do nothing to improve the distribution of income that now exists in capitalist countries would, however, be too pessimistic. There is, in the more affluent Western nations, a good deal of scope for reducing pay differentials before the point is reached at which significant numbers of people begin to think of emigrating. This is, of course, especially true of those countries, like the United States, where pay differentials are presently very great. It is here that pressure for a more equitable distribution can best be applied.

What of the problems of redistribution within a single nation? There is a popular belief that if we did not pay people a lot of money to be doctors or university professors, they would not undertake the studies required to achieve these positions. I do not know what evidence there is in support of this assumption, but it seems to me highly dubious. My own salary is considerably higher than the salaries of the people employed by the university to mow the lawns and keep the grounds clean, but if our salaries were identical I would still not want to swap positions with them—although their jobs are a lot more pleasant than some lowly paid work. Nor do I believe that my doctor would jump at a chance to change places with his receptionist if their salaries did not differ. It is true that my doctor and I have had to study for several years to get where we are, but I at least look back on

---

[1]According to one observer, salary differentials in China are quite steep, in some areas steeper than in Western nations. For instance, a full professor gets almost seven times as much as a junior lecturer, whereas in Britain, Australia, or the United States, the ratio is more like three to one. See Simon Leys, *Chinese Shadows* (New York, 1977).

my student years as one of the most enjoyable periods of my life.

Although I do not think it is because of the money that people choose to become doctors rather than receptionists, there is one qualification to be made to the suggestion that payment should be based on need rather than ability. It must be admitted that the prospect of earning more money sometimes leads people to make greater efforts to use the abilities they have, and these greater efforts can benefit patients, customers, students, or the public as a whole. It might therefore be worth trying to reward *effort*, which would mean paying people more if they worked near the upper limits of their abilities, whatever those abilities might be. This, however, is quite different from paying people for the level of ability they happen to have, which is something they cannot themselves control. As Jeffrey Gray, a British professor of psychology, has written, the evidence for genetic control of IQ suggests that to pay people differently for 'upper-class' and 'lower-class' jobs is 'a wasteful use of resources in the guise of "incentives" that either tempt people to do what is beyond their powers or reward them more for what they would do anyway'.

We have, up to now, been thinking of people such as university professors, who (at least in some countries) are paid by the government, and doctors, whose incomes are determined either by government bodies, where there is some kind of national health service, or by the government protection given to professional associations like a medical association, which enables the profession to exclude those who might seek to advertise their services at a lower cost. These incomes are therefore already subject to government control and could be altered without drastically changing the powers of government. The private business sector of the economy is a different matter. Business people who are quick to seize an opportunity will, under any private enterprise system, make more money than their rivals or, if they are employed by a large corporation, may be promoted faster. Taxation can help to redistribute some of this income, but there are limits to how effective a steeply progressive tax system can be—there almost seems to be a law to the effect that the higher the rate of tax, the greater the amount of tax avoidance.

So do we have to abolish private enterprise if we are to eliminate undeserved wealth? That suggestion raises issues too large to be discussed here; but it can be said that private enterprise has a habit of reasserting itself under the most inhospitable conditions. As the Russians and East Europeans soon found, communist societies still had their black markets, and if you wanted your plumbing fixed swiftly it was advisable to pay a bit extra on the side. Only a radical change in human nature—a decline in acquisitive and self-centred desires—could overcome the tendency for people to find a way around any system that suppresses private enterprise. Since no such change in human nature is in sight, we shall probably continue to pay most to those with inherited abilities, rather than those who have the greatest needs. To hope for something entirely different is unrealistic. To work for wider recognition of the principle of payment according to needs and effort rather than inherited ability is both realistic and, I believe, right. . . .

REVIEW AND DISCUSSION QUESTIONS

1. Explain how Rawls understands equality, and why Singer thinks that view is mistaken.

2. According to Singer, of what significance for equality, if any, is IQ? Does it matter to him that some groups score higher or lower on such tests?

3. What are the major psychological differences between men and women? What significance do they have, according to Singer?

4. Why does Singer reject equality of opportunity in favor of equality of consideration?

5. Does Singer's understanding of equality solve the "dilemma of difference" that Minow discussed? How might Minow respond to Singer's argument?

Affirmative Action: An Exchange

Ronald Dworkin and Respondents

The words "affirmative action" were first used by President John Kennedy in 1961. His Executive Order 10925 required that contractors working for the federal government take "affirmative action to ensure that applicants are employed without regard to their race, creed, color, or national origin." Over the next decade, however, this requirement moved slowly away from racial neutrality toward preferences and quotas, as the government tried to expand the opportunities for minorities. In 1965 President Lyndon Johnson's secretary of labor issued guidelines for hiring federal contractors that included "goals and timetables" to achieve increased minority employment. As originally understood, affirmative action is largely uncontroversial, requiring only that recruitment of minorities be seriously undertaken, and hiring should be done without regard to race and only strictly on the basis of ability to perform. Now, however, affirmative action means more than that: it includes special minority scholarships and set-asides of jobs and contracts; preferences for minorities to jobs, contracts, and admissions; and sometimes explicit quotas in hiring and admission. The most important of the Supreme Court cases to consider affirmative action is Regents of the University of California v. Bakke *(1978).*

Allan Bakke was turned down for admission to the University of California at Davis medical school, which had set aside sixteen of its hundred slots for "disadvantaged" students. The evidence at his trial showed that although in theory whites could be admitted under the affirmative action program, none in fact were. It also showed that Bakke's overall grade-point average was 3.46, while the average for the affirmative action program was 2.62. His Medical College Aptitude Tests percentile scores were verbal, 96; quantitative, 94; and science, 97. These compared with 34, 30, and 37, respectively, for the affirmative action admittees. Bakke also received an overall rating of 94 out of possible 100 in his interview. As to the regular admission process, that year there were one African American, six Mexican Americans, and thirty-seven Asian Americans admitted.

In this essay, written before the Supreme Court handed down its decision in the case, Ronald Dworkin analyzes three potential arguments Bakke's lawyer might have made (including the one he in fact did make), arguing that Bakke had no case. We also include a sample of the letters received in response to Dworkin's original essay.

On October 12, 1977 the Supreme Court heard oral argument in the case of *The Regents of the University of California v. Allan Bakke.* No lawsuit has ever been more widely watched or more thoroughly debated in the national and international press before the Court's decision. Still, some of the most pertinent facts set before the Court have not been clearly summarized.

The medical school of the University of California at Davis has an affirmative action program (called the "task force program") designed to admit more black and other minority students. It sets sixteen places aside for which only members of "educationally and economically disadvantaged minorities" compete. Allan Bakke,

white, applied for one of the remaining eighty-four places; he was rejected but, since his test scores were relatively high, the medical school has conceded that it could not prove that he would have been rejected if the sixteen places reserved had been open to him. Bakke sued, arguing that the task force program deprived him of his constitutional rights. The California Supreme Court agreed, and ordered the medical school to admit him. The university appealed to the Supreme Court.

The Davis program for minorities is in certain respects more forthright (some would say cruder) than similar plans now in force in many other American universities and professional schools. Such programs aim to increase the enrollment of black and other minority students by allowing the fact of their race to count affirmatively as part of the case for admitting them. Some schools set a "target" of a particular number of minority places instead of setting aside a flat number of places. But Davis would not fill the number of places set aside unless there were sixteen minority candidates it considered clearly qualified for medical education. The difference is therefore one of administrative strategy and not of principle.

So the constitutional question raised by *Bakke* is of capital importance for higher education in America, and a large number of universities and schools have entered briefs *amicus curiae* urging the Court to reverse the California decision. They believe that if the decision is affirmed then they will no longer be free to use explicit racial criteria in any part of their admissions programs, and that they will therefore be unable to fulfill what they take to be their responsibilities to the nation.

It is often said that affirmative action programs aim to achieve a racially conscious society divided into racial and ethnic groups, each entitled, as a group, to some proportionable share of resources, careers, or opportunities. That is a perverse description. American society is currently a racially conscious society; that is the inevitable and evident consequence of a history of slavery, repression, and prejudice. Black men and women, boys and girls, are not free to choose for themselves in what roles—or as members of which social groups—others will characterize them. They are black, and no other feature of personality or allegiance or ambition will so thoroughly influence how they will be perceived and treated by others, and the range and character of the lives that will be open to them.

The tiny number of black doctors and professionals is both a consequence and a continuing cause of American racial consciousness, one link in a long and self-fueling chain reaction. Affirmative action programs use racially explicit criteria because their immediate goal is to increase the number of members of certain races in these professions. But their long-term goal is to *reduce* the degree to which American society is overall a racially conscious society.

The programs rest on two judgments. The first is a judgment of social theory: that America will continue to be pervaded by racial divisions as long as the most lucrative, satisfying, and important careers remain mainly the prerogative of members of the white race, while others feel themselves systematically excluded from a professional and social elite. The second is a calculation of strategy: that increasing the number of blacks who are at work in the professions will, in the long run, reduce the sense of frustration and injustice and racial self-consciousness in the black community to the point at which blacks may begin to think of themselves as individuals who can succeed like others through talent and initiative. At that future point the consequences of nonracial admissions programs, whatever these consequences might be, could be accepted with no sense of racial barriers or injustice.

It is therefore the worst possible misunderstanding to suppose that affirmative action programs are designed to produce a balkanized America, divided into racial and ethnic subnations. They use strong measures because weaker ones will fail; but their ultimate goal is to lessen not to increase the importance of race in American social and professional life.

According to the 1970 census, only 2.1 percent of US doctors were black. Affirmative action programs aim to provide more black doctors to serve black patients. This is not because it is desirable that blacks treat blacks and whites treat whites, but because blacks, for no fault of their own, are now unlikely to be well served by whites, and because a failure to provide the doctors they trust will exacerbate rather than reduce the resentment that now leads them to trust only their own. Affirmative action tries to provide more blacks as classmates for white doctors, not because it is desirable that a medical school class reflect the racial makeup of the community as a whole, but because professional association between blacks and whites will decrease the degree to which whites think of blacks as a race rather than as people, and thus the degree to which blacks think of themselves that way. It tries to provide "role models" for future black doctors, not because it is desirable for a black boy or girl to find adult models only among blacks, but because our history has made them so conscious of their race that the success of whites, for now, is likely to mean little or nothing for them.

The history of the campaign against racial injustice since 1954, when the Supreme Court decided *Brown v. Board of Education*, is a history in large part of failure. We have not succeeded in reforming the racial consciousness of our society by racially neutral means. We are therefore obliged to look upon the arguments for affirmative action with sympathy and an open mind. Of course, if Bakke is right that such programs, no matter how effective they may be, violate his constitutional rights then they cannot be permitted to continue. But we must not forbid them in the name of some mindless maxim, like the maxim that it cannot be right to fight fire with fire, or that the end cannot justify the means. If the strategic claims for affirmative action are cogent, they cannot be dismissed simply on the ground that racially explicit tests are distasteful. If such tests are distasteful it can only be for reasons that make the underlying social realities the programs attack more distasteful still.

The New Republic, in a recent editorial opposing affirmative action, missed that point. "It is critical to the success of a liberal pluralism," it said, "that group membership itself is not among the permissible criteria of inclusion and exclusion." But group membership is in fact, as a matter of social reality rather than formal admission standards, part of what determines inclusion or exclusion for us now. If we must choose between a society that is in fact liberal and an illiberal society that scrupulously avoids formal racial criteria, we can hardly appeal to the ideals of liberal pluralism to prefer the latter.

Professor Archibald Cox of Harvard Law School, speaking for the University of California in oral argument, told the Supreme Court that this is the choice the United States must make. As things stand, he said, affirmative action programs are the only effective means of increasing the absurdly small number of black doctors. The California Supreme Court, in approving Bakke's claim, had urged the university to pursue that goal by methods that do not explicitly take race into account. But that is unrealistic. We must distinguish, as Cox said, between two interpretations of what the California court's recommendation means. It might mean that the university should aim at the same immediate goal, of increasing the proportion of black and other minority students in the medical school, by an admissions procedure that on the surface is not racially conscious.

That is a recommendation of hypocrisy. If those who administer the admissions standards, however these are phrased, understand that their immediate goal is to increase the number of blacks in the school, then they will use race as a criterion in making the various subjective judgments the explicit criteria will require, because that will be, given the goal, the only right way to make those judgments. The recommendation might mean, on the other hand, that the school should adopt some nonracially conscious goal, like increasing the number of disadvantaged students of all races, and then hope that that goal will produce an increase in the number of blacks as a by-product. But even if that strategy is less hypocritical (which is far from plain), it will almost certainly fail because no different goal, scrupulously administered in a nonracially conscious way, will in fact significantly increase the number of black medical students.

Cox offered powerful evidence for that conclusion, and it is supported by the recent and comprehensive report of the Carnegie Council on Policy Studies in Higher Education. Suppose, for example, that the medical school sets aside separate places for applicants "disadvantaged" on some racially neutral test, like poverty, allowing only those disadvantaged in that way to compete for these places. If the school selects these from that group who scored best on standard medical school aptitude tests, then it will take almost no blacks, because blacks score relatively low even among the economically disadvantaged. But if the school chooses among the disadvantaged on some basis other than test scores, just so that more blacks will succeed, then it will not be administering the special procedure in a nonracially conscious way.

So Cox was able to put his case in the form of two simple propositions. A racially conscious test for admission, even one that sets aside certain places for qualified minority applicants exclusively, serves goals that are in themselves unobjectionable and even urgent. Such programs are, moreover, the only means that offer any significant promise of achieving these goals. If these programs are halted, then no more than a trickle of black students will enter medical or other professional schools for another generation at least.

If these propositions are sound, then on what ground can it be thought that such programs are either wrong or unconstitutional? We must notice an important distinction between two different sorts of objections that might be made. These programs are intended, as I said, to decrease the importance of race in the United States in the long run. It may be objected, first, that the programs will in fact harm that goal more than they will advance it. There is no way now to prove that that is so. Cox conceded, in his argument, that there are costs and risks in these programs.

Affirmative action programs seem to encourage, for example, a popular misunderstanding, which is that they assume that racial or ethnic groups are entitled to proportionate shares of opportunities, so that Italian or Polish ethnic minorities are, in theory, as entitled to their proportionate shares as blacks or Chicanos or American Indians are entitled to the shares the present programs give them. That is a plain mistake: the programs are not based on the idea that those who are aided are entitled to aid, but only on the strategic hypothesis that helping them is now an effective way of attacking a national problem. Some medical schools may well make that judgment, under certain circumstances, about a white ethnic minority. Indeed it seems likely that some medical schools are even now attempting to help white Appalachian applicants, for example, under programs of regional distribution.

So the popular understanding is wrong, but so long as it persists it is a cost of the program because the attitudes it encourages tend to a degree to make people more rather than less conscious of race. There are other possible costs. It is said, for example, that some blacks find affirmative action degrading; they find that it makes them more rather than less conscious of prejudice against their race as such. This attitude is also based on a misperception, I think, but for a small minority of blacks at least it is a genuine cost.

In the view of the many important universities who have such programs, however, the gains will very probably exceed the losses in reducing racial consciousness overall. This view is hardly so implausible that it is wrong for these universities to seek to acquire the experience that will allow us to judge whether they are right. It would be particularly silly to forbid these experiments if we know that the failure to try will mean, as the evidence shows, that the status quo will almost certainly continue. In any case, this first objection could provide no argument that would justify a decision by the Supreme Court holding the programs unconstitutional. The Court has no business substituting its speculative judgment about the probable consequences of educational policies for the judgment of professional educators.

So the acknowledged uncertainties about the long-term results of such programs could not justify a Supreme Court decision making them illegal. But there is a second and very different form of objection. It may be argued that even if the programs *are* effective in making our society less a society dominated by race, they are nevertheless unconstitutional because they violate the individual constitutional rights of those, like Allan Bakke, who lose places in consequence. In the oral argument Reynold H. Colvin of San Francisco, who is Bakke's lawyer, made plain that his objection takes this second form. Mr. Justice White asked him whether he accepted that the goals affirmative action programs seek are important goals. Mr. Colvin acknowledged that they were. Suppose, Justice White continued, that affirmative action programs are, as Cox had argued, the only effective means of seeking such goals. Would Mr. Colvin nevertheless maintain that the programs are unconstitutional? Yes, he insisted, they would be, because his client has a constitutional right that the programs be abandoned, no matter what the consequences.

Mr. Colvin was wise to put his objections on this second ground; he was wise to claim that his client has rights that do not depend on any judgment about the likely consequences of affirmative action for society as a whole, because if he makes out that claim then the Court must give him the relief he seeks.

But can he be right? If Allan Bakke has a constitutional right so important that the urgent goals of affirmative action must yield, then this must be because affirmative action violates some fundamental principle of political morality. This is not a case in which what might be called formal or technical law requires a decision one way or the other. There is no language in the Constitution whose plain meaning forbids affirmative action. Only the most naïve theories of statutory construction could argue that such a result is required by the language of any earlier Supreme Court decision or of the Civil Rights Act of 1964 or of any other congressional enactment. If Mr. Colvin is right it must be because Allan Bakke has not simply some technical legal right but an important moral right as well.

What could that right be? The popular argument frequently made on editorial pages is that Bakke has a right to be judged on his merit. Or that he has a right to be judged as an individual rather than as a member of a social group. Or that he has a right, as much as any black man, not to be sacrificed or excluded from any opportunity because of his race alone. But these catch phrases are deceptive here, because, as reflection demonstrates, the only genuine principle they describe is the principle that no one should suffer from the prejudice or contempt of others. And that principle is not at stake in this case at all. In spite of popular opinion, the idea that the *Bakke* case presents a conflict between a desirable social goal and important individual rights is a piece of intellectual confusion.

Consider, for example, the claim that individuals applying for places in medical school should be judged on merit, and merit alone. If that slogan means that admissions committees should take nothing into account but scores on some particular intelligence test, then it is arbitrary and, in any case, contradicted by the long-standing practice of every medical school. If it means, on the other hand, that a medical school should choose candidates that it supposes will make the most useful doctors, then everything turns on the judgment of what factors make different doctors useful. The Davis medical school assigned to each regular applicant, as well as to each minority applicant, what it called a "benchmark score." This reflected not only the results of aptitude tests and college grade averages, but a subjective evaluation of the applicant's chances of functioning as an effective doctor, in view of society's present needs for medical service. Presumably the qualities deemed important were different from the qualities that a law school or engineering school or business school would seek, just as the intelligence tests a medical school might use would be different from the tests these other schools would find appropriate.

There is no combination of abilities and skills and traits that constitutes "merit" in the abstract; if quick hands count as "merit" in the case of a prospective surgeon, this is because quick hands will enable him to serve the public better and for no other reason. If a black skin will, as a matter of regrettable fact, enable another doctor to do a different medical job better, then that black skin is by the same token "merit" as well. That argument may strike some as dangerous; but only because they confuse its conclusion—that black skin may be a socially useful trait in particular circumstances—with the very different and despicable idea that one race may be inherently more worthy than another.

Consider the second of the catch phrases I have mentioned. It is said that Bakke has a right to be judged as an "individual," in deciding whether he is to be admitted to medical school and thus to the medical profession, and not as a member of some group that is being judged as a whole. What can that mean? Any admissions procedure must rely on generalizations about groups that are justified only statistically. The regular admissions process at Davis, for example, set a cutoff figure for college grade-point averages. Applicants whose averages fell below that figure were not invited to any interview, and therefore rejected out of hand.

An applicant whose average fell one point below the cutoff might well have had personal qualities of dedication or sympathy that would have been revealed at an interview, and that would have made him or her a better doctor than some applicant whose average rose one point above the line. But the former is excluded from the process on the basis of a decision taken for administrative convenience and grounded in the generalization, unlikely to hold true for every individual, that those with grade averages below the cutoff will not have other qualities sufficiently persuasive. Indeed, even the use of standard Medical College Aptitude Tests (MCAT) as part of the admissions procedure requires judging people as part of groups because it assumes that test scores are a guide to medical intelligence which is in turn a guide to medical ability. Though this judgment is no doubt true statistically, it hardly holds true for every individual.

Allan Bakke was himself refused admission to two other medical schools, not because of his race but because of his age: these schools thought that a student entering medical school at the age of thirty-three was likely to make less of a contribution to medical care over his career than someone entering at the standard age of twenty-one. Suppose these schools relied, not on any detailed investigation of whether Bakke himself had abilities that would contradict the generalization in his specific case, but on a rule of thumb that allowed only the most cursory look at applicants over (say) the age of thirty. Did these two medical schools violate his right to be judged as an individual rather than as a member of a group?

The Davis Medical School permitted whites to apply for the sixteen places reserved for members of "educationally or economically disadvantaged minorities," a phrase whose meaning might well include white ethnic minorities. In fact several whites have applied, though none has been accepted, and the California Court found that the special committee charged with administering the program had decided, in advance, against admitting any. Suppose that decision had been based on the following administrative theory: it is so unlikely that any white doctor can do as much to counteract racial imbalance in the medical professions as a well-qualified and trained black doctor can do that the committee should for reasons of convenience proceed on the presumption no white doctor could. That presumption is, as a matter of fact, more plausible than the corresponding presumption about medical students over the age of thirty, or even the presumption about applicants whose grade-point averages fall below the cutoff line. If the latter presumptions do not deny the alleged right of individuals to be judged as individuals in an admissions procedure, then neither can the former.

Mr. Colvin, in oral argument, argued the third of the catch phrases I mentioned. He said that his client had a right not to be excluded from medical school because of his race alone, and this as a statement of constitutional right sounds more plausible than claims about the right to be judged on merit or as an individual. It sounds plausible, however, because it suggests the following more complex principle. Every citizen has a constitutional right that he not suffer disadvantage, at least in the competition for any public benefit, because the race or religion or sect or region or other natural or artificial group to which he belongs is the object of prejudice or contempt.

That is a fundamentally important constitutional right, and it is that right that was systematically violated for many years by racist exclusions and anti-Semitic quotas. Color bars and Jewish quotas were not unfair just because they made race or religion relevant or because they fixed on qualities beyond individual control. It is true that blacks or Jews do not choose to be blacks or Jews. But it is also true that those who score low in aptitude or admissions tests do not choose their levels of intelligence. Nor do those denied admission because they are too old, or because they do not come from a part of the country underrepresented in the school, or because they cannot play basketball well, choose not to have the qualities that made the difference.

Race seems different because exclusions based on race have historically been motivated not by some instrumental calculation, as in the case of intelligence or age or regional distribution or athletic ability, but because of contempt for the excluded race or religion as such. Exclusion by race was in itself an insult, because it was generated by and signaled contempt.

Bakke's claim, therefore, must be made more specific than it is. He says he was kept out of medical school because of his race. Does he mean that he was kept out because his race is the object of prejudice or contempt? That suggestion is absurd. A very high proportion of those who were accepted (and, presumably, of those who run the admissions program) were members of the same race. He therefore means simply that if he had been black he would have been accepted, with no suggestion that this would have been so because blacks are thought more worthy or honorable than whites.

That is true: no doubt he would have been accepted if he were black. But it is also true, and in exactly the same sense, that he would have been accepted if he had been more intelligent, or made a better impression in his interview, or, in the case of other schools, if he had been younger when he decided to become a doctor. Race is not, in, *his* case, a different matter from these other factors equally beyond his control. It is not a different matter because in his case race is not distinguished by the special character of public insult. On the contrary the program presupposes that his race is still widely if wrongly thought to be superior to others.

In the past, it made sense to say that an excluded black or Jewish student was being sacrificed because of his race or religion; that meant that his or her exclusion was treated as desirable in itself, not because it contributed to any goal in which he as well as the rest of society might take pride. Allan Bakke is being "sacrificed" because of his race only in a very artificial sense of the word. He is being "sacrificed" in the same artificial sense because of his level of intelligence, since he would have been accepted if he were more clever than he is. In both cases he is being excluded not by prejudice but because of a rational calculation about the socially most beneficial use of limited resources for medical education.

It may now be said that this distinction is too subtle, and that if racial classifications have been and may still be used for malign purposes, then everyone has a flat right that racial classifications not be used at all. This is the familiar appeal to the lazy virtue of simplicity. It supposes that if a line is difficult to draw, or might be difficult to administer if drawn, then there is wisdom in not making the attempt to draw it. There may be cases in which that is wise, but those would be cases in which nothing of great value would as a consequence be lost. If racially conscious admissions policies now offer the only substantial hope for bringing more qualified black and other minority doctors into the profession, then a great loss is suffered if medical schools are not allowed voluntarily to pursue such programs. We should then be trading away a chance to attack certain and present injustice in order to gain protection we may not need against speculative abuses we have other means to prevent. And such abuses cannot, in any case, be worse than the injustice to which we would then surrender.

We have now considered three familiar slogans, each widely thought to name a constitutional right that enables Allan Bakke to stop programs of affirmative action no matter how effective or necessary these might be. When we inspect these slogans, we find that they can stand for no genuine principle except one. This is the important principle that no one in our society should suffer because he is a member of a group thought less worthy of respect, as a group, than other groups. We have different aspects of that principle in mind when we say that individuals should be judged on merit, that they should be judged as individuals, and that they should not suffer disadvantages because of their race. The spirit of that fundamental principle is the spirit of the goal that affirmative action is intended to serve. The principle furnishes no support for those who find, as Bakke does, that their own interests conflict with that goal.

It is of course regrettable when any citizen's expectations are defeated by new programs serving some more general concern. It is regrettable, for example, when established small businesses fail because new and superior roads are built; in that case people have invested more than Bakke has. And they have more reason to believe their businesses will continue than Bakke had to suppose he could have entered the Davis medical school at thirty-three even without a task force program.

There is, of course, no suggestion in the program that Bakke shares in any collective or individual guilt for racial injustice in America; or that he is any less entitled to concern or respect than any black student accepted in the program. He has been disappointed, and he must have the sympathy due that disappointment, just as any other disappointed applicant—even one with much worse test scores who would not have been accepted in any event—must have sympathy. Each is disappointed because places in medical schools are scarce resources and must be used to provide what the more general society most needs. It is hardly Bakke's fault that racial justice is now a special need—but he has no right to prevent the most effective measures of securing that justice from being used.

TO THE EDITORS:

As somebody who has recently been refused an interview for an openly advertised post in a state university explicitly on grounds of my color, I would be grateful for the opportunity to comment on Professor Dworkin's lucid and interesting article (*NYR*, November 10).

Broadly, Professor Dworkin argues that those who find themselves excluded from education or employment because of the operation of affirmative action programs should console themselves with two thoughts: first, that all administrative actions and distinctions contain an element of arbitrariness; second, that, as long as they are not being rejected as members of a group habitually treated as inferior, they have no legitimate reason for complaint. Apart from that, Dworkin says, rather coldly, that, of course, we must have sympathy for Bakke, as for all who suffer incidentally from national policies, but that, after all, he had very little invested and was rather old to be starting a career (thirty-three).

He also makes a curious analogy with the highway construction industry, to the effect that Bakke is the victim of technological progress.

In fact, one of the features of affirmative action programs is that they disproportionately hurt those who are fairly young and almost never touch those who have, as tenured professors, put their investments beyond risk. In my own experience, the employer (the State University of New York) made no attempt to indicate racial preference when advertising but refused to provide any information about the post (the chairmanship of its Africana Studies Program): I was merely told, five weeks later, that only blacks were to be interviewed and that my qualifications were, nevertheless, "very impressive." As with Professor Dworkin, no attempt to explain or sympathize. (All this, I might say, after fourteen years in the field and a post-graduate degree from an African university!)

Surely the most equitable implementation of affirmative action programs would be, at least in employment, to review all posts, senior and junior, in accordance with its principles. As matters stand, those who are excluded are dismissed as necessary casualties (including by Professor Dworkin who, elsewhere, brands as a "meaningless maxim" the notion that the end can justify the means) and are attacked as "racists" by the left and such bodies as the NAACP if they utter the mildest cheep of complaint.

I have every sympathy with the principles of affirmative action, but, as a foreigner, I would despair of its ever contributing to racial harmony, given the insensitivity of its radical and liberal protagonists toward those designated for sacrifice. They have much to say about and against casualties such as Alan Bakke; nothing, it seems, to say to them.

Martin Staniland
Pittsburgh, Pennsylvania

TO THE EDITORS:

In "Why Bakke Has No Case," Dworkin defends the position that affirmative action quotas do not violate the rights of whites excluded from programs on grounds of race. An individual's rights are violated, he contends, only when the tests employed to exclude him involve prejudice or contempt for a group of which that individual is a member. The affirmative action quotas express no such contempt for white males, but use race only to promote the laudable reduction of racial consciousness in America.

Let it be granted that at least part of the point of protecting individuals from exclusion from public benefits on the grounds of race alone is to protect groups, usually minorities, from public insult. Is it clear that this is the *only* point? Surely it is at least as much a concern that the value and dignity of individuals be protected, and this value and dignity *is* undercut by practices such as exclusion from public benefits by irrelevant tests such as race (or religion, or sex, or sexual preference). And just as surely, an individual's worth and dignity can be threatened by such tests in individual cases, irrespective of their impact on groups.

What has encouraged the view that exclusion on irrelevant grounds violates a person's rights only in those cases involving contempt or prejudice for a group? Perhaps it is that unfair exclusion is tolerated in case no readily identifiable group is involved. But this does not establish the point that only the protection of groups is at issue. Historically, individuals have been excluded unjustifiably, on the basis of race, religion, or sex, and it is natural that concern for the worth of individuals should emerge in the form of the right *not* to be excluded on these grounds. The law cannot proscribe every form of injustice of this sort, but it can identify the most common forms and prohibit them. Here, as often, the law does what it can. If this is correct, then Bakke does have a right to be judged on his own merits even though, should he not be so judged, he will not suffer from contempt or prejudice. (I pass over without comment Dworkin's desperate claim that, in being excluded on grounds of race, Bakke *is* being judged on his merits.)

If Bakke's rights are being denied by affirmative action, it is crucial to examine the program. What is its point, and what are its prospects of success? Dworkin denies that blacks and other minorities are *entitled* to preferential treatment (though on this he is fuzzy—by page 15 he has slipped into describing the goal of affirmative action as an "attack on present and certain injustice"), so the only issue can be that of individual rights balanced against the probable social benefits of affirmative action.

Here I cannot share even the guarded optimism Dworkin allows himself. The program will generate a black professional class which will better serve blacks, it is claimed. But what guarantee have we that a black professional class will willingly foresake more lucrative practices, if they can get them, to work in black areas? (One must beware of succumbing to what Bertrand Russell once called the myth of the moral superiority of the oppressed). It is suggested that black professionals are needed to provide "role models" for black children. But it is difficult to assess how to balance this consideration against the plain fact that quotas generate resentment among those whose rights, as I have argued, must be overridden; and also difficult to balance the advantage against the self-doubts that quotas must arouse in those who benefit from them.

These problems might be set aside if we had assurance that quotas are only temporary. Dworkin offers such assurance, but I can see no reason to believe that reasons for instituting quotas will not be reasons for continuing them, if it should appear likely that discontinuing them would erode the gains blacks make under them. Since the under-representation of blacks in the professions is caused in the main by conditions that quotas themselves will do nothing to correct, such as poverty and a history of oppression, there seems no reason to think that quotas once introduced will not be required for as long as these conditions prevail. And indeed, it would be cruel to provide blacks with "role models" in the professions, thus raising their expectations as well as, perhaps, their self-assurance, and then to remove the conditions on which realizing these expectations depend.

John Robertson
Syracuse University
Syracuse, New York

TO THE EDITORS:

. . . Dworkin is correct when he asserts that merit is difficult to define, and that individuals are rarely judged as such in any pure philosophical sense: we are always categorizing and grouping in the course of making judgments. Yet this does not mean that all characteristics put forth as possible components of "merit" or all treatments of an individual as a member of a group, have equal legal or moral claims for all cases. Historical experience and empirical common sense, operating through the processes of legislation and judicial interpretation, have established a consensus on a number of theoretical principles denoting the best in the Western liberal-democratic tradition. One such principle is that except for the rarest of rarest exceptions (males cannot be wetnurses), ascribed traits such as race, religion, and one hopes sex, may play no role in the public life (housing, education, employment) of citizens. A historic toll of blood and oppression, as well as the understanding that skin color bears no intrinsic relationship to the ability to hit a baseball or interpret an electrocardiogram, have shaped this consensus. Other traits, such as age, are complex and need reflection; still others such as height, or strength, enter our notions of merit without violating our sense of justice or fairness, in limited cases (basketball players, jockeys). There is little reason, other than capricious relativism, why remaining ambiguities in these latter cases need undermine the hard-won recognition of the illegality of the former.

Morton Weinfeld
McGill University
Montreal, Canada

TO THE EDITORS:

In your issue of November 10, Ronald Dworkin announced that "Bakke has no case." Constitutional lawyers are deeply divided on the issue, and many militant Blacks are so fearful of a decision in favor of Bakke that a major effort was launched to persuade the Court to deny certiorari, i.e., to let the California decision stand without passing on the merits. Bakke may indeed lose; the Court may set its imprimatur on racial handicapping. If so, it will not be on Dworkin's grounds.

Perhaps Dworkin's failure to see any case for Bakke stems from his misperception of the issue. He starts his argument by declaring that Bakke "applied for one of the remaining eighty-four places"—i.e., those left over after sixteen places had been preempted for non-Whites. Bakke did no such thing; he applied for one of the full hundred available slots, not supposing that he could be barred by a state institution from *any* available opportunities solely on the ground of color.

Much of Dworkin's essay is directed at showing that affirmative action is necessary in order to make opportunities equally available to all groups. *That is not the issue.* There is virtually unanimous agreement on the legality and desirability of affirmative action. The only issue is as to one rare and radical form of affirmative action: a quota from which Whites are excluded. The California Supreme Court in deciding for Bakke outlawed only that; and it outlawed that only because other effective forms of affirmative action are available.

Among forms of affirmative action [that] the California decision permits and encourages are:

1. actively seeking Black applicants.

2. supplementary training to qualify Black applicants affected by surviving racial disadvantages in schooling and employment.

3. preferring Blacks over higher ranking applicants to the extent that a poly-racial setting improves medical training of all students.

4. preferring Blacks over higher ranking applicants to the extent that Black applicants commit themselves to serve underprivileged Black communities more frequently than Whites.

The California decision even permits preferential Black admissions on the highly dubious basis that it is a function of state education to bring about an allocation of "leadership" positions in society on an ethnically proportioned basis.

Although Bakke had not proved that he would have been admitted to medical school if the sixteen places reserved for Blacks had been available to him (i.e., there might have been more than sixteen Whites higher on the admissions list than Bakke), the California Court recognized that he had been wronged by the reservation of sixteen places for Blacks. He would have been admitted if he were Black, since his qualifying scores were much higher than Blacks who were admitted. His chances of being admitted from the White "queue" were reduced by the reduction in the total of White admissions. Finally, he was excluded from the "Black" queue without any comparison with Black admittees, even by the criteria which led to the creation of a separate Black queue. A White would be barred from the Black queue even if he was married to a Black, had adopted Black children, was a civil rights activist, was a student of Black history and culture, was a veteran of VISTA in Africa, and gave bond to practice in a Black community. Conversely, a Black would have been admitted although he was ignorant of and hostile to uniquely Black culture, fully integrated into the White community, and dominated by bourgeois "White" aspirations.

It is clear that the California Court did not mandate "racially neutral means" of selection, as Dworkin erroneously states. The United States Supreme Court will not be mandating "racially neutral means" because that's not at issue in the case, and because the Court has many times sustained racially sensitive governmental action to improve the lot of minorities.

The heart of Dworkin's argument is that Blacks will get into professional schools *only* if quotas are set aside for them. This contradicts experience at many schools where nonquota systems are working. The Dworkin argument also constitutes the ultimate White insult and condescension: that Blacks cannot get in by any conceivable rational set of admissions criteria, however sensitive to racial and social factors. Skin color is the only test by which they can

prevail. That devastating put-down is rejected by many Blacks, including a colleague of mine who has declared himself against "special admissions" as stigmatizing. What is wanted is a broader view of the way qualifications should be measured. Aptitude tests and college grades are useful selection aides, but they are crude guides at best. There are dimensions of personality including commitment, stability, human sympathy, and unique social point of view that should and do enter into all student admissions programs. The Dworkin view that only the skin-test will respond to such factors is ridiculous.

Dworkin's argument that the unfortunate impact of racial handicapping on Bakke should not be allowed to stand in the way of an "experiment" on the way to the distant goal of a prejudice-free society betrays an insensitivity to the significance of constitutional litigation. The Supreme Court is not asked to weigh its sympathy for Bakke against the desirability of racial justice. Bakke is simply the accidental protagonist in a critical controversy over the shape of our democracy. The issue is whether we as a nation shall move from a policy against discrimination to a "race policy" explicitly addressed to assuring ethnic proportional representation not only in the schools, but in the professions, in Congress, and perhaps in the White House, where racial and religious changeovers on the model of the old Lebanese government would be the order of the day.

I write as one whose whole career has been identified with promotion of civil liberties, especially of Blacks, opposition to the death penalty, restraint on police abuses, and with effective affirmative action. I chaired the Faculty Committee which first succeeded in recruiting Black professors. I cringe at the notion that my Black colleagues should be regarded as "inferior" scholars or teachers, whom we had to accept to carry out a social or political policy.

Louis B. Schwartz
Benjamin Franklin University
Professor of Law
University of Pennsylvania
Philadelphia, Pennsylvania

REVIEW AND DISCUSSION QUESTIONS

1. Dworkin says affirmative action programs rest on two premises. Explain them.

2. How does Dworkin answer critics of those two goals?

3. How does Dworkin respond to the claim that Bakke's right to be judged on the basis of "merit" was infringed?

4. How does he respond to the claim that Bakke was not "judged as an individual"?

5. In fact Bakke's lawyer claimed he had a right not to be excluded from medical school based on race. How does Dworkin answer that charge?

6. Which of the respondents makes the best argument? Explain the argument, then Dworkin's likely response. Indicate who you think is right and why.

7. Setting aside questions of justice or rights, describe the potential social and economic advantages and disadvantages of affirmative action policies.

8. How might it be argued that some people have a *right* to affirmative action programs? Are those groups you mention the same ones that benefit from such a program? Explain.

9. Sociologist Charles Moskos wrote (*Atlantic Monthly*, May 1986) that nearly 10 percent of the Army's officers are black, and although they still believe they must work harder than whites to succeed, they oppose introduction of affirmative action programs into the army. Why would they think that?

10. How might it be argued that affirmative action programs actually harm relations between minorities and others? How might it help?

Wartime Internment of Japanese Americans

Korematsu v. United States

Fear of invasion and of the power of the Japanese army were widespread after Japan conquered much of the Western Pacific, having already destroyed most of the United States naval fleet at Pearl Harbor. At the same time, there was growing pressure along the West Coast of the United States for the military to do something about the minority population of Japanese Americans. Some argued they could aid an invading army; others feared for the welfare of people of Japanese descent at the hands of angry mobs; and, finally, there was also a fair amount of economic advantage to be gained if these successful, hard-working people were forced to sell or otherwise lose their businesses and homes. Although people in both military intelligence and in the Federal Bureau of Investigations disputed the claims that Japanese Americans posed a danger, Franklin Roosevelt nevertheless signed a bill into law allowing the military to establish "military zones" from which any persons could be excluded and that validated the military's already established curfew on both Japanese citizens and American citizens of Japanese descent living on the West Coast.

In Hirabayashi v. United States *(1943), the Supreme Court had upheld the conviction of a University of Washington student, Gordon Hirabayashi, for violating the curfew. Military leaders went on to enforce Roosevelt's order aggressively by requiring that persons of Japanese ancestry living on the West Coast be sent to internment camps.*

---

323 U.S. 214 (1944). Some citations omitted.

Fred Korematsu was a native-born citizen of the United States of Japanese ancestry. After Pearl Harbor he volunteered to join the army but was rejected due to ill health. He then worked for the civilian defense industry as a welder. Korematsu was convicted of refusing to report to the authorities for eventual internment in a camp. He appealed to the Supreme Court, which after bitter internal disputes refused to overturn the military's judgment and allowed the camps. Some justices wanted to allow only the curfew but not the camps; others refused to second-guess the president, Congress, and the military at all. One of the eventual dissenters, Justice Murphy, after reading a draft of an opinion from another potential dissenting justice, sent a copy of the draft to his clerk with the following note: "Gene: Read this and perish! The Court has blown up over the Jap case—just as I expected it would."

The economic costs for Japanese Americans were staggering. They lost both their homes and their livelihoods. But even more important, perhaps, were the emotional consequences of their treatment at the hands of fellow citizens.

Mr. Justice Black delivered the opinion of the Court:

It should be noted, to begin with, that all legal restrictions which curtail the civil rights of a single racial group are immediately suspect. That is not to say that all such restrictions are unconstitutional. It is to say that courts must subject them to the most rigid scrutiny. Pressing public necessity may sometimes justify the existence of such restrictions; racial antagonism never can. . . .

In the light of the principles we announced in the *Hirabayashi* case, we are unable to conclude that it was beyond the war power of Congress and the Executive to exclude those of Japanese ancestry from the West Coast war area at the time they did. True, exclusion from the area in which one's home is located is a far greater deprivation than constant confinement to the home from 8:00 P.M. to 6:00 A.M. Nothing short of apprehension by the proper military authorities of the gravest imminent danger to the public safety can constitutionally justify either. But exclusion from a threatened area, no less than curfew, has a definite and close relationship to the prevention of espionage and sabotage. The military authorities, charged with the primary responsibility of defending our shores, concluded that curfew provided inadequate protection and ordered exclusion. They did so, as pointed out in our *Hirabayashi* opinion, in accordance with Congressional authority to the military to say who should, and who should not, remain in the threatened areas. . . .

Like curfew, exclusion of those of Japanese origin was deemed necessary because of the presence of an unascertained number of disloyal members of the group, most of whom we have no doubt were loyal to this country. It was because we could not reject the finding of the military authorities that it was impossible to bring about an immediate segregation of the disloyal from the loyal that we sustained the validity of the curfew order as applying to the whole group. In the instant case, temporary exclusion of the entire group was rested by the military on the same ground. The judgment that exclusion of the whole group was for the same reason a military imperative answers the contention that the exclusion was in the nature of group punishment based on antagonism to those of Japanese origin. That there were members of the group who retained loyalties to Japan has been confirmed by investigations made subsequent to the exclusion. Approximately five thousand American citizens of Japanese ancestry refused to swear unqualified allegiance to the United States and to renounce allegiance to the Japanese Emperor, and several thousand evacuees requested repatriation to Japan.

We uphold the exclusion order as of the time it was made and when the petitioner violated it. . . . In doing so, we are not unmindful of the hardships imposed by it upon a large group of American citizens. . . . But hardships are part of war, and war is an aggregation of hardships. All citizens alike, both in and out of uniform, feel the impact of war in greater or lesser measure.

Citizenship has its responsibilities as well as its privileges, and in time of war the burden is always heavier. Compulsory exclusion of large groups of citizens from their homes, except under circumstances of direst emergency and peril, is inconsistent with our basic governmental institutions. But when under conditions of modern warfare our shores are threatened by hostile forces, the power to protect must be commensurate with the threatened danger. . . .

It is said that we are dealing here with the case of imprisonment of a citizen in a concentration camp solely because of his ancestry, without evidence or inquiry concerning his loyalty and good disposition towards the United States. Our task would be simple, our duty clear, were this a case involving the imprisonment of a loyal citizen in a concentration camp because of racial prejudice. Regardless of the true nature of the assembly and relocation centers—and we deem it unjustifiable to call them concentration camps with all the ugly connotations that term implies—we are dealing specifically with nothing but an exclusion order. To cast this case into outlines of racial prejudice, without reference to the real military dangers which were presented, merely confuses the issue. Korematsu was not excluded from the Military Areas because of hostility to him or his race. He *was* excluded because we are at war with the Japanese Empire, because the properly constituted military authorities feared an invasion of our West Coast and felt constrained to take proper security measures, because they decided that the military urgency of the situation demanded that all citizens of Japanese ancestry be segregated from the West Coast temporarily, and finally, because Congress, reposing its confidence in this time of war in our military leaders—as inevitably it must—determined that they should have the power to do just this. There was evidence of disloyalty on the part of some, the military authorities considered that the need for action was great, and time was short. We cannot—by availing ourselves of the calm perspective of hindsight—now say that at that time these actions were unjustified.

Affirmed.

Mr. Justice Murphy, dissenting:

This exclusion of "all persons of Japanese ancestry, both alien and non-alien," from the Pacific Coast area on a plea of military necessity in the absence of martial law ought not to be approved. Such exclusion goes over "the very brink of constitutional power" and falls into the ugly abyss of racism.

In dealing with matters relating to the prosecution and progress of a war, we must accord great respect and consideration to the judgments of the military authorities who are on the scene and who have full knowledge of the military facts. . . .

At the same time, however, it is essential that there be definite limits to military discretion, especially where martial law has not been declared.

That this forced exclusion was the result in good measure of this erroneous assumption of racial guilt rather than bona fide military necessity is evidenced by the Commanding General's Final Report on the evacuation. . . . In it he refers to all individuals of Japanese descent as "subversive," as belonging to "an enemy race" whose "racial strains are undiluted," and as constituting "over 112,000 potential enemies . . . at large today." . . . In support of this blanket condemnation of all persons of Japanese descent, however, no reliable evidence is cited to show that such individuals were generally disloyal, or . . . constitute[d] a special menace to defense installations or war industries, or had otherwise by their behavior furnished reasonable ground for their exclusion as a group.

Justification for the exclusion is sought, instead, mainly upon questionable racial and sociological grounds not ordinarily within the realm of expert military judgment, supplemented by certain semi-military conclusions drawn from an unwarranted use of circumstantial evidence. Individuals of Japanese ancestry are condemned because they are said to be "a large, unassimilated, tightly knit racial group, bound to an enemy nation by strong ties of race, culture, custom and religion." They are claimed to be given to "emperor worshipping ceremonies" and to "dual citizenship." Japanese language schools and allegedly pro-Japanese organizations are cited as evidence of possible group disloyalty, together with facts as to certain persons being educated and residing at length in Japan. . . .

The main reasons relied upon by those responsible for the forced evacuation . . . [are] largely an accumulation of much of the misinformation, half-truths and insinuations that for years have been directed against Japanese Americans by people with racial and economic prejudices—the same people who have been among the foremost advocates of the evacuation. A military judgment based upon such racial and sociological considerations is not entitled to the great weight ordinarily given the judgments based upon strictly military considerations. Especially is this so when every charge relative to race, religion, culture, geographical location, and legal and economic status has been substantially discredited by independent studies made by experts in these matters.

No adequate reason is given for the failure to treat these Japanese Americans on an individual basis by holding investigations and hearings to separate the loyal from the disloyal, as was done in the case of persons of German and Italian ancestry. It is asserted merely that the loyalties of this group "were unknown and time was of the essence." Yet nearly four months elapsed after Pearl Harbor before the first exclusion order was issued; nearly eight months went by until the last order was issued; and the last of these "subversive" persons was not actually removed until almost eleven months had elapsed. Leisure and deliberation seem to have been more of the essence than speed. And the fact that conditions were not such as to warrant a declaration of martial law adds strength to the belief that the factors of time and military necessity were not as urgent as they have been represented to be.

Moreover, there was no adequate proof that the Federal Bureau of Investigation and the military and naval intelligence services did not have the espionage and sabotage situation well in hand during this long period. Nor is there any denial of the fact that not one person of Japanese ancestry was accused or convicted of espionage or sabotage after Pearl Harbor while they were still free, a fact which is some evidence of the loyalty of the vast majority of those individuals and of the effectiveness of the established methods of combating these evils. It seems incredible that under these circumstances it would have been impossible to hold loyalty hearings for the mere 112,000 persons involved—or at least for the 70,000 American citizens—especially when a large part of this number represented children and elderly men and women. . . .

I dissent, therefore, from this legalization of racism. Racial discrimination in any form and in any degree has no justifiable part whatever in our democratic way of life. It is unattractive in any setting but it is utterly revolting among a free people who have embraced the principles set forth in the Constitution of the United States. All residents of this nation are kin in some way by blood or culture to a foreign land. Yet they are primarily and necessarily a part of the new and distinct civilization of the United States. They must accordingly be treated at all times as the heirs of the American experiment and as entitled to all the rights and freedoms guaranteed by the Constitution.

Mr. Justice Jackson, dissenting:

Korematsu was born on our soil, of parents born in Japan. The Constitution makes him a citizen of the United States by nativity and a citizen of California by residence. No claim is made that he is not loyal to this country. There is no suggestion that apart from the matter involved here he is not law-abiding and well disposed. Korematsu, however, has been convicted of an act not commonly a crime. It consists merely of being present in the state whereof he is a citizen, near the place where he was born, and where all his life he has lived.

Even more unusual is the series of military orders which made this conduct a crime. They forbid such a one to remain, and they also forbid him to leave. They were so drawn that the only way Korematsu could avoid violation was to give himself up to the military authority. This meant submission to custody, examination, and transportation out of the territory, to be followed by indeterminate confinement in detention camps.

A citizen's presence in the locality, however, was made a crime only if his parents were of Japanese birth. Had Korematsu been one of four—the others being, say, a German alien enemy, an Italian alien enemy, and a citizen of American-born ancestors, convicted of treason but out on parole—only Korematsu's presence would have violated the order. The difference between their innocence and his crime would result, not from anything he did, said or thought, different than they, but only in that he was born of different racial stock.

Now, if any fundamental assumption underlies our system, it is that guilt is personal and not inheritable. Even if all of one's antecedents had been convicted of treason, the Constitution forbids its penalties to be visited upon him, for it provides that "no attainder of treason shall work corruption of blood, or forfeiture except during the life of the person attainted." But here is an attempt to . . . make an otherwise innocent act a crime merely because this prisoner is the son of parents as to whom he had no choice, and belongs to a race from which there is no way to resign.

. . . [T]he "law" which this prisoner is convicted of disregarding is not found in an act of Congress, but in a military order. Neither the Act of Congress nor the Executive Order of the President, nor both together, would afford a basis for the conviction. . . . And it is said that if the military commander had reasonable military grounds for promulgating the orders, they are constitutional and become law, and the Court is required to enforce them.

It would be impracticable and dangerous idealism to expect or insist that each specific military command in an area of probable operations will conform to conventional tests of constitutionality. . . . The armed services must protect a society, not merely its Constitution. The very essence of the military job is to marshal physical force, to remove every obstacle to its effectiveness, to give it every strategic advantage. Defense measures will not, and often should not, be held within the limits that bind civil authority in peace. . . .

But if we cannot confine military expedients by the Constitution, neither would I distort the Constitution to approve all that the military may deem expedient. . . . I cannot say . . . that the orders of General DeWitt were not reasonably expedient military precautions, nor could I say that they were. But even if they were permissible military procedures, I deny that it follows that they are constitutional. If, as the Court holds, it does follow, then we may as well say that any military order will be constitutional and have done with it. . . .

Much is said of the danger to liberty from the Army program. . . . But a judicial construction of the due process clause that will sustain this order is a far more subtle blow to liberty. . . . A military order, however unconstitutional, is not apt to last longer than the military emergency. Even during that period a succeeding commander may revoke it all. But once a judicial opinion rationalizes such an order to show that it conforms to the Constitution, or rather rationalizes the Constitution to show that the Constitution sanctions such an order, the Court for all time has validated the principle of racial discrimination in criminal procedure and of transplanting American citizens. The principle then lies about like a loaded weapon ready for the hand of any authority that can bring forward a plausible claim of an urgent need. . . . All who observe the work of courts are familiar with what Judge Cardozo described as "the tendency of a principle to expand itself to the limit of its logic." A military commander may overstep the bounds of constitutionality, and it is an incident. But if we review and approve, that passing incident becomes the doctrine of the Constitution. There it has a generative power of its own, and all that it creates will be in its own image. Nothing better illustrates this danger than does the Court's opinion in this case.

It argues that we are bound to uphold the conviction of Korematsu because we upheld one in *Hirabayashi*. . . .

In that case we were urged to consider only the curfew feature. . . . We yielded, and the Chief Justice guarded the opinion as carefully as language will do. He said: " . . . We decide only the issue as we have defined it—we decide only that the *curfew order* as applied, and at the time it was applied, was within the boundaries of the war power." . . . Now the principle of racial discrimination is pushed from support of mild measures to very harsh ones, and from temporary deprivations to indeterminate ones. And the precedent which it is said requires us to do so is *Hirabayashi*. The Court is now saying that in *Hirabayashi* we did decide the very things we there said we were not deciding. Because we said that these citizens could be made to stay in their homes during the hours of dark, it is said we must require them to leave home entirely; and if that, we are told they may also be taken into custody for deportation; and if that, it is argued they may also be held for some undetermined time in detention camps. How far the principle of this case would be extended before plausible reasons would play out, I do not know.

I should hold that a civil court cannot be made to enforce an order which violates constitutional limitations even if it is a reasonable exercise of military authority. The courts can exercise only the judicial power, can apply only law, and must abide by the Constitution, or they cease to be civil courts and become instruments of military policy.

. . . I would not lead people to rely on this Court for a review that seems to me wholly delusive. . . . If the people ever let command of the war power fall into irresponsible and unscrupulous hands, the courts wield no power equal to its restraint. The chief restraint upon those who command the physical forces of the country . . . must be their responsibility to the political judgments of their contemporaries and to the moral judgments of history.

My duties as a justice . . . do not require me to make a military judgment as to whether General DeWitt's evacuation and detention program was a reasonable military necessity. I do not suggest that the courts should have attempted to interfere with the Army in carrying out its task. But I do not think they may be asked to execute a military expedient that has no place in law under the Constitution. I would reverse the judgment and discharge the prisoner.

Review and Discussion Questions

1. Explain the reasoning behind Justice Black's opinion for the Court.

2. Justice Black begins his opinion with a brief indication how he approaches the case, mentioning both "suspect" restrictions and "strict scrutiny." These have now become the centerpiece of Equal Protection analysis. Explain what he means.

3. Describe the basis of Justice Murphy's dissent.

4. Justice Jackson's dissent focuses on due process rather than equal protection. Explain how that aspect of Justice Jackson's position differs from Justice Murphy's.

5. On whose shoulders does Justice Jackson think rests the possibility of avoiding future abuses of authority by the military? Explain.

6. Justice Jackson's conclusion has been described as an example of judicial "nihilism." Explain that comment, indicating if you agree.

7. In later years Justice Douglas, who had reluctantly gone along with the majority, came to regret his decision and believed *Korematsu* was a grave mistake. He also said, however, that he thought any of the many courts he served on during his long career would have ruled the same way. Justice Black, on the other hand, continued to believe that Congress had not exceeded its power in delegating authority to the military to intern Japanese Americans. Many today think the case represents how far the Court and Congress are willing to go in bending the Constitution in time of war. Still others see it as an indication that the racism infecting society has not been limited to blacks. How would you assess the case?

Gender Discrimination

Michael M. v. Sonoma County Superior Court

This case concerns equality between the sexes. A seventeen-year-old man was convicted under California law for the statutory rape of a sixteen-year-old female. Men, but not women, are liable under the statute, which makes it illegal to have sex with a female under eighteen, whether or not she consents. Justice Rehnquist, writing for a plurality of the Supreme Court, upheld the California law, maintaining that it does not discriminate against men or women. In a dissenting opinion, Justice Brennan argues that California has not shown that this law will reduce pregnancies more effectively than one that does not make any distinction based on sex.

Mr. Justice Rehnquist:

[We] have not held that gender-based classifications are "inherently suspect" and thus we do not apply so-called "strict scrutiny" to those classifications. Our cases have held, however, that the traditional minimum rationality test takes on a somewhat "sharper focus" when gender-based classifications are challenged. In *Reed v. Reed*, for example, the Court stated that a gender-based classification will be upheld if it bears a "fair and substantial relationship" to legitimate state ends, while in *Craig v. Boren*, the Court restated the test to require the classification to bear a "substantial relationship" to "important governmental objectives."

Underlying these decisions is the principle that a legislature may not "make overbroad generalizations based on sex which are entirely unrelated to any differences between men and women or which demean the ability or social status of the affected class." But because the Equal Protection Clause does not "demand that a statute necessarily apply equally to all persons" or require "things which are different in fact to be treated in law as though they were the same," this Court has consistently upheld statutes where the gender classification is not invidious, but rather realistically reflects the fact that the sexes are not similarly situated in certain circumstances. . . .

Applying those principles to this case, the fact that the California Legislature criminalized the act of illicit sexual intercourse with a minor female is a sure indication of its intent or purpose to discourage that conduct. Precisely why the legislature desired that result is of course somewhat less clear. . . .

The justification for the statute offered by the State, and accepted by the Supreme Court of California, is that the legislature sought to prevent illegitimate teenage pregnancies. . . .

We are satisfied not only that the prevention of illegitimate pregnancy is at least one of the "purposes" of the statute, but also that the State has a strong interest in preventing such pregnancy. . . .

We need not be medical doctors to discern that young men and young women are not similarly situated with respect to the problems and the risks of sexual intercourse. Only women may become pregnant, and they suffer disproportionately the profound physical, emotional, and psychological consequences of sexual activity. The statute at issue here protects women from sexual intercourse at an age when those consequences are particularly severe.

[Although petitioner concedes that the State has a "compelling" interest in preventing teenage pregnancy, he contends that the "true" purpose of [the statute] is to protect the virtue and chastity of young women. As such, the statute is unjustifiable because it rests on archaic stereotypes. What we have said above is enough to dispose of that contention. The question for

450 U.S. 464 (1981). Some citations omitted.

us—and the only question under the Federal Constitution—is whether the legislation violates the Equal Protection Clause of the Fourteenth Amendment, not whether its supporters may have endorsed it for reasons no longer generally accepted.]

The question thus boils down to whether a State may attack the problem of sexual intercourse and teenage pregnancy directly by prohibiting a male from having sexual intercourse with a minor female. We hold that such a statute is sufficiently related to the State's objectives to pass constitutional muster.

Because virtually all of the significant harmful and inescapably identifiable consequences of teenage pregnancy fall on the young female, a legislature acts well within its authority when it elects to punish only the participant who, by nature, suffers few of the consequences of his conduct. It is hardly unreasonable for a legislature acting to protect minor females to exclude them from punishment. Moreover, the risk of pregnancy itself constitutes a substantial deterrence to young females. No similar natural sanctions deter males. A criminal sanction imposed solely on males thus serves to roughly "equalize" the deterrents on the sexes. . . .

[We] cannot say that a gender-neutral statute would be as effective as the statute California has chosen to enact. The State persuasively contends that a gender-neutral statute would frustrate its interest in effective enforcement. Its view is that a female is surely less likely to report violations of the statute if she herself would be subject to criminal prosecution. . . .

There remains only petitioner's contention that the statute is unconstitutional as it is applied to him because he, like [his partner], was under 18 at the time of sexual intercourse. Petitioner argues that the statute is flawed because it presumes that as between two persons under 18, the male is the culpable aggressor. We find petitioner's contentions unpersuasive. Contrary to his assertions, the statute does not rest on the assumption that males are generally the aggressors. It is instead an attempt by a legislature to prevent illegitimate teenage pregnancy by providing an additional deterrent for men. The age of the man is irrelevant since young men are as capable as older men of inflicting the harm sought to be prevented.

Justice Brennan, dissenting:

The State of California vigorously asserts that the "important governmental objective" to be served by [the statute] is the prevention of teenage pregnancy. It claims that its statute furthers this goal by deterring sexual activity by males—the class of persons it considers more responsible for causing those pregnancies. [In a remarkable display of sexual stereotyping, the California Supreme Court stated: "The Legislature is well within its power in imposing criminal sanctions against males, alone, because they are the *only* persons who may physiologically cause the result which the law properly seeks to avoid."] But even assuming that prevention of teenage pregnancy is an important governmental objective and that it is in fact an objective of [the statute], California still has the burden of proving that there are fewer teenage pregnancies under its gender-based statutory rape law than there would be if the law were gender neutral. To meet this burden, the State must show that because its statutory rape law punishes only males, and not females, it more effectively deters minor females from having sexual intercourse. . . .

A State's bare assertion that its gender-based statutory classification substantially furthers an important governmental interest is not enough to meet its burden of proof. . . . Rather, the State must produce evidence that will persuade the Court that its assertion is true. [Even] assuming that a gender-neutral statute would be more difficult to enforce, the State has still not shown that those enforcement problems would make such a statute less effective than a gender-based statute in deterring minor females from engaging in sexual intercourse. Common sense, however, suggests that a gender-neutral statutory rape law is potentially a *greater* deterrent of sexual activity than a gender-based law, for the simple reason that a gender-neutral law subjects both men and women to criminal sanctions and thus arguably has a deterrent effect on twice as many potential violators. Even if fewer persons were prosecuted under the gender-neutral law, as the State suggests, it would still be true that twice as many persons would be *subject* to arrest.

Until very recently, no California court or commentator had suggested that the purpose of California's statutory rape law was to protect young women from the risk of pregnancy. Indeed, the historical development of [the statute] demonstrates that the law was initially enacted on the premise that young women, in contrast to young men, were to be deemed legally inca-

pable of consenting to an act of sexual intercourse. Because their chastity was considered particularly precious, those young women were felt to be uniquely in need of the State's protection. In contrast, young men were assumed to be capable of making such decisions for themselves; the law therefore did not offer them any special protection. . . .

I would hold that [the statute] violates the Equal Protection Clause of the Fourteenth Amendment. . . .

REVIEW AND DISCUSSION QUESTIONS

1. Explain the basic legal question before the Court in this case.

2. Does Justice Rehnquist see this as a case of discrimination against males or females, do you think? What were Justice Rehnquist's reasons for upholding the law?

3. The dissenters offer two arguments. Describe them.

4. Of what importance is the fact that California could have made all informers, male or female, exempt from the law?

5. Arguably *both* sides missed an important aspect of this case: It puts a burden on young women it does not place on men. Explain.

6. Why do you think California passed this law?

Speech Creating a "Hostile Environment"

Harris v. Forklift Systems

This case involves the interpretation of Title VII of the Civil Rights Act of 1964. In the earlier case of Meritor Savings, *the Supreme Court had held that employers who maintain a "hostile work environment" were guilty of sex discrimination. In this case, the Court again addressed the question of what constitutes a "hostile work environment" and which forms of speech lack constitutional protection for that reason.*

Justice O'Connor delivered the opinion of the Court:

In this case we consider the definition of a discriminatorily "abusive work environment" (also known as a "hostile work environment") under Title VII of the Civil Rights Act of 1964.

114 S.Ct. 367 (1993).

I

Teresa Harris worked as a manager at Forklift Systems, Inc., an equipment rental company, from April 1985 until October 1987. Charles Hardy was Forklift's president.

The Magistrate found that, throughout Harris' time at Forklift, Hardy often insulted her because of her gender and often made her the target of unwanted sexual innuendoes. Hardy told Harris on several occasions, in the presence of other employees, "You're a woman, what do you know" and "We need a man as the rental manager"; at least once, he told her she was "a dumb ass woman." Again in front of others, he suggested that the two of them "go to the Holiday Inn to negotiate [Harris'] raise." Hardy occasionally asked Harris and other female employees to get coins from his front pants pocket. He threw objects on the ground in front of Harris and other women, and asked them to pick the objects up. He made sexual innuendoes about Harris' and other women's clothing.

In mid-August 1987, Harris complained to Hardy about his conduct. Hardy said he was surprised that Harris was offended, claimed he was only joking, and apologized. He also promised he would stop, and based on this assurance Harris stayed on the job. But in early September, Hardy began anew: while Harris was arranging a deal with one of Forklift's customers, he asked her, again in front of other employees, "What did you do, promise the guy . . . some [sex] Saturday night?" On October 1, Harris collected her paycheck and quit.

Harris then sued Forklift, claiming that Hardy's conduct had created an abusive work environment for her because of her gender. The United States District Court for the Middle District of Tennessee, adopting the report and recommendation of the Magistrate, found this to be "a close case," but held that Hardy's conduct did not create an abusive environment. The court found that some of Hardy's comments "offended [Harris], and would offend the reasonable woman," but that they were not "so severe as to be expected to seriously affect [Harris'] psychological well-being. A reasonable woman manager under like circumstances would have been offended by Hardy, but his conduct would not have risen to the level of interfering with that person's work performance. . . . Neither do I believe that [Harris] was subjectively so offended that she suffered injury. . . . Although Hardy may at times have genuinely offended [Harris], I do not believe that he created a working environment so poisoned as to be intimidating or abusive to [Harris]."

. . . We granted certiorari, to resolve a conflict among the Circuits on whether conduct, to be actionable as "abusive work environment" harassment (no quid pro quo harassment issue is present here), must "seriously affect [an employee's] psychological well-being" or lead the plaintiff to "suffe[r] injury."

II

Title VII of the Civil Rights Act of 1964 makes it "an unlawful employment practice for an employer . . . to discriminate against any individual with respect to his compensation, terms, conditions, or privileges of employment, because of such individual's race, color, religion, sex, or national origin." As we made clear in *Meritor Savings Bank v. Vinson*, this language "is not limited to 'economic' or 'tangible' discrimination. The phrase 'terms, conditions, or privileges of employment' evinces a congressional intent 'to strike at the entire spectrum of disparate treatment of men and women' in employment," which includes requiring people to work in a discriminatorily hostile or abusive environment. When the workplace is permeated with "discriminatory intimidation, ridicule, and insult," that is "sufficiently severe or pervasive to alter the conditions of the victim's employment and create an abusive working environment," Title VII is violated.

This standard, which we reaffirm today, takes a middle path between making actionable any conduct that is merely offensive and requiring the conduct to cause a tangible psychological injury. As we pointed out in *Meritor*, "mere utterance of an . . . epithet which engenders offensive feelings in an employee" does not sufficiently affect the conditions of employment to implicate Title VII. Conduct that is not severe or pervasive enough to create an objectively hostile or abusive work environment—an environment that a reasonable person would find hostile or abusive—is beyond Title VII's purview. Likewise, if the victim does not subjectively perceive the environment to be abusive, the conduct has not actually altered the conditions of the victim's employment, and there is no Title VII violation.

But Title VII comes into play before the harassing conduct leads to a nervous breakdown. A discriminatorily abusive work environment, even one that does not seriously affect employees' psychological well-being, can and often will detract from employees' job performance, discourage employees from remaining on the job, or keep them from advancing in their careers. Moreover, even without regard to these tangible effects, the very fact that the discriminatory conduct was so severe or pervasive that it created a work environment abusive to employees because of their race, gender, religion, or national origin offends Title VII's broad rule of workplace equality. The appalling conduct alleged in *Meritor*, and the reference in that case to environments "so heavily polluted with discrimination as to destroy completely the emotional and psychological stability of minority group workers," merely present some especially egregious examples of harassment. They do not mark the boundary of what is actionable.

We therefore believe the District Court erred in relying on whether the conduct "seriously affect[ed] plaintiff's psychological well-being" or led her to "suffe[r] injury." Such an inquiry may needlessly focus the factfinder's attention on concrete psychological harm, an element Title VII does not require. Certainly Title VII bars conduct that would seriously affect a reasonable person's psychological well-being, but the statute is not limited to such conduct. So long as the environment would reasonably be perceived, and is perceived, as hostile or abusive, there is no need for it also to be psychologically injurious.

This is not, and by its nature cannot be, a mathematically precise test. . . . But we can say that whether an environment is "hostile" or "abusive" can be determined only by looking at all the circumstances. These may include the frequency of the discriminatory conduct; its severity; whether it is physically threatening or humiliating, or a mere offensive utterance; and whether it unreasonably interferes with an employee's work performance. The effect on the employee's psychological well-being is, of course, relevant to determining whether the plaintiff actually found the environment abusive. But while psychological harm, like any other relevant factor, may be taken into account, no single factor is required.

III

Forklift, while conceding that a requirement that the conduct seriously affect psychological well-being is unfounded, argues that the District Court nonetheless correctly applied the *Meritor* standard. We disagree. Though the District Court did conclude that the work environment was not "intimidating or abusive to [Harris]," it did so only after finding that the conduct was not "so severe as to be expected to seriously affect plaintiff's psychological well-being," and that Harris was not "subjectively so offended that she suffered injury." The District Court's application of these incorrect standards may well have influenced its ultimate conclusion, especially given that the court found this to be a "close case." We therefore reverse the judgment of the Court of Appeals, and remand the case for further proceedings consistent with this opinion.

So ordered.

REVIEW AND DISCUSSION QUESTIONS

1. Describe the facts of this case.
2. The Court said it was taking a "middle path" in this case. Explain.
3. The Court acknowledges that its test is not "mathematically precise." Do you see any problem with its test? Explain.
4. How might Minow and Singer respond to this case?

Campus Speech Codes

Doe v. University of Michigan

Some U.S. campuses have instituted "speech codes" designed to prevent racist, sexist, and other forms of speech, and in doing so have brought the values of equality and free speech into apparent conflict. One of the most restrictive of these codes was found at the University of Michigan. The policy outlawed conduct that "stigmatizes or victimizes" students on the basis of "race, ethnicity, religion, sex and sexual orientation." This suit was brought by a student who wished to remain anonymous to protect himself from adverse publicity and is therefore referred to only as "John Doe." As a teaching assistant in an advanced psychology class on animal behavior, Doe wanted to discuss mental differences between men and women and their potential impact on career choices. Because some regard his theories as sexist, he said, he feared being charged under the university's speech code and brought suit claiming the code violated the First Amendment.

1. INTRODUCTION

It is an unfortunate fact of our constitutional system that the ideals of freedom and equality are often in conflict. The difficult and sometimes painful task of our political and legal institutions is to mediate the appropriate balance between these two competing values. Recently, the University of Michigan at Ann Arbor (the University), a state-chartered university, . . . adopted a Policy . . . in an attempt to curb what the University's governing Board of Regents (Regents) viewed as a rising tide of racial intolerance and harassment on campus. The Policy prohibited individuals, under the penalty of sanctions, from "stigmatizing or victimizing" individuals or groups on the basis of race, ethnicity, religion, sex, sexual orientation, creed, national origin, ancestry, age, marital status, handicap or Vietnam-era veteran status. . . .

2. FACTS GENERALLY

According to the University, in the last three years incidents of racism and racial harassment appeared to become increasingly frequent at the

---

721 F. Supp. 852 (F.D.Mich. 1989). Some citations omitted.

University. For example, on January 27, 1987, unknown persons distributed a flier declaring "open season" on blacks, which it referred to as "saucer lips, porch monkeys, and jigaboos." On February 4, 1987, a student disc jockey at an on-campus radio station allowed racist jokes to be broadcast. At a demonstration protesting these incidents, a Ku Klux Klan uniform was displayed from a dormitory window. . . .

On December 14, 1987, the Acting President circulated a confidential memorandum to the University's executive officers detailing a proposal for an anti-discrimination disciplinary policy. The proposed policy prohibited "[h]arassment of anyone through word or deed or any other behavior which discriminates on the basis of inappropriate criteria." The Acting President recognized at the time that the proposed policy would engender serious First Amendment problems, but reasoned that

just as an individual cannot shout "Fire!" in a crowded theater and then claim immunity from prosecution for causing a riot on the basis of exercising his rights of free speech, so a great many American universities have taken the position that students at a university cannot by speaking or writing discriminatory remarks which seriously offend many individuals beyond the immediate victim, and which, therefore detract from the necessary educational climate of a campus, claim immunity from a campus disciplinary proceeding. I believe that position to be valid.

The other "American universities" to which the President referred . . .were not identified at any time. Nor was any document presented to the Court in any form which "valid[ates]" this "position." . . .

3. THE UNIVERSITY OF MICHIGAN POLICY ON DISCRIMINATION AND DISCRIMINATORY HARASSMENT

A. THE TERMS OF THE POLICY

The Policy established a three-tiered system whereby the degree of regulation was dependent on the location of the conduct at issue. The broadest range of speech and dialogue was "tolerated" in variously described public parts of the campus. Only an act of physical violence or destruction of property was considered sanctionable in these settings. Publications sponsored by the University such as the *Michigan Daily* and the *Michigan Review* were not subject to regulation. The conduct of students living in University housing is primarily governed by the standard provisions of individual leases, however the Policy appeared to apply in this setting as well. The Policy by its terms applied specifically to "[e]ducational and academic centers, such as classroom buildings, libraries, research laboratories, recreation and study centers[.]" In these areas, persons were subject to discipline for:

1. Any behavior, verbal or physical, that stigmatizes or victimizes an individual on the basis of race, ethnicity, religion, sex, sexual orientation, creed, national origin, ancestry, age, marital status, handicap or Vietnam-era veteran status, and that

   a. Involves an express or implied threat to an individual's academic efforts, employment, participation in University sponsored extracurricular activities or personal safety; or

   b. Has the purpose or reasonably foreseeable effect of interfering with an individual's academic efforts, employment, participation in University sponsored extra-curricular activities or personal safety; or

   c. Creates an intimidating, hostile, or demeaning environment for educational pursuits, employment or participation in University sponsored extra-curricular activities.

2. Sexual advances, requests for sexual favors, and verbal or physical conduct that stigmatizes or victimizes an individual on the basis of sex or sexual orientation where such behavior:

   a. Involves an express or implied threat to an individual's academic efforts, employment, participation in University sponsored extracurricular activities or personal safety; or

   b. Has the purpose or reasonably foreseeable effect of interfering with an individual's academic efforts, employment, participation in University sponsored extra-curricular activities or personal safety; or

   c. Creates an intimidating, hostile, or demeaning environment for educational pursuits, employment or participation in University sponsored extra-curricular activities. . . .

B. HEARING PROCEDURES

Any member of the University community could initiate the process leading to sanctions by either filing a formal complaint with an appropriate University office or by seeking informal counseling with described University officials and support centers. . . .

C. SANCTIONS

The Policy provided for progressive discipline based on the severity of the violation. It stated that the University encouraged hearing panels to impose sanctions that include an educational element in order to sensitize the perpetrator to the harmfulness of his or her conduct. The Policy provided, however, that compulsory class attendance should not be imposed "in an attempt to change deeply held religious or moral convictions." Depending on the intent of the accused student, the effect of the conduct, and whether the accused student is a repeat offender, one or more of the following sanctions may be imposed: (1) formal reprimand; (2) community service; (3) class attendance; (4) restitution; (5) removal from University housing; (6) suspension from specific courses and activities; (7) suspension; (8) expulsion. The sanctions of suspension and expulsion could only be imposed for violent or dangerous acts, repeated offenses, or a willful failure to comply with a lesser sanction. The University President could set aside or lessen any sanction.

D. INTERPRETIVE GUIDE

Shortly after the promulgation of the policy in the fall of 1988, the University Office of Affirmative Action issued an interpretive guide (Guide) entitled *What Students Should Know about Discrimination and Discriminatory Harassment by Students in the University Environment.* The Guide purported to be an authoritative interpretation of the Policy and provided examples of sanctionable conduct. These included:

> A flyer containing racist threats distributed in a residence hall.
>
> Racist graffiti written on the door of an Asian student's study carrel.
>
> A male student makes remarks in class like "Women just aren't as good in this field as men," thus creating a hostile learning atmosphere for female classmates.
>
> Students in a residence hall have a floor party and invite everyone on their floor except one person because they think she might be a lesbian.
>
> A black student is confronted and racially insulted by two white students in a cafeteria.
>
> Male students leave pornographic pictures and jokes on the desk of a female graduate student.
>
> Two men demand that their roommate in the residence hall move out and be tested for AIDS.

In addition, the Guide contained a separate section entitled "You are a harasser when . . ." which contains the following examples of discriminatory conduct:

> You exclude someone from a study group because that person is of a different race, sex, or ethnic origin than you are.
>
> You tell jokes about gay men and lesbians.
>
> Your student organization sponsors entertainment that includes a comedian who slurs Hispanics.

> You display a confederate flag on the door of your room in the residence hall.
>
> You laugh at a joke about someone in your class who stutters.
>
> You make obscene telephone calls or send racist notes or computer messages.
>
> You comment in a derogatory way about a particular person or group's physical appearance or sexual orientation, or their cultural origins, or religious beliefs.

It was not clear whether each of these actions would subject a student to sanctions, although the title of the section suggests that they would. . . .

4. STANDING

Doe is a psychology graduate student. His specialty is the field of biopsychology, which he describes as the interdisciplinary study of the biological bases of individual differences in personality traits and mental abilities. Doe said that certain controversial theories positing biologically-based differences between sexes and races might be perceived as "sexist" and "racist" by some students, and he feared that discussion of such theories might be sanctionable under the Policy. He asserted that his right to freely and openly discuss these theories was impermissibly chilled, and he requested that the Policy be declared unconstitutional and enjoined on the grounds of vagueness and overbreadth. . . .

. . . The Policy prohibited conduct which "stigmatizes or victimizes" students on the basis of "race, ethnicity, religion, sex, sexual orientation" and other invidious factors. However, the terms "stigmatize" and "victimize" are not self defining. These words can only be understood with reference to some exogenous value system. What one individual might find victimizing or stigmatizing, another individual might not.

. . . The record clearly shows that there existed a realistic and credible threat that Doe could be sanctioned were he to discuss certain biopsychological theories.

. . . [T]he University attorney who researched the law and assisted in the drafting of the Policy, wrote a memorandum in which he conceded that merely offensive speech was constitutionally protected, but declared that

[w]e cannot be frustrated by the reluctance of the courts and the common law to recognize the personal damage that is caused by discriminatory speech, nor should our policy attempt to conform to traditional methods of identifying harmful speech. Rather the University should identify and prohibit that speech that causes damage to individuals within the community.

The record before the Court thus indicated that the drafters of the policy intended that speech need only be offensive to be sanctionable.

The Guide also suggested that the kinds of ideas Doe wished to discuss would be sanctionable. The Guide was the University's authoritative interpretation of the Policy. It explicitly stated that an example of sanctionable conduct would include:

A male student makes remarks in class like "Women just aren't as good in this field as men." thus creating a hostile learning atmosphere for female classmates.

Doe said in an affidavit that he would like to discuss questions relating to sex and race differences in his capacity as a teaching assistant in Psychology 430, Comparative Animal Behavior. He went on to say:

An appropriate topic for discussion in the discussion groups is sexual differences between male and female mammals, including humans. [One] . . . hypothesis regarding sex differences in mental abilities is that men as a group do better than women in some spatially related mental tasks partly because of a biological difference. This may partly explain, for example, why many more men than women chose to enter the engineering profession.

Doe also said that some students and teachers regarded such theories as "sexist" and he feared that he might be charged with a violation of the Policy if he were to discuss them. In light of the statements in the Guide, such fears could not be dismissed as speculative and conjectural. The ideas discussed in Doe's field of study bear sufficient similarity to ideas denounced as "harassing" in the Guide to constitute a realistic and specific threat of prosecution.

. . . A review of the University's discriminatory harassment complaint files suggested that on at least three separate occasions, students were disciplined or threatened with discipline for comments made in a classroom setting. These are . . . discussed *infra*. At least one student was subject to a formal hearing because he stated in the context of a social work research class that he believed that homosexuality was a disease that could be psychologically treated. As will be discussed below, the Policy was enforced so broadly and indiscriminately, that plaintiff's fears of prosecution were entirely reasonable. Accordingly, the Court found that Doe had standing to challenge the policy.

5. VAGUENESS AND OVERBREADTH

. . . While the University's power to regulate so-called pure speech is . . . limited, . . . certain categories can be generally described as unprotected by the First Amendment. It is clear that so-called "fighting words" are not entitled to First Amendment protection. *Chaplinsky v. New Hampshire*, 315 U.S. 568 (1942). These would include "the lewd and obscene, the profane, the libelous, and the insulting or 'fighting words'— those which by their very utterance inflict injury or tend to incite an immediate breach of the peace." *Id.* at 572. Under certain circumstances racial and ethnic epithets, slurs, and insults might fall within this description and could constitutionally be prohibited by the University. In addition, such speech may also be sufficient to state a claim for common law intentional infliction of emotional distress. Credible threats of violence or property damage made with the specific intent to harass or intimidate the victim because of his race, sex, religion, or national origin is punishable both criminally and civilly under state law. Similarly, speech which has the effect of inciting imminent lawless action and which is likely to incite such action may also be lawfully punished. . . .

What the University could not do, however, was establish an anti-discrimination policy which had the effect of prohibiting certain speech because it disagreed with ideas or messages sought to be conveyed. *Texas v. Johnson*. As the Supreme Court stated in *West Virginia State Board of Education v. Barnette*, 319 U.S. 624 (1943):

> If there is any star fixed in our constitutional constellation, it is that no official, high or petty, can prescribe what shall be orthodox in politics, nationalism, religion, or other matters of opinion or force citizens to confess by word or act their faith therein.

Nor could the University proscribe speech simply because it was found to be offensive, even gravely so, by large numbers of people. *Texas v. Johnson, supra*. . . . These principles acquire a special significance in the university setting, where the free and unfettered interplay of competing views is essential to the institution's educational mission. With these general rules in mind, the Court can now consider whether the Policy sweeps within its scope speech which is otherwise protected by the First Amendment.

OVERBREADTH

Doe claimed that the Policy was invalid because it was facially overbroad. It is fundamental that statutes regulating First Amendment activities must be narrowly drawn to address only the specific evil at hand. . . .

The Supreme Court has consistently held that statutes punishing speech or conduct solely on the grounds that they are unseemly or offensive are unconstitutionally overbroad. In *Houston v. Hill*, the Supreme Court struck down a City of Houston ordinance which provided that "[i]t shall be unlawful for any person to assault or strike or in any manner oppose, molest, and abuse or interrupt any policeman in the execution of his duty." . . . In *Papish v. University of Missouri*, (1973), the Supreme Court Ordered the reinstatement of a university student expelled for distributing an underground newspaper sporting the headline "Motherfucker acquitted" on the grounds that "the mere dissemination of ideas—no matter how offensive to good taste—on a state university campus may not be shut off in the name alone of conventions of decency." *Id.* at 670. Although the Supreme Court acknowledged that reasonable restrictions on the time, place, and manner of distribution might have been permissible, "the opinions below show clearly that [plaintiff] was dismissed because of the disapproved *content* of the newspaper." *Id.* Most recently, in *Texas v. Johnson, supra*, the Supreme Court invalidated a Texas statute prohibiting burning of the American flag on the grounds that there was no showing that the prohibited conduct was likely to incite a breach of the peace. These cases stand generally for the proposition that the state may not prohibit broad classes of speech, some of which may indeed be legitimately regulable, if in so doing a substantial amount of constitutionally protected conduct is also prohibited. This was the fundamental infirmity of the Policy. . . .

VAGUENESS

Doe also urges that the policy be struck down on the grounds that it is impermissibly vague. A statute is unconstitutionally vague when "men of common intelligence must necessarily guess at its meaning." A statute must give adequate warning of the conduct which is to be prohibited and must set out explicit standards for those who apply it. . . .

Looking at the plain language of the Policy, it was simply impossible to discern any limitation on its scope or any conceptual distinction between protected and unprotected conduct. . . . The operative words in the cause section required that language must "stigmatize" or "victimize" an individual. However, both of these terms are general and elude precise definition. Moreover, it is clear that the fact that a statement may victimize or stigmatize an individual does not, in and of itself, strip it of protection under the accepted First Amendment tests.

. . . Students of common understanding were necessarily forced to guess at whether a comment about a controversial issue would later be found to be sanctionable under the Policy. The terms of the Policy were so vague that its enforcement would violate the due process clause.

REVIEW AND DISCUSSION QUESTIONS

1. What, exactly, were the provisions of the speech code? What were the penalties?

2. Describe the "Interpretive Guide" the university provided to assist students in understanding the code.

3. On what basis did Doe gain "standing" to bring suit?

4. Describe the limits on speech that the Court says a public university *can* restrict.

5. What is "overbreadth"? Why does the Court hold that the code is overbroad?

6. Why does the Court argue that the code is "vague"?

7. Does it matter, legally, that the University of Michigan is a public institution? Why?

8. Explain whether or not this case presents a conflict between equality and free speech.

9. Suppose you are told to redraft the university's code in a way that deals with the most egregious instances of racist and sexist speech yet is consistent with this decision. How would such a code be worded?

10. Compare this case with the *Harris* decision. Are the findings consistent?

Appendix

THE BILL OF RIGHTS
AND THE FOURTEENTH AMENDMENT

AMENDMENT I

Congress shall make no law respecting an establishment of religion, or prohibiting the free exercise thereof; or abridging the freedom of speech, or of the press; or the right of the people peaceably to assemble, and to petition the Government for a redress of grievances.

AMENDMENT II

A well regulated Militia, being necessary to the security of a free State, the right of the people to keep and bear Arms, shall not be infringed.

AMENDMENT III

No Soldier shall, in time of peace be quartered in any house, without the consent of the Owner, nor in time of war, but in a manner to be prescribed by law.

AMENDMENT IV

The right of the people to be secure in their persons, houses, papers, and effects, against unreasonable searches and seizures, shall not be violated, and no Warrants shall issue, but upon probable cause, supported by Oath or affirma-

tion, and particularly describing the place to be searched, and the persons or things to be seized.

AMENDMENT V

No person shall be held to answer for a capital or otherwise infamous crime, unless on a presentment of indictment of a Grand Jury, except in cases arising in the land or naval forces, or in the Militia, when in actual service in time of War or public danger; nor shall any person be subject for the same offence to be twice put in jeopardy of life or limb; nor shall be compelled in any criminal case to be a witness against himself; nor be deprived of life, liberty, or property, without due process of law; nor shall private property be taken for public use, without just compensation.

AMENDMENT VI

In all criminal prosecutions the accused shall enjoy the right to a speedy and public trial, by an impartial jury of the State and district wherein the crime shall have been committed, which district shall have been previously ascertained by law, and to be informed of the nature and cause of the accusation; to be confronted with the witnesses against him; to have compulsory process for obtaining witnesses in his favor, and to have the Assistance of Counsel for his defence.

AMENDMENT VII

In suits at common law, where the value in controversy shall exceed twenty dollars, the right of trial by jury shall be preserved, and no fact tried by a jury shall be otherwise reexamined in any Court of the United States, than according to the rules of the common law.

AMENDMENT VIII

Excessive bail shall not be required, nor excessive fines imposed, nor cruel and unusual punishment inflicted.

AMENDMENT IX

The enumeration in the Constitution, of certain rights, shall not be construed to deny or disparage others retained by the people.

AMENDMENT X

The powers not delegated to the United States by the Constitution, nor prohibited by it to the States, are reserved to the States respectively, or to the people.

AMENDMENT XIV

Section 1. All persons born or naturalized in the United States, and subject to the jurisdiction thereof, are citizens of the United States and of the State wherein they reside. No State shall make or enforce any law which shall abridge the privileges or immunities of citizens of the United States; nor shall any State deprive any person of life, liberty, or property, without due process of law; nor deny to any person within its jurisdiction the equal protection of the laws. . . .

ACKNOWLEDGMENTS

Lawyers' Ethics in an Adversary System: From Monroe H. Freedman, *Lawyers' Ethics in an Adversary System* (Indianapolis: Bobbs-Merrill Company, 1975). Reprinted by permission of the author. Some footnotes omitted.

Building Power and Breaking Images: Critical Legal Theory and the Practice of Law: From Peter Gabel and Paul Harris, "Building Power and Breaking Images: Critical Legal Theory and the Practice of Law," 11 *NYU Review of Law and Social Change* 369 (1982–1983). Reprinted by permission of the authors and *NYU Review of Law and Social Change.* Footnotes omitted.

The Lawyer as Friend: From Charles Fried, "The Lawyer as Friend: The Moral Foundations of the Lawyer–Client Relation," *Yale Law Journal,* 85 (1976), 1060–75 and 1087–89. Reprinted by permission. Some notes omitted.

The Lost Lawyer: Reprinted by permission of the publisher from *The Lost Lawyer* by Anthony Kronman, Cambridge, Mass: Harvard University Press, Copyright © 1993 by the President and Fellows of Harvard College.

Magnitude and Importance of Legal Science: From David Dudley Field, "Magnitude and Importance of Legal Science." Address at the opening of the Law School of the University of Chicago. From I. Sprague, ed., *Speeches, Arguments, and Miscellaneous Papers of David Dudley Field,* 517–533 (1884).

Eight Ways to Fail to Make Law: From Lon L. Fuller, *The Morality of Law* (New Haven: Yale University Press, 1964). Copyright © 1964 by Yale University Press. Reprinted by permission.

The Problem of the Grudge Informer: From Lon L. Fuller, *The Morality of Law* (New Haven: Yale University Press, 1969). Reprinted by permission.

Grudge Informers and the Rule of Law: From H. L. A. Hart, "Positivism and the Separation of Law and Morals," 71 *Harvard Law Review* 90, 616–20 (1958). Copyright 1958 by the Harvard Law Review. Excerpts reprinted by permission of the Harvard Law Review Association.

The Rule of Law and Its Virtue: From Joseph Raz © 1979, "The Rule of Law and Its Virtue." Reprinted with permission of the author from *The Authority of Law: Essays on Law and Morality* by Joseph Raz, Oxford University Press, 1979.

Crito: From Plato, *The Dialogues of Plato,* 3d ed., trans. Benjamin Jowett (London: Oxford University Press, 1892).

The Justification of Civil Disobedience: Originally presented at the meetings of the American Political Science Association, September 1966. Some revisions have been made and two paragraphs have been added to the last section. Copyright © 1968 by John Rawls. Reprinted by permission.

On Not Prosecuting Civil Disobedience: From Ronald Dworkin, *Taking Rights Seriously* (Cambridge: Harvard University Press, 1977), pp. 206–222. Reprinted by permission.

On Interpretation: The Adultery Clause of the Ten Commandments: From Sanford Levinson, "On Interpretation: The Adultery Clause of the Ten Commandments," *Southern California Law Review* 58, no. 2 (1985). Reprinted with the permission of the *Southern California Law Review.*

Stare Decisis: The Use of Precedent: From C. Gordon Post, "Stare Decisis: The Use of Precedent," in *An Introduction to the Law* (Englewood Cliffs, NJ: Prentice Hall, 1963). Copyright © 1963 by Prentice Hall. Some footnotes omitted.

Rules of Interpretation: From William Blackstone, *Commentaries* on the *Laws of England* (1765–69). Vol. 1. Copyright © 1807 by Thomas B. Waitand Company.

A Case Study in Interpretation: The Man Act: From Edward H. Levi *An Introduction to Legal Reasoning* (Chicago: University of Chicago Press, 1948). Copyright © 1948 University of Chicago Press. Reprinted by permission.

Summa Theoligica: Selections from *Summa Theologica,* reprinted from Anton C. Pegis, ed., *The Basic Writings of Saint Thomas Aquinas* (New York: Random House, 1945); used by permission of the A. C. Pegis Estate. Footnotes omitted.

The Province of Jurisprudence Determined: From John Austin, "The Province of Jurisprudence Determined," *Lectures on Jurisprudence,* 5th ed., vol. 1 (R. Campbell, 1885).

Preface to Cases on the Law of Contracts: From Christopher Columbus Langdell, *Cases on the Law of Contracts* (1871).

A Treatise on the Conflict of Laws: From Joseph H. Beale, *A Treatise on the Conflict of Laws* (1935).

The Path of the law: From Oliver Wendell Holmes, "The Path of the Law," *Harvard Law Review*, Vol. 10 (1897), pp. 457–68.

Realism and the Law: From Jerome Frank, *Law and the Modern Mind* (New York: Doubleday and Co., 1963). Copyright 1930, 1933, 1949 by Coward McCann, Inc., and copyright 1930 by Brentano's Inc., from Anchor Books Edition, 1963. Copyright renewed in 1958 by Florence K. Frank. Reprinted by arrangement with the estate of Barbara Frank Kristein.

Interpretation: From Tony Honoré, *About Law* (Oxford: Clarendon Press, 1995). Reprinted by permission of Oxford University Press.

Positivism and the Separation of Laws and Morals: From H. L. A. Hart, "Positivism and the Separation of Law and Morals," *71 Harvard Law Review* 593 (1958). Copyright © 1958 by the Harvard Review Association. Reprinted by permission.

Law as the Union of Primary and Secondary Rules: From H. L. A. Hart, *The Concept of Law* (New York: Oxford University Press, 1961). Copyright © 1961 by Oxford University Press. Reprinted by permission of Oxford University Press.

The Model of Rules: From Ronald Dworkin, *Taking Rights Seriously* (Cambridge, MA: Harvard University Press, 1977). Reprinted by permission. Some notes omitted.

"Natural" Law Revisited: From Ronald A. Dworkin, "'Natural' Law Revisited," *University of Florida Law Review* 34 (1982). Reprinted by permission of the *University of Florida Law Review*.

The Economic Approach to Law: Reprinted by permission of the publisher form Richard A. Posner, *The Problems of Jurisprudence* (Cambridge, Mass: Harvard University Press, Copyright © 1990 by the President and Fellows of Harvard College.

Law and Economics: An Analysis and Critique: From *Arguing About Law, 1st edition*, by A. Altman. © 1996. Reprinted with permission of Wadsworth Publishing, a division of Thomson Learning.

Critical Legal Studies: From Robert Gordon, "Law and Identity," *TIKKUN*, vol. 3, no. 1, p. 14. Reprinted with permission.

Toward a Theory of Law and Patriarchy: From Janet Rifkin, "Toward a Theory of Law and Patriarchy," *Harvard Women's Law Journal*, 83. Copyright © 1980 by the President and Fellows of Harvard College and the Harvard Women's Law Journal. Reprinted with permission.

Jurisprudence and Gender: From Robin West, "Jurisprudence and Gender," *The University of Chicago Law Review* 55, no. 1 (Winter 1988). Copyright © 1988 by the University of Chicago. Reprinted by permission.

Legal Realism, Critical Legal Studies, and Dworkin: From Andrew Altman, "Legal Realism, Critical Legal Studies, and Dworkin," *Philosophy & Public Affairs* 15, no. 3 (1986). Copyright © 1986 by Princeton University Press. Reprinted by permission of Princeton University Press.

Skepticism, Objectivity, and Democracy: From Ronald A. Dworkin, "'Natural' Law Revisited," *University of Florida Law Review* 34 (1982). Reprinted by permission of the *University of Florida Law Review*.

Who Should Be Punished? From *The Case of the Dog Provetie.* Reported in *The South African Law Journal*, Vol. 24 (1907): 232–234.

The Utilitarian Theory of Criminal Punishment: From Richard B. Brandt, *Ethical Theory* (Englewood Cliffs, NJ: Prentice-Hall, 1959). Reprinted by permission of the author.

Persons and Punishment: From Herbert Morris, "Persons and Punishment," *The Monist* 52, no. 4 (October 1968). Copyright © 1968 by *The Monist*, La Salle, Illinois. Reprinted by permission of the *The Monist*.

Restitution: A New Paradigm of Criminal Justice: From Randy E. Barnett, "Restitution: A New Paradigm of Criminal Justice," *Ethics* 87, no. 4 (July 1977). Copyright © 1977 by the University of Chicago Press. Reprinted by permission of the University of Chicago Press. Some footnotes omitted.

Survival on a Lifeboat: From *Law Reports, Queen's Bench Division*, vol. 14 (1884–85) (London: William Clowes and Sons, 1885).

The Principals of Criminal Law: From Richard B. Brandt, *Ethical Theory* (Englewood Cliffs, NJ: Prentice-Hall, 1959). Reprinted by permission of the author.

Intention: From H. L. A. Hart, *Punishment and Responsibility* (New York: Oxford University Press, 1969). Copyright © 1969 by Oxford University Press. Reprinted by permission.

Rape: From Susan Estrich, "Rape," *Yale Law Journal* 95, no. 6 (May 1986). Reprinted by permission of the Yale Law Journal Company and Fred B. Rothman & Company.

The Battered Woman's Defense: From *The American University Law Review*, Vol. 36 (1986), pp. 33–56. Reprinted by permission of the publisher.

Is the Insanity Test Insane?: From R. J. Gerber, "Is the Insanity Test Insane?" *The Journal of American Jurisprudence* 20 (1975). Reprinted by permission. Some footnotes omitted.

What Is So Special about Mental Illness? From Joel Feinberg, *Doing and Deserving: Essays in the Theory of Responsibility* (Princeton: Princeton University Press, 1970). Copyright © 1970 by Princeton University Press. Reprinted by permission of Princeton University Press.

The Cultural Defense in the Criminal Law: Copyright © 1986 by the Harvard Law Review Association. This was published as an unsigned note.

Convicting the Innocent: From James McCloskey, "Convicting the Innocent," *Criminal Justice Ethics* 8, no. 1 (winter-spring 1989). Copyright © 1989 by *Criminal Justice Ethics*, 899 Tenth Avenue, New York, NY 10019. Reprinted by permission.

A Debate on the Exclusionary Rule: From Malcolm Richard Wilkey and Stephen H. Sachs, "The Exclusionary Rule: A Prosecutor's Defense," *Criminal Justice Ethics* 1, no. 2 (summer–fall 1982). Reprinted by permission of the author and *Criminal Justice Ethics*. Some footnotes omitted.

Criminal Justice and the Negotiated Plea: From Kenneth Kipnis, "Criminal Justice and the Negotiated Plea," *Ethics* 36 (1976). Copyright © 1976 by the University of Chicago Press. Reprinted by permission of the author and the publisher. Some footnotes omitted.

The Race Card and Jury Nullification: Reprinted by permission from *Race, Crime, and the Law*. Copyright © 1997 by Randall Kennedy. Some notes omitted.

Negligence: From William Prosser, *The Law of Torts*, 4th ed. (West Publishing Company, 1971). Reprinted by permission of the West Publishing Company.

Tort Liability and Corrective Justice: Reprinted by permission from Jeffrie G. Murphy and Jules L. Coleman, *The Philosophy of Law*, rev. ed. Copyright © 1990 by Westview Press. Reprinted by permission of Westview Press, a member of Perseus Books, L. L. C.

Property: From John Locke, *The Second Treatise of Government: An Essay Concerning the Origin, Extent and End of Civil Government* (1690).

Property and Sovereignty: From Morris Raphael Cohen, "Property and Sovereignty," 13 *Cornell Law Quarterly* 8 (1927). Copyright © 1927 by Cornell University. All rights reserved. Reprinted by permission.

The Basis of Contract: From Morris Raphael Cohen, "The Basis of Contract," 46 *Harvard Law Review* 553 (1933). Copyright © 1933 by Harvard Law Review Association. Reprinted by permission.

Contract as Promises: From Charles Fried, *Contact as Promise: A Theory of Contractual Obligation* (Cambridge, MA: Harvard University Press, 1981). Copyright © 1981 by the President and Fellows of Harvard College. Reprinted by permission. Notes omitted.

The Political Meaning of Constitutionalism: British, French, and American Perspectives: From Ulrich K. Preuss, "The Political Meaning of Constitutionalism," *Constitutionalism, Democracy and Sovereignty: American and European Perspectives*, ed. Richard Bellamy (Aldershot, UK: Avebury Publishing Co., 1996). Reprinted by permission.

The Notion of a Living Constitution: From William H. Rehnquist, "The Notion of a Living Constitution." Originally published in 54 *Texas Law Review* 693–706 (Texas Law Review Association, May 1976). Copyright 1976 by the Texas Law Review Association. Reprinted by permission.

Constitutional Cases: From Ronald Dworkin, *Taking Rights Seriously* (Cambridge, MA: Harvard University Press, 1978). Copyright © 1978 by Ronald Dworkin. Reprinted by permission of the author.

Precommitment and Disagreement: From Jeremy Waldron, in *Constitutionalism: Philosophical Foundations*, ed. Larry Alexander. Copyright © 1998 Cambridge University Press. Reprinted by permission of Cambridge University Press.

Democracy, Judicial Review, and the Special Competency of Judges: From John Arthur in *Constitutionalism, Democracy and Sovereignty: American and European Perspectives*, ed. Richard Bellamy (Aldershot, UK: Avebury Publishing Co., 1996). Reprinted by permission.

A Letter Concerning Toleration: From John Locke, *A Letter Concerning Toleration* in *John Locke on Politics and Education*, ed. Howard R. Penniman (New York: Van Norstrand Company, 1947).

On Liberty: From John Stuart Mill, *On Liberty* (1859).

Privacy, Homosexuality, and the Constitution: From John Arthur, *The Unfinished Constitution* (Belmont, CA: Wadsworth Pub. Co., 1989). © John Arthur.

Justice Engendered: From Martha Minow, "Justice Engendered," *Harvard Law Review*, Vol. 101, p. 10. Copyright © 1987 by the Harvard Law Review Association. Reprinted by permission of the publisher and the author.

Equality, Race, and Gender: From Peter Singer, *Practical Ethics*, 2d edition. Copyright © 1995. Reprinted with permission of Cambridge University Press.

The Rights of Allan Bakke: An Exchange: From Ronald Dworkin, "Why Bakke Has No Case," *New York Review of Books*, Nov. 10, 1977. Copyright © 1977, Nyrev, Inc. Reprinted by permission of *The New York Review of Books*.